P9-APH-226

THE TRANSFORMATION OF GOVERNANCE

INTERPRETING AMERICAN POLITICS

Michael Nelson, Series Editor

THE TRANSFORMATION OF GOVERNANCE

Donald F. Kettl

Public Administration for Twenty-First Century America

The Johns Hopkins University Press

BALTIMORE AND LONDON

Printed in the United States of America on acid-free paper
9 8 7 6 5 4 3 2 1

The Johns Hopkins University Press
2715 North Charles Street
Baltimore, Maryland 21218-4363
www.press.jhu.edu

Library of Congress Cataloging-in-Publication Data

Kettl, Donald F.
The transformation of governance : public administration for twenty-first century America / Donald F. Kettl.
p. cm.—(Interpreting American politics)
Includes bibliographical references and index.
ISBN 0-8018-7048-8 (hardcover : alk. paper)—
ISBN 0-8018-7049-6 (pbk. : alk. paper)
1. Administrative—United States—Management. 2. Bureaucracy—United States 3. United States—Politics and government. 4. Public administration—United States. I. Title II. Series.
JK421.K483 2002
351.73—DC21

2001007420

A catalog record for this book is available from the British Library.

CONTENTS

SERIES EDITOR'S FOREWORD

The United States may be the only country in the world whose constitutional plan of government can be read in the map of its capital city. The Constitution's separation of powers, for example, was expressed physically by the city's planners when the Capitol and the Executive Mansion were separated from each other by a considerable distance. The idea that Washington's main reason for being was to represent the rest of the country was displayed in the wide avenues that radiate from the city in all directions, inviting citizens to come and be heard. No space was left for the construction of large commercial enterprises: just as constitutional government was to rest on the consent of the governed, so would Washington survive as a city only through their financial support.

Yet the original capital plan was hazy about where the administrative departments would be housed. To locate the departments on the outer reaches of the various avenues would suggest that they would take their direction from the people and the states, implying a bottom-up model of bureaucratic accountability. To cluster the departments together in their own part of town would suggest that they would be largely self-governing, an inside-out model of accountability. To place them near the president and Congress would suggest a top-down model, in which the departments would take their marching orders from their elected superiors.

In practice, the approach taken by the new government during Washington's early years as a city favored the last of these three strategies of building and governing the bureaucracy, the top-down model. As Donald F. Kettl shows in this book, the top-down model of bureaucratic accountability continued to dominate American public administration for more than a century and a half, reigning supreme at least until the time of the Allied victory in World War II. The way top-down administration worked, Kettl writes, was that "policymakers, elected by citizens, would craft public decisions and delegate responsibility to administrators." In turn, these "higher-level bureaucrats would use authority to control what their subordinates did" in carrying out the decisions of the elected policymakers. Public administration was meant to work "almost like a vending machine, into which [policymakers] put money and out of which they expected results."

As Kettl demonstrates, the last half-century has witnessed great strains on the top-down model of bureaucratic accountability. Most of the programs created by elected policymakers in recent decades have been designed to be implemented by state and local governments, or by private contractors. Because those outside Washington were given a share of the responsibility for making the policies work, these programs necessarily implied a weakening of top-down accountability in favor of bottom-up accountability. A further weakening has come from the contemporary idea, imported from the business world, of making the customer (citizens) the boss.

Policymakers have also injected doses of inside-out accountability into the workings of public administration in recent years. Most prominently, the "reinventing government" movement that caught fire in the 1990s was, as Kettl points out, "a strategy founded on an assumption that managers know how to do their jobs and that top officials ought to get out of the way and let them perform."

To complicate matters even more, the emergence of the inside-out and bottom-up models has not displaced the traditional top-down model of public administration. In times of crisis such as the September 11, 2001, terrorist attacks on New York and Washington, the universal impulse is still to put someone in charge of the far flung activities of, in this case, homeland security, then hold that person accountable for the government's performance. In short, modern bureaucracy, like the map of contemporary Washington, is the furthest thing from simplicity and coherence. Although visitors to the city will still find some departments and agencies located near the Capitol and White House, they also will find others headquartered on the broad avenues leading out of town and still others clustered together in neighborhoods of their own.

Michael Nelson

PREFACE

Public administration is built on the foundation of a theory of hierarchy and authority that is clear and straightforward, with a tradition that has continued for millennia. The actual work of public administration, however, has grown increasingly out of sync with the theory guiding it. While the theory is built on the foundation of hierarchy and authority, the structure of public work has become less and less hierarchical. Managers manage less through authority and more through a wide variety of other strategies. Moreover, the very nature of American democracy—the force that makes American public administration *public*—has shifted dramatically as well.

As a result, public administration—in theory and practice—has sagged under the strain. Managers have cobbled together new approaches without sufficient theoretical support. Many managers have followed what appeared to be lonely pathways only to discover other managers on the same road. Other managers have wandered down blind alleys. The field's lack of a guiding compass has thwarted the pursuit of efficiency that long was its reason for being. Even worse, the "ad hocracy" that emerged from the erosion of the theoretical foundation has posed huge challenges to democratic accountability. Elected officials find themselves delegating authority in traditional ways but discovering that the old mechanisms for ensuring accountability often work poorly, if at all. Instead they work increasingly through loose networks of service providers, but often, as government practitioners, they struggle to maintain government's legitimacy—to retain their roles as the leader of the network instead of just one participant among others.

The challenge to public administration theory thus is more than just an academic exercise. It has profound implications for the effectiveness and efficiency of government. It defines the conduct of American democracy. It shapes the relationship between government and its citizens. Public administration is in trouble because it does not match up well, either in theory or in practice, with the problems it must solve.

Public administration, especially in the United States, has for a long time been built on a tight theory of hierarchy and authority. Citizens elect officials to govern them. These elected policymakers frame policy and delegate the administrative details to unelected administrators. Delegation is inevitable—the work of government is too complex for elected officials to supervise every detail. Even if they had the time, they could not possibly have the skill or training to oversee the wide-ranging work of government. Relying on a career civil service allows government to build the capacity it needs to get the job done, and to get it done efficiently. Holding public administration responsible for that delegation, moreover, is the keystone of democratic accountability—for limiting the power of administrators and ensuring that administration pursues the goals that policymakers set. But as public administration has become less hierarchically organized and authority controlled, the shifting realities have challenged its traditions.

Such intellectual struggles, of course, are nothing new to American administration or democracy. Since the nation's first years, America's leaders have recognized that public administration is a fundamental manifestation of governmental power. They have advanced different—and conflicting—ideas about how to shape and control it. Over the centuries, policymakers and theorists alike have periodically reexamined which values and practices deserve the most emphasis. The process was much like the maddening Rubik's cube, a puzzle cube with different colors on different sides that could be rearranged in a vast number of combinations—43,252,003,274,489,856,000, in fact. What has changed is that public administration is no longer simply a matter of rearranging the dominant values of the American system. Rather, public administration has changed so fundamentally, if quietly, that the traditional values provide weak guidance.

Consider, for example, the September 11, 2001, terrorist attack on New York's World Trade Center and Washington's Pentagon. Traditional bureaucratic strategies proved a poor match for detecting and preventing such attacks or for deploying a coordinated response. The burning and collapsing buildings demonstrated that effective management of the crisis depended on coordinating very different agencies. In probing possible intelligence failures before the attacks, analysts quickly focused on the old rivalries between the CIA and the FBI. They poked into the historic division of responsibility, between the FBI's emphasis on domestic terrorists and the CIA's focus on international problems. The proposals for a single national antiterrorist agency to coordinate terrorist policy recall the challenges that came from the post–World War II plan that combined the various military services into a single Department of Defense.

During the attack and its aftermath, the coordination problem boiled over. Federal officials bluntly admitted that they had no procedure for notifying federal agencies in Washington about a possible attack. Washington Mayor Anthony A. Williams complained that federal officials failed to inform him quickly enough about critical decisions they were making, while District of Columbia officials discovered they lacked a citywide antiterrorist plan. New York's emergency management officials discovered that they had planned for many contingencies but didn't anticipate having their communications system virtually wiped out. Creative managers there proved almost unimaginably inventive in salvaging communications. Around the country, local officials discovered that their emergency response plans, devised for hurricanes or floods, were inadequate to manage a terrorist threat.

The terrorist attacks and the government responses were unprecedented. This book argues, however, that they were especially tragic examples of a far broader and deeper problem: that the way we think about and study public administration is out of sync with the way we practice it. The result of this disjunction is a serious challenge to the cost, effectiveness, and responsiveness of American government.

At the core is an emerging gap between *government* and *governance*. *Government* refers to the structure and function of public institutions. *Governance* is the way government gets its job done. Traditionally, government itself managed most service delivery. Toward the end of the twentieth century, however, government relied increasingly on nongovernmental partners to do its work, through processes that relied less on authority for control. We have advanced theories about government, how it works, and how we can make it work better. Our theory for understanding the relationship between government and the nongovernmental partners who play a critical role in executing government policy, on the other hand, is underdeveloped. The gap between how we have traditionally thought about government and governance itself has widened. That poses fundamental challenges to ideas that reach back to Jefferson and Hamilton—and to management practice that stretches out into the twenty-first century. Sorting through those challenges is the aim of this book.

The book's principal aim is to examine the historical traditions of American public administration, to identify the challenges facing it, and to chart the tensions between what it has to do and its capacity to do it. This volume will not attempt to offer comprehensive solutions, although it concludes with a blueprint of ten basic strategies for building a new approach to the field. Rather, its goal is to frame a research agenda: why theory and practice have increasingly failed to connect with the problems of American public administration—and why attacking these problems head-on is a critical and inescapable challenge for twenty-first century American government.

ACKNOWLEDGMENTS

In preparing this book, I was fortunate to have received generous financial assistance from the Smith Richardson Foundation, the University of Wisconsin–Madison's Robert M. La Follette School of Public Affairs, and the university's Graduate School, for support of the book's research and writing. I am deeply indebted to them for their assistance.

Two anonymous readers contributed the kind of thorough comments about which authors can only dream. They forced me to think even more carefully about the book's themes and arguments, and I am truly grateful to them for prodding me to straighten the furrows the book has plowed. Moreover, my editor at Johns Hopkins, Henry Tom, has proven more patient and helpful than any author has a right to expect. Series editor Michael Nelson contributed great insight and unflagging support. The book's copyeditor, Alice Honeywell, discovered the hidden meanings of some phrases that were struggling to see the light. They all have my deep thanks.

An earlier version of chapter 6 appeared as "The Transformation of Governance: Globalization, Devolution, and the Role of Government," in *Public Administration Review*, vol. 60 (November/December 2000), pp. 488-97. This paper, in turn, grew out of work done by the Priority Issues Task Force of the National Academy of Public Administration. The Task Force engaged in spirited and stimulating debate about the future of the field. Its members spurred me to consider carefully the links between the field's deep traditions and its emerging challenges: Mark Abramson, Donald Borut, Jonathan Breul, Peter Harkness, Steven Kelman, Valerie Lemmie, Naomi B. Lynn, David Mathews, David Mathiasen, Brian O'Connell, and Susan Schwab.

Finally, my wife, Sue, provided constant support and encouragement. I'm more grateful to her than she could know.

THE TRANSFORMATION OF GOVERNANCE

ADMINISTRATIVE PARADOXES ||| 1

Toward the end of 2000, junkfoodaholics suffered through a major crisis. The puffy corn munchies adored by millions of snackers suddenly disappeared from store shelves. Why? Producers feared that genetically engineered corn, approved for animal feed but not for human consumption, had found its way into the manufacturing process. Rather than risk harm to consumers—and a public relations debacle—the producers took the puffs off the market until they could check the manufacturing lines. Some consumers complained of a "puff paucity," but grocery store owners reassured buyers that crunchy snacks were still available, and they outsold the puffy ones by a ratio of twenty to one.[1] Snackers were relieved, but recalls of corn-based products swept the nation's grocery stores. Kellogg's shut down production at a Memphis plant, Kraft asked that its taco shells be removed from the shelves, and even Japanese merchants soon joined the product recalls. The cheese puff problem had become a genuine foreign policy crisis.

The problem flowed from the invention of a new genetically engineered brand of corn named "StarLink." Farmers had long been plagued by the European corn borer, a pest that devoured the grain before it could reach market. American farmers annually lost hundreds of millions of dollars in corn to the insect's voracious appetite. Organic farmers, however, had discovered that a natural insecticide called "Bt" would kill the corn borer, and long-term research had shown Bt to be safe. Genetic scientists at Aventis, a biotech company employing upwards of 95,000 people in more than 120 countries, discovered a way to implant a bacteria gene in corn to produce Bt. Farmers could simply plant the new breed of corn—StarLink—and allow the grain's genes to do the work instead of using an expensive hit-or-miss spray that also carried greater environmental risk.

Although farmers saw the seed as a huge boon, health experts worried that the corn could cause harm. In addition to the Bt, the bioengineered corn also contained a protein, Cry9C, which had caused allergies in some people. Aventis scientists did not believe that the small concentrations of Cry9C posed any real health danger, but to be on the safe side, government regulators initially approved the seed for use only as animal feed. In addition, the Environmental Protection Agency (EPA) mandated a 660-foot buffer zone around all fields containing StarLink to prevent cross-pollination with corn grown for human consumption.

In marketing StarLink, Aventis had counted on a long-term winner. By 2000, the bioengineered seed already accounted for about 1 percent of the 80 million acres of corn grown in the United States. Soon, however, the reports of contaminated corn chips began, followed by recalled corn tortillas and shutdowns of the corn flakes line among cereal producers. Some farmers complained that seed salespeople never told them of the mandated buffer zone. Some farmers even said that the salespeople never informed them that StarLink was not yet approved for human consumption. Because of careless planting, some of which was inadvertent, pollen from the StarLink corn blew into fields with corn being grown for human use. Some corn grown for human consumption became cross-pollinated with StarLink, while other corn that had been separated from StarLink was later shipped on barges or in rail cars or stored in silos that, in turn, contained contaminated corn. Once any StarLink corn became mixed with corn certified for human consumption, screening tests for Cry9C would show that the entire shipment was suspect.

Some of this corn found its way into American factories. Other supplies spread through the food and grain transportation systems as well. Japanese officials, for example, discovered that a corn flour mix sold for home baking contained StarLink residue. That was triple trouble for American farmers. Japan was the single biggest importer of U.S. agricultural products. Japan had approved StarLink for neither human nor animal consumption, and Japanese citizens were especially leery about bioengineered food products. The domestic problem thus quickly became an international crisis as well.

Aventis managers saw the problem primarily as a technical one that they could solve through a regulatory waiver. If the EPA would temporarily permit StarLink to be sold for human consumption, they would no longer risk violating the regulations. Because of the low concentrations of Cry9C, the company's scientists suspected that the corn was highly unlikely to cause any problems for humans in any event. They thought they could resolve the international issues by having the U.S. Department of Agriculture (USDA) test all corn shipments bound for Japan for StarLink residue. The Japanese government, in addition, pledged to conduct random tests to ensure that no StarLink corn entered the country. This combined strategy, Aventis hoped, would end the embarrassing headlines and get the corn back to market.

But the problems continued. Even after the import ban, traces of StarLink were found again in Japan. In the United States, the product continued to pop up throughout the food chain. Archer Daniels Midland (ADM), one of the largest U.S. agricultural giants, announced that its plants would no longer accept bioengineered crops that did not have worldwide approval. In many European nations, citizen concern about bioengineered crops was rising. Governments were considering proposals to require more labeling about the source and content of food items, and ADM simply did not want to risk its worldwide business by purchasing StarLink products.

Aventis argued that the health worries were overblown, but the international complaints had created an escalating public relations disaster. In January 2001, Aventis staged a retreat: It announced that it was asking the EPA to cancel StarLink's registration, which would effectively withdraw the product from the market. Aventis also announced a plan, costing hundreds of millions of dollars, to compensate farmers and grain elevators in seventeen states whose crops were contaminated with StarLink and were thus unmarketable. These steps, Aventis hoped, would put the problem quickly behind them. Japanese officials, however, soon discovered even more StarLink in imported corn. American brewers found traces of StarLink in cornmeal used in making beer. Once the corn crept into the human food chain, Aventis officials found it unexpectedly difficult to remove. StarLink researchers argued that normal food processing would destroy any Cry9C residue that might make its way into supply chains, but the science failed to reassure worried consumers. Food producers had no wish to risk their reputations on corn that might provoke a consumer backlash and backed away from StarLink.

The StarLink episode was the quintessential twenty-first century policy problem. New technology offered great advances, but it also created huge uncertainty and potential risk. Faced with scientific uncertainty and political attack—some critics labeled bioengineered produced like StarLink "Frankenfoods"—the ground shifted under food producers. No matter how small the risk, the *perceptions* of danger drove the policy agenda. When scientists discovered even small traces of Cry9C in corn used for corn chips and other products, worried manufacturers recalled the product. Once recall fever started, further scientific research mattered little. From Japanese corn to American cheese puffs, public concern about the safety of the food supply pushed the issue squarely onto the policy agenda, and citizens literally around the world demanded that their governments respond.

The StarLink problem defied any effort to assign responsibility for solving it. StarLink was produced by Aventis, a French-based global corporation, and marketed by its agricultural division, Aventis CropScience, with American operations based in North Carolina's Research Triangle. In announcing the creation of CropScience in December 1999, the company's president proudly said, "Our objective is to bring to the North American farmer the innovative and effective products that are solutions to the challenges he faces—and in the process, create an effective partnership with him."[2] Within a year, the StarLink problem had seriously scarred its reputation, and the company's efforts to market the new product ended, at least for a while.

Within American government, multiple agencies regulated the product. The EPA granted the initial approval to use StarLink for animals but not for humans. The USDA's Grains Inspection, Packers, and Stockyards Administration oversaw corn shipments, including exports to Japan. Its Kansas City laboratories tested samples for traces of Cry9C. The Food and Drug Administration (FDA) conducted voluntary screening of bioengineered food and, in general, monitored the safety of the food supply. The Centers for Disease Control, part of the U.S. Department of Health and Human Services, along with the FDA, examined the cases of forty-four people who blamed Cry9C for allergic reactions along with possibly life-threatening anaphylactic shock. These regulators shared jurisdiction. In addition, unlike in most countries around the world, the EPA sometimes granted "split approval," which could approve the use of a product for animal feed but not for consumption by humans. The EPA said the decision was a halfway step that allowed initial production of StarLink as researchers completed research into the grain's effects on humans. Critics, however, worried that corn approved for animals would find its way into the human food chain. The result, however, was a public relations nightmare for Aventis. It was a biotech scare for many consumers. It was a foreign relations dilemma for American regulators. And it was an extraordinarily complex regulatory problem for three federal agencies.

THE STUDY OF ADMINISTRATION

The StarLink case was, in short, the prototype for twenty-first century management problems. It was a problem that demanded a solution, but no agency had the responsibility or the leverage to solve it. Government's response by necessity had to involve teamwork among a host of regulatory agencies as well as cooperation of private companies, from Aventis and food manufacturers to food shippers and individual farmers. Americans had to satisfy both the Japanese government and Japanese consumers. Even these efforts could not truly "solve" the problem. The Americans could only contain the problem and, in the end, hope it would ebb as StarLink gradually disappeared from the food and distribution chains. Those hopes were frustrated by continuing discovery of StarLink corn in the food chain, even months after regulators thought they had solved the problem.

Government agencies thus could not truly solve, control, or even manage the problem. At best, they could collaborate in framing a response. Neither was it an issue for which the theories of public administration offered an adequate solution. For a century, the field had built its approach on service delivery, basing that service delivery on theories of hierarchy and authority. The StarLink case grew out of a complex problem that simply did not fit standard hierarchical, authority-based systems. As a result, the case presented policymakers with problems for which neither they nor the theory on which they operated were prepared. Government found itself ill equipped for the problems it had to solve, and administrative theory proved a poor match for the world in which it attempted to operate.

Boundaries and Public Administration

The theory and practice of modern American public administration date from the end of the nineteenth century. The rise of the industrial age had gradually pushed aside the agrarian lifestyle and put large, complex private corporations at the center of American economic life. As the market grew for cheap, standardized goods, the budding corporations developed new systems of mass production, including the assembly line and other new processes. Entrepreneurs discovered the advantages of monopoly. Citizens complained that the muscle of corporate trusts drove prices up, limited market choice, and weakened citizens' autonomy. They complained that private utilities ignored some neighborhoods and that other companies produced unsafe products. Tough market competition produced wildly fluctuating interest rates, especially between the heavy borrowing season (for spring planting) and the heavy repayment season (during fall harvest). The concentration of capital, especially in the East, enraged those who needed it for development, especially in the West. In these and scores of other cases, the rise of corporate power created new demands for a stronger government.

The Progressives responded by arguing for a more powerful government, one powerful enough to tackle these demands and yet be insulated from political influence. In 1883, Congress took the first step toward forming a modern public administration by creating the federal civil service system. By the turn of the twentieth century, this modern public administration was in full flower.[3] Frank J. Goodnow, whom Paul P. Van Riper views as "the effective founder of academic public administration in the United States," wrote influential works on administrative law and the relationship of politics and administration.[4] The Taft Commission, which recommended a consolidated executive budget in its 1912 report, included such public administration notables as Frederick A. Cleveland (as chairman), W. F. Willoughby, and Goodnow.[5] Congress later enacted the commission's key recommendations. As governor of Wisconsin, Robert M. La Follette pressed the Progressive agenda, which embodied a positive role for government and the need for an effective government to play that role. In 1911, a training program was created to prepare public administrators to meet government's new responsibilities. That program later grew into Syracuse University's Maxwell School of Citizenship, now the oldest academic public administration program in the country.

The Progressive movement espoused a belief in strong government, a government that pursued both administratively efficient and politically accountable strategies. Furthermore, the Progressives aimed to create a government that solved public problems at the lowest cost for taxpayers—and that ensured government would ultimately be accountable to citizens, not to large corporate interests. The Progressives' belief in effective government led, in turn, to a theory of public administration built on principles of technical professionalism and political neutrality. The Taft Commission's proposal for a comprehensive executive budget, for example, advanced the norms of rational-comprehensive analysis and executive-centered control. Goodnow's work underlined the role of administrative law as a way of establishing clear, uniform, procedural standards for administrative action. Following on the Teapot Dome and other late-nineteenth-century scandals, the field's early thinkers insisted on strong ethics.

The rise of public administration also brought new technologies to government, like the Burroughs adding machine, punch cards for automating the census, typewriters, and a decimal system (invented by

Melvil Dewey) for classifying library books—a system later adapted for filing papers in the War Department. Army engineers accomplished what had been thought nearly impossible—digging a canal across the Panamanian isthmus. The result, in the early part of the twentieth century, was what Paul P. Van Riper has called "an heretical and explosive idea," the thought "that the modern administrative state, properly directed, could accomplish almost anything it might envision and at reasonable cost."[6]

They built a new civil service system and created independent regulatory agencies. They constructed a unified executive budget that pulled decision-making into one place and gave the president power to shape the government's overall fiscal policy. In many ways, for better or worse, they built the foundation for the modern federal establishment—on a commitment to a strong government that worked well but that ultimately was accountable to elected officials. They were not devoted to an expansion of government power as much as they were committed to solving the people's problems. Well schooled in the warnings of the founders about the potential abuse of executive power, they nested the more-powerful executive in the balance-of-powers system created to ensure that no branch of government could misuse its power at the expense of the citizenry.

But if they were not devoted to expanding administrative power as an end in itself, the direct product of their work was indeed a stronger executive. They were cognizant of the risks, so they drew elaborate boundaries to prevent, they hoped, the strong executive from straying too far into political decisions or abuses of individual liberty. In fact, the creation of orthodox public administration by the Progressives at the turn of the twentieth century was as much about building boundaries as strengthening administrative structures—restraining government power to make it accountable while empowering government to make it effective.[7] Its proponents struggled with a central dilemma—how to make government administration strong enough to cope with the increasingly complex problems of the modernizing world. On the other hand, they shared the worries of the nation's founders—worries well founded in their experience with the British king—that strong government could rob citizens of their liberty. The Progressives thus struggled first to define and then to solve the central problem of the modern administrative state as it operated in a democracy: How could it be made strong enough to work without risking tyranny? Their answer, in general, was to strengthen administration but also to limit its power.

For the Progressives, the most important boundary was between policy*making* and policy *administration.* Policymakers, elected by citizens, would craft public decisions and delegate responsibility to administrators. They defined clearly what each agency's job was and, by extension, what it was not. The principle of hierarchy defined clearly each administrator's responsibilities. Complex missions could be separated into their individual components, each component could be assigned to individual administrators, and administrators would know what they were—and were not—charged with doing. The principle of authority would hold everyone in the system accountable. Policymakers delegated authority to the bureaucracy, and higher-level bureaucrats could use authority to control what their subordinates did. The application of these two principles—hierarchy and authority—would promote efficiency by allowing the creation of sophisticated bureaucracies full of highly skilled workers. It would promote accountability by specifying the relationship of each worker to policymakers. It would remove administration from the political chaos that had often crippled it in the past. And it would do all of these things by carefully structuring the work within clear boundaries.

This approach dominated both the theory and practice of American public administration throughout most of the twentieth century. When the Depression brought a new wave of problems, Franklin D. Roosevelt's New Deal created new government reforms in the Progressive spirit. New problems led to new government programs, and new programs spawned new government agencies. When the Brownlow Committee concluded that "the president needs help," the new Executive Office of the President emerged to supervise better the executive branch's expanded domain.[8]

World War II helped bring orthodox public administration to the apex of its influence. Its experts built the Pentagon in an extraordinarily short time and then worked from the Pentagon to manage the war effort. Many of the nation's best public administrationists—professionals trained in the art and science of managing government programs—came to Washington to help run the war effort. They ensured that the Progressives left an indelible mark on American government. Their success in the vast complexity of mounting and winning a two-front war sealed the Progressives' legacy. So it was scarcely surprising that, when the war ended, President Truman, a Democrat, appointed Herbert Hoover, a Republican engineer-as-president-as-government-efficiency-expert, to chair two long-running commissions, which, in turn, transformed how government worked.[9] It had become unthinkable to build a government without simultaneously worrying about how to make it work, to plan government policy without thinking about how best to manage it, or to consider how best to manage it without consulting the best thinkers of American public administration.

The postwar high point of orthodox public administration, however, did not anticipate emerging crises, both pragmatic and intellectual. The field had few good answers about how to manage new programs intended to eliminate poverty or urban blight. Frustrated elected officials began turning to other sources for advice in designing and running programs. Meanwhile, beginning in the 1950s, the social sciences in general devoted themselves to becoming more scientific. Orthodox public administration, long as much art as science and as much philosophy as theory, found itself increasingly squeezed from the central role it had played for three generations. Its scholars lamented the erosion of respect, while practitioners looked far more broadly for guidance. Public administration was suffering from a genuine intellectual crisis.[10] The boundaries that had limited both theory and practice for three generations no longer seemed appropriate for the nation's emerging problems.

Boundaries and Political Science

Among public administration theorists, this crisis could not have been more jarring. Public administration, after all, had been one of the original subfields of the American Political Science Association when it was established in 1903, along with comparative government (as applied to the governance of colonies), public law (through constitutional law and jurisprudence), international law, and political theory. The association's first president was perhaps the most prominent public administrationist of the day, Frank J. Goodnow. Goodnow preached the critical connection between theory and practice.[11]

For the next generation, public administration helped shape the emerging discipline of political science. The field proved attractive to students, and in 1940, public administration accounted for one-fifth of all Ph.D.'s awarded in political science.[12] Franklin D. Roosevelt gave the field's thinkers a front-line education by bringing them to Washington to help run the New Deal and World War II. All in all, it had been a stunning half century: one that helped to give birth to a new discipline, shaped that discipline's development, and brought the field's knowledge to policymakers.

By the 1960s, all that had changed. The social sciences put a far greater emphasis on the development of scientific knowledge. That, in turn, shifted the focus of much administrative theory from the traditional focus on organizational structure to human interactions, especially the power relationships and motivations that drive them. Herbert Simon, a social scientist who won the Nobel Prize for economics, argued that decision-making, not organizational structure, was the central problem of administration.[13] The emerging focus on decisions and power ran counter to orthodox public administration's focus on organizational structure and process. Rooted so deeply in that orthodoxy, public administration found it hard to change, and even sympathetic analysts despaired about whether public administration could ever truly become a science.[14]

These worries about public administration surfaced precisely as political science, sociology, and especially economics together sought a more scientific footing. A new generation of postwar social sciences wanted more rigor: theories that produced predictions, predictions that could be tested, tests that could be replicated. The search for more science in the social sciences brought, in particular, new statistical methods. These methods were especially hard on public administration. Public administration researchers had been used to working at the organizational level and, within the organization, on administrative process. To be valid and reliable, the new statistical methods demanded large numbers of units to study. Organizations typically occurred in groups of just a few, and organizational processes proved hard to model. The traditional study of public administration thus did not match the new analytical techniques sweeping the social sciences, so as they rose in influence, the study of public administration became more marginal.

At that high level of analysis, moreover, the same circumstances rarely repeat themselves. Unlike the scientific approaches the other social sciences were beginning to champion, traditional public administration rarely sought to predict outcomes. Rather, public administration grew from the "scientific management" movement of the late nineteenth and early twentieth centuries, which was led by analysts like Frederick W. Taylor.[15] The legacy of the scientific management approach infuriated the postwar social scientists. They tended to view public administration as little more than a collection of fuzzy proverbs that sometimes conflicted and that, in any event, provided weak guides for both theory and action.[16] The new social scientists looked longingly at their colleagues in the natural sciences, where advances in everything from biochemistry to nuclear physics fueled an explosive growth in theory and in government financial support.

In political science, this new work focused on the behavior of individuals. Berelson, Lazarsfeld, and McPhee's classic 1954 study, *Voting*, brought statistical research to voting behavior.[17] Dahl's *Who Governs?* shaped the study of small-scale pluralistic influences on political life.[18] Analysis of institutions, especially of the bureaucracy, fell in prestige within political science. In the view of the emerging orthodoxy, bureaucracies were too few to be analyzed statistically, whereas there were millions of voters whose decisions could be studied. Public administration theory yielded too vague a set of hypotheses for careful testing. As statistical methods and individual-level analysis became more popular in political science, public administration dramatically slipped in prestige. One of the field's giants, Dwight Waldo, sadly noted the split between the emerging political science orthodoxy and the traditional approach to public administration. That, Waldo believed, was ironic, given public administration's central role in helping found the discipline of political science: "It is now unrealistic and unproductive to regard public administration as a subdivision of political science. . . . The truth is that the attitude of political scientists (other than those accepting public administration as their 'field') is at best one of indifference and is often one of undisguised contempt or hostility. We are now hardly welcome in the house of our youth."[19]

At the beginning of the twentieth century, public administration and political science were inseparable. By the century's midpoint, the two fields were asking different questions (searching for predictability instead of prescription) using different levels of analysis (individuals instead of institutions) and different analytical methods (statistics instead of common sense). In a little more than half a century, the two fields went from seamless connection to a strained relationship. In the view of some public administration scholars, the stress was leading to an outright divorce.

Boundaries and Public Policy

Similar problems plagued public administration's efforts to train practitioners. The practical side of the field had always had an uneasy place within political science. In the American Political Science Association's first decade, public administrationists made an abortive effort to launch a training program. In the end, they decided to stay within political science, in part because they had no other discipline to which they could go. Still, public administrationists worried that political scientists had little appreciation for the need to train individuals in the practice as well as the study of government. For their part, political scientists worried that a focus on training would deflect energy from the more important task of building the intellectual foundation for the new field. They made an uneasy but highly productive truce, and in every major university around the country, public administration proved one of the cornerstones of the political science department.

The New Deal and its administrative challenges scratched the pragmatic itch of many public administrationists. In 1939, these pragmatists formed the new American Society for Public Administration (ASPA), largely because they believed they needed a new institutional home in which to train public servants more effectively. Faced with the enduring question of whether they were pursuing science or practice, the ASPA embraced all the competing perspectives by dedicating itself to the "science, process, and art of public administration." ASPA leaders played critical roles in governments throughout the country, especially during World War II.

The same forces that eroded public administration's place in political science soon reduced its influence in training public servants as well. In the early 1960s, the Kennedy administration's "whiz kids" brought a new commitment to policy analysis and an argument that microeconomics provided a powerful—indeed, a superior—analytical tool for producing efficiency. Orthodox public administration sought efficiency through structure and process. Microeconomics pursued Simon's argument that decisions mattered most and sought to use rigorous methods to prescribe the right policy judgments. At the very least, microeconomics had a patently reassuring feel to it. It was exacting. It grew from a straightforward theory and led to relatively unambiguous prescriptions. As public administration was criticized for offering flimsy proverbs and platitudes, microeconomics rose to present clear guidance. That is not to say that the guidance was always useful or correct. One of the whiz kids' central projects, the development of a new tactical fighter to be shared by the navy and the air force, thus slashing development and procurement costs, failed. Both services continued to add requirements until the plane eventually worked for neither. But in the face of public administration's reputation for fuzziness, there was something powerful and persuasive about an approach that gave clear answers.

Many major universities had long-established public administration programs that became the centerpieces of orthodox public administration. Syracuse University's Maxwell School of Citizenship and Public Affairs, for example, began in 1924 with six students. The program focused on training "teachers of citizenship" and "practitioners of public affairs."[20] The Maxwell program, and scores like it, produced thousands of graduates who went into government service. Such programs also housed the field's best scholars and produced a generation of scholarship that defined the field and helped run the country.

In the 1960s, however, the desire for stronger economics-based prescriptions fueled the rise of public policy schools in direct competition with—indeed, rejection of—public administration programs. For example, Harvard's Littauer Graduate School of Public Administration, established in 1936 with the same mission as Syracuse's Maxwell School, gradually shifted to the Simon-based decision-making approach. In the spirit of the Kennedy administration's whiz kids, the program incorporated more microeconomics and policy analysis. Friends of the Kennedy family created the Institute of Politics and, eventually, a school renamed in the assassinated president's honor.

The public policy movement grew from an assumption that orthodox public administration had reached a dead end. Its enthusiasts agreed with Simon that decisions were central and that most of the field's theory was excruciatingly simplistic. The field's scholars started essentially from scratch by creating a new approach, which they named "public management." The field rejected the orthodox public administration focus on organizational structure and process. The public policy movement rejected the field's emphasis on the organization of the unit of analysis as its method of drawing insights from common sense. Instead, public policy focused on public decisions (What fighter plane should we buy? How does the State Department shape foreign policy?) and individual policy areas (like transportation, welfare, housing, or defense). It drew its method from the business school practice of extracting insights from close analysis of cases.

The touchstone of public policy was Richard Neustadt's *Presidential Power*. He built on the decision-based approach of Herbert Simon and the power-based approach of Norton Long. Neustadt's preface was seductive to scholars seeking to build a new field: "My theme is personal power and its politics: what it is, how to get it, how to keep it, how to use it."[21] The president's power built on the "power to persuade." For the new students of public policy, that focused their work on the personal interactions of high-level players, instead of the front-line activities of administrative minions. To gain insights about how this worked, they wrote case studies that provided rich detail of such decisions.

Graham Allison's classic on the Cuban missile crisis, *Essence of Decision*, became the model for how case analysis could illuminate the study of public decisions. He developed three alternative models for explaining decisions in the crisis. "Model I" presented a classical model of rational actors making rational decisions. "Model II" explained decisions in terms of basic organizational theory and standard operating procedures. "Model III" put the case in the context of bureaucratic politics. Allison quite carefully explained that these were alternative models and that none of them presented the "correct" approach.[22] Nevertheless, his readers—especially in the new public policy community—immediately gravitated to Model III. Model I's "rational actor" approach conveyed the basic journalistic who-what-when-how story and provided few new insights. Model II's "standard operating procedures" approach laid out the pathologies of bureaucratic action, especially how the standard operating procedures of the military on both sides almost led to major irremediable miscalculations—and nuclear war. It was Model III that produced the new insights: central players make the important decisions; the places where they sit affect the decisions they make; and government decisions can be understood as political results. It was clear that the political instincts of the key players, especially John and Robert Kennedy, had helped shape the key decisions at the critical moments, and it was also clear that these instincts ran against the interpretations suggested by Models I and II.

In one stroke, Allison portrayed the behaviors stimulated by orthodox public administration as pathologies to be managed—that management had to come through skilled leaders who could negotiate bureaucratic politics. This approach proved a serious, nearly fatal blow to orthodox public administration. It reinforced the emerging belief that orthodox public administration had led to inflexible, rules-oriented organizations that frustrated the ability of leaders to lead. It strengthened the case of analysts who argued the need for stronger leaders who could cure the pathologies of administration. It supported the budding movement toward a decision-based, case-driven management approach.

In fact, analysts argued that there was a "missing link" in the study of public policy—bringing decisions to action.[23] Pressman and Wildavsky's instant classic, *Implementation*, sealed the argument. They explained that in preparing the book, they assumed that "there is (or there must be) a large literature about implementation in the social sciences. . . . It must be there; it should be there; but in fact it is not."[24] That surprised orthodox public administrationists, who had always believed that their field had been exploring these questions for generations. If the problem was not new, the movement and its approach were. The implementation movement rejected the primarily structural and procedural approach of orthodox public administration in favor of a policy-based approach. And it began with an assumption that the fledgling movement needed to start from scratch.

Some of the problem, moreover, flowed from how public administration tended to approach administrative problems. Rooted far more than most political science in pragmatism, public administration focused much more on *prescriptions*. And much more than most political actions, administration is full of vast complications, irresolvable conundrums, and eternal dilemmas. Should managers decentralize to increase the responsiveness of their programs or centralize to improve accountability? Should they organize by function to improve specialization or by area to strengthen coordination?

Even in its more recent search for theoretical rigor, pragmatic imperatives have driven the field. In part, this is because many of the scholars who craft its literature also teach students who have (or seek) public-sector jobs. Trying to build theory from the work of public managers has always proven difficult, Behn argues, because managers manage by "groping along."[25] The complexity of public problems and the multiple strategies of the public officials who wrestle with them have made finding, or even imposing, predictable patterns difficult. The constant tensions between administrative theories and public events have, on one hand, always kept public administrationists busy. On the other hand, struggling with difficult problems and uncertain solutions has made the search for predictable patterns an endless and, ultimately, frustrating one. It seeks to give practitioners grounding in coping with their daily lives; students a foundation for the careers they hope to explore; and scholars a precision in how they understand administrative action.

Every academic discipline, and especially every social science field, grapples with such problems. Fields constantly search for "the next big idea," a concept that can both resolve ongoing theoretical battles and powerfully shape future work. Sociology, for example, has dealt with structuralism, deconstruction, poststructuralism, psychoanalysis, postcolonialism, historicism, and empire.[26] Within economics, the study of macro-level behavior ebbed as microeconomics rose—and critics complained that the model-driven approach of some microeconomics had torn the soul out of the field. Political science, torn between an instinct to become more scientific and the urge to ground itself more deeply in the realities of politics, felt the pressure from both sociology and economics. These pressures affected public administration as well, where the simplifying urge of more formal social science theory was at odds with the growing complexity of administrative action. Theorist Edgar H. Schein argued that the "theory in use" tends to endure until reality intervenes with problems and scandals "that cannot be hidden, avoided, or denied."[27] When theories and problems fall out of sync, pressures build for recasting the theory. Among all the areas of social science, public administration has perhaps taken pragmatic problems most seriously. It has always sought a theory to guide practice.

Toward the end of the twentieth century, the growing complexity of public policy problems and the governmental response increasingly confounded theory. In particular, these trends challenged the field's roots in hierarchy and authority; boundaries that once seemed secure became porous. At the same time, public administration's sister fields—political science, economics, and sociology—all pressed toward more rigorous theories. Public administration found itself trying to span growing gaps: between its own intellectual heritage and the emerging realities of twenty-first century administration; and between its own intellectual pursuits and those of the other social sciences.

The tensions have also come from the search for *prescriptions* amid academic pursuits based on *predictions.* The goal of political science—and related fields, like public management—is to have a strong analytical framework that generates replicable propositions. What are the central, repeating patterns of political life? How will voters vote, judges decide, legislators legislate—or administrators manage? Predictions build on an effort to simplify reality. Prescriptions, on the other hand, flow from an understanding of the rich complexity of political and administrative life. The search for answers to the basic questions—What do we know? What should we do?—lead in opposite directions. Those seeking prescriptions are often surprisingly comfortable with ambiguity and complexity; they often look for *how to think about* issues as much as *what to do.* The search for simple, straightforward, replicable, verifiable propositions leaves little room for ambiguity and the "It's complicated!" approach to analysis.

That, at its core, defines public administration's basic problem. For a century, it has sought both an accepted place in academic theory and a voice in the debate over important policy puzzles. These goals have always pulled public administration in opposite directions, toward theoretical parsimony and pragmatic richness. In the last half of the twentieth century, these tensions pushed public administration near the breaking point. The social sciences have worked to make their research more scientific. The policy world has become more intricate, with more federal-state-local partnerships, more public-private linkages, and more transnational action. The demands for parsimony have grown even as complexity has increased. Rooted fundamentally in difficult theoretical puzzles, public administration has struggled as well with practical problems that have become even harder.

It is tempting to attack these problems by moving away from public administration's roots—by seeking *either* pragmatic policy advice *or* theoretical rigor. That course is surely the road to intellectual defeat, however. Theory without the ability to predict and understand something real and important is not worth having. Political action without theoretical structure is dangerous, especially in the American political system, where political traditions and ideas have always had great sway. Public administration without a guiding theory is risky; administrative theory without connection to action is meaningless. That dilemma is the foundation of a genuine intellectual crisis in public administration.

This is more than just a quaint intellectual debate among academics. Public trust in government depends, at least to some degree, on government's ability to produce results. Effective oversight of administration by elected officials hinges on their ability to understand the management systems they create to implement policy. Global economic and political systems pose challenges that participants only dimly understand. Solving tough problems thus requires substantial intellectual capital. Efforts to govern without investing in that intellectual capital will inevitably be impoverished. That is surely all the more true as tight budgets make it harder for governments to devise new programs and where much of the action lies inevitably in making existing programs work better.

Meanwhile, new interdisciplinary public policy programs sprang up in the late 1960s and early 1970s. These programs focused sharply on how to improve the performance of public programs and on how to make public managers more effective in managing these programs. Traditional public administration had focused, for nearly a century, on the structure of government organizations and the processes (especially budgeting and personnel systems) that drove them. The intellectual leaders of the new public policy movement did not find the traditional approaches useful, and they self-consciously pushed them aside in creating their new programs.

While some public policy scholars like Pressman and Wildavsky worried about "why it's amazing that federal programs work at all," as the subtitle of their book read in part, others asked how effective leaders could produce strong results. Implementation scholars focused on the program as the unit of analysis (just as public administrationists looked at structure and process). In many of the new public policy schools, analysts used case studies to understand how individuals—especially high-level officials in government agencies—could make a difference. "Leadership counts" was the watchword.[28] Unlike the implementation scholars, they saw the solution in individual leadership rather than analysis of programs. Like the implementation scholars, however, they found public administration sorely lacking. They developed, instead, a new focus—"public management"—to replace a discipline they found tired and disconnected from the theoretical challenges facing both theory and practice.

In addition to dodging salvos from political science and public policy, public administration found itself under attack from the practitioner community as well. Public cynicism, rising expectations, more complicated programs, and political crossfire combined to create imposing challenges for government managers. Many of the old theories seemed to fit poorly, and hard-pressed managers scrambled for fresh insights. When they looked to public administration theory, they found few answers that fit their new challenges well. Many managers, in fact, felt strangely alone, jury-rigging tactics to fit their own situations. They had little sense of which managers shared their problems and which solutions fit which problems best. While many public administration scholars rejected the lively arguments in Osborne and Gaebler's *Reinventing Government*, many practitioners eagerly embraced their message of hope. The result was a growing gap between those who *taught* public administration and those who *lived* it.

Private managers and business theorists have seized the intellectual lead in management practice. They invented new ideas like total quality management, customer service, reengineering, and a host of others. Some produced quick results. Others soon failed. Many proved to be fads that ebbed away. Regardless of their ultimate success, however, the energy created a flood of new ideas—and, with the vacuum of engaging new approaches in public administration, the private sector ideas quickly swept through public management as well. The more private sector ideas took hold, the weaker public administration's theoretical claims became. At the same time, many of the private ideas worked no better in government agencies than they had in corporations. That left public administration adrift, without a strong set of its own cutting-edge theories yet saddled with private sector ideas that, at best, were a poor fit.[29] Administrative theory often found itself not one but two bounces behind.

It was scarcely the case that administration had become less important, either in American society or in the academy. If anything, policy goals had become more ambitious, tight budgets made it harder to create new programs, and the execution of existing programs became more complicated. Administration was more, not less, central to the aspirations of citizens and elected officials alike. Public administration, however, was less sure about how to speak to these issues.

In a century, public administration had gone from playing a central role in academic research to being a relatively marginal player. Political science's push toward behavioralism and formal theory left public administration on the sidelines. Practitioners complained that it provided weak guidance to those on government's front lines, and they sought solutions elsewhere. To provide better training—and, they would argue, better research—scholars in the public policy schools put most of public administration aside in favor of new approaches to implementation, leadership, and public management.

It is hard to dispute the sense that the field lost its intellectual footing—that it struggled for respect from those for whom, a century before, it had been vital and central. Indeed, public administration found itself stranded between two problems: it possessed a theoretical tradition that no longer fit reality, and it faced tough new policy problems for which the theory had few good answers. To make matters worse, it was hard to escape a nagging sense that public administration was lagging behind the intellectual curve, with ideas and innovations from the practice of administration far in advance of most of the field's literature. That, in fact, was the underlying message of the StarLink problem.

Public administration scarcely slid away. It continues to claim one of the largest contingents of scholars within the American Political Science Association. The American Society for Public Administration continues to publish a first-rate journal, *Public Administration Review*, and its annual meetings continue to attract hundreds of practitioners and scholars alike. New journals, like the *Journal of Public Administration Research and Theory*, have produced significant theoretical advances. Even a casual look at the academic scholarship shows that the field's intellectual energy and dynamism continues to grow. Intellectual inquiry in public administration, in fact, began an important renaissance as the twentieth century ended.

Along with the rise of the public management movement came greater compartmentalization of the field. Political scientists focused on the study of elected executives, especially presidents, governors, and mayors. Public management scholars focused on appointed executives, like cabinet officials, senior advisers, and other key policymakers. Public administrationists focused on career executives and front-line administrators. The same compartmentalization occurred within the respective disciplinary homes of these scholars: the American Political Science Association for students of the executive; the Association for Public Policy Analysis and Management for students of appointees; and the National Association of Schools of Public Affairs and Administration for students of careerists. As Laurence Lynn Jr. has perceptively noted: "The partitioning of the domain distorts the study of public management and, ultimately, our understanding of it. Scholars in the two largest academic provinces, public policy and public administration, have tended to be—there is no better word for it—provincial. Sociologically they fraternize or collaborate infrequently, and intellectually they cite each other's work irregularly."[30]

This fragmentation has created new boundaries in the field's research and training. Political scientists studying executives have focused on broad historical trends as well as more systematic analysis of presidential decisions. They have not worried much about training. For public management scholars, leadership by political appointees is what counts, so they have concentrated heavily on understanding the personal attributes and skills of effective leaders.[31] Public administration continues doggedly to train thousands of public servants a year, but its struggles to regain a toehold in political science, cope with the rising tide of public management, and compete with the public policy schools have led to genuine soul-searching.[32]

Boundaries and Civic Life

The different approaches to analysis have rarely intersected, and the proponents of each one have stuck to what they knew. In part, this fragmentation reflects the increasing balkanization of academia in general. In part, it also reflects public administration's instincts for self-preservation. Within political science, the pressure for a more formal, more scientific, model-driven approach has become increasingly powerful. In the 1980s and 1990s, public administrationists occupied a stronger place within political science, but they rarely found their way into the field's governing councils. And within public policy schools, public management scholars encountered serious problems as well. Policy analysis, driven by microeconomics and microeconomists, became increasingly influential. The field offered a clear, persuasive theory of decision. It was a theory derived from widely accepted assumptions, like the individual pursuit of self-interest, and it provided a scheme for both understanding and shaping public decisions. While public policy schools accepted the need to offer public management, it was no secret that many microeconomists viewed public management as a theoretically weak sibling to be tolerated out of necessity but not fed with new resources. As the twenty-first century dawned, each of the major approaches to the study of administration was struggling for legitimacy: struggling with each other for intellectual primacy, struggling within their disciplinary homes for respect, and struggling for a foothold in the public mind.

One sign of this tug-of-war was the rise of the "reinventing government" movement. The best-seller by Osborne and Gaebler became a phenomenon—at least within government circles.[33] It provided ten steps for transforming government, making it more innovative and improving its responsiveness. It fueled the Clinton administration's sweeping reform, led by Vice President Al Gore, and a host of similar initiatives throughout the country. The book had an impact on government unlike anything since the Hoover Commission reports of the 1950s. But unlike the studies produced by academic experts during the heyday of orthodox public administration, *Reinventing Government* was the product of a journalist—David Osborne—and a former city manager—Ted Gaebler. Academics had little to do with either the book or its implementation throughout government. When asked about which academics they relied on for insights, though, Elaine Kamarck, Gore's senior domestic policy adviser, paused, thought carefully, and replied, "Well, really—none."[34]

Thus, the study of administration, management, implementation, and public policy became fragmented and neglected, and it no longer had the impact on decisions that had prompted the development first of public administration and later of public management. This intellectual laryngitis could not have come at a worse time. America's effort to reinvent government was in fact part of a global management reform movement that struggled to help government do more with less. That movement had begun a decade earlier, first in New Zealand and then spreading through the United Kingdom, Canada, international organizations like the World Bank, and even into developing nations.[35] Governments were reforming their administrative systems, simultaneously and on a massive scale, unlike anything seen since the turn of the twentieth century. Unlike in the transition to the twentieth century, led by the Progressives and orthodox public administration, public officials were charting their own course into the twenty-first century, largely without intellectual or moral support from academia.

THE FUTURE OF PUBLIC ADMINISTRATION

The challenge facing government administrators in the twenty-first century is that they can do their jobs by the book and still not get the job done. They can issue regulations as required by Congress and discover that the problems they were seeking to prevent occur nonetheless. They can audit taxes only to discover that they upset taxpayers when they get it right and enrage members of Congress when they get it wrong. They can produce programs that work better and cost less only to discover more demands that they work even harder and spend even less. They can run airport security systems by the book only to have terrorists slip by and crash airplanes into office buildings. The challenge is to rewrite the book to get the job done.

Complicating the task is the fact that government administration—and public administrators—have never remained very popular for very long. Even Jesus raised local eyebrows when he chose a local bureaucrat, Matthew the tax collector, as one of his twelve apostles. Administrators tend to make people happy only when they are providing services (and usually only when the level of service is generous and the cost is low). When services are lower than people expect, or if the costs are too high, people complain. In fact, while wandering in the desert, the Israelites constantly grumbled about Moses' leadership. Why had they not remained in Egypt? they asked.

Administrative reformers move between tinkering and transforming institutions fundamentally. In the American political tradition, the transformations occurred with the creation of the executive branch by the founders; with the Progressive period along with its new processes and structures; and with the generation-long changes that followed World War II. As America entered the twenty-first century, another transformation was in the works. It was subtler than its predecessors. The founders and the Progressives each contributed long tracts to provide intellectual leadership for their reforms. By contrast, the twenty-first century transformation emerged from the triumph of bottom-up pragmatism. Front-line administrators struggled to cobble together new tactics for solving the problems they faced, but new problems often surfaced faster than their solutions could be applied. Administrative orthodoxy became increasingly disconnected from administrative realities. The twenty-first century reformers faced nothing less than the intellectual and governmental crises of the Progressives, and they reached to frame solutions that would prove just as enduring.

Food and Drug Administration (FDA) regulators discovered the problem the hard way. For eight years during the 1990s, the FDA had warned pharmaceutical companies not to use products from cattle in countries plagued by mad cow disease, a fatal brain-based illness that spread from cows to humans in some European countries. Despite the warnings, however, the FDA discovered that five drug companies had continued to use bovine-based ingredients from these countries. In some cases, blood might have been used to grow cultures in the lab. In other cases, vaccine manufacturers might have made gelatin from the hooves or bones of cows. The FDA also worried that suspect ingredients might have found their way into supplements for humans that claimed to improve memory or stimulate sexual vitality. Even though scientists calculated that the risk was very small, "it's just insane not to have greater safeguards," one senior FDA official said, especially for the supplements. A wide variety of vaccines, including polio, diphtheria, and tetanus administered to children, were affected.[36]

The FDA had recognized the risks very early. It had warned manufacturers not to use the suspect ingredients. In fact, some companies complained they had a hard time keeping up with the FDA's advisories. The FDA had done its job as it was supposed to—yet problems occurred despite its work. As with the StarLink corn episode, a mismatch occurred between how the government did its work and the problems it was trying to solve. As with StarLink, government managers had made clear what they expected private companies to do, but for a variety of reasons, serious problems developed. Citizens and policymakers alike, in the treasured tradition of holding government managers accountable for the results of government programs, had not reduced their expectations.

Policymakers tend to think of government management as a matter of framing decisions, delegating responsibility to administrators, and holding government administrators accountable for results. That approach, of course, defines two centuries of American democracy as well as the driving theory for bureaucracy in most of the world's governments, democratic or not. Policymakers tend to convey a simple and straightforward view of how the administrative process works—almost like a vending machine, into which they put money and out of which they expect results. When the desired product does not pop out of the machine, their instinct is to summon the machine's builders and mechanics and demand to know why. In the early decades of the Progressive period, this model proved a reasonable fit. The builders could construct a machine that operated through hierarchy and authority; the mechanics could fix problems by adjusting the machine's structure and process.

In the last decades of the twentieth century, however, government's policymakers retained the same expectations, but its machinery worked far differently. More of what government—especially the federal government—did no longer fit the hierarchical model of authority-driven government. As in the StarLink and vaccine cases, government needed close and active partnerships with nongovernmental partners to accomplish its purposes. Government could do its part, but without effective partnerships it could not achieve the results it desired. Because policymakers rarely looked inside the machines responsible for public policy, they had little sense that the insides had so dramatically changed. Their instincts remained the same: When trouble brews, haul the responsible government managers before legislative committees and demand an accounting. In the early decades of the Progressive period, these managers were responsible for the results and could adjust the machines to produce better outcomes. In the last decades of the twentieth century, however, they had control over only some elements of the machine and relied increasingly on their partners to produce results. Thus, not only did administrative theory become more distant from administrative reality; so, too, did political decisions become more distant from the results of those decisions. Policymakers—elected officials—understandably became more critical of the administrative system as the growing complexity of the administrative process frustrated their ability to transform their bold ideas into results.

These problems did not fit well with the approaches of orthodox public administration or its more modern challengers. To an increasing extent, from regulating StarLink corn to finding a way to make government work better while costing less, government officials and academic theorists worked on different planes. The problems are not just the field's struggles to adjust to maturity and some hardening of the intellectual arteries. They are more fundamental and flow from the roots of American approaches to public administration. They flow as well from the mismatch of a system created on principles of control—and an administrative system that can no longer control the problems it was fashioned to solve. Public administration grew on the principle of establishing boundaries, especially around hierarchy and authority. New issues, however, strained the existing boundaries and challenged public administration's theory and practice. The "theory in use," as Schein put it, ran headlong into problems it did not fit.[37]

It is time to reclaim public administration and refashion it for a new century's problems. Its deep historic roots establish the field—and its questions—as among the oldest and most important in human inquiry. Its centrality to politics makes understanding its functions essential to understanding government. Its role in bringing government decisions to life constructs a framework for understanding the relationships between government and society. Public administration is inescapably central to both academic inquiry and government practice. The field's difficulties in cracking both problems are not so much a sign of its intellectual weaknesses—though problems have abounded throughout its history—but, rather, are a reflection of the challenges society must solve.

Reclaiming public administration requires matching these new problems with new approaches. Finding the new approaches requires adapting the great administrative traditions to new issues. It requires understanding that fundamental transformations have occurred in governance, and that these transformations challenge both administration and politics. They pose stark challenges for the administrative traditions as well. Exploring these traditions and transformations, and their implications for the transformation of governance, is the aim of this book.

2 ||| ADMINISTRATIVE TRADITIONS

Public administration—the art of turning big policy ideas into solid results—ranks among the very oldest of intellectual disciplines. Public administrators were managing government programs long before Plato and Aristotle worried about how they *ought* to do so. Aaron Wildavsky's lively study of the Torah powerfully makes the case that Moses needs to be understood not only as a religious leader but also as a political leader, one who struggled to transform the Jews from runaway slaves into a coherent nation.[1] Much of the Bible's first five books is a study of organization, rule-making, and other forms of bureaucratization to ensure that the Israelites walked in God's ways. Caesar's commentary on the Gallic wars describes the administrative and political challenges he faced in subduing the Gauls, conquering Britain, and keeping strong the lines to Rome. Indeed, as long as humans have been writing, they have been writing about administration. It is a safe bet that they were worrying about administration long before they started writing about it.

Administration is about organizing people to do complex jobs. *Public* administration is about organizing people to do complex jobs in pursuit of a broader, government-defined interest. It is, in short, about applying the public interest to the management of work. The thread of public administration has wound through human history from its beginning, as long as difficult social jobs and multiple players have required coordination. In fact, public administration—its study and practice—predates democracy and its debates. Its very centrality, however, has also ensured constant conflict. Public administration is not only about getting government to work well, but it is also about managing—both promoting and limiting—the exercise of governmental power. Through the centuries, despots have sometimes misused that power. Ineffective leaders have produced poorly managed programs, which caused their citizens to suffer. Over the centuries, citizens have frequently disagreed over what government should do—and how. They have wanted a strong and effective government, but they have resisted a government so strong and effective as to threaten their liberty.

Political conflict has thus always been an inevitable component of public administration, around the world and especially within the United States. So too are complaints about administrative mismanagement. Those who think that complaints about waste, fraud, and abuse in government programs are a new phenomenon have only to look at General George Washington's letters from the field. Officers in units at the rear often stopped wagons heading for the front. They unloaded the supplies they needed for their own men and left front-line troops chronically undersupplied. Some of the government's own purchasing agents encouraged defense contractors to bid up prices, which increased their own commissions.[2] The much-repeated news reports of the last decades of the twentieth century—of overpriced screws and toilet seats—have a rich tradition in American political history.

Americans, on the other hand, have always called on government at the first sign of trouble. When nineteenth-century riverboat steamers exploded, citizens demanded that government toughen safety standards. More recently they complain about government spending, but they plead with elected officials not to cut Medicare. They criticize IRS tax collectors, but they insist on good weather forecasts, safe air-traffic control, and effective treatment of anthrax. Since the days of King George III, Americans have loathed public administration because it represents the exercise of governmental power. New innovations constantly create the demand for rules, Deborah Spar argues.[3] As columnist David Wessel explains, it is an eternal cycle. On the other hand, Americans have expected high levels of public service in exchange for the taxes they dutifully paid: "A revolutionary new technology emerges—the compass, the telegraph, the radio, the Internet, the mobile phone, the science of cloning. Pioneers profit, enjoying the gold rush. Pirates arrive. Pioneers seek to protect their property rights. Problems of coordinating emerge. Government looks impotent." Eventually, the demand for rules of the game becomes inescapable and government typically supplies them.[4]

Public administration thus is paradoxical, caught between citizens' antipathy toward government and their insistence on government services and protection. It is an eternal paradox for all public administration, but it is especially deeply rooted in American democracy. In part this is because armed revolt against government power gave birth to the nation. In part, though, it is because fierce individualism has long driven American culture. And in part it is because conflicting expectations between tax collections and government services, between the abuse of government power and the benefits of using it, have been particularly fierce in this nation. Citizens—especially American citizens—resent the exercise of government power almost as much as they rail at its inefficiency.

This paradox also appears in the academic study of public administration. On one hand, there can be no understanding of government and politics without a study of public administration. Ambitious public goals are empty without the capacity to meet them, so it is impossible to study government adequately without also studying how it is administered. On the other hand, the study of public administration has long struggled to find a seat at the academic table. In part, this is because its work is mundane, especially in comparison with more lofty debates about the meaning of human rights and the tragedy of the commons. In part, this is because its work is messy, because it deals with the constant complications of human behavior in complex organizations. In part, this is because the complexity of administrative action creates enormous methodological problems that frustrate the creation of robust theory.

Orthodox public administration conquered these problems long enough to enjoy a truly golden age in the first half of the twentieth century. By the end of the century, however, both the theory and practice of public administration had fallen onto hard times. As an academic field of study, public administration had an uncertain intellectual home. Its students struggled for acceptance within traditional academic disciplines (although by the 1990s public administration began a notable resurgence). In practice, public administrators struggled to cope with rising expectations of performance, declining public enthusiasm for taxes, growing complexity in doing ever-harder things, and increasing calls for fundamental "reinvention" of their operations. From ending welfare as we know it to providing a healthy cradle-to-grave environment, public administrators have found themselves constantly exhorted to do more with less. They have sought more insight from theory just as theory struggled to reestablish its former prominence.

The founders created American constitutional government to limit government's power. Public administration is about making the exercise of government power effective. Governments and citizens everywhere, at all times, have quarreled over the use of such power. While Moses spent forty days on Mount Sinai receiving the Ten Commandments from God, his people broke God's law by building a golden calf to worship. They had found the law too hard to follow, and they rejected

Moses' attempts to enforce it. Of course, these were the same people who had previously welcomed God's power, exercised through Moses, to lead them out of bondage in Egypt.[5] In twenty-first century consultant-speak, Moses' first try to promulgate the commandments failed because of the lack of constituent buy-in. For millennia since then, people have sought the exercise of political power to advance their aims but have struggled against that power when its burdens limited their freedom. Add to this age-old mix America's special antipathy toward government power and its historic devotion to the motto "give me liberty or give me death." The result is the profound tension within the peculiarly American form of public administration.

The tension springs from four fundamentally different intellectual traditions: a *Hamiltonian* tradition that seeks an effective government, that promotes top-down government, and that favors a strong executive; a *Jeffersonian* tradition that celebrates America's agrarian roots, that promotes bottom-up government, and that seeks a weak executive; a *Madisonian* tradition that tries to balance political power among competing forces; and a *Wilsonian* tradition that prefers to concentrate administrative power in hierarchically structured organizations.[6] In this chapter and the next, we examine these traditions.

THE HAMILTONIAN TRADITION

Administrative historians credit Alexander Hamilton as the true founder of the American administrative state.[7] Leonard D. White's sweeping history of American bureaucratic development, for example, concludes simply, "Hamilton was the administrative architect of the new government."[8] While many leaders shaped the new republic, Hamilton's voice was loudest when it came to devising an administrative scheme for the new nation. He made a forceful case for a strong executive—a case, in fact, he often made so strongly that he stirred anger among many political leaders. At the Constitutional Convention in 1787, he made an impassioned case for an elected monarchy. When the delegates rejected that idea, he continued to argue for a strong and powerful national government.

Hamilton built his case on the manifest failures of the Articles of Confederation. The confederation was a masterpiece of over-devolution. The Continental Congress had rejected John Dickinson's plan for a strong national government and in its place constructed a plan to give the states maximum discretion. It took the states years even to ratify these limited rules, and in the meantime, they quarreled over everything from boundaries to commerce. After the victorious new nation won the Revolutionary War, its leaders were embarrassed by their failure to get the states to live up to the terms of the Treaty of Paris, which had ended the war. Some states created their own foreign policies while others disputed who had control of the western lands. The states squabbled over paying for an army, and some leaders worried that this type of spending might open the frontier to poaching by the Spanish and British. By 1787, nearly everyone agreed that the Articles had not worked and that some stronger national government was needed.

The central problems proved the enduring ones: making the national government strong enough to be effective; creating an executive powerful enough to make the government strong; yet preventing a concentration of power that would threaten liberty. Hamilton's was the most important voice in making the case for a strong executive. As the nation's first treasury secretary, he wrote reports on public credit, national banking, and manufacturing that ultimately created the framework for the modern executive branch.

Three basic principles drove Hamilton's views on public administration: independence, power, and responsibility.[9] He recognized that the law, as passed by Congress, bound the executive branch. He also strongly believed that the executive needed independence in implementing the law. Within its own sphere, he said, the Constitution gave the executive freedom of action. In *Federalist* 71, he pointed out that "it is one thing to be subordinate to the laws, and another to be dependent on the legislative body." In essence, Hamilton was making two points. One was the need for separation of powers. A too-powerful legislature could thwart government just as could a too-powerful executive. He embraced the notion of balance to counter this danger. The other was the need for delegation. Once Congress passed a law, Hamilton believed, it needed to allow the executive flexibility in determining how best to administer it. He recognized that one of the most important roles for the executive was concentrating the expertise required to administer the law well. If the executive was to do so, it needed to rely on this expertise as it managed public programs.

From there, Hamilton argued the need for executive power. In perhaps his most-quoted passage, Hamilton contended in *Federalist* 70 that "energy in the executive is a leading character in the definition of good government." The Articles had clearly demonstrated that weak government produced poor policy and worse results. The new Constitution, he believed, required a government that could act decisively over the long haul to pursue the national purpose. Failing to do so—creating a government that was ineffective—was unwise and ultimately threatening to democratic government. If the people were to rule and be served, Hamilton argued, they needed a government strong enough to protect their interests and fulfill their ambitions.

In *Federalist* 70, he outlined what "energy in the executive" required. His analysis was perhaps the first textbook in American public administration, and it set the foundation for public administration orthodoxy that emerged in its fullest form a century later. Energy first requires *unity*, he said. There must be a single top administrator, the president, with clear lines of authority to those charged with managing government programs. This executive must have *duration*. There must be consistency in administration over time. The argument for duration was, of course, a not-so-subtle suggestion that the legislature, driven by popular opinion, could not produce a sufficiently strong foundation for effective government management. Finally, he said, there must be adequate *competence*. The executive needed to have enough expertise to know how to carry policy ideas forward to achieve effective results.

On one level, of course, *Federalist* 70 lays out the central elements of any effective administrative system, elements that the Progressives rediscovered a century later. On another level, however, Hamilton's argument raised many of the same worries that had stalled Dickinson's argument for a strong central government a decade before. A unified, long-term, highly competent executive brought worries about the risks of a too-strong executive—worries that were to surface periodically throughout American history.

Hamilton's third basic principle, in addition to independence and power, was responsibility. This was his argument about keeping administration accountable and preventing it from becoming too powerful. If the executive was to be empowered to act independently of Congress, it would also ultimately be subject to its oversight. For example, Hamilton accepted the power of Congress to investigate the executive departments' actions and to impeach the chief executive. He clearly was not happy about surrendering authority to the legislature; he would surely have preferred a far stronger executive branch and less chance of congressional intrusion into legislative affairs. But he accepted these provisions as central tenets in the new system's balance-of-powers structure.

Hamilton worked hard to translate these principles into practice. As treasury secretary, he led the battle for national assumption of the states' revolutionary war debt and the creation of the First Bank of the United

States. His "Report on Manufactures" laid out his long-term vision for a manufacturing-driven economy, one strongly supported by government. James Madison observed that his views were a coherent package that came together "like the links of a chain." Hamilton biographer Richard Brookhiser explained, "Settling America's debts would fortify its credit; credit would allow manufactures to develop; a diverse and flourishing economy would generate the revenue that would ensure the debt's proper funding."[10] Underlying it all was a grand vision for a brash, ambitious new country. It was a country that would rise above its agrarian foundation to play a major role in global commerce. A strong national government, led by a powerful executive, would support this economic transformation and, in turn, generate jobs and economic growth for citizens.

This ambitious vision caused Hamilton unending problems, especially with the Jeffersonians. In the end, it led to his death in a duel with Jefferson's vice president, Aaron Burr. As Brookhiser puts it, "He had been trading partisan shots with the man who killed him for twelve years before they traded real ones."[11] His personal life, from a high-profile sex scandal to his ongoing feud with the Jeffersonians, was puzzling. But his long shadow across American government is unmistakable. He made the case for strong government, structured with unitary command and managed with skill. He recognized, if reluctantly, the need for a balance of power while asserting the executive's preeminence. He contended that unlike the legislature, with elected representatives moving in and out, the executive needed long-term capacity and leadership. He made the case for a strong executive branch, run from the top down but also responsible to the other branches and, ultimately, to the people. In vision, writing, and practice, Hamilton truly was the father of the modern administrative state.

THE JEFFERSONIAN TRADITION

If Hamilton shaped the American administrative state, Thomas Jefferson cast a vastly longer shadow over the American political tradition. The gentleman farmer from Virginia is well known as author of the Declaration of Independence, president of the United States, and founder of the University of Virginia, as his tombstone says simply. His home, Monticello, is a notable tourist attraction and great architectural achievement—one celebrated, in fact, on the back of the nickel, with Jefferson's own image on the other side. Hamilton trumps Jefferson in the currency department: His image on the ten-dollar bill is better known, by contrast, than Jefferson's on the little-seen two-dollar bill. But Hamilton's statue in front of the Treasury Department pales in comparison with Jefferson's impressive memorial on the shore of Washington's Tidal Basin. Daniel J. Boorstin notes, "The vitality of Thomas Jefferson is one of the striking features of modern American history. He always has something to say to us, and the nation always seems ready to listen."[12]

On government, Jefferson's view was simple: It was not, according to Boorstin, "the expression of political theory, but the largely unreflective answer of healthy men to the threat of tyranny."[13] The threat of abuse of power—especially executive power—hung heavy over Jefferson. Unlike Hamilton's early background in commerce and accounting, Jefferson came of age as a gentleman farmer in Virginia. He drew his strength from the love of the land. The British crown was a very long way from his mountaintop house. The exercise of its power had perennially poached on his freedom, and he was determined that the new American nation would never again risk losing liberty. His Declaration of Independence is a ringing expression of his rejection of tyranny.

When the new Constitution replaced the Articles of Confederation, Jefferson joined George Washington's cabinet as secretary of state. His relationship with treasury secretary Hamilton was constantly tumultuous. They engaged in a long-running policy feud over the question of federal power. For Jefferson, power came from the land and from the people. Hamilton distrusted popular rule out of his fear that it would retard commerce and industry. When Hamilton proposed the creation of a national bank, Jefferson fought it thinking that the bank would encourage speculation and undermine agriculture. Hamilton believed the bank would provide the federal government with the power it needed. Jefferson was a staunch advocate of the limitations on federal power embodied in the Tenth Amendment. The differences helped spawn the first American political parties, Hamilton's Federalists and Jefferson's Democratic-Republicans. Yet despite their differences and because Hamilton despised Aaron Burr, Hamilton supported Jefferson in the 1800 presidential campaign.

Jefferson and Hamilton could not have been more different. If Hamilton celebrated the nation's commercial, manufacturing, and banking future, Jefferson venerated the nation's agrarian roots. Where Hamilton argued vigorously for a strong national government with a powerful executive and a limited citizen role, Jefferson believed in local government, a strong legislature, and popular control. Jefferson argued for limited government, while Hamilton pursued an energetic government. Their philosophical disagreements erupted over the Bank of the United States and continued for more than a decade until Hamilton's death.[14]

Jefferson's almost religious belief in limited government has resonated throughout American history. His instinct, especially as captured in his early writings, was to keep as much power in the people's hands as possible. If government needed to exercise power, it ought to be state and local governments, he argued, not the federal government. And if the federal government needed to exercise power, Congress, with its roots in popular will, ought to be supreme. Jefferson championed federalism because it established the predominance of state governments in the American system. He was a champion of the separation of powers because it provided checks on executive functions. Like many of the founders, he worried constantly that monarchy might reassert itself, and he saw a monarchist threat in Hamilton's incessant arguments for an energetic executive. The foundation of society, he believed, ought to be individual liberty. Government's foremost responsibility was to promote that liberty. Accountability in the system had to come from the bottom up.

In practice, however, Jefferson's philosophical approach did not much inform his approach to public administration. Jefferson had a "speculative rather than an administrative mind," Leonard D. White concluded. In fact, he writes, "Jefferson was not interested . . . in the normal process of day-by-day administration." Jefferson, in his own words, believed "there are no mysteries in it." It simply calls for "common sense and honest intentions." He compared government administration to running a farm, and "we all know that a farm, however large, is not more difficult to direct than a garden, and does not call for more attention or skill." White was incredulous and argued that such a statement could scarcely have been made by anyone familiar with the difficulties of keeping even a modest government running.[15] The model fit neither practical reality nor Jefferson's own approach to the presidency. He feared power, but "he nevertheless found himself forced to exercise it ruthlessly," White noted. "His preferences were frustrated by circumstances that compelled him to abandon his own theories."[16] He enforced the embargo extending the Alien and Sedition Acts. He negotiated the purchase of Louisiana, whose constitutionality was questioned, and he dispatched Lewis and Clark to survey that vast expansion of American territory. As a philosopher, Jefferson believed in a weak government and in strong individual liberty. As president, however, he was truly Hamiltonian in supporting a strong and energetic presidency.

These conflicts—between Jefferson and Hamilton as political philosophers, and between Jefferson the philosopher and Jefferson the president—have long engaged historians. Over time, however, the Hamiltonian foundations of Jefferson's presidency have largely been forgotten. A romantic reading of his intellectual tradition, of his reverence for liberty, and his life as the gentleman farmer of Monticello have more powerfully defined the Jeffersonian tradition. His almost theological arguments for limited government have echoed in conservative minds throughout the centuries. These themes drove the South's revolt against Lincoln during the Civil War as much as they did the conservative congressional Republicans' short-lived Contract with America during the 1990s. In these cases, as in Jefferson's life, the romantic themes have always collided with pragmatic realities. The North bitterly fought to preserve the Union in the 1860s, and in the 1990s Americans discovered that they did not really want the more limited government that the congressional Republicans promised. One can debate—endlessly—the struggles between Jefferson's ideas and actions. One can also debate how to factor his thoughts into the quest to make government, whatever its size and reach, truly effective. Jefferson's paradoxical life helps underline two big quandaries—what government *ought to do* and *how best to do it.* But throughout the ensuing debates, Jefferson's ideas have held sway. His ideas have made a lasting case for limiting government power, for keeping governmental power more in the hands of the legislature than in the administration, and for maximizing individual liberty. They have defined a counterpoint to Hamilton's argument for a powerful executive branch.

THE MADISONIAN TRADITION

James Madison's work defines a third American administrative tradition. It is, in fact, not so much a theory of administration as a more general approach to politics in America's republican government. Madison was the architect of America's balance-of-power system and thus a designer of the tactics that Americans have used for centuries to keep an uneasy peace between the conflicting Hamiltonian and Jeffersonian forces. Madison's influence on the Constitution is unquestioned. The notes he kept on the Constitutional Convention's deliberations remain the best record of the debate. His was the most influential voice in crafting the Constitution and the strongest voice for developing the separation of powers. Later, he joined with Hamilton and John Jay to write the *Federalist Papers*, but his contributions are perhaps the best known. In particular, *Federalist* 10 is the definitive explanation of the linkage of government power and economic power. Economic differences among the states could breed conflict. A strong, effective, well-balanced national government, on the other hand, could bring stability and prosperity.

Like Jefferson, he differed with Hamilton over just the how strong the executive ought to be. But unlike Jefferson, whose more doctrinaire position held that power ought to be left in the hands of the people and the local governments, Madison developed a subtler approach that hinged on balancing power among the major players. He worried about the "mischiefs of faction" and the risks that economic and political competition could undermine both social order and the new federal government. He also worried about the risk that a too-strong government could promote tyranny. To resolve these problems, he hewed a pragmatic middle position between Hamilton and Jefferson. The new system was a larger and more complex republic than thinkers had often considered wise, but he concluded that the system offered more internal balance, more diverse institutional roles, and more factions—all the better to balance the ambitions of any faction and block its ability to exercise monarchical power.[17]

In *Federalist* 51, Madison argued, "It is evident that each department [that is, branch of government] ought to have a will of its own." To prevent "a gradual concentration of the several powers in the same department," he contended that the key lies in "giving to those who administer each department, the necessary constitutional means, and personal motives, to resist encroachments of the others. The provision for defense must in this, as in other cases, be made commensurate to the danger of attack. Ambition must be made to counteract ambition." Then comes the most famous piece of *The Federalist:* "If men were angels, no government would be necessary. If angels were to govern men, neither external nor internal controls on government would be necessary. In framing a government which is to be administered by men over men, the great difficulty lies in this: You must first enable the government to control the governed; and in the next place, oblige it to control itself." The legislature, he argued, ought to predominate in a republican government. To prevent legislative tyranny, legislative power was divided between two houses. His biggest worry, however, which he shared with most of the founders, was preventing renewed executive tyranny. Separating government powers provided dual checks, through the legislative and judicial branches, on executive power.

In fact, of course, the founders never fully subscribed to a complete separation of powers among the branches. For them, it was more a matter of blending powers. The president can veto acts of Congress, Congress can impeach and remove a president, the president appoints Supreme Court justices, and Congress confirms them. In *Federalist* 48, Madison pointed to the "partial mixture" of powers as a safeguard—indeed, an enhancement—of republican government.[18] The inherent messiness of the American constitutional system prevented the abuse of power. That also made its effective exercise difficult, as Hamilton often later pointed out. But it provided the safeguards for which a new nation yearned.

Madison devoted most of his contributions to *The Federalist* to reassuring his fellow citizens that the new Constitution did not create a government so strong as to threaten their liberty. He pointed to the risks that continuing the Articles of Confederation would bring, and he energetically led the charge for the new form of government. Like Jefferson, however, he worked to protect liberty by ensuring that no part of this new government became too powerful. He saw great virtue in federalism, especially as stated in the Tenth Amendment, which reserved powers to the states. Most of all, Madison devised an approach to government founded on a separation—actually a blending—of powers. Administration and bureaucracy did not preoccupy him. Like Jefferson, he did not focus heavily on the execution of government powers but worried more about government's overall architecture.

Like Jefferson, Madison had bitterly fought Hamilton's plans for a strong national government. In part, as with Jefferson, his differences lay along North-South lines, with Hamilton championing commerce and the two Virginians, Jefferson and Madison, promoting agrarian interests. He opposed Hamilton's proposal for federal assumption of state debts. Virginia had retired most of its debt, but Hamilton's New York had not. He objected to Hamilton's plans for a new tariff and a national bank. By the end of his presidency, however, Madison, like Jefferson, had become more Hamiltonian. He came to support both the national bank and a tariff to protect American industries. In the broad sweep of American political thought, however, Madison's separation-of-powers ideas have had much more influence than his more pragmatic adaptation of Hamilton's views to the presidency.

Unlike Hamilton, who had an administration-based view of government, Madison's ideas were fundamentally political. The basic political features of the system—the institutions created to exercise government power and how to balance power among them—were for Madison its most important elements. Thus, he did not develop an explicit theory of administration. Rather, he built a political theory in which administration was subservient, in practical operation and in theoretical understanding, to political power. He was a political scientist to Hamilton's public administrationist and Jefferson's political theorist.

THE WILSONIAN TRADITION

The fourth major theme of American administrative thought did not develop until more than two generations later. Toward the end of the nineteenth century, American government had suffered embarrassing breakdowns. Development of the West presented new opportunities for corruption, and greedy developers eagerly took advantage. Stunning new technologies, from electric lights to the telegraph and telephone, offered new conveniences, but market competition left some areas unserved and other areas tangled with spaghetti-like masses of wires. Corporate trusts brought huge concentrations of private power and new threats to public well-being.

In response, a new political movement, Progressivism, sprang up with a twin messages: Government had a positive role to play in shaping, balancing, and controlling corporate power; to play that role, government needed to be strong enough to be effective. In many ways, the Progressives were children of Hamilton. It had taken a century for Hamilton's vision of a mercantile America to emerge. When it did mature, however, it came with a concentration of power and threat to republican government that Hamilton had not anticipated.

Unlike the theorists of a century before, the Progressives had a tightly integrated approach to the relationship between political and administrative power. With the American Revolution a distant memory of more than a century before, the specter of George III was not so frightening. But with the emergence of corporate monopolies, the threats of unfettered market competition loomed large indeed. In the face of those monopolies, the Progressives argued the need for a stronger government, both to rein in the abuses of corporate power and to bring Americans a better life: quicker transportation, better communication, protection from an ever-more-dizzying collection of external threats. With American "manifest destiny" secure—with the United States stretching from the Atlantic to the Pacific Oceans—the next step lay in developing the land between. That meant a government that could secure a continental railroad, make credit available for citizens who needed to borrow for their businesses, and redefine the historic commitment to the common welfare.

The Progressives saw a strong government as a balance to the corporate world and as the natural next step to prosperity. They worried, however, that building a stronger government would open a new route for private power to capture control of the public agenda. Political machines celebrated their invention of "honest graft" and profoundly dishonest tactics for gaining leverage over municipal governments. If government was to be stronger, the Progressives needed to keep it from being captured by narrow interests. They found themselves squarely in the middle of the same debate that had preoccupied the founders. This time, however, instead of fears that a monarchist administration might dominate American government, the Progressives worried that king-like corporate titans and corruption might control the political system. They saw a stronger, better-organized government—and a more effective public administration—as essential to a new balance of political power.

A stronger federal government, however, raised the familiar problem of how to keep a more powerful government from undermining democratic government. In response to this issue, a thirty-one-year-old professor at Princeton University, Woodrow Wilson, wrote an article suggesting how this balance ought to be struck. The author was not yet famous and the 1887 article, "The Study of Administration," was not much read. Only when Leonard D. White's famous 1950 textbook discussed it extensively did scholars pay it serious attention.[19] Since then, however, Wilson's article has become a classic as the first American statement of modern public administration. Scholars have celebrated his argument about the relationship between political institutions and public administration. "It is the object of administrative study," he wrote, "to discover, first, what government can properly and successfully do, and, secondly, how it can do these proper things with the utmost efficiency and at the least possible cost either of money or of energy."[20] Determining what government could do best and how it could best do it were the central questions for the Progressives' approach to government.

Wilson began his article by noting that "at the same time that the functions of government are every day becoming more complex and difficult, they are also vastly multiplying in number."[21] As he famously pointed out, "It is getting harder to *run* a constitution than to frame one."[22] That is why, Wilson argued, "there should be a science of administration which shall seek to straighten the paths of government, to make its business less unbusinesslike, to strengthen and purify its organization, and to crown its duties with dutifulness."[23]

American government, he suggested, had grown quickly, like a child who had become taller but more awkward at the same time. For clues about how to manage a modern state effectively, Wilson looked to Europe, especially the Prussians and French. The English and Americans, by contrast, had "long and successfully studied the art of curbing executive power to the constant neglect of perfecting executive methods." The concern had been far more with making government "just and moderate" than "well-ordered and effective."[24] Wilson sought to marry the Anglo-American strategies for controlling administrative power with Franco-Prussian strategies for enhancing it.

The lesson that Wilson drew from these other nations was that "the field of administration is a field of business . . . removed from the hurry and strife of politics."[25] To be sure, the great truths that drive the political process lie at the core of administration as well. But Wilson believed that "administration lies outside the proper sphere of *politics.* Administrative questions are not political questions. Although politics sets the tasks for administration, it should be not suffered to manipulate its offices." His evidence? Wilson pointed to the Germans, for example, who had made such a separation the bedrock of an effective administrative system.[26] That did not mean Wilson wanted to make the American system more German, or more like any other system dominated by monarchist traditions. "If I see a murderous fellow sharpening a knife cleverly, I can borrow his way of sharpening the knife without borrowing his probable intent to commit murder with it." He concluded that we could learn from others how to administer our own system more effectively without "getting any of their diseases into our veins."[27]

Wilson's formulation, especially his argument about separating administration and politics, has defined the central battle of modern public administration. He argued that public administration could be made stronger and more effective by borrowing the best practices from administrators around the world. It could be made more accountable by separating administration from politics, empowering administration to follow political direction, and making administrators ultimately responsible to policymakers. In making this argument, he sought to resolve the field's eternal dilemma. Separating administration from politics could free administrators from political interference in their work and thus enhance administrative efficiency. Separating politics from administration could strengthen the ability of elected officials to oversee administration and thus enhance accountability.

Orthodox public administrationists seized on Wilson's formulation. Wilson's argument made the case for a separate field of study in public administration and suggested, at least implicitly, a methodology. It was one that fit neatly into the orthodoxy that had emerged in the first half of the twentieth century: focus on the process and structure of government organizations; explore strategies to make them more efficient; keep them separate from political institutions to ensure their effectiveness; but ultimately hold them accountable to elected officials for their exercise of power. As powerful as some public administrationists found the argument, many political scientists argued it was hopelessly naive to pretend that one could actually separate administration from politics. If public administrationists used Wilson's article as a manifesto to define the field, many political scientists seized on it as a justification for dismissing it. The emerging public policy schools likewise saw in Wilson's article—and the field's embrace of it—a validation of their efforts to invent a new approach. To his critics, Wilson neither got to the core of effective program implementation nor made the critical linkages to bureaucratic politics.

Wilson's small article was barely read for sixty years, but it emerged in the intellectual debates just as critical boundaries were beginning to form. If his article did not broadly shape the Progressive tradition, it certainly captured its most important administrative ideas. It explained the Progressives' efforts to strengthen bureaucracy without threatening democracy. At the same time, it clearly defined the target at which political scientists and public policy scholars shot when they took aim at the field.

What should we make of Wilson's politics-administration separation? Even a casual observer of politics and administration would quickly reject the idea that the two are truly separate. A senior official in a major American city once told me that his department had a special plan to help Democrats in case of a major snowstorm on election day: city plows went first to the wards that had the highest percentage of Democratic voters to make sure they made it to the polls. There can be no clearer case of administration having political impact—or of political incentives shaping administrative decisions.

Moreover, the administration of law inevitably involves the exercise of discretion. Exercising discretion inevitably requires value choices, and value choices are without doubt political decisions. No law can ever detail all the decisions that administrators on the front lines must make, and sometimes even the smallest of front-line decisions can have great political implications. Witness the election-day snow removal plan: which streets get plowed first can influence which voters end up at the polls. Other administrative decisions, from how to translate tax legislation into regulations or which road proposals to fund, involve both discretion and value choices. For many observers, therefore, Wilson's argument was not only naive, but it hid the implicit (or explicit) political judgments made by administrators and limited the ability of elected officials to hold them accountable for the exercise of discretion.

Wilson's argument, actually, was much more fundamental. Like other Progressives, he believed that government needed to play an important role in a society that was becoming ever more complex. To play that role, public administration needed to be strong and effective. He argued that Americans, preoccupied with high-profile constitutional issues, had paid far too little attention to figuring out how to *run* their constitution, especially by comparison with many European nations. He believed that Americans could learn important lessons from the European experience while maintaining American democratic principles. Perhaps most important, he believed that effective democracy required competent, politically impartial administrators, who could work free from political interference.

Wilson was scarcely naive. Nor was he alone in asserting the politics-administration dichotomy. Indeed, the American Political Science Association's first president, Frank Goodnow, wrote a book in 1900 that made the same argument.[28] Wilson, Goodnow, and their colleagues grew out of a tradition in which public administration had received relatively little attention, either from elected officials or from scholars. New social problems were emerging that the existing administrative system could not solve effectively. Special interests were infiltrating government administration and were threatening to steer government action to private, not public, interests. Their argument was not so much to wring politics from the study or practice of administration, though. Wilson quite explicitly recognized the role of constitutional politics in the administrative system, and he had earlier written a more famous work, titled *Congressional Government.* For Wilson, Congress was "the central and predominant power of the system."[29] His argument, rather, was that, to be effective, administration had to be protected from political interference. Just *how* that ought to be done remained a constant dispute. In fact, it ultimately caused a fundamental schism between public administration and the rest of political science and a break between the field of public administration and the public policy community.

Wilson's work nevertheless was—and continues to be—an enormous influence on American public administration. It was fully compatible with Madison's separation-of-powers argument, but unlike Madison's approach it had an explicit role for administration. Like Jefferson, he recognized the importance of responsiveness and local governance, but Wilson shared with Hamilton a strong belief in effective administrative power. Wilson had much in common with Hamilton, but he came to the issue with less commitment to *national* power and with the more subtle sense of government's complexity that a century of experience helped nurture. Like Hamilton, he laid an important cornerstone in the intellectual construct of public administration.[30]

IRRECONCILABLE DIFFERENCES

These four traditions represent the basic approaches that have framed both the study and practice of American public administration since the beginning of the twentieth century. Over time, these traditions have risen and fallen in importance and emphasis. Indeed, the history of American public administration has identified three recurring themes. First, at the core of public administration rests important and enduring ideas. Second, these ideas push both theory and practice in opposite directions. Third, the balance among these ideas has shifted over time, so no approach has defined orthodoxy for long. It is scarcely surprising, then, that the field of public administration has always found itself amidst political conflict and intellectual tumult. The conflicts center in part on whether the bureaucracy is seen, by both practitioners and scholars, as the primary actor or a supporting cast member in public affairs. They focus as well on whether the approach to the bureaucracy presumes a relatively strong executive insisting on top-down accountability, or whether the approach builds accountability from the people—from the bottom up—and presumes a weaker executive. Hamilton believed in a strong executive managing from the top down; Jefferson argued for a weak executive held accountable from the bottom up. Madison's balance-of-powers model made the executive just one of the players, and the bureaucracy did not play a role; Wilson concentrated on the role of the permanent bureaucracy in making the case for the separation of policy and administration. Jefferson and Madison shared their concern over the broad architecture of the American system, while

TABLE 2-1 ***Administrative Ideas in the American Political Tradition***

	Wilsonian *Bureaucracy-centered*	***Madisonian*** *Balance-of-power-centered*
Hamiltonian *Strong-executive/ Top-down*	• Centered on executive • Principle: strong executive function • Top-down accountability • Hierarchical authority	• Centered on non-bureaucratic institutions • Principle: separation of powers • Focus on political power • Top-down accountability
Jeffersonian *Weak-executive/ Bottom-up*	• Centered on local control • Principle: weak executive with devolved power • Bottom-up accountability • Responsiveness to citizens	• Centered on non-bureaucratic institutions • Principle: federalism • Focus on local control • Bottom-up responsiveness

Hamilton and Wilson concentrated on the mechanisms of administrative action.

As table 2-1 shows, these four traditions produced radically different, and fundamentally irreconcilable, administrative traditions. These traditions, in turn, have fueled centuries of debate and conflict in American public administration. Where should power be centered? How should executive power be balanced with other institutions? How should accountability work? The conflicting traditions have resulted in very different answers to these questions.

Americans have struggled for more than two hundred years to resolve these differences—and they have proven singularly unsuccessful in doing so. The conflicts are likely to continue as long as American democracy does because the American approach to bureaucracy embodies two important sets of tradeoffs: about how bureaucracy ought to work—from the bottom up or from the top down; and how bureaucracy ought to be integrated into American republican government—whether bureaucracy is central or peripheral. These issues shape the arguments in the chapters to come. In the meantime, three questions frame the conflict.

Administration and Hierarchy

First, *what is the role of hierarchy in public administration?* Strong bureaucracies have always built on strong hierarchies. They provide a highly organized way of completing complex tasks—structured along a chain of command and controlled by authority. Ancient Rome's conquest of much of the Western world, and its ability to maintain control for centuries, hinged on the strength of its military power and the hierarchical structure that directed it. The Roman centurion, for example, was the linchpin of the imperial army, the critical "middle management" man in charge of 100 soldiers. The Middle Ages that followed suffered, at least in part, because that powerful arrangement disintegrated.

Since the earliest days, American public administration has always had a hierarchical structure. The structure, moreover, has built primarily on functionally organized departments—Departments of State, Treasury, War, and Post Office, with others added in the centuries since the Washington administration. As the government grew, the practice of organizing by function and managing through hierarchy became strongly entrenched. In the early years of the twentieth century, however, this foundation came under assault. Social psychologists conducted experiments that suggested hierarchy was not the only—or even the most important—tool to use in shaping administrative action. For example, researchers at Western Electric's Hawthorne plant found in the late 1920s that behavioral incentives could radically affect productivity.[31] The Hawthorne experiments stunned managers because they established, for the first time, the case for managing complex organizations through mechanisms other than hierarchical authority. New government programs further eroded the roles of authority and hierarchy as the basic building blocks. The pragmatic demands for fighting World War II led the federal government to create GOCOs—government owned, contractor operated facilities—to manufacture weapons. The GOCO was an administrative hybrid, with the government producing goods and services through an indirect contractor network.

In the decades that followed the war, the pattern continued. In the 1950s, the federal government managed urban renewal through grants to local governments and built the Interstate Highway System through grants to state governments. It fought much of the 1960s War on Poverty through grants to local governments that ultimately went to nongovernmental organizations, like neighborhood associations. Private contractors managed most of the Medicare and Medicaid programs, while the 1970s federal effort to restore the environment operated largely through contractors and the states. In the 1990s, the federal government "ended welfare as we know it" by giving the job to the states. In fact, the federal government managed every major post–

World War II policy initiative through nonhierarchical, nonauthority-based strategies. To a lesser but still substantial degree, this movement toward using indirect tools of government spilled over into state and local governments as well.[32]

These trends sharpened a tough problem: How could its hierarchically structured, authority-managed agencies effectively manage increasingly nonhierarchical, nonauthority-based administrative systems? Hierarchy and authority worked, more or less well, in an era in which the government produced most of its goods and services itself. As government employed more indirect tools, however, the management strains grew. So, too, did the challenge to ensuring the accountability of administration.

Politics and Administration

Second, *what is the linkage between politics and public administration?* Wilson's article is most famous for framing the battle lines. The question, however, dates back to Hamilton's battles with the Jeffersonians, who quarreled for decades over the proper spheres of administrative and political power. If administration is central to government, as Wilson argued in the less-cited portion of his famous paper, neither political science nor public administration can be complete without embracing the other. At least since World War II, however, political science and public administration have been on uneasy terms with each other. The public policy schools, increasingly grounded in microeconomics and policy analysis, have grown uneasy with politics. Are politics and administration truly inseparable? If so, how have analysts managed so successfully to separate them? And if they are to be joined, what linkages make the most analytical and practical sense?

The reform tradition in American politics, always bubbling but especially strong in the Progressive period, has long sought to prevent political interference in administration. Toward the end of the twentieth century, reformers led by the "reinventing government" movement sought to empower bureaucrats and, thus, to give administrators more political discretion. The field's efforts to provide prescriptions have often been ignored by politicians, while politicians have frequently criticized administrators for their inability to deliver results. Some academics, in their search for stronger predictive theory, have moved further from practical prescriptions. Other academics see little need for theoretical predictions from which pragmatic implications have been wrung. Understanding these linkages remains one of public administration's toughest problems.

Administration and the People

Third, *what is the connection between public administration and citizens?* Evidence abounds that public trust and confidence in government declined significantly in the last half of the twentieth century. In 1964, three-fourths of Americans said that they trusted government to do the right thing. By the end of the twentieth century, the number dropped to one-fourth. Cultural and political conflicts, worsened by a cynical news media, had deepened public cynicism and reduced trust.[33] Most Americans were frustrated with government, especially with its elected officials. Citizens in 1998, for example, trusted federal workers more than elected officials to do the right thing (by a margin of 67 percent to 16 percent). More citizens held a favorable view of government workers than in the past—69 percent favorable in 1998, compared with 55 percent in 1981. Nevertheless, the eroding public trust in government corroded government's ability to perform—and performance problems undermined public confidence.[34] Meanwhile, Robert D. Putnam wrote tellingly of the decline of "social capital" and community in American society.[35] How, he asked, could we rebuild the bonds between citizens and social organizations, especially government?

The trust-in-government scores shot upward in the aftermath of the September 11, 2001, terrorist attacks. Of those surveyed, 64 percent trusted the government in Washington to do what was right, three times the proportion in a 1994 poll.[36] In their heroic response to the attacks, firefighters and police officers renewed Americans' faith in at least some government workers. Analysts carefully watched the surveys to determine whether this marked the end of a decades-long slide in public trust of government or a short-lived response to the tragedy. Either way, the polls made clear, popular opinion about government was closely tied to the public's sense of how government, pragmatically and effectively, helps citizens solve problems.

ADMINISTRATION AND POLITICS

In its early years of the twentieth century, public administration sought strength by insulating itself from politics. Indeed, its leaders presented a strong public administration as a defense from corruptions of political power. By the end of the century, political problems had soiled administration along with the rest of the American political system. Politicians have discovered great success in mounting antigovernment (read: antibureaucracy) campaigns. Reformers tried to "reinvent" bureaucracy, but they did so with unorthodox strategies and tactics. The century began and ended with a quarrelsome linkage between administration and politics, with deep uncertainty about whether both were stronger or weaker if tied together theoretically and pragmatically. Critics and analysts alike were uncertain about how administrative pathologies might have weakened public trust in politics—and how the behavior of political institutions might spawn administrative problems.

These issues are both profound and inescapable, for they lie rooted in the enduring tradeoffs of the American political traditions. The tensions have only been worsened by new trends, discussed in the next chapter, that layer new dilemmas on top of old ones. The connection between politics and administration, on one level, is clear. Without an adequate administrative foundation, bold policy ideas will fail in execution, or at least will stumble erratically in ways that further erode the public's trust in government. Theories about political relationships and institutions will be fatally flawed without an understanding of how administration shapes political possibilities and results. Moreover, in ways that even elected officials often fail to appreciate, changes in administration are redefining fundamental political relationships: between and among nation states, between the national and state and local governments; and between government and the private and nonprofit sectors.

Nevertheless, both academics and politicians have lurched ahead without adequately thinking through these connections. Elected officials—and especially candidates for elected office—launch bold policy proposals without thinking through how they will carry them out. The mass media rarely hold them to account for the mismatch of their ambitions and their results, and when problems occur, they blame the administrative machinery instead of its policy designers.

Many of the key players work from a vending-machine model of public policy. They frame big ideas. They then assume that they can carry them out by putting money into the top of the machine and waiting for services to pop out the bottom. The failure of this model in describing either how public administration *does* or *should* operate helps explain the mismatch between public problems and the administration we use to solve them.

That is why reclaiming public administration is so essential. Without a theory of administration that is a theory of politics, and a theory of politics that is informed by administration, the basic connection between citizens and their government simply cannot be understood. Meeting that challenge means grappling with the three central linkages—of administration with hierarchy, politics, and citizens. It also means understanding the fundamental transformation that occurred in governance at the end of the twentieth century and how that transformation undermined the sense of boundaries that had helped sustain public administration for a century. We turn to that puzzle next.

3 ||| ADMINISTRATIVE DILEMMAS

The four enduring traditions of public administration paint a rich tableau against which Americans have developed their dreams. The traditions, however, have provided weak guidance about just *how* to fulfill those dreams. Compared with some other social science theories, theories of public administration have often been lacking. Microeconomics, for example, holds an explicit theory of efficiency built on markets and how individuals use markets to maximize their preferences (although economist Arthur Okun warns that conflicting values about efficiency and equality plague microeconomics more than its advocates typically admit).[1] The pursuit of efficiency in microeconomics leads to a single best approach for problem-solving.

By contrast, public administration builds on recurring tradeoffs: responsiveness and efficiency; centralization and decentralization; strong executives and separation of powers; federal control and federalism. Resolving those tradeoffs in the short run has always been difficult; settling them permanently has been impossible. America's leaders and citizens have traditionally wanted both responsiveness and efficiency, both centralization and decentralization, and so on—and they have wanted different measures of each at different times. While microeconomics built its theory on maximizing one value—efficiency—public administration has grown up struggling with multiple and conflicting values. There is no prospect that either theorists or politicians will find an enduring balance among these values any time soon, so there is little hope that public administration will ever be able to match the theoretical precision of microeconomics. The inherent conflicts buried deep in these traditions have long posed big problems for theorists and practitioners alike: finding short-term accommodations among the four traditions; developing theoretical insights to bring clarity to the complexity of administrative action; and offering practical guidance to improve how government works.

NEW TRENDS IN OLD TRADITIONS

The field's four major intellectual traditions each built on basic assumptions about how public administration can pursue efficiency in a democratic republic. Hamilton's case for a strong executive assumed that executives could command without threatening accountability. Jefferson's argument for responsive local government assumed that the governments could be insulated from large-scale pressures. Madison's balance-of-power proposition assumed that the delicate political balance would produce workable policy, while Wilson's case for accountability rested on an assumption of a bureaucracy shaped by hierarchical authority. The traditions still powerfully shape the way Americans think about and act upon American public administration. Within each of these traditions, however, new challenges have arisen that pose fundamental problems.

The Wilsonian Dilemma

Wilson's approach to public administration laid out a neat strategy for organizing administrative work: elected officials defined policy and delegated the details to top-level administrators; these administrators worked within a hierarchy to organize the work; and authority within the hierarchy ensured that the exercise of administrative discretion remained consistent with policymakers' goals. His theory guided public administration for a century. He intended it as a mechanism for promoting both efficiency (by building hierarchies and controlling them through authority) and accountability (by separating elected officials who make policy from administrators who carry it out). Even though analysts have long attacked this approach as a thin reed on which to build theory or practice, Wilson's ideas have dominated the public administration community.

In the last third of the twentieth century, however, government began relying on new tools, especially grants, contracts, and loans, which undermined Wilson's theory.[2] Unlike direct delivery of services by government bureaucracies, these tools operated more through incentives and partnerships with nongovernmental players than through governmental management with hierarchical authority. With the erosion of traditional tactics, government managers had to devise new mechanisms to ensure effectiveness and accountability. As Lester M. Salamon put it, "Instead of the centralized hierarchical agencies delivering standardized services that is caricatured in much of the current reform literature and most of our political rhetoric, what exists in most spheres of policy is a dense mosaic of policy tools, many of them placing public agencies in complex, interdependent relationships with a host of third-party partners."[3] For example, one study of human service programs in sixteen communities revealed that government itself delivered only 40 percent of public programs in 1982. As partnerships for welfare and other social service programs spread in the 1990s, the government's direct service provision shrank further. The more such indirect tools rose in importance, the less traditional theory provided guidance for managing the already problematic traditions of public administration. Such tools were often more complex to manage, and government found itself struggling to manage them without the reassuring intellectual framework that a century of administrative theory had provided for directly managed programs.

Getting a clear fix on the scale of this movement is difficult because government keeps its books according to how much it spends, not who does its work. Moreover, the full financial implications of some indirect tools, like loan and tax programs, do not show up in standard budget scorekeeping. In fact, that is one of the political attractions of these new tools. Policymakers can expand government programs without their full cost appearing in the budget. Nevertheless, by the end of the twentieth century, indirect tools had become the dominant form of federal administrative action. In 1999, Lester M. Salamon analyzed the full range of federal activity that year, including spending, loan, insurance, and regulatory programs. He estimated that at least 83 percent of all federal financial activity occurred using indirect tools like contracts, grants, loans, and regulation. Of the 17 percent of the federal government's remaining financial activity, 9 percent went for income support (mostly for Social Security) and 4 percent went for interest on the debt (for payments to individuals and organizations holding federal securities). That left only about 3 percent of all federal financial activity for goods and services, from air traffic control to management of the national parks, that the federal government administered itself.[4] In the last two decades of the twentieth century, federal spending through indirect methods has increased while federal spending through direct provision of goods and services has shrunk—probably by half.[5] Direct spending for goods and services at the state and local levels is greater, since a much larger share of their budgets goes for police, fire, emergency, and education services, all of which are provided by government employees. However, even in local government, contracting out has grown significantly, especially for road construction and maintenance, social services, and support services.

Wilson's administrative tradition was founded on the direct government administration of public services. The government's changing strategies and tactics, therefore, pushed the actual management of public programs out of sync with the theories that had long guided them. The sources of this trend vary greatly. Ideologues have argued that shifting service provision from government to the private sector would improve efficiency and reduce the incentives for an ever-burgeoning government. Pragmatists have argued the need for greater flexibility in service delivery.[6]

But beyond its roots, three things are clear. First, in many ways, there is nothing new here. Governments have relied on contractors for millennia. Indeed, the Roman legions relied on their own defense contractors as they conquered most of the land within reach. The "ideal type" of direct government administration has never really described the full range of scope of governmental activity.

Second, even though governments have always relied on contractors, the scope and scale of this contracting out increased significantly in American government toward the end of the twentieth century. The balance between indirect and direct governmental tools significantly shifted, and American governments showed no signs that the trend would reverse. The linkage between the dominant Wilsonian idea and reality thus became increasingly strained, and more public administration occurred outside the fundamental theoretical framework.

Third, this change brought significant administrative implications. Analysts have debated whether indirect tools are harder to manage than direct ones. However, at the very least, managing government's set of indirect tools requires a *different* collection of people skills, organizational processes, and control mechanisms. These different tactics, in turn, require different people skills and, perhaps, even different people. The comptroller general of the United States, David M. Walker, called this issue the government's "human capital problem" and found that the government's "human capital management has emerged as the missing link in the statutory and management framework that Congress and the executive branch have established to provide for more businesslike and results-oriented federal government."[7]

Authority still matters, but at the start of the twenty-first century it mattered less than a century earlier, when Wilson's tradition ruled.[8] At the same time, it continues to provide the basic framework for the structure of government agencies and how they relate to other political institutions. The intellectual challenge lies in updating government's tools to fit these new realities. The Wilsonian tradition simply could not account for most of how the federal government—and, to a growing degree, state and local governments as well—performed its functions. As a result, American government increasingly found itself focused on governmental tools that had become much less important. It was poorly equipped to handle the emerging tools that increasingly dominated government activity. As the twenty-first century dawned, a yawning gap had emerged between government's dominant management technologies, founded on traditional Wilsonian principles, and the tools it used to deliver government services, which were distinctly non-Wilsonian. That poses the Wilsonian dilemma: *How can we secure efficient and responsive public administration when there is no chain of hierarchical authority linking policymakers with those who deliver public services?*

The Madisonian Dilemma

American public administration has always struggled to accommodate its pursuit of efficient management with the political system's idiosyncratic diffusion of power. Managerial efficiency seeks strategies to produce high value at the lowest costs, but for any of the strategies to work, managers must know what goals they are seeking. That is always a tall order in the public sector, but it is all the more the case in the United States.

In part, this is because the American separation-of-powers system is exquisitely balanced to ensure that no one ultimately is in charge of anything. The founders worried about an over-concentration of power in any branch of government. In particular, a too-strong president would raise the old worries about monarchical power; a too-strong Congress would bring to the surface worries about the recurring ineffectiveness that plagued the Articles of Confederation. The founders balanced power among the institutions and put the judiciary in a position to keep an eye on both the other branches. That has indeed secured a remarkable political balance over the centuries, but it has created an ongoing administrative predicament. The balance-of-powers approach builds on the art of compromise, and compromise blurs the objectives of public policy.

Compromise, of course, is part of politics everywhere, but the Madisonian features of American democracy introduce peculiarly American dilemmas for public managers. The interplay of the three branches means that no decision is ever truly final. Congress passes a bill, usually after negotiating at least quietly with the president and his staff. The executive branch administers the law, but rarely without at least subtle consultation with Congress and its committees. Anyone who disagrees with the way a law emerges from Congress can take the case to the executive branch and hope to bend rules and procedures more to his or her liking. And anyone who disagrees with those twists can seek leverage through congressional oversight and budgetary action. Those who lose in either forum can seek redress through the courts. As a result, decisions are rarely ever absolute. Every decision is subject to reinterpretation and revision as administration evolves. This dance of implementation has helped the government adapt and endure, despite the huge problems the nation has encountered and the vast pluralism of the interests at play. But it regularly proves frustrating to administrators who seek a clear sense of direction to guide their work.

The great genius of the Founders, captured in Madison's elegant arguments for balance, lay in creating a system that could survive, even thrive, among the pressures and counterpressures of modern society. The system's great administrative problem, however, grew directly from its political strength. The very elements that promoted political steadiness made it difficult to strengthen the system's administration and improve its results. As the Clinton administration sought to "reinvent" American government, for example, administration officials and analysts compared their efforts with the New Zealand reforms, widely viewed as the world's most aggressive.[9] In New Zealand, the connection between political decisions and administrative action was relatively straightforward. Parliament set the policy goals and delegated implementation to government ministers. The ministers signed management contracts with chief executives, who had great flexibility in managing the programs as long as they delivered the outputs defined in the contracts. As the New Zealand Treasury argued in a report to help guide the 1987 transition for a new prime minister,

> Making the right choices about the nature and form of government intervention is the key to effective economic and social management.... Where the Government makes an intervention in some area it is important that it be done well. The design of efficient and effective institutions is difficult. Careful consideration must be given to the specification of objectives (to avoid ambiguous or conflicting objectives), to the scope of the authority given to managers (it must be sufficient to allow the manager to manage effectively), to effective lines of accountability, an effective way of assessing performance (which is not easy if the institution's shares are not publicly traded), and above all else to the way in which incentives can be designed to ensure that the objectives of managers and other employees are aligned with the institution's objectives.[10]

The contrast with the American system could scarcely be greater. The New Zealand reforms built on the clarity of goals and accountability of managers. The American reforms built on the search for political consensus. Some American reformers wistfully visited New Zealand and wished for the opportunity to import that system to the United States.[11] New Zealand reformers visited the United States and wondered how the country managed to run anything at all.

This is not to say that the New Zealand system—or, indeed, any other system—is superior to the American one. Indeed, the New Zealanders have constantly tinkered with their reforms. They have struggled, in particular, to link the output-based focus of management—what should agency managers do?—to the outcome-based focus of politics—what results do these programs have? None of the management reforms introduced around the world during the 1990s proved stable because all of them struggled to balance the connection between policy and its administration. No system proved inherently superior—and every nation struggled to strengthen the connection between its political decisions and its management processes.

Compared with virtually any other nation's, America's political and administrative systems are highly fragmented. That does not necessarily mean that the quality of management is worse in the United States. It does mean that the separation of powers and federalism place extra burdens on both elected officials and administrators: to translate broad, sometimes conflicting political goals into goals clear enough for administrators to follow; to hold administrators accountable for goals that often shift underneath them; and to link administrative structures with the peculiarly American diffusion of responsibility. That shapes the Madisonian dilemma: *How can we secure efficient and responsive public administration, which presumes clear lines of authority, when the constitutional separation-of-powers system diffuses responsibility? Who is in charge when no one is in charge—or if everyone is in charge?*

The Jeffersonian Dilemma

That brings in the Jeffersonian dilemma. As president, even Jefferson was not a Jeffersonian. Through the Louisiana Purchase, the gentleman farmer from Virginia produced the greatest expansion of federal reach in American history. That only underlines the profound irony of Jefferson's administrative tradition. Perhaps none of the four administrative traditions has historically been more honored but less followed.

Nowhere has that been truer than in the ongoing debate over devolution of responsibility within American federalism. As the federal role expanded, so too did its partnerships with state and local governments and the opportunities for leveraging policy decisions. The antipoverty programs of the 1960s, the pollution control programs of the 1970s, the social service programs of the 1980s, and the welfare reform of the 1990s all relied heavily on state and local government implementation of federal standards. In each case, the argument was that governments closer to the people could be far more politically and administratively responsive to local needs. Furthermore, these strategies allowed a substantial growth in federal programs without increasing federal employment or multiplying the number of federal agencies. Federalism, of course, has been an underlying principle of American government since its inception. Conflict over federalism has been just as deeply rooted, whether the conflict was armed (as in the Civil War) or legal (as in the struggle over civil rights).

In vastly multiplying the loci of action, in explicitly giving state and local governments authority to adjust national goals to local conditions, and in adding their contributions to federal money, the federalism strategy has made it far more difficult to determine what the "goal" of any program is or to assess what results they produce. This process provides an uncommon level of flexibility, one of the central virtues of the American system. In the federal Medicaid program, for example, different states add different supplements to fund different levels of service. No two states, in fact, have identical versions of the same federal entitlement program. The same is true of welfare reform, environmental policy, and other national programs. The counterpoint to local flexibility is wide variation in the goals pursued and the results achieved, and that further fogs accountability in the process. The enduring reality—the great political strength and administrative nightmare—is that no policy decision in the United States is ever final.

Jefferson anticipated neither the hyperdevolution that has resulted in so many national responsibilities being shared with local governments nor the intrusion of globalization into the fabric of American government. Jefferson's bucolic image of local self-government was of a self-contained government. The facts of twenty-first century governance have removed the few remaining bits of romance from that idyllic vision. That shapes the Jeffersonian dilemma: *How can we secure efficient and responsive government in an era when the federal government devolves so much responsibility to state and local governments and, at the same time, finds itself swept along by broader globalizing trends? Is it possible to secure accountability when there is no locus for accountability and where responsibility is spread across the entire political landscape?*

The Hamiltonian Dilemma

Hamilton imagined a pragmatic solution to Jeffersonianism. He never believed that Jefferson's reverence for local self-government could ever work in practice, and he sought instead to strengthen the nation's ability to craft and sustain a strong commercial footing. Hamilton was a pragmatist and viewed his argument for a strong federal executive as the essential and inevitable prerequisite for a strong national economy and for a rich quality of life for America's citizens.

In many ways, Hamilton anticipated America's future. If the Constitution created a three-way separation of powers, the president has clearly become first among equals. If the Tenth Amendment reserved powers to the states, the federal government has set the agenda for much state action (even if the states pursue infinite variations on that agenda). The federal executive—especially the presidency—is the fulcrum on which American government sways. The power of different players might rise and fall, but the president is never far from the center. As the twentieth century wore on, American government increasingly became presidential government, to the point that Nixon's critics fretted over his "imperial presidency."[12] Concentrated on a single person, in contrast to Congress, which has 535 members, and with unequaled ability to command the media, the presidency is both the symbol and focus of American government.

If Americans have almost all become Hamiltonians, Hamiltonians have struggled to make sense of fundamental changes in governance. Hamilton argued the need for a strong government to shape commerce and a strong president to command the government. What he never anticipated was the government's broad sharing of its power with nongovernmental partners and the difficulty of integrating them into the conduct of public policy. Neither did he anticipate the flood of global influences into American public policy. He always saw government shaping commerce, not the other way around. In short, what Hamilton never expected was the importance of *governance* as well as *government.*

As Hamilton had hoped, the executive has become the center of American government. But the executive does not hold sway over American governance. Power has become broadly shared with nongovernmental partners; federal power is shared with state and local partners; and no important problem remains within the boundaries of any local government for long. Transnational problems intrude constantly on American government. Citizens expect government to respond, but government cannot control the tools of action. These changes frame the Hamiltonian dilemma: *How can we secure efficient and responsive government when government is only one player among many? No matter how efficient and responsive government might be, how can it solve problems it cannot control?*

FUZZY BOUNDARIES

Each of these four dilemmas presents a common problem—"fuzzy boundaries." The administrative orthodoxy of the twentieth century depended on drawing clear lines of responsibility, especially who was in charge of setting policy and who was in charge of implementing which pieces of policy. The four dilemmas all demonstrate different difficulties in setting boundaries. These problems, of course, have affected nations around the world, and because American government was founded with deliberate sharing of responsibility and multiple channels of access, it was better positioned than most of the world's governments for the transformations that occurred at the dawn of the twenty-first century. American government nevertheless faced the challenge of devising new strategies to cope with the administrative implications of this transformation.

The fuzzy boundary problem confounds the central task of administration—building coordinated efforts to solve complex problems. Administration, in both public and private life, is a search for coordination. It is about how leaders pull together widely disparate resources—money, people, expertise, and technology—to do complex things. The implementation of public programs requires an intricate performance, whether it is the dispatch of highly trained firefighters to the scene of a disaster or the high-tech ballet that safely separates planes in the air-traffic control system. Indeed, as Harold Seidman points out, coordination is the "philosopher's stone" of public management.[13] Medieval alchemists believed that if they could find the magic stone, they would find the answers to human problems. Coordination, Seidman argues, has the same appeal for managers and reformers. "If only we can find the right formula for coordination," he writes, "we can reconcile the irreconcilable, harmonize competing and wholly divergent interests, overcome irrationalities in our government structures, and make hard policy choices to which no one will disagree."[14] Coordination becomes the answer to government's problems; the lack of coordination is the diagnosis for its failures.

As responsibility for implementing public programs has become more broadly shared, however, devising effective coordination strategies has become more difficult. Moreover, as authority has become a less effective tool with which to solve problems, managers have struggled to determine what can best replace it. Twenty-first century bureaucracy thus faces a host of new coordination problems. With responsibility for management so broadly shared, no bureaucracy can completely encompass, manage, or control any problem that really matters. Pursuing either efficiency or responsiveness is far more difficult when no one is fully in charge of anything.

When partners share responsibility for managing programs, how well the programs work depends on how well the partnerships work. Managing government programs effectively thus increasingly depends on bridging the fuzzy boundaries that separate those who make policy from those in the complex interdependent chain of those who share responsibility for implementing it. Six fuzzy boundaries, in particular, are important in managing public programs:

1. *Policymaking versus policy execution.* With responsibility for policy so diffuse, where does the boundary lie between policymakers and policy administrators?
2. *Public versus private versus nonprofit sectors.* With responsibility for results fundamentally shared among the sectors, where do the boundaries between the sectors lie?
3. *Layers within the bureaucracy.* With efforts afoot to flatten the bureaucracy and trim middle management, where does responsibility for the critical management and administrative decisions lie?
4. *Layers between management and labor.* Tensions between management and labor in government, as in the private sector, abound. How do these tensions affect the performance of public programs?
5. *Connections between bureaucracies.* With service recipients and policy reformers alike demanding more service coordination between and among bureaucracies, how can managers sort out the responsibilities of each bureaucracy?
6. *Connections with citizens.* With reformers seeking to treat citizens more as "customers," what *is* the proper relationship between government agencies and the citizens they serve?

Policymaking versus Policy Execution

Wilson, Goodnow, and their colleagues set the stage for the century-long battle over whether one can truly distinguish policy execution from policymaking. Since then, of course, scores of political scientists have contended that political decisions have meaning only in administrative action. Matthew Holden Jr., for example, argued in his 1999 American Political Science Association presidential address, "If students of politics, in this country and around the world, wish to observe power in action, then the crucial focus is discretion regarding the actual use of information, money or its surrogates, and force." Indeed, Holden argued simply, "administration is the lifeblood of power."[15] It is one thing to declare that safe streets or high-quality public education ought to be available to all citizens. It is quite another to make it happen. To do so requires discretion—whether to do more of one thing than another or to decide which thing is appropriate to do first. The exercise of discretion, in turn, requires a choice among competing values, and that means administrators inevitably make political judgments in managing programs.

The government reform movements of the 1990s took very different routes toward resolving this problem. The reforms launched in Australia, the United Kingdom, and especially New Zealand, built on the assumption that politics and administration can—and should—be separated. The American reforms, by contrast, drew no such sharp line between politics and administration. The Clinton administration's "reinventing government" effort, for example, argued the need to give front-line managers more flexibility so they could better meet the needs of citizens. It was a strategy founded on an assumption that managers know how to do their jobs and that top officials ought to get out of the way and let them perform. It built on a blurring of the lines of policy and administration.

The differences in the reform techniques underline just how slippery a concept "policy" has become. A definition of "policy" limited to the decisions of elected officials is ludicrously inadequate. On the other hand, a definition extended through the long chain of decisions required to carry it out would be impossibly broad. This has complicated the task of separating administration from policy and of determining who is responsible for what.

Public, Private, and Nonprofit Sectors

Even more than citizens in most countries, Americans have never much liked government. Since the dawn of time, taxing has never been popular, and no level of public service is ever really adequate. But the American republic was founded on a rebellion against government, even if it was a monarchical government, and its framers wrote the American Constitution to put strong limits on government's power. In many but certainly not

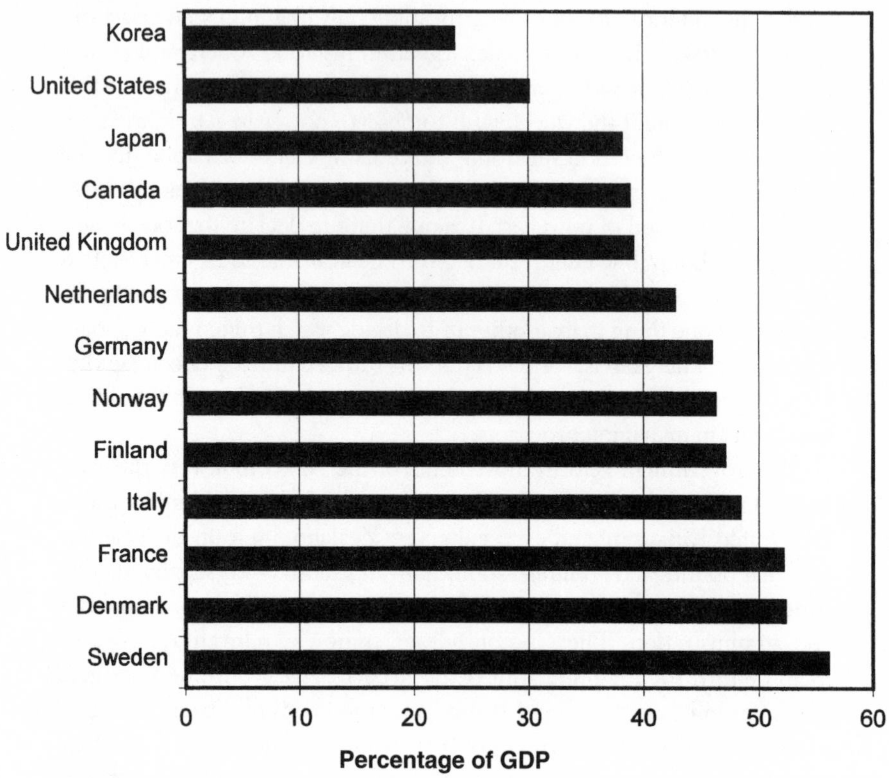

FIGURE 3-1 General Government Total Outlays
Source: Organization for Economic Cooperation and Development, *OECD Economic Outlook* 68 (December 2000), p. 236.

all parts of American society, the instinct has been to criticize government endlessly for its failings and to contend continuously that the private sector could do any job better. Despite the criticisms, Americans over time have asked government to take on an ever-lengthening list of responsibilities. Nevertheless, as figure 3-1 shows, American government, at least as measured by the percentage of the gross domestic product devoted to public spending, ranks almost at the bottom of industrialized nations. With government spending at 30 percent of its gross domestic product compared with Sweden, which spends more than 50 percent, the United States has still found itself criticized for its size of government despite being among the smallest of the world's leading governments. It has taken on more responsibilities without growing disproportionately.

The public-private sector dichotomy likewise has obsessed both analysts and policymakers in the United States. Americans have never much liked government and, like reformers around the world, have often argued that markets produce better solutions than public power does. If government seemed inefficient or unresponsive, then market competition might offer the hope of giving consumers more choice at lower cost. The Reagan administration produced a report, based on a private sector survey, on how the government could reduce its costs through more privatization.[16] The Clinton administration's "reinventing government" campaign continually re-echoed the need to teach the government lessons from the nation's best-run private companies.[17] Both Bush administrations aggressively pursued public-private partnerships, tax cuts to shrink the government, and turning more responsibility over to the private sector. Other nations have likewise expanded government's relationship with the private sector. Reformers have not only copied the British and New Zealand strategy of converting state-owned enterprises to market-driven private companies or public-private hybrids. They have also followed the American contracting-out model even more aggressively.

Americans, in particular, have long argued the need to fix clear boundaries between public and private power. Such boundaries offered the Jeffersonian hope of protecting individual liberty from the threat of governmental tyranny, but the reality has never matched the rhetoric. In the eighteenth century, settlers asked for government protection on the frontier. In the nineteenth century, travelers clamored for government regulation of private enterprises, from steamboats whose boilers blew up far too often to trusts whose monopolies gouged consumers. In the twentieth century, calls for a stronger governmental role occurred even more often than complaints about overreaching public power. By the end of the century, television newsmagazines regularly alternated "give me a break!" features about government gone amuck with plaintive stories of citizens in need—along with a tag line such as "Why isn't the government protecting us?" The calls for more government, in fact, reached unprecedented levels following the September 11, 2001, terrorist attacks on New York and Washington.

As government's reach expanded with stronger public-private partnerships, government sought to retain its sovereignty over crucial decisions while sharing more power with nongovernmental partners. It worked to ensure that its partners managed programs efficiently while it lost the traditional leverage that came through hierarchy and authority.[18] The rhetoric calling for sharper boundaries between government and the private sector continued to grow out of the Jeffersonian tradition. The administrative tactics, however, produced boundaries between government, business, and nonprofit organizations that were ever fuzzier.

Layers within the Bureaucracy

Fuzzy boundaries exist within the bureaucracy as well as outside it. For example, the 1986 space shuttle *Challenger* tragedy stemmed in large part from communication problems across boundaries—between NASA and its contractors but also across boundaries within NASA. The night before the fatal launch, engineers working for Morton Thiokol, the contractor that built the shuttle's solid rocket motors, warned that launching the shuttle in freezing weather posed serious risks. These warnings, however, never reached top NASA officials charged with the launch decisions. Low-level NASA engineers shared the worries of their Morton Thiokol colleagues, but mid-level NASA managers decided that the concerns were not serious enough to stop the launch and did not inform top agency officials. The project had suffered a series of embarrassments, from an inability to keep to the schedule to, on one occasion, difficulty in finding the right tools to pop open the shuttle's hatch following a launch cancellation. Top officials worried that more such problems would erode public support, and they put heavy pressure to get the *Challenger* into orbit. These internal boundary problems in the end proved tragically fatal.[19]

James Q. Wilson's classic, *Bureaucracy*, argues that most government agencies must cope with these three very different internal cultures. "Operators," Wilson wrote, perform the basic work of government agencies. What they do and how they do it define the organization's culture. "Managers" help organizations cope with the constraints imposed by the political environment. "Executives," finally, seek to maintain their organization's "turf" and autonomy.[20] These three levels are important because the roles of officials at each level are different. These different roles lead to different organizational perspectives.

Because officials at each organizational level have different functions, sociologist Talcott Parsons concluded, the gaps between the levels can interrupt the chain of command.[21] As the *Challenger* accident illustrated, these different perspectives can in turn hinder communication—by making lower-level officials cautious about speaking and higher-level officials deaf in hearing. The boundaries separating operators from managers and managers from executives are certainly fuzzy, but the three cultures are very real and important for the management of public organizations. Bridging those boundaries is one of the most critical jobs that government officials have. Moreover, as the tasks and relationships of public management become more complex, the gaps between the three cultures have threatened to expand, and the job of bridging them has become more important.

When the "government bureaucracy" interacts with its external partners, therefore, it is not just as a monolithic entity. The "bureaucracy" is really composed of different individuals at different levels with different instincts and goals. These officials interact, in turn, with counterparts in other bureaucracies who share similar characteristics. Officials at different levels tend to behave differently; as they interact with other officials at different levels in different bureaucracies, problems in communication, performance, and accountability often arise. Top-level executives must manage the programs for which they are responsible. They must also span the boundaries between different types of officials within the bureaucracy to prevent failures that could prove politically embarrassing. Mid-level managers must ensure that the operators perform their tasks and serve as a shock absorber between external forces (transmitted from top-level executives) and internal pathologies (generated by operators). The operators must do the organization's work within the resource limits imposed on them. Failure to bridge the boundaries between levels can create temporary breakdowns, chronic performance problems, political embarrassments, and, sometimes, great tragedies.

Layers between Management and Labor

With the exception of the occasional outbreaks of labor-management tensions like the 1981 air-traffic controllers strike, the federal government has been spared the virulent worker-management battles that have plagued many private companies, some state and local governments, and many foreign governments. The lack of high-profile struggles has tended to hide enduring labor-management tensions, however. When congressional hearings in 1997 and 1998 highlighted problems in the IRS, treasury officials struggled with reforms because of the monumental task of changing the behavior of the service's 95,000 employees. In the 1980s and 1990s, downsizing the Pentagon became enmeshed in ongoing disputes over protecting the jobs and transforming the work of civilian employees. The Clinton administration's "reinvention" effort centered on shrinking the federal workforce and on reducing the number of bureaucratic layers. While the number of federal employees who belong to public employee unions is closely held, the percentage of federal employees represented by unions is especially high in agencies like the IRS, Social Security Administration, and other agencies with large numbers of clerical employees. Federal managers tend to view the unions as an impediment to flexible operations, and it is a constant refrain among federal managers that labor-management tensions span a set of very well-protected boundaries.

The Clinton "reinventing government" initiative recognized the importance of these tensions: the substantial number of employees covered by collective bargaining agreements; the tremendous political problems that Ronald Reagan had after breaking the air-traffic controllers union; the special bonds that the Democratic Party had enjoyed with unions, especially public employee unions; and the damage that strong union opposition could have inflicted on the National Performance Review (NPR) at its very start. To counter these problems, the administration created the National Partnership Council, composed of top-level managers and union representatives. Charged with reinventing labor-management relations as the administration tried to reinvent government, the council in fact accomplished relatively little beyond defusing the potential of initial strong union opposition to the NPR's downsizing. Many government managers, moreover, complained that downsizing disrupted labor-management relations and made it even harder to manage effectively.

The George W. Bush administration tried a different tack. In 2000, the Office of Management and Budget (OMB) ordered agencies to develop plans to reduce the number of layers between top policymakers and citizens and to put more workers into positions where they could serve citizens.[22] The goal certainly was admirable: Who could object to structuring government agencies so that they best served citizens? In many federal agencies, however, from the Federal Aviation Administration to the Centers for Disease Control and from most of the State Department to the National Institutes of Health, most federal employees do not have contact with citizens. Their job is to do the background work that makes programs function. Moreover, the government is most thickly layered at the very top, with many levels of political appointees, and the administration did not propose to reduce the layers by trimming the number of these appointments.[23] The OMB's directive simply did not match the changing realities of federal management.

Other nations included more explicit labor-management changes in the 1980s as part of their reforms. New Zealand, for example, dramatically changed those relationships along with the move to government-by-contract and, in 2000, launched a "partnership for quality" between government and its employees.[24] In the United Kingdom, the government pursued a more collaborative effort as part of the "Next Steps" initiative. The strategy, among other things, decentralized bargaining substantially and gave a great deal of negotiating authority to agency officials.

No nation's management reforms have solved the labor-management conundrum. New dilemmas, moreover, lay over the horizon. Given the limits on public employee unions' rights within government, could the unions find new strength by organizing workers in nongovernmental organizations that have come to play a larger role in service delivery? Can managers devise innovative ways to motivate and discipline employees to improve their ability to deliver results? Can government develop a better match between its management needs and the capacity of its employees? As Comptroller General David M. Walker argued, "No organization can maximize its economy, efficiency, and effectiveness without having up-to-date, state-of-the-art, human capital strategies that are integrated with its overall strategic plan. People are assets in which one has to invest, in which one expects a return, in which one has to manage the risk. People are not an unlimited resource one can consume and throw away."[25] Americans, like the citizens of most nations, have never much liked bureaucrats, but the importance of good managers, well-trained, has never been greater.

Connections between Bureaucracies

The policy-administration, public-private-nonprofit, bureaucratic-level, and labor-management fuzzy boundaries create substantial coordination problems. But the biggest coordination problem—the one for which organizational alchemists have for millennia sought the philosopher's stone—is coordination *between* bureaucracies. If this coordination problem is ageless, it increased in the last third of the twentieth century as a product of both the growing ambition of government and the transformation of governance in seeking to serve that ambition.

Some coordination problems occur within government. In the aftermath of the September 2001 terrorist attack, for example, President Bush named Pennsylvania Governor Tom Ridge to head a new Office of Homeland Security. Ridge's mission was to coordinate both the government's intelligence information and its operational response. Critics pointed, for example, to the problems of pulling together facts and analysis from such disparate sources as the FBI, the CIA, and the National Security Agency. A unified response required uniting the efforts of the Coast Guard, Border Patrol, and the Immigration and Naturalization Service, among other agencies. The problem was clear and the need was great. On the other hand, many government agencies shared responsibility for pieces of work, and no agency had responsibility for it all. Like most public problems, the government's antiterrorist policy played out through a network of agencies. Each agency, in turn, was part of multiple networks working on a host of different problems. If there were but one problem, policymakers could simply reorganize government agencies to focus on that problem. But as problems proliferated, so too did the networks—and the impossibility of drawing clear boundaries around any of them.

Other coordination problems occurred between government and its nongovernmental partners—and among those partners as well. The American welfare reform initiative of the 1990s, for example, depended on moving welfare recipients to productive long-term employment. That required assessing a welfare recipient's job skills; providing job training to help the recipient be more employable; securing transportation to get the recipient to training and, eventually, to a new job; finding a good job to put those new skills into practice; securing day care for the recipient's children; and frequently ensuring health care, subsidized housing, and Food Stamps through the transition to work. The recipient's children might be troubled at school and require remedial work, and too often the children stumble into problems with the law and require attention from the juvenile justice system. Children of newly working parents might need after-school care and could well benefit from new recreational and educational help. Welfare reform thus was not one program but the complex amalgamation of perhaps a dozen or more different programs, each run by a different agency. It could not succeed unless each of those programs supported the overall mission, much as different pieces of an orchestra combine to produce fine music—except that in the case of welfare reform and other complex programs, the orchestra plays without a conductor.

Recurring jokes focus on how much time government managers spend in meetings. Everyone agrees that managers spend more time in meetings than they need to, but one of the reasons meetings have proliferated is that officials need face-to-face conversations to resolve the nonroutine issues that routinely develop across organizational boundaries. That is where much of any organization's hardest work takes place—and where, if the boundaries are not understood well and spanned carefully, citizens can fall through the cracks.

Relationships with Citizens

Reformers, finally, have eagerly sought to redefine government's relationships with its citizens. The Clinton administration built its strategy on the notion that "taxpayers are customers too." Private-sector managers and consultants, in fact, challenged the federal government to become "raging inexorable thunderlizard evangelists of customer service," as management guru Tom Peters put it.[26] In fact, turning citizens into customers and making the customer's—not the bureaucracy's—needs the goal of government agencies was the centerpiece of the reinventing government movement. Reinvention advocates David Osborne and Ted Gaebler argued that "while businesses strive to please customers, government agencies strive to please interest groups." As a result, citizens become irritated with "the arrogance of the bureaucracy." Reform, they concluded, requires "getting close to the customer" and "putting the customer into the driver's seat."[27]

In other nations, the customer service movement has been even more aggressive. The British government created "citizens' charters," which sought to guarantee citizens a prescribed level of service. Signs at British railway stations listed the on-time performance of different trains, and regular riders received rebates if a train's performance did not meet standards. Similar customer-service initiatives drove reforms in both New Zealand and Australia. Improving citizen satisfaction with government programs was a central goal of most government reform efforts.

The customer-service movement, however, enraged many academic analysts.[28] Individuals are citizens and taxpayers, not "customers," the argument went. It would be hard to suggest that government should not be as responsive as possible to the needs of its citizens, and surely anything that improves the quality of government services is a good thing. Shorter waiting lines at customs and immigration facilities and more on-time delivery from the Postal Service can scarcely be a bad idea. Simple IRS forms and friendlier Social Security offices would certainly receive warm taxpayer welcomes. But such notions only begin to explore the issues implicit in the customer-service approach. Five unresolved problems make it difficult to use "customer service" as a touchstone for management reform.[29]

1. *Who is the customer?* The customer-service advocates typically proceed as if everyone knew just who government's customers are and what they want. That, however, is rarely the case. There are at least four different perspectives on the citizen-as-customer. As *service recipients,*

citizens naturally want large (sometimes even unlimited) high-quality services at low (even no) cost. If it snows, citizens want their streets plowed—immediately. If a pothole develops, they want it filled before they break an axle on their car. They want parks that are clean and safe, schools that teach kids to read and write well, police that arrest criminals quickly, and food inspection services that keep dangerous germs away from their stomachs. In short, they want a responsive government. This perspective most closely matches the total-quality-management approach of the private sector: find out what customers want and find a way to give it to them.

Citizens, however, often are *partners in service provision* as well. More government programs, from welfare reform and social services to environmental protection and recreation, require citizens to be active participants in the process. As these partnerships grow, the need for coordinating services among the partners multiplies. Citizens want programs that work effectively, where service provision is seamless regardless of bureaucratic boundaries. As customers of these services, citizens must play a strong role very different from the more passive role suggested by the customer-as-service-recipient one.

Third, citizens are *"owners" of the government* and expect accountability. If there are problems, they expect that they will be solved. In the American system, this means acting through the formal process of republican democracy: elections, administrative oversight, judicial review, and the other strategies and tactics that drive American political life. The relationship is not as direct as it is in transactions between a business and its customers. The relationship, rather, is more like that between a company's stockholders and its management. Stockholders can be customers, too, but the relationship and expectations are different.

Finally, citizens are *taxpayers*, and as such they pay the government's bills. As service recipients, they might expect virtually unlimited service; as taxpayers, they expect tough management, high efficiency, and minimal waste, fraud, and abuse. These standards, moreover, are as much political as managerial. Fraud is a legal term, but "waste" often is in the eye of the beholder. One person's waste is often money that flows into someone else's favorite program. Senior citizens sometimes criticize agricultural subsidies, while farmers wonder why Medicare costs so much. Thus, not only do the interests of citizens-as-service-recipients often conflict with their interests as citizens-as-taxpayers, but citizens rarely agree on how their tax dollars can best be spent.

It is clear that government should try hard to serve the needs of its citizens and to do so responsively. It is also clear that government has a long way to go. But it is often deceptively difficult to define clearly what "customer service" truly means. The relationships between citizens and their government in a democratic society are far more intricate and difficult than those between a customer and the private organization seeking the customer's business. Customer service thus is a valuable target but in actuality is perhaps only one of several.

2. *How should connections with customers be designed?* The customer-service model, drawn as it is from the private sector, presumes a straightforward connection between customer and organization. In the private sector, the market transaction is the fundamental building block for customer service. In the public sector, however, the transactions not only are typically not market-based, but the connections between elected policymakers, government agencies, and the proxies who produce many of government's goods and services are at best attenuated. Most federal agencies and many state agencies do not deal directly with citizens. Their business, rather, is with each other and with government's proxies. In most public programs, moreover, organizations do not have a choice about which services they will provide customers. Programs and priorities are fixed in law.

That scarcely makes the customer-service concept useless. Many imaginative public managers, for example, have created the notion of "internal customers" to describe those within government whose needs they are responsible for meeting. They suggest, for example, that personnel managers must think of the needs of the agencies for which they recruit personnel instead of the dictates of their own procedures. They suggest that contract managers must work toward high performance by their contractors instead of mere compliance with internal paperwork. The nature of government's administrative strategies and tactics, however, make it hard to import private-sector notions of customer service to its operations. Many private-sector companies, of course, work through proxies as well. But the multiple boundaries within areas of public service provision create stark and very different challenges.

3. *How can government avoid hypersensitivity to customers' wishes?* Much of government's problem is not so much insensitivity but hypersensitivity to citizens' demands. Elected officials, naturally, wish to please their constituents. Indeed, one of Congress's first acts upon learning that the budget was to be balanced in fiscal year 1998 was to pass a massive trans-

portation bill that provided highway improvements to virtually every congressional district. From higher Social Security checks and new dams to cleanup of waste dumps, the relationship between voters and elected officials can swell government spending and make it hard to judge where customer service stops and waste begins. The 2001 debate over a fiscal stimulus plan brought forth ideas to funnel tax cuts and spending increases to virtually every political constituency.

These pressures, of course, are scarcely a phenomenon limited to the United States. Moreover, some critics have suggested that government is already hypertuned to microlevel needs yet lacks the capacity or incentives to deliver broad, sustained, high-level performance.[30] George Frederickson has contended that genuine reinvention of government that focuses only on reinventing the administrative process will fail. He argues for "total quality politics" to supplement "total quality management."[31]

4. *How can government balance top-down and bottom-up pressures?* Historical notions of governmental accountability, along with traditional public administrative practice, build from the top down. In the traditional model, citizens vote for elected officials. These officials make policy and delegate administrative responsibility to executive-branch agencies. These agencies implement their own policy in accordance with the policy set at the top. If citizens object to administrative behavior, the standard course of action is to work through their elected officials. Redress of grievances is a top-down affair, which turns tradition on its head. It argues that front-line government workers ought to identify and respond directly to citizens' needs. It contends that the rest of the bureaucracy ought to be structured to make this connection as effective as possible. Most important, it makes accountability bottom-up instead of top-down.

This raises two difficult problems. First, it squeezes government managers between two perspectives—the traditional top-down approach to rational-legal accountability and the bottom-up approach to greater citizen satisfaction. Such a squeeze often proves uncomfortable at best and creates impossible dilemmas at worst. Second, it raises a stark challenge to the rule of law and accountability on which American government is based. The more grassroots administrators adjust their practice to accommodate the needs and demands of citizens, the more elected officials can become marginalized. The more elected officials insert themselves into the transactions between front-line administrators and citizens, the more administrators often struggle to provide customer service. Elected officials thus can find themselves squeezed between the top-down process (citizens as voters) and the bottom-up process (citizens as customers). The customer-service approach makes their role anything but clear and creates the potential for great tension.

Especially when coupled with the other problems surrounding the customer-service movement, the top-down or bottom-up dilemma is a difficult one for public managers. Improved responsiveness of government to citizens/customers/taxpayers is, of course, an ideal toward which all democratic governments strive. The customer service movement, however, complicates as much as it guides by leaving critical questions unanswered and boundaries even fuzzier.

5. *How should government balance responsiveness through customer service with other governance objectives?* It is impossible to argue that government should not provide services in a responsive and friendly way. It is equally impossible to suggest that government does so all the time. Responsive-ness, however, is not the only goal that Americans expect government to achieve. They expect an efficient government as well; maximizing responsiveness (for example, ensuring that every telephone call from a citizen is answered within two rings) does not necessarily maximize efficiency (since building enough slack into systems to provide rapid telephone response can prove very costly).

Moreover, citizens expect government to treat citizens equitably. Although airlines accommodate their frequent flyers with special check-in lines, it would be inconceivable for the IRS to provide fast-track treatment (like a special-service telephone number or expedited refunds) for rich taxpayers.[32] Applying the private sector's customer service ap-proaches to government would often violate the public's expectations of how the government ought to behave, at least in part. Add to that the fact that, in public programs, the "sellers" have no choice of what to sell, and the "buyers" frequently have no alternative place for buying. The metaphor thus becomes unrecognizable. Indeed, it is the public's multiple and often-conflicting expectations that make public management fundamentally different, and harder, than private-sector management.

ASSESSING THE FUZZY BOUNDARY PROBLEM

American public administration thus finds itself swirling. Four great administrative traditions shape both the practice and theory of public administration, but the traditions lead in conflicting directions. One cannot simultaneously embrace Jeffersonian and Hamiltonian principles, or Madisonian and Wilsonian principles. Just as Americans have always simultaneously sought the advantages of centralization *and* decentralization, administrators and administrative theorists must eventually make strategic choices that emphasize some values over others. No choice has ever endured for long because Americans' preferences among the underlying values have shifted over time. The one sure feature of every new presidential administration, for example, is a new "new federalism" that swings back and forth between national dominance and local discretion. Similar swings have driven reform in all areas of administrative practice.[33] By the end of the twentieth century, it was not only impossible to find a comfortable middle ground between Madisonian and Wilsonian ideas, or between Hamiltonian and Jeffersonian impulses, but it was also impossible to embrace and follow *any* of the traditions because the transformation of governance, in each case, undermined each tradition's guiding principles. That further confounded the search for both practical and theoretical guidance.

At the core of this issue lies the fuzzy boundary problem. Each of the four traditions grew from efforts to draw lines defining the roles and responsibilities of each of the players. The transformation of governance, in each case, blurred those historic boundaries. It proved impossible to draw useful new boundaries to replace the old ones. Moreover, experience in both the United States and other nations soon proved that the transformation was unlikely to be a short-lived phenomenon. As first the United Kingdom, then Europe, and finally the rest of the globe struggled to deal with "mad cow" and hoof-and-mouth disease in the first years of the twenty-first century, the world learned that traditional boundaries could no longer contain big problems. The world's nations learned that they could not impose solutions on problems that grew from complex interactions among hosts of players.

That, in turn, framed the central problem of American public administration. Administration, in general, is about defining the nature of work; breaking work down into its component pieces; developing expertise for managing each of those pieces; and matching expertise to the job to be done. Administration is about devising and honing routines to accomplish complex tasks. That requires fixing responsibilities and drawing boundaries. However, the American version of *public* administration, from the very beginning, dealt with these principles. The founders were political men dealing with difficult political problems. They worried about making government strong enough to protect citizens and promote the common good without making it so strong as to threaten individual liberty. Their political answer was an institutional one, founded on a separation of governmental power into three branches. They did not so much seek a long-term strategy for government management as much as a short-term balance of political pressures. Their genius lay in charting the basic cross-pressures and in devising remarkably elastic systems for resolving them—a system that could constantly bend without breaking.

For most of the founders, with the notable exception of Hamilton, determining how to manage the details of the new government was not a first-order question. It is not that they were not practical men. They were, in fact, idealists with a powerful sense of the pragmatic. Rather, it was hard enough simply crafting the new political institutions. Making the institutions work created more questions that were even more difficult, and their genius extended in not biting off too much at once. As a result, however, very different ideas emerged about just how government should administer itself. The tradeoffs implicit in the design of the institutions multiplied throughout the administrative system. Strong and fundamentally conflicting traditions grew up around basic questions: What functions should government perform? Who should perform them? As the nation grew, the four fundamental traditions—Jeffersonian, Hamiltonian, Madisonian, and Wilsonian—emerged, and American public administration shifted uneasily among them.

Administration has always struggled to create and manage the boundaries that contain it. That has been true through the ages wherever administrators have practiced, whether in private or public enterprises. The particular balancing act of the American republic, however, has put the search for administrative boundaries in a distinctive political setting. It has involved not only finding a match between administrative tasks and political values but constantly readjusting that match to the endlessly shifting balance among the political traditions.

As this chapter illustrates, the growing complexity of the administrative process has added another layer to the issue. Administrative boundaries, both within public agencies and between those agencies and the broader environment, have multiplied and become fuzzy. The old dilemmas: balancing the Jeffersonian instinct for self-government with the Hamiltonian pursuit of a strong executive; balancing the Madisonian separation of powers with the Wilsonian models of effective administration—have not disappeared. Indeed, these lasting ideas have powerfully shaped how Americans, academic theorists and public officials alike, have approached new issues. What has emerged, however, are new pressures that increasingly stress the fundamental problem of administration—balancing the instinct of administration to create boundaries with the need to pursue broad social goals of political institutions. Theorists have devised numerous approaches to accommodate the fundamentals of administration, the enduring American administrative traditions, and the emerging fuzzy boundary problems. The next two chapters chart those approaches.

BOUNDARIES WITHIN THE BUREAUCRACY ||| 4

The fuzzy boundary problem compounded public administration's practical difficulties. Public administration, especially in the Wilsonian tradition, built its case for strong administration on the assumption that it could devise strategies for elected officials to oversee administrative decisions effectively. These strategies all depended on drawing clear boundaries between policymaking and policy administration. Meanwhile, the number of boundaries within the system multiplied and became fuzzier. For a field founded on drawing clear boundaries, that proved a serious problem. As government relied more on partnerships with the private sector, the problems multiplied. Government not only needed to devise new techniques to manage the emerging tools, it also needed to create new strategies for securing democratic accountability.

As public administration tried to solve these puzzles, the twentieth century's advances in social sciences raised the theoretical bar. Public administration theory quite thoroughly charted the competing choices that managers faced. By the middle of the century, however, that was no longer enough. Theorists wanted to know more than that rival approaches posed contradictory implications. They wanted to know which approaches produced the best outcomes, and social scientists became increasingly impatient with the tradeoffs that traditional public administration posed.

Other models, including emerging formal models that grew out of economics, also built on tradeoffs, but they had greater respect in many quarters. In part, the difference lay in the method. Many of the social sciences favored newer, inductive approaches, derived from basic assumptions about human behavior and then formed carefully into hypotheses and theories. New social science research methods emerged, and those that allowed advanced statistical analysis increasingly gained favor. To use data analysis, researchers needed large samples. That, in turn, led researchers away from qualitative research on organizations or programs—which each presented small samples—to the behavior of individuals, especially bureaucrats and policymakers, where the numbers of research subjects were far larger. These methods posed real problems for traditional public administration, which had long relied on case studies about individual programs and analysis of public agencies. Traditional theory-building had been deductive, with propositions drawn out of such small samples. This approach tended to emphasize variations more than similarities, and it tended to produce conclusions that emphasized tradeoffs more than general theoretical propositions.

These methodological problems have proven especially difficult for public administration. The big public policy battles have brought to the surface the big political values, and scholars have often found it more alluring to examine these issues than to probe the tough, intricate process of moving from decisions to results. That has produced a stronger bias in favor of studying how public policy is made than how it is implemented.

Moreover, the scholars who have studied the administration and management of public programs have often not been at the center of their fields. Political scientists, who focus on institutions, often have not worked with public administrationists, who concentrate on organizational structure and process. Public management scholars at public policy schools give their attention to decision-making, especially by top-level officials. Economists who analyze the decision-making and evaluation processes have tended to dominate those schools. Different scholarly backgrounds lead scholars from different traditions, such as organizational sociologists, to ask different questions and use different analytical techniques. Their work crosses without a sense that they share the same problems. Not only does the work from these different disciplines fail to be cumulative, but the disagreements about basic problems, approaches, and conclusions tend to feed the more widespread belief among some cynical academics that there really is no theory in the field at all.

These conflicts also are deeply rooted in the four American administrative traditions. These traditions have powerfully guided research in public administration and related fields, even if scholars pursuing formal methods might not recognize the intellectual provenance of their work. A careful look at the state of theory, however, shows that these four traditions help organize much of what Americans have contributed to the study of public bureaucracy. In turn, the inherent conflicts in the traditions help explain the ongoing tensions in the academic literature: over the questions they ask as well as the ones they do not, the answers they reach, and the methods they use to explore. This disparate work fails to connect because of these differences—and because the instincts embodied in these traditions and the ways in which they combine tend to take scholars down very different roads.

As Norton Long once argued, administration is about power—who has it and how they use it.[1] John Gaus reminds his readers that how one feels about power depends on whether one has it: "When you are out of power, you want to limit the powers of those who are in; but your zeal (or rather, that of your wiser and shrewder leaders) will be cooled by the consideration that you want to leave a loophole through which you can respectably undertake the same activities when you in turn achieve power."[2] Public administration theory, in all its variations, revolves around the strategies for structuring and exercising political power.

Public administrationists have long celebrated the field's diversity in analyzing questions of political power. In the leading textbook of the mid-twentieth century, *Introduction to the Study of Public Administration*, Leonard D. White wrote, "There are many ways to study the phenomenon of public administration. . . . All of these approaches are relevant and from all of them come wisdom and understanding."[3] For public administration's critics, however, that is precisely the problem—a "complacent, undiscriminating eclecticism," as Herbert Storing put it, which frustrated the search for enduring theory.[4] If any approach could be useful, then no approach could be central. If the field could not focus on a central theory, then critics wondered if there was really any intellectual center to the field. Public administration's eclecticism, especially in the middle of the twentieth century, undermined its theory and its reputation in the social sciences. It was little wonder that Leonard D. White, perhaps the leading student of administration from the 1920s to the 1950s, ended his career not with grand theories but with administrative histories.[5] It was almost as if he felt compelled to begin again at the beginning, to rebuild the field on a new foundation with fresh interpretations.

Public administration, as well as the competing approaches to administrative theory, all must grapple with the application of power. They must do so in the setting of political institutions and in the crossfire of political conflicts. By necessity, that means that they must wrestle with the enduring administrative traditions of American democracy and how they combine. The big issues of administrative theory constantly present themselves in new ways, but they inevitably must deal with the big puzzles:

— How strong should the executive function be?
— Should the executive exercise its influence from the top down or the bottom up?

— Should administrative theory focus on hierarchical relationships within the bureaucracy?
— How should the executive connect with the other political institutions in the American balance-of-powers system?

These questions play out in different combinations of the four basic traditions: Hamiltonian, Jeffersonian, Wilsonian, and Madisonian. Scholarship on public organizations sorts itself out into the combinations these traditions define.

THE HAMILTONIAN-WILSONIAN CONNECTION

The Hamiltonian and Wilsonian traditions combine to frame the classic approach to strong administration. The Hamiltonian tradition presents the executive as a strong leader who works from the top down to ensure efficiency and control. The Wilsonian tradition explains *how* managers can do so, especially within the constraints of American constitutionalism. Together, they frame the classical approach to public administration. They have also framed many of the principal administrative reforms that practitioners developed toward the end of the twentieth century.

"Traditional" Public Administration

The modern study of public administration dates from the Progressive era. Modern theorists traced the launch of traditional public administration from the publication of Wilson's "The Study of Administration" in 1887, although as noted in chapter 2, his article did not achieve "classic" status until the 1950s. Frank J. Goodnow and other prominent political scientists championed the same cause, however, drawing a clear line between administration and politics. They argued that administration matters; that by intruding into the practice of administration, politics had undermined the efficient and effective pursuit of government policy; that insulating administrative practice from political influence could significantly improve the results of government programs; and that this separation would improve democratic accountability. Indeed, they were not so much interested in taking administration out of politics as in taking politics out of administration. Wilson, Goodnow, and others argued that this would improve administration by allowing administrators to focus more on efficiency. This, in turn, would improve democracy by clarifying the relationship between policy decisions and administrative results.

By the end of the nineteenth century, theorists were in a bind. The industrialization of the economy and the rise of corporate trusts had brought the need for stronger government regulation, but the federal government that emerged from the Civil War was not remotely up to the task. Reformers faced a knotty problem—creating a stronger administrative system to tackle the problems of industrialization and the trusts without courting tyranny and threatening democratic accountability. The Wilson/Goodnow solution was simple and elegant. Separating policy administration from policymaking provided a way to hold administrators ultimately accountable to policymakers. If administrators could be held accountable, then their power could grow without sacrificing accountability. For Wilson, the task was strengthening government so it could properly do its job. Government might be a "necessary evil," but "it is no more an evil than is society itself." In fact, Wilson argued following an extensive study of governments throughout history and around the world, "It is the organic body of society: without it society would be hardly more than a mere abstraction." In fact, "government is the indispensable organ of society." Government's crucial role is "to assist in accomplishing the objects of organized society."[6] Wilson's view was of a strong society. A strong society needed a strong government. His argument for a separation of politics from administration grew directly out of his long-term research and his belief that the Progressives' approach to administration was critical for taking the United States into the twentieth century.

The decades that followed showed how hard it was in practice to pursue these theoretical ideas. Not everyone agreed on the need for a strong public administration, and certainly not everyone agreed on giving administrators their head. Nevertheless, traditional public administration provided a neat, elegant approach to the problem of government. It provided the intellectual foundation for the stronger administration that inevitably accompanied the Progressives' views of a vigorous government.

This theoretical solution proved short-lived. Soon after the public administrationists helped found the American Political Science Association, some pragmatists tried to split off in a separate movement to train public managers. That effort failed, but not before planting the seeds of ongoing theoretical strife that was to plague public administration for the next century. Practitioners wanted to develop programs to teach future administrators. Public administration theorists wanted a secure seat in budding academic departments. As the decades wore on, though, the policy-administration dichotomy troubled more of their political science colleagues. To many political scientists, public administration seemed a peculiarly apolitical theory of politics. Public administration, however, had no other intellectual base, and at least in the American Political Science Association's early years, the considerable strength of public administration nurtured the new field. For better or worse, political science became the theoretical home for the study of public administration.[7]

These strains worsened as public administration developed. Frederick W. Taylor led the movement toward management efficiency. He devoted himself to "scientific management" and his famous search for the "one best way" to perform work.[8] Taylor helped popularize time-and-motion studies, in which researchers carefully studied the motions of workers, examined alternative ways of performing the same task, and recommended techniques that could do the work most quickly, easily, and cheaply. The scientific management movement revolutionized assembly lines and clerical work alike. Critics complained that Taylorism reduced workers to mere cogs in huge machines, an image Charlie Chaplin made memorable in his classic 1936 film, *Modern Times.* Defenders countered that Taylorism improved the lives of workers by reducing physical strain and increasing output, which in turn increased wages.

Traditional public administration thus inevitably posed problems as it grew and developed. It sought to resolve a fundamentally irresolvable problem—creating an administration strong enough to be effective but not so strong as to endanger accountability. It sought to do so by creating a theory of public administration insulated from the pressures of politics. As Roscoe Martin explained in 1952, "'Politics' was anathema—not the politics practiced by administrators, but the politics of the 'politicians.'" The rise of Wilson's approach to public administration in the early twentieth century was also a triumph of Hamiltonianism. Hamilton would have recognized, and perhaps applauded, the approach of traditional public administration—"not only impatience but also profound distrust" about the politics of legislation, as Martin put it.[9] Proponents of the scientific management school built on the Wilsonian and Hamiltonian traditions. They saw virtually no barrier to the ability of public administration to improve government—if only government administrators could be protected from political meddling.

By the time Franklin Roosevelt appointed the Brownlow Committee in 1937 to help him reorganize the Office of the President, traditional public administration was triumphant. The committee's three members—Louis Brownlow, Charles Merriam, and Luther Gulick—were in the pantheon of public administrationists.[10] Brownlow had helped establish the city manager movement, whose efforts to create a cadre of professional, nonpartisan, local administrators grew directly out of the Wilsonian approach. Merriam vigorously supported scientific management, and Gulick's "Notes on the Theory of Organization" was perhaps the field's definitive catechism. The young scholars who staffed the committee in turn became the field's next generation of intellectual leaders. Future stars like James W. Fesler, Arthur W. Macmahon, Schuyler C. Wallace, Harvey Mansfield, Paul T. David, and Robert H. Connery staffed the commission.[11]

The field's growing practical influence, however, did nothing to soothe the intellectual tensions. Within the American Political Science Association, scholars squabbled about whether public administration was a science, process, or art—indeed, about whether public administration even belonged within political science. Several political scientists led another breakout effort in 1939 by forming a new association, the American Society for Public Administration (ASPA). A new institutional home, they concluded, was needed to train new public servants better. They embraced all of the competing perspectives by committing the ASPA to the "science, process, and art of public administration." Even if its seat within political science was an uncomfortable one, traditional public administration demonstrated its strength by helping craft the management strategies for winning World War II. The field continued to enroll large numbers of students in the nation's universities.

The war brought two big problems to the field, however. On one hand, as the social sciences attempted to become more scientific, traditional public administration lagged far behind. Some public administrationists focused on improving practice and simply rejected the effort. Their approach to "science" was scientific management—the pursuit of efficient administration, not scientific theory—the search for more rigorous models. The social scientists struggling to bring more rigor to the field found that the new statistical techniques worked far better for studying voting behavior and polling, where they could collect large quantities of data, than for studying public programs and government agencies, which resisted the application of statistical techniques. *How* scholars studied political behavior increasingly defined *what* they studied. The rise of these new research techniques squeezed public administration off the lists of top-rank social science issues and high-profile social science fields.

Meanwhile, traditional public administration began losing ground on its own soon after World War II. Public administration became more fundamentally power-related and less executive-centered. David Rosenbloom, for example, argues that the passage of the Administrative Procedure Act in 1948 marked the rise of a legislative-centered public administration, with Congress shaping the structure, process, and behavior of administration.[12] Norton Long's argument that administration was about the exercise of power reshaped the theoretical foundation of the field.[13] Public administrationists took a more compelling view of their field by recognizing that attempting to separate politics and policy from administration was a fool's errand. They attempted to rebuild theory that explicitly recognized the link between politics and administration.[14]

If traditional public administration became more politically aware during the 1950s, the erosion of the politics-administration dichotomy threatened the field's intellectual foundation.[15] With the downfall of traditional administrative theories and the rise of a new political science, Allen Schick concluded, "Public administration had come apart and could not be put back together."[16] While many within public administration vigorously fought separatist tendencies, public administration and political science moved apart.[17] Many public administrationists sought refuge from political science, especially in the American Society for Public Administration and in schools of public administration separate from political science departments. For their part, many political scientists saw little merit in studying administrative institutions in their search for a new theory of politics. In 1904, public administration had been a critical pillar in Goodnow's vision of political science, and the field had been central in defining and leading the association itself. By 1962, when the American Political Science Association issued "Political Science as a Discipline," a special report on instruction in the discipline, public administration was mentioned only in passing as a subfield of American government.[18]

Allen Schick forcefully argued that "public administration can no more escape political science than it can escape politics." He concluded, "Until it makes peace with politics, public administration will wander in quest of purpose and cohesion."[19] Public administrationists have disagreed among themselves about the prospects for resolving this crisis, especially within the discipline of political science. Dwight Waldo's John M. Gaus Lecture before the American Political Science Association contended, "*Estrangement* is perhaps too mild to characterize the relationship of public administration to other fields of political science." Waldo suggested that for most political scientists, "public administration concerns the lower things of government, details for lesser minds."[20] Herbert Kaufman, in his Gaus Lecture, worried that public administration and political science were reaching "the end of alliance."[21] To solve the problem, James W. Fesler concluded in a third Gaus Lecture that the worlds of governance and of political science "should not be far apart."[22]

Despite these admonitions, traditional public administration continued to struggle for acceptance within other social science disciplines. It did not develop the rigor that economics, sociology, and political science expected. It continued to search for a way to bridge the gulf between the administrative power embodied in the Hamiltonian and Wilsonian approaches and the political accountability required by American democracy. Much of the instruction in public administration remained remarkably similar to that in the salad days of the 1940s and early 1950s. Courses continued to focus on issues like personnel, budgeting, and organizational structure. These issues undoubtedly remain important. In fact, neglect of these important issues has seriously weakened other approaches to administrative theory. But traditional public administration suffered serious blows in the 1950s and 1960s, most notably in the intellectual rigor of its theory and in its difficulty in grappling with the connection between politics and administration. In the next half century it showed only halting signs of recovery.

Formal Theories

Despite its manifest problems, traditional administration's solution to the dilemma of empowering bureaucrats without creating an unresponsive bureaucracy proved remarkably long-lasting. By the 1960s, however, political science had grown markedly impatient with its intellectual problems. Traditional public administration gradually was squeezed out of the field's mainstream and its premier journal, the *American Political Science Review*. Bureaucracy was an institution of unquestioned power. How could this power be reconciled with accountability—and how could the inquiry regarding it be made more scientific?

Some political scientists responded by borrowing heavily from the formal theories that had transformed microeconomics. The formal theories focused primarily on individuals, what motivates them, and how those motivations shape their behavior when they join in organizations. The theory started by asking: Why do employees of complex organizations behave as they do? Traditional public administration tended to assume that authority relationships between superiors and subordinates provided at least part of the answer. Individuals did what they did because superiors asked them to do it. The formal approach, by contrast, applied economics principles. Microeconomics assumes that individuals seek their self-interest—to maximize their utility. Workers agree to work because the work provides them rewards, such as pay and fulfillment. Employers agree to pay workers to get the job done. The market determines how much employers must pay and what employees agree to accept. These basic assumptions led to theories that saw bureaucracies as networks of contracts rather than systems of hierarchies and authority.[23]

Such contracts, theorists argued, identified the key relationships in bureaucracy and key problems that officials had to solve. In particular, Nobel laureate Ronald Coase argued in 1937, such relationships created "transaction costs" for supervisors in managing these contracts, and Oliver Williamson further advanced that work during the 1970s.[24] Their work suggested that theory builders not only needed to focus on contracts, written and implicit, between superiors and subordinates, but they needed as well to understand what incentives best shaped the behavior that supervisors wanted to shape.

Closely related to this work was principal-agent theory. This approach developed models for describing the contracts between superiors and subordinates. A top-down alternative to hierarchical authority, the approach stipulated that higher-level officials—principals—initiated the contracts and that they then hired subordinates—agents—to implement them. It also provided an alternative theory of accountability. Workers (agents) would be responsible to top-level officials (principals) not because they were ordered to do so but because they negotiated contracts in which they agreed to pursue specific actions in exchange for specific rewards. Principal-agent theory thus provided a more elegant and theoretically powerful solution to the problems with which traditional public administration had been struggling for nearly a century. The task of devising the most efficient organizational structure and the best operating processes became a matter of constructing the best contracts. In both cases, the measure of "best" was the same—the ability of the organization to produce the most efficient and responsive goods and services possible.

Because principals and agents operate through contracts, results will be only as good as the contracts. Theorists contended that predictable problems grow out of any contractual relationship. To write a good contract requires good information. But principals can never know enough about their agents to make sure they have selected the best ones. That can produce "adverse selection" problems, in which ill-chosen agents cannot or choose not to do what their principals want. Moreover, principals can never observe their agents' behavior closely enough to be sure that their performance matches the terms of the contract. That can produce "moral hazard" problems, in which agents perform differently than the principals had in mind.

Agency theory thus focuses on information and the incentives for using that information as the critical problems of public administration. Principals need to learn the right things about their agents before hiring them. They can improve their monitoring of agents' behavior to learn what results they produce. They can use this improved knowledge to adjust agents' incentives and to redesign organizations to reduce the risks from adverse selection and moral hazard. And because conventional wisdom and formal theory alike predict that bureaucrats resist change, principals can use this analysis to improve performance and oversight. For public administration, this produces a straightforward theory: Institutions headed by elected officials, such as the presidency and Congress, create bureaucracies; that is, bureaucracies can be viewed as agents for the principals' (elected officials') wishes. The principals design bureaucracies' incentives and sanctions to enhance their own control. When the principals detect bureaucratic behavior that does not match their policy preferences, they use these incentives and sanctions to change that behavior. Among the important sanctions are the president's appointment power and the budgetary leverage that the branches share.[25]

Not only did principal-agent theory introduce a more theoretically elegant solution to the enduring puzzle, but with the theory of contracts, it also provided important insight into the linkage between organizations and their results. Moreover, principal-agent analysis provided an inductive approach to theory-building. Starting with a simple assumption—that individuals seek their self-interest—the theorists built propositions about why individuals join organizations, how organizations structure their work, and what problems can emerge from such relationships. Those propositions, in turn, produced hypotheses—for example, that rational bureaucrats seek to maximize their budgets—that seemed to explain much commonly observed administrative behavior. Principal-agent theory not only helped develop an alternative explanation of bureaucratic behavior in the Hamiltonian-Wilsonian tradition, but it also identified the pathologies that, especially by the late 1970s, seemed so often to afflict bureaucratic behavior.

Political science seized on it as an answer to the theoretical problems that had long plagued the field. It provided both clear analysis and strong predictions that could be empirically tested. It coupled important political institutions with an approach that enjoyed a strong theoretical base. For public administration, this spelled trouble. Increasingly estranged from the association they had helped found, public administrationists found it difficult to counter either the mathematical rigor of the principal-agent approach or the zeal with which its proponents espoused it. The schism grew greater because few public administrationists were trained in applied calculus and formal models, so they were unprepared to fight back. The principal-agent challenge drove some public administrationists out of political science into public policy and public administration schools. A considerable number of public administrationists remained in their traditional home, but by the 1980s, they found themselves scraping for intellectual traction and struggling for acceptance. The formal approach has had tremendous intellectual appeal and great influence within political science. For a field seeking to keep up with the theoretical advances in economics, the combination of economic, transaction-cost, principal-agent, and related theories led to formal approaches to the field. Its supporters claimed that these approaches, in turn, established a strong movement that would soon become the dominant method for studying public administration.[26]

Its very popularity, however, also stirred heavy criticism, especially from theorists who contend that the search for rationality robs the study of organizations of their very life. Economic theories of organization, Charles Perrow contends, represent "a challenge that resembles the theme of the novel and movie *The Invasion of the Body-Snatchers*, where human forms are retained but all that we value about human influence and resentment of domination has disappeared."[27] Even one of formal theory's strongest voices, Terry M. Moe, agrees. He argues that the inner workings of bureaucracies tend to evaporate from most of these models. Instead, they appear "as black boxes that mysteriously mediate between interests and outcomes. The implicit claim is that institutions do not matter much."[28] Traditional public administrationists often add that the same goes for the people inside these institutions.

A more serious dispute arose within political science. Donald P. Green and Ian Shapiro charged that "rational choice scholarship has yet to get off the ground as a rigorous empirical enterprise." Indeed, they argue, "many of the objections that rational choice theorists characteristically advance against rival modes of social science turn out to be applicable to their own empirical work."[29] Kenneth A. Shepsle and Mark S. Bonchek counterattacked by admitting that "political science isn't rocket science." However, they argued, the formal models provide "purposely stripped-down versions of the real thing." These models, they wrote, provide greater rigor than the storytelling approach that characterized much of the post–World War II literature in political science.[30] They contended that solid study of bureaucracy requires embedding it in larger political systems; therefore, any effort to separate politics from administration is folly.

They argued that the relationships between bureaucrats and the rest of the system can be modeled as a bargaining process. From this work they spin three different (and conflicting) alternatives to explain bureaucratic behavior. First, because the bureaucracy has huge information advantages over elected officials, they exploit their knowledge to produce budgets that are too big, bureaucracies that are too numerous, and results that are inadequate. This approach builds on William A. Niskanen's 1971 work that argues politicians have insufficient information and incentives to provide better oversight.[31] Second, because politicians can be proactive and well informed, they can use their information to bargain effectively with bureaucrats over results. Improved information can reduce moral hazard.[32] Finally, they review the argument that information asymmetries might actually favor politicians. Elected officials can know more about key assets, especially the dynamics of political support, and can use their advantages to control effectively the behavior of bureaucrats.[33]

These conflicting propositions lead to several important conclusions about the formal approaches to bureaucracy. First, although they are intriguing, they are not theoretically mature. Their proponents frankly acknowledge that large holes remain in their arguments and that far more work needs to be done. In particular, even though the approach builds from models of individual behavior, many of the models are peculiarly people-free. Public administration, at the least, demonstrated that bureaucratic behavior matters, and if theory-builders are to be successful, the approach will need to become more sophisticated about modeling that behavior. Second, the approach leads in different, even contradictory, directions. The theorists have engaged in lively, even heated, arguments among themselves about which formal approach is most useful, and the battles are nowhere close to being over. Third, the theoretical propositions are far more elegant than their empirical tests. The behaviors they seek to model are extremely complex and not easily reducible to equations and statistics. To conduct empirical tests, the formalists must impose large constraints and look only at pieces of the puzzle. That, they contend, is a natural part of theory-building.

Traditional public administrationists have found the assumptions and models arbitrary and unrealistic. Especially for practically inclined researchers and practitioners, the formal models have proven unpersuasive. The formal approaches provide little guidance to administration-in-action. They also provide scant guidance, at best, about what they ought to do about it. In a previous research project, I interviewed one of the governors on the Federal Reserve Board. He laughed hard when talking about efforts by formal analysts to model his decision making. Those models, he said, bore little resemblance to what he actually did on the job.

The formal approaches thus have become far more advanced and sophisticated, but they have not yet won the day within political science. Nor have they bridged the gap between administrative theory and practice. Despite these criticisms, the theories introduced new approaches and developed new explanations that had largely escaped traditional public administration in the past. They provided, in particular, a far richer explanation of the linkages between bureaucrats and bureaucracies, on the one hand, and the larger political system on the other. They advanced the debate by framing some central questions far more sharply. In particular, formal theory provided an especially imaginative approach to resolving the Hamiltonian-Wilsonian dilemma. It is an approach that did not resort to artificial distinctions between politics and administration and that did produce a more scientific approach to the field. Public administration has learned it cannot ignore formal theory's significant contributions—even if it does not completely accept its approaches.

Reinventing Government

In the 1980s, a very different front opened in the effort to solve the Hamiltonian-Wilsonian dilemma. Unlike traditional public administration and formal theory, which academics launched, the new strategy emerged from pragmatic tactics government officials developed to cope with budgetary stress and complaints about public performance. In fact, theorists struggled to keep up with a blizzard of reforms in the United States and around the world: to sort the efforts into analytical categories, to gauge their results, and to assess their implications for administrative theory and practice. Unlike the Progressive reforms of a century before, the American "reinventing government" effort grew from the experiments of front-line administrators, popularized by journalists who covered them. For example, in 1988, journalist David Osborne celebrated a new breed of American governors, including a then little-known Arkansas chief executive, Bill Clinton.[34] His next book, in 1992, written with former city manager Ted Gaebler, fueled a broad-scale movement. They embraced "a new form of governance" created by "public entrepreneurs" around the country. These entrepreneurs, Osborne and Gaebler concluded, were reinventing government using ten strategies, ranging from "steering rather than rowing" to "meeting the needs of the customer, not the bureaucracy."[35]

The book described what some managers had been doing for years. In part, it was a critique of existing administrative practice. Traditional public administration, Osborne and Gaebler argued, hamstrung government managers because it did not allow them the flexibility to do their jobs. As a result, the performance of government suffered. In part, the book was also a polemic that made the case for a fundamentally reinvented government. In the best of the Hamiltonian-Wilsonian tradition, it argued that reinventing government required giving government managers, especially on the front lines, more responsibility for managing their programs. It was a claim that these managers knew best how to do their jobs—and that they would do those jobs well if they were given flexibility and were motivated.

Their work caught the eye of the 1992 Democratic candidates, Bill Clinton and Al Gore, who made Osborne and Gaebler's argument the government management theme of their campaign. Soon after Clinton's inauguration, he named Gore to head a "National Performance Review" (NPR) to apply Osborne and Gaebler's model to reinventing the federal government. Their book quickly moved from being a bestseller to a how-to guide for the new administration's program. The NPR pursued hundreds of recommendations and an aggressive downsizing of the federal bureaucracy. The Clinton administration did indeed produce substantial accomplishments, and it shrank the federal workforce by more than 350,000 positions. Some parts of the federal government were largely unaffected by the reinvention effort, and some federal employees criticized the effort as not so much a positive effort to improve the federal government and motivate as a negative strategy to reduce the number of government employees.[36]

Some of "reinventing government's" reforms were Jeffersonian-style bottom-up initiatives, like "empowering" lower-level employees and pursuing a major customer-service initiative to make government programs more responsive to citizens' needs. For the most part, however, reinventing government was a Wilsonian-Hamiltonian initiative that sought to strengthen bureaucracy and reduce the number of levels to strengthen the hierarchy. The reinventing government model replaced the traditional administrative model, but it was more a rebuff to the rigidity it had spawned than a revolt against its principles. Indeed, the movement grew directly out of Wilson's argument to separate politics and administration. Osborne and Gaebler made a strong case for administrative competence and discretion.

It was scarcely surprising, therefore, that modern Madisonians roundly attacked the NPR as they had attacked other variations of the Hamiltonian tradition. As editor of public administration's leading journal, *Public Administration Review*, David Rosenbloom warned reformers, "Don't forget the politics!"[37] Congressional Research Service analyst Ronald C. Moe contended that the NPR threatened serious damage to democracy by seeking to uproot public administration's roots in administrative law and constitutional practice.[38] Frustrated with the drumbeat of private-sector models, H. George Frederickson argued strongly that public administration is *public* and ought not be confused with private-sector strategies.[39] Indeed, the NPR's arguments for "customer service" and "entrepreneurial government" enraged Madisonians. Not only did they see the public and private sectors as so different that private reforms simply were not transferable to government, they also believed that private-sector approaches threatened democratic accountability.

The conflicts were deeply rooted. Madisonians have scrapped with Hamiltonians for generations over where the balance of power in the American political system ought to lie. Moreover, the Hamiltonian and Jeffersonian forces within the NPR led to a constant tug-of-war among its elements: Should the reinventers stress downsizing or customer service, performance-driven control or employee empowerment? Administrative reform movements are hard-wired into the national political culture. Indeed, perhaps no other nation has so consistently pursued such reform, especially during the twentieth century. The NPR was very different, compared with the others. Its intellectual provenance came from a best-seller produced from outside academe, not from its theoretical leaders. Its instincts, however, contained internal contradictions. Its Hamiltonian and Jeffersonian features ensured both internal conflict and attack from academics, who had been marginalized in the debate and who often found themselves opposed to at least some of the NPR's tactics.

The New Public Management

America's NPR was but part of a broader, global management reform movement christened "the new public management."[40] The movement grew out of a strategy devised by a liberal New Zealand government and a conservative British government to shrink government's size and improve its performance. These governments self-consciously sought to drive government administration by models of market-like, self-interested behavior. In fact, the reformers borrowed heavily from principal-agent theory, to the point that phrases like "moral hazard" and "adverse selection" regularly popped up in conversations among government officials. Together, these reforms—and others occurring in a surprising array of nations around the world—comprised "the new public management."[41]

While scholars debated whether it, in fact, represented a new paradigm or part of a continual battle to reconcile old ideas, there was little doubt that it represented an approach substantially different from public administration.[42] It focused on management rather than social values; on efficiency rather than equity; on mid-level managers instead of elites; on generic approaches rather than tactics tailored to specifically *public* issues; on organizations rather than processes and institutions; and on management rather than political science or sociology.[43] It also provoked a substantial new literature with a strong comparative focus.[44]

The New Zealand reforms became the very center of the new public management. In the early 1980s, the country faced staggering economic problems. The economy stagnated, inflation soared, the currency was in crisis, and the nation could not afford its expansive welfare state. The nation's leaders launched perhaps the world's most aggressive management reforms. Policymakers would clearly define the outputs they wanted to buy and sign contracts with managers to deliver them. The managers would have great flexibility in deciding how to do so. They would receive financial rewards for meeting the targets, and their jobs would be in jeopardy if they did not. The government also privatized many formerly government-owned enterprises and deregulated many industries.[45]

Thus, the reformers quite explicitly borrowed from the formal models of bureaucracy. The New Zealand reformers attempted to substitute markets for traditional governmental mechanisms, and contracts for authority. The reformers not only followed the formal model, they embraced its theoretical propositions. Even in casual conversations, New

Zealand Treasury officials spoke easily about principal-agent problems and moral hazard. Indeed, in explaining the reforms, two former government officials wrote, "The goal for designers of public sector institutions and processes is to avoid public choice problems and minimize agency costs."[46] In fact, New Zealand officials sometimes joked about how closely they followed the principal-agent model. They told stories about American public choice economists who visited to study their experiences. "We developed this model," they quoted the economists as joking, "but we never expected anyone to follow it."[47]

These changes dramatically transformed New Zealand's government. For reformers, the New Zealand experiment was a beacon of change—privatizing public assets, substituting markets for governments, giving managers more flexibility but holding them accountable for results.[48] Careful and balanced assessments have found that the reforms in fact produced substantial improvements. The market strategy encountered some problems, especially because some public services had no private markets to use for comparison, because managers tended to rely on a "checklist" mentality of meeting narrow output goals without necessarily fulfilling the broader public purpose, and because the new competition model imposed its own compliance costs. As Allen Schick pointed out in his definitive analysis of the New Zealand reforms, "No other country has accomplished what New Zealand has in building accountability into the framework of government." Indeed, Schick finds, "it is a singular accomplishment in the development of modern public administration." Moreover, "taking accountability seriously is a genuine triumph of New Zealand public management."[49]

Despite New Zealand's substantial progress, however, Schick found that the process-based accountability, which in turn was based on defining each manager's responsibility for outputs, created substantial gaps in performance. The problem became especially serious "when unspecified matters escape accountability," especially issues not anticipated in management contracts, for which clear responsibilities cannot be defined in advance or for which outputs cannot clearly be measured after the fact. Greater efforts to write contracts in more detail, Schick worried, might "split government into seemingly airtight compartments" that would leave important issues out. The problem, Schick explained, is that "in practice, the boundaries between . . . accountabilities are somewhat fuzzy." Focusing more on specific outputs, Schick also worried, might undermine a government's ability to build "the capacity to achieve its larger political and strategic objectives."[50]

The Hamiltonian-Wilsonian approach produced tremendous results. Indeed, it is perhaps most responsible for the energy and accomplishments of American government, as well as some of its most significant reform ideas. But it has long proven unsatisfying to theorists because of the messy intellectual problems it leaves behind, and it has never resolved the fuzzy-boundary dilemma of how to create enough capacity in bureaucracy to do the job without so strengthening it that its power threatens democracy.

From Wilson to the new public management, practitioners and analysts alike have struggled to reconcile these competing aims. At both the beginning and the end of this period, as well as much of the time between, academics provided the intellectual foundation for many of the reforms. The Progressives built on the orthodox view of public administration that Wilson, Goodnow, and Taylor helped create. The modern executive branch then built on their efforts, through the Brownlow Committee and World War II. As that orthodoxy came under increasing attack, practitioners looked for other solutions. The search for a new pragmatism ironically relied on the more abstract view of public administration embodied in formal theory. That theory provided a critique of traditional public administration. It also provided straightforward remedies—understanding decisions as the central administrative act, information as the central element in decisions, and information pathologies as the central administrative problem. Finally, it prescribed how to improve administrative practice—substitute markets and competition for authority and hierarchy.

The new public management and reinventing government grew directly from these roots. They were very different reform movements than those that previously had emerged in the twentieth century, which had built exclusively on the orthodox approach spun out by Wilson, Goodnow, Taylor, and others. They were scarcely atheoretical. But they grew from roots grafted onto practice from microeconomics, not political science. Especially in the United States, they tended to grow more from ad hoc experimentation than from the more coherent philosophy that shaped the Progressive influence. Both forces crippled traditional public administration's ability to grapple with the big ideas of the new public management and reinventing government. Because they grew out of a fundamentally different discipline, public administrationists had a difficult time defending their ideas. And because practitioners pursued their reforms in such an ad hoc fashion, inspired in part by formal theory but often not fully informed by it, analysts often lacked clear categories into which to sort the efforts, let alone to examine them carefully. Traditional public administration, formal theory, and reinventing government efforts thus found themselves strange bedfellows, often without realizing that they even shared the same bed.

ASSESSING THE HAMILTONIAN-WILSONIAN CONNECTION

Beyond those tensions lay the basic problem with the Hamiltonian-Wilsonian approaches, which Schick's argument revealed. The approaches all relied on being able to draw clear boundaries. The increasing fuzziness of those boundaries, however, undermined the effort. How can administrators build sufficient administrative capacity to make government effective without making it so strong that it threatens democratic accountability? The variations on the Hamiltonian-Wilsonian approach, from separating politics from administration through the variations of reinventing government and, ultimately, to New Zealand's creation of a contract-driven model of management, share the same problem—attempts to protect democracy by carefully circumscribing the discretion of bureaucrats ultimately fail. Many theorists have tried to strengthen administrative theory by drawing clearer boundaries, but these efforts have come at precisely the time that policy strategies have made boundaries ever fuzzier.

In contrast, traditional public administration has a long and noble tradition of research on the fuzzy boundaries of discretion. Woodrow Wilson's work focused fundamentally on that problem—how to strengthen administrators without risking an administration going out of political control. By World War II, traditional public administration had developed two standard but conflicting perspectives on accountability. One perspective, following Carl J. Friedrich, contended that accountability had to come from an administrator's own integrity and thus was largely a product of professional training and experience.[51] Herman Finer strongly disagreed and argued that accountability essentially had to flow from control by outside forces with legal oversight powers, such as Congress, the president, and the courts.[52] This debate has never been, and indeed never can be, resolved. Both personal qualities and legal prescriptions inevitably are part of the accountability process, and the balance between them can never be finally fixed.

The policy problems that emerged at the end of the twentieth century, however, illustrated that even seeking an equilibrium between checks internal and external to the administrator is insufficient. As policy problems have become more complex, as divided party government has become a fixture in American politics, as the role of interest groups has increased, as policy administration has become more interconnected with the private sector, as bureaucratic politics has become more complex and less formalized, as organizational networks have departed more from standard chains of command, as bureaucratic structures have simultaneously become more centralized and decentralized, and as politics generally has become more volatile, accountability has become more elusive.[53] Control can come from within an agency or from the outside. The kind and context of the policy, furthermore, can make the degree of control relatively high or low. Accountability can therefore flow through different channels: bureaucratic control by supervisors; legal control by formal overseers, such as Congress or the president; control through the norms of professional groups; and political control through democratic pressures imposed on administrators.[54] In American democracy, no concept is more central to the role of bureaucracy than accountability. As the conduct and context of policy has become more complex, however, ensuring accountability has likewise become more difficult.[55]

This tradition grows from public administration's firm foundation in public law, which seeks to guide administrative discretion without a strong reliance on constitutional government.[56] When tough policy problems challenge public law, public administration reformers have long suggested broadening public participation in the administrative and political processes. When process becomes hard to manage, reformers have tended to focus more on results, especially equity in public policy decisions.[57] Other approaches, including many of the public management and reinvention perspectives, have tended toward silence on these issues. They have focused little on public law and concentrated more on empowering administrators. But with administrators increasingly charged with bridging fuzzy boundaries, the puzzle of how to structure and manage discretion has become even more difficult, and the need to respond has grown markedly.

Theorists therefore built alternatives that focused on a more self-consciously political approach to government management. These alternatives often conflicted, but they shared one central premise—that effective study and practice of administration had to begin on the outside, unlike the inside-out approach of the Hamiltonians and Wilsonians. Moreover, they put politics, not administration, at the center of things. Administration was not so much the fulcrum from which politics swung, as sometimes seemed the case for the Hamiltonians and Wilsonians. Rather, administration was but one aspect of American politics. If some theories painted a richer, more textured picture of administration's role, the alternatives struggled far more with the challenge of devising a prescriptive model of administration. Given the realities of politics, what should administrators do? And given the imperatives of democratic government, how can administrative power be held accountable?

BOUNDARIES OUTSIDE THE BUREAUCRACY ||| 5

The issue of administrative accountability—the challenge of controlling bureaucratic power in a democratic republic—depends most on managing the boundaries between bureaucracy and the political institutions beyond it. Each of the four administrative traditions has developed its own approach, and policymakers have struggled constantly to balance the competing instincts of the different traditions. Moreover, the basic problem has itself grown as the boundaries have become fuzzier. All of the traditions have increasingly focused on the importance of building politics into the model, but the enormous uncertainties and variations in politics have taken them into an increasingly tumultuous analytical and pragmatic world.

THE HAMILTONIAN-MADISONIAN CONNECTION

Some scholars have sought to marry Hamilton's strong-executive model to Madison's distinctively political approach to government. However, instead of following Wilson's strategy of making bureaucracy the center of the analysis, they have built an approach focused fundamentally on America's constitutional balance-of-power system. In the Hamiltonian-Wilsonian approach, what was important was what bureaucracies did. The Hamiltonian-Madisonians, by contrast, rejected the politics-administration dichotomy in favor of an explicitly political model. Because their approach grew so strongly from political reality, they produced richly detailed analyses of how things actually work. The very richness of the analyses, however, made it hard for them to produce normative recommendations or sharp theoretical propositions. The political instinct to probe the system's vast complexities ran headlong into the administrative imperative for clear guidance.

American political thought has a rich Madisonian tradition built on two elements. First, politics depends on compromise, political compromise flows from power, and the power of political institutions depends on balance. Madison worried about balancing executive power with Congress and the courts to shrink the risk of tyranny. Second, administration is secondary to politics. Madison wrote little about administration, but he implicitly made the case for subordinating administration to politics. The great struggles to balance political power came first, and administrative issues followed later. That differed sharply from the Hamiltonian-Wilsonian approach, which made administration central to the analysis.

Bureaucratic Politics and Implementation

In the 1970s and 1980s, some American political scientists used the Hamilton-Madisonian model to develop a new "bureaucratic politics" approach to administration. They saw administrative behavior in largely pathological terms, the product of tensions in the administrative process as it implemented public programs. In particular, they reacted to the perceived failures of so many of the Johnson administration's Great Society programs—suggesting that they seemed to have so little to show for themselves. In the extended subtitle to their classic, *Implementation*, Jeffrey L. Pressman and Aaron B. Wildavsky frame the problem: "How Great Expectations in Washington Are Dashed in Oakland; Or, Why It's Amazing that Federal Programs Work at All, This Being a Saga of the Economic Development Administration as Told by Two Sympathetic Observers Who Seek to Build Morals on a Foundation of Ruined Hopes."[1]

Indeed, the subtitle captured the major themes of the bureaucratic politics literature. Bureaucratic politics sought to explain why public programs so often produce disappointing results. That often gave the literature a distinctly pathological touch, since much of it focused on case studies explaining policy failures.[2] Indeed, Brian W. Hogwood and B. Guy Peters explicitly borrowed the pathology metaphor from medicine to create a typology of why programs get sick and die.[3] The roots of failure, the analysts argued, lie in the complexity of the system. Federalism and a flood of interest-group cross-pressures, coupled with balance-of-powers politics, made it hard to build a consensus in favor of doing anything. These forces, in turn, made it easy to derail ambitious policy proposals. As Pressman and Wildavsky explained, if a policy process required seventy different approvals and the chance of a successful agreement at each step was very high at 99 percent, there was nevertheless less than a fifty-fifty chance of success.[4] It was little wonder, they concluded, that so many governmental programs failed so often.

Bureaucratic politics did not focus exclusively on postmortem research. Although complexity was endemic and failure common, the scholars who framed the bureaucratic politics movement believed that a richer understanding of the administrative system's politics could improve its results. For Morton H. Halperin, for example, improving the management of the State Department required understanding first the cross pressures operating on it.[5] All this assumed that administrators actually wanted to pursue the program's goals. The implementation game was so complex that they enjoyed many chances to scuttle it.[6]

Thus, the implementation researchers believed that the disappointing results of Johnson's Great Society's programs demanded a fresh interpretation that went beyond traditional public administration. The study of implementation provided the "missing link," as Erwin C. Hargrove put it, which helped connect ambitious ideas and effective results.[7] The approach's insight was positively anti-Wilsonian. "No one is clearly in charge of implementation," Randall B. Ripley and Grace Franklin concluded. Therefore, they said, "domestic programs virtually never achieve all that is expected of them."[8] The work created a depressing forecast of the prospects for success.

Like newspaper reporters, analysts tended to be drawn to interesting stories. As in journalism, the most intriguing stories were programs that seemed not to work well. This approach produced an elaborate inventory of the causes of failures, but they did not yield a very sharp sense of what separated failures from successes. In fact, from air-traffic control to delivering Social Security checks, many programs do work very well, but this approach did not help explain why.

Moreover, much of this literature focused heavily on intergovernmental programs that involved state and local implementation of federal programs. In fact, nearly 80 percent of all of the entries for programs and organizations in one standard implementation textbook were for programs and organizations that have an important intergovernmental dimension.[9] That focus is scarcely surprising, given the predominantly intergovernmental nature of the strategies the federal government used in launching the Great Society programs of the 1960s. The literature did not capture the rich range of other policy strategies. Neither did it fully depict the sharing of power that was central to intergovernmental programs, in which state and local governments adapt federal money and programs to their local needs. Indeed, funding state and local experimentation, adaptation, and variation was precisely the object of many of these programs. Any attempt to build local discretion and a shift of power into federal programs was bound to produce conflict—and it did. By contrast, much of this literature took the top-down, goal-driven approach characteristic of Hamiltonian analysis. From that perspective, conflicts over program goals seemed chaotic. The Hamiltonian approach, moreover, has no room for dynamic change as different players in the system tinker with program goals along the extended implementation chain. Much of the implementation literature combined a Hamiltonian approach with Jeffersonian cases. It succeeded far better in capturing the enduring conflicts between these traditions than in advancing new ideas about how to resolve them.

By the mid-1980s, a new stage of implementation research emerged, as scholars searched for the systematic variations that separated success from failure.[10] They contended that public programs could in fact succeed. The conditions that produced success and failure varied over time and across levels of government. Implementation, therefore, depended on its political context. Critics pointed out that this second phase of implementation illustrated but could not prove their propositions. The literature remained grounded in case studies of individual programs, but the propositions they developed remained invalidated by comparison.[11] That led to a third stage of implementation research, led by scholars like Laurence J. O'Toole Jr., which sought a more systematic investigation of implementation and a better sense of what conditions produced which results.[12] This shift helped implementation advance past the presumption of failure that dominated the first stage and the broad synthetic work of the second stage. It also focused on what administrators do—manage programs—instead of how they do it. That, in turn, separated implementation from traditional public administration.

By the 1990s, the implementation approach helped frame a distinctly Madisonian alternative. It also undermined traditional public administration. In pointing to manifest failures, it armed an attack on traditional administrative approaches. If so many programs worked so badly, could the underlying theory survive? It also argued that any attempt at theory-building had to build on very different intellectual and political traditions. Implementation established that government programs were hard to manage and that the political setting of these programs helped explain why. However, with the notable exception of sophisticated analysis by scholars like O'Toole, much of the literature did not provide very clear guidance about what either analysts or managers could do about it.[13] The rise of the reinventing government movement made managers less patient for analysis that focused on complexity. They searched for a sharp sword with which to cut the Gordian knot, not a thicker knot that resisted assault.

Public Management

Within the rise of public policy schools in the 1970s, a new "public management" approach emerged. Public management sought to understand what administrators—especially top-level executives—could do to make programs work. Unlike implementation, it focused less on programs than on managers. Unlike public administration, it focused on decision-making more than on organizational processes and structures. And unlike formal theory, it reveled in the complexity of the management process instead of seeking to impose order upon it. In fact, as Laurence E. Lynn Jr. contends, "there is no intellectual alternative to regarding the experience of each public executive as a unique case." Since managers always find themselves in different positions, generalizable principles are impossible.[14] The search for teachable truths therefore leads to broad propositions, guideposts for public managers to check. Public management used case studies to understand the behavior of top administrators, typically political appointees such as cabinet secretaries and agency administrators, and to understand how best to craft management strategies.[15]

For public management scholars, "leadership counts," as Robert Behn put it.[16] Solving problems depends on "managerial craftsmanship" to "break through bureaucracy."[17] Its proponents self-consciously distinguished public management from public administration.[18] Public management teaches that managers must develop strategies and that their strategies must solve three problems. First, they must devise a strategy for overseeing their programs and for the administrators who manage them. Second, since in the Madisonian tradition managers find themselves in conflict about what they should do and how, they must build political support—within and outside their agency—for their strategy. Finally, they must maintain their agency's health—its credibility and capacity—and obtain the resources they need to do their job—especially legislation, funding, and skilled personnel.[19] The public management movement developed along three fronts. Its researchers focused first on building the leadership skills of top managers.[20] In looking to the outside world, its researchers then examined relations between top executives and other political forces, especially the president, Congress, and interest groups.[21] In looking within public agencies, they finally built on the pathological approach of implementation to chart the games that bureaucrats play in frustrating the strategies of top officials.[22]

Public management, often implicitly, sometimes explicitly, rejected public administration and related Hamiltonian-Wilsonian approaches. Public management scholars, in fact, typically referred to "traditional public administration," with "traditional" as a pejorative term. Instead, these scholars focused heavily on the Madisonian and political dimensions of administrative behavior. For example, two public management experts from Harvard's Kennedy School pointedly argue, "Public managers are negotiators," and "public managers are leaders." By contrast, "Public administrators are experts."[23] Traditional administration has a place in the management of public programs, but the public management movement holds that it is subordinate to the leadership of top managers. There is rich irony in public management's rejection of public administration, for most of the public policy programs grew from the foundations of earlier public administration programs. For example, the premier public management program, at Harvard's Kennedy School, came from the Graduate School of Public Administration, originally established in 1936 as part of the field's training movement. Public administration scholars like Francis E. Rourke had for decades championed the importance of a political understanding of public administration, but the public management programs sought to replace the old traditions with a new approach.[24]

The public-management movement has made useful contributions to the study of public policy and administration. Far more than implementation, it celebrates the art of the possible. Far more than traditional public administration, it focuses on the unique role played by top-level administrators and on the special problems they face. Perhaps most important, it builds on its Madisonian roots to describe, in top-down Hamiltonian fashion, how managers can simultaneously be powerful and politically shrewd. Public management helped solve some of the knottiest problems of the Hamiltonian-Wilsonian approach to government management. It did so, however, by minimizing the role of organizational structure and administrative processes, which lay at the core of the Wilsonian approach. It also replicated, without building the linkages, the arguments that scholars like Rourke had made within public administration for a generation. As a result, faculty members at public policy programs often pointedly wondered what theoretical structure public management brought to policy debates.

Institutional Choice

Meanwhile, a variant of the formal modeling approach developed within political science. Christened the "institutional-choice approach," it introduced a more Madisonian perspective to the microeconomic models by incorporating the influence of political players outside of the bureaucracy. It examined the basic interactions among bureaucracies, politicians, and interest groups, and it postulated bureaucracy as an agent of political forces.[25] The institutional approach thus fundamentally changed the role that bureaucracy plays in the analysis. Bureaucracy was no longer central. Nor did it play the primary role in others. It is one player among others and an instrument others within the political system create with which to pursue their own political ends. The formal approach eliminates the policy-administration dichotomy by placing bureaucracy squarely in the middle of its political environment. Institutional-choice theory thus completes the steps, in rigorous form, first made by bureaucratic politics. It replaces the traditional public administration view of bureaucracy-as-actor, as independent variable, with a new view of bureaucracy-as-acted-upon, as dependent variable. Organizations are not designed to promote efficiency but, rather, to reflect the power of political interests.

Institutional-choice analysts conclude that the power of bureaucracies is the result of an equilibrium that contending political forces produce. Different organizational strategies produce different configurations of political forces and different kinds of uncertainty. Therefore, policymakers can shift policy results by making the institutional choices most likely to produce the results they seek.[26] Thus, it is scarcely surprising that bureaucracies so often seem to be inefficient. Institutional-choice theory contends that they are not fundamentally designed to be efficient. They are not so much policy instruments as the product of rules, implicit and explicit, shaped by political forces. These rules can be discovered, influenced, and changed. Any attempt to reform bureaucracy thus must take account of, not just efficiency (which might not even be accounted for at all), but also the political forces that will create the rules under which the bureaucracy must operate.

Some research in this tradition, such as John E. Chubb and Terry M. Moe's controversial study on reform of local schools, builds on economic theories to recommend more choice as a way to make bureaucracies more responsive.[27] Other analyses have become even more sophisticated both in modeling bureaucratic behavior and in specifying outcomes. Morris's examination of the Federal Reserve, for example, carefully assesses the "independence" of Fed policymaking. He compares the Fed's decisions with presidential and congressional policy preferences to conclude that monetary policy results from a highly interactive system.[28]

By changing focus from bureaucracy-as-actor to bureaucracy-as-acted-upon, institutional-choice analysis fundamentally shifts the inquiry. It seeks not so much to understand bureaucracies in order to improve their efficiency and results but, rather, to understand how the power of political interests shapes bureaucratic behavior. By extension, improving government performance thus is a matter of making the right institutional choices to produce the most productive bureaucratic incentives (hence the label "institutional choice"). Moreover, the theory suggested that the key to holding bureaucracies politically accountable lies in strong administrative oversight by elected officials. Why does bureaucracy so often seem unaccountable? Formal theorists had a ready explanation. As David Mayhew concluded, members of Congress engage in little oversight because they have few incentives for doing so. Their constituents care much less about overseeing government bureaucracies than they do constituency casework and policymaking.[29] Thus, the theory of incentives not only determines how bureaucrats-as-agents behave, it shapes the behavior of elected-officials-as-principals as well.[30]

Institutional choice thus provides a mechanism for asking—and answering—whether elected officials can change bureaucratic results. Is the bureaucracy so intransigent that bureaucrats resist efforts by presidents and Congress to shift policy? Or can elected officials find the right incentives to shift bureaucratic behavior? Several scholars have found that elected officials can actually shift bureaucratic outcomes.[31] In fact, B. Dan Wood and Richard W. Waterman conclude, "elected leaders can and do shape bureaucratic behavior in systematic ways."[32] This analysis has tended to focus on the process, rather than the outcome, of bureaucratic behavior. For example, analysts tend to study the number of seizures by drug enforcement agencies or the level of enforcement activity by regulatory agencies. Those numbers are easier to gather, and they fit more neatly into the models' predictions. The analysis tends not to focus, however, on the results the activity produces.

Of course, this is an old problem—one that traditional public administration did not deal with any better. In drug enforcement, for example, thousands of small dealers can be put out of business without affecting the large suppliers; a large number of seizures can produce high levels of activity without demonstrating effectiveness. Likewise, hundreds of small antitrust cases can pale by comparison with the implications of a single case, such as the divestiture of AT&T or the breakup of Microsoft. Thus, statistical links between independent variables, such as changes in presidential administrations, and dependent process measures, such as the number of seizures or inspections, may in fact say very little about bureaucratic outcomes. That weakens the argument for a clear principal-agent connection between the preferences of elected officials and the activities of government bureaucracies. It undermines the power of the formal approach. It also underlines the critical information problems that afflict inferences about the whole process. But it does little to sap the great intellectual appeal and power of the straightforward formal model, which derives clear, testable propositions from simple, clear assumptions.

That is why, in the view of institutional choice scholars, bureaucratic structures often do not promote efficiency and too often produce ineffective results. Poor performance comes from poor design. Bureaucracies are the result of rules, implicit and explicit, that are, in turn, the result of political forces. These rules can be discovered, influenced, and changed. Any attempt to reform bureaucracy thus must take account not just (and perhaps not even) of efficiency but, rather, of the constellation of political forces that will create the rules under which the bureaucracy must operate. That has enhanced the appeal of the institutional-choice model within political science.

Assessing the Hamiltonian-Madisonian Connection

Hamilton long ago made the case for a strong and effective public administration. For analysts, the question has always been whether to start building from the inside out or the outside in. Orthodox public administration and its Wilsonian alternatives took the former approach. They tended to view political pressures from outside the bureaucracy as a problem to be dealt with—as a possible drag on efficiency but as a necessary element of democratic accountability. Students of implementation and its variants took precisely the opposite approach. They began by recognizing the reality of crosscutting political forces and the American separation-of-powers system for balancing them. Bureaucracy tended to be more the source of pathologies that frustrated the accomplishment of public purpose than a tool for executing the public will. Reconciling administration with the inevitable power of politics was the central problem for the Wilsonian variants. The Madisonians, on the other hand, struggled to devise strategies to make bureaucracy effective within the constraints of political reality.

Both of these Hamiltonian approaches, however, shared a fundamentally top-down view of bureaucracy. For Wilsonians, this was a natural product of their focus on hierarchy. For Madisonians, it flowed from a model of political accountability that held administrators responsible to elected officials. The long Jeffersonian tradition, however, spun out two alternatives that built bureaucracy instead from the bottom up.

THE JEFFERSONIAN-WILSONIAN CONNECTION

The Jeffersonian dimension to public administration has not developed with nearly the richness of the Hamiltonian variants. In large part, this is because the Jeffersonian influence in American politics has been more religion than reality, more ideology than practice. Indeed, as chapter 2 pointed out, as president, even Jefferson himself was more a Hamiltonian. Moreover, the American administrative tradition has been most strongly dominated by the two top-down variants of Hamiltonianism: working from the inside to make bureaucracies strong and effective; or working from the outside to hold them accountable. The bottom-up approach has historically carried little influence. Top administrators have found little to tell them how to manage their agencies better; elected officials have found little to help them hold administrators more accountable; and the top-down approach has most captured scholars' attention. Thus, despite the reverence for the Jeffersonian tradition, there has been relatively little work, by either practitioners or academics, to develop it.

Street-Level Bureaucrats and Customer Service

One notable effort by Michael Lipsky focused on the role and behavior of "street-level bureaucrats." Lipsky built an elegant analysis of administrative behavior by focusing on how police officers, social workers, legal aid lawyers, and other front-line workers translate governmental policy into action. Like other Wilsonians, he focused on the bureaucratic context—the pressures that street-level bureaucrats face in trying to manage complicated services while coping with insatiable demands. Lipsky found that ambiguous expectations and enormous caseloads pose huge challenges for these government officials. They cope by rationing services and struggling to match expectations with demands. They thus exercise genuine discretion and enjoy substantial autonomy from the organization's authority. Agency "policy" becomes defined by how their individual decisions add up. For Lipsky, politics and policy become joined in the behavior of these front-line managers. Both policy and behavior build at least as much from the bottom up as from the top down.[33]

That recognition of the importance of front-line workers spilled over into the government reform movement of the 1990s, especially into one part of the Clinton administration's "reinventing government" campaign. The administration's efforts to improve customer service and "empower" lower-level administrators, in particular, followed the bottom-up philosophy. These initiatives elaborated on David Osborne and Ted Gaebler's proposal that government meet "the needs of the customer, not the bureaucracy." They argued, "The greatest irritant most people experience in their dealings with government is the arrogance of the bureaucracy." Private companies were investing more energy in trying to satisfy their customers, and government, they concluded, had no alternative but to do the same. For government, that required "turning agency-driven government on its head," by putting the needs of citizens first—over the convenience of government administrators. Customer-driven systems, they contended, make governments more accountable, stimulate more innovation, and improve efficiency. Government officials often have to change their behavior to make this happen—to make government officials more entrepreneurial and to empower lower-level administrators.[34]

The federal government launched a major customer-service initiative to improve government's relations with citizens. In the last year of the Clinton administration, the government applied the American Customer Satisfaction Index, a joint product of University of Michigan Business School, Arthur Andersen, and the American Society for Quality, to federal programs. The survey found that customer satisfaction with many government services compares favorably with the private sector and that the range of satisfaction scores was roughly similar in the public and private sectors.[35] While some critics objected to the "customer" metaphor, there was little doubt that focusing more attention on how well the government performed was helping to improve government's service.

Focusing on service, however, required reengineering government's service systems from the bottom up instead of from the top down. For example, the efforts of several states to improve their drivers' license bureaus led them to study patterns in the demand for help, to cross-train workers so they could meet variations in those demands, and in some cases even to relocate license offices to shopping malls and to expand their hours. That further underlined the service function and gave front-line operators more discretion in solving problems.

Assessing the Jeffersonian-Wilsonian Connection

Although Americans have celebrated the Jeffersonian ideal of local self-government for centuries, in the bureaucratic tradition it has been honored far more in the abstract than in practice. The Wilsonian approach, which has long focused on the role and behavior of bureaucracies, contains a natural bias toward top-down analysis. Lipsky's book proved a major breakthrough by turning bureaucratic behavior on its head and looking at administrative functions from the outside in and from the bottom up. With few exceptions, like Richard Elmore's analysis of implementation as "backward mapping," from the desired result to the process that produced it, the Hamiltonian top-down analysis has proven far more powerful than the Jeffersonian bottom-up variant.[36]

THE JEFFERSONIAN-MADISONIAN CONNECTION

Other theorists have understood that authority and hierarchy have traditionally rested at the very core of traditional organizational theory. They also have recognized, however, that many of government's most important strategies, especially since World War II, have involved more partnerships between governments, more government contracting with nongovernmental organizations, and more multiorganizational partnerships within government. These partnerships grew not so much because of an explicit policy choice but from pragmatic strategies devised to help government cope with the growing complexity of public programs.[37] Public managers built these partnerships to assemble those who had a piece of the policy action, to incorporate expertise that the government lacked, and to avoid growing the government bureaucracy as government programs expanded. The government's pragmatic responses developed first; analysts' efforts to describe and categorize them followed, especially in network theory and a more advanced approach to devolution. These new approaches emerged as government's behavior traveled further from its traditional roots in hierarchical authority and, thus, posed growing problems for describing how public administration worked—and how it ought to work.

Networks and Governance

Analysts, for example, discovered that government relied more on a wide variety of partnerships with nonprofit and voluntary organizations.[38] The result, H. Brinton Milward and others argued, was a trend toward a "hollow state," with government organizations providing essential services but with most of the production taking place outside the bureaucracy's walls, through relationships with nongovernmental partners.[39] These increasing connections among public, private, and nonprofit organizations profoundly disrupt traditional notions of administration. In fact, such interorganizational relationships epitomize the ultimate "fuzzy boundary" problem. Successfully bridging the boundaries requires different strategies and fresh tactics to ensure effective and responsive programs.[40]

Public administrationists responded by developing new ideas founded on networks and informal relationships instead of hierarchy and authority. Its contributors have disagreed about whether "networks" constitute an approach, a theory, or a loose construct. What they did share is a focus on the relationships among the players in the network.[41] Those players focus not on the network's structure, as in traditional bureaucracy, but on the purposes they share. Moreover, these networks are not fixed with unchanging players. Different relationships spring up around different programs. Grants, contracts, and money tie the players together. The partners in each network might well find themselves working with each other often on different projects, but perhaps never in the same network configuration twice. The network approach, in fact, represents the virtual bridge from traditional hierarchy to the knowledge-driven information society. Some government agencies, like the Occupational Safety and Health Administration, have restructured themselves to make their organization more "horizontal" than "vertical."[42]

This work has made several important contributions. First, it helped public administration escape the pathologies of theory deeply rooted in hierarchical authority. Second, the reality-driven features of the network approach presented a theoretical structure that far better matched developing administrative practice. Third, the network approach has led to intriguing new methods for coordination that do not rely solely on authority.[43] The primary force behind authority had always been its power to secure coordination. Networks presented a genuine alternative for both theory and practice. Fourth and most important, it linked the notion of *governance* with an understanding of the workings of *government*. This last contribution is the most important because, as H. George Frederickson argues, this provides the critical connection "to the big issues of democratic government. It is in governance theory that public administration wrestles with problems of representation, political control of bureaucracy, and the democratic legitimacy of institutions and networks in the time of the fragmented and disarticulated state."[44] For Laurence E. Lynn Jr., Carolyn J. Heinrich, and Carolyn Hill, "governance" consists of "regimes of laws, administrative rules, judicial rulings, and practices that constrain, prescribe, and enable governmental activity."[45] This approach, coupled with careful investigation of the web of relationships within government, provides a strong foundation on which to build future theoretical advances.

The terrorist attacks in September 2001 underlined the importance of the network approach. The attacks themselves emerged out of a closely coordinated network of terrorist cells that were supported, in turn, by a loose network of terrorist organizations. In the first minutes following the attacks, emergency forces in both New York and Washington used long-developed network-based approaches to forge a response pulling together firefighters, police officers, emergency medical technicians, hospital workers, doctors, and nurses into a vast network of help. Part of the Bush administration's response to the attacks was to devise a new cabinet-level Office of Homeland Security. President Bush named Pennsylvania Governor Tom Ridge to coordinate the office's activity—as, essentially, a czar to bring together the diverse elements of the domestic antiterrorist network. Meanwhile, the president's foreign policy team built a coordinated effort to undermine the terrorists' financial, military, and diplomatic support. In short, what emerged from the terrorist attacks was a front-line network to cope with the attacks' immediate aftermath, a high-level domestic network to reduce the risk of future attacks, and an international network to undermine the terrorists—who themselves operated through a network. In the aftermath of that sad day, reports identified numerous problems in the short- and long-term response. But it is impossible to escape the fact that the network approach proved far better than competing administrative theories in charting the major issues and in taking the first steps in framing a response. Indeed, a careful empirical study by Thad E. Hall and Laurence J. O'Toole Jr. demonstrates that public programs have been consistently and unambiguously network-based, with heavy reliance on networks since at least the 1960s.[46]

Thus, networks have provided a framework for understanding the growing connections between varied organizations that find themselves working together to implement public policy. They have also helped public administration gain fresh purchase on the question that has occupied it since its founding—and, indeed, the nation since its creation: how best to understand the connections between political power and representative democracy. Network-based analysis has not yet approached the status of theory. But it does provide a framework for defining a central problem, understanding how organizations operate with each other across the boundaries they share. It has framed the first steps toward providing effective tools for managing networks, which could significantly improve public policy. Achieving the approach's promise, however, awaits further work to develop and confirm theoretical propositions about the way networks behave.

Complexity

Beginning in the mid-1980s, political scientist Robert Axelrod used game theory to advance a formal model of how individuals and organizations cooperate. It brought together formal models, governmental institutions, evolutionary biology, computer science, and social interactions. Important, complex relationships change over time because those involved in them learn. Following the lead of Darwinian evolution, he argued that "whatever is successful is likely to appear more often in the future."[47] Evolution is most successful when many new things are tried and when feedback provides good evidence of what works. In time, everyone involved would learn what works best for them and settle on a "collective stability" that makes everyone better off.[48] Axelrod took this simple concept and applied it to how individuals cooperate—and how cooperation can thrive. That, in turn, led him to speculate that his approach could be used for everything from designing institutions to shaping leadership. If individuals can speed up evolution—the interplay of trial and error—they can speed up the development of cooperation.[49]

Axelrod built his insight into a considerable movement, christened "complexity" theory.[50] He designed it to prescribe how many players, working from different perspectives, could collaborate. That then led him to identify a dozen concepts, ranging from strategies to performance measures, from which managers could work in building cooperation in complex systems. The hope, he and coauthor Michael D. Cohen explained, was "to contribute a coherent approach to designing interventions in a complex world."[51] Some critics countered that the approach, while intriguing, was simply a reframed view of outdated systems thinking, a translation of inputs into outputs. With the growth of the knowledge economy, the critics contend, information—getting it and managing it—has become more important.[52]

This debate has joined some of the more abstract foundations of formal theory with clear and lively recommendations for improving administration, among many other forms of complex human interactions. It has not yet produced prescriptions as sharply focused on practicing managers as public management, the reinventers, or mainstream public administration, and many theorists in the field have not thoroughly explored its theoretical insights. Complexity theory, however, provides a formal framework that complements the network approach. Indeed, they are different lines of argument flying in close formation. As theorists and practitioners alike seek new ways to understand how multiple players sharing the same mission can interact and collaborate, the two approaches offer great potential.

Devolution

The network approach built on America's rich tradition of intergovernmental relations. Like most of the richly textured elements of the American constitutional system, it has undergone constant change and reform. In 1938, Jane Perry Clark Carey noted "the rise of a new federalism" with Roosevelt's New Deal programs.[53] Since then "new" new federalisms have reappeared periodically and predictably, with the Eisenhower administration's foray into interstate highways and urban renewal; the Johnson administration's Great Society; the Nixon administration's block grants; the Carter administration's strategy to restructure federal grants; the Reagan administration's rollback of federal aid to state and local governments; and the Clinton administration's devolutionary welfare reform.[54]

American federalism combines the Jeffersonian and Madisonian traditions—Jefferson's commitment to pushing government to the lowest possible level and Madison's careful balance of competing forces. Indeed, since the days of the Articles of Confederation, American federalism has teetered back and forth between an emphasis on state control and national power. From the Civil War to the Great Society, to rollback in federal aid and devolution of welfare, American government has never constructed a stable balance of power. Federalism is, of course, a political, not an administrative theory. State and local governments have been participants in the service delivery network, but they have been much more. As American opinion has swung from an emphasis on local autonomy to an insistence on national uniformity, federalism has been the battleground. But the administrative implications of federalism—especially the recurring call for devolution matched by repeated efforts to pull power back to Washington—have long been the arena for playing out the Jeffersonian-Madisonian administrative themes.

Assessing the Jeffersonian-Madisonian Connection

Of all the administrative approaches in the American administrative tradition, the Jeffersonian-Madisonian approach is at once the most deeply rooted and the least prescriptive. The long tug-of-war over federalism has provided less a clear answer to the problems of American administration than it has touchstones for the struggle. The network approach to governance has not built a new theory as much as it has suggested problems with the dominant authority-driven model and provided a new framework for understanding the central problems. Both network and federalism approaches provide more a road map for understanding the complex crosscurrents in the American political system than an administrative guide.

Thus, it is scarcely surprising that neither networks nor federalism produce strong normative models for either theory or practice. In the case of federalism, it is because the approach depends ultimately on balancing federal and state power. The beauty of the American political system is not setting that balance but creating a mechanism for resetting it often without fundamentally disrupting the system. The network approach offers considerable potential. Developed toward the end of the twentieth century, it provided a way to understand the nonhierarchical forces that increasingly were responsible for service delivery. The approach promised to develop both theoretical and practical alternatives to the limits and pathologies of authority and hierarchy.

COMPETING SOLUTIONS FOR THE CENTRAL PROBLEMS

Public administration's biggest challenge at the beginning of the twenty-first century was to resolve the fuzzy boundary problem—to develop new theoretical and practical tools for understanding the boundary-spanning issues that have become the field's knottiest and most important problems. The fuzzy boundary problem had not replaced earlier administrative dilemmas. Rather, it became a new one layered on top of the enduring issues that had shaped debate in American public administration for more than two decades. The four basic traditions had not evaporated. Their primary instincts remained key themes: whether to manage from the bottom up or from the top down; to have a strong or a weak executive branch; to view the executive branch as the center of the analysis or as a political player in the constitutional balance-of-power system; and whether to make authority or market mechanisms the building block of bureaucratic analysis. Moreover, as table 5-1 shows, they produced a rich—if often competing—set of arguments about how to proceed.

In the twentieth century, both practitioners and academics developed even more intricately textured approaches, from the Progressive move-

TABLE 5-1 ***Public Administration Theory and the American Administrative Traditions***

	Wilsonian *Hierarchical*	***Madisonian*** *Balance-of-power*
Hamiltonian *Strong-executive/ Top-down*	• "Traditional" public administratration • Principal-agent theory • New public management • Reinventing Government (procedural reforms)	• Bureaucratic politics • Implementation • Public management • Formal theory
Jeffersonian *Weak-executive/ Bottom-up*	• Reinventing Government (employee empowerment and customer service)	• "New" federalism • Network theory

ment through reinventing government and from scientific management through formal economically driven models. As befits a field struggling to provide descriptive and normative analysis of the way government works, public administration at the start of the twenty-first century was vastly more complex than at the end of the nineteenth century. Moreover, the level of conflict within the field remained high as the level of outside support for its work fell. It was scarcely the case that public administration had become less important, but confidence in its ability to speak truth to power had unquestionably fallen.

Moreover, as Lynn pointed out, the field lost its moorings. It "seems to have let lapse the moral and intellectual authority conferred by its own recognition that enacting democracy in our constitutional order requires us to confront the dilemmas of reconciling capacity with control."[55] Lynn sadly concluded, "As a result, the profession mounts an unduly weak challenge to various revisionists and to the superficial thinking and easy answers of the policy schools and the ubiquitous management consultants." The problem, he wrote, was that the battles missed a "recognition that reformers of institutions and civic philosophies must show how the capacity to effect public purposes and accountability to the polity will be enhanced in a manner that comports with our Constitution and our republican institutions."[56] Thus, not only had public administration theory and practice become more conflict-ridden and less clear in its voice, but, Lynn argued, many of the competing theories had been less true to important theoretical traditions and less sound a guide. In short, Lynn believed, the new ideas had failed to serve America's political traditions and constitutional expectations. For its part, public administration had lost its compass. Many analysts would contest Lynn's arguments, especially about reinventing government and the public policy approaches. Indeed, these approaches gained ground because they offered fresh insight into problems where orthodox public administration had seemed to run dry.

But beyond these disputes are three larger themes that frame the basic challenge of this book. First, public administration faced important unresolved issues that it had to tackle. Second, the field has diverged widely, both on theoretical approaches and on practical solutions. Given the competing cross-pressures of complex public policies, there is little prospect that a consensus, in theory or practice, will soon emerge. Third, any approach must at least confront, if not resolve, the basic administrative traditions embodied in Hamiltonian, Jeffersonian, Wilsonian, and Madisonian ideas. The challenge is how to pursue these themes to resolve the field's basic dilemmas—and to produce fresh insight for tackling the fuzzy boundary problem. Compounding that challenge was a fundamental change in the strategies and tactics of government that vastly multiplied the boundaries, made them even fuzzier, and posed profound new challenges for democratic government.

6 ||| ADMINISTRATION AND GOVERNANCE

All four administrative traditions seek a solution to the enduring problem of bureaucratic power in a democratic republic. How can government—especially its administrative arm—be made strong enough to do the job without threatening individual liberty? Hamiltonians believed that a strong executive would promote commerce. Jeffersonians struggled to limit government's power. Madisonians worried about balancing political power while Wilsonians sought a powerful administration balanced by political accountability. For more than two hundred years, Americans worked to balance competing ideas about how best to solve the enduring problem. If they never came to a solution that remained stable for long, they came at least to agree, at least implicitly, on where the battle lines lay.

Toward the end of the twentieth century, those battle lines began to erode. The processes of government spilled out into strategies of governance. In doing their work, American governments at all levels became increasingly interconnected with private corporations and nongovernmental organizations (NGOs) that share in the task of delivering public services. Government policy thus became the product of how government managed its relationships with an increasingly devolved system. In framing its role, the national government became intertwined with broad global forces, including multinational organizations, corporations and ngos with global reach, and other sources of multinational influence. Theorists once built their views about government's role on a foundation of national sovereignty, but the rise of globalization in its numerous forms has, at least, transformed the meaning of national sovereignty and, at most, substantially eroded it.

The rising importance of these twin forces—devolution and globalization—has fundamentally altered the foundation on which the four dominant traditions were based. No longer was it possible to frame the big questions in terms of how to structure administration's internal relationships or its linkages with the rest of government. The four traditions concentrated on administration's relationship with government. The transformations of governance that emerged toward the end of the twentieth century focused on government's relationship with the rest of American society—indeed, with the rest of the world. In 1950, John Gaus argued, "A theory of public administration means in our time a theory of politics also."[1] To that we can add: A theory of public administration means in our time a theory of governance as well.

"Governance" is a way of describing the links between government and its broader environment—political, social, administrative. It is also a way of capturing the initiatives that governments around the world have deployed to shrink their size while struggling to meet their citizens' demands. As Jon Pierre and B. Guy Peters have put it, governance is about government's "changing role in society and its changing capacity to pursue collective interests under severe external and internal constraints."[2] For Robert O. Keohane and Joseph Nye, governance is "the processes and institutions, both formal and informal, that guide and restrain the collective activities of a group."[3] "Government," they explain, is the portion of the activity that "acts with authority and creates formal obligations." "Governance" describes the processes and institutions through which social action occurs, which might or might not be governmental.[4]

The concept is slippery indeed. It is not new—the French have been using the term *gouvernance* since the fourteenth century.[5] Toward the end of the twentieth century, however, governments and scholars have used it to capture the stress on governmental institutions: the inescapable pressures on government to do more with less; the increasingly complex partnerships governments have been building to do their work; and the search for intellectual guidance through these extremely difficult practical problems. Not only did government officials feel the heat from the growing burdens they faced, but they struggled for guidance on how best to deal with them. Western Europeans more directly confronted the theoretical implications of the transformation. Americans, by contrast, proved more energetic in devising new strategies. In both cases, governments are struggling for the insights and practical steps to cope with the challenges they face. "Because societies are ever more complex the analytical tools currently used to tackle problems of governance are outmoded," Robert Cameiro wrote in 2001. Moreover, he argued, "it is hard to believe that improved government performance in the next [twenty-first] century will be compatible with the government models of the 19th century."[6]

This transformation has strained the traditional roles of all the players. For decades, the United States has debated privatizing and shrinking government. While the debate raged, however, the nation incrementally made important policy decisions that have rendered much of the debate moot. Government has come to rely heavily on for-profit and nonprofit organizations for delivering goods and services ranging from antimissile systems to welfare reform. These changes have scarcely obliterated the roles of Congress, the president, and the courts. State and local governments have become even livelier. Rather, these changes have layered new challenges on top of the old ones, under which the system already mightily struggled.

New process-based problems have emerged as well: How can hierarchical bureaucracies, created with the presumption that they directly deliver services, cope with services increasingly delivered through multiple (often nongovernmental) partners? Budgetary control processes that work well for traditional bureaucracies often prove less effective in gathering information from nongovernmental partners or in shaping their incentives. Personnel systems designed to insulate government from political interference have proven less adaptive to these new challenges, especially in creating a cohort of executives skilled in managing indirect government. Public administration orthodoxy simply is a poor match for these problems.

Consequently, government at all levels has found itself with new responsibilities but without the capacity to meet them effectively. The same is true of its nongovernmental partners, which now find themselves under heavy public scrutiny as they implement public policy through their older organizational cultures. Moreover, despite these transformations, the expectations placed on government—by citizens and often by government officials—remain rooted in a past that no longer is relevant. Citizens simply expect that their problems will be solved; they care little about who solves them. Indeed, nothing more frustrates most citizens than to complain about a problem and be told, "Sorry, that isn't my job." Elected officials tend to take a similar view: They create programs and appropriate money. They expect government agencies to deliver the goods and services. When problems emerge, their first instinct is to reorganize agencies or to impose new procedures. That, they hope, will streamline administration and clarify responsibility. The problem is that this instinct no longer fits reality. As management responsibilities have become more broadly shared, it has become harder to define clearly who is in charge of what, as the StarLink corn case makes clear. The performance of American government—its effectiveness, efficiency, responsiveness, and accountability—depends on devising new solutions to this problem.

Consider the case of Wen Ho Lee, arrested in December 1999 and charged with mishandling classified nuclear secrets on his computer. For two decades, Lee had been a researcher at the Department of Energy's (DOE) Los Alamos National Laboratory. As an analyst in the secret "X Division," he had access to the secrets and had moved massive amounts of data—806 megabytes—to unsecured computers. Intelligence analysts believed that the Chinese government had captured the secrets of the W-88 warhead, America's most advanced nuclear device, and they searched for how it had done so. The analysts concluded that Lee, either by intentionally spying or making the information accessible through sloppy handling of secret data on his computer, had provided some of the nation's most valuable secrets to the Chinese.

Federal agents could not prove that Lee had leaked the data. In fact, they could not even demonstrate that data had leaked—or whether the Chinese had somehow managed to replicate the design on their own. The investigation itself had been sloppy. It had focused prematurely on Lee, and that precluded a close look at other possible suspects. At the very least, however, the agents believed that the Chinese had obtained the information, and they concluded that Lee, one way or another, had made the system vulnerable to Chinese spying.[7]

Congress responded in typical fashion. In a series of hearings, members of Congress expressed outrage at the problem and resolved to take firm action. They concluded that the DOE could not be trusted to plug the leaks on its own. Members asked pointedly, "What can we do to solve this problem?" Congress's answer: Split off the security issues into a new, quasi-independent National Nuclear Security Administration. If the DOE could not ensure the security of nuclear secrets, Congress resolved to create a new agency that could. Congress responded with a strategy steeped in tradition: in response to a separation-of-powers problem, it sought to restructure the function to improve accountability.

This instinct, however, did not match the challenge. It was not clear that there even was a problem, or that if there was a problem it was with Lee, or that if the problem was Lee's whether restructuring the DOE would fix it. In fact, Lee was not even a federal employee. He worked for the Los Alamos National Laboratory, which was a subcontractor to the University of California, Berkeley. Nuclear research had been conducted there since World War II. To the degree there was a problem with Lee, it lay in the DOE's ability (or inability) to manage its contractor—the University of California—and the contractor's ability (or inability) to manage its subcontractor, the Los Alamos National Laboratory. The DOE's contractor employee list is vast. Paul Light, for example, has estimated that there are thirty-five contractor employees for every DOE worker.[8]

The DOE's management of its contractors depends not on traditional hierarchy but on a hybrid marketplace built on two generations of contracting. Transforming the organizational structure would not necessarily give top DOE officials any greater leverage over the contractor network. Given the inevitable disruptions that always accompany restructuring, such a move could even make it worse. But Congress had responded in reflexive fashion to the appearance of administrative problems. It misidentified the problem: it saw it as a structural problem within the DOE instead of the department's management of its nongovernmental partners. It solved the problem poorly—by reorganizing instead of strengthening the department's leverage over its partners. Suggestions that the solution failed to fit the problem were ignored. Congress did what it was used to doing. What it was used to doing, however, failed to match how the rest of the federal government was doing its work.

On one hand, more responsibility for both making and implementing policy has flowed to state and local governments and to for-profit and nonprofit service partners. In many communities, small-scale, quasi-governments are managing everything from education to arts districts. Some governance mechanisms have become computer-based, neighborhood-based, or both. In many communities, the welfare reform initiative of the late 1990s sought to use new computer technologies to integrate a large, disparate collection of services. To deliver those services, governments relied increasingly on nongovernmental agents, including for-profit contractors and social-service-based nonprofits. In the course of three decades, from the mid-1960s through the late 1990s, the entire fabric of the American administrative state had been substantially transformed.

On the other hand, the global linkages affecting American governance had multiplied dramatically. State and local governments had, in many cases, developed their own foreign policies through strategies to promote trade and attract foreign investment. Organizations like the World Trade Organization (WTO), World Bank, and the International Monetary Fund (IMF) have taken a strong hand in shaping international relations. Ad hoc international structures have managed the world's response to recent ethnic conflicts, from the Kosovo peacekeeping operation to the intense bombing campaign in Serbia. Foreign—or shared—command of American troops proved a hot domestic issue, but it has become increasingly common in the deployment of military forces. Other policy arenas that used to be domestic, from telecommunications to the environment, now have major international components. More decisions have flowed from the national to the international levels—and at the international level to both ad hoc and multinational organizations. Permanent organizations like the State Department have struggled to build the capacity to cope with these changes, while ad hoc ones never institutionalize. Maintaining national sovereignty while effectively pursuing international policy has become an increasingly difficult challenge.

In short, America's preeminent policy strategies have tended to grow beyond the nation-state, to linkages with international organizations, and to focus below it, on partnerships with subnational, for-profit, and nonprofit organizations. Supranational organizations have grown to take on new but poorly understood functions. Subnational partnerships have transformed the role of state and local governments. As we have debated "privatizing" government, we have paradoxically also governmentalized a substantial part of the for-profit and nonprofit sectors. The federal government's institutions, political and administrative, find themselves with yet more challenges, from orchestrating these partnerships to shaping the national interest. The roles of all of these players have changed dramatically.

Managing these roles requires capacity that lies far beyond the standard responses, structures, and processes that have gradually accumulated within American government. It requires, in particular, devising new strategies to deal with four basic transformations of governance: the devolutionary and globalizing forces that grew out of the changing world scene; the merger of function and place as administrators struggled to deal with the consequences of fuzzy boundaries; and a hyperpluralism in politics and administration that shaped the changing politics of a transformed government. The challenges are substantial, for both theory and practice. But to a surprising degree, governmental institutions have shown remarkable resilience in adapting. In this chapter and the next, I explore the challenges and chart some of the most promising solutions.

DEVOLUTION

As I noted in chapter 2, devolution has dominated the practice of American public management since World War II. The federal government has managed every major policy initiative through grants, contracts, and other indirect tools. H. Ross Perot, who gained national attention as a maverick presidential candidate in 1992, became a millionaire by running a company that helped develop computer systems that, in turn, helped manage Medicare and Medicaid. These programs rank as some of the most complex the federal government has ever created. A small federal agency with just over 4,000 employees, the Department of Health and Human Service's Centers for Medicare and Medicaid Services, runs both programs. Together, they are budgetary giants—$221 billion for Medicare and $108 billion for Medicaid (in fiscal year 2001).

For example, a senior citizen might receive treatment from a local doctor or hospital. The health care provider submits the bill to a private company, which manages reimbursement procedures on behalf of the government. Computer links, typically provided by another private company, transfer the information. The private management companies collect payments from the federal government and distribute them to the health care providers. The federal government neither provides care nor manages the providers. Rather, it manages the managers and attempts to oversee the system. For low-income individuals who receive care through Medicaid, the process is similar. The federal government sets basic standards and monitors the programs. State governments tailor Medicaid to local tastes—and contribute about 43 percent of total Medicaid spending. The states have followed the federal government's course in contracting with financial intermediaries, often the same ones used in the Medicare program, to manage the reimbursements. The government has thus built an extensive publicly funded health-care system without making it publicly run.

The system has grown rapidly and it works remarkably well. But as in welfare, responsibility is broadly shared while no one is fully in charge. And as the General Accounting Office has noted, the complex management strategy poses huge challenges. In analyzing Medicare, the GAO concluded:

> Even though Medicare is a complicated program for the agency to administer through its more than 50 contractors, HCFA [the Health Care Financing Administration, the predecessor agency charged with managing the programs] cannot devote all its attention to Medicare because it is also responsible for administering Medicaid and other state-centered programs. In addition, frequent changes in HCFA lead-

> ership make it difficult for the agency to develop and implement a consistent long-term vision. Finally, constraints on HCFA's ability to acquire human capital expertise and shortcomings due to its aged information systems limit the agency's capacity to modernize Medicare's existing operations and carry out the program's growing responsibilities.[9]

The combination, the GAO concluded, makes Medicare vulnerable to waste, fraud, and abuse—to the point that, by one 1999 estimate, one in twelve dollars spent on the program's fee-for-service payments was improper.[10] The point is not so much that the government has mismanaged the program but that the government has chosen to manage the program through a vast network of private contractors so as to avoid creating a huge expansion of the government bureaucracy.

This complexity increases the difficulty of managing the program. Moreover, the program does not fit the strategies and tactics of twentieth century administrative orthodoxy. Although the HCFA operates through hierarchical authority, its relationships with state governments, private contractors, and health care providers are neither hierarchical nor authority-driven. The HCFA has had to devise different strategies for those who deliver the services, and Congress has had to develop new ways for overseeing the HCFA.

Devolving Welfare

The same is true of the radical transformation of the nation's welfare program in 1996, through the Personal Responsibility and Work Opportunity Reconciliation Act. President Clinton celebrated the change as an "end to welfare as we know it." But "welfare as we knew it" ended largely by passing the administrative burdens to the states, after they had complained for years about federal constraints and some states had advanced new strategies. The act built especially on Wisconsin's experience in the "Wisconsin Works" program—W-2—widely hailed for its dramatic reduction in the welfare rolls. The reforms depended on state, local, and nonprofit partnerships. Wisconsin's state government, for example, divided the state into eighty W-2 areas. County governments administered the program in most areas; in eleven areas, for-profit or nonprofit organizations ran the program. Native American tribes managed the program in three areas. Many county governments subcontracted the program to other private and nonprofit organizations. The program's administrative chain, from Washington to the front lines, where officials worked to get welfare recipients off welfare and into jobs, built a complex network of governmental and nongovernmental partners.

Nowhere was this truer than in the state's largest city, Milwaukee. Officials divided Milwaukee County (with roughly the same boundaries as the city) into six regions and collected bids for the work. In four regions, nonprofit organizations won the job. For-profit organizations—one based in Virginia—won two of the contracts. In all six regions, community steering committees, designed to link private employers and others in the network of services such as transportation, provided advice on how best to manage the transition from welfare to work. The government had to determine which contractors were equipped to do the job. It had to maintain competition among them to prevent the criticisms of government monopoly, which plagued traditional welfare programs. It had to devise new systems of oversight, especially of auditing the contractors' financial records. It had to determine what level of profit was acceptable. Reports of excessive profits produced criticisms that the contractors were squeezing the poor. The effort enjoyed remarkable success in its first years, with far more welfare recipients moving to jobs than the program's advocates had dared hope. That, in turn, led to questions about appropriate benchmarks: What level of performance was expected and desirable in welfare reform?

Welfare reform surely ranks as one of the most complex policy initiatives American government has ever attempted. It sought nothing less than ending generations-long cycles of poverty and dependence on government programs by moving welfare recipients to long-term employment. That, in turn, required an uncommon coordination of services, from screening welfare recipients for job skills to helping them find good jobs. It often also required coordinating a broad array of support, from health care and transportation to day care for children and social services to help address family problems. For the effort to succeed, the network had to perform without allowing serious problems to slip through unaddressed. The government's nongovernmental partners had to synchronize their own missions to the program's goals. The government's federal, state, and local partners had to align their different perspectives. And government had to transform its role from service provider to service arranger and coordinator. Government faced the challenge of allowing partners enough flexibility to do the job, on the one hand, while holding them accountable for federal goals, on the other.[11]

The result was an extended chain of implementation. A vastly complex network produces the program; no one is in charge of everything. In Milwaukee, the typical welfare recipient does not even encounter a government employee—federal, state, or local—in the journey from welfare to work, except for workers who qualify as recipients for Medicaid and Food Stamp programs. In a subtle, unplanned way, W-2 became the model for welfare reform, and welfare reform was but part of a broader transformation of governance in the United States.

In short, welfare reform turned the existing system on its head. Government workers found themselves managing contractors instead of delivering services. Contractors, many of whom had substantial experience managing social services but did not have a track record running such a broad or ambitious effort, had to find employees and develop mechanisms for the new program. The success driven by a rapidly growing economy with low unemployment helped disguise the underlying management issues that Milwaukee and the state struggled to resolve. Other local governments hired private companies to serve as general contractors to manage the entire program. These contractors, in turn, hired subcontractors to conduct front-line operations. Understanding welfare reform required an understanding of the networked programs that supported it. Understanding what helped make welfare reform work required building a theory to explain the administration of this network.

Devolutionary Strategies

Contracting out for urban social services, of course, is nothing new. The practice dates from the 1960s, when Model Cities and other antipoverty programs supported neighborhood organizations—even religious organizations—around the country. Federal government officials worried that cities were unresponsive to the needs of their citizens—and especially of their poor. They gave local governments grants with the expectation that the communities, in turn, would develop service-delivery partnerships with neighborhood groups. The funding helped institutionalize these groups, as well as the pattern of service partnerships. Nongovernmental organizations have become partners with local governments in managing federal- and state-funded programs.

Welfare reform marks the maturing of a generation-long trend that fundamentally transformed community governance. It is a trend with great political attraction: It wires local nongovernmental groups directly into the service system, and it allows government to increase its reach without increasing its size. It spreads administrative responsibility and, hence, political risk. It provides a way to tailor broad programs to community needs. Having forged partnerships that serve so many interlocking purposes, it would be hard for governments to undo them.

At the state and local levels, more partnerships have developed. Mayor Steve Goldsmith launched major reforms of Indianapolis's government through his "Yellow Pages" test. If the local Yellow Pages contained at least three entries for a service the city provided, the city would contract it out.[12] Phoenix won an award as one of the world's best-run cities by pursuing an aggressive contracting-out approach.[13] Driven by the legacies of the federal Model Cities, Comprehensive Employment and Training Act, Community Development Block Grant, and Title XX block grant programs, state and local governments have contracted out most of their social service programs. Local "smart growth" initiatives have led to new partnerships among local governments. And state governments also have tended to manage their highway construction programs through contracts.

In general, the lower the level of government in the United States, the more the government is engaged in direct service delivery. At every level, however, partnerships with both other governmental and nongovernmental units have proliferated at an accelerating rate. That has made government both *horizontal*—in search of service coordination and integration with nongovernmental partners in service provision—and *vertical*—through both traditional, hierarchical bureaucracies and multilayered federalism. It is not so much that the horizontal relationships have supplanted the vertical ones, but rather that the horizontal links have been added to the vertical ones. That, in fact, was one of the implicit precepts of the reinventing government movement of the 1990s.

After a decade-long emphasis on strengthening performance within the United Kingdom, the Blair government moved to a greater emphasis on "joined-up government." British officials discovered that the "new public management"–style reforms had in fact produced efficiency gains, but they also created new problems. Managers focused narrowly on the specific outputs they were charged with producing. They tended to do well on the outputs that political officials explicitly identified. Problems that didn't fit neatly into such output-based structures, however, tended to be managed poorly if at all. A series of serious train accidents, for example, revealed that strong pressures for on-time performance led to a neglect of safety and maintenance. A 1999 white paper committed the government to integrated policy—to "tackle the issues facing society—like crime, drugs, housing and the environment—in a joined up way, regardless of the organisational structure of government."[14] The new strategies focused more on service delivery to meet the needs of citizens, not on the narrow functions that preoccupy bureaucrats.

Over the last several decades, the federal government's work has increasingly been carried out through an elaborate network of contracting, intergovernmental grants, loans and loan guarantees, regulations, and other indirect administrative approaches. As the case of W-2 shows, the same is true of state and local governments, especially in human services.[15] The federal government manages most of its domestic programs through such indirect partnerships. It mails entitlement checks directly, handles air traffic control, and runs the national parks. From Medicare to Medicaid, and environmental to transportation policy, the federal government shares responsibility with state and local governments and with for-profit and nonprofit organizations.[16] Indirect tools have gradually and subtly risen in prominence. In part, this represents a conscious strategy to avoid increasing the size of the federal government while expanding its programs. In part, it represents an unconscious strategy to wire civil society ever more directly into public programs. As Light has shown, the federal government's "shadow" employees, in the state and local governments as well as in the for-profit and nonprofit sectors, outnumber federal workers by nine to one.[17]

The Challenge of Devolution

Therein lies a central challenge for domestic governance. Reformers have focused on reorganizing administrative structure and reshaping organizational processes (especially budgeting and personnel). Elected policymakers have seen in these vertical relationships the cornerstone of bureaucratic responsibility—delegation of authority to administrators in exchange for accountability for results. They have tried to strengthen the hierarchical chain, driven by authority, to provide the critical linkage between front-line workers and policymakers. But the pragmatic realities of public policy innovation have not mirrored these approaches. For public administration, the challenge is reconciling the management and accountability challenges of these networks with the bedrock ideas that hierarchical authority has long provided. How can government ensure accountability in extended service networks where administrative responsibility is widely shared and where no one is truly in charge?

How can government, structured and staffed for an era when vertical relationships dominated, build the capacity to manage horizontal partnerships effectively?

The devolution movement has not been just an American phenomenon. At the end of the twentieth century, the United Kingdom's government gave in to growing demands for devolution of power to Scotland and Wales. As Eastern European nations struggled to regain their footing after two generations of communist rule, they sought to push power down to local governments. Japan committed itself to delivering more services through NGOs.[18] Around the world, more governments have contracted out service delivery. In sum, as the Organization for Economic Cooperation and Development (OECD) pointed out, "Government has become just one player among many seeking to represent and serve the public."[19] The United States might well have devolved more programs faster than other countries, but nations around the world have quickly followed the same trail, for both pragmatic and ideological reasons.

GLOBALIZATION

The United States and the European Union (EU) brought in the new millennium with an ongoing banana battle. The row did not involve bananas grown in either place. The EU had created rules that favored growers in territories of EU countries, including the Caribbean. Those rules, the United States charged, discriminated against bananas grown in Latin America by American companies, like Chiquita Brands International. The United States won its case before the WTO and imposed sanctions on imports from the EU. The EU revised its import license procedures, but American trade representatives complained that would in fact change nothing. In retaliation, the Bush administration signaled it was ready to impose a 100 percent import duty on EU imports to the United States—doubling their price—and shift to a different product every six months. The sanctions would begin with products including lead-acid batteries and cardboard packaging and would rotate in carousel fashion to other products, the administration warned. The threat infuriated EU officials, who promised to take their case to the WTO. They threatened to retaliate with their own sanctions if they were unsuccessful before the WTO.[20] Although the dispute was resolved early in 2001 by creating a new import license system, other issues, including an EU ban on hormone-treated beef, continued to fester.

It was a prototypical twenty-first century globalization policy puzzle. It involved two multinational organizations—the EU and the WTO. It involved governmental policy over trade relations and mainstream products. In this case, the product had not even originated from within the two warring bodies. Like the Aventis case, it involved products that ordinary citizens used all the time. It defied any effort to draw clear boundaries.

Debates about globalization have ranged from French complaints about McDonald's "burger imperialism" to American worries about StarLink corn. International disputes over imports, quotas, and tariffs, of course, are nothing new. American colonists protested against Britain's long colonial reach by tossing tea into Boston Harbor. What changed was the rapid spread of globalizing forces at the end of the twentieth century and the widespread recognition, by both public officials and citizens, of the trend. London School of Economics Director Anthony Giddens noted that globalization "has come from nowhere to be almost everywhere." In the early 1990s, the term was little used. By the turn of the millennium, no speech was complete without it—even if those who used the term agreed on little more than the fact "that we now all live in one world."[21]

Globalization as Movement, Market, and Ideology

"Globalization" is poorly defined. Most often, the term is synonymous with the galloping expansion of the worldwide marketplace. But it is much more. It includes political, technological, and cultural forces. It is an ideology that defines basic expectations about the roles and behaviors of individuals and institutions. Giddens suggests, in fact, that globalization is about "action at a distance"—the increasing "interpenetration" of individual lives and global futures.[22] For some, it is an ideology of hope and potential—a belief that the global marketplace can improve the living conditions and economic well-being of all.[23] For others, it is an ideology that warns of the threat unrestrained megacompanies can pose for individual welfare. As the UN report on the 2000 Millennium Summit succinctly put it, "The benefits of globalization are obvious—faster growth, higher living standards, new opportunities. Yet a backlash has begun, because these benefits are so unequally distributed, and because the global market is not yet underpinned by rules based on shared social objectives."[24]

These issues quickly sprang from widely disparate roots.[25] The sudden end of the Cold War left the United States as the world's remaining superpower. By uprooting a generation of ideologies and power relationships, that change also scrambled relationships among all the world's nations. The major conflicts since the end of the Cold War have been not international but rather subnational and ethnic ones. These conflicts have posed tough dilemmas: How much do internal conflicts threaten international stability? How can—and should—the world's nations respond to such conflicts? These nations have delicately picked their way through the battles. When they have responded, they have tended to do so by forging multinational alliances. In the 1999 bombing campaign against Serbia, for example, nearly 30 nations negotiated which targets to bomb and when to bomb them. American pilots found themselves under the de facto command of a loose, ad hoc multinational coalition. The coalition shored up international support but made it far harder to fight the war. Other multinational peacekeeping operations have struggled to reduce conflict in places as different as Somalia and Bosnia. In each case, the essential war-fighting strategy was surrender of national autonomy in exchange for (more or less) international unity. Nations acted awkwardly together because no nation could—or desired to—act alone.

Behind these military actions, however, lies the accelerating globalization of world markets. Manufacturers debate "global sourcing," where manufacturing and marketing know no national boundaries. Indeed, Nike manufactures and markets its shoes around the world. The company has reduced its market presence to a single, universally known symbol—its unique swish. Hungry travelers can enjoy Burger King in Australia or Pepsi in Moscow. The French resent the spread of Disney and McDonald's but visit both anyway. Street corner cafes in Berlin advertise "genuine American pizza" from Pizza Hut. Global trade, of course, does not flow one way. Corporate mergers have sometimes become mania, especially in consolidation of communications industries across national borders. Scandinavian companies distribute two of the fastest-selling cellular phones in the United States—Nokia (from Finland) and Ericsson (from Sweden). No American television factories exist any longer. Classic American clothing from the Lands' End catalog might come from North Carolina, Scotland, or Thailand—and be sold through the Internet from Wisconsin to Tokyo. Some analysts have gone so far as to suggest that globalization "is increasingly forcing us to live in an economy rather than a society"—with shrinking national political power and "with government's role in economic affairs now deemed obsolete."[26]

While that might be going a bit far, it is impossible to ignore the fact that it is at least a debatable proposition. With on-line stock, futures, options, and commodity trading, along with the world's rotating time zones, the markets never close, and no nation can insulate its finances in the world economy. Capital markets are global, and hiccups in one region can quickly spread to everyone else, as the "Asian flu" in 1997 and 1998 painfully proved. The Clinton and Bush campaigns to wipe out the national debt produced surprising spillovers. The U.S. Treasury's thirty-year bond has long been the world's interest-rate benchmark. International investors have worried that if the national debt declines sharply—or even disappears—so too will the bedrock of investor security. While it surely is better to develop a new touchstone than to lean too heavily on an expansive old one, the worldwide ripples flowing from the treasury's decision showed how tightly linked the world's economic finances have become.

The markets have become more important than national governments in setting the economic rules. Nations can choose to go their own way, but the markets exact retribution for policies that run afoul of the global marketplace. No country is exempt. It was a U.S. policy decision to rescue the Mexican peso in 1995, for example. But once the United States made the decision, it lost control about *how* to do so. The bond markets, not national governments, ultimately set the terms for the rescue.[27] Corporations are outgrowing the world's governments, some observers suggest.[28]

Global Communication

At the core of the globalization movement are the lightning-fast communication systems—especially the Internet—that have developed over the last decade. The communications revolution has made it possible to spread information around the world quickly and easily and cheaply. It has not only fueled the twenty-four-hour financial markets, it has also transformed governance. For the price of a local telephone call to connect to the Internet, organizations around the world can instantly exchange information. As Jessica Mathews argued in *Foreign Affairs*, "Widely accessible and affordable technology has broken governments' monopoly on the collection and management of large amounts of information and deprived governments of the deference they enjoyed because of it. In every sphere of activity, instantaneous access to information and the ability to put it to use multiplies the number of players who matter and reduces the number who command great authority.

The effect on the loudest voice—which has been government's—has been greatest."[29] The result—so far, at least—has been rampant fragmentation of norms, ideologies, values, and institutions. "We are at the beginning of a fundamental shake-out of world society," Giddens bluntly suggests, "and we really do not know where it is going to lead us."[30]

Globalization and Nongovernmental Organizations

Instantaneous communication has already fueled an important transformation. Nongovernmental organizations have quickly acquired great influence, in the United States and around the world. (In the United States, they are better known as nonprofit organizations, for their tax-exempt status.) When nations debated trade liberalization in the 1986 Uruguay round of talks, twelve NGOs registered to follow the proceedings. Seattle's 1999 WTO meeting drew so many NGO representatives that they crammed the city's symphony hall to plot strategy. About 1,500 NGOs signed an anti-WTO protest declaration created online by Public Citizen. The Internet allowed organizers to share ideas and tactics instantly. They overwhelmed the Seattle police who found themselves using 1970s-era crowd-control strategies in trying to tame twenty-first century organizers.[31]

These nongovernmental organizations are powerful engines for organizing and driving policy change. Their influence has been impressive. At the 1992 Earth Summit in Rio de Janeiro, they exerted public pressure for governments to commit to reducing greenhouse gases. In 1994, they dominated the World Bank's fiftieth anniversary meeting and forced the bank to rethink its goals and techniques. In 1998, a coalition of environmentalist consumer rights activists pressed for the end of the Multilateral Agreement on Investment, a draft treaty under the auspices of the OECD meant to improve foreign investment rules. In the late 1990s, Princess Diana's much-publicized campaign to outlaw land mines was part of a broader movement, which, in just that year, led to substantial success. The Jubilee 2000 campaign elevated the push to forgive the debts of the world's poorest countries. The number of international NGOs behind these and other movements grew from 6,000 in 1990 to more than 26,000 at the end of the decade. The total number of NGOs around the world, from neighborhood-based groups to large international organizations, surely is in the millions.[32] Moreover, not only have these NGOs been important in political organizing, they have in many countries (including the United States) become important as well in delivering public services.

International Organizations

Add to this the widely recognized and growing power of formal, quasi-governmental, international organizations like the World Bank, IMF, WTO, and the EU. The IMF played a powerful (and much-criticized) role in steering Asian nations through their brutal but short-lived economic storms. In Seattle, the WTO stumbled into a vicious political battle as it attempted to transform international trade. The UN has had intermittent success in launching peacekeeping missions. The EU has reshaped everything from environmental policy and drug manufacturing to agricultural policy and transportation in Europe. Its policies are coming in America's back door through the international companies that do business in both places.

Risk

As the terrorist assault on America on September 11, 2001, showed, globalization has a dark and dangerous side. The terrorists did more than demonstrate the nation's—indeed, the world's—vulnerability to an exquisitely planned attack. It confirmed as well that globalization brings great risk as well as opportunity. The more interconnected social and economic forces are, the more easily disruptions in any part of the global network can reverberate throughout it. Indeed, the 2001 attack echoed other risks that worked through the global system. The United Kingdom's 2001 struggles with mad-cow disease not only closed down much of its animal export market. It also mobilized worldwide forces to prevent the disease's spread. Genetically modified crops, like the Aventis bio-corn that created the American agricultural crisis, have likewise created policy issues that have spread throughout the world.

Globalization has provided great opportunity for businesses, governments, and citizens. But it has also brought new, and often unexpected, risks that in turn have challenged governments' abilities to respond.[33] The challenges have not only been substantive—fending off terrorism or preventing the spread of disease, but they have also cut to the heart of the role and sovereignty of government. They have, moreover, introduced new uncertainties into public affairs. Many of these problems have emerged from channels outside the usual course of public policy. They can, in turn, be solved only by adopting new, collaborative strategies that draw together governmental and nongovernmental partners alike.

Globalization thus has transformed government not only by posing new administrative challenges but also by introducing new risks and uncertainties in solving these challenges. Public administration has always been about far more than managing public programs. The cross-pressures of globalization have multiplied the challenges for success and magnified the costs of failure.

Governance and Government

Amid galloping globalization, the United States has found itself squarely in the middle of an international paradox: It has become the world's only superpower but has found itself unable, for political and pragmatic reasons, to act alone. It has struggled to craft a policy to accommodate these new realities, to organize its governmental apparatus to cope with them, and to help lead the redefinition of the international community.

To deal with this paradox, American government has sought to answer two questions. First, what is the role of the American national government at a time when international organizations—formal organizations like the WTO and the UN, informal organizations like the NGOs, and multinational corporations—have become so strong? The rise of these organizations has limited policymakers' discretion about both what to do and how to do it. National sovereignty, even for the world's remaining superpower, has eroded. At least in relative terms, the federal government has become more marginalized in the international debate. It has found itself drawn into the debate, which first bubbled up from the governments comprising the EU, about what role nation-states will play in the globalized world.

Second, what capacity does the federal government need to play this emerging role? Following a forty-two-year career in the State Department, outgoing Assistant Secretary of State Phyllis Oakley worried in 1999 that America's ability to conduct foreign policy had become "threadbare." The State Department itself lacked people skilled in dealing with the issues of globalization. Its budget stagnated while the CIA and Pentagon budgets grew. Special envoys took important jobs that previously would have gone to senior career foreign service officers. "The only thing we have left is the military," she complained, "so we use it in Iraq and Kosovo." Consequently, the nation tends toward "using military means for diplomatic purposes."[34]

Some critics might dismiss Oakley's comments as the parochial complaints of a long-term State Department official bruised by too many budget wars. Her worries about the nation's capacity to cope with new issues, however, took on new and pressing meaning following the 2001 terrorist attack. Former Clinton administration reinventing government official Elaine Kamarck pointed out, for example, that homeland defense requires careful coordination between the Immigration and Naturalization Service (INS) and the Customs Service, as well as with the Coast Guard, FBI, and CIA. She pointed to longstanding tensions between the INS and Customs: "They took lunch breaks at different times; they didn't share information; even their dogs hated each other."[35] Globalization, as Oakley and Kamarck both pointed out, is not the province of any cabinet department. Indeed, in addition to the usual suspects in the State, Defense, and Treasury Departments, no cabinet department is untouched by globalization. Its implications strike at issues ranging from the Department of Health and Human Service's health care programs to the Environmental Protection Agency's (EPA) clean air standards, from the Labor Department's job security programs to the Commerce Department's efforts to help American businesses compete. Ad hoc White House and interagency teams have sprung up to deal with crises, but they have failed to build long-term capacity to anticipate and cope with tough problems. Executive-branch political leadership has often been lacking. Congress, for its part, has scarcely proven equal to the task of framing policies to cope with this trend.

Globalization has helped homogenize cultures. The phenomenon is far broader than the spread of American fast food and movies. The Internet has helped establish English as the global language and has fueled rapid communication. Because these forces are so decentralized, from information to markets, governments cannot hope to control this trend. At best, they can learn to cope and take advantage of the synergism it offers. They can also work to shape the process and redress some of its risks. For example, governments can devise policies to ensure that the rampant spread of electronic communications technology does not create an underclass without a knowledge of or access to communication systems.

In many ways, however, globalization has sparked an emerging system of governance without government, management, or control. Shared values that shaped governmental policies in the past have yet to emerge. National sovereignty has shrunk along with government's capacity to understand and shape the emerging issues and the conflicts that underlie them. European concerns about American "Frankenfoods," products incorporating genetically modified organisms, have shaped a new generation of public policy problems. So, too, has the rise of global warming, ethnic conflict, international currency flows, and multinational business mergers. The puzzle is how to build the administrative capacity, in sustained rather than ad hoc fashion, for tackling these problems. Equally difficult is how to strengthen the ability of our political institutions, especially Congress, to frame the policies the nation will need for negotiating the problems and utilizing the potential of globalization.

FUNCTION AND PLACE

A final transformation epitomizes how government administration is organized. For deeply historic and practical reasons, most of American government is organized by function, with separate bureaucracies for jobs such as health, environment, defense, and transportation. As policy problems have become more complex and interrelated, government has needed to frame policy solutions that likewise are more interconnected. Citizens expect that government will solve their problems, and they think about how problems affect their neighborhoods. They want the road department to work with the sewer and water departments to avoid repeatedly digging up and repaving the same highway. When cars collide at the border between two communities, they expect that the right mix of emergency units will promptly arrive. In short, citizens expect that a government organized primarily by *function* will be well coordinated in each *place*. Such coordination tasks have always been important. The spread of globalization, devolution, hyperpluralism, and ever more-complex problems have made it both more important and harder to accomplish.

Coordinating Administrative Action

At first blush, this kind of coordination might not seem any different from any of the other coordination problems that government must address. As Luther Gulick argued, however, in his classic 1937 paper, "Notes on the Theory of Administration," the problem cuts to the core of public administration.[36] Franklin D. Roosevelt appointed Gulick as a member of the famous Brownlow Committee, charged with reorganizing the executive branch. Gulick asked: Is there an ideal form of organization? He concluded that, in fact, there were four basic alternatives in organizing government bureaucracies: organization by process (such as engineering or medicine); by clientele (the people served, such as veterans or children); by place (such as region of the country); or by major purpose (such as water supply or crime control).

Gulick contended that policymakers could not simply pick bits of each approach. The task of management inevitably required top officials to emphasize one approach over the others. They were conflicting, indeed contradictory, strategies, moreover, and each one had its own advantages and disadvantages. For example, focusing on process could bring all the accountants into one office and put all the scientists into another office. That would make supporting their operations much easier and cheaper, since the government could create a single accounting computer center and just one scientific laboratory. The purpose of both accounting and science, however, is to support the government's policy decisions, not to make life easier for the accountants and scientists. Governments therefore have tended to focus more on function, like environmental policy or job training, than on process. That has required more investment in process and has, perhaps, led to process-based support that is less useful than might otherwise be the case. But the functions receive far stronger support, and that, in turn, has improved governments' pursuit of their basic goals.

Policymakers have had to choose which organizational advantages to pursue and which disadvantages to tolerate. That, Gulick observed, was more a matter of value choice than of scientific management. Policymakers simply had to choose what balance of costs and benefits they could accept. However, Gulick concluded, researchers could not predict very accurately which combination of costs and benefits any particular administrative strategy would produce. As a result, he said, "we must rest our discussion primarily on limited observation and common sense, because little scientific research has been carried on in this field of administration."[37]

That sets up tough dilemmas. Policymakers want to pursue certain goals, but there are different strategies for achieving them. Choosing one option forecloses others. Every strategic choice has advantages and disadvantages, but it is impossible to know all implications in advance. Public administration thus inevitably is doomed to suboptimization. Some alternatives surely will prove better than others, but it is hard to predict in advance which alternatives will produce the best results. These basic principles have not changed since Gulick's time, and they set up a recurring pattern. The administrative pursuit of public policies leaves some groups unsatisfied because they disagree with the administrative balance of benefits and costs—or unanticipated problems arise and they object. Reformers reform by selecting a different administrative strategy, which in turn creates new problems. Cynics suggest that it is simply a case of bureaucracy gone bad again; realists recognize that public administration is the pursuit of political aims through political choices, and such choices inevitably create friction. As a result, few administrative patterns remain stable.

In the last decades of the twentieth century, however, new organizational problems became layered on top of these traditional ones. With more policy problems crossing bureaucratic boundaries, it has become harder for any government bureaucracy to own or control administrative solutions. With more policy problems involving collaboration among federal, state, and local governments, as well as among governmental organizations and NGOs, it has become more important for these partners to coordinate their efforts. And with more policy problems stretching across both functions and places, it has become more important for government managers to develop strategies that enhance both functional specialization and place-based effectiveness.

Managing Environmental Policy

In environmental policy, for example, the EPA has traditionally been organized by function, with separate pollution-control offices for water, air, solid waste, and toxic chemicals. These functional offices enabled the EPA's staff to build the considerable scientific expertise needed to regulate the different sources of pollution. As a result, the EPA made substantial progress in reducing pollution. In focusing on the individual "media," or sources, however, the EPA was less effective in reducing pollution that crossed media lines. Substantial water pollution, for example, comes as rain falls through contaminated air, and streams collect contaminated runoff from farms. Media-based efforts risk missing pollution problems that cross these organizational boundaries, as well as "nonpoint-source" pollution like contaminated storm water runoff from parking lots and urban streets where a specific pollution source cannot be identified.

After its considerable success in its first generation, the EPA faced a "second generation" of environmental problems, such as nonpoint-source pollution, global warming, and cross-media challenges. As the EPA has waded into these "second-generation" problems, its "first-generation" tactics, including inspections and litigation, proved less effective. The agency found it had to rely far more extensively on innovative strategies implemented through partnerships with other players.[38]

Since the EPA manages many of its programs through partnerships with state governments, it faced further coordination problems. Statehouses were not subsidiary field offices of the EPA but, rather, quasi-independent entities with their own environmental programs and policies. At the same time, through incentives and requirements of the EPA's programs, the states took on legal responsibility for enforcing the EPA's standards. For the state agencies, the job was melding the EPA objectives and requirements with their own programs and goals. For the EPA, the job was ensuring that the states enforced policies set in federal law, that the states uniformly enforced standards intended by Congress to be uniform, and that the EPA allowed the states flexibility where pursuit of national goals made that possible. Those problems multiplied as environmental agencies began shifting more emphasis to nonpoint-source and other pollution problems, problems that earlier strategies left relatively untouched.

Put bluntly, citizens wanted their neighborhoods—the air they breathed, the water they drank, the ground on which they walked—to be free from pollution. For the EPA, this meant crafting a way to make a functionally based agency work effectively on problems that increasingly were place-based. The EPA had tried a host of reorganization strategies only to discover what Gulick had predicted: a new strategy could help solve the problems of the past effort, but it created new ones in turn. "We've tried almost everything," one senior EPA official said, "and we still haven't been able to solve this problem."[39] At its most basic level, organizing the EPA's efforts by place—for example, focusing on a state-by-state approach—risked undermining the agency's functional expertise. Continuing the EPA's organization by function had already weakened its ability to coordinate disparate programs as they affected individual communities. The agency continued to experiment with new organizational strategies, but frustrated managers concluded that they were unlikely ever to crack the problem fully.

This is not just a problem for the EPA. As globalization and devolution have become more widespread, the boundaries that once constrained problems and shaped solutions have become less useful. On the other hand, the boundaries created long ago for political and administrative convenience can get in the way of solving problems. Wallace Stegner's intriguing biography of geologist John Wesley Powell, for example, compellingly explains why managing the American West has long proven so difficult. The state boundaries were drawn from long distance by people who did not understand the land, its strengths, and its problems. When they sketched out the states, they did so in ways that separated responsibility over the region's most valuable resource—water—into many jurisdictions. Governments in the area have struggled ever since to coordinate their policies for controlling the flow and managing the use of water.[40]

Public managers face the challenge of improving coordination among agencies within their own level of government, since fewer public problems fit neatly within any one agency's jurisdiction. They face the challenge of strengthening ties to governments at other levels with which they share responsibility for solving problems. They must improve their relations with their nongovernmental partners in administering public programs. They need to devise tactics for linking functionally organized programs with place-based impacts—for connecting air, water, and soil programs, for example, to create clean and livable communities. As a result, the strain between the vertical processes of government (represented in function-based departments) and its horizontal processes, however, has been growing. The problem, recognized ages ago by public administration's best scholars, has emerged as one of the field's most pressing ones.

HYPERPLURALISM

Madison long ago recognized the importance and proliferation of political interests. As the country grew older, his warning about the "mischiefs of faction" in *Federalist* 10 proved even truer. And as the nation entered its third century, the factions of its founding had grown into hyperpluralism. The number of political interests multiplied. More of the interests became better organized, with full-time lobbyists and extensive staffs. More of the interests also became partners with the government in delivering public services.

In fact, the rise of globalization and devolution elevated the issue. With more responsibility for public programs shared more broadly, no one was fully responsible for anything, and many more players became responsible for everything. Moreover, the technological revolution has further decentralized information, lowered the cost of access to political debate, and accelerated hyperpluralism. The federal government could not frame international policy except by consulting with other nations and by working through international organizations. It could not implement domestic policy except in concert with state and local governments and with its for-profit and nonprofit contractors. At the state and local level, the same held true. Of course, uncertain responsibility has always been one of the guiding principles (and enduring frustrations) of American democracy in general and American federalism in particular. What happened toward the end of the twentieth century, however, was a quantum increase in the scale and scope of the sharing of responsibility—and of its advantages and pathologies. Moreover, this sharing occurred not only within the constitutional framework of American federalism but, increasingly, through an extraconstitutional skeleton that provided limited, often underdeveloped mechanisms for ensuring accountability.

As American governments pursued more public policy through nongovernmental partners, public policy increasingly became entangled in private goals and norms. Government, for example, relied more on private and nonprofit contractors to train welfare recipients for new jobs. But those contractors were not solely governmental agents. They each had their own missions, operating procedures, and other projects—frequently nongovernmental ones—that they pursued as well. It was hard enough for government to manage nongovernmental contracts to administer governmental programs well. It was far harder ensuring that their parallel private missions did not distort their pursuit of public goals.

Hyperpluralism and Environmental Protection

Nowhere was this truer than in environmental protection. Since its creation in 1970, the EPA has faced an ongoing dilemma. Although it was nominally in charge of framing, coordinating, and enforcing the nation's environmental standards, it did very little of the work itself, and it did not have a strong hand on the steering wheel. In fact, a National Academy of Public Administration (NAPA) panel found that "the nation's environmental 'system' is so rich and complex that no one institution—not Congress, not EPA, not the states or Wall Street, or even the myriad NGOs and private companies—controls the system."[41] The Justice Department litigates on its behalf. Private contractors clean toxic-waste sites in the Superfund program. State governments do much of the enforcement. Congress mandates the EPA to set national environmental standards, and the EPA conducts some enforcement activity. Despite its image in the popular (and sometimes congressional) mind, the EPA does most of what it does by working with partners elsewhere in the federal government, in the states, and among private contractors.

To some degree, of course, the EPA has relied on such partnerships since its creation. The states asked for more flexibility in fulfilling their responsibilities under federal laws. They worked to integrate federal requirements with their own policy goals and to tailor environmental approaches that matched the needs of individual communities. In concert with the EPA, they created the National Environmental Performance Partnership System, which set measurable goals in exchange for granting the states more operating freedom. American multinational companies, driven to compete with EU companies, have sought uniform environmental standards so they did not have to face widely differing rules in different countries. They were especially eager to import the ISO 14001 approach from Europe, which gives companies greater flexibility to create environmental management systems in exchange for agreements to meet environmental standards. The EPA has thus found itself pulled toward more devolution while its policy strategies have faced increasingly global pressures.[42]

Environmental problems piled up quickly and demanded quick reaction from EPA administrators, but any effective action required linking a host of different organizations both within and outside government. The NAPA panel bluntly argued that these problems were extremely serious:

> The nation's current environmental protection system cannot deliver the healthy and sustaining world that Americans want. Absent significant changes in America's environmental governance, the accumulation of greenhouse gases will continue to threaten the stability of the global climate and all the systems that depend on it; the uncontrolled runoff of fertilizers and other pollutants will continue to choke rivers, lakes, and estuaries with oxygen-depleting algae; smog will continue to degrade the health of millions of Americans. The regulatory programs in place in this country simply cannot address those problems at a price America can afford.

Instead, the panel concluded, what is needed is a "transformation of the nation's environmental governance. From the EPA through states and communities, from regulatory agencies to businesses, individuals and organizations with an impact on the environment need to adopt new roles and accept new responsibilities."[43]

The panel recommended a multipart strategy. The EPA, the panel said, should focus on a handful of the most strategically important issues, invest in the information required to understand the issues, and chart policy and build partnerships with the states that hold them accountable for results. But beyond these steps, NAPA also found that the EPA needed to work aggressively to revamp its management culture and rely more on regional offices as the crucial bridge between functionally organized national policy and place-based integration of environmental results. Indeed, the panel found, "the challenge is not merely technological." It is also "organizational: EPA will have to change, as will state environmental agencies, businesses, and the many other organizations that comprise the nation's system of environmental governance." The panel argued, in short, that linking vertical functions with horizontal coordination was central to environmental policy, and that successfully pursuing that policy depended on the government's building strong partnerships with its partners in governance.[44] The EPA has enjoyed considerable success in the past, but existing strategies were unlikely to allow the agency to satisfy those who expected an effective and coordinated future attack. Moreover, as the EPA gradually moved past the early environmental goals into second-generation problems, the fit of its organizational strategy to its policy goals became far worse. It not only faced harder problems but growing difficulty in structuring itself to solve them.

Maintaining Governmental Sovereignty

THE EPA and many other government agencies share the problem of encouraging other governmental organizations as well as private and nonprofit organizations to become productive partners in delivering public services. That means setting government's goals clearly enough so that others can pursue them. It means finding incentives attractive enough to redirect the attention of the partners. Those incentives must be large enough to cement the partnership without being so large as to create inefficiency. It means giving government's partners enough operating flexibility to do the job well without the government's surrendering control over policy and process to the partners.

Formal organizational theory recognizes these issues clearly: it is the "moral hazard" problem, the risk that the goals of principals and agents will not coincide and that, therefore, agents' work might distort the goals of the principals. Hyperpluralism incorporates that issue as well as the deeper challenge that springs from the distinctly *public* nature of public services. Government's foremost job is to focus society on achieving the public interest. To do so requires enough leverage to maintain its sovereignty over its partners without exercising so much leverage that it crushes individual liberty. As the number and importance of government's partners has grown, so too has the challenge of finding that balance between sovereignty and threats to liberty. American government, especially in the Madisonian tradition, has always celebrated political interests. With growing devolution, however, government has sliced its programs ever more thinly. With globalization, multinational corporations have become even more powerful, and international organizations have taken on more responsibility for framing public policy. The movement toward more contracting out has further accelerated this trend. As governments have, for good and pragmatic reasons, relied more on partners to deliver public services, they have increasingly had less autonomy in managing their policies. To manage these partnerships, they have increasingly relied more on market-like controls through contracts and performance agreements.

Although the evidence is only suggestive, the New Zealand experience raises cautions about the implications of slicing government into smaller slivers and relying on market-based controls for accountability. The reforms separated public services into more discrete packages managed through performance contracts. These changes unquestionably produced substantial gains in efficiency, but some New Zealand analysts have worried that this approach also reduced the "social capital"—the civic engagement, mutual trust, and opportunities for debate about community concerns required for a healthy community. Such output-based contracts might well lead to less broad sharing of information, greater difficulty in translating narrow outputs to the broader outcomes that are the focus of public concerns, and less ability to manage the broader networks on which successful public programs and vital communities depend.[45]

Although the answers are far from clear, these reforms do define a critical problem. Government strategies to increase control and sovereignty over public programs might in fact increase leverage over outputs, but they risk weakening government's ability to manage the networks on which effective implementation of public programs depend. They also risk eroding the already weak base of social capital. This does not mean governments should abandon the reforms that helped strengthen public management in the 1990s. It does suggest, however, that the reforms are at best only partial remedies for the complex problems of managing hyperpluralism in both politics and administration.

IMPLICATIONS FOR GOVERNANCE

Government must not only devise new strategies for managing public programs effectively in a globalized and devolved policy world, but it must also build the capacity for pursuing these strategies. This is the first and most central challenge for governance in the twenty-first century. Most government bureaucracies remain structured and staffed to manage traditional direct programs through traditionally structured and staffed bureaucracies. As the government's strategies and tactics have changed, however, its structures and process—especially its personnel systems—have not. Governance of twenty-first century American government is more likely to resemble the complex partnerships of W-2 in Milwaukee and of the Medicare and Medicaid programs than traditional administrative orthodoxy.

If government must devise new strategies for working effectively in this world, public administration must devise new theories to explain and guide it. Public managers worked with little theoretical guidance to cope with the twin challenges of devolution and globalization. That has hurt both the practice and the study of government. It is the central challenge to which twenty-first century public administration must rise. This certainly does not mean abandoning the traditional public administration model. As chapter 2 showed, the model builds on centuries-old principles of separation of powers and democratic accountability. It *does* mean updating it to deal effectively with the horizontal networks that have been layered on top of the traditional system. Thus, the first governance problem is *adaptation:* fitting traditional vertical systems to the new challenges of globalization and devolution; and integrating new horizontal systems into the traditional vertical ones.

The second governance problem is *capacity*—enhancing government's ability to govern and manage effectively in this transformed environment. Devolution and globalization have undermined the traditional foundations of administration, especially delegating power to the bureaucracy in exchange for accountability through the hierarchy. Government faces the challenge of building new strategies for effective management and accountability. The federal civil service system, for example, is built on the assumption of direct service delivery. It performs more poorly in developing and rewarding a cadre of skilled contract managers.[46] The federal budget system simply does not track well the number and dollar volume of contracts awarded. The data that are available are rudimentary and require great interpolation. How can government strengthen its ability to govern and manage while maintaining democratic accountability?

This is also a problem of education. Many, perhaps most, of the nation's schools of public affairs, public administration, and public policy have not adjusted themselves to cope with the challenges well under way in public institutions. Consequently, future public servants, who will pursue the public interest both within and outside the government, might well fail to receive the education they need. Increasingly, the pursuit of public value occurs in the nongovernmental institutions that manage many of government's programs. It is also increasingly the case that the careers of many public affairs' program graduates take them, at least for part of their professional life, into NGOs. Public affairs education needs to broaden its perspective to the emerging tools of government action—and to the transforming environment in which managers use them.

Closely related is a third governance problem, *scale*—sorting out the functions of different levels of governance and, in particular, redefining the role of the federal government. As Daniel Bell argued in his prescient 1988 forecast, "Previewing Planet Earth in 2013":

> The common problem, I believe, is this: the nation-state is becoming too small for the big problems of life, and too big for the small problems of life. It is too small for the big problems because there are no effective international mechanisms to deal with such things as capital flows, commodity imbalances, the loss of jobs, and the several demographic tidal waves that will be developing in the next twenty years. It is too big for the small problems because the flow of power to a national political center means that the center becomes increasingly unresponsive to the variety and diversity of local needs. In short, there is a mismatch of scale.[47]

Some problems, like welfare reform, are better suited to devolved systems. Other problems, like international capital flows and regional security policy, might best fit globalized systems. The federal government, like other national governments, risks finding itself in a squeeze for relevance. The rise of global pressures in international (and even domestic) policies, coupled with the increasing importance of state-local governments and nongovernmental partners in implementing domestic programs, raises sharp questions about what role the federal government should play.

The problem, as World Bank Vice President Jean-Francois Rischard pointed out, is that "inherently global issues," from global warming and water problems to education and disease, are becoming increasingly important. The problems are serious, solutions are urgent, and actions inevitably are slow. Moreover, Rischard worries that "there's no pilot in the cockpit" for most of these issues. Governmental institutions have not risen to their challenges. Indeed, he argued, the lack of boundaries and the "urgency" of inherently global issues conflict with the "territorial and hierarchical nature of the traditional institutions that are supposed to solve them, that is, the nation-states." As a result, he continued, "current ways of handling IGIs [inherently global issues] are essentially bankrupt, if they ever worked at all."[48]

Washington politics already shows the strain of trying to cope with these questions. The executive establishment has increasingly relied on "ad hocracy," especially in the Executive Office of the President. Decisions have leaked from the executive departments. That has made it harder for the vast reservoir of the executive branch's policy expertise to find its way into major decisions. As a result, the executive's machinery for coping with cutting-edge issues risks atrophy. Whatever capacity accumulates in the ad hoc machinery can quickly leak away when crises end. Most major policy issues cannot be the province of any single agency or department, so ad hoc mechanisms tailored to important problems are inevitable. To improve public performance, government agencies must strengthen their capacity to manage such ad hoc tactics. Meanwhile, Congress too often finds itself trapped in gridlock, unable to take more than symbolic stands on a host of important issues. Some of this undoubtedly flows from the bitter politics of divided party government and, in particular, the fallout from the Clinton impeachment battle. The tensions and inaction on Capitol Hill are a sign of the mismatch of congressional behavior and the mission that is expected of it in the twenty-first century. There is indeed a mismatch of scale. Its symptoms show up regularly enwrapped in Washington's dysfunctional politics.

The United States is scarcely alone in facing this problem. A worldwide survey by the OECD in 1998 found that there is "more interdependence between levels of government as the problems to be addressed become more complex and difficult to resolve unilaterally. Divisions of responsibility for the design, implementation and evaluation of programmes are changing; and the distinction between who finances, delivers, and administers is increasingly unclear in many programmes. The search for greater flexibility in managing public programmes can blur lines of accountability."[49] These changes, the OECD concluded, produced three dichotomies:

— encouraging more *autonomy* at lower levels of government, while providing overall *direction;*
— allowing for *differentiation* through flexibility, yet ensuring some minimum degree of *uniformity;* and
— providing for more *responsiveness* to local needs, but not to the detriment of *efficiency* and *economy.*

The OECD's analysis surely applies to the United States as much as to any of the world's nations. The United States has become increasingly intertwined in the world's governance, and global governance problems increasingly apply to the United States as well. The federal government shares domestic policy with state and local governments and with NGOs—and state and local governments do the same. These changes are not the result of an explicit policy decision; rather, they grew gradually and imperceptibly from hundreds of tactics decisions over two generations of public policy. They have accumulated, however, into a fundamental transformation of governance—a transformation that poses substantial challenges for public institutions, how we manage them, how we study them, and how we prepare the nation's future public servants.

WHO GOVERNS— AND HOW? 7

Since the dawn of the human race, administration has been about building expertise to accomplish complex tasks. *Public* administration has been about building expertise to accomplish tasks defined by government on behalf of the people. Within democracies, the challenge has been to translate public wants and needs into policy, to marshal expertise to answer the wants and provide for the needs, but then to limit that expertise so the very power required for effective administration does not threaten individual liberty. That frames a basic paradox for public administration in a democracy. It is a discipline focused constantly on a search for strong and stable tools, but the more successful it is the more it potentially threatens the democratic forces charged with controlling it.

This paradox has frustrated public officials and scholars alike. Harry S. Truman famously once called for a one-armed economist. He was tired, he said, of constantly getting the "on the one hand" but "on the other hand" advice. This has been even more true of public administration. When public officials have wanted clear advice, they have tended to receive warnings about complexity. When they get strong recommendations, equally compelling arguments on the other side invariably emerge. The field's traditional roots in America, in fact, have long been framed by the eternal conundrums—centralization versus decentralization, efficiency versus responsiveness. Public administration and its related disciplines have struggled for greater precision, and some approaches have indeed produced sharper theoretical focus. The various economics-based formal approaches, in particular, have struggled to push aside the field's traditional tradeoffs for clear and replicable propositions. But the field has never been able to move far from the basic, irresolvable tradeoffs, and that has frustrated managers and theorists alike.

The problem flows in part from issues inherent in public administration. When problems fall through the cracks—when fire companies cannot agree on whose jurisdiction is responsible for fighting a fire, or when intelligence agencies fail to share information adequately—calls for better coordination arise. Coordination is hard to achieve, however, because it is hard to get different agencies with different missions and different organizational cultures to work together.[1] Moreover, agencies cannot simultaneously coordinate all activities at all times. They have to concentrate on something in order to build the capacity to do anything. In addition, coordination is expensive: it requires substantial investment by supervisors and public officials to build and nurture the required links. Coordination on some missions risks weakening capacity to achieve others. Strengthening coordination between and among agencies also is difficult to achieve without undermining the very strengths within each organization that policymakers hope to capitalize on.

The problem also flows in part from issues inherent in American democracy. Public administration is not a freestanding entity; it is the creature of a political system and is designed to accomplish its ends. All of the tradeoffs that are endemic to American republicanism occur throughout public administration also. Public administration seeks to accomplish public goals, but American democracy is exquisitely designed to ensure that policy goals are neither defined in detail nor fixed for long. Furthermore, Americans have never been consistent in their eagerness for a strong government. The Bush administration in early 2001 had sought to pick up the Reagan administration's downsizing-government banner. Soon after the September 11 terrorist attacks, however, presidential spokesman Ari Fleischer told reporters, "People need help, and in a time of war, it is principally the government that is the best instrument to help people."[2] The United States does not have just one rich tradition shaping the relationships between public administration, American democratic institutions, and the public. It has four, and the balance among them has constantly shifted.

American public administration, in theory and practice, thus, is not so much a matter of finding stable models but in adapting its various tools to fit shifting political and administrative goals. It never has and never will be a field of study that systematically builds clear, replicable propositions. In practice, it inevitably will produce ammunition for critics who will point to problems and breakdowns. Public administration is a complex business and problems constantly occur. Efforts to redress past problems plant the seeds for future ones. The emphasis on some values de-emphasizes others, and that spurs complaints. It is little wonder that Pressman and Wildavsky plaintively noted that "it's amazing that federal programs work at all."[3] The constant tradeoffs and recurring complaints often seem to make public administration just as depressing as Thomas Carlyle's "dismal science" characterization of political economy.

The tradeoffs and complaints, rooted in the very business of public administration and in the political forces shaping it, have become magnified by the increasingly fuzzy boundaries shaping the field. Administration draws its strength from boundaries: defining functions, building capacity, focusing narrowly on the job to be done, and getting it accomplished. Fuzzy boundaries challenge public administration. The forces of fuzziness have multiplied, both within the bureaucracy, between bureaucracies, and between the administrative system and democratic institutions. Devolution and globalization have tugged bureaucratic theory in opposite directions. The old tradeoffs between function and place have become sharper. Efforts to resolve the tradeoffs have become vastly more complex because of the hyperpluralism in the political system.

On one level, these are issues facing public administration around the world. The special traditions and forces within American democracy, however, pose special problems for American public administration. In considering these traditions and forces, it is impossible to escape one profoundly important conclusion: *At the dawn of the twenty-first century, neither the theory nor the practice of American public administration proved sufficient for the problems it has to solve.* The same was true at the dawn of the twentieth century, and public administration underwent a major transformation, driven by the Wilsonian tradition, to catch up. The field needs to transform itself again, just as completely. Less clear is how it ought to do so.

Front-line pragmatists have been cobbling together new tactics on top of old ones. In the 1996 welfare reform, for example, neither the federal nor the state governments decided as a matter of policy that they would rely on nongovernmental organizations (NGOs) to manage the program. Faced with tough challenges, tight budgets, and a public not eager to expand public bureaucracies, the quasi-privatized approach was simply a pragmatic response to a pressing problem. In areas as far-ranging as environmental policy and local land use, ad hocracy trumped strategic thinking. Unlike reformers in New Zealand and the United Kingdom, who drafted white papers to chart a revolution, American officials avoided writing a master plan. They worried less about plans than solving problems, less about theory than balancing challenging cross-pressures.

Even at their most tumultuous, however, the struggles of American public administration have built on powerful foundations. The strong guiding power of the great administrative traditions meant that the revolutions were merely evolutionary and that no new idea was ever fully new. When Lyndon Johnson launched his "Great Society," public administrators saw a theoretical foundation in ageless Jeffersonian debates about decentralization. When Ronald Reagan proposed to downsize government by privatizing key programs, they recognized the old Hamiltonian debates about the balance of public and private power. Richard Nixon's failed plan to restructure the executive departments built on the Wilsonian traditions of government efficiency, while Bill Clinton's reinventing government swirled around the old Madisonian balance-of-power battles. Public administrationists often contended that nothing was really new; they were not so much cynics as intellectual historians. Indeed, much of recorded history—from Moses' struggle to organize the children of Israel in their flight from Egypt and Roman emperors' efforts to conquer and organize the world—is a story of recurring themes about organization and administration.

In its relatively short life, American public administration has added two important elements to these ageless debates about administration. First, Americans introduced a self-conscious tension between individual liberty and government power. All basic values in the American republic, including the role of public administration, rest in intricate balance. Second, the American Constitution mirrored this tension by balancing political power among governmental institutions. The genius of politicians was to find everything a lasting strategy to capture different political values and to manage conflict among them. Public administration grew as endless twists on old ideas.

Nevertheless, with the start of the twenty-first century, it was clear indeed that this time-proven approach to public administration had developed large fissures. In their efforts to become more scientific, the social sciences rejected the old approach as too relativistic and directionless for the social sciences. One could always find some combination of old themes that fit new situations, but the theory could not predict what approaches would produce which results. Meanwhile, when practitioners faced increasingly complex problems, they looked to public administration theory for answers. It was scarcely the case that public administration had nothing to offer. The field had deep roots in the nation's great political traditions. But practitioners who faced tough new problems found little there that appealed to them. Instead, they turned to journalists and other practitioners who told them how to "reinvent" their activities. Some sought the counsel of consultants grounded in private-sector management practice. Theorists, however, worried that reinvention pushed public administration off its constitutional foundations and risked surrendering public power to private interests.

The great insight of the founders was to discover that they could not control or end such conflict, but they could channel and manage it. As historian Joseph J. Ellis argues in *Founding Brothers*, the American republic that emerged "was really an improvisational affair in which sheer chance, pure luck—both good and bad—and specific decisions made in the crucible of specific military and political crises determined the outcome."[4] The genius of the American revolutionaries was that they "found a way to contain the explosive energies of the debate in the form of an ongoing argument or dialogue that was eventually institutionalized and rendered safe by the creation of political parties." The political history that followed became "an oscillation between new versions of the old tension." As a result, "the debate was not resolved so much as built into the fabric of our national identity." Indeed, Ellis argues, "we are really founded on an argument" about what Jefferson's Declaration of Independence really means.[5]

By the end of the twentieth century, the arguments had become more pointed and the oscillations more rapid. Moreover, the Constitution and the politico-administrative system it generated had become less useful in capturing and channeling the conflict. In 1999, protesters in Seattle trashed much of the downtown to argue that the World Trade Organization was undemocratic. The world's governments, they said, were surrendering their sovereignty to large businesses. Globalization, in short, had created new policy venues over which the Constitution held less sway and in which important new decisions were being made. American governments devolved more decisions to state and local governments and, in many cases, they spun more programs out to NGOs. At the same time, however, these governments had not sufficiently strengthened their capacity to manage the devolution they created. In welfare reform, many program recipients and managers complained that devolution of welfare reform to the states and the states' privatization of welfare management to NGOs had wrung the public interest from publicly funded programs. Far too much money went into profits for NGOs, they charged, and far too little into public services.

Functionally organized governments—by health, environment, labor, and commerce, for example—strained to cope with the coordination demands of a world with fuzzy boundaries, in which no important problem would agree to stay within the lines of any governmental agency.

Coordination among government agencies has always been both important and difficult, but by the end of the twentieth century the problem had increased substantially. Cross-agency task forces and coordination teams became more important. At the same time, local officials and citizens worried as much as ever about how decisions made in far-off government agencies would affect them and where they lived. Matching functional expertise with place-based impact is one of public administration's eternal challenges, but increasingly fuzzy boundaries enormously complicated that problem.

As American governments struggled to manage these forces, they fractionated their management approaches. They sliced programs more thinly to increase management control. They experimented with performance-based management as a substitute for traditional hierarchical authority. They privatized and contracted out. Ever-thinner slices, however, presented the grave difficulty of reassembling them into a coherent whole. Perhaps even more important, they created new arenas for conflict and action that lie at—or beyond—the fringes of the American constitutional system, like devolution and globalization. American government often had neither the administrative capacity nor the political institutions for channeling conflict and ensuring democratic accountability. That is why twentieth-century governance increasingly grew out of sync with administrative practice and theory.

Periodically throughout American history, and especially in times of great economic transformation, governance problems and public administration theory have become mismatched. That was the case at the end of the nineteenth century, when the rise of business monopolies concentrated political power just as the people's expectations for more public functions grew. Government risked being captured by narrow interests and becoming less accountable even as its role grew more important. The Progressives charted a strategy for government to be more capable while becoming more accountable. Their approach—advanced hierarchy with authority-based control—fed a theory that increased administration's power while holding it more responsible to policymakers. Through two world wars, the Great Depression, and the rise of the nation's global power, that approach proved remarkably resilient.

By the end of the twentieth century, however, the transformation of governance had rendered that approach obsolete. New economic forces—this time, global ones—threatened to capture public power. Government struggled to build the capacity to manage transformed strategies. Americans showed no eagerness to abandon the traditions that had guided political and administrative practice for more than two centuries. Less clear, however, was how those traditions ought to guide political and administrative practice for the future. As boundaries became fuzzier, how could government effectively coordinate public programs? As NGOs became increasingly important in governmental service delivery, how could government hold them accountable? How could the living Constitution adapt to manage and channel conflicts that strained existing institutions?

Among these questions, one is most important. As responsibility for public programs becomes more broadly shared—where no one is fully responsible for anything and many players are responsible for everything—how can American government pursue the timeless values that have guided the nation since its founding? This is an echo of the question Robert A. Dahl posed plainly in his classic 1961 book, *Who Governs?:* "In a political system where nearly every adult may vote but where knowledge, wealth, social position, access to officials, and other resources are unequally distributed, who actually governs?" For Dahl, political power was pluralist, with power distributed among a wide range of interests, and dynamic, with patterns of power shifting over time.[6] Dahl's argument helped move political science from an institutional approach to politics—one that built theories of political power on the formal organizations empowered by law and the Constitution to make decisions—to a process-driven approach—one that analyzed political power by who exercised it and how. That approach helps frame the answer to how American government can best cope with the transformation of governance.

In many ways, Dahl anticipated by a generation a similar transformation of the study of public administration. During the twentieth century, public administration prospered with a theory built on organizational structure. Clearly framing administration's role and function—and defining what its role was not—helped make government larger and more effective without sacrificing the pursuit of democratic accountability. John Gaus's 1950 article in *Public Administration Review* argued, "A theory of public administration means in our time a theory of politics also."[7] To that we can add, "No theory of politics is complete without a theory of administration." Building a theory of public administration that is true to the realities of politics has become both more critical and more difficult because constraints on and expectations of public administration grew significantly in the last half of the twentieth century. Citizens and elected officials expected administrators to eradicate poverty, manage rapid transportation systems, provide high-quality, low-cost health care, and clean up the environment. On the other hand, building a theory of politics that embraces the central role of administration has become far more critical, because turning policy aspirations into reality has, by any measure, become more difficult. Indeed, more than ever before, administration has become the essence of political reality. On many fronts, politics has become less a battle over what government ought to do and more a battle over how it can do it better and cheaper.

THE RISE OF A NEW GOVERNANCE

If the problems of public administration seem daunting and the prospects for resolving them seem small, it is important to remember two things. One is that while many of the cross-pressures are new, the inescapable reality of making tradeoffs is not. The great strength of American democracy and public administration is its almost infinite ability to flex, transform, and adapt to new realities—and to do so in ways consistent with the nation's enduring values and traditions. Indeed, American public administration has been remarkable in its intellectual and pragmatic elasticity, to stretch its approaches without losing its basic norms.

The other is that, despite the manifest problems, most of government works pretty well most of the time. The news media focus on news, and success stories rarely make the headlines. The Social Security Administration, for example, correctly posts 99 percent of wage earners' contributions, and 82 percent of citizens rate the SSA's service as "good" or "very good."[8] The U.S. Department of Transportation's regulatory and grant programs have brought down the number of gas pipeline explosions.[9] New York City's performance system has reduced crime and improved the productivity of city agencies.[10] Problems dominate the news, not the system's overall high level of performance, and that can make discussion of the transformation of governance seem a rather gloomy affair.

Thus, the basic issue is not to rue government's failures. Rather, given the constant and inevitable swings among traditions and strategies in American government, which approaches are most likely to help government cope with the transformation of governance? What new approaches must public administration forge to cope better with the inescapable challenges facing government and governance?

Americans have never been fully satisfied with the performance of their governments. Of course, performance can always be improved. Higher performance can always produce lower taxes or more service for the same level of taxes. Moreover, what Americans want often changes. At the core, Americans have always wanted more government services without having to pay higher taxes. But just *how* best to deliver those services and *which* problems government needs to solve have changed constantly.

If the nineteenth-century challenge was the rise of corporate power that threatened to swamp the public interest, the challenge at the beginning of the twenty-first century was the diffusion of administrative action, the multiplication of administrative partners, and the proliferation of political influence outside government's circles. American politics has always been famous—or notorious—for the multiple channels it provides citizens to participate in the process and for the intricate balance the constitutional framework provides. Citizens can seek redress from their local, state, or national governments. They can press their views in the legislative, executive, and judicial branches. It is a rare policy decision in the American system that is ever truly final. The American political tradition, however, made government the arbiter of policy. Americans have always debated just how far government ought to reach into their lives, but those battles were fought with the ground rules the constitutional system established.

These puzzles multiply Dahl's basic question: Who governs—and how? How can we make effective public policy? How can we implement it well? And how, in the course of administration, can we pursue the goals of American democracy that have for centuries been the bedrock of the political system? The questions certainly are not new. Neither is conflict in how best to answer them. As Ellis pointed out in his study of America's "founding brothers," new oscillations in the old patterns develop. Each new oscillation presents new challenges of finding an equilibrium among the old cross-pressures. With the transformation of governance at the end of the twentieth century, these challenges had grown. Meanwhile, the ability of America's political institutions to find that new equilibrium—to channel and to manage conflict—had shrunk.

Government thus finds itself with several complex, interwoven problems. It faces new service demands from citizens, but citizens usually show little enthusiasm for paying higher taxes. It is deploying increasingly complex public programs, but no one really wants to increase the size of government bureaucracies. To solve these problems, it has devised new management strategies, but it is struggling to build the capacity to manage the strategies and to cope with unexpected side effects, such as a possible reduction in social capital. Practitioners have struggled to cobble together new solutions to these problems—and to speed the learning curve so that they could quickly appropriate successful strategies from other practitioners. However, unlike during the Progressive movement, when Wilson, Goodnow, and other thinkers helped lead the effort, theorists at the end of the twentieth century lagged behind the transformation of governance. Together, they struggled to devise new strategies for the new governance:

to develop an effective government without sacrificing accountability, to pursue efficiency without sacrificing the public good. The transformation of governance thus frames five big issues:

1. *Challenges.* American government is stretching to perform tasks that no government has attempted before. Terrorist attacks demand new strategies for safeguarding travel, work, home, and play. New health threats, like mad-cow disease, easily cross international borders, while bioengineered food presents unprecedented regulatory demands. The Internet and other tools for instantaneous communication and networking provide great opportunities but also new challenges. None of these problems easily fits within the province of existing bureaucracies, and it would be hard to imagine how to create a bureaucracy that could encompass them. The challenges require new administrative strategies and tactics.

2. *Capacity.* Many of these challenges require government to develop and deploy new skills as well as to expand existing ones significantly. The capacity problem not only involves finding and hiring smart people but also means devising effective strategies to tackle the new problems of governance. As government relies more on nongovernmental partners to deliver services, it increases its own need to define sharply what it is trying to accomplish. It also increases its need for tools to supervise grantees, contractors, and other third parties who work on its behalf. Finally, government must be able to gauge the success of its complex chain of action. Because much of government remains deeply rooted in traditional command-and-control techniques and direct-service strategies, it faces the twin task of escaping the bounds of its existing culture and building capacity to meet its emerging challenges.

3. *Legitimacy.* American government's increasing dependence on nongovernmental partners—and their increasing dependence on government programs and cash—highlight important problems for the legitimacy of public power. As Fritz W. Scharpf argues, the more government and its partners become interdependent, the more its policy options are constrained and the more previous policies "become less effective, more costly, or downright unfeasible—which must be counted as a loss of democratic self-determination even if new options are added to the policy repertoire."[11] Political interests help frame governmental policy but then also become important in administering it. That shifts the balance of political forces, because some interests become far more tightly wired into both the making and the administration of governmental policy. It makes it harder for those outside this network to oversee that policy. And it changes government's role from one of hierarchical supremacy to that of one player in a broader network. This disrupts the age-old notions of gov-

ernment's role and of the workings of democratic accountability. How does influence over public policy work? Are all voices equal? What should government do when a place within the administrative network privileges some political voices over others?

4. *Sovereignty.* Government also needs to devise new strategies to ensure that its voice is not just one among many in the network. Especially with the simultaneous rise of devolution and globalization, the federal government's role has become far less clear. To rule effectively, government must first attain and then exercise sovereignty. It must be able to chart its course and ensure that that course is followed. Hyperpluralism, policy networks, devolution, and globalization have all greatly diffused power. Government might retain its legal position, but exercising practical sovereignty amid such diffused power presents a major challenge to twenty-first century government. It requires government both to know what it wants to accomplish and to devise strategies for doing so. Government is not just one participant in policy networks, working on the same level as others. It has a responsibility to the law and to the public interest and must, therefore, ensure it has the capacity to steer the behavior of the policy systems that produce public programs.

5. *The public interest.* Perhaps the strongest argument of traditional public administration is its particular focus on the public interest—the use of administration to pursue programs to advance the interests and to solve the problems of citizens. The Hamiltonian and Wilsonian traditions, in particular, have always carried a heavy public-interest argument. Administration needed to be strong enough to allow government to do what citizens wanted done. Of course, defining "the public interest" has always been the most daunting of practical and theoretical problems. The diffusion of sovereignty has made the tough job even tougher. Nevertheless, public administration—in all its competing theories and traditions—remains single-mindedly committed to what Waldo calls "the good life."[12] Indeed, White believed that "in its broader context, the ends of administration are the ultimate ends of the state itself—the maintenance of peace and order, instruction of the young, equalization of opportunity, protection against disease and insecurity, adjustment and compromise of conflicting groups and interests, in short, the achievement of the good life."[13] The Brownlow Committee in 1937 echoed that argument by concluding, "By democracy, we mean getting things done that we, the American people, want done in the general interest."[14] Public administration thus stands among the highest traditions of American government—and squarely in the middle of its biggest tests. Its task is to rise to the challenge of the transformation of governance.

STRATEGIES FOR TRANSFORMING GOVERNANCE

What would strategies for twenty-first century governance look like? American governments face three capacity problems: fine-tuning their traditional, hierarchical systems to work more productively in managing direct service systems; creating new nonhierarchical approaches for managing indirect service systems; and, perhaps most daunting, configuring those systems to operate effectively side by side, without the authority-based system disrupting the network and without the network disrupting the authority-based system. In particular, the expansion of both contracting out and federalism as administrative strategies brings new burdens.

Capacity

Government strategies, especially grants and contracts, do not manage themselves. Rather, they require the cultivation of new skills to specify program goals, negotiate good contracts, and oversee the results. Moreover, the contract system requires the development of markets that could supply the goods and services the government wanted to buy; replacing a public monopoly with a private monopoly scarcely could increase the efficiency of service delivery.[15] In assessing the government's "high-risk programs," the U.S. General Accounting Office identified contract management as one of its most difficult problems.[16] The rise of this contractor workforce raises important challenges to the federal workforce and fuels its "human capital" problem. Comptroller General Walker argued, "The problem is not federal employees, it's the policies, procedures and legislative framework that guide federal human capital actions."[17]

The rise of intergovernmental relations as both a political and an administrative system has complicated this problem. The federal government has long managed many of its operations through direct systems, such as Social Security and air traffic control. As the scope of its activities expanded through the last decades of the twentieth century, the federal government began relying more on state and local governments as front-line field agents to deliver federal programs, from interstate highways and antipoverty programs to Medicaid and environmental programs. The federal government relied on state and local governments in part because they provided useful administrative intermediaries. The federal government also, however, relied on subnational governments to share decision-making and make government programs more responsive. The history of American federalism has always rendered the federal-state-local administrative relationship complex. Federalism has long sought to define uniform national policies and to give state and local government responsibility to tailor those policies to local conditions. Determining where federal goals leave off and local policy discretion picks up has long been a difficult puzzle.

The rise of these strategies—contracting and intergovernmental relations—requires the federal government to shape policy and measure results without intruding on administrative flexibility. These activities require greater skill in negotiation and information management than does direct service delivery. The federal government must develop these skills—enhancing its "human capital"—without undermining its ability to manage direct programs, which continue to rely on hierarchy and authority. When a department uses both strategies, such as the U.S. Department of Transportation's air traffic control and highway grant systems and the EPA's enforcement and Superfund cleanup systems, it faces the task of constructing parallel administrative systems. These systems have vastly different organizational cultures but must be cultivated by the same senior management team. Building the skills to manage these strategies is a substantial challenge. Leading them in parallel is an even bigger one.

Add to that an additional challenge: America's local governments have maintained more direct service delivery than the federal government. So not only must America's administrative system develop parallel direct and indirect management systems. It must also accommodate the different rules of different levels of government, an issue as much political as administrative.

Coordination

No problem is more central to administration than coordination. Hierarchy and authority have long offered two great advantages in solving this problem. They allow top managers to break complex jobs into smaller, manageable pieces. They also allow top managers to assign precise responsibilities to each administrator and thereby hold them accountable for results. With the transformation of governance, these approaches had scarcely become less widespread or useful. Rather, they solved a smaller share of government's management problems. As more organizations shared responsibility for producing results, American government at all levels sought additional strategies and tactics to supplement hierarchy and authority—to solve the problems that the traditional approaches left unresolved.

For example, the path-breaking welfare reform strategy Wisconsin Works (W-2) taught an important lesson about helping welfare recipients get off welfare and into productive long-term employment. In three years ending in September 2000, the number of people on cash assistance had dropped by half. Most of the front-line work was done by for-profit and nonprofit organizations and, in fact, the typical welfare recipient never saw a government employee in the journey from welfare to work. In the program that became the model for the 1996 federal welfare reform legislation, devolution was the driving strategy.

Reducing the welfare rolls was one thing. Getting welfare recipients into good jobs and keeping them there was quite another. As a 2001 Wisconsin state legislative audit report showed, one-third of the 2,129 individuals who left the W-2 program in the first three months of 1998 did not file a 1999 income tax return.[18] Experts suspected that they were not earning enough money to file. Another third had incomes below the poverty level, while one-third had incomes above the poverty level when benefits from the earned income tax credit were included. Many participants cycled into and out of the program. A little more than one-fourth of those who left the program returned by July 2000. In Milwaukee, which had the lion's share of Wisconsin's case load as well as many of its most difficult cases, 42 percent of W-2 clients were back in the program because work had not worked out.

What strategies proved most successful in getting people off welfare, keeping them off, and helping them climb above the poverty level? The W-2 alumni with the highest incomes were those who had received extensive job training and other support services and then moved on to unsubsidized private-sector jobs. Those who went into subsidized jobs did not fare nearly as well. Those with the greatest success benefited from "case management," in which service coordinators working for one of the NGOs pulled together job training, child care, housing and food support, health care, and the other services that families need to make the jump from welfare to work.

Service delivery has become less a process by which government agencies convert inputs (including money, people, and expertise) into outputs and more a process by which many agencies, in government and outside, share responsibility for producing services. To the traditional command-and-control functions of management have been added new functions of building and managing partnerships. Although the job varies tremendously by level of government—direct service delivery continues to predominate in local governments while the government by proxy dominates federal programs—the functions of public management have subtly but dramatically changed since the Progressive era. In dealing with citizens, effective government managers are increasingly case managers; in coordinating different agencies and programs, government managers are increasingly service integrators.

This heightens the value of the network approach that emerged in public management research during the 1990s. If it has not yet become a fully developed theory, it has at least provided an important step toward understanding the complexity of the service system and charting strategies for operating effectively within it. Moreover, the coordination imperative increased the importance of information technology and electronic government.[19] Information strategies and tactics that move seamlessly across those boundaries offer great potential.[20]

Control

When demonstrators swarmed Seattle in 1999 to protest the meeting of the World Trade Organization, they joined the issues of globalization and democratic accountability. Amid the tear gas and broken glass, they argued that large multinational corporations and organizations like the WTO were taking power away from citizens. If the proposition was debatable, it was surely true that the rise of global trade and multinational organizations stretched the boundaries of constitutional government. Behind the headlines, the demonstrations focused attention on big issues: assessing the power of groups like the WTO; determining how to hold it accountable to democratic governments and their people; and structuring patterns of popular participation in critical decisions such organizations make. It was an important case of how constitutional democracy had lagged behind the forces shaping critical decisions.

Within devolved systems, similar issues surfaced without the glass-shattering impact of the Seattle demonstrators. As NGOs took on greater responsibility for service delivery, critics worried about how to hold them accountable. Government reformers countered that market-style contracts and incentives were the key. But when large declines in the Wisconsin welfare rolls produced big profits for the contractors, interest groups representing the poor complained that the money should have gone instead to provide better services to more welfare recipients. Since Dwight D. Eisenhower's warning about the military-industrial complex—indeed, since George Washington warned the Continental Congress that military contractors were stealing desperately needed provisions from his troops—thoughtful observers have worried about the leakage of public power and money into private hands.

In the American administrative traditions, the dominant approach to this problem has always rested in the delegation doctrine: voters elect public officials; they make policy; they delegate the management of complex issues to administrators; and the administrators are accountable through the chain of command to elected officials. In fact, the doctrine of delegation tightly controls administrative behavior. In the private sector, managers may do anything not prohibited by law. In the public sector, managers may do only what the law allows. Responsiveness to the public occurs from the top down through the electoral process. Elected officials have not always been eager to exercise their responsibility, but the fabric of bureaucratic power in the American republic depends on this relationship.

The transformation of governance has unraveled that fabric, however. Elected officials might delegate power to administer programs, but the real task of administration is coordination—weaving together separate programs into a sensible policy. That coordination results in responsibility shared among administrators at different agencies, at multiple levels of government, and among nongovernmental partners. Hyperpluralism means that no one is fully in charge of anything and that nearly everyone ultimately shares responsibility for results. That does not mean that accountability through the delegation process has evaporated. It does mean that it is less effective, both in drawing a clear link between policy decisions and the ultimate results and in ensuring that the administration of individual programs meshes to produce sensible policy. As in bureaucratic organizations that use hierarchy and control through authority, the traditional approaches have not disappeared. But the transformation of governance has created a powerful need to layer new systems on top of the old to ensure democratic accountability.

In the best Jeffersonian tradition, moreover, citizens expect to have direct influence on public administrative decisions. Citizens would quickly reject a theory that worked only from the top down and through elected officials. From decisions about local zoning to disposal of nuclear waste, citizens expect to be able to speak and to have their words heard. With so many front-line decisions made by NGOs and with supranational organizations making other decisions, the process for incorporating citizen involvement is anything but clear. It was this worry that drove frustrated demonstrators to violence in Seattle and at subsequent meetings of international bodies in Washington and Quebec City.

The problems, at their most basic level, involve how to apportion responsibilities among the elements of complex policy networks; how to hold individual members of the networks responsible for their contributions; and how to ensure that these contributions combine into prudent policy. Reformers in nations like the United Kingdom and New Zealand have experimented with market-based accountability mechanisms, by transforming public programs into competitive arrange-ments and relying on competition and self-interest to promote the public interest. In the United States, advocates of the reinventing government movement have argued similar approaches. More broadly, reformers have argued the value of a performance-based approach, in which elected officials would manage accountability by judging results instead of the process that produced them.

In global networks, there is an additional concern—how to ensure adequate participation in and accountability for decisions shaped by multinational organizations—some public, some private—over which the different constitutional systems of individual nation-states have limited leverage. Nation-states have structured the ground rules for these organizations, and they have voting rights for their policies and chief officials. The effectiveness of such accountability mechanisms, especially in the face of the rising power of global corporations, however, is anything but clear.

Complex public-private networks raise vastly different accountability questions than programs managed directly through government bureaucracies. They require creative strategies that build on the strengths of time-honored traditions while incorporating new tactics that work effectively to shape the behavior and results of the networks. Perhaps more than any other element of the transformation of governance, the control issue raises most sharply the tough problem of who governs—and how.

GOVERNANCE FOR THE PUBLIC INTEREST

American public administration has never had—and it never will have—a steady state. The field, in its study and practice, is the product of an uneasy and dynamic balance between four very different and competing administrative traditions. Americans have never embraced any of them for long. Meanwhile, competing economic, political, and social forces have constantly presented new challenges that require new—and always uneasy—fits between management tools and political goals, between administrative organizations and political institutions. To explore public administration in either theory or practice is to make oneself a captain of a ship on a sea where the waves never settle. But as anyone who has devoted hours of serious research to studying the patterns of tides and waves on a beach can testify, the same patterns never recur in precisely the same ways. The administrative process is always undergoing change.

Every once in a while, however, storms churn up the waves and dramatically rearrange the shoreline. Engineers once built a bridge on North Carolina's Outer Banks to connect two barrier islands. Within a decade, a large part of the bridge was over dry land because ocean storms filled in sand from the opposite side of the island. Administration is about coordination, and twenty-first century coordination is increasingly about bridge-building. The transformation of governance calls for new bridges built in new and imaginative ways—bridges that will cross wide divides and that will endure. Ten principles suggest how to build these bridges:

1. *Hierarchy and authority cannot and will not be replaced, but they must be fitted better to the transformation of governance.* From the earliest days of human history, managers have used hierarchy and authority to coordinate solutions to complex problems. The governance problems of the twenty-first century do not reverse that basic truth. Hierarchy and authority provide enduring strategies for both coordination and accountability in democratic governments.

2. *Complex networks have been layered on top of hierarchical organizations, and they must be managed differently.* Despite the enduring power of hierarchy, managers need to adapt its tools to the interorganizational networks that increasingly drive administrative action. They need to harness their hierarchies to manage those networks, often side by side with traditional programs that continue to be managed through authority-driven structures.

3. *Public managers need to rely more on interpersonal and interorganizational processes as complements to—and sometimes as substitutes for—authority.* Whatever their weaknesses, authority and hierarchy provide stable and useful mechanisms for structuring and controlling the behavior of administrators. The more managers rely on networks, the more they need to find substitutes—or supplements—for coordinating action. The more informal or dynamic those networks are, the more managers need new mechanisms. Traditional administration relied primarily on organizational structure to shape administrative action. The more fluid administrative action becomes, the more administrators are likely to need to shift from structure to process for leverage.

4. *Information is the most basic and necessary component for the transformation of governance.* Many processes, including financial and personnel systems, offer the potential for control and influence. In twenty-first century government, however, information has become essential. As computerized information technology and e-government spread, and as more government work occurs across organizational boundaries, information offers the most effective bridge. Information technology makes possible instantaneous, boundary-free communication, and that communication is necessary for coordinating twenty-first century work.

5. *Performance management can provide a valuable tool for spanning fuzzy boundaries.* Of the different forms of information, performance-based information can be the most important. When multiple organizations share responsibility for producing public programs, it can become difficult for citizens, government managers, or elected officials to determine who is in charge of what—and who contributes what to the overall outcomes of governmental policy. Performance-based management systems can strengthen administration by allowing administrators to allocate responsibility for broad outcomes among members of the service network, by assessing how the outputs of each part of the network supports the broader goals of public policy, and by encouraging elected officials to examine the links between their policy decisions and the results the system produces. Performance management thus is not only a potential mechanism for managing networks but also a tool for accountability.

6. *Transparency is the foundation for trust and confidence in government operations.* Communication that is transparent—accessible in real time to everyone—can increase the trust and confidence of citizens in governmental work. With the rise of global corporations, many citizens have feared that private power will swamp the public interest. With increasing reliance on devolution, many citizens have worried that the real decisions about managing public programs will be pushed into invisible, nongovernmental nooks and crannies. Both fears have often combined to reduce public trust and confidence in government's work. Information technology, including the Internet and e-government, makes possible rapid and broad distribution of knowledge about what government is doing and how. That, in turn, can help strengthen citizens' relations with an increasingly indirect government.

7. *Government needs to invest in human capital so that the skills of its workers match the jobs they must perform.* Many of these tools, however,

require high skill levels, especially in the government managers who must coordinate them. Moreover, these skills are often very different from the ones traditionally developed for command-and-control programs. The bridge-building required to manage the transformation of governance will require, in turn, a retooling of government's personnel systems so that public employees have the skills their jobs require. Many of the tasks of twenty-first century government, especially its critical coordination challenges, are at their core people-based challenges. Solving them will require skilled managers who can negotiate the constantly shifting forces of the administrative systems.

8. *The transformation of governance requires new strategies and tactics for popular participation in public administration.* Although the American republic anticipates top-down administrative accountability through elected officials, citizens increasingly expect more bottom-up responsiveness from public services and the employees who run them. In part, this flows from the customer service movement encouraged in the private sector. In part, it comes from the movement launched through the 1960s Great Society programs to empower citizens and make programs more responsive to their needs. The rise of e-government and other forms of boundary-spanning communication also promotes bottom-up responsiveness. As citizens gain new channels for influence and communication, they can rely less on top officials as problem-solvers and more on going directly to those who manage the programs that affect them. That, in turn, requires a rethinking of the linkages between citizens and governments.

9. *Civic responsibility has become the job of government's nongovernmental partners.* The same holds true for the public's relations with the for-profit and nonprofit organizations that increasingly play a central role in service delivery. Government needs more effective mechanisms to ensure that citizens receive the same basic and consistent treatment regardless of whether governments or NGOs provide services. The government's nongovernmental partners are no longer agents-for-hire who can maintain their traditional missions. By becoming partners in public service provision, NGOs assume responsibilities for how they treat citizens. That requires, in turn, the development of mechanisms to promote the responsiveness, flexibility, and efficiency that nongovernmental partners can offer without sacrificing the basic standards that citizens expect from government—and that the Constitution guarantees.

10. *Americans need to devise new constitutional strategies for the management of conflict.* The basic transformation of governance has not so much

created brand new paradigms as it has layered new issues on top of old ones. That calls not so much for a new Constitution as for fresh strategies based on the old one. The Constitution has proven remarkably resilient over its history, but periodically new pressures have built up that have required new tactics. The great genius of the Founders lay in framing a Constitution that could adapt; the genius of the nation's leaders since has lain in their ability to manage that adaptation as new pressures have demanded. For a century, the patterns devised by the Progressives shaped the relationships between economic and political interests and between administrative and political power. These adaptations have occurred especially when economic power threatened to swamp the public interest. That spurred the Progressives' reforms of government at the end of the nineteenth century—and the same issues framed the tensions government faced at the end of the twentieth century.

It is always tempting to seize on any new administrative practice and to declare it a revolution, to examine a new theoretical idea and proclaim a new paradigm. In the case of American administrative practice, that is especially dangerous. For centuries, American government and its administrative systems have evolved through endless adaptations. Its basic administrative strategies have grown on foundations that stretch back hundreds, if not thousands, of years. In many ways, therefore, there is nothing really new in the story of the transformation of governance. It simply represents the latest change—one new tide in the waves that constantly have washed across the American political system.[21]

In the transformation of governance, however, lie two basic truths. One truth is that the context truly is new. The rise of globalization and devolution, the stress between government's horizontal and vertical dimensions, and hyperpluralism all combine to create fresh tensions for which government's existing structures and strategies proved a poor match. The other truth is that this transformation plays itself out within the four traditions—Hamiltonian, Jeffersonian, Wilsonian, and Madisonian—that have long shaped America's basic administrative instincts. Neither the context nor the traditions remain stable for long. The system has long been resilient enough to accommodate big changes in context with modest changes in administration. But periodically, the tensions have grown serious. Reformers created new twists on the existing traditions that proved a better and, at least temporarily, more stable fit for the problems they faced. Some of America's most difficult times preceded these adjustments; some of America's most intense periods of economic prosperity and social content have followed these shifts. The new puzzles that emerged at the end of the nineteenth century helped set the stage for America's remarkable twentieth century. The puzzles that surfaced at the end of the twentieth century set the stage for a similar transformation. America's economic prosperity and social welfare depend on cleverly crafting a new match between the emerging policy puzzles and the enduring administrative traditions.

NOTES

CHAPTER ONE: ADMINISTRATIVE PARADOXES

1. Judy Newman, "Chee-Tos Lovers May Find Themselves in Puffy Crunch," *Wisconsin State Journal*, 9 December 2000.

2. "Aventis CropScience Is Created in North America," company press release, Aventis CropScience, 15 December 1999. See www.biotech-info.net/aventis.html (accessed January 30, 2001).

3. See Paul P. Van Riper, "The American Administrative State: Wilson and the Founders," in Ralph Clark Chandler, ed., *A Centennial History of the American Administrative State* (New York: Free Press, 1987), 3–36.

4. See Frank J. Goodnow, *Comparative Administrative Law: An Analysis of the Administrative Systems, National and Local, of the United States, England, France, and Germany* (New York: G. P. Putnam's Sons, 1893); and *Politics and Administration: A Study in Government* (New York: Russell and Russell, 1900).

5. Willoughby's central text is *The Government of Modern States* (New York: Century Co., 1919). For Cleveland's work, see *The Budget and Responsible Government* (New York: Macmillan, 1920).

6. Van Riper, "The American Administrative State," 24.

7. On the empowerment of government, see Willoughby, *The Government of Modern States*. For a discussion, see Dwight Waldo, *The Administrative State: A Study of the Political Theory of American Public Administration* (New York: Ronald Press, 1948), 112–13.

8. President's Committee on Administrative Management, *Report with Special Studies* (Washington, D.C.: U.S. Government Printing Office, 1937).

9. For an analysis of these changes, see Barry D. Karl, *Executive Reorganization and Reform in the New Deal* (Cambridge: Harvard University Press, 1963); Paul C. Light, *The Tides of Reform: Making Government Work, 1945–1995* (New Haven: Yale University Press, 1998).

10. Vincent Ostrom, *The Intellectual Crisis in American Public Administration* (University: University of Alabama Press, 1973).

11. See Goodnow, *Politics and Administration*; see also Goodnow's presidential address at the annual meeting of the American Political Science Association, "The Work of the American Political Science Association," *Proceedings of the American Political Science Association, 1904* (Lancaster, Pa.: Wickersham Press, 1994), 35–46.

12. Roscoe C. Martin, "Political Science and Public Administration: A Note on the State of the Union," *American Political Science Review* 46 (1952): 662.

13. Herbert Simon, *Administrative Behavior* (New York: Macmillan, 1947).

14. Robert Dahl, "The Science of Public Administration: Three Problems," *Public Administration Review* 7 (1947): 1-11.

15. See Frederick W. Taylor, *Principles of Scientific Management* (New York: Harper and Brothers, 1911). For an analysis of the influence of Taylor's work, see Robert Kanigel, *The One Best Way: Frederick Winslow Taylor and the Enigma of Efficiency* (New York: Viking, 1997).

16. See, for example, Herbert Simon, "The Proverbs of Administration," *Public Administration Review* 6 (1946): 53-67.

17. Bernard R. Berelson, Paul F. Lazarsfeld, and William N. McPhee, *Voting: A Study of Opinion Formation in a Presidential Campaign* (Chicago: University of Chicago Press, 1954).

18. Robert A. Dahl, *Who Governs? Democracy and Power in an American City* (New Haven: Yale University Press, 1964).

19. Quoted in Allen Schick, "The Trauma of Politics: Public Administration in the Sixties," in Frederick C. Mosher, ed., *American Public Administration: Past, Present, Future* (University: University of Alabama Press, 1975), 160.

20. See www.maxwell.syr.edu/deans/ (last accessed February 5, 2001).

21. Richard E. Neustadt, preface to *Presidential Power: The Politics of Leadership* (New York: John Wiley, 1960).

22. Graham T. Allison, *Essence of Decision: Explaining the Cuban Missile Crisis* (Boston: Little, Brown, 1971).

23. Erwin C. Hargrove, *The Missing Link: The Study of the Implementation of Social Policy* (Washington, D.C.: Urban Institute, 1975).

24. Jeffrey L. Pressman and Aaron Wildavsky, *Implementation* (Berkeley: University of California Press, 1973), 166. In fact, there already was a small but important literature on implementation when Pressman and Wildavsky wrote their pathbreaking book. See, for example, Stephen K. Bailey and Edith K. Mosher, *ESEA: The Office of Education Administers a Law* (Syracuse: Syracuse University Press, 1968); and Jerome T. Murphy, "Title I of ESEA: The Politics of Implementing Federal Educational Reform," *Harvard Educational Review* 41 (1971): 35-63.

25. Robert D. Behn, "Management by Groping Along," *Journal of Policy Analysis and Management* 7 (Fall 1988): 643-63.

26. For an examination of such a battle within sociology, see Emily Eakin, "What Is the Next Big Idea? The Buzz Is Growing," *New York Times*, 7 July 2001, 7(B).

27. Edgar H. Schein, *Organizational Culture and Leadership: A Dynamic View* (San Francisco: Jossey-Bass, 1987), 289.

28. See, for example, Robert D. Behn, *Leadership Counts: Lessons for Public Managers from the Massachusetts Welfare, Training, and Employment Program* (Cambridge: Harvard University Press, 1991).

29. See John Micklethwait and Adrian Wooldridge, *The Witch Doctors: Making Sense of the Management Gurus* (New York: Times Books, 1996).

30. Laurence E. Lynn Jr., *Public Management as Art, Science, and Profession* (Chatham, N.J.: Chatham House Publishers, 1996), 3.

31. See Lynn, *Public Management as Art, Science, and Profession;* and Behn, *Leadership Counts.*

32. See, for example, the "Symposium on the Advancement of Public Administration," *Journal of Public Affairs Education* 5 (April 1999): 119-66.

33. David Osborne and Ted Gaebler, *Reinventing Government: How the Entrepreneurial Spirit Is Transforming the Public Sector from Schoolhouse to Statehouse, City Hall to the Pentagon* (Reading, Mass.: Addison-Wesley, 1992).

34. Personal interview with Elaine Kamarck.

35. See Donald F. Kettl, *The Global Public Management Revolution: A Report on the Transformation of Governance* (Washington, D.C.: Brookings Institution Press, 2000); and Christopher Pollitt and Geert Bouckaert, *Public Management Reform: A Comparative Analysis* (Oxford: Oxford University Press, 2000).

36. Melody Petersen and Greg Winter, "5 Drug Makers Use Material with Possible Mad Cow Link," *New York Times*, 8 February 2001, 1(C), 5(C).

37. Schein, *Organizational Culture and Leadership*, 289.

CHAPTER TWO: ADMINISTRATIVE TRADITIONS

1. Aaron Wildavsky, *The Nursing Father: Moses as a Political Leader* (Tuscaloosa: University of Alabama Press, 1984).

2. Erna Risch, *Supplying Washington's Army* (Washington, D.C.: Center of Military History, U.S. Army, 1981).

3. Deborah L. Spar, *Ruling the Waves: Cycles of Discovery, Chaos, and Wealth from Buccaneers to Bill Gates* (New York: Harcourt Brace, 2001).

4. David Wessel, "The Market Demands Rules," *Wall Street Journal*, 29 November 2001, 1(A).

5. Wildavsky, *The Nursing Father*, 99-106.

6. Other authors have examined the powerful influence of such traditions on American public administration. In particular, see Richard J. Stillman, chap. 7 in *The American Bureaucracy: The Core of Modern Government* (Chicago: Nelson Hall, 1987).

7. See Leonard D. White, *The Federalists: A Study in Administrative History* (New York: Macmillan, 1948); Lynton K. Caldwell, *The Administrative Theories of Hamilton and Jefferson* (Chicago: University of Chicago Press, 1944); and Van Riper, "The American Administrative State," 34.

8. White, *The Federalists*, p. 127.

9. See White, *The Federalists*, chap. 8.

10. Richard Brookhiser, *Alexander Hamilton, American* (New York: Free Press, 1999), 101.

11. Ibid., 6.

12. Daniel J. Boorstin, *The Lost World of Thomas Jefferson* (Chicago: University of Chicago Press, 1981), ix, 237.

13. Ibid., 237.

14. See White, *The Federalists,* 222-23. More generally on Jefferson, see Leonard D. White, *The Jeffersonians: A Study in Administrative History, 1801-1829* (New York: Macmillan, 1951).

15. White, *The Jeffersonians,* 4.

16. Ibid., 5.

17. See Brookhiser, *Alexander Hamilton, American,* 70.

18. John A. Rohr, "The Administrative State and Constitutional Principle," in Ralph Clark Chandler, ed., *A Centennial History of the American Administrative State* (New York: Free Press, 1987), 127-29. See also John A. Rohr, *To Run a Constitution: The Legitimacy of the Administrative State* (Lawrence: University Press of Kansas, 1986).

19. See Van Riper, "The American Administrative State," in Chandler, ed., *A Centennial History of the American Administrative State,* 9. White's textbook is *Introduction to the Study of Public* Administration, 3rd ed. (New York: Macmillan, 1950).

20. Woodrow Wilson, "The Study of Administration," *Political Science Quarterly* 2 (June 1887): 197.

21. Ibid., 200-1.

22. Ibid., 200.

23. Ibid., 201.

24. Ibid., 206.

25. Ibid., 209.

26. Ibid., 210.

27. Ibid., 220.

28. See Frank J. Goodnow, *Politics and Administration: A Study in Government* (New York: Russell and Russell, 1900).

29. Woodrow Wilson, *Congressional Government: A Study in American Politics* (New York: Houghton Mifflin, 1885), xiii; see also Leonard D. White, *The Republican Era: 1869-1901* (New York: Macmillan, 1958), 46-48; and Stephen Skowronek, *Building a New American State: The Expansion of National Administrative Capacities 1877-1920* (Cambridge: Cambridge University Press, 1982), 42-46.

30. Deil S. Wright, "A Century of the Intergovernmental Administrative State: Wilson's Federalism, New Deal Intergovernmental Relations, and Contemporary Intergovernmental Management," in Chandler, ed., *A Centennial History of the American Administrative State,* 233.

31. For a discussion of the Hawthorne experiments and, more generally, of the broader human relations movement, see Charles Perrow, chap. 3 in *Complex Organizations,* 3d ed. (New York: Random House, 1986).

32. See Lester M. Salamon, ed., *The New Governance and the Tools of Public Action: A Handbook* (New York: Oxford University Press, 2001); and Donald F. Kettl, *Government by Proxy: (Mis?)Managing Federal Programs* (Washington, D.C.: Congressional Quarterly Press, 1988).

33. Joseph S. Nye Jr., Philip D. Zelikow, and David C. King, *Why People Don't Trust Government* (Cambridge: Harvard University Press, 1997).

34. Pew Research Center for the People and the Press, *Deconstructing Distrust: How Americans View Government* (Washington, D.C.: Pew Research Center, 10 March 1998).

35. Robert D. Putnam, *Bowling Alone: The Collapse and Revival of American Community* (New York: Simon and Schuster, 2000).

36. Dana Milbank and Richard Morin, "Public Is Unyielding in War Against Terror," *The Washington Post*, 29 September 2001, 1(A).

CHAPTER THREE: ADMINISTRATIVE DILEMMAS

1. See Arthur Okun, *Equality and Efficiency: The Big Tradeoff* (Washington, D.C.: Brookings Institution Press, 1975).

2. See, for example, Frederick C. Mosher, "The Changing Responsibilities and Tactics of the Federal Government," *Public Administration Review* 40 (November/December 1980): 541-48; Lester M. Salamon, "Rethinking Public Management," *Public Policy* 29 (Summer 1981): 255-75; and Donald F. Kettl, *Government By Proxy: (Mis?) Managing Federal Programs* (Washington, D.C.: Congressional Quarterly Press, 1988).

3. Lester M. Salamon, "The New Governance and the Tools of Public Action: An Introduction," in Lester M. Salamon, ed., *The New Governance and the Tools of Public Action: A Handbook* (New York: Oxford University Press, forthcoming), chap 1.

4. Ibid.

5. See also Mosher, "Changing Responsibilities."

6. See E. S. Savas, *Privatization and Public-Private Partnerships* (New York: Chatham House Publishers, 2000); and Jeffrey L. Brudney, Laurence J. O'Toole, and Hal G. Rainey, *Advancing Public Management: New Developments in Theory, Methods, and Practice* (Washington, D.C.: Georgetown University Press, 2000).

7. Statement of David M. Walker, *Managing in the New Millennium: Shaping a More Efficient and Effective Government for the 21st Century*, GAO/T-OCG-00-9 (March 29, 2000), 37.

8. See Harlan Cleveland, "Control: The Twilight of Hierarchy," *New Management* 3 (1985): 14-25.

9. For a review of the New Zealand reforms, see Jonathan Boston, John Martin, June Pallot, and Pat Walsh, *Public Management: The New Zealand Model* (Auckland: Oxford University Press, 1996).

10. New Zealand Treasury, "Introduction," *Government Management: Brief to the Incoming Government, 1987, Vol. 1,* 2-3, at www.treasury.govt.nz/briefings/1987/big87-1-intro.pdf (last accessed March 19, 2001).

11. See David Osborne and Peter Plastrik, *Banishing Bureaucracy: The Five Strategies for Reinventing Government* (Reading, Mass.: Addison-Wesley, 1987).

12. See, for example, Arthur M. Schlesinger Jr., *The Imperial Presidency* (Boston: Houghton Mifflin, 1973).

13. Harold Seidman, *Politics, Position, and Power: The Dynamics of Federal Organization* (New York: Oxford University Press, 1998), 142.

14. Ibid.

15. Matthew Holden Jr., "The Competence of Political Science: 'Progress in Political Research' Revisited," *American Political Science Review* 94 (March 2000): 7. Compare Norton Long, *The Polity* (Chicago: Rand McNally, 1962).

16. President's Private Sector Survey on Cost Control, *Report* (Washington, D.C.: GPO, 1983).

17. Al Gore, *Businesslike Government: Lessons Learned from America's Best Companies* (Washington, D.C.: GPO, 1997).

18. See Donald F. Kettl, *Sharing Power: Public Governance and Private Markets* (Washington, D.C.: Brookings Institution Press, 1993).

19. Presidential Commission on the Space Shuttle *Challenger* Accident, *Report to the President* (Washington, D.C.: GPO, 1986); see also Barbara S. Romzek and Melvin J. Dubnick, "Accountability in the Public Sector: Lessons from the *Challenger* Tragedy," *Public Administration Review* 47 (1987): 227-38.

20. James Q. Wilson, *Bureaucracy: What Government Agencies Do and Why They Do It* (New York: Basic Books, 1989), 27-28. The analysis builds on similar work by James D. Thompson, *Organizations in Action: Social Science Bases of Administrative Theory* (New York: McGraw-Hill, 1967); and, ultimately, by Talcott Parsons, *Structure and Process in Modern Societies* (New York: Free Press, 1960). Parsons and Thompson label these layers "technical," "managerial," and "institutional."

21. See Parsons, *Structure and Process in Modern Societies,* 65. Compare Thompson, *Organizations in Action,* 11.

22. Office of Management and Budget, "Workforce Planning and Restructuring," Bulletin 01-07 (May 8, 2001), at www.whitehouse.gov/omb/bulletins/b01-07.html (last accessed May 31, 2001).

23. On the layers of government, see Paul C. Light, *Thickening Government: Federal Hierarchy and the Diffusion of Accountability* (Washington, D.C.: Brookings/Governance Institute, 1995).

24. New Zealand State Services Commission and New Zealand Public Service Association, "Partnerships for Quality: Guidelines for Departments and PSA Organisers" (September 2000), at www.ssc.govt.nz/siteset.htm (last accessed March 22, 2001).

25. David M. Walker, "Government in the 21st Century," Lecture cosponsored by the PricewaterhouseCoopers Endowment for the Business of Government, the Council for Excellence in Government, and the National Academy of Public Administration (March 23, 1999).

26. Gore, *Businesslike Government*, 7, 11.

27. David Osborne and Ted Gaebler, *Reinventing Government: How the Entrepreneurial Spirit Is Transforming the Public Sector from Schoolhouse to Statehouse, City Hall to the Pentagon* (Reading, Mass.: Addison-Wesley, 1992), 167, and more generally, chap. 6.

28. In addition to the discussion on the National Performance Review cited earlier, see also Evan M. Berman, "Dealing with Cynical Citizens," *Public Administration Review* 57 (March/April 1997): 105-12; and Gerald E. Smith and Carole A. Huntsman, "Reframing the Metaphor of the Citizen-Government Relationship: A Value-Centered Perspective," *Public Administration Review* 57 (July/August 1997): 309-18.

29. The discussion that follow builds on Donald F. Kettl, "Building Lasting Reform," in Donald F. Kettl and John J. DiIulio Jr., *Inside the Reinvention Machine: Appraising Governmental Reform* (Washington, D.C.: Brookings Institution Press, 1995); and John J. DiIulio Jr., Gerald Garvey, and Donald F. Kettl, *Improving Government Performance: An Owner's Manual* (Washington, D.C.: Brookings Institution Press, 1993).

30. See Jonathan Rauch, *Demosclerosis: The Silent Killer of American Government* (New York: Times Books, 1994).

31. George Frederickson, "George and the Case of the Government Reinventors," *PA Times* 17 (January 1, 1994): 9.

32. I am indebted to conversation with Joel Aberbach of the University of Michigan for this point.

33. See James W. Fesler, *Area and Administration* (University: University of Alabama Press, 1949); and Paul C. Light, *The Tides of Reform: Making Government Work, 1945-1995* (New Haven: Yale University Press, 1997).

CHAPTER FOUR: BOUNDARIES WITHIN THE BUREAUCRACY

1. Norton Long, "Power and Administration," *Public Administration Review* 9 (1949): 257-64.

2. John Merriman Gaus, *Reflections on Public Administration* (University: University of Alabama Press, 1947), 135.

3. Quoted by Herbert J. Storing, "Leonard D. White and the Study of Administration," *Public Administration Review* 25 (1965): 50.

4. Ibid.

5. Leonard D. White, *The Federalists* (New York: Macmillan, 1948); White, *The Jeffersonians* (New York: Macmillan, 1951); White, *The Jacksonians* (New York: Macmillan, 1954); White, *The Republican Era* (New York: Macmillan, 1958).

6. Woodrow Wilson, *The State: Elements of Historical and Practical Politics* (Boston: D.C. Heath, 1898), 631, 633.

7. Lynton K. Caldwell, "Public Administration and the Universities: A Half-Century of Development," *Public Administration Review* 25 (1965): 52-60; and Nicholas Henry, "The Emergence of Public Administration as a Field of Study," in Ralph Clark Chandler, ed., *A Centennial History of the American Administrative State* (New York: Free Press, 1987), 37-85.

8. Frederick W. Taylor, *Principles of Scientific Management* (New York: Harper and Brothers, 1911). For a study of his work and influence, see Robert Kanigel, *The One Best Way: Frederick Winslow Taylor and the Enigma of Efficiency* (New York: Viking, 1997).

9. Roscoe Martin, "Political Science and Public Administration: A Note on the State of the Union," *American Political Science Review* 46 (1952): 667.

10. Barry D. Karl, *Executive Reorganization and Reform in the New Deal* (Cambridge: Harvard University Press, 1963).

11. E-mail to the author from James W. Fesler, 6 April 2001. See also James W. Fesler, "The Brownlow Committee Fifty Years Later," *Public Administration Review* 47 (1987): 291-96.

12. See David H. Rosenbloom, *Building a Legislative-Centered Public Administration: Congress and the Administrative State, 1946-1999* (Tuscaloosa: University of Alabama Press, 2000).

13. Norton Long, "Power and Administration."

14. See, for example, Paul Appleby, *Big Democracy* (New York: Alfred A. Knopf, 1945); Dwight Waldo, *The Administrative State*, 2d ed. (New York: Holmes and Meier, 1984); and James W. Fesler, "The State and Its Study: The Whole and Its Parts," in Naomi B. Lynn and Aaron Wildavsky, eds., *Public Administration: The State of the Discipline* (Chatham, N.J.: Chatham House Publishers, 1990), 84-96.

15. See Orion F. White Jr. and Cynthia J. McSwain, "The Phoenix Project: Raising a New Image of Public Administration from the Ashes of the Past," *Administration and Society* 22 (1990): 3-38.

16. Allen Schick, "The Trauma of Politics: Public Administration in the Sixties," in Frederick C. Mosher, ed., *American Public Administration: Past, Present, Future* (University: University of Alabama Press, 1975), 157.

17. Roscoe C. Martin, "Political Science and Public Administration: A Note on the State of the Union," *American Political Science Review* 46 (1952): 660-76.

18. American Political Science Association, Statement by the Committee on Standards of Instruction of the American Political Science Association,

"Political Science as a Discipline," *American Political Science Review* 56 (1962): 417-21.

19. Schick, "The Trauma of Politics," 160.

20. Dwight Waldo, "A Theory of Public Administration Means in Our Time a Theory of Politics Also," in Lynn and Wildavsky, *Public Administration*, 74 (emphasis in original).

21. Herbert Kaufman, "The End of an Alliance: Public Administration in the Eighties," in Lynn and Wildavsky, eds., *Public Administration*, 483-94.

22. Fesler, "The State and Its Study," 85.

23. See Harrison C. White, "Agency as Control," in John W. Pratt and Richard J. Zeckhauser, eds., *Principals and Agents: The Structure of Business* (Boston: Harvard Business School Press, 1985), 187-212.

24. Ronald H. Coase, "The Nature of the Firm," *Economica* 4 (1937): 386-405; and Oliver E. Williamson, *Markets and Hierarchies: Analysis and Antitrust Implications* (New York: Free Press, 1975).

25. See B. Dan Wood and Richard W. Waterman, "The Dynamics of Political Control of the Bureaucracy," *American Political Science Review* 85 (1991): 801-28.

26. Terry M. Moe, presentation at American Political Science Association Annual Meeting, August 31, 2001.

27. Charles Perrow, "Economic Theories of Organization," *Theory and Society* 15 (1986): 41.

28. Terry M. Moe, "An Assessment of the Positive Theory of 'Congressional Dominance,'" *Legislative Studies Quarterly* 12 (1987): 475-520.

29. Donald P. Green and Ian Shapiro, *Pathologies of Rational Choice Theory: A Critique of Applications in Political Science* (New Haven: Yale University Press, 1994), 7; see also Fritz W. Scharpf, *Games Real Actors Play: Actor-Centered Institutionalism in Policy Research* (Boulder, Colo.: Westview, 1997).

30. Kenneth A. Shepsle and Mark S. Bonchek, *Analyzing Politics: Rationality, Behavior, and Institutions* (New York: W. W. Norton, 1997), 8-9. See also Jeffrey Friedman, ed., *The Rational Choice Controversy: Economic Models of Politics Reconsidered* (New Haven: Yale University Press, 1996).

31. William A. Niskanen, *Bureaucracy and Representative Government* (Chicago: Aldine Publishers, 1971).

32. See Gary J. Miller and Terry M. Moe, in Herbert F. Weisberg, ed., *Political Science: The Science of Politics* (New York: Agathon Press, 1986), 167-98.

33. Mathew McCubbins, Roger Noll, and Barry Weingast, "Administrative Procedures as Instruments of Political Control," *Journal of Law, Economics, and Organization* 3 (1987): 243-79; and Mathew McCubbins, Roger Noll, and Barry Weingast, "Structure and Process, Politics and Policy: Administrative Arrangements and the Political Control of Agencies," *Virginia Law Review* 75 (1989): 431-83.

34. David Osborne, *Laboratories of Democracy: A New Breed of Governor Creates Models for National Growth* (Boston: Harvard Business School Press, 1988).

35. David Osborne and Ted Gaebler, *Reinventing Government: How the Entrepreneurial Spirit Is Transforming the Public Sector from Schoolhouse to Statehouse, City Hall to the Pentagon* (Reading, Mass.: Addison-Wesley, 1992), xi.

36. See Donald F. Kettl, *Reinventing Government: A Fifth-Year Report Card* (Washington, D.C.: Brookings Institution Press, 1998).

37. David Rosenbloom, "Editorial: Have an Administrative Rx? Don't Forget the Politics!" *Public Administration Review* 53 (1993): 503-7.

38. Ronald C. Moe, "Let's Rediscover Government, Not Reinvent It," *Government Executive* 25 (June 1993): 46-48; and Ronald C. Moe, "The 'Reinventing Government' Exercise: Misinterpreting the Problem, Misjudging the Consequences," *Public Administration Review* 54 (1954): 125-36.

39. H. George Frederickson, "Painting Bull's-Eyes around Bullet Holes," *Governing* (October 1992): 13.

40. See Donald F. Kettl, *The Global Public Management Reform Revolution: A Report on the Transformation of Governance* (Washington, D.C.: Brookings Institution Press, 2000).

41. See Christopher Hood and Michael Jackson, *Administrative Argument* (Aldershot: Dartmouth, 1991); Christopher Hood, *The Art of the State: Culture, Rhetoric, and Public Management* (Oxford: Clarendon Press, 1998); and Lawrence R. Jones, Kuno Schedler, and Stephen W. Wade, eds., *Advances in International Comparative Management* (Greenwich, Conn.: JAI Press, 1997).

42. See, for example, Sandford Borins, "What the New Public Management Is Achieving: A Survey of Commonwealth Experience," in Jones, Schedler, and Wade, *Advances in International Comparative Management*, 49-70; and Laurence E. Lynn Jr., "The New Public Management as an International Phenomenon: A Skeptical View," in Jones, Schedler, and Wade, *Advances in International Comparative Management*, 105-22.

43. Fred Thompson, "Defining the New Public Management," in Jones, Schedler, and Wade, *Advances in International Comparative Management*, 3.

44. See Hood, *The Art of the State;* B. Guy Peters and Donald Savoie, *Taking Stock: Assessing Public Sector Reforms* (Montreal: McGill-Queens University Press, 1998); Frieder Naschold, *New Frontiers in Public Sector Management: Trends and Issues in State and Local Government in Europe* (New York: Walter De Gruyter, 1996); and Peter Aucoin, *The New Public Management: Canada in Comparative Perspective* (Quebec: Institute for Research on Public Policy, 1995).

45. See Colin James, *The State Ten Years On from the Reforms* (Wellington, New Zealand: State Services Commission, 1998); Graham Scott, Ian Ball, and Tony Dale, "New Zealand's Public Management Reform: Implications for the United States," *Journal of Policy Analysis and Management* 16 (1997): 357-81; Jonathan Boston and June Pallot, "Linking Strategy and Performance: Developments in the New Zealand Public Sector," *Journal of Policy Analysis and Management* 16 (1997): 382-404; Jonathan Boston, John Martin, June Pallot,

and Pat Walsh, *Public Management: The New Zealand Model* (Wellington, New Zealand: Oxford University Press, 1996).

46. Scott, Ball, and Dale, "New Zealand's Public Management Reform," 360.

47. Interview with New Zealand Treasury official.

48. See, for example, David Osborne and Peter Plastrik, *Banishing Bureaucracy: The Five Strategies for Reinventing Government* (Reading, Mass.: Addison-Wesley, 1997).

49. Allen Schick, *The Spirit of Reform: Managing the New Zealand State Sector in a Time of Change* (Wellington: New Zealand State Services Commission, 1996), 84, 86, 87.

50. Ibid., 87.

51. Carl J. Friedrich, "Public Policy and the Nature of Administrative Responsibility," in Carl J. Friedrich and E. S. Mason, eds., *Public Policy* (Cambridge: Harvard University Press, 1940).

52. Herman Finer, "Administrative Responsibility in Democratic Government," *Public Administration Review* 1 (1941): 335-50.

53. See Moe, "An Assessment of the Positive Theory of 'Congressional Dominance'"; and Francis E. Rourke, "American Bureaucracy in a Changing Political Setting," *Journal of Public Administration Research and Theory* 1 (1991): 111-29.

54. Barbara Romzek and Melvin J. Dubnick, "Accountability in the Public Sector: Lessons from the *Challenger* Tragedy," *Public Administration Review* 47 (1987): 227-38.

55. Judith Gruber, *Controlling Bureaucracies: Dilemmas in Democratic Governance* (Berkeley: University of California Press, 1987); James L. Sundquist, "Needed: A Political Theory for the New Era of Coalition Government in the United States," *Political Science Quarterly* 103 (1988): 613-35; John P. Burke, *Bureaucratic Responsibility* (Baltimore: Johns Hopkins University Press, 1986); and John Rohr, *To Run a Constitution: The Legitimacy of the Administrative State* (Lawrence: University Press of Kansas, 1986).

56. For an application to contract management, for example, see Phillip J. Cooper, *Public Contract Management: After Advocacy and Beyond Bidding* (Washington, D.C.: CQ Press, forthcoming 2002).

57. For example, see Gary L. Wamsley et al., *Refounding Public Administration* (Beverly Hills, Calif.: Sage, 1990); and Charles T. Goodsell, *The Case for Bureaucracy: A Public Administration Polemic,* 3d ed. (Chatham, N.J.: Chatham House Publishers, 1994).

CHAPTER FIVE: BOUNDARIES OUTSIDE THE BUREAUCRACY

1. Jeffrey L. Pressman and Aaron B. Wildavsky, *Implementation* (Berkeley: University of California Press, 1973).

2. See, for example, Martha Derthick, *New Towns In-Town* (Washington, D.C.: Urban Institute, 1972); Eugene Bardach, *The Implementation Game* (Cambridge: MIT Press, 1977); Paul Berman, "The Study of Macro- and Micro-Implementation," *Public Policy* 26 (1978): 157-84; Richard Elmore, "Organizational Models of Social Program Implementation," *Public Policy* 26 (1978): 185-228; and Carl E. Van Horn, *Policy Implementation in the Federal System: National Goals and Local Implementation* (Lexington, Mass.: Lexington Books, 1979).

3. Brian W. Hogwood and B. Guy Peters, *The Pathology of Public Policy* (Oxford: Clarendon Press, 1985).

4. Pressman and Wildavsky, *Implementation*, 107.

5. Morton H. Halperin, *Bureaucratic Politics and Foreign Policy* (Washington, D.C.: Brookings Institution Press, 1974).

6. Bardach, *The Implementation Game*.

7. Erwin C. Hargrove, *The Missing Link: The Study of the Implementation of Social Policy* (Washington, D.C.: Urban Institute, 1975).

8. Randall B. Ripley and Grace Franklin, *Policy Implementation and Bureaucracy*, 2d ed. (Chicago: Dorsey Press, 1986), 12.

9. Calculated by the author from Ripley and Franklin, *Policy Implementation and Bureaucracy*.

10. For example, see Helen Ingram and Dean E. Mann, "Policy Failure: An Issue Deserving Analysis," in Helen Ingram and Dean E. Mann, eds., *Why Policies Succeed or Fail* (Beverly Hills, Calif.: Sage, 1980); Daniel A. Mazmanian and Paul A. Sabatier, *Implementation and Public Policy* (Glenview, Ill.: Scott, Foresman, 1983); and Ripley and Franklin, *Policy Implementation and Bureaucracy*.

11. See Malcom L. Goggin, Ann O'M. Bowman, James P. Lester, and Laurence J. O'Toole Jr., *Implementation Theory and Practice: Toward a Third Generation* (Glenview, Ill.: Scott, Foresman/Little, Brown, 1990).

12. See, for example, the work of Laurence J. O'Toole Jr.: "Policy Recommendations for Multi-Actor Implementation: An Assessment of the Field," *Journal of Public Policy* 6 (1986): 181-210; Laurence J. O'Toole Jr., "Goal Multiplicity in the Implementation Setting: Subtle Impacts and the Case of Wastewater Treatment Privatization," *Policy Studies Journal* 18 (1989): 1-20; Laurence J. O'Toole Jr., "Alternative Mechanisms for Multiorganizational Implementation: The Case of Wastewater Management," *Administration and Society* 21 (1989): 313-39. See also Goggin et al., *Implementation Theory and Practice;* and Helen Ingram, "Implementation: A Review and Suggested Framework," in Naomi B. Lynn and Aaron Wildavsky, eds., *Public Administration: The State of the Discipline* (Chatham, N.J.: Chatham House Publishers, 1990), 462-80.

13. See, for example, Thad E. Hall and Laurence J. O'Toole Jr., "Structures for Policy Implementation: An Analysis of National Legislation, 1965-1966 and 1993-1994," *Administration and Society* 31 (January 2000): 667-86.

14. Laurence E. Lynn Jr., *Managing Public Policy* (Boston: Little, Brown, 1987), 5.

15. John M. Bryson, *Strategic Planning for Public and Nonprofit Organizations* (San Francisco: Jossey-Bass, 1988).

16. Robert Behn, *Leadership Counts: Lessons for Public Managers from the Massachusetts Welfare, Training, and Employment Program* (Cambridge: Harvard University Press, 1991).

17. See Eugene Bardach, *Managerial Craftsmanship: Getting Agencies to Work Together* (Washington, D.C.: Brookings Institution Press, 1998); and Michael Barzelay with Babak J. Armajani, *Breaking through Bureaucracy: A New Vision for Managing Government* (Berkeley: University of California Press, 1992).

18. Laurence E. Lynn Jr., *Public Management as Art, Science, and Profession* (Chatham, N.J.: Chatham House Publishers, 1996).

19. See Laurence E. Lynn Jr., *Managing the Public's Business* (New York: Basic Books, 1981); Lynn, *Managing Public Policy;* Laurence E. Lynn Jr., Carolyn J. Heinrich, and Carolyn Hill, "Studying Governance and Public Management: Why? How?" in Laurence E. Lynn Jr. and Carolyn J. Heinrich, eds., *Governance and Performance: Models, Methods, and Results* (Washington, D.C.: Georgetown University Press, 1999), xx; and Philip B. Heymann, *The Politics of Public Management* (New Haven: Yale University Press, 1987).

20. Behn, *Leadership Counts.*

21. Heymann, *The Politics of Public Management.*

22. Lynn, *Managing the Public's Business;* Lynn, *Managing Public Policy;* and Robert Behn, "The Nature of Knowledge about Public Management: Lessons for Research and Teaching from Our Knowledge about Chess and Warfare," *Journal of Policy Analysis and Management* 7 (1988): 200-12.

23. Michael Barzelay and Linda Kaboolian, "Structural Metaphors and Public Management Education," *Journal of Policy Analysis and Management* 9 (1990): 600.

24. Most notably, see Francis E. Rourke, *Bureaucracy, Politics, and Public Policy*, 3d ed. (Boston: Little, Brown, 1984).

25. See Terry M. Moe, "The Politics of Structural Choice: Toward a Theory of Public Bureaucracy," in Oliver E. Williamson, ed., *Organization Theory: From Chester Barnard to the Present and Beyond* (New York: Oxford University Press, 1995), xx.

26. Jonathan Bendor and Terry M. Moe, "An Adaptive Model of Bureaucratic Politics," *American Political Science Review* 79 (1985): 755-74; Jack H. Knott and Gary J. Miller, *Reforming Bureaucracy: The Politics of Institutional Choice* (Englewood Cliffs, N.J.: Prentice-Hall, 1987); Terry M. Moe, "The Politics of Bureaucratic Structure," in John E. Chubb and Paul E. Peterson, eds., *Can the Government Govern?* (Washington, D.C.: Brookings Institution Press, 1989), 267-329; and Murray J. Horn, *The Political Economy of Public Administration: Institutional Choice in the Public Sector* (Cambridge: Cambridge University Press, 1995).

27. John E. Chubb and Terry M. Moe, *Politics, Markets, and America's Schools* (Washington, D.C.: Brookings Institution Press, 1990).

28. Irwin L. Morris, *Congress, the President, and the Federal Reserve: The Politics of American Policy Making* (Ann Arbor: University of Michigan Press, 1999).

29. David Mayhew, *Congress: The Electoral Connection* (New Haven: Yale University Press, 1974).

30. See Terry M. Moe, "Regulatory Performance and Presidential Administration," *American Journal of Political Science* 26 (1982): 197-224; Barry R. Weingast and Mark J. Moran, "Bureaucracy Discretionary Congressional Control? Regulatory Policymaking by the Federal Trade Commission," *Journal of Political Economy* 91 (1983): 765-800; Terry M. Moe, "Control and Feedback in Economic Regulation: The Case of the NLRB," *American Political Science Review* 79 (1985): 1094-1116; and B. Dan Wood and Richard W. Waterman, "The Dynamics of Political Control of the Bureaucracy," *American Political Science Review* 85 (1991): 801-28.

31. The underlying debate in institutional-choice theory is whether the very nature of bureaucracy creates reservoirs of political power that, in turn, allow bureaucrats to resist attempts by elected officials to control their behavior. In that sense, the institutional-choice movement is an effort to impart more rigor to the arguments initially framed in the implementation movement. Unlike the implementation movement, which focused on programs, institutional-choice theory focuses on the bureaucracy as the unit of analysis.

32. Wood and Waterman, "The Dynamics of Political Control of the Bureaucracy," 801.

33. Michael Lipsky, *Street-Level Bureaucracy: Dilemmas of the Individual in Public Services* (New York: Russell Sage Foundation, 1980).

34. David Osborne and Ted Gaebler, *Reinventing Government* (Reading, Mass.: Addison-Wesley, 1992), chap. 6, esp. 166-67, 186-87.

35. See www.nhq.nrcs.usda.gov/NPR/index.htm (last accessed April 11, 2001).

36. See Richard Elmore, "Backward Mapping: Implementation Research and Policy Decisions," in Walter Williams and others, *Studying Implementation: Methodological and Administrative Issues* (Chatham, N.J.: Chatham House, 1982), 18-35.

37. See Frederick C. Mosher, "The Changing Responsibilities and Tactics of the Federal Government," *Public Administration Review* (1980): 541-48; Lester M. Salamon, "Rethinking Public Management: Third-Party Government and the Changing Forms of Government Action," *Public Policy* 29 (1981): 255-75; Donald F. Kettl, *Government by Proxy: (Mis?)Managing Federal Programs* (Washington, D.C.: Congressional Quarterly Press, 1988); and Lester M. Salamon, ed., *The Tools of Government: A Public Management Handbook for the Era of Third-Party Government* (New York: Oxford University Press, forthcoming).

38. Christopher C. Hood, *The Tools of Government* (Chatham, N.J.: Chatham House, 1983); Ruth Hoogland DeHoog, *Contracting Out for Human*

Services: Economic, Political, and Organizational Perspectives (Albany: State University of New York Press, 1984); Harold Seidman and Robert Gilmour, *Politics, Position, and Power: From the Positive to the Regulatory State*, 4th ed. (New York: Oxford University Press, 1986); and Jeffrey L. Brudney, "Expanding the Government-by-Proxy Concept," *Nonprofit and Voluntary Sector Quarterly* 19 (1990): 62-73.

39. H. Brinton Milward et al., "Managing the Hollow State," paper presented at the 1991 annual meeting of the American Political Science Association, Washington, D.C.

40. Bruce L. R. Smith, "Changing Public-Private Sector Relations: A Look at the United States," *Annals of the American Academy of Political and Social Sciences* 466 (1983): 149-64.

41. See E. S. Savas, *Privatization and Public-Private Partnerships* (New York: Seven Bridges Press, 2000); Laurence J. O'Toole Jr., "Treating Networks Seriously: Practical and Research-Based Agendas in Public Administration," *Public Administration Review* 57 (1997): 45-52; Laurence J. O'Toole Jr., "The Implications for Democracy in a Networked Bureaucratic World," *Journal of Public Administration Research and Theory* 7 (1997): 443-59; H. Brinton Milward and Louise Ogilvie Snyder, "Electronic Government: Linking Citizens to Public Organizations Through Technology," *Journal of Public Administration Research and Theory* 6 (1996): 261-75; H. Brinton Milward and Keith Provan, "A Preliminary Theory of Network Effectiveness: A Comparative Study of Four Mental Health Systems," *Administrative Science Quarterly* 40 (1995): 1-33; H. Brinton Milward and Keith G. Provan, "Principles for Controlling Agents: The Political Economy of Network Structure," *Journal of Public Administration Research and Theory* 8 (1998): 203-21; and Fritz W. Scharpf, *Games in Hierarchies and Networks: Analytical and Empirical Approaches to the Study of Governance Institutions* (Boulder, Colo.: Westview, 1993).

42. See Frank Ostroff, *The Horizontal Organization: What the Organization of the Future Looks Like and How It Delivers Value to Customers* (New York: Oxford, 1999).

43. Charles R. Wise, "Public Service Configurations and Public Organizations: Public Organization Design in the Post-Privatization Era," *Public Administration Review* 50 (1990): 141-55; Harlan Cleveland, "Control: The Twilight of Hierarchy," *New Management* 3 (1985): 14-25; and Donald Chisholm, *Coordination without Hierarchy: Informal Structures in Multiorganizational Systems* (Berkeley: University of California Press, 1989).

44. H. George Frederickson, "The Repositioning of American Public Administration," John Gaus Lecture, American Political Science Association Annual Meeting (September 3, 1999).

45. Lynn, Heinrich, and Hill, "Studying Governance and Public Management."

46. Hall and O'Toole, "Structures for Policy Implementation."

47. Robert Axelrod, *The Evolution of Cooperation* (New York: Basic Books, 1984), 169.

48. Ibid., 170.

49. Ibid., 191.

50. See, for example, Robert Axelrod, *The Complexity of Cooperation: Agent-Based Models of Competition and Collaboration* (Princeton: Princeton University Press, 1997). See also John H. Holland, *Hidden Order: How Adaptation Builds Complexity* (Cambridge: Perseus Books, 1995).

51. Robert Axelrod and Michael D. Cohen, *Harnessing Complexity: Organizational Implications of a Scientific Frontier* (New York: Basic Books, 2000), 159.

52. See, for example, Ralph D. Stacey, *Complex Responsive Processes in Organizations: Learning and Knowledge Creation* (London: Routledge, 2001).

53. Jane Perry Clark Carey, *The Rise of a New Federalism: Federal-State Cooperation in the United States* (New York: Columbia University Press, 1938).

54. See, for example, Frank Smallwood, ed., *The New Federalism* (Hanover, N.H.: Dartmouth Public Affairs Center, 1967); Michael D. Reagan, *The New Federalism* (New York: Oxford University Press, 1972); Timothy J. Conlan, *New Federalism: Intergovernmental Reform from Nixon to Reagan* (Washington, D.C.: Brookings Institution Press, 1988).

55. Laurence E. Lynn Jr., "The Myth of the Bureaucratic Paradigm: What Traditional Public Administration Really Stood For," *Public Administration Review* 61 (March/April 2001): 155.

56. Ibid.

CHAPTER SIX: ADMINISTRATION AND GOVERNANCE

1. John Gaus, "Trends in the Theory of Public Administration," *Public Administration Review* 10 (1950): 161-68.

2. Jon Pierre and B. Guy Peters, *Governance, Politics, and the State* (New York: St. Martin's Press, 2000), 7.

3. Robert O. Keohane and John D. Donahue, eds., *Governance in a Globalizing World* (Washington, D.C.: Brookings Institution Press, 2000), 12.

4. Ibid.

5. See Pierre and Peters, *Governance, Politics, and the State*, 1, 7.

6. Robert Cameiro, "A Changing Canon of Government: From Custody to Service," Organization for Economic Cooperation and Development, *Government of the Future* (Paris: OECD, 2001), 92, at www.oecd.org/publications/e-book/420008 1e.pdf (last accessed March 5, 2001).

7. For a thorough exploration of these issues, see the *New York Times* series on the affair: Matthew Purdy, "The Making of a Suspect: The Case of Wen Ho Lee," *New York Times*, 4 February 2001, 1; and Matthew Purdy with James Sterngold, "The Prosecution Unravels: The Case of Wen Ho Lee," *New York Times*, 5 February 2001, 1.

8. Paul C. Light, *The True Size of Government* (Washington, D.C.: Brookings Institution Press, 1999).

9. U.S. General Accounting Office, *Major Management Challenges and Risks: Department of Health and Human Services*, GAO-01-247 (2001), 7.

10. Ibid., 8.

11. For an overview of the W-2 program, see Thomas Kaplan, "Evaluating Comprehensive State Welfare Reforms: An Overview," *Focus* 18 (Spring 1997): 2.

12. William Fanaras, "Focusing on Outputs: Competition for City Services in Indianapolis" (Washington, D.C.: Brookings Institution Working Paper, 2000); William R. Potapchuk, Jarle P. Crocker, Bill Schechter, "Systems Reform in Two Cities: Indianapolis, Indiana, and Charlotte, North Carolina," *National Civic Review* 87 (Fall 1998): 213; and Jon Jeter, "A Winning Combination in Indianapolis: Competitive Bidding for City Services Creates Public-Private Success Story," *Washington Post*, 21 September 1997, 3(A).

13. Jim Flanagan and Bob Wigenroth, "Phoenix Manages for Performance Results," *PA Times*, 1 March 1996, 1, 3; and Jim Flanagan and Susan Perkins, "Public/Private Competition in the City of Phoenix, Arizona," *Government Finance Review* 11 (June 1995): 7-12.

14. Prime Minister and Cabinet Office, *Modernising Government* (London, 1999), 10, at www.cabinet-office.gov.uk/moderngov/download/modgov.pdf (last accessed October 2, 2001).

15. See Frederick C. Mosher, "The Changing Responsibilities and Tactics of the Federal Government," *Public Administration Review* 40 (1980): 541-48; Lester M. Salamon, "Rethinking Public Management: Third-Party Government and the Changing Forms of Government Action," *Public Policy* 29 (1981): 255-75; Lester M. Salamon, ed., *Beyond Privatization: The Tools of Governmental Action* (Washington, D.C.: Urban Institute, 1989); Donald F. Kettl, *Government by Proxy: (Mis?)Managing Federal Programs* (Washington, D.C.: Congressional Quarterly Press, 1988); and Lester M. Salamon, ed., *The Tools of Government: A Public Management Handbook for the Era of Third-Party Government* (New York: Oxford University Press, 2001).

16. Donald F. Kettl, *Sharing Power: Public Governance and Private Markets*, (Washington, D.C.: Brookings Institution Press, 1993).

17. Light, *The True Size of Government.*

18. Akira Nakamura and Kosaku Dairokuno, "The Age of Public Management Reform: The Rise of Non-Profit Organizations in Japan's Local Public Administration," in National Institute for Research Advancement and National Academy of Public Administration, *The Challenge to New Governance in the Twenty-First Century: Achieving Effective Central-Local Relations* (Tokyo: National Institute for Research Advancement, 1999), 97-109.

19. Organization for Economic Cooperation and Development, *Government of the Future* (Paris: OECD, 2000), 12.

20. Adrian Croft, "EU, Washington in New Clash over Bananas," March 8, 2001, at http://dailynews.yahoo.com/h/nm/20010308/ts/us_bananas_dc_2.html (last accessed March 8, 2001).

21. Anthony Giddens, BBC Reith Lectures, "Lecture 1: Globalisation," at www.lse.ac.uk/Giddens/reith_99/week1/week1.htm (last accessed March 8, 2001). See also Anthony Giddens, *Runaway World: How Globalisation Is Reshaping Our Lives* (London: Profile Books, 1999).

22. Ibid.

23. John Micklethwait and Adrian Wooldridge, *A Future Perfect: The Challenge and Hidden Promise of Globalization* (New York: Times Books, 2000).

24. United Nations, *We the Peoples: Executive Summary* (New York: United Nations, 2000), at www.un.org/millennium/sg/report/summ.htm (last accessed March 8, 2001).

25. See David Held, Anthony McGrew, David Goldblatt, and Jonathan Perraton, *Global Transformations: Politics, Economics and Culture* (Stanford: Stanford University Press, 1999).

26. Claude Smadja, "Time to Learn from Seattle," *Newsweek International*, 17 January 2000.

27. Jessica Mathews, "Power Shift," *Foreign Affairs* 76 (January/February 1997): 50-66.

28. Ross Gelbspan, "A Good Climate for Investment," *Atlantic Monthly* 281 (June 1998): 22.

29. Mathews, "Power Shift."

30. Quoted in United Nations Research Institute for Social Development, *Report of the UNRISD International Conference: Globalization and Citizenship* (Geneva, 1996).

31. "The Non-Governmental Order," *The Economist* 353 (9 December 1999): 20-21; and Sebastian Mallaby, "Big Nongovernment" *Washington Post*, 30 November 1999, 29(A).

32. Mathews, "Power Shift."

33. See, for example, Giddens, *Runaway World.*

34. Jane Perlez, "Career Diplomat, Yes, but She Shoots from the Hip," *Washington Post*, 26 September 1999, 26(1).

35. Elaine Kamarck, "Homeland Defense Requires Trust, Will," *Newsday*, 26 September 2001, at www.ksg.harvard.edu/news/opeds/kamarck_homeland_defense_nd_092601.htm (last accessed October 3, 2001).

36. Luther Gulick, "Notes on the Theory of Administration," in Luther Gulick and L. Urwick, eds., *Papers on the Science of Administration* (New York: Institute of Public Administration, 1937), 1-45.

37. Ibid., 21.

38. See Donald F. Kettl, ed., *Environmental Governance: A Report on the Next Generation of Environmental Policy* (Washington, D.C.: Brookings Institution, forthcoming 2002); and Mary Graham, *The Morning after Earth Day: Practical Environmental Politics* (Washington, D.C.: Brookings Institution Press, 1999).

39. Interview with EPA official.

40. Wallace Stegner, *Beyond the Hundredth Meridian: John Wesley Powell and the Second Opening of the West* (New York: Penguin, 1954, 1992).

41. National Academy of Public Administration, *Environment.gov: Transforming Environmental Protection for the 21st Century* (Washington, D.C.: NAPA, 2000), 183. The author served as a member of this NAPA panel.

42. National Academy of Public Administration, *Setting Priorities, Getting Results: A New Direction for EPA* (Washington, D.C.: NAPA, 1995); *EPA: Resolving the Paradox of Environmental Protection* (Washington, D.C.: NAPA, 1997); and *Environment.gov*.

43. NAPA, *Environment.gov*, 11.

44. Ibid., esp. 17-18.

45. See, for example, David Robinson, "Introduction," in David Robinson, ed., *Social Capital in Action* (Wellington, New Zealand: Institute of Policy Studies, Victoria University of Wellington, 1999), 9; and Paul Curry, "Commentary," in Robinson, *Social Capital in Action*, 110. More generally on the issue of social capital, see Robert D. Putnam, *Bowling Alone: The Collapse and Revival of American Community* (New York: Simon and Schuster, 2000).

46. See Donald F. Kettl, Patricia W. Ingraham, Ronald P. Sanders, and Constance Horner, *Civil Service Reform: Building a Government that Works* (Washington, D.C.: Brookings Institution Press, 1996).

47. Daniel Bell, "Previewing Planet Earth in 2013," *Washington Post*, 3 January 1988, 3(B).

48. Jean-Francois Rischard, "High Noon: The Urgent Need for New Global Governance Solutions" (World Bank, 2000), 5, at www.worldbank.org/research/abcde/eu_2000/pdffiles/rischard.pdf (last accessed February 4, 2001).

49. Organization for Economic Cooperation and Development, *Managing Across Levels of Government: Executive Summary* (Paris: OECD, 1998), at www.oecd.org//puma/malg/malg97/summary.htm (last accessed March 22, 2001).

CHAPTER SEVEN: WHO GOVERNS—AND HOW?

1. See, for example, Anne Khademian, *Putty in Your Hands? Managing the Roots of Public Program Culture* (Washington, D.C.: CQ Press, forthcoming 2002).

2. Keith Koffler, "White House Defends Increased Federal Role," *Govexec.com Daily Briefing* (October 5, 2001), at www.govexec.com/dailyfed/1001/100401cd1.htm (last accessed October 5, 2001).

3. Jeffrey L. Pressman and Aaron Wildavsky, *Implementation* (Berkeley: University of California Press, 1973).

4. Joseph J. Ellis, *Founding Brothers: The Revolutionary Generation* (New York: Alfred A. Knopf, 2001), 5.

5. Ibid., 15, 16.

6. Robert A. Dahl, *Who Governs? Democracy and Power in an American City* (New Haven: Yale University Press, 1961), 1.

7. John Gaus, "Trends in the Theory of Public Administration," *Public Administration Review* 10 (1950): 161-68.

8. Social Security Administration, *Social Security: Performance and Accountability Report for 2000* (Washington, D.C.: GPO, 2000), 25.

9. U.S. Department of Transportation, *DOT Performance Plan (FY 2002) and Report (FY 2000)* (Washington, D.C.: GPO, 2001), 44.

10. See New York City Accountability Program at http://home.nyc.gov/portal/index.jsp?pageID=nyc_stat_reports&catID=1724 (last accessed October 5, 2001).

11. Fritz W. Scharpf, "Interdependence and Democratic Legitimation," in Susan J. Pharr and Robert D. Putnam, eds., *Disaffected Democracies: What's Troubling the Trilateral Countries?* (Princeton: Princeton University Press), 115.

12. Dwight Waldo, *The Administrative State* (New York: Ronald Press, 1948), chap.7.

13. Quoted in ibid., 69n.

14. Ibid., 69

15. See Donald F. Kettl, *Sharing Power: Public Governance and Private Markets* (Washington, D.C.: Brookings Intitution Press, 1993).

16. U.S. General Accounting Office, *GAO's Performance and Accountability Series and High Risk Update 2001: A Governmentwide Perspective* (Washington, D.C.: GAO, GAO-01-241, 2001).

17. David M. Walker, "Government Challenges in the 21st Century" (Speech, National Press Club, April 23, 2001), at www.gao.gov/cghome/ncspch.html (last accessed April 23, 2001).

18. Wisconsin Legislative Audit Bureau, *Wisconsin Works (W-2) Program* (April 2001), at www.legis.state.wi.us/lab/Reports/01-7tear.htm (last accessed May 14, 2001).

19. See Organization for Economic Cooperation and Development, "E-government for Democracy and Development," *Focus: Public Management Newsletter* (March 2001), at www.oecd.org/puma/focus/num19.pdf (last accessed May 14, 2001).

20. See Accenture, *Rhetoric versus Reality: Closing the Gap* (2001), at www.accenture.com/xd/xd.asp?it=enWeb&xd=industries\government\gove_study.xml (last accessed May 14, 2001).

21. See Paul C. Light, *The Tides of Reform: Making Government Work, 1945-1995* (New Haven: Yale University Press, 1997).

INDEX

BOOKS IN THE SERIES

The Logic of Lawmaking: A Spatial Theory Approach
GERALD S. STROM

Executive Privilege: The Dilemma of Secrecy and Democratic Accountability
MARK J. ROZELL

With Reverence and Contempt: How Americans Think about Their President
THOMAS S. LANGSTON

The Two Majorities: The Issue Context of Modern American Politics
BYRON E. SHAFER AND WILLIAM J. M. CLAGGETT

The Selling of Supreme Court Nominees
JOHN ANTHONY MALTESE

The Foundation of Merit: Public Service in American Democracy
PATRICIA WALLACE INGRAHAM

Shaping Constitutional Values:
Elected Government, the Supreme Court, and the Abortion Debate
NEAL DEVINS

Bureaucracy and Self-Government:
Reconsidering the Role of Public Administration in American Politics
BRIAN J. COOK

Uncertain Guardians: The News Media as a Political Institution
BARTHOLOMEW H. SPARROW

Political Parties and Constitutional Government: Remaking American Democracy
SIDNEY M. MILKIS

The Institutional Presidency, 2d ed.
JOHN P. BURKE

Regulatory Politics in Transition, 2d ed.
MARC ALLEN EISNER

The Transformation of Governance:
Public Administration for Twenty-First Century America
DONALD F. KETTL

PENGUIN REFERENCE BOOKS

R37

THE PENGUIN COMPANION TO LITERATURE 4

The Penguin Companion to Literature

-4-

CLASSICAL AND BYZANTINE

Edited by D. R. Dudley

ORIENTAL AND AFRICAN

Edited by D. M. Lang

PENGUIN BOOKS

Penguin Books Ltd, Harmondsworth, Middlesex, England
Penguin Books Inc., 7110 Ambassador Road, Baltimore, Maryland 21207, U.S.A.
Penguin Books Australia Ltd, Ringwood, Victoria, Australia

—

First published 1969

—

—

Made and printed in Great Britain
by Hazell Watson & Viney Ltd
Aylesbury, Bucks
Set in Linotype Times

CONTENTS

CONTRIBUTORS

(s.o.a.s.=School of Oriental and African Studies, University of London)

AKI	A. K. Irvine, Lecturer in Semitic Languages, s.o.a.s
APB	A. P. Brink, Lecturer in Afrikaans, Rhodes University
APGM	A. P. G. Manuud, Associate Professor, University of Manila
AST	A. S. Tritton, Emeritus Professor of Arabic, s.o.a.s.
BNP	B. N. Pandey, Lecturer in Modern Indian History, s.o.a.s
BWA	G. W. Andrzejewski, Reader in Cushitic Languages, s.o.a.s.
CB	C. R. Bawden, Reader in Mongolian, s.o.a.s.
CH	C. Hookyaas, Reader in Old Javanese, s.o.a.s.
CHBR	C. H. B. Reynolds, Lecturer in Sinhalese Studies, s.o.a.s.
CJD	C. J. Dunn, Reader in Japanese, s.o.a.s.
DEP	D. E. Pollard, Lecturer in Modern Chinese, s.o.a.s.
DEWW	D. E. W. Wormell, Professor of Latin, Trinity College, Dublin
DJW	D. J. Wiseman, Professor of Assyriology, s.o.a.s.
DLD	D. L. Duguid
DLS	D. L. Snellgrove, Reader in Tibetan, s.o.a.s.
DML	D. M. Lang, Professor of Caucasian Studies, s.o.a.s.
DRD	D. R. Dudley, Professor of Latin, University of Birmingham
ECD	E. C. Dimmock, Professor of Bengali, South Asia Language and Area Centre, University of Chicago
ECGB	E. C. G. Barrett, Lecturer in Malay and Indonesian Language and Literature, s.o.a.s.
EE	Dr Elizabeth Eppler
EG	Edwin Gerow, Assistant Professor of Sanskrit and Indic Literature, University of Washington
EHSS	E. H. S. Simmonds, Reader in Thai Languages and Literatures, s.o.a.s.
EMB	Mary Boyce, Professor of Iranian Studies, s.o.a.s.
GA	G. Atkins, Lecturer in Bantu Languages, s.o.a.s.
GBM	G. B. Milner, Reader in Oceanic Languages, s.o.a.s.
GTA	G. T. A. Atangana
GTWH	G. T. W. Hooker, Lecturer in Classics, University of Birmingham
HC	Father H. de la Costa, former Professor of History, University of Manila
HLS	H. L. Shorto, Reader in Languages and Literatures of South East Asia, s.o.a.s.
IMPR	I. M. P. Raeside, Lecturer in Marathi and Gujarati, s.o.a.s.
JAR	J. A. Ramsaran, Lecturer in English, University of Ibadan, Nigeria
JCB	The late J. C. Bottoms, formerly Lecturer in Malay, s.o.a.s.

JCG	Professor Jonas Greenfield, Department of Near Eastern Languages, University of California
JDC	J. D. Chinnery, Senior Lecturer in Chinese, Edinburgh University
JGD	J. G. Davies, Professor of Theology, University of Birmingham
JMJ	Judith M. Jacob, Lecturer in Cambodian, S.O.A.S.
JRM	J. R. Marr, Lecturer in Tamil and Indian Music, S.O.A.S.
JWAO	J. W. A. Okell, Lecturer in Burmese, S.O.A.S.
LPH	Lyndon Harries, Professor of Swahili Language and Literature, University of Wisconsin
ORD	O. R. Dathorne, UNESCO, Freetown, Sierra Leone
PJH	P. J. Honey, Reader in Vietnamese Studies, S.O.A.S.
PT	P. Thomson, Lecturer in Drama, University of Manchester
RA	R. Antonissen, Professor of Afrikaans, Rhodes University, Cape Town
RB	Robert Browning, Professor of Classics, Birkbeck College, University of London
REA	R. E. Asher, Senior Lecturer in General Linguistics, Edinburgh University
RFH	R. F. Hosking, Assistant Keeper, Department of Oriental Printed Books and Manuscripts, British Museum
RR	R. Russell, Reader in Urdu, S.O.A.S.
RSM	R. S. McGregor, Lecturer in Hindi, Cambridge University
SMNA	Syed M. Naguib al-Attas, Lecturer in Malay, University of Malay
TAD	T. A. Dorey, Senior Lecturer in Latin, University of Birmingham
VLM	V. L. Ménage, Reader in Turkish, S.O.A.S.
WHW	W. H. Whiteley, Professor of Bantu Languages, S.O.A.S.

ABBREVIATIONS

ACL. Ante-Nicene Christian Library.

ACW. Ancient Christian Writers series.

Andrzejewski and Galaal, *SPC*. B. W. Andrzejewski and Musa H. I. Galaal, 'A Somali Poetic Combat', in *Journal of African Languages*, Vol II, i-iii (1963).

Andrzejewski and Lewis, *SPI*. B. W. Andrzejewski and I. M. Lewis, *Somali Poetry – An Introduction* (1964).

Arberry, *CPL*. A. J. Arberry, *Classical Persian Literature* (1958).

Arnim, *SVF*. *Stoicorum veterum fragmenta*, ed. H. von Arnim (3 vols., Leipzig, 1903).

AWA. Akademie van Wetenschappen, Amsterdam.

Bardon, *ELL*. H. Bardon, *Les empereurs et les lettres latines* (Paris, 1940).

BAW. Bayerische Akademie der Wissenschaften.

Beare, *RS*. W. Beare, *The Roman Stage* (1935; 3rd edn, 1965).

Bowra, *EGE*. C. M. Bowra, *Early Greek Elegists* (1938).

Bowra, *GLP*. C. M. Bowra, *Greek Lyric Poetry from Alcman to Simonides* (1926; 2nd edn, 1961).

Brower and Miner, *JCP*. R. H. Brower and E. Miner, *Japanese Court Poetry* (Stanford University, 1961).

Browne, *LHP*. E. G. Browne, *A Literary History of Persia* (4 vols., 1906–24).

CSEL. Corpus Scriptorum Ecclesiasticorum Latinorum (Vienna).

CSHB. Corpus Scriptorum Historiae Byzantinae (Bonn).

Diehl, *ALG*. *Anthologia lyrica graeca*, ed. E. Diehl (3 vols., Teubner, Leipzig, 3rd edn, 1951–4).

Diels, *FV*. *Die Fragmente der Vorsokratiker*, 3rd edn, ed. and German comm. H. Diels and W. Kranz (Berlin, 1954).

Dobson, *GO*. J. F. Dobson, *The Greek Orators* (1919).

Dudley, *HC*. D. R. Dudley, *A History of Cynicism* (1937).

Duff, *MLP*. *Minor Latin Poets*, ed. and tr. J. W. and A. M. Duff (Loeb, 1934).

Edmonds, *FAC*. *The Fragments of Attic Comedy*, ed. J. M. Edmonds (3 vols., Leiden, 1957–61).

E of I. *Encyclopaedia of Islam* (5 vols., 1908–38).

Harries, *SP*. Lyndon Harries, *Swahili Poetry* (1962).

Hughes and Reygnault, *AAM*. *Anthologie africaine et malgache*, ed. Langston Hughes and Christiane Reygnault (Paris, 1962).

Jacoby, *FGH*. *Die Fragmente der griechischen Historiker*, ed. F. Jacoby (Berlin, Leiden, 1923–).

Jebb, *AO*. R. C. Jebb, *The Attic Orators from Antiphon to Isaeos* (2 vols., 1893).

JHS. *Journal of Hellenic Studies*.

JRS. *Journal of Roman Studies*.

Keene, *AJL*. *Anthology of Japanese Literature*, ed. Donald Keene (1956; Penguin Classics, 1968) (English translations).

Keene, *MJL*. *Modern Japanese Literature*, ed. Donald Keene (1957) (English translations).

Klausner, *HMHL*. J. G. Klausner, *A History of Modern Hebrew Literature, 1785–1930* (1932).

LCC. Library of Christian Classics.

MGH. Monumenta Germaniae Historica, Auctores Antiquissimi (Berlin).

Migne, *PG*. *Patrologiae cursus completus, series graeca*, ed. J. P. Migne (162 vols., Paris, 1857–1912).

Migne, *PL*. *Patrologiae cursus completus, series latina*, ed. J. P. Migne (221 vols., Paris, 1844–64).

Moore, *SAW*. Gerald Moore, *Seven African Writers* (1962).

Moore and Beier, *MPA*. *Modern Poetry from Africa*, ed. Gerald Moore and Ulli Beier (Penguin African Library, 1963).

Morel, *FPL*. *Fragmenta poetarum latinorum*, ed. W. Morel (Teubner, Leipzig, 1927, Stuttgart, 1963).

Morris, *MJS*. *Modern Japanese Stories*, ed. I. Morris (1961) (English translations).

Müller, *FHG*. *Fragmenta historicorum graecorum*, ed. C. W. Müller (Paris, 1883).

Nicholson, *LHA*. R. A. Nicholson, *A Literary History of the Arabs* (1903; re-issued 1953).

Nicholson, *SIP*. R. A. Nicholson, *Studies in Islamic Poetry* (1921).

NPF. Select Library of Nicene and Post-Nicene Fathers (New York).

OAS. *Bulletin of the School of Oriental and African Studies, London University*.

OCT. Oxford Classical Texts.

Page, *PMG*. D. L. Page, *Poetae Melicae Graeci* (1962).

Peter, *HRR*. *Historicorum romanorum reliquiae*, ed. H. Peter (2 vols., Vol. I, 2nd edn, 1914, Vol. 2, 1906).

Pickard-Cambridge, *DTC*. A. W. Pickard-Cambridge, *Dithyramb Tragedy and Comedy* (1962).

PVG. Papiro Vaticano Greco (Vatican City).

Reed and Wake, *BAV*. *A Book of African Verse*, ed. John Reed and Clive Wake (1964).

Rutherfoord, *DL*. *Darkness and Light*, ed. Peggy Rutherfoord (1958).

Rypka, *IL*. J. Rypka, *Iranische Literaturgeschichte* (Leipzig, 1959).

Sarton, *HS*. George Sarton, *A History of Science* (2 vols., Cambridge, Mass., 1953–9).

Senghor, *PNM*. *Anthologie de la nouvelle poésie nègre et malgache*, ed. L. S. Senghor (Paris, 1953).

Warmington, *ROL*. *Remains of Old Latin*, ed. and tr. E. H. Warmington (Loeb, 1935–40).

Waxman, *HJL*. M. Waxman, *A History of Jewish Literature* (4 vols., New York, 1930–41).

WES. Wisdom of the East Series.

Winstedt, *CML*. Sir Richard Winstedt, *A History of Classical Malay Literature*, *Journal* of the Malayan Branch of the Royal Asiatic Society, Vol. 31, pt 3 (Singapore, 1961).

Winternitz, *GIL*. Moriz Winternitz, *Geschichte der Indianischen Literatur* (3 vols., 1905–20; tr. S. Ketkar, 2 vols., Calcutta, 1927–33).

PUBLISHER'S NOTE

Bibliographies

The bibliographies in small type which generally follow an entry are arranged as follows. The first paragraph lists editions of texts and of translations of texts not already dealt with in the entry itself. The second paragraph lists critical works concerning the subject of the entry. In cases where only one paragraph is given, it will be clear from the titles of the works listed whether they are texts or criticism.

Except in the case of four standard series in the Classical and Byzantine section, the nature of the text is indicated by the following abbreviations: ed. = edited by, tr. = translated by, comm. = commentary by. The four exceptions are Loeb, Teubner, Budé and the Penguin Classics series. The reader should therefore bear in mind that the Loeb series gives text and English translations, Teubner gives text only, Budé gives text and French translations, and the Penguin Classics English translations.

The list of critical works is deliberately selective – further bibliographical information can usually be found in the listed works themselves.

Places of publication are given only for works published outside the British Isles.

Abbreviated titles are explained in the List of Abbreviations on pages 9–10.

Bibliographies have been compiled by the contributors of the relevant articles – their initials are placed before the bibliographies only for convenience.

Cross-references

Cross-references (⇨=see, ⇨⇨= see also) from one article to another are made in the following cases: (a) when relevant information can be found in the articles cross-referred to; (b) when the writer cross-referred to is comparatively minor and the reader may wish to know who he is, even though he has not much relevance to the article in which cross-reference occurs. (A fruitless search is thus avoided – if a minor figure is not cross-referred to it can be assumed that there is no article under his name.)

Classical and Byzantine

EDITORIAL FOREWORD

The general plan of this series provides for articles on individual authors, chosen on their merits as literature. It has not proved altogether easy to apply to Greek and Latin literature. So much is lost that many of the great classical authors appear in an artificial isolation: they cannot be understood without reference to contemporaries who are known to us from fragments, or perhaps, only by name. Thus Aristophanes needs to be placed against other writers of Old Comedy and Catullus set firmly among the *poetae novi.* Again, the classical feeling for form was so strong and the influence of literary *genres* so pervasive that it has been essential to have articles on such topics as dithyramb, tragedy, satyric drama, Greek and Roman historiography, and so on. As for individual authors, some have found a place because of their relevance to a major figure – for example, Virgil brings in the commentators Servius and Donatus. Others, again, command admission in their own right. How could Socrates, who wrote nothing, be excluded from any account of Greek literature, or the great patron Maecenas omitted from Latin because only a few lines of his poetry survive? None the less, the principle has been applied to thin the ranks of the grammarians, rhetoricians, and other writers of technical works, and also, especially, of the early Church Fathers. If Christian authors appear with much greater frequency in the Byzantine section, it is because they are an integral part of that literature. Whatever the test applied, there are bound to be some marginal cases: my rule has been to admit when in doubt.

At the end of most entries there will be found a brief bibliography, usually listing an edition, commentary, and books for further reading. For the convenience of the general reader, the books cited are, so far as possible, chosen from works published in English. He should be reminded, however, that this method can only give a very unfair impression of the merits of Continental scholarship. And, in the Byzantine section, it would have been impossible to apply, even were it extended to English, French, German, and Italian. Byzantine literature, it should be said, could not have been treated at all had not Professor Robert Browning, in the double role of editor and contributor, made himself responsible for its special, and, to me, intractable problems. Thanks to him, it has been possible to cover Greek literature from Homer to the fall of Constantinople in 1453. In Latin, save in a very few cases, no author is included after the end of the Western Empire in A.D. 476.

I am grateful to my pupils, Miss Maureen Rowlands and Mr Alan Peacock, for their help in preparing the manuscript.

The contributors hope that this volume, besides being useful in schools and universities, may win many new readers from the general public for Greek and Latin literature. They know that they will have done less than their duty to the writers of Greece and Rome if they have failed to make clear their high standing among the great literatures of the world.

D. R. DUDLEY

CLASSICAL

A

Accius, Lucius (170–*c.* 85 B.C.). Roman tragic poet. Born in Umbria, the son of a former slave, Accius became the friendly rival and eventual successor of ♢ Pacuvius. Titles and about 700 lines survive from over 40 of his tragedies on Greek themes and 2 ♢ *fabulae praetextae*. Energetic, versatile and somewhat careless, he was considered less learned but more vigorous than Pacuvius, and equally impressive and dignified. His violently emotional characters made Roman tragedy increasingly melodramatic, but he was admired for his rhetoric and repartee, and inspired Virgil with his pathos and compassion. His plays remained popular until the Augustan period. (♢ Tragedy, Roman.) [G T W H]

Loeb: Warmington, *R O L*, ii.
Beare, *R S*.

Acilius, Gaius (fl. 155 B.C.). Roman historian. Senator and philhellene of 2nd century B.C. He was probably related to M. Acilius Glabrio, consul of 191 and supporter of Scipio Africanus. In 155 he acted as interpreter for the Greek philosophers Critolaus, Diogenes and Carneades, sent on a mission to the Senate by Athens. He was possibly a member of the ♢ Scipionic circle. He wrote a history of Rome in Greek (*c.* 142) from the earliest times to his own day, and believed that Rome was a Greek foundation. He recorded the story of the meeting between Scipio and Hannibal at Ephesus. His work was used as an important source by ♢ Claudius Quadrigarius. [T A D]

Peter, *H R R*, i.

Aelius Herodianus. ♢ Herodian.

Aelius Tubero, Quintus (fl. *c.* 50 B.C.). Roman historian. Fought for Pompey in Civil War, then was reconciled to Caesar. He abandoned forensic oratory for jurisprudence after failure in a case in 46. He is quoted by Pomponius as an eminent jurist, and wrote a history of Rome from the earliest times to his own day, in rather old-fashioned language. He used the 'Linen Books' (♢ Macer) as a historical source. [T A D]

Peter, *H R R*, i.

Aenesidemus. ♢ Sceptics.

Aeschines (*c.* 390–*c.* 314 B.C.). Athenian orator. Demosthenes' arch-enemy. Family circumstances curtailed his education and early made him independent. He served with distinction in the armed forces. His political career began under the aegis of Eubulus, *c.* 357. Though cooperating in the attempt to organize panhellenic resistance to Macedonia in 348, he soon became convinced a settlement was needed. With Demosthenes he was one of the mission which negotiated the Peace of Philocrates. Demosthenes' subsequent attempt to show that Aeschines was bribed by Philip misfired when Aeschines prosecuted his joint accuser Timarchus and convicted him of immorality. When Demosthenes reopened the attack, however, in 343, Aeschines was barely acquitted. In 339 he characteristically sidetracked charges brought by the Amphissans against Athens by furiously denouncing them for cultivating the Crisaean plain, thus precipitating the Sacred War. In 337 he moved the rejection of Ctesiphon's decree to confer a crown on Demosthenes for services to Athens. Philip's death postponed a decision until 330, when Aeschines' attempt to eliminate Demosthenes from public life eliminated Aeschines. He withdrew to Rhodes, where he practised as a rhetor.

Of his speeches 3 have survived: (1) *Against Timarchus* (345); (2) *On the Embassy* (343), a successful rebuttal of Demosthenes' attacks; (3) *Against Ctesiphon* (330), persuasive when arguing the technical illegalities of the proposal, but inadequate as a general attack on Demosthenes' record.

Aeschines, with his shrewdness and opportunism, was formidable, especially in opposition, and perhaps surpassed Demosthenes in understanding the art of the possible. His estimate of Athens' chances in a war with Macedon was unflattering, but was borne out. He had great natural endowments as an orator – a fine voice and presence, a witty, lively well-stored mind, and impassioned eloquence, enriched by illustration from poetry and myth. He lacked in oratory, as in politics, judgement, taste, and moral authority. At his best he is persuasive and moving. [DEWW]

Loeb: C. D. Adams (1919).
Dobson, *G O.*

Aeschines of Sphettus (4th cent. B.C.). Greek philosopher. One of Socrates' most faithful disciples, known to have attended his trial and death. Later, he emigrated to Syracuse, but returned to Athens in 356. Like Xenophon, Plato and other Socratics, he gave a picture of the life and teaching of the Master by writing dialogues in which he was the central figure. Antiquity judged him to have been a faithful recorder; regrettably only fragments survive of the 7 dialogues which can be confidently assigned to him. [DRD]

Ed. and comm. H. Dittmar (1912).

Aeschylus (*c.* 525–456 B.C.). Greek tragic poet. Born of a noble family at Eleusis in Attica, Aeschylus patriotically fought the Persian invaders at Marathon (where his brother was killed in action), and probably at Salamis. He was once accused of revealing the Eleusinian Mysteries in a play, but he seems not to have been initiated, for he is said to have secured acquittal by proving that he had offended unwittingly. He began exhibiting tragedies early in the 5th century, and won his first victory in 484. The earliest extant play is the *Persians* (produced 472). The *Seven against Thebes* appeared in 467, and the *Oresteia* (*Agamemnon, Libation Bearers,* and *Eumenides*) in 458: and the 2 undated plays, the *Suppliant Women* and *Prometheus Bound,* seem to belong to the late 460s. He went to Sicily probably twice on visits to the court of Hieron of Syracuse, whose wealth, enterprise and culture were attracting many leading Greek artists. On the first visit he produced the *Women of Etna* in honour of Hieron's new city of that name and repeated his recent production of the *Persians.* He was back in Athens by 468, when he was defeated in the tragic contests by Sophocles, and went to Sicily again after 458. He died there in 456, near Gela. His epitaph, said to be his own composition, records proudly that he fought the Persians, but says nothing of his poetry. He won 13 tragic victories in his lifetime, and more after his death, posthumous revivals of his works being permitted by special decree. He left about 80 plays, of which 7 survive; the remainder are known only from titles and fragments, some of them recently discovered on papyri. The extant plays, representing a short list selected by Alexandrian and Byzantine scholars, include some of Aeschylus's most famous works and his greatest trilogy.

The *Persians* belonged to a tetralogy of apparently unrelated plays – *Phineus, Persians, Glaucus of Potniae* and a satyric *Prometheus.* In it Aeschylus presents recent history in tragic form, but gives it a suitable remoteness by setting the play in the exotic opulence of the Persian royal court. The theme is the homecoming of the defeated Xerxes, who appears at the end in utter dejection. Aeschylus does not gloat; the disaster is seen from the Persian point of view.

The *Seven against Thebes* was part of a tetralogy chronicling the fortunes of the royal house of Thebes, generation by generation: first came the *Laius,* next the *Oedipus,* and then the extant play, on the rivalry of Eteocles and Polynices; the satyr-play, the *Sphinx,* returned to the story of Oedipus. There is little action in the *Seven,* but a pageant of heraldry and growing tension as Eteocles assigns seven Theban warriors one by one to face the Argive champions at the seven gates. Inevitably the two brothers meet at the seventh gate, and both are killed.

The date of the *Suppliant Women* has been much disputed, but recently discovered evidence suggests that it was produced after 468. The play was the first of a tetralogy on the legend of Danaus. The chorus of suppliants are his 50 daughters, who flee to Argos to escape marriage with their cousins, the 50 sons of Aegyptus, and are there given asylum. The action is slight and inconclusive; the play is in effect only the first act of a larger drama. The girls who reject marriage in the first play were forced into it in the second, the *Egyptians.* All murdered their bridegrooms except one, who was then accused of treachery in sparing her husband; but in the third play, the *Daughters of Danaus,* she was apparently acquitted, and persuasion succeeded with her sisters where force could not, when Aphrodite, goddess of love, reconciled them to their natural role in marriage. The satyric *Amymone,* on the adventures of another daughter of Danaus, probably completed the tetralogy.

The date of the *Prometheus Bound* is also uncertain, but is probably fairly late. The plan of the trilogy and the order of its plays are unknown, but possibly it embodied the same pattern of conflict and ultimate reconciliation as the Danaid trilogy and the *Oresteia,* with *Prometheus the Fire-Bearer* showing the original crime of Prometheus, *Prometheus Bound* the deadlock between a vengeful Zeus and his defiant victim, and *Prometheus Unbound* the final settlement. Nothing certain is known of the satyr-play. The *Prometheus Bound* opens strikingly with Prometheus (perhaps represented by a lay figure) being nailed to a lonely rock at the ends of the earth as a punishment for stealing fire for mankind. There he is left, immovable, and the rest of the play shows the impact of visits by a succession of other characters: the chorus, the gentle daughters of Oceanus: Oceanus himself, a time-server: the tormented Io, another victim of Zeus; and lastly Hermes, his lackey. Prometheus knows a secret on which the future of Zeus depends, but when ordered by Hermes to reveal it he defiantly refuses. Finally a thunderbolt from Zeus hurls him and the chorus beneath the earth.

The plot of the *Oresteia*, the only complete trilogy extant, is taken from the legend of the royal house of Atreus, in which crime bred crime through many generations. The first part of the action takes place at the palace of Agamemnon, son of Atreus, at Argos, and it begins in an atmosphere of mingled hope and foreboding. The end of the Trojan War is near; but before he sailed for Troy Agamemnon had to sacrifice his own daughter Iphigenia to obtain a fair wind, and for 10 years the bereaved mother Clytemnestra has brooded over this deed in his absence, sending their son Orestes away and ruling over Argos with her lover Aegisthus. Now comes the news, flashed by a chain of beacons, that Troy has fallen. Clytemnestra is jubilant, but the chorus of Argive elders think of the crime that started the war and the price that has been paid for victory. Presently the victorious king appears, with a captive Trojan girl, Cassandra, in his train. It is a strained reunion. Clytemnestra is fulsome, Agamemnon cold and wary, but eventually she entices him in to meet his death; and Cassandra, after seeing horrifying visions of the crimes of the house of Atreus, past and imminent, despairingly follows her master. Soon the interior of the palace is revealed, and the chorus are aghast to see Clytemnestra standing over the bodies of Agamemnon and Cassandra. She answers their protests by recalling the sacrifice of Iphigenia, and when Aegisthus appears he overawes them by a show of force. They can only hope that one day Agamemnon's son will avenge him.

In the *Libation Bearers* Orestes returns to Argos with a companion, Pylades, after years of exile, under Apollo's explicit orders to avenge his father's death. He sees his sister Electra, with a number of slave-women (the chorus), taking libations to pour at Agamemnon's tomb. After a hesitant recognition Electra joins him in an awe-inspiring invocation of their dead father's spirit, until they are fired with a passion for revenge. Orestes contrives to kill Aegisthus and then, sword in hand, faces his mother. For a moment he falters, but Pylades sternly reminds him of Apollo's command, and they take her into the palace. Again the interior is thrown open, and Orestes in his turn is seen standing over the bodies of Clytemnestra and Aegisthus. He is justifying his vengeance when he sees avenging furies appearing to haunt him, and he flees to seek purification at Apollo's shrine at Delphi.

The opening scene of the *Eumenides* is set in Delphi, and the Furies form the chorus. The suppliant Orestes, surrounded by the sleeping Furies, is reassured by Apollo and sent away to Athens for judgement and acquittal by Athena. The ghost of Clytemnestra angrily rouses the Furies, and they set off on his trail. The scene now changes to Athens, before Athena's temple on the Acropolis. The Furies and Orestes submit their claims to Athena, whereupon she founds the homicide court of the Areopagus to hear the case. The Furies prosecute, and Apollo defends; the judges are evenly divided, but Athena gives her casting vote to Orestes. She then calms the enraged Furies, persuading them to take on a new function and settle in Attica as revered and beneficent powers, the Eumenides or Kindly Ones, and they are conducted in a procession to their underground sanctuary on the Areopagus.

Aeschylus founded classical Greek tragedy by taking over from ⇨ Phrynichus a relatively simple form of art and raising it to a level of heroic and unsophisticated magnificence that his successors scarcely tried to emulate. His introduction of a second actor made the dialogue independent of the chorus, increasing its dramatic potentialities; and he developed, if he did not invent, the trilogy and tetralogy as vehicles for drama on the largest scale. He was noted for creating suspense by letting one character stay impressively silent, and he made much use of spectacular effects. Gods, Titans and heroes trod his stage in actions determining the fate of whole cities and dynasties, and even of Zeus himself. His fondness for the outlandish in settings, action, descriptions and scenic devices led him to perilous heights of Wagnerian grandeur and absurdity.

The style of Aeschylus matched his drama: high-flown and rich in weighty compound words and massed epithets; at times bombastic to the point of bathos; and abounding in metaphors, often extremely bold. The choral element bulks large in his dramas, and despite a tendency to portentous platitude and obscurity his major odes are masterpieces of concentrated, darting thought, sharply focused imagery and intense feeling. Their rhythms were later criticized as excessively dactylic; but the extant lyrics achieve powerful emotional effects with other metres also, although the music is lost. Since drama on the superhuman Aeschylean scale is necessarily simple, his brief plots move straight ahead, with little subtlety of characterization. Naturally the choruses are types – fanatical virgins, anxious elders, the indescribable Furies – even when they play a positive part in the action; but most of the individual characters, too, appear in outline rather than in the round. The main exceptions are in the *Oresteia*, the poet's latest work: the demonic personality of Clytemnestra, the woman with the heart of a man, who dominates the *Agamemnon*; perhaps Cassandra, in her frenzy and pathos; and two vivid thumbnail sketches of a humble watchman and nurse. Aeschylus perhaps showed most originality in his instinct for good 'theatre'. He has ghosts, messenger speeches, interiors suddenly revealed, and a king reduced to rags; these were probably traditional features of Greek tragedy, but he exploits them with good effect. Where he seems to show his own hand is in his famous silent characters, the massed movements of the *Suppliant Women*, the cataclysm at the finale of the *Prometheus Bound*; and above all in the *Oresteia*, in Clytemnestra's temptation of Agamemnon, the ghastly pack of Furies, and the tremendous crescendo of the great trial scene and final procession.

Aeschylean morality, simple, harsh and grand, is curiously reminiscent of the Old Testament. For Aeschylus there is danger in great prosperity, since it may lead a man into presumptuous insolence, *hubris*; and then retribution, perhaps long delayed but ultimately inevitable, will destroy him or his descendants. The innocent may suffer, too, but the design of Providence will in the end prove just and beneficent. A man who sins taints his whole house with guilt, and his children and children's children will be haunted by the curse; yet by virtue, by avoidance of *hubris*, by learning wisdom through suffering, they may escape. But violence breeds violence without end, until it yields to persuasion, as it must at last. That is a law which governs god and man alike: Zeus was once a tyrant himself, but even he had to learn this lesson. Here Aeschylus, deeply but unconventionally religious, makes his boldest and most imaginative bid to establish a moral basis for the fantastic and often gruesome mythology of the Greeks. (⇨ Satyric Drama; Tragedy, Greek.) [G T W H]

OCT: G. Murray (1955). Fragments: H. J. Mette, *Supplementum aeschyleum* (Berlin, 1959). Commentaries: H. J. Rose (Amsterdam, 1957–8); *Persians*, H. D. Broadhead (1960); *Seven Against Thebes*, *Suppliant Women*, with tr., T. G. Tucker (1908, 1889); *Prometheus Bound*, *Oresteia*, with tr., G. Thomson (1932, 1966); *Agamemnon*, with tr., E. Fraenkel (1962); J. D. Denniston and D. Page (1957). Verse tr.: Loeb, with new fragments, H. W. Smyth and H. Lloyd-Jones (2 vols., 1922, 1957); P. Vellacott (Penguin Classics, 1956, 1961); D. Grene and R. Lattimore, *The Complete Greek Tragedies* (1959). Prose tr.: W. and C. E. S. Headlam (1909).

G. Murray, *Aeschylus: The Creator of Tragedy* (1962); H. W. Smyth, *Aeschylean Tragedy* (Berkeley, Cal., 1924); A. Lesky, *Greek Tragedy* (1965).

Aesop. ⇨ Fables.

'Aetna'. ⇨ Appendix Virgiliana.

Afranius. ⇨ Comedy, Roman.

Agathon (*c.*445–*c.*399 B.C.). Greek tragic poet. He won his first prize for a tragedy in 416, and celebrated it with the party described in Plato's *Symposium.* An effeminate dandy, he was both mocked and admired for his beauty and poetic talent. He left Athens about 407 to reside at the court of Archelaus of Macedon.

Several titles of his tragedies are known, but only fragments survive; these reveal an artificial, epigrammatic style, evidently accurately hit off by Plato. Aristophanes' burlesque (in *Thesmophoriazusae*) implies a certain complexity and voluptuousness in his lyrics. An innovator in Greek tragedy, Agathon treated choral odes as mere irrelevant interludes in the action, introduced more florid music, and invented a romantic story of his own for his *Antheus* instead of drawing on the traditional legends. His example was influential; and Aristotle, though critical of his plot-construction, treats him as ranking next to the three great tragedians of Athens. [G T W H]

Ed. A. Nauck, *Tragicorum graecorum fragmenta* (Leipzig, 1889).

Agias. ⇨ Epic Cycle.

Agrippa, Marcus Vipsanius (63–12 B.C.). Roman statesman and general. Augustus's minister of war and for a time his chosen successor. He wrote an *Autobiography* (now lost) justifying his part in the Civil War. As consul he carried out a great programme for the embellishment of Rome; there was also to have been a map of the Roman Empire engraved on a portico. Agrippa collected the material for this map and wrote a *Commentary,* extensively used by later geographers, to illustrate it. [D R D]

M. Reinhold, *Marcus Agrippa* (Geneva, N.Y., 1933).

Albinovanus Pedo (early 1st cent. A.D.). Roman poet. A friend of Ovid and author of an epic poem on the Theseus legend, he took part in the northern campaigns of Germanicus in A.D. 15 and 16. These he described in a poem whose title is unknown. But the elder Seneca (*Suasoriae,* I: 15) quotes a fragment of some 20 lines, describing the great storm in the North Sea which scattered the Roman fleet (see Tacitus, *Annals,* II: 23, 24, which may be derived from it). Roman accounts of the world beyond the Empire are rare, and these splendid lines arouse sharp regret for the poem's loss. [D R D]

Fragment in Tacitus, *Annals,* ed. H. Furneaux (2nd edn, 1896), i, p. 386.

Alcaeus (b.*c.*620 B.C.). Greek lyric poet. Born of an aristocratic family at Mytilene in Lesbos. His life mirrors the disturbed age in which it fell; his favourite allegory of the state as a ship battling with stormy seas symbolizes his own tempestuous career. He fought for his country against Athens at Sigeum (where he lost his shield and fled) and also against his fellow-countrymen. Too young to help his kinsmen under Pittacus's leadership in overthrowing the tyrant Melanchrus, in the aristocratic struggle for supremacy he clashed violently with the new tyrant Myrsilus, and finally with the strong man Pittacus, who ultimately came to power. Extrovert and aggressive, better at hating than loving, he lived and drank hard. His years in exile at Pyrrha in Lesbos or overseas may account for his visiting Boeotia and Egypt; probably, like his brother Antimenidas, he enlisted as a mercenary. He seems to have served for a time with the Lydian army.

The Alexandrians knew not less than 10 books of his poetry. No complete poem survives, though our knowledge of his versatility and accomplishment has been much enlarged by papyri. His dialect is the Lesbian vernacular with occasional epic enrichment. His metrical virtuosity is matched by his variety of theme; he ranges from the almost slick transposition into lyric form of a passage from Hesiod, through convivial drinking songs, to the dramatic monologue of a love-sick girl. His political poems, violent in tone, are controlled in technique, with a self-discipline missing from his life. His hymns to the gods are vivid and individual. In many ways he and his contemporary Sappho, addressed in one poem, complement each other. He was admired and creatively imitated by Horace, and merges through him with the main stream of the European lyric tradition. [D E W W]

E. Lobel and D. L. Page, *Poetarum lesbiorum fragmenta* (1955).
Bowra, *G L P;* D. L. Page, *Sappho and Alcaeus* (1955).

Alcman (mid 7th cent. B.C.). Greek choral lyric poet, the earliest known to us. Lived at Sparta. He came perhaps from Sardis in Lydia, but he writes the Laconian vernacular with only occasional epic borrowings, and is completely assimilated to his Spartan environment. Alexandrian scholars edited his lyrics in 6 books. A papyrus has restored to us most of a *Partheneion,* some hundred verses composed in 14-line responding stanzas, sung by 10 girls competing against a rival choir at a festival of Artemis Ortheia. The sombre retribution of the gods in the mythical past is contrasted with the beauty of the choir-leaders in the present. Here is the zest and *joie de vivre* of early Sparta, before the iron had entered her soul. Otherwise only fragments survive: passages from various hymns, a few hexameters (apparently preludes to epic-verse recitations), and an outstanding short evocative description of Nature, animate and inanimate, sunk in sleep. Alcman loves colour, festivity, the beauty and spontaneity of young living things, human or animal. The archaic simplicity of his metre and diction discipline and strengthen his sustained lyricism, and the economy of his style is the perfect medium for his fresh, delicate and exquisitely apt imagery. [D E W W]

Page, *P M G; The Partheneion,* ed. tr. and comm. D. L. Page (1951); Bowra, *G L P* (translates representative passages and gives critical assessment).

Alexander the Great (356–323 B.C.). King of Macedon. Alexander III of Macedon was the son of King Philip II and Olympias. On his accession he determined to carry out a persistent Greek ambition, the liberation of the Greek cities of Asia Minor from Persian domination and Persia's destruction as a Mediterranean power. These primary objectives were accomplished by the defeat of the Persians under Darius III; then, after consolidating his hold on Syria and Egypt, Alexander penetrated into the heart of the Persian Empire, defeated Darius again, seized the chief Persian cities, and on the death of Darius assumed the title of King of Persia. During the next few years he penetrated as far as the Hindu Kush and the Punjab before disaffection among his troops compelled him to return to Persia. In his last years he tried to establish an Empire based on a multi-racial partnership between all his various Greek and Asiatic subjects and encouraged intermarriage, but his schemes were encountering ever-increasing difficulties, due mostly to the opposition of his victorious Macedonian troops, when he died of fever. His conquests spread Greek civilization all over the Middle East, and indirectly led to establishing the important seats of learning at Alexandria and Pergamum.

Alexander made a greater impact on literary tradition than any other man in the ancient world. There were countless biographies of him and histories of his campaigns, ranging from the sober, reliable works of ◊ Ptolemy, ◊ Aristobulus and ◊ Arrian to the more romantic sagas of ◊ Callisthenes, ◊ Onesicritus, ◊ Cleitarchus, ◊ Plutarch and ◊ Curtius, full of exaggerations and sometimes malicious propaganda. In the Middle Ages popular knowledge of Alexander was drawn from the *Alexander Romance*, ultimately derived from a collection of stories and fictitious documents written in Greek in Egypt in the 2nd century A.D. and falsely attributed to Callisthenes. It was translated into Latin by Julius Valerius in the 3rd century, and subsequently epitomized; the epitome was used by Vincent de Beauvais in the 12th century, but this version was superseded by another rendering of the pseudo-Callisthenes, the *Historia de proeliis*, composed in the 10th century by Leo of Naples. The *Alexander Romance* was a complete farrago of stories, based on fact in a few cases, but mostly fictitious or completely fabulous. [T A D]

Alexandrian Poetry. The extension of Macedonian control over mainland Greece marked the end of an epoch; and literary decline accompanied political decay. A major readjustment was necessary if poetry was to survive. Under the Ptolemies Alexandria grew rapidly in size, power and prestige. Here, in an environment uninhibited by the past, the pattern of a new culture, fundamentally Greek, but less introspective and more cosmopolitan, could evolve. Sophisticated court circles provided patronage, and the enlightened policy of the Ptolemies in founding the Museum and Library attracted men of letters and learning. Many were recruited from parts of the Greek world that still enjoyed political freedom or a measure of it – Syracuse, Rhodes and Cos. The characteristic poetic genres of the Hellenistic age were New Comedy, which for all its Attic flavour had some of the universal deracinated appeal of the modern cinema, and Epigram, in which flawless mastery of a minor art form was attained.

Philetas, Simias and ⇨ Asclepiades were among the forerunners; but the tone of the new movement was largely set by ⇨ Callimachus, who dominated the literary scene during the period of greatest creativity (280–240 B.C.). He preached perfection in miniature, combining a depth of erudition intelligible only to a limited cultured audience with a new technical accomplishment and formal discipline: and he practised what he preached. Though his views were challenged, on the whole they prevailed and determined the lines of poetic development. These include the choice of exotic and recondite subject-matter, and the rehandling of familiar themes in an unfamiliar way – a conscious departure from and reblending of the traditional in form, dialect and vocabulary. The personal subjective element acquires a new prominence, and erotic motives are exploited. Among Callimachus's contemporaries are ⇨ Aratus, famous for his *Phaenomena*, a didactic poem on astronomy, and ⇨ Theocritus, whose *Idylls* begin the long tradition of European pastoral, a poetry of escape from the artificiality of urban civilization into a countryside which itself in time becomes stylized. In addition, ⇨ Herodas in his mimes achieves realism of character-drawing, dialogue and situation, within a disciplined verse form. He is almost the only surviving witness to the flourishing literary drama of Alexandria – the poets of the tragic Pleiad are mere names to us. Finally, ⇨ Apollonius Rhodius's romantic epic, the *Argonautica,* is a consciously provocative assault on Callimachus's aesthetic position.

There are also numerous fragments, often of anonymous authorship (conveniently assembled by J. U. Powell, *Collectanea alexandrina*, 1925), which testify to a widespread literary ferment. But with Callimachus's death the movement rapidly lost its initial impetus. In the 2nd century, erudition tended to crush inspiration under a dead weight of learning, as in ⇨ Lycophron. Yet the tradition lived on with sufficient vitality to initiate a 1st-century revival, in which Meleager was outstanding, and to give a new impulse to Latin poetry. [D E W W]

W. W. Tarn and G. T. Griffith, *Hellenistic Civilisation* (3rd edn, 1952).

Alexandrianism, Latin. The fashion of writing in the Alexandrian style was adopted by a number of Roman poets from the beginning of the 1st century B.C. to the death of Augustus. It began with ⇨ Laevius and ⇨ Catulus, whose works are lost, and was one of the chief marks of the group of young poets from Cisalpine Gaul which included Catullus. Their models were, especially, ⇨ Callimachus, ⇨ Philetas and ⇨ Euphorion in whom they admired mythological learning, skill and versatility in the handling of metre, and a high degree of polish. The ⇨ *epyllion*, or short epic poem, was in a genre which they were eager to exploit. From their Greek models they may also have learned to write on personal subjects, but to these such Roman writers as ⇨ Catullus and Propertius brought an intensity of feeling quite alien to the scholarly intellectuals of Alexandria. The mythological learning which reappears in Virgil and Ovid may be considered an Alexandrian strain. (⇨ *Neoterici.*) [D R D]

Ambrose (A.D. 339–97). Christian Latin writer. Son of the *praefectus praetorio Galliarum,* Ambrose, after a rhetorical and legal training, achieved high public office, becoming *c.*370 the governor of Liguria and Aemilia, with his residence at Milan. In 374, despite his objections, he was consecrated bishop of Milan and forthwith devoted himself to care of his diocese and to theological studies. He was active against the western Arians, even opposing the Empress-Mother Justina, who was their patroness. He exercised influence over the Emperor Gratian and interceded on behalf of his successor with the usurper Maximus. Ambrose's sturdy independence was evident in his dealings with Theodosius I, whom he even compelled to do penance for the massacre at Thessalonica in 390.

Most of Ambrose's writings were the outcome of his pastoral work and are homiletic in origin; in true Roman manner, he was essentially practical and engaged little in dogmatic speculation, being content to reproduce the views of others when necessary. His exegetical writings include 6 books on the *Hexameron*, containing brilliant descriptions of nature and owing not a little to ⇨ Basil, and the *Commentary on Luke's Gospel* in 10 books. Amongst his moral-ascetical works there is *On the Duties of the Clergy*, based upon Cicero's *De officiis*; there is an identical arrangement of material but the antithesis between the morality of the pagan and that of the Christian are most striking. His dogmatic treatises were largely directed against the Arians – such was *On Faith* and *On the Holy Spirit*, the latter owing much to Basil's treatment of the same subject, both written at the request of Gratian. His sermons and letters are of high literary merit, the most famous of the former being his funeral discourses on Valentinian II and Theodosius the Great. Ambrose introduced congregational singing into the liturgy and composed a number of hymns, the earliest dating from 386. They are written in iambic dimeters, divided into four-line verses.

Ambrose's style is frequently of oratorical vigour and poetic beauty and abounds in classical allusions, particularly to the writings of Virgil. It is characterized by a brevity and a simplicity that have earned him a deserved reputation. [J G D]

Migne, *P L*, 13–17; *On Faith, On the Holy Spirit, Sermons* and *Letters*, tr. H. de Romestin (N P F, 1896).
F. H. Dudden, *The Life and Times of St Ambrose* (1935).

Amelesagoras. ⇨ Atthis.

Ammianus Marcellinus (b. *c.*A.D. 330). Roman soldier and historian. Born in Antioch of an upper-middle-class family, he joined the Roman army and served as a staff-officer in Gaul and in the East, encountering stirring experiences in the Persian Wars of Constantius II and Julian. After Julian's death he left the army and devoted himself to literature, living in Antioch till 378, when he went to Rome. There, encouraged no doubt by his friend ⇨ Symmachus, the leading literary figure in the city, he wrote and published his *History*. He seems to have died some time after 394.

The *Res gestae* of Ammianus cover the period from the death of Domitian in A.D. 96 to the death of Valens in 378. It is thus a continuation of the *Histories* of Tacitus. It originally consisted of 31 books, but only the last 18 have survived, starting with the year 353. Ammianus is a historian of great ability. He has the necessary practical knowledge of soldiering and imperial administration; he was accurate in collecting and presenting his facts; and although he is ready to praise or blame, he is free from prejudice. He can write a thrilling narrative, especially of events he himself took part in, and his character-studies have great power. This is particularly noteworthy in his famous description of the Huns (XXXI: 2) – wild, savage nomads, little better than animals, who spend almost their whole lives on horseback and whose only homes are their waggons.

His style, though vigorous, is at times obscure. Greek was his native language, and the Latin that he first learnt was the colloquial Latin of the camp. Later he read widely among classical Latin authors, and he seems to have based his style largely on Tacitus, though there are traces of an attempt to imitate Livy. But the ornate literary language is never fully mastered, and the colloquialisms and Graecisms are continually showing through. Some of his usages, for example the indiscriminate use of the comparative, the use of *quod* with the indicative to express indirect statement, and the lack of precision in tenses and moods, all foreshadow the Latin of the Middle Ages. [T A D]

Loeb: *Res gestae*, J. C. Rolfe (3 vols., 1935–7).
E. A. Thompson, *The Historical Work of Ammianus Marcellinus* (1947); ed. T. A. Dorey, *Latin Historians* (1966).

Ammonius Saccas. ⇨ Neo-Platonism.

Anacreon (*c.*570–*c.*485 B.C.). Greek lyric poet. Born at Teos. His career reflects the menacing emergence of Persian power in the Near East. The Teans, beleaguered by the Great King's forces, abandoned their city and sought refuge in Abdera. Thence Anacreon was invited by Polycrates to Samos; tyrant and poet became close friends. When Persia destroyed Polycrates, Anacreon accepted Hipparchus's patronage at Athens. The fall of the Peisistratids forced him temporarily to transfer to the court of Echecratidas at Pharsalus. Eventually he returned to Athens, which reciprocated his affection – his statue was later shown on the Acropolis.

Aristarchus edited Anacreon's poetry in 6 books. The lyrics are mostly banqueting songs celebrating love and wine in a straightforward Ionic vernacular and metrically uncomplicated (the simple Anacreontic is appropriately named after him). The satirical attack on Artemon shows that he was not lightly crossed, and this is borne out by the iambic fragments. The elegiac epigrams are slight yet moving in their economy and restraint. The genial façade of Anacreon's poetry conceals a fastidious sensibility, and a capacity for self-criticism which finds expression in irony and wit; like Horace he contemplates his life and loves with a wry detachment. The passionate eloquence of early monody is replaced by a warmth and limpidity which have an immediate and universal appeal. [DEWW]

Page, *PMG*.
Bowra, *GLP* (tr. and discussed).

Anaxagoras (*c.*500–*c.*428 B.C.). Greek philosopher. Born at Clazomenae in Ionia. As a *metic* (resident alien) he lived and taught at Athens for 30 years, the first philosopher to do so. He became the friend of Pericles, who defended him when he was prosecuted (perhaps twice) for impiety. He withdrew to Lampsacus, where he founded a school. Fragments amounting to some 1,000 words survive of the single book he wrote. He worked, like the atomists, on the problems raised by ⇨ Zeno and ⇨ Parmenides but he reached opposite conclusions. His thought was imperfectly understood in antiquity, and perhaps now cannot be reconstructed. The much-discussed term 'Homoiomeries' (things with like parts), associated with him by Aristotle and Lucretius, does not seem to have been used by him. We do know that he thought (1) that matter is infinitely divisible, and (2) that the cosmic process began when Mind 'the finest and purest of all things' set up a rotatory process resulting in the separating-out of opposites. We also know something of his speculation on growth, nutrition, sense-perception, and astronomy ('the sun is a stone larger than the Peloponnesus'). [DRD]

Diels, *FV*, 59.

Anaximander (fl. *c.*560 B.C.). Greek philosopher. Born at Miletus. Traditionally the pupil of ⇨ Thales. He seems to have propounded a bold and far-reaching cosmology of which only portions are known. For him, the basic substance of the Universe is the Unlimited, i.e. not one of the existing elements. From this separate off 'innumerable worlds', each containing the opposites Hot–Cold, Wet–Dry. He speculated about the size and orbits of the sun and moon, and the evolution of living creatures from the sea. He drew a map of the world, and invented the gnomon. These views were set out in a book entitled (probably) *On Nature*. [DRD]

Diels, *FV*, 12.

Anaximenes (fl. *c.*546 B.C.). Greek philosopher. Third of the Ionian physicists, he is said to have been the pupil of ⇨ Anaximander. Following up the work of Thales and Anaximander, he chose Air as his underlying substance, accounting for its transformations by the processes of rarefaction and condensation. Perhaps he reached this view by analogy – as the 'breath-soul' (*pneuma*) is to our bodies, so is Air to the Cosmos. He is said to have written a book, of which Theophrastus quotes a sentence. [DRD]

Diels, *FV*, 13.

Andocides (*c.*440–*c.*390 B.C.). Attic orator. Of aristocratic origins, with a family tradition of public service. Accused in 415 of complicity in the mutilation of the Hermae and the sacrilegious parody of the Eleusinian mysteries, he failed to clear himself on the first charge. Imprisoned, he revealed as much as he knew, and despite a promise of immunity, forfeited some of his citizen-rights and left Athens, engaging in commerce abroad. He sought restoration in 411, and again in 410, but only with the general amnesty of 403 was he allowed to return. He resumed an active political career, defending himself in 399 on a charge of impiety. In 391 he participated in an unsuccessful peace mission to Sparta. Subsequently he appears to have been exiled a second time.

The *De reditu* (411), *De mysteriis* (399) and *De pace* (391) survive. Andocides was not a professional advocate – his speeches were composed for himself and delivered in person, and this gives them a compelling immediacy. Less of a conscious artist than any other Greek orator, he has a natural fluency and liveliness (modulating on occasion into personalities), a manly vigour, and a gift for narrative. Untutored and sometimes undisciplined, he is best when he is simplest, adopting a conversational tone, but speaking with a force and candour that command attention. [D E W W]

Loeb: K. J. Maidment, *Minor Attic Orators*, i (1941).
Jebb, *A O*, i; Dobson, *G O*.

Androtion (fl. 4th cent. B.C.). Athenian politician and writer. A pupil of Isocrates, a right-wing politician, and an opponent of Demosthenes. He wrote an ◊ *Atthis* which was used by Aristotle as one of the main sources of his *Constitution of Athens*. [T A D]

Müller, *F H G*.

Annales Maximi. The name given to the official records of the Pontifex Maximus (Tabulae Pontificum) after their publication *c.* 123 B.C. by the then Pontifex Maximus, P. Mucius Scaevola. They contained the names of magistrates, events of religious importance (e.g. festivals, triumphs, dedications), and accounts of portents and their expiation. The information contained was meagre, but they were of great importance in providing a convenient chronological framework for later historians. [T A D]

Annalists. The name given to the native Roman historians of the Republic. They represented a tradition that was in many places exaggerated and inaccurate, as opposed to the more reliable tradition of ◊ Polybius. [T A D]

Anniceris. ◊ Cyrenaics.

Anthology, Greek. As we have it, a collection of short poems in 15 books, compiled by the learned Byzantine, Constantinus Cephalas, in the 10th century. Since the manuscript was found in the library of the Elector Palatine at Heidelberg, it is often known as the Palatine Anthology. There is an expurgated version, compiled in the 14th century by the monk Planudes. Cephalas incorporated several earlier collections of the classical period, notably the *Garland* of Meleager (fl. *c.* 90 B.C.), and re-arranged their contents in an order which is somewhat fanciful. The great majority of the poems are in the elegiac metre; they include poems on love, death, and nature, satiric verses, and a great range of other *vers d'occasion*. There is some rubbish and much that is trivial, but also many of the most beautiful and unforgettable poems in Greek. Some great names appear – Aeschylus, Bacchylides, Plato, Simonides, Theocritus. Of the professional epigrammatists ◊ Leonidas of Tarentum (3rd century B.C.), Meleager (1st century B.C.), ◊ Palladas (fl. *c.* A.D. 400) and Paulus Silentiarius (*c.* A.D. 560) are especially noteworthy. That the elegiac epigram was handled with skill by poets for more than a millennium and a half is one of the most striking instances of the continuity of Greek literature. [D R D]

Loeb: W. R. Paton (5 vols., 1916–18); *Select Epigrams from the Greek Anthology*, ed. and tr. J. W. Mackail (3rd edn, 1911); *The Greek Anthology, Hellenistic Epigrams*, ed. A. S. F. Gow and D. L. Page (1965).

Anthology, Latin. The basis of the Latin Anthology is a collection made in Africa in the 6th century A.D. The contents of a number of later manuscripts, notably the Thuaneus (9th cent.), have been added. It contains much agreeable minor verse, such as the poems of ◊ Petronius and ◊ Tiberianus, and one great prize, the ◊ *Pervigilium Veneris*. It was much read in the Middle Ages. [D R D]

Loeb: Duff, *M L P* (selections).

Antimachus. ◊ Epic Cycle.

Antipater. ◊ Epigram.

Antiphon (*c.* 480–411 B.C.). Athenian *logographos*. The earliest Greek professional speech-writer. He took no part in public life, never addressed the Assembly, and rarely appeared in court. Aristocratic in sympathies, he emerged in 411 as the chief organizer of the revolution of the Four Hundred. When the conspiracy collapsed the ringleaders fled, but three, including Antiphon, were tried and executed. Thucydides (VIII: 68) describes his defence as the finest ever heard from one facing a capital charge; unfortunately only a few brief fragments of it survive.

Three speeches are extant: *On the Murder of Herodes,* defending a Mytilenean accused of killing an Athenian; and two poisoning cases, *On the Choreutes* and *Against a Stepmother* (almost certainly authentic). Two of the lost speeches were on behalf of subject states against Athens; clearly Antiphon had little liking for Athenian democracy. Finally there are 3 tetralogies, rhetorical exercises each comprising 4 short speeches on the same imaginary homicide case; but language peculiarities make it hard to accept their attribution to Antiphon.

Archaic austerity of tone, vocabulary tinged with poeticisms, and periodic structure maintaining balance of thought, pattern, rhythm and sound, characterize Antiphon's style. His material is simply but powerfully deployed. He refuses to stoop to personalities, but is master of a dignified slow-moving eloquence, not always in keeping with the character of his client, but clearly impressive and effective in court. [D E W W]

Loeb: K. J. Maidment, *Minor Attic Orators,* i (1941).
Jebb, *A O,* i; Dobson, *G O.*

Antisthenes (*c.*443–*c.*366 B.C.). Athenian philosopher. A faithful follower of Socrates (he appears in the *Symposium* of Xenophon) and author of Socratic dialogues now lost. The titles of his works, as preserved by Diogenes Laertius, cover ethics, logic, politics and metaphysics, and he was interested in rhetoric and the interpretation of Homer. His writings were noted in antiquity for their literary merit. In his ascetic life he laid great emphasis on 'toil' – exemplified by such figures as Heracles and Cyrus – as the highway to virtue. As the author of Socratic dialogues stressing asceticism, he was the obvious choice for the first figure in that apostolic succession which later Stoics and Cynics invented to link themselves with Socrates. Hence the tradition of Antisthenes as the founder of ◊ Cynicism, a distinction probably belonging to Diogenes of Sinope. [D R D]

Fragments ed. A. W. Winckelmann (1842).
Dudley, *H C.*

Antonius, Marcus (143–87 B.C.). Roman orator and statesman. As praetor in 102 he defeated the pirates and annexed Cilicia. He became consul in 99, censor in 97, and supported the Senatorial party. He was put to death by Marius. He was grandfather of Mark Antony. With L. Licinius ◊ Crassus, Antonius raised Roman oratory to a level with that of the Greeks. His style was noted for its vigour and he posed as a man of little learning, though he had, in fact, a wide knowledge of Greek. He was greatly admired by Cicero. [T A D]

Cicero, *De oratore,* tr. E. W. Sutton and H. Rackham (Loeb, 1942).

Apicius. The name attached to the principal surviving Roman cookery book, which dates from the late Empire, though the proverbial gourmet of that name lived under Augustus. It gives a large number of recipes, both ordinary and exotic, and provides a practical handbook for savouring the Roman cuisine. [D R D]

Barbara Flower and E. Rosenbaum, *The Roman Cookery Book: A Critical Translation of the Art of Cooking for Use in the Study and Kitchen* (1958).

Apollodorus of Carystus (fl. *c.*285 B.C.). Greek poet of the New ◊ Comedy. From him Terence took his *Phormio* and *Hecyra.* Only fragments survive. [D R D]

Ed. A. Meineke, *Fragmenta comicorum graecorum,* iv.

Apollodorus of Gela (fl. *c.*315 B.C.). Greek poet of the New ◊ Comedy. He is to be distinguished from Apollodorus of Carystus. [D R D]

Ed. A. Meineke, *Fragmenta comicorum graecorum,* iv.

Apollonius of Tyana (1st cent. A.D.). Greek philosopher. A neo-Pythagorean sage and thaumaturge, whose supernatural powers included clairvoyance, knowledge of the language of birds and animals, and the 'understanding of tongues'. Born at Tyana in Cappadocia, he became a wandering holy man, visiting Persia, India and Egypt. He was in Rome in Nero's reign and again in Domitian's, when he became involved in the persecution of the philosophers. He died, in extreme old age, under Nerva (96–98), and was 'translated to Heaven'. A cult of Apollonius developed in Asia and Syria as a counterblast to Christianity; it was fostered by the Syrian dynasty in Rome, especially by the pietistic Empress Julia Domna, for whom ⇨ Philostratus wrote the *Life of Apollonius of Tyana*. He was attacked as a charlatan by ⇨ Lucian and ⇨ Eusebius. Some letters are attributed to him, on very doubtful grounds. [DRD]

Letters and *Life* in Loeb: *Philostratus*, ed. F. C. Conybeare (2 vols., 1912).

Apollonius Rhodius (*c.* 295 B.C.–after 247 B.C.). Alexandrian scholar and epic poet. Two ancient *Lives* of Apollonius are extant; between them they manage to throw almost every detail of his life into hopeless confusion. He was certainly sometime Librarian at the Museum in Alexandria, lived at Rhodes, and had a blazing personal and literary quarrel on the nature of poetry with ⇨ Callimachus, of which some records survive. Callimachus contended that epic poetry was wholly obsolete in the Hellenistic world. Apollonius tried to prove him wrong by a vast epic on the Argonauts, revealing deep familiarity with Homer, founded on long study and passionate admiration, and much learning of the Alexandrian kind, especially in mythology and geography. The result, 4 books of nearly 6,000 lines, is a medley. Judged as an epic, the *Argonautica* is a failure. It lacks unity; its hero lacks character; the action is always breaking down; and it cannot be read straight through. But there are many passages of interest, and one whole book (III) of high poetic quality. As with Ovid, Apollonius's gifts were for the portrayal of romantic love, especially from the woman's side. He gives a subtle and moving account of the young Medea's first passion for Jason. The contrast between the tender, sensitive Medea and the wooden Jason is striking. It was the most brilliant study of the moods of a woman in love in classical literature, until Virgil turned it into something greater with Dido. The Argo's return is of interest, though it (and its description!) is intolerably roundabout. For, with a unique knowledge of the waterways of Central Europe, Jason brings her back, with no portage overland, by the Danube, the Adriatic, the Po, the Rhône and the coasts of North Africa! [DRD]

OCT: H. F. Fränkel (1961); Loeb: R. C. Seaton (1912); comm. G. W. Mooney (1912); comm. M. R. Gillies (1928) (Book III); tr. E. V. Rieu (Penguin Classics, 1959).

Appendix Virgiliana. Suetonius and Servius mention the names of a number of poems said to be the *Juvenilia* of Virgil. About the question of their authenticity there has been much controversy, as a result of which few, if any, can now be accepted as Virgilian beyond doubt. The *Catalepton* ('Trifles') is a collection of 14 short poems, strongly influenced by Catullus. No. 5, a farewell to poetry by one embarking on the study of Epicureanism, may well be by Virgil as a student. The *Copa* ('The Barmaid') is a delightful genre poem, a perfect evocation of a hot summer's day, and the attraction to the traveller of the little inn and its charming hostess. The comment that it is 'too cheerful to be ascribed to Virgil' is not wholly convincing. The *Ciris* is a short epic (⇨ *Epyllion*) on the legend of Nisus and Scylla; it has been ascribed to Cornelius ⇨ Gallus. It was probably written shortly after Virgil's death. The *Culex* ('The Gnat') tells of the ungrateful shepherd, who, warned by the gnat's sting of the approach of a snake, kills them both. Later the gnat's ghost reproaches him with its fate. A silly theme, and a rather silly poem, it seems on stylistic grounds to belong to the Silver Age. The *Moretum* ('The Salad') has much merit; it describes with realism the household of a peasant and the preparation of his simple breakfast before he goes off to plough. The *Dirae* was probably associated with Virgil because it mentions the confiscation of land for veterans. The *Aetna*, a hexameter poem of some 600 lines, shows zeal for the study of nature. Its date and authorship have been much disputed; most likely it belongs to the early Silver Age, and it must be earlier than the eruption of Vesuvius in A.D. 79. [DRD]

Loeb: H. R. Fairclough, Virgil ii (1934); OCT: W. J. Clausen etc. (1966) (includes *Aetna*); *Aetna*, ed. F. D. R. Goodyear (1965). A. Rostagni, *Virgilio minore* (Turin, 1933).

Appian (fl. *c.* A.D. 140). Greek historian. Appian was a native of Alexandria who rose to a high position in his own country before coming to Rome. At Rome he was a barrister, probably attached to the Imperial treasury, and eventually became Procurator through the influence of Fronto, the tutor and friend of Marcus Aurelius.

Appian wrote a history of Rome from the arrival of Aeneas in Italy to the Battle of Actium (31 B.C.); the statement of Photius that he extended his work in summary form to the times of Trajan is probably incorrect. Appian did not follow the normal annalistic method of dealing with events year by year, but divided his work into books according to the locality of the events described. Thus there are 3 books dealing with the extension of Roman power throughout Italy (the Regal Period, the Italian Wars, and the Samnite Wars), 1 book dealing with the Gallic Wars from Brennus to Caesar, further books dealing with wars in Sicily and other islands, the Spanish Wars, the Hannibalic War, the Punic Wars, the Macedonian Wars, the Wars in Greece, the Syrian Wars, the Mithridatic Wars, the Illyrian Wars, and finally 5 books of Civil Wars, covering the period from the Gracchi to Actium. Some of these books, especially those dealing with the early period, survive only in excerpts made in the Middle Ages.

The value of Appian depends on the source that he is following for any particular period. For the Second Punic War, for example, he uses a very poor source, and his account is a combination of nationalistic fiction and gross inaccuracy. For the first half of the 2nd century B.C. he probably used ◊ Polybius, and his account of the Macedonian Wars and the Third Punic War is more reliable. For much of his book of Illyrian Wars he seems to have used the contemporary account of Octavian, while his first book of the Civil Wars, which covers a period for which there is no other continuous record, also seems to have been taken from a very good author. But even when he is using sound material, he often gravely distorts his narrative by condensation, and he is often guilty of serious omissions. [TAD]

Loeb: H. White (4 vols., 1912–13).

Apuleius, Lucius (?) (b. *c.* A.D. 127). Roman writer and orator. Born at Madaurus in Africa. The most interesting Latin writer of the age of the Antonines. Educated at Carthage and Athens, he lectured and travelled widely, and visited Rome. A trip to Oea (Tripoli) involved him in marriage with a wealthy widow, Pudentilla, and a complicated law-suit, in which he successfully defended himself against the charge of having won her by magic. His speech, the *Apologia*, is extant. But his fame rests on the *Metamorphoses* or *Golden Ass*, based apparently on a Greek story by Lucius of Patras, and the only Latin novel to survive entire. It describes how Lucius, a sorcerer's apprentice, is accidentally changed into an ass, the many adventures, reputable and otherwise, which he met, thus translated, and his final deliverance by the goddess Isis. It contains the wholly delightful tale of Cupid and Psyche; the scenes describing the mysteries of Isis are written in a Latin that is at once strange, beautiful and compelling. He is also the author of 3 minor philosophic works, and of the *Florida*, an anthology of passages from his speeches. [DRD]

Metamorphoses, ed. R. Helm (1931); tr. Robert Graves (Penguin Classics, 1950); *Apologia*, ed. H. E. Butler and A. S. Owen (1914); *Cupid and Psyche*, ed. L. C. Purser (1910).

Aratus (*c.* 315–240 B.C.). Greek scholar and poet. Author of the most widely read of Hellenistic didactic poems. Born at Soli in Cilicia, he studied Stoicism at Athens under ◊ Zeno, his fellow-countryman. Introduced (probably) by him to Antigonus Gonatas, he went to the Macedonian Court in 276. There, at the king's suggestion, he wrote his poem entitled *Phaenomena* ('Things Seen in the Sky'), which used the astronomical systems of Eudoxus of Cnidos for scientific background and ◊ Hesiod for a poetic model. It describes the constellations and recounts the legends associated with them, and then goes on to deal with weather signs. It was very popular in Hellenistic and, still more, in Roman times, being translated by Cicero, influencing Virgil and being quoted by St Paul. It was popular in the Renaissance, though little read now. Aratus spent some time at the Court of Antiochus I of Syria, where he is said to have edited the *Odyssey*, but he returned to Macedonia in his later years. [DRD]

Loeb: G. R. Mair, *Callimachus, Lycophron and Aratus* (1921).
W. W. Tarn, *Antigonus Gonatas* (1913).

Arcesilaus. ◊ Sceptics.

Archilochus (*c.* 680–*c.* 640 B.C.). Greek iambic and elegiac poet. Born in Paros. He was the bastard son of an aristocrat Telesicles and a slavewoman Enipo. Out of luck and money he moved to Thasos, but returned to Paros *c.* 650. His ruinous affair with Neobule, Lycambes' daughter, preceded the total eclipse of the sun in 648, which he describes. He died in battle. His surviving fragments show extreme metrical virtuosity. His subject-matter is equally varied. A mercenary, familiar with poverty and defeat, he has no romantic illusions about war, no qualms about jettisoning his shield. He turns a sharply satirical gaze on the world, and expresses what he sees and feels with unsurpassed vividness. Except in his elegies, where epic influence is strong, his vocabulary is colloquial, his dialect Ionic vernacular. He uses homely metaphors and recounts fables drawn from folk-tale, with echoes of camp-fire talk. He achieves a complete break with the objectivity, idealization, and aristocratic code of epic, freely expressing his own personality, critical of his own and others' weaknesses, judging men by what they are, not by what they profess to be. Antiquity recognized him as an explosively original genius; what little survives gives no cause to dispute that verdict. [D E W W]

Diehl, *A L G*, i.
A. Hauvette, *Archiloque* (1905); Bowra, *E G E.*

Archimedes (287–212 B.C.). Greek scientist. Born at Syracuse. Perhaps the greatest name in Greek science – certainly its greatest mathematician and physicist. After a period of research in Alexandria, he returned to Syracuse to become chief scientific adviser to King Hieron II. He was killed at the siege of Syracuse. His surviving works illustrate the range and depth of his interests. Those on mathematics include *On the Sphere and Cylinder, The Measurement of a Circle, On Spirals, On the Equilibrium of Plane Surfaces* and *The Sand-Reckoner.* This last deals with the problem of expressing very large numbers; it shows that the number of grains of sand in the universe, far from being infinite, may on certain assumptions be expressed as 10^{63}. His work *On Floating Bodies* laid the foundation of the science of hydrostatics. Much of his work was concerned with the problems of levers and their application: hence the siege-engines he built for the discomfiture of the Roman besiegers. His grasp of fundamental principles is expressed in the famous saying 'Give me a place to stand, and I will move the earth'. He also invented the water-screw, calculated the value of π to a very narrow margin, and constructed a planetarium, which still survived in the time of Cicero. [D R D]

Teubner: J. L. Heiberg (Leipzig, 1910–15); *The Works of Archimedes*, ed. and tr. T. L. Heath (1897).
Sarton, *H S*, ii.

Arctinus. ◊ Epic Cycle; *Titanomachia.*

Arion. ◊ Dithyramb.

Aristarchus (*c.* 217–*c.* 143 B.C.). Hellenistic grammarian. Born in Samothrace. Librarian at Alexandria (*c.* 160–145). He combined scientific method and intuition in the manner of all the great textual critics and was known as 'The Great Grammarian'. Much of his best work was done on Homer, whom he stoutly maintained to be the author of the *Iliad* and the *Odyssey.* Also wrote commentaries on Pindar, Aeschylus, Sophocles, Herodotus, etc. [D R D]

D. B. Munro, *Homer's Odyssey*, Appendix (1901).

Aristides, Aelius (A.D. 117 or 129–189). Greek orator. Aristides stands with ◊ Dio Chrysostom as the chief representatives of the 'Second Sophistic', a feature of the revival of Greek learning in the late 1st and 2nd centuries A.D. Educated in Pergamum and Athens, he lectured to large appreciative audiences in the chief intellectual centres of the Greek world, and was in Rome in 156. The great majority of the 55 orations that have been preserved are public addresses on ceremonial occasions. The best known of these is the famous *Speech to Rome*, an eloquent tribute to the mistress of the world from a Greek intellectual. There is also a fine eulogy of Athens. Another, supporting Smyrna's claims to pre-eminence among Asian cities, would do credit to any publicity bureau. His obsession with his own health caused him to say a good deal about the cult of Asclepius, and the various treatments prescribed for those who consulted the God. In his work form is invariably superior to content; but that is the defect of his times and class. [DRD]

Teubner: W. Schmid (Leipzig, 1926).
A. Boulanger, *Aelius Aristide et la sophistique dans la province d'Asie* (Paris, 1923).

Aristobulus (fl. *c.*320 B.C.). Greek historian. Officer who served under Alexander the Great and wrote a history of his campaigns that was used by ◊ Arrian and ◊ Strabo. [TAD]

Ariston. ◊ Zeno.

Aristophanes (*c.*450–*c.*385 B.C.). Greek comic poet. Little is known of his life. Though he came of an Athenian family his citizen status was questioned, probably because he lived in Aegina. He is not known to have held any public office at Athens, but clearly took a lively interest in contemporary politics and intellectual movements. Plato portrays him in the *Symposium* as a friend of Agathon, Alcibiades and Socrates, and a jovial and clear-headed drinking companion, whose wryly fantastic wit masks seriousness and compassion. He wrote some 40 plays, of which 11 are preserved, with titles and fragments of most of the rest. In his own day he seems to have been less popular than ◊ Cratinus and ◊ Eupolis, for he won considerably fewer prizes (only 3 are recorded); possibly his weakness was not so much in writing as in production. He did not produce his early plays personally, deterred, he says, by youthful diffidence; but he continued to have occasional comedies presented by others throughout his career.

The two earliest plays of Aristophanes, the *Banqueters* (427; placed second) and *Babylonians* (426), made his name as a comic poet, but have not survived. The *Banqueters* seems to have been a social satire, contrasting old and new fashions in education. The *Babylonians* was political, attacking the authorities and the demagogue Cleon, and ridiculing the demos for its gullibility in dealing with wily allies; it stung Cleon into denouncing the poet before the Athenian Council. The earliest extant comedy is the *Acharnians* (425), an anti-war play which won the prize. It concerns Dicaeopolis, a war-weary old countryman who obtains a private peace for himself. He meets opposition both from the chorus, belligerent old men from Acharnae, whom he wins over with an audacious speech in defence of the enemy, and from the war-mongering general Lamachus; but Lamachus is called out on frontier duty in the snow just as Dicaeopolis is invited to a public feast. The contrast is farcically emphasized, and the play ends with Lamachus returning wounded and half-frozen, and Dicaeopolis tipsy after winning a drinking competition.

With the *Knights* (424), the first play he produced in his own name, Aristophanes renewed his attack on Cleon and again won the prize. Here he depicts the demagogue as the rascally slave of Demos, a gullible old man who personifies Athenian democracy. Cleon dominates the whole household until the appearance of an even greater villain, a disreputable sausage-seller who brazenly outdoes him in all a demagogue's tricks. Cleon acknowledges defeat in tragic style, and the sausage-seller takes Demos in hand; he magically rejuvenates the old man behind the scenes, and leads him out in triumph, young and handsome as a bridegroom.

Famous as it now is, the *Clouds* was unsuccessful when produced in 423; the extant play is a revised version. The hero is Strepsiades, a simple-minded old countryman plagued with his son's extravagance. He decides to go to Socrates's school to learn how to make the worse argument appear the better, and so baffle his creditors; but after being initiated into the mysteries and absurdities of this bizarre establishment he is found excessively stupid and eventually expelled. He then sends his son, who proves so apt a pupil that he can soon justify beating his own father; and finally the exasperated Strepsiades and his slaves burn the school down.

The *Wasps,* placed second in 422, satirizes the Athenian system of trial by mass jury and the addiction of waspish old men like Philocleon ('Cleon-lover') to paid jury service. His son Bdelycleon ('Cleon-loather'), unable to cure him, shuts him up at home, and then gets him to try the family dog on a charge of cheese-stealing. The old man acquits the defendant by mistake, and faints from the shock. To console him Bdelycleon grooms him for smart society and takes him out; but he becomes drunk and disorderly, and ends the play by leading a wild dance. The *Wasps* was imitated by Racine in *Les plaideurs*.

The hope of an armistice inspired the *Peace* (placed second, 421), in which Trygaeus, an honest countryman rendered destitute by the war, flies up to heaven on a gigantic dung-beetle and finds that the gods have left in disgust and that War has hidden Peace in a pit and is about to pound the Greek cities up in a huge mortar. While War is looking for a pestle Trygaeus summons all good men to come and unearth Peace, who is hauled out of her pit with two beautiful handmaids. Trygaeus returns to earth, hands over one girl to the Athenian Council, and triumphantly prepares to marry the other, meanwhile dismissing several visitors with a vested interest in the war.

The *Birds* (placed second) was produced in 414, when the fate of the Sicilian expedition was still in the balance. It is an escapist fantasy in which two Athenians, Pisthetaerus and Euelpides, dissatisfied with Athens, go in search of somewhere better; they join forces with the birds, the original lords of creation, and build a new city, Cloudcuckooland, in mid-air. They soon dominate mankind, and by cutting off the nourishing steam of sacrifices force the gods to surrender Zeus's sceptre to the birds and his lovely colleague Basileia ('Sovereignty') as a bride for the exultant Pisthetaerus.

Produced in the aftermath of the Sicilian disaster, the *Lysistrata* (411) is a hilariously bawdy yet fundamentally serious play, depicting a revolt of women against war: on the initiative of Lysistrata of Athens their representatives meet and swear to refuse intercourse with men until peace is made, and simultaneously her followers seize the Acropolis. Despite some comic backsliding the women resist all the men's efforts to dislodge them, and an over-eager husband is artfully tantalized and left in acute frustration. Meanwhile consternation spreads throughout Greece, until envoys arrive from Sparta, a conference is held, and peace is made.

In the *Women at the Thesmophoria,* produced soon after the *Lysistrata,* Euripides learns that the women of Athens are planning revenge on him for blackening their character in his tragedies. When the effeminate Agathon refuses to go and defend him, an elderly relative, Mnesilochus, attends disguised as a woman, but tactlessly points out how much worse Euripides's aspersions might have been. Mnesilochus is detected and arrested, and Euripides makes farcically unsuccessful attempts to save him by re-enacting appropriate recognition and rescue scenes from his tragedies. Eventually the women agree to a truce, and Mnesilochus is released.

The hero of the *Frogs* (405) is Dionysus himself, who goes down to Hades disguised as Heracles to bring back a tragic poet; for with Euripides and Sophocles lately dead there are no good ones left at Athens. After many ludicrous alarms and adventures, in part occasioned by his disguise, he arrives at the palace of Pluto and there adjudicates in a poetic contest between Aeschylus, hitherto supreme, and Euripides, who is challenging his position. Despite his original partiality for Euripides, he decides in favour of Aeschylus and returns with him to the upper world. The parabasis of the play contains a moving appeal to the Athenians to close the ranks in the face of imminent disaster. The last and perhaps the finest extant example of Old ◊ Comedy, it won the prize and also the rare honour of a second performance.

With little personal satire, no parabasis, and the rest of the choral part considerably reduced, the last two surviving plays of Aristophanes mark the beginning of Middle ◊ Comedy. *Women in Parliament*, produced about 392, takes up ideas on communism and equality between the sexes soon to be given expression in Plato's *Republic,* and shows the women of Athens packing the Assembly, disguised as men, and voting themselves into power under their leader Praxagora. They introduce a new regime in which wives, children and property are to be held in common, and old women given priority in marriage; a romantic young man who comes to meet his sweetheart is accordingly pounced upon by three old hags claiming their rights; and finally a communal dinner is announced. The *Plutus* (388), a revised version of an earlier production, presents Plutus, the god of wealth, as a ragged, blind old man, exploited by rogues and terrorized by Zeus. The poor but honest hero Chremylus, who deplores seeing scoundrels prosper, befriends and encourages Plutus, and in spite of the protests of Poverty has his blindness cured at the temple of Asclepius.

Honest men are thereupon enriched; and the discomfiture of the dishonest, and even of the now disregarded gods, is farcically illustrated. Aristophanes composed two further comedies, now lost, but let his son Araros produce them. One, the *Cocalus,* anticipated ⇨ Menander in introducing a rape, a recognition and other stock incidents of New ⇨ Comedy; the other, the *Aeolosicon,* ridiculed contemporary tragedy and dispensed with choral songs and a parabasis.

The loss of the comedies so often judged superior to those of Aristophanes unfortunately precludes any effective comparison with his contemporaries; but as a leading poet who superseded Cratinus and out-lived Eupolis, and whose range of work extended from the maturity of Old Comedy to the beginnings of New, he must have exercised a major influence on the development of Greek comedy. In the parabasis of the *Clouds* he claims that his comedies were better than his rivals' in construction, variety and originality, with more wit, less slapstick and less obscenity. His comparative lack of success in competition suggests that he may sometimes have aimed too high for his public. His comedies, belonging to a traditional but still evolving genre, contain many recurrent elements in structure and in plot, without conforming to any set pattern. In the *Lysistrata* and *Frogs* there are two choruses instead of one; in the latest plays the chorus's part becomes nominal. After the *Peace* of 421 the undramatic parabasis is made dramatic by allowing the chorus to speak in character, or omitted; but the *Frogs* of 405 has an old-style parabasis and seems, like the *Bacchants* of Euripides, to have reverted to type for a special occasion. For each of his plots – 'all different, and all clever' – Aristophanes conceived a separate satiric fantasy based on contemporary life, and developed it with an astonishing fertility of invention. His satire is largely political in the earlier plays, but after the oligarchic revolution of 411 it turns to literature, philosophy and finally mild social criticism; the first pair of romantic young lovers, precursors of New Comedy, appear early in the 4th century, in the *Women in Parliament.* There was no revolution in Greek comedy during Aristophanes' career, but rather a gradual loss or domestication of its disorderly, fantastic nature.

Brilliant in realistic dialogue, Aristophanes can command almost any other style at will – rhetorical, legal, hieratic, epic, tragic or lyric. As a lyric poet he can match, in a lighter vein, the beauties of tragedy, achieving a particularly haunting charm in the *Clouds* and *Birds.* His favourite character seems to be an elderly Athenian with a rustic blend of simplicity and shrewdness, an earthy, amiable fool who yet comes out on top in his absurd adventures; but like the other Aristophanic characters, this hero is a type, not an individual. Indecency abounds in Old Comedy as a natural and even necessary part of the original fertility ritual. Aristophanes exploits it frankly, and even with gusto, but is not preoccupied with it; in time he toned down the worst excesses, if only because they were a feeble form of humour. His wit operates at every level from the crudest to the most sophisticated. He is a master of verbal jokes and comic situations, but much of the humour of characterization necessarily escapes him. His satire, vigorous rather than savage, embraces gods and men, things old and new. He saw himself wielding it like a poetic Heracles, to rid his country of pests and monsters; but the only lasting results of his labours seem to have been the caricature of Socrates in the *Clouds* and a famous catch-phrase from the *Frogs.*

At once conservative and critical by temperament, Aristophanes admired a past when life was simpler and more honest, and distrusted modernity. His political sympathies were with the aristocratic landowners and country folk, who wanted to live in peace; he opposed the demagogues and their war policy, and without disapproving of the principle of democracy deplored its contemporary perversions. Innovations in music, drama and philosophy provided him with abundant comic material; but his friendship with Agathon, Socrates and Plato, and his love-hate relationship with Euripides, whom he cannot refrain from quoting, make it uncertain how far he was personally hostile to much of what he mocked. His impartial ridicule of both gods and atheists suggests no very profound concern with religion; what does emerge from his comedies is his genial sympathy with ordinary human nature. (⇨ Comedy, Greek.) [G T W H]

O C T (with fragments): F. W. Hall and W. M. Geldart (2 vols., 1906, 1907). Commentaries: B. B. Rogers (1902–16); *Frogs*, W. B. Stanford 1958); *Peace*, M. Platnauer (1964). Translations: Loeb, B. B. Rogers (1924); D. Barrett (Penguin Classics, 3 plays, 1964); P. Dickinson, *Aristophanes against War* (3 plays, 1957); W. Arrowsmith (ed.), *The Complete Greek Comedy* (1961–); Edmonds, *F A C*, i.

G. Murray, *Aristophanes* (1933); V. Ehrenberg, *The People of Aristophanes* (1962); C. H. Whitman, *Aristophanes and the Comic Hero* (Cambridge, Mass., 1964).

Aristophanes of Byzantium (*c.* 257–180 B.C.). Alexandrian scholar. Head of Library in 191 B.C. Perhaps the most distinguished product of Alexandria in the humanities, he was so esteemed by Ptolemy Epiphanes that he was put in prison to prevent him from accepting an invitation to the Library at Pergamum. He produced editions of Homer, Hesiod, Pindar, Alcaeus, Euripides and Plato, and the first critical edition of Aristophanes. He also worked out a system for the punctuation and annotation of texts, and compiled a Greek lexicon. His lists of the best authors greatly influenced Hellenistic literary canons, and indeed helped to formulate the whole concept of 'classical' authors. [D R D]

F. G. Kenyon, *Books and Readers in Ancient Greece and Rome* (1931).

Aristotle (384–322 B.C.). Greek philosopher and scientist. He was born at Stagira in Thrace; his father Nicomachus had been court physician to Amyntas II, King of Macedon. His parents died when he was young, and at 17 he went to Athens to study at the Academy under Plato. From then there are three periods in his life. First, 20 years at the Academy, ended by Plato's death – sufficient to refute the stories of estrangement between the two, which are no more than gossip. But probably Aristotle was out of sympathy with the increasing ascendancy of mathematics in the Academy: when one of that group, Speusippus, was elected to succeed Plato, he may have felt it time to go. There followed a period of travel. First, with fellow-students, he set up a kind of breakaway Academy at Assos in Asia Minor, then under the rule of a former Academic, Hermeias. Here Aristotle found a wife in Pythias, daughter of Hermeias; he may also have become interested in politics, for the philosophers were called in to advise the ruler, and Jaeger claims that the project which Plato had failed to carry through in Sicily was here realized in miniature. Aristotle did not stay long in the Troad: in 344 he accepted an invitation from ⇨ Theophrastus to visit Lesbos, where there were excellent facilities for marine biology. A major commission came his way in 342, as tutor to the young prince Alexander at the Macedonian court at Pella. Posterity has over-dramatized the contact of the great philosopher with the greatest of kings: for both, their real work was to come. But Aristotle will have taught Alexander Homer, and politics; he may have imbued him with his own anti-Persian sentiments, evoked by the cruel death of his friend Hermeias at Persian hands. It is uncertain whether he saw much of Alexander after he became regent in 340; but even after Alexander left for the east in 334 contact was not wholly lost, and scientific specimens were sent back to Aristotle as the expedition crossed Central Asia to India.

In 335 Aristotle returned to Athens, where the pro-Macedonian party was in the ascendant, for his most fruitful years. He rented a property near the grove of Apollo Lyceius for the great institute which he intended to establish in the intellectual capital of the world. Hence the name Lyceum (the other name, the Peripatetic School, came from the covered courtyard or *peripatos*). Clearly, the Lyceum derives from the Academy, but its broader programme reflects the more catholic interests of Aristotle. Something is known of its organization and methods. There was a library, a museum and a map collection. Research students came from many parts of the Greek world to work on the projects which Aristotle directed. His own formal lectures for Lyceum students were given in the mornings; in the afternoons there were extension courses for a wider public. These were years of high achievement. But Alexander died in 323, and the nationalist party revived. Aristotle thought it wiser to leave Athens. He retired to Chalcis, where he died within a year. His will survives; a grave excavated in 1890 at Eretria may just possibly be his.

The long list of titles, known or ascribed, comprises the following: (1) works addressed to a general audience, many in dialogue form and bearing Platonic titles and therefore to be dated to his term at the Academy. None has survived, but substantial parts of the best known, the *Protrepticus*, have been preserved by Cicero and Iamblichus; (2) collections of research materials, e.g. the *Customs of the Barbarians*, or the 158 *Constitutions of Cities*. Of all this, only the *Constitution of Athens* survives; (3) the Aristotelian *corpus* in the form in which it has reached us, i.e. works on a wide range of scientific and philosophical topics whose style shows that they were not works of literature meant for publication, but notes or outlines for lectures. It is no longer thought that they all belong to the Lyceum period: the *Organon*, *Physics*, *Eudemian Ethics*, *De anima* and part of the *Metaphysics*, *Politics*, and *Historia animalium* are now dated 347–335. They fall into groups that cover these fields of knowledge: Logic and Analysis, Physics, Biology, Metaphysics, Ethics, Politics and Literature. Only the most important individual works can be named. The *Organon* is the great treatise on logic that dominated the later Middle Ages. The *Physics* deals with problems of natural philosophy – matter, movement, time, place – and sets out the doctrine of the four causes of physical change, the material, the formal, the efficient, and the final cause. Much of his finest work was done in biology, and the treatise *Historia animalium*, as well as special studies such as the *De partibus animalium* and *De generatione*, were greatly admired by Darwin. Closely associated with these is the *De anima*; its treatment of sensation, thought, imagination and reason makes it the first definitive work on psychology. All these studies of the world of nature led on, for Aristotle, to the *Metaphysics*, the study of the 'real as such', the highest rungs of the great ladder of nature, culminating in Theology or the study of God. The chief sciences concerned with man are Ethics and Politics. The 10 books of the *Nicomachean Ethics* contain Aristotle's most mature thought on this topic. The *Politics* (8 books) is the last great work of Greek political thought, although the institution which had produced it, the Greek city-state, was already obsolescent. But some of its conclusions are valid in any society, such as the proposition that 'men came together into cities for the sake of life: they continue for the sake of the good life'. Two important works deal with oratory and literature: the *Rhetoric* is an analysis of the art of persuasion; the *Poetics* of epic and tragedy. The latter is a classic of literary criticism. If its influence has at times been cramping, this is due to the tendencies of critics – especially in France – to read universal principles into observations that relate to one form of literature at one period of time.

This whole *corpus* was bequeathed to ⇨Theophrastus after Aristotle's death. It was lost – or hidden – for nearly two centuries, then sold and badly edited; finally it was rescued by Sulla, who brought it to Rome – one of his most enduring acts. The editions on which ours are based were made in Rome late in the 1st century B.C. So the popular works have gone, and we must judge Aristotle on his technical writings – the opposite of what happened with Plato. A further divergence is one of outlook. Plato's mathematical interests led him to the search for universals and to withdrawal from the visible world. Aristotle, as a biologist, saw reality in the particular, and his care was ever to 'save the phenomena'. Where Plato excelled in bold speculation and imaginative insight, Aristotle's gifts were for classification and order. He could codify anything, even the philosophy of Plato.

Only the briefest mention can be made of his influence. The work of generations of commentators, Greek, Latin and Arabic, transformed his philosophy into the closed, authoritarian system that dominated the later Middle Ages. When St Thomas Aquinas reconciled Christian doctrine and Aristotelian philosophy, it was thought to be the ultimate synthesis of human knowledge. The inevitable challenge came with the Renaissance. If much of the scientific knowledge of the last 400 years appears as a struggle against Aristotle, it is an ironic fate to have overtaken the work of one of the greatest creative minds of antiquity. There were, of course, limits to his genius. Neither his mathematics nor his astronomy was of a high order. But no mind of comparable range has appeared since, save that of Leonardo da Vinci. Now that knowledge has become so specialized, there will be no other.

Philosophy, theology and indeed scientific and intellectual thought in general owe to Aristotle most of their vocabulary and many of the distinctions with which they operate. (⇨ Literary Criticism.) [D R D]

OCT: *Ars rhetorica*, W. D. Ross (1959); *Atheniensium respublica*, F. G. Kenyon (1920); *Categoriae et Liber de interpretatione*, L. Minio-Paluello (1949); *De anima*, W. D. Ross (1956); *De arte poetica*, I. Bywater (1911); *De caelo*, D. J. Allan (1936); *Ethica nicomachea*, I. Bywater (1849); *Fragmenta selecta*, W. D. Ross (1955); *Metaphysica*, W. Jaeger (1957); *Physica*, W. D. Ross (1950); *Politica*, W. D. Ross (1957); *Topica et Sophistici elenchi*, W. D. Ross (1958). Other texts: *Metaphysics*, ed. W. D. Ross (2 vols., 1924); *On Coming-to-be and Passing-Away*, ed. H. H. Joachim (1922); *Constitution of Athens*, ed. J. E. Sandys (1912). Translations: *The Oxford Translation of Aristotle*, ed. J. A. Smith and W. D. Ross (12 vols., 1908–31); Loeb (25 vols.); *The Ethics*, tr. J. A. K. Thomson (Penguin Classics, 1953); *The Politics*, tr. J. A. Sinclair (Penguin Classics, 1962); *On the Art of Poetry*, tr. Lane Cooper (Cornell, 1962).

Werner Jaeger, *Aristotle* (paperback edn, 1954); W. D. Ross, *Aristotle* (2nd edn, 1930); D. J. Allan, *The Philosophy of Aristotle* (1952).

Arnobius (fl. A.D. 327). Pagan rhetorician who turned Christian. Born at Sicca in Numidia. His book *Adversus nationes* (*c.*305) is a violent attack on pagan beliefs and customs, in the ornate Latin characteristic of African prose writers. In Lucretius he finds a ready weapon to hand. Some valuable material on early Roman religion probably derives from ⇨ Varro. [D R D]

Ed. C. Marchesi (Turin, 1934).

Arrian (Flavius Arrianus) (2nd cent. A.D.). Greek historian. Born at Nicomedia in Bithynia. In his youth he was a pupil and friend of the Stoic philosopher Epictetus. He entered public life at Rome, became Consul, and was appointed by Hadrian as governor of Cappadocia, a unique distinction for a Greek. He seems to have been a man of considerable military experience, and defeated the Alani when they tried to invade his province. He subsequently lived for some years at Athens, where he was appointed Archon, and finally retired to Nicomedia to write.

Arrian wrote books on hunting, tactics and military history, a description of the coast of the Black Sea, some biographies, and an account of the wars that followed the death of Alexander the Great. But his importance rests on two works of totally dissimilar types. He had made notes of the teachings of Epictetus, and wrote them up and published them in 8 books of *Dissertations*, of which 4 survive; he later produced a condensed version of the *Dissertations*, entitled the *Encheiridion* (*Handbook*). Secondly he wrote a history of the campaigns of Alexander the Great, the *Anabasis*, in 8 volumes, of particular value because Arrian based it on the first-hand contemporary accounts of ⇨ Ptolemy and ⇨ Aristobulus and he showed considerable critical judgement in evaluating his material. The last book is also called the *Indica*, and is an account of the peoples of India, based on Megasthenes, a Greek who had visited India *c.*300 B.C.; it also describes the voyage of the Macedonian fleet from the Indus to Susa, using mainly the report of ⇨ Nearchus. [T A D]

Loeb: E. I. Robson, *History of Alexander and Indica* (2 vols., 1929); *The Life of Alexander the Great*, tr. A. de Sélincourt (Penguin Classics, 1958).

Asclepiades (fl. *c.*270 B.C.). Greek epigrammatist. Born on Samos. Leader of a group including Posidippus and Hedylus which by its sensibility and accomplishment breathed new life into the epigram, he was in touch with his contemporaries of the Coan school, and Theocritus (7, 40) pays tribute to him, under his pen-name Sicelidas, along with ⇨ Philetas. Some 40 epigrams ascribed to him survive in the Greek ⇨ Anthology, though several have double attribution and are of doubtful authenticity. He sings of love and wine with a limpid economy of means, an imaginative brilliance, and an unsurpassed feeling for the rhythmic and musical potentialities of the elegiac couplet. It is the art of the impressionistic miniature, but flawless of its kind. Callimachus (with whom he had critical controversy) and Dioscorides are deeply in his debt. The Asclepiadean metre, named after him, shows that he also wrote lyric – perhaps in the same genre as Theocritus 29 and 30. [D E W W]

Loeb: W. R. Paton, *The Greek Anthology* (5 vols., 1916–18); *The Greek Anthology. Hellenistic Epigrams*, ed. A. S. F. Gow and D. L. Page (1965).

Asellio, Sempronius (fl. *c.* 100 B.C.). Roman historian. He served as military tribune under Scipio at Numantia in 134 B.C. He wrote a history of his own times, probably from *c.* 150 to 90 B.C. He drew a clear distinction between the annals, which merely record events year by year, and history, which explains the causes of events and the motives of participants, and aims at influencing its readers morally. [T A D]

Peter, *H R R*, i.

Atellan Farce. *Fabula atellana,* an improvised Italian sketch performed by grotesquely masked players. Developed early among the Oscans of Campania, it became popular with amateur performers in Rome about the end of the 3rd century B.C. It appeared in a more sophisticated form under the late Republic, with written plot and professional performers, but retained a rustic coarseness of language and incident. The stock characters were Maccus and Bucco, two fools; Pappus, a ridiculous old man; and Dossennus, a wily hunchback, possibly indentical with Manducus, a glutton with great gaping jaws and clashing teeth. Under the Empire, despite a brief revival, it was eclipsed by pantomime. (⇨ Comedy, Roman; Mime.) [G T W H]

Fabularum atellanarum fragmenta, ed. P. Frassinetti (Turin, 1955).
Beare, *R S.*

Athanasius (A.D. 295–373). Greek Christian writer. Born at Alexandria, Athanasius was present at the Council of Nicaea in 325 and became bishop of his native city in 328. His stormy career was mainly occupied with his struggle against the Arians, who denied the divinity of Christ, in the course of which he was repeatedly exiled, only the concluding seven years of his life being spent in comparative peace. Most of his writings are concerned with his defence of the faith of Nicaea; his style is clear and simple but is marred by a lack of arrangement of material and by diffusiveness. His study of *The Incarnation of the Word of God* remains a classic of its kind, while in his *Life of Antony* he created a new biographical form that served as a model for later Greek and Latin hagiographers. [D R D]

Migne, *P G*, 25–28; *The Incarnation of the Word of God,* tr. a religious of the C.S.M.V. (1944); *Life of Antony,* tr. R. T. Meyer (A C W, 1950).
J. Quasten, *Patrology*, iii (1960).

Athenaeus (? early third cent. A.D.). Greek writer. Author of the *Deipnosophistae* ('Learned Dining-Club'). Nothing is known of him except that he came from Naucratis in Egypt, and the inference that he wrote later than the reign of Commodus, which would put him in the early 3rd century A.D. His book stands in a tradition of literary banquets which derive from the *Symposium* of Plato. But, lacking Plato's realism, Athenaeus makes his inordinate meal extend through several days and over some 30 books (15 even in the abridged form which survives). The learned company discuss with unflagging zeal a wide range of topics, especially those to do with banquets. Like that other great miscellany, Pliny's *Natural History,* the book is often fascinating in detail, but it is indigestible at length. Its value lies in the preservation of much out-of-the-way information, besides substantial fragments of lost authors, notably of the Middle and New Comedy. [D R D]

Loeb: C. B. Gulick (7 vols., 1927–41).

Atomists. The Atomic theory, the greatest intellectual achievement of pre-Socratic thought, was the work of Leucippus (fl. *c.* 440 B.C.) and Democritus (*c.* 460–*c.* 370 B.C.). Ancient authorities usually mention them together; modern scholarship has tried to distinguish their contributions, ascribing to Leucippus, in reaction against the views of ⇨ Parmenides, the fundamentals of the theory, to Democritus its elaboration and extension. Very little is known of the life of Leucippus. He was probably born at Miletus, and visited Elea; whether he worked with Democritus is uncertain. He is credited with 2 books, *The Great World-System* and *On Mind*, of which only one authentic fragment survives. Democritus is better attested. Born at Abdera in Thrace, he spent his considerable fortune on travel and research, visiting Egypt, Babylon, Persia and perhaps India. On his return to Greece he set up a philosophical school at Abdera. A list in Diogenes Laertius (IX: 46) credits him with 70 books, covering physics, logic, mathematics and astronomy, of which some 200 fragments survive.

In the Atomic theory, the universe contains only atoms and space. Atoms are infinite in number, indestructible, indivisible and solid. Different combinations of atoms make up all the phenomena of the world shown by our senses. The processes of nature are mechanical and determinist; there is no providence, no creation. The theory was taken up by ◊ Epicurus to provide the scientific basis of a comprehensive system of philosophy. [D R D]

Diels, *F V*, 68.
C. Bailey, *The Greek Atomists and Epicurus* (1928).

Atthis. The Atthis was the collective name given by Alexandrine scholars to a series of histories of Athens written in the 4th and 3rd centuries B.C. They were based on a chronological framework supplied, where possible, by a yearly list of magistrates, and contained considerable information about the mythology and very early history of Attica, as well as many details about religious cults. They all seem to have been independent works, covering the whole span of history and pre-history down to the writer's own times.

The Atthidographers, as they were called, included ◊ Cleidemus, ◊ Androtion, Demon, Philochorus, Phanodemus, Melanthius, Amelesagoras and Ister, though the last-named did not write a true Atthis but a compilation from the mythological sections of his predecessors' works. Most took an active part in Athenian political life, or held important priesthoods. [T A D]

F. Jacoby, *Atthis* (1949).

Attic Orators. The canonical 10 classical Attic orators were: ◊ Antiphon, ◊ Andocides, ◊ Lysias, ◊ Isocrates, ◊ Isaeus, Lycurgus, ◊ Aeschines, ◊ Demosthenes, ◊ Hypereides and Dinarchus. It is uncertain who first compiled this list, but it bears the hall-mark of Alexandrian criticism. We have no grounds for challenging the critic's choice. Plaintiff and defendant in an Athenian court of law nominally conducted their own cases; in reality they pronounced a speech composed for them by a professional *logographos*. It cannot have been easy to strike a mean between subtlety in argument and an approach in conformity with the client's personality, the first appealing to the jury's intellect, the second to its sense of dramatic appropriateness. The first generally prevails over the second, but the ablest orators combine the two. Private and public speeches alike tend to obscure the issue by calumniating the other side, and by emotional appeals, to an extent that would not be tolerated today. In political oratory, speeches were written in advance and committed to memory. Thus the text of Demosthenes' addresses to the Athenian assembly, though doubtless revised, reproduces substantially the actual words of the orator. This made for subtlety and elaboration of style and prose-rhythm, but must have meant a loss in spontaneity and in closeness of sympathy between speaker and audience. [D E W W]

Jebb, *A O*; Dobson, *G O*.

Atticus, Titus Pomponius (109–32 B.C.). Roman man of letters. He was the intimate friend of Cicero. He spent much of his life in Greece, practised strict neutrality in politics, and was on friendly terms with members of all parties. In the struggles that followed Caesar's death, he gave shelter and protection to people on both sides. He was an important banker and publisher. He worked out and published an accurate chronology of Rome, dating the foundation to 753 B.C. Also wrote a number of family histories, and an account of Cicero's consulship. [T A D]

Loeb: Nepos, *Life of Atticus*, J. C. Rolfe (1929); Loeb: Cicero, *Letters to Atticus*, E. O. Winstedt (1912).

Attius. ◊ Accius, Lucius.

Aufidius Bassus (fl. 1st cent. A.D.). Roman historian. Debarred from public life by weak health, he wrote a *History of the German War*, probably covering the period down to the triumph of Germanicus in A.D. 17, and also a *History of Rome* that included the death of Cicero and probably ended in A.D. 31. His style is somewhat artificial, but he is praised by Quintilian, and his work was used by the 6th-century epitomizer Cassiodorus. [T A D]

Peter, *H R R*, ii.

Augustine, Saint (Augustinus, Aurelius) (A.D. 354–430). Christian Latin writer. Augustine was born at Tagaste in Numidia, his father, Patricius, being a municipal official and a convert only late in life to Christianity, unlike his mother, Monica, who was a devout believer. In his *Confessions*, written 397–401, Augustine has described his intellectual and moral development from earliest childhood to his mother's death in 387. A literary masterpiece and something new in the history of Christian writing, it records his education first in his native town and then at Carthage (371). Soon after his arrival at the university, he contracted a liaison which lasted for some 12 years and gave him a son, Adeodatus. In 373 Augustine read Cicero's *Hortensius*, which made him long for 'an immortality of wisdom', and, attracted by the rational claims of the Manichees, he joined their sect. Returning to Tagaste, 375, he set up as a teacher of rhetoric, soon removing back to Carthage in the same capacity.

Augustine's growing doubts concerning the truth of Manicheism reached a climax in 383 when he met one of their leaders, Faustus of Milevi, whom he found to be eloquent but ignorant. No final breach took place immediately and he remained in touch with the Manichees after he had gone to Rome in 383. A year later he was appointed to a chair of rhetoric at Milan, where he came under the influence of Ambrose, being profoundly impressed by the bishop's exposition of the scriptures. Augustine's intellectual development was further stimulated by his introduction to neo-Platonic thought, and in 385 he decided to become a Christian, retiring to Cassiciacum, a friend's estate near the city, to prepare for baptism.

It was here that Augustine wrote 4 philosophical works, of which *Against the Academics*, an attack upon the scepticism of the new academicians, reveals his conviction of the knowability of truth. Baptized on 24 April 387, Augustine set out for home only to stay a further year in Rome, delayed by his mother's death. During this time he wrote another philosophical treatise, *On the Greatness of the Soul*, to prove the soul's immortality, and continued work on an anti-Manichean study, the first of several he was to publish over the next decade. These included *On Free Will* and the 33 books *Against Faustus the Manichee*, and sought to refute the Manichean dualism, establish that evil is a negation and demonstrate that the Old and New Testaments are not contradictory.

By the autumn of 388 Augustine was back in Tagaste, where he lived in monastic retirement for some three years, until ordained priest by bishop Valerius of Hippo, becoming his co-adjutor in 395 and soon succeeding him. Augustine continued the monastic community life with his clergy and became a zealous preacher, but above all an untiring literary protagonist. The struggle with Manicheism persisted, and as late as 404 he had a public disputation with one Felix, publishing the acts in 2 books. Meanwhile the Donatist controversy occupied him and in another spate of treatises, mainly in 400–6, he endeavoured to show the errors of this schismatic group, which maintained that the efficacy of a sacrament depends upon the personal worthiness of its minister and that the Catholic ministry had been irretrievably compromised by defections in its ranks during the Diocletian persecution. In *On Baptism Against the Donatists* (7 books, 400–1) Augustine argued powerfully for his understanding of the sacraments, and in *Against the Letter of Parmenianus* he gave his version of the schism to show that if the Catholic party was compromised, so was the Donatist.

The year 412 saw the publication of Augustine's first writing against Pelagius, who was asserting that human perfection is attainable without the assistance of divine grace. *On the Spirit and the Letter*, his second anti-Pelagian tract, was Augustine's answer in the form of a careful and profound study of the meaning of grace. *On the Grace of Christ and on Original Sin* reveals by its title the scope of its contents, as does *On Grace and Free Will* (427), an answer to the questioning of some monks of Hadrumetum, which was the prelude to the semi-Pelagian controversy.

While Augustine's dogmatic-polemical works fall into clearly defined periods, his other writings span his whole life, some of them taking many years to complete. *On the Trinity* (399–419) crystallized western teaching on the subject and sought to penetrate the mystery intellectually by a series of analogies, above all those of the human mind. *City of God* (published in instalments, 413–26) was an apology against the revived charge, consequent upon Alaric's capture of Rome, that Christianity was responsible for the misfortunes of the Roman Empire. It contains the first outline of a theology of history, in terms of the struggle between faith and unbelief – the two cities – and its basic ideas largely determined the Church's politics in the Middle Ages.

Augustine's biblical writings include *On Christian Learning* (mostly written 396–7, completed 426) which set out the requirements for the fruitful study of the Bible and attempted a synthesis between Christian and ancient learning. Many of those treatises relating to the books of the Bible were originally in the form of homilies; such were his *Sermons on the Psalms* and his tractates on the fourth Gospel. His sermons (some 400) were taken down by stenographers and are notable for their compactness, logic and simplicity. His letters deal with philosophical and theological problems, but some contain pastoral advice and convey solace in trial or misfortune.

By 427, Augustine claimed he had written 93 literary works and 232 books, and only 10 of those that he discusses in his *Retractions* have been lost; nor does this list include sermons and letters. This vast output reveals Augustine to be a master of the written and spoken word, capable both of polished diction, using all the rhetorical devices, and of vulgar speech, when he wished to be understood by the common people. His versatility as a stylist is only matched by the breadth of his interests that show a mind remarkable for logical acuteness and speculative depth. His originality is unquestionable, his influence on later thought inestimable. [J G D]

Migne, *P G*, 32–47; Teubner: *Confessions*, F. Skutella (1934); Translations: *Confessions*, R. S. Pine-Coffin (Penguin Classics, 1961); *Against the Academics*, J. J. O'Meara (A C W, 1951); *On the Greatness of the Soul*, Joseph M. Colleran (A C W, 1950); *On Free Will*, Dom Mark Pontifex (A C W, 1955); *Against Faustus the Manichee*, R. Sthoert (1872); *On Baptism against Donatus*, J. R. King (1872); *On the Spirit and the Letter*, W. J. Sparrow Simpson (1925); *On Grace and Free Will*, M. Dods (1934); *On the Trinity*, John Burnaby (L C C, 1955); *City of God*, M. Dods (1934); *On Christian Learning*, J. F. Shaw (1883); *Sermons on the Psalms*, S. Hebgin and F. Corrigan (A C W, 1960–1); *Letters*, M. Dods (2 vols., 1872).

Ed. Thomas F. Burns, *A Monument to St Augustine* (1930); F. van der Meer, *Augustine the Bishop* (1961).

Augustus (Gaius Octavius) (63 B.C.–A.D. 14). Roman Emperor (31 B.C.–A.D. 14). It is no accident that attaches the name of Augustus to the greatest period of Latin literature. More than any other Emperor, he won the support of poets and writers for his policy. An imperial patron, at the head of a regime dedicated to peace and reform, he opened new vistas for the destiny of Rome and her work in the world. He could discern and foster talent, and, in his best days, as the central figure of a circle which included such patrons as Pollio and Maecenas, such writers as Virgil, Horace, Propertius and Livy, gave it a fair measure of independence. Later, Ovid was to strain his tolerance beyond its limits.

The customary education of the young Roman aristocrat had given him a lucid oratorical style, and the ability to write. Of his lost works we should mention (1) the *Commentaries*, dedicated to Agrippa and Maecenas, a work of apology which recounted the story of his own life to 24 B.C., (2) the *Life of Drusus* (? 8 B.C.), (3) a tragedy (? unfinished) called *Ajax*, and (4) a hexameter poem *Sicily*, dealing presumably with the history and geography of the island.

His surviving work is the *Res gestae* or *Monumentum ancyranum*, so called from the inscription discovered at Ancyra (Ankara) in 1553, which gives the Latin text and a Greek translation. Composed to be affixed to the Mausoleum in the Campus Martius, and probably reproduced in all the principal cities in the provinces, it is one of the most important political documents of antiquity – being Augustus's own account of his long stewardship for the Roman People. [D R D]

Ed. and comm. E. G. Hardy (1923); Loeb: F. W. Shipley (1924) (with Velleius Paterculus).
Bardon, *E L L*.

Aurelius, Antoninus Marcus (A.D. 121–180). Roman emperor and Stoic philosopher. Son of Annius Verus, he came from an aristocratic family long established in Spain. Marcus was early picked out by his fellow-countryman, the Emperor Hadrian, as a possible future ruler for the Roman world. His education was carefully planned and entrusted to the best professors of literature, rhetoric and philosophy. Some details have been preserved in his correspondence with ◊ Fronto. From his early twenties, he deserted other studies for philosophy; Stoicism, as preached and practised by ◊ Epictetus, was henceforth to dominate his life. In 138 he was adopted by Antoninus Pius, who treated him as a confidant and helper throughout his reign. When Marcus succeeded in 161, it seemed that the Roman world was to enjoy the blessings Plato foresaw for the State where philosophers are kings. In fact, his reign was marked by lamentable disasters on a scale unknown for centuries. There was war with Parthia, and the victories won by the great general Avidius Cassius were cancelled by an epidemic of the plague which his armies brought back from the East. In the north, a confederation of barbarians swamped the Roman defences on the Danube in 166. For 13 years all Marcus's energies were absorbed into pushing them back and establishing a better frontier. Success was in his grasp when Avidius Cassius rebelled (175). He set to work again, and had come close to completing his grand design when he died of fever in the camp at Vindobona (Vienna). His gains were thrown away by his worthless successor Commodus.

His *Meditations,* in Greek, in 12 books, were written in army camps; thus Book I is headed 'This among the Quadi on the Gran', Book II 'Written at Carnuntum'. They are not a systematic exposition of Stoicism, but the self-communings of a lonely man bearing a terrible burden, trying to bring philosophy to bear to help him in his duty 'as a man, a Roman, and an Emperor'. 'Say to yourself each morning "Today I shall meet the officious, the thankless, the overbearing, the treacherous, the envious, the selfish. All this has happened to them because they do not know the difference between good and bad."' He returns again and again to certain themes: an absolute trust, which he learned from Epictetus, in Providence; a reverence for Reason, our ruling principle and an emanation from God; the example of Antoninus in the discharge of imperial duties (I:16; VI:30); a sense of the insignificance of all human affairs before the immensities of time and space (IV:32; VI:36).

The Life of Marcus in the ◊ *Historia Augusta* contains useful facts but adds nothing to the understanding of his inner life. But from the *Meditations,* and from two Roman monuments, the column which commemorates his victories in the Marcomannic Wars and the equestrian statue on the Capitol, it is possible to form some idea of the personality of this remarkable man. [D R D]

Loeb: C. R. Haines (1915); ed., tr. and comm. A. S. L. Farquharson (2 vols., 1944).

Aurelius Victor, Sextus (fl. A.D. 389). Roman historian. Governor of Pannonia 361, Praefectus Urbi 389. He wrote *Lives of the Caesars,* modelled on Suetonius, covering the period from Augustus to Constantius II. This work is combined with the *Origo gentis romanae* and *De viris illustribus* in the *Historia tripertita.* [T A D]

Teubner: R. Gruendel (Leipzig, 1961).

Ausonius, Decimus Magnus (d. probably *c.* A.D. 395). Latin poet. His life shows the kind of career possible for an intellectual in the Late Empire. Born at Burdigala (Bordeaux), educated there and at Tolosa (Toulouse), he taught for 30 years in his native city, then a main cultural centre of Gaul. A summons to the Imperial Court at Trèves to act as tutor to Gratian was the turning point of his career. Imperial patronage led to a number of high posts in the State service, including the governorship of Gaul and of Africa, and in 379 the consulship. He retired to Bordeaux after the murder of Gratian in 383. With considerable gifts for writing verse, and none for self-criticism, he was a voluminous writer. A full edition of his work was published after his death by his son Hesperius. It includes (1) the *Parentalia,* 30 epigrams on friends and relatives, written with extravagant adulation; (2) the *Commemoration of the Professors of Bordeaux,* in the same vein, and portraying a very complacent senior common-room, but of interest in the history of education. More important are (3) the exchange of letters with his friend and pupil ◊ Paulinus of Nola, which give an insight into the conflict between Christian and pagan culture; and (4) the *Mosella,* a charming descriptive poem of the river Moselle and the adjacent country, full of a sensitive feeling for nature. It has been claimed as the first poem in French literature: certainly it may stand beside Drayton's *Polyolbion*. The *List of Noble Cities* and the *Ephemeris*, a picture of daily life, ought also to be mentioned. [D R D]

Loeb: H. G. Evelyn-White (2 vols., 1919–21); *Mosella*, ed. C. Hosius (3rd edn, 1926).

Avienus, Rufus Festus (fl. *c.* A.D. 375). Latin didactic poet. Born at Volsinii, Avienus wrote on geography and astronomy. There survive: (1) *Descriptio orbis terrae*, an adaptation of Dionysius 'Periegetes'; (2) the *Ora maritima*, a description of the coasts between Marseilles and Cadiz, preserving some interesting accounts of early voyages of exploration in the Western Mediterranean and beyond the Straits of Gibraltar including the earliest reference to Britain and Ireland; and (3) and (4) the *Aratea phaenomena* and *Aratea prognostica*, which translates and expands ◇ Aratus on astronomy and meteorology. [D R D]

Ed. A. Holder (1887).

B

Babrius (Valerius?) (2nd cent. A.D.?) Nothing is known of his life. He wrote in Greek 10 books of *Aesop's Fables in Verse* (of which 2 survive); these were widely read in the late empire. [D R D]

Ed. W. G. Rutherford (1883); Teubner: O. Crusius (Leipzig, 1897).

Bacchylides (*c.* 516–*c.* 450 B.C.). Greek choral lyric poet. Born on Ceos, a nephew of ◇ Simonides. His earliest poems celebrate successes by local athletes in the minor games, but he soon established connexions with Thessaly and Macedon, and subsequently attracted the patronage of the Aeginetan aristocracy. His uncle's influence helped him to gain the *entrée* to Hiero's court at Syracuse. Bacchylides wrote the first of 3 odes in his honour when Hiero's horse Pherenicus won at Olympia in 476, and the series culminates in the celebration of his victory in the Olympic chariot race of 468. ◇ Pindar, who composed some of his finest poetry for Hiero, may have been piqued by the competition of Simonides and Bacchylides, but they were more than his match in the arts of diplomacy. The death of Simonides in 468 and of Hiero a year later ended the Sicilian connexion. Unlike Pindar, Bacchylides failed to find alternative patronage at other tyrants' courts, and was forced to resume the glorification of his compatriots' successes. His exile for a time to the Peloponnese was probably associated with the rise of democracy at Ceos.

The Alexandrians knew 9 books of Bacchylides' poetry. Apart from scanty fragments nothing had survived; but in 1896 an Egyptian papyrus was discovered containing part of 14 epinikia and 6 dithyrambs. From ancient times critics have tended to judge Bacchylides by comparison with Pindar. The Cean nightingale, however melodious, cannot soar and stoop like the Theban eagle. For passion and profundity he substitutes sureness of touch and a fresh, charming lyricism. He has, however, the Ionian gift of vivid and colourful narrative, a genuine feeling for and joy in the contests he celebrates, and a capacity for moralizing with equable simplicity. His dithyrambs have a special interest, since our knowledge of this form of lyric is tenuous. No. 16, describing Theseus's acceptance of Minos's challenge to hurl himself into the sea and so prove Poseidon is his father, is the liveliest piece of sustained narrative in Bacchylides. No. 17, a dialogue between the Chorus and Aegeus, is the only dramatic dithyramb surviving in its entirety, though it is not certain whether this is a reversal to an earlier form of dithyramb (such as was postulated by Aristotle), or an experiment in a new manner. ◇ Dithyramb. [D E W W]

Teubner: B. Snell (1949); ed., tr. and comm. R. C. Jebb (1905).

Basil the Great (A.D. *c.* 330–79). Greek Christian writer. Born and brought up at Caesarea in Cappadocia, Basil attended the universities of Constantinople and Athens, returning home *c.* 356. He was then baptized and made a tour of the ascetic communities throughout the Middle East, withdrawing into solitude not far from Neocaesarea to practise the same devotions. In 364 he was summoned by the bishop of Caesarea, ordained priest, and succeeded him in 370. A staunch opponent of the Arians, he withstood the Emperor Valens and worked constantly for better relations between all Christian parties.

Basil's writings include dogmatic, ascetic, homiletic and liturgical treatises. His study *On the Holy Spirit* (375) was the first complete work to be devoted to this subject. His ascetic books show him as the organizer of eastern monasticism. In his *Admonition to Young Men on the Profitable Use of Pagan Literature* he argued that the classical writings were admirable for training the intellect until it was able to grasp the deeper sense of holy scripture. His homilies reveal a generous borrowing of the style of the Second Sophistic, in the use of ecphrasis, metaphor, Gorgianic figures and parallelism. The 9 books *On the Hexameron* are outstanding for their rhetorical beauty. Photius was particularly impressed by Basil's style, referring to it as pure, persuasive and brilliant, to be compared with anything written by Plato and Demosthenes. [J G D]

Migne, *P G*, 29–32; *The Ascetic Works*, tr. W. K. L. Clarke (1925); *Admonition to Young Men on the Profitable Use of Pagan Literature*, tr. F. M. Padelford (1902); *On the Hexameron*, tr. B. Jackson (N P F, 1895).

J. M. Campbell, *The Influence of the Second Sophistic on the Style of the Sermons of St Basil the Great* (1922); M. M. Fox, *The Life and Times of St Basil the Great as Revealed in his Works* (1939).

Basilides. ♢ Gnosticism.

'Batrachomyomachia' or **'Battle of the Frogs and Mice'** (perhaps 5th cent. B.C.). Greek mock-heroic epyllion popularly attributed in antiquity to Homer, describing a war provoked by the drowning of a mouse. The fighting is fierce. The diminutive warriors bear appropriate names like Physignathos (Puff-cheek) and Tyrophagos (Cheese-eater), but are incongruously heroic in speech and action. Eventually Zeus intervenes to rescue the hard-pressed frogs by sending an army of crabs which rout the mice, and end the 'one-day war'. The humour of the poem is obvious enough, but the prefabricated phrases and incidents of Greek epic are effectively used. [G T W H]

O C T: *Homeri Opera*, v, ed. T. W. Allen (1912); Loeb: H. G. Evelyn-White, *Hesiod, The Homeric Hymns and Homerica* (1936).

'Bellum Alexandrinum'. A book written to continue Caesar's work *De bello civile*, possibly but not certainly by Aulus ♢ Hirtius. The surviving 68 chapters tell the story of the Egyptian and Asian campaigns as far as the victory over Pharnaces at the battle of Zela in 47 B.C. [D R D]

Loeb: A. G. Way (1955).

Berossus (fl. *c.*290 B.C.). Babylonian historian. A Hellenized native, High Priest of Marduk, he was commissioned by Antiochus I to produce a history of Babylon. The 3 volumes of his *Babyloniaca* covered a period from the Creation to Alexander the Great, which he reckoned as 468,215 years. This long perspective is due to Babylonian astronomy which, together with the sister 'science' of astrology, he popularized in the Greco-Roman world. Some of his historical work can be reconstructed from ♢ Josephus. [D R D]

Müller, *F H G*, ii.

Bibaculus, Marcus Furius (born, according to Jerome, 103 B.C.). Mentioned with Catullus as the author of lampoons against Caesar and his party. Perhaps the Furius cited by Horace (*Satires*, I: 10: 36 ff.) as the author of a famous 'bad line' (*Iuppiter hibernas cana nive conspuit Alpes* – 'Jupiter bespat the wintry Alps with hoary snow'), which seems to come from an epic on the Gallic wars. But the name may cover one poet, or two, or three. [D R D]

Biography. Biography, and its kin the Memoir, appears late as a literary form in Greece, developing probably from the historical monograph, and from the character sketches in continuous histories. In the 4th century B.C. the *Cyropaedia, Memorabilia* and *Agesilaus* of ♢ Xenophon approximate to true biography, as does the *Evagoras* of ♢ Isocrates, though in none of these is the primary purpose the writing of history. The school of Aristotle had interests in biography and evolved a formula for its composition, though none of their products survives. There are only fragments from the Hellenistic period, where the genre was largely employed by philosophers.

At Rome the native traditions of the funeral eulogy (*laudatio*) and commemorative inscription (*tituli*) provided a base for a development, which was usually directed to political or historical ends. (For the *tituli* cf. the inscriptions on the statues of the *triumphatores* in the Forum of Augustus.) A very large number of Roman statesmen wrote to explain or commend themselves to posterity; hence the claim of Latin literature to the invention of the autobiography. Memoirs were written by great Republican figures such as Gaius Gracchus, Rutilius Rufus and Sulla, and under the Empire by Augustus, Tiberius, Claudius and Hadrian. All are lost. Of surviving biographies the most important are those of ◊ Cornelius Nepos (1st cent. B.C.), the *Agricola* of ◊ Tacitus, the *Lives of the Twelve Caesars* by ◊ Suetonius Tranquillus (1st and 2nd century A.D.) and the ◊ *Historia Augusta*, a collection of the lives of 30 Roman emperors (? late 4th century A.D.).

In Greek there are the *Lives of the Philosophers* by ◊ Diogenes Laertius (3rd century A.D.) and, far more important, ◊ Plutarch's *Parallel Lives of the Noble Greeks and Romans* (2nd century A.D.). For the combination of psychological insight, historical acumen, and literary merit Plutarch stands easily first among ancient biographers.

The only autobiography we have is the *Confessions* of ◊ Augustine, earliest and greatest of its kind. [D R D]

D. R. Stuart, *Epochs of Greek and Roman Biography* (Berkeley, Cal., 1928); ed. T. A. Dorey, *Latin Biography* (1967).

Bion (*c.*325–*c.*255 B.C.). Greek philosopher. Born at Borysthenes (Olbia), on the Black Sea. Son of a fishmonger and a prostitute, a combination to which a German scholar has attributed his remarkable familiarity with vulgar phraseology. The whole family was sold into slavery for fraud, but Bion managed to get an education and win his freedom. Arriving in Athens some time before 314 he made the round of the philosophical schools, including the Academy and the Peripatetics, but was most influenced by Crates the Cynic (◊ Cynics). Later he wandered the Greek world as a travelling sophist, living on pupils' fees. He made prolonged stays at Rhodes and at Pella, where (later than 276) he won the favour of Antigonus Gonatas. He is said to have died at Chalcis. As a philosopher Bion was an eclectic in whose teachings Cynicism was dominant. As a development of the spoken lecture, he popularized the written diatribe, or sermon, which can reach a wider audience. His writings, of which fairly extensive fragments survive, had a wide influence, notably on the satires of Lucilius and Horace. They are characterized by anecdotes, quotations, short dramatic passages, character sketches and animal similes. Many of his sayings have passed into common usage – the simile of Man the actor on the stage of the world, of life as a Feast which one should leave as a sated guest, the story of the dying frog: 'This may be fun to you, but it's death to me.' [D R D]

Life in Diogenes Laertius, iv; L. Fiske, *Lucilius and Horace* (Madison, 1920); Dudley, *H C.*

Bion of Smyrna (probably fl. *c.*100 B.C.). Greek pastoral poet. Worked in Sicily. Six *Idylls* and a number of fragments survive, slight but graceful, erotic rather than true pastoral poems. The most notable is the 'Lament for Adonis' (if indeed it is by Bion). Of the others, III 'The Seasons', IV 'Love and the Fowler', V 'The Tutor of Love', and XI 'The Evening Star', are pretty poems. In a very different vein is IX, a lament for the sorrows of human life. [D R D]

Budé: Ph. E. Legrand, *Bucoliques grecs*, ii (Paris, 1927): tr. A. Lang, *Theocritus, Bion, and Moschus* (1928).

Boethius, Anicius Manlius Severinus (A.D. *c.*480–524). Roman philosopher. In both his life and his writings, Boethius is one of the last authentic representatives of the classical world. He came of a family which had held high office in the decaying Western Empire, was Consul in 510, and was a trusted political adviser to Theodoric the Ostrogoth. Later he became involved in a conspiracy, was imprisoned, and was executed at Ravenna. In prison he wrote his famous work *De consolatione philosophiae*. Written, like the satires of ◊ Menippus, in a mixture of verse and prose, it is a dialogue between himself and philosophy, and draws largely on Stoic and Platonic ideas. He also wrote commentaries on works of Aristotle and Cicero, besides text-books on arithmetic and music, and a number of works on theology. He was one of the most influential Latin authors for the next thousand years, and his works were chosen for translation by Alfred the Great. [DRD]

Loeb: H. F. Stewart and E. K. Rand, *De consolatione* and selected theological works (1918).

C

Caecilius (1st cent. B.C.). Roman poet. A friend of Catullus and author of a poem on Cybele. Almost all our knowledge of him derives from Catullus XXXV, a warmly affectionate verse letter inviting Caecilius to set out post-haste from Novum Comum for a meeting in Verona. The date must be after 59 B.C., when Comum was resettled and took its new name. Pliny the Younger's father was a Caecilius from Novum Comum, but there is no evidence that this is more than a coincidence. [DEWW]

Loeb: Warmington, *R O L*, i.

Caecilius Statius. ◊ Comedy, Roman.

Caelius Rufus, Marcus (83–48 B.C.). Roman orator. He was a prominent member of the dissolute but brilliant upper-class social set in which Catiline and subsequently Clodia Pulchra (probably the 'Lesbia' of Catullus) were leaders. He made a name as an orator by his successful prosecution of C. Antonius in 59, but later was prosecuted on a charge of attempting to poison Clodia, who had shortly before been his mistress; the defence was conducted by Caelius himself, Crassus and Cicero, whose speech is extant. Caelius was aedile in 50, when he made a speech attacking the evaders of the water-regulations which is highly praised by Frontinus. Following his own cynical *dictum* that in a civil war, whatever one's previous allegiance, one should join the side that seems most likely to win, he joined Caesar in 49. He was made praetor in 48, but quarrelled with Caesar over the question of relieving debt and was killed while attempting a *coup d'état*.

Caelius was an orator of the first rank, though better in attack than in defence. Quintilian preserves his wonderful description of how a Roman proconsul was surprised by the enemy while sleeping off the effects of an orgy. But he is known best as a correspondent of Cicero when the latter was governor of Cilicia in 51/50. His letters are written in vivid, racy style, with much use of contemporary metaphors; they show shrewd political judgement as well as giving interesting details about the social scene. [TAD]

Cicero, *Ad familiares* VIII; *Cicero's Correspondence*, Tyrrell and Purser, iii.

Caesar, Gaius Julius (100–44 B.C.). Roman general and statesman. Caesar belonged to an ancient patrician family that had achieved little distinction in later generations. Connected by birth and marriage to the anti-senatorial party of Marius and Cinna, he consistently opposed the claim of the senatorial aristocracy to a monopoly of power. He first appears in Roman politics in the mid-sixties, as an associate of Crassus in his intrigues for greater personal power, but he gained real eminence only in 63. In that year he was, partly through immense bribery, elected Pontifex Maximus, and by his prosecution of Rabirius and his speech against inflicting the death penalty on the Catilinarian conspirators without a proper trial he upheld the view that the Senate could not empower its magistrates to put Roman citizens to death. After a year as governor in Spain he was elected consul for 59, and by reconciling the two inveterate enemies, Pompey and Crassus, he formed an irresistible combination. In this First Triumvirate Caesar's executive authority as consul was backed by Crassus's money and by strong-arm methods from Pompey's veteran soldiers. All opposition, whether from Caesar's fellow-consul Bibulus or from the senatorial leaders, was crushed; Pompey achieved the ratification of his settlements in the East and grants of land to his discharged troops; Crassus obtained certain business concessions; while Caesar got for himself a large-scale and long-term command in Gaul.

In the next nine years Caesar conquered Gaul, penetrated into Britain and Germany, subdued a series of Gallic revolts, and wrote the first 7 books of his *Commentaries*. Strains that had begun to appear in the Triumvirate owing to the ineradicable hatred of Crassus for Pompey had been eased, and Caesar's command had been prolonged; but in 53 the death of Crassus robbed Caesar of a firm ally, while after the death of Caesar's daughter Julia, who had been married to Pompey, the latter proceeded to marry the daughter of Metellus Scipio, and to draw closer and closer to Caesar's enemies.

In 50, as Caesar's command in Gaul began to expire, the question arose whether he would be able to start on a second consulship without previously laying down his command in Gaul, or whether his opponents could compel him to come to Rome as a private individual, when he could be prosecuted. Throughout that year, Caesar was able to get any decision of the Senate adverse to his interests vetoed by one of the tribunes, but at the beginning of January 49 the Senate refused to acknowledge the right of tribunes continually to obstruct their decisions, and peremptorily ordered Caesar to lay down his command; they were supported by Pompey, who was now jealous of Caesar's successes.

Caesar won the civil war that ensued (49–45), and Pompey and his leading supporters were killed. Caesar had at first gained wide support as a result of his moderation and refusal to allow unnecessary bloodshed; many of the Pompeian supporters were won over and served under him later in the war. But his increasingly autocratic behaviour bred hostility and resentment, and the realization that he had no intention of abdicating his autocratic powers resulted in a conspiracy among a group of nobles who wished to restore the power of the senatorial aristocracy. Caesar was murdered at a meeting of the Senate on 15 March 44, when about to set out on a war against Parthia.

Caesar was an orator of great distinction, one of the leading exponents of the plain, unadorned Attic style. But his literary fame rests on his *Commentaries on the Gallic War*, in 7 books, and *On the Civil War*, in 3 books. The eighth book of the *Gallic War* is by his staff-officer, Hirtius, as is probably the *Alexandrine War*; the *African War* and the *Spanish War* are by unknown officers.

Caesar's *Commentaries* are written in a simple, straightforward style; the sentence-structure tends at times to become montonous, and the precision of the language, with stereotyped phrases and stock words repeated to describe similar events, makes little concession to variety. But in the unembellished terms of a military despatch Caesar tells a gripping narrative; the events described obtain a vividness from the very simplicity of their portrayal, and the men who take part in the events come to life and appear far more like real men than do the rhetorical lay-figures of Livy or the psychopaths of Tacitus. The story is told in the third person, and gives an artfully contrived impression of objectivity. In the *Gallic War* there seems to be little deliberate factual distortion, though in many cases enemy losses were greatly exaggerated; in parts of the *Civil War*, especially in the opening chapters of the first book, there is a great deal of propaganda, as Caesar deliberately sets out to present his side of the question to the Roman public. The *Civil War* also differs from the earlier work in that the language flows more freely and admits more variety; the style as a whole shows greater maturity.

Caesar also wrote a book on the proper formation of words (*De analogia*), a number of poems, and an attack on his great rival Cato Uticensis (*Anticato*). [TAD]

OCT: R. L. A. Du Pontet, *Bellum gallicum* (1900), *Bellum civile* (1901); Loeb: H. J. Edwards, *Gallic War* (1930); A. G. Peskett, *Civil War* (1921); A. G. Way, *Alexandrian, African and Spanish Wars* (1955); *The Conquest of Gaul*, tr. S. A. Handford, (Penguin Classics, 1951).

T. Rice Holmes, *Roman Republic* (1923), *Caesar's Conquest of Gaul* (1911); R. Syme, *Roman Revolution* (1939); J. Buchan, *Julius Caesar* (1932); F. Adcock, *Caesar as a Man of Letters* (1936); ed. T. A. Dorey, *Latin Historians* (1966).

Callimachus (*c.*305–*c.*240 B.C.). Greek poet and scholar. He was the son of Battus, a name suggesting descent from the founder of his native Cyrene. In early youth he moved to Alexandria, and taught at a suburban school. Under Ptolemy Philadelphus he worked in the Library. He became involved in embittered literary controversy with rival critics and authors, including his pupil ◊ Apollonius Rhodius. Though moving freely in court society under the Ptolemies, he was twice passed over when the Librarianship fell vacant.

Antiquity ascribed 800 volumes to him. Apart from the hymns and epigrams only fragments survive, though papyri have greatly enlarged our knowledge. He compiled the first systematic library catalogue (the *Pinakes,* in 120 books), and published a series of learned prose works on an encyclopedic range of subjects. His poetry too suggests a restless creative activity. His masterpiece, the *Aetia,* recounted the causes and origins of religious festivals, monuments and practices, in 4 books of elegiacs. The *Lock of Berenice* (originally a separate poem) was incorporated in the final version of Book IV. Among other elegiac poems were the *Ibis* (a bitter invective), the fifth hymn, and a group of perfectly turned epigrams. The scanty lyrical fragments show extreme metrical diversity – also a feature of the *Iambi,* short pieces of occasional verse with very varied themes, including literary and aesthetic criticism, satirical description and fable. The epyllion *Hecale* digresses characteristically from an episode in the adventures of Theseus into a description of the old woman who shelters him for the night. It is in hexameters, as are five of the hymns – literary compositions designed to be read or recited, and illustrating Callimachus's gift of describing with sympathy and insight religious beliefs and usages alien to himself.

Callimachus makes possible a new literary development attuned to the cosmopolitan and sophisticated society of a new era. He aims at mastery of a limited medium, small-scale perfection. The controversies which he precipitated arose from his criticisms of Antimachus and Apollonius for writing epic rather than epyllion, which to him was the only living poetry in this genre. He has a half-humorous detachment, a cultivated poise and elegance reminiscent of the 18th century (Pope too wrote a *Rape of the Lock*). His erudition helps to establish the ideal of the learned poet, at once scholar and man of taste. Though his appeal is more to the head than the heart, his approach is profoundly original, and his accomplishment dazzling. His influence on Catullus and Propertius, and through them on the Latin and European literary tradition, was profound. English poetry between the wars owed more to him than it realized. [DEWW]

Ed. R. Pfeiffer (2 vols., 1949 and 1953; Loeb: *Hymns and Epigrams,* A. W. Mair (1921); *Fragments,* A. C. Trypanis (1958).

U. von Wilamowitz-Moellendorff, *Hellenistische Dichtung* (2 vols., 1924).

Callinus (fl. *c.* 650 B.C.). The earliest Greek elegist. He lived at Ephesus. The one considerable surviving fragment is a stirring appeal to the young to take up arms and if need be die for their country. The barbaric Cimmerian and Trerian invaders had overrun much of Asia Minor, and sacked the famous temple of Ephesian Artemis at the city's gates. With complete mastery of the new verse medium, Callinus succeeds in recapturing the temper of the heroic age and adapting it to the deeper loyalties and broader-based patriotism of the city-state. [DEWW]

Bowra, *E G E.*

Callisthenes (d. 328 B.C.). Greek historian and philosopher. He was born at Olynthus, and was the nephew or cousin of Aristotle and became his pupil. He accompanied Alexander the Great on his expedition to Asia, but he made many enemies as a result of his outspoken manner of speech, which he never attempted to control. At last he gave offence to the king, and was put to death as being implicated in a conspiracy. His main work was an account of Alexander's campaign, but he also wrote a history of Greece from 387 to 357 B.C. He was severely criticized by later writers for his inaccuracy and poor style. [TAD]

Müller, *F H G.*

Calpurnius Siculus, Titus (fl. *c.* A.D. 50). Latin pastoral poet. His life and works have been the subject of controversy, but it now seems established (1) that he wrote in the reign of Nero, and (2) that of the 11 poems that bear his name in the manuscript, the last 4 are by ◊ Nemesianus. Of the others, 3 are on court themes: I, a prophecy of a Golden Age, like the Fourth *Eclogue* of Virgil; IV, thanks to an imperial patron; VII, a description of a spectacle in the Circus of Gaius and Nero. The rest are on conventional pastoral themes, with many echoes of Virgil. His poetry is derivative, and on a level far below that of the *Eclogues,* but the verse is pretty enough. [DRD]

Loeb: Duff, *M L P* (1934).

J. Hubaux, *Les thèmes bucoliques dans la poésie latine* (Paris, 1930).

Calvus, Gaius Licinius Macer (82–47 B.C.). Roman orator and poet. Catullus's younger contemporary and closest friend, son of the orator and historian Licinius ⇨ Macer. He was a small man, impulsive, warm-hearted, lovable. Little of his verse or prose survives. His poetry had much the same range as Catullus's – epyllion, epithalamium, epigram, elegy (including the famous lament for his wife Quintilia, untimely dead). He and Catullus are often linked by later writers as representatives of the ⇨ *neoterici.* Calvus also ranked high as an orator; indeeed his speeches with their 'Attic' economy of style were still read when his poetry was forgotten. [D E W W]

Ed. H. Malcovati, *Oratorum romanorum fragmenta* (Turin, 1930); Teubner: Morel, *F P L.*

Cassiodorus, Flavius Magnus Aurelius (*c.* A.D. 487–583). Roman statesman. In his long life, he had two careers, first as a public figure in the Ostrogothic kingdom, then, after his retirement *c.* 550, as a monk in the monastery he founded at Vivarium in his native Bruttium. An indefatigable worker, he is important in both pagan and Christian learning.

As Latin secretary to Theodoric, he corresponded with all the great personages of the day, and his letters are an invaluable source for 6th-century history. They are in 12 books, entitled *Variae Epistulae.* The *History of the Goths* survives only in fragments, but it is the chief source used by Jordanes. The *Chronica,* a general history of the world from Adam to A.D. 519, was well known in the Middle Ages. Fragments survive of his *Orationes.*

The chief work of his later period is the *Institutiones,* a guide to divine and secular learning compiled for the general education of monks. It deals with the seven liberal arts, and also instructs scribes in the copying of manuscripts, in which Vivarium was a pioneer. The copying by monks of classical texts, with all that it has meant for the preservation of ancient literature, is due to Cassiodorus above any other man. [D R D]

Chronica, ed. T. Mommsen (M G H, 1894); *Variae* and *Orationes,* ed. T. Mommsen (M G H, 1894); *Institutiones,* ed. R. A. B. Mynors (1937).

Cassius Hemina, Lucius (fl. *c.* 146 B.C.). Roman historian. One of the earliest Latin annalists. He wrote history of Rome from time of Aeneas down to his own day, probably in 4 books. His treatment is sketchy, but he shows interest in religious antiquities. [T A D]

Peter, *H R R,* i.

Cato, 'Censorius', Marcus Porcius (234–149 B.C.). Roman statesman, orator and historian. Born at Tusculum of an old Italian family, Cato had an active and distinguished military career. Elected consul in 195, he won a triumph for a campaign in Spain. Elected censor in 184 in the face of strong opposition, his term of office was memorable for the sternness of his behaviour. He vigorously attacked the growth of luxury and of Greek influence at Rome, as bringing inevitable corruption. A bitter enemy of Scipio Africanus, he helped to bring about his downfall. Towards the end of his life he became concerned by the growth of Carthaginian power, and his influence helped to precipitate the Third Punic War. A hard-headed man of business, he had the puritanical streak often found in such men; ruthless in public life, he was devoted to his children; a resolute enemy of all things Greek, he yet learnt Greek in his later years.

Cato followed many activities. He was a great orator, and the first Roman to write up and publish his own speeches. He wrote the *Origines,* a history of Rome and the other Italian peoples; he composed manuals on various subjects including law and medicine; his handbook on agriculture (*De re rustica*), written in a formless disjointed style, still survives, our earliest substantial piece of Latin prose. In this he describes not merely methods of agriculture, horticulture and stock-keeping, but also rules of domestic behaviour, religious observances, ways of curing ailments and the use of cabbage for purges. [T A D]

Origines, Peter, *H R R,* i; Speeches: H. Scullard, *Roman Politics* (1951); Loeb: W. D. Hooper and H. B. Ash, *De re rustica: Cato and Varro* (1934).

E. Badian, in *Latin Historians,* ed. T. A. Dorey (1966).

Catullus, Gaius Valerius (*c.* 84–*c.* 54 B.C.). Latin poet. Born at Verona, he became the dominant figure among the ⇨ *neoterici,* the New Poets of the late republic. His father was of sufficient means and standing to entertain Julius Caesar. Catullus never mentions his parents, but was devoted to his brother. He had a villa near Tibur, and another at Sirmio on the shore of Lake Garda; but he lived mostly at Rome, and it was there that he met Lesbia, the inspiration of his finest poetry. Her true name was Clodia; she was almost certainly the wife of Q. Metellus Celer, and sister of Cicero's arch-enemy P. Clodius Pulcher. In 57/6 when G. Memmius was in office as governor of Bithynia, Catullus accompanied him to the Near East, where he probably visited his brother's grave in the Troad.

The manuscripts present Catullus's poems in 3 groups roughly classified by length and metre. (1) 1–60 comprise short pieces with much metrical variety, but predominantly hendecasyllabic and choliambic. (2) 61–68 consist of long poems, one in lyric stanzas, one galliambic, the rest in hexameters or elegiacs. (3) 69–116 are a series of shorter elegies, the longest 26 lines long, the rest mostly epigrams, some only a single couplet. Catullus planned to publish a collection of his poetry, and composed the opening dedicatory poem. What survives, however, is certainly not his book, but the work of a much later editor.

Catullus lived in a disturbed and revolutionary era, and the excitement of new ideas and experiments communicates itself to his poetry. He and his group are conscious innovators, deliberately breaking as far as possible with the Roman past, avoiding drama and epic as outmoded, and seeking fresh inspiration from Greece. The model is mostly Alexandrian, but for the language of passion Catullus with sure insight goes back to Sappho. He maps new fields of experience, the ecstasy and degradation of love, the despair of the rejected and abandoned, the hysteria of religious enthusiasm. His poetry shows extreme metrical variety and accomplishment. His hexameters have a novel freshness and lyricism. He breaks new ground with his sapphics and monodic stanzas, which point the way for Horace. He writes pure iambics of extraordinary lightness and rapidity; and introduces into Latin priapeans, asclepiads, and galliambics, with each of which metres he experiments only once but most successfully. He starts the long and brilliant tradition of Latin erotic elegy; and his brief elegiac epigrams show unique pungency and vehemence. And he writes with supreme mastery in his favourite simple and relaxed rhythms, hendecasyllables and choliambics, which are close to the movement of everyday speech.

This metrical virtuosity is only one aspect of an extraordinary versatility, ranging from the discipline and structural patterning of the longer poems to the studied inconsequence and conversational simplicity of his informal style. His greatest lyrics are for Lesbia, and the sequence of 25 poems about her, many of them short and slight, modulates from the sunlit serenity of the early days to disillusionment, quarrels and reconciliations, despair, and ultimately to vitriolic hatred. Their affair was unusual in that she was socially his superior, and his idealization of her qualities, and quest for a permanent relationship in which depth of feeling might be united with mutual loyalty and understanding, made his final repulse the more humiliating. The filth to which he has recourse in moods of savage bitterness is the counterpart to the limpid lyricism of his hours of happiness. It too is sometimes used with consummate art, as in his poem of farewell, but his thought and language can be those of the gutter. The depth of feeling and passionate sincerity of his love lyrics are matched by the warmth and affection of his occasional poems, many of which have the uninhibited simplicity and directness of verse letters. Even in his most casual verse Catullus raises the prosaic and colloquial word, or usage, or metre, to the level of great poetry. Similarly the shorter elegies, though unpolished by Ovidian standards, more than compensate by their vigour. The longer poems show more artifice; he is closest here to Alexandria with its sophisticated courtiers, its cult of erudition, its polish and glitter. Catullus translates the *Coma Berenices,* is aware of himself as a *doctus poeta,* and composes an epyllion, the *Peleus and Thetis,* characterized by extreme pictorial brilliance, in which he seeks to acclimatize to Latin not only a Greek literary genre, but the syntax, movement, words and sounds of the Greek language.

Catullus gave the neoteric movement its driving force and is its justification. By his restless experiment with new themes and forms and by bringing poetry more directly into contact with life as he lived it and Greek literature as he knew it, in fact by showing Greek literature to be an integral part of that life, he gave a new vitality to Latin and helped to make possible the achievement of the Augustans. Their severer and narrower canon of taste rejected as extravagant some features of his style, notably his fondness for diminutives and for compound epithets. But the mature as well as the youthful Virgil is deeply in his debt, and for all their differences in temperament and outlook Horace and Martial each owed much to him. He died young. Had he lived, he might well have modified the whole development of Latin elegy. As it was he blazed the trail for Cornelius Gallus, Tibullus, Propertius and Ovid, all in the neoteric tradition. The loose-knit texture of his verse, his instinct for living speech, his personal subjective approach and passionate involvement in his art, above all his immediacy and spontaneity have made him a major influence on European literature, and give him a direct appeal to the modern reader. (⇨ Lyric Poetry, Latin.) [DEWW]

OCT: R. A. B. Mynors (1958); comm. C. J. Fordyce (1961) (omitting 35 poems); concise German annotated ed., W. Kroll (Stuttgart, 1959); tr. P. Whigham (Penguin Classics, 1966).

A. L. Wheeler, *Catullus and the Traditions of Ancient Poetry* (Berkeley, Cal., 1934); K. Quinn, *The Catullan Revolution* (1959).

Catulus, Quintus Lutatius (d. 87 B.C.). Roman statesman and man of letters. Catulus was consul in 102 and in the following year helped C. Marius defeat the Germanic invaders at Vercellae. As leader of the senatorial aristocracy he was forced by Marius to commit suicide. Catulus was the leader of the most important literary circle at Rome. He is praised by Cicero as an orator with an elegant and polished style. He was a philosopher; he wrote his memoirs in a style based on that of Xenophon; and he composed a number of love poems in the Alexandrian manner, of which two survive. [TAD]

Peter, *HRR*, i.

Celsus, Aulus Cornelius (early 1st cent. A.D.). Roman encyclopedist. Celsus wrote in the reign of Tiberius (A.D. 14–37) on medical matters (*De re medicina*). This is the only surviving portion of what seems to have been an encyclopedia. It contains a digest of Hellenistic and Roman practice, together with an account of the history of medicine. The section on surgery (VII) is of especial interest; it describes operations for goitre and stone in the bladder, tonsillectomy and many procedures of oral and dental surgery. Written in excellent Latin, the work of Celsus had an influence in the Renaissance comparable with that of Vitruvius in architecture. [DRD]

Loeb: W. G. Spencer (3 vols., 1936–8).

Cercidas of Megalopolis (*c.*290–*c.*220 B.C.). Two men of that name are known. Prior to 1906 it was uncertain which of them was the 'excellent lawgiver and meliambic poet' mentioned by the Byzantine writer Stephanus. In that year the discovery at Oxyrhynchus of a papyrus containing 7 longish fragments of 'the meliambic poems of Cercidas the Cynic' made it highly probable that the poet was also the Cercidas active in the political affairs of the Peloponnesus in the latter half of the 3rd century B.C. In 226 he was sent to enlist the help of Macedon against the revolutionary Spartan king Cleomenes. In the war that followed Cleomenes destroyed the city of Megalopolis (223), but was finally defeated at the battle of Sellasia (222) in which Cercidas led the Megalopolitan contingent. But Cercidas was no reactionary. Fragment IV, a remarkable outburst against social inequality, shows his sympathies for the party of reform in the agitation for the redistribution of land. They are urged not to wait for the vengeance of Heaven to overtake the rich, but to act themselves under the inspiration of a new triad of divinities – Paean and Sharing (Metados) and Nemesis. This would suit the context of the refounding of Megalopolis in 217. The subjects of other fragments are sexual desire and its gratification, the praise of Diogenes, the effects of music, the degeneracy of the Stoics and an address to his soul in old age. Cercidas was the inventor of meliambic poetry, in which lyric metres are used for satire. He was strongly influenced by the Cynics ⇨ Diogenes and ⇨ Bion. [DRD]

Loeb: A. D. Knox, *Herodes, Cercidas and the Greek Choliambic poets* (1929).

Dudley, *HC*.

Chrysippus (*c.*280–207 B.C.). Greek philosopher. From Soli in Cilicia, he was the pupil of ◊ Cleanthes (Master 263–232 B.C.) and in effect second founder of the Stoic school (◊ Stoicism). At a time when Stoic dogmatism was beginning to wilt under the remorseless attacks of the Academy, Chrysippus completely overhauled its logic and dialectics, and gave it a coherent structure which needed very little repair for over a hundred years. An industrious writer credited with 705 'books', he cared little for style, repeated his arguments *ad nauseam*, and quoted from other writers at undue length. [D R D]

Arnim, *S V F*, ii and iii.
M. Pohlenz, *Die Stoa* (2 vols., Göttingen, 1948).

Chrysostom, John (A.D. *c.* 350–407). Greek Christian writer. Trained in rhetoric under ◊ Libanius at Antioch, John was made deacon in 381 and ordained priest in 386. He was appointed to the special duty of preaching and for 12 years discharged this office with distinction. His orations, which earned him the title of 'golden-mouthed', are notable for their Attic qualities and contain much information of value to theologians, historians and archaeologists. In 398 John was consecrated bishop of Constantinople, but his reforming zeal aroused such opposition, including that of the Empress, that in 404 he was exiled to Cucusus in Lesser Armenia. Three years later he was sent further into exile but died of exhaustion on the journey to Pityus, on the Black Sea. [J G D]

Migne, *P G*, 47–64; *Orations* tr. W. R. W. Stephens and others (6 vols., 1888–93).
D. Attwater, *St John Chrysostom* (1939).

Cicero, Marcus Tullius (106–43 B.C.). Roman orator and statesman. He was born at Arpinum, of a wealthy local family, and taken to Rome for his education, presumably with the idea of a public career. After studying under the best teachers, Roman and Greek, he started as a barrister, and made his name in 81 by his defence of Sextus Roscius of Ameria on a charge of parricide fabricated by two creatures of Sulla. Cicero's forensic career was interrupted by a visit to Rhodes, for both health and advanced study, but on his return he went from strength to strength, and in 70 established himself as the leading barrister in Rome by his successful prosecution of Verres for gross misgovernment in Sicily.

During this time Cicero had got well started on his political career, and was elected praetor for 66. This was normally the highest office obtained by a man from outside the Roman aristocracy, but Cicero was ambitious, and in that year delivered his first public political oration, in support of the proposal to confer on Pompey the command in the war against Mithridates. Cicero's attachment to Pompey was one of the most permanent features of his political career. It may have started from self-interest, but it was continued because Cicero felt convinced that Pompey was the one man who could preserve Rome not only from enemies without but also from lawlessness within, and who would, reconciled to the senatorial aristocracy, guarantee Cicero's ideal – the unchallenged right of the senate to exercise all the powers of government.

Cicero was elected consul for 63, partly as a result of sudden alarm among the aristocracy over the revolutionary policies of his most dangerous rival, Catiline; and he showed outstanding skill and judgement in crushing the subsequent attempt at a *coup d'état* by Catiline and Lentulus Sura; but by his execution of the conspirators without proper trial he ranged himself alongside the most reactionary section of the aristocracy, lost the support of the masses, and estranged himself from Pompey. During the next few years various attempts to arrange a working agreement between Pompey, now returned from the east, and the senatorial aristocracy proved unsuccessful, and it was left to Caesar to form a coalition between himself, Crassus and Pompey to divide between themselves political power at Rome. Cicero was invited to join this coalition, but, rightly regarding both its aims and its methods as utterly unconstitutional, he refused, and, being too dangerous an opponent to leave at large, was driven into exile.

After eighteen months, Cicero was restored in 57, and at once tried to split the coalition by driving a wedge between Pompey, to whom he was now wholly reconciled, and Caesar. This attempt was thwarted by the prompt action of Caesar, and Cicero was compelled to give a written recantation of his attacks on him, and to put his services at Caesar's disposal in the law-courts and in the senate. His position was made less humiliating by the courtesy and generosity of Caesar, who all through his career went out of his way to try and enlist Cicero's support, while Cicero drew some consolation from the reflection that the leaders of the senatorial aristocracy, whose cause he had tried to champion, had always failed to give him resolute support.

In the Civil War, after a long period of indecision, Cicero went to Greece to join Pompey's forces, but his relations with Pompey and the other senatorial leaders were strained, and after the battle of Pharsalus he was able to make peace with Caesar and return to Italy. From then on until Caesar's death he took little part in politics, apart from making a number of pleas for the pardoning of exiled Pompeians. Most of this period he devoted to literature, but the death of his beloved daughter Tullia early in 45 plunged him into a grief that was almost inconsolable. After the murder of Caesar in 44, Cicero took a leading part in establishing a compromise settlement between Antony and Brutus and Cassius, but during most of the summer, while Antony unscrupulously built up his own power, he withdrew into private life. However, when Antony left Rome for Cisalpine Gaul, Cicero put himself at the head of the remnants of the senatorial party, and, burning with a fierce desire to revenge himself for all the years of impotence spent under Caesar's domination, he delivered a series of stirring attacks on Antony. Early in 43 he persuaded the senate to send the two consuls with an army against Antony, who was blockading Decimus Brutus, one of the murderers of Caesar, in Mutina. In a successful engagement they compelled Antony to abandon the siege, but both lost their lives. However, Cicero's triumph was shortlived, for the spearhead of the senatorial army had been provided by Caesar's nephew and heir, Octavian, at the head of Caesar's veterans, whom he had personally raised and commanded. Octavian realized that he had more to hope for from Antony than from the Senate; he joined forces with him, and together their power was irresistible. One of their first acts was to procure the death of their chief enemies, and Cicero's name stood highest on the list.

Cicero has often been blamed for weakness and vacillation. But it is not weakness to submit to overwhelming force, and when faced with a choice he always chose the more dangerous path. His greatest failing as a politician was his consistent refusal to compromise; as a statesman his ideals were more honourable and unselfish than those of his contemporaries.

Cicero was the greatest orator that the Romans, a nation of orators, ever produced. He possessed to the fullest extent all the equipment then considered necessary. He had a wide range of technique, could rise to the greatest heights in emotional passages, pour ridicule on his opponents, make full use of wit, irony, innuendo and repartee, hold the attention of his hearers by his powers of narrative, and carry them with him in the unfolding of his argument. He always tried to fight a case on ground of his own choosing by persuading the court that the crucial issue was one on which the facts could be made to favour his client.

Cicero's greatest asset was his exceptional command of the Latin language. His diction was pure and elegant, avoiding archaism and colloquialism. His mastery of words enabled him to build up a complex period structure of logically developed sentences, in combinations of long and short syllables that provided a rhythm which appealed to the ear. The mere sound of it delighted the young Petrarch. His style owed much to the great Greek writers of prose, and he combined the vigour and power of Demosthenes with the rhythmical sentences of Isocrates and the richness of Plato's vocabulary.

Cicero's forensic speeches were mostly delivered for the defence. Of them the most important were those made on behalf of Roscius, mentioned above; of Cluentius (in which he based his whole argument on a blatant fallacy – and succeeded); on behalf of Murena, consult-elect in 63, charged with (and almost certainly guilty of) electoral corruption (this Cicero almost condones, provided that the result is the election of the best man as consul, and pokes fun both at the formalism of Roman lawyers and the rigid creed of the Stoics); on behalf of Caelius Rufus, charged with conspiracy to murder an Egyptian envoy and the attempted poisoning of his former mistress, a lady of high society whose reputation Cicero tears to shreds in open court; and, finally, the defence of Milo on a charge of murdering his political rival

Clodius, a speech which Cicero never actually delivered in anything like its present form, but subsequently wrote up and published. Of his political speeches, the best are the *Pro Lege Manilia,* a panegyric on Pompey delivered before the popular assembly in 66, the 4 *Catilinarian Orations* of 63, and the 14 *Philippics,* delivered against Antony in 44 and 43. Many of his other political speeches suffer from the fact that where his own emotions were involved he allowed invective to descend to crude vituperation.

Cicero followed the common practice of publishing his speeches, but he also produced a large number of works on the theory and practice of rhetoric, on religion, and on moral and political philosophy. His two most interesting rhetorical works were the *De oratore,* a treatise on the whole range of oratory, and the *Brutus,* a survey of famous speakers of the past. On philosophy, his most important works were the *Republic,* containing an outline of the ideal constitution and including the famous 'Dream of Scipio', and the *Laws,* an account of Roman public and religious laws; the *De officiis,* a discussion on moral duty, and the *De finibus,* an examination of the ideas held by the various Greek schools of philosophy on the nature of the Supreme Good; and the two shorter works on *Friendship* and *Old Age.* Many of these works were cast in the form of a dramatic dialogue. Cicero did not claim to be an original philosopher – 'I only supply the words, and I have plenty of those.' But it was popularization of a very high order, it was important in preserving the views of various Greek philosophers, and it had considerable influence on the early Church.

Although the satirist Juvenal scoffs at Cicero's verses, he played a leading part in the development of the Latin hexameter, and had some influence on Lucretius and Catullus. But perhaps the most interesting of all his work is the collection of letters, nearly 900 in number, written in most cases with complete spontaneity and not published till long after his death. These letters not only contain a first-hand account of social and political life in the upper classes at Rome, but also reflect the changing personal feelings of an emotional and sensitive man. Ironically, they have served to compromise his reputation by comparison with contemporaries whose inner feelings we do not know in this way. (⇨ Oratory and Rhetoric; Letters, Latin.) [T A D]

O C T: *Epistulae,* L. C. Purser, D. R. Shackleton Bailey, W. S. Watt (3 vols., 1901, 1958); *Orationes,* A. C. Clark, W. Peterson (6 vols., 1905–18); complete works in Loeb (26 vols.); *Ad Atticum,* xi–xiii, ed. and comm. D. Shackleton Bailey (1966); *Selected Works,* tr. Michael Grant (Penguin Classics, 1960); *Brutus,* tr. A. E. Douglas (1966).

Introduction to *Selected Letters,* ed. A. Watson, rev. W. W. How and A. C. Clark 1925–6.)

Cicero, Quintus Tullius (102–43 B.C.). Roman administrator and man of letters. Younger brother of Marcus. Praetor 62, and Governor of Asia 61–59. He was a staff-officer under Pompey in Sardinia 57–55, under Caesar in Gaul 54–51, and under his brother in Cilicia 52–51. He joined Pompey in the Civil War, but made his peace with Caesar and took no further part in public life. He was killed in proscriptions. Quintus had wide literary interests. He wrote a history, and also a number of tragedies, some in Gaul and Britain, mainly free translations from Greek models. A pamphlet on electioneering (*Commentariolum petitionis*) is attributed to him, though this may be of later date. [T A D]

Commentariolum petitionis, see Cicero's *Letters,* tr. E. S. Shuckburgh, i (1899).

R. G. M. Nisbet, *Journal of Roman Studies,* (1961).

Cinaethon. ⇨ Epic Cycle.

Cinna, Gaius Helvius (*c.* 70–44 B.C.). Roman poet. An adherent of Caesar, tribune in 44, Cinna is supposed to be the person lynched by the Roman mob in mistake for his namesake (Plutarch, *Brutus,* 20) or 'for his bad verses' (Shakespeare!). Author of a poem on *Smyrna,* marked by Alexandrian learning, a *Propempticon* addressed to Pollio, and erotic poems. Too little survives to assess his standing in the group of young poets around ⇨ Catullus. [D R D]

Claudian (Claudius Claudianus) (A.D. *c.* 370–404). Latin poet. Poet-laureate of his hero Stilicho, and the last major classical poet of Rome. Born at Alexandria he felt himself to be an Egyptian, and his early verse was in his native Greek. After his move to Rome, however, in 395, his poetry shows a complete mastery of Latin. He speaks of a four years' absence from the capital, and from 395 to 400 he was probably in attendance at the imperial court in Milan. On his return to Rome in 400 his poem on Stilicho's consulship won him patrician status and the honour of a statue in Trajan's forum (the inscribed base survives). He married in 404: his wife, whom he met through Serena (the adopted daughter of Theodosius and married to Stilicho), was of African origin. His latest datable poem was addressed to Serena while he was on honeymoon in Africa. He must have died shortly afterwards. He was probably a Christian, at least nominally, though this is denied by Augustine.

In Greek two fragments of a *Gigantomachia* ascribed to Claudian may be his, as may a majority of the epigrams bearing his name in the Palatine Anthology. His works in Latin, with probable dates of composition, comprise: (1) A series of *Panegyrics* in hexameters often introduced by short elegiac prefaces: (a) on the joint consulship of the brothers Probinus and Olybrius (395); (b) on the third, fourth and sixth consulships of the Emperor Honorius (396, 398, 404); (c) on the consulship of Theodosius (398); (d) on the consulship of Stilicho, in 3 books (400). (2) An *Epithalamium* in hexameters with elegiac preface, and associated Fescennine verses in lyric metres, on the marriage of Honorius and Maria (398). (3) Descriptive historical poems in hexameters: (a) on the war against Gildo (398; the poem was left uncompleted); (b) on the Gothic war (402). (4) Poems of satirical invective: (a) *In Rufinum*, an elegiac preface followed by 2 books of hexameters describing the insurrection of the pretorian prefect and his murder by disaffected troops (396); (b) *In Eutropium*, 2 books of hexameters, the second with elegiac proem, describing the rise to power and fall of the eunuch consul (399). (5) Collected short poems, 52 in all, ranging in length from 2 to 200 lines, and in subject from the description of a lobster to an epic fragment, all in hexameters or elegiacs except the first, which is in anapaests. (6) *The Rape of Proserpine*, an unfinished descriptive poem with mythological theme in 3 books of hexameters with brief elegiac introduction to the first 2 (395–7).

The ten years of Claudian's life as a Latin poet were extraordinarily productive, yet he is far removed from superficiality. The panegyric might seem a form of highly artificial court poetry; but he revitalizes it and writes with great eloquence and dignity and with a sonority that had hardly been heard in Latin since Virgil's death. He lapses occasionally into Silver Latin conceits and banality, but the high seriousness of his temperament is matched by descriptive power, and although steeped in the writings of his predecessors, he has a marked originality of his own. Thus his account of the Cave of Time (*Stilicho*, 2, 424 ff.) is a beautifully realized piece of romantic scene-painting. He brightens his narrative with dialogue, has the gift of personifying abstractions and touching them to life, and deploys an epic divine machinery with considerable success. Surprisingly the unfinished *Gigantomachia* and *De raptu Proserpinae* are less convincing than some of the panegyrics. The intensity of the satirical poems is almost Juvenalian. His best poetry is in hexameters although he can write accomplished elegiacs, as in the best known of his shorter poems about the smallholder of Verona (*c.m.* 52). Though some of the minor poems suggest that he may have paid lip-service to Christianity, his temperament and outlook are non-Christian, and his poetry is a not unworthy swan-song of dying paganism. ⇨ Epic Poetry, Roman. [D E W W]

Ed. T. Birt (M G H, 1892); Loeb: M. Platnauer (2 vols., 1922).

Claudius (Tiberius Claudius Nero Germanicus) (10 B.C.–A.D. 54). Roman Emperor A.D. 41–54. Deeply read in Greek and Latin, Claudius had made a mark as a scholar before his unexpected accession to the throne. As a historian, he had produced with the encouragement of Livy a *History of Rome, a pace civili* – from 27 B.C. He is also credited with a *History of the Etruscans*, in 20 books, a *History of Carthage*, in 8, and an *Autobiography*. Only fragments of his historical work survive. As a grammarian, he added 3 letters to the Latin alphabet. Latin literature did not flourish in his reign, but he fostered the Museum at Alexandria for the encouragement of science and scholarship. The *Table of Lyon* and the *Letter to the Alexandrians* are authentic administrative documents. [D R D]

Peter, *H R R*, ii; *Documents to Illustrate the Reigns of Claudius and Nero*, i, ii, v, ed. M. P. Charlesworth (1939).

Claudius Quadrigarius, Quintus (fl. *c.*80 B.C.). Roman historian. He wrote a history of Rome from the capture of the city by the Gauls (390) to the dictatorship of Sulla (82). He had a pleasant style and used everyday language, but was very prone to exaggeration and is often unreliable. Probably to be identified with the Claudius who translated into Latin the Greek history of G. ◊ Acilius. [T A D]

Peter, *H R R*, i.
E. Badian, in *Latin Historians*, ed. T. A. Dorey (1966).

Cleanthes (331–232 B.C.). Greek philosopher. Cleanthes of Assos was Zeno's pupil and the second Master of the Stoic school (263–232). He developed the religious aspect of ◊ Stoicism, teaching that the universe is a living being, with God as its soul. Stobaeus (*Ed. phys.*, I: i: 12) preserved 28 lines of his famous 'Hymn to Zeus', one of the noblest expressions of religious feeling in the Greek language.

'Lead me, O Zeus, and thou, O Destiny,
Wherever is ordained by your decree . . .'

This Zeus is master of the cosmos: 'Nothing is done apart from Thee in Heaven, on the earth, nor in the sea, save only what the wicked perform in their folly.' The hymn was known to St Paul. [D R D]

Arnim, *S V F*.
E. R. Bevan, *Later Greek Religion* (1927).

Cleidemus (fl. *c.*350 B.C.). Athenian writer. Cleidemus was the first Athenian to write an ◊ Atthis. He also wrote a book on religious ritual. [T A D]

Müller, *F H G*.

Cleitarchus (fl. *c.*280 B.C.). Greek historian. Cleitarchus of Alexandria wrote an account of the campaigns of Alexander the Great. He is criticized by later writers for lack of truthfulness, and his work, which was used by Q. ◊ Curtius, seems to have aimed at the sensational. [T A D]

Jacoby, *F G H*, ii.

Clement of Alexandria (Titius Flavius Clemens) (A.D. *c.*150–*c.*214). Greek Christian writer. Born in Athens, a student of rhetoric and philosophy, he was converted to Christianity and became head of the catechetical school at Alexandria. Withdrawing in the face of the Severan persecution of 202, he took up residence in Cappadocia. His principal writings form a trilogy: the first, *Exhortation to the Greeks*, was intended to convert the reader to Christianity; the second, the *Paedagogus*, to instruct in the Christian way of life; and the third, the *Stromata*, was a collection of diffuse material describing the ideal of a complete Christian.

Of comprehensive education, well versed in the classics, from which he quotes no fewer than 360 passages, Clement sought to reconcile Christianity and secular learning. His works are a mine of information on the social practices of his day. [J G D]

Migne, *P G*, 8–9; tr. W. Wilson (A C L, 1868–9).
R. B. Tollinton, *Clement of Alexandria* (2 vols., 1914).

Clodius Licinus, Gaius (fl. A.D. 4). Roman historian. Suffect consul A.D. 4. Historian and friend of G. Julius ◊ Hyginus, whom he helped financially. [T A D]

Peter, *H R R*, ii.

Cluvius. ◊ Rufus, Marcus Cluvius.

Coelius Antipater, Lucius (fl. *c.*120 B.C.). Roman jurist and historian. Leading teacher of rhetoric, who wrote a history of the Second Punic War in 7 books introducing to Rome the historical monograph. He paid great attention to style, used a more ornate language than his predecessors, and was the first writer to treat history as a form of literary composition rather than a mere record of events; in this he pointed out the way to subsequent Roman historians. His work was characterized by an excessive love of the miraculous and the supernatural. He made use of the work of Silenus of Calatia, who had accompanied Hannibal. [T A D]

Peter, *H R R*, i.

Colluthus. ◊ Epic Poetry, Greek.

Colotes. ◊ Epicureanism.

Columella, Lucius Junius Moderatus (1st cent. A.D.). Latin writer on agriculture. Born at Gades (Cadiz) in Spain, he served in the army (an inscription shows him as an officer in the Sixth Legion *Ferrata* in

Syria), and then settled to farm his estate at Ardea in Italy. His work on agriculture, *De re rustica,* was published about A.D. 60. Its object was to arrest the decay of Italian agriculture, which he regarded as being due to too much imported corn and too few owners farming their own lands. Making full use of earlier agricultural writers (⇨ Cato, ⇨ Varro, etc.) its 10 books extend beyond the usual corn–vines–olives–cattle pattern to such topics as poultry-keeping, fish-ponds and orchard-trees. As a graceful tribute to Virgil, Book X is written in verse, and deals with gardening, a subject only sketchily treated in the *Eclogues*. Columella has a good prose style, and though his purpose is practical his manner is never dull. He is one of the best of the Latin technical writers, and it is a pity that his book has fallen into an undeserved neglect. [D R D]

Loeb: H. B. Ash, E. S. Forster and E. Heffner (4 vols., 1941 ff).
W. E. Heitland, *Agricola* (1921).

Comedy, Greek. Comedy originated among the ancient Greeks, in the often obscene seasonal revelry forming part of the Dionysiac fertility cult (⇨ Dionysia). Its early history was not recorded, but by the 5th century B.C. it had assumed two main forms: non-choral Sicilian comedy, developed by ⇨ Epicharmus out of a simple farce or mumming-play current among the Dorians of the Peloponnese and Magna Graecia; and Attic comedy, a choral performance apparently derived from a blend of Dorian farce with a native carnival characterized by badinage between groups of revellers in disguise. Sicilian comedy proved short-lived, but the Attic variety flourished and was officially admitted to the Athenian dramatic competitions in 486 B.C. Ancient critics distinguished two (and later three) stages in the subsequent development of comedy; the first, that of Old Comedy, lasted until the downfall of Athens in 404.

Old Comedy has a distinctive tripartite structure which usually includes a development based on a set contest or dispute; an undramatic interlude, the parabasis, in which the poet addresses the audience through the chorus; and a concluding section consisting of consequential comic scenes and a triumphant finale. It was mainly devoted to personal lampoon until about 450, when plots of a more general character were introduced by Crates. The leading poets of the Old Comedy were ⇨ Cratinus, an older contemporary of Crates, and ⇨ Eupolis and ⇨ Aristophanes in the generation of the Peloponnesian War, when comedy, stimulated by the stresses of wartime, was in its heyday. In the extant plays, all by Aristophanes and all dating from the 420s or later, the plot is simple, making some ludicrous or fantastic idea the vehicle for social, political or literary satire; the action is a richly fanciful and erratic burlesque in which startling indecencies may appear side by side with lyrics of great charm, and gods, heroes, animals and personified abstractions such as Peace are mingled with real or imaginary characters from everyday life.

The enervation of defeat at Athens was reflected in the transition, about 400 B.C., to the tamer Middle Comedy, represented by the latest surviving plays of Aristophanes. Obscenity gave way to innuendo, fantasy to ironic realism, and political satire was largely replaced by burlesque of mythology and contemporary intellectual movements. With the increasing assimilation of comedy to the structure of tragedy, the parabasis disappeared, the remaining choral part dwindled, and the plot became more complex and coherent. By about 330, soon after the final loss of Greek independence, the transformation into New Comedy was complete. A range of stock characters was firmly established, each with its recognizable mask; and in the sentimental love-plot with sub-tragic complications, serious in tone, often pathetic and given to moralizing, which became almost universal, comedy and tragedy virtually coalesced. New Comedy flourished at Athens in the late 4th and early 3rd centuries; its two most eminent poets, ⇨ Philemon and ⇨ Menander, enjoyed such popularity that some of their plays were revived after their death.

Comedies were produced twice a year at Athens at the same festivals and under much the same conditions as tragedy (⇨ Tragedy, Greek). Normally five poets were selected to compete, each with one play. In Old Comedy the chorus often appeared in some bizarre animal disguise, from which the play took its title; later it usually represented a troop of revellers. The actors, three in number and all men, were masked like the chorus, and in Old

Comedy sported a conspicuous leather phallus and grotesque padding fore and aft; otherwise they wore ordinary dress. In metrical technique, as in scenic devices and conventions, comedy followed the example of tragedy, but with appropriately greater freedom.

The brilliance and extravagance of Old Comedy were astonishing while it lasted, but too idiosyncratic to be influential, except eventually as a model for Roman ◊ satire. The more pedestrian but polished New Comedy, however, combining the humour of everyday life and the unfailing interest of the love-story with a happy ending, had a universal and lasting appeal, and strongly influenced the literature both of Rome and of modern Europe. [G T W H]

Pickard-Cambridge, *D T C*; G. Norwood, *Greek Comedy* (1931); K. Lever, *The Art of Greek Comedy* (1956); T. B. L. Webster, *Studies in Later Greek Comedy* (1953), and *Greek Theatre Production* (1956); M. Bieber, *The History of the Greek and Roman Theater* (1961).

Comedy, Roman. Among the Romans comedy was the only indigenous form of drama. In early times the native Italian tradition of comedy was represented by two forms, both of unknown antiquity: the so-called Fescennine verses, consisting of bantering dialogue in impromptu verse, and the more elaborate ◊ Atellan farce of the Oscans in Campania. At Rome itself young men seem to have engaged in improvised exchanges similar to Fescennine verses, but the first organized theatrical performances, *ludi scaenici*, were given in 364 B.C. by players from Etruria, who danced without song or mime in a propitiatory ceremony. Roman performers combined these dances with their own repartee, and gradually developed a composite stage show with a prepared libretto which included song, dance and a musical accompaniment in a medley or *satura* of different rhythms. The decisive step from this medley to a play with a plot was taken by ◊ Livius Andronicus, who in 240 produced the first Latin versions of a Greek comedy and a Greek tragedy. His initiative established comedy from Greek sources, the ◊ *fabula palliata*, on the Roman stage, and for some 80 years it was exploited by a series of able poets. Of these ◊ Naevius, a highly versatile writer, and ◊ Plautus, a specialist in comedy, were both lively, prolific and popular playwrights, who did much to adapt their Greek material to Roman tastes; but their successors Caecilius Statius (*c.*219–168) and ◊ Terence, though praised by cultured critics, lost favour with the Roman public as their work approximated more closely to the Greek originals. In the latter part of the 2nd century B.C. the *fabula palliata* was eclipsed by the *fabula togata*, or comedy with an Italian setting. The chief exponent of this native comedy was Afranius (b. *c.*150), whose work long remained popular. In the 1st century B.C. both the *palliata* and the *togata* continued in revivals, but new writing practically ceased. Contemporary critics, summing up the history of Roman comedy, ranked Caecilius and Plautus highest, with Naevius and Terence somewhat lower. The Atellan farce, in a new literary form, and the ◊ mime now came into vogue; and the latter, with the more serious and sophisticated pantomime, dominated the Roman theatre under the Empire.

Roman comedies included both spoken dialogue, in iambics, and *cantica*, passages of recitative and song in a variety of metres probably inherited from the old *satura*. The *cantica* were delivered by the actors, or by a special singer off-stage; there are few traces of a chorus in Roman comedy. The performances were given in the open air, in a makeshift auditorium; there was no permanent theatre building at Rome until 55 B.C. Plautus and Terence afford ample evidence of the difficulties of entertaining their turbulent audiences in these conditions, especially in competition with rival attractions. The scene of the comedies usually represented the fronts of two or three houses in a street, and consequently all the action took place out of doors. The stage had little depth but considerable width, which facilitated the use of artificial conventions such as the aside and one character's failure to notice another. The actors almost certainly wore masks, with Greek dress in the *fabula palliata* and Roman in the *togata*. They were mostly slaves and freedmen, for professional acting was at first not permitted to Roman citizens, and the prejudice against it died hard. But with the relaxation of standards in the late Republic success on the stage was allowed to compensate for lack of breeding, and under the Empire the adulation of leading actors at times became hysterical. (⇨ Comedy, Greek.) [G T W H]

The Complete Roman Drama, tr. G. E. Duckworth (New York and Toronto, 1942).

G. E. Duckworth, *The Nature of Roman Comedy* (Princeton, 1952); Beare, *R S*; M. Bieber, *The History of the Greek and Roman Theater* (1961).

Corax. ⇨ Oratory and Rhetoric.

Cordus. ⇨ Cremutius Cordus.

Corinna (late 6th cent. B.C.). Greek lyric poetess. Born at Tanagra, Pindar's elder contemporary and rival, she composed narrative poems drawn from Boeotian saga for a feminine audience. Two fragments recovered from a papyrus describe respectively a contest in song between Cithaeron and Helicon, won by Cithaeron (an allegory?), and a speech concerning the daughters of Asopus by the prophet Acraephen. The unsophisticated narrative and simple metre match the Boeotian dialect. Judging from the orthography the poems were transcribed in their present form *c.*200 B.C. The theory that Corinna lived at this date cannot be disproved, but it seems on balance unlikely. [D E W W]

Page, *P M G*.

Cornelius Gallus. ⇨ Elegiac Poetry.

Cornelius Nepos (*c.*99–*c.*24 B.C.). Roman biographer. A native of Cisalpine Gaul, he spent most of his life at Rome. He was a friend of Catullus, who dedicated his book of poems to him, of Cicero, and in particular of ⇨ Atticus, at whose house on the Quirinal he was a frequent guest.

Nepos wrote some love poems, a book of anecdotes and other useful information (*Exempla*), a summary, in 3 books, of world history (*Chronica*), described by Catullus as 'learned and laborious', and a series of *Lives of Famous Men*; of these *Lives*, 25 survive, mostly of Greek generals, such as Themistocles, Miltiades, Epaminondas and Pausanias, but also including Hannibal and Hamilcar. The most valuable is the *Life of Atticus*, of whom Nepos can speak with intimate knowledge; in this, Nepos defends Atticus's policy of political neutrality, which the author himself shared. The style of these *Lives* is dull and tedious, and their historical value is generally slight; but Nepos himself declared that he is not attempting to write history; their main purpose is to eulogize the subject and to point a moral. [T A D]

Loeb: J. C. Rolfe (1929).

Cornificius, Quintus (1st cent. B.C.). Latin poet. Younger contemporary and friend of Catullus, who addresses him in poem 38. His public career was distinguished: after commanding Caesar's forces in Illyricum in 48, he was governor successively of Cilicia in 46–44 (when he corresponded with Cicero), and of Africa Vetus in 44. After Caesar's death he supported the Senate, and clashed with T. Sextius, governor of Africa Nova, finally falling in battle near Utica in 41. He wrote an epyllion entitled *Glaucus*, and hendecasyllables. Almost nothing of his poetry survives, but he was clearly one of the ⇨ *neoterici*, as is confirmed by Ovid (*Tristia*, II: 431). [D E W W]

Crassus, Lucius Licinius (140–91 B.C.). Roman orator and statesman. As consul he ordered the expulsion from Rome of all non-citizens, an act which was one of the causes of the revolt of the Italians in 90. He was censor in 92. The following year he vigorously championed the Senate against the attacks of Marcius Philippus, but died, probably from a heart-attack brought on by excessive strain. He lived in great luxury. With ⇨ Antonius, Crassus was the first of the great Roman orators. He had a smooth polished style. He was a pupil and friend of ⇨ Coelius Antipater, and supervised Cicero's early studies. [T A D]

Cicero, *De oratore*, E. W. Sutton and H. Rackham (Loeb, 1942).

Crates. ⇨ Comedy, Greek.

Crates of Thebes. ⇨ Cynics.

Cratinus (*c.*484–*c.*420 B.C.). Greek comic poet. The earliest of the three Athenian masters of Old Comedy, he began presenting plays about 453, was still a formidable competitor, though noted for his drunkenness, when Aristophanes described him in the *Knights* (424) as senile and forgotten, and won the prize in the following year with his reply, the *Wine-Flask*, probably his last work. He wrote

21 plays, of which only titles and fragments now survive, and won the prize 9 times. He indulged freely in personal and political satire, often through the medium of mythological burlesque, with Pericles as the principal target. In the *Odysseuses,* however, he avoided satire and confined himself to burlesque of the *Odyssey,* thereby anticipating Middle Comedy. Modern discoveries of papyri have yielded a synopsis of his *Dionysalexander,* a farcical version of the Judgement of Paris in which Dionysus himself impersonated Paris and eloped with Helen to Troy, only to panic when the Greeks arrived in pursuit; the play was an attack on Pericles, represented by Dionysus, for provoking the Peloponnesian War. In the *Wine-Flask* Cratinus satirized himself as a poet who deserted his lawful wife, Comedy, in favour of his mistress, Drink, and whose friends tried to induce him to mend his ways. Ancient critics noted an imaginative, Aeschylean quality in his work, and his best lyrics were on everyone's lips. His plots lacked coherence, but his satire was bitter and powerful; Aristophanes compared him to a torrent sweeping all before it. (⇨ Comedy, Greek.) [G T W H]

Edmonds, *F A C*, i.

Cremutius Cordus, Aulus (d. A.D. 25). Roman historian. During the reign of Augustus, Cordus wrote an outspoken history of the Civil Wars in which he refrained from praising Caesar or Augustus, but went out of his way to eulogize Cicero, Brutus and Cassius. This history gave no offence to Augustus, but in A.D. 25, under Tiberius, it was made the grounds of a charge of treason brought by two henchmen of Sejanus, whom Cordus had antagonized. Despairing of acquittal, Cordus starved himself to death; his books were burnt, but some copies survived and were later republished in modified form. [T A D]

Peter, *H R R*, ii.

Ctesias (late 5th cent. B.C.). Greek doctor and writer. Ctesias of Cnidos was personal physician to King Artaxerxes of Persia. He wrote a *History of Persia* in 23 books which was used by Diodorus Siculus and Plutarch, and also a description of India in one book. Both of these works were abridged by Photius. [T A D]

Fragments ed. J. Gilmore (1888).

Curiatius Maternus (1st cent. A.D.). Roman tragic poet. He is chiefly known from his appearance in Tacitus's *Dialogues.* A distinguished senator with a natural gift for oratory, he is represented as prudently preferring seclusion and poetry to the dangers of public life under the emperors. He wrote 2 tragedies on Greek themes, *Medea* and *Thyestes,* and 2 ⇨ *fabulae praetextae, Cato* and *Domitius*; all are now lost. (⇨ Tragedy, Roman.) [G T W H]

R. Syme, *Tacitus* (1958).

Curtius Rufus, Quintus (fl. A.D. *c.* 50). Roman historian. Probably to be identified with the teacher of rhetoric mentioned in the index of Suetonius's *De viris illustribus.* Some time in the middle of the 1st century A.D., he wrote the *History of Alexander the Great*; the work was in 10 volumes, of which the first 2 and parts of the others are lost.

The *History of Alexander* is more important as literature than as history. It is a work drawn indiscriminately from all sources, both good and bad, some favourable to Alexander, some hostile. It is difficult to determine in what proportion Curtius used ⇨ Ptolemy and ⇨ Aristobulus, the *Ephemerides* (diaries of the campaign), ⇨ Cleitarchus, and the Peripatetics. Yet the work is very readable, the treatment romantic, the language elegant though somewhat rhetorical and the speeches vigorous. But there is little attempt to trace the development of Alexander's character, and the narrative consists of a series of dramatic incidents skilfully presented in such a way as to appeal to the emotions. [T A D]

Loeb: J. C. Rolfe (2 vols., 1946).
H. McQueen, in *Latin Biography*, ed. T. A. Dorey (1967).

Cynaethus. ⇨ Homeric Hymns; Homeridae.

Cynics. Traditionally the Cynics traced their ancestry to Socrates through his 'pupil' Antisthenes. But this is probably a fabrication, and the real founder of the movement (it was never strictly a school of philosophy) was Diogenes (*c.* 400–*c.* 325 B.C.). Diogenes' father is said to have been a mint-official of Sinope, ruined through having debased the currency. The son apppeared as an exile at Athens about 340 B.C. Here, and perhaps at Corinth and elsewhere, he set up as a philosopher of an unusual kind, preaching the need to 'alter the currency' in another sense, to strike out of circulation false values and standards of all kinds. The ingredients of his practice were an ascetic life, complete freedom of speech, complete shamelessness of action. From the last, he derived his nickname of the Cynic or 'the dog'. Most of the stories about him are apocryphal (? the retorts to Alexander), but he was clearly a man of striking personality and caustic wit. The best-known of his successors are: Crates of Thebes (*c.* 365–285 B.C.), who threw away his wealth to take up the vagrant life and who became a 'public consultant to Athens'; his wife, the 'female philosopher' Hipparchia: ⇨ Onesicritus, who went to India with Alexander, and saw in the fakirs so many Cynics; and 3 writers of some note, ⇨ Bion, ⇨ Cercidas and ⇨ Menippus. Cynicism became widespread in the earlier Hellenistic period, but we hear little of it in the 2nd and 1st centuries B.C. With the Roman Empire came a revival; admiration for the movement as a kind of left-wing Stoicism appears in the writings of ⇨ Musonius Rufus, ⇨ Dio Chrysostom, ⇨ Epictetus and Marcus ⇨ Aurelius. The Cynic Demetrius (A.D. *c.* 10–*c.* 80) is associated with the Stoic opposition to Nero, and was banished from Rome by Vespasian. Cynics were also involved in the expulsion of philosophers in A.D. 94. In the 2nd century A.D. they were numerous in the Eastern provinces of the Empire, and are known through fragments of Oenomaus of Gadara (preserved by Eusebius), and through the works of Lucian, who admired the Cynic Demonax and disliked the charlatan Peregrinus (d. A.D. 167). The Emperor Julian attacked the immorality of the Cynics. Even as late as the 5th century, a certain Sallustius is found leading the vagrant Cynic life. The movement probably survived into Byzantine times.

Basically, Cynicism was an attempt to show that life can be lived at a minimum level of material, emotional and spiritual needs. As such, its intellectual content was slight, and incapable of development. But it had a social effect comparable to that of the ascetic orders of the Middle Ages and its influence on literature was considerable. Needing a vehicle for popular propaganda, the Cynics evolved a kind of writing called the 'serious-comical': the main genres were the diatribe or lay sermon, the anecdote (*chreia*) and the kind of satire-writing represented by Menippus. These in turn influenced Stoic and even Christian writers. [D R D]

Dudley, *H C*; F. G. Sayre, *Diogenes of Sinope* (1938).

Cyprian (Caecilius Cyprianus) (A.D. *c.* 200–258). Latin Christian writer. Born at Carthage, a rhetor by profession, Cyprian was converted to Christianity *c.* 246 and became bishop two years later. His episcopate was disturbed by the Decian persecution (250), during which he went into hiding, and by the disciplinary problems to which this gave rise, including various schisms. In the persecution under Valerian he was beheaded.

Cyprian's writings reflect his practical activities, each one being produced for a specific occasion. His letters – 65 from his own pen and 16 addressed to him or to the Carthaginian clergy – are valuable for the history of the times and, although largely conversational, they form an outstanding monument of Christian Latin. His treatises, 13 in number including one on the *Unity of the Church* (251), have a polished style and reveal the brilliance of the former rhetor. [J G D]

Migne, *P L*, 3–5; tr. R. E. Wallis (A C L, 1868–9).

E. W. Watson, 'The Style and Language of St Cyprian', in *Studia biblica et ecclesiastica*, iv (1896); E. W. Benson, *Cyprian: His Life, His Times, His Work* (1897).

Cyrenaics. A school of philosophers which flourished in Cyrene in the 4th and early 3rd centuries B.C. They taught a system of hedonism, in which 'the pleasure of the moment' is the end of action. They are sometimes traced to Socrates through his friend and pupil Aristippus, but possibly the Socratic Aristippus has been confused with his grandson of the same name. Other members of the school were Hegesias, Theodorus 'the Atheist' and Anniceris. None of their writings survives. [D R D]

Theodore Gomperz, *Greek Thinkers*, ii (tr. 1905).

D

Damascius. ⇨ Neo-Platonism.

Damasus I (Pope A.D. 366–81). Christian Latin writer. Damasus played an important part in the ecclesiastical politics of his day, both in obtaining acceptance of the jurisdiction of the bishop of Rome and in attempting to reconcile East and West, torn by the Arian troubles. Justly famous as the one who ordered ⇨ Jerome's revision (the Vulgate) of the Old Latin Bible text, Damasus has left several letters and some 59 genuine epigrams – inscriptions engraved on marble slabs by Philocalus and used to adorn the catacombs and various churches and chapels in Rome. [J G D]

Migne, *P L*, 13; *Christian Inscriptions*, tr. H. V. P. Nunn (1951) (19 epigrams).

'Dares'. A 5th-cent. A.D. (?) Latin version, perhaps based on a Greek original, of the Trojan War, ascribed to Dares of Phrygia, priest of Hephaestus with the Greeks at Troy. It was much used as a source by medieval writers on the Trojan War. (⇨ *Dictys; Ilias Latina*.) [D R D]

Teubner: P. Meister (Leipzig, 1873).

'De Viris Illustribus'. A series of 86 epitomized biographies of famous men and women from Romulus and Remus to Antony and Cleopatra, by an unknown author. It contains some glaring mistakes; for example, it confuses C. Flaminius, consul in 187 B.C., with T. Quinctius Flamininus. The *De viris illustribus* was at some time combined with the *Origo gentis romanae*, also of an unknown author, and the *Liber de Caesaribus* of Aurelius Victor (A.D. *c.* 360), into a work known as the *Historia tripertita*. [T A D]

Teubner: *Historia tripertita*, R. Gruendel (Leipzig, 1961).

Demetrius of Phaleron (*c.* 350–283 B.C.). Athenian statesman. He was a member of the Peripatetic School, and the first Librarian at Alexandria. Expelled from Athens in 307, he took refuge with Ptolemy Soter in Egypt, whom he assisted in political affairs and in the foundation of the Museum and Library. He wrote on a wide range of political, historical and ethical subjects. None of his works survives. Diogenes Laertius in his *Life* (v, 527–37) gives a list of titles. [D R D]

W. S. Ferguson, *Hellenistic Athens* (1911).

Demetrius the Cynic. ⇨ Cynics.

Democritus. ⇨ Atomists.

Demon. ⇨ Atthis.

Demonax. ⇨ Cynics.

Demosthenes (384–322 B.C.). Greatest of Greek orators. Son of Demosthenes, a well-to-do Athenian of the deme Paeania, and of Cleobule, who had Scythian blood in her veins. From his mother he may have inherited some of his fiery intensity; from his father, who died when he was 7, he should have inherited a considerable estate. But his guardians abused their trust, and he was forced to fight for the remains of his patrimony. Traditionally he was a lonely bookish boy, struggling to overcome his physical and temperamental handicaps. Aloofness always prevented his mixing easily, and his oratory lacks the common touch. He studied rhetoric and judicial procedure under ⇨ Isaeus. The protracted dispute with his guardians was finally brought into court when he came of age. The 3 speeches *Against Aphobus* and the 2 *Against Onetor* show already a disciplined style and a strength of will beyond his years. He next took up the profession of speech-writer, and continued to practise it for most of his active career. More than half the surviving private speeches are unauthentic; but enough genuine work remains to show that his success lay in his intellectual grasp of each case's complexities and in a formidable gift of exposition and argument. The collection, ranging from trespass, forgery and embezzlement to assault and battery, gives a colourful cross-section of the life of the courts.

Success in private cases led to public prosecutions and ultimately to a political career. *Against Androtion* and *Against Timocrates* were spoken by Diodorus, but *Against Leptines* by Demosthenes in person. All are concerned with finance; they were well received and encouraged Demosthenes to come forward as spokesman for foreign affairs. The speeches of 354–351, *On the Symmories, For the Megalopolitans, On the Freedom of Rhodes*, and *Against Aristocrates*, constituted a survey of the whole range of Athenian foreign relations, supporting the policy of Eubulus and advocating a balance of power. But Demosthenes was among the first to realize that Philip's emergence changed the whole political landscape, since Greek independence could be maintained only by a panhellenic coalition, with Athens and Thebes dominant, and with Persian support if possible. The great political speeches date from 351 to 340, those down to 344 being spoken in opposition. The *First* and *Second Philippics* and the 3 *Olynthiacs* warn the Athenians of their danger – the help given to their allies has been too little and too late. The first phase of the struggle ended in 346 with the Peace of Philocrates, which Demosthenes accepted only as a necessary breathing-space. The impeachment of Aeschines, *On the Embassy*, in 344, was unsuccessful, but the margin for acquittal was narrow, and from now until 338 Demosthenes and the anti-Macedonian party were in the ascendant. The *Third Philippic* (Demosthenes' most masterly speech on foreign affairs) dates from 341, and the *Fourth Philippic* follows shortly after. He did force through the alliance with Thebes, though only when victory was unattainable. Chaeroneia meant the end of Greek independence, but at least Greece had gone down fighting.

The *Epitaphios*, commemorating the battle victims, is probably authentic. But the real speech on the fallen came in 330, when Aeschines' attempt to withhold the golden crown voted to Demosthenes for his services elicited the *De corona*, a triumphant vindication of his character and conduct. In 324 the arrival in Athens of Harpalus, who on a rumour of Alexander's death had absconded with his treasure, caused Demosthenes to emerge from retirement. Harpalus distributed money lavishly, and after his departure Demosthenes was impeached, and on conviction withdrew to Aegina. His integrity is above suspicion; he had possibly been indiscreet. Alexander's death roused Athens to strike a last blow for freedom, and Demosthenes was recalled. But the dream of independence vanished at Crannon. Demosthenes, hunted down by Antipater's agents, took poison to avoid arrest.

The speeches were no doubt revised before publication, but survive substantially as delivered. The 56 prooemia attributed to Demosthenes are probably authentic; the 6 letters almost certainly forgeries. Demosthenes was at his best in the great debates on foreign policy, when the seriousness and conviction of his style, together with his grasp and understanding of the situation and issues, combine to produce passages of irresistible eloquence. He has a dynamic and elemental force which sweeps all before it, and may blind us to the controlled artistry, product of long years of training and experience, which disciplines and moulds his sentences and periods. Much of his power lies in his feeling for prose rhythm and his ear for the stately music of the spoken word. His effects may be calculated, but he contrives to give an impression of unelaborated spontaneity, just as in the structure of his speeches he appears to deploy his materials simply, but in fact marshals his arguments subtly to achieve maximum effectiveness. He is less at ease in the more intimate court-room atmosphere; his intellect, though powerful, is not agile, and his attempts at humour sometimes misfire. One can well believe that he was not a good impromptu speaker, and that he broke down in an unprepared address to Philip. But the fiery spirit of the man still glows in his public speeches, and his steely determination and moral earnestness grip the imagination. The last Greek for centuries to breathe the air and speak the language of liberty, he gave worthy expression to the ideals of a free Athens, for which he laid down his life, and which perished with him. [DEWW]

Loeb: A. T. Murray, C. A. and J. H. Vince, N. W. and N. J. De Witt (7 vols., 1926–49).
Dobson, *GO*; A. W. Pickard-Cambridge, *Demosthenes and the Last Days of Greek Freedom* (1914); W. Jaeger, *Demosthenes* (1938).

Dialogue. Dialogue was an important element in several forms of Greek literature in the 5th century B.C. – tragedy, comedy, mime and history. But as a specific *genre* it developed mainly from the discussions of the philosophers and, above all, from those of ⇨ Socrates. The main aim of writers of 'Socratic discourses' such as ⇨ Plato, ⇨ Xenophon, Phaedo and ⇨ Antisthenes was to give a lively picture of their master in action. The dialogue was indeed the main vehicle for the thought of Plato, who used it with skill and flexibility. Some of his earlier dialogues are 'reporting' of the highest possible level. Each character is drawn in the round and plays his appropriate part: the give-and-take of the conversation is easy and natural. In the later dialogues the emphasis is usually on philosophical exposition – characterization is weak; the argument is in the hands of one or two main speakers; conversation is a fossilized convention. None of Aristotle's dialogues survives, but they seem to have been of this second type.

The Romans, with their forensic bent, found the dialogue form congenial. ⇨ Cicero used it extensively in his works on philosophy, politics and rhetoric. The *Dialogus de oratore* of ⇨ Tacitus is of this kind; the *Octavius* of ⇨ Minucius Felix and the *De consolatione* of ⇨ Boethius carry Latin dialogue into the later Empire.

There are two notable examples of its use by later Greek authors; ⇨ Plutarch revived it for philosophy, and ⇨ Lucian employs it most effectively for satire. [D R D]

Dicaearchus (fl. *c.* 300 B.C.). Greek scholar and writer. Born at Messana in Sicily, he spent most of his life in Greece. He was a pupil of Aristotle and a friend and contemporary of Theophrastus. He had a very wide range of interests and wrote on political and social history, geography, philosophy and literature. His ideas on mixed constitutions probably influenced Polybius and Cicero. His summaries of the plots of Sophocles and Euripides were used by Byzantine scholars. As a philosopher, he denied the immortality of the soul. [T A D]

Jacoby, *F G H*, ii.

'Dictys'. A Latin rendering, by one Lucius Septimius (4th century A.D.), of a Greek book, itself a forgery (? 2nd century A.D.). The latter purported to be an eye-witness account of the Trojan War by Dictys of Crete, companion of the Cretan hero Idomeneus at Troy. It was used as a source by writers on the Trojan war in the Middle Ages, when it was widely read. (⇨ *Dares; Ilias Latina.*) [D R D]

Teubner: F. Meister (Leipzig, 1872).

Didymus (*c.* 80 B.C.–A.D. *c.* 10). Alexandrian philologist, grammarian and textual critic. His prodigious output earned him the name of Chalcenteros ('Brazen-guts'). He is credited with some 4,000 works – so many that he himself forgot what he wrote. His best work seems to have been done in commentaries on Homer, Thucydides and the Attic orators. Much of his material found its way into later editions. [D R D]

Fragments ed. M. Schmidt (1854).

Dinarchus. ⇨ Attic Orators.

Dio Cassius (Cassius Dio Cocceianus) (A.D. *c.* 155–*c.* 235). Greek historian. He was born in Bithynia, the son of Cassius Apronianus, who was governor of Cilicia and Dalmatia, and probably the maternal grandson of ⇨ Dio Chrysostom. Coming to Rome in about the year 180, he entered the Senate under Commodus; he held the praetorship in 193, and the consulship some years later. He seems to have spent most of the reign of Septimius Severus in retirement, preparing and writing his history, but returned to public life under his successors, holding various administrative posts, including the proconsulship of Africa and the governorships of Dalmatia and Pannonia, crowning his official career with a second consulship in 229, with the emperor Alexander Severus as his colleague. He passed the last few years of his life in Bithynia.

Apart from a biography of Arrian and an account of the portents that foretold the reign of Septimius Severus, Dio's great literary work was his *Roman History*, covering the period from the arrival of Aeneas to his own second consulship in 80 books, written in Greek. Of this work, the books dealing with the period from the Second Mithridatic War (69 B.C.) to the reign of Claudius (A.D. 46) have survived intact, and there are fragments containing the last years of the Second Punic War and the reigns of the Emperors Caracalla and Macrinus. The rest survives only in excerpts in medieval collections and in epitomes made by Zonaras

(12th century) and **Xiphilinus** (11th century). Dio's history is useful in supplementing other earlier sources for the Late Republic and the Early Empire. His books contain much interesting detail not found elsewhere, but in many cases it may be derived from scurrilous propaganda, a fact of which Dio himself was aware. As history, therefore, his work should be used with caution – he had a clear understanding of imperial administration and practical political experience, but he had no opportunity for evaluating his historical sources. [T A D]

Loeb: E. Cary (9 vols., 1914).

Dio Chrysostom (Dio Cocceianus) (A.D. *c.*40–*c.*115). Greek orator and philosopher. Dio's public career is divided into three stages. Born of wealthy parents at Prusa in Bithynia, he won fame as an orator and an ardent Hellenist. This brought him excellent connexions at Rome, notably the emperor Titus and his stepson Flavius Sabinus. He was involved in the conspiracy of Sabinus against Domitian (82), and sentenced to exile from Rome, Italy and his native province. His career in ruins, he asked the advice of the oracle at Delphi, and was told: 'Do the near-by thing with all earnestness, until you come to the ends of the earth.' During the next 14 years he wandered through the north-eastern portions of the Roman world, and we hear of him in Greece, Pontus and the Danube lands. He earned his living in a variety of humble occupations, acting always as a philosopher-missionary in the Cynic tradition. He became interested in the barbarian peoples outside the Roman frontiers, especially the Dacians and their great king Decebalus. On Domitian's death his exile was ended by Nerva, and he enjoyed high favour under Trajan. His reputation as philosopher and Hellenist enabled him to speak as a representative of the educated classes of the Greek half of the Roman world, to express their hopes of the new regime, and to expound the social problems of the day.

No less than 80 of his speeches survive, though unfortunately his *History of the Getae* is lost. Of these the most popular are (1) The *Rhodian Oration*, a programme for a Greek cultural revival (*Or.* 31), (2) *Or.* 6, 8, 9, 10, from the period of exile, Cynic discourses with Diogenes as the central figure, (3) *Or.* 1–4 on kingship, and delivered in the presence of Trajan, setting out the concept of the ideal king, modelled on Hercules, the servant of mankind. In the *Alexandrian Speech* (*Or.* 32) he addresses the turbulent populace of that city as the emperor's unofficial representative; in the *Euboean Speech* (*Or.* 7), he takes up the problems of poverty and the means to a virtuous life for the poor. *Or.* 52 is a comparison of the three great Greek tragedians. [D R D]

Teubner: G. de Budé (2 vols., 1912–19); Loeb: J. W. Cohoon and H. Lamar Crosby (5 vols., 1932–51).

H. von Arnim, *Leben und Werke des Dion von Prusa* (1898).

Diodorus Siculus (fl. 60–30 B.C.). Greek historian. Diodorus was born at Agyrium in Sicily. Little is known about his life, though he claims to have travelled widely to collect material for his work.

Diodorus wrote a history of the Mediterranean world, *The Library of History*, in 40 volumes, from mythological times to the Ciceronian age. The only books that survive entire are Books I–V (legendary material and folk-lore), and XI–XX (480–302 B.C.). The rest only survive as excerpts or paraphrases in Byzantine or medieval collections. Diodorus is most useful for 479–431 B.C. – the gap between the end of Herodotus and the start of the main narrative of Thucydides; and for 362–302 B.C., where there is no other continuous literary account. He is also important for the history of Sicily. As a historian, Diodorus had little critical ability, and his value depends on the source used. Fortunately, for the wars following Alexander the Great's death his sources were particularly reliable. Diodorus employs a complex chronological framework based on Olympic Festivals, Athenian archons, and Roman consuls, but often he cannot adjust his material to his framework and so often makes gross chronological errors. He also moralizes excessively. [T A D]

Loeb: C. H. Oldfather (12 vols., 1933).

Diogenes Laertius (early 3rd cent. A.D.). Author of the *Lives and Opinions of the Eminent Philosophers*. Of his own life we know almost nothing. He was neither a philosopher nor an original thinker, but an energetic compiler and collector. More than 200 authors are cited as sources in his book. His method is to arrange the philosophers in the 'schools' or 'successions' to which they belong. Thus Book I deals with the Seven Wise Men, II with the Ionian succession from Thales to Socrates, III with Plato, IV the Academy, V the school of Aristotle, VI the Cynics, VII the Stoics (incomplete), VIII the Italian succession, IX a mixed bag of unclassifiables, and X Epicurus. He retails anecdotes about his philosophers rather than expounding their thought; he has no sense of historical development, and not much insight into character; he wrote for a public that preferred to read philosophy in digests. But the almost complete loss of the authors he cites has given his book a greater importance, for us, than its intrinsic merits could claim. Many of the biographical details and lists of works contained are not otherwise known. Weak on the pre-Socratics, Diogenes gives us good lives of Socrates, Plato, Aristotle and the Stoics; but perhaps his most valuable service is that he quotes extensively, in Book X, from the original writings of Epicurus. A number of his epigrams are in the Greek ⇨ Anthology. [D R D]

OCT: *Vitae philosophorum*, H. S. Long (2 vols., 1963); Loeb: R. D. Hicks (2 vols., 1925).

Diogenes of Apollonia (fl. *c.*440–430 B.C.). Greek philosopher. One of the last of the pre-Socratics. His wide range of interests and the scanty fragments surviving make it hard to estimate his influence. He seems to have revived the 'monist' principle, developing Anaximenes' theory of Air as the underlying substance for a new assault on the pluralists. This gave particular interest to his views on physiology and biology; he practised dissection, described the vascular system, and dealt with problems concerning the semen and the embryo. He thus influenced the medical writers of the school of ⇨ Hippocrates. [D R D]

Diels, *F V*, 64.

Diogenes of Oenoanda. ⇨ Epicureanism.

Diogenes the Cynic. ⇨ Cynics.

Dionysia. Rites or festivals of Dionysus, the Greek god of wine and vegetation, and the embodiment of the life force in nature generally. His cult was widespread throughout the Greek world in antiquity, but we have few details from anywhere but Athens. There the name Dionysia was applied to three festivals, distinguished by locality as the Dionysia in the country, at the Lenaeum (a sanctuary), and in the city. The first, the Rural Dionysia, was organized in midwinter by various local communities in Attica, and included processions in which model phalli were carried and carnivals with contests between groups of revellers in disguise, whose competitive and indecent buffoonery may have been a source of Greek ⇨ comedy; in the 4th century, tragedies, comedies and dithyrambs were also performed. The Dionysia at the Lenaeum, or Lenaea, took place a month later; little is known of the programme, except that from the late 5th century onwards, and perhaps earlier, it included a dramatic competition with performances of comedy and tragedy. The City Dionysia, or Great Dionysia, were held in late spring, and attended by many delegations and visitors from abroad. The festival included a great procession in which model phalli were carried and numbers of bulls led to the sacrifice, a carnival and a progressively enlarged programme of competitions in tragedy, dithyramb and comedy, ultimately lasting several days. There were similar dramatic festivals in other parts of Greece, as the remains of theatres testify, but the success and splendour of the City Dionysia in the 6th and 5th centuries made Athens the chief centre of drama in the whole Greek world. (⇨ Comedy, Greek; Dithyramb; Tragedy, Greek.) [G T W H]

A. W. Pickard-Cambridge, *The Dramatic Festivals of Athens* (1953).

Dionysius of Halicarnassus (fl. 30–8 B.C.). Greek scholar and writer. Dionysius came to Rome *c.*30 B.C. and became a teacher of rhetoric and the leading figure in one of the literary circles at Rome. As a recompense for the welcome he received he composed a history of Rome from the earliest origins of the Roman race to the beginning of the First Punic War, where the history of Polybius begins. He chose this period because earlier historians who had dealt with it had touched on it in a very summary manner without careful investigation of the evidence. Dionysius did not appreciate that the reason for this neglect was that there was little trustworthy material available. Therefore much of the early books of his *Roman Antiquities* consists of a series of very scholarly discussions of conflicting theories all based on unsupportable evidence (e.g., he goes to great lengths to prove that the Romans were descended from Greeks). The *Roman Antiquities* contained 20 books, of which the first 11 survive almost entire, and the rest in fragments, mostly in the form of 10th-century excerpts. The narrative is long-winded, tedious, often moralizing and frequently interrupted by lengthy speeches, which are a free-composition of the author. It takes Dionysius 10 books to cover a period that Livy dealt with in 3. His main value lies in his preservation of accounts by previous historians.

To us, however, his most useful writings are his *Scripta rhetorica,* letters and essays on literary criticism written at various times while he was still engaged on his historical work. They include criticisms of Plato, whose popularity as a model for style Dionysius attacks, of historians such as Herodotus, Thucydides and Xenophon, and of orators such as Isocrates, Lysias, Isaeus and Demosthenes. He also discusses the correct order of words. He adopted and developed the method of comparative criticism, setting the faults and virtues of one writer against those of another. In his earlier works he lacks original thought, and merely applies the traditional rules for the judgement of style in respect to such qualities as purity of language, clarity, brevity and adornment; but in his later works he develops his own ideas, and discusses not merely style but also treatment of subject-matter. His work is always characterized by a very thorough and systematic analysis, his strongest point as a critic. He was an exponent of the 'Middle' style of oratory, and he followed Cicero in advocating Demosthenes as the supreme master of style. [T A D]

Loeb: *Roman Antiquities*, E. Cary (7 vols., 1937); *Three Literary Letters*, tr. W. R. Roberts (1901); *On Literary Composition*, tr. W. R. Roberts (1910).
S. F. Bonner, *Dionysius of Halicarnassus* (1939).

Dionysius Thrax (b. *c.* 166 B.C.). Greek grammarian. Pupil of ⇨ Aristarchus of Samothrace at Alexandria, and later taught at Rhodes. He wrote an *Art of Grammar*, which has had an enduring influence as a textbook, comparable to Euclid's. Taken up in Rome by ⇨ Remmius Palaemon, it was widely used in the Renaissance, and was not abandoned in some English schools until the 19th century. [D R D]

Teubner: G. Uhlig, *Grammatici graeci* (Leipzig, 1883).

Dioscorides of Anabarzus (fl. A.D. *c.* 50). Greek botanist. The greatest of ancient herbalists. He lived in the reign of Claudius and Nero. Apparently he was a doctor in the Roman Army. Dioscorides drew on his own extensive travels and his knowledge of previous authorities to draw up a comprehensive *Materia medica* (published A.D. *c.* 65). It describes 600 plants, and sets out the uses of nearly 1,000 drugs. Frequently translated into Latin, Arabic and all the main vernacular languages, and often accompanied by fine illustrations, it became one of the most important books known to the medieval world. [D R D]

Ed. M. Wellman (3 vols., 1907–14); *The Greek Herbal of Dioscorides*, tr. R. T. Gunther (1934).

Diphilus (*c.* 355?–*c.* 288 B.C.). Greek comic poet. Diphilus of Sinope was the son of an immigrant, but established himself at Athens as a leading writer of New Comedy. He wrote about 100 plays; nearly 60 titles are preserved, some mythological but most suggesting domestic comedy. Of the surviving fragments a great many are concerned with food, cooks and parasites. Despite jokes in antiquity about his frigid comedies Diphilus had a considerable influence on the Roman stage: ⇨ Plautus adapted the *Casina*, *Rudens* and *Vidularia* from his plays and ⇨ Terence a scene in the *Adelphi*. (⇨ Comedy, Greek; Comedy, Roman.) [G T W H]

Edmonds, *F A C*, iii, A.
T. B. L. Webster, *Studies in Later Greek Comedy* (1953).

Dithyramb. A form of Greek choral lyric associated with the cult of Dionysus, and sung by a 'cyclic' chorus (one arranged in a circle). The meaning of the name and the early history of the form are obscure. Initially a kind of processional song particularly cultivated in the Peloponnese, the dithyramb was first reorganized as a static performance and given a literary form by Arion at Corinth about 600 B.C., and was promoted at Athens under the tyrants by Lasus of Hermione. Official dithyrambic competitions were instituted at Athens *c.* 509 B.C. The chief masters of the dithyramb in the early 5th century were ⇨ Simonides, who won over 50 prizes; Lasus himself; ⇨ Pindar, the composer of a famous dithyramb for the Athenians, of which a richly florid fragment survives; and ⇨ Bacchylides, whose extant work includes a unique dithyramb in dialogue form. At this period the dithyramb seems to have normally been a narrative lyric on a mythological theme, with a regular antistrophic structure. But from *c.* 470 B.C. onwards, under the influence of modernist composers such as Melanippides, Philoxenus, Cinesias and Timotheus, the music assumed greater importance at the expense of the words; the correspondence of strophe and antistrophe was abandoned for greater freedom of expression, lyric solos were introduced, and the language became more elaborate and affected until the dithyramb was a byword for sound without sense. The dithyramb continued until Roman times, but ceased to be a significant form of art after the 4th century B.C. (⇨ Dionysia.) [G T W H]

Pickard-Cambridge, *D T C*; Bowra, *G L P*.

Domitius Marsus (*c.* 54–*c.* 4 B.C.). Latin epigrammatist. A contemporary of Ovid, much esteemed by Martial, but now represented only by meagre fragments (one on the death of Tibullus). [D R D]

Teubner: Morel, *F P L*.

Donatus, Aelius (fl. 4th cent. A.D.). Latin grammarian and literary critic. Donatus was one of the leading scholars of his time, and ⇨ Jerome was his pupil. His grammatical works were 'known to every schoolboy' throughout the Middle Ages, and are the foundation of all Latin grammar. They comprised (1) the *Ars minor*, a brief introduction to grammar, and (2) the *Ars secunda*, dealing with accidence and stylistics. Of the literary works, the commentary on Terence survives (incomplete) in a later compilation. We have the *Life* of Virgil and the commentary on the *Eclogues*. Much of the rest of his Virgilian commentary is re-used by ⇨ Servius. [D R D]

Ed. in H. Keil, *Grammatici latini*, iv (Leipzig, 1880).

Dracontius, Blossius Aemilius (late 5th cent. A.D.). Christian Latin poet. He lived under the Vandal rule in North Africa, and was imprisoned by Gunthamund. His shorter poems, mostly on classical mythology, go under the title of *Romulea*, and include an epyllion on Medea. A tragedy on the Orestes theme is now attributed to him. The Christian poems consist of an *Apologia*, in elegiac couplets, addressed to the King, and 3 books of hexameters, whose correct title appears to be *De laudibus Dei*. His works are interesting for the light they throw on the survival of Roman culture in Africa in that dim period rather than for their own literary merits. [D R D]

Teubner: F. Vollmer, *Poetae latinae minores*, v (Leipzig, 1914).

Duris (*c.* 340–260 B.C.). Greek historian and critic. Duris of Samos claimed descent from Alcibiades. He was a pupil of ⇨ Theophrastus and for a time was tyrant of Samos. He wrote a *History of Greece* from 370 to 281 B.C., a *History of Agathocles* (the tyrant of Syracuse), a *History of Samos* and various works on art and music. As a historian he was inclined towards the sensational. [T A D]

Jacoby, *F G H*, ii.

E

Eleatics. The school of monist philosophers who taught at Elea in south Italy in the 6th and 5th centuries B.C. Perhaps found by ⇨ Xenophanes: later representatives included ⇨ Parmenides, ⇨ Zeno and ⇨ Melissus. [D R D]

Elegiac Poetry, Greek and Latin. A heterogeneous body of poetry written over many centuries, which has a common feature the use of the elegiac metre – that is, the distich of a dactylic hexameter followed by a pentameter (⇨ Metre). The word perhaps derives from a non-Greek word for the Phrygian flute, so that elegies are flute-songs. Hence it is natural that they should cover a wide range of emotions as they first appear in Greek literature – the martial songs of ⇨ Tyrtaeus, the personal poems of ⇨ Archilochus, drinking-songs, love-songs, laments and narrative. ⇨ Solon, ⇨ Mimnermus, ⇨ Theognis and ⇨ Simonides are other early Greek elegists.

In the Hellenistic world the *genre* was frequently used for narrative, and especially for mythological poems. Here the great names are ⇨ Callimachus and Philetas. They are also associated with love-elegy, though little of it survives.

But the great flowering of love-elegy was at Rome, in the period of rather more than half a century which covers ⇨ Catullus, ⇨ Propertius, ⇨ Tibullus and ⇨ Ovid. We might understand its evolution better if we had the works of Cornelius Gallus (d. 26 B.C.), whom his peers speak of with the highest respect. As it is, we can grant that the work of the four poets mentioned (to which we must add scanty fragments of Sulpicia) constitutes one of the most brilliant achievements of Latin literature – an exploration of 'the realm of Venus' as bold, personal and felicitous as that of any literature in the world. After Ovid Latin elegy is of no great account, though there are some graceful poems by Petronius. (⇨ Metre; Anthology, Greek and Latin.) [D R D]

T. Hudson-Williams, *Early Greek Elegy* (1926); Bowra, *E G E*; Georg Luck, *The Latin Love Elegy* (1959).

Empedocles (*c.* 493–*c.* 433 B.C.). Greek philosopher. A key-figure in the development of Greek philosophy before Socrates. Like Pythagoras, he was a statesman, philosopher and mystic; unlike him, he expanded his system in writing, of which too little survives to allow a coherent reconstruction. By birth he belonged to the aristocracy of Acragas (Agrigento) in Sicily, but he was a democrat in politics, and played a leading part in the events which brought that party to power in 471. A turn of political fortune drove him into exile. His travels took him to south Italy and to Greece. That he committed suicide by leaping into the crater of Etna is one of several traditions about his death.

He wrote (1) a poem of 5,000 hexameters *On Nature* (some 350 lines survive), and (2) the *Purifications* (*Katharmoi*). The first contained his views on natural philosophy, which had the merit of making a fresh start after the impasse created by ⇨ Parmenides. Briefly, he postulated four indestructible elements, contained within a spherical universe, and operating through a cycle of four stages under the influence of the forces of Love and Strife (attraction and repulsion?), each of which is dominant in turn. He also concerned himself with medicine and with rhetoric. Aristotle had a high regard for him as a thinker, and Lucretius saw in him a forerunner as a scientific poet. [D R D]

Diels, *F V*, 31.

Ennius, Quintus (239–169 B.C.). Roman epic and tragic poet. Ennius, the 'father of Roman poetry', was born of Messapian stock in Magna Graecia at Rudiae, near Brundisium, and spoke Greek, Oscan and Latin. After serving with the Roman army in Sardinia he was brought to Rome by the elder ⇨ Cato in 204, and made a modest living as a teacher and playwright. He became friendly with several leading patricians, accompanied one abroad in the Aetolian campaign of 189, and obtained Roman citizenship in 184. His epic poetry seems to have been the work of his later years. He remained active but poor till he died, confident of lasting fame. He reveals himself in his works as a genial companion, humane, scholarly and discreet; an eclectic in beliefs, he combined a measure of Greek rationalism and advanced thinking with a conviction that he was a reincarnation of Homer.

The works of Ennius survive only in fragments. His dramas were mainly tragedies, adapted from the Greek; 20 titles and some 400 lines are preserved, but even these scraps conjure up moments of terror, pathos or despair, or the splendour of a starry night, with the power of a great poet, and with characteristically Roman rhetorical effect. He also appears to have written two *fabulae praetextae* and some comedies, his least successful form of drama. Other minor works included his *Satires,* or poetical medleys, *Scipio*, a poem on his patron's conquests; didactic poems on natural philosophy, gastronomy and mythology; translations from ⇨ Sotades; and some choice epitaphs in verse.

By far his most influential work was

the *Annals,* an epic chronicle of Rome in 18 books (some 550 lines remain). Narrating events in chronological order, it was artless and episodic; in so far as there was any central character it was Rome itself. In metre the poem was revolutionary, for instead of the native saturnian verses Ennius used the hexameter of Greek epic, thereby consciously challenging comparison with Homer. Naïve and clumsy as he often was in fitting, or forcing, accentual Latin into quantitative Greek rhythms, he achieved great power and dignity in the new medium, blending the high heroic tone, similes and other descriptive touches of Homer with Roman alliteration, predilection for word-play and rhetoric. In this rugged, massive masterpiece the Romans found their history grandly and vividly retold; fundamentally religious in its conception of their predestined greatness, it became their national epic.

Ennius was the last and greatest of the versatile poets of early Rome, and to the end of the Golden Age was revered as the founder of Roman poetry in its classical form. Lucretius and Virgil in particular acknowledged his pre-eminence in epic and didactic poetry, and Cicero ardently admired his dramas; his poetry permeated the language almost as Shakespeare and the Authorized Version have permeated English. Under the Empire he was respected, or at times derided, as the ancient monument of Roman literature until archaic Latin returned to favour in Hadrian's time. His achievement in naturalizing quantitative verse was decisive, and confirmed once and for all that Roman poetry and thought would thenceforth be Greco-Roman. (⇨Epic, Roman; Tragedy, Roman.) [G T W H]

Ed. J. Vahlen, *Ennianae poesis reliquiae* (Leipzig, 1928); Loeb: Warmington, *R O L*; *Annals*, ed. E. M. Steuart (1925).

Beare, *R S*; O. Skutsch, *The Annals of Q. Ennius* (1951); R. E. Smith, *The Failure of the Roman Republic* (1955).

Ephorus (*c.*405–*c.*330 B.C.). Greek historian. Born at Cyme in Asia Minor, Ephorus came to Athens and was a pupil of ⇨ Isocrates. He wrote a *Local History of Cyme,* 2 books of *Discoveries* containing interesting mythological and antiquarian information, and a history in 30 books, the last book of which was completed after his death by his son Demophilus. His work survives only in fragments quoted by Strabo and Diodorus Siculus, though he is also the source of Books XI–XV of Diodorus.

The history of Ephorus embraced the whole of the Greek world from the Dorian invasion to the siege of Perinthus by Philip of Macedon. It is rhetorical in tone, is strongly didactic, and each book starts with a preface in which Ephorus expresses his own views. He has little knowledge of military matters, is undiscriminating in his use of sources, and has a strong pro-Athenian bias, but he was highly estimated in classical times and was one of the best of the many historians of the 4th century B.C. [T A D]

Jacoby, *F G H*, ii.

G. L. Barber, *The Historian Ephorus* (1935).

Epic Cycle. The name given by Greek writers of the late classical period to a group of early epic poems by poets other than Homer and Hesiod, independently composed at various dates but collectively forming an ordered series and providing a history of the world in myth and legend from the birth of the gods to the end of the Heroic Age. The poems themselves are now lost, but fragments and some abridged prose synopses survive.

The Epic Cycle began with the union of Heaven and Earth, and the conflicts of their descendants, leading to the supremacy of the Olympian gods under Zeus; the earliest poems were apparently a *Theogony*, a *Gigantomachy,* and the ⇨ *Titanomachia.* To relieve Earth of the burden of the human race Zeus brought about first the Theban War and then the Trojan War; hence both Theban and Trojan poems had a place in the Epic Cycle. The Theban sequence consisted of the *Oedipodeia* or *Story of Oedipus*, ascribed to Cinaethon of Lacedaemon (perhaps 8th century); the *Thebais* (8th century), an anonymous poem on the expedition of the Seven against Thebes; and the *Epigoni* or *After-Born*, ascribed to Antimachus of Teos (perhaps 8th century), on the second expedition by the sons of the Seven. The *Thebais* was much admired, and Plutarch considered it the next best to the *Iliad* and *Odyssey*.

In the Trojan sequence the *Cypria* (perhaps 8th century), a poem of uncertain authorship on the abduction of Helen and the opening stages of the war, led up to the *Iliad,* and the *Aethiopis,* ascribed to Arctinus of Miletus (8th century), provided a sequel which continued to the death of Achilles. Following this, the *Little Iliad*, probably by Lesches of Mytilene (7th century), and the earlier *Sack of Ilium*, also ascribed to Arctinus, overlapped; only the *Little Iliad* included the strategem of the Wooden Horse, but both described the destruction of Troy. Next came the *Homecomings*, attributed to Hegias, or Agias, of Troezen (probably 7th century), a companion piece to the *Odyssey* recording the fate of Agamemnon among others; and finally a sequel to the *Odyssey*, the *Telegonia* ascribed to Eugammon of Cyrene (6th century). This continued the story to the death of Odysseus and the marriage of his two sons, in a settlement which marked the end of the Trojan saga, the Epic Cycle and the Heroic Age.

Even the scanty remains of the Cycle suffice to indicate its wealth of myth and legend. The barbaric elements in the poems, the monsters, brutalities, superstitions and human sacrifices, betrayed their primitive sources more clearly than the more polished *Iliad* and *Odyssey,* whose superiority was generally acknowledged. In time the cyclic poems were valued less for their excellence than for their sequence of stories; and Aristotle condemned their lack of dramatic movement and unity of action. But they remained a treasury of themes which were a perennial inspiration to subsequent generations, and particularly to the Greek lyric and tragic poets, and to later writers of epic, both Greek and Latin. [G T W H]

Testimonia and fragments in O C T *Homeri Opera*, v, ed. T. W. Allen (1912); Loeb: H. G. Evelyn-White, *Hesiod, The Homeric Hymns and Homerica* (1936).

Epic Poetry, Greek. Epic poetry, large-scale narrative poetry of high seriousness on heroic themes, with the hexameter as its characteristic metre, is the oldest surviving form of Greek literature. The only extant early examples are the *Iliad* and the *Odyssey* of ◊ Homer, and their survival confirms Aristotle's verdict of outstanding excellence. They provide the main evidence of the origin and character of pre-Homeric epic, but they are scarcely typical of the genre.

For the evolution of Greek epic, which Aristotle suggests was derived from hymns and *encomia* (songs of praise), the essential prerequisites were a compelling motive and an occasion for recitation; a large stock of material; a highly developed poetic technique; and time – probably many centuries. Homer's own picture of an epic poet as an after-dinner entertainer suggests far too trivial a motive for the creation of something so deeply rooted in Greek life and thought. Nor, probably, would the relatively brief and recent Mycenaean period, with its aftermath, have allowed enough time. There are in fact probably links in Greek epic with a much more distant past: the fairy-tale element recalls the Sumerian story of Gilgamesh in the third millennium, and the epic heroes themselves, although certainly presented as Bronze Age warriors, still retain some of the characteristics of neolithic divine kings, or would-be kings – semi-divine parentage, magical invulnerability, miraculous weapons and the protection of Athena. This association of Athena with epic is especially significant. Athena was the ally and mentor of the epic hero; epic poetry was ceremonially recited at her festivals; and she was the tutelary deity of boys and youths. This suggests that epic poetry grew up with her cult (itself probably of neolithic origin), and that its primary object was not entertainment but the indoctrination of young men with the traditions of the community. Greek epic poetry, in short, was fundamentally didactic; hence its use in antiquity as the instrument of education, and the ancient tradition of the poet as teacher.

If this was the nature of pre-Mycenaean epic, the coming of the Mycenaeans revolutionized it. For being alien to its traditions they used it as a secular entertainment, and it accordingly came to reflect their interests and achievements in craftsmanship, piracy and war – above all, the Trojan War; the late Bronze Age milieu became conventional, and the saga of Troy overlaid and embodied many local legends of heroes. During the succeeding Dark Age migrations probably led to further mingling of legends; and in Asia Minor epic was refined and elaborated into a work of conscious art, until it reached the perfection associated with the name of Homer, probably in the 8th century B.C. Later and lesser poets completed the tale of Troy, from the birth of the gods to the death of Odysseus, in a number of epics, now lost, which were eventually arranged in a series to form the ◇ Epic Cycle; and there were also cycles or single epics on many other legends. The didactic purpose of the genre was made more explicit by ◇ Hesiod, who applied it to a non-heroic theme in his *Works and Days*. With the disappearance of the kingship in Greece, and the introduction of writing, whose use destroys the powers of oral poets, royal bards were succeeded by rhapsodes who preserved the existing epics but did not compose more. Among these were the ◇ Homeridae of Chios, inheritors of the Homeric poems. The excellence of the two great epics outshone the rest; we hear of their introduction into Sparta, Athens and also Syracuse, and they seem to have ultimately superseded most local epics, becoming the common heritage of the Greek world. To this period also belong the Ionian ◇ *Homeric Hymns*, composed in Homeric vein as preludes to recitations of epic.

Early Greek epic was oral poetry, composed and preserved without the aid of writing, but not necessarily wholly improvised. The composition could have been premeditated, and the poet's memory would be filled from boyhood with a large store of ready-made components: traditional lays, stock incidents, and a whole vocabulary of poetic formulae providing for almost every requirement of narrative and metre. Given these resources he could add much or little of his own according to his talents, and produce anything from a simple cento to works as monumental, fine and essentially original as the Homeric poems. In the absence of writing the text remained fluid: a poem might grow and develop throughout the composer's career, and for long afterwards among his successors. Each recitation was to some extent a new creation, so that it would be difficult to single out the original composer of most poems or even to draw a line between composers and mere reciters.

By the 6th century at latest the creative period of Greek epic was over. New epics were indeed composed by literate poets in the 5th century, including the philosophers ◇ Parmenides and ◇ Empedocles; but none of their works survives. In the Alexandrian period the epic was revived in a new form, romantic rather than heroic, by ◇ Apollonius of Rhodes with his *Argonautica*; but in general the large-scale poem did not suit contemporary taste. The final flowering of Greek epic came in the 4th and 5th centuries A.D., in poems which are still extant. ◇ Quintus Smyrnaeus, Colluthus and Tryphiodorus went back for inspiration to Homer and the saga of Troy; but Musaeus used a romantic theme in his *Hero and Leander*, a love story effectively told, and ◇ Nonnus assembled a mass of myths about Dionysus in his elaborate and rhetorical *Dionysiaca*. [G T W H]

Musaeus, ed. A. Ludwich (Bonn, 1912); see Loeb for other authors cited.

C. M. Bowra, *Heroic Poetry* (1964); G. Murray, *The Rise of the Greek Epic* (1960); G. S. Kirk, *Homer and the Epic* (1965); F. A. Wright, *A History of Later Greek Literature* (1951).

Epic Poetry, Roman. Epic poetry in Latin seems to have begun, as in Greek, with heroic lays or ballads. Their medium was the native saturnian verse, their subject-matter the praise of famous men, and their purpose protreptic; but they did not survive into the classical period. The first written epic in Latin was a translation of the *Odyssey* into saturnians, produced as a school-book by ◇ Livius Andronicus in the 3rd century B.C. The first Roman epic was the *Bellum punicum* of his younger contemporary ◇ Naevius, a chronicle of recent history, and also some legends, in saturnians. A generation later ◇ Ennius virtually refounded Roman epic with his *Annals*, using the quantitative hexameter of Greek epic which revolutionized the character of Latin verse. This too was a chronicle, but on the grandest scale, extending from the heroic age to his own times. Both poems, founded on a conception of Roman history as a divinely ordained advance to world dominion, deeply influenced later Roman thought and literature.

In the last century of the Republic Roman patricians took to literature, and several wrote historical epics, whether as panegyric or as political memoirs. For the *dilettante* an alternative much in vogue was the writing of epic in the Greek style on hackneyed legendary themes. It remained for ⇨ Virgil, at the beginning of the Augustan age, to combine both kinds of epic in one harmonious whole. He had attempted historical epic early in his career, and found the subject-matter intractable; but half-way through the *Georgics,* in a striking digression, he announced a plan for a new kind of epic, Greek in form, Roman in substance, and centred on Octavian. His plan changed considerably as it matured: in particular, he set the action in the heroic past, transforming Octavian into Aeneas, and by the imaginative use of prophecy introduced a vista of Roman history from the Alban kings to the Augustan peace. He died before the work was complete, but the most highly finished parts are magnificent; taken as a whole, the *Aeneid* is the high-water mark of Latin poetry, and the supreme affirmation in Latin literature of the destiny of Rome.

In the shadow of the *Aeneid* Virgil's successors reverted to earlier types of epic. ⇨ Lucan's unfinished poem, *On the Civil War,* written in Nero's reign, represents the reaction in its most extreme form. Ostensibly a realistic historical epic, it dispenses with the traditional machinery of divine intervention, but melodramatically exploits the supernatural and makes the recent past incredible with its inordinate rhetoric. The Flavian period produced 3 notable epic poets. ⇨ Valerius Flaccus, a Virgilian without his master's essential magic, but able enough, wrote an unfinished and now underrated mythological epic, the *Argonautica,* freely adapted from Apollonius Rhodius. ⇨ Statius, also drawing on Greek legends, produced a *Thebais,* on the Seven against Thebes, which provided romantic and striking set-pieces for public recitation, but lacks unity; his unfinished *Achilleis* contains the opening episodes of something otherwise unknown in Latin poetry, an epic biography. ⇨ Silius Italicus, in the *Punica,* incongruously and tediously employed all the traditional apparatus of mythological epic for a poetic chronicle of the Second Punic War. Some 300 years later Roman epic was briefly revived in the unfinished *Rape of Proserpine* by the Greek ⇨ Claudian, who rivalled the Silver Age in polish and charm. (⇨ Epic Poetry, Greek.) [G T W H]

R. E. Smith, *The Failure of the Roman Republic* (1955); B. Otis, *Virgil: A Study in Civilized Poetry* (1964), and *Ovid as an Epic Poet* (1966); H. E. Butler, *Post-Augustan Poetry* (1909); F. A. Wright and T. A. Sinclair, *A History of Later Latin Literature* (1931).

Epicharmus (6th–5th cent. B.C.). Greek comic poet. Epicharmus, the traditional founder of Greek ⇨ comedy, was a Dorian by descent, who is said to have been born in Cos, but spent most of his life at Syracuse. With another comic poet, Phormis, he introduced plot into the hitherto loosely organized farce or mumming-play of the Dorian Greeks, and so created comedy. His achievement was proudly commemorated by the Syracusans for generations afterwards. He apparently wrote some 50 comedies in the Doric dialect, but only titles and scanty fragments remain. Many of his apparently very brief plays were burlesques of gods and heroes with comic potentialities, such as Hephaestus, Heracles and Odysseus; others were based on stock characters or on a debate with a somewhat philosophic tone. They were distinguished from Attic Old Comedy of a generation later by their lack of satire and personal lampoon, and the absence of a chorus; but they anticipated the Attic poets in many details of subject-matter and comic treatment. Epicharmus's works were known in Athens, being echoed in some late 5th-century comedies and praised by Plato; a critical edition was produced by an Alexandrian scholar in the 2nd century B.C. He was much admired in antiquity as a dramatist and moralist, and Horace notes that Plautus was considered to have been inspired by him. [G T W H]

Ed. A. Olivieri, *Frammenti della commedia greca e del mimo* (Naples, 1946–7); Diels, *F V*, 23.

Pickard-Cambridge, *D T C*.

Epictetus (A.D. *c.* 55–135). Stoic philosopher. Of Phrygian origin, he was a slave of the freedman Epaphroditus, who held important posts under Nero and Domitian. Recognizing his abilities, his master allowed him to attend the lectures of ⇨ Musonius Rufus, and gave him his freedom. Epictetus set up a school in Rome, and when Domitian in 89 expelled philosophers from the city, he transferred it to Nicopolis in Epirus. Here he taught to large numbers of pupils, of all social classes, for the remainder of his life. Thanks to one of these, the historian ⇨ Arrian, some of his writings are preserved. Arrian collected his *Discourses* and published them after his death (4 books survive), and also wrote a *Handbook* (*Encheiridion*) as a guide to his philosophy. These are the most important documents of Stoicism under the empire. They are notable for their deeply religious outlook – enjoining an absolute trust in Divine Providence, to be maintained through every misfortune. The philosopher is the missionary of Providence to mankind; his role is like that of the Cynic in its austerity, but without all the grosser features of the historic Cynicism. The aspirant to such a profession must 'think the matter over carefully, know himself, ask of God, and do nothing without his consent'. Again 'he has taken all mankind for his children: the women he has for daughters, the men for sons; in that spirit he approaches and cares for them all. . . . He reproves them as a father, as a brother, as the servant of God, who is the Father of us all . . . '. His teachings were the main formative influence on the Stoicism of Marcus ⇨ Aurelius. [DRD]

Loeb: W. A. Oldfather (2 vols., 1938).
D. S. Sharp, *Epictetus and the New Testament* (1914).

Epicureanism. The followers of ⇨ Epicurus were known, beyond all the Hellenistic philosophers, for their faithfulness to their Master's teaching. Moreover, the first generation of the school had produced a vast literature for its defence and propagation. Hence the school was never marked by such reforms as overtook ⇨ Stoicism in the 2nd century B.C., and though in ⇨ Lucretius it produced one of the world's greatest poets, it gave rise to little or no original thought after Epicurus. The duty of later adherents was to proselytize and to defend their doctrine against attack, especially that of the Stoics, their chief rivals after about 200 B.C. In the first they were very successful – literary sources assert (and epitaphs using Epicurean formulae confirm) that the school found adherents in all parts of the Hellenistic world, and, in Roman times, in Italy and Africa, though not in the western provinces. The chief schools known to us were those of: (1) Athens – where 14 successive heads of the school are known to the time of Julius Caesar, and the Garden of Epicurus was maintained to at least the reign of Hadrian; (2) Antioch, where under Philonides the school was highly influential *c.* 175 B.C. Probably from Antioch Epicureanism reached the hellenized cities of Judaea: it influenced the writer of Ecclesiastes and was known to St Paul (1 Cor. xiii); (3) Naples, where in the 1st century B.C. Siro and Philodemus of Gadara (see below) attracted many Roman pupils. Atticus, the friend of Cicero, and Maecenas were converts to Epicureanism; Horace, Virgil and Julius Caesar came under its influence.

The chief surviving writings and documents after Epicurus are: (1) The works of Colotes of Lampsacus (a pupil of Epicurus), author of 2 pamphlets against Plato – *Against the Lysis, Against the Euthydemus*. The titles of other polemical works are known. (2) (Much more important), the works of Philodemus of Gadara (110–*c.* 30 B.C.), part of whose library was discovered in a charred condition in the excavations at Herculaneum. He wrote a general account of Greek philosophy, a *Life* of Epicurus, a book *On the Management of an Estate*, a treaty on aesthetics, and various books on logic and ethics. He also wrote epigrams, 25 of which are in the Greek Anthology. (3) The enormous inscription of (300 ft of it!) which Diogenes of Oenoanda (2nd century A.D.) 'being about to die' had carved for the edification of posterity on the wall of a colonnade in his native town. Discovered in 1884, it gives a straightforward account of Epicurean doctrine in ethics and physics.

The school survived until the 4th century A.D., and was on hostile terms with Christianity. Its influence and reputation have known strange vicissitudes in modern times. Admired by the rationalists of the 18th century, it is responsible via Thomas Jefferson for the mention of the Pursuit of Happiness in the American Declaration of Independence. More recently the 'anti-religious' teachings of Epicurus have led to his canonization as a Marxist saint. [DRD]

Colotes: ed. W. Crönert, *Kolotes und Menedemos* (Leipzig, 1906); Philodemus: see his bibliography in *Oxford Classical Dictionary*; Diogenes: ed. and comm. J. Williams (Leipzig, 1907).
N. W. de Witt, *Epicurus and His Philosophy*

(Minneapolis, 1954); Gilbert Murray, *Five Stages of Greek Religion* (1935).

Epicurus (341–271 B.C.). Greek philosopher. Son of Neocles, an Athenian settled in Samos, and founder of one of the most successful of Hellenistic missionary philosophies. After spending two years in Athens (323–321) Epicurus migrated with his family and lived in several cities of Asia, notably Teos, where he studied philosophy with the atomist Nausiphanes. He began to work out his own philosophical system in Colophon, and set up a school first in Mytilene (311–310), then at Lampsacus (310–306). Finally he moved to Athens in 306, where he purchased a house and the famous Garden ('the Garden' became a synonym for ◊ Epicureanism, as 'the Porch' for Stoicism). There he taught until his death. The organization of the Epicurean school was remarkable. Its pupils included women and slaves; they shared a common life, including regular discussion groups and monthly banquets; they followed an integrated curriculum apparently designed to rival the programme of the Academy of Plato. It was also designed as a publishing-house, engaged on the writing and copying of various grades of text-books for propaganda. With his more advanced students, Epicurus undertook to survey and analyse all previous Greek philosophy. He himself is said to have written over 300 books – a generally hostile tradition has seen to it that little survives. By far the best exposition is the great poem *De rerum natura* of ◊ Lucretius, but for all his devotion Lucretius did not always understand his Master's teaching. Hence the importance of the authentic writings preserved in Book x of ◊ Diogenes Laertius. These consist of (1) the *Letter to Herodotus,* a simple exposition of physics, (2) the *Letter to Pythocles,* on celestial phenomena, and (3) the *Letter to Metrodorus,* an exposition of ethics, and of the right attitude to the gods, death, pleasure and pain. In the same book are contained the *Kuriai doxai* or *Sovereign Maxims,* a set of 40 aphorisms to be memorized by students on problems of ethics, and also the Will of Epicurus. In 1888 a further set of 80 aphorisms was discovered in a Vatican manuscript.

What emerges from all sources is an integrated rationalist system of physics, psychology and ethics. Its basis is the old atomic theory of Leucippus and Democritus (◊ Atomists), refurbished and provided with a modified form of free-will. To this is geared a system of ethics which offers a life of tranquillity and happiness, free from fear of the gods, of death and of the accidents of life. The price is the renunciation of worldly aims, political activity, even family life. In the changed conditions of the Hellenistic world it was possible to practise this kind of quietism, and many did so. But the anti-religious and anti-political standpoint of Epicureanism earned it the displeasure of authority in both Hellenistic and Roman times, and the hostility, sometimes envenomed, of other philosophies. [D R D]

Teubner: *Epistulae tres et ratae sententiae,* P. von der Mühll (Leipzig, 1922).

N. W. de Witt, *Epicurus and His Philosophy* (Minneapolis, 1954); B. Farrington, *Science and Politics in the Ancient World* (1939).

Epigram. The word implies an inscription, and early Greek epigrams were composed (usually in elegiac couplets) for monuments and, especially, as epitaphs. ◊ Simonides achieved a high reputation in this line. In the Hellenistic world a distinctive literary genre was evolved, that of the short poem composed for a wide range of moods and 'occasions', real or imaginary, still using the elegiac metre. ◊ Callimachus, ◊ Leonidas, Antipater, Meleager and many others worked this vein. There were collections of epigrams like those now incorporated in the Greek ◊ Anthology.

In Rome the successive phases are less clearly marked. There are early epitaphs – those of the Scipios date from the 3rd century B.C. – but ◊ Ennius and his contemporaries, under Greek influence, also used the literary form. With ◊ Catullus and his circle the epigram became associated with satire and invective, and a wide variety of metres was employed – hendecasyllables, iambic, scazons, as well as elegiacs. This form became very popular in Rome and the fullest development of the Latin epigram is to be found in ◊ Martial. Unity of subject, lightness of touch, and a sting in the tail are his characteristics; and they are found in the Renaissance writers who copied him, and especially in that associated form, the pasquinade. (◊◊ Anthology, Greek and

Latin; Elegiac Poetry, Greek and Latin.) [D R D]

'Epinikion'. ◊ Games.

'Epyllion' ('Miniature epic'). A literary genre of Alexandrian invention. A few hundred hexameter lines in length (600 seems to have been the upper limit), these poems dealt with a single personage or topic (*Hecale, Heracles the Lion-killer* etc.); they were diversified by dialogue and descriptive passages; the convention of a digression allowed the introduction of another legend. ◊ Callimachus and ◊ Euphorion are the great names, but their *epyllia* are lost and the only Greek examples to survive are in the poems of Theocritus. It was taken up enthusiastically by the Latin poets affected by ◊ Alexandrianism, especially ◊ Catullus and his friends. His *Marriage of Peleus and Thetis* (No. 64) and the lost *Io* of Calvus were well known. None handled it with greater skill than ◊ Virgil, in whom *epyllia* are incorporated in longer poems, as the *Aristaeus* story in the Fourth Georgic, and that of *Hercules and Cacus* in Book VIII of the *Aeneid*. ◊ Ovid found it invaluable for the legends of the *Metamorphoses*. [D R D]

M. M. Crump, *The Epyllion from Theocritus to Ovid* (1931).

Eratosthenes (*c.*275–*c.*194 B.C.). Greek geographer and polymath. After education in Athens, Eratosthenes of Cyrene accepted an invitation from Ptolemy III Euergetes to a fellowship at the Museum in Alexandria. Here he worked in several fields, geology, astronomy, mathematics and literary criticism. It was an age of specialists, who did not care for Eratosthenes and called him 'Beta' (the second-rater) and 'Pentathlos' (the all-rounder), as not being in the first rank in any field. In fact he was an excellent geographer: he established the sphericity of the earth, measured its diameter to within 4 per cent, and wrote on descriptive geography. He also worked on the size and distances of the sun and moon. In mathematics he investigated the problems of prime numbers; in history he tried to establish a scientific chronology; in literary studies he wrote 12 books *On Ancient Comedy*. He was appointed Librarian at Alexandria in 235, the first scientist to hold that office. None of his writings survives, but much of his geographical material was used by ◊ Strabo and ◊ Ptolemy. [D R D]

Jacoby, *F G H*, ii.
Sarton, *H S*, ii.

Erinna (early 3rd century B.C.). Greek poetess. From Telos. She was probably connected with the Coan literary movement – ◊ Asclepiades edited her collected poetry, and ◊ Theocritus influenced her versification, vocabulary and dialect (Doric with Aeolic elements). She died at 19. Her best-known work was *The Distaff* (a symbol of spinsterhood). Of the original 300, 60 fragmentary hexameters have been recovered from a papyrus. Erinna laments the untimely death of her friend Baucis, and recalls the girlhood joys and sorrows they shared. She writes with delicacy, freshness and deep feeling. Three accomplished epigrams also survive. [D E W W]

Diehl, *A L G*.

Euclid (fl. *c.*300 B.C.). Greek geometer. Author of the *Elements*, the most widely read and enduring of all text-books. Little is known of his life. His main work was done in Alexandria, but it is uncertain whether he held an official post at the Museum. The *Elements* summarizes and supersedes all previous work in geometry. Books I–VI deal with plane geometry, VII–X with arithmetic and the theory of numbers, XI–XIII with solid geometry. Two additional books are spurious, XIV being by Hypsicles (2nd century B.C.), and XV belonging to the 7th century A.D. There were numerous ancient commentaries, the most important by Proclus. The *Elements* were translated into Syriac, Hebrew, Latin, Arabic and all the principal languages of the West, and are still regarded as serviceable. Euclid also wrote on astronomy and music. [D R D]

Teubner: I. L. Heiberg and H. Menge (8 vols., Leipzig, 1883–1916); Sir Thomas Heath, *Euclid's Elements in English* (3 vols., 1926).
Sarton, *H S*, ii.

Eudoxus (*c.*408–355 B.C.). Greek astronomer and mathematician. Eudoxus of Cnidos founded scientific astronomy, and was the first mathematician of his age. After studying, as a poor scholar, at the Academy of Plato, he worked in Egypt,

Cyzicus and Halicarnassus. He built observatories in Egypt and at Cnidos. He had a thorough grasp of Egyptian astronomy: how much he knew of Babylonian is uncertain. His own major contribution to astronomy – one of the greatest triumphs of Greek rationalism – was to show how all the movements of the sun, moon and planets can be explained by postulating 27 concentric spheres, each revolving on its own axis. In mathematics, his chief work was on irrationals, and on the 'theory of Exhaustion'. He also wrote on geography and astronomy: a book entitled *Phaenomena* was later used by ⇨ Aratus. [D R D]

Sarton, *H S*, i.

Eugammon. ⇨ Epic Cycle.

Eumelus. ⇨ *Titanomachia.*

Euphorion (b. *c.*275 B.C.). Greek poet. Born at Chalcis in Euboea, he studied at Athens, and may never have visited Alexandria, his spiritual home. Late in life he became librarian at Antioch, on the invitation of Antiochus the Great. He died in Syria.

Euphorion's poetry, apart from a few epigrams, consists almost entirely of ⇨ *epyllia.* His subject-matter was mythological and recondite; and although he strikes a more personal note in his poems of malediction, here too mythological illustration was prominent. The papyrus fragments fit readily into this framework, and the known titles of his works mostly indicate the same restricted range. Only the *Replies to Theodoridas* suggests something new and different – an experiment with a verse-letter. He also published results of his literary and historical researches in prose.

The fragmentary evidence makes an assessment hazardous. He followed where ⇨ Callimachus led, but without Callimachus's fastidiousness and detachment. His over-elaboration of detail must have thrown his poems out of balance. His cult of obscurity and ambiguity, absurdly far-fetched etymologies and bizarre neologisms make it easy to dismiss him as insincere, affected and pedantic. Against this must be set his profound influence on Catullus, Gallus and the youthful Virgil. Cicero's contemptuous criticism of the ⇨ *neoterici* as 'Euphorion's songsters' suggests that his poetry had a music which captivated some of his Roman readers. [D E W W]

Ed. J. U. Powell, *Collectanea alexandrina* (1925); Loeb: D. L. Page, *Greek Literary Papyri*, i (1950) (new fragments).

Eupolis (*c.*455–*c.*410 B.C.). Greek comic poet. One of the three Athenian masters of Old Comedy, he exhibited his first play at the age of 17. He is said to have been thrown into the sea on the expedition to Sicily by Alcibiades, whom he lampooned in the *Baptizers,* but he eventually died in a shipwreck in the Hellespont a few years later; thereafter the Athenians debarred their poets from serving abroad. He won victories with 7 plays out of a probable total of 17, of which only titles and brief fragments remain. The *Nancy-boy* presented the demagogue Hyperbolus in the title role, and gratuitously brought in his mother in a lewd and drunken dance; Aristophanes complained that this travestied his own *Knights,* but Eupolis claimed that he had written part of the *Knights* himself. The *Flatterers* satirized a notorious spendthrift and his hangers-on, and one fragment presents the first extant portrait of a famous stock character, the parasite. The *Baptizers* depicted Alcibiades and his friends, disguised as women, worshipping Cotytto, a Thracian goddess, with orgiastic rites. Modern discoveries of papyri in Egypt have added to our knowledge of the *Demes,* in which famous Athenian statesmen of the past reappeared from the dead to intervene in the city's affairs. A lively and verbally ingenious comic poet, Eupolis was judged superior to Aristophanes in charm; he was also noted for scurrility and indecency, even by the standards of Old Comedy, and in this provided a model for Roman satire. (⇨ Comedy, Greek.) [G T W H]

Edmonds, *F A C*, i.

Euripides (*c.*484–406? B.C.). Greek tragic poet. In spite of the jeers and scurrilities of the comic poets, Euripides came of a respectable family in Attica, perhaps *bourgeoisie* rather than landed gentry. He had a good education, distinguishing himself as an athlete and associating with the leading philosophers and sophists of the day, whose influence probably moulded him into the advanced thinker he became.

He held a local priesthood at Phlya, but otherwise played little part in public affairs; bookish and retiring, and so regarded as an unsociable oddity, he mostly lived and wrote in seclusion in Salamis. He first competed in a tragic contest in 455, and won his first victory in 441. Sensational as many of his plays were, they were not often successful in the contests, and his controversial views won him notoriety rather than approval. Late in life, in 408 or 407, he left Athens in dissatisfaction and went to the court of Archelaus in Macedon. There he produced an *Archelaus* in the king's honour, and died in the winter of 407/6. He left behind the *Bacchants* and other plays, which were later produced in Athens by his son, the younger Euripides.

Later Euripides was by far the most popular of the three great tragedians, and so a greater proportion of his work has survived. He composed 92 plays, few of them satyric, but won only 4 victories in his lifetime. Altogether 19 plays are now extant under his name, and we have titles and fragments, some substantial, of most of the rest. Not all the surviving plays are dated, but they can be placed in chronological order with fair certainty.

The earliest dated surviving play is the *Alcestis,* a tragi-comedy produced as a substitute for the satyr-play in a tetralogy which was placed second in 438. Based on a folk-tale, it presents Admetus as the man whom the gods allow to postpone his death if he can find someone to take his place; his aged parents refuse, and only his wife Alcestis will volunteer. She duly dies, but Heracles, an untimely and boisterous guest, discovers why Admetus is secretly mourning and brings her back from the dead. Plot and characterization provide piquant and ironic humour throughout the play.

The *Medea* (431) and the *Hippolytus* (428) belong to the period when Greek tragedy was in its prime, and are relatively orthodox by Aristotelian standards. The former is a more powerful treatment of a theme probably already used by ◊ Sophocles in his *Women of Trachis* – the reactions of a wife discarded in favour of a younger rival. Here the injured heroine is a fiery barbarian princess who destroys her rival and, in an agonizing scene, kills her own children by the unfaithful Jason, leaving him physically unharmed but desolate. In the *Hippolytus,* where sexual passion and asceticism are shown in irreconcilable conflict, Euripides presents another tormented heroine, Phaedra, whose unwilling but violent love for her fanatically chaste stepson Hippolytus leads to the death of both. A third play, the *Heracles,* with its bitter, moving story of undeserved calamity, has a similar tragic character, although it is usually dated, albeit tentatively, to about 416. It shows Heracles, at the moment of his greatest triumph, plunged into irremediable disaster by his implacable enemy Hera, who sends him mad.

Events of the Peloponnesian war are reflected in a group of 'political' plays for which Euripides chose legendary themes with a topical interest. The *Children of Heracles* (*c.*429), an undistinguished drama, presents Athens as the protector of Heracles' children, whose ungrateful descendants are now her enemies. In the *Suppliant Women* (probably *c.*420) Theseus recovers the bodies of the fallen Seven against Thebes on behalf of their Argive mothers, who are the suppliants, and earns the gratitude of Argos, the ally of Athens in 420. The *Andromache* (*c.* 419), a somewhat shapeless and un-tragic piece not produced at Athens, deals with the rivalry between Andromache, the captive of Neoptolemus, and his Spartan wife Hermione, and is marked by sharp hostility towards the Spartan character and the pro-Dorian oracle at Delphi. Two other plays express hatred of war in more general terms. The magnificent *Hecuba* (*c.*425), another study of a woman in anguish, shows the widow of Priam treacherously bereft of her last surviving son after the fall of Troy, and taking a hideous revenge on his murderer. The *Trojan Women* (415) was produced shortly after the Athenians had massacred the male population of Melos, a would-be neutral in the war; it contains a heart-rending series of scenes depicting the plight of the Trojan women, their menfolk dead, in the hands of the victors.

At this point, perhaps because the Athenians had had their fill of calamity in real life, Euripides turned to a lighter and more romantic type of tragedy, pleasantly exciting, sentimental, at times humorous, and ending happily. Such was the *Iphigenia in Tauris* (*c.*411), in which Iphigenia, as a priestess of Artemis, finds that the intended victims of human sacrifice are her brother Orestes and his friend, and outwits a barbarian king in organizing an exciting escape. Similarly the *Ion* (*c.*411) is clearly a forerunner of New Comedy, with its wronged heroine and her long-lost child, finally recognized by birth-tokens. There are complications of jealousy and attempted murder, but all ends well enough, except that Apollo, the father of the child and stage-manager of the whole intrigue, is thoroughly discredited. The *Helena* (412) is another escape story, almost a comedy-thriller. Menelaus, shipwrecked in Egypt, is astonished to find that Helen is living there, only a phantom having gone to Troy; she too outwits the barbarian king, and both get away safely.

An alternative line of development, or decline, led to melodrama, whose excitements are found in several of Euripides' latest plays. The *Electra* (413) virtually presents the legend of Orestes' revenge in modern dress, displaying the ancient matricide realistically as a contemporary crime. The principal characters in this striking but painful play are necessarily odious, and arouse no sympathy. The story is continued in the *Orestes* (408), a successful play, in which Orestes, now intermittently mad, is anachronistically put on trial and condemned to death with his sister. By the time he has seized a hostage to protect himself and she has set their palace on fire, only the *deus ex machina* can restore the plot to order. The *Phoenician Women* (*c.*408) is a rambling and sensational chronicle of the attack of the Seven on Thebes, and probably contains some additions by another hand. Euripides did not live to complete the *Iphigenia at Aulis,* but it was produced posthumously with supplements which are now lost. It shows an irresolute Agamemnon preparing to sacrifice his daughter, and much embarrassed by the presence of Clytemnestra; in the lost finale Iphigenia was probably rescued by Artemis.

In the *Bacchants* Euripides produced his masterpiece, and the last great Greek tragedy. For his theme he went back to the very source of tragedy, the sufferings of the king in the orgiastic cult of Dionysus. He depicts the coming of the god himself to Thebes. The women surrender to the mass hysteria which he inspires, but their king Pentheus sees its dangers and is determined to stamp it out; and Dionysus takes revenge on him by contriving that the women, led by the king's own mother, shall tear him to pieces in their frenzy. The tragedy is at once horrible and beautiful, an astonishing study of the irrational element in human nature. The chorus, nearly redundant in some previous plays, here comes into its own again, and is given lyrics of extraordinary loveliness and power.

One satyric drama by Euripides has survived – the *Cyclops*, of unknown date, the only complete extant example of the genre. Based on the Homeric story of the blinding of Polyphemus, with Silenus and the chorus of satyrs brought in as his slaves, it is a brief but lively farce whose illogicalities and improbabilities increase rather than diminish the comic effect. The *Rhesus,* a tragedy, is also attributed to Euripides, but its authorship is very uncertain. A melodramatic version of the Homeric night raid in which Odysseus and Diomedes kill Rhesus in the Trojan lines and capture his horses, it contains some furious argument and lively scenes, and the novelty of action taking place in the dark.

In his choice of subjects for drama Euripides ranged widely over the Greek legends, and in the more romantic or melodramatic plots of his later plays, in particular, he freely invented variations of his own. The realism with which he is often credited arises from a somewhat Shavian tendency to take a legend at its face value and work out its logical implications in terms of real life, with disconcerting and revealing results. He constantly dwells on the behaviour of the individual, especially in extreme, even sensational, situations – not out of a desire for the sensational, but rather because of his intense interest in exploring the farthest reaches of the human character. Above all he is interested in the character of women, and his insight into their minds and hearts was unprecedented in his day; his contemporaries, scandalized and fascinated by turns, clearly felt that he laid bare almost too much. The impact of his tragedies was all the greater because most of them ended unhappily. It is only by chance that happy endings preponderate in his extant works: for Aristotle he was the most tragic of poets.

A conspicuous feature of Euripidean

tragedy is the use of prologues and epilogues, many of them delivered by gods. Often criticized as inartistic, they nevertheless enable Euripides to concentrate in between on the real business of his play, and to set it in relation to the divine government of the world; in a number of epilogues he also links the action with the foundation of some ancient Athenian institution. Some of his plots are masterly, as in the *Hippolytus* and the lighter tragedies, but he was apt to sacrifice excellence of plot if his interest lay elsewhere. Often his play turns on the traditional recognition scene, for which he was famous; he handles this and the equally traditional descriptive messenger-speech with brilliant effect. Less dramatic, though suited to the contemporary taste for rhetoric, are his tirades expressing his personal antipathies, and his debates or discussion scenes, another Shavian feature of his works. In his dramas of intrigue the continual presence of the chorus, demanded by tradition, is apt to be an embarrassment. Increasingly, until the *Bacchants,* his choral odes become mere interludes with little relevance to the action, more loosely constructed, and with the words more subordinated to the music. In all this critics have seen signs of decadence; yet the songs of Euripides exercised an immense fascination in his own day. The language of his plays is naturalistic, even commonplace, in ordinary dialogue and rhetorically forceful in argument, but in his lyrics it rises to great heights of descriptive power and imaginative beauty; he has been compared to Ibsen in his penchant for combining the prosaic and the sublime. His music is unfortunately lost, but we know that its modernism aroused much controversy with its various novel effects, its abandonment of form and symmetry, and its highly emotional quality.

Euripides belonged to a generation which was primarily interested in the study of man, and found its rationalism turned to scepticism by the calamities of war. Hence his critical attitude to the traditional mythology. If he presents gods in their conventional form, it is only to show that they could not, or should not, have acted as the myths relate. Equally often he makes them personifications of psychological or natural forces; and then he neither attacks nor defends them, but demonstrates their tragic effects. As a citizen Euripides took pride in Athens, and hated her enemy Sparta. But it was an idealized Athens, the champion of freedom and democracy, that he admired; he had no love for Athens the imperialist power and the home of demagogues. Above all he hated war, and the misery and human degradation that it entailed.

In the hands of Euripides Greek tragedy became more tragic than ever before, and then died out. In a sense his last play, the *Bacchants,* was a throwback to a species already extinct. The disappearance of true tragedy was largely a natural process: the vein was becoming worked out, and times had changed; Sophocles also ceased to write it at about the same time. But in part the change was due to the genius of Euripides himself and his mastery of the new kinds of drama. Although his work received a mixed reception in his lifetime, his popularity was soon unrivalled after his death. His dramas of intrigue paved the way for New Comedy; and as a pioneer of romance in literature he became one of the most influential writers of the ancient world. (⇨ Satyric Drama; Tragedy, Greek.) [G T W H]

OCT: G. Murray (3 vols., 1902–13). Fragments and *Life*: H. von Arnim, *Supplementum euripideum* (Bonn, 1913); D. L. Page, *Greek Literary Papyri* (Loeb, 1942); *Hypsipyle*, ed. G. W. Bond (1963). Commentaries: F. Paley (1872–80); the Oxford *Plays of Euripides* (1938–); *Hippolytus*, W. S. Barrett (1964). Translations: Loeb, A. S. Way (1912); P. Vellacott (Penguin Classics, 11 plays, 1953, 1954, 1963); R. L. Green, *Two Satyr Plays* (Penguin Classics, 1957); D. Grene and R. Lattimore, *The Complete Greek Tragedies* (1959).

G. Murray, *Euripides and His Age* (1965); G. M. A. Grube, *The Drama of Euripides* (1961); A. Lesky, *Greek Tragedy* (1965).

Eusebius Pamphili (A.D. 263–339). Greek Christian writer. Often called the 'Father of Ecclesiastical History'. Born in Palestine and educated at Caesarea under Pamphilus, Eusebius fled at the outbreak of the persecution in 303, but was imprisoned in Egypt. On his return (*c.* 313) he was made bishop of Caesarea and was soon involved in the Arian controversy, the complex issues of which he did not really appreciate. At Nicaea (325) he concurred in the condemnation of Arius, but at later synods supported the Arian cause, agreeing to the deposition of Athanasius in 335. An ardent admirer of the Emperor Constantine, he delivered the official panegyric on the thirtieth anniversary of his accession.

Eusebius's voluminous literary remains may be grouped under four heads: (1) Historical. The *Ecclesiastical History* comprises 10 books covering the period from the foundation of the Church to the defeat of Licinius in 324. Apologetic in that it seeks to prove the Church was created and guided by God to final victory, it nevertheless contains original historical material of the first importance and is an eminently readable, if selective, account of the times. The story of the last persecution is supplemented by the *Martyrs of Palestine* and the historical background by the *Life of Constantine*. (2) Apologetic. A *Preparation for the Gospel*, in 15 books (312–22), shows that Christians rightly prefer Judaism to paganism, and its continuation, the *Proof of the Gospel*, shows how the Christian religion is the fulfilment of the Old Testament. (3) Biblical. Under this head is to be noted the *Onomasticon*, a gazetteer of Bible sites, and his *Commentary on the Psalms*, of which only fragments remain. (4) Dogmatic, in particular his 2 books *Against Marcellus*.

Sometimes termed the 'Christian Herodotus', Eusebius has earned legitimate fame as *the* historian of Christian antiquity. [J G D]

Migne, *P G*, 19–24; *Ecclesiastical History*, tr. H. J. Lawlor and J. E. L. Oulton (1927); *Martyrs of Palestine, Life of Constantine*, tr. A. C. McGiffert (N P F, 1890); *Preparation for the Gospel*, tr. E. H. Gifford (1903); *Proof of the Gospel*, tr. W. J. Ferrar (1920).

F. J. Foakes-Jackson, *Eusebius Pamphili. A Study of the Man and His Writings* (1933).

Eutropius (fl. A.D. 370). Roman historian. He served in Julian's expedition against Persia in 363 and later held an official post under Valens. He wrote a summary of Roman history in 10 books, from the foundation of Rome to A.D. 364, the early part of which (Books 1–7) was based on the *Epitome* of Livy. [T A D]

Teubner: H. R. Dietsch (Leipzig, 1875).

F

Fabius Pictor, Quintus (fl. 216 B.C.). Roman historian. Senator during the Second Punic War. In 216, after the defeat at Cannae, the Senate sent Fabius to consult the Delphic Oracle and find some means of ending the Roman reverses. Fabius had previously taken part in the Gallic War in 225.

The *Annals* of Fabius contained a history of Rome from the time of Aeneas to the Second Punic War. Fabius wrote in Greek, partly because Latin prose was not yet an adequate literary language, partly to explain the policies of Rome to the Greeks. In this he was followed by the next three Roman historians, L. Cincius, ⇨ Acilius and A. Postumius. He treated the foundation of Rome in detail, and then proceeded rapidly to events of his own day. His style is described as bare. He was regarded as an important authority by Livy because he was the earliest source, and a contemporary of many of the events described. Polybius criticizes his pro-Roman prejudice, but admits that he never deliberately falsified. However, no ancient historian appreciated that Fabius was biased in favour of members of his own *gens*, a bias responsible for the distortions in the history of the early years of the Second Punic War, when Fabius Maximus is portrayed as infallible, and his political opponents blamed for all the Roman disasters. [T A D]

Peter, *H R R*, i.

E Badian, in *Latin Historians*, ed. T. A. Dorey (1966).

Fabius Rusticus (A.D. *c.*30–110). Roman historian. Protégé of Seneca, and later a friend of the younger Pliny. He wrote a history of Rome that certainly covered Nero's reign and may have dealt with the period from the Battle of Actium to the death of Nero. He is praised by Tacitus as the most eloquent historian of recent times, and he may be the unnamed historian so warmly commended by Quintilian in Book X. [T A D]

Peter, *H R R*, ii.

Fables, Greek and Latin. In both literatures the fable, usually with animal characters and always with a moral, was an enduring part of popular tradition. Originating in peasant folk lore, it found early expression as a literary genre, the oldest and best-known collection being associated with Aesop, who seems to belong to the 6th century B.C., though nothing is known of his personal life. His Roman equivalent, ⇨ Phaedrus, is undoubtedly a historical figure. A freedman of Augustus, he used the fable for educational and political ends, like the modern cartoonist. Phaedrus wrote in iambic verse. Later a prose version of his fables was collected under the name of Romulus. ⇨ Babrius (? 2nd century A.D.) compiled 10 books of *Fables after Aesop*, of which two survive.

Besides the professional writers of fables, one should note the part played by this rich and familiar common stock in education and in popular philosophy. It was drawn on freely by writers such as ⇨ Hesiod ('The Hawk and the Nightingale'), ⇨ Aristophanes ('The Dung-Beetle') in the *Peace* and ⇨ Horace ('The Town Mouse and the Country Mouse'). [D R D]

Teubner: Aesop, K. Halm (1889); Babrius, W. G. Rutherford (1883); Phaedrus, L. Müller (1903); Romulus, G. Thiele (1910).
W. R. Halliday, *Greek and Roman Folklore* (1927).

'Fabula'. 'Talk' or 'story', the usual Roman term for a play. The Romans commonly classified *fabulae* according to the costume worn by the actors, and drew a broad distinction between drama in Greek dress, the *fabula palliata* (from *pallium*, a Greek cloak), and drama in Roman dress, the *fabula togata* (from the formal toga of Roman public life), using both terms more for comedy than for serious drama. Beyond this there was no generally recognized classification, and there seems to have been considerable variation and confusion of definitions both in the classical period and among later grammarians. Like the *palliata*, the *fabula crepidata* (from *crepida*, an open shoe) derived its name from a typical article of Greek dress; both terms usually denoted a Roman comedy adapted from a Greek original and retaining the Greek setting and characters. Introduced by ⇨ Livius Andronicus in the 3rd century B.C., the *fabula palliata* was the most successful form of Roman comedy, and the one in which ⇨ Plautus and ⇨ Terence excelled. *Fabula togata* usually meant native Roman comedy with Italian scenes and characters, but was something of a misnomer since the toga was seldom worn in country towns, where the action took place; the term *fabula tabernaria* ('domestic comedy', from *taberna* in the sense of 'a private house') was a more accurate alternative. The *fabula trabeata* (from *trabea*, the knight's formal robe) was a variant of this, invented in the Augustan age and dealing with middle-class life. (For the *fabula atellana*, ⇨ Atellan Farce, and for the *fabula riciniata*, ⇨ Mime.)

There appears to have been no vernacular term for a Roman version of a Greek tragedy. The *fabula praetexta* or *praetextata* (from *praetexta*, the purple-bordered toga worn by Roman magistrates) was the native Roman equivalent, a historical drama introduced by ⇨ Naevius and based on Roman characters. (⇨ Comedy, Roman; Tragedy, Roman.) [G T W H]

Beare, *R S*.

Fannius, Gaius (fl. 122 B.C.). Roman orator and historian. Son-in-law of C. Laelius Sapiens, pupil of the Stoic Panaetius. He fought in the Third Punic War and in Spain, and was consul in 122. He was a successful orator, and wrote *Annals*, probably dealing with events of his own times, which were epitomized by Brutus. [T A D]

Peter, *H R R*, i.

Favorinus (A.D. *c.* 80–*c.* 150). Greek orator and polymath. Favorinus of Arles was one of the most notable figures in the revival of Greek learning under Hadrian. The pupil of ⇨ Dio Chrysostom, he taught ⇨ Herodes Atticus, ⇨ Fronto and ⇨ Gellius. He is known to have written an encyclopedic work entitled *Miscellaneous History*, also a book of *Memoirs*. A speech *On Exile* has been found in papyrus; it is based on personal experience, for Hadrian banished him to Chios. [D R D]

Fragments in Müller, *F H G*, iii; *On Exile* (P V G, Vatican City, 1931).

Fenestella (52 B.C.–A.D. 19). Roman historian and poet. None of his poems has survived; quotations from his Annals indicate that his historical writings covered the last century of the Republic, and they seem to have been a rich store of general information. [TAD]

Peter, *HRR*, ii.

Fescennine Verses. ◊ Comedy, Roman.

Florus, Annaeus (or Lucius) (fl. A.D. *c.* 140). Roman poet and historian. Florus was a friend of Hadrian, who exchanged witty epigrams with him. He wrote an *Epitome of the Wars of the Roman People,* in 2 books; it is of some interest, but is rhetorical and inaccurate. He also wrote a *Dialogue* on whether Virgil is an orator rather than a poet, and a number of short poems in various metres, some of which have considerable elegance and charm. [TAD]

Teubner: *Epitome,* O. Rossbach (Leipzig, 1896), *Epitome and Dialogue,* C. Halm (Leipzig, 1879); Loeb: *Epitome,* E. S. Forster (1929), Duff, *MLP* (1934).

Frontinus, Sextus Julius (A.D. *c.* 30–100). Roman soldier and administrator. Consul in 73. He governed Britain 74–78, subdued the Silures in South Wales, and may have taken part in Domitian's German campaign. On the accession of Nerva in 96, he was one of the small group of senior senators who acted as the new emperor's close advisors. He was consul again in 98 and 100. In 97 he was appointed Curator Aquarum, in charge of the whole water system at Rome. He wrote a number of technical manuals on strategy, on land-surveying, and on other similar matters, but the only ones surviving are *On Stratagems* and *On Aqueducts.* The *Stratagems,* in 3 books (the fourth is a late addition), sets out practical examples of wartime strategic devices, classified according to subject-matter, and strictly utilitarian in aim. The *Aqueducts,* in 2 books, written for his own guidance at the start of his administration of the Cura Aquarum, is a comprehensive account of the whole Roman water system, historical, legal, administrative and technical. These two works have no pretensions to literary style, but the material is set out in a plain, logical manner. [TAD]

Loeb: *Stratagems and Aqueducts,* C. E. Bennett and M. B. McElwain (1925).

Fronto, Marcus Cornelius (A.D. *c.* 100–*c.* 166). Roman writer. He was the most famous Roman orator of the 2nd century A.D. Born at Cirta in North Africa – then a flourishing centre of Latin culture – he came to Rome for a public career which culminated in the consulship (143). His fame as an orator led to his appointment as tutor to the young princes Marcus Aurelius and Lucius Verus; his close relations with the imperial household continued until his death. Ancient critics speak of his powers in such terms that it was natural to think of the complete loss of his works as a major gap in Latin literature. But when a manuscript of his correspondence with Marcus Aurelius was discovered in 1815, expectations were disappointed. Why an intimate correspondence between master and pupil should call for the pulling out of all the rhetorical stops is not clear, but Fronto is often paired with Menander as one who falls (on our evidence) far short of his ancient reputation. In fact, the correspondence gives a useful insight into the life of the imperial family in a period not well documented. It also enables us to see something of what Fronto meant by the New Style (*elocutio novella*) of Latin prose, which he invented. Reacting against the standard Latin of Cicero's speeches and (more violently) the prose of Seneca, the New Style blended popular speech and the archaic Latin of such writers as Cato and Gaius Gracchus. It is found in his contemporary and fellow-countryman ◊ Apuleius but had no lasting vogue. [DRD]

Loeb: C. R. Haines (1920).

M. D. Brock, *Studies in Fronto and His Age* (1911).

G

Galen (A.D. *c.* 129–?199). Greek medical writer. The greatest name in Greek medicine after Hippocrates; certainly its leading anatomist and physiologist. After study in Greece and Alexandria he practised first in his native Pergamum, then (162) in Rome. Here he taught medical students, gave public demonstrations, and conducted an extensive practice, including attendance on the Emperor Marcus

Aurelius. He is charged with having left Rome in 166, when the soldiers of Avidius Cassius brought back the plague from the East, but he returned in 169. He carried out many experiments, and evolved a comparative anatomy based on the dissection of animals. On the muscular system, the cranial nerves, and the spinal column his work is outstanding. A firm belief in teleology – see the passage *On the Hand* – commended him to the Middle Ages. His voluminous writings cover every aspect of the history, theory and practice of medicine. They have had an enormous influence, both directly and through Arabic translations. Very little is translated into English. [D R D]

Teubner: C. G. Kühn (20 vols., Leipzig, 1821–33); Loeb: *On the Natural Faculties*, A. J. Brock (1916); *On the Hand*, tr. T. Bellott (1840).

Charles Singer and C. Rabin, *A Prelude to Science* (1946); *Oxford Classical Dictionary* (for bibliography).

Gallus, Gaius Asinius (d. A.D. 33). Roman orator. Son of Asinius ⇨ Pollio. Consul 8 B.C. His marriage to Vipsania, whom the Emperor Tiberius had been compelled to divorce, aroused the enmity of Tiberius, which Gallus did nothing to mollify by his veiled attacks on Tiberius and which his reputation for excessive ambition helped to stimulate. He was arrested in A.D. 30 and died in prison. He wrote a number of epigrams, and a work on oratory, comparing his father Pollio with Cicero, to the latter's detriment. [T A D]

Gallus, Gaius Cornelius (*c.* 69–26 B.C.). Roman poet and man of affairs. Born at Forum Iulii (Fréjus), probably of native stock. His official career culminated in 30 B.C., when Octavian rewarded his wartime services against Antony by appointing him Prefect of Egypt. But he proved unequal to viceregal office, was recalled in disgrace, and committed suicide. His poetry comprised ⇨ *epyllia* and 4 books of elegies in the ⇨ neoteric manner (probably entitled *Amores*) in honour of Lycoris. Almost nothing survives, but his range may be inferred from Virgil *Eclogue* X (especially 31–49). He helped to establish erotic elegy as a literary genre. [D E W W]

Gallus, Marcus Fadius (fl. *c.* 45 B.C.). Roman writer. Intimate friend and fellow-townsman of Cicero, who wrote to him a number of letters. He wrote a *Life of Cato Uticensis*, which seems to have contained a strong attack on Caesar. [T A D]

Cicero, *Ad fam.*, *VII*: 23–26.

Games (Olympic, Pythian, Isthmian, Nemean). Athletic contests were a feature of Greek aristocratic society from the earliest times. They reflect a spirit of rivalry and the cult of physical fitness as rewarding in itself and militarily desirable. The great games were associated with religious centres and festivals, and attracted competitors and spectators from all over the Greek world. The Olympic games enjoyed the highest prestige. Founded traditionally in 776 B.C. in honour of Olympian Zeus, they were celebrated every 4 years uninterruptedly until abolished by Theodosius I. Lists of victors down to A.D. 217 have survived, and the Greeks tended to reckon their chronology by Olympiads. The full festival lasted for 5 days and included chariot- and horse-racing, and separate contests for boys and men. The Pythian, Isthmian and Nemean games, honouring respectively Delphic Apollo, Poseidon and Zeus of Nemea, were established or re-established with panhellenic status some 200 years after the first Olympiad. The Pythian were the most important of the three games, celebrated on a 4-year cycle (whereas the Isthmian and Nemean games recurred biennially) and supplementing the normal athletic contests with competitions in music and literature. The prize for success was a plain crown of wild olive, bay or wild celery; but cities welcomed the victors with lavish rewards. The simple song of rejoicing at this festive home-coming was developed by Simonides and Pindar into the *epinikion*, a new and brilliant genre of choral lyric. [D E W W]

Gellius, Aulus (A.D. *c.* 123–*c.* 165). Roman writer. Little is known of his life, save that he had a legal career in Rome. His only work, the *Noctes atticae*, is a collection of essays in 20 books on literary, historical and philosophical themes which he made while studying in Athens. His quotations from a very wide range of Greek and Latin authors preserves much material that would otherwise have been lost, especially for earlier Latin writers. Not a man of first-rate talent, this learned and amiable barrister is nevertheless one of the most attractive of minor Latin authors. [DRD]

Loeb: J. C. Rolfe (3 vols., 1927–8).

Gellius, Gnaeus (*c.* 150 B.C.). Roman historian. Gellius wrote a *History of Rome* from earliest times to his own day. He included much mythological and legendary material, and was quoted by later grammarians for his use of peculiar grammatical forms. [TAD]

Peter, *HRR*, i.

Germanicus, Julius Caesar (15 B.C.–A.D. 19). Roman general and poet. Elder brother of the emperor Claudius, he was adopted as heir by the emperor Tiberius in A.D. 4. After a series of spectacular but not completely successful campaigns in Germany (13–16), he was recalled to Rome and later sent out to the East. He died in somewhat mysterious circumstances at Antioch. He was a poet of considerable reputation. He wrote some plays, in Greek, but his reputation chiefly depends on his translation into Latin hexameters of the astronomical poems of ⇨ Aratus, the *Phaenomena* and the section called *Prognostica*. [TAD]

Teubner: A. Breysig (Leipzig, 1899).

Gigantomachy. ⇨ Epic Cycle.

Gnosticism. A term of convenience used to cover a number of esoteric and mystic sects which flourished in the 2nd and 3rd centuries A.D. alongside of, and often in opposition to, apostolic Christianity. All sought access to divine revelation (*gnosis*), promised life after death to their initiates, and (in most cases) provided a cult and ritual symbolizing these beliefs. Their systems were formed as syntheses from a wide range of constituents – ⇨ Plato, and especially the *Timaeus*, Stoicism, especially ⇨ Posidonius, the arcane Jewish wisdom, astrology, the eastern mystery cults, especially the dualism of Persia, and the Christian scriptures, especially St Paul. The best-known persons associated with Gnosticism are :(1) Simon Magus, who appears as the opponent of the Apostles (Acts viii, 9–24), but who may be confused with the 2nd-century heresiarch Simon of Gitta; (2) Basilides, who taught in Alexandria A.D. 120–40, and formulated a doctrine of creation by Absolute Being 'out of that which is not' that greatly influenced the thinking of the Church; (3) Marcion (d. A.D. *c.* 160), who was the son of a bishop of Sinope, taught in Rome A.D. *c.* 140 and was expelled from the Church in A.D. 144. He discarded the Old Testament as a source of revelation, tried to establish a limited canon of 'inspired' or trustworthy books of the New Testament, and denied the doctrine of the incarnation of Jesus Christ; (4) Valentinus, who taught in Rome A.D. *c.* 136–165, left the Christian community, and established a sect of his own with numerous followers. Their influence is also seen in the great Persian heresiarch Mani. Much of our material about them comes from their Christian opponents, ⇨ Irenaeus, ⇨ Tertullian, etc. There is also the Corpus Hermeticum, a collection of Egyptian origin, in which several anonymous Gnostic tracts are preserved together with other occult and astrological material; others exist in Coptic and Syriac. But when such discoveries as the Gnostic texts found at Nag Hammardi in Upper Egypt (1946) have been studied, they may bring into sharper focus what seems at present a puzzling and amorphous episode. [DRD]

E. de Faye, *Gnostiques et gnosticisme* (2nd edn, Paris, 1925); F. C. Burkitt, *Church and Gnosis* (1932).

Gregory of Nazianzus (A.D. *c.* 330–*c.* 390). Greek Christian writer. Life-long friend of ⇨ Basil the Great, whom he first met at Caesarea in Cappadocia, Gregory continued his studies at Caesarea in Palestine, Alexandria and Athens. Returning home *c.* 357, he withdrew into monastic retirement. In 362 he was forcibly ordained a priest by his father, bishop of Nazianzus, whom eventually, after a second period of withdrawal, he assisted in the administration of his see. He was consecrated bishop of Sasima (*c.* 371) by Basil but failed to secure entrance to his territory, and in 374 took over the control of Nazianzus, after his father's death. In 379 he accepted a summons from the orthodox party in Constantinople and in 381 was made bishop, only to resign shortly afterwards because of intrigues against him. The final years of his life were spent on the family estates, where he devoted himself exclusively to literary pursuits.

Outstanding among his writings are his 45 orations, most of them from 379–81, when he was at Constantinople. These works have earned him the title of the 'Christian Demosthenes' and in them are displayed all the devices of the Second Sophistic. Amongst his 400 or so poems is an autobiographical study in 1,949 iambic trimeters. His 245 letters are notable for their epistolary style which, according to him, should be characterized by brevity, clarity, charm and simplicity. [J G D]

Migne, *P G*, 35–38; *Orations*, tr. C. G. Browne and J E. Swallow (N P F, 1894); *Select Poems of Synesius and Gregory of Nazianzen*, tr. H. S. Boyd (1814).
J. Quasten, *Patrology*, iii (1960).

Gregory of Nyssa (A.D. *c.* 335–94). Greek Christian writer. Initially a teacher of rhetoric, Gregory was eventually consecrated bishop of Nyssa, under the jurisdiction of his elder brother, Basil the Great. Arian opposition culminated in his deposition in 375, but after the death of Valens (378) Gregory returned to his diocese. Elected metropolitan of Sebaste in 379, he attended the Council of Constantinople two years later, paying further visits to the capital to deliver the funeral orations of the Empress Flacilla and of her daughter Pulcheria.

A versatile author, writing dogmatic, exegetical and ascetic works, together with orations, sermons and letters, Gregory was much indebted to the contemporary sophistic, revealing a predilection for ecphrasis, metaphor and oxymoron, and for Atticisms. His style however lacks charm and tends to obscure the profundity of his thought. [J G D]

Migne, *P G*, 44, 46; selection tr. W. Moore and H. A. Wilson (N P F, 1893).
B. Altaner, *Patrology* (1960).

H

Hadrian (Publius Aelius Hadrianus) (A.D. 76–138). Roman Emperor A.D. 117–38. As a writer, Hadrian is represented merely by a poem addressed, on his death-bed, to his soul (*animula vagula blandula* etc.), and by an exchange of trifles with the poet ◊ Florus. Among lost works, we hear of 12 speeches, a collection of letters, and an autobiography. An inscription (CIL, viii, 2352) preserves a substantial part of an address to the troops at Lambaesis; another from Jarrow (CIL, vii, 488) a tiny fragment of a similar address to the troops in Britain.

His deep interest in Greek literature and his taste for archaism ('he preferred Cato to Cicero, Ennius to Virgil') exercised an important influence on taste. He founded the *Athenaeum* in Rome (? A.D. 134–35) for the encouragement of Latin literature; Juvenal may have been a beneficiary. [D R D]

Bardon, *E L L.*

Hecataeus (fl. *c.* 500 B.C.). Greek historian and geographer. Hecataeus of Miletus was one of the leaders of the Ionian revolt against Persia, though he had at first opposed the revolt, possibly from personal hostility towards Aristagoras. He wrote the *Genealogiae*, a mythological history tracing back the lineage of various important families, and the *Periegesis*, a description of the inhabited world. He was criticized by his successors for inaccuracy and for failing to distinguish between fact and fiction, but he was regarded as a pioneer in the development of prose style. He is important as the composer of the earliest prose history and geography. [T A D]

Jacoby, *F G H*, i.
L. Pearson, *Early Ionian Historians* (1939).

Hegesias. ◊ Cyrenaics.

Hegias. ◊ Epic Cycle.

Heliodorus (? 3rd cent. A.D.). Greek novelist. From Emesa in Syria, where he was probably attached to the Temple of the Sun-God. Author of one of the more readable of the 5 extant Greek novels – the *Aethiopica, or Theagenes and Charicleia.* The heroine (ingeniously conceived as the white daughter of the King and Queen of Ethiopia) preserves her virtue through a series of incredible adventures that take her from Delphi to Meroe. In the end the lovers marry, and live happily ever after. It was much read in the 16th century, especially in the French translation of Amyot. [D R D]

Budé: R. M. Rattenbury, T. W. Lumb and J. Maillon (3 vols., Paris, 1935–43); Everyman: Sir Walter Lamb (1961).

Hellanicus (*c.* 490–*c.* 405 B.C.). Greek historian. Hellanicus of Lesbos wrote various works on mythology, ethnology and history, of which the most important were a *History of Attica* and a chronological list of the Priestesses of Hera at Argos. He was the earliest historian to work out some kind of chronological framework, though according to Thucydides it was not very accurate for the period 480–430 B.C. [T A D]

Jacoby, *F G H*.
L. Pearson, *Early Ionian Historians* (1939).

Heracleides Ponticus (*c.* 390–*c.* 310 B.C.). Greek philosopher. Born at Heraclea in Pontus, he joined the Academy *c.* 367, and soon became one of its leading members, acting as Plato's deputy on his third voyage to Sicily (361–360). When the Mastership fell vacant in 338 Heracleides was an unsuccessful candidate, after which he opened his own school in Pontus. He wrote on many subjects, some of his dialogues on mythology being known to Cicero, and he was greatly interested in the mysticism of Pythagoras. His best scientific work was in astronomy, where he made an advance towards the heliocentric theory by suggesting that Mercury and Venus revolve round the sun. Fragments only survive. [D R D]

Müller, *F H G*, ii.
Sarton, *H S*, i.

Heraclitus (fl. *c.* 500 B.C.). Greek philosopher. Born at Ephesus. There is little trustworthy evidence concerning his life: the numerous anecdotes seem invented to illustrate the arrogance and obscurity for which he was famed. Socrates complained that 'it needs a sponge-diver to bring up the truth from those depths'. The obscurity derives from his cryptic, oracular style. Later commentators such as Aristotle and the Stoics misunderstood him, but about 120 authentic fragments survive of his book (*On Nature*?), revealing the main features of a bold and comprehensive cosmology. These are: 'Fire is the underlying element: the world is an ever-living fire.' There is a continual process of change in the world: 'All things are exchanged for fire, and fire for things; as goods for gold and gold for goods.' 'Opposites', such as love-strife, health-sickness, pleasure-pain, are constantly at war, but connected by an essential unity, 'a tension of opposites, like that of a bow or a lyre'. Finally, wisdom consists in understanding the Formula (*Logos*) by which the world works. The clue to this is through self-knowledge. 'I searched within myself.' [D R D]

Diels, *F V*, 22.
G. S. Kirk, *Heraclitus, The Cosmic Fragments* (1954).

Herillus. ⇨ Zeno.

Herodas or Herondas (3rd century B.C.). Greek mime writer. Nothing was known of him until the discovery, in 1890, of a papyrus containing 8 mimes, written in iambic scazons, and now the most considerable representative of their genre (⇨ Mime). Their setting recalls the low-life scenes of New Comedy – a world of bawds, pimps, jealous mistresses, charlatans and petty crooks. The language is racy, the characters realistically portrayed, warts and all, with a keen eye for their amorous peculiarities. It is thought that they were written for solo performance – which must have been entertaining. (⇨ Alexandrian Poetry.) [D R D]

Ed. and tr. W. Headlam and A. D. Knox (1922); Loeb: A. D. Knox (with Theophrastus, *Characters*) (1929).

Herodes Atticus (A.D. *c.* 101–177). The Greek multi-millionaire of his day, and a great philanthropist. Some of his benefactions, such as the Odeon at Athens, survive, together with numerous inscriptions in honour of his wife, Regilla. He kept a day-book or library journal, and delivered public addresses. One of these, *On the State*, survives, together with fragments of his other writings. [D R D]

Herodian (fl. *c.* A.D. 230). Greek historian. Said to have been of Syrian origin, and (less certainly) to have held an official post in Rome. He belongs, with ⇨ Dio Cassius, to that group of Greek authors who, with Thucydides as their model, wrote on the Roman Empire. His 8 books cover the period from Marcus Aurelius to Gordian III (A.D. 180–238), and he writes as a contemporary observer. His authority is generally preferable to that of the *Historia Augusta*, and is a useful supplement to Dio Cassius. The speeches are verbose and uninteresting, but the narrative is lively and even dramatic. His comparative neglect is due to our undue concentration on the history of the late Republic and early Empire rather than to his own defects.

He is to be distinguished from the grammarian Aelius Herodianus, a contemporary of Marcus Aurelius. [DRD]

Teubner: K. Stavenhagen (Leipzig, 1922); tr. Edward Echols (Berkeley, Cal., 1961).

Herodotus (*c.*484–*c.*420 B.C.). Greek historian. Son of Lyxes, he was born at Halicarnassus in Asia Minor. As a result of political troubles he migrated to Samos, and then moved to Athens, where he probably composed and published some of his work. He took part in the foundation of the Athenian colony of Thurii, in south Italy, and died there, though possibly he returned to Athens for a time before his death. Herodotus travelled continually, and he records journeys to Egypt, the Black Sea and Scythia, the Euphrates and Babylon, and Cyrene and the North African coast, as well as to the various parts of the Greek Mediterranean and Asia Minor. Some of these travels were for trade, others clearly for collecting information.

It is uncertain when and in what order Herodotus composed his *History*, but probably it was not written in the order in which it has reached us. It has been very plausibly suggested that the account of the Persian Wars was written first and the other sections, on the rise of the Persian Empire and the various digressions, were added later, with Book II, the description of Egypt, being written last. The present division into 9 books was made several hundred years after the historian's death.

Herodotus's purpose was to give the complete story of the struggle between Europe and Asia, culminating in the invasion of Greece by Xerxes. In Book I he tells the story of Croesus of Lydia and his disastrous attack on Cyrus, and the rise of the Persian Empire under Cyrus; Book II contains the long digression about Egypt; Book III describes the conquests of Cambyses and Darius; Book IV deals with the digression on Scythia and North Africa and the account of the Scythian expedition of Darius; Book V with the Ionian Revolt; Book VI with Marathon; Book VII with the invasion of Xerxes and the battle of Thermopylae; Book VIII with the sea-battle of Artemisium and the Greek victory at Salamis; and Book IX with the final victories at Plataea and Mycale. Throughout the narrative relevant historical events in Greece have been referred to and described, with increasing frequency as the scene shifts to Greece.

As a historian, Herodotus has defects. He is too ready to accept the miraculous, especially in early history, and to include without qualification stories of some romantic interest but of little historical value or authenticity. However, it is wrong to accuse him of excessive credulity, as often he makes it clear that he is not vouching for the truth of what is obviously legendary or fabulous. But his main fault is lack of real military or political understanding – he failed to show any intelligent appreciation of strategy in the Persian Wars, and took a figure based on the total of the full-scale muster-roll of the whole Persian Empire as the number of the Persian troops in Greece; he tended to attribute events to personal motives, and to confuse the occasion of an event with its underlying cause; he had little idea of political or economic causes. But these defects, which are so often pointed out, are far outweighed by his merits as a historian, which are not. He was impartial and remarkably free from racial prejudice; he had a natural interest in the physical world and in his fellow-men, and acute powers of observation; above all, he set down a faithful record of all the information he obtained, gave alternative versions where available, did what he could to balance the evidence by estimating the comparative value of his various sources, and was not too proud to include accounts or explanations that he personally did not believe, so making it possible for later readers to exercise their own judgement.

Herodotus had a keen interest in geography, but he was a compiler of geographical information rather than a real geographer. Many of his anthropological details, at one time derided, are now fully accepted in the light of modern scientific knowledge. However, his explanation of climatic phenomena is nearly always at fault.

Whatever his faults as historian or geographer, as a storyteller Herodotus was superb. His narrative of events always sustains the reader's interest, while his portrayal of character, though often not based on any sound tradition, is dramatically satisfying. His literary skill is all the more remarkable in that prose-writing was in its infancy. He was the first writer to produce in prose, rather than in poetry, a work on so vast a scale, dealing with so large and varied a theme, to which it brings an epic dignity.

Herodotus wrote in a form of the Ionic dialect. The sentences are straightforward and unadorned, though the various clauses in the sentences are not always properly subordinated, a sign of a primitive stage in prose-writing development. But the story flows swiftly, the writer being intensely interested in what he is writing and confident that his readers will share his interest. [T A D]

O C T: K. Hude (2 vols., 1927); Loeb: A. D. Godley (4 vols., 1920–24); comm. W. W. How and J. Wells (1912); tr. Aubrey de Sélincourt (Penguin Classics, 1954).

Herondas. ⇨ Herodas.

Hesiod (800 B.C.? 700 B.C.?). Greek poet. From Ascra in Boeotia, he was the earliest of Greek poets after Homer. There has been much controversy about his date; a view now widely accepted would place him about 800 B.C., which is not much later than the date given by Herodotus. His father, an emigrant from Ionia, acquired a small holding near Mt Helicon – 'a bad place in winter, stuffy in summer, good at no season of the year'. When it came to be divided and his brother Perses – 'that silly man' – tried to claim more than his fair share, he drew on himself (besides a lawsuit) the long admonitory verse epistle which bears the title *Works and Days*. The 'works' are the operations of farming year, the 'days' the astrologically lucky and unlucky days of the lunar month. But there are other ingredients of the poem – the story of Pandora's box, the Five Ages of the world, the fable of the Hawk and the Nightingale, a rather perfunctory excursus on sea-faring, much moralizing on country lore, and some fine descriptive passages, notably that on winter (503 ff.). Such apparently incongruous elements have led to attempts to split the poem between several authors. These are not convincing. Uniformity of tone and a discernible thread of argument speak in favour of a single author. His is the authentic voice of the Balkan peasant, living on the bare edge of subsistence, often the victim of injustice, viewing Nature without sentiment and his fellows without illusions, but sustained by the dignity of hard work, not devoid of pleasure, and responsive to poetry. The poem is in the Ionian dialect, with Boeotian elements.

An impressive list of classical authors – though not the local tradition – also ascribe to Hesiod the *Theogony*, a poetic account of the origins of the world, the genealogy of the gods, and their more important myths. The prologue, invoking the Muses and telling how they brought Hesiod the gift of song as he fed his sheep on Mt Helicon, is a classical statement of early views of poetical inspiration. The poem as a whole is basic for all later Greek mythology.

Like Homer, Hesiod fostered a school of poets who worked in his tradition. They are the most likely authors of such poems as the *Shield of Heracles* (480 lines survive), the fragments of the *Catalogue* (of heroines), and of various works on astronomy and mythology. (⇨ Epic Poetry, Greek.) [D R D]

Loeb: H. G. Evelyn-White (1936); *Works and Days*, ed. T. A. Sinclair (1932); *Theogony*, ed. and comm. M. L. West (1966).
K. von Fritz and others, *Hésiode et son influence* (Paris, 1960).

Hieronymus (fl. 300 B.C.). Greek historian. Born at Cardia, he took an active part in the wars that followed the death of Alexander the Great. He served successively Eumenes of Cardia, Antigonus, Demetrius and Antigonus Gonatas in various administrative and diplomatic posts, including that of governor of Boeotia. He is said to have lived over 100 years. Hieronymus wrote a *History of the Wars of the Successors*, from the death of Alexander (323 B.C.) to the death of Pyrrhus (272 B.C.). Apart from some prejudice against Pyrrhus and Lysimachus he is a very reliable historian, and his work was used as a source by Arrian, Diodorus and Plutarch. [T A D]

Müller, *F H G*.

Hieronymus, Saint. ⇨ Jerome.

Hipparchus (fl. *c.* 130 B.C.). Greek astronomer and mathematician. Hipparchus of Nicaea worked in Alexandria (161 – 126?)

and at Rhodes (after 128). None of his works survives, and most of our information about him comes from ◊ Ptolemy. But he was clearly the most influential of Hellenistic astronomers: his *Table of Chords* is the first work on trigonometry; he discovered the precession of the equinoxes, and compiled a catalogue of 850 fixed stars. He also noted the appearance of a *nova* in 134. [D R D]

Sarton, *H S*, ii.

Hippocrates of Cos (*c.*460–? 380 B.C.). The most famous of ancient physicians, and the founder of Greek scientific medicine. The standards attained by Greek medicine at its best are largely due to him; he influences modern practice through the Hippocratic oath, and through the work of the International Hippocratic Foundation at Cos. Little is known of his life, and none of the extensive Hippocratic *corpus* is certainly by him. The Hippocratic school is associated with the great healing shrine of Asclepius on Cos (excavated by the German and Italian archaeologists), but Hippocrates himself practised in many parts of the Greek world, especially in the north. He died at Larissa in Thessaly.

The 53 works in the Hippocratic *corpus* belong to several periods, and are of varying scientific value. All are in the Ionian dialect, and the *corpus* may well represent the library of the Coan school as known in Alexandrian times. They deal with surgery, epidemiology (notably of malarial diseases), therapeutics, pharmacology and medical ethics. The most important – probably belonging to the age of Hippocrates – constitute a landmark in the history of scientific thought. We may mention: (1) *On the Sacred Disease*: a classic demonstration that the 'Sacred Disease' (epilepsy) is to be ascribed to natural causes like all other disorders, 'Its supposed origin being due to man's inexperience, and their astonishment at its characteristics.' (2) *Epidemics* (esp. Books I and III). These contain the celebrated 'case-book' studies of 42 cases of illness (mostly serious, though one describes an epidemic of mumps, with attendant orchitis). They show remarkable skill in observation – much importance was attached to prognosis in the Hippocratic system. (3) *Airs, Waters and Places*. 'The first attempt at medical climatology', with some impressive observations on anthropology and on the distribution of disease. (4) *The Oath of Hippocrates*, taken by medical students before admission to the guild. [D R D]

Ed. E. Littré (10 vols., Paris, 1839–61); Loeb: W. H. S. Jones and E. T. Withington (4 vols., 1923–31).

L. Edelstein, *The Hippocratic Oath* (Baltimore, 1943); Sarton, *H S*, i; P. Schazmann, *Asklepieion* (Berlin, 1932) (for the shrine of Asclepius).

Hipponax (fl. second half 6th cent. B.C.). Greek iambic poet. His name suggests aristocratic origins: traditionally he was banished by the tyrant of his native Ephesus, and went into exile at Clazomenae. The surviving fragments suggest extreme and embittered impoverishment. He launches outspoken attacks on Arete, his mistress, on the sculptors Bupalus and Athenis (whom he was alleged to have driven to suicide), on the painter Mimnes, and on the otherwise unknown Sannus. Satirical and savagely uninhibited, he can on occasion be broadly indecent. He created the 'limping iambus' (*scazon* or *Choliambus*) in which the iambic trimeter is made to end with a spondee, creating a violently disturbed rhythm matching the content of much of his work. He also writes limping trochaic tetrameters, normal iambic trimeters, iambic epodes reminiscent of Archilochus, and (in a mock-heroic parody of epic) dactylic hexameters. His vocabulary is colourfully colloquial, including Lydian loan-words. His consuming hatred is redeemed by a sense of humour which never wholly deserts him, and his coarse hard-hitting realism is communicated with gusto and a crisp vigour of style. [D E W W]

Diehl, *A L G*, i.

A. D. Knox, *The Greek Choliambic Poets* (1929).

Hirtius, Aulus (d. 43 B.C.). Roman writer. He was staff officer of Caesar in Gaul, though his duties seem to have been administrative rather than military. Well known as a *bon vivant*, after the Civil War he was on close terms with Cicero, who gave him lessons in oratory in exchange for instruction on how to enjoy the pleasures of the table. As consul in 43 he shared command of the senatorial forces sent against Antony in Cisalpine

Gaul, but was killed in the battle of Mutina.

Hirtius wrote Book VIII of Caesar's *Gallic Wars*, describing the last two campaigns, 51–50 B.C. He also probably wrote the *Alexandrine War*, which describes the end of the war at Alexandria and the short campaign in Asia Minor, serving as a continuation of the *Civil Wars*. The *African War*, describing the campaign against Cato and Metellus Scipio that ended at Thapsus, is sometimes attributed to Hirtius, but with little probability. This book, and the *Spanish War*, which describes in very bad Latin the campaign that led up to the battle of Munda, may have been rough drafts that Hirtius had made by soldiers in the campaigns, and which he would have written up more elaborately if he had lived. [T A D]

Works published as part of the Caesarian *corpus* (◊ Caesar).

'Historia Augusta'. The *Historia Augusta* is the name given to a series of biographies of Roman Emperors (Augusti), heirs to the throne (Caesares), and pretenders (*tyranni*), from Hadrian to Carinus. These biographies contain a mixture of good historical tradition (in the earlier Lives, at any rate), anecdotal gossip and poor-quality biographical material, and records of speeches, documents and proclamations, mostly forgeries. In some cases the 'Minor Lives' – those of the Caesars or Pretenders – contain no historical material not in the 'Major Lives' of the relevant Augusti.

The various biographies purport to be the work of 6 authors, Aelius Spartianus, Julius Capitolinus, Vulcacius Gallicanus, Aelius Lampridius, Trebellius Pollio and Flavius Vopiscus. Most of the Lives are dedicated either to Diocletian or to Constantine, and it was long assumed that they had been written and published in the reigns of these Emperors. However Dessau maintained that the whole *Historia* was fabricated by a single author in the reign of Theodosius at the end of the 4th century A.D., who gave it an appearance of verisimilitude by attributing it to 6 earlier authors. Since then, innumerable interpretations of the problem have appeared, and it is now accepted that the biographies cannot be assigned to the various authors whose names are appended to them. It is, however, agreed that several different authors were probably involved, and that the work was composed later than was first supposed. The prevalent theory is that it was put out during the reign of Julian the Apostate (A.D. 360–3), as propaganda for his social and religious reforms – the main themes that run through the *Historia* (the supremacy of the Senate and the frequent succession of good emperors by unworthy sons) fit in well with the atttude of Julian towards the family of Constantine, whom he supplanted, as does the frequent praise of old-fashioned philosophic virtues. [T A D]

Loeb: D. Magie (3 vols., 1922–32) (vol. ii discusses composition).

N. H. Baynes, *The Historia Augusta, Its Date and Purpose* (1926); A. Birley, in *Latin Historians*, ed. T. A. Dorey (1966).

Historiography, Greek. Accounts of events in very early days were recorded in verse, and the earliest historical information was provided by the epic poets. It was not until about 500 B.C. that, under the influence of philosophic and scientific thought in Ionia, the first prose histories began to appear. ◊ Hecataeus of Miletus played a leading part in their development.

The various types of Greek histories can be classified under three main headings. (1) Local histories, dealing with one particular city or family. These include the collections of official lists of magistrates for Athens, Sparta and Argos, compiled in the 5th century B.C., which helped to establish a chronological framework; the local histories of Attica (◊ Atthis), one of which forms the basis of the historical sections of Aristotle's *Constitution of Athens*; and such works as the *Local History of Cyme* by ◊ Ephorus. They often contained much mythological information. (2) The scientific histories, on a rather larger scale and based on careful observation and inquiry; their purpose was to ascertain the truth and explain the real causes of events. Of this type the main examples were ◊ Thucydides, ◊ Hieronymus of Cardia and ◊ Polybius. Most historians of this type had practical experience in political and military affairs. (3) Those histories whose primary aim was to provide entertainment or edification. Thucydides, in his preface, criticizes certain 5th-century historians for writing what pleases the ear rather than what is true, and this type is frequently found in the 3rd century, notable examples being ◊ Duris of Samos and ◊ Cleitarchus of Alexandria. But an even greater inducement to distort historical truth was provided by the teachings of ◊ Isocrates, under whose inspiration history became the vehicle of moral instruction and political propaganda. His disciple ◊ Ephorus regarded praising and blaming as one of the historian's chief functions. This school had great influence on Roman historians, particularly Livy.

In its earliest form, Greek history was a manifestation of scientific thought, and in spite of the many other distracting influences these origins were always reflected in the serious attitude to history taken by the best Greek historians. [T A D]

M. I. Finley, *The Greek Historians* (1959).

Historiography, Roman. The Greeks were interested in theory, and tended to regard history as a branch of either science or philosophy; the Romans were more practical, and treated history merely as a form of literary production, or at times as an exercise in the art of persuasion. Quintilian said that history was closely akin to poetry, while Cicero described it as a part of rhetoric, and maintained that the most important qualification of the historian was a command of language. In fact, the Romans regarded the composition of history as less important than that of a political or forensic speech; to them it was a form of literature designed to give pleasure, and nearly all the comments made by Roman literary critics on history concern style.

Cicero, Quintilian and even Tacitus stress the need to avoid partiality or prejudice. However, it seems that in practice Roman historians merely paid lip-service to the principle of impartiality. The influence of rhetoric, which made it second nature for a Roman writer to take sides, made impossible any really objective approach.

The publication of the ◊ *Annales Maximi* established a convenient chronological framework, and as a result most Roman historians used the annalistic method, describing events as they happened year by year (though Tacitus deals with the provinces or foreign wars several years at a time).

Roman historians paid more attention to the presentation of their material than to its collection, and original research was felt to be the antiquarian's task rather than the historian's. Cicero, however, went to very great pains in his works on philosophy or oratory to get his historical facts completely right.

Finally, it is wrong to regard Roman historiography and Latin historiography as synonymous. The earliest Roman historians wrote in Greek, as Latin prose had not developed as a literary medium at the start of the 2nd century B.C. (e.g. ◊ Fabius Pictor; ◊ Cato). Under the Empire, many Greeks settled in Rome and took an active part in its literary and political life; educated Romans were as fluent in Greek as in Latin, and some of the more important histories under the Principate were written in Greek (e.g. ◊ Appian; ◊ Dionysius of Halicarnassus; ◊ Dio Cassius), though ◊ Ammianus Marcellinus is an example of a Greek who wrote in Latin although it was not his native tongue. [T A D]

Ed. T. A. Dorey, *Latin Historians* (1966).

Homer (probably 8th cent. B.C.). Greek epic poet. He was traditionally regarded as the author of the *Iliad* and *Odyssey*; the ◊ *Margites* and ◊ *Batrachomyomachia* and other epic poems were also popularly attributed to him, but the best ancient authorities reject the attribution. There was much uncertainty even in antiquity about Homer's date and birthplace. Many different dates were suggested, ranging from the time of the Trojan War to 500 years later, and the number of his alleged birthplaces was a byword; practically every city, it was said, claimed him. Herodotus confidently dated Homer to about 850 B.C., and that is possible; but modern scholars tend to favour the end of the 8th century. At all events, the Homeric poems, in their present form, were composed in the main long after the events they describe, but probably before alphabetic writing came into use for literary purposes about the middle of the 7th century B.C. Their largely Ionic dialect, and some evidence of local knowledge, support the tradition that Homer lived in Ionia; the most likely places seem to be Smyrna and especially Chios, the home of the ◊ Homeridae.

Of Homer's life we have several ancient accounts but little reliable information. The most circumstantial *Life,* attributed to Herodotus, represents Homer as a wanderer not unlike his own hero Odysseus: born in Smyrna, he voyaged to many parts of Greece (including Ithaca), suffered poverty, blindness and lack of appreciation in the course of many vicissitudes, and finally died on Ios. This career, however apocryphal in detail, would at least account for Homer's evident first-hand knowledge of men and the sea.

It was generally believed in antiquity that the *Iliad* and the *Odyssey* were the work of a single poet, but some Alexandrian grammarians, the 'Separators', argued there were two. Modern scholars have even doubted whether Homer existed at all. Since the end of the 18th century there has been much controversy over this 'Homeric question'. It is generally agreed that *Iliad* and *Odyssey* embody a number of earlier and shorter lays, contain many inconsistencies, and were composed largely of traditional formulae handed down in an oral technique which makes it difficult to determine the contribution of any individual to an evolving poem (◊ Epic Poetry, Greek). On the other hand there is a marked unity of structure and style in each poem, as Aristotle recognized; inconsistencies are inevitable in a long poem orally composed; and the almost universal ancient belief in 'one Homer' must carry great weight. Opinions continue to differ on the Homeric question, but it is still possible to hold that the *Iliad* and *Odyssey* are substantially the earlier and later work of one man using traditional material; or, more cautiously, that there was one 'main poet' for each poem.

It seems doubtful whether the *Iliad* and *Odyssey* were committed to writing before the 6th century B.C., when they were introduced to Athens and reduced to proper order in a written text for use at the Panathenaea. For centuries thereafter garbled variant versions, perhaps originally pirated from the official recitations, formed a composite vulgate text, of which fragments survive on papyri; and from this our own text is ultimately derived. The scholars of Alexandria, and later of Constantinople, collected and compared different copies, including probably the Panathenaic version, and laboured to establish an authentic text and explain it, though without substantially affecting the vulgate. Each poem, as we have it now, has 24 books, an arrangement apparently made by the Alexandrians; before their time the poems were divided somewhat differently into major episodes, each with its own title.

The *Iliad* is the poem of Ilium (Troy). Its theme, stated at the outset, is the wrath of Achilles, the champion of the besieging Greeks, and its disastrous consequences. The action covers only a few weeks in the last year of the siege, but the poet contrives to bring in much of the previous course of the Trojan War, as seen from both sides, and all the principal characters in the saga, Greek and Trojan, human and divine. The story opens with a clash of personalities, when Agamemnon, the Greek commander-in-chief, publicly offends his proud ally Achilles by a high-handed assertion of authority, and Achilles thereupon refuses to take any further part in the siege. His hope that this will lead to the discomfiture of the Greeks is fulfilled all too well. He rejects a handsome offer of compensation from Agamemnon, and stubbornly nurses his wrath until the Greeks are in such dire straits that his friend Patroclus goes to their help and is killed. The shock of bereavement ends the wrath, or rather redirects it against the Trojans: he comes to terms with Agamemnon, joins the fighting again in vengeful fury, and kills the Trojan champion Hector. Still unsatisfied, he maltreats Hector's corpse day after day, until the old king Priam comes by night from Troy and begs to be given his son's body for burial. Then the wrath of Achilles fades at last as he reflects that he too must soon die; the two men mourn their dead together, and Achilles returns the body of his enemy. The tragic central theme is interwoven with many episodes which diversify the poem and enhance the total effect – reviews of the opposing forces at Troy; the exploits of individual heroes; the very human debates and intrigues of the gods; Hephaestus forging new armour of miraculous workmanship for Achilles; and the great funeral games for Patroclus. As a foil to the picture of the Greek warriors in the field and in camp, there are the Trojan scenes: Helen, the cause of the war, beautiful as ever and uneasily nostalgic, watching the Greeks from the walls of Troy; Paris, a contemptible figure, at home; the doomed Hector taking leave of his wife and baby son; and his aged parents, Priam and Hecuba, looking on in despair as he awaits the fatal single combat with Achilles.

The *Odyssey,* named after its hero Odysseus, tells the story of his return home from the Trojan War. His wanderings lasted ten years, but the action of the *Odyssey* covers only the final six weeks. The poet tells the latter part of the story first, in the proverbial Homeric fashion, and brings in the rest by means of a flashback. When the poem opens Odysseus is a castaway, longing for home, in the island paradise of the goddess Calypso, who has kept him there as her lover for nearly eight years; while at home in Ithaca his son Telemachus is almost a grown man, and his wife Penelope is overrun with unwanted guests, her suitors, feasting at the house's expense, continually pressing her to marry again, and after being fobbed off for three years insisting that she should at last make her choice. Odysseus's plight is due to the hostility of Poseidon, father of the Cyclops who was blinded by Odysseus early in his wanderings; but in Poseidon's absence the other gods are persuaded by Athena to take pity on Odysseus and help him, and so the plot is set in motion. Athena prompts Telemachus to visit Pylos and Sparta in search of news of his father, and Zeus orders Calypso to let Odysseus go. Odysseus builds a raft and sets sail; Poseidon raises a storm and wrecks the raft, but Odysseus is eventually cast up on the shore of Scheria, a Bronze Age Utopia inhabited by the estimable and highly civilized Phaeacians. Here, in a charming and famous episode, Odysseus meets the princess Nausicaa, whose parents entertain him royally in their palace of bronze and gold, with its door framed in silver. During the feasting he describes his adventures since setting out from Troy, in a narrative that embodies a number of familiar folk-tales. He tells of many strange and perilous encounters – with the Lotus-Eaters, with cannibals, monsters, whirlpools and clashing rocks, with Aeolus, god of the winds, with the enchantress Circe, the ghosts of the dead, and the cattle of the Sun-god; and how at the last he was cast up on Calypso's island, the sole survivor of his company. When his tale is told the Phaeacians transport Odysseus back to Ithaca, where, in the guise of a beggar, he learns about the suitors. Athena brings Telemachus back from Sparta, and father and son, reunited at last, plan to destroy them. At his house no one recognizes Odysseus except his faithful dog and his aged nurse; but when Penelope proposes a final contest in archery for the suitors before making her choice, only he can string the bow. The suitors are slaughtered, Penelope is convinced of her husband's identity, and Odysseus is established in his kingdom once more.

Epic poetry should be distinguished, according to Aristotle, by high seriousness and nobility, unity of action combined with variety of incident, dramatic vividness, and self-effacement on the part of the author; and in all these qualities he judged Homer to be pre-eminent. Nor has any other poet surpassed him to this day. The speed and simplicity of Homer's poetry carries him easily along, and his narrative technique is masterly: the end is continually kept in view, yet continually postponed as delays and digressions, with an interest and an end and consequences of their own, are introduced to draw out the story to a majestic length. Homer's heroic conception of his characters was an inspiration to poet and audience alike, and taught a not ignoble morality to all the ancient world, since his poems formed the basis of Greek and Roman education. Children learned them by heart, and men's minds were as much saturated by the language of Homer in antiquity as by the language of the Bible in later ages. Homer's influence on Greek and Latin literature was all-pervasive; his characterization, plots and language all made their mark on Greek lyric, drama and history, and on almost all Latin poetry. The Latin translation of the *Odyssey* by ⇨ Livius Andronicus virtually marked the foundation of Latin literature, and more than one vernacular literature of modern Europe had similar beginnings.

Translations of Homer have generally reflected as much of the translator and his age as of the original. The famous verse translations by Chapman (ed. Allardyce Nicoll, 1957), which were an inspiration to Keats, and by Pope, which presented the Trojan War in 18th-century dress, are works of literature in their own right. The standard modern English translations have long been the prose versions of the *Iliad* by Lang, Leaf and Myers (1883) and of the *Odyssey* by Butcher and Lang (1879), written deliberately in an archaic English as artificial as the Epic dialect itself. More recently there has been an idiosyncratic prose translation of the *Odyssey* by T. E. Lawrence (1955), and business-like prose versions of both *Iliad* (1950) and *Odyssey* (1946) in plain English by E. V. Rieu in the Penguin Classics series; but in these, as in all prose translations, the poetry has evaporated. The most successful modern attempt to do justice to the Homeric hexameter in English verse is Richmond Lattimore's translation of the *Iliad* (Chicago, 1962). (⇨ Epic Poetry, Greek). [G T W H]

OCT: D. B. Munro and T. W. Allen (5 vols., 1912–20); Loeb: A. T. Murray (4 vols., 1919–24); *Hesiod, The Homeric Hymns and Homerica*, H. G. Evelyn-White (1936).

G. Murray, *The Rise of the Greek Epic* (1960); G. S. Kirk, *Homer and the Epic* (1965); E. T. Owen, *The Story of the Iliad* (1947); A. J. B. Wace and F. H. Stubbings, *A Companion to Homer* (1962).

'Homeric Hymns'. A collection of 33 Greek poems in epic style and metre, addressed to gods and demi-gods. Though commonly attributed to Homer in antiquity, they were excluded from the Homeric canon by the Alexandrian grammarians; they seem to be later than ⇨ Homer, ⇨ Hesiod and some poems of the ⇨ Epic Cycle, and to belong mostly to the period from the 8th to the 6th centuries B.C. The authors were evidently rhapsodes, and all are anonymous; but one refers to himself in the *Hymn to Apollo* as 'a blind man living in rocky Chios', and is identified by a later authority as Cynaethus of Chios, one of the ⇨ Homeridae. When the collection was formed is not known.

Formally the *Homeric Hymns* are no more than preludes to recitations of epic poetry, in which rhapsodes competed at religious festivals; nearly all end with a phrase announcing 'another song'. Many consist of only a few lines of praise and invocation, but in a few the prelude has outgrown these limits and virtually become an epyllion narrating the adventures of the god invoked. The *Hymn to Demeter* (ii) relates the famous myth of Persephone, carried off by Hades to be his queen, of the vain search for her by her grief-stricken mother Demeter, and of the famine which Demeter caused until Persephone was allowed to return to the upper world every spring. The story is imaginatively and eloquently told, and the poem is one of the best in the collection. The *Hymn to Apollo* (iii) falls into two parts, the first describing the god's birth on Delos and the second his establishment of his oracle at Delphi; whether the poem is really two hymns or one is uncertain. There is an element of burlesque in the *Hymn to Hermes* (iv), translated by Shelley as the hymn *To Mercury,* which depicts the god as a highly precocious infant who on the day of his birth invented the lyre and, after stealing the cattle of his brother Apollo, used it as a gift to placate him. In the *Hymn to Aphrodite* (v) an able poet shows the goddess humbled by Zeus to punish her for her depredations, and yielding unwillingly to the power of love, which even she cannot resist. The *Hymn to Dionysus* (vii) more briefly tells the story of the god's capture by pirates, and the miracles he performed until they leapt overboard in terror and were turned into dolphins; and the even shorter *Hymn to Pan* (xix) describes Pan as a hunter roaming the wilds, and tells of his birth and the quaint pride of Hermes in his goat-footed son.

The *Homeric Hymns* represent the last phase of early Greek epic poetry. They inevitably lack the grandeur of the Homeric poems, and in the handling of the epic formulae the authors sometimes become mechanical and repetitive; but the collection is varied and interesting, and has a romantic charm of its own. (⇨ Epic Poetry, Greek.) [G T W H]

Ed. and comm. T. W. Allen, W. R. Halliday and E. E. Sikes (1963); Loeb: with Hesiod, H. G. Evelyn-White (1936).

G. S. Kirk, *Homer and the Epic* (1965).

Homeridae. 'Sons of Homer', originally a clan of rhapsodes claiming descent from Homer, which later developed into a guild including others not related to him. They possessed the knowledge of the Homeric poems as their hereditary property, with the right to recite them publicly, and preserved esoteric traditions of Homer in secret verses. Their headquarters, at least as early as the 6th century B.C., were at Chios, which claimed to be Homer's birthplace. They spread the knowledge of the Homeric poems through the Greek world; one of them, Cynaethus of Chios, is said to have introduced the poems into Syracuse. (⇨ Epic Poetry, Greek.) [G T W H]

A. J. B. Wace and F. H. Stubbings, *Companion to Homer* (1962); G. S. Kirk, *Homer and the Epic* (1965).

'Homerus Latinus'. ⇨ *Ilias Latina.*

Horace (Quintus Horatius Flaccus) (65–8 B.C.). Latin lyric poet and satirist. Born at Venusia in Apulia, where his father, a freedman, had a modest property. His mother is unknown. His father's affairs prospered, and he could afford to educate his son at Rome and later at Athens. In 44 Horace enlisted in Brutus's army and fought at Philippi as a military tribune. Physically unscathed, he returned to Rome friendless and penniless; poverty, he says, drove him to poetry. His early verse brought new contacts; Virgil and Varius introduced him to ⇨ Maecenas early in 38. Nine months later he was invited to join Maecenas's circle; and their friendship ripened steadily. *Satires* I appeared *c.*35. Maecenas gave Horace his Sabine farm, a small estate in hilly country, about this time. *Satires* II and the *Epodes* followed *c.*30. Actium had been fought by now, and Horace at last found peace of mind and poetic fulfilment. *Odes* I–III were published in 23. Their reception was luke-warm, and Horace, bitterly mortified, renounced lyric. *Epistles* I dates from 20, and in 20–17 fall the letters *To Florus* and *To the Pisones* (*Ars poetica*). In 17, however, Augustus commissioned a hymn for the Secular Games; and with this official recognition as poet laureate the lyric mood revived. Augustus's invitation to become his private secretary was tactfully declined; but his half-humorous complaint (*c.*14) that no Epistle had been addressed to him elicited II i, and Horace added the two long Letters already in circulation to complete *Epistles* II, following it in 13 with *Odes* IV. Maecenas died in the year 8, and Horace, as he had prophesied, did not long outlive him.

The *Epodes,* predominantly in iambic metres, are freely modelled on ⇨ Archilochus. Despite their vigorous invective, direct personal attacks are avoided, identities being concealed under pseudonyms. Politics, love and melodrama are among the themes explored, as Horace feels his way with growing mastery towards a new form of Latin lyric.

Satires I range over moral and literary criticism, personal memories (including touching tributes to Horace's father), and dramatic vignettes foreshadowing the dialogue form in which *Satires* II is almost wholly cast. These informal conversations succeed in catching in hexameters the cadence of colloquial Latin. Horace bases himself on Lucilius, but without his savagery, roughness and bitter personalities. What does emerge is a portrait of the author, his quirks and prejudices, likes and dislikes, set mostly against a colourful back-drop of the streets and crowds and teeming life of Rome, but with one radiant glimpse of country peace.

In the *Odes* Horace takes his metres and often his themes from Greek monody; he owes most here to ⇨ Alcaeus. But the emotional impulse whether from life or literature is shaped and transmuted by his subtle imagination and balanced personality into a poetry fresh and alive, but poised and sophisticated. He is keenly aware of the contemporary revival of Roman greatness, so that the achievement of Augustus, and of those helping to shape his policies, inspire some of Horace's finest work. He responds also to the momentary mood, to his friends, to love, as it was in youth, as it is in middle age, to wine and good company, to the beauty of the countryside, to the fleeting loveliness of spring. Much of the charm of his poetry derives from his unique blend of sense with sensibility, passion with irony, a happy-go-lucky disposition with a considered philosophy of life. From his profound understanding of the genius of Latin, with its pregnant brevity, highly flexible word-order, and sonorous vowels, he fashions a disciplined lyricism, with a new economy of words, an inexhaustible metrical virtuosity, a music akin to that of modern Italian. The *Carmen saeculare,* specially commissioned and designed to be sung, not read, stands a little apart. It is a stately poem, instinct with gratitude for what Augustus has accomplished and with the sense of a great religious occasion. Its success encouraged Horace to compose *Odes* IV, and though his lyrical impulse is declining, this book contains some of his most moving work.

The latest *Satires* already foreshadow the *Epistles*. Some of these may be authentic verse letters, slight, crisp, witty. Others elaborate a new genre, accomplished in versification and phrasing, easy and relaxed in tone, drawing freely, as the *Satires* had done, on fable, anecdote, and reminiscence, free from hatred, rarely touched with acrimony, with something of the attractiveness of a confidential diary, lit by the mature wisdom and poetic insight of the author, and illuminating the circle of his friends as though he were conducting us through a portrait gallery. Book II primarily defines his literary attitudes. He had spoken of abandoning poetry for philosophy; but the *Ars poetica* is a statement of aesthetic principles for the guidance of contemporary writers, and II i, is a reaffirmation of the part the poet must play in the evolution of the new society, in the poetic as well as the moral regeneration of the world.

The formal discipline of the *Odes* and the informality of the *Satires* and *Epistles* complement each other in a way which corresponds to a fundamental tension and equipoise in the Roman character. It is no accident that Horace is the most quoted author of antiquity. He is the supreme interpreter to subsequent generations of Augustan culture, and this, together with his own special qualities of imagination and temperament, make him the first European, appealing more directly and to a wider range of readers of every age and at every age than any other ancient poet. (⇨ Lyric Poetry, Latin.) [D E W W]

OCT: E. C. Wickham (2nd edn 1912); ed. A. Kieszling and R. Heinze, with German comm. (3 vols., 1914–30); Loeb: C. E. Bennett and H. R. Fairclough (2 vols., 1914, 1926); *Odes*, tr. into verse E. Marsh (1941); *Odes*, tr. James Michie (Penguin Classics, 1967); *Satires and Epistles*, tr. into verse J. Conington (1905).

L. P. Wilkinson, *Horace and His Lyric Poetry* (1945); E. Fraenkel, *Horace* (1957).

Hortensius (Quintus Hortensius Hortalus) (114–50 B.C.). Roman orator. Cicero's great rival at the Roman bar, who sometimes opposed him, as in the trial of Verres (70 B.C.), and sometimes helped him, as in the cases of Sulla (62) and Sestius (56). He belonged to the ornate 'Asianic' style of rhetoric: contemporaries said his speeches were better to hear than to read. We are in no position to judge, for so completely has he been eclipsed by Cicero that fragments only survive. [D R D]

Ed. H. Malcovati, *Oratorum romanorum fragmenta* (2nd edn 1905).

Hyginus. The name attached to a collection of mythographical material, the *Genealogiae* or *Fabulae,* which appears to date from the 2nd century A.D. Confused and inaccurate, it is thought to derive from a Greek original, translated by someone with a poor knowledge of Greek. An astronomical poem is attributed to the same person. Style and content rule out any association with the Hyginus of the next entry. [D R D]

Ed. H. J. Rose (Leiden, 1934).

Hyginus, Gaius Julius (fl. 10 B.C.). Roman scholar and writer. Hyginus was a Spaniard, a freedman of Augustus and librarian of the Palatine Library. He was a friend of ⇨ Clodius Licinus and Ovid. He was a man of antiquarian interests, and wrote *Lives of Famous Men, Families of Troy,* and *Origins of the Cities of Italy,* as well as works on agriculture and religion, a commentary on Virgil, and other works of scholarship. Two other collections of mythological legends, the *Fabulae* (*Books of Fables*) and the *Astronomica,* are also attributed to him. These, however, were probably compiled in the 2nd century A.D. [T A D]

Peter, *H R R*, ii.

Mary A. Grant, *Hyginus* (Kansas, 1960).

Hypereides (*c.* 390–332 B.C.). Attic orator. Of good Athenian stock, he traditionally studied under Isocrates and Plato. He was a well-known *bon vivant.* Starting his career as a *logographos,* he soon launched into politics and became a protagonist in the struggle against Macedonia. He served with the Athenian fleet at Euboea and

Byzantium in 340. After Chaeronea political activity was paralysed, but he continued to practise as an advocate. In 324 he participated in the impeachment of his old ally Demosthenes in connexion with the Harpalus-scandal, but later the two were reconciled. He was largely responsible for the conduct of the Lamian war, delivering the speech on the fallen in 322. When Athenian resistance collapsed he was condemned to death, arrested by Antipater's agents, and executed.

Substantial portions of 6 of his speeches have come to light on papyri, the most representative being *Against Athenagoras.* He combines extreme intellectual ability with a wide and tolerant knowledge of human nature. He makes an outstanding advocate: his urbanity and tact engage the sympathies of the judges, and he is master of the art in which restraint, good taste and lightness of touch count for everything. His language is racily colloquial, his usage already looks forward to the Greek of a later age. We can well understand that he was widely read and admired in the Hellenistic world. [D E W W]

Loeb: J. O. Burtt, *Minor Attic Orators,* ii (1954).
Dobson, *G O.*

I

Iamblichus (A.D. *c.* 250–*c.* 325). Greek neo-Platonist philosopher. A native of Syria, he studied under Porphyry in Rome, then returned to Syria to open a school of his own, probably at Apamea. He wrote extensively on astrology and mysticism; his commentaries on Plato and Aristotle were – to judge from the extracts in Proclus – highly misleading. Extant works are (1) *On the Life of Pythagoras,* (2) the *Protrepticus* and (3) 3 books on mathematics. Shallow in themselves, they contain some useful information on Pythagoreanism. A work *De mysteriis* is now generally attributed to him. [D R D]

Teubner: *Pythagoras,* ed. L. Deubner (Leipzig, 1937) and *Protrepticus,* ed. H. Pistelli (Leipzig, 1888); *De mysteriis,* German tr. and comm. Th. Hopfrer (Leipzig, 1922).
E. R. Dodds, *Proclus' Elements of Theology* (1933).

Iambulus (date unknown). Greek writer of the Hellenistic period. Author of the *Oceanica,* a book of travellers' tales parodied by ◊ Lucian in the *Vera historia.* An outline is preserved by ◊ Diodorus Siculus (II, 55–60): it tells of a Utopian society of primitive communism in a group of tropical islands. [D R D]

Ibycus (b. *c.* 600 B.C.). Greek lyric poet. Born at Rhegium. His father Phytius may have played a part in local politics. Ibycus himself refused the proffered tyranny in his native city and withdrew to the brilliant cosmopolitan court of Polycrates in Samos. Ultimately he returned to Rhegium and was buried there. The story of his violent death and of the birds revealing the identity of his murderers is Hellenistic melodrama.

Alexandrian scholars edited Ibycus's poetry in 7 books. The fragments are supplemented by a papyrus which preserves 50 lines from an encomium of Polycrates the younger, almost certainly attributable to Ibycus. In theme and treatment the early poetry shows the influence of Stesichorus, who dominated the contemporary literary scene in Magna Graecia. The move to Samos meant a profound change. In the encomium Ibycus is pouring new wine into old bottles. In form his poem is choral lyric with the normal triadic structure. Yet in content it is wholly secular, consciously renounces epic narrative, and culminates in a personal tribute to the prince's beauty. It reflects Ibycus's evolution into a predominantly erotic poet, fresh and spontaneous, and with an imaginative and evocative imagery and symbolism. He has the artist's eye for the colourful and picturesque. It is part of his lyrical response to the beauty of nature that he observes and records the life of birds and plants with sympathy and humour. [D E W W]

Page, *P M G.*
Bowra, *G L P.*

'Ilias Latina' ('Homerus Latinus'). A poem, well known in the Middle Ages, which gives an epitome of the *Iliad* in about 1,000 Latin hexameters. On internal evidence, the author's name seems to be Baebius Italicus, the date not later than

A.D. 68. Of no literary merit, it none the less kept alive some knowledge of Homer, along with ⇨ *Dares* and ⇨ *Dictys*, at a time when Greek was lost in the West. [D R D]

Teubner: F. Vollmer, *Poetae latini minores*, ii (Leipzig, 1913).

Irenaeus (2nd cent. A.D.). Greek Christian apologist. From Asia Minor, he came to Gaul before 177, and was subsequently bishop of Lugdunum (Lyons). His work *Adversus haereses* is chiefly an attack on the currently powerful sect of the Gnostics (⇨ Gnosticism). It was much used by later Christian controversialists. Although the Greek original survives in fragments only, there is a Latin translation (4th century A.D.?), and also a version in Armenian. [D R D]

Isaeus (*c.* 413–*c.* 343 B.C.). Attic orator. Born at Chalcis in Euboea. He was probably not an Athenian, but a resident alien; hence his lack of interest in politics. He is said to have studied under Isocrates. He himself taught rhetoric, and traditionally Demosthenes was a pupil. Certainly Demosthenes' early work owes something to Isaean influence. His main career was as *logographos*, a highly professional composer of speeches for others in the law-courts.

Antiquity knew 50 genuine speeches by Isaeus, and an *Art of Rhetoric* was also attributed to him. Of his orations, 11 have survived complete. All deal with family quarrels over wills and legacies; clearly Isaeus specialized in testamentary law. He excels at the lucid exposition of legal technicalities and intricate family relationships. The effect is of complete mastery of a complicated subject expressed in simple vigorous language and with a judicial objectivity drained of emotion and even of humour. Closer examination reveals that he is a clever and not over-scrupulous advocate manipulating the evidence, suppressing the truth and suggesting the false. But his effectiveness is undeniable, and there is little doubt that his clients generally won their cases. [D E W W]

Ed. W. Wyse (1904); Loeb: E. S. Forster (1927).
Jebb, *A O*, ii; Dobson, *G O*.

Isocrates (436–338 B.C.). Greek educator, publicist and orator. He came from a well-to-do Athenian family, and traditionally studied under Prodicus, Protagoras and Gorgias. Socrates, according to Plato, spoke highly of his promise. Impoverished by the Peloponnesian War, he took up the profession of *logographos*. His natural diffidence and weak voice debarred him from politics, and he resolved to influence opinion by teaching and writing. From *c.* 392 his school provided a systematic advanced literary training lasting three or four years. It was highly successful, rivalling Plato's Academy in attracting pupils from all over the Greek world; many achieved distinction in politics or literature. All his subsequent writings are ultimately related to his educational thought, since his aim was to secure the survival and, if possible, the wider diffusion of Greek cultural values. His conviction that civil strife was destroying the city-state led him to advocate enlightened monarchy; and his belief that inter-city warfare was ruining Hellas persuaded him that the Greeks must merge their differences in a common cause. Hence his successive appeals to the chief Greek states and their rulers to organize and lead a panhellenic crusade against Persia. Throughout a long and active life Isocrates continued to teach and to write. He died at the age of 97, when Philip appeared to be about to realize the programme he had advocated.

Of Isocrates' forensic speeches (which he himself preferred to forget) 6 have survived. His educational views are sketched in the early essay *Against the Sophists* (390), and elaborated 36 years later in the largely autobiographical *Antidosis*. The *Busiris* (391) and *Helen* (390) are school exercises in the handling of legendary themes. The most constructive of his political pamphlets are the *Panegyricus* (380) and the *Philippus* (346). He draws a portrait of the ideal ruler and his relationship to his subjects in the *Demonicus* (doubtfully authentic), the *To Nicocles*, and the *Nicocles* (374–372). The *Evagoras* (365), a panegyric on the ruler of Salamis, belongs to the same group. There are also numerous pamphlets commenting on the contemporary political scene – *Plataicus* (373), *Archidamus* (366), *Areopagiticus* (355), *De Pace* (355), and *Panathenaicus* (339). A majority, perhaps all, of the 9 letters attributed to Isocrates are authentic.

Isocrates' prose represents the periodic style in its most developed form, with elaborate balance of thought, phrasing, rhythm and sound. He is careful to avoid the clash of vowels in hiatus, or of dissonant syllables; aiming at a smooth unbroken flow. He is highly sophisticated in his sense of rhythm. The artifice seldom obtrudes, and although his periods are sometimes overloaded, he reveals in general complete mastery of a disciplined and integrated prose medium. [D E W W]

Ed. G. E. Benseler (rev. F. Blass) (2 vols., 1878–9); Loeb: G. B. Norlin and L. Van Hook (3 vols., 1928–45).

Jebb, *A O*, ii; Dobson, *G O*; W. Jaeger, *Paideia*, iii (1945); G. Mathieu, *Les idées politiques d'Isocrate* (Paris, 1925).

Ister. ◇ Atthis.

J

Jerome, Saint (Sophronius Eusebius Hieronymus) (A.D. *c.* 348–420). Christian Latin writer. Born of wealthy parents at Strido in Dalmatia, Jerome received a grammatical, rhetorical and philosophical education at Rome, his teacher of the first being the famous grammarian Aelius ◇ Donatus. After further study at Trèves, he moved to Aquileia and then, in 373, went on a pilgrimage to the Holy Land. Halted by illness at Antioch, he withdrew to the desert upon his recovery to practise the ascetical life. In 379 he was ordained priest and visited Constantinople, where he attended the lectures of ◇ Gregory of Nazianzus. In 382 he was invited to a synod at Rome by ◇ Damasus and became the friend and secretary of the pope, who charged him with the revision of the texts of the Latin Bible. His strictures upon the moral laxity of the Romans aroused much opposition and, soon after the death of his patron, he set out for the Middle East, eventually settling at Bethlehem (385), with the direction of a monastery, built by a wealthy friend, Paula. Here he stayed, engaged in literary activity, for the remaining 34 years of his life, his peace at times disturbed by his own excursions into controversy, as when he attacked Vigilantius in 404, and was himself physically assailed by the Pelagians in 416.

Of Jerome's excellence as a scholar there can be no question, and pre-eminent among his many works are his translations. The first stage of his monumental task of providing a Latin version of the Bible was soon completed with the publication of the four Gospels in 383, to be followed almost immediately by a revision of the Psalter. His first work after settlement in Bethlehem was another text of the Psalter, on the basis of Origen's *Hexapla*. Next came Job and other books, but Jerome was dissatisfied with the Greek text and, after learning Hebrew, began a new version which was completed by 405. His aim as a translator was to produce an accurate rendering of the original in the idiom of popular speech without being slavishly literal. The measure of his success is apparent from the way in which his version gradually ousted all rivals, coming fully into its own in the 8th and 9th centuries and being known as the Vulgate (*vulgata editio*) from the 13th. Jerome also translated a considerable number of the works of Origen, and others by ◇ Eusebius and ◇ Didymus.

Jerome produced numerous commentaries on the books of the Bible, and while many show traces of haste – he dictated his study of Matthew in a fortnight – he reproduces the opinions of previous scholars, both Jewish and Christian, thus preserving much valuable material. Jerome continued the new biographical form created by ◇ Athanasius and wrote a *Life of Paul the Monk* (376) as well as accounts of Malchus and Hilarion (*c.* 390). His interest in history is further indicated by his *Of Illustrious Men* (392), modelled on the work of Suetonius and consisting of brief records of all those who had written on the sacred scriptures from the death of Christ to the date of compilation.

Jerome's dogmatic treatises are all polemical and are notable for their acidity and directness. He sought to repel attacks upon ecclesiastical tradition and so wrote *Against Helvidius* (383), who had denied the perpetual virginity of Mary; *Against Jovinian* (393), who taught *inter alia* that fasting was worthless and that the heavenly rewards would be the same for all; *Against Vigilantius* (406), who opposed the veneration of saints and relics and the monastic ideal, and his 3 books *Against the Pelagians* (415), whose doctrine of sin and grace he believed to be defective.

It is above all in his letters that Jerome is seen to have been an attractive writer. The collection comprises 150 epistles, of which 117 are genuine. They cover the whole period of his literary activity and relate to personal and family affairs, to ascetic and polemical questions and to matters of scholarly concern. They are polished compositions and full of epigrammatic phrases.

For erudition few can be compared with Jerome, and if he lacked profundity of thought, his works have a formal excellence all but equal to those of ⇨ Lactantius. His influence on later ecclesiastical Latin was profound and he became the master of Christian prose for all later centuries. [J G D]

Migne, *P L*, 22–29; tr. W. H. Freemantle (N P F, 1893) (major works).

F. X. Murphy, *A Monument to St Jerome* (1952); J. N. Hritzu, *The Style of the Letters of St Jerome* (1939).

Josephus (b. A.D. 37/8). Jewish historian. Josephus was one of the Jewish leaders at the time of the revolt of the Jews in the reign of Nero. He commanded in Galilee, was captured by the Romans, but his life was spared, he became a friend of Titus and Vespasian, and spent the rest of his life at Rome, where he was given Roman citizenship.

At Rome Josephus wrote his 2 important works, the *Jewish War*, originally composed in Aramaic and then translated into Greek, and the *Jewish Antiquities*, a history of the Jews since the Creation, also in Greek. Of peculiar interest is the detailed, and at times contradictory, information they give on the accession of the Emperor Claudius, in which Herod Agrippa is prominent. Josephus also wrote 2 shorter works, an autobiography, mainly concerned with the defence of his conduct as commander in Galilee, and the *Apion*, a vindication of the Jewish race against attacks made by an Alexandrian scholar of that name. [T A D]

Loeb: H. Thackeray and R. Marcus (9 vols., 1928 and 1934); *The Jewish War*, tr. G. A. Williamson (Penguin Classics, 1959).

H. Thackeray, *Josephus: The Man and the Historian* (1929).

Julian (Flavius Claudius Julianus) (A.D. ? 331–363). Roman Emperor A.D. 361–3. 'The Apostate' of Christian tradition. Younger son of Julius Constantius, he and his brother survived the massacre of their family in 337. Imprisoned in the lonely castle of Macellum in Cappadocia (337–42) he became an avid student of Greek literature and philosophy. Later, in Constantinople and Asian cities, he came under the influence of leading pagan teachers like ⇨ Libanius and Themistius. His passion for Hellenic culture caused his secret conversion to paganism (?351). After his brother's murder, he was appointed Caesar (355), with the gigantic tasks of expelling the invading Alamanni from Gaul, restoring the Rhine defences, and bringing back financial stability in the Gallic provinces. He was outstandingly successful. In 361 he became sole Emperor, and at once embarked on a policy of restoring the pagan cults and depriving the Christians of their special privileges. With only the first stages implemented, he mounted the great expedition against Persia which resulted in the capture of Ctesiphon and his death. The pagan reaction abruptly collapsed.

Much survives of his voluminous writings. The 80 *Letters* contain much historical material. Of the 8 *Orations*, the most important are the panegyrics on Constantius (i) and Eusebia (ii), the prose hymns in honour of King Helios (iv) and the Mother of the Gods (v), and the 2 speeches (vi and vii) on Cynicism, contrasting the affectations of the modern brand with the true version of Diogenes. The *Caesares* is a satire, in the style of Lucian, on Julian's imperial predecessors from Augustus to Constantine, who enter a contest in which the gods are the judges. Marcus Aurelius wins. The *Misopogon* or *Anti-Beards* is a ferocious attack on the people of Antioch for their high living and antipathy to philosophy. The *Commentaries* on his Gallic campaigns are lost. So too is the notorious work *Against the Christians*, which was destroyed by the emperor Theodosius II, although the general argument perhaps survives in the letter *Against the Galilaeans*. His style is derivative – a rather affected classicism, overloaded with quotations – but his views are often startlingly individual. His versatility – scholar, statesman, mystic, soldier, religious reformer – makes him one of the most gifted of Roman emperors, fit to be compared with some great Renaissance prince. [DRD]

Loeb: W. C. Wright (3 vols., 1913–23).
J. Bidez, *La vie de l'Empereur Julien* (Paris, 1930).

Juvenal (Decimus Junius Juvenalis) (A.D. ?60–?130). The greatest of Roman satirists. Sources for his biography are unsatisfactory, but he is probably the man mentioned in an inscription (CIL, 10, 5382 – now lost) from Aquinum. If so, it would seem that he came from a well-to-do local family, took an army appointment as the first step in an official career, and held a municipal magistracy. From the internal evidence of the *Satires,* he fell foul of the Emperor Domitian, received a punishment (perhaps exile to Egypt), and was living in Rome in middle age in a state of poverty and dependence. Later his situation improved – probably thanks to the Emperor Hadrian – and in *Satires* XI we find him living in Rome in modest comfort, and owning a small country property. There are no details of his death, but it must have been later than 130.

His 16 *Satires* are arranged in 5 books, published between 110 and 130. Book I (Satires i–v) appeared about 110. Satire i announces his reason for writing satire – his bitter indignation at the degeneracy of Roman society – and his intention to confine his attacks on individuals to those who lived under Domitian. Satires ii and v deal with the characteristic vices of the Roman aristocracy – homosexuality, greed and parsimony to their clients; iv is a brilliant burlesque of a meeting of the Emperor's Privy Council; iii deals with Rome itself – Megalopolis – as the seat of vice and corruption (imitated in Johnson's *London*). Book II came out about 116, and consists of a single satire, a sustained invective (nearly 700 lines) on marriage, one of the most effective expressions of misogyny ever written. In these two books we find Juvenal's powers at their height, with the full armoury of sarcasm, irony, innuendo and invective which gave a new dimension to Roman satire, and set him by the side of Swift. Book III came out in about 120, and its tone is more mellow. Satire vii deals with the miseries of the impoverished intellectual; viii is a reproof of aristocratic snobbery; ix reverts to the theme of ii. Book IV (date uncertain, probably *c.* 125) contains in Satire x one of Juvenal's finest poems, a magnificent sermon on the proper objects of prayer (or, as Johnson entitled it, *The Vanity of Human Wishes*). Satire xi is a charming invitation to dinner, xii deals with friendship. In Book V (not before 127) xiii is a *consolatio* to a friend who cannot endure being the victim of embezzlement, xiv is a disquisition on the duties of parents, XV describes a nasty scene of fanaticism in Egypt, xvi (which breaks off short) is about life in the army.

Juvenal's work is one of the most impressive and original achievements in Roman literature. Few satirists of the Middle Ages, and not many of modern times, have escaped his influence. [DRD]

OCT: W. V. Clausen (1959); Loeb: G. G. Ramsay (1925) tr. Peter Green (Penguin Classics, 1967).
G. Highet, *Juvenal the Satirist* (1955).

L

Laberius, Decimus (*c.* 110–43 B.C.). Roman knight and writer of mimes. He was the first to give ◊ mime a written form at Rome. Of his work 42 titles and some 140 lines survive. The subjects were varied, but many were already familiar in comedy, especially the ◊ *fabula togata.* The scanty fragments include part of the dignified prologue to his command performance of his own mimes for Julius Caesar, the shaming penalty for his freedom of speech. His language was criticized as too boldly informal and at times vulgar. Cicero found his mimes boring, and Horace implies that they were notoriously unpoetic. (◊◊ Comedy, Roman.) [GTWH]

Romani mimi, ed. M. Bonaria (Rome, 1965).
Beare, *RS.*

Lactantius, Lucius Caecilius Firmianus (A.D. *c.* 250–*c.* 320). Christian Latin rhetorician. An African by birth and a disciple of ◊ Arnobius, he was summoned by the emperor Diocletian to Nicomedia as a teacher of Latin rhetoric, but was compelled to resign at the outbreak of the persecution of 303. In impecunious retirement he wrote *The Divine Institutes* (304–13) in 7 books, which was intended to demonstrate the falsity of pagan religion and serve as an introduction to the principal doctrines of Christianity. It was the first attempt at a Latin *summa* of Christian thought and, while lacking depth and cogency, its stylistic elegance has earned its author the title of 'the Christian Cicero'. Lactantius published an abridged re-edition of it, the *Epitome, c.* 315.

Leaving Bithynia between 305 and 306, Lactantius is next and finally heard of at Trèves, whither he had been called by the emperor Constantine (*c.* 317) as tutor to his eldest son Crispus. It is probably to this period, after his arrival in Gaul, that *The Death of the Persecutors* is to be assigned. After an introduction devoted to the early persecutions, Lactantius vividly describes events from the final years of Diocletian to Licinius's victory in 313. It is an extremely important historical source. Amongst his extant shorter works notice should be taken of *On God's Workmanship* (*c.* 304), which Lactantius declares to be a complement to and a more thorough investigation of the discussion on the nature of man in Book IV of Cicero's *Republic. The Anger of God* was written *c.* 313 to refute the Epicurean and Stoic teaching on the impassibility of God and to defend the existence and necessity of the divine wrath. *The Bird Phoenix*, a poem in 85 distichs, recounts the well-known story of the legendary bird and treats it as a symbol of the resurrection of Christ; while its attribution to Lactantius is not certain, the language and style favour his authorship. [J G D]

Migne, *P L*, 6–7; tr. W. Fletcher (A C L, 1871); *Phoenix* in Loeb: Duff, *M L P*.
J. Quasten, *Patrology*, ii (1953); R. Pichon, *Lactance* (Paris, 1901).

Laevius (fl. *c.* 100 B.C.). A student of Alexandrianism who wrote a collection of poems under the title of *Erotopaignia* ('Fantasies on Love'). He used a wide variety of metres, and was bold in coining words. Clearly of some importance in the development of Latin lyric, but too little survives for any estimate of quality. [D R D]

Teubner: Morel, *F P L*.

Lasus. ⇨ Dithyramb.

'Laus Pisonis'. A hexameter poem by an unknown author in honour of a certain Calpurnius Piso, himself not certainly identified, but probably the man concerned in the conspiracy against Nero, who committed suicide in A.D. 65. The authorship has been claimed for Lucan, and for ⇨ Calpurnius Siculus, but on no very firm grounds. [D R D]

Loeb: Duff, *M L P*.

Leo I, the Great (A.D. *c.* 400–61). Pope from 440 to his death. Leo, who came from Toscana, was an influential deacon in the papal curia under Celestine I (422–32). While on an embassy to Gaul on behalf of Sixtus III, the pope died and Leo was elected to succeed him. His 96 genuine sermons post-date his consecration on 29 September 440, some being delivered on the anniversary of his enthronement, others on fast days, and others in Passiontide. They are remarkable for their purity of language, their clarity of thought and elevated and solemn style; they reveal a rhetorical training.

Leo's letters (422–60) number 173, but 20 are spurious and 30 are addressed to him; the remainder, official in character and largely concerning doctrine and discipline, were probably not written by Leo himself but by the papal chancery. During an active pontificate, he persuaded Attila, at Mantua in 452, to abandon his designs on Rome, and Geiseric, in 455, to spare its citizens' lives. He intervened in the Monophysite troubles of the East and in his 28th letter, to Flavian, gave a classic formulation of Christological doctrine that was endorsed by the Council of Chalcedon (451). [J G D]

Migne, *P L*, 54–56; sermons tr. C. L. Feltoe (N P F, 1895).
W. J. Halliday, *The Style of Pope St Leo the Great* (1939); T. Jalland, *The Life and Times of St Leo the Great* (1941).

Leonidas (fl. *c.* 280 B.C.). Greek poet. Leonidas of Tarentum is one of the most graceful, accomplished and versatile of the writers of Greek elegiac poetry; more than a hundred of his poems are in the Greek ⇨ Anthology. Among his patrons was King Pyrrhus of Epirus. Many of his poems deal with the life of the poor (fishermen, sailors, shepherds, divers, farm-labourers) in the Hellenistic world. Much admired by the Roman writers of the Augustan age, his influence is seen in Propertius and in the *Moretum* (◊ Appendix Virgiliana). [D R D]

Ed. and tr. E. Bevan (1931).

Lesches. ◊ Epic Cycle.

Letters, Greek. There are in Greek literature a number of collections of letters, ascribed to various well-known persons. Most are obvious forgeries, such as the *Letters of Phalaris*, exposed (1699) by the great Richard Bentley in his best knock-down fashion. Of those that are both authentic and important, the most notable belong to the 4th century B.C. – the 9 *Letters* of ◊ Isocrates on political and moral issues, the 3 *Letters* of ◊ Epicurus, which give a popular exposition of his philosophy, and some of the *Epistles* of ◊ Plato, the only groups to include some genuine personal letters. Much later, the letters of the Emperor ◊ Julian and the sophist ◊ Libanius are valuable for the history of the Roman Empire in the late 4th century A.D. [D R D]

Letters, Latin. The Romans had a gift for expressing themselves in writing with clarity and elegance. This is particularly noticeable in their letter-writing. The wide-spread and lively business and political activity of the 1st century B.C. increased the volume of correspondence, and in the Ciceronian collection are letters not only from ◊ Cicero himself, but also from Caesar, Mark Antony, Pompey, Cato, Brutus, Pollio, Vatinius, Caelius, Servius Sulpicius and many others. The letters from Cicero's own pen cover a wide field. Some are pure news-letters, giving a detailed account of the political situation; in others, such as those to Trebatius or Papirius Paetus, he writes in a humorous vein to cheer up the recipient; others contain the type of moral exhortation often given to a younger man by an older one; some are purely formal letters of recommendation or congratulation; others contain an exchange of gossip, or even scandal; while one small group of letters represents those pieces of special pleading in which any active politician must from time to time indulge, as when he writes to Lucceius asking for a history of his consulship to be written as soon as possible, or when he gives Lentulus Spinther a very uncomfortable explanation for his recent political *volte-face*.

Nearly all Cicero's letters, however short or informal, have a high literary value, although, with very few exceptions, they were never intended for publication. This was not the case with the next Roman letter-writer whose work survives in any quantity, ◊ Pliny the Younger. With the exception of his official correspondence with the Emperor Trajan, when he was governor of Bithynia, all his letters were deliberately written as literary pieces, designed to build up his reputation as a leading man of letters and to project a suitable 'image' of his personality. Therefore, although Pliny's letters make him appear rather self-conscious and vain, they do not expose his innermost feelings to the critical judgement of posterity, as Cicero's had done.

Pliny's correspondence gives an interesting picture of political, social, and literary life in the Roman aristocracy in the reign of Trajan. The letters of M. Cornelius ◊ Fronto, two generations later, are far more personal in their contents, and are completely spontaneous. Fronto was the tutor to Marcus Aurelius and L. Verus, and his correspondence gives valuable information about the personal family life of the Imperial household in the age of the Antonines.

Other collections of letters, now lost, include those of Augustus, which are quoted on several occasions by Suetonius, and of Virgil. [T A D]

A Book of Latin Letters, ed. R. G. C. Levens (2nd edn, 1955).

Leucippus. ◊ Atomists.

Libanius (A.D. 314–93). Greek sophist and rhetorician. His voluminous writings are a valuable source for 4th-century social and cultural life. An education in the pagan schools of Athens gave him a lifelong enthusiasm for the philosophy and literature of classical Greece. When he tried to set up a school at Constantinople, the holders of the publicly endowed chairs had him expelled as a dangerous competitor. There followed a period of teaching at Nicomedia, where the young prince ◊ Julian was a pupil. In 354 he returned to Antioch, to become the leading figure in its intellectual life.

Students – pagan and Christian – came from all parts of the Greek world; they included ◊ Basil, John ◊ Chrysostom, and the historian ◊ Ammianus Marcellinus. He won the patronage of Roman emperors, notably Julian, and was an important influence in the pagan revival of that reign.

His high reputation in Byzantine times accounts for the survival of his works on a massive scale – more than 60 orations, numerous rhetorical treatises, 1,600 letters. The most notable speeches are those on the death of Julian, the eulogies of Constantius and Chlorus, the autobiographical speech *On His Own Fortune*, and Oration XI, a well-known description of Antioch. Many of the letters to famous contemporaries are of historical importance. Students of Demosthenes value his *Life* of that orator (whom he took as a model), and the summaries of his speeches. Very little of the *corpus* has been translated into English. [D R D]

Teubner: R. Förster (12 vols., Leipzig, 1905–22).

A. J. Festugière, *Antioche paienne et chrétienne* (Paris, 1959).

Libraries. The Tyrants of Greece in the 6th century B.C., such as Pisistratus of Athens, seem to have been the first owners of private libraries, of which there must have been a number in 5th-century Athens. ◊ Aristotle made a systematic collection of books for the use of his School. The first public libraries date from the Hellenistic period, and the finest was the royal foundation of the Ptolemies at Alexandria, the greatest library of the ancient world. It is said to have possessed 700,000 items – whether this means manuscripts or books is uncertain. The work of its scholars and copyists was of crucial importance for the survival of classical Greek literature. It was damaged by fire in Caesar's Alexandrian War (47 B.C.). There were fine libraries in other Hellenistic cities such as Pergamum. Aemilius Paullus brought the library of Perseus to Rome after Pydna (168 B.C.); many wealthy Romans of the late Republic had private collections. Augustus founded two public libraries in Rome for Greek and Latin literature. His example was followed by later Emperors, notably Trajan. Private benefaction endowed numerous public libraries in the cities of the Roman Empire, such as those found by archaeologists at Ephesus and Timgad. All were reference and not lending libraries. [D R D]

F. G. Kenyon, *Books and Readers in Ancient Greece and Rome* (2nd edn, 1951).

Literary Criticism, Greek and Latin. The Greeks seem to have been too busy creating a literature to find time for sustained serious criticism before the 4th century B.C. Certain critical attitudes became familiar, however: thus the Hesiodic view that the poet is primarily a teacher starts a chain reaction including in its links the attack on Homer (whose attitude to poetry is hedonistic) as immoral, Plato's banning of poets from his Republic, and the allegorical interpretation of offending passages. Similarly, popular contests in poetry and drama begin a tradition which culminates in Aristophanes weighing Aeschylus against Euripides in the *Frogs*; merged with the doctrine of poetry as Imitation it issues in the pitting of author against author – a besetting vice of much ancient criticism. Though Aristophanes and Plato show flashes of extreme insight, often conveyed through parody, Greek literary criticism comes of age with ◊ Aristotle. His *Poetics* (preserved in the form of lecture notes, and incomplete) is a systematic and comprehensive investigation into the nature and purpose of the supreme Greek literary art forms, drama and epic. Reacting strongly against the didacticism of Plato's approach, though never denying that the poet is in some sense a teacher, he asserts that all poetry has its own pleasure as goal. He takes over the doctrine of Imitation, utilized by Plato as a stick to beat the poets, and gives it a new active and creative force. In psychological understanding and sense of historical perspective he is impressively original; he asks the right questions even when his answers appear mistaken. The Alexandrians specialized in formal and verbal criticism, and with the increasing spread of Hellenism westwards attention focused on stylistic analysis. ◊ Dionysius of Halicarnassus, with his subtle studies of oratorical and historical prose style, and ◊ Demetrius represent this movement at its best. The last major Greek critic is ◊ 'Longinus', who succeeds in formulating and communicating a sensitive response to great writing.

The Greeks in general refrained from criticizing Latin literature, but inevitably Roman literary criticism started from Greco-Roman concepts. ⇨ Cicero's preoccupation with the history and theory of Latin oratorical prose corresponded with the widespread Roman interest in the one branch of literature under the Republic in which Latin was felt to rival Greek. In general the Romans, accepting the Greek view of poet as teacher, degraded literary criticism to be the handmaid of rhetorical education. In the *Epistles* and *Ars poetica* ⇨ Horace advocates a neo-classicism based on Greek models, and he himself best realizes his doctrine in practice. The decay of letters under the Empire became a chief topic of criticism. ⇨ Tacitus's *Dialogus* gives a profound diagnosis of the sickness in the Roman soul. ⇨ Quintilian's *Institutio* seeks to reverse the trend by educational reform. His comparison of Greek and Roman authors in his tenth book (an annotated reading course) has been overpraised; but his detailed assessments of Cicero and Seneca are balanced and suggestive. [DEWW]

J. W. H. Atkins, *Literary Criticism in Antiquity* (1934); G. M. A. Grube, *The Greek and Roman Critics* (1965).

Livius Andronicus (?284–?204 B.C.). Roman poet. Latin literature begins with this Greek ex-slave from Tarentum, captured perhaps while a child in the wars against Pyrrhus. Schoolmaster, translator, playwright, actor, he was the prototype of the versatile Greek of Juvenal's Third Satire. He was first employed as tutor in the house of his owners, the Livii; on being set free he set up a school for the sons of Roman nobles. This induced him to make a Latin translation of the *Odyssey* in Saturnian metre; it was a schoolbook for more than two centuries. He also wrote tragedies, comedies, and *saturae* or 'medleys', in which he both acted and sang. As one of the few literary craftsmen in Rome, he received a number of public commissions, and in 207 B.C. founded a theatre guild. Of his *Odissia* (which began '*virum mihi Camena insece versutum*') 46 lines remain, also isolated lines from some half-dozen plays. (⇨ Lyric Poetry, Latin.) [DRD]

Loeb: Warmington, *R O L*, ii.
Beare, *R S*.

Livy (Titus Livius) (59 B.C.–A.D. 17). Roman historian. Livy was born at Padua. Little is known of his life; he came to Rome as a young man and by the time he was 30 had undertaken the task of writing a large-scale *History of Rome*; it took up nearly the whole of his life. Livy's history was written in 142 books, from the arrival of Aeneas in Italy to the death of Drusus in 9 B.C. Of these, only 35 books are completely extant: I–X cover the early history of Rome to the beginning of the 3rd century B.C., and the final stages of the Samnite Wars; XXI–XXX contain the Second Punic War; XXXI–XLV include the Third Macedonian War and end in 166 B.C. Of the other books a few short fragments and the Epitomes of later writers survive.

Even in the generation before Livy it had been pointed out that no adequate history of Rome had then been written; none of the previous historians had had the ability or command of language to do his theme justice. It was to make good this deficiency that Livy wrote his history. His methods were those established by Isocrates and re-stated by Cicero: the historian must keep strictly to the truth and be impartial, but the truth must be elaborated and given literary form; it was not enough to record actions in themselves; a full description must be given of the time, place and circumstances of the actions, the preceding deliberations, the nature of the results, and the motives, character and lives of the chief participants; the whole must be clear and intelligible; where the raw material is insufficiently clear, the historian must expand it and, where necessary, add his own explanations of events and causes; the result must edify and enlighten the reader. In short, the purpose was literary and didactic rather than scientific.

Livy achieved instant success because he fulfilled these requirements consummately; he produced the very type of history for which the Romans had long been waiting, and no subsequent Latin writer ever attempted to improve on what he did. By our standards Livy has numerous faults, not wilful falsification or deliberate prejudice, but uncritical use of sources, mis-handling and at times misunderstanding of his material, and complete lack of practical knowledge of politics or war. Where his sources vary, he usually shows sound judgement, giving alternative versions and either leaving the matter open or indicating his reasons for supporting one of them – that it is, for example, the version of the oldest source, or the least exaggerated, or the most inherently probable. But where his sources agree, he never looks behind them. For example, in Book XXII he fails to observe that all surviving accounts of Roman military and political activity are derived from Fabius Pictor, who was intensely biased in favour of his kinsman Fabius Maximus and against the popular leaders, Varro, Flaminius and Minucius. Livy's handling of his sources also led him into difficulty at times; he would use material from one source, and then, for contemporaneous events in a different field, would turn to another, often leaving a faulty 'join' in the narrative – in this way he omitted a vital part in the manoeuvres preceding the Battle of Cannae. This method would also be likely to cause difficulties in chronology, especially where one source might date events by the Roman official year, from March to March, and the other by the Greek year, from October to October. But Livy's most serious failing is his lack of practical acquaintance with the activities he describes. He had not the first-hand knowledge of war and politics of many of his despised predecessors. He is thus often guilty of errors and anachronisms – he equates the smallholders who made up the plebs in the early Republic with the urban proletariat of his own day; in his account of Zama, he misinterprets the adjective 'Italian' which Polybius applies to the Carthaginian third line, and assumes it was composed of Italians, not realizing that Polybius was referring to Hannibal's veteran army that had just been brought back from Italy; in the same battle he does not realize that these troops were stationed a long way back to act as a strategical reserve, but supposes that their loyalty was suspect and that they were deliberately kept out of the fighting; this vitiates his whole account of the engagement. This lack of practical knowledge may have been what Asinius ◊ Pollio meant when he criticized Livy for '*patavinitas*' – the type of *naïveté* to be expected from a provincial from Padua.

Otherwise, Livy is reasonably accurate. In the first decade his material is unreliable, and is based either on legend or on the self-glorification of family histories. Here he is perhaps closer to epic than to history. But in the later books he is more reliable; the parts based on Polybius have particular claim to veracity, limited mainly by his inability to understand fully what the Greek historian was saying. Other parts based on Roman official records have a good claim to authenticity. But where he follows one of the later Annalists, such as Valerius Antias, there is usually much exaggeration and embroidery – the last engagement of the Second Punic War, the clash with Vermina, has been magnified from a trifling cavalry skirmish into a battle of first-rank importance.

Considering the varied nature of his material, Livy carried out his task with conscientiousness and skill. But what made him a great historian was his manner of presentation. His language has a sustained grandeur – another aspect of its epic quality – and he is unsurpassed in his description of great exploits. Although he pays lip-service to the fashionable doctrine of contemporary decadence, it does not make him cynical or unduly pessimistic, and throughout his work he displays a belief in the inherent nobility of human nature, and of the splendid destiny of Rome. [TAD]

OCT: I–X, XXI–XXX, R. S. Conway, S. K. Johnson, C. F. Walters (1914–35); XXXI–XXXV, A. H. McDonald (1966); Teubner: G. Weissenborn, M. Müller, G. Heraeus (1858–1914); Loeb: B. O. Foster, F. G. Moore, E. T. Sage, A. C. Schlesinger (14 vols., 1919–59); I–V ed. R. M. Ogilvie (1965); tr. Aubrey de Sélincourt, *The Early History of Rome* and *The War with Hannibal* (Penguin Classics, 1960, 1965).

A. H. McDonald, 'The Style of Livy', in *JRS*, 1957; P. G. Walsh, *Livy, His Historical Aims and Methods* (1961); ed. T. A. Dorey, *Latin Historians* (1966).

'Longinus' (mid 1st cent. A.D. ?). Greek author of *On the Sublime*. Cassius Longinus was a 3rd-century B.C. Greek rhetorician, minister of Zenobia, queen of Palmyra. Critics misled by the inscription on the manuscripts attributed to him the treatise *On the Sublime*, which is now generally ascribed to an unknown author writing in the mid 1st century A.D. The discourse (whose theme is really 'great writing') replies to an essay on the subject by one Caecilius, and analyses the sublime in literature, tracing 5 sources from which it derives: lofty conceptions, passionate feeling, the correct formation of figures of thought and speech, nobility of diction and dignified composition. The author is one of the sanest and most discerning critics of antiquity, and he has the rare gift of communicating his own enthusiasms. He keeps his eye firmly focused on the passage and writer he is discussing – we owe to his quotation the survival of one of Sappho's greatest odes. He is not afraid to take an independent line, and is refreshingly outspoken when adverse comment is called for. He excels at assessing quality: his comparison of Demosthenes and Hypereides is particularly penetrating. Many of his *obiter dicta* linger in the memory: sublimity is 'the echo of a great soul'; and 'in the *Odyssey* Homer may be likened to a setting sun'. The breadth of his literary interests is reflected in the quotation from the beginning of Genesis. [D E W W]

Ed. and tr. W. Rhys Roberts (1899); ed. D. A. Russell (1964).

Lucan (Marcus Annaeus Lucanus) (A.D. 39–65). Latin epic poet. He was born at Corduba in Spain, his father being the wealthy Roman knight M. Annaeus Mela, brother of Seneca the philosopher, and his mother Acilia, from whose father Acilius Lucanus he took his *cognomen*. In 40 the family moved to Rome, where Lucan enjoyed the best possible education; among his teachers was the Stoic L. Annaeus Cornutus (a freedman of the Senecas), among his friends the satirist Persius. He acquired a reputation for precocious brilliance at declaiming in Greek and Latin. In 59 Nero recalled him from Athens, where he was completing his education, made him quaestor and augur, and for a time became his friend. Lucan's marriage to Polla Argentaria took place *c.* 60; she was a prominent and respected figure in Roman society long after his death. Having essayed many literary genres he embarked on an historical epic, on the Civil War between Pompey and Caesar, the first 3 books being issued in 62/3. His subsequent estrangement from Nero, who forebade him to publish or recite his poems, was due to his growing sympathy with Stoicism. Lucan became involved in Piso's conspiracy against the Emperor, and on its betrayal was forced to commit suicide.

Only insignificant fragments of Lucan's early work survive. The *Bellum civile*, or *Pharsalia*, as it came to be known, is incomplete, as the smaller number of lines in Book X sufficiently shows. It was probably intended to extend to 12 books and to culminate in the death of Caesar. There is a marked change in tone from the adulation of Nero in Book I to the barely veiled innuendoes of the later books. Lucan shows judgement in reverting to the tradition of historical epic instead of attempting to follow the *Aeneid* too closely. As a Stoic he discards the traditional epic divine machinery, substituting a depersonalized Fate or Fortune for the Olympians. His poem has been criticized as lacking a hero, but his place is taken by the spirit of republican liberty, which transforms the Pompey of Book I into a great leader, and inspires Cato on Pompey's death, and the sons of Pompey after Cato's suicide. Lucan has great natural gifts. He has a torrential spate of words, his epigrams are memorable, and he achieves lines and passages of forceful eloquence – there are over 100 speeches in his epic. His death as a youthful martyr to tyranny makes him specially sympathetic, but it was also his literary quality which appealed to poets as different as Dante and Shelley, and critics as diverse as Southey and Macaulay. Immaturity and impetuosity, however, lead him into faults of taste, realism degenerating into grotesqueness, pathos into sentimentality. He has perhaps the strictest metrical discipline of any Latin poet, but the result is rhythmical monotony. He lacks above all self-criticism; at his worst he sinks into artificiality, bombast and bathos. (⇨ Epic Poetry, Roman.) [D E W W]

Ed. A. E. Housman (1926); annotated ed. C. E. Haskins, with introduction by W. E. Heitland (1887); Loeb: J. D. Duff (1928); tr. Robert Graves (Penguin Classics, 1956). M. P. O. Morford, *The Poet Lucan* (1967).

Lucian (A.D. *c.* 115?–*c.* 180). Greek writer. Born at Samosata in Syria, and perhaps not a Greek, Lucian received an education in rhetoric, and at first earned a successful living as a public lecturer. His travels took him to Asia, Greece, Italy and Gaul, but later he deserted rhetoric for philosophy. About 155 he was studying in

Athens; at some time he held a post in the Roman administration in Egypt. He wrote copiously, in excellent Attic, and in several genres – essays, speeches, dialogues, letters, stories which are really short novels. About 80 works are ascribed to him. It is only possible to date them very roughly on the assumption that the purely rhetorical works are early, that the philosophical works are later, and that certain works marked by a strong vein of satire and contempt for human folly – such as the *Peregrinus* and *Alexander* – belong to his last years. He was essentially a publicist, not an original thinker. He had wit, inventiveness, formidable powers of parody and a rooted dislike of cant and superstition. With these qualities, and drawing on his knowledge of the Old Comedy, Platonic dialogue, and the satires of ⇨ Menippus, he was able to draw up a scathing indictment of the human conditions of his day, though he lacks Juvenal's force. Among his best works are: *The True History*, a most amusing parody of travellers' tales (including a journey to the Moon), introduced by the words: 'Every word of this is a lie, and my readers should put no trust in it at all'; *The Dialogues of the Dead* and the *Sale of Lives*, in which the old Cynic Menippus returns from the underworld to unfold a tale; *Peregrinus*, and *Alexander*, which expose respectively a Cynic-Christian fanatic and a religious imposter; the *Charon, Descent into Hades* and *Menippus*, which deal with human folly as seen from the underworld; the *Cock*, the admonitions of a wise bird who is a reincarnation of Pythagoras. *The Dialogues of Courtesans* is worthy of its lively subject. Of the numerous works on literary themes the best is the short but well-known *How to Write History*. A novel, *Lucius* or *The Ass*, is doubtfully ascribed to him; it deals with the same theme as that of ⇨ Apuleius. [D R D]

Loeb: A. M. Harmon, K. Kilburn and M. D. Macleod (8 vols., 1913 ff.); selection tr. Paul Turner, *Satirical Sketches* (Penguin Classics, 1961).

Lucilius, Gaius (*c.* 180–*c.* 102 B.C.). The first Roman satirist. That of his 30 books only fragments (some 1,300 lines) survive is a major loss to Latin literature. Born of a wealthy family in Suessa Aurunca, he came to Rome to win a place among the statesmen, philosophers, historians, poets and lawyers of the ⇨ Scipionic circle. He served with Scipio at the siege of Numantia in 133. His work as a satirist belongs to his last 30 years – the period of the Gracchan revolution and its aftermath. In 105 he returned to Naples, where he died.

At first he used a variety of metres, but his mature work is in hexameters, which he established as the standard metre for Roman satire. The books as we have them are grouped according to metre. The order of publication would seem to be (1) 26–30, about 124 B.C., (2) 1–21, about 120 B.C., (3) 22–25, between then and his death. 'Lucilius lashed the city' – the society he satirized was the Rome which had conquered the Mediterranean world, grown rich and corrupt, with a wide gulf between the social classes. He attacked it as a 'liberal' conservative, sharing the political views of his Scipionic friends, and deeply affected by Greek literature, especially Old Comedy and Stoic philosophy. His themes dealt with private and public morality, literary style, and popular philosophy; they include a mock trial, a Council of the Gods, a journey to Sicily, a burlesque of Ulysses' return to Penelope. Quintilian stresses his learning, his freedom of speech and the invective that went with it, and his wit. He influenced later satirists, especially Horace, and was read until the end of the Empire. [D R D]

Loeb: Warmington, *R O L*.
G. C. Fiske, *Lucilius and Horace* (Madison, Wis., 1920); J. Wight Duff, *Roman Satire* (1937).

Lucius Septimius. ⇨ *Dictys*.

Lucretius (Titus Lucretius Carus) (*c.* 95–*c.* 55 B.C.). Roman philosophical poet. The external evidence for his life disintegrates under analysis. Jerome asserts that Lucretius was driven mad by a love potion and died by his own hand after composing in the lucid intervals of his insanity some books which Cicero later corrected. There is no support in classical sources for this story (which has every appearance of being a Christian attempt to discredit the poem and its author), and it is not borne out by the internal evidence of the *De rerum natura*, which show no traces of an unbalanced mind, but furnishes on every page compelling evidence of an unusually purposeful and powerful intellect.

Nothing can safely be inferred from Cicero's mention of Lucretius when writing to his brother in Gaul in 54, beyond the fact that both had read with appreciation some lines of Lucretius. The poem itself reveals that Lucretius dedicated his work to Memmius, presumably before his disgrace in 53, and that the poet did not live to complete his task.

De rerum natura comprises 6 books, some 7,400 hexameters in all. It expounds, with a wealth of illustrative detail and a magnificent range of metaphor and imagery, the main teaching of Epicurus (⇨ Epicureanism) concerning the nature of the physical world, and is designed to liberate mankind from the crippling fear of the gods and of death. The first two books are largely concerned with atomic physics. Book I, after the superb opening invocation of Venus, goddess of peace and of creative life, demonstrates that the universe consists solely of small particles of matter and of void, and that the particles are in fact atoms, completely solid, indivisible and indestructible; and it concludes with a refutation of earlier physicists and a demonstration that the universe is infinite in extent. Book II introduces the doctrine of the atomic swerve (which enabled Epicurus to break with determinism), and argues that atoms possess only size, shape and mass, all other qualities perceived by the senses in material objects being secondary. The existence within the universe of an infinite number of worlds like our own is also demonstrated. Books III and IV deal with the nature of mind and soul (which are, of course, material), the psychology of man's sensation and thought, and aspects of his bodily mechanism. After piling proof on proof of the mortality of the soul, the argument of Book III concludes with an exultant hymn of triumph over the fear of death. Book IV is concerned with the Epicurean theory of vision, sensation and mental processes, discusses the assimilation of food, the function of sleep, the meaning of dreams, and culminates in a violent satirical attack on physical passion, the great destroyer of Epicurean peace of mind. Books V and VI have as their theme our world, its creation, astronomical situation and the beginnings of vegetable, animal and human life, followed by a treatment of unusual meteorological and terrestrial phenomena. Although beginning with some of the more ingenuous Epicurean astronomical speculations, Book V amply compensates by its brilliantly imagined account of primitive man, and of the evolution of human civilization and society. Book VI, the most loose-knit and unfinished part of the poem, deals with the wonders of heaven and earth, storm, earthquake, waterspouts, volcanoes and so on, concluding with pestilence and culminating in the horrific account of the plague at Athens. It is a feature of the poem that each book has its own proem, not always fully integrated into the structure of the whole, but containing some of Lucretius's finest writing. His imagination is fired at the thought of Epicurus, the vanquisher of superstition, the purveyor of peace, the benefactor of mankind, the moral teacher who shows men how to confront the normal challenges of life and even natural disasters with serenity. This recurrent theme links the proems together, and the link is strengthened by the repeated symbolism of the triumph of light over darkness, the coming of peace after storm, the cleansing by philosophy of the stain which mars human life.

Lucretius is above all a man with a mission. He writes his poem initially to convince Memmius of the truth of his philosophy. It was Epicurean practice to aim first at the conversion of individuals. But Lucretius is of course also aware of the prevalence of human suffering and is committed ultimately to the liberation of mankind from superstition and the fear of the unknown. His own acceptance of Epicureanism had some of the emotional power of a religious conversion, and he speaks of Epicurus himself as divine. At the same time he shows a firm intellectual grasp of what is often a complex and abstruse philosophical argument. He has the artist's intense sensory awareness of the world about him, a feeling for nature, a sympathy with animals and children and all unspoilt things, a compassionate understanding of humanity almost Christian in its range and depth. His moral involvement in his subject and his sense of the ludicrous make it easy for him to modulate into satire. He is a superbly endowed artist wrestling triumphantly with intractable material, writing with a vigour and gusto hardly found in Latin after the end of the republic. He uses repetition, alliteration, assonance and rhyme with extreme freedom to hammer home his argument in hexameters with more bite and attack than any others in Latin. At the same time his high seriousness of temperament moulds the hexameter to a new and majestic dignity with an austere archaic music. He is aware of his own originality, of the difficulties involved in treating philosophy as subject-matter for poetry; he has something of the loneliness of the pioneer as well as of the creative artist. But his theme is ultimately life itself as he had realized it in Epicurean terms, since Epicurus alone had made life richly rewarding. By poetically relating philosophy to life, Lucretius in fact makes the philosophy itself more dynamically alive. [D E W W]

Ed., tr. and comm. C. Bailey (3 vols., 1947); verse tr. R. C. Trevelyan (1937); tr. R. E. Latham (Penguin Classics, 1951).

C. Martha, *La poème de Lucrèce* (Paris, 1869); O. Regenbogen, *Lukrez, seine Gestalt in seinem Gedicht* (*Neue Wege zur Antike*, Heidelberg, 1932); E. E. Sikes, *Lucretius* (1936); ed. D. R. Dudley, *Studies in Latin Literature and Its Influence* (1965).

Lycophron (b. *c.* 320 B.C.). Greek scholar and poet. He was born at Chalcis in Euboea, came to Alexandria under Ptolemy Philadelphus, and was employed in cataloguing the comedies in the Library. He wrote a dissertation on Comedy in at least 9 books. He became famous as a dramatist, and was one of the 7 poets of the tragic Pleiad. His *Cassandreis* and the satyr-play *Menedemus* had a contemporary setting. A fragment from his *Pelopidae* survives. In addition the *Alexandra,* a dramatic monologue in 1,474 iambic trimeters, is preserved entire. A messenger recounts to Priam the prophecies of Cassandra (Alexandra) ranging from the fall of Troy to events which occurred in Lycophron's lifetime. The apparent forecast of Rome's victory at Cynoscephalae in 197 and subsequent imperial destiny is puzzling. Possibly, however, the allusion is to the triumph over Pyrrhus; and the arrival of a Roman embassy at Alexandria in 273 may well have focused attention on the clouds gathering in the West.

The riddling obscurity of the oracular style wedded to Alexandrian erudition produces a poem every line of which challenges the reader's ingenuity. Its outlandish vocabulary, unnatural idiom, recondite subject-matter and deliberate obscurantism would make much of the *Alexandra* unfathomable, but for the excellence of the ancient commentators. It has value, however, as illustrating what can happen to literature if it loses contact with life. [D E W W]

Loeb: A. W. Mair (1921).

Lycurgus. ⇨ Attic Orators.

Lygdamus (b. 43 B.C.). *Nom de plume* of a minor Latin elegist. He is the author of the first 6 poems in Book III of the *Corpus tibullianum.* He addresses himself to Neaera, and seeks to win back by his poetry the favour he has forfeited. We cannot penetrate behind these pseudonyms. His wealth, his amateurish attempts at poetry and his membership of Messalla's circle perhaps point to a Roman of good family. A few of his lines are borrowed from (or by) Ovid, but their relationship remains unfathomable. He writes pedestrian love-poetry, without warmth or wit. [D E W W]

Lyric Poetry, Greek. Greek lyric is poetry composed to be sung to the accompaniment of the lyre. It is thus clearly distinguished from epic (designed for recitation) and elegy (accompanied originally by the flute). Until the rise of Alexandria brought a fusion and confusion of poetic styles, Greek lyric falls into two genres: poetry composed for the single voice (monody), and poetry composed for a choir. Choral lyric may take the form of a solo by the leader answered by the chorus (sometimes in a refrain); but if so, the style of the solo is assimilated to the style of the choral passages, and is different in character from monody, which is simpler in metre and manner. Poetry was sung before it was recited or read; indeed song is probably the mother not only of music and verse, but also of speech itself. Thus the origins of both forms of Greek lyric lie in prehistory. Monody evolved from folk-song, occasionally religious in character, but more often secular, and dealing with such primordial themes as love or work or play; hence its characteristic spontaneity, directness, and simplicity of vocabulary and structure. Choral lyric, on the other hand, was predominantly religious in character, composed for a specific public occasion and accompanied by dancing. Hence came its exalted tone, poetic vocabulary and complex metrical structure; and the division of the choir into parts, and its dialogue with its leader, made possible a longer and more elaborate composition than could be sustained by the single voice.

Homer is already familiar with ballads and lays for the solo singer, which are forms of monody, and with dirges, hymns, maiden-songs, marriage-songs and mimetic dance-songs (*hyporchemes*), which are choral. The processional song (*prosodion*) also goes back to remote antiquity. Later, the worship of Dionysus brought with it a new form of choral lyric, the dithyramb, in which, according to Aristotle, the dialogue between leader and choir contained the seeds of tragic drama. Composition in a balanced metrical scheme of strophe and antistrophe seems to go back to the beginnings of choral lyric. Other features common to most Greek choral poetry are: (1) direct reference to the occasion of the poem; (2) myth, in origin no doubt connected with the religious context of the performance; (3) gnomic moralizing, linking and interpreting the past as reflected in the myth to the present. The poet was allowed great freedom in handling these constituents, and there is a strong subjective element in choral lyric no less than in monody.

Alexandrian scholarship admitted 9 Greek lyric poets to its classical canon: Alcman, Stesichorus, Alcaeus, Sappho, Simonides, Ibycus, Anacreon, Pindar, Bacchylides (⇨ under these names). There was an extraordinary flowering of monody in Lesbos during the early 6th century B.C., when Alcaeus and Sappho created masterpieces of personal lyric; and their tradition lived on in Anacreon. In choral lyric, Stesichorus seems to have introduced the triadic form (strophe, antistrophe, epode), which became a common structural feature. The progressive secularization of what had been predominantly religious poetry is illustrated in the emergence of the *epinikion*, celebrating victory in the Games, and of the *encomium*, praising the exploits of an individual man. Although Pindar gave the *epinikion* emotional depth and dignity, he could do nothing to arrest the decline of the aristocracy whose exploits inspired his poetry. Monody too seems to have withered as aristocratic codes of conduct and feeling became obsolete. Choral lyric lived on in the dithyramb, and found a new vitality by merging in tragedy. Monody survived in the nome, in which the music became increasingly the dominant partner, and the words were reduced to the status of libretto. In the Hellenistic age, when poems were read, rather than sung, the old formal distinctions no longer applied, and lyric tended to become either an artificial exercise in a dying genre, or sank back into its origins in religious hymn and folk-song. [D E W W]

Bowra, *G L P*.

Lyric Poetry, Latin. Fragments of folk-song, of prayers and traditional hymns, and of magical or religious incantations (*carmina*), together with allusions to early dirges, suggest that there was some promise of an indigenous Latin lyric poetry. But the tidal wave of Greek influence determined the lines of Latin development here as elsewhere. Even ⇨ Livius Andronicus's hymn for a girls' choir, though 'uncouth and unpolished', dating as it does from 207 B.C., must have followed Greek models. Almost all Latin lyric is designed for reading, not for singing (the only exceptions apart from Livius's *Partheneion* and Horace's *Carmen saeculare* are the dramatic lyrics of tragedy and comedy, and popular poetry, such as soldiers' marching songs). Classical Roman literature knows only two major lyric poets. ⇨ Catullus experiments in lyric with great audacity and accomplishment (poems 11, 17, 30, 34, 51 and 61 show a command of 5 different metres). In addition he wrote in hendecasyllables and choliambics poems whose directness and vitality make them rank, whatever their formal classification, among the finest lyrics of antiquity. ⇨ Horace, in the *Odes*, displays an extraordinarily severe and varied metrical discipline, and a matching variety of mood and tone, ranging from deeply committed utterances of high seriousness on themes of national significance at one extreme, to slight but beautifully poised subjective lyrics at the other. His mastery of a medium was such that few cared or dared to follow his lead, and after him the lyric note sounds rather in Latin elegy than in the traditional metrical forms. ⇨ Statius included two rather frigid lyrics in his

Silvae, and there were experiments with the lyric form and manner in the 2nd century, but it was only when the coming of Christianity brought a new fire and passion that personal and choral lyric finally achieved its magnificent late flowering in the increasingly accentual rhythms of medieval Latin. [DEWW]

W. Beare, *Latin Verse and European Song* (1957).

Lysias (*c.* 459–*c.* 380 B.C.). Attic orator. Son of the prosperous Syracusan Cephalus, who at Pericles' invitation settled in Athens. There is a fascinating picture of the family at the beginning of Plato's *Republic*; the dramatic setting is the house of Polemarchus, the eldest son, who together with Cephalus participates in the opening discussion. On his father's death Lysias moved to Thurii in South Italy, where he studied rhetoric. A political upheaval followed the failure of the Sicilian expedition, and Lysias returned to Athens. In the revolution of the Thirty, Polemarchus was executed; but Lysias escaped to Megara, and from there supported the democratic counter-revolution. Thrasybulus tried to confer citizenship on Lysias in 403, but was defeated on a technicality, and Lysias remained a resident alien. He appears to have taught rhetoric and composed speeches and letters as school exercises – the *Eroticus* quoted by Plato in the *Phaedrus* belongs to this genre. As a *logographos* Lysias proved outstandingly successful. Antiquity knew over 200 speeches written by him. His latest attested work dates from 380; traditionally he died at the age of 80.

Of his speeches 35 survive (among these vi, viii and xx are certainly spurious); only 23 are preserved entire. Papyri have considerably increased the number of fragments. As a resident alien Lysias could not appear in court. Only his masterpiece *Against Eratosthenes*, describing his experiences under the Thirty, addressed perhaps to an official court of inquiry, the *Epitaphios*, on the fallen in the Corinthian War, and the *Olympiacus* (a mere fragment), warning against the dangers of disunity, were spoken by him in person; all have touches of formality which are uncharacteristic. His other speeches show remarkable diversity of interest, illuminating the seamier side of contemporary social, economic, and political life, and ranging through murder, adultery, high treason, sacrilege, embezzlement, bribery, false pretences and military desertion.

Lysias was recognized in antiquity as the master of the simple style, and his language was rated the purest Attic Greek. His speech derives from the colloquial idiom of the society in which he moved, but is a sublimation of it with an individual and characteristic elegance, precision and clarity. His organization of his materials is simple and straightforward; his introductions, always most carefully considered, lead logically on to narrative, proof and peroration. He excels at vivid reporting of situations and actions. He has also in the highest degree the faculty of *ethopoeia*, the art, akin to that of the dramatist, of adapting vocabulary, idiom, style and manner of approach to the age, temperament and special circumstances of his client, so that he speaks convincingly in character. In the subtlety of his insight and in the restrained persuasiveness of his eloquence Lysias remains unsurpassed. [DEWW]

Loeb: W. R. M. Lamb (1930).
Jebb, *A O*, i; Dobson, *G O*.

M

Macer, Gaius Licinius (d. 66 B.C.). Roman orator and historian. He was demagogic tribune of the plebs in 73, praetor *c.* 68, and in 66 condemned for provincial misgovernment and committed suicide. As an orator, he is criticized by Cicero for his lack of learning and poor style. He also wrote a history of Rome from earliest times, using as one of his sources the Linen Books (*Libri lintei*), an early, though not always accurate, list of magistrates. Macer's history is followed by Livy for large parts of Books IV and V. [TAD]

Peter, *H R R*, i.
R. Ogilvie, 'Livy, Licinius Macer, and the Libri Lintei', *J R S* (1958).

Macrobius, Ambrosius Theodosius (fl. A.D. *c.* 400). Known to have had a public career, the writer is probably the Macrobius who was *praefectus Africae* in A.D. 410. Little else is known of his life.

He is the author of: (1) A *Commentary on the Dream of Scipio*, i.e. the *Dream* in the last book of the *De republica* of Cicero. Written from the neo-Platonist standpoint, this book was widely influential in the Middle Ages. (2) The *Saturnalia*, a symposium of a group of *savants* at the time of the great winter festival. Their discussions range over many literary, philological and antiquarian themes, and are valuable because they preserve much earlier material, notably fragments of ⇨ Ennius and ⇨ Lucilius. There is some interesting criticism of Virgil. He also wrote a grammatical work. [D R D]

Teubner: F. Eyssenhardt (Leipzig, 1893).
T. Whittaker, *Macrobius* (1923).

Maecenas, Gaius (d. 8 B.C.). Roman patron and writer. If he holds a central place in the history of Latin literature, Maecenas does so as a patron, not as an author. Of an ancient Etruscan royal lineage, he became Augustus's political advisor and close personal friend. Of his many services, none was worth more, in the long run, than his talent for finding and encouraging writers of promise. Enlisted in the service of the regime, they found in him insight into their needs, respect for their talents and regard for their feelings. Horace, Virgil and Propertius were his *protégés*. Only fragments survive of his poetry and prose; critics find in their mannered style a reflection of his own complex personality. Certainly they show what Augustus meant when he spoke of the 'scented curls' of his verse. [D R D]

Ed. P. Lunderstedt (Leipzig, 1911).

Manetho (fl. 280 B.C.). An Egyptian high-priest who wrote and published in Greek an account of the religious beliefs of the Egyptians, and also a *History of Egypt* which was epitomized by Eusebius and Julius Africanus. [T A D]

Müller, *F H G*; Loeb: W. G. Waddell (1940).

Manilius, Marcus (fl. early 1st cent. A.D.). Latin poet. Author of the *Astronomica*, a didactic treatise in Latin hexameters about astrology. Nothing is known of his life, but on internal evidence it is clear that the poem was composed in the last years of Augustus and the first of Tiberius. Its subject was at that time enjoying an alarming vogue in the Roman world. The absence of any contemporary reference to Manilius may be due to Tiberius's decree against the astrologers in A.D. 16. Five books survive, of which I deals with creation, the vault of heaven and its astrological divisions, II and III the signs of the zodiac and their influence on individuals, IV (mainly) the different parts of the world, and V the astrological importance of other constellations. His recondite subject and many textual problems have attracted editors rather than readers, but Manilius is an accomplished versifier who can sometimes rise higher, and his Stoic views are in interesting and perhaps deliberate contrast to Lucretius. [D R D]

Ed. and comm. A. E. Housman (5 vols., 1903–30; shorter edn, 1932); Book II, ed. and tr. H. W. Garrod (1911).

Marcion. ⇨ Gnosticism.

Marcus Aurelius. ⇨ Aurelius, Marcus.

'Margites'. The title of a lost early Greek comic poem, named after its hero. Written in hexameters irregularly interspersed with iambics, it was commonly regarded in antiquity as a youthful experiment by Homer, but some authorities attributed it to Pigres of Halicarnassus (5th century B.C.). Margites ('Madman') was an ancient Simple Simon whose utter foolishness became proverbial – he could not count beyond five; as a grown man and husband he remained unbelievably naïve; 'he knew many things but knew them all badly'. Aristotle, who accepted the poem's attribution to Homer, saw in its absurdity the germ of Greek comedy. [G T W H]

Testimonia and fragments in O C T *Homeri Opera*, V, ed. T. W. Allen (1912).

Marsus, Domitius. ⇨ Domitius Marsus.

Martial (Marcus Valerius Martialis) (A.D. *c.* 40–*c.* 104). Latin epigrammatist. Son of Fronto and Flaccilla, he was born at Bilbilis in Spain on 1 March (hence the *cognomen*). Almost the whole of his creative life (*c.* 64–98) was lived in or near Rome. His compatriots, Seneca and Lucan, may have helped him initially; after their deaths he was dependent on the hazards of patronage, but his fortunes slowly improved. Several of his acquaintances stood close to Domitian, and he alludes in friendly terms to most of his literary contemporaries. His house on the Quirinal and his country villa at Nomentum (perhaps a legacy from Seneca) were unpretentious. On Nerva's succession Martial found the atmosphere at Rome less congenial, and retired to Spain, his patroness Marcella providing him with a small property, where he died soon after publishing his last book of epigrams.

The earliest surviving work is *Liber spectaculorum* (80), 32 short elegies celebrating the gladiatorial games held by Titus in the newly completed Colosseum. Next in time come the *Xenia* (now Book XIII) and the *Apophoreta* (now Book XIV), 2 collections of brevities (83–86) consisting almost entirely of single elegiac couplets, 350 in all, meant to accompany presents at the Saturnalia, ancestors of the mottoes in Christmas crackers. Martial was himself responsible for the revision and arrangement of the 12 books of epigrams proper, generally prefixing introductory prose letters or poems to each. Books I and II were published in 86; III–XI followed at approximately annual intervals. An expurgated selection from X and XI appeared in 97, and X was reissued in its present bowdlerized form in 98. Book XII, breaking a three years' silence, was published in 101 after his retirement to Spain.

Martial, the greatest Latin epigrammatist, shows insight into his own powers and limitations in restricting himself to this form. He writes by preference in elegiacs, but also uses hendecasyllables, choliambics, and occasionally iambics and hexameters. Some 1,500 short poems survive, ranging from a single line to an extreme limit of 51 verses, but mostly brief and pungent. In him Latin conciseness acquires a cutting edge; our concept of the epigram as a compact witticism with a sting in its tail derives largely from him. At heart a satirist he prefers the stiletto to the bludgeon, or indeed to the rapier, and avoids personal attacks on the living. He has also an attractive vein of lyricism, a genial humanity, and writes with warmth and tenderness of children and pets, and of the countryside. He excels, however, in his unique cross-section of Roman society, sharply observed and described with dispassionate realism. He has been accused of obsequiousness and obscenity. The first was a condition of survival under Domitian. The second arises from the jaded palate of the reading public he had to secure and hold, and is largely justified by the satirical undertones. Martial's awareness of his own shortcomings as poet and moralist is highly characteristic. His best work has a classic economy of style in which every word tells. [D E W W]

Ed. and German comm. L. Friedländer (2 vols., 1866); Loeb: W. C. A. Ker (2 vols., 1919–20).

Martianus Capella (probably early 5th cent. A.D.). Latin encyclopedist. Born at Carthage. The one book he is known to have written had a great vogue, for educational reasons, in the Middle Ages. Entitled the *Disciplinae* or *De nuptiis Philologiae et Mercurii*, it is an elaborate and, to modern tastes, tedious allegory on the marriage of Business and Learning, at which the 'Seven Liberal Arts' serve as bridesmaids. There are 9 books, in a mixture of prose and verse, 2 for the married pair, 1 each for the bridesmaids. The Seven Liberal Arts as described by Martianus Capella are the *Trivium* (Grammar, Dialectic, Rhetoric) and *Quadrivium* (Music, Arithmetic, Geometry, Astronomy) of the medieval curriculum. [D R D]

Teubner: F. Eyssenhardt (Leipzig, 1866).

Maximus of Tyre (A.D. *c.*125–*c.*185). Greek sophist. Like ⇨ Dio Chrysostom and Aelius ⇨ Aristides, he made a living by delivering public lectures in the great intellectual centres of the Roman world. Like them, he is represented by a substantial body of work (41 of his lectures survive, all apparently given in Rome in the time of Commodus), to which little attention is now paid. This is because their thought is neither profound nor original – Maximus borrows freely from Plato, Stoicism and Cynicism. But at least they give an insight into the moral problems of their age, and to the solutions available. For example, the fifth lecture discusses the reasons for prayer, which is to be undertaken, not for the granting of requests, but for communion with the gods. Lecture 36 is on the life of the Cynic, which is declared to be that of man in the Golden Age. [D R D]

Teubner: H. Hobein (Leipzig, 1910).

Melanthius. ⇨ Atthis.

Meleager. ⇨ Alexandrian Poetry; Anthology, Greek; Epigram.

Melissus (fl. *c.* 440 B.C.). Greek philosopher. Melissus of Samos was a pupil of ⇨ Parmenides and last of the Eleatic school. He commanded the Samian fleet in a successful action against the Athenians in 440; otherwise no biographical details are known. He defended the system of Parmenides against attack from many quarters, being particularly concerned with problems of limit, of sense-perception and of change. His statement 'if things are Many, they must be as I have shown the One' paved the way for the ⇨ Atomists. [D R D]

Diels, *F V*, 30.

Menander (341–290 B.C.). Greek comic poet. Antiquity doted on him as the supreme writer of New Comedy. An Athenian of good family, and nephew of another comic poet, Alexis, he produced over 100 plays – the first while still under age – but won only 8 prizes, being often defeated by his rival ⇨ Philemon. Over 1,000 fragments of his work survive, but only one complete play, the *Dyscolus* (*Misanthrope*), which won the prize in 316 B.C. Recovered from an Egyptian papyrus in 1958, this slight piece depicts the discomfiture of an embittered recluse who violently rejects his daughter's suitor until he is demoralized by falling down a well and being rescued with the young man's help, and finally swept willy-nilly into the wedding celebrations. Pan, the god of a neighbouring sanctuary, delivers the prologue and benevolently sets the simple plot in motion. The plots of several other plays can be at least partially reconstructed, including 4 of which substantial portions, with a paraphrase, were recovered in another papyrus find in 1905. The *Arbitration,* of uncertain date, depicts a newly married couple estranged by the husband's discovery that the bride has had a baby and exposed it shortly before the wedding; the child is rescued by two rustics, and the trinkets exposed with it eventually prove that the father is the husband himself. From the *Hero* (314) one scene remains, notable for a nobly self-sacrificing slave. The *Shorn Girl* (*c.* 310) turns on the action of a soldier who cuts off his mistress's hair in a jealous fury; she turns out to be the long-lost daughter of his wealthy neighbour, and reconciliation and marriage follow. The *Woman from Samos* (308) concerns the foreign concubine of an Athenian citizen who returns from abroad to find her nursing a baby; the true parentage of the child is established only after much suspicion and confusion. Newly deciphered fragments of the *Man from Sicyon* have revealed a complicated plot with no less than three recognition scenes, in which a brother and sister and their father, long separated and unknown to each other, are eventually reunited with the help of an enterprising parasite.

In the plays of Menander tragedy and comedy converge, to be blended in a new comedy of manners. He extended and refined the range of stock characters in comedy, borrowed themes freely from tragedy (especially the recurrent motif of the exposure and ultimate recognition of a child), and improved on both in plots so constructed as to produce their own denouement. His style is easy and natural, suited to the characters, yet recognizably his own. His best characters are subtly portrayed individuals, often unconventional, and even developing as the action progresses; these, and not his stereotyped situations, won him his reputation for holding up a mirror to life. Mildly humorous rather than broadly funny, his comedy is characterized by gentle irony and moralizing, with a detective-story element in the revelation of unknown identities to lend it piquancy; its preoccupation with domestic life, its indulgent morality and its slightly tame and enervated air were appropriate to the twilight of Athens. More admired by posterity than by his contemporaries, Menander's plays were revived at Athens after his death and adapted for the Roman stage by ⇨ Plautus and ⇨ Terence, through whom they strongly influenced modern European literature. (⇨ Comedy, Greek.) [G T W H]

Teubner: A. Koerte and A. Thierfelder (2 vols., 1957–9); Edmonds, *F A C*, iii, B; Loeb: F. C. Allinson (1959); *Dyscolus*: O C T, H. Lloyd-Jones (1960); ed. and comm., E. W. Handley (1965); tr. (*The Bad-Tempered Man*), P. Vellacott (1960); *Man from Sicyon*, ed. and Latin comm., R. Kassel (Berlin, 1965).

T. B. L. Webster, *Studies in Menander* (1960); Beare, *R S*.

Menippus (first half of 3rd century B.C.). Cynic philosopher. Menippus of Gadara was a slave who bought his freedom, came to Thebes, and became a pupil of the Cynic Metrocles. As a writer he used his considerable comic gifts to mock the follies of mankind, regarding the world as a vast madhouse, in which the trappings of wealth, the vanity of beauty and the pedantry of learning are equally absurd. He developed for comic purposes two genres previously reserved for philosophy – the dialogue and the letter. In form his writings were a mixture of prose and verse, in tone of the comic and the serious. The titles of 13 of his books are known; they include such topics as *The Sale of Diogenes, A Journey to the Underworld, Epistles from the Gods, An Attack on Scientists, Mathematicians, and Philologists, The Wills of the Philosophers*. They were sufficiently distinctive to give their name to a subdivision of satiric writing, which reappears in the *Satirae menippeae* of ⇨ Varro and the *Apocolocyntosis* of ⇨ Seneca the Younger. Menippus was greatly admired by ⇨ Lucian, who used several of his themes. [D R D]

Diogenes Laertius, VI, 95, 99–101.
Dudley, *H C*.

Messalla, Valerius. ⇨ Valerius Messalla.

Messalla, Vipstanus (fl. A.D. 69). Roman historian. As a young man of distinguished family he was military tribune in command of a legion in the Flavian army in 69. He was greatly admired by Tacitus, who introduced him as one of the speakers in his *Dialogus de oratoribus*, in which he is shown as the supporter of 'the good old days'. He wrote a history, or memoirs, to which Tacitus refers twice during his account of the Civil War of A.D. 69. Little else is known about him, and he probably died young. [T A D]

Peter, *H R R*, ii.

Metre, Greek. All classical poetry is composed in quantitative metres, whose pattern is determined by the succession or alternation of long and short syllables punctuated by pauses. The unit of quantitative measurement is the single short element ⏑. The long element — is equivalent to two shorts. All syllables are scanned long or short. From a long element (or its equivalent two shorts) and at least one other element is built the foot, the smallest entity which can indicate the rhythm. Common basic feet are: iambus (⏑ —), trochee (— ⏑), dactyl (— ⏑⏑), spondee (— —), anapaest (⏑ ⏑ —), cretic (— ⏑ —), choriambus (— ⏑⏑ —). In iambic metres the odd, in trochaic the even, feet might be spondees, and the unit of metrical measurement (metron) here is not the foot, but the dipody (⏓ — ⏑ — iambic metron, — ⏑ — ⏓ trochaic metron). Similarly the anapaestic metron is the dipody, spondees and dactyls being freely substituted for anapaests. From metra are built units of uniform length and movement ending with the end of a word, the lines into which recited or spoken poetry naturally falls. Such lines are divided internally by word-endings occurring at fixed places: division between words occurring within a foot is called caesura, division coinciding with the end of a foot diaeresis. Greek lyric verse also is sometimes composed in repeated lines. Normally, however, the largest entity within the overall structure of the lyric poem is the stanza or strophe, which may be elaborately and intricately built, but can be broken down into metrical units, cola in monody and dramatic lyric, and periods in non-dramatic choral lyric, especially in Pindar. A colon is a rhythmic sequence sufficiently long to be apprehended as a metrical entity with its own distinctive structure, and sufficiently short and homogeneous to be apprehended as a single such entity (e.g. — — — ⏑⏑ — ⏑ —). A period is a long, composite, rhythmic sequence extending between one pause and the next within the strophe, the end of the sequence coinciding with the end of a word (e.g. — ⏑⏑ — ⏑ — ⏑ — ⏑⏑ — — ⏑ ⏓). On occasion it is only through strophic responsion (continuous aaa . . ., triadic aabaab . . . (probably an invention of Stesichorus), dyadic aabbcc . . . (as normally in drama)) in a balanced metrical structure that the period can be determined. Such responsion is integral to most choral lyric.

Epic is the earliest Greek poetry to have survived. It was composed for recitation in dactylic hexameters, which became the standard metre for didactic and pastoral, as well as heroic, poetry. (— ⏖ — ⏖ — |(2) ⏓ |(1) ⏓ — |(3) ⏖ — ⏑⏑ — ⏓. Caesura at (1) is commonest, at (2) is frequent, at (3) is relatively rare.) Elegy, in origin a song sung to a flute accompaniment, was composed in couplets, a pentameter, consisting of two half-hexameters separated by diaeresis (— ⏖ — ⏖ — | — ⏑⏑ — ⏑⏑ —), complementing and alternating with the hexameters. It was an adaptable metre, suitable for convivial, gnomic and martial poetry, and proving the ideal medium for epigram. The iambic trimeter (⏓ — ⏑ — ⏓ |(1) — ⏑ |(2) — ⏓ — ⏑ ⏓ ; caesura at (1) is commonest, at (2) is frequent), closest to the rhythms of everyday speech, is the metre of the iambographers and of dramatic dialogue. A variant is the scazon or choliambus, with a spondee in the last foot giving a limping movement to the end of the line, not found in drama other than mime, and reflecting mostly a despondent or satirical mood. The trochaic tetrameter catalectic (— ⏑ — ⏓ — ⏑ — ⏓ | — ⏑ — ⏓ — ⏑ ⏓) is employed by dramatists in emotional and exciting scenes, and a sequence of anapaests, originally a marching metre, often bridges the gap between dialogue and the lyrical choruses. The metres of lyric monody, composed in repeated single lines, couplets, or three- or four-line stanzas, are mostly straightforward enough. Choral lyric is much more complex; the choruses of tragedy and old comedy are subtly articulated, and Pindar is uniquely daring and brilliant in his elaborate metrical invention. (For a lucid analysis of dactylo-epitrites and 'aeolic' rhythms, Pindar's two main groups of composite metres, see D. S. Raven, *Greek Metre* (1962).) No doubt, in performance the accompaniment of music and dancing helped to sustain the rhythm. [D E W W]

P. Maas, *Greek Metre*, tr. H. Lloyd-Jones (1962).

Metre, Latin. All Latin metres are borrowings or adaptations from the Greek, with one exception. The Saturnian, used for epic by Livius Andronicus and Naevius, and occurring also in early epitaphs, appears to be an indigenous Italian verse form. So far it has defied analysis on either a quantitative or an accentual basis. The line clearly falls into balancing halves, the first a little longer than the second. In Latin dramatic verse the main novelty is the substitution of the foot for the dipody as the significant metrical unit in iambics and trochaics, a change due to the slower and more spondaic movement of Latin. Thus the iambic trimeter is replaced by the iambic senarius, the only metre used for spoken dialogue, and the trochaic tetrameter catalectic by the trochaic septenarius, Plautus's favourite metre. Both admit spondees in all but the final foot, and have very free resolution of long syllables (iambic senarius ⏓ ⏖ | ⏓ ⏖ | ⏓ | ⏖ | ⏓ ⏖ | ⏓ ⏖ | ⏑ ⏓ ; trochaic septenarius ⏖ ⏓ | ⏖ ⏓ | ⏖ ⏓ | ⏖ ⏓ | ⏖ ⏓ | ⏖ ⏓ | ⏖ ⏑ | ⏓). Plautus also uses iambic septenarii, iambic and trochaic octonarii, and a wide range of lyric metres deployed with characteristic audacity and exuberance. All his metres, except the senarius, had a musical accompaniment. Dactylic hexameters too are notably more spondaic in Latin than in Greek. (— ⏖ — |(3) ⏖ — |(1) ⏓ |(4) ⏓ — |(2) ⏖ — ⏑⏑ — ⏓. Caesura at (1) is normal; at (2) frequent, if accompanied by caesura at (1) or (3); at (4) (the favourite position in Homer) a rare Grecism. The ◊ *neoterici* are partial to a spondaic fifth foot in imitation of their Alexandrian models. In elegy, the chief change is in the final half-line of the pentameter, which comes to end regularly with a dissyllabic word. Catullus extends the range of hendecasyllables (— — ⏑⏑ — ⏑ — ⏑ — ⏓) and choliambics in what amount to lyrics of great immediacy and power, and Martial further exploits these metres for epigram. Catullus also experiments with assurance in traditionally lyric Greek metres, and Horace shows mastery in assimilating to Latin the stanza form of Greek monody for personal and formal lyric. Thus a metrical discipline derived from Greece and reshaped to fit the genius of Latin made possible the creation of classical Roman poetry with its solemn music and formal perfection. [D E W W]

W. Beare, *Latin Verse and European Song* (1957).

Mime. A simple dramatic performance akin to mumming-plays, widespread in Greece and Italy from early times, and generally consisting of an improvised, farcical short scene from daily life, based on stock themes and characters. Sophron of Syracuse (5th century B.C.) first gave the mime literary form, producing 'men's mimes' and 'women's mimes' in rhythmic prose in the Doric dialect, which were imitated by Plato, Theocritus and Herodas. By the 3rd century various kinds of popular mime were performed in the Greek theatre alongside the formal drama; for more cultivated audiences at Alexandria ⇨ Theocritus and ⇨ Herodas produced their literary mimes – humorous, realistic sketches, probably composed as semi-dramatic monologues. At Rome the mime, long known in various parts of Italy, appeared in the theatre from the 3rd century B.C. onwards as the farcical, topical and indecent ⇨ *fabula riciniata* (from *ricinium*, a woman's mantle). Acted without masks by both male and female performers, it became popular as a supplementary item on the programme. It was first given written form in Latin by ⇨ Laberius in the 1st century B.C. A variant, the pantomime, in which a more serious theme was presented by a single masked actor playing several parts in dumb-show, accompanied by a chorus and musicians, was introduced in 22 B.C. and enjoyed a tremendous vogue under the Empire. Mime also was favoured by emperors and groundlings alike, and the two genres between them dominated the later Roman stage. (⇨ Atellan Farce; Comedy, Greek; Comedy, Roman.) [G T W H]

Sophron, ed. G. Kaibel, *Comicorum graecorum fragmenta* (Berlin, 1958); D. L. Page, *Greek Literary Papyri*, i (Loeb, 1942); M. Bonaria, *Romani Mimi* (Rome, 1965).
J. R. A. Nicoll, *Masks, Mimes and Miracles* (1931); *The World of Harlequin* (1963).

Mimnermus (fl. end of 7th cent.). Greek elegist. Of Colophon and Smyrna, he flourished towards the close of the 7th century B.C. The ancients knew 2 books of his poetry. One of these, called *Nanno* after a flute-girl whom he loved, was a long and presumably loose-knit sequence of miscellaneous verse with mythological and historical content, and no doubt some more personal erotic elements. Callimachus ranked it below his shorter poems. The *Smyrneis*, a historical poem on Smyrna, may have formed part of the *Nanno*. Some 80 lines have survived. They include beautifully realized laments on the passing of youth and its fleeting pleasures, a vivid picture of the sun journeying at night in a magic bowl to his rising, and a stirring portrait of a doughty fighter on the field of battle. Mimnermus is an aristocrat who seasons melancholy with a touch of the heroic temper and disciplines escapism with regard for reality. He writes with a profound feeling for the rhythm and music of the elegiac couplet, and with a refined hedonism reflecting the slightly overripe civilization of the Ionian coastal cities. [D E W W]

Diehl, *A L G*, i.
Bowra, *E G E*.

Minucius Felix (fl. A.D. *c.*200). Christian Latin writer. Almost nothing is known of his life. His *Octavius* is one of the most readable Christian apologetics. Set on the shore near Ostia, the book records the conversation of Octavius and Minucius, two Christian converts, and Caecilius, a Roman lawyer, who stands for educated paganism. He puts forward an attack on Christianity from the standpoint of philosophical scepticism; this is refuted by Octavius, who disposes of many current slanders against the conduct of Christians, and finally converts Caecilius himself to the faith. From it we gain an insight into a debate that must have taken place in the minds of many intelligent people as Christianity spread in the Roman world. [D R D]

Loeb: G. H. Rendall (1931); tr. J. H. Freese (1918).

Moschus (probably fl. *c.*150 B.C.). Greek pastoral poet. From Syracuse. Of the 9 *Idylls* attributed to him some are suspect. These include the short epic on *Europa and the Bull* (II), and also the famous *Lament for Bion* (III). Since Bion was a full generation later than Moschus, this must be by one of his pupils. It is at any rate one of the finest of all Greek bucolic poems. The poems which can safely be given to Moschus show a pleasant talent, even though it falls far below that of Theocritus. [DRD]

Budé: Ph. E. Legrand, *Bucoliques grecs*, ii (Paris, 1927); tr. A. Long, *Theocritus, Bion, Moschus* (1928).

Mucianus, Gaius Licinius (fl. A.D. 70). Roman statesman and writer. As governor of Syria in 69 he played the part of 'king-maker' to put Vespasian on the imperial throne. Rich, cultivated and dissolute, he was three times consul and was Vespasian's chief adviser. Tacitus refers to him as the author of books of antiquarian interest, while he is quoted more than 30 times in Pliny's *Natural History* for information on geographical matters. [TAD]

Peter, *HRR*, ii.

Musaeus. ◊ Epic Poetry, Greek.

Musonius Rufus, Gaius (A.D. *c.*30–*c.*100). Roman Stoic philosopher. He came of an equestrian family from Volsinii, in Etruria. Nothing is known of his education, but by 60 he had a prominent place among the Stoics who formed the 'philosophic opposition' to Nero. When Rubellius Plautus went into voluntary exile Musonius followed him to Asia; two years later he urged him to commit suicide. Musonius returned to Rome, but as a political suspect was exiled after the conspiracy of Piso (66) to the penal island of Gyaros, but he was able to continue his teaching, and attracted many pupils. He returned to Rome on Nero's death, intervened (unsuccessfully) in political affairs in the year 69, and for a while stood high in Vespasian's favour. Later, he survived a second banishment, but was recalled by Titus (79–81). We know nothing of his later years, but he is unlikely to have prospered under Domitian. Like Socrates, Musonius wrote nothing, but numerous sayings and some of his discourses have been preserved (in Greek) by his pupils, the most notable of whom was ◊ Epictetus. His teachings concern conduct and ethics, and almost exclude other aspects of philosophy. He advocated two levels of austerity: one for philosophers, which approached the asceticism of the Cynics, one for their disciples, who 'need not exceed normal limitations'. They should, however, practise simplicity of diet, dress and housing, and some simple form of manual labour, preferably on the land. His advocacy of higher education for women is a striking feature of his teaching. [DRD]

Teubner: O. Hense (Leipzig, 1905).
M. P. Charlesworth, *Five Men* (Harvard, 1936); Dudley, *HC*.

N

Naevius, Gnaeus (*c.*270–*c.*201 B.C.). Roman dramatist and epic poet. Probably a Campanian by birth, he fought for Rome in the First Punic War, and began producing plays in 235. He wrote both tragedies and comedies, but excelled in comedy based on Greek models, the ◊ *fabula palliata*; he also produced 2 historical dramas on the legend of Romulus and on contemporary events, thus founding the ◊ *fabula praetexta*. His outspokenness in comedy led to his imprisonment for persistent abuse of Roman patricians; he was released after a recantation, but later exiled. It was probably then that he turned from drama to epic and wrote the *Bellum punicum*, on the antecedents and history of the First Punic War. He died at Utica, in Carthaginian territory, leaving an epitaph in which he proudly claimed that after his death men forgot how to speak in the Latin tongue at Rome.

Only titles and brief fragments of Naevius's work survive. In his 34 *palliatae* he revealed a lively and even bawdy talent that infused Greek New Comedy with Roman realism, topicality and verbal humour. His tragedies, mostly on Trojan themes, were less successful, handling the strong emotions of Greek drama with awkward restraint. His most important work was the *Bellum punicum*, an original Roman epic in the native saturnian metre. In this he seems to have digressed from the history of the war to introduce the story of Aeneas and describe the legendary beginnings of Rome, and perhaps also of Carthage. Although criticized in antiquity as prosaic and inelegant, the *Bellum punicum* greatly influenced ⇨ Ennius and particularly Virgil, who borrowed freely from it for the *Aeneid*. Despite his originality and independence Naevius founded no independent school of native Latin poetry. Greek culture was already taking Rome captive, and Naevius's epitaph was virtually an admission that the cause was lost. (⇨ Comedy, Roman; Epic Poetry, Roman; Tragedy, Roman.) [G T W H]

Teubner: W. Strzelecki, *Bellum punicum* (Leipzig, 1964); Loeb: Warmington, *R O L*.
T. B De Graff, *Naevian Studies* (New York, 1931); Beare, *R S*.

Namatianus, Claudius Rutilius (fl. A.D. 416). Latin poet. The last Roman pagan poet of any stature. Born, probably at Toulouse, of a Gallo-Roman family with a tradition of public service, he held high office in Rome under Honorius, and was City Prefect in 414. But the disasters of the barbarian invasions of Gaul forced him to go back there, and his elegiac poem *De reditu suo* (in 2 books, incomplete) describes his homeward journey as far as Luna on the bay of La Spezia. The farewell lines to Rome – the valedictory of history to the dying capital of the West – are famous. The poem contains some charming descriptions of the Tuscan coast and its cities. In his dislike of Jews and Christians – especially monks – and his devotion to Rome and her glorious past we hear the authentic voice of the pagan aristocracy for the last time. [D R D]

Loeb: Duff, *M L P*.
E. S. Duckett, *Latin Writers of the Fifth Century* (New York, 1930).

Nearchus (d. 312 B.C.?). Greek sailor. Nearchus of Crete was a close friend of Alexander the Great, and the admiral of his fleet. His most famous exploit was the successful completion of a voyage through unknown seas from the mouth of the Indus to the head of the Persian Gulf, in ships built for use in rivers rather than on the ocean. His account, which included a description of India, was used by Arrian and Strabo. [T A D]

Jacoby, *F G H*, ii; Arrian, *Anabasis*, VIII.

Nemesianus, Marcus Aurelius Olympius (late 3rd century A.D.). Latin poet. From Carthage. Known only as the author of (1) *Eclogues*, 4 short pastorals, once ascribed to Calpurnius Siculus, from whom and from Virgil they derive and (2) the *Cynegetica* (*Hunting with Dogs*), A.D. 283–4, a didactic poem (incomplete) of rather over 300 lines. His talents are slight, but the age was so barren for Latin poetry that he must have some credit. [D R D]

Loeb: Duff, *M L P*.

Neo-Platonism. This is the term modern scholarship has chosen to apply to the last great movement of classical Greek philosophy. It began A.D. *c.* 200, and continued until closing of the schools of Athens by Justinian in A.D. 529. As champions of the pagan intellectual tradition, the neo-Platonists fought on two fronts, against the dualism of ⇨ Gnosticism and against Christianity. The first struggle they won; although they lost the second, they left a deep and enduring mark on the thought of their opponents, as can be seen in St Augustine and in the Platonists of the Renaissance. The founder was probably Ammonius Saccas, who taught in Alexandria early in the 3rd century, but who wrote nothing. His pupil, Plotinus (A.D. 205–70), was the first and greatest expositor. He taught in Rome from 244 to his death, was the head of a brilliant intellectual circle, and won the favour of the Emperor Gallienus. A project for the founding of a Utopian community in Campania was never carried out. His system was more than a revival of Platonism: it blended Plato, Aristotle and earlier Greek philosophy into a new formulation. How much it owed to Eastern thought is a matter of conjecture; the influence of oriental religion (unlike Gnosticism) is negligible. It is known to us through the collection made by Porphyry, and arranged in 6 groups of 9 books each – hence the title of the *Enneads*. This work – one of the classics of mysticism – expounds the doctrine of the expansion of the One into Matter, through the World–Soul, the World–Mind, and Nature. The philosopher should be a spiritual athlete, striving to attain through asceticism and contemplation the beatific vision, in which the Self becomes united with the One. This Plotinus had attained thrice in his life. Porphyry (A.D. 232–302), born in Tyre, studied in Rome under Plotinus, and later taught in Sicily. A polymath in the old

Alexandrian tradition, he wrote commentaries on Plato and Aristotle, lives of Homer and Pythagoras, and discussed the problem of Homeric scholarship. A polemical work in 15 books *Against the Christians* was publicly burned in A.D. 448.

In the 4th century, separate neo-Platonist schools grew up in Rome and in the great intellectual centres of the eastern provinces such as Alexandria, Antioch and Athens. The most notable head of the Syrian school was ⇨ Iamblichus; Proclus (A.D. 410–85), born at Constantinople, became head of the Athenian school. He was a strange combination – possible in that age – of philosopher, logician, mathematician and mystic. Neo-Platonism gave to the intellectual of the last phase of paganism a metaphysical religion, which became linked with the cult of the Sun-God. The figure of the sage gazing upwards in contemplation is often found on late imperial sarcophagi. The last head of the Athenian school, Damascius, went to Persia when the school was closed by Justinian in A.D. 529 as a pagan institution. [D R D]

E. R. Dodds, *Select Passages Illustrating Neoplatonism* (1924); Plotinus: Budé, E. Bréhier (Paris, 1924–38); *Enneads*, tr. Stephan MacKenna (2nd edn, 2 vols., 1956); Proclus: *Elements of Theology*, ed., tr. and comm. E. R. Dodds (1933); Damascius: *Lectures on the Philebus*, ed. and tr. L. G. Westerink (Amsterdam, 1959).

'Neoterici'. A late Latin word used to designate the brilliant group of New Poets (Cicero's *poetae novi*), many of them from Cisalpine Gaul, who gave fresh direction and impetus to Latin poetry early in the 1st century B.C. Turning away from epic and drama as outdated, they sought inspiration from other Greek literary traditions, especially from the ⇨ Alexandrians, who seemed closer to them both in time and in outlook. ⇨ Valerius Cato, *savant*, teacher and poet, was in some sense the focus of a *coterie* which included ⇨ Catullus and his friends, ⇨ Calvus, ⇨ Cinna, ⇨ Cornificius, ⇨ Bibaculus and ⇨ Caecilius. Their aims, deriving from ⇨ Callimachus, were: perfection in miniature, free experiment in metre and language, a blend of erudition and good taste, a strict metrical discipline and high polish. Romantic and erotic themes had a special appeal, and they followed their Hellenistic models in exploring human psychology in conditions of emotionalism and overstrain. They borrowed freely from Greece, not only metrical forms and mannerisms, especially spondaic hexameter endings, but also idioms, words and in particular proper names, with which they sought to introduce a strange and foreign music into Latin. The youthful Cicero and Virgil were profoundly influenced, though both reacted later. Horace seems to have been consistently hostile. But the movement lived on as an influence on the tradition of the elegists, Cornelius Gallus, Tibullus, Propertius and Ovid. The leaders of the poetic revival under Hadrian were also called *neoterici*, and modelled themselves to some extent on the earlier group – Hadrian's well-known address to his soul itself shows clear affinities. [D E W W]

Nepos, Cornelius. ⇨ Cornelius Nepos.

Nero (Nero Claudius Caesar) (A.D. 37–65). Roman Emperor A.D. 54–68. A *dilettante* of literature as of all the arts, Nero combined the parts of actor, singer and poet in his role of *artifex*. He wrote tragedies, and on the theme of Attis; also a poem on the Trojan legend (*Troica*). The *Capture of Troy* may or may not have been a part of this (this is the poem which a false tradition represents him as declaiming at the Great Fire of Rome). His works survive in a few doubtful fragments, and the literary tradition is generally critical. Yet the revival of Latin literature in his reign was a solid achievement (⇨ Seneca, Lucan, Petronius, Calpurnius Siculus etc.), and probably owed more to his patronage and encouragement than his detractors allow. [D R D]

Bardon, *E L L.*

New Testament. The second part of the Christian Bible, consisting of 27 documents written in Greek A.D. *c.*48–*c.*130. They may be divided into 4 categories: (1) Letters, (2) Gospels, (3) Acts, (4) Apocalypses – there being only single examples of the third and fourth.

(1) *Letters.* The Pauline corpus of epistles contains the earliest writings. Paul, originally a Pharisee, was converted to Christianity some two years after the crucifixion of Jesus, and, making Antioch the centre of his operations, set out on

his first missionary journey A.D. *c.*46. From that year onwards his letters were written, mainly to the Christian communities he had formed, to answer questions, give directions and supplement his verbal teaching. Returning to his base, he sent what is probably the first of his epistles to the Galatians. In A.D. 50 he began his second journey and during an 18-month stay in Corinth wrote I and II Thessalonians. From Ephesus in 55, on his third mission, he sent I and II Corinthians (in fact probably a conflation of 3 and possibly 4 epistles), and from Corinth, the following year, his letter to the Romans, of which the final chapter is a separate commendatory note given to a certain Phoebe who was going to visit the Church in Ephesus. There followed his final visit to Jerusalem, his arrest and eventual deportation to Rome, where, in captivity (*c.*60), he wrote Colossians, Philemon and Philippians. With this collection may be included the epistle to the Ephesians, which many scholars regard as non-Pauline, issued between 75 and 80 by one of Paul's own disciples. The epistle to the Hebrews, while bearing Paul's name in many versions, has no direct connexion with him; its real authorship, destination and date are uncertain (reasonable limits would be between 60 and 90). Also ascribed to Paul are the so-called Pastoral Epistles, I and II Timothy and Titus, compilations possibly containing some scattered genuine Pauline fragments, and to be assigned to the early 2nd century. The General or Catholic Epistles is the title given to the remaining 7 letters in the New Testament – 'general' because they do not name an individual addressee, 'catholic' because they appear to have been written to the Church at large and not to particular churches. James bears the name of, and is traditionally assigned to, the brother of Jesus, who became leader of the Jerusalem community. This ascription is possible and would date the work between 50 and 60. According to its address I Peter was written by the apostle to persecuted Christians in the north-west province of Asia Minor. If Silvanus, who is named as secretary, is responsible for the polished Greek, this is possible and the date would be *c.*64, immediately prior to the Neronian persecution. I, II and III John are usually regarded as from the pen of the author of the Fourth Gospel and therefore belong to the end of the 1st century. Jude purports to be by the brother of James and could well have been written between 60 and 85. Some scholars however, partly because the writer seems to look back to the days of the apostles as to a period long past, assign it to the 2nd century. A large part has been copied and included in II Peter, certainly not by the apostle, and produced several decades after the turn of the century.

(2) *Gospels.* To the early Christians there was only *one* Gospel, which had been preserved in a fourfold form, the first account being that of John Mark, who according to a reasonable tradition based his work on the reminiscences of Peter and wrote it down after the apostle's death in the Neronian persecution. Mark would therefore have been composed A.D. *c.*65. In addition to the evidence of eyewitnesses, the evangelist probably drew upon a *catena* of Old Testament proof texts, had access to a collection of the sayings of Jesus, of the type preserved in the Oxyrhynchus papyrus, and possessed a continuous narrative of Jesus's passion. Luke, written by a companion of Paul, was an enlarged edition of Mark, A.D. 80–90, and used further material. Matthew, of unknown authorship, compiled between A.D. 70 and 100, was also based upon Mark, and used a source available to Luke, usually known as Q, together with various other traditions. John, the last to be completed (*c.*100), possibly by a disciple of the apostle John and bearing the same name, is a more independent work which seeks to draw out the meaning of Jesus's words and deeds in the form of a meditation. These writings were not intended to be biographies; they do not attempt to trace the course of Jesus's life or the development of his personality. They represent a unique literary form and are best described as kerygmatic history, i.e. proclamation of good news, that something has happened – that God's promises, contained in the Old Testament, the fulfilment of which was eagerly expected, were being realized through Jesus of Nazareth. The evangelists did not view Jesus as a figure of the past, but rather as the risen Lord present in his power and work, so that in relating his minis-

try they proclaim who he is and not who he was. Similarly they reproduce his sayings not as a recollection out of the past but as directions for the present and future. So the Gospels are both the testimony of the Church's faith in Jesus and the narrative, however summary, of his history.

(3) *Acts.* One of the evangelists, Luke, has also left a second volume, the Acts of the Apostles. He drew in part upon his own reminiscences, represented by the so-called 'we-passages', which indicate participation by the use of the first person plural. Acts is the only book of its kind in the New Testament, in that it alone tells the story of the Church's progress from the first days in Jerusalem to its secure establishment in Rome some 30 years later. Nevertheless' Acts is not a straightforward account produced in accordance with the canons of modern historical study. Luke was less concerned to record exactly what happened than to justify the Gentile mission to both Christians who were uneasy about it and pagans who were interested in it. The driving power of the Holy Spirit, the main stages, as he saw them, of the outward movement from the place of Jesus's execution and resurrection – these were his interests. If the work is the sequel to and continuation of the Gospel, it must be dated *c.*85.

(4) *Apocalypse.* The book of Revelation is the sole representative of this class of literature in the New Testament. In style and content it is of the same class as Daniel, in the Old Testament – a series of visions of the future revealed to the writer. The name of its author is given as John, traditionally identified with John the son of Zebedee, but the objections to this identification, first formulated by Dionysius of Alexandria in the mid 3rd century, are so weighty that it can have little sound basis. During what persecution it was written is unknown. Some assign it to Nero's reign, others to Domitian's latter years, others again to 112, when the Christians in Bithynia are known to have suffered under Pliny and his imperial master Trajan – a late 1st-century date seems the most appropriate.

The language in which the New Testament documents were written was the 'common Greek' (*koine*) spoken throughout the Middle East and the Mediterranean lands as a result of the conquests of Alexander. It was largely the language of the common man; it was not a separate dialect but reproduced the forms and vocabulary found in the many papyri, of both commercial and personal character, discovered in the present century. There is noticeably a large number of Hebraisms; these are partly the result of a literal rendering of Aramaic, the language spoken by Jesus, and partly a reflection of the style of the Septuagint, the Greek translation of the Old Testament chiefly known and used by the first Christians. The individual writers have their own characteristics: thus Hebrews is written in very polished Greek; James and I Peter show close acquaintance with the classical style; the Johannine epistles, like the Gospel, appear to be written in the *koine* by one whose native thought and speech were Aramaic. Jude and II Peter are tortuous and the latter has been accused of Atticizing. Mark is quite simply written in the tongue of the common man, and his style is improved in both Luke and Matthew. The Greek of Revelation is curious, and may in part be explained as a translation from Hebrew or Aramaic orginals. [J G D]

For the authorship, date and contents of the several books see H. F. D. Sparks, *The Formation of the New Testament* (1952); for a translation of the Gospels see E. V. Rieu, *The Four Gospels* (1952) and for Acts C. H. Rieu, *Acts of the Apostles* (1957). The latest English rendering is *The New English Bible: New Testament* (1961).

Nicander (probably late 2nd cent. B.C.). Greek poet. Nicander of Colophon was the author of a number of didactic poems on scientific subjects. He probably flourished in the late 2nd century B.C., but was perhaps a century earlier. There survive (1) the *Theriaca* (*On Poisonous Animals*) and (2) the *Alexipharmaca* (*Antidotes to Poison*). He also wrote on bee-keeping and on farming. These poems influenced Virgil. A mythological work may have influenced the *Metamorphoses* of Ovid. Nicander seems to have been a mere versifier, but his poems contain (besides many archaisms) some interesting pieces of folk-lore and medical information, including a description of lead-poisoning. [D R D]

Ed. and tr. A. S. F. Gow and A. F. Scholfield (1953).

Nicolaus of Damascus (end of 1st cent. B.C.). Greek historian. He was a friend and courtier of Herod the Great, whom he represented on various diplomatic missions, in the course of which he won the friendship of Augustus. At Herod's instigation he wrote a *Universal History* in 144 books, from early times to the death of Herod. He also wrote an autobiography, a *Life of Augustus,* some tragedies and comedies, from one of which nearly 50 lines survive, and various philosophical works. [T A D]

Jacoby, *F G H*, ii.

Nonnus (5th cent. A.D.). Greek epic poet. He belongs with ◊ Quintus Smyrnaeus to the revival of interest in epic poetry that marks Greek literature in the Late Empire. His chosen theme was the *Dionysiaca* ('History of Dionysus'); it pursues the legends connected with Dionysus through 48 books, paying special attention to his numerous love affairs. Nonnus's use of the hexameter is of interest to students of metre. He probably worked at Alexandria. (◊ Epic Poetry, Greek.) [D R D]

Loeb: W. H. D. Rouse (3 vols., 1940).

'Nux Elegia', 'The Nut-tree's Lament'. A short elegy of 182 lines, in which a nut-tree planted by the highway complains of stones thrown at it by the passers-by. It is attributed to Ovid in the manuscripts, and its elegance and accomplishment are not unworthy of him. Critics have often accepted it as an Ovidian allegory of his sufferings in exile. It is more likely to be the work of a very skilful imitator writing towards the end of the 1st century A.D. [D E W W]

A. G. Lee, 'The Authorship of the *Nux*', in *Ovidiana*, ed. N. I. Herescu (1958).

O

Oenomaus. ◊ Cynics.

Onesicritus (3rd cent. B.C.). Greek historian. Onesicritus of Astypalaea was a Cynic philosopher who accompanied Alexander the Great on his campaigns and was appointed his chief pilot. In that capacity he acted as second-in-command to ◊ Nearchus in the long voyage from the mouth of the Indus to the Persian Gulf. He wrote a biography of Alexander that was criticized by later writers for inaccuracy and exaggeration. [T A D]

Jacoby, *F G H*, ii.

Oppian. The name is attached to two Greek didactic poems: one, in 5 books, *On Fishing* (*Halieutica*), and the other, in 4 books, *On Hunting* (*Cynegetica*). It seems likely that they are by separate authors, the first from Cilicia, the second from Syria. Both attracted the patronage of the Emperor Caracalla (A.D. 211–17). [D R D]

Loeb: A. W. Mair (1958).

Oratory and Rhetoric. No activity so engrossed the intellectual energy of the ancient world as rhetoric, the study of the art of persuasion, and oratory, its practical application. From the Persian Wars onwards, politics and law in most cities of Greece offered the highest rewards to men with a mastery of the spoken word; demand created a supply of those who professed to be able to teach it. The earliest professors, Corax and Tisias, appear in Sicily before 450 B.C. Gorgias brought this Sicilian import to Athens in 427 B.C. Rhetoric indeed was a large part of the stock-in-trade of the ◊ sophists; they studied figures of speech, semantics, prose rhythm and the means of rousing emotion. Socrates and still more Plato criticized all this as superficial – a knack, and not an art based on real knowledge. Here is the beginning of the long quarrel between rhetoric and philosophy. In the 4th century B.C. there came a counter-offensive from ◊ Isocrates. Starting from the premiss that 'all things that are done with intelligence are done with the aid of speech', he elevated rhetoric into a many-sided liberal education, producing men who could bring a trained intelligence to bear on political issues. The next major stage is marked by ◊ Aristotle's study of the whole phenomenon. To him is probably due the three-fold divisions of oratory as judicial or political or epideictic (i.e. for purposes of display).

No actual speech of any of the great political figures of the 5th century B.C. is extant; the Funeral Speech in ⇨ Thucydides (II: 35–46) probably preserves the high style of Pericles. We know a good deal about political and forensic oratory in Athens in the 4th century B.C. thanks to the canon of Ten (Antiphon, Andocides, etc. – ⇨ Attic Orators) set up probably in Hellenistic times. Of these, the political speeches of ⇨ Aeschines and ⇨ Demosthenes display Attic oratory at the highest level it attained.

The Hellenistic world did not give much scope for political oratory; philosophers, especially the Stoics and Epicureans, continued to be hostile to rhetoric. But its educational importance was unabated, and famous schools flourished at Athens, Rhodes and Pergamum. The two major 'styles' of ancient oratory crystallized at this time – the rich, flowing, exuberant Asiatic, and the simple, lucid Attic style, modelled on ⇨ Lysias.

A native Roman tradition of oratory may be traced back at least as far as the 4th century B.C., evoked by the demands of the courts and the popular assemblies. When, in the 2nd century B.C., contact with Greece brought a knowledge of Greek rhetoric, all Rome, as Cicero says (Brutus, I: iv: 14–15), 'was seized with an incredible zeal for speaking'. Romans flocked to Greek schools; Greek professors set up in Rome; handbooks were specially produced for the Roman market, such as the *Rhetorica ad Herennium* (81 B.C.). ⇨ Cicero wrote several works on the theory of his art. Yet the long line of Roman orators reviewed in the *Brutus* owed more to the institutions of the Republic than to any coaching from their Greek masters. The Roman Senate in the late Republic must have been the finest arena for political oratory ever known. Here the great political issues were debated and decided before an audience of connoisseurs. Of all this immense corpus, we have complete only the speeches of Cicero, its greatest master.

Under the Empire all was changed. Though debates in the Senate continued to attract attention (Tacitus shows an acute sensitivity to individual styles), the great decisions were taken elsewhere. Oratory could no longer scale the heights reached by Demosthenes and Cicero. But rhetoric was too deeply embedded in education to be dislodged, though it now taught for the courts or for display. With the Roman gift for large-scale organization, public chairs of rhetoric were endowed in all large cities, on the model of that founded in Rome by Vespasian. ⇨ Quintilian, first holder of the Roman chair, produced in his *Institutio oratoria* the major Roman work on the education of the orator – an attempt to revive the debased oratory of the day by a return to the best features of an earlier tradition. In the 2nd century A.D. famous speakers like ⇨ Dio Chrysostom and Aelius ⇨ Aristides could tour the Empire and draw audiences as large as those for a modern sporting event. Rhetoric was by now almost synonymous with higher education, and continued to be so in the late Empire. Many of the best-known figures of later antiquity were either orators (⇨ Ambrose, ⇨ Symmachus) or teachers of rhetoric (⇨ Augustine, ⇨ Basil, ⇨ Gregory of Nazianzus).

No single verdict can be pronounced on ancient rhetoric. What Isocrates, Cicero and Quintilian had conceived as a great liberal discipline might be trivial, sterile and mechanical as taught by a provincial schoolmaster. Yet the whole phenomenon permeates classical culture so deeply that, without it, we cannot understand its education, literature or literary criticism. [D R D]

S. F. Bonner, *Roman Declamation in the Later Republic and Early Empire* (1949); D. L. Clark, *Rhetoric in Greco-Roman Education* (New York, 1957); M. L. Clarke, *Rhetoric at Rome* (1953); George Kennedy, *The Art of Persuasion in Greece* (1963).

Origen (A.D. *c.* 185–253). Greek Christian writer. Born at Alexandria, Origen came to the fore in 202 when he succeeded ⇨ Clement as head of the catechetical school and continued in this capacity until 231. In this latter year he was condemned by Demetrius for accepting ordination at the hands of another bishop and for castrating himself. He thereupon removed to Caesarea, where previously he had been made presbyter, and continued his teaching until arrested and tortured in the persecution under Decius, dying of his sufferings at Tyre in his seventieth year.

Of immense influence in the sphere of theological thought, Origen did not possess great literary talent and only a small proportion of his vast literary output has been preserved, some in Latin translation. His *Hexapla* (a six-fold Bible) was the first attempt to establish a critical text of the Old Testament. His *First Principles* was the first manual of dogma to be produced, and his *Against Celsus*, an apologetic work, illuminates the struggle between paganism and Christianity and is a monument to its author's erudition. [J G D]

Migne, *PG*, 11–17; *First Principles*, tr. G. W. Butterworth (1936); *Against Celsus*, tr. H. Chadwick (1953).

G. L. Prestige, *Fathers and Heretics* (1948); H. Chadwick, *Early Christian Thought and the Classical Tradition* (1966).

Orphism and Orphic Literature. Orphism was a mystery religion, said to have been founded by the Thracian bard Orpheus, who may or may not be a real person. It had a very long life – from the 6th century B.C. to the 4th century A.D. In its early phases it was closely associated with Pythagoreanism; in its later, with neo-Platonism. Its initiates practised asceticism, and its central doctrine was concerned with rebirth and life after death. There is a large corpus of Orphic and kindred literature, some under the names of Orpheus and Musaeus. The famous tablets of gold found in graves in Rome, Petelia and Crete belong to initiates; they contain instruction for the soul after death. The frescoes in the underground basilica by the Porta Maggiore in Rome may also be Orphic. [D R D]

Ed. E. Abel, *Orphica* (1885); ed. O. Kern, *Orphicorum fragmenta* (1922).

J. E. Harrison, *Prolegomena to the Study of Greek Religion* (3rd edn, 1922); W. K. C. Guthrie, *Orpheus and Greek Religion* (1935), *The Greeks and Their Gods* (Boston, Mass., 1951).

Ovid (Publius Ovidius Naso) (43 B.C.–A.D. 17 or 18). Roman poet. He came from Sulmo in the territory of the Paeligni. Of equestrian status by birth, he was educated at Rome, and rounded off his studies with the Grand Tour of Greece, Asia Minor and Sicily. He probably thought of an official career – legal phraseology is common in his work – but his poetry won immediate success, and he early devoted himself to literature. He married three times; his only daughter was probably by his second wife. There was some connexion between his third wife and the aristocratic family of Paullus Fabius Maximus. Ovid had become a leading figure in the literary and social life of Rome, when in A.D. 8 Augustus suddenly banished him to Tomis (Constanza), a remote half-barbarized outpost on the Black Sea. Ovid gives two reasons for his exile – a poem and a blunder. The poem was the *Ars amatoria*, which gave so great offence that all Ovid's works were banned from the public libraries. The blunder was that he had witnessed something which should not have happened, and to which he cannot allude except obliquely (perhaps the affair of the younger Julia with Silanus). Ovid continued to write at Tomis, vainly hoping that Augustus might relent. After Tiberius's succession, the visit of his nephew Germanicus, himself a poet, to the Near East in A.D. 17 revived Ovid's hopes; but he died in exile.

Ovid's poetry falls into 3 groups, chronologically and otherwise. (1) Early period, erotic poems (16 B.C.–A.D. 2): (i) *Amores*. Short elegies, many addressed to Corinna, hardly a real person but a composite imaginary mistress, collected into 5 books shortly after 16 B.C. A revised edition in 3 books was published *c.* 2 B.C.; (ii) *Heroides*. Elegiac letters addressed by women to absent husbands or lovers. Ovid's friend Sabinus composed replies to 6 of the original 15 epistles, and his success encouraged Ovid to add poems 16–21 (3 additional letters and replies) in an enlarged edition. Propertius had experimented with the verse love-letter. Ovid breaks new ground in these fictitious and sophisticated soliloquies by setting them in the past and treating them as dramatic studies of women in love; (iii) *Medicamina faciei femineae*. An incomplete elegiac text-book on cosmetics and the art of make-up; (iv) *Ars amatoria*. An elegiac poem in 3 books of which I–II describe how a man may win and keep a mistress, and III advises how a woman may win and hold a lover. This is perhaps Ovid's most accomplished early work, with an assured mastery of the verse medium and an unflagging inventiveness and zest; (v) *Remedia amoris*. Instructions on how to terminate an affair –

the last of the didactic series of erotic elegies. In this period also falls Ovid's tragedy *Medea*, of which next to nothing survives, but which was highly praised in antiquity.

(2) Middle period (A.D. 2–8). These years were devoted to the *Fasti* and the *Metamorphoses*. The *Fasti* was planned as an aetiological elegy in 12 books, one for each month of the year, explaining the Roman Calendar. Only the first 6 books had been completed when the sentence of banishment was pronounced, and Ovid lacked the antiquarian material, and the heart, to complete the poem in exile. The *Metamorphoses* is a loosely linked series of tales from ancient mythology in 15 books of hexameter verse. With supreme skill Ovid contrives a unity out of legends whose only point of contact is that all are concerned with change of shape. In his hands the hexameter acquires a new speed and lightness, and his narrative gift here flowers to perfection. Ovid's greatest poem has always been popular, and it profoundly influenced European art and literature during the Middle Ages and since the Renaissance. According to his own account he destroyed the manuscript when the news broke of his banishment; but his friends had copies and Ovid's masterpiece survived.

(3) Poems of exile (A.D. 8–17/18). The *Tristia* in 5 books, and *Epistulae ex Ponto* in 4, consist mostly of short elegies, though *Tristia* II is a carefully composed single poem in defence of his career. The technical mastery remains, but there is some monotony in the recurrent nostalgic pleas for recall. The *Ibis*, a venomous sustained elegiac curse of an unknown enemy, written soon after his exile, has something of the old accomplishment.

Ovid marks the culmination and end of the movement begun by the ◊ *neoterici*. Through him Latin verse achieves a grace, rapidity and flexibility rivalling Greek. The ease and polish of his hexameters, the poise of his elegiacs, are a constant joy. Wittiest of Roman poets, epigrammatically brilliant, his spontaneity and simplicity conceal a strict metrical discipline and stylistic control. His personal history reminds us of Wilde, but he has deeper affinities with the 18th century. The triumph of reason and taste creates a climate killing to love poetry; but Ovid would rather be entertaining than sentimental. His lighthearted cynicism pricked the bubble of Augustan bourgeois respectability. To the Emperor his wit seemed frivolous, his attitude to his art irresponsible; but to posterity he appears amoral rather than immoral, and his poetry has been a perennial source of delight, entertainment and inspiration. [D E W W]

Erotic poems ed. E. J. Kenney (1961); *Amores, Ars Amatoria*: German comm. P. Brandt (Leipzig, 1911 and 1902); *Remedia amoris, Medicamina faciei:* German comm. F. W. Lenz (1960); *Heroides*: ed. and comm. A. Palmer (1898); *Fasti:* ed., tr. and comm. J. G. Frazer (5 vols., 1929); *Metamorphoses*: ed. and German comm. R. Ehwald (2 vols., 1915–16); tr. Mary M. Innes (Penguin Classics, 1955); *Tristia, Epistulae ex Ponto etc.:* ed. S. G. Owen (1915); *Tristia* II: ed., tr. and comm. S. G. Owen (1924); *Ibis:* ed. and comm. R. Ellis (1881).

L. P. Wilkinson, *Ovid Surveyed* (1962); A. G. Lee, 'Tenerorum lusor amorum,' in *Critical Essays on Roman Literature, Elegy and Lyric*, ed. J. P. Sullivan (1962); Brooks Otis, *Ovid as an Epic Poet* (1966).

Oxyrhynchus Historian. The name given to the author of a papyrus fragment of about 900 lines discovered at Oxyrhynchus in Egypt. The fragment is part of a history of Greece, probably extending from 411 to 394 B.C., and it gives a detailed account of the years 396–395 B.C., with a careful chronological arrangement. It was probably written between 387 and 346 B.C. There has been considerable dispute about the identity of the author; both ◊ Theopompus and ◊ Ephorus have been suggested, but there are very strong arguments against its being the work of either, and it should probably be attributed to some unidentified but highly competent Greek historian. It is probable, however, that this work was used by Ephorus as one of his sources. [T A D]

E. A. Walker, *Hellenica Oxyrhyncha* (1913).

P

Pacuvius, Marcus (220–*c.* 130 B.C.). Roman tragic poet. A nephew of ◊ Ennius, and like him of South Italian descent, he had a long career at Rome as a painter as well as a dramatist. The first poet to specialize in serious drama, he wrote 12 tragedies adapted from Greek sources and one ◊ *fabula praetexta*; the titles and some 400 lines survive. His style was luxuriant but unpolished, admitting solecisms and grotesque compound words, his characters impressively brave and noble. His dignified, rhetorical drama, with its strong situations, remained popular long after his death. He and ◊ Accius were considered the greatest of Roman tragic poets. [G T W H]

Loeb: Warmington, *R O L*, ii.
Beare, *R S*.

Palladas (fl. A.D. *c.* 400). Greek poet and schoolmaster. Embittered by the poverty common in his profession, Palladas of Alexandria developed a vein of satiric pessimism that makes him one of the most individual and forceful of Greek epigrammatists. The Greek ◊ Anthology contains more than 150 of his poems, many of them variants of the theme 'vanity of vanities . . .'. [D R D]

Palladius, Rutilius Taurus Aemilianus (4th cent. A.D.). Latin writer. Palladius is known only by his *Opus agriculturae*, a treatise on farming. This contains an introduction and a book for each month of the farming year, the last being in verse. A book on veterinary science is also attributed to him. [D R D]

Teubner: J. C. Schmitt (Leipzig, 1898).

Panaetius (*c.* 185–*c.* 109 B.C.). Stoic philosopher. From Lindos in Rhodes, he was a principal agent in the 2nd century B.C. synthesis of Greek and Roman culture. After studying Stoicism at Pergamum and Athens, he came to Rome *c.* 145, and was admitted to the group of statesmen and *savants* around Scipio Aemilianus, and accompanied Scipio on his diplomatic mission to Greece and the East (141–139). He thus had a unique opportunity to assess Roman world supremacy. After Scipio's death (129) he returned to Athens to become head of the Stoic school. Panaetius thus had two groups of pupils – Roman nobles and Greek philosophers. His work with the former was by far the more important. On their behalf he redesigned Stoicism for export to the Roman market. His knowledge of Plato and Aristotle, his practical experience of political life in Rhodes, gave him an interest in politics very different from that of the Asiatic Greeks who had founded Stoicism. In his system – the Middle Stoa – the Roman constitution is extolled as the most perfect, the 'old Roman virtue' is incorporated into his ethics, and the traditional Roman religion left untouched. But rigorous demands faced its adherents – the subordination of personal ambitions to the good of the state, the suppression of luxury, conformity to a code which regulated conduct in private and public life. This was expanded in the most important of his treatises *On Duties*, known to us through the *De officiis* of Cicero, and widely read in the 1st century B.C. (◊◊ Stoicism; Scipionic Circle.) [D R D]

Fragments ed. and Fr. comm. M. von Straaten (Amsterdam, 2nd edn, 1962).
E. Arnold, *Roman Stoicism* (1911).

Panegyric, Greek and Latin. Two speeches by ◊ Isocrates (the *Panegyricus* and *Panathenaicus*) are the best surviving examples of the Greek panegyric, a speech delivered to the public, drawn from every part of the Greek world, at one of the great athletic festivals, and (in these two instances) expounding a high political theme. In Latin the form is used for the eulogy of a person, living or dead, and especially for *gratiarum actio*, the speeches which newly elected consuls were required to deliver in honour of the Emperor. There is extant a collection of 12 of these under the title of *Panegyrici latini*. The first is Pliny's address before Trajan in A.D. 100; the others all belong to the late Empire, four of them to the time of Constantine. In these later speeches the language is fulsome and nauseating to modern taste, but they are not devoid of historical interest. [D R D]

Teubner: G. Baehrens, *Panegyrici veteres* (Leipzig, 1911); O C T: *XII Panegyrici latini*, ed. R. A. B. Mynors (1964).

Pantomime. ◊ Mime.

Parmenides (fl. *c.* 450 B.C.). Greek philosopher. Parmenides, of Elea in south Italy, was one of the most important of the pre-Socratics. He is said to have met Socrates on a visit to Athens. Plato admired him and gave his name to a dialogue. His views on philosophy were set out in a remarkable hexameter poem, much of which was preserved by Simplicius. This is divided into 3 parts, the Prologue, the Way of Truth and the Way of Opinion. The Prologue is cast as a mystic revelation, introducing a goddess who expounds the two Ways. That of Truth is a remorseless examination of the logical consequences of the statement 'it is'. It leaves us with a reality which is indivisible, motionless, finite and spherical. Clearly this is not the world our senses reveal: therefore our senses are wrong. The Way of Opinion is therefore a 'likely' exposition of the world of sense-perception. In confining 'knowledge' to the sphere of the One and Unchanging, Parmenides deeply influenced Plato. [D R D]

Diels, *F V*, 28.
J. Beaufret, *La poème de Parménide* (Paris, 1965).

Parthenius (1st cent. B.C.). Greek novelist. Author of the *Amatory Tales*, a summary of the plots of famous love-stories. Taken prisoner in Bithynia in the Third Mithridatic War (74–66 B.C.), he was taken to Rome, where he met Cornelius ⇨ Gallus, for whom his collection was intended. He also wrote elegiac poems now lost. [D R D]

Loeb: S. Gaselee (1916).

Pastoral Poetry, Greek and Latin. 'The pastoral' has had a long run in the literature of Europe, and some of its products are artificial to a degree. But its ancient origins were in real life – the songs of the shepherds of the mountain pastures of Sicily and Greece, a form of popular art not extinct even now. As a literary *genre* it first appears, fully developed, in the *Idylls* of ⇨ Theocritus (*c.* 315–250 B.C.); it is a matter of controversy whether there was some intermediary stage, perhaps in bucolic scenes in Sicilian popular drama. Theocritus's poems about the loves and rivalries of shepherds won immediate favour in the great Hellenistic cities, where people were nostalgic for the countryside they had lost. He was followed by the slighter talents of ⇨ Bion and ⇨ Moschus.

In Rome, again, it is uncertain what bucolic elements may have preceded the *Eclogues* of ⇨ Virgil, which were published between 42 and 37 B.C. Whatever they were, they were overshadowed by this second and greater exemplar. For while some of the *Eclogues* are simple pastoral poems, others in 'a somewhat loftier strain' use the pastoral convention for literary, allegorical or political themes. Here is the point of departure for *Lycidas, Adonais* and *The Scholar Gypsy* on the one hand: for Marie Antoinette and the gambols of the Petit Trianon on the other. The enormous prestige of Virgil led to a tradition of Latin pastoral, running from ⇨ Calpurnius Siculus and the author of the 'Einsiedeln Eclogues' in the 1st to ⇨ Nemesianus in the 3rd century A.D. [D R D]

R. J. Cholmeley, *The Idylls of Theocritus* (1919); H. J. Rose, *The Eclogues of Virgil* (Berkeley, Cal., 1942); J. Hubeaux, *Les thèmes bucoliques dans la poésie latine* (Brussels, 1930).

Paulinus of Nola, Meropius Pontius (A.D. 353–431). Christian Latin writer. Born at Burdigala of a wealthy Gallo-Roman family, and educated by his fellow-townsman ⇨ Ausonius. He entered the public service, becoming consul in 378, and later governor of Campania. But he and his wife became convinced that their duty as Christians was to give up their wealth to do good work among the poor. Paulinus settled at the shrine of St Felix. Later he was made bishop of Nola. His writings include (1) 51 *Letters,* of which those to his friend Ausonius show the difference between the devout and the conventional Christian, and (2) 33 poems, mostly composed for the Feast of St Felix (14 January). These place him in the forefront of Christian Latin poets; the *Epithalamium* ('Wedding-Song') and the *Consolatio* addressed to the parents of a dead boy are especially noteworthy. [D R D]

Ed. W. von Hartel (C S E L, Vienna, 1894).

Pausanias (fl. *c.* 150 A.D.). Greek traveller and writer. Probably born in Lydia, and lived during the reigns of the Antonines. He travelled in Asia Minor, Syria, Palestine, Egypt and Greece, and had been to Rome. His fame rests on his *Description of Greece*, in 10 books. Book I deals with Athens and Attica, and Megara, II with Corinth, Argos and the surrounding country, III with Sparta, IV with Messenia, V–VI with Elis and Olympia, VII with Achaia, VIII with Arcadia, IX with Thebes and Boeotia, and X with

Phocis and Delphi. The *Description of Greece* is not a work of geography or topography, but a guide-book for tourists, intended to describe what was most worth seeing. Pausanias shows little interest in natural scenery, and concentrates on buildings, tombs, statues and other works of art, giving such information as he thinks would be useful or interesting. He also adds considerable historical or mythological information. For example, reference to the statues of the Ptolemies, Lysimachus and Pyrrhus at Athens leads up to a brief account of the wars between the generals of Alexander the Great after his death; the mention of the tomb of Medea's children at Corinth gives Pausanias an opportunity to refer to various stories about Medea and Jason; and he goes on after describing the portrait of the Argive poetess Telesilla to tell how she defended Argos after the Argive army had been destroyed by Cleomenes of Sparta. He also gives a brief history of most of the cities included. What interested Pausanias most were places with religious associations and works of art, especially paintings. He gave a very detailed description of the pictures by the great artist Polygnotus at Delphi, and he always included information about any unusual religious ritual.

Pausanias was an honest and accurate writer. Without his work, it would be impossible to understand what many of the ruins of Ancient Greece were meant to be. In Victorian times his book was a regular companion for the well-educated visitor to Greece. [TAD]

Loeb: W. H. S. Jones, H. A. Ormerod and R. Wicherly (5 vols., 1918); tr. and comm., J. G. Frazer (6 vols., 1898).

Peregrinus. ◊ Cynics.

Persius Flaccus, Aulus (A.D. 34–62). Latin satirist. Born at Volterrae in Etruria, and educated in Rome, Persius joined the group of Stoics headed by the senator Thrasea Paetus, which included the poet ◊ Lucan and the philosopher ◊ Musonius Rufus. The Stoicism he learned from his tutor Cornutus was the dominant influence on his life; he wrote satire, modelled on Lucilius and Horace, as an engaged poet, to spread the Stoic evangel. After his early death, his minor works were suppressed on the advice of Cornutus, and his reputation rests on his 6 satires, published in a single book. Of these, I attacks the poetry fashionable at Nero's court, II deals with the right use of prayer, III, in the form of a tutor's exhortation to a wealthy, idle student, gives a clinical picture of the effects of vice on the soul; IV exhorts the young Alcibiades (whom some scholars indentify with Nero) to choose the path of virtue, V is a tribute to Cornutus and to Stoicism as the key to the virtuous life, VI is on the right use of wealth. We are told that Persius wrote 'seldom and slowly', and clearly he knew books rather than life. By imitating writers of comedy, mime, diatribe and satire he makes his own style an incongruous medley; he never uses an easy word where an obscure one will do; his earnest solemnity is not enlivened by any touch of wit or humour. As a result, he is the least read of the Roman satirists – not that that would have distressed him. Yet he has something to say and, in short passages, says it memorably. Many have found his priggishness intolerable in so young a man, but it must be remembered that it is raised against the frivolous immorality of the court of Nero. There can be no doubt that his morality was sincere, and it helps us to understand the later advance of Christianity in Roman society. [DRD]

OCT: W. V. Clausen (1959); Loeb: G. G. Ramsay (1918); verse tr. J. Tate (1930).
J. Wight Duff, *Roman Satire* (1937).

'Pervigilium Veneris'. The title of a poem of unknown authorship and uncertain date (probably late 3rd century A.D.), but of a quality unique in Latin. The setting is Sicily, the occasion the eve of the spring festival of Venus. In 93 trochaic lines of haunting beauty the poet describes the triumph of spring, the surge of passion and new life in flower and beast and man, and the festival that is to take place the next day. The poem ends with the nightingale's song, and with a poignant expression of personal sorrow – *'illa cantat; nos tacemus; quando ver venit meum?'* – 'She is singing; we are silent; will my springtime never come?' The sensuous and exquisite description of nature, the passionate refrain, and the wonderful harmony of metre and theme set this poem by the side of the *Primavera* of Botticelli. [DRD]

Loeb: with Catullus, J. W. Mackail (1912); ed., comm. and tr. Sir Cecil Clementi (1936).

Petronius Arbiter, Gaius (?) (probably 1st cent. A.D.). Latin satirist. The author of the *Satyricon*, usually assumed to be the same Petronius Arbiter to whose life and death Tacitus devotes two brilliant chapters (*Annals*, XVI: 18, 19). 'His days he passed in sleep, his nights in the business and pleasures of life. The reputation that most men win by energy he achieved by idleness. Yet as governor of Bithynia, and later as consul, he showed himself fully equal to his duties.' Later he became a favourite of Nero's, and as 'Arbiter of Taste' directed the pleasures of the court. His enemy Tigellinus, Prefect of the Guard, saw to it that he fell a victim to the Terror which followed the Conspiracy of Piso (A.D. 66). He committed suicide, but not before he had written a detailed account of Nero's vices, sent it to him under seal, and smashed a precious vase which he knew the Emperor wanted. The *Satyricon* is a huge picaresque novel, of which only parts of Books XV and XVI survive. A medley of prose and verse, on the model of the satires of ⇨ Menippus, it describes the adventures of three disreputable young men in the taverns and low haunts of Campania and Magna Graecia. Encolpius, the narrator, his friend Ascyltos, and the boy Giton are devoid of morals but not of intelligence; their escapades are told with a merciless realism that records but does not judge. It has been suggested that the whole forms a parody of the *Aeneid* (as Joyce's *Ulysses* of the *Odyssey*) but this is not established. The chief episode of the books we possess, the *Cena*, is a description of a dinner given (probably at Cumae) by a *nouveau-riche*, Trimalchio. The multi-millionaire himself, his wife Fortunata, their friends, their household and their way of life present a classic example of the economics of conspicuous waste. The gastronomic absurdities of the dinner, a drunken brawl, a dog-fight and two ghost stories round off one of the most fascinating and original passages in Latin. Besides his sharp eye for the portrayal of characters – all of them disreputable, none wholly unsympathetic – Petronius has a sharp ear for vulgar Latin. Only in the plays of Plautus can we get a comparable idea of the flavour and raciness of popular speech. The *Satyricon* has at various times been compared with the *Golden Ass* of Apuleius, and with the writings of Rabelais, Fielding, Balzac, Flaubert and Maupassant. There is something in all these comparisons, but in truth the *Satyricon* stands on its own not merely in Latin, but in all European literature.

Petronius is also the author of a small collection of lyric and elegiac poems. [DRD]

Loeb: M. Heseltine (1913); tr. J. Sullivan (Penguin Classics, 1965); *Cena:* ed. W. B. Sedgwick (1925).

G. Bagnani, *Arbiter of Elegance* (Toronto, 1954).

Phaedo. ⇨ Dialogue.

Phaedrus (Phaeder) (fl. early 1st. cent. A.D.). Latin fabulist. He wrote in the reign of Tiberius and Caligula. Little is known of his life, except that he was of Macedonian origin, and a freedman of Augustus. His fables are modelled on Aesop, and also draw on the diatribes of the philosophers. They are no mere children's tales. The animal-fable can be an effective vehicle of social satire (as in Orwell's *Animal Farm*, or the work of modern cartoonists), and Phaedrus's satire was sufficiently near the bone to earn him the hostility of Sejanus. He suffered punishment of some kind, but was still writing in old age. Of the fables 5 books survive; to these may be added some 30 individual prose pieces contained in a 15th-century collection. Phaedrus wrote in iambic senarii, and used a terse and vigorous Latin. A prose version of the fables was made in the Late Empire, under the name of *Romulus*. This it was that attained an immense vogue in the Middle Ages, and placed Aesop and Phaedrus side by side as the two great exponents of the tale that ends 'and the moral of that is . . .'. [DRD]

Ed. L. Havet (14th edn, 1923); Budé: A. Brenot (Paris, 1924).

Pherecydes (fl. 456 B.C.). Greek historian. Pherecydes of Athens, also called Pherecydes of Leros, wrote a mythological *History* in 10 books, dealing mainly with the great families of the Heroic Age. He is often confused with Pherecydes of

Syros (*c.* 550 B.C.), an early philosopher. [T A D]

Jacoby, *F G H*, i.

Philemon (*c.* 361–262 B.C.). Greek comic poet. A native of Syracuse, he spent his long career at Athens, where he was granted citizenship, and at Alexandria. As a highly successful writer of Middle and New Comedy, he produced nearly 100 plays, among them the originals from which ⇨ Plautus adapted the *Mercator, Trinummus* and *Mostellaria*, and perhaps also the *Captivi* and *Truculentus*. Often preferred in his own lifetime to his Athenian rival, ⇨ Menander, he was however judged inferior by later critics, though praised for his wit, neat plots and apt characterization. (⇨ Comedy, Greek; Comedy, Roman.) [G T W H]

Edmonds, *F A C*, iii, A.

T. B. L. Webster, *Studies in Later Greek Comedy* (1953).

Philetas. ⇨ Alexandrianism, Latin; Elegiac Poetry.

Philo Judaeus (*c.* 30 B.C.–A.D. *c.* 45). Greek-Jewish writer. Not much is known of his life, save that he was a member of a leading Jewish family in Alexandria, was perhaps a Roman citizen, and took part in the (unsuccessful) mission sent by his community to prevent Gaius from imposing Emperor-worship on them. Deeply imbued with Greek culture, particularly philosophy, and yet loyal to the intellectual heritage of Judaism, it was Philo's life-work to blend these two great traditions into a new view of God and of the world. Drawing freely from Plato, Posidonius and the mystery religions on the one hand, and from the Torah on the other, he adumbrates for his proselytes a contemplative life whose end is the mystical vision of God. Hence his deep influence on neo-Platonism and on medieval philosophy.

His writings were on several levels, and addressed to many different audiences. Part of the *corpus* is lost, part survives only in Armenian. The most important works in Greek are (1) the *In Flaccum* and the *Embassy to Gaius*, written as an apologia for the Jewish cause for the benefit of Roman administrators, (2) *On the Contemplative Life*, describing the Therapeutae, a sect of Jewish anchorites, (3) the *Life of Moses*, in which Moses appears as the ideal legislator, the embodiment of the natural law, (4) the *Exposition of the Law*, a commentary on the Pentateuch, for Gentiles, and (5) the *Allegory*, a series of works giving, for an inner group of initiates, an allegorical interpretation of the Biblical text. [D R D]

Ed. L. Cohn and P. Wendland (7 vols., Berlin, 1896–1930); Loeb: F. H. Colson and G. H. Whitaker (10 vols., 1939–62).

E. R. Goodenough, *An Introduction to Philo Judaeus* (1926); H. A. Wolfson, *Philo* (2 vols., 1948).

Philochorus. ⇨ Atthis.

Philodemus. ⇨ Epicureanism.

Philostrati. The identity of several men called Philostratus, and the works to be ascribed to each, is a long-standing problem. Scholarship has now disentangled:

(1) Philostratus Verus, a sophist of the 2nd century A.D.

(2) Flavius Philostratus (son of the above A.D. *c.* 170–*c.* 245). He was a protégé of the Empress Julia Domna, and his most important works are (1) the *Life* of ⇨ Apollonius of Tyana, the notorious thaumaturge, and (2) the *Lives of the Sophists*, a series of anecdotal biographies of the leaders of the New Sophistic.

(3) Philostratus of Lemnos (son-in-law of 2, born A.D. *c.* 191) who wrote (among others) books of *Eikones* or descriptions of pictures, supposed to be in a collection at Naples and dealing with mythological subjects.

(4) The grandson of the above, who added a third book of *Eikones*. [D R D]

Loeb: F. C. Conybeare, *Life of Apollonius* (2 vols., 1912).

W. C. Wright, *Lives of the Sophists* (1922); A. Fairbanks, *Eikones* (1931).

Phocylides (fl. mid 6th cent. B.C.). Greek gnomic poet. Phocylides of Miletus composed brief versified maxims in hexameters (occasionally in elegiacs). Some begin with the formula 'This too is by Phocylides . . .' – a stamp of authenticity which prevented his work being lost in the anonymous mass of proverbial literature. Thirty-four lines survive; they reflect the aristocratic code – praises of the symposium fit in well with the rest of the collection. The fragments show a neat turn of epigrammatic phrase, though the thought hardly rises above the homely commonplace. [D E W W]

Diehl, *A L G*, i.

Phrynichus (*c.* 540–*c.* 470 B.C.). Greek tragic poet. An Athenian, he won his first prize for tragedy in 511 and another in 476, when Themistocles was his choregus. Following the lead of ◊ Thespis, he extended the scope of the dialogue in tragedy by introducing female characters for the first time, although the lyrics remained the predominant element. His work, of which only fragments survive, included an *Alcestis* and 2 historical dramas: the *Capture of Miletus* (suppressed as too painful a reminder of recent events) and the *Phoenician Women*, on the defeat of Xerxes. A pioneer of classical Greek tragedy, Phrynichus prided himself on the variety of his choreography, and was long remembered for the honeyed sweetness of his lyrics. [G T W H]

A. Nauck, *Tragicorum graecorum fragmenta* (Leipzig, 1889).
Pickard-Cambridge, *D T C*.

Phylarchus (fl. *c.* 215 B.C.). Greek historian. Phylarchus of Athens wrote a *History of Greece* from 272 to 220 B.C., including events in Asia and Egypt. He is criticized by Polybius (Book II) for his prejudices and for attempting to play upon the emotions of his readers. [T A D]

Jacoby, *F G H*, ii.

Pindar (518–438 B.C.). Greek choral lyric poet. Born at Cynoscephalae, a village in Theban territory. As a boy he was sent to Athens to be educated in music and poetry. Of noble birth, he will have moved in aristocratic Athenian society. Character and temperament, origins and upbringing combined to shape his beliefs and attitudes: his patrons were kings and nobles, his poetry expresses the traditional aristocratic code of values and conduct. No doubt the youthful poems which spread his fame outside Boeotia were addressed to gods rather than men; but these have perished. The earliest surviving ode, composed for the Aleuadae of Thessaly in 498, already shows stylistic maturity. Eight years later Xenocrates of Acragas, brother of the tyrant Theron, commissioned a poem, promising contacts with the exciting new world of the West. Megacles, an exiled Alcmaeonid, possibly known to Pindar from his boyhood at Athens, and Agesidamus of Epizephyrian Locri were also among his early patrons, as were the Aeacides of Aegina, whose wealth, sporting interests, and cultivated taste made them especially congenial. The Persian invasion confronted Pindar with an agonizing dilemma of divided loyalties, his sense of solidarity with the medizing Theban aristocracy conflicting with his sympathy for free Greece in her heroic resistance. His connexions in Aegina proved friends in need, and in the immediate post-war years he celebrates Aeacid and Boeotian successes and emphasizes the links between Aegina and Thebes. But it was ◊ Simonides, not Pindar, who commemorated the sacrifices and victories of the Persian war.

Pindar's visit to Sicily in 476–474 marks the re-establishment of his position. Theron of Acragas and Hiero of Syracuse welcomed him to their courts, and he celebrated some of their greatest victories. Simonides and his nephew were also in Sicily at the time. Hiero and Pindar understood and respected each other; but Simonides with his ripe knowledge of men and affairs and supple intelligence will have fitted more easily into the court environment. Pindar's disdainful resentment echoes in his poetry; but especially after his return to Greece his prestige in Sicily declined, and Hiero's victory in the chariot race at Olympia in 468 was commemorated by Bacchylides. In the rest of the Greek world, however, he enjoyed a great and growing reputation. The mainland cities (Athens, Argos, Corinth, Opus), the islands (Rhodes, Tenedos, Ceos), ultimately the remotest parts of the Greek world from Abdera and Macedon in the north to the temple of Zeus Ammon in the south knew his work. In 474 he celebrated a victory by Telesicrates of Cyrene, and this may have led to his connexion with the royal house. The fourth *Pythian* (462) is among Pindar's masterpieces, but his attempt to intercede on behalf of the exiled Damophilos may have given offence, and he was not commissioned to celebrate Arcesilas's Olympic victory of 459. He remained staunchly loyal to Thebes, and defends himself against critics and detractors in the ninth *Pythian.* Above all Aegina retained her primacy in his affections; it is appropriate that his latest surviving poem (*Pythians,* VIII, 446) commemorates an Aeacid victory. As Pindar grew older the shadows lengthened around him; the old order in Boeotia and Aegina was visibly passing under the impact of Athenian imperialism and rationalism; he must have lived in a world of memories.

The ancients knew 17 volumes of Pindar's poetry, embracing every kind of choral lyric. We have the 4 books of his *Epinikia,* 44 poems in all, together with numerous fragments, recently supplemented by papyri which have greatly enlarged our knowledge of the paeans, dithyrambs and partheneia. The new evidence suggests that the *Epinikia* are fully representative of Pindar's exalted style, being probably the most elaborate and highly wrought of all his poems.

Pindar and ◊ Hesiod are the only two Boeotians who rank as major figure in Greek literary history. Temperamentally they are poles apart, but they have in common deep religious convictions, a high sense of their poetic calling as prophets, the inspired mouthpieces of a divine message, and a certain brusque uncompromising outspokenness. Though the *epinikion* was a traditional genre, there is little doubt that Pindar transformed it, giving it a new depth and seriousness, and imposing a new unity. Details of the contest are eliminated as unworthy of the dignity of the theme, and the victory is put in the setting of a hymn of praise and thanksgiving to the gods. The myth linking past and present is sketched impressionistically, the relevant parts of a familiar story being touched in with a sure sense of the dramatic and the picturesque. The gnomic moralizing, often of great profundity and beauty, is directly related to the occasion and expressed in a concise laconic style, owing much to the teaching and manner of the Delphic oracle. Thus unity is achieved by compression and integration, and also by elaboration and exaltation of language. The dialect is literary, artificial and eclectic. The metres, though the strophic or triadic form is strictly observed, are extraordinarily complex and varied, and no two poems are metrically identical (*Isthmian,* III and IV, are a single composition). The profusion of vivid epithets, the exuberant sentence structure, the splendour of imagery and metaphor, the poet's feeling for the shimmer and play of light, for the excitement and colour of a great occasion, all contribute to the richness of texture. Pindar makes extreme demands on the imagination and understanding of the modern reader; but one can glimpse the personality behind the poetry, proud of his birth, his race and his gifts, which permit him to address his patrons on terms of equality. The aristocratic society and values which gave life its meaning to him were crumbling, but in his poetry he recreates an almost vanished world and immortalizes it. (◊ Dithyramb) [D E W W]

Ed. C. M. Bowra (1947); verse tr. R. Lattimore (1947).

U. von Wilamowitz-Moellendorff, *Pindaros* (Berlin, 1922); G. Norwood, *Pindar* (1945); C. M. Bowra, *Pindar* (1964).

Piso Frugi, Lucius Calpurnius (fl. 133 B.C.). Roman orator and historian. As tribune of the plebs in 149 he established a permanent court to try cases of provincial mis-government. He was consul 133, and later censor. He published some of his speeches, and wrote *Annals* covering the history of Rome from earliest times to his own day. He tries to give rationalistic explanations of the early legends, and intersperses his history with anecdotes. [T A D]

Peter, *H R R,* i.

Plato (*c.* 429–347 B.C.). Greek philosopher. Plato is one of the greatest figures of Greek literature: with him, Greek prose reaches its fullest range of expression. He stands, with his master ◊ Socrates and his pupil ◊ Aristotle, as one of the shapers of the whole intellectual tradition of the West. Both his parents came from families long prominent in Athenian politics. His step-father, Pyrilampes, was an intimate of Pericles. It would have been natural for him to enter politics, but his first chance came when the reactionaries were in power after the defeat of Athens in 404, and he declined to come forward as their protégé. The execution of Socrates in 399 by the restored democracy sickened him for ever of Athenian politics. Since the formative influence of his own youth and early manhood had been his friendship with Socrates, he turned to philosophy as offering more hope of regenerating society. He began with a period of travel, which perhaps took him to Cyrene and Egypt, certainly to Italy and Sicily. He did not care for the affluent society of the Western Greeks, but made important contacts with Pythagoreanism, while a friendship with Dion, brother of Dionysius I of Syracuse, was to have political consequences. On his return to Athens (possibly in 387, but perhaps as late as 370) he founded the Academy, the first permanent institution devoted to education and research, and the prototype of all western universities. Advanced studies were concentrated on the fields of mathematics, jurisprudence and political theory, the aim being to produce experts for the service of the state. The rival establishment of ◊ Isocrates sought to produce practical politicians through an education largely based on rhetoric. Teaching, research and writing in Athens took up the last 40 years of his life, save for two visits to Sicily. The first was in 367, when he accepted the invitation of Dion to go to Syracuse to undertake the education of the new 'tyrant', Dionysius II. The optimum conditions for the production of the philosopher-ruler seemed to be present, but the result was a dismal failure. Plato returned to Athens in 360. Even so, he did not lose all concern with the tortuous and violent politics of Syracuse till 354, when Dion was murdered. Little is known of his last years, which must have been largely devoted to writing the *Laws*.

Plato's literary activity lasted for more than half a century, and, so far as we know, all that he wrote has survived, together with some material that is apocryphal, though probably contemporary. When this is taken away, we are left with (1) the *Apology* and 25 dialogues, (2) 13 *Epistles* (probably only I and XII are spurious), and (3) some at least of the poems that go under the name of Plato in the Greek Anthology. The first group stands for what Plato has meant to the world. But Plato himself regarded his writings as less important than his formal teaching at the Academy, and they do not form a coherent 'system' of philosophy; such a thing was alien to Plato's cast of mind. But, in broad outline, they do present a picture of the development of his thought and interests. No detailed chronological order can be established; close dating is only possible with the *Theaetetus*, published in 368 B.C. However, considerations of stylometry and content enable us to distinguish two, possibly three, periods of production: (1) An early group of Socratic dialogues, including the *Apology, Crito, Euthyphro, Hippias Minor, Laches* and *Lysis*. (2) More elaborate Socratic works, such as the *Gorgias, Meno, Protagoras, Phaedo, Symposium, Phaedrus* and *Republic*. Both these groups were probably written before the founding of the Academy. (3) After a gap of some 20 years, the later works – *Theaetetus, Parmenides, Politicus, Sophistes, Philebus, Timaeus* and *Laws*.

The purpose of the first group is to portray the personality and methods of Socrates. In the simplest cases, we see him trying to reach a satisfactory definition of some commonly accepted 'good', e.g. 'courage' (*Laches*), 'friendship' (*Lysis*). Examples brought forward by his interlocutors are tested and found wanting, and we are left feeling that no advance can be made until the underlying reality, 'the good in itself', can be defined. Of the rest, the *Cratylus* is a brilliant and light-hearted discussion of linguistics and etymology, the *Euthydemus* a skit on the methods of the ◊ sophists. The *Gorgias*, a work of ample scale, leads on from the nature and aims of rhetoric to the problem of right and wrong in public life, and contains a spirited exposition by Callicles of the claims of the superman. The *Meno* is concerned with 'goodness', and whether it can be taught. Four dialogues are devoted to the prosecution of Socrates and its sequel. The *Euthyphro* – in view of the charge brought against him – deals with piety. The *Apology* gives the historic defence Socrates presented in the court, and also an *apologia* or vindication of his way of life. The *Crito* shows why he refused to escape from prison. The *Phaedo*, written several years later, and belonging to the middle group, describes his last day in prison, his speculation with his friends about the immortality of the soul, and his death. Plato's dramatic powers are fully shown in two dialogues – the *Symposium*, where Socrates, Alcibiades, Aristophanes and the other contemporaries are brilliantly parodied as they discuss, at a banquet, the nature of love, and the *Protagoras*, where Socrates and a number of famous sophists talk about the relation of virtue and knowledge. The *Phaedrus* unites the themes of the *Gorgias* and the *Symposium*. The 10 books of the *Republic* provide an ample canvas for a leisurely treatment of the state and of the nature of justice in society. The first great piece of 'Utopian' writing, it raises issues of fundamental importance for all students of education and of politics. In all these dialogues, stress is laid on the theory of Forms or Ideas – the archetypes which underlie the phenomena of the world we see about us, and which are the only true objects of knowledge. In the third book there is a discussion of literary censorship, and the famous attack on poetry is in Book x.

The tone of the later group is very different. Their dramatic content is slight. Socrates is a recessive figure – in the *Laws*, he does not appear at all. The theory of Forms is absent from the *Parmenides*. The general trend is to the rigorous examination of major problems. Thus the *Theaetetus* deals with epistemology, the *Sophistes* with Being and not-Being, or (to use modern jargon) with significant negative predication, the *Philebus* with pleasure and knowledge, and the *Politicus* with the functions of the statesman. The *Timaeus* is concerned with cosmology and anthropology, and is the only work of Plato where the interest is on natural science. It contains the famous description of the *Demiurgos* or 'creator-god'; the *Critias*, a kind of appendix, tells the story of the lost civilization of Atlantis. The *Laws* returns to the problem of politics, but no longer with the idealism of the *Republic*. Instead, we are given a blueprint for the Greek *polis* of the ordinary kind, incorporating improvements suggested by the disillusionment of Sicily, and the practical experience of legislation accumulated by the Academy.

This bald summary cannot, of course, do justice to the marvellous achievement represented by Plato's writings. Nor could one that was much richer and fuller. Plato's dialogues – any more than Shakespeare's plays – are not apprehended by a recital of their contents. For he is the greatest master of Greek prose, commanding an astonishing range of tone and emotion, from the grave simplicity of the end of the *Phaedo* to the sumptuousness of the parts of the *Symposium* and *Phaedrus*. There is a dexterous use of simile and metaphor – e.g. the chariot of the soul in the *Phaedrus*, the parable of the cave in the *Republic*. The second group of dialogues is notable for the occurrence of the 'myth' – a device, perhaps taken from the Pythagoreans, which Plato uses to transcend logic and reason. In such myths as those of the *Phaedo*, the *Symposium*, *Phaedrus* and *Republic*, his presentation takes on the heightened intensity of great poetry. But Plato did not think that the highest philosophy could ever be communicated in writing. 'There is not, nor will there ever be, any treatise of mine on this subject. It cannot be reduced to formulae, as with other branches of knowledge. Only as a result of long meditation on the problem itself, and of a life lived in common, is a light suddenly kindled, as it were, in the soul by a spark that leaps from another: thereafter, it feeds itself' (*Ep.* VII: *c.*341). [DRD]

OCT: J. Burnet (5 vols., 1903–15); Loeb: W. R. N. Lamb, H. N. Fowler, R. G. Bury, Paul Shorey (12 vols, 1914 ff.); *Gorgias*, ed. E. R. Dodds (1959); *Timaeus*, comm. A. E. Taylor (1928); *Laws*, comm. Glen R. Morrow, *Plato's Cretan City* (Princeton, 1960); *Philebus and Epinomis*, comm. A. E. Taylor (1956); *Sophist and Philebus*, comm. A. E. Taylor (1961); *Theaetetus* and *Sophist*, comm. F. M. Cornford, *Plato's Theory of Knowledge* (1935); *Gorgias*, tr. W. Hamilton, *The Last Days of Socrates*, tr. H. Tredennick, *Protagoras and Meno*, tr. W. K. C. Guthrie, *The Republic*, tr. A. D. P. Lee, *The Symposium*, tr. W. Hamilton (Penguin Classics, 1960, 1954, 1956, 1955, 1951).

A. E. Taylor, *Plato, the Man and His Work* (5th edn, 1948); C. M. A. Grube, *Plato's Thought* (1933); G. C. Field, *Plato and His Contemporaries* (1930).

Plato of Athens (*c.*450–*c.*388 B.C.). Greek comic poet. A writer of both Old and Middle Comedy at Athens, he produced his first play about 428. He was credited with 28 comedies whose titles are preserved and many others besides; he claimed to have written comedies for others because he was poor. The titles suggest both political satires and mythological burlesque, and an ingeniously indecent passage survives from the *Phaon*, on the story of

Sappho's unhappy passion. Other remaining fragments are meagre and unrevealing, but one ancient critic described his style as brilliant, and another judged him the best writer of Middle Comedy. (⇨ Comedy, Greek.) [G T W H]

Edmonds, *F A C*, i.

Plautus, Titus Maccius (*c.* 254–184 B.C.). Roman comic poet. There was uncertainty even in antiquity about his name, his background and the authenticity of his works. Apparently a self-made man, born in modest circumstances in northern Umbria, he worked as a craftsman in the theatre at Rome and suffered setbacks and poverty before he took to writing plays in middle life, and became the most successful adapter of Greek New Comedy for the Roman stage. Of the 130 plays attributed to him 21 were accepted as authentic in the Augustan period – no doubt the 21, all ⇨ *fabulae palliatae*, which survive today.

The *Amphitruo*, described by Plautus as a tragi-comedy, and possibly adapted from ⇨ Philemon, burlesques the story of Alcmena's seduction by Jupiter, impersonating her husband Amphitryon. Farcical complications develop when the real husband appears, but Alcmena's innocent dignity remains unshaken. This play inspired the comedies by Molière, Dryden, and, more recently, Giraudoux. The *Aulularia* (*The Pot of Gold*), adapted from ⇨ Menander, studies the effect on Euclio, a poor elderly Athenian, of discovering a buried hoard of gold; obsessively suspicious, he distrusts even his daughter's suitor, and betrays his secret by his own anxiety; but all ends happily. The pathetically miserly Euclio was the original of Harpagon in Molière's *L'avare*. The *Captivi* (*The Prisoners of War*), recommended by Plautus as unusually edifying, concerns an old Greek, Hegio, who buys up prisoners of war in the hope of exchanging one for his captured son. Two such prisoners, master and slave, secretly exchange identities; the master is released to negotiate, and brings back Hegio's son, and the slave's self-sacrifice is rewarded when he is identified as Hegio's other son, kidnapped in childhood. Strong in dramatic irony, and dignified by the gallant behaviour of the two prisoners, this is one of Plautus's best plays. In the *Menaechmi* he farcically exploits the possibilities of confusion between identical twins, a theme often used in Greek New Comedy, and elaborated by Shakespeare in *The Comedy of Errors*. The *Miles gloriosus* (*The Boastful Soldier*), is based on a familiar stock figure, the model for the braggart captain of the Elizabethan stage. His foolish bombast and the cynical effusiveness of his toady, exaggerated to the point of caricature, enliven a farce in which he is ingeniously fooled by his mistress and her young lover. The *Mostellaria* (*The Ghost*) is a comedy of improvisation by a quick-witted slave, Tranio, to conceal the dissipation of his young master when the latter's niggardly father returns unexpectedly from abroad. Though found out in the end Tranio remains impudently self-assured, and finally obtains an unexpected pardon. The *Rudens* (*Rope*) beings strikingly with a prologue by the star Arcturus, an unusual setting on the rocky North African coast, and an opening scene of storm and shipwreck. But thereafter the plot, adapted from ⇨ Diphilus, is trite enough: the free-born heroine is rescued from a villainous pimp, and the salvage of her trinkets leads to her recognition by her father as his long-lost daughter.

The remaining plays are variations on the theme of a lover abetted by his resourceful slave and frustrated by a rival, a pimp, or a stern father; often the heroine is a slave or courtesan who eventually proves to be free-born after all. In the *Asinaria* (*Asses' Tale*), a father and son are allies in the intrigue; in the *Casina* and the *Mercator* (*The Merchant*), they are rivals. The slave is the central character in the *Bacchides*, where he contends with confusion over two courtesans both named Bacchis, and in the *Persa* (*The Persian*), where he is himself the lover; he has the title-role in the complicated *Epidicus*, Plautus's own favourite play, and in the *Pseudolus* (*The Trickster*), which is also distinguished by the richly revolting character of Ballio the pimp. The nick-name of a parasite, who conducts the intrigue, similarly gives the title to the *Curculio* (*The Weevil*). Heroines who were foundlings, or kidnapped in childhood, and whose recognition forms the climax of the plot, appear in several of these plays, as also in the highly sentimental *Cistellaria* (*The Tale of a Trinket-Box*), and the *Poenulus* (*The Little Carthaginian*), where the principal characters are Carthaginians; while in the cynical *Truculentus* (*The Boor in Love*) the central figure is a courtesan, who heartlessly exploits three lovers in turn. Family comedy is the main interest of the slight *Stichus*, and in the moral but dull *Trinummus* (*The Fiver*), in which the unexpected return of a father saves a spendthrift son from himself. Of the *Vidularia* (*The Tale of a Trunk*) only fragments remain.

What Plautus achieved was the re-creation in Latin of a foreign form of drama, and its popularization with an uncultured Roman public unfamiliar with its conventions, in a makeshift theatre and in competition with rival attractions. His success was due to his own vigorous genius and the rough-and-ready freedom with which he handled his Greek originals, as much as to the originals themselves. From a convention-ridden genre he chose the most varied and lively plays; the restrained art of Menander provided relatively few models. To these, as adapter rather than translator, he added much of his own. He retained the Greek setting, but introduced anachronisms and incongruous Roman allusions. He revelled in comic language and song, alliteration and word-play, congenial to Latin but alien to Greek, and converted a performance consisting almost entirely of dialogue into something akin to comic opera, with some two thirds of the dialogue replaced by songs and recitative in a wide variety of metres. He found his plots and characters in his Greek originals; there is little evidence of independent invention here, although he liked complicated intrigues and irrepressibly articulate and resourceful slaves. His own contribution was his boisterous humour, his gift for dialogue and amusing songs, and the comic force and sheer gusto that made the plays a popular success. He was greatly admired as a comic poet in the late Republic and early Empire, and his work exercised a considerable influence on comedy in England and France in the 16th and 17th centuries. (⇨ Comedy, Roman.) [G T W H]

O C T: W. M. Lindsay (2 vols., 1904–5). Commentaries: *Captivi*, W. M. Lindsay (1924); *Rudens, Mostellaria*, E. A. Sonnenschein (1901, 1907); *Miles gloriosus*, M. Hammond and others (1963). Translations: Loeb, P. Nixon (5 vols., 1928–38); E. F. Watling (Penguin Classics, 7 plays, 1964, 1965).

F. A. Wright, *Three Roman Poets* (1938); Beare, *R S*.

Pliny the Elder (Gaius Plinius Secundus) (A.D. 23–79). Roman administrator and writer. Born at Comum of an equestrian family, he held a succession of posts as commander of auxiliaries or of cavalry units in Germany and as Imperial financial official in various provinces. In 79 he was commander of the Roman fleet at Misenum. He died from suffocation at the eruption of Vesuvius, where he had gone to conduct rescue operations and obtain first-hand information of the unique phenomena.

Apart from a number of shorter works on grammar, rhetorical training, the use of the javelin by cavalry, and a biography of Pomponius Secundus, Pliny's 3 most important works were a *History of the German Wars* in 20 books, in which the campaigns of Drusus seem to have played a prominent part; a continuation of the *History* of ⇨ Aufidius Bassus, both used by Tacitus; and the 37 books *On Natural History*, which alone have survived. The *Naturalis historia*, Pliny claimed, contained a record of 20,000 facts worthy of note, compiled from 146 Roman and 327 non-Roman authors. Book I contains the table of contents, II deals with the Universe, III–VI with physical geography, VII with physiological peculiarities, VIII–XI with animals, fishes, birds and insects, XII–XXVII with trees, plants, flowers and herbs and their medicinal properties, XXVIII–XXXII with drugs to be obtained from animals and fishes, and XXXIII–XXXVII with metals and precious stones. The work shows a love of observation rather than a true scientific spirit.

Pliny was regarded as an important scientific authority in the Middle Ages; unfortunately, what he said was often subjected to travesty and exaggeration, and the strange things he described were frequently used by moralists as the basis for religious symbolism. [T A D]

Peter, *H R R*, ii; Loeb: *Naturalis historia*, H. Rackham, W. H. S. Jones and D. E. Eichholz (11 vols., 1938–).

Pliny the Younger (Gaius Plinius Caecilius Secundus) (A.D. 61/2–before 114). Roman man of letters and affairs. Born at Comum, he lost his father L. Caecilius Cilo during boyhood, the great soldier Verginius Rufus becoming his guardian. He was adopted by his uncle, ◊ Pliny the Elder, to whom he owed his name, his wealth and much by way of precept and example. He had the best education Rome could offer, Quintilian being among his teachers. After pleading his first case at an early age, he served as military tribune in Syria. On his return to Rome he achieved success in the courts as a specialist in property cases, and advanced steadily in his official career, rising to be prefect of the military and later of the civil treasury. As consul suffect in 100, he expressed his gratitude to the Emperor in the *Panegyricus* – his only extant speech. Though diffuse and fulsome it has characteristic fluency, and is a valuable source for the early history of Trajan's reign. Pliny was also put in charge of the drainage system of Rome, and later was made an augur. He was leading counsel in important political trials, prosecuting the notorious informer Marius Priscus, and defending two ex-governors of Bithynia accused of extortion. His expert knowledge of Bithynian affairs and grasp of financial administration made him the logical choice as Trajan's legate when the Emperor removed the province from senatorial control. He took up his appointment in 112, and died before 114, probably in office.

The first 9 books of Pliny's correspondence, comprising 247 letters, were given to the public during his lifetime, appearing in groups of 3 books between 97 and 109. Designed for publication, they are a kind of unpretentious social history, a series of vivid and varied pictures of life in an age of good taste and civilized values, viewed from above – the satirists view it exclusively from below. These are models of the literary letter, informal, lively, eminently readable. His circle includes the major figures of the day – Tacitus, Suetonius and Martial; and surprisingly members of the Stoic opposition are among his friends. He excels at anecdote or describing a scene, and combines both gifts in the best ghost story from antiquity. The gentle charm of his own kindly and generous personality pervades the whole. Book X stands quite apart from the rest of the correspondence, a posthumously published file from the imperial archives, containing Pliny's letters to Trajan, and in many cases the official replies. They are primary source material for the history of provincial administration in the 2nd century A.D., and include the famous account of the early Christians. The contrast between Pliny the over-conscientious civil servant and Trajan the man of action is particularly illuminating. (◊ Letters, Latin.) [D E W W]

Letters and Panegyricus, ed. M. Schuster (1933); Book X ed. and comm. E. G. Hardy (1889); Loeb: tr. Melmoth, rev. W. M. L. Hutchinson (2 vols., 1921, 1927); *The Letters of the Younger Pliny*, tr. Betty Radice (Penguin Classics, 1963).

Plotinus. ◊ Neo-Platonism.

Plotius Tucca. Chosen with ◊ Varius Rufus to edit the *Aeneid*, left incomplete at Virgil's death. His qualifications were that he was an intimate friend (*contubernalis*) of Virgil and Horace, and perhaps a poet in his own right, though nothing is known of his work. [D R D]

Plutarch (A.D. *c.*46–*c.*127). Greek biographer and essayist. Born at Chaeronea in Boeotia, Plutarch combined academic studies with multifarious civic activities. Through friendships formed on an official visit to Rome, he was made procurator of Achaea by Hadrian, and he also held a priesthood at Delphi. Yet much of his time he devoted to his school at Chaeronea and to his literary works.

Plutarch wrote a large number of essays and dialogues on philosophical, scientific and literary subjects (the *Moralia*), including his well-known diatribe *The Malignity of Herodotus*, a violent and unreasonable attack on that historian for his criticism of certain Greek states. His philosophical standpoint was that of a Platonist and he frequently attacked both Stoics and Epicureans. He is best known for his *Parallel Lives*, 50 biographies of eminent Greeks and Romans, generally composed in pairs, one Greek and one Roman, followed by a comparison between the two. His interest is with character rather than career – he emphasizes any changes in his hero's personality – but in character assessment he is influenced more by the prejudice of his sources than by his own critical judgement. Little attention is paid to chronology, and the historical value of the material varies considerably according to the source used; Plutarch sees nothing incongruous in coupling Thucydides with some obscure late historian as if they were of equal weight. However, he is interesting about personal and family life, and is rich in anecdote. Plutarch's *Lives* were very popular in the Elizabethan Age, and their translation by Sir Thomas North gave Shakespeare the subject-matter for his Roman plays. [T A D]

Loeb: *Moralia*, F. C. Babbitt, W. C. Helmbold, B. Einarson, P. H. de Lacy, P. A. Clement, H. B. Hoffleit, E. L. Minar, F. H. Sandbach, H. N. Fowler, L. Pearson, J. B. McDiarmid, H. Cherniss (15 vols., 1927 ff.); *Lives*, B. Perrin (11 vols., 1914–26); *Lesvies parallèles*, ed. R. Flacelière (Paris, 1957, 1961); *Fall of the Roman Republic*, tr. Rex Warner, *The Rise and Fall of Athens* and *The Makers of Rome*, tr. Ian Scott-Kilvert (Penguin Classics, 1958, 1960, 1964) (selections).

Pollio, Gaius Asinius (76 B.C.–A.D. 5). Roman orator and historian. He fought for Caesar in Gaul and in Civil War and supported Antony after Caesar's death, but remained neutral at Actium. He was a consul in 40, and a friend of Catullus, Horace and Virgil, who dedicated Fourth (Messianic) *Eclogue* to him. He founded the first public library in Rome and started the custom of giving public recitations of his own works.

Pollio was notable as an orator, poet, writer of tragedies, historian and critic. He wrote the *History of the Civil Wars from 60 B.C.* His style of language was plain and unadorned. As a critic he was severe; he criticized Caesar for lack of accuracy, Sallust for the use of archaisms, Livy for 'provincialism' (*patavinitas*), and Cicero for lack of consistency and courage in his political career. [T A D]

Peter, *H R R*, ii; Cicero, *Ad fam.*, x: 31–33.

Polybius (*c.*203?–*c.*120 B.C.). Greek historian. Polybius of Megalopolis, in Arcadia, was the son of Lycortas, leading statesman of the Achaean League and close associate of Philopoemen. He took an active part in Achaean military and political activities, and was elected Master of the Horse for the League in 169/8. However, his family had always shown an independent attitude towards Rome, and after the Roman victory over Perseus in 168 the Senate, encouraged by the pro-Roman politicians in Achaea, removed to Rome for indefinite detention all those Achaean leaders who had in any way opposed Roman interests. At Rome, by a fortunate chance, Polybius met the young Scipio Aemilianus, and soon became his close friend and adviser. This gave Polybius entry into the ◊ Scipionic circle, and secured for him great freedom of movement – it seems that he was even able to make journeys outside Italy, to Africa, Spain and Gaul. In 150 his official detention was ended, and he returned to Greece. But he still associated closely with Scipio, and accompanied him to Carthage in the Third Punic War, and possibly to Numantia. He died reputedly from a fall from his horse.

Apart from minor works, such as a *Life of Philopoemen*, a *Treatise on Tactics*, and a *History of the Numantine War*, Polybius wrote a history in 40 books, describing the events in the Mediterranean world that led up to the supremacy of Rome. He starts his main narrative from 220 B.C., but the first 2 books give an introductory account of earlier events, including the First Punic War and the Cleomenic War in Greece. The work was to have concluded with the end of the Third Macedonian War in 168 B.C., but it was extended to 145 B.C. to include the destruction of Carthage and the capture of Corinth. The first 5 books survive intact, the rest as extracts of various lengths made by later writers, while much of Livy XXXI–XLV is a fairly close translation of Polybius.

The style of Polybius is poor, lacking in grace and full of circumlocutions and periphrases; but as a work of scientific history, written by a man of great intelligence with a wide practical experience of top-level political and military affairs, largely free from national prejudices and dedicated to the pursuit of the truth, it is of inestimable value.

His expressly stated aim is to write a history of practical benefit to future statesmen. This is frequently stressed, and is contrasted with the empty pleasure provided by other histories written in a rhetorical vein or embellished with miraculous elements. Polybius attaches great importance to the causes of events, with the distinction carefully made between the real causes, the pretexts, and the preliminary incidents. As well as the historical narrative, Polybius includes a comparison between the Roman and Greek types of constitutions (Book VI) and an excursus on geography (XXXIV). His account of events is generally very accurate, partly because he was a contemporary of many of them and obtained information from eye-witnesses; he had, for example, talked with the elder Laelius and Masinissa. He viewed the struggle between Rome and Carthage impartially; as regards affairs in Greece, he shows considerable animosity against the Achaean League's enemies, notably the Aetolians, and also against the social-reform movements, typified by Cleomenes, Agis and Nabis in Sparta. But there is no reason to believe that his national or class prejudices ever led to an inaccurate account of any event.

Polybius used a variety of sources, the most important being ◊ Fabius Pictor, Philinus of Acragas, the *Memoirs* of ◊ Aratus, and one of the Greek writers, possibly Silenus of Calatia, who accompanied Hannibal. He also made full use of documentary evidence, such as the treaties between Rome and Carthage and Hannibal's inscription on the Lacinian promontory, recording the number of his forces. [T A D]

Loeb: W. R. Paton (6 vols., 1922–7); tr. E. S. Shuckburgh (1889); comm. F. W. Walbank, Books 1–6 (1957).

Porphyry. ◊ Neo-Platonism.

Posidonius (*c.*135–*c.*50 B.C.). Stoic philosopher and polymath. Posidonius of Apamea in Syria was the most influential Greek thinker of his time, and one of the chief mediators of Hellenistic culture to Rome. After studying under ◊ Panaetius in the Stoic school at Athens, he travelled extensively in the Mediterranean world, doing research in astrology, geography and meteorology. Early in the 1st century B.C. he became head of the Stoic school at Rhodes: he paid at least two visits to Rome, and probably died there. His influence on the thought of his age was deep and many-sided, but it is not easy to define. In geography he visited and described the customs of semi-civilized peoples in Gaul, Spain and Germany (a visit to Britain is improbable); gave the first full account and explanation of the Atlantic tides; measured the circumference of the earth; and first suggested the idea (so fruitful in the Renaissance) that India can be reached by sailing across the Atlantic. In the 52 books of his *Historia* (planned as a continuation of Polybius) he followed the tradition of Panaetius by providing a philosophical justification for the world. This view is reflected in the *Somnium Scipionis* of Cicero, and may have influenced the conception of the Augustan principate. A mystical element pervaded his teaching: its basis was the doctrine of the parallel between the macrocosm of the Universe and the microcosm of the individual soul, maintained by their common possession of the 'divine fire'. Associated with this was his interest in occultism of all kinds, especially astrology. Since only fragments of his writings survive, we can only guess how his system formed a coherent structure. (◊ Stoicism.) [D R D]

Jacoby, *F G H*, ii.
K. Reinhardt, *Kosmos und Sympathie* (Munich, 1926); A. Pauly, G. Wissowa, W. Kroll, *Real-Encyclopädie der Klassischen Altertumwissenschaft* (1897 ff.).

Pratinas. ◊ Satyric Drama.

'Priapeia'. Poems addressed to Priapus, god of fertility, whose image, a manikin with an enormous phallus, was commonly placed in gardens. Greek poems were written to him, but the name usually applies to a collection of 85 Latin poems, mostly written in the age of Augustus. Such names as Tibullus, Virgil and Ovid are attached to some of the pieces. They usually deal – in language of ritual obscenity – with the fate in store for those who, like the Nero of ◊ Petronius's *Satyricon*, have offended against the divinity. [D R D]

Teubner: E. Baehrens, *Poetae latini minores*, i (Leipzig, 1879).

Priscian (fl. A.D. *c.*500). Roman grammarian. Born at Caesarea, later professor of Latin at Constantinople. His

18 books of *Institutiones grammaticae* draw on the learning of all previous Greek and Latin grammarians, and show a grasp of the comparative grammar and syntax of the two classical languages. For the Middle Ages it became an authority on correct Latin usage: in various commentaries and abridged editions it was a widely used (and much-hated) school book. He also wrote a poem in praise of the emperor Anastasius, and a geographical poem modelled on the *Periegesis* of Dionysius Periegetes. [D R D]

Ed. H. Keil, *Grammatici latini*, iii (1855–1923); Teubner: E. Baehrens, *Poetae latini minores*, v (Leipzig, 1883) (poems).

Proclus. ◊ Neo-Platonism.

Propertius, Sextus (54/48–*c.* 16 B.C.). Roman elegiac poet. He was born at Assisi in Umbria. His father, who died when he was a boy, was of equestrian status, and the poet belonged to one of the leading families of a small Italian town. Part of their estate was forfeited in the confiscations after Philippi. Propertius had lasting memories of the Perusine War in which a relative died. It is uncertain when he came to Rome; he was destined for a legal career, but early decided to devote himself to poetry. His circle included Virgil and Ovid and a group of wealthy and cultured young aristocrats. His relationship with the imperial house is difficult to assess, but its closeness is attested by his poems on the deaths of Marcellus and Cornelia. His early poetry is dominated by his affair with Cynthia (a pseudonym for Hostia), which began probably in 30 and lasted at least 5 years. She was an accomplished courtesan; marriage was never envisaged, or indeed possible. She was of course unfaithful to him; the Illyrian praetor is not a fantasy of the imagination. But for all his complaints and bitterness Propertius makes her credible and even sympathetic.

Book I, dedicated to his friend Tullus, was published in 29 or 28. Its poems are directly linked to real events, often addressed to a friend or circle of friends, and half-epistolary in character. It is dominated by Cynthia's personality and was named after her. The book had a great success, and Maecenas now became Propertius's patron; to him the poet may have owed his house on the Esquiline. In Book II, published in 25, the erotic theme still predominates, but the lyrical note of rapture is muted and disillusionment is creeping in. Rome, his friends, the whole physical setting, recede into the background as the poet introspectively explores the psychology of passion. Book III followed in 22. There is a progressive decline in subjectivity corresponding to the cooling of the poet's feeling for Cynthia. He now claims to speak for all lovers, and his poetry becomes increasingly generalized and abstract. Cynthia is mentioned by name, however, in the brutal final poems ending the affair, intended as his farewell not only to her but to poetry. He breaks silence again however in Book IV, published after 16. The freshness of his early work now finally gives place to a harder and more brilliant manner, and apart from miscellaneous poems and extracts from a planned but abandoned aetiological sequence, the book contains four masterpieces (4, 7, 8 and 11, 'the queen of elegies'), all character studies of women portrayed with extreme sympathy and insight. Poem 8 in particular, with its vivid pictures of town and country and its unique humour, foreshadows Petronius. The date of Propertius's death is unknown, but it seems unlikely that he would not have followed up these successful experiments had he lived.

Propertius's love-poetry ranges from ecstasy to baffled rage and dejection. His lyrical early manner produces poems whose sensuous beauty of sound and imagery is unsurpassed. He presents an unforgettable picture of a man of sensibility in the grip of passion. His intuitive understanding of the past, his sense of place and atmosphere, his feeling for the supernatural and for the grim inevitability of death give depth and evocative colour to his poetry. Despite his Umbrian origins he is as essentially urban as Ovid. His poetry, like himself, is anchored in Rome. When he escapes from the distractions of his affair he finds refuge in the peace not of Nature but of Art. Allusions to painting and sculpture abound in his work – when he praises the natural complexion of ancient heroines he characteristically compares their colouring to Apelles' palette. He frequently idealizes his passion by comparing his love with the amours of the heroes and heroines of the legendary past. But unlike his Alexandrian models he keeps mostly to familiar themes (many can be paralleled from Pompeian wall-paintings), and here too his inspiration seems often visual rather than literary. In this respect he is poles apart from Tibullus, who seeks an ideal world of peace and beauty in the countryside, or from Ovid, who introduces gods and heroes into his poetry rather as if they were members of his circle. This intense visual imagination conditions all Propertius's poetry, which is frequently a sequence of brilliantly realized pictures succeeding each other with bewildering rapidity. No doubt this is partly conscious art, meant to mirror the shifting moods and feverish excitement of lovers. But it corresponds also to something fundamental in Propertius's personality. His verse has an extraordinary strength and power, especially in the pentameters, which are made to carry their full weight, a technique very different from the formal patterning of ebb and flow in the Ovidian couplet. He is among the most difficult of ancient poets because of his daring and violent manipulation of Latin, the abruptness of his changes of mood and theme, and the fact that he gives the reader the minimum of help in following the far from logical sequence of his thought. He creates a mannered and intensely personal style, and like Tacitus in prose strains Latin almost to breaking point in the process. At the same time he is fully aware of being in the Alexandrian tradition. He repeatedly claims to be the Roman Callimachus, and is consciously following and extending the range of the neoteric movement. His last book points the way for Ovid, in themes and treatment. [D E W W]

Ed. and comm H. E. Butler and E. A. Barber (1933); Loeb: H. G. Butler (1912); Book I, III and IV, ed. and comm. W. A. Camps (1961); tr. A. E. Watts (Penguin Classics, 1966); Ezra Pound, *Homage to Sextus Propertius* (1934) (lively, and though sometimes misusing Propertius's matter captures much of his manner).

Protagoras (*c.*485–*c.*415 B.C.). Greek sophist. Protagoras of Abdera in Thrace began to teach *c.*455 B.C., and made much money in Athens and in Sicily during his professional career. He professed to teach *arete* (virtue) – the efficiency leading to worldly success. His philosophy was based on the subjectivity of all human knowledge: 'Man is the measure of all things, of things that are, that they are, of things are not, that they are not.' He despised mathematics and science, and thought theology unknowable. 'Of the gods I know nothing, whether they exist or do not exist: nor what they are like in form. Many things stand in the way of knowledge – the obscurity of the subject, the brevity of human life.' His best-known writings (lost) were *On Truth* and *On the Gods*. He appears as the opponent of Socrates in the Platonic dialogue which bears his name. [D R D]

Diels, *F V*, 80.
Kathleen Freeman, *The Pre-Socratic Philosophers* (1946).

Prudentius (Aurelius Prudentius Clemens) (A.D. 384–410). Christian Latin poet. He was born at Calahorra (?) in northern Spain. His education gave him a good knowledge of Latin culture, but little or no Greek. A distinguished career in the public service included possibly a provincial governorship, and certainly high office at the court of Theodosius. Like many of the best spirits of the age he grew weary of the service of the world and longed for that of God. A visit to Rome – where he saw the catacombs, and the martyr shrines in their new splendour – confirmed his decision to retire, and to devote his talents as a poet to the Church. So much we know from his own writings.

His poems comprise (1) *Cathemerinon*, a collection of hymns (some still in use) for various occasions and festivals, (2) *Peristephanon* (*The Martyrs, Crowns*), poems in praise of martyrs, especially those of Spain, (3) *Apotheosis* (*On the Nature of God*), (4) *Hamartigenia* (*The Origin of Sin*), (5) *Contra Symmachum*, written in support of the Christian cause in the last great debate against paganism and (6) *Psychomachia* (*The Battle for the Soul*), an allegory of the spiritual struggle within the soul of man. This last was well known in the Middle Ages, and frequently apears in the art of that period. A work called *The Double Testament* (*Dittochaeon*) may also be his. To a mastery of a wide range of Latin metres, he brought poetic gifts of a high order. If he is sometimes over-earnest and credulous, these are the faults of the age. Certainly no list of Latin lyric poets can omit his name. [D R D]

Ed. W. Bergman (C S E L, Leipzig and Vienna, 1926); Loeb: H. J. Thomson (2 vols., 1949).

Ptolemy (Claudius Ptolemaeus) (fl. A.D. 121–151). Greek astronomer and geographer. Claudius Ptolemaeus was born at Ptolemais in Egypt and probably spent most of his life at Alexandria. He composed various works on astronomy, the most important being the *Great Collection* or *Almagest*, in which he set out and improved on the system developed by Hipparchus, using spherical trigonometry as the basis of his calculations. He also wrote on music, optics, mechanics and astrology. However, his most important work was his *Geography*, in 8 books, in which he laid down the principles and set out the necessary data for the construction of a map of the world.

Writing in the middle of the 2nd century A.D., when the British Isles had been circumnavigated and military and commercial penetration had made big advances into Asia and Africa, Ptolemy had available far more information than had his predecessors, and it was his great merit that he set it all out in systematic form, giving the latitude and longitude of all the places he mentions. However, although his work constitutes a great advance it has serious defects. The geographical positions he lists were not, apart from a very few, based on astronomical observation, but on bearing and distance derived from the calculations of travellers, who tended grossly to over-estimate distances. Moreover, by taking too small a figure for the circumference of the earth he made his degrees of longitude too small, and as a result represented the continent of Asia as extending to 180°. Included in Ptolemy's work was a map of the world and a series of sectional maps. Ptolemy's *Geography* was regarded as a work of definitive authority until comparatively recent times. His other works were held in high regard by the Arabs, and in some cases the only version extant is a Latin rendering of an Arabic translation. [T A D]

Ed. and Latin tr. C. Müller and C. T. Fischer (3 vols., 1883–1901); ed. and comm. P. J. Fischer, *Cl. Ptolemaei . . . codex Urbinas Graecus* (3 vols., 1932).
E. H. Bunbury, *History of Ancient Geography* (1883).

Ptolemy Soter (*c.* 367/6–283/2 B.C.). Greek historian. Ptolemy Soter, son of Lagus, was a close friend and general of Alexander the Great. After Alexander's death he became governor of Egypt, and later declared himself king and founded the Ptolemaic dynasty that ended with Cleopatra. He wrote what was regarded as the most reliable of the histories of Alexander. His work was the chief source used by ⇨ Arrian. [T A D]

Pyrrhon. ⇨ Sceptics.

Pythagoras (fl. *c.* 530 B.C.). Greek philosopher. Pythagoras of Samos is said to have been expelled from Samos by the tyrant Polycrates, and to have visited Egypt and Babylon. He settled at Croton in south Italy, where he founded the scientific-religious order named after him, which won many adherents in the Greek cities of Italy and Sicily. It is hard to separate his teachings from those of his followers, as described by Aristotle. On the religious side, his order resembled the mystery cults (⇨ Orphism etc.) which then flourished. It taught the transmigration of souls and the kinship of all living things, and practised ascetism. In science his chief work was in mathematics; he discovered the harmony of the octaves, and saw in Number (i.e. mathematical relationships) the underlying principle of the universe. He may actually have discovered the geometrical proposition that bears his name. It is uncertain whether he left any writings. [D R D]

Diels, *F V*.
Sarton, *H S*, i.

Pytheas (*c.* 310–*c.* 306 B.C.). Sea-captain and explorer. Pytheas of Massilia made the most enterprising of all ancient voyages in northern waters. Sailing through the Straits of Gibraltar and the Bay of Biscay, he passed Ushant, Land's End, and, by way of the west (?) coast of Britain, reached Orkney and 'Thule' (Faroes? Iceland? Norway?). He may have got as far as the mouth of the Elbe or even the Vistula. His report told of the tin-mines of Cornwall, the tides of the Atlantic, the size and shape of the 'Bretannic' islands (he was the first Greek to use the name), and the melting ice of the northern seas. Unfortunately, only fragments survive, quoted with disbelief by ⇨ Diodorus, Strabo and Pliny. [DRD]

J. A. Thomson, *History of Ancient Geography* (1948).

Q

Quintilianus, Marcus Fabius (A.D. 30/40–*c.* 100). Roman rhetorician and educationist. He was born at Calagurris in Spain. His father was probably a teacher. Quintilian was sent to Rome in boyhood to be educated; among his teachers were Domitius Afer and Julius Africanus. He returned to Spain probably in 58 on Domitius Afer's death, but accompanied Galba to Rome in 68. He soon became the acknowledged head of the teaching profession, being encouraged by Vespasian, who gave him official status and a salary. He taught and practised at the Bar for 20 years, retiring *c.* 90. Pliny the younger was proud of having been his pupil and Juvenal and Martial speak well of him. He collected the fruits of his experience in the *Institutio oratoria* (*Education of an Orator*), published between 93 and 95. Domitian had made him the tutor of his grand-nephews, the sons of Flavius Clemens and Flavia Domitilla, and his book was probably meant as an educational programme for the young princes and for Quintilian's own children. But Quintilian married late in life, his young wife predeceased him, and his two sons died in childhood. Clemens and Domitilla were charged with atheism in 95, Clemens being executed and Domitilla exiled. It is almost certain that they were Christians (Quintilian may allude to the parable of the sower in I: 3, 4–5). The date of his death is unknown.

None of his speeches has survived. The *Pro Naevio Arpiniano* was the only oration published by him, but other speeches and some of his lectures were in circulation in pirated editions deriving from shorthand notes. On his retirement he composed an essay on the reasons for the decline in oratory, which has not survived, and the *Institutio oratoria* in 12 books. The core of the work lies in Books III–XI, a technical treatise on rhetoric, III–VII, dealing with subject matter and arrangement, and VIII–XI, dealing with style and delivery. A good deal is arid and uninteresting ('much wormwood and too little honey', as he himself puts it), but at least Quintilian is a practising advocate and an experienced teacher who refuses to allow abstract theory to triumph over personal knowledge and commonsense. The modern reader is likely to find books I, II and X the most rewarding. Book I is an extraordinarily perceptive account of childhood education, sympathetic, balanced and in some respects (notably in its attitude to corporal punishment) in advance of modern practice. Book II includes a stimulating discussion on the nature and functions of oratory and rhetoric. Book X contains *inter alia* a discussion of reading suitable for an orator and the well-known comparative survey of Greek and Latin literature. Book XII presents a picture of the educated orator, the good man skilled in speaking, which it is Quintilian's aim to produce. Much of what he says has been absorbed into the European educational tradition. His enthusiasm, dedication and fundamental human decency and wisdom suggest a teacher who was also his pupils' friend; and his style is the man, clear, vigorous, unaffected, yet polished. (⇨ Literary Criticism; Oratory and Rhetoric.) [DEWW]

Loeb: H. E. Butler (4 vols., 1921); annotated eds: I F. H. Colson (1924), X W. Peterson (1891), XII R. G. Austin (1948).

M. L. Clarke, *Rhetoric at Rome* (1953); A. Gwynn, *Roman Education from Cicero to Quintilian* (1926).

Quintus Curtius. ⇨ Curtius Rufus, Quintus.

Quintus Smyrnaeus (? fl. A.D. *c.* 400). Greek poet. Author of an epic poem, in 14 books, called the *Posthomerica*, which tells the events of the Trojan war between the end of the *Iliad* and the beginning of the *Odyssey*. Written by a man steeped in Homer, and remarkably successful, considering his late date, in his use of Homeric diction, the poem has some literary merit, though it deals with themes often much better handled in the ⇨ Epic Cycle or by Virgil. Since the manuscript was found at Otranto in Calabria, the author is sometimes called Quintus Calaber, but he himself says he came from Smyrna. (⇨ Epic Poetry, Greek.) [D R D]

Loeb: A. S. Way (1913).

R

Remmius Palaemon, Quintus (1st cent. A.D.). Grammarian and schoolmaster. In the first capacity he wrote a compendious treatise, now lost, which was used by all later grammarians. In the second, his immorality was such that two emperors (Tiberius and Claudius) warned parents against committing their sons to his charge. [D R D]

Reposianus (probably 3rd or early 4th cent. A.D.). Latin poet. Author of a poem of 182 lines preserved in the codex Salmasianus. Its theme is the loves of Mars and Venus; the style, delicate and charming, recalling that of the ⇨ *Pervigilium Veneris* without its passionate intensity. [D R D]

Loeb: Duff, *M L P*.
Bardon, *E L L* (for possible connexion with Poussin).

Rufus, Marcus Cluvius (fl. A.D. 68). Roman historian. He was consul some time before 41 and a friend of Nero. He was eloquent, but did not misuse his eloquence by bringing prosecutions. He kept the friendship of subsequent emperors. He governed Spain at the start of 69, but joined Vitellius and was present at the conversations with Flavius Sabinus at which a settlement of the civil war was sought. He lived on some years under Vespasian. Cluvius wrote a history of Rome that covered the reign of Gaius, Claudius, Nero and probably the accession of Vespasian. He was an outspoken man of moderate views, and was praised by Tacitus. [T A D]

Peter, *H R R*, ii.

S

Sallust (Gaius Sallustius Crispus) (86–*c.* 34 B.C.). Roman politician and historian. In his youth an active supporter of the anti-senatorial party, Sallust was tribune of the plebs in 52, and after the death of the demagogue Clodius took an active part in fomenting the riots which resulted in the burning down of part of the Senate House. For this, though nominally for gross immorality, he was expelled from the Senate by the Censors in 50. He was restored by Caesar during the Civil War and as a reward for some military successes was made governor of Numidia. However, he was apparently so blatant at enriching himself at the expense of the provincials that he had to retire from public life, and he devoted the rest of his life to literature at his beautiful home in the Gardens of Sallust, built with his newly acquired wealth.

Sallust's main work was a *History of Rome* in 5 books, covering the period 78–66 B.C. Apart from a few short excerpts this has perished, and his reputation rests on his 2 monographs, the *Catiline,* describing the Conspiracy of Catiline in 63 B.C., and the *Jugurtha,* dealing with the war against Jugurtha, King of Numidia, from 111 to 105 B.C. Both these outstanding pieces of literature are written in a forceful style and they contain many moral and philosophical disquisitions, and a number of violent attacks on the corruption of life at Rome and particularly of the senatorial aristocracy. But the chronology is careless and at times confused, and there are inaccuracies in detail. Sallust's style is partly based on that of Thucydides; it had considerable influence on Tacitus. Its chief characteristics were variety, brevity and a love of archaisms. Some scholars regard Sallust as a serious philosophic historian; others as a mere political propagandist. But his philosophical judgements are nearly always second-hand, at times insincere, and often out of place, though his wit is sometimes shrewd. Those who maintain that the *Catiline* is primarily an attempt to exonerate Caesar from complicity in the plot have failed to make out a good case. Most probably Sallust's great motivating force was a desire for glory; balked in politics, he resolved to win a great name in literature, and by combining moralizing with sensationalism succeeded beyond all his hopes.

Sallust's greatest contribution to Latin literature was the development of the historical monograph. He is also notable for the dramatic nature of his narrative, in which events are presented as a series of vivid scenes, and for his interest in the psychological causes for men's actions. In both these respects he was followed by Tacitus. [T A D]

Loeb: J. C. Rolfe (1921); tr. S. A. Handford (Penguin Classics, 1963).

D. C. Earl, *The Political Thought of Sallust* (1961); R. Syme, *Sallust* (1965).

Sappho (b. *c.* 612 B.C.). Greek poetess. She was born at Eresos, in Lesbos, of aristocratic parentage. Her father, Scamandronymus, fell apparently in the fighting between Athens and Lesbos for Sigeum. Sappho lived mostly at Mytilene, the native city of her mother Cleïs. In her childhood political disturbances drove her briefly into exile in Sicily. She was married and writes lovingly of her daughter, whom she named Cleïs, after her own mother. Charaxus, Sappho's brother, had an affair with a Thracian slavewoman Doricha, and acquired some notoriety by purchasing her freedom for an exorbitant sum. The familiar story of Sappho's love for Phaon, and suicide by leaping into the sea from the Leucadian cliff, is a transparent later fabrication.

Sappho was the dominating figure amid a group of girls held together by the power of her personality in a relationship of passionate erotic undertones, based on shared emotional sensibility and devotion to poetry (they were the audience for whom most of her personal lyrics were composed). The analogy drawn in antiquity with Socrates and his circle is illuminating.

The Alexandrian editors arranged Sappho's poetry in 7 books. Her reputation rests on a handful of poems, the majority fragments preserved on papyri. Only the address to Aphrodite is certainly complete. Her subject-matter appears limited almost entirely to the personal world of her family and friends, and of her emotional and religious life. But the range and intensity of her feeling, which fires her imagination to a white heat in which all dross is burnt away, is unlimited. Her poetry has its roots in Lesbian folk-song; her dialect is the Lesbian vernacular. The marriage songs are exceptional; here too she can be colloquial in tone, but more often they are formal compositions and draw on epic conventions of subject and usage. She has extreme metrical versatility and accomplishment, composing freely in 4- and 3-line stanzas, in couplets, or with the single line for unit. The strength and poignancy of her greatest poems, their deceptively simple sensuous beauty of phrase, rhythm and sound, have something of the instantaneous appeal, the immediate magical power of a Mozart aria. Catullus, with sure insight, took Sappho's picture of the jealousy of love as his model in portraying passion. ⇨ Alcaeus, her slightly senior contemporary, was also a Mytilenean. Between them they created the subjective personal lyric, and began a tradition transmitted by Catullus and Horace, expanded and developed by a long sequence of European poets, and still intensely alive today. [D E W W]

Poetarum lesbiorum fragmenta, ed. E. Lobel and D. L. Page (1955).

Bowra, *GLP*; D. L. Page, *Sappho and Alcaeus* (1955) (both contain translations of chief fragments).

Satire, Roman ('Satura'). The well-known claim to Roman supremacy in satire ('*satura quidem tota nostra est*', Quintilian, X: 1:93) is admissible if its terms are understood. There were strong satirical elements in several forms of Greek literature, notably in Old Comedy (e.g. Aristophanes' attacks on Pericles, Cleon, Lamachus, Socrates, etc.), and also in the Cynic-Stoic diatribes of ⇨ Bion of Borysthenes and ⇨ Menippus. But to have developed satire as a literary genre in its own right, with a loose form of the hexameter as its appropriate metre, to have equipped it with a varied armoury of weapons, and to have directed them on themes compelling enough to engage the full attention of a succession of powerful writers – all this is perhaps the most striking original achievement of Latin literature.

It is now widely agreed, after much controversy, that *satura* derives from *satur*, meaning 'full' or 'stuffed', with gastronomic sense of a *melange*, hodgepodge, or mixed stuffing. Thus Livy uses '*saturae*' to describe a kind of primitive dramatic performance in vogue in Rome in the 4th century B.C., a medley of prose and verse, song and dialogue, on a wide range of themes. These crude forms of entertainment gave ground before the influence of Greek drama. But the name reappears as a title of certain writings of Ennius (239–169 B.C.), again in the sense of medley.

For ⇨ Ennius satire was a *parergon*. The first author to devote himself wholly to the *genre* was ⇨ Lucilius (*c.* 180–*c.* 102 B.C.), who produced no less than 30 books, constituting a formidable indictment on Roman life and morals. He used various metres, but eventually chose the hexameter. All later Roman satirists refer to Lucilius as the father of their line; it is a grave loss that only fragments remain.

In the next century ⇨ Varro (116–27 B.C.) revived the medley of verse and prose. The *Satires* of ⇨ Horace (65–8 B.C.) blend the Lucilian literary form with the sermonizing of the Greek philosophers. But where Lucilius lashed vice, Horace turned a tolerant smile on eccentricity. Something of the Lucilian tone was revived in the 6 satires of ⇨ Persius (A.D. 34–62), a little muffled by the primness of the author and the obscurity of the style. There is a strong satirical element in ⇨ Lucretius, and an even stronger one in the *Apocolocyntosis* of ⇨ Seneca the Younger and the *Satyricon* ('satirical-novel') of ⇨ Petronius.

But the *chef d'œuvre* of this Roman tradition is the 16 satires of ⇨ Juvenal – one of the greatest of satirists, magnificently endowed with that *saeva indignatio* indispensable to the best effects. They are an indictment of Roman society under the early Empire as powerful as that in the historical writings of Tacitus. In both cases, the work of modern apologists has done no more than show that the mark is indelible. [D R D]

Gilbert Highet, *Juvenal the Satirist* (1954), *The Anatomy of Satire* (1962).

Satyric Drama. A type of Greek drama similar to tragedy in form and subject-matter, but fanciful and light-hearted in treatment. It was named after the chorus, who were dressed as satyrs, the wanton, unruly creatures, part man and part horse, associated with Dionysus and led by their Falstaffian father, the wise old Silenus. The relationship of satyric drama to early tragedy is uncertain. Pratinas, a dramatic poet from the Peloponnese, is said to have invented satyric drama, and probably introduced it into the tragic contests at Athens late in the 6th century B.C. Early in the 5th century the last play in each competitor's tetralogy was customarily a satyr-play, but later only one satyr-play was produced at each contest.

Any legend suitable for humorous treatment might be used. The satyr-plays of ⇨ Aeschylus were the most highly esteemed, then those of Pratinas and his son. Numerous fragments remain of the *Net-Haulers* of Aeschylus, from his tetralogy on the Perseus legend; it appears to have been a work of considerable charm, showing the satyrs as fishermen rescuing Danae and her baby Perseus from the sea. Part of the *Trackers* of ⇨ Sophocles is also preserved, but the *Cyclops* of ⇨ Euripides is the only complete satyr-play extant. The genre seems to have remained alive until Roman times, and ⇨ Horace includes some rules for its composition in his *Ars poetica*, remarking that it is distinct from both tragedy and comedy, and should have a dignity of its own. (⇨ Tragedy, Greek.) [G T W H]

Two Satyr Plays, tr. R. L. Green (Penguin Classics, 1957).
Pickard-Cambridge, *D T C*; A. Lesky, *Greek Tragedy* (1965).

Sceptics. The Greek sceptics represent not so much a school of philosophy as a tradition of empiricist or agnostic opposition to various forms of dogmatic teaching. Their more important representatives are: (1) Pyrrhon of Elis (*c.* 360–*c.* 270 B.C.), who is said to have been on the scientific staff that accompanied the expedition of Alexander. On his return he taught in Elis, maintaining the impossibility of 'true' knowledge, and the need to conduct life on a theory of probability. (2) Arcesilaus (*c.* 315–241 B.C.), who became head of the New Academy in 264, and his successors. They launched a frontal attack on the key Stoic doctrine of sense-perception as the basis of knowledge. (3) Aenesidemus, a contemporary of Cicero, who, in the tradition of Pyrrhon, taught 'suspension of judgement'. (4) Sextus Empiricus (fl. A.D. *c.* 180) to whose extant writings we owe our knowledge of Greek scepticism. The chief of these are (1) the *Outline of Pyrrhonism* (3 books), (2) *Against the Dogmatists* (5 books), and (3) *Against the Schoolmasters* (6 books), a critical examination of the subject of general education. [D R D]

Loeb: *Sextus Empiricus*, R. G. Bury (4 vols., 1933–).
M. M. Patrick, *The Greek Sceptics* (1929).

Scipionic Circle. A convenient label for the group of statesmen and intellectuals (Greek and Roman) which gathered round Scipio Aemilianus (185–129 B.C.), the son of the philhellene Aemilius Paullus who brought the royal library of Macedon to Rome in 167 B.C. Prominent in Roman politics throughout his adult life, and predominant from about 145 to his death, Scipio was well placed to encourage men to domesticate the best in Greek culture at Rome. With Scipio and his friend Laelius, both leading orators, the group included the historian ◊ Polybius, the Stoic philosopher ◊ Panaetius, the satirist ◊ Lucilius, and the dramatists ◊ Terence and ◊ Pacuvius. Besides their contributions to literature, religion and philosophy, they fostered such important general concepts as that of *concordia*, as the ideal for the conduct of domestic politics, and of *humanitas*, the bond uniting all men, irrespective of nationality, colour or race. Through the work of such eminent jurists as Q. Mucius Scaevola these ideas were in some measure embodied in Roman law. The death of Scipio and the great political crisis of the Gracchi ended the collective influence of the group. But its outlook survived for another generation in Rutilius Rufus and other individual members. It held a powerful attraction for Cicero in the last age of the Republic. [D R D]

Scylax (fl. 5th cent. B.C.). Greek explorer. Scylax of Caryanda, in Caria, explored the Indus for King Darius of Persia and then sailed across the Indian Ocean to the Red Sea. The *Periplus*, a description of certain countries of Europe, Asia and Africa, is a later work, compiled some time in the 4th cent. B.C. [T A D]

V. Müller, *Geographici graeci minores* (1855); Herodotus, IV: 44.

Seneca, Lucius (?) Annaeus, the Elder (55 B.C.–A.D. ?40). Roman rhetorician. Called 'The Elder' (or 'The Orator') to distinguish him from his son, Seneca the Younger. Born at Corduba in Spain, he came to Rome as a young man, and acquired a considerable fortune, perhaps by trade. His intellectual interests lay in the art of rhetoric, of which he was a connoisseur: the experience of a lifetime is contained in the anthology of rhetorical practice which he drew up for his three sons. It contained 10 books of *Controversiae* (debating themes on points of law, of which 1, 2, 7, 9 and 10 are complete, the rest in epitome), and 2 or more (1 survives) of *Suasoriae*, speeches of advice to historical characters. Here lies embalmed all that is known of Roman rhetoric in the reigns of Augustus and Tiberius, besides much incidental information on Latin authors now lost. Moreover, we gain a better understanding of Silver Latin literature from Seneca's portrayal of its main formative influence. Nor are his own merits negligible. He shows remarkable skill in representing the individual styles of a hundred or so orators, his anecdotes are pithy and well told, his literary judgements penetrating. He adheres steadily to the dignity and good sense of Cicero as a corrective to more facile trends of his own day. [D R D]

Teubner: A. Kiessling (Leipzig, 1872); *Suasoriae*, ed. and tr. W. A. Edward (1928).
S. F. Bonner, *Roman Declamation in the Late Republic and Early Empire* (1949).

Seneca, Lucius Annaeus, the Younger (4 B.C.–A.D. 65). Roman statesman, philosopher and man of letters. Second son of ◊ Seneca the Elder. Born at Corduba in Spain of a wealthy equestrian family, he came in early childhood to Rome, and showed precocious literary and philosophical promise. Never very robust, he impaired his health by excessive austerity; a visit to his aunt, who was married to Galerius, prefect of Egypt, helped him to find himself physically and emotionally. He rapidly made his name as orator and author. His official career began (and nearly ended) under Caligula. In 41 Claudius banished him to Corsica on a charge of adultery with Julia Livilla; but in 49 Agrippina secured his recall and appointment as Nero's tutor. On Nero's succession Seneca with Burrus was initially the power behind the throne, being consul suffectus in 56. The murder of Agrippina in 59 marked the waning of his influence; the story that he composed Nero's speech of self-justification is probably apocryphal. After Burrus's death in 62 he sought safety in retirement, but in 65 was ordered to commit suicide, and died with Stoic fortitude. He has been accused of temporizing and cowardice in his public career; but as he watched the corruption of Nero's character by power he may have felt it his duty to exercise such restraining influence as he could. He can at least claim credit for his share in the five years of good government – the *quinquennium Neronis*.

Though the speeches are lost a representative selection of his prose and verse has survived. (1) Philosophical works. (a) 12 books of 'dialogues', mostly treatises with frequent interruption by an imaginary interlocutor, expounding Stoic morality; (b) More extensive essays, the *De clementia*, and the *De beneficiis* (in 7 books); (c) *Epistulae morales*, 124 brief sermons in letter form, perhaps the freshest of his philosophical writings. (2) *Naturales quaestiones* (in 7 books), dealing with strange phenomena and written with strong moralistic undertones. (3) The *Apocolocyntosis*, or 'Pumpkinification', of the Emperor Claudius; a Menippean satire blending prose and verse and maliciously amusing on the theme of Claudius's deification. (4) 9 tragedies: *Hercules Furens, Troades, Phoenissae, Medea, Phaedra, Oedipus, Agamemnon, Thyestes* and *Hercules Oetaeus* (this is of doubtful authenticity). Designed for reading and recitation, they are melodramatic and emotional, with only occasional flashes of poetry and dramatic feeling. A tenth play, the *Octavia*, is no longer attributed to him. (5) It is possible that some 50 of the epigrams ascribed to Seneca are authentic.

Seneca is a master of the pointed style, writing in short stabbing sentences with a vocabulary enriched by poetic, archaic and colloquial elements, and striving for paradox and epigram to such an extent as often to defeat his own purpose. The measure of his achievement is that he paved the way for Tacitus. Philosophically he is essentially a popularizer, lacking deep conviction or scientific curiosity. As poet and dramatist he is only spasmodically moving, though hidden somewhere beneath the elaborate and inscrutable façade is a genuine poetic impulse. But he set the tone for the Silver Age, and profoundly influenced subsequent Latin and European literature. [D E W W]

Loeb: tragedies F. J. Miller (2 vols., 1916–17), philosophical writings J. W. Basore (3 vols., 1932–5), epistles R. M. Gummere (3 vols., 1917–25), *Apocolocyntosis* W. H. D. Rouse (1913); *Naturales quaestiones*, tr. and comm. A. Geikie and J. Clarke (1910); 4 tragedies tr. E. F. Watling (Penguin Classics, 1966).

C. W. Mendell, *Our Seneca* (1941); G. Lloyd-Evans, 'Seneca, Shakespeare, and the Kingdom of Violence', in *Roman Drama*, ed. D. R. Dudley (1965).

Servius (late 4th cent. A.D.). Roman grammarian and scholar. One of the two most important ancient commentaries on Virgil (the other being that of ◊ Donatus, of which only a portion survives) is ascribed to him. 'Servius' now exists in two forms, (a) a shorter version and (b) the so-called *Servius Auctus* or *Servius Danielis*, incorporating much earlier material. This version is valuable in its own right, besides as a sample of the educational methods of the late Empire. [D R D]

Sextius (Quintus Sextius Sextians) (b. *c.* 70 B.C.). Founder of a Roman school of Stoic philosophy, which had some distinguished pupils. His works (now lost) were written in Greek. [D R D]

Sextius Niger (fl. *c.* 10 B.C.) Son (?) of the above, writer on botany and medicine, quoted by ◊ Dioscorides. [D R D]

Sextus Empiricus. ◊ Sceptics.

Sidonius Apollinaris (A.D. *c.* 430–*c.* 480). Latin Christian writer. Sidonius saw the final collapse of Roman power in Gaul, and his writings are among the most important sources for social conditions in 5th-century Gaul. High birth, eloquence and powerful connexion won him favour with three of the last feeble emperors of the West, Avitus, Majorian and Anthemius, to each of whom he addressed a panegyric. But he was no mere time-server: as Bishop of Arverna (Clermont) he organized the last brave resistance of the Gallo-Romans of Auvergne to the Visigoths, which was betrayed when to his disgust the imperial authorities ceded the province to the Gothic king Euric (475). Imprisoned for a time, Sidonius returned to his see, and to life on his country estate, which seems to have been surprisingly peaceful and comfortable for such troubled times. His writings comprise (1) *Poems*, including the 3 panegyrics, and secondly and more important, the *Letters*, of which there are 9 books. Modelled on those of Pliny, and like his composed with an eye to publication, they deal with a wide range of social, political and literary topics, and deserve to be more widely read. [DRD]

Loeb: W. B. Anderson (1936) (poems and letters 1 and 2); *Letters*, tr. O. M. Dalton (1915).

C. E. Stevens, *Sidonius Apollinaris and His Age* (1933).

Silius Italicus, Tiberius Catius Asconius (A.D. ?26–?101). Roman poet. Author of the longest (12,200 lines) and certainly the dullest of Latin poems. Senator, consul (68), and informer under Nero, he supported Vitellius in the Civil War, and was Governor of Asia in 77. In a long retirement on his estates in Campania he indulged his tastes as art-collector and bibliophile, and pursued the cult of Virgil with more enthusiasm than discretion. To restore Virgil's tomb was an act of piety, to compose an epic on the model of the *Aeneid* was not, for Silius had no poetic talent. His *Punica* (in 17 books, composed 88–98) is a tedious application of the conventions of literary epic to a historical theme. Pliny has said the last word on it – that it was written '*maiore cura quam ingenio*', 'with more diligence than talent'. For all its diligence, it does not really tell us anything fresh about the Punic Wars. (⇨ Epic Poetry, Roman.) [DRD]

Loeb: J. D. Duff (2 vols., 1927, 1934).

Simias. ⇨ Alexandrian Poetry.

Simon Magus. ⇨ Gnosticism.

Simonides (*c.*556–*c.*468 B.C.). Greek lyric poet and epigrammatist. Born on Ceos, he lived for a time as Hipparchus's guest at Athens. When the tyranny fell he moved to Thessaly, enjoying the patronage of the Scopads. Before Marathon he returned to Athens and later became a supporter and friend of Themistocles. The great victories of the Persian Wars were all commemorated by him. In 476 with the waning of Themistocles' ascendancy Simonides transferred to Sicily. His tact healed the breach between Theron and Hiero, and secured him an established position. He was joined by his nephew ⇨ Bacchylides – their poetic successes nettled ⇨ Pindar, also in Sicily at this time. He died at Acragas.

Simonides developed the *epinikion* from a short improvised song of welcome to the victor into a large-scale choral composition, though humorous touches show him less on his dignity than Pindar. The simple pathos of his dirges was famous. His epigrams, especially his epitaphs, were unsurpassed. He also composed hymns, dithyrambs, drinking-songs and elegies. The graceful Ionic fluency of his early lyric develops into a powerful close-knit style with an almost lapidary quality, owing something to the discipline of epigram. His famous dictum that poetry is painting in words accords well with the pictorial quality of his verse. Age brought a riper humanity and deeper wisdom, with little if any lessening in his poetic powers. (⇨ Dithyramb.) [DEWW]

Page, *PMG*.
Bowra, *GLP*.

Siro. ⇨ Epicureanism.

Sisenna, Lucius Cornelius (d. 67 B.C.). Roman orator and historian. Praetor in 78. He served as a legate of Pompey in the campaign against the pirates and died while on mission to Crete. He wrote a history of the Social War, and the Civil War between Sulla and Marius. His work receives qualified praise from Cicero, who describes it as the best history written so far, but a long way short of the ideal. As an orator his style is commended by Cicero, but he is ranked below Sulpicius and ⇨ Hortensius. [TAD]

Peter, *HRR*, i.

Socrates (?469–399 B.C.). Greek philosopher. Socrates wrote nothing. But so potent was the influence of his life and teaching that he must rank as a major figure in Greek literature; in that of philosophy he is, of course, central. He was the son of a sculptor and a midwife, and there was enough money in the family to give him a good education. He was at first attracted to natural science, especially as taught by Archelaus and Anaxagoras, but later turned in disillusion to investigate the problems of morals and conduct. The ◊ sophists were doing the same thing; to contemporaries such as Aristophanes, Socrates appeared as a sophist, though Plato portrays him as their first adversary. But the sophists were professional teachers, and aliens. Socrates was a citizen of Athens; he fought for his country in the Peloponnesian war at Potidaea, Delium and Amphipolis, and showed bravery in action. He was also to show political courage of a high order in the hysterical years of Athens' collapse. But his life's main work was a sort of philosophical mission to his fellow-citizens, which he regarded as a duty imposed by the Delphic oracle, when it declared that there was no man wiser than he. This, and the divine sign which is said to have warned him on critical occasions in his life, are hard to understand in a man otherwise removed from conventional piety and mysticism. Of the nature of his mission there can be no doubt. He formed no philosophical school and had no regular pupils. But he went everywhere in Athens – the gymnasia, the markets, private gatherings – talking and discussing, examining the bases of morality and convention, and 'following the argument wherever it led'. He claimed to follow his mother's profession, and to be a midwife of ideas. Above all, he attracted the young, from all ranks of society – Alcibiades, ◊ Plato, ◊ Xenophon, non-Athenians like Simmias of Thebes and Euclides of Megara. He must have trampled on many prejudices and upset many dignities. In 399 old scores were paid off. The democracy was now restored and many of Socrates' friends discredited. Socrates was accused on a twofold charge – impiety, and the corruption of the young. His reply can be read in the *Apology* of Plato. Perhaps it was not intended to press the charges home, but Socrates was uncompromising, and a sentence of death was passed. There was thirty days' stay of execution. It is likely that he could have escaped from prison, as his friends urged him to do. But in the *Crito* we see how, believing that this would falsify his whole life, he remained absolute for death. The *Phaedo* describes his last talks with his friends, and the taking of the hemlock, in words which it would be impertinent to praise.

After his death, many of his friends thought it their duty to set down in writing a picture of the master at work and a record of his teaching. Of these there survive only the dialogues of Plato and the *Apology, Symposium* and *Memorabilia* of Xenophon. The problem is to know how much of the historical Socrates stands behind these literary portraits. It is unlikely that the last word on this subject has been said. But the general trend of modern scholarship – in contrast to that of the last century – has been to regard the earlier Socratic dialogues of Plato (those before the foundation of the Academy) as a faithful portrayal by an observer of insight and genius, and to attach less value to the jejune impressions of Xenophon. [D R D]

A. E. Taylor, *Socrates* (1932); G. C. Field, *Plato and His Contemporaries* (1930); W. Jaeger, *Paideia* (tr. 1939).

Socrates Scholasticus (A.D. *c.* 380– after 439). Greek Christian historian. A lawyer of Constantinople, in his *Ecclesiastical History* he continued the record of Eusebius for the period 305–439. In 7 books, Socrates' account frequently reproduces original documents verbatim, carefully detailing the sources, and it is remarkable for its objectivity. The work is an invaluable store of information for the historian and makes lively reading for the non-expert. [J G D]

Migne, *P G*, 67; tr. A. C. Zenos (N P F, 1890). F. J. F. Jackson, *A History of Church History* (1939).

Solon (*c.* 640–*c.* 560 B.C.). Athenian statesman and the first Athenian poet. The climax of his political career was in 594–3, when as archon he carried through a programme of agrarian, legal and constitutional reforms which left a lasting mark on the Athenian state. Later he travelled extensively in Greece, Asia Minor and Egypt. He returned to Athens shortly before Pisistratus became tyrant. His poems, chiefly in iambic and elegiac metre, contain, besides some general moralizing, his reflections on current politics and an *apologia* for his political actions. Though only fragments survive, they have a high value as the authentic voice of a great statesman. [D R D]

Diehl, *A L G*, i.
W. J. Woodhouse, *Solon the Liberator* (1938); Bowra, *E G E.*

Sophists. Properly those professional teachers who travelled the cities of the Greek world in the 5th and early 4th centuries B.C. They taught many subjects, especially the art of rhetoric, and charged high fees. The word *sophistes* originally meant 'good craftsman' or 'experts'; its pejorative meaning was largely due to Plato; by the time of Demosthenes it had become a term of abuse. Plato's quarrel with them was that they were interested in persuasion, not in truth; he sets against them the disinterested inquiry of Socrates. In Aristophanes, Socrates himself appears as a sophist. Modern critics stress the services they rendered to Greek education; their pupils valued them as providers of the means to success in practical life. (⇨ Protagoras.) There was a similar movement in the Roman Empire in the 1st and 2nd century A.D. (⇨ Aristides, Dio Chrysostom, Favorinus, etc.), but its practitioners gave displays of oratory and little else. [D R D]

Diels, *F V.*
Werner Jaeger, *Paideia* (tr. 1939).

Sophocles (*c.*496–406 B.C.). Greek tragic poet. Sophocles was born at Colonus, just outside Athens, the son of a prosperous arms manufacturer. A handsome youth, he won distinction early by his musical gifts. He played the leading role, as was then customary, in at least two of his own dramas; but his voice was too weak for the theatre, and he became the first tragic poet to give up the practice. His long life spanned the rise and decline of the Athenian Empire; he was a friend of Pericles, and though not an active politician held several public offices, both military and civil. As a priest of a minor healing deity he welcomed the cult of Asclepius to Athens in 420, and for this he was honoured as a hero after his death. He was the leader of a fellowship of the Muses, or literary circle, and a friend of Herodotus the historian; he was interested, as his studied art suggests, in poetic theory as well as practice, and he wrote a prose treatise *On the Chorus*. He seems to have been content to spend all his life at Athens, and is said to have refused several invitations to royal courts. When he died his genial charm was greatly missed, as Aristophanes testifies. His last work was produced posthumously by his grandson, the younger Sophocles, also a tragic poet.

Sophocles first won a prize for tragedy in 468, defeating the veteran Aeschylus amid scenes of great excitement. Altogether he is said to have composed 123 plays, or perhaps more, and to have won 24 victories (presumably with 96 plays); he was often second in the contests, but never third. Only 7 tragedies and part of a satyr-play are now extant, but titles and fragments of many other plays remain, showing that he drew on a wide range of themes, with the Theban and Trojan legends predominating. Plutarch reports that he distinguished three successive styles in his work: (1) high-flown, in the Aeschylean manner; (2) more independent, but austere and artificial; and (3) highly expressive of character and best suited to drama. All the extant tragedies belong to the last phase. The dates of four are uncertain, but the *Ajax* is perhaps the earliest, followed by the *Antigone* (probably in 440); *Oedipus the King* and the *Women of Trachis* probably belong to the 420s, and the *Electra* to the following decade; the *Philoctetes* was produced in 409, and the posthumous *Oedipus at Colonus* in 401.

The action of the *Ajax* takes place at the Greek camp before Troy. The pride of Ajax was so outraged when the armour of Achilles was awarded to his rival Odysseus that he set out to murder his comrades in their sleep; but the goddess Athena, already offended by his arrogance, sent him mad, and he slaughtered some livestock instead. The tragedy displays his madness, his recovery (which brings no remorse, but only an overwhelming sense of humiliation), his suicide at a lonely place on the seashore, and the dispute over his burial. The Greek commanders condemn him to lie unburied – the ultimate dishonour – but his half-brother Teucer defies them. The impasse is resolved by a magnanimous appeal from Odysseus. Throughout the dispute the body of Ajax remains on the scene, a mute but powerful participant.

The *Antigone* develops a similar theme more fully, and with a woman as the leading character. After the attack of the Seven on Thebes, Creon, who is now king, declares their dead leader Polynices a traitor and forbids anyone on pain of death to give him burial. Antigone, Polynices' sister, disobeys, claiming a higher authority than Creon's. There is thus a conflict of principle. Antigone is condemned to death and kills herself; Creon, at first conscientiously resolute, eventually gives way, but is too late to save her or prevent the suicide of his son, betrothed to Antigone, and of his wife. He is led away, a broken man. This is his tragedy as well as Antigone's.

In *Oedipus the King* Sophocles turns to an earlier stage in the Theban legend. Oedipus has been king of Thebes for several years, having left his home in Corinth to escape the fulfilment of an oracle that said he would kill his father and marry his mother. He now has to investigate the murder of the previous king, Laius, by persons unknown, and step by step he discovers that Laius was a man he once killed himself, that Laius and not the king of Corinth was his true father, and that his queen Jocasta is also his mother. The oracle has after all been fulfilled. Jocasta commits suicide; Oedipus blinds himself in his distraction, takes leave of his two daughters, and is led away. This is Aristotle's model tragedy; yet, admirable as the construction is, the catastrophe is due less to the hero's character than to circumstances contrived by the gods.

The leading characters in the *Women of Trachis* are Deianira and her formidable husband Heracles, and the action turns on her devotion to him despite his infidelities, and her disastrous attempt to win him back with a supposed love-philtre which turns out to be a violently corrosive poison. Cursed by her son as a murderess, she kills herself without offering any defence. The dying Heracles is next brought in, helpless and in agony; he forces his son to agree to burn him alive on a great pyre and take over his new mistress, and is then escorted away to the pyre. The appearance of Heracles is no mere appendage to the tragic story of Deianira, but rather its climax, for his superhuman personality looms in the background throughout the earlier scenes.

The *Electra* has the same theme as the *Libation Bearers* of Aeschylus – the return of Orestes to avenge his father by killing his mother Clytemnestra and her lover Aegisthus; but there is less emphasis on the hereditary curse of the house of Atreus, and no Furies haunt Orestes after the deed is done. The main interest in the play is centred on the character of Electra, who despite all ill-treatment has stubbornly cherished the memory of her father and the hope that her brother would return. Her despair at the false report of Orestes' death is exploited in some striking scenes. Her recognition of Orestes brings her joy, not disaster, and the play as a whole is melodramatic rather than tragic.

The scene of the *Philoctetes* is the uninhabited coast of Lemnos, where the wounded Philoctetes was abandoned by his comrades years before, on the way to Troy. Odysseus and Neoptolemus, son of Achilles, now arrive to induce him to rejoin the Greeks with his bow and arrows, inherited from Heracles, since the city cannot be taken without them. Philoctetes, an embittered cripple, is outmanoeuvred by the wily tactician Odysseus, but at the last minute the scruples of his young and ingenuous companion frustrate the plot. Nothing will persuade Philoctetes to help the Greeks until Heracles himself appears in Euripidean style and bids him go to Troy, to play his part in taking the city.

Sophocles' last and greatest tragedy, *Oedipus at Colonus,* contains a minimum of plot. It describes how the aged Oedipus, a blind, helpless and squalid beggar, arrives after years of wandering at Colonus near Athens; how he is received there, in a series of encounters involving little action but much recapitulation and justification by Oedipus of his tragic career, and finally, summoned by peals of thunder, leads the way with majestic confidence to the spot where his mysterious apotheosis takes place, witnessed by no one but Theseus the king. A messenger reports his passing; Theseus returns with the two mourning daughters of Oedipus, and agrees to convey them home to Thebes. Profoundly moving, yet scarcely tragic in the ordinary sense, *Oedipus at Colonus* is one of those masterpieces which transcend the limits of their genre.

Of the satyr-play, the *Trackers*, a substantial and lively fragment has been recovered from papyri in modern times. The subject is the precocious exploits of the infant Hermes, as described in the ◊ *Homeric Hymns*. The trackers are the chorus of satyrs, searching for Apollo's stolen cattle. They hear a strange noise, which a nymph explains as the sound of Hermes' new invention, the lyre; this evidence of his resourcefulness convinces them that he must be the cattle-thief, and they report him to Apollo.

A moderate innovator in the art of tragedy, Sophocles increased the importance and complexity of the dialogue by introducing a third actor. He abandoned the Aeschylean practice of composing connected trilogies or tetralogies on a single theme, and made each play an independent drama with a more rapidly moving plot built round a single character. Where the fate of the central character is settled before the end of the play, as in the *Ajax, Antigone* and *Women of Trachis,* some sense of lack of unity and even anti-climax is inevitably felt (though it should not be exaggerated); but in the others unity of action is complete. Events in a Sophoclean tragedy are the necessary or probable consequence of what has gone before, as Aristotle recommended. Improbabilities or inconsistencies in the legend are adroitly suppressed, or placed outside the plot as part of the situation assumed at the outset. Like Homer, with whom he has much in common, Sophocles is a self-effacing artist, content to tell a story for its own sake. Such is his concentration on his dramatic theme that it is hard to detect many allusions in his plays to contemporary affairs. The structure of his tragedies, in its distribution of dialogue and lyrics, is orthodox and often – even at the most dramatic moments – deliberately symmetrical. His prologues are genuinely dramatic, and no mere programme-notes such as Euripides sometimes uses; indeed, his dramatic technique generally shows little sign of Euripidean influence.

Dialogue, not lyric, is Sophocles' main vehicle of dramatic expression. Although scarcely realistic, since it is all couched in the conventional Attic Greek, it is in his hands dignified, subtle and admirably responsive, even in the unnaturally rigid but traditional line-for-line exchanges of *stichomythia*. A device for which Sophocles won great fame was his use of dramatic irony in dialogue, whereby a speaker's words were given some special and usually terrible significance of which he himself was unaware. The Sophoclean chorus, consisting of ancillary characters, are seldom more than sympathetic bystanders: neither indispensable, as in some Aeschylean dramas, nor yet embarrassingly redundant. They share the emotions aroused by the action, and give them lyric expression; they may advise, argue, appeal and warn, but they do not take the initiative; they contribute to the dramatic effect of the action rather than to the action itself. If at times they merely moralize, in many odes they achieve lyric poetry of the highest order. Dramatic irony appears in their lyrics as well as in the dialogue, for odes of rejoicing over triumph or deliverance often prove to be premature and precede disaster.

Although Sophocles is said to have remarked that he depicted people as they ought to be, Euripides as they are, his characters are not wholly idealized. Noble they certainly are, and rather larger than life, as heroes were; but they also have their faults, conforming to Aristotle's formula, 'like us, only finer'. Yet the hero's fault is seldom fatal; perhaps only in the *Ajax* is it the sole cause of disaster. What Sophocles generally does is to present heroic characters in tragic or potentially tragic situations, and display their reactions to the circumstances and to one another. In the process he creates a notable gallery of heroes, and of heroines too.

Sophoclean language, the product of conscious technique, avoids extremes of grandeur and naturalism alike; and every word tells. There are a pervasive epic colouring and traces of Aeschylean influence, but no bombast. If Sophocles does admit some idiosyncrasies of expression, it is not at the expense of clarity, aptness or dignity. His lyrics are for the most part unobtrusively fine in imagery, structure and rhythm, often breathing a slight air of detachment, and lacking both the intensity and the obscurity of Aeschylus; his most famous ode of all, in praise of Colonus, is both relevant and intricately beautiful.

To attempt to deduce a philosophy of life from the dramas of Sophocles is an unprofitable exercise, whose fruits are little more than commonplaces. By and large he accepts the conventional religion of the day, and takes life as he finds it. He sees the element of drama in the traditional legends and presents it without trying to reveal underlying principles, without rationalization or protest or comment – unless it was a comment to return in extreme old age, and in the last act of his city's own tragedy, to the story of Oedipus, the most tragic of heroes. (⇨ Satyric Drama; Tragedy, Greek.) [G T W H]

O C T: A. C. Pearson (1928). Fragments: A. C. Pearson (3 vols., 1917); D. L. Page, *Greek Literary Papyri* (1942). Commentaries: with prose tr., R. C. Jebb (1883–96); J. C. Kamerbeek (Leiden, 1953–); *Ajax*, W. B. Stanford (1963). Verse tr.: Loeb, F. Storr (2 vols., 1913); E. F. Watling (Penguin Classics, 1947, 1953); R. L. Green, *Two Satyr Plays* (Penguin Classics, 1957); D. Grene and R. Lattimore, *The Complete Greek Tragedies* (1959).

C. M. Bowra, *Sophoclean Tragedy* (1965); A. J. A. Waldock, *Sophocles the Dramatist* 1951); A. Lesky, *Greek Tragedy* (1965).

Sophron. ⇨ Mime.

Sotades (fl. *c.*340 B.C.). Greek comic poet. Only a few fragments survive. [D R D]

Ed. A. Meineke, *Fragments comicorum graecorum*, iii (1939–57).

Sotades of Maronea (3rd cent. B.C.). Greek poet. Said to have been put to death for a lampoon against the marriage of Ptolemy II and Arsinoë (276–275 B.C.). He invented a metre called, after him, the 'sotadean', in which he wrote a version of (? portions of) the *Iliad*, also a poem addressed to Priapos (⇨ *Priapeia*). [D R D]

Fragments in J. U. Powell, *Collectanea alexandrina* (1933).

Sozomen, Salaminius Hermias (early 5th century A.D.). Greek Christian historian. Originally a native of Palestine and eventually a resident in Constantinople, Sozomen, like ⇨ Socrates Scholasticus, whose work he copied, wrote an *Ecclesiastical History* in 9 books, as a continuation of the pioneer work by Eusebius, to cover the period A.D. 324–425. His literary style is superior to that of Socrates, but his critical judgement is weak. [J G D]

Migne, *P G*, 67; tr. rev. C. H. Hartrauft (N P F, 1890).

F. J. F. Jackson, *A History of Church History* (1939).

Sphaerus. ⇨ Zeno.

Statius, Publius Papinius (A.D. *c.*45–*c.* 96). Latin epic poet. He was born in Naples. His father, himself a poet and successful teacher, who transferred his school to Rome, supervised his son's education and lived to see his early successes. Statius enjoyed a growing literary reputation and gave recitals of his poetry in the capital, his patrons including the emperor himself. He was successful in the competition for poetry at the Alban games in *c.*89, but was defeated at the Capitoline contest in 94. His health failing he retired to Naples in 95, and predeceased Domitian.

His chief work is the *Thebaid*, an epic in 12 books published in 92 after a dozen years' work. It describes the fulfilment of Oedipus's curse on his sons culminating in the expedition of the Seven against Thebes and the duel to the death between Eteocles and Polynices. A loose-knit sequence of scenes and speeches, mostly sensational or pathetic, gives full scope to Statius's genuine feeling for stirring action, movement and colour, and to a descriptive and dramatic power the consciousness of which may have attracted him initially to epic. His style, however, is always allusive, recondite and constrained, and the elaborate artificiality of his diction gives the impression that it has been gone over so often that it is irretrievably overdone, with the ornament stifling rather than enriching the poetry. He did not live to finish the second projected epic, the *Achilleid*, whose theme was to have been the life of Achilles and his death in the Trojan War. This would require a full 12 books; as it is, the poem ends abruptly, at II: 167. What we have is more freshly written than the *Thebaid*, perhaps because it lacks a final revision. The *Silvae*, 32 informal pieces dating from the last years of Statius's life, supposedly written under time-pressure and without his normal finish, are mostly in hexameters with a few excursions into lyric metres. Typical subjects are birthdays, weddings, funeral lamentations, festivals, fine buildings, *objets d'art*, favourite pets and slaves. They range from obsequious flattery of the emperor to the famous invocation of Sleep (V: 4). Even in these short occasional verses Statius tends to reject simplicity and directness as unworthy of poetry, but they have more appeal to the modern reader than his more formal compositions and throw valuable light on Roman society in the last years of Domitian. (⇨ Lyric Poetry, Latin.) [D E W W]

OCT: *Thebaid* and *Achilleid*, H. W. Garrod (1906), *Silvae*, J. S. Phillimore (1917); *Achilleid*, ed. O. A. W. Dilke (1954); Loeb: J. H. Mozley (2 vols., 1928).

Stesichorus (end 7th cent. to mid 6th cent B.C.). Greek choral lyric poet. He was born at Mataurus in the toe of Italy and made his home at Himera. For a time he lived in mainland Greece, perhaps as a refugee from Phalaris's tyranny; he knew Boeotia, Sparta and Arcadia. But the atmosphere of Magna Graecia uninhibited by the dead weight of tradition was his natural milieu, and he died at Catana in his native Sicily.

The Alexandrians knew 26 books of Stesichorus's poetry; we have just 26 fragments. The introduction of the balanced triadic structure of strophe, antistrophe and epode is attributed to him. His chief innovation, however, was in subject-matter, in the treatment of epic themes in lyric manner. The fact that his poems are known by name, and his influence on contemporary art, suggest the ability to select the vivid moments of dramatic climax. He boldly reshaped legend to his ends; most famous was the palinode in which he retracted his previous condemnation of Helen. He broke wholly new ground in drawing on Sicilian folk-lore for the tragic stories of Daphnis and of Calyce. These romantic themes foreshadow faintly and distantly the emergence of pastoral. Stesichorus was a profoundly original creative artist who composed on an epic scale lyric poetry with a lofty nobility of temper and a sustained dignity of style. [D E W W]

Page, *PMG*.
Bowra, *GLP*.

Stesimbrotus (fl. late 5th cent. B.C.). Greek scholar and writer. He was born at Thasos, but taught at Athens. He wrote a book on Homer, one on the Mysteries of Samothrace, and a biographical work on Themistocles, Pericles and Thucydides (son of Melesias) frequently used by Plutarch. [T A D]

Jacoby, *FGH*, ii.

Stoicism. Of the great philosophical systems which grew up to meet the changed conditions of the world after Alexander, Stoicism – if not intellectually the most profound – had the longest life and exerted the widest influence. Though Athens was for long the headquarters of the school, its leading figures at first were all Asiatics. The founder, ⇨ Zeno (335–263 B.C.) from Citium in Cyprus, came to Athens *c.* 313, and after studying with Crates the Cynic (⇨ Cynics), and at the Academy, set up his own school in a lecture hall of the Stoa Poikile (whence the name Stoic, or, in English, the Porch). He combined logic, 'physics' (natural science) and ethics into a coherent system of philosophy, which enabled the Stoic disciple to live a virtuous life, 'in harmony with nature', under any circumstances that might befall him. We know the names and dates of 6 of his successors as Master of the school, and many followers, in the next 150 years. The most important are ⇨ Cleanthes of Assos (Master 263–232 B.C.), who enlarged the conception of divine government of the world, making Zeus virtually a monotheistic deity, and ⇨ Chrysippus of Soli (Master 232–207 B.C.), who had to meet the full blast of the attack on Stoicism by Arcesilaus and the Academy. He overhauled Stoic logic and physics, and indeed so refurbished the system that he became regarded as its second founder. Since only fragments of Zeno and Chrysippus remain, it is hard to distinguish their doctrines. But it is certain that in this period Stoicism gained a hold on many of the best minds of the Hellenistic world, notably on such rulers as Antigonus Gonatas of Macedon (284–239) and Cleomenes III of Sparta (235–219 B.C.).

This political aspect became more marked in the next phase, when ⇨ Panaetius of Rhodes tried to naturalize Stoicism in Rome. From *c.* 145 he was, like the historian Polybius, the intimate of the group of enlightened Roman nobles round Scipio Aemilianus (⇨ Scipionic Circle). Concentrating on ethics and politics, he tailored the original Greek garment of Stoicism to fit a Roman figure. In this new system – known as Middle Stoicism – emphasis has shifted from the wise man in the universe to the citizen in the framework of society, and the object is to provide for the good government of the world by educating the Roman nobility to a sense of its duties. In the next century ◊ Posidonius of Apamea made a new synthesis of the natural sciences, and did original work in history and ethnography. His concept of Natural Law as the Will of God had a far-reaching influence on Roman jurisprudence. He also did much to revive the pseudo-science of astrology.

The course of Roman politics in the 1st century B.C. put paid to the dream of rule by the enlightened nobles. Roman adherents of Stoicism now swim against the stream, or, like Brutus, Cato the Younger and Marcus Favonius, die in the last ditch to support the losing cause of republicanism. Stoic endurance supports their intransigence – *victrix causa deis placuit, sed victa Catoni.*

In the 1st century A.D., Stoicism animates the 'philosophic opposition' to the Empire. There is a symbiosis of Stoic sage (◊ Musonius Rufus, etc.) and Roman noble, as in the circle of Paetus Thrasea under Nero, and of Barea Soranus under Domitian. Reduced by now to a system of ethics, Stoicism taught not merely a virtuous life but an edifying death; Tacitus recounts the deaths of the Stoic martyrs in moving scenes. There was also another strain of Stoicism, whose leading representative is the statesman and multi-millionaire ◊ Seneca.

After the death of Domitian, Stoicism became the philosophy of the establishment. For four successive reigns it provided a code of conduct and a concept of service for the Roman Emperor, and, at the last, a Stoic emperor in the person of Marcus ◊ Aurelius. The writings of ◊ Epictetus and of Marcus Aurelius are the main source for Stoic doctrine in this last creative phase. Morever, Stoicism was very widely diffused: it gave a philosophy of life to many intelligent persons of the middle and even – through its ally Cynicism – of the lower class. After this period, Stoicism produced no major figure, but it was one of the most powerful forces in the eclecticism which marked the final stage of pagan philosophy, and it deeply influenced the Fathers of the Church, notably Augustine. [D R D]

Arnim, *S V F.*

E. Bevan, *Stoics and Sceptics* (1913); M. Pohlenz, *Die Stoa* (2 vols., Göttingen, 1948) and *Stoa und Stoiker* (Zurich, 1950); M. Hadas, *Essential Works of Stoicism* (New York, 1961).

Strabo (64/63 B.C.–after A.D. 21). Greek geographer. Strabo was born at Amaseia in Pontus, a member of a family that had risen high in the service of the kings of Pontus. He seems to have been very wealthy, as he was able to devote his life to study, writing and travelling. He came to Rome in 44, and studied under the most eminent Greek teachers there; possibly his interest in geography was aroused by Tyrannion. In philosophy he was a Stoic, and he had almost uncritical admiration for the Romans, perhaps owing to the influence of ◊ Polybius and ◊ Posidonius, or possibly to the hereditary disposition of his family to back the winning side. Few details of Strabo's life are known, but he visited Rome several times, travelled extensively in Asia Minor and Egypt, and probably spent the last years of his life in Amaseia.

Strabo's earliest work was a history in 47 books, nothing of which has survived. He then wrote 17 books on geography. This work was probably first published *c.*7 B.C., and later republished in revised form. Strabo regarded geography as a branch of philosophy, defining philosophy as a wide knowledge embracing things human and divine, and his object was to write what would be useful and helpful to men occupying high positions in public life. It is undecided whether the select audience for whom he wrote were Greeks in his native Pontus, or Romans.

Strabo based his geography on ◊ Eratosthenes, though he did not hesitate to criticize both him and other writers on geography. He regarded the earth as a sphere, with the inhabited world forming an island surrounded by the ocean and occupying a quadrilateral in the northern hemisphere. In his first two books he deals with the dimensions of the inhabited world, its positions and limits, the situation of various places (e.g. Marseilles, the mouth of the Dnieper) with reference to a simple graticule of meridians and parallels of latitude, and criticizes his predecessors' views. In subsequent books he surveys the physical and political geography of the various countries of the inhabited world, beginning with Western Europe and proceeding through Eastern Europe, Asia Minor and Asia to Egypt and Africa. His description includes a brief account of the history and customs of their peoples; thus, in his account of Palestine he mentions Moses and Jewish religious beliefs, and when he relates the founding of Tarentum he refers to the circumstances that arose in Sparta as a result of the Second Messenian War. [T A D]

Loeb: H. L. Jones (8 vols., 1917–33).
E. H. Bunbury, *History of Ancient Geography* (1907).

Suetonius Paulinus, Caius (fl. A.D. 69). Roman soldier As governor of Africa in 41 he was the first Roman to penetrate the Atlas mountains, and he wrote an account of what he saw. After his consulship (*c.* 42), he governed Britain (59–61), conquered Anglesey, and suppressed the revolt of Boudicca; but his severity towards the rebels led to his recall. In 69 he fought for Otho against Vitellius. [T A D]

Peter, *H R R*, ii.

Suetonius Tranquillus, Gaius (A.D. *c.* 69–*c.* 140). Roman biographer. Suetonius was a man of equestrian family and did not himself rise above an equestrian career. He was a friend and probably a contemporary of the younger ◊ Pliny, and for some years was one of Hadrian's secretaries. On being dismissed for some indiscretion involving the Emperor's wife, Sabina, he went into retirement and seems to have devoted the rest of his life to literature.

Suetonius wrote a number of biographies, and also works on the antiquities of Rome, on natural science, and on literary and linguistic matters. All that have survived are his *Lives of the Twelve Caesars* and his *Lives of Famous Men.* The latter was probably his earliest work. It consisted of a number of short lives of important literary figures, including orators, poets, philosophers, teachers of rhetoric and teachers of literature ('grammarians'). Much is now lost, but Lives of Terence, Virgil and Horace survive.

The *Lives of the Caesars* begins with Julius Caesar and ends with Domitian. Each biography follows roughly the same pattern: first the family history and early life of the subject is described, then his public career, then his physical appearance; details of his private life are set out, and there is a list of his virtues and vices. The picture of the man is very piecemeal, without any attempt at a balanced character judgement. There is little effort made to weigh the various pieces of evidence, which are all presented with equal force, and little attention is paid to chronology. Imperial problems are often dismissed with very scant reference, as, for example, Caesar's campaigns in Gaul and Claudius's conquest of Britain – far more space is given to the madcap soldiering of Gaius. But it is on the details of his subjects' private lives that the interest of the writer is concentrated, and much of the material to which Suetonius had access in the Imperial archives would otherwise have been lost. Suetonius was widely read in the Middle Ages; he was the model of Einhard's *Life of Charlemagne,* and through him influenced Asser's *Life of Alfred.* [T A D]

Teubner: R. Dietsch (Leipzig, 1882); Loeb: J. C. Rolfe (1924); tr. Robert Graves (Penguin Classics, 1957).

Sulpicia (fl. late 1st cent. B.C.). Roman poetess. Granddaughter of Servius Sulpicius Rufus, the distinguished jurist and friend of Cicero. She was the niece and ward of Valerius Messalla Corvinus. Six brief elegies by her, none more than 10 lines long, have survived in the *Corpus tibullianum* (III: 13–18). They give frank expression to her passion for Cerinthus, the pseudonym of a Roman of approximately the same age and social standing as herself. This handful of utterly sincere, unaffected, ingenuous poems gives a fascinating glimpse into the personal world of an aristocratic Roman girl who is deeply in love. Publication must have been delayed until long after the affair was over, possibly until after Sulpicia's death. [D E W W]

Sulpicius Severus (A.D. *c.* 350–*c.* 425). Christian historian. Born in Gaul, Sulpicius had a successful legal career, but later became a monk at the behest of St Martin of Tours. The *Life* of St Martin is his best-known work, but there is also the

Universal History, which begins with the Creation and passes by way of scriptural history to the great persecutions and heresies of the Empire. Sulpicius wrote a good clear Latin, and gives a useful idea of the intellectual interests of the educated Christian of his day. [D R D]

Ed. and comm. C. F. von Halm (Vienna, 1866).

Symmachus, Quintus Aurelius (A.D. *c.* 340–*c.* 402). Roman statesman and orator. A member of one of the great aristocratic families of the Late Empire, and with a distinguished career in public life (governor of Africa 373, city prefect 384, consul 391), Symmachus was a spokesman of the pagan party in Rome in its last extremity. He played a part in the famous debate over the restoration of the statue of Victory to the Senate House after its removal by Gratian in 382. The restoration, opposed by St ♦ Ambrose and ♦ Prudentius, was not carried out. The third of Symmachus's *Relationes* describes his part in the affair. His letters were edited by his son in 10 books, 9 of private correspondence, of no great interest; the tenth, *Relationes* (official correspondence), contains some useful historical material. [D R D]

Ed. O. Seeck (Berlin, 1883).

T

Tacitus, Cornelius (b. *c.* A.D. 55). Little is known of his family, which was probably from North Italy or Gallia Narbonensis. The Cornelius Tacitus mentioned in an inscription as finance officer of Gallia Belgica is almost certainly his father. More is known of his public career. After holding minor magistracies, he was given senatorial rank by Vespasian, was praetor in 88, consul in 97. In 112–13 he was governor of Asia. To fill the gaps, Syme suggests a 4-year period as commander of a legion *c.* 90, and another provincial governorship, perhaps of one of the German provinces, shortly after 100. In his private life we should note his marriage to the daughter of Julius Agricola (77), friendship with the younger ♦ Pliny, and high reputation as an orator, shown in his selection to deliver the funeral oration for Verginius Rufus (97), and to prosecute Marius Priscus (100). That he saw at close quarters the reign of terror in the last years of Domitian was of paramount importance in determining his attitude to the Empire.

His earliest work is the *Dialogus de oratoribus*, published *c.* 80. Four distinguished contemporaries (two of them from Gaul) discuss the decline in Roman oratory, and its future prospects. It reveals those powers of characterization fully displayed in the historical writings. He published no more under Domitian. In 98 came 2 historical monographs, the *Agricola* and the *Germania*. The *Agricola* is a biography of his father-in-law, written as a tribute to his memory. The peak of Agricola's career was his governorship of Britain (?77–?84), so there is a brief account of the earlier history of the province, and a fairly full one of Agricola's campaigns, especially in Caledonia. Infuriating to the student of Roman Britain by its avoidance of detail and of place-names, the *Agricola* gives an invaluable picture of the better type of provincial governor. Its last chapter is one of the noblest pieces of Latin prose. The *Germania* is an ethnographical account of Rome's most formidable enemies – the Germanic peoples beyond the Rhine and Danube frontiers. Though aware of the defects of the Germans, Tacitus accords them something of the colouring of the Noble Savage, in contrast to the corrupt Roman world.

His major historical works were composed under Trajan and Hadrian. The *Histories* came out between 104 and 109, the *Annals* not earlier than 117. Between them, they covered the period from the death of Augustus to the death of Domitian (14–96). There survive of the *Histories* Books I–IV, and part of V, of the *Annals* Books I–VI (incomplete), parts of XI and XVI, and XII to XV. A project for the work on the reigns of Nerva and Trajan, 'which I am reserving for my old age' (*Histories* I: 1), did not materialize.

Senator, historian, orator – all three contribute. As senator – and perhaps especially as a new man – he preferred the Old Republic at its worst to the Principate at its best. But he had played a part in the working of the great imperial machine. He knew it had come to stay. The problem was to secure a good man at the top. As a historian he shared the common Roman view (◊ Historiography, Roman) that it is human beings who count: the pattern of history is determined by the characters of those who wield power. The function of the historian is to reward virtue and punish vice at the bar of posterity (*Annals* III: 65). To do so required an elevation of thought and style, the true property of *eloquentia*. One of the greatest masters of Latin, Tacitus evolved a style uniquely fitted to his purpose. We can point to the influence of Sallust here or an echo of Virgil there, but the product is more than its ingredients. Intense, complex, subtle and sustained, it defies translation and reserves its full flavour for the connoisseur. But all can derive pleasure from his irony, wit and innuendo, and admire the dignified pessimism of his outlook 'so precarious is the condition of man in all the affairs of life' (*Annals* III: 18).

The surviving books of the *Histories* justify his description of a period 'rich in catastrophe, fearful in its battles, fertile in mutinies – bloody even in peace'. The terrible events of the year of the Four Emperors (69), the great battles, the burning of the Capitol, the rebellions in Gaul, are brilliantly described. The characters of contenders for power and their principal lieutenants stand out in vivid colours.

But his full powers are reserved for the *Annals*, especially the first six books, which deal with the reign of Tiberius (14–37). The claim that they are written 'without bias or partisanship' is not accepted. Seeing in Tiberius the archetype of Domitian, Tacitus builds up against him a tremendous indictment, whose details may be discredited without erasing the total impression. Some of the other leading characters in these and the later books – Sejanus, Messalina, Agrippina, Nero – are unforgettable. Carefully selected, the secondary characters are drawn with firm but economical strokes – members of the Imperial family, Roman commanders, the chieftains of the barbarian north, eastern kings and princes. There are group characters, the Roman common soldier, in triumph or disaster, the Senate, collectively supine, yet containing men who know how to die. The scenes alternate between Rome and the frontiers (Germany, Britain, the Euphrates), the world of the court and capital, and that of the army camps. There is little about the peaceful life of the provinces, the real glory of the *pax romana*.

Criticism has been directed against Tacitus's use of his sources, his defects as a military historian, and his settled bias against the Empire. He is vulnerable on all these counts. But the trend of modern scholarship is to try to reach a fuller understanding of those positive qualities which set him in the very front rank of historians. [D R D]

OCT: *Annales* C. D. Fisher (1906), *Historiae* C. D. Fisher (1911), *Opera minora* H. Furneaux (1900); *Annals* i–vi, ed. H. Furneaux (1896), xi–xvi, ed. H. Furneaux, H. F. Pelham and C. D. Fisher (1907); Loeb: *Agricola, Germania* M. Hutton (1914); *Dialogus* W. Peterson (1914), *Histories* C. H. Moore (2 vols., 1925–31), *Annals* J. Jackson (3 vols., 1931); *Agricola, Germania*, tr. H. Mattingly (Penguin Classics, 1948); *Annals*, tr. M. Grant (Penguin Classics, 1956), tr. D. R. Dudley (1966).

R. Syme, *Tacitus* (2 vols., 1958); Clarence E. Mendell, *Tacitus, the Man and His Work* (New Haven, 1957).

Terence (Publius Terentius Afer) (?195–159 B.C.). Roman comic poet. Born at Carthage, but of Libyan parentage, he was brought to Rome as a young slave. His talents and good looks won him an education, manumission, and entry to a patrician literary circle, with whose encouragement he wrote 6 plays, produced between 166 and 160. Although he became, after ◊ Plautus, the leading adapter of Greek New Comedy for the Roman stage, only one of his plays, the *Eunuchus*, was a popular success, for his art appealed mainly to connoisseurs. Rivals accused him of 'contaminating' his Greek sources, but in his prologues he defended himself, besides denouncing the stupidity of an unappreciative public. He died in 159 during a visit to Greece.

All Terence's plays were ◊ *fabulae palliatae*, mainly taken from ◊ Menander. In the *Andria* (*The Girl from Andros*, 166), two love-intrigues are interwoven, and the main plot is resolved by the discovery that the supposed Andrian girl is the long-lost daughter of an Athenian. The *Hecyra* (*The Mother-in-Law*, 165), with its sentimental plot of a ravished heroine and her young husband's ultimate discovery that he is the father of her child, resembles the *Arbitration* of Menander. The *Heauton Timorumenos* (*The Self-Punisher*, 163) amusingly contrasts two fathers, one formerly excessively harsh but now remorseful, the other all too indulgent, and the love-affairs of their respective sons. The *Eunuchus* (*The Eunuch*, 161) combines the love-intrigues of two brothers with the deception of a braggart soldier and his toady. The *Phormio* (161) concerns two cousins who fall in love while their fathers are abroad, and is named after a resourceful parasite who helps them to circumvent the father's opposition. The *Adelphoe* (*The Brothers*, 160) interestingly contrasts the upbringing of two brothers by a strict father and an indulgent uncle respectively; when strictness fails, the father, in a curious volte-face perhaps derived from the Greek original, becomes embarrassingly genial.

The accusation of 'contamination' against Terence is traditionally, and probably rightly, interpreted as meaning that he conflated his Greek sources, as he claims to have done in the *Andria, Eunuchus* and *Adelphoe*. The stereotyped character of Greek New Comedy no doubt reduced the difficulty of transposing characters or incidents, but Terence showed considerable skill in reconstruction, invention and rewriting. He is more refined than Plautus, with a corresponding loss of comic vigour; his characters are no longer farcical caricatures, but are depicted with Menandrean restraint and realism. Adapting structure, not content, Terence did not romanize, but presented Greek New Comedy with its Athenian setting and conventions intact, and with no concessions to Roman parochialism or popular taste. He reproduced the Attic style of the originals in Latin equally pure and elegant, without the native verbal humour that Plautus exploited to such effect. Inevitably his somewhat bloodless comedy was eclipsed by the cruder amusements of contemporary Roman festivals; but his refinement was greatly admired by sophisticated critics in the late Republic and early Empire. Universally known and studied in the Middle Ages and later, his work inspired the Christian comedies of Hroswitha and deeply influenced the comedy of manners in modern European literature. (⇨ Comedy, Roman.) [G T W H]

OCT: R. Kauer and W. M. Lindsay (1959). Commentaries: S. G. Ashmore (1910); *Andria*, G. P. Shipp (1959); *Phormio*, R. H. Martin (1959); *Hecyra*, T. F. Carney, *Proceedings of the African Classical Associations*, Suppl. ii (1963). Translations: Loeb, J. Sergeaunt (2 vols., 1914); L. Echard, ed. R. Graves (1963); B. Radice (Penguin Classics, 3 plays, 1965).

G. Norwood, *The Art of Terence* (1923); Beare, *RS*.

Terpander (fl. *c.* 675 B.C.). Greek musician and poet. From Antissa in Lesbos. His well-attested victory at the Carneia in Sparta was in 676–673. He reintroduced the 7-string lyre to the Greek world, and dominated the contemporary musical scene. He composed nomes (settings of epic words, whether his own or others', to the lyre); preludes (introducing the singing of epic); and drinking-songs. His prestige was such that others' work became attached to his name, as happened also with Homer. It is unlikely that any of the surviving fragments attributed to him are authentic. [D E W W]

Tertullianus, Quintus Septimius Florens (A.D. *c.* 160–*c.* 225). Latin Christian writer. Trained in jurisprudence and an advocate of repute at Rome, Tertullian returned to his native Carthage after his conversion to Christianity *c.* 193, and embarked upon a literary career in the service of his new faith. At the latest by 207, he broke with the Church and became a member of the rigorist Montanist sect, finally leading a party of his own, the Tertullianists, which survived until the days of Augustine. His death must be placed after 220.

Well versed in law, philosophy and Greek and Latin letters, Tertullian was an enthusiast with a gift for biting satire and passionate eloquence; his dialectic is dazzling rather than convincing, owing to his impatience and his inclination to extremes. His mastery of Latin was remarkable and it has been estimated that he invented some 982 new words. To call him 'the creator of ecclesiastical Latin' is probably to go too far, since the older translations of the Bible provided him with part of his vocabulary, but his many neologisms did become part of the technical language of dogma.

Of Tertullian's treatises 31 have survived, and while some may be dated with a measure of certainty, most can be no more than assigned to his Catholic or Montanist periods. These works, all polemical in character, may be divided into three groups: apologetic, controversial and moral-ascetic.

To the first group belongs his earliest essay, *To the Heathen* (197), an attack on paganism and a defence of Christianity, which may be regarded as a provisional draft for the *Apology*. The latter is Tertullian's masterpiece. Juridical in form and restrained in expression, it refutes the charges of contempt for the State religion and of high treason. In the vein of the Hellenist philosophers such as Posidonius, Tertullian argues for the existence of God in *The Testimony of the Soul* (197) and the same breadth of vision characterizes *To Scapula* (212), with its assertion that 'it is a fundamental human right, a privilege of nature, that every man should worship according to his own convictions', and hence Tertullian's attack on the Proconsul of Africa for his persecution of Christians.

Tertullian's legal training is evident in the first of his controversial treatises, *The Prescription of Heretics* (*c.*200). He invokes the law of *praescriptio*, which is a juridical objection to bar a suit in the form in which the plaintiff enters it, and he argues that the heretics have no basis for their teaching, since the Bible to which they appeal is not theirs by right. Tertullian was nevertheless prepared to attack heretical ideas one by one and his *Against Marcion* (207–12) is a main source for the beliefs of that gnostic, since it refutes him point by point. Other gnostics were in his purview when he wrote *Against Hermogenes*, and *Against the Valentinians*, while the docetic strand in their teaching was opposed in *On the Flesh of Christ* and *The Resurrection of the Flesh*. *On Baptism* (198–200) is also anti-heretical, in that it attacks the views of the sect of Caius, but it is more justly famous as the sole ante-Nicene treatise on any of the sacraments. *Against Praxeas* (213) defends the doctrine of the Trinity against the modalistic monarchians.

To his pre-Montanist period probably belongs a number of his moral writings, such as *To the Martyrs*, an encouragement to steadfastness; *The Shows*, a vigorous condemnation of public games on the grounds of their immorality and idolatrous associations; *On the Dress of Women*, which applies Christianity to the smallest details of everyday life; and *Concerning Prayer*, which is not philosophical but essentially practical in its advice. After his defection to Montanism, Tertullian expressed his extreme rigorism in *On the Soldier's Chaplet* which discusses the participation of Christians in military service; in *Concerning Flight in Persecution* (212), which contends that no escape should be attempted, and in *Monogamy* (217), which condemns second marriages.

Tertullian's writings reveal his familiarity with rhetorical techniques and his indebtedness to the 'Asianic' manner of Greek orators. He has a predilection for short sentences, which frequently produce memorable epigrams. Questions and brief answers, antitheses and even puns abound. His brevity occasionally renders his thought obscure, but his position in the history of Christian Latin cannot be denied. [J G D]

Ed. F. Oehler (Leipzig, 1853); tr. S. Thelwall and others (N P F, 1868–70); Loeb: *Apology*, T. R. Glover (1931).

J. Quasten, *Patrology*, ii (1953).

Thales (fl. *c.*585 B.C.). Greek philosopher. Thales of Miletus was first of the great Ionian physicists. He is said to have visited Egypt, speculated about the Nile floods, and found how to measure the height of the pyramids. Herodotus says that he predicted the solar eclipse of 585 B.C. He was the first to ask the question. 'What is the basic substance of which the universe is made?' His answer, water, presumably derives from his study of meteorology. Tradition varies as to whether he wrote anything. [D R D]

Theocritus (*c.*310–250 B.C.). Greek pastoral poet. Born at Syracuse, Sicily was the scene of his early life and writings. Soon after 275 he went to Cos, to join the 'School of Poets' associated with Philetas. For a few years (*c.*270) he was in Alexandria, where he won favour at the court of Ptolemy Philadelphos. He probably returned to Cos, where he worked for the rest of his life.

It is not really possible to date his poems, and it is best to group them by subject and setting. Poems I, III, IV, V, VI, X, XI and XXVII are the true pastoral poems – the fountain-head, indeed, of that whole genre, which has had so long and diversified a career among the literatures of Europe. This, now, suggests artificiality; it is all the more necessary to insist that behind the poems of Theocritus lies the real and timeless world of the pastoral uplands of Sicily and southern Italy. Moreover, as the peasant culture of the West of Ireland lies behind the plays of Synge, so does that of the shepherds, fishermen and goatherds of Sicily behind Theocritus. Such a popular culture is still to be found in the ballads of modern Greece or Yugoslavia. Written in a literary Doric, the pastoral poems of Theocritus were highly popular in the great cities of the Hellenistic world. Cos is the setting of VII, a wonderful evocation of a summer day and the harvest in the Aegean; XVI and XVII are court poems, addressed to Hiero of Syracuse and Ptolemy Philadelphos respectively; II, 'The Love Charm', is one of Theocritus's finest; XV, the 'Women at the Festival of Adonis', is a witty and realistic picture of two Syracusan ladies, now suburban housewives in Alexandria. Of the others, XXIV and XXV deal with the myth of Heracles, XXVI with that of Pentheus; XIX is a Wedding-Song, XXII a Hymn to the Dioscuri; VIII, IX, XIII, XX and XXIII of our corpus are probably not by Theocritus. There are a number of epigrams by him, mostly written for tombs and statues. [D R D]

Ed., tr. and comm. A. S. F. Gow (2 vols., 1952); Loeb: J. M. Edmonds, *The Greek Bucolic Poets* (1912).

R. J. Cholmely, *The Idylls of Theocritus* (1919).

Theodorus. ⇨ Cyrenaics.

Theognis (second half of 6th cent. B.C.). Greek gnomic elegist. Some 1,390 lines attributed to him survive in a series of short elegies, mostly 1 to 6 couplets long. Much of this is by other hands; borrowings can be identified from ⇨ Tyrtaeus, ⇨ Mimnermus and ⇨ Solon. Theognis's own work must have been expanded into this anthology of varied date and provenance, but with general similarity of theme (thus the poems of the brief second book are all erotic and of Athenian provenance). The collection expresses the aristocrat code of behaviour in short but accomplished elegiac poems perhaps intended for singing or recitation at symposia. The personality of Theognis himself emerges most clearly in the opening 254 lines of Book I, which form a unity and include the 'seal' of authenticity (probably the mention of the author's name). He reveals himself as a Megarian living in the second half of the 6th century B.C., and facing with resolute despair a changing world and the destruction of his class and its traditions. He addresses himself to the youthful Cyrnus; their close friendship, with its erotic undertones, is characteristic of Theognis and of the Greek aristocratic society he represents. He records his feelings, mostly of fear, disillusionment and bitterness, with candour and sincerity, in a fresh and lively style, showing a fluent and easy command of the elegiac medium. [D E W W]

Diehl, *A L G*, i.

Bowra, *E G E*.

'Theogony'. ⇨ Epic Cycle; Hesiod.

Theophrastus (?372–?288 B.C.). Greek Peripatetic philosopher. President of the School after Aristotle. A native of Lesbos, studied philosophy at Athens, at first as a pupil of Plato. From him he probably learned the principle of classification as a guide to knowledge, exemplified in all his work. Later he became the friend and colleague of Aristotle, who left him his library and his Athenian estate – the Lyceum – in his will. From 322 to his death Theophrastus was President of the School, said to have had more than 2,000 students from all parts of the Greek world. His phenomenal powers of work enabled him to lecture and write on all the subjects studied in the School – politics, ethics, religion, education, rhetoric, mathematics, botany, astronomy, logic, meteorology. The titles of some 270 works attributed to him are known. Of those that survive, the works on botany are much the most important. The *Enquiry into Plants* (9 books) and the *Aetiology of Plants* (6 books) form the first great systematic botany; between them they give a description and classification, with notes on the habitat and physiology, of the plants of the eastern Mediterranean and parts of western Asia. For the first group the field-work seems to have been done by Theophrastus's pupils, for the second, by the scientists attached to Alexander's Persian expedition. The style is dry and technical: they may well be lecture notes. The *Characters* (published 319 B.C.) attempt a typology of human characteristics on the same lines. It has been plausibly suggested that they are a *jeu d'esprit*, written for entertainment at the monthly dinners of the School. Since Theophrastus is said to have been a skilful mimic, the specimens submitted were no doubt soon identified. The characters seem to have been collected in 2 volumes, the Good and the Bad, of which only the Bad survive. There are 30 of them (Beastliness, Grossness, Garrulity, Arrogance, Superstitiousness, Meanness, Late Learning, etc.), and they are amusing. There are also some short treatises on miscellaneous scientific problems. [D R D]

O C T: *Characters*, H. Diels (1909); *Characters*, tr. and comm. Sir Richard Jebb and J. E. Sandys (1909); Loeb: *Enquiry into Plants*, A. F. Hort (2 vols., 1916), *Characters*, J. M. Edmonds (1929); *Characters*, tr. P. Vellacott (Penguin Classics, 1967).
T. Gomperz, *Greek Thinkers*, iv (tr. 1912).

Theopompus (b. *c.* 378 B.C.). Greek historian. Born in Chios, he was exiled for some years on account of the pro-Spartan sympathies of his father Damasistratus. He was restored by Alexander, but was expelled again some time after Alexander's death and fled to Egypt.

He was a pupil of ⇨ Isocrates at Athens, who encouraged him to turn from oratory to history. He was a rich man, able to travel widely to collect material. His 2 most important works were the *Hellenica*, in 12 books, continuing the history of Thucydides from 411 to 394 B.C., and the *Philippica*, a history of Greece under Philip of Macedon, but containing many digressions. Of his works there survive only fragments quoted by later authors.

Theopompus was a learned man who went to great trouble in carrying out first-hand research, but his value as a historian is impaired by violent prejudices. For example, he attacks most of the Athenian political leaders for venality and corruption, and, having chosen Philip of Macedon as the hero of his work, he accuses the king and his associates of every kind of vile practice. [T A D]

Jacoby, *F G H*, ii.

Thespis (6th cent. B.C.). Greek poet. Tradition credits him with the invention of ⇨ tragedy. A native of Icaria in Attica, he may have begun his career as early as 560, but he produced a tragedy in a competition at Athens for the first time about 534. He was the first to appear in tragedy as an actor playing a part and delivering a prologue and set speech. He experimented with various facial disguises, perhaps to permit changes of role, and finally adopted a mask of linen. By admitting dialogue into a hitherto choral performance he converted it into a rudimentary form of drama. [G T W H]

Pickard-Cambridge, *D T C*.

Thucydides (*c.* 455/460–*c.* 399 B.C.). Greek historian. His father, Olorus, was probably the grandson of the Thracian king Olorus who was the maternal grandfather of Cimon, son of Miltiades. It is significant that Thucydides had property in Thrace and was buried in Cimon's family vault. He was also probably related to the old opponent of Pericles, Thucydides son of Melesias. In politics he was, by family connexions at any rate, a right-wing democrat, but he became a strong admirer of Pericles and his support for him may have increased as Pericles moved into a more central position in Athenian politics on the rise of extreme democrats like Cleon. Elected general in 424, Thucydides was given the task of protecting the Thracian coast, but he failed to save the treasured Athenian colony of Amphipolis against Brasidas, was condemned in his absence, and compelled to withdraw into exile. He did not return to Athens until 404, at the end of the Peloponnesian War, and he died a few years later.

Thucydides wrote a *History of the Peloponnesian War* in 8 books. He had intended to carry it down to the capture of Athens in 404, but breaks it off in the winter of 411/410. He started collecting material for his work at the very outset of the war, for he realized that the struggle, which in company with other Athenian leaders he may well have foreseen, would be violent and protracted. Spending three quarters of the war in exile, he made full use of this admirable opportunity to get first-hand information from both sides. His acknowledged purpose is to provide an accurate record of the conflict, of permanent value to future generations. In his introduction

(I: 22), he claims that his record of events is the result of careful investigation and the examination of eye-witnesses. For the speeches (which illustrate public opinion, the morale of the troops, and the political issues at stake at various stages of the war), he does not claim such accuracy, but maintains that he set out the arguments that he thought the speakers would have used while keeping as closely as possible to the substance of what was actually said. It is often argued that the speeches are his own free compositions, based solely on what seemed appropriate in the circumstances; but this disregards the plain statement of Thucydides himself, and it seems better to believe that the speeches were actually delivered, and their substance was reproduced by Thucydides as accurately as could be expected.

Of the 8 books written, Book I contains an introduction, giving the author's motives for writing his history, a brief summary of early Greek history to substantiate his claim that the present war was more important than any that had preceded it, a description of the military incidents at Corcyra and Potidaea and the diplomatic exchanges that led up to the outbreak of hostilities, and an account of the growth of Athenian power from the end of the Persian War; this latter illustrates his contention that it was the Spartan fear of the growth of Athenian power that was the chief cause of the war; it also serves as a direct continuation of the history of ⇨ Herodotus. Books II–IV describe the main events of the Archidamian War, with the Plague (from which Thucydides himself suffered) and the Funeral Speech (Pericles presenting an idealized picture of Athens) in II, the revolt of Lesbos in III, and the capture of the Spartan garrison on Sphacteria and the loss of Amphipolis to Brasidas in Book IV. Book V contains the deaths of Brasidas and Cleon, the Peace of Nicias, the Mantinean War and the subjugation of Melos. Books VI and VII describe the Sicilian expedition, and VIII, unfinished, the revolt of the Athenian allies and the naval warfare off the coast of Asia Minor. The work was probably not finally completed until after Thucydides' return to Athens in 404.

Thucydides is a very great historian. He aims at, and achieves, a high degree of accuracy; he is generally impartial and free from prejudice; as an experienced soldier he is able to convey a full understanding of the battles that he describes, and his comments on the vicious effects of the war upon the characters of the Greeks are intelligent and illuminating, without any trace of sermonizing. It has been said, with some truth, that his appreciation of higher strategy is faulty; for example, he gives the impression that the strategy of Pericles at the start of the war was wholly defensive, and ignores the determined attempt to isolate Corinth by the attack on Epidaurus. It has also been argued recently that in his picture of Cleon he is guilty of the same deliberate distortion of facts as Tacitus was in his portrayal of Tiberius. But these criticisms are of little importance when set against the general merits of the historian.

Thucydides wrote in a plain, austere style, well suited to the narration of great events. In his speeches, his love of abstract expressions and the obscurity of some of his antitheses make his meaning difficult to follow at times, especially in comparison with the lucidity of his narrative prose.

The history of Thucydides is that of the clash between the two great powers of the Greek world. The subject is always handled at a very high level, and there is no room for the plethora of gossip, scandal and anecdote that became so popular with later writers. The historian's interest in individuals was focused on the part they played in the struggle he was describing rather than on their personalities; his treatment of his theme was closer to the dramatic than to the heroic, and the world that he portrayed was an adult world which never lost touch with reality. [T A D]

OCT: H. Stuart Jones and J. G. Powell (2 vols., 1942); comm. A. W. Gomme (1945); Loeb: C. F. Smith (4 vols., 1919–23); tr. Rex Warner (Penguin Classics, 1954).

G. B. Grundy, *Thucydides and the History of His Age* (2nd edn, 2 vols., 1948).

Tiberianus (fl. A.D. 335). Latin poet. Little is known of his career, and his poems survive only in fragments, the best of which is a passage of 20 trochaic tetrameters describing a river (*amnis ibat*) and the scenery along its banks. It is marked by a feeling for nature, but the suggestion that its author also wrote the much finer ⇨ *Pervigilium Veneris* is not generally accepted. [D R D]

Fragments in Loeb: Duff, *M L P.*

Tibullus, Albius (?48–19 B.C.). Roman elegist. Of equestrian rank, handsome, cultured and well-to-do. Although some of his family estate was confiscated after the Civil War, he retained his property at Pedum and his complaints of poverty are not to be taken seriously; he addresses his patron Messalla on terms of equality. He accompanied Messalla on his Aquitanian campaign, and on a mission to the Near East during which Tibullus fell ill and was left behind on Corcyra. Horace and Ovid were personal friends.

Three books of poetry (the *Corpus tibullianum*) have come down from antiquity under his name (the subdivision of III into 2 separate books dates from the Renaissance). Book I, published *c.*26 B.C. contains 5 elegies (1, 2, 3, 5, 6) inspired by Delia (a pseudonym for Plania); in Ovid her name stands for Book I, as does Nemesis for Book II. Three elegies (4, 8, 9) are concerned with love of a boy, Marathus. In addition there are poems in honour of Messalla's birthday (7), and in praise of peace and condemnation of war (10). Book II comprises only 6 elegies; three (3, 4, 6) about Nemesis, a much harder and less sympathetic mistress than Delia. The opening poem, a description of the *Ambarvalia* but skilfully linked with the erotic theme, is Tibullus's masterpiece. There are also birthday greetings to Cornutus (2), and rejoicings at the installation of Messalinus as *quindecimvir* (5).

Book III is a collection of minor poetry by various hands, the bond linking them together being membership of Messalla's circle. The first 6 elegies are by Lygdamus; next follows the anonymous *Panegyric of Messalla* in 211 pedestrian hexameters, obsequious, ingratiating and tasteless. The 5 short poems of *Sulpicia's Garland* come next, sympathetically recording her affair with Cerinthus, and leading on to her own 6 brief elegies which follow immediately. The author of the *Garland* is a considerable poet. There are grounds for identifying him with Tibullus, though Ovidian echoes suggest a later author. The final erotic elegy and epigram which round off the collection may be authentic early Tibullan work.

Tibullus achieves a loose-knit simplicity of thought and language which conceals his artistry. Avoiding Alexandrian erudition, mythological illustration and rhetorical overstatement, he escapes into the unspoiled life of the countryside, much as Virgil does in the Eclogues. The ebb and flow of his thought reflects perfectly the wavering moods of the lover oscillating between rapture and despair. No Latin poet moves more easily from fantasy to reality and back again. The warmth of his personality and his unaffected pleasure in the simple good things of life enlist the reader's sympathies; he finds and communicates some of the peace he seeks in a war-distracted world. [D E W W]

Ed. and comm. K. F. Smith (1913); Loeb: J. P. Postgate (1913).

Timaeus (*c.*356–260 B.C.). Greek historian. The son of Andromachus, who made himself tyrant of Tauromenium in Sicily. He was expelled from Sicily by Agathocles, the tyrant of Syracuse, *c.*315, and spent the next 50 years at Athens, where he studied rhetoric and wrote his histories. His most important work was a history of Sicily in 38 volumes, extending down to 264. He established an accurate system of chronology, based on the 4-year Olympic periods, but he was violently attacked by ⇨ Polybius (XII) for inaccuracy, false statements, superstition, inadequate knowledge of geography and lack of practical experience of political and military affairs. These criticisms are probably overdone, and Cicero describes Timaeus as learned and eloquent. He seems to have been a typical arm-chair historian with no real critical ability and a taste for rhetoric who did his best by rather limited standards. [T A D]

Jacoby, *F G H*, iii.

Timocreon (fl. *c.*475 B.C.). Greek lyric and elegiac poet. Timocreon of Rhodes was celebrated for his gluttony, his boxing and his bitter tongue, and after the Persian invasion was exiled for medizing. He wrote lyrics, scolia and epigrams. He was a good hater, and his poetry was his weapon. Themistocles and ⇨ Simonides were among his antagonists; the latter immortalized him with the terse and deadly mock-epitaph preserved in the *Palatine Anthology* (VII: 348). His scanty surviving fragments have a sharp and vigorous tone, and are enlivened by the language of comedy and the beast-fable. [G T W H]

Loeb: J. M. Edmonds, *Lyra graeca*, ii (1924). Bowra, *G L P.*

Tisias. ⇨ Oratory and Rhetoric.

'Titanomachia' ('Battle of the Titans'). A lost Greek epic of uncertain date and authorship, variously attributed by ancient authorities to Arctinus of Miletus or Eumelus of Corinth (both probably 8th century B.C.), or to an anonymous poet. The theme was the struggle in which the youngest generation of the gods, Zeus and the other Olympians, overthrew their elders, the Titans, as rulers of the universe. The poem formed an early part of the ⇨ Epic Cycle. It consisted of at least 2 books, but only scanty fragments survive. [G T W H]

Testimonia and fragments in O C T *Homeri Opera*, v, ed. T. W. Allen (1912); Loeb: H. G. Evelyn-White, *Hesiod, The Homeric Hymns and Homerica* (1936).

Tragedy, Greek. The early history of Greek tragedy is obscure, but it seems to have developed out of a form of choral song commemorating the death of a king, performed in the cult of Dionysus in several parts of Greece. At Athens in the 6th century B.C. a tragedy competition was included in the newly organized festival of Dionysus, the Great ⇨ Dionysia, and ⇨ Thespis introduced a dramatic element into the performance. Thereafter, spurred by competition, development was rapid; the number of actors progressively increased, plots grew in complexity, and tragedy became more dramatic and less choral, until the lyrics were no more than interludes. In the hands of Phrynichus and the three great masters, ⇨ Aeschylus, ⇨ Sophocles and ⇨ Euripides, Athenian tragedy became the dominant form of 5th-century Greek literature. After a phase of Aeschylean grandeur it reached its highest perfection, by Aristotelian standards, under Sophocles about mid-century. Later it became less tragic, developing into political plays, tragicomedies and melodramas, mostly Euripidean; then, in the final years of the century, its creative period ended with two tragic masterpieces, and a period of decline set in, from which virtually nothing has survived.

Tragedy, like comedy, was performed only twice a year at Athens, at the Dionysiac festivals in the late winter and spring. The theatre was a vast open-air auditorium on the southern slope of the Acropolis, with the circular dancing floor for the chorus at its focal point; its great scale, and the masks and cumbersome costumes worn by the actors, precluded intimacy or precise nuances. Three tragedies and a ⇨ satyric drama were presented at a single performance, lasting several hours, by each of the three competing poets on successive days. All the parts, male and female, were played by men; their performance, in which episodes of dialogue alternated somewhat irregularly with choral song and dance to a flute accompaniment, has affinities with ballet, grand opera and Christian liturgy scarcely less than with modern poetic drama. The choral parts, whose metres varied subtly with the emotions expressed, were in elevated language in a conventional Doric dialect; most of the dialogue was in the more conversational iambics, and in a substantially Attic dialect. The unities of time and place were not strictly observed: a choral ode might mask an interval ranging from hours to weeks, and occasionally a complete change of scene. The setting varied, but generally represented a palace façade; scene-painting, probably simple, was used. Gods could appear on an upper level, above the human characters; other devices were the 'machine' or crane for flying entrances and exits, and the *ekkyklema*, which revealed an interior scene in a tableau.

According to Aristotle's famous definition, tragedy is a representation of a series of events in which the hero, who is neither saint nor villain, brings disaster on himself through error, and not through accident or wickedness; and the disaster should come about unexpectedly through a sudden change of circumstances, or a recognition of someone hitherto unrecognized, or (better still) both together. This was a counsel of perfection, and seldom fully achieved. Nevertheless tragedy was, as Aristotle indicates, a supremely impressive and potent form of art. It provided a collective emotional release for the audience in the contemplation of a fellow man in the toils of destiny, and deepened their understanding of the nobility and pathos of their human condition. [G T W H]

A. W. Pickard-Cambridge, *D T C*, and *The Theatre of Dionysus in Athens* (1946), A. Lesky, *Greek Tragedy* (1965); H. D. F. Kitto, *Greek Tragedy* (1961); R. Lattimore, *The Poetry of Greek Tragedy* (1958); T. B. L. Webster, *Greek Theatre Production* (1956); M. Bieber, *The History of the Greek and Roman Theater* (1961).

Tragedy, Roman. Tragedy first appeared at Rome, already fully evolved, in 240 B.C., when ⇨ Livius Andronicus began presenting Greek tragedies in translation. In these he adapted the metres of his Greek models to Roman practice, and established a regular form. His younger contemporary ⇨ Naevius similarly produced adaptations of Greek tragedy, and also founded a native counterpart in the ⇨ *fabula praetexta,* a Roman historical drama. He produced two such plays, based respectively on the early legends and recent history of Rome, but in a theatre in which the audience looked eagerly for topical allusions, and the authorities forbade praise or blame of any living person, it was difficult for his successors to follow his example, and few other *praetextae* are recorded. Tragedy, however, remained in vogue at Rome until the end of the Republic. ⇨ Ennius and then ⇨ Pacuvius continued the romanization of Greek originals, and chose their models carefully to suit the Roman taste for noble fortitude and dignified rhetoric; late in the 2nd century B.C. their successor ⇨ Accius sacrificed restraint to rhetorical effect, and made Roman tragedy increasingly melodramatic. The plays of all three were popular, and were often revived or read as classics. After the death of Accius, *c.* 85 B.C., the vein was worked out, and the production of new tragedies practically ceased. The writing of tragedy became a literary hobby for cultured amateurs. Under the Empire ⇨ Ovid wrote a *Medea* which was highly praised but probably not performed in the theatre, and tragedy for reading rather than acting was further developed by the younger ⇨ Seneca. His 9 surviving tragedies, based on the familiar, lurid Greek legends, use all the resources of Silver Age rhetoric to meet the requirements of performance by recitation, and with some success. The anonymous *Octavia,* on the fate of Nero's first wife, was written in a similar style soon after the emperor's death. The sole extant example of a *fabula praetexta,* it also marks the end of Roman tragic drama.

Tragedy at Rome was produced at major festivals and celebrations under the same makeshift conditions as Roman ⇨ comedy. The actors wore Greek costume in tragedy proper, and Roman dress in the *fabula praetexta*; in the former, at least, the performers were masked, and there was a chorus which, unlike the Greek chorus, took part in the action. Although tragedy was not as widely popular at Rome as comedy, it survived on the stage for some two centuries. Derivative as it was, and never wholly naturalized, it appealed to Roman audiences with its rhetoric and melodramatic extremes of vice and virtue. The surviving tragedies of Seneca, which preserve these qualities in concentrated form, strongly influenced the drama of the Renaissance and the Elizabethan theatre. (⇨ Tragedy, Greek.) [G T W H]

The Complete Roman Drama, tr. G. E. Duckworth (New York and Toronto, 1942).
Beare, *R S*; M. Bieber, *The History of the Greek and Roman Theater* (1961).

Trogus, Pompeius (fl. *c.* 10 B.C.). Roman historian. A Gaul from Gallia Narbonensis, son of Caesar's confidential secretary. He wrote works on natural history, and also a history of the non-Roman world in 44 books, epitomized by Justinus. [T A D]

L. E. Halberg, *De Trogo Pompeio* (1869).

Tryphiodorus. ⇨ Epic Poetry, Greek.

Tyrtaeus (7th cent. B.C.). Greek elegiac poet. His military command in the Second Messenian War and his dialect, Ionic but with Doric colouring, show that he was a Spartan. Parts of 9 poems survive. Their themes include the Messenian War, the divinely sanctioned Spartan constitution, and the praises of the good soldier – not the individual champion but the warrior fighting shoulder to shoulder with his peers in the hoplite phalanx. These are marching-songs breathing a martial spirit and the chauvinistic pride which was Sparta's strength and weakness. [D E W W]

Diehl, *A L G*, i.
Bowra, *E G E*.

V

Valentinus. ◊ Gnosticism.

Valerius Antias (fl. *c.* 80 B.C.). Roman historian. He wrote history of Rome from its foundation to his own day. His style is described as unattractive, but his worst fault is his disregard for the truth. Livy, himself no stern critic, is outspoken about his gross exaggerations, especially as regards enemy casualties, and his chronology is often confused. [T A D]

Peter, *H R R*, i.

Valerius Cato, Publius (b. *c.* 100 B.C.). Latin teacher, critic and poet. Born in Cisalpine Gaul, orphaned in childhood, and deprived of his patrimony under the Sullan proscriptions, he made an uncertain living by teaching and writing, and became the acknowledged leader of the ◊ *neoterici*. His grammatical studies and his interest in personal subjective poetry led him to interpret, perhaps to edit, ◊ Lucilius. His original work included the *Indignatio*, a protest against persecution by his enemies, an ◊ *epyllion* entitled *Diana* or *Dictynna*, and the *Lydia*, a love poem blending mythological erudition and eroticism in the Alexandrian tradition. [D E W W]

Valerius Flaccus (d. A.D. *c.* 90). Little is known of his life; on internal evidence he seems to have been a member of one of the great priestly colleges. His *Argonautica* survives, incomplete, in 8 books; it was started in about 70. The model is ◊ Apollonius Rhodius, but there are original episodes. Parallels with the *Aeneid* are frequent (e.g. the underworld scene in Book I); the verse style is close to the hexameters of Ovid. But Valerius has merits of his own. He is good in descriptive passages. His Medea is flesh and blood, though she owes much to Dido. It has been supposed that, in the later books, he intended to bring Jason home via the Danube, the Rhine and the North Sea, thus allowing a description of Britain out of compliments to Vespasian (or Domitian?). (◊ Epic Poetry, Roman.) [D R D]

Loeb: J. H. Mozley (1934).

Valerius Maximus (fl. A.D. *c.* 31). Roman historian and moralist. Friend and protégé of Sextus Pompeius (consul A.D. 14), whom he accompanied to Asia when the latter was proconsul *c.* 27. Some time after his return, probably after the downfall of Sejanus in 31, he wrote his 9 books of *Memorabilia* – 'Noteworthy Words and Deeds' – a series of unconnected historical anecdotes collected for the purpose of illustrating human vices and virtues. The style of the work is rhetorical, the treatment of the material superficial, and the moralizing that fills much of it insincere. Valerius rarely considers whether the incidents he records as examples of a particular trait really call for praise or blame; and he has a narrow, shallow nationalism that gives an air of pompous priggishness. But some of his anecdotes are of historical interest, and he was popular during the Roman Empire and the Middle Ages. [T A D]

Teubner: C. Kempf (Leipzig, 1888).

Valerius Messalla Corvinus, Marcus (64 B.C.–A.D. 8). Roman general, administrator, orator and patron of letters. Of aristocratic birth he was studying at Athens with his contemporary Horace in 44. He supported Brutus at Philippi, joining forces later with Antony, and finally switching to Octavian, for whom he fought at Actium in 31, when they shared the consulship. Augustus made full use of his administrative and military gifts, which brought him a triumph over the Aquitani in 27, and a series of important governmental posts. Characteristically he resigned in 26 as prefect of the city, within a week of assuming office, on the grounds that it offended his republican principles. In fact he steered a skilful course through stormy waters – it was he who proposed the conferring of the title 'Father of his country' on Augustus in 2 B.C. With ◊ Pollio he was the leading orator of the day, speaking in a muted Ciceronian style but with an aristocratic candour and charm. He dabbled in literature, displaying his philhellenism and mastery of two languages by composing Greek prose and poetry, and in his later years wrote his memoirs and published works of antiquarian and grammatical research. His patronage was in the republican tradition of generous assistance on a personal basis. Tibullus and Ovid were the two great artists to benefit, but there must have been many lesser figures, and Book III of the *Corpus tibullianum* is a miscellaneous collection held together by the bond of his personality. [D E W W]

Valgius Rufus (1st cent. B.C.). Roman scholar and elegiac poet. He was a friend of Horace, Virgil and Maecenas. His book on herbs was cited by Pliny. Horace praises the sensuous melancholy of his *Elegies,* of which a few lines only survive. [D R D]

Teubner: Morel, *F P L.*

Varius Rufus (1st cent. B.C.). Roman writer. He was highly praised by his friends Horace and Virgil. He wrote a poem on the death of Caesar and a panegyric on Augustus. His tragedy *Thyestes* (performed 29 B.C.) was, with Ovid's *Medea,* thought to stand comparison with Greek tragedy. After Virgil's death, he was ordered, with Plotius Tucca, to edit the *Aeneid* for publication. [D R D]

Teubner: Morel, *F P L.*

Varro, Marcus Terentius (116–27 B.C.). Roman polymath. Born at Reate, he studied at Rome under Aelius Stilo, and at Athens under Antiochus of Ascalon. Long-lived and hard-working, he achieved a prodigious output. He is credited with more than 600 books on a vast range of subjects, including grammar, linguistics, rhetoric, literary criticism, archaeology, history, religion, agriculture, law and mathematics – yet he was no cloistered scholar. He followed a public career that took him as far as the praetorship, saw service in the field under Pompey, had the courage to oppose the First Triumvirate, and the sense to make his peace with Caesar when there was no alternative. An appointment in 47 as the first public librarian in Rome left him free to devote all his energies to scholarship, probably with the help of several research assistants.

Of his immense output there survive (1) 3 books *On Agriculture,* a practical guide to Italian farming, based on the experience of running his Sabine estates, and begun when the author was 80, and (2) 5 books *On the Latin Language,* of interest mainly because they preserve fragments of earlier authors now lost.

Of his other works the most important seem to have been (1) the *Menippean Satires,* an early work, a satiric medley of prose and verse in the style of the Cynic ⇨ Menippus of Gadara, whose wit and humour come through in the fragments that survive, (2) the *Antiquitates,* a vast treasure-house of information on ancient customs and religious observance, (3) the *Imagines,* said to be the first illustrated book, containing 700 biographies of notable Greeks and Romans, and (4) the *Disciplinae,* an encyclopedia of the liberal arts, which gave rise to the *trivium* and *quadrivium* of medieval education. Varro's influence for the next thousand years was deep and far-reaching, though we lack the means for a more precise estimate than is contained in Quintilian's judgement – 'the most learned of the Romans'. [D R D]

Loeb: *On Agriculture,* W. D. Hooper and H. B. Ash (with Cato, 1934), and *On the Latin Language,* R. G. Kent (1938).

J. Wight Duff, *Roman Satire* (1937) (for the *Menippean Satires*).

Vegetius Renatus, Flavius (?) (fl. A.D. *c.* 400). Author of a military manual (*Epitoma rei militaris*). Written not earlier that A.D. 383, its 4 books deal with (1) training of recruits and construction of camps, (2) the legion and the duties of officers, (3) logistics and battle-tactics, (4) siege warfare and naval tactics. There is no evidence that Vegetius had a distinguished military record, and his work is largely a compilation from earlier writers, but it is logical and informative. [D R D]

Teubner: C. Lang (Leipzig, 1885).

Velleius Paterculus, Gaius (c. 19 B.C.–after A.D. 31). Roman historian. Born of a distinguished equestrian family, Velleius followed a military career, and served for some years as one of Tiberius's generals in Germany and Illyricum. He was quaestor in A.D. 7 and praetor in 15, but did not advance further. Little else is known of his life.

Velleius wrote a *History of Rome* from earliest times to A.D. 30, to celebrate the consulship of his friend M. Vinicius in that year. It is a patchy, uneven work, with little attention paid to chronology; the chief interest of the writer was not in the events but in the man who performed them, and he has left a number of vivid character-sketches of some of the leading personalities in Roman history – that of Pompey is particularly enlightening. Velleius also contains useful first-hand information of the wars in Germany and the Balkans, and corrects the prejudiced picture of Tiberius given in Tacitus. The style of the work is highly rhetorical, with many exclamations, exaggerations and laboured antitheses. [T A D]

Loeb: F. W. Shipley (1924).

Vespasian (Titus Flavius Vespasianus) (A.D. 9–79). Roman Emperor A.D. 69–79. In deliberate reaction against the policy of Nero in all points, Vespasian did not seek to make his mark as an author. His *Memoirs* (now lost) served a political purpose, the justification of his career. But he fostered literature, especially the historians (◊ Josephus, Pliny the Elder, Fabius Rusticus). He also found public chairs of Greek and Latin rhetoric in Rome – one of the first holders was ◊ Quintilian. How far he tried to stimulate higher education in the provinces is a matter of dispute. [D R D]

Bardon, *E L L.*

Virgil (Publius Vergilius Maro) (70–19 B.C.). Roman poet. (There is no doubt that Vergilius is the correct Latin form, but the misspelling Virgil is long domesticated in English.) The greatest of Roman poets was born at the village of Andes near Mantua, probably but not certainly the modern Pietole. The land was then part of Cisalpine Gaul, not Italy. A vigorous frontier province with a thriving agriculture, prosperous cities and a flourishing Latin culture, it had already produced such writers as ◊ Catullus, ◊ Caecilius and ◊ Cornelius Nepos. Virgil's parents were farmers, with means enough to give the boy a good literary education, first at Cremona and then at the provincial capital, Mediolanum (Milan). Later he unsuccessfully went to learn rhetoric at Rome, and left to study philosophy with Siro at the famous Epicurean school near Naples (◊ Epicureanism). That philosophy, and especially the work of its great expositor Lucretius, left its mark on him, though later it was inadequate for his deeper vision of life. Poor health seems to have debarred him from military service in the Civil Wars, and he devoted his time to reading and writing. This tenor of life looked like being shattered when, in 42, his estate became involved in the confiscations necessary to provide land-grants for discharged soldiers. Somehow – the details are obscure – Virgil's lands were returned to him, thanks to an appeal to Octavian.

A number of poems are ascribed to him as *juvenilia,* on more or less doubtful grounds (◊ Appendix Virgiliana). But his first authentic work bears the title of *Bucolics* (*Pastoral Poems,* also known as the *Eclogues*), and was written between 42 and 37. Poems in the tradition of ◊ Theocritus, they portray the singing-matches, loves and quarrels of shepherds and goatherds, against an idealized landscape which is a blend of Sicily, Arcadia, Campania and northern Italy. Such are II, III, VI, VII and VIII. These are poems of escape; elsewhere reality intrudes: I and IX deal with the evictions and their consequence (Octavian's generosity to Virgil is not allowed to gloss over the hard fate of the dispossessed); V is probably occasioned by the commemoration of the death of Julius Caesar; X (the latest) is in honour of the poet's friend Cornelius Gallus, to console him for a lost love and to predict for him fame as a poet; IV stands apart from the rest. Striking 'a somewhat louder strain', it is a polyphony in which the voices of the Sibyl, the oracle, and the nurse, are blended to foretell the birth of a miraculous child, who is to usher in peace and renew the Golden Age. This is the famous 'Messianic Eclogue', which seemed to the Middle Ages to prophesy the birth of Christ. With Virgil's contemporaries the *Eclogues* were an immediate success. The modern reader is likely to approach them more warily (IV excepted), having in mind the artificiality of so much later pastoral. Indeed, even in the *Eclogues,* it is sometimes wiser not to investigate too closely, and to forget that the dead shepherd lad of V is probably

Julius Caesar, while the romantic agonies of X undoubtedly represent the end of an affair between an ambitious politician and an expensive call-girl. Still, even here, the limpid sweetness of the verse and the genuine feeling for nature may induce a willing suspension of disbelief. The rest (apart again from IV) we may take at Virgil's own estimate of the pastoral *genre,* slight but charming.

By now Virgil enjoyed the patronage of ⇨ Maecenas, who gave him a house near Naples. He was also in touch with Octavian, and willingly subscribed to the larger hopes of the new regime. The connexion between the *Georgics* (published 29 B.C.) and Octavian's plans for the revival of Italian agriculture is clear, but they are a poet's vision and not a piece of imperial propaganda. They purport to be didactic poems, on the model of the *Works and Days* of ⇨ Hesiod. Book I deals with corn, II with vines and olives, III with cattle and horses, IV with bees (whose honey was a staple in the absence of sugar) – all the main aspects of Italian agriculture except market-gardening. But the debt to Hesiod is slight, and the *Georgics* much more than a farmer's handbook. They derive from Virgil's conception, finely expressed in the Second Georgic, of Italy as *Saturnia tellus,* 'mighty mother of crops and men', the land uniquely fitted for agriculture. The best life for man is that of the Italian farmer, harsh and laborious, prone to setbacks and disappointments, but bringing the rewards of peace, true worth and honest content – and the only firm basis for the greatness of the state. Virgil's enthusiasm for his glorious theme makes the *Georgics* perhaps the supreme achievement of Latin poetry. Varied in tone but flawless in diction, alert to the particularity of bird and beast and flower, open to the changes of weather and season, they reach out beyond the Italy of Augustus and speak directly to all who care for life on the land.

The last 10 years of his life were devoted to his most ambitious project – an epic poem in honour of Rome. There had been earlier hints of the Civil War as a theme. A wiser choice was the legend of Aeneas, the Trojan hero who survived the fall of Troy, sailed westward with his father Anchises and his son Iulus to Italy, and married an Italian princess, to become the ancestor of the *gens Julia* and founder of Alba Longa. Its advantages were great. It provided a link with the Homeric poems without directly challenging Homer. Within the framework of a well-known legend there was ample room for new material. In Rome and Italy, Virgil could gather the legends dear to local and regional patriotism. But its very immensity drove Virgil, always acutely self-critical, to the edge of despair. He often said that he had been mad to undertake it, and he did not live to complete it. In 19 B.C. he left for a tour of Greece and the East to gather new material, caught a fever at Megara on his homeward voyage, and died soon after landing in Italy. He was buried near Naples, where his tomb soon became the object of pilgrimage. Disregarding the *proviso* in his will that the *Aeneid* should be destroyed, Augustus appointed his friends Varius and Tucca to edit and publish it, while forbidding them to add anything.

Despite some 60 unfinished lines and certain passages in draft only, the *Aeneid* in its 12 books is substantially complete. Book I, after introducing the poem's main theme, describes the great storm which brought Aeneas and his followers to the coast of Carthage and the hospitality of Dido. In a long after-dinner story Aeneas recounts, in Book II, the fall of Troy, in III, wanderings from Troy to Sicily. Book IV is devoted to the tragic love of Dido and Aeneas, which for a time seems likely, in defiance of fate, to link the destinies of Rome and Carthage. But Aeneas, in obedience to instructions from Jupiter himself, sails on, and Dido kills herself. Book V, a description of the funeral games for Anchises, provides a break in the tension. It builds up again in VI, when Aeneas, with the Sibyl of Cumae as his guide, goes down to the Underworld to receive from the spirit of Anchises the great revelation of the future of Rome. It is the turning-point of the poem. Aeneas finds the justification for all his suffering, the reader Virgil's final revelation of the divine plan for the world. In VII the Trojan fleet reaches the Tiber, and the Italian peoples muster for war. In VIII Aeneas sails up the river to the future site of Rome, and spends his first night ashore in the humble abode of Evander, on the very spot where

Augustus's own house was to stand. Vulcan forges for him a magic shield – the counterpart of the Homeric shield of Achilles – whose designs reveal a second prophecy of the future of Rome, and bear in the centre a picture of the battle of Actium. The last four books are devoted to the wars of the Trojans and the Latins. After many vicissitudes, the Italian cause is lost with the death of their great hero Turnus at the end of Book XII. We have been left in no doubt of the grandeur and universality of Rome's mission in the world. In the deaths of Dido, of Turnus, of Camilla, of Pallas, of Lausus and Euryalus, we have also learned something of its price.

The *Aeneid* moves on more than one level. At its simplest, it narrates the *res gestae* of Aeneas and his followers. Beyond that, it shows the men and the qualities required to make Rome great, as well as their opposites. Aeneas, as he develops into the ideal leader, may be seen as the archetype of Augustus; and certainly there is something of Cleopatra in Dido. On a deeper level still, it deals with the ultimate problems of human life and destiny. Criticism of the poem, in the main, is directed against its hero. Aeneas is said to be dull and priggish, a static character, stamped with the damning adjective *pius*, and in his treatment of Dido no more than a cad. Such views are imperceptive; they arise because, all too often, the poem is not read as a whole. To do this is to see Aeneas as a developing character, by no means devoid of human aims or personal weakness, but always, in the long run, able to subordinate them to a mission which he recognizes conscientiously but, at first, without enthusiasm. A man, in fact, who grows greater with his responsibilities, who comes in the end to accept freely the terrible burden placed on him, and who at last shakes off the Trojan past to face the Roman future. Even in the Dido episode, he can be defended. These are not young lovers, a Romeo and a Juliet, with nothing at stake beyond themselves. They are leaders – the fate of nations hangs on what they do. Nor does their relationship end with Book IV. We must not forget their last meeting in Book VI (455 ff.). Virgil has left no loose ends, and in this last encounter it is not Aeneas who is in the better case.

The *Aeneid* placed Virgil supreme among Roman poets, and a kind of Virgilian cult grew up. It also fostered a revival of epic poetry, but on the Silver Latin poets like ◇ Statius, ◇ Silius Italicus and ◇ Valerius Flaccus the unassailable majesty of the *Aeneid* had rather a stultifying effect. To the early Middle Ages Virgil was the greatest poet in the world; he dominates education as well as literature. He was also, through the fourth Eclogue, the 'prophet of the Gentiles', and the magician and thaumaturge of Neapolitan legend. In the later Middle Ages and the Renaissance there came a succession of great poets – Dante, Tasso, Camoens, Milton – on whom his influence was fruitful. Devoted to Virgil, they had something fresh and great to say, and they could meet him as one master meeting another. Because of his intrinsic merits, his many-sided influence, and his place in the majestic succession Homer–Virgil–Dante–Milton, Virgil stands closer than any other poet to the very heart of the culture of the West. [DRD]

OCT: Arthur Hirtzel (1900); Loeb: H. R. Fairclough (2 vols., 1916, 1934); *Aeneid:* ed. J. W. Mackail (1930); Book I, ed. R. S. Conway (1935); II, ed. R. G. Austin (1964); III, ed. R. D. Williams (1962); IV, ed. R. G. Austin (1955); VI, ed. E. Norden (4th edn, 1957); XII, ed. W. S. Maguinness (1953); tr. W. F. Jackson Knight (Penguin Classics, 1956); verse tr. C. Day Lewis (1952); *Bucolics*: tr. E. V. Rieu (Penguin Classics, 1949); verse tr. C. Day Lewis (1963); *Georgics:* verse tr. C. Day Lewis (1940).

W. F. J. Knight, *Roman Vergil* (1944); E. K. Rand, *The Magical Art of Virgil* (Cambridge, Mass., 1931); V. Pöschl, *The Art of Virgil*, tr. G. Seligson (1962); W. Warde Fowler, *Aeneas at the Site of Rome* (2nd edn, 1913); Brooks Otis, *Virgil: A Study in Civilized Poetry* (1963); Michael C. J. Putnam, *The Poetry of the Aeneid* (1965).

Vitruvius Pollio, Marcus (probably end of 1st cent. B.C.). Roman writer on architecture. He was, in all probability, a contemporary of Augustus. He is only known to have built the basilica at Fanum, and his importance derives from his writings. The *De architectura*, dedicated to the Emperor, 'contains all the branches of architecture, in ten books'. It is in fact a complete guide to Hellenistic and Roman practice in town-planning, architecture and civil engineering. Book I deals with architect's education (about which he had high ideals) and with town-planning, II with building materials, III with temples, IV with the Orders, V with fora and basilicas, baths, theatres, harbours, VI with siting, exposure and proportions of houses, VII with lime, stucco, frescoes and their colouring materials, VIII with water-supply, aqueducts, cisterns, etc., IX with astronomy, meteorology and the measurement of time, X with machines used in civil and military engineering. Though scarcely a work of literature, few books have been so influential. As the only surviving work on the architecture of antiquity, Vitruvius was accepted as an authority by the great architects of the Renaissance such as Bramante, Michelangelo, Palladio and Alberti. Through their influence, and that of their followers, buildings are to be found modelled on his precepts in many parts of the world, from St Petersburg to Louisiana, and from Scotland to the Dutch colonies of the Cape. [D R D]

Loeb: F. Granger (2 vols., 1931, 1934); tr. M. H. Morgan (New York, 1960).
Encyclopedia Britannica.

X

Xanthus (fl. *c.* 450 B.C.). Greek historian. Xanthus of Lydia wrote a *History of Lydia* in 4 books, and possibly a *Life of Empedocles* and a work on the Persian Magi. He is said by Ephorus to have inspired Herodotus to write history. [T A D]

L. Pearson, *Early Ionian Historians* (1939).

Xenocrates (339–315 B.C.). Greek philosopher. The third Head of the Academy. Xenocrates of Chalcedon seems to have been chiefly concerned in systematizing the philosophical legacy of Plato, and defending it against attack. His own interests – to judge from the titles of his works, all lost – lay in the fields of ethics and theology. [D R D]

Sarton, *H S*, ii.

Xenophanes (*c.* 570–*c.* 460 B.C.). Greek philosopher. Driven out of Ionia by the Persian invasion (545? B.C.) Xenophanes of Colophon went to western Greece, and travelled widely, though spending most of his time in Sicily, where he was one of the earliest teachers of philosophy. His views were set out in poems which he recited in public. He was especially well known for his attack on the anthropomorphic conception of the deity, and for the stories about the gods found in Homer and Hesiod. 'If horses or cattle had hands and could draw, they would draw the gods like horses and cattle. . . .' But in reality 'God is one, the greatest among gods and men, in no respect like mortals in body or thought.' Other fragments show his interest in the natural phenomena of Sicily, volcanic eruptions, the fossils in the quarries of Syracuse etc. [D R D]

Diels, *F V*, 21.

Xenophon (*c.* 430–*c.* 354 B.C.). Greek historian. Xenophon is best known for the leading part that he took in one of the greatest military exploits of the ancient world – the retreat of the Ten Thousand. A force of Greek hoplites, enlisted by Cyrus in his attempt to gain the Persian throne from his brother Artaxerxes, found themselves leaderless in the heart of Persia after the death of Cyrus in battle and the treacherous murder of their commanders; but they chose new generals, Xenophon and Chirisophus, and under their leadership fought their way out to reach the Greek cities on the southern shores of the Black Sea (400 B.C.).

Xenophon was an Athenian, but he spent most of his life in Sparta, to which he was greatly attached, and eventually died at Corinth. He seems to have been continually drawn towards men of strong personality, for he was a disciple of Socrates in his youth, attached himself to the Persian prince Cyrus, and for much of his life was a close personal friend of the great Spartan king Agesilaus.

Xenophon was a prolific and versatile writer. His most important works were: the *Anabasis*, an account of his adventures with the Ten Thousand; the *Hellenica*, a history of Greece from 411 (where Thucydides breaks off) to 362 B.C.; the *Cyropaedia*, an idealized biography of Cyrus the Great; the *Memorabilia*, anecdotes concerning Socrates; the *Apology*, a fictitious defence of Socrates, which gives further information about the real nature of the charges; the *Symposium*, an account of an imaginary party at which Socrates was present; the *Oeconomicus,* a pleasant discussion on household and estate management with interesting information on the position of women at Athens; *Hiero,* a dialogue on the art of being a beneficent ruler; a laudatory biography of Agesilaus and a laudatory account of the Spartan constitution; and various works on horsemanship, cavalry tactics, finance and hunting. The *Constitution of Athens,* which was ascribed to Xenophon, is a political pamphlet by an earlier writer.

As a historian, Xenophon is sometimes guilty of partiality and serious omissions. As a philosopher and moralist, he is superficial and borrows much from other writers. On military matters, however, he has an expert's knowledge and communicates an expert's interest. He can tell a good story well, his portrayal of character is skilful, his style is straightforward, and his books are enjoyable. [T A D]

OCT: E. C. Marchant (5 vols., 1900–21); Loeb: *Cyropaedia,* Walter Miller (2 vols., 1914), *Hellenica, Anabasis, Apology, Symposium,* C. L. Brownson and O. J. Todd (3 vols., 1918–22), *Memorabilia, Oeconomicus* E. C. Marchant (1923); *The Persian Expedition* and *Hellenica,* tr. Rex Warner (Penguin Classics, 1949 and 1966).

Z

Zeno (335–263 B.C.). Greek philosopher. The founder of Stoicism. Son of Mnaseas, of Citium in Cyprus, but perhaps of Semitic origin (Mnaseas = Manasseh?). He came to Athens to study philosophy in 313, and was at first attracted to Crates the Cynic (⇨ Cynics), then attended lectures at the Academy. Finally he set up his own school in the Stoa Poikile (hence the name Stoic). It flourished and attracted many disciples, the best known of whom were ⇨ Cleanthes, Herillus, Ariston and Sphaerus. He always remained sympathetic to Cynicism, and its influence was strong in his famous *Republic,* perhaps the first portrayal in literature of the World State of which all men are citizens, bound together by obedience to Universal Law. But his system was of a deeper intellectual content: it combined logic, physics and ethics into a new synthesis well suited to the changed conditions of the Hellenistic world, and destined for a vigorous life of at least five centuries. Only fragments of his writings survive. (⇨ Stoicism.) [D R D]

Arnim, *S V F.*
M. Pohlenz, *Die Stoa* (2 vols., Göttingen, 1948).

Zeno of Elea (fl. *c.* 450 B.C.). Greek philosopher. Zeno of Elea, in southern Italy, was a pupil of ⇨ Parmenides, in whose company he visited Athens *c.* 450. He is said to have died in a conspiracy against the tyrant Nearchus. His one book defended the system of Parmenides against the attacks of the pluralists by showing that his opponents' theses led to absurd conclusions. The fragments we have deal with problems of magnitude, space and motion. The well-known 'paradoxes' of Achilles and the tortoise, and of the flying arrow, belong to him. [D R D]

Diels, *F V,* 29.

Zenodotus (*c.* 325–*c.* 234 B.C.). Greek grammarian. Zenodotus of Ephesus, a pupil of Philetas, was appointed by Ptolemy Philadelphus as the first librarian at Alexandria (284). It fell to him to direct the library's first major research project, the production of standard texts of the Greek poets. Zenodotus worked on Theogius, Pindar, Hesiod and, especially, Homer. He collected manuscripts, obelized doubtful lines, and divided the *Iliad* and the *Odyssey* into 24 books. To accompany his editions he produced the *Homeric Glossary.* [D R D]

D. B. Munro, *Homer's Odyssey,* Appendix (1901).

RECOMMENDED READING

The following is a short list of books for further reading, selected from works published in English. Since it is limited, it cannot hope to be comprehensive, but in many cases good bibliographies will be found in the books mentioned here.

LITERATURE AND LANGUAGE

C. M. Bowra, *Landmarks in Greek Literature* (1966)

A. Lesky, *A History of Greek Literature* (1966)

J. W. Duff and A. M. Duff, *A Literary History of Rome to the Close of the Golden Age* (rev. impression 1962)

J. W. Duff and A. M. Duff, *A Literary History of Rome in the Silver Age* (3rd edn, 1964)

W. B. Stanford, *The Ulysses Theme: A Study in the Adaptability of a Traditional Hero* (1954)

M. Hadas, *Hellenistic Culture: Fusion and Diffusion* (1959)

T. B. L. Webster, *From Mycenae to Homer. Greek Art and Literature 700–530 B.C.* (1959)

T. B. L. Webster, *Hellenistic Poetry and Art* (1964)

J. Whatmough, *Poetic, Scientific and Other Forms of Discourse: A New Approach to Greek and Latin Literature* (1956)

L. P. Wilkinson, *Golden Latin Artistry* (1963)

L. R. Palmer, *The Latin Language* (1954)

G. Thomson, *The Greek Language* (1960)

H. I. Marrou, *A History of Education in Antiquity* (1956)

R. R. Bolgar, *The Classical Heritage and its Beneficiaries* (1954)

G. Highet, *The Classical Tradition, Greek and Roman Influences on Western Literature* (1949)

HISTORY AND SOCIAL LIFE

General Histories

The Cambridge Ancient History (Vols. IV–XII, 1926–39)

History of the Greek and Roman World. Greece: Vol. II (479–323 B.C.), M. L. W. Laistner (2nd edn, 1947); Vol. III (323–126 B.C.), M. Cary (2nd edn, 1951); Rome, 753–146 B.C., H. H. Scullard (2nd edn, 1951); 146–30 B.C., Frank Burr Marsh (2nd edn, 1953); 30 B.C.–A.D. 138, Edward P. Salmon (3rd edn, 1957); A.D. 138–A.D. 337, H. M. D. Parker (1935)

N. G. L. Hammond, *A History of Greece to 322 B.C.* (1959)

M. Rostovtzeff, *Social and Economic History of the Hellenistic World* (1941)

M. Rostovtzeff, *Social and Economic History of the Roman Empire* (2 vols., revised by P. M. Fraser, 1957)

A. H. M. Jones, *The Later Roman Empire* (3 vols., 1964) (now published in a shorter version as *The Decline of the Ancient World*, 1966)

C. G. Starr, *A History of the Ancient World* (1965)

C. G. Starr, *Civilization and the Caesars: The Intellectual Revolution in the Roman Empire* (1954)

M. I. Finley, *The Ancient Greeks* (Penguin Books, 1966).

D. R. Dudley, *Civilization of Rome* (Paperback edn, 2nd printing 1962)
M. Grant, *The World of Rome, 133 B.C.–A.D. 217* (Paperback edn, 2nd printing 1964)

Early Greece

M. I. Finley, *The World of Odysseus* (1956)
A. R. Burn, *The Lyric Age of Greece* (1960)

The Greek City-States

A. Andrewes, *The Greek Tyrants* (1956)
V. Ehrenburg, *The Greek State* (1960)
A. R. Burn. *Pericles and Athens* (1948)
A. E. Zimmern, *The Greek Commonwealth* (5th edn, 1951).
T. Hill, *The Ancient City of Athens* (1953)

Alexander and the Hellenistic World

W. W. Tarn, *Alexander the Great* (1948)
W. W. Tarn and G. T. Griffith, *Hellenistic Civilization* (3rd edn, 1952)

Early Rome

R. Bloch, *The Origins of Rome* (1960)
M. Pallottino, *The Etruscans* (Penguin Books, 1955)

The Republic

H. H. Scullard, *From the Gracchi to Nero* (1959)
R. E. Smith, *The Failure of the Roman Republic* (1955)
A. N. Sherwin-White, *The Roman Citizenship* (1939)

The Roman Empire

R. Syme, *The Roman Revolution* (Paperback edn, 1960)
A. Momigliano, *The Emperor Claudius and His Work* (1934)
A. H. M. Jones, *The Cities of the Eastern Roman Provinces* (1939)
T. Mommsen, *The Provinces of the Romans* (2 vols., 1909)
G. H. Stevenson, *Roman Provincial Administration* (1939)
A. Alföldi, *The Conversion of Constantine and Pagan Rome* (1948)
Tenney Frank, *Economic Survey of Ancient Rome* (5 vols., 1933–40)

Christianity

P. Carrington, *The Early Christian Church* (2 vols., 1957)
C. N. Cochrane, *Christianity and Classical Culture* (Paperback edn, 1957)
A. D. Nock, *Conversion, The Old and the New in Religion from Alexander to Augustine* (1933)

Rome

E. Nash, *Pictorial Dictionary of Ancient Rome* (2 vols., 1961)
M. Scherer, *The Marvels of Ancient Rome* (1955)
J. Carcopino, *Daily Life in Ancient Rome* (Penguin Books, 1956)

WORKS OF REFERENCE, ATLASES, ETC.

Oxford Classical Dictionary (1949; a new edn in preparation)
Nairn's Classical Handlist (1953)
N. Lewis and M. Reinhold, *Roman Civilization* (source-material, 2 vols., 1955)
Atlas of the Classical World, ed. A. A. M. Van der Heyden and H. H. Scullard (1959)
Atlas of the Early Christian World, ed. F. Van der Meer and C. Mohrmann (1958)

BYZANTINE

A

Acominatus, Michael. ⇨ Choniates, Michael.

Acominatus, Nicetas. ⇨ Choniates, Nicetas.

Acropolites, George (1217–82). Byzantine historian. After holding high civil and military office under the Nicaean emperors John II Vatatzes and Theodore II Lascaris (whose tutor he was), Acropolites returned to Constantinople in 1261 as Rector of the newly restored university. His diplomatic missions took him as far as Lyons and Trebizond. His history of the Nicaean Empire, largely based on first-hand observation, covers the years 1203–61. Sober, intelligent and well informed, he does not quite make good his claim to impartiality. His style is archaizing but lucid. A number of minor rhetorical and theological works also survive. [R B]

Teubner: A. Heisenberg (2 vols., Leipzig, 1903).

Agathias (*c.*536–82). Byzantine historian and poet. Born in Myrina in Asia Minor, he studied in Alexandria and practised as an advocate in Constantinople. His unfinished *History of the Reign of Justinian* starts where ⇨ Procopius stopped, in 552, and goes on to 558, dealing mainly with the military operations of Narses against Ostrogoths, Vandals and Persians. His sources are mainly eye-witness accounts, though he says he also had Persian texts translated for him. He is in general favourable to Justinian's policy of expansion. He lacks Procopius's judgement and experience of affairs; and his florid, poetic style and delight in elaborating rhetorical commonplaces sometimes make his meaning obscure. But he provides a detailed, contemporary and very valuable account of the penultimate decade of Justinian's reign.

Agathias was a member of a circle of poets close to Justinian's court interested mainly in the occasional poem or epigram. He published a collection of these by his contemporaries and himself, many of which, including 100 by Agathias, appear in the Greek Anthology (⇨ p. 26). Fertile in imagination and a skilled versifier, he is too long-winded to be a successful epigrammatist. His best – and shortest – poems are his love-poems; many of the rest – epitaphs, dedications, descriptive poems etc. – are brief elegies rather than epigrams. The prologue to his collection, in 133 lines, throws an interesting light on the literary movement of his time. [R B]

Teubner: L. Dindorf, *Historici graeci minores*, II (Leipzig, 1871); *Agafij, O tsarstvovanii Yustiniana*, tr. M. V. Levchenko (Moscow, 1953) (the only complete translation in a modern language since the 17th century).

Anna Comnena (1083–*c.*1153). Byzantine historian. Eldest child of the Emperor Alexius I and his wife Irene Ducas, Anna was from her earliest childhood in daily contact with the leading figures of the Empire. Through her parents' care and her own passion for knowledge, she obtained an education in literature and philosophy vouchsafed to few women in the Middle Ages. Betrothed in childhood to Constantine Ducas, son of her father's defeated rival, she could count on succeeding to power in due course. But Constantine died, and her younger brother John became her father's heir. Anna was married to Nicephorus ⇨ Bryennius, son or grandson of an unsuccessful pretender to the throne, to whom she bore at least four children. When Alexius I died in 1118 Anna and her mother did all they could to prevent John II succeeding his father, and a little later Anna was apparently involved in a clumsy attempt to assassinate her brother. As a result she and her mother were forced to retire to a convent, where Anna spent the rest of her days. Defeated in the struggle for power, she turned to scholarship and organized a group of philosophers who stimulated the revival of Aristotelian studies. After the death of her husband in 1138 she continued his *History*. The result, completed after 1148, was the *Alexiad*, a history of her father's reign in 8 books. Anna was uniquely well informed and immensely erudite, and she had a rewarding theme: the restoration of Byzantine fortunes by a brilliant and forceful ruler, successful wars against Seljuk Turks, Pechenegs and Norman invaders, the unexpected challenge of the First Crusade, bitter theological disputes, and a splendid renaissance of art and letters. But she was a woman who loved and hated passionately, and who had cherished for thirty years a grudge against fate and its instruments. Accordingly, her history is something of a panegyric upon her father, whom she idealizes; and those she dislikes, above all the Normans Robert Guiscard and his son Bohemund, and the leaders of the Crusaders, are given less than their due. Her brother, the future John II, is hardly mentioned, and then only in the coldest of tones. Her military accounts incline to vagueness, and much of interest is omitted. Nevertheless the *Alexiad* is a vivid, detailed and on the whole trustworthy narrative, every page of which reveals the writer's passionate personality. Something of a cultural snob, Anna writes in an elaborately classicizing Greek, full of literary allusions and rare words. She apologizes for sullying her pages with the names of western barbarians. For all its shortcomings, the *Alexiad* is a uniquely valuable source, particularly as it provides a very different picture of the Crusade from that of western historians. And it is a fascinating example of the imaginative reconstruction of the life of the writer's own youth, before the power for which she yearned had been snatched for ever from her hands. [R B]

Ed. and Fr. tr. B. Leib (3 vols., Paris, 1937–45); tr. E. A. S. Dawes (1928).

Georgina Buckler, *Anna Comnena, A Study* (1929).

Areopagite, Pseudo-Dionysius the. ◊ Pseudo-Dionysius.

Arethas of Caesarea (*c.* 850–?*c.* 944). Byzantine theologian, scholar and bibliophile. Born in Patras, he studied in Constantinople, probably under ◊ Photius, and later took orders as a deacon. About 902 he became Metropolitan of Caesarea, but continued to live mainly in Constantinople. He negotiated the complex ecclesiastical politics of the early 10th century in a way that seemed to some unprincipled, and may have been deposed shortly before his death in very old age. His works include a commentary on the *Apocalypse* and a series of exegetical homilies, dogmatic treatises, panegyrics on saints, speeches on ceremonial occasions, and a collection of letters, many of them 'open letters' on disputed questions of canon law and ecclesiastical polity, and many of great historical interest. His chief claim to fame, however, lies in the care he took to seek out manuscripts of rare classical works, have them copied in the new minuscule hand, and supply them with marginal commentaries. Many of the copied manuscripts survive, often with his own exegetical and other notes. Among these are the D'Orville Euclid of 888 and the Clark Plato of 895, both in the Bodleian Library at Oxford, the Harley Lucian of 913–14, in the British Museum, the Vatican Aristotle of 900, and the Paris manuscript of the Greek Christian Apologists, copied in 913–14. The Venice manuscript (No. 454), our oldest witness to the text of the *Iliad*, a Herodotus manuscript in Florence, and others have been plausibly connected with him. All reveal his scholarship and his delight in beauty. In addition to surviving manuscripts, copies made by Arethas are clearly the originals of our later manuscripts of many other authors, such as Marcus Aurelius, Dio Chrysostom, Epictetus, Thucydides and Plutarch. He seems to have been uninterested in the classical dramatists, but he had copies of Pindar and Callimachus containing more than now survives. This worldly prelate with a talent for intrigue did as much as any man to save works of classical and early Christian literature after the long 'dark age' of the 7th to early 9th centuries. Many of the entries in this book would be missing but for him. Arethas's writings are scattered in a multitude of publications. [R B]

Bibliography in H. G. Beck, *Kirche und theologische Literatur im byzantinischen Reich* (Munich, 1959).

S. Kugeas, *Ho Kaisareias Arethas kai to ergon autu* (Athens, 1913); E. Zardini, 'Sulla biblioteca dell'arcivescovo Areta di Cesarea', *Akten des XI Internationalen Byzantinisten-Kongresses* (Munich, 1960); P. Karlin-Hayter, 'New Arethas Documents', i–v, in *Byzantion* 25/27–34 (1957–64), and 'New Arethas Texts for the Historical Study of the *Vita Euthymii*', in *Byzantion* 31 (1961).

Argyropulos, John. ⇨ John Argyropulos.

Attaliates, Michael (second half of 11th cent.). Byzantine historian. Attaliates was by profession a lawyer, and rose to high judicial office under Romanus IV (1067–71) and Michael VII (1071–8). His *History,* written in 1079–80, covers the years 1034–79, largely on the basis of personal observation and eye-witness accounts. It is a trustworthy source on political and military history. The style and language are archaizing and mannered. A compendium of law dated 1072, and the statutes of a monastery and almshouse founded by him in 1077, of great interest to the social historian, also survive. [R B]

Ed. W. Brunet de Presle and I. Bekker (C S H B, 1853); *Acta et diplomata graeca medii aevi*, ed. F. Miklosich and J. Müller, v (Vienna, 1887).

B

Bessarion (1403–72). Byzantine theologian and humanist. Born in Trebizond, he studied in Constantinople and under George Gemistus ⇨ Plethon at Mistra, and by 1437 had become Archbishop of Nicaea. At the Council of Florence in 1438 he was the leading partisan of church union, and soon migrated permanently to Italy, where in 1439 he was created a cardinal. After the fall of Constantinople in 1453 he became patron and protector of many refugee Greek scholars and defender of Greek culture, and collected a magnificent library of manuscripts, which he bequeathed to the Library of St Mark in Venice. His works include numerous polemical theological treatises, some of which he provided with a Latin translation, a collection of letters, a defence of Plato, and historical and rhetorical writings. [R B]

Migne, *P G*, 161.
L. Mohler, *Kardinal Bessarion als Theologe, Humanist und Staatsmann* (3 vols., Paderborn, 1923–42).

Blemmydes, Nicephorus (*c.*1197–*c.*1272). Byzantine scholar and man of letters. Leaving his native Constantinople after the Latin conquest in 1204, he was educated in various towns of Asia Minor, entered the Church in Nicaea, and became tutor to the future emperor Theodore II Lascaris. Later he became abbot of a monastery near Ephesus. He was offered, but refused, the Oecumenical Patriarchate. He writes on philosophy, theology, geography, medicine, rhetoric, education, etc. His principal works are: (1) a handbook of logic and natural philosophy; (2) several entirely derivative geographical treatises; (3) an address to his imperial pupil on a monarch's duties; (4) a fascinating autobiography in which, in spite of his care to show himself always in a favourable light, he reveals his own prickly character and gives a vivid picture of life in the Nicaean empire; (5) a collection of poems and occasional writings; (6) dogmatic treatises, ascetic works, biblical commentaries and other theological works. Blemmydes was the centre of intellectual life in the Nicaean empire, and is in his weakness and his strength a very typical Byzantine figure. Thanks to his autobiography we know him more intimately than most Byzantines. [R B]

Migne, *P G*, 142; *Curriculum vitae et carmina,* ed. A. Heisenberg (Leipzig, 1896) (with a valuable introduction).

Bryennius, Nicephorus (1062–1138). Byzantine historian. Son of Nicephorus Bryennius, unsuccessful claimant to the throne in 1078, Bryennius enjoyed the favour of Alexius I Comnenus (1082–1118), whose eldest daughter, ⇨ Anna Comnena, he married in 1097. Promoted to the dignity of Caesar, he held many high military and civil posts under Alexius I and his son John II (1118–43). His *History* covers the period 1070–9; he intended to continue it to include his father-in-law's reign, but was prevented by death. Although his main purpose is to narrate the rise to power of the Comnenus family, he is a careful writer and preserves much valuable historical material. He writes in classicizing Greek. [R B]

Ed. A. Meineke (C S H B, 1836); Fr. tr. H. Grégoire in *Byzantion* 23 (1953).

Byzantine Hagiography. The early Christian church preserved the documentary records (Acts) of the trial and condemnation of its martyrs for the edification of succeeding generations. From this root, under the influence of ancient biography, aretalogy (e.g. Philostratus's *Life of Apollonius of Tyana*), the ancient novel, and other literary genres, there soon grew a vast body of texts on the lives and virtues of those recognized by the church as saints, martyrs or confessors. These texts varied from sober factual accounts to tangles of legend, myth and miracle; they were composed in various linguistic forms, from the most ornate classicizing Greek to near-vernacular; they might be written by eye-witnesses, or a thousand years later; and they might take the form of strict biography or of panegyric. Older texts were often worked over by later writers. A palmary example is the rewriting in more literary Greek of a great corpus of saints' lives by Symeon the Metaphrast in the 10th century. Such rewritten texts tend to replace hard facts by pious reflections, and to omit much that does not seem to the reviser sufficiently elevated in tone.

Hagiographical texts are often preserved as separate works for private reading, but they principally survive in collections designed for liturgical use. Such collections are the *Menaea*, in 12 volumes, containing the lives of saints for each day of the year, the *Synaxaries* and *Menologies*, containing in a single volume shorter lives for the whole year, *Homiliaries*, containing encomia and panegyrics upon saints for each day of the year, and so on.

Saints' lives often contain valuable historical information, particularly on social and economic matters. But they must be treated critically; one must use the oldest version of the text, and have some idea when and by whom it was written; one must set aside legendary and other tralatitious motifs; and one must be reasonably sure that the text is not simply a pious construction, designed to provide a plausible background to an otherwise jejune note in the liturgical calendar. Many are admirable as literature, particularly those that have escaped the dead hand of the reviser. Not a few are of theological interest.

The earliest recognizable saint's life – as distinguished from the Acts of the Martyrs – is Athanasius's *Life of St Antony* (4th century). In the 6th century we have a group of interesting lives by ◊ Cyril of Scythopolis. The century of the Iconoclasts (mid 8th to mid 9th) produced much of historical interest and literary merit. In the later 9th and 10th centuries the Greek communities of Sicily and southern Italy produced many valuable lives of local saints. From the 11th century, Byzantine hagiography is spoiled by the pursuit of literary elegance and edification at all costs, but there are occasional jewels. [R B]

Acta sanctorum (from 1643) (principal collection of texts, supplemented annually since 1882 *by Analecta Bollandiana*); *Bibliotheca hagiographica graeca* (3rd edn, 3 vols., Brussels, 1957) (complete bibliography of lives); *Lives of the Saints*, ed. A. Butler and N. H. Baynes (12 vols., 1926–38) (largest collection of English translations); *Three Byzantine Saints*, tr. E. Dawes and N. H. Baynes (1948).

R. Aigrain, *L'hagiographie, ses sources, ses méthodes, son histoire* (Paris, 1953); H. Delehaye, *Sanctus* (Brussels, 1927); A. Ehrard, *Überlieferung und Bestand der hagiographischen und homiletischen Literatur der griechischen Kirche* (3 vols., 1937–52) (incomplete).

Byzantine Hymnography. Christians brought up in the pagan literary tradition occasionally composed devotional poetry in the classical quantitative metres and the old literary forms. Examples are the hymn of Clement of Alexandria (◊ p. 55), the hymn to the Virgin of Methodius of Philippi (died *c.* 311), the paraphrase of the Psalter in Homeric hexameters of Apollinaris of Laodicea (*c.* 310–*c.* 390), the poetry of Gregory of Nazianzus (◊ p. 84), and the hymns of Synesius. Such classicizing religious poetry continued to be written throughout the Byzantine age, but it had always an artificial character, and never – with one exception, mentioned below – found liturgical use.

The hymnody of the early Church grew out of that of the Synagogue. It was in Aramaic-speaking Syria that it developed most rapidly and extensively; in the early centuries A.D. we find there a kind of homily in verse sung as part of the liturgy. In the Greek-speaking world short rhythmical responses (*troparia*) – the vowels of Greek had become homochronous by the 2nd century A.D., and the basis of quantitative metre was destroyed – were sung after the Psalms or lessons. Some consist of a succession of lines with the same accentual rhythm, others are more complex.

In the 6th century a new hymn-form, the *kontakion*, appeared in the Greek world, certainly under the influence of the Syriac-speaking church. (There was a large bilingual population in Syria, which had close cultural links with Constantinople.) The *kontakion* was an expansion of the *troparion*, and consisted of 20 or more similar stanzas, often embodying an acrostic; each stanza was built out of a succession of similar or dissimilar periods, each a unit of sense, accentual rhythm and melody; responsion between stanzas was strict; all stanzas usually ended with the same short refrain. Thus there had grown up an art form, based on accentual and not on quantitative metre, which recalled in its complexity the choral lyric of classical Greece. The *kontakion* usually recounted some event of Biblical history or the lives of saints or martyrs, with moral or dogmatic reflections. It often contained passages of dramatic dialogue. In language and imagery it adhered closely to the Septuagint and New Testament models, and the better-known patristic texts. We cannot as a rule reconstruct the music.

The greatest composer of *kontakia*, perhaps the greatest Christian hymnographer, was ◊ Romanus the Melode. Others were Anastasius, Cyriacus, Dometius, ◊ Theodore of Studium, the emperor Justinian, and the 9th-century Sicilian hymnographer Joseph; most are mere names to us. The most famous *kontakion*, though one somewhat abnormal in form, is the *Akathistos Hymn*, addressed to the Virgin, and still in liturgical use in the Orthodox Church.

However, by the early 8th century the *kontakion* began to be replaced by a more complex hymn-form, the *kanon*. The *kanon* is a series of 9 – or later 8 – odes, each the equivalent of a *kontakion*, with its own melody and rhythmical pattern repeated throughout its successive stanzas. Each ode recalled or referred to one of the 9 Biblical odes. The *kanon* offered greater musical scope than the *kontakion*, but it fostered the Byzantine tendency to verbosity and repetitiousness. Modern taste finds the *kontakia* more pleasing than the *kanones*. The content of the *kanon* was similar to that of the *kontakion*, and was closely linked with the particular feast for which it was composed.

The greatest composers of *kanones* were Andrew of Crete, ◊ John of Damascus (who wrote *kanones* in quantitative iambic metre as well as in accentual rhythm) and Cosmas of Maiuma in the 8th century, ◊ Theodore of Studium, Theophanes Graptus, Joseph of Thessalonica, Metrophanes of Smyrna, the nun Casia and the emperor Leo VI in the 9th century, and John ◊ Mauropus in the 11th. By the end of the 11th century the ecclesiastical authorities forbade the introduction of new hymns into the liturgy, and development was henceforth limited to enrichment of the music of hymns already in use. In the Basilian monasteries of southern Italy, however, new hymns were written until the 13th century.

The music of pre-9th-century hymns is probably irrevocably lost. But from then on we have manuscripts with musical notation, in a succession of different systems. The decipherment of these is very complex. But in recent years an international group of Byzantine musicologists has made great headway, and we can now reconstruct a number of the melodies with some certainty. They are comparable with those of Gregorian plainchant as restored by the Motu proprio *Inter pastoralis officii* of 1903. As time went on a more and more ornamented style of execution prevailed, and in the centuries of Turkish rule strong influence was exercised by Islamic music. [R B]

Anthologia graeca carminum christianorum, ed. W. Christ and M. Paranikas (Leipzig, 1871, repr. 1962) (Greek texts); *Eklogē hellēnikēs orthodoxu hymnographias*, ed. P. N. Trempelas (Athens, 1949) (Greek texts); E. Wellesz, *The Akathistos Hymn* (*Monumenta Musicae Byzantinae. Transcripta* ix) (Copenhagen, 1957); *Initia hymnorum ecclesiae graecae*, ed. E. Follieri (5 vols., Vatican City, 1960–65) (in course of publication); *Hymns of the Eastern Church*, tr. J. M. Neale (2nd edn, London, 1863) (translations).

E. Wellesz, *A History of Byzantine Music and Hymnography* (2nd edn, 1961) (admirable; full references to earlier literature); E. Wellesz, 'The Akathistos. A Study in Byzantine Hymnography', in *Dumbarton Oaks Papers*, 9/10 (1956).

Byzantine Verse Romances. The romantic novels of the late Hellenistic world, in particular those of Achilles Tatius and

Heliodorus, were read by Byzantine scholars, for whom they had perhaps the same kind of ambivalent attraction as that of Ovid upon Western medieval monks. But for centuries no more were written; it would have been difficult to fit them into a Christian frame of reference, apart from other problems.

Finally, in the pre-renaissance of the mid and later 12th century, when classical models were more freely copied and pagan thought more readily accepted and absorbed, a number of new romantic novels were composed, slavishly reproducing the plots, motifs and manner of their Hellenistic models. The theme is always the fate of a pair of lovers, separated and united again after a series of hair-raising adventures, and always involves descriptive set-pieces, letters, speeches, trial scenes, capture by pirates, loyal slaves and so on. The scene is always the classical, pre-Christian world. These 12th-century works are in literary Greek, and the authors all men of learning. All but one is in Byzantine 12-syllable verse; the classical feeling for the appropriateness of form to content had long been lost. These poor and derivative novels are: *Aristandros and Callithea* by ⇨ Constantine Manasses, of which only excerpts survive; *Rhodanthe and Dosicles* by ⇨ Theodore Prodromus; *Drosilla and Charicles* by Nicetas Eugenianus, a pupil of Prodromus, from whose pen there also survive speeches and other minor rhetorical works; and the prose novel *Hysmine and Hysminias* by Eustathius Makrembolites, who also left a collection of riddles in verse.

The Latin capture of Constantinople in 1204 and the half-century of Latin rule broke up the cultural milieu in which these learned pastiches had been written and read. After the 1261 Byzantine restoration the verse romance flourished again, but in very different conditions. The writers are, with one possible exception, unknown; the language is no longer classicizing literary Greek, but strongly reflects the spoken vernacular; the metre is the popular 15-syllable line; and in theme and treatment they are very strongly influenced by the western romance of chivalry – some being little more than adaptations of western models (recent research, however, has shown that even the most derivative include much that is specifically Byzantine, as well as oriental elements, imported directly from the Arab world or via Georgia).

These new romances were written by and for a lower social stratum than the learned novels of the age of the Comneni (though they are not, of course, folk poetry). Some may have been composed in parts of the former Byzantine world then ruled by Franks, such as Crete, Rhodes, Cyprus, the Cyclades or the Morea. At any rate they belong to a world of great cultural interpenetration. Like so many popular poems belonging to the world of oral poetry, they tend to show a different text in each successive copy; hence it is sometimes difficult to reconstruct the original form and usually impossible to date them. The scene is set in a timeless world which has yet many features of the late Middle Ages. The theme is love, treated in a hedonistic fashion as an end in itself. There is constant exaggeration – everything is much larger than life – frequent use of the supernatural, and much reflection of the western Mediterranean ideology of chivalry. But there is also much derived, perhaps at several removes, from the Byzantine and classical literary tradition.

The surviving examples of the late Byzantine verse romance are: *Callimachus and Chrysorrhoe* (2,607 lines), perhaps by Andronicus Comnenus Ducas, a cousin of Andronicus II (1282–1328); *Belthandros and Chrysantza* (1,348 lines); *Lybistras and Rhodamne*, surviving in 4 slightly variant recensions, averaging 3,500 lines; *Imperios and Margarona*, surviving in 3 recensions varying from 800 to 1,000 lines, of which one is, after the western fashion, in rhymed couplets (this poem is an adaptation, though not a direct one, of the Provençal story of *Pierre de Provence et la belle Magueloune*); *Phlorios and Platsiaphlora* (1,874 lines), an adaptation of the Tuscan *Canzone di Florio e Biancifiore*, itself derived from a Provençal model. In three other poems the erotic element is slightly less prominent, but the general treatment is similar to that of the preceding works. They are: *The Story of Achilles* (in two redactions, of 761 and 1,820 lines); *The Romance of Alexander* (6,117 lines), a remote and scarcely recognizable descendant of Pseudo-Callisthenes' *History of Alexander*; and *The Story of Belisarius* (in 3 redactions, one rhyming, varying from 500 to 1,000 lines), a treatment of a purely Byzantine theme, perhaps originally preserved in popular songs. These verse romances, together with vernacular poems attributed to ⇨ Theodore Prodromus, mark the beginning of Modern Greek literature. [R B]

R. Hercher, *Scriptores erotici graeci*, ii (Leipzig, 1859) (Manasses, Prodromus, Eugenianus, Makrembolites); M. Pichard, *Le roman de Callimaque et de Chrysorrhoé* (Paris, 1956) (text and Fr. tr.); E. Legrand, *Bibliothèque grecque vulgaire*, i (Paris, 1880) (*Belthandros and Chrysantza*); I. A. Lambert - van der Kolf, *Le roman de Lybistros et Rhodamné* (A W A, N.R. 35, Amsterdam, 1935); Sp. Lambros, *Collection de romans grecs en langue vulgaire et en vers* (Paris, 1880) (*Imperios and Margarona*); D. C. Hesseling, *Le roman de Phlorios et Platzia Phlore* (A W A, N.R. 17, Amsterdam, 1917); D. C. Hesseling, *L'Achilleide byzantine* (A W A, N.R. 19, Amsterdam, 1919); W. Wagner, *Trois poèmes grecs du moyen âge* (Berlin, 1881) (Alexander Romance); W. Wagner, *Carmina graeca medii aevi* (Leipzig, 1874) (*Belisarius*).

B. Knös, *Histoire de la littérature néo-grecque* (Stockholm, 1962).

C

Cameniates, John (beginning of 10th cent.). Byzantine historian. Cameniates was a priest in Thessalonica. His *Capture of Thessalonica* is a graphic eye-witness account of the capture of the city by the Arab corsairs from Crete under Leo of Tripolis on 31 July 904, in which Cameniates himself was taken prisoner. He is no historian, and his conception of causality is almost exclusively theological. But he writes with vigour and directness under the impression of events, and his detailed account of his native city, its people and their occupations is something rare in Byzantine literature. His language and style are modelled on those of the Greek Bible. [R B]

Theophanes Continuatus, Ioannes Cameniata, Symeon Magister, Georgius Monachus, ed. I. Bekker (C S H B, 1838); R. A. Nasledova, S. V. Polyakova, I. V. Felenkovskaya, 'Ioann Kameniata, Vzyatie Fessaloniki', in *Dve vizantijskie Khroniki X veka* (Moscow, 1959) (Russian translation - the only one in any modern language - with valuable introduction and notes).

Cantacuzenus, John VI (d. 1382). Byzantine emperor and historian. A member of a rich feudal family, he held high military office under Andronicus II (1282–1328) and Andronicus III (1328–41). After the latter's death he was proclaimed emperor in rivalry with Andronicus's son and heir John V. Only after 6 years of civil war did he gain possession of Constantinople in 1347. Driven out in 1354 he turned to the Turkish rulers of Asia Minor for help, but in vain. In 1355 he entered a monastery, under the name Ioasaph, and devoted himself to theology, philosophy and history. His *History* covers the years 1320–56. Its apologetic purpose comes out particularly in the many fictitious speeches. But in spite of his eagerness to justify his own lost cause, Cantacuzenus is a careful, accurate and reliable narrator, who made good use of his own diaries and official documents. His *History* and that of Nicephorus ⇨ Gregoras complement one another. His many theological works are also partly apologetic in intent, seeking to justify the doctrine of Gregory ⇨Palamas and the Hesychasts, whom he had supported as emperor; they also include anti-Moslem and anti-Jewish treatises; not all have been published. Another product of his long retirement is a paraphrase of Books 1–5 of Aristotle's *Nicomachean Ethics*. [R B]

Ed. J. Schopen (3 vols., C S H B, 1828–32).

V. Parisot, *Cantacuzène, homme d'état et historien* (Paris, 1845).

Casia (Ikasia) (first half of 9th century A.D.). Byzantine poetess. Daughter of a Byzantine notable, she took part in the bride show for the emperor Theophilus (*c.* 830), but her sharp tongue lost her the throne, and she spent the rest of her life in a convent. Her epigrams - never more than a line or two in length - show warmth of feeling but lack literary skill. They are in 12-syllable metre, and perhaps modelled on the pseudo-Menandrean *Monosticha*. Several of her rhythmical hymns are in liturgical use in the Orthodox Church. [R B]

K. Krumbacher, *Kasia* (B A W, Munich, 1897).

Cecaumenus (mid 11th cent.) Byzantine military writer, probably to be identified with Catacalon Cecaumenus, who held various commands from 1038 onwards. His *General's Handbook* (*Stratēgikon*), addressed to his son, is a discursive guide to conduct in military and public affairs, illustrated by many personal reminiscences and historical examples. It contains much valuable historical and ethnographical information. It illustrates vividly the ideals and attitudes of an upright, realistic, rather old-fashioned provincial landowner, a type little represented in Byzantine literature. The language is literary Greek, but with few stylistic adornments. [R B]

Ed. B. Vasil'evskij and V. Jernstedt (St Petersburg, 1896); German tr. H. G. Beck (Graz, 1956).

Cedrenus, George (11th cent.). Byzantine historian. Cedrenus was probably a monk, but nothing is known of his life. His *Chronicle*, from the Creation to 1057, is entirely compilatory. For the earlier period his sources, which he puts together quite mechanically, include some not now surviving. For the years 811–1057 he transcribed almost verbatim the work of ◊ Scylitzes. His work has therefore no independent value. But occasionally he copies from sources now lost, and he enables us to detect interpolations and corruptions in the manuscripts of his surviving sources. [R B]

Ed. I. Bekker (2 vols., C S H B, 1838–9).

Chalcocondyles, Laonicus (*c.* 1423–*c.* 1490). Byzantine historian. Cousin of Demetrius Chalcocondyles the humanist, Chalcocondyles was born in Athens, studied at Mistra under Gemistus ◊ Plethon, and later lived in Constantinople, which he left shortly before 1453; the circumstances of his later life are unknown. His *Historical Demonstrations* narrate the history of the years 1298–1463; his theme is the growth of Turkish power to fill the political vacuum created by the decline and final destruction of the Byzantine Empire. Coldly objective, critical, generally reliable on facts but vague in chronology, he is an interesting historian with an eye for the large movements of history. His style is archaizing, involved and obscure. [R B]

Ed. E. Darkó (2 vols., Budapest, 1922, 1927); Fr. tr. Blaise de Vigenère (Paris, 1577, and many reprints).

W. Miller, 'The Last Athenian Historian: Laonikos Chalkokondyles', *J H S* 42 (1922).

Choniates, Michael (Michael Acominatus) (*c.* 1138–*c.* 1222). Byzantine man of letters. Born in Chonae (the ancient Colossae), elder brother of Nicetas ◊ Choniates, Michael was educated in Constantinople and held various high appointments on the Patriarch's staff. In 1182 he became Metropolitan of Athens, where he remained until his expulsion by the Latins in 1204. Until 1217 he lived on Ceos, within sight of Attica, then retired to a monastery near Thermopylae, where he died. His literary works include a series of moral sermons, festal homilies, an interesting inaugural homily on his arrival in Athens, funeral orations on contemporaries (including his brother Nicetas the historian and ◊ Eustathius of Thessalonica), a large collection of letters, and a number of poems, in particular that on the degenerate state of Athens in his day. His letters are often lively and informative, and tell us much about contemporary intellectual life. As he played a leading part in political life, his works are important historical sources. Of immense and varied learning – he was one of the last men to read the lost *Hecale* of Callimachus, and in old age we find him dissecting pigs to verify the statements of Galen – Michael writes in a simpler, more straightforward style than most of his Byzantine contemporaries. Along with his teacher Eustathius, he is one of the most attractive figures of the 12th-century renaissance. [R B]

Ed. S. P. Lampros (2 vols., Athens, 1879–80).

G. Stadtmüller, *Michael Choniates, Metropolit von Athen* (Vatican City, 1934).

Choniates, Nicetas (Nicetas Acominatus) (*c.* 1150–1213). Byzantine historian. Born at Chonae (the ancient Colossae), younger brother of Michael ◊ Choniates, he studied at Constantinople and entered the government service. He became secretary to the emperor Isaac Angelus, governor of the province of Philippopolis from 1189, and chief minister before 1204. After the Latin capture of Constantinople he took refuge in Nicaea and held high office under the emperor in exile Theodore Lascaris. His works include a *History* of the period 1118–1206, a number of ceremonial speeches delivered 1180–1210, a poem on the marriage of Isaac Angelus and the daughter of Béla III of Hungary, and a vast handbook on heresies, the *Treasury of Orthodoxy*.

His *History* recounts briefly the reign

of John II (1118–43) and in more detail the period from the accession of Manuel I (1143) until after the Latin capture in 1204. His position gave him access to many sources, which he used with objectivity and intelligence, though not always critically. Though coloured throughout by ecclesiastical and theological interests, his approach is sophisticated and humane. His countless character sketches are penetrating and occasionally malicious. His bitterness towards the Latins is understandable in one who had lived through the events of 1204. His account of the monuments destroyed by the Latins is important for art history. His ornate and allusive style, overladen with learning, makes him difficult to read. But those who make the effort will find in his work a circumstantial and sympathetic account of the catastrophic decline from the glories of Manuel's reign to the irremediable disaster of 1204. The closing books of his *Treasury of Orthodoxy* (not yet all published) provide valuable material on the theological and philosophical movements of 12th-century Byzantium. The speeches are of interest only as historical sources. [R B]

Historia, ed. I. Bekker (C S H B, 1835); German tr. F. Gräbler, *Byzantinische Geschichtsschreiber*, 7–9 (Graz, 1958) (with useful introduction); *Recueil des historiens des croisades, historiens grecs*, ii, ed. E. Miller (Paris, 1881) (speeches); *Mesaionike Bibliotheke*, i, ed. K. Sathas (Venice, 1872) (speeches); *Treasury of Orthodoxy* in Migne, *P G*, 139, 140; complete edn of all works, ed. J. A. J. van Dieten, in preparation.
F. Gräbler, 'Nikolas Choniates als Redner', in *Jahrbuch der österreichischen byzantinischen Gesellschaft* 11/12 (1962–3).

Christopher of Mytilene (*c.* 1000–50). Byzantine poet. A government official, he finally became chief judge of Paphlagonia. His collection of epigrams in 12-syllable verses and hexameters is largely of personal inspiration. His caustic wit, irony and occasional sense of humour raise his poetry far above the run of Byzantine verse. He is also author of religious calendars in verse which are used liturgically by the Orthodox Church. [R B]

Ed. E. Kurtz (Leipzig, 1903); *Megas Synaxaristēs pantōn tōn hagiōn*, ed. K. Dukakes (12 vols., Athens, 1889–97) (liturgical poems).

'Christus Patiens'. Byzantine dramatic poem on the Passion of Christ in 2,640 lines. The central figure is the Virgin, depicted with profound human sympathy. The poem is largely a cento of verses from classical tragedy, mainly from Euripides. Though attributed in the manuscripts to Gregory of Nazianzus (⇨ p. 84), it is almost certainly of the 11th or 12th century. It is designed for reading, not for acting, though the author was clearly inspired by classical drama. [R B]

Teubner: J. G. Brambs (Leipzig, 1885).
V. Cottas, *Le théâtre à Byzance* (Paris, 1931); G. La Piana, *Speculum*, ii (1936).

Chrysoloras, Manuel. ⇨ Manuel Chrysoloras.

Cinnamus, John (*c.* 1144–*c.* 1203). Byzantine historian. Cinnamus was confidential secretary of the emperor Manuel I (1143–80) and probably also held office under his successor. His *Epitome*, composed 1180–3, covers the years 1118–76. For the years from 1143 onwards he relied mainly on eye-witness accounts, personal observation and official documents. Military operations, which he thoroughly understood, figure largely. He is an objective historian, factually reliable, though he omits much that we should like to know. The surviving text may be an abbreviation of the original. His language is archaizing and classical. There survives also a rhetorical exercise (*Ethopoeia*), probably composed in his early years. [R B]

Ed. A. Meineke (C S H B, 1836).
C. Neumann, *Griechische Geschichtsschreiber und Geschichtsquellen im zwölften Jahrhundert* (Leipzig, 1888); M. M. Freidenberg, 'Trud Ioanna Kinnama kak istoricheskij istochnik', in *Vizantijskij Vremennik* 16 (1959).

Climax (Climacus), John. ⇨ John Climax.

Comnena, Anna. ⇨ Anna Comnena.

Constantine Manasses (d. *c.* 1187). Byzantine historian, poet and orator. He was a government official, who later entered the church and died as Metropolitan of Naupactus. His *Historical Synopsis*, from the Creation to 1081, in 6,733 15-syllable accentual verses and dedicated to a princess of the Comnenus family, marks a new attempt to dress universal history in an attractive guise. It is entirely derivative in content, and only very occasionally draws upon sources not accessible to us. But it is adorned with set speeches, images, literary allusions and descriptive passages, all handled with verve and taste. Its popularity is attested by the large number of manuscripts, the existence of a prose paraphrase in vernacular Greek and an Old Slavonic translation made in Bulgaria about 1350. Another poem in some 800 12-syllable lines describes the poet's adventures on a diplomatic mission to Antioch, Jerusalem and Tripolis. A verse romance, *Aristandros and Callithea,* survives only in excerpts. We have also some speeches by Manasses made on ceremonial occasions, rhetorical exercises and letters. Not all are published, and the authorship of some is problematic. All are in the flowery, involved, literary prose of the 12th century, which Manasses handles with consummate skill. A moralizing poem in 916 15-syllable lines has been attributed to Manasses but is probably not his. [R B]

Breviarium historiae metricum, ed. I. Bekker (C S H B, 1837) (new edition in preparation by O. Lampsides); Speeches etc. in a variety of learned journals – see Gy. Moravcsik, *Byzantinoturcica* (2nd edn, vol. I, Berlin, 1958).

K. Horna, 'Das Hodoiporikon des Konstantinos Manasses', *Byzantinische Zeitschrift* 13 (1904).

Constantine VII Porphyrogenitus (905–59). Byzantine emperor and man of letters. Son of Leo VI by his fourth marriage, Constantine was a child when his father died in 912. His minority was turbulent, and by 920 the usurper Romanus Lecapenus seized imperial power. Though Romanus married his daughter Helena to the young prince and proclaimed him co-emperor, Constantine was kept in the background, without real power, until Romanus's fall in December 944. Only for his last 15 years was he emperor in fact as well as in name.

Of antiquarian and artistic tastes, said to have been a painter and to have trained church choirs, he spent his long years of impotence in amassing a superb library, in antiquarian research and in organizing and supervising the compilation of a series of encyclopedic works; these activities he continued after his accession to power. As with other exalted authors, it is sometimes difficult to distinguish between what he wrote himself and what he commanded to be written, but the following works are wholly or mainly his own: (1) The life of his grandfather Basil I, which forms part of ⇨ *Theophanes continuatus.* (2) The *De administrando imperio,* a handbook on Byzantine foreign policy prepared for his son, the future Romanus II. Imbedded in the imperial author's instructions concerning relations with the various powers beyond the frontiers are many excerpts from documents and reports in the state archives, some already several centuries old. The whole forms a priceless source for Eastern European history in the early middle ages. The sections on Russia, on the southern Slavs, on the steppe peoples north of the Black Sea and on the Hungarians are particularly valuable. (3) The *De thematibus,* a survey of the Byzantine empire, province by province, with ethnographical, historical and antiquarian notes. A work of Constantine's youth, and somewhat remote from the political realities of the 10th century, much of its information relates to a period several centuries earlier. (4) The *De caerimoniis aulae byzantinae,* a vast and detailed compilation on Byzantine court ceremonial, including many protocols and reports of coronations, visits of foreign potentates, departures for campaigns, etc. Many are of great historical interest. There is much detailed information on the administrative structure, state hierarchy, and titulature of the Byzantines, and on the topography of the Great Palace and of Constantinople in general. (5) We hear also of ceremonial speeches and liturgical poetry composed by Constantine, but these have not survived.

Of the compilatory works inspired and supervised by the emperor, the following are the most noteworthy: (1) The *Historical Excerpts,* a gigantic anthology of passages from Greek historians from Herodotus to the 9th century A.D., arranged by subject-matter under 53 heads, in order, as Constantine puts it in his preface, to save readers the trouble of consulting the originals. The whole would have occupied tens of thousands of printed pages. There survive the section 'On Embassies' and considerable portions of those 'On Virtues and Vices', 'On

Wise Sayings', 'On Plots against Monarchs', 'On Stratagems', and 'On Addresses to Troops'. They preserve many substantial extracts from historical works now lost. (2) An encyclopedia on tactics. (3) The *Geoponica*, an anthology of passages from writers on agriculture. (4) Encyclopedias on medicine, veterinary science and zoology.

Constantine wrote literary Greek in his life of his grandfather, but the other works, in particular the *De administrando imperio*, a top-secret document not for publication, are written in a loose style, with many echoes of vernacular speech.

Constantine is an original and attractive character, seriously concerned about education and the preservation of knowledge – he refounded or reorganized the University of Constantinople – and he saved a great deal that would otherwise be lost. His vices, longwindedness and pedantry, are the counterpart of his virtues. [R B]

De administrando imperio, ed. Gy. Moravcsik, tr. R. J. H. Jenkins (Budapest, 1949); *De administrando imperio*, comm. R. J. H. Jenkins and others (London, 1962); *De thematibus*, ed. A. Pertusi (Vatican City, 1952); *De cerimoniis aulae byzantinae*, ed. I. I. Reiske (2 vols., C S H B, 1829–30); *Le livre des cérémonies*, ed., Fr. tr. and comm. A. Vogt (4 vols., Paris, 1935–40) (incomplete, covering only ch. 1–92 of Book I).

A. Rambaud, *L'empire grec au dixième siècle, Constantin Porphyrogénète* (Paris, 1870).

Constantine of Rhodes (first half of 10th cent. A.D.). Byzantine poet. A native of Lindos in Rhodes, he held a court appointment in Constantinople. He is best known for his *Description of the Church of the Holy Apostles in Constantinople* in 981 12-syllable lines, composed 931–44. Verbose and vague, it cannot be compared with the similar poem by ⇨ Paul the Silentiary, but art historians have extracted useful information from it. A series of epigrams by Constantine are of little merit. [R B]

E. Legrand, 'Constantin le Rhodien. Description des œuvres d'art et de l'église des Saints Apôtres, suivie d'un commentaire par Th. Reinach', *Revue des études grecques* 9 (1896).

G. M. Downey, 'Constantine the Rhodian, His Life and Writings', *Late Classical and Mediaeval Studies in Honour of A. M. Friend, Jr* (Washington D.C., 1955).

Cosmas Indicopleustes (first half of 6th cent. A.D.). Byzantine theologian and geographer. A merchant and sea-captain from Alexandria, Cosmas voyaged to the ports of East Africa, the Persian Gulf and perhaps India and Ceylon. In his retirement he composed his *Christian Topography*, in which he attacked the Ptolemaic system of geography and astronomy, and sought to prove that the universe was shaped like Noah's Ark. His physics and his theology are alike derivative, naïve and absurd. But his topographical and ethnological information is often first-hand and of the utmost value for understanding early Byzantine trade relations and foreign policy, and for the history of the Near and Middle East. He was an eye-witness of the Axumite expedition against the Yemen in 579. His theoretical expositions are turgid and sometimes scarcely comprehensible; but his descriptive and narrative passages are written in a racy Greek which owes more to living speech than to literary tradition. There is a cycle of illustrations to his work which are of great value to the art historian. [R B]

Ed. and comm. E. O. Winstedt (Cambridge, 1909); tr. J. W. McCrindle (London, 1897).

W. Wolska, *La topographie chrétienne de Cosmas Indicopleustès* (Paris, 1962).

Critobulus, Michael (*c.*1400–after 1467). Byzantine historian. A member of a noble family of Imbros, Critobulus early entered the service of the Ottoman Turks, under whom he became governor of his native island; he may have earlier been Sultan Mohammed II's private secretary. His *Histories*, covering the years 1451–67, are a panegyric of the Ottoman Empire and of Mohammed II in particular. One-sided, occasionally inaccurate, often silent on matters unfavourable to the Turks, he preserves much unique material and tells the story of the capture of Constantinople from an unfamiliar, if unattractive, point of view. He writes heavy, archaizing Greek, in imitation of Thucydides. [R B]

Ed. V. Grecu (Bucharest, 1963); tr. C. T. Riggs (Princeton, 1954).

Cydones, Demetrius (*c.*1324–97/8). Byzantine theologian and man of letters. Born in Thessalonica, he became a minister of state under John VI ⇨ Cantacuzenus, learned Latin and was accepted into the Roman Catholic church. His last years were spent in voluntary exile in Venice and Crete. His writings include Greek translations of the works of St Thomas Aquinas and other western theologians, polemical treatises attacking the doctrines of Gregory ◊ Palamas, defences of his own theological position, speeches and, most interesting today, a collection of letters which give a vivid picture of Byzantine intellectual life in the second half of the 14th century. [R B]

Correspondance, ed. R.-J. Loenertz (2 vols., Vatican City, 1956, 1961).

Cyril of Scythopolis (*c.*524–*c.*560). Byzantine hagiographer. Born at Scythopolis (Bethsan) in Palestine, he became a monk in the great monastery of St Sabbas at Jerusalem. He wrote lives of the notable Palestinian monks of the two preceding generations, including those of Sabbas, Euthymius, John the Hesychast and Cyriac. Though without a literary education, Cyril had a gift for sharp observation and vivid description, a love of accuracy, an ability to impose order on his complex material, and a sympathetic understanding of his subjects' aims and ideals. His lives, together with the stories of ◊ John Moschus, give us a clear and unidealized picture of 6th-century monastic life and of the monk's place in society. [R B]

Ed. E. Schwartz (Leipzig, 1939).

D

Damascene, John. ◊ John of Damascus.

Demetrius Cydones. ◊ Cydones, Demetrius.

Demetrius Triclinius (*c.*1280–*c.*1340). Byzantine scholar. He was a teacher of grammar and rhetoric, probably in Thessalonica, but virtually nothing is known of his life. His commentaries on classical lyric and dramatic poetry break new ground by their attempt to analyse the complex lyric metres and to emend the text of lyric passages on metrical grounds. We possess several autograph manuscripts of Triclinius and can thus follow his method of editing and commenting on a classical text. He is in many ways a forerunner of the Renaissance humanist scholar. [R B]

R. Aubreton, *Démétrius Triclinius et les recensions médiévales de Sophocle* (Paris, 1949); W. J. W. Koster, *Autour d'un manuscrit d'Aristophane écrit par Démétrius Triclinius* (Leiden, 1957).

'Digenēs Akritēs'. Byzantine epic poem. The poem survives in several recensions, differing in linguistic form and in the details of the episodes included; but all show substantially the same plot and most episodes are common to all. In addition to these recensions in 15-syllable accentual verse without rhyme, there is a rhymed version composed in 1670 by a monk of Chios, Ignatios Petritzes, a Greek prose paraphrase of the same period, and an Old Russian prose version probably from the 13th century and heavily interpolated with folk-tale motifs.

The nucleus of the story is as follows: The daughter of a Byzantine prince of the Dukas family is kidnapped from her Cappadocian home by a raiding Arab emir, himself of Greek blood but captured in childhood by the Arabs. The girl's brothers pursue the emir, defeat him in battle, and bring him back to Byzantine territory, where he becomes a Christian and marries the girl. In time a son is born to them, whom they call Basil Digenes Akrites (=The borderer of dual race, i.e. Greek and Arab). The emir returns to Muslim territory, having many adventures on the way, and brings back his mother and all his family. The young Basil learns letters and the use of arms, and on his first hunt kills two bears and a lion. Grown to manhood, he has various adventures with bands of *apelatai* or rievers. After a romantic courtship he elopes with Eudokia, the daughter of a Byzantine border baron, and goes to live with her in the wild border lands, killing bandits and imposing peace. The emperor himself hears of his fame and visits him, to be entertained by a display of Basil's physical prowess. There follows a long passage in which Basil narrates in the first person some of his adventures, including a passage of gallantry with the daughter of an emir (which shocked the late W. P. Ker), the rescue of Eudokia from a dragon, and a single combat with a formidable lady warrior, who after being defeated tries in vain to seduce him. Then Basil builds a great castle with a marvellous garden, and his life there is described with many curious details. Finally he falls ill, calls Eudokia and in a long speech recalls their happy life together. As she prays for him he dies, and she drops dead beside him. His funeral and his great tomb are described, and the poem concludes with a moralizing passage on the vanity of worldly glory.

The language is Byzantine literary Greek. The style is marked by felicitous imagery, precision of description and many lively speeches and dialogue passages. Some of the descriptive set-pieces are long-winded; and the speeches occasionally incline to sententiousness. There is no development of character. But the authors – for the poem was clearly rewritten again and again, as was the way with such works in the Middle Ages – show immense inventiveness in detail.

The dramatic scene and date are the Byzantine–Arab frontier regions in the 9th and 10th centuries. But the poem is hardly historical epic in the strict sense, though it may have been built out of shorter, orally transmitted lays dealing with particular persons and events. Some of these, including the struggle with the Paulician heretics in the 9th century, can be dimly discerned still beneath the poem's even texture. In its present general form it was probably put together in the 11th century in Asia Minor by an educated man in the service of some great feudal baron, as an imaginative reconstruction of the glories of a still-remembered past.

The Akritic ballads surviving still in various parts of Greece give nothing to the poem, and are probably quite unlike the lays from which it may have been composed 1,000 years ago. [R B]

Ed. P. P. Kalonaros (2 vols., Athens, 1941–2) (gives the various versions); Fr. tr. P. Pascal, *Byzantion* 10 (1935) (old Russian version); Grottaferrata MS tr. and comm. John Mavrogordato (1956).

S. Kyriakides, 'Forschungsbericht zum Akritas-Epos', in *Berichte zum XI Intern. Byzantinisten-Kongress* (Munich, 1958); B. Knös, *Histoire de la littérature néo-grecque* (Stockholm, 1962). (To the bibliographies add a series of Russian articles by A. Ya Syrkin, *Vizantijskij Vremennik* 17 (1960), 18 (1961), 19 (1961), 20 (1961)).

Dionysius the Areopagite. ⇨ Pseudo-Dionysius the Areopagite.

Ducas (*c.* 1400–*c.* 1470). Byzantine historian. Probably born in Asia Minor, he was for most of his life in the service of the Gattilusio family, Genoese overlords of Lesbos, for whom he carried out many diplomatic missions. He supported the union of western and eastern Churches. His *History* covers the years 1341–1462, and deals with both the growth of the Ottoman Empire and the last century of Byzantium. Noteworthy is his vivid, detailed and moving account of the capture of Constantinople in 1453. His wide experience of affairs, his impartiality and his narrative skill make it a major source for 15th-century eastern European history. He writes plain and lucid Greek. [R B]

Ed. V. Grecu (Bucarest, 1958).

V. Grecu, 'Pour une meilleure connaissance de l'historien Doukas', *Mémorial Louis Petit* (Bucarest-Paris, 1948).

E

Eugenius of Palermo (*c.* 1130–1203). Sicilian Greek poet, mathematician and statesman. He held a series of high offices under the Norman kings of Sicily, was imprisoned in Germany by the emperor Henry VI, and finally returned to south Italy as a papal official. He is the author of 24 short poems in Greek, including a panegyric on King William I or II, a discourse on monarchy, several descriptive pieces, and a complaint from prison. He also revised an earlier translation from Arabic to Greek of a collection of fables of Indian origin, and translated Arabic mathematical works into Latin. He is probably also author of a Latin history of Sicily under the Normans, attributed to one Hugo Falcandus. He is an interesting representative of the trilingual culture of Norman Sicily. [R B]

L. Sternbach, 'Eugenius von Palermo', *Byzantinische Zeitschrift* 11 (1902); E. Jamison, *Admiral Eugenius of Sicily* (1957).

Eustathius of Thessalonica (d. *c.* 1195). Byzantine scholar and theologian. Eustathius taught literature and rhetoric in the patriarchal school in Constantinople for many years, and in 1175 became archbishop of Thessalonica, displaying vigorous and many-sided pastoral activity. When the city was sacked by the Normans from Sicily in 1185 he remained at his post and was for some time a prisoner. Opposition in Thessalonica led to his recall in 1191 to Constantinople, where he seems to have stayed until 1194. He was soon regarded as a saint by the Orthodox church, though never formally canonized: his portrait in fresco appears in the early-14th-century church at Gračanica in Yugoslavia. His works fall into three groups: (1) grammatical and literary, written before his elevation to the archbishopric; (2) theological and pastoral; (3) historical and occasional works. To the first group belong his lengthy surviving commentaries on the *Iliad* and *Odyssey* and on the geographical poems of Dionysius Periegetes, together with those on Pindar, of which only the introduction survives, and on Aristophanes, now lost. Eustathius preserves in these some information now lost. But their principal interest is in the light they throw on Byzantine literary scholarship and teaching, for they are substantially the texts of his lectures. They are marked by fullness and painstaking attention to detail, fair citation of conflicting views, frequent digressions and constant illustration from contemporary analogies and from vernacular speech. To the second group belong a series of Lenten Homilies, a treatise on the reformation of monasteries, several works attacking religious hypocrisy and exaggerated ascetic practices, a number of hagiographical works, and a long commentary – similar in style to those on Homer – on liturgical hymns of John Damascene. To the third group belong a number of addresses made to distinguished personages on ceremonial occasions, a funeral oration on Manuel I, a collection of letters and his account of the Norman capture of Thessalonica. Apart from the last, these are of interest only as historical sources. The *Capture of Thessalonica* is a lucid and moving eye-witness account of the sack of a great city, marked by detachment, humanity and courage. It was written within a few months of the events which it describes. Eustathius is one of the most attractive characters of the Byzantine world, and a noble product of the 12th-century renaissance, with its renewed interest in the classical tradition, its rationalism, and its high artistic standards. He merits a full length study. [R B]

Commentarii ad Homeri Iliadem, ed. G. Stallbaum (4 vols., Leipzig, 1827–30, repr. Hildesheim, 1960); *Commentarii ad Homeri Odysseam*, ed. G. Stallbaum (2 vols., Leipzig, 1822–6, repr. Hildesheim, 1960); ed. C. Müller, *Geographi graeci minores*, ii (Paris, 1882) (commentary on Dionysius); A. B. Drachmann, *Scholia vetera in Pindari carmina*, iii (Leipzig, 1927); Migne, *P G*, 135–136 (theological works); *Opuscula*, ed. T. L. F. Tafel (Frankfurt, 1832) (speeches etc.); *La espugnazione di Tessalonica*, ed. S. Kyriakidis (Palermo, 1961) (with Italian tr.); *Die Normannen in Thessalonike. Die Eroberung von Thessalonike*, German tr. H. Hunger (Graz, 1955); R. Browning 'The Patriarchal School at Constantinople in the Twelfth Century', in *Byzantion* 23 (1963) (complete list of works).

G

Gazes, Theodore. ◊ Theodore Gazes.

Gemistus Plethon, George. ◊ Plethon, George Gemistus.

Genesius, Joseph (mid 10th cent.). Byzantine historian. Of noble birth, Genesius held a high position in the Imperial Chancellery under Constantine VII Porphyrogenitus (912–59). His *History*, covering the years 813–86 (accession of Leo V to death of Basil I), was written in 944–59, at the behest of Constantine VII. Based on oral tradition and upon a variety of narrative and hagiographical material now lost, it is a valuable source. Like all historians of the period, Genesius is strongly prejudiced against the Iconoclast emperors and in favour of Basil I, the grandfather of his patron. He writes in would-be classicizing Greek, with many learned and irrelevant digressions. [R B]

Ed. C. Lachmann (C S H B, 1834).

George Acropolites. ◊ Acropolites, George.

George Cedrenus. ◊ Cedrenus, George.

George Gemistus Plethon. ◊ Plethon, George Gemistus.

George the Monk (George Hamartolus) (mid 9th century A.D.). Byzantine chronicler. Nothing is known of his life. His *Chronicle*, from the Creation to A.D. 842, is a typical production of Byzantine monastic piety. His purpose is edification, his interest predominantly ecclesiastical, and his conception of historical causation entirely theological. His sources are varied and not always identifiable, and he copies them quite uncritically and occasionally stupidly. For the Byzantine period he relies mainly upon John ◊ Malalas and ◊ Theophanes, but also in part upon lost ecclesiastical histories. Only for the first half of the 9th century has his chronicle much independent value. His language and style are popular and simple; as he says, 'it is better to stammer the truth than to lie in the tongue of Plato'. The work was highly esteemed by his successors, and was translated into Old Slavonic in the 10th or 11th century and into Georgian in the 11th or 12th. A continuation, carrying the narrative up to 948, was written in the 10th century, probably by an adherent of the deposed emperor Romanus Lecapenus, and was later re-edited with copious interpolations from the history of ◊ Genesius; it too was translated into Old Slavonic. Both original and continuation were much drawn on by later chroniclers, lexicographers and others. [R B]

Teubner: C. De Boor (2 vols., Leipzig, 1904); *Theophanes continuatus, Ioannes Cameniata, Symeon Magister, Georgius monachus*, ed. I. Bekker (C S H B, 1838) (the continuation).

George Pachymeres. ◊ Pachymeres, George.

George of Pisidia (first half of 7th century A.D.). Byzantine poet. He was deacon and chartophylax (=archivist) of Hagia Sophia in Constantinople in the reign of Heraclius (610–41). His poems, which are with one exception in 12-syllable lines, fall into two groups, historical and religious. The historical poems comprise an account of Heraclius's Persian campaign (1,093 lines), a poem on the Avar attack on Constantinople in 626 (541 lines), a panegyric on Heraclius (471 lines), a poem on the recovery of the Cross by Heraclius in 628 (116 lines), and some shorter compositions. The religious poems include the *Hexaemeron*, on the creation of the world (1,910 lines), a polemic against the heretic Severus of Antioch (726 lines), and a poem on the vanity of life, after the manner of Ecclesiastes (262 lines). We have also some epigrams on a variety of themes, religious and historical. His style is clear and refined, rising at times to grandeur. His copious vocabulary is employed with fine discrimination; his imagery striking and harmonious. Though he knew the Greek tragedians, and particularly their messengers' speeches, he is no mere imitator. He observes the ancient vowel quantities, no longer brought out in pronunciation, but also has a regular pattern of stress accent at the caesura and the end of the line. He is thus the perfecter, if not the originator, of the Byzantine 12-syllable metre, the descendant of the classical iambic trimeter. He was much esteemed in the Byzantine world, and later critics compared him with advantage to Homer and Euripides. Chroniclers used him as a source for Heraclius's campaigns. The *Hexaemeron* was translated into Armenian and Old Slavonic. [R B]

Claudii Aeliani varia historia, ii, ed. R. Hercher (Leipzig, 1866) (*Hexaemeron*); *Panegirici epici*, ed. and Italian tr. A. Pertusi (Ettal, 1959).

Th. Nissen, 'Historisches Epos und Panegyricus in der Spätantike', in *Hermes* 75 (1940).

George Sphrantzes. ◊ Sphrantzes, George.

George Syncellus (d. between 810 and 814). Byzantine chronicler. A monk, George spent many years in Palestine and later became private secretary (*syncellus*) to the Byzantine Patriarch Tarasius (784–806). His *Chronicle* extends from the Creation to A.D. 284 and consists largely of long, detailed chronological tables. He drew upon many lost historians and chronologists who welded together Greco-Roman and Judaeo-Christian history in a single chronological framework. [R B]

Ed. G. Dindorf (C S H B, 2 vols., 1829).

Glycas, Michael (Michael Sikidites) (mid 12th cent.). Byzantine historian, theologian and poet. Probably born in Corcyra, he lived in Constantinople, was sentenced to be blinded in 1159 for his heretical views, and survived, still active, until after 1185. His *Chronicle*, from the Creation to 1118, is a trivial work of no historical value. His *Problems of Holy Scripture* is a systematic commentary of great learning, marked by scepticism and historical sense. There survive also a poem in vernacular Greek written in prison and some letters. [R B]

Annales, ed. I. Bekker (C S H B, 1836); *Michaēl tu Glyka eis tas aporias tēs theias graphēs kephalaia*, ed. I. Eustratiades (2 vols., Athens, 1906, Alexandria, 1912).

K. Krumbacher, *Michael Glykas. Eine Skizze seiner Biographie und seiner literarischen Thätigkeit* (B A W, Munich, 1895).

Gregoras, Nicephorus (1290–1360). Byzantine historian, polymath and statesman. Born in Paphlagonia, Gregoras came to Constantinople as a young man, became a pupil of Theodore ◊ Metochites, and from 1326 was in the thick of the political and theological controversies of his time. He was a principal opponent of Gregory ◊ Palamas and the Hesychasts, and so from 1351 to 1355 was confined to a monastery; but it had a magnificent library, and Gregoras's literary output was undiminished. His surviving writings include rhetorical, grammatical, philosophical and mathematical works, speeches, poems, a collection of letters, and a *Roman History* covering the years 1204–1359. His *History* depends in its earlier portion in part on lost sources, in its later mainly on his own observation. It has the faults of the age – over-emphasis of theological and ecclesiastical controversies, an uncompromisingly partisan attitude to the events of his own time, and a tiresome archaizing style, in which even place-names are disguised. But it is conceived on a grand scale (the years 1320–59 occupies 30 books), it embodies many documents and other source-material, and the author tries to discern general principles beneath the mass of confusing details. Used with discretion it is a most valuable source for the second quarter of the 14th century, a period of grim civil wars and bitter ideological controversy. Among his many other works, not all published, his letters are the most interesting. He was one of the leading mathematicians and astronomers of his age, forecasting eclipses and proposing a reform of the calendar which anticipated in many points the Gregorian reform (cf. his *History*, VIII: 13). Among his works in this field that of greatest interest to historians of science is his treatise on the construction of the astrolabe. Gregoras was clearly one of the greatest intellects of the 14th century, a man of immense energy and width of interest, and a passionate controversialist. His account of his own times is sometimes of absorbing interest. [R B]

Historia, ed. L. Schopen, I. Bekker (C S H B, 3 vols., 1829–55) (there are Italian and French translations dating from the 16th and 17th centuries, and a Russian translation, St Petersburg, 1862); *Correspondence*, ed. and Fr. tr. R. Guilland (Paris, 1927).

R. Guilland, *Essai sur Nicéphore Grégoras. L'homme et l'œuvre* (Paris, 1926); I. Ševčenko. 'Some Autographs of Nicephorus Gregoras', in *Zbornik radova Vizantološkog instituta* 8 (1963).

Gregory of Cyprus (*c.* 1241–after 1289). Byzantine theologian and man of letters. Born in Cyprus, he went to Constantinople in 1261 to study under George ◊ Acropolites. After a long career on the staff of the Patriarchate, he became Patriarch himself in 1283, but was forced to resign in 1289. At first a partisan of union with Rome, he early changed sides, but finally lost the support of all parties in the complex ecclesiastical politics of the time. Besides his polemical theological works and panegyrics upon saints, he wrote ceremonial speeches, an interesting autobiography and some letters. The autobiography and the letters throw much light on the intellectual life of the Byzantine empire after the expulsion of the Latins. [R B]

Migne, *P G*, 142; *Autobiography*, Fr. tr. W. Lameere (Rome, 1937).

Gregory Palamas. ◊ Palamas, Gregory.

I

Ikasia. ◊ Casia.

Ignatius the Deacon (early 9th cent.). Byzantine poet and hagiographer. Ignatius was a deacon on the staff of the Patriarch of Constantinople, and later became Metropolitan of Nicaea. His poetry includes a rendering in 12-syllable tetrastichs of the fables of Aesop, and a curious dramatic dialogue between Adam, Eve, God and the Serpent, certainly designed for reading rather than acting. He is a heavy and awkward versifier. His prose works include lives of the patriarchs Tarasius (784–806) and Nicephorus (806–15), and of St Gregory Dekapolites. [R B]

Migne, *P G*, 117; *Nicephori archiepiscopi Constantinopolitani opuscula historica*, ed. C. de Boor (Leipzig, 1880) (Life of Nicephorus); ed. J. A. Heikel, *Acta societatis scient. Fennicae* 17 (1889) (Life of Tarasius); *La vie de S. Grégoire le Dêcapolite et les slaves macédoniens au IXe siècle*, ed. F. Dvornik (Paris, 1926).

Italus, John (second half of 11th cent.). Byzantine philosopher. A south-Italian Greek, he studied in Constantinople under Michael ⇨ Psellus, whom he succeeded as professor of philosophy. His uncompromising dialectic led him into theological positions which could be regarded as heretical; this, together with political opposition, led to his synodal trial and condemnation in 1082; he renounced his errors but seems not to have been permitted to continue teaching. A less pliant character than Psellus, and with none of his master's literary elegance, Italus in his commentaries on Aristotle and other philosophical works was feeling his way towards a new Christian-Platonist synthesis. His influence showed itself in a continuing Platonist current of thought throughout the 12th century, which constantly clashed with Christian orthodoxy. [R B]

Quaestiones quodlibetales, ed. P. Joannou (Ettal, 1956).
P. Joannou, *Christliche Metaphysik in Byzanz. I: Die Illuminationslehre des Michael Psellos und Joannes Italos* (Ettal, 1956).

J

John Argyropulos (d. 1487). Byzantine humanist. After teaching for some years in Constantinople he emigrated to Italy and by 1441 was teaching Greek in Padua. In 1456 he was invited to Florence by the Medici, and after 1470 to Rome by Pope Sixtus IV. His teaching influenced a wide circle in Renaissance Italy and beyond. His works include numerous Latin translations, particularly of Aristotle, and theological works in Greek. [R B]

G. Cammelli, *I dotti bizantini e le origini dell'umanesimo. II, Giovanni Argiropulo* (Florence, 1941) (full references to published works).

John Cameniates. ⇨ Cameniates, John.

John Cantacuzenus (John VI). ⇨ Cantacuzenus, John VI.

John Cinnamus. ⇨ Cinnamus, John.

John Climax (John Climacus) (born 2nd half of 6th cent., d. *c.* 670). Byzantine theologian. After some years in monasteries, probably in Egypt, he spent 40 years as a hermit on Mount Sinai and later became abbot of the monastery of St Catherine there. His *Stairway to Paradise* is a treatise on the ascetic's spiritual development, of great influence in Byzantine monastic life for many centuries. It was also translated during the Middle Ages into Syriac, Georgian, Latin and Arabic. A cycle of illustrations is found in many manuscripts. John also wrote a handbook for heads of monasteries, the *Liber ad pastorem*. [R B]

Migne, *P G*, 89; *Scala Paradisi: The Holy Ladder of Perfection*, tr. Father Robert (1858).

John of Damascus (John Damascene) (*c.* 675–*c.* 750). Byzantine theologian. Born of a rich Christian family of Damascus – his father was a high financial officer under the Umayyad caliphs – John as a young man entered a monastery near Jerusalem, where he spent the rest of his life. He was prominent in theological disputes, and was theological adviser to successive patriarchs of Jerusalem and Antioch. Living in Moslem territory, out of reach of the long arm of the Iconoclast emperors of Constantinople, he became the principal defender of image-worship in the Orthodox Church. He is regarded as a saint by both eastern and western Churches.

He was a prolific writer; his reputation during his lifetime and after his death caused many works to be wrongly attributed to him. There are therefore many complex problems of authenticity in connexion with his works, and no complete list can be given here. Undoubtedly authentic is his *Fountain of Knowledge*, a great dogmatic treatise in 3 parts, the first dealing with philosophical problems and terminology, the second with the refutation of heresies, and the third with the exposition of orthodox doctrine. It has had immense influence in both eastern and western Churches, and has been compared with the *Summa* of St Thomas Aquinas. It is supplemented by minor dogmatic works on particular questions. John also wrote a number of polemical treatises directed against Nestorians, Jacobites, Manichaeans and above all the Iconoclasts; a series of Biblical commentaries, largely derivative in character, and not all certainly authentic; a number of moral and ascetic treatises; a series of Homilies, which present many difficult problems of authorship; several saints' lives and panegyrics upon saints; and hymns in both quantitative and accentual metre, which are still in liturgical use. Among the longer works whose attribution is uncertain the most important are the *Sacra parallela*, a vast anthology of Biblical and patristic excerpts arranged under ethical categories, and the *Story of Barlaam and Joasaph*, a Christianized Greek version, via Persian and Arabic or Georgian intermediaries, of the story of Buddha, itself translated into Latin and many western European languages in the Middle Ages.

John of Damascus himself disclaims all originality. But he had a sovereign command both of earlier Christian literature and of the Aristotelian tradition of the ancient world, as filtered through the neo-Platonist and Christian commentators of late antiquity; he had an unerring eye for the crux of a complex problem; and he could set out a difficult argument with clarity and elegance. He stands head and shoulders above his fellows in a dark age, much as does his contemporary Bede. [R B]

Migne, *P G*, 94–96; H. G. Beck, *Kirche und theologische Literatur im byzantinischen Reich* (Munich, 1959) (full bibliography); *Fountain of Knowledge*, German tr. D. Stiefenhofer (Kempten-Munich, 1923); Pt III tr. S. D. F. Salmond (N P F, 1899). D. Ainslee, *John of Damascus* (4th edn, 1906); J. M. Hoeck, 'Stand und Aufgaben der Damaskenos-Forschung', in *Orientalia christiana periodica* 17 (1957) (a fundamental study).

John Italus. ⇨ Italus, John.

John Kyriotes Geometres (10th cent.). Byzantine poet. A court dignitary, he later became Metropolitan of Melitene. He wrote a large number of short occasional poems, in 12-syllable verses, hexameters, and elegiac couplets, on many themes – personal, historical, mythological, literary, religious, sepulcral, descriptive, etc. – and also a long verse encomium of St Panteleimon, 5 hymns to the Virgin, a paraphrase of the Song of Solomon, prose homilies, commentaries on Church Fathers, etc. His command of language and style, his wide culture and his warm, sincere personality make him one of the most sympathetic of Byzantine poets. Though his language is classicizing, and his verse-forms traditional, he handles them with un-Byzantine directness and brevity. [R B]

J. Sajdak, *Ioannis Kyriotis Geometrae Hymni in SS. Deiparam* (Poznan, 1931) (poetry bibliography); H. G. Beck, *Kirche und theologische Literatur im byzantinischen Reich* (Munich, 1959) (prose bibliography).

John Malalas. ⇨ Malalas, John.

John Mauropus. ⇨ Mauropus, John.

John Moschus (d. 619). Byzantine theologian. As companion and friend of the future patriarch ⇨ Sophronius he visited monastic settlements and hermitages throughout the Near East, and went to Rome in 614, where he stayed until his death. His *Spiritual Meadow* (*Pneumatikos Leimon*) is a series of edifying stories of monks and hermits, full of biographical detail and vividly presented topical information, and so throwing much light not only on spiritual ideals and ascetic practices, but also on the social and economic history of the time. Their language is close to the vernacular. There are Latin, Old Slavonic and Arabic translations. [R B].

Migne, *P G*, 87; *Morceaux choisis du pré spirituel de Jean Moschos*, ed., Fr. tr. and comm. D. C. Hesseling (Paris, 1931).
N. H. Baynes, *Byzantine Studies and Other Essays* (1955).

John Philoponus. ◊ Philoponus, John.

John Scylitzes. ◊ Scylitzes, John.

John Tzetzes (*c.*1110–*c.*1180). Byzantine scholar and man of letters. Born in Constantinople of a family that had seen better days, he received a good education and obtained a post as secretary to a provincial governor. But he was soon dismissed as a result of some adventure involving the governor's wife, and worked for some time as a secretary in Constantinople. For most of the rest of his life he gained a poor livelihood by teaching and writing, though for a time he enjoyed the patronage of a lady of the imperial family, and had the sons of distinguished men as his pupils. In later life he was attached in some way to a monastery of imperial foundation, though not as a monk. His wide contacts in the worlds of affairs and letters are reflected in his correspondence. Tzetzes was a very erudite man, and at the same time as vain and touchy as a child. Reduced by poverty to selling his library, he relied a great deal on his extraordinary memory, of which he was very proud; but it often let him down. He is outspoken in his dealings with the great, and justly proud of his own ability. His principal works are: (1) Commentaries on many classical Greek poems, from Homer to Oppian, in which he shows an originality new in this field; notable among them is a long allegorical commentary on the *Iliad* and *Odyssey* in 15-syllable verses; (2) Hexameter poems on the Trojan war, its antecedents and its consequences, to which he wrote a commentary himself; (3) A mythological poem in 15-syllable verses, the *Theogony;* (4) A collection of 107 letters, some of which appear to be rhetorical models rather than actual missives; they are an interesting source for the social and intellectual life of the period, as well as a mine of obscure literary and historical allusions; (5) The *Historiae* or *Chiliads,* a versified commentary on his letters in 12,674 15-syllable lines, in which he elucidates 660 points of mythology, history, geography and literary history alluded to in the letters. He later composed a prose commentary on his commentary. The Chiliads contain much information not available elsewhere, but Tzetzes' hasty way of working and his reliance on his memory make much of it suspect; (6) A number of occasional poems on personalities and events of his own time; (7) Introductions in verse to dramatic and bucolic poetry, which preserve some of the literary theory of late antiquity. Most of these works are by-products of Tzetzes' activity as a teacher, either used as text-books by himself or composed to the order of distinguished patrons. The use of verse in so many of them is a mnemonic device rather than the outcome of any poetic inspiration.

Tzetzes is of interest to the classical scholar for the numerous citations from lost commentaries, handbooks and occasionally works of literature, e.g. the poems of Hipponax, which are embedded in his writings. But he also merits study in his own right, as a colourful, original, somewhat querulous personality, and as an example of a teacher of literature and his aims and methods, in one of the most productive periods of Byzantine letters. His sincerity of purpose and love of truth are beyond question, though his too great facility of composition and the difficult conditions in which he worked led him to make many slips. We have learned now to appreciate him more than did 19th-century scholarship. [R B]

Ed. P. Matranga, *Anecdota graeca*, i (Rome, 1850) (allegorical commentaries on the *Iliad* and first half of the *Odyssey*, and the *Theogony*); H. Hunger, *Byzantinische Zeitschrift* 48 (1955) (the newly discovered allegorical commentary on the rest of the *Odyssey*); *Commentarii in Aristophanem*, ed. L. Massa Positano and others, 1–3 (Groningen, 1960–62); *Antehomerica, Homerica et Posthomerica*, ed. I. Bekker (Berlin, 1816); *Epistolae*, ed. T. Pressel (Tübingen, 1851); *Historiarum variarum chiliades*, ed. T. Kiessling (Leipzig, 1826, repr. Hildesheim, 1963).

Article 'Tzetzes' by C. Wendel in Pauly-Wissowa, *Real-Encyclopädie* 7 A (Stuttgart, 1942).

John Zonaras. ◊ Zonaras, John.

Joseph Genesius. ◊ Genesius, Joseph.

K

Kyriotes Geometres, John. ◊ John Kyriotes Geometres.

L

Lascaris, Theodore. ⇨ Theodore Lascaris.

Leo Diaconus (end of 10th cent.). Byzantine historian. A native of Caloe in Asia Minor, Leo held ecclesiastical office and took part in Basil II's Bulgarian campaign in 986. His *History* recounts in considerable detail the years 959–76, and is mainly based on eye-witness accounts and personal observation. It is a reliable and valuable source. Leo, a man of wide reading, writes an archaizing and artificial Greek, full of classical tags and allusions, which sometimes obscure rather than illuminate his narrative. There survives also a panegyric by Leo upon Basil II. [R B]

Ed. C. B. Hase (C S H B, 1828).

F. Loretto, *Nikephoras Phokas, 'Der bleiche Tod der Sarazener' und Johannes Tzimiskes, Die Zeit von 959–976, in der Darstellung des Leon Diakonos* (Graz, 1961).

Leo VI (866–912). Byzantine emperor and writer. He succeeded his father Basil I in 886. A pupil of ⇨ Photius, of scholarly tastes and weak health, he took no part in the military campaigns of his reign, but in his own lifetime was nicknamed 'the Wise'. His numerous writings include a compilatory handbook on tactics, a funeral oration on his father, theological works of various kinds, iambic poems, etc. The great Byzantine legal code, the *Basilica,* was prepared under his direction, and many special enactments were issued by him. A collection of oracles circulating in the 14th and 15th century was falsely attributed to him. A colourless character, Leo yet typifies the renewed scholarly interests and encyclopedic spirit which found its best expression in his son ⇨ Constantine VII. [R B]

Migne, *P G*, 107; *Tactica*, ed. R. Vári (2 vols., Budapest, 1917–22); *Leonis VI sapientis problemata*, ed. A. Dain (Paris, 1935).

Leontius of Neapolis (d. *c.* 650). Byzantine theologian. A friend and colleague of the Cyprian-born Patriarch of Alexandria, John the Almsgiver (610–19), Leontius became bishop of Neapolis in Cyprus. His *Life of John the Almsgiver,* written in popular language and style, is a precious source for the social and economic history of the times, and incidentally mentions trade between Egypt and Britain in the 7th century. In his *Life of St Symeon of Edessa* there is less information and more concern with the miraculous. There survive also an anti-Jewish dialogue (published only in part) and some sermons of dubious authenticity. [R B]

Migne, *P G*, 86, 93; *Leben des Heiligen Johannes des Barmherzigen*, ed. H. Gelzer (Freiburg-Leipzig, 1893); *Life of John the Almsgiver*, tr. E. Dawes and N. H. Baynes, in *Three Byzantine Saints* (1948) (slightly abbreviated); *Ausgewählte kleine Schriften*, ed. H. Gelzer (Leipzig, 1907).

L. Rydén, *Das Leben des heiligen Narren Symeon von Leontios von Neapolis* (Stockholm, 1963).

M

Machaeras, Leontius (first half of 15th cent.). Cypriote historian. A Greek in the service of the Latin rulers of Cyprus, for whom he undertook a diplomatic mission to the Turks in 1452, Machaeras wrote a history of Cyprus from 1359 to 1432. He used good sources, including those in western languages, for the earlier part, and his own observation for the later. Strongly influenced by medieval French historiography, he stands quite outside the Byzantine tradition. His language is basically the Cypriote vernacular, but is overloaded with French and Italian loan words, and his style is awkward and obscure. [R B]

Ed. and tr. R. M. Dawkins (2 vols., 1932).

R. M. Dawkins, *The Nature of the Cypriot Chronicle of Leontios Makhairas*, The Taylorian Lecture 1945 (1945).

Magister, Thomas. ⇨ Thomas Magister.

Malalas, John (*c.* 491–*c.* 578). Byzantine historian. Nothing definite is known of his life. He was probably of Syrian origin and a native of Antioch, and may be identical with the Byzantine Patriarch John III Antiochius (565–77). His

Chronicle, from the Creation to 565, includes Biblical history, Greek mythology, and the history of oriental peoples as well as Greek, Roman and Byzantine political history. It is an uncritical compilation from a great variety of sources, full of absurd errors. Trivial curiosities and isolated episodes are graphically described; Malalas always knows exactly what historical or mythological figures looked like. Events in Antioch are kept in the foreground. A tone of rather primitive Christian apology prevails, and provides the author with his only frame of reference. Nevertheless Malalas in his later sections preserves much information from lost sources, in particular from a local chronicle of Antioch. Used carefully he is a valuable source for the first half of the 6th century. The style is simple and the language reflects the spoken tongue of the time. The Greek text, which survives in a single manuscript in the Bodleian library, has been slightly abbreviated, and a fuller version is in a 10th- or 11th-century Old Slavonic translation. There was also a Georgian translation. Malalas was immensely popular in the Byzantine world and was used directly or indirectly by all succeeding writers of universal history.

Ed. L. Dindorf (CSHB, 1831); Books VIII–XVIII, tr. M. Spinka and G. M. Downey (Chicago, 1940).

G. M. Downey, *A History of Antioch in Syria* (Princeton, 1961); K. Weierholt, *Studien im Sprachgebrauch des Malalas* (Oslo, 1963).

Manasses, Constantine. ⇨ Constantine Manasses.

Manuel Chrysoloras (*c.* 1350–*c.* 1414). Byzantine humanist and diplomat. A pupil of Demetrius ⇨ Cydones he became like his master a Roman Catholic convert. After carrying out several diplomatic missions in Italy for Manuel II he settled in Florence, where he taught Greek for many years. He later taught in Paris, Rome and elsewhere, and died at the Council of Constance. He gave the first stimulus to Greek studies in Renaissance Italy, and numbered many scholars and men of letters among his pupils. His works include theological treatises, letters and a Greek grammar. [RB]

Migne, *PG*, 156.

G. Cammelli, *I dotti bizantini e le origini dell'umanesimo. I, Manuele Crisolora* (Florence, 1941).

Manuel Moschopulus. ⇨ Moschopulus, Manuel.

Manuel II Palaeologus (1350–1425). Byzantine emperor and man of letters. Succeeding his father John V in 1391 he fought persistently to save the dwindling and threatened Byzantine empire from the Turks. In 1399–1402 he visited Italy, France and England. Widely cultured, he left a mass of letters, occasional speeches, poems, a treatise on the duties of a king, and a number of theological works, apologetic, dogmatic and homiletic. Not all have been published. Manuel is an attractive character, a scholar of ability and a pleasing writer, though hindered rather than helped by the classicizing literary tradition of Byzantium. Several portraits exist from his Italian visit. [RB]

Migne, *PG*, 156; *Lettres*, ed. E. Legrand (Paris 1893, repr. Amsterdam, 1962).

S. Lampros, *Palaiologeia kai Peloponnēsiaka*, iii (Athens, 1926).

Mauropus, John (11th cent. A.D.). Byzantine poet and scholar. Born in Paphlagonia about 1000, he was appointed to the Chair of Rhetoric in the refounded University of Constantinople in 1045, and a few years later became Metropolitan of Euchaita in Pontus. He returned to a monastery in the capital in his old age. His writings comprise a collection of epigrams on a variety of themes, about 150 liturgical hymns in accentual rhythm (some perhaps not authentic), a lexicon in verse, 77 letters, 13 homilies and a saint's life. He combined wide and humane culture with simple piety, and is one of the most attractive figures of the middle Byzantine period. The short poem in which he prays to Christ to save Plato and Plutarch from damnation typifies his outlook. [RB]

P. de Lagarde and J. Bollig, *Johannis Euchaitarum metropolitae quae supersunt in cod. Vaticano graeco 676* (Berlin, 1882); H. G. Beck, *Kirche und theologische Literatur im byzantinischen Reich* (Munich, 1959) (for publication of other works).

J. M. Hussey, 'The Writings of John Mauropus', in *Byzantinische Zeitschrift* 44 (1951).

Maximus Confessor (580–662). Byzantine theologian. Maximus was secretary of State to the emperor Heraclius (610–41), and after becoming a monk about 613 lived in monasteries in Asia Minor, North Africa and Rome. In the great 7th-century Christological controversy he attacked, and by his writings demolished, the view that although there were two activities in Christ there was but a single will (Monothelism). In 653 the long arm of the monothelite emperor Constans II reached him in Rome, and he was haled off to Constantinople, tried and banished to Thrace; a year later he was sentenced to have his tongue cut out and his right hand amputated and banished to a remote spot on the eastern frontier, where he died. His writings cover every branch of theology, and include several collections of metaphysical problems with their answers, commentaries on biblical texts, a long series of dogmatic treatises; a collection of mystical and ascetic treatises, and a corpus of letters of great importance for the history of 7th-century theology. There are many unsolved problems of authenticity. In his dogmatic writings Maximus combines complete command of the writings of the Church Fathers with trenchant logic and debating skill; he made extensive use of the Pseudo-Dionysiac writings (➪ Pseudo-Dionysius the Areopagite). His mystical writings are at the root of most subsequent Byzantine religious mysticism. He writes clear, flowing Greek, with little attempt at ornamentation for its own sake. He has been called the last independent thinker in the eastern Church. [R B]

Migne, *P G*, 90–91; *The Ascetic Life. The Four Centuries in Charity*, tr. P. Sherwood (1955).

P. Sherwood, *An Annotated Date-List of the Works of Maximus the Confessor* (Rome, 1952).

Maximus Planudes. ➪ Planudes, Maximus.

Mazaris (early 15th cent.). Hero of an anonymous Byzantine account of a descent to Hades, the dramatic date of which is 1414–15. There are 3 sections, the descent to Hades proper, a scene in the Peloponnese in which various characters appear to Mazaris in a dream, and a pair of letters. Like the ➪ *Timarion*, it is an imitation of Lucian's *Necyomanteia*. The work is a satirical pamphlet, and many of the allusions cannot now be understood. Much of it consists of virulent and often crude abuse of individuals and classes. The language shows many traces of vernacular speech. [R B]

Ed., German tr. and comm. A. Ellissen, *Analekten der mittel- und neugriechischen Litteratur*, iv (Leipzig, 1860).

Meliteniotes, Theodore. ➪ Theodore Meliteniotes.

Menander Protector (second half of 6th cent.). Byzantine historian. Born in Constantinople, studied and practised law, later became a military officer attached to the court of the emperor Maurice (582–602). His *History*, a sequel to that of ➪ Agathias, from 558 to at least 582, is based on eye-witness accounts and official documents, many of which he quotes. It survives only in excerpts. Plain and unpretentious in style and reliable factually, it is a uniquely valuable source for the last decade of Justinian's reign and those of him immediate successors, and embodies much fascinating ethnographical material. [R B]

Ed. L. Dindorf, *Historici graeci minores*, ii (Leipzig, 1871); *Byzantinische Diplomaten und östliche Barbaren. Aus den Excerpta de legationibus des Konstantinos Porphyrogennetos ausgewählte Abschnitte des Priskos und Menander Protector*, tr. E. Doblhofer (Graz, 1955).

Metochites, Theodore (d. 1332). Byzantine statesman and polymath. Son of George Metochites, theologian and champion of church union, he was educated in Constantinople and entered the state service. He soon became the close friend and chief minister of the emperor Andronicus II. On the fall of his imperial patron he retired to the monastery of Chora (now the Kariye Cami), which he had earlier had restored and decorated with the finest example of late Byzantine fresco paintings. Theodore was renowned for his width of learning; his works, many still unpublished, include rhetorical exercises and speeches, extensive paraphrastic commentaries on Aristotle, a hand-book of astronomy, letters, panegyrics upon saints, minor poems, etc. The two works still of interest are his collection of 120 miscellaneous essays on philosophical, historical and literary subjects, and his series of 20 long hexameter poems on personal and contemporary themes. The former reveal independent thinking on traditional problems, and to some extent systematically criticize the whole Byzantine intellectual tradition; he has been called a forerunner of Renaissance humanism. The latter are informative on events and personalities, the author's great library, his monastery life, and his lively and sincere interest in culture. [R B]

Miscellanea, ed. M. C. G. Müller and Th. Kiessling (Leipzig, 1821); *Dichtungen*, ed. M. Treu (Potsdam, 1895).

H. G. Beck, *Die Krise des byzantinischen Weltbildes im 14. Jahrhundert* (Munich, 1952); R. Guilland, 'Les poésies inédites de Théodore Métochite', in *Études byzantines* (Paris, 1959); I. Ševčenko, *Études sur la polémique entre Théodore Métochite et Nicéphore Choumnos* (Brussels, 1962).

Michael Acominatus. ⇨ Choniates, Michael.

Michael Attaliates. ⇨ Attaliates, Michael.

Michael Choniates. ⇨ Choniates, Michael.

Michael Critobulus. ⇨ Critobulus, Michael.

Michael Glycas. ⇨ Glycas, Michael.

Michael Panaretos. ⇨ Panaretos, Michael.

Michael Psellus. ⇨ Psellus, Michael.

Moschopulus, Manuel (b. *c.*1265). Byzantine scholar. He was a pupil of Maximus ⇨ Planudes and probably his successor as head of a school in Constantinople, where he taught throughout his life. A mysterious excursion into politics led to his imprisonment for a time. His works include a grammar and lexicon, commented editions of selections from classical poetry, letters, a treatise on the mathematical properties of magic squares and an anti-Latin theological tractate. As an editor he made many false conjectures, but also cleared up many long-standing errors in the traditional texts. His comments, when original, are mainly lexicographical. [R B]

R. Aubreton, *Démétrius Triclinius et les recensions médiévales de Sophocle* (Paris, 1949); I. Ševčenko, 'The Imprisonment of Manuel Moschopoulos', in *Speculum* 27 (1952).

Moschus, John. ⇨ John Moschus.

N

Nicephorus (*c.*750–829). Byzantine patriarch and historian. Born of a distinguished family in Constantinople, he became imperial secretary, like his father before him, and later became a monk and founded a monastery. Elected patriarch in 806, he was deposed in 815 by the Iconoclast emperor Leo V, and remained in exile until his death. Besides a number of polemical theological treatises directed against the Iconoclasts, some still unpublished, Nicephorus wrote 2 historical works: his *Chronicle*, a brief chronological list of rulers and church dignitaries from the Creation to 829 with jejune historical notes; his *Breviarium*, a history of the years 602–769. Like ⇨ Theophanes he draws on many sources now lost. His approach is theological and his interest lies in picturesque details rather than in the broad sweep of history. But he faithfully reproduced what he found in his texts and is, along with Theophanes, a principal source of our knowledge of eastern-European history in the Dark Ages. A 9th-century manuscript in the British Museum appears to preserve an earlier version of the first part of the *Breviarium*. Though Nicephorus, as can be seen from his theological works, was a learned man, the *Breviarium* is written in plain style, with few literary adornments, and in a language which shows many popular features: it was probably composed for monastic reading. It was translated into Latin by the papal librarian Anastasius *c.*870, and there is also an Old Slavonic translation dating from *c.*900. There is a contemporary biography of Nicephorus by his pupil, the deacon ⇨ Ignatius. [R B]

Opuscula historica, ed. C. De Boor (Leipzig, 1880); Migne, *P G*, 100 (theological works).

P. J. Alexander, *The Patriarch Nicephorus of Constantinople* (1958).

Nicephorus Blemmydes. ◊ Blemmydes, Nicephorus.

Nicephorus Bryennius. ◊ Bryennius, Nicephorus.

Nicephorus Gregoras. ◊ Gregoras, Nicephorus.

Nicetas Acominatus. ◊ Choniates, Nicetas.

Nicetas Choniates. ◊ Choniates, Nicetas.

P

Pachymeres, George (1242–*c.* 1310). Byzantine historian and polymath. Born in Nicaea, he came to Constantinople in 1261 and held a succession of high offices in church and state. His *History*, covering the reigns of Michael VIII and Andronicus II (1261–1308) and based largely on his own observation, is the main narrative source for the period. The prominence given to theological disputes and the involved, allusive, archaizing style make for difficult reading. Other surviving works are: rhetorical and theological texts, poems, an outline of the philosophy of Aristotle, and a vast compendium of the mathematical sciences, important for the history of science. [R B]

De Michaele et Andronico Palaeologis, ed. I. Bekker (2 vols., C S H B, 1835); *Le Quadrivium de Georges Pachymère*, ed. P. Tannery (Vatican City, 1940).

Palamas, Gregory (1296/7–1359). Byzantine theologian. Born and educated in Constantinople, he spent many years as a monk on Mount Athos, in Thessalonica, and in Berrhoea, and was initiated into the mystical doctrines and practices of the Hesychasts, who sought by divers techniques direct individual experience of God, and tended to scorn both the intellectual element in Christianity and the organization of the church. Drawn into ecclesiastical controversies in the 1330s, he was soon the acknowledged leader and spokesman of the Hesychasts, and deeply involved in political struggles. The victory of John VI ◊ Cantacuzenus, whom the Hesychasts supported, brought him the metropolitan see of Thessalonica. Later he was captured by Turkish pirates, who held him for several years until he was ransomed.

His writings, many still unpublished, are mainly polemical, arising out of his day-to-day controversies. Together they form a powerful, persuasive account of the mystical, anti-intellectual side of late Byzantine monasticism. They have had a great influence upon Orthodox Church thought, which venerates Palamas as a saint. We have also a large collection of his homilies. Palamas, like the Hesychasts whose spokesman he was, turns his back not only on the Byzantine synthesis of ancient philosophy and Christian revelation, but also on the whole 14th-century Byzantine intellectual movement, which was one of the precursors of Renaissance humanism, and of which he himself was a product. [R B]

Migne, *P G*, 150, 151; *Défense des saints hésychastes*, ed., Fr. tr. etc. J. Meyendorff (2 vols., Louvain, 1959).

J. Meyendorff, *Introduction à l'étude de Grégoire Palamas* (Paris, 1959, abbreviated tr., *A Study of Gregory Palamas*, 1964) (full bibliography).

Panaretos, Michael (first half of 15th cent.). Byzantine historian. Nothing is known of his life. His brief history of the Empire of Trebizond covers the period 1204–1426, is a unique source for the history of the independent Trebizond empire, and contains much valuable material on the early history of the Ottoman Turks. [R B]

Ed. I. T. Pampukes (Athens, 1947).

Paschal Chronicle. Byzantine chronicle, covering the period from the Creation to A.D. 627, and compiled by an unknown cleric in Constantinople shortly after 628. It is a vast chronological table filled out, particularly in the later years, with historical information and misinformation, from various sources. The concluding section (600 onwards) is fairly full and based on personal observation and eyewitness accounts; it alone is of any value. The style is unadorned and the language popular. [R B]

Ed. L. Dindorf (C S H B, 1832).

Paul the Silentiary (6th cent.). Byzantine poet. By profession a gentleman-usher (*silentiarios*) at the court of Justinian, Paul was a member of the literary circle of ◊ Agathias. His best-known work is his *Description of the Church of the Hagia Sophia* in 887 hexameters, to which the 'Description of the Pulpit (*Ambon*)' of the church, in 275 hexameters, is an appendix. In style and metre he is a follower of Nonnus (◊ p. 124). Descriptive poetry is rarely successful, but Paul's poem is an exception. His rich, almost verbose, style and his felicitous imagery in no way diminish the precision of his description, and his poem has been fruitfully studied by archaeologists. It belongs to a genre – the epic ecphrasis – which was much cultivated in late antiquity; a pagan pendant to Paul's Christian poem is the description of an allegorical mural painting by his contemporary John of Gaza. We have in addition 78 short poems by Paul, included by Agathias in his anthology. About half are erotic; the rest vary in theme. But all are elegant and in good taste, and avoid the occasional long-windedness of Agathias. Paul is among the last Greek poets in the classical tradition, to which he forms a not unworthy conclusion. [R B]

Johannes von Gaza und Paulus Silentiarius; Kunstbeschreibungen justinianischer Zeit, ed. P. Friedländer (Leipzig, 1912); epigrams in the Greek Anthology (◊ p. 26); *Epigrammi*, ed. G. Viansino (Turin, 1963).

P. Lamma, *Ricerche sulla storia e cultura del sesto secolo* (Brescia, 1955).

Philes, Manuel (*c.* 1275–*c.* 1345). Byzantine poet. A native of Ephesus, he held a court appointment in Constantinople, took part in diplomatic missions to Russia, Persia, the Arab world and possibly India, but later was disgraced and imprisoned for a time. His surviving poetry amounts to some 25,000 lines. The bulk consists of short occasional poems – epigrams on stock mythological and religious themes, requests, complaints of poverty, encomia on benefactors, epitaphs, descriptive pieces, etc. But there are several longer poems: dramatic dialogues between a man and the spirit of a dead friend, and between the poet and his soul, didactic zoological poems, a paraphrase of the Akathistos Hymn in 12-syllable verses, etc. His favourite metre is the Byzantine 12-syllable line, which he employs with a new metrical strictness; he also writes hexameters and 15-syllable accentual lines (political verses). Despite his technical skill as a versifier, Philes has no poetic vein, and his work is nearly all pedestrian stuff. He repeats motifs and even entire passages from poem to poem, and he evidently had a stock of honorific addresses ready, to which he added a line or two specifying the occasion and the name of the dedicatee. His poetry, if such it can be called, is of interest largely for the incidental information it contains on prosopography, art history, etc. He writes exclusively in literary Greek, eschewing the vernacular. [R B]

Carmina, ed. E. Miller (2 vols., Paris, 1855–57); *Carmina inedita*, ed. E. Martini (Naples, 1900).

Philoponus, John (first half of 6th cent.). Byzantine philosopher. Born in Caesarea in Palestine, he studied in Alexandria under Ammonius, and perhaps succeeded him as head of the Alexandrian school. A Monophysite Christian and an Aristotelian, Philoponus found himself in open conflict with the still pagan and Platonizing school of Athens (◊ p. 120). Many of his commentaries on Aristotle survive. Although verbose, they still repay study; they have many flashes of penetration, and Philoponus had a sharp eye for analogies offered by the technology of late antiquity. His *De aeternitate mundi* is a polemical treatise addressed to the Athenian Proclus refuting the neo-Platonist view that the universe exists timelessly; it avoids specifically Christian arguments. A long commentary on the Biblical account of the Creation sought to make it comprehensible in terms of Aristotelian metaphysics and physics. Many other theological works are now lost, though read by ◊ Photius in the 9th century; others survive only in Syriac translation. Philoponus played a major role in welding together Judaeo-Christian tradition and pagan philosophical thought into a synthesis which provided an intellectual frame of reference for the Byzantines for many centuries. But to the Orthodox Church he was a heretic, and later generations often hesitated to acknowledge their debt to him. The Aristotelian commentators of the early 12th century were particularly indebted to Philoponus. [R B]

Commentaria graeca in Aristotelem, 13–17 (Berlin, 1887–1909); Teubner: *De aeternitate mundi*, H. Rabe (Leipzig, 1899); *De opificio mundi*, ed. G. Reichardt (Leipzig, 1897). S. Sambursky, *The Physical World of Late Antiquity* (London, 1962).

Photius (*c.* 820–*c.* 893). Byzantine patriarch and scholar. Born in Constantinople of a prominent family persecuted under the Iconoclasts, he acquired – we do not know how or where – a wide and profound acquaintance with all branches of knowledge cultivated in his time. After the restoration of icon-worship he combined service as imperial secretary with varied and extensive teaching activities in the newly refounded university. On the dismissal of the rigid zealot Ignatius, Photius, although still a layman, was called to the Patriarchal throne (25 December 858). The partisans of Ignatius obtained the support of Pope Nicholas I, and in 867 Photius was deposed and exiled. He was soon back in Constantinople as tutor to the future emperor ◊ Leo VI, and when Ignatius died in 877 Photius became Patriarch again. On the death of the emperor Basil I (886), Photius's opponents again prevailed, and he was deposed a second time. His stormy patriarchate marked the beginning of the schism between the eastern and western Churches, which was however patched up in his own lifetime. He furthered the conversion of Bulgaria and the beginnings of Byzantine Christianity in Russia, and in 9th-century European diplomatic history he played a prominent part. But it is as a scholar and man of letters that he is today remembered. His principal works are: (1) The *Bibliotheca* or *Myriobiblon*, an account of 280 books read in a reading circle conducted by Photius; besides a summary of the contents, each entry contains a critical judgement and often extensive excerpts. More than half the works discussed do not survive. They include theological writings of all kinds, historians from Herodotus to Photius's own day, the Attic orators and the rhetorical writers of the second sophistic, the Greek novelists, medical writers, grammarians, natural historians, etc. Little can be inferred from the absence of individual authors, but the almost complete absence of poetry and philosophy betokens the limited scope of Photius's own interests. The *Bibliotheca* is priceless not only for the information it supplies on lost works, but also for the light which it throws on the critical principles and methods of the Byzantine revival of learning after the Dark Ages. (2) A *Lexicon* of rare words and expressions met with in classical literature, supported by many quotations, often from works now lost. The full text was discovered in a Greek monastery library in 1959 and is unpublished. (3) A collection of over 250 letters, some official documents of historical interest, others telling us much of the intellectual and social life of the time. (4) 19 homilies, some, e.g. that on the Russian attack on Constantinople in 860, valuable sources for the historian.

There are traces of many other works, biblical commentaries, commentaries on patristic texts, polemical treatises, juristic studies, etc., and much that is spurious has been attached to his name. Photius is one of the greatest intellectual figures of the Middle Ages, at the very centre of the Byzantine renaissance of learning, whose effects were felt all over Europe. [R B]

Migne, *P G*, 101–104 (most works except the *Lexicon*, and much of doubtful authenticity); *Bibliothèque*, ed. and Fr. tr. R. Henri (4 vols., Paris, 1959–65); *Homiliai*, ed. B. Laourdas (Thessalonica, 1959); *Lexicon*, ed. S. A. Naber (2 vols., Leiden, 1864–5); *The Library of Photius*, tr. J. H. Freese (1920) (first part of *Bibliotheca*).

J. Hergenröther, *Photius, Patriarch von Konstantinopel* (3 vols., Regensburg, 1867–9) (still fundamental); F. Dvornik, *The Photian Schism, History and Legend* (1948); L. Politis, 'Die Handschriften des Klosters Zavorda und die neuaufgefundene Photios-Handschrift', in *Philologus* 105 (1961).

Pisides, George. ◊ George of Pisidia.

Planudes, Maximus (*c.* 1255–*c.* 1305). Byzantine scholar and man of letters. Born in Nicomedia as younger son of a provincial landowner, he was educated in Constantinople, and became successively an imperial secretary, a monk in Constantinople, and titular abbot of a monastery near Scutari. But he was primarily a teacher. He early became head of a school in which a complete education, from reading and writing to philosophy and higher mathematics, was given. Though housed successively in two monasteries in Constantinople, it enjoyed government subventions and was probably a part of the imperial university. Sent on a delicate diplomatic mission to Venice in 1296, he was arrested for a time by the Venetian authorities, and captured by pirates on his return journey.

Planudes was a polymath; language, literature, mathematics and theology all fell within his competence. He was one of the earliest Byzantine scholars to have a thorough acquaintance with Latin, and he translated many Latin works into Greek, mainly for pedagogical purposes. His letters reveal much about his interests and activities: seeking out copies of rare texts and old manuscripts of common texts, searching in libraries in odd corners of the empire for rarities, arranging for a supply of first-grade vellum from army booty, pondering on the problems of the theory of numbers, and writing testimonials for his former pupils.

His works, which reflect the width of his interests, include: (1) text-books of accidence, syntax and lexicology; (2) editions and commentaries on classical texts read in school; (3) an edition of the *Dionysiaca* of Nonnus, which he seems to have rescued from oblivion – Planudes' text, in a poetic miscellany compiled under his supervision, is the ancestor of all other manuscripts of the poem; (4) an edition of the complete works of Plutarch, compiled over a number of years from a variety of manuscripts; (5) an edition of the *Geography* of Ptolemy, a work for which he sought for many years, and for which he probably reconstructed a set of maps; (6) an edition of the first half of Diophantus's *Arithmetic*, accompanied by a commentary showing a high level of mathematical understanding; (7) a handbook of astronomical computation using positional numerals; (8) A compilatory text-book of rhetoric; (9) an anthology of short poems of classical and Byzantine authors, based on the anthology of Constantine Cephalas, but containing supplementary material (☞ Greek Anthology, p. 26); (10) a collection of letters far more informative than most Byzantine epistolography; (11) polemical theological treatises and homilies; (12) translations of Cicero's *Somnium Scipionis* with Macrobius's commentary, Caesar's *Gallic War*, Ovid's *Metamorphoses* and *Heroides*, Donatus's *Ars minor*, Augustine's *De Trinitate*, the *Distichs* attributed to Cato, and Boethius's *De consolatione philosophiae*.

Planudes combines wide-ranging vision, minute attention to detail, and great intellectual power. He taught most 14th-century Byzantine humanists, was a pioneer in bridging the intellectual gap between east and west, and had a warm, sympathetic personality. Most of his works are highly technical, but his letters repay reading by the non-specialist. [R B]

Epistulae, ed. M. Treu (Breslau, 1890, repr. Amsterdam, 1960).

Article, 'Planudes' by C. Wendel in Pauly-Wissowa, *Real-Encyclopädie* 20 (1950); J. Irigoin, *Histoire du texte de Pindare* (Paris, 1952); A. Turyn, *The Byzantine Manuscript Tradition of Euripides* (Urbana, 1957); C. Gallavotti, 'Planudea', in *Bollettino della Commissione per la Preparazione dell'Edizione Nazionale dei Classici Greci e Latini*, N.S. 7 (1959); 8 (1960).

Plethon, George Gemistus (1353–1452). Byzantine humanist and philosopher. He taught and held high office for many years at Mistra, the capital of the semi-independent Despotate of the Morea; in 1438–9 he was one of the Byzantine delegates to the Council of Ferrara and Florence, and gave public lectures in the latter; he returned to Mistra some years before his death. Plethon was steeped in neo-Platonism; in challenging the Christian-Aristotelian synthesis which provided the philosophical background to most Byzantine thought he directly conflicted with Christianity. He did not flinch, but constructed a whole neo-pagan religious and philosophical system, with a Platonist core; but he owed many of the trappings to the antiquarian scholarship of the last centuries of the Byzantine empire. It was no doubt the collapse of the whole Byzantine system of values, and the imminent fall of the Byzantine state itself, that made him throw overboard so much of Byzantine thought.

His works include the *Laws*, a vast systematic treatise modelled on Plato's *Laws*, of which only fragments survive, all copies having been burned by the ecclesiastical authorities; a treatise on political and economic reform in the Morea; a geographical handbook; a work on the differences between Plato and Aristotle; and numerous speeches and occasional writings. Plethon's influence in the Orthodox post-Byzantine world was slight; but in Italy his revelation of the idealist tradition of ancient philosophy made a profound and lasting impression. The Platonic Academy in Florence was largely the result of his inspiration, and Italian art and literature of the mid 15th century are full of echoes of the impact which his teaching made. [R B]

F. Masai, *Pléthon et le platonisme de Mistra* (Paris, 1956) (full references to the literature and to the very scattered publications of Plethon's works); C. Alexandre, *Plēthōnos nomōn syngraphēs ta sōzomena* (Paris, 1858).

Procopius (b. *c.* 500). Byzantine historian. A native of Caesarea in Palestine, he studied rhetoric and law, and by 527 held a high civilian post on the staff of Justinian's great marshal, Belisarius. He accompanied Belisarius on his Persian campaign (527–31), on his reconquest of Africa from the Vandals (533–4), and on his victorious campaign against the Ostrogoths in Italy (536–40). In 542 he was back in Constantinople, where he probably continued his official career and became Prefect of the City in 562.

His works comprise a *History of the Wars of Justinian* in 8 books, an account of Justinian's buildings, and the so-called *Secret History*. The *History of the Wars* covers the years 527–53, and deals primarily with Justinian's campaigns in east and west; but there are many digressions on the political scene in Constantinople, the most celebrated being the account of the Nika revolt of 532. Procopius had direct and comprehensive acquaintance with military affairs during most of this period, and could interrogate eye-witnesses of what he had not himself seen. His history principally rests upon these sources, but he also used written sources in Greek, Latin and Syriac. He was a man of high intelligence, balanced judgement and love of truth, and the account which he gives is sober, reliable and clear. Belisarius is his hero, and he is cool towards Justinian and Theodora and those responsible for Byzantine government policy. His language is classicizing, and in style he particularly imitates Thucydides. The work on Justinian's buildings was composed after the *History*, and probably at the emperor's request. Its panegyric tone contrasts strangely with that of the *History*; but it is a first-class source on the geography, topography and art of the period. Procopius overcomes the difficulties of architectural description skilfully. The third work, the *Secret History*, probably written *c.* 550, is a virulent, scurrilous, scabrous and sometimes well-grounded attack upon Justinian and Theodora, their advisers and their policy. It goes over, from a very different point of view, the ground covered in the *History*. The undiscriminating nature of Procopius's attack upon Justinian, who is blamed for everything from insolvency to earthquakes, rather blunts the edge of his well-informed and telling criticism of certain features of the emperor's financial and foreign policy. The *Secret History* can never have been published, and scarcely even shown to trusted friends, during Justinian's reign. Its presence in his desk as he wrote the fulsome panegyrics of the *Buildings* offers an interesting problem to the psychologist. Whatever the verdict on Procopius's complex character, as a historian he comes only a little behind the greatest of antiquity. J. B. Bury called him the best Greek historian since ◊ Polybius. He is the principal source for the first two thirds of Justinian's reign. [R B]

Ed. J. Haury (3 vols., Leipzig, 1905–13); ed. and tr. H. B. Dewing, G. Downey (Loeb, 8 vols., 1914–1940); *The Secret History*, tr. G. A. Williamson (Penguin Classics, 1966).

B. Rubin, *Prokopios von Kaisareia* (Stuttgart, 1954); P. N. Ure, *Justinian and His Age* (Penguin Books, 1951).

Prodromus, Theodore. ◊ Theodore Prodromus.

Psellus, Michael (1018–1096 or 7). Byzantine philosopher, historian and man of letters. Born in Constantinople of a family in modest circumstances, he was something of an infant prodigy in his schooldays, and attracted the notice of influential patrons. He entered the government service, and was soon imperial secretary. As one short-lived emperor succeeded another – often through the whim of the elderly, passionate and unbalanced empress Zoe – Psellus's influence grew, and in the reign of Constantine IX Monomachus (1042–55) he was in virtual control of certain departments of State. The restoration at this time of the imperial university, in which Psellus became professor of philosophy, was largely his inspiration. Falling into disfavour on Constantine IX's death, Psellus for a time became a monk in Asia Minor, but soon found he had no vocation. Returning to court he played a leading role under

Isaac I Comnenus (1057–9), Constantine X Ducas (1059–67) and Romanus Diogenes (1067–71), and became under Michael VII Ducas (1071–8) chief minister of the empire. He probably returned to monastic life in his old age, more from necessity than choice.

In character a pliant, time-serving courtier, Psellus was nevertheless an intellectual giant, driven by a passion for knowledge and a compulsive need to teach and write. More than any other single man he laid the groundwork for the 12th-century flowering of art, letters and science. Though there was no branch of knowledge, from grammar to medicine, which he did not touch, his main contribution was twofold – a new and deeper understanding of the Platonist, idealist tradition of ancient philosophy, and a new attention to style and elegance of expression. Many of the succeeding generation's most influential figures were his pupils.

His literary output was immense, and not all of it has been identified, let alone published. Much is of a technical character – manuals of rhetoric, discussion of problems in meteorology, astronomy and medicine, etc. The following are those of more general interest in his own time and today: (1) The *Chronography*, a history of the years 976–1078; the latter portion is based on personal observation, and Psellus constantly appears on the stage himself. Brilliant, sometimes malicious, delineation of character, graphic descriptions, and elegant style, make the reader forget the rather superficial character of Psellus's historical analysis, which turns largely on court personalities. But as literature, the *Chronography* is superb. (2) A collection of speeches, some merely formal panegyrics, but others, like the funeral orations on his mother, his daughter, his colleague Nicetas, the patriarch Michael Cerularius, Constantine Leichudes and John Xiphilinus, valuable both for their factual information and for the light they throw on Byzantine mentality. (3) About 500 letters, private and official, more informative than most Byzantine epistles. (4) The *De omnifaria doctrina*, a collection of 193 answers to theological, philosophical and scientific problems posed by pupils and friends.

Psellus's work marks the first break in the old Christian–Aristotelian synthesis which had provided the philosophical and intellectual framework for the Byzantine world since late antiquity. And his no longer merely imitative, but actually creative, use of the classical literary heritage paved the way for stylists like ◊ Anna Comnena and Nicetas ◊ Choniates, as well as for the revived Lucianic satire of the 12th century. Above all, he was the teacher of a brilliant generation. [R B]

Chronographie, ed. and Fr. tr. E. Renauld (2 vols., Paris, 1926–8); *Mesaiōnikē Bibliothēkē*, ed. K. N. Sathas, v (Athens-Paris, 1875) (speeches and letters); *Scripta minora magnam partem adhuc inedita*, ed. E. Kurtz and F. Drexl (2 vols., Milan, 1936–41) (further speeches and letters); *De omnifaria doctrina*, ed. L. G. Westerink (Utrecht, 1948); *Chronographia*, tr. E. R. A. Sewter (1952; Penguin Classics, 1966).

J. M. Hussey, *Church and Learning in the Byzantine Empire 867–1185* (1937).

Pseudo-Dionysius the Areopagite. Author of 4 books, *Divine Names, The Heavenly Hierarchy, The Ecclesiastical Hierarchy, Mystical Theology*, and 10 letters attributed to Dionysius the Areopagite, a convert of St Paul (Acts 17:34; Eusebius, *Ecclesiastical History*, 3:4; 4:23). The works expound in neo-Platonic terms the nature of the universe, its divine government, and the relation of the Church in heaven to that on earth. All is hierarchically arranged, the lesser proceeding from and depending upon the greater. Accepted by the Byzantines as a genuine document of apostolic Christianity, Pseudo-Dionysius enjoyed immense influence, particularly among mystics, who found in his hierarchical arrangement a path to divinity; even so worldly a character as ◊ Anna Comnena relied heavily upon him.

The true authorship and date of the Pseudo-Dionysiac corpus has been discussed inconclusively since the Renaissance. It is first mentioned in 553, which provides a lower date limit. The upper limit is furnished by the many borrowings from the 4th-century fathers, particularly Gregory of Nazianzus (◊ p. 84) and Gregory of Nyssa (◊ p. 85) and from Cyril of Alexandria, who died in 444. Recent research suggests dependence on the Athenian philosopher Proclus (◊ p. 121), and a date about A.D. 500. The author was probably a Syrian Greek, but his identity is likely to remain unknown. His work is perhaps the most successful forgery in the history of literature. Byzantine theologians one and all took it at its face value. Latin translations were made about 800 and were influential in the western Church, for whom Pseudo-Dionysius was *'doctor hierarchicus'*. Syriac, Armenian and Arabic translations are also known. All medieval cosmology and mysticism is indebted to the Pseudo-Areopagite. [R B]

Migne, *P G*, 3–4; tr. C. E. Rolt (*The Spiritual Body*) (1920); Fr. tr. M. de Gandillac (Paris, 1943).

R. Roques, *L'univers dionysien* (Paris, 1954); A. von Ivánka, *Plato Christianus* (Einsiedeln, 1964).

R

Romanus the Melode (first half of 6th cent.). Byzantine hymnographer. Born of Jewish parents at Emesa (Homs) in Syria, he became a deacon at Berytus (Beirut) and went to Constantinople in the reign of Anastasius I (491–578), where he became a member of the clergy of one of the churches. There, according to the legend, he was visited one Christmas eve by the Virgin, patroness of his church, who gave him a scroll to eat; and the next day he intoned from the pulpit his famous Christmas hymn. From then on he composed hymn after hymn with such fertility that he was credited with more than a thousand. He died shortly after 555.

Romanus's hymns are *kontakia* (⇨ Byzantine Hymnography); and he is said to have invented this poetic form in a moment of inspiration. In view of the formal perfection of all his *kontakia*, this is unlikely. What he probably did do, however, was to adapt to Byzantine taste and requirements an existing Syriac form, the *memrā* or poetic homily, with which he was doubtless familiar from his youth.

The fame of Romanus, who was canonized by the Orthodox Church – his feast is celebrated on 1 October – resulted in the eventual attribution to him of many *kontakia* composed by others. It is thus difficult to identify all his authentic hymns. Style, contemporary allusions and acrostic (if any) are the principal internal criteria; the study of the dates and descent of the manuscripts provides the external criteria. The authentic hymns probably number about 80; no complete edition has yet been published. The best known of all Byzantine hymns, the *Akathistos Hymn*, is probably by Romanus, but the question remains open.

Romanus's hymns are marked by simplicity and clarity of language, dramatic use of dialogue, frequent polemical outbursts against heretics and pagans, extensive use of assonance, rhyme and word-play, vivid and fresh descriptions and depth of feeling; the occasional passages of dogmatic argument were no doubt to his contemporaries' taste; and he avoids on the whole the besetting Byzantine vice of verbosity. His theological position was central, opposed alike to Monophysitism and to Nestorianism, against both of which he polemizes.

The sources from which he draws his themes and their expression are first the Bible, then the homilies of Ephraim the Syrian, and to a lesser extent the works of the 4th-century Fathers. His dependence on Ephraim is often very close.

The music of his hymns is unfortunately lost, so we cannot judge them as his contemporaries could. He is outstanding among Byzantine hymnographers, but to call him a 'Christian Pindar' is to exaggerate. [R B]

Ed. P. Maas and C. A. Trypanis (1963) (further volume, of dubious and spurious hymns, in preparation); ed. N. B. Tomadakis (4 vols., Athens, 1952–61) (in course of publication); ed. and Fr. tr. J. Grosdidier de Matons (3 vols., Paris, 1964–6) (in course of publication); H. J. W. Tillyard, *Byzantine Music and Hymnography* (1923) (includes some English translations); J. M. Neale, *Hymns of the Eastern Church* (2nd edn, 1863) (includes some English translations).

G. Cammelli, *Romano il Melode* (Florence, 1930); E. Mioni, *Romano il Melode* (Padua, 1937).

S

Scylitzes, John (second half of 11th cent.). Byzantine historian. Scylitzes held high military offices, and survived at least until 1092. His *Historical Synopsis*, an uncritical but full chronicle, covers the years 811–1057; a continuation in some manuscripts to 1079 is probably not his. Most of Scylitzes' work is derivative, but he used historical narratives now lost (he names some); only the last portion depends on observation and eye-witness accounts. Scylitzes' work has never been published, and is accessible only in the transcription of George ◊ Cedrenus. Portions of it, in particular his history of the 11th century, are of great value in the absence of other sources. Scylitzes' chronicle is one of the few Byzantine profane texts illustrated (in a 13th-century manuscript) by a series of miniatures of great interest. [R B]

Ch. Diehl, *Manuel d'art byzantin* (2nd edn, 1925–6) (on the cycle of miniatures).

Sikidites, Michael. ◊ Michael Glycas.

Simocatta, Theophylact (first half of 7th century). Byzantine historian. Egyptian Greek by birth, Theophylact held a series of high legal offices in Constantinople. His *History*, a continuation of ◊ Menander Protector's, covers the reign of Maurice (582–602). Sincere, writing in the ancient historiographical tradition, and having access to many sources, narrative and documentary, including Persian documents, Theophylact is reliable but not profound. His high-flown style, overloaded with imagery and countless digressions, is not to modern taste. A collection of rhetorical letters and a dialogue on physics also survive. [R B]

Historiae, ed. C. De Boor (Leipzig, 1887); *Epistolographi graeci*, ed. and Latin tr. R. Hercher (Paris, 1873); *Questioni naturali*, ed. L. Massa Positano (Naples, 1953).

Simplicius (first half of 6th cent.). Byzantine philosopher. Born in Cilicia, he studied in Athens under Damascius and accompanied him to Persia when Justinian closed the Athenian school (529). Returning to Byzantine territory a few years later, he devoted himself to writing. He composed commentaries on a number of Aristotle's works and on the *Handbook* of Epictetus (◊ p. 72). His aim was to show that ancient pagan philosophers were basically in agreement. The copious and careful citation from earlier philosophers makes his commentaries valuable. Without Simplicius's misconceived and pedestrian textbooks we should know very much less about Aristotle's predecessors than we do. [R B]

Commentaria graeca in Aristotelem, vols. 7–11 (Berlin, 1882–1907).

J. Geffcken, *Der Ausgang des griechisch-römischen Heidentums* (Heidelberg, 1920).

Sophronius (*c.* 560–638). Byzantine poet and theologian. Born in Damascus, he was a teacher of rhetoric, later became a monk in Palestine and in 633–4 Patriarch of Jerusalem, and lived to see the capture of the city by the Caliph Omar. His 23 religious poems in anacreontic metre are really versified sermons. Despite their neatness, they lack the warmth and sincerity of the anacreontic hymns of Synesius. The metre is already part quantitative and part accentual. Of his prose theological writings only a few festal homilies, some saints' lives and a synodal epistle survive. [R B]

Ed. M. Gigante (Rome, 1957).

Th. Nissen, *Die byzantinischen Anakreonteen* (B A W, Munich, 1940).

Sphrantzes, George (1401–after 1478). Byzantine historian. In the service of the Byzantine emperors from 1418, and employed on many diplomatic missions, Sphrantzes was chief minister of Constantine XII in 1453. Imprisoned by the Turks, he escaped first to the Peloponnese and later to Corfu, where he died. His *Chronicle* covers the years 1413–78 – an expanded version, the *Chronicon maius*, covering 1258–1478, is not by him – and recounts mainly Byzantine political and diplomatic history. It is valuable for its accuracy of detail and chronological precision, and an eye-witness account of the capture of Constantinople (1453). [R B]

Ed. J. B. Papadopulos (Leipzig, 1935) (vol. 1 only); ed. I. Bekker (C S H B, 1838); *Die letzten Tage von Konstantinopel*, German tr. E. von Ivánka (Graz, 1954).

Studites. ◊ Theodore of Studium.

'Suda' ('Suidas') (compiled in second half of 10th cent.). Byzantine literary encyclopedia. The unknown compiler, inspired perhaps by the encyclopedic works sponsored by Constantine VII Porphyrogenitus, drew on ancient and medieval lexica, commentaries on classical texts, historical narratives, and the lost literary history of

Hesychius Illustrius (6th century A.D.). The work, of some 30,000 entries alphabetically arranged, contains, along with much that is trivial or wrong, a mass of priceless information on the lives and writings of classical and early Byzantine writers. Without it, our knowledge of Greek literary history would be very much poorer. The name 'Suda' means 'palisade'; the mythical author 'Suidas' is an invention of later generations. [R B]

Ed. Ada Adler (5 vols., Leipzig, 1928–38).

Symeon Magister (mid 10th cent.). Byzantine historian. A chronicle, most often attributed to Symeon (probably Symeon Metaphrastes the hagiographer), but also going under the names of Theodosius of Melitene, Leo Grammaticus, etc., covers the period from the Creation to A.D. 948. Its core is a chronicle extending to *c.* 690, which was then worked over and continued by a series of editors. It was translated into Old Slavonic in the 14th century. This chronicle would be of great importance for determining the interrelations of the various medieval Greek and Slavonic chronicles, had we an adequate edition. [R B]

Leonis Grammatici chronographia, ed. I. Bekker (C S H B, 1842).

Symeon the New Theologian (949–1022). Byzantine theologian and mystic. A native of Paphlagonia, he was a monk in the monasteries of Studius and then St Mamas in Constantinople, becoming abbot of the latter. But his innovations led to his expulsion from each in turn. Drawing on the traditions of the earlier church, particularly ◊ Pseudo-Dionysius and ◊ Maximus Confessor, he built up a systematic theory and practice of mysticism, open to cleric and layman alike, and culminating in direct perception of the divine light. His is the groundwork on which all later Byzantine mysticism is built. His views are set out and illustrated in a body of 34 catecheses, numerous other prose-works, and 57 poems in 15-syllable accentual verse describing ecstatic experiences. He writes with directness, lack of pretension and great insight into the psychology of mystic experience. [R B]

Migne, *P G*, 120; *Chapitres théologiques, gnostiques et pratiques*, ed. J. Darrouzès (Paris, 1957); *Catéchèses 1–5*, ed. B. Krivochéine. Fr. tr. J. Paramelle (Paris, 1963) (to be completed in 3 vols.); G. Beck, *Kirche und theologische Literatur im byzantinischen Reich* (Munich, 1959) (for bibliography).

J. M. Hussey, *Church and Learning in the Byzantine Empire 867–1185* (1937); I. Hausherr, *Syméon le nouveau théologien* (Rome, 1928).

Syncellus, George. ◊ George Syncellus.

T

Theodore Gazes (*c.* 1400–76). Byzantine humanist. Born in Thessalonica, he emigrated to Italy about 1435, and became the first Professor of Greek at Ferrara. Later he moved to Rome, Naples and Calabria. His works include Latin translations of works of Aristotle and Theophrastus, a Greek grammar and a mass of letters and occasional writings. Among his pupils and friends were many leading Renaissance figures from Italy and beyond the Alps. He played a major role in the revival of Greek studies in western Europe. [R B]

Migne, *P G*, 161.

L. Mohler, *Aus Bessarions Gelehrtenkreis* (Paderborn 1942); L. Mohler, 'Theodoros Gazes. Seine bisher ungedruckten Schriften und Briefe', in *Byzantinische Zeitschrift* 42 (1943–9).

Theodore Lascaris (1222–58). Byzantine emperor. Born in Nicaea, son of the emperor in exile John III Vatatzes, Theodore studied under Nicephorus ◊ Blemmydes. He succeeded his father in 1254. Both before and after his accession he wrote a stream of works on dogmatic and pastoral theology (only partly published). He also composed a series of orations for ceremonial occasions of some interest to the historian, and a body of religious poetry. He is best known for his collection of letters to high officials and men of learning – a fascinating glimpse of culture in the Nicaean empire. [R B]

Epistulae ed. N. Festa (Florence, 1898); Migne, *P G*, 140.

J. B. Papadopulos, *Théodore II Lascaris, empereur de Nicée* (Paris, 1908).

Theodore Meliteniotes (d. *c.* 1390). Byzantine poet, theologian and polymath. He held a succession of high offices in the patriarchal staff at Constantinople. His works include an allegorical poem of several thousand 15-syllable lines *On Temperance* displaying his encyclopedic erudition, a vast commentary on the Gospels, of which only a portion survives, and an immense manual of astronomy, drawing not only on Ptolemy and Theon, but also Persian and Arabic sources in translation. Only the preface has been published. [R B]

Ed. M. E. Miller, 'Poésie allégorique de Méliténiotès, *Notices et extraits de la Bibliothèque Nationale*, 19, ii (1857); Migne, *P G*, 149.

Theodore Metochites. ◊ Metochites, Theodore.

Theodore Prodromus (d. *c.* 1166). Byzantine poet and man of letters. He seems to have been a teacher in the Patriarchal school in Constantinople and a colleague of Michael Italicus, future archbishop of Philippopolis. His literary output is astonishingly varied. Not everything attributed to him has yet been published, and there are many difficult problems of authenticity. His poems include: (1) the verse romance *Rhodanthe and Dosicles* (◊ Byzantine Verse Romances); (2) the *War of the Cats and Mice*, a dramatic parody in 384 12-syllable lines; (3) an astrological poem in 593 15-syllable lines, addressed to the daughter-in-law of John II Comnenus; (4) several sets of short poems on feasts of the ecclesiastical calendar; (5) satirical poems; (6) a very large collection of occasional poems on historical events, addressed to various dignitaries from the emperor downwards; many of these are lightly veiled requests for patronage. In a special category are the poems in vernacular Greek attributed to Ptochoprodromus (= poor Prodromus). One complains of a nagging wife and begs for help from John II, another asks a prince for money to pay the food bill, a third is a young monk's complaint about the scandalous conditions in his monastery, addressed to Manuel I, another depicts the wretched life of a poor intellectual, and so on. These may not all be by the same author, and possibly none is by Prodromus. These lively poems are among the earliest examples of modern Greek literature.

Prodromus's prose works include: (1) several dialogues after the manner of Lucian (◊ p. 107) on philosophical and literary subjects; (2) grammatical works; (3) an extensive commentary on the liturgical hymns of ◊ John of Damascus and Cosmas of Maiuma (published only in part); (4) a collection of letters; (5) many speeches delivered, or purporting to be delivered, on ceremonial occasions – marriages, funerals, inaugurations etc. Problems of authenticity are particularly difficult in this last category, and many texts, anonymous in the manuscripts, have been plausibly attributed to Prodromus.

Prodromus, the contemporary of ◊ John Tzetzes and a generation older than ◊ Eustathius, is typical of the 12th-century literary and philosophical renaissance. The begging poems, by which he is best known to many, are a tiny part of his output. Of wide literary culture, he moves at ease in the classical tradition. His rationalist standpoint is unaffected by theological preconceptions. He has a certain detachment from his subject-matter which permits him to treat it with irony and occasional mordant wit. If some of the Ptochoprodromus poems are by him, then he was one of the first men to break through the stifling classical literary tradition, which extended back for two millennia, and to write on everyday life in the language of the people. His facility was his undoing, however, and there is much repetition of motives and tricks of style from one work to another. And like all the productions of the 12th-century Byzantine renaissance, Prodromus's works are written for a coterie, and therefore sometimes hard to understand today. As a historical source he is often of great value. [R B]

Ed. R. Hercher, *Scriptores erotici graeci*, ii (Leipzig, 1859) (*Rhodanthe and Dosicles*); *Catomyomachia*, ed. R. Hercher (Leipzig, 1873); E. Miller, *Notices et extraits de la Bibliothèque Nationale* 23 (1872) (astrological poem); *Poèmes prodromiques en grec vulgaire*, ed. D. C. Hesseling and H. Pernot (Amsterdam, 1910); *Commentarios in carmina sacra melodorum Cosmae Hierosolymitani et Ioannis Damasceni*, ed. H. Stevenson (Rome, 1888); Migne, *P G*, 133; bibliography in Gy. Moravcsik, *Byzantinoturcica*, i (2nd edn, Berlin, 1958) (to which should be added C. Giannelli, *Analecta Bollandiana* 75 (1957), and *Studi in onore di Luigi Castiglioni* (Florence, 1960), where two major collections of religious poems are published for the first time).

C. Diehl, *Figures byzantines*, ii (8th edn,

Paris, 1927); B. Knös, *Histoire de la littérature néo-grecque* (Stockholm, 1962); A. P. Kazhdan, 'Dva novykh pamyatnika XII stoletiya', in *Vizantijskij Vremennik* 24 (1964). (There are only two full-length studies of Prodromus. One was published in Russian in Odessa in 1905 by G. D. Papadimitriu; the other is a Paris doctoral thesis by M. Kyriakis (1952), existing only in a few copies consultable in certain French libraries. Details will be found in Moravcsik – see above.)

Theodore of Studium (Studites) (759–826). Byzantine theologian. As a young man he entered a monastery founded on his family estate in north-west Asia Minor, and by 794 had become abbot of the community. In 798, before the threat of an Arab invasion, Theodore and his monks moved to the deserted monastery of Studios in Constantinople, which they made into a centre of monastic reform. By the early years of the 9th century Theodore had become the acknowledged leader of the Zealot party in the Orthodox Church, which refused all concessions to the temporal power, and had already been twice banished and imprisoned. With the resurgence of Iconoclasm in 815 Theodore became the leading propagandist of image worship, and was banished for a third time. He died in the Prince's Islands in the Sea of Marmara. He is recognized as a saint by eastern and western Churches.

His most interesting work is his collection of some 550 letters, many of them 'open letters'. They shed a brilliant light on the theological controversies of the time, and upon Constantinople intellectual movements and everyday life. His two *Catecheses* – Greater and Lesser – embody his ideals of monastic life and activity. There survive also a collection of festal homilies and panegyrics upon saints, a number of hymns, several minor works on monastic discipline, anti-Iconoclast treatises, and an interesting series of iambic poems on the various functionaries of his monastery. An uncompromising theologian, a gifted organizer and a tireless controversialist, Theodore is yet a warm, humane character, with a deep regard for the classical tradition, which many of his partisans despised. He writes clear workmanlike Greek, with little attempt at ornamentation. [R B]

Migne, *PG*, 99; *Analecta sacra spicilegio Solesmensi parata*, ed. J. Pitra, i (Paris, 1876) (hymns).

A. Gardner, *Theodore of Studium, his Life and Times* (1905); I. Hausherr, *Saint Théodore Studite: l'homme et l'ascète* (Rome, 1926).

Theodulus. ◊ Thomas Magister.

Theophanes (*c.*752–818). Byzantine historian. Born of a rich family in Constantinople, after a brief marriage he became a monk in the monastery which he had founded at Sigriane on the Sea of Marmara. He was a leader and spokesman of the Iconodule party in the church, and was as a result imprisoned by the Iconoclast emperor Leo V (813–20) and banished to the island of Samothrace, where he died. He is venerated as a Confessor by the Orthodox Church. His *Chronography,* written in 810–14 at the request of his friend ◊ George Syncellus, whose *Chronicle* it continues, covers the years 284–813. It follows a rigid chronological scheme, every event being narrated under a particular year. As his sources were not all arranged annalistically, his dates are sometimes unreliable. He had at his disposal many narrative sources now lost, including Iconoclast chronicles. For the concluding portion he depended on first-hand observation and eye-witness accounts. Naïve, uncritical and devout, he has no interest in the deeper problems of motivation and historical causation, but merely narrates one event after another. He tends to see in disasters punishments for heresy, and in successes rewards for orthodoxy, and theological edification is clearly his main purpose. Within his limitations, however, he diligently reported what he found in his sources, including much that is trivial. He is the principal narrative source for the Byzantine 'Dark Age' of the 7th and 8th centuries, and was excerpted and abbreviated by many later Byzantine historians and chroniclers. A Latin translation made in 873–5 by the Papal librarian Anastasius was similarly used by western historians. Thus his chronography is one of the foundations upon which the history of the early Middle Ages is built. He writes a plain Greek close to the popular speech of his time, and free from classical tags and literary allusions, to suit the education and taste of his mainly monastic readers. He has a certain talent for straightforward narrative, and is more readable than most Byzantine historians. [R B]

Ed. C. De Boor (Leipzig, 1883).

L. Breyer, *Bilderstreit und Arabersturm in Byzanz. Das 8 Jahrhundert (717–813) aus der Weltchronik des Theophanes* (Graz, 1957).

'Theophanes Continuatus'. Greek chronicle, compiled under the direction of the emperor ◊ Constantine VII Porphyrogenitus. Continuing where the *Chronography* of Theophanes left off, it covers the period 813–961. The fifth book, dealing with the reign of Basil I (867–86), is the work of Constantine VII himself. The sixth book, covering 886–961, is a later addition. The sources of the first 5 books are uncertain; the writer or writers had official documents and the very rich imperial library at their disposal. But there is much similarity with the history of ◊ Genesius. The sixth book agrees very closely with the continuation of the *Chronicle* of ◊ George the Monk, and may have been written by Theodore Daphnopates, a high official and man of letters of the mid 10th century. Books 1–5 are strongly partisan in tone, seeking to diminish the reputation of the predecessors of the Macedonian dynasty, and to exalt that of its founder Basil I. However, there is no falsification of fact, and the work's precision and detail makes it a valuable source for the 9th century. The theological approach which had dominated Byzantine historiography for three centuries is replaced by a more sophisticated and flexible analysis of character and motive, which owes much to renewed study of classical models. The language is much more classicizing than that of Theophanes, and the style owes more to literary tradition. [R B]

Ed. I. Bekker (C S H B, 1838); ed. O. Jurewicz (in preparation).

A. P. Kazhdan, 'Iz istorii vizantijskoj khronografii x *v*. I: O sostave tak nazyvaemoj khroniki Prodolzhatelya Fedfana', in *Vizantijskij Vremennik* 19 (1961).

Theophylact of Achrida (d. *c.*1108). Byzantine theologian and man of letters. A native of Euboea, he became a pupil of Michael Psellus in Constantinople, taught rhetoric in the Patriarchal school, became teacher to the young son of Michael VII Ducas, and *c.*1090 was appointed archbishop of Bulgaria, with his cathedral at Achrida (modern Ohrid, in Yugoslav Macedonia). His Biblical commentaries – many still unpublished – are largely derivative, but those on the Pauline Epistles are a new attempt to evaluate and arrange the vast mass of traditional exegesis. We have also a number of festal sermons and polemical anti-Latin works, and an interesting life of his 9th-century predecessor St Clement of Achrida. Outside theology, he wrote an address to his imperial pupil Constantine, which develops elegantly, but with little originality, the stock theme of a monarch's education; a panegyric on Alexius I Comnenus, containing information on the peoples then threatening the frontiers of the empire; a few poems; and a great collection of letters. These last, mostly written from Bulgaria and addressed to leading figures in Church and State in Constantinople, are a mine of information on prosopography, on Byzantine culture and on the social and economic conditions in a Byzantine province whose population was largely non-Greek. Theophylact is typical of the middle Byzantine period, the man of learning who crowns a long career in the capital with an archbishopric in the provinces, a post carrying new and heavy responsibilities (cf. Michael ◊ Choniates, ◊ Eustathius). [R B]

Migne, *P G*, 123–126.

P. Gautier, 'L'épiscopat de Théophylacte Héphaistos archevêque de Bulgarie', in *Revue des études byzantines* 21 (1963).

Theophylact Simocatta. ◊ Simocatta, Theophylact.

Thomas Magister (first half of 14th cent.). Byzantine scholar and man of letters. He seems to have lived and taught in both Thessalonica and Constantinople; and he had contact with the literary circle of Manuel ◊ Moschopulus, Theodore ◊ Metochites and Nicephoras ◊ Gregoras, and with the emperor Andronicus II (1282–1328). He later became a monk under the name Theodulus. His works include a lexicon of literary Greek words and expressions, much studied in the Renaissance; commentaries on classical drama and lyric poetry; and a collection of speeches and letters, some of which are of historical interest. [R B]

Ecloga, F. Ritschl (Halle, 1832); Migne, *P G*, 145 (speeches and letters); F. W. Lenz, 'Eine bisher ungedruckte Rede Thomas Magisters', in *Parola del passato* 17 (1962).
J. Irigoin, *Histoire du texte de Pindare* (Paris, 1952).

'Timarion'. Anonymous Byzantine satire of the mid 12th century. The theme is the descent to the underworld of one Timarion, who meets there not only traditional mythological figures, but several recently deceased personages of the Byzantine literary world. In the earlier part there is a famous description of the annual fair at Thessalonica. The work is modelled on the satires of Lucian (◊ p. 107), who was much read and imitated in the 11th and 12th centuries. [R B]

Ed. and German tr. A. Ellissen, *Analekten der mittel- und neugriechischen Literatur*, iv (Leipzig, 1860).
H. F. Tozer, *J H S*, 2 (1881).

Tzetzes, John. ◊ John Tzetzes.

Z

Zonaras, John (first half of 12th cent.). Byzantine historian. A high court official, he later became a monk on an island in the Sea of Marmara. His *Historical Epitome*, a universal history from the creation to A.D. 1118, is on a much higher level than the other Byzantine world-chronicles. Zonaras went to great pains to find sources, and treated them, up to a point, critically. He had access to some sources now lost, such as the complete text of Dio Cassius (◊ p. 63) and several Byzantine historians; and he reproduced his sources at greater length and in greater detail than other compilatory chroniclers. He is thus valuable not only for the history of his own time – he is a useful check on ◊ Anna Comnena – but also for that of the Roman Empire and the early Byzantine period up to the death of Justinian. In language and style he is midway between the elaborate, archaizing, literary prose of his day, and the spoken language. His *Epitome* was translated into Old Slavonic in the 14th century. He is also the author of a *Lexicon* of difficult Greek words, a number of homilies and lives of saints, commentaries on liturgical poems of the Orthodox Church, and a great treatise on Canon Law in which he comments upon and interprets the Canons of the Apostles, and of the Oecumenical Councils and Synods, and the canonical rulings of the Fathers of the Church. He was a man of many-sided learning and balanced judgement. [R B]

Epitomae historiarum libri, ed. M. Pinder, Th. Büttner-Wobst (C S H B, 3 vols., 1841–97); *Lexicon*, ed. J. A. H. Tittman (2 vols., Leipzig, 1808).

Zosimus (last half of 5th cent.). Byzantine historian. A government official in later life, he may have studied in Gaza, where there was a flourishing school of rhetoric and philosophy. His *New History* covers the period 295–410, and is bitterly anti-Christian in tone, drawing on the lost pagan histories of Olympiodorus and Eunapius. For Zosimus the decline of the Roman empire is the direct consequence of giving up the old religion. His dry account of events is not always reliable, but is the only surviving Greek narrative source for the period. [R B]

Ed. L. Mendelssohn (Leipzig, 1887); German tr. Seybold and Heyler (2 vols., Frankfurt, 1802–4).

RECOMMENDED READING

LITERATURE

K. Krumbacher, *Geschichte der byzantinischen Literatur von Justinian bis zum Ende des oströmischen Reiches (527–1453)* (2nd edn, Munich, 1897). (Fundamental and detailed, though in many respects out of date.)

H. G. Beck, *Kirche und theologische Literatur im byzantinischen Reich* (Munich, 1959). (Replaces Krumbacher for all theological and ecclesiastical literature.)

Gy. Moravcsik, *Byzantinoturcica* (2nd edn, vol. I, Berlin, 1958). (Up-to-date information and exhaustive bibliographies on all Byzantine historians.)

F. Dölger, *Die byzantinische Dichtung in der Reinsprache* (Berlin, 1948, repr, with additions in *Χαριστήριον*, Dölger, Thessalonica, 1962.)

C. A. Trypanis, *Mediaeval and Modern Greek Poetry* (1961). (Anthology with brief introduction.)

R. Cantarella, *Poeti bizantini* (2 vols., Milan, 1948). (Anthology with detailed biographical and bibliographical notes.)

G. Montelatici, *Storia della letteratura bizantina* (Milan, 1916). (A slight work.)

E. Wellesz, *Byzantine Music and Hymnography* (2nd edn, 1961).

B. Knös, *L'histoire de la littérature néo-grecque. La période jusqu'en 1821* (Stockholm, 1962). (Excellent for late Byzantine literature in demotic Greek.)

B. Tomadakes, *Eisagōgē eis tēn byzantinēn philologian* (2nd edn, Athens, 1956).

B. Tatakis, *La philosophie byzantine* (Paris, 1949).

GENERAL

J. M. Hussey, *The Byzantine World* (1957).

N. H. Baynes, *The Byzantine Empire* (1925).

S. Runciman, *Byzantine Civilisation* (1933, repr. 1961). (Three excellent short introductions to the subject.)

N. H. Baynes and H. St L. B. Moss, ed., *Byzantium. An Introduction to East Roman Civilisation* (1948, repr. 1961). (A series of essays by various scholars.)

Ch. Diehl, *Figures byzantines* (2 vols., Paris, 1906, 1908).

J. Lindsay, *Byzantium into Europe* (1952).

L. Bréhier, *Le monde byzantin* (3 vols., Paris, 1947–50). (On political history, organization and administration, and culture; reliable but rather heavy going.)

G. Ostrogorsky, *History of the Byzantine State* (1956). (The best straight-forward political history.)

A. A. Vasiliev, *History of the Byzantine Empire* (Madison, 1952; repr. 1958). (A less penetrating but more discursive history.)

H. W. Haussig, *Kulturgeschichte von Byzanz* (Stuttgart, 1959). (Lively and wide-ranging.)

M. Y. Levtchenko, *Byzance des origines à 1453* (Paris, 1949). (Translated from the Russian edition of 1940.)

PARTICULAR ASPECTS

J. M. Hussey, *Church and Learning in the Byzantine Empire, 867–1185* (1937).

P. N. Ure, *Justinian and his Age* (Penguin Books, 1951).

S. Runciman, *The Eastern Schism* (1956).

E. Barker, *Social and Political Thought in Byzantium* (1957).

K. M. Setton, *The Byzantine Background to the Italian Renaissance*, Proceedings of the American Philosophical Society, vol. 100, No. I (Baltimore, 1956). (Clear survey with detailed bibliography.)

Oriental and African

EDITORIAL FOREWORD

The main purpose of the Oriental and African sections of the Penguin Companion is to provide Western general readers, and school and University students, with a handy and readable 'Who's Who' of the most significant writers of Asia and Africa, from ancient times to the present day. A special attempt has been made to include authors whose works are available in translation into some Western language, or whose names are likely to crop up in periodical articles or broadcast talks. Where no outstanding authors occur, short surveys of certain lesser known national literatures have been prepared for the sake of completeness, but this is by way of exception to the book's general layout. Many famous Eastern epics and ethical classics are of course anonymous, and these will be found under their respective titles. Our aim has been above all to combine clarity with brevity and concision; we have had of necessity to be selective, since we could not hope to be complete.

As editor of this portion of the Penguin Companion, I owe a tremendous debt to friends and colleagues in many countries, who have given generously of their advice, in addition to writing the actual articles. Special tribute is due to the late John Bottoms, Lecturer in Malay at the School of Oriental and African Studies, London, who planned and supervised the entire South-East Asian section before his untimely death, and to O. R. Dathorne, who did the same for the African section. I would also thank particularly Dr Ron Asher of the University of Edinburgh, who has acted as regional editor and coordinator of the India, Pakistan and Ceylon section – an involved and demanding task.

To all whose names feature in the list of contributors to this volume I extend cordial thanks for their unfailing enthusiasm and scholarly expertise. We have tried between us to provide a key to unlock some at least of the rooms in the treasure house of Oriental and African literatures. Time and experience will show to what extent we have succeeded.

DAVID MARSHALL LANG

School of Oriental and African Studies
University of London, London WCI

ORIENTAL

A

Abdul Rauf (of) Singkel (?1615–93). Sumatran ◊ Malay theologian and Muslim mystic. This Sumatran-born writer worked and taught in Acheh under royal patronage from 1661, after extensive travels and studies in the Hedjaz and Yemen.

He made a Malay translation of Baidawi's commentary on the Koran (Constantinople, 1884) and his best-known works are *Mir'at a't-Tullab fi Tashil Ma'rifat al-Ahkam a'sh Shar'iyyah li Malik a'l-Wahhab* and *Umdat al-muhtajia,* the latter with autobiographical details. The former is a book of Shafiite jurisprudence, but also deals generally with social, political and religious life. In theology, Abdul Rauf was an orthodox mystic with similar views to those of ◊ Nuruddin. [J C B]

D. A. Rinkes, *Abdoerraoef van Singkel* (Heerenveen, 1909).

Abdullah bin Abdul Kadir Munshi (1796–1854). ◊ Malay memoirist. Abdullah was born in Malacca of mixed Arabic, South Indian and Malay parentage, his father being a writer and language teacher. He grew up as a Malay and very early became interested in languages and language teaching. He was amanuensis and secretary to Sir Stamford Raffles in Malacca and Singapore and many of his ideas and interests came from this association.

His best-known work is the *Hikayat Abdullah,* the first true autobiography in Malay, completed in 1845 (tr. A. H. Hill, *Journal,* Malayan Branch Royal Asiatic Society, Vol. 28, Pt 3, Singapore, 1955) and important for the historical material it contains – particularly about the coming of British influence to Malacca and Singapore – and also for the new note of contemplative individuality it struck in Malay literature. *Kesah Pelayaran Abdullah* (tr. A. E. Coope, Singapore, 1949) is a pleasant account of a journey up the relatively primitive East Coast of Malaya in 1838, and he also wrote at least one short narrative poem about contemporary events: *Sha'er Singapura Dimakan Api.* He is the best-known Malay writer of the 19th century and may be regarded both as a traditionalist formally grounded in classical Malay language and literature and as an innovator, since his writings are the first which took account of the impact of western influences in Malaya.

His style can be prolix and prosy but is usually vivid, and the quality of thought and observation as well as the writer's curiosity about his surroundings make his prose works good reading. [J C B]

Winstedt, *C M L.*

Abraham ibn Ezra. ◊ Ibn Ezra.

Abu Nuwās, Hasan ibn Hānī' (762–*c.* 815). Arab poet. One of the greatest poets in Arabic literature, he was actually of half Persian birth. He became a favourite of the caliph Harun al-Rashid, but was constantly on the verge of imprisonment or execution on account of his free speech.

Abu Nuwās's poetry represents an intermediate stage between the Traditional and the 'Modern' styles (◊ Imru'u'l-Qais and al-Mutanabbī). He broke away from the traditional themes and language of the pre-Islamic poets, abandoned the *qasīda,* the long ode, then and for many years afterwards still regarded by some as the real test of a poet's proficiency, and turned to more lyrical love poetry, wine songs, panegyric and satire; a spectacular success was his revival of the Beduin hunting song as an art form. Many of these genres had been used in the preceding century, but Abu Nuwās is regarded as the greatest exponent of them who had yet appeared. He was one of the last poets to learn his craft by association with his predecessors and with desert Arabs; his successors were generally trained in schools of philology, and so were more concerned with linguistic innovations and survivals than with the subject matter of their poetry.

Abu Nuwās also appears frequently in the ◊ *Arabian Nights,* as a salacious member of Harun al-Rashid's court rather than as a poet. Many anecdotes are told about him in Arabic literature (as with most great Arab literary figures); in most he appears unfavourably, but it is unjust to any Arab author to judge him by such anecdotes. [A S T]

W. H. Ingrams, *Abu Nuwas in Life and in Legend* (Mauritius, 1933); Nicholson, *L H A*; *E of I*.

Abu'l-'Alā, Ahmad ibn 'Abdullāh, al-Ma'arri (973–1058). Arab poet. Born near Aleppo. He lost his sight from smallpox as a child, and spent nearly all his life in northern Syria. Having gained some local fame, he tried the literary world of Baghdād, but soon returned home unsuccessful. He was an ascetic, a vegetarian, and he never married, since he did not wish to wrong anyone by bringing him into the world. He was too poor to give financial help to his students, but many came to him for advice.

Abu'l-'Alā was to a certain extent an adherent of the 'Modern' school of poetry (◊ al-Mutanabbī), particularly in his early poems, *Sparks from Flint and Steel*. In his later work, however, for all the artifice of his language, he stands apart from all Arab poets, Traditional or 'Modern'. In the *Luzūmiyyāt* ('The Making Necessary of What is Not Necessary' – so called because of his imposing on himself stricter rules of rhyme than were obligatory) (tr. A. F. Rihani, *The Quatrains of Abu'l-Ala*, 1904, New York, 1920), he passes a harsh and almost atheistical judgement on the world, and fearlessly and rationally attacks injustice, hypocrisy and superstition. Orthodox Muslims, displeased by these extraordinary poems, have frequently judged his earlier work to be better.

Abu'l-'Alā also wrote *Risālat al-Ghufrān* ('The Epistle of Forgiveness. A Divine Comedy', tr. G. Brackenbury, 1943), the description of a journey through Heaven and Hell, in which the author discusses literary matters with the famous poets he meets. We also have a volume of his letters, in rhymed prose, and part of an odd and almost incomprehensible work entitled *Paragraphs and Periods*, a mixture of pious exhortations and pessimistic comments, also in rhymed prose. [A S T]

The Diwan of Abu'l-Ala, tr. H. Baerlein (Wisdom of the East Series, 1908 etc.); *The Letters of Abu'l-'Alâ*, ed. and tr. D. S. Margoliouth (1898).
H. Baerlein, *Abu'l Ala the Syrian* (W E S, 1914); Nicholson, *S I P*.

Abu'l-Faraj, 'Alī ibn Husain, al-Isfahānī (879–967). Arab writer. A descendant of the last Ummayad caliph (the Abbasid dynasty overthrew the Ummayads in 750). He was prolific, but is known today principally for a large literary encyclopedia entitled *Kitāb al-Aghānī* ('Book of Songs'), never translated. It is a history of Arabian poetry down to Abu'l-Faraj's own time, based on a collection of 100 poems that had been set to music for Harun al-Rashid. Abu'l-Faraj added others of his own choice, and interspersed the biographical and other information that he supplied with a great deal more poetry, both ancient and modern.

The *Kitāb al-Aghānī* is one of our chief sources for information concerning life, culture and social conditions in Pre-Islamic and early Muslim Arabia. It became so popular in the Muslim world that one leading statesman, accustomed to travelling with a camel-load of books, restricted himself to it alone. ◊ Ibn Khaldūn said, 'It is the final resource of the student of belles-lettres, for he can desire nothing more.' [A S T]

F. Rosenthal, *Humor in Early Islam* (Leiden, 1956); *E of I*.

Achehnese Literature. The Achehnese of North Sumatra, although possessing a distinct language, have traditionally used ◊ Malay or Arabic for works of learning; these languages have now been replaced by ◊ Indonesian. Poetry almost alone has been written in the Achehnese language. This includes *pantōn* (quatrains), *rasib* and *kisah* (recitations forming part of religious performances called *ratéb*) and, the most important Achehnese literary form, *hikayat* – long stories and legends, and religious tracts in verse. To this must be added much 'unwritten prose' – *haba* transmitted by the story-tellers in more colloquial language and relating to the past history of Acheh, fables and other stories. The most notable of the *hikayats* are the anonymous work, the *Hikayat Malém Dagang*, celebrating an episode in a 17th-century war with the Dutch, and the *Hikayat Pochut Muhamat* by

Teungku Lam Rokam, dealing with the dynastic wars of the following century. [E C G B]

C. Snouck Hurgronje (tr. A. W. S. O'Sullivan), *The Achehnese* (Leiden, 1906).

Adivar, Halide Edib (1883–1964). Turkish novelist. She was educated at the American Girls' College, Üsküdar; she was thus one of the few prominent figures of her generation to be educated in an Anglo-Saxon, rather than a French, milieu. She became known as an ardent patriot and feminist because of her impetuous political novels *Yeni Turan* (1912; German tr. F. Schrader, *Das neue Turan: ein türkisches Frauenschicksal,* 1916) and *Khandan* (1912). After the First World War she and her husband (Adnan Adivar, a notable scholar, author of *La science chez les Turcs ottomans,* Paris, 1939) joined Mustafa Kemâl in Anatolia and worked devotedly for the nationalist cause; her experiences at this time produced the novel *Ateşten Gömlek* (1922; Eng. tr. M. Yakub Khan, *The Daughter of Smyrna,* Lahore, 1933; German tr. H. Dorn, *Das Flammenhemd,* Vienna, 1923). After the proclamation of the republic she and her husband lived abroad – in France, England, U.S.A., and for a time in India – until 1938, when she returned to Turkey to become Professor of English Literature at the University of Istanbul. During these years she wrote 2 books of reminiscences, *Memoirs of Halidé Edib* (New York–London, 1926), her life to 1918, and *The Turkish Ordeal* (1928), her experiences during the War of Independence, invaluable pictures of the Turkey of those years seen through the eyes of a Western-educated Turkish patriot. Istanbul life at the turn of the century and the tension between the oriental and the occidental outlooks are portrayed in *The Clown and his Daughter* (1935, later published in Turkish as *Sinekli Bakkal*). [V L M]

Turkey Faces West (New Haven, 1930); *Conflict of East and West in Turkey* (Delhi, 1936); *Inside India* (1937). (All in English.)

E. Saussey, *Prosateurs turcs contemporains* (Paris, 1935); O. Spies, *Die türkische Prosaliteratur der Gegenwart* (Leipzig, 1943); A. Bombaci, *Storia della letteratura turca* (Milan, 1956); *Philologiae Turcicae Fundamenta,* ii (Wiesbaden, 1964).

Agnon, Samuel Joseph (1888–). Hebrew novelist and short-story writer. Born at Buczacz in Galicia he settled in Palestine in 1909, where he has since lived except for a period (1912–23) in Germany. His family name was Czaczkes, which he changed to Agnon after the success of his first story published in Palestine – *Agunot* ('Deserted Wives'). Agnon's Galician childhood and youth had a great influence on his writing. He has a gift for combining symbolism with reality, and is regarded as the great epic writer of modern Hebrew. In his fiction he avoided much of the innovation used by some of the earlier writers of modern Hebrew, and based his style more on that of children's stories with a skilful blending of elements from the Biblical and Talmudic literature.

Perhaps Agnon's greatest novel is *Hakhnasath Kallah* (1922; *The Bridal Canopy,* tr. I. M. Lask, Garden City, N.Y., 1937), which is rich in the folklore of early 19th-century Jewish Galicia. In *Oreah natah lalun* (1945; 'A Wayfarer Tarries the Night') the ruin of a Jewish village in Galicia between the wars is depicted. Even when the setting is in Israel, as in *Temol Shilshom* (1947; 'The Day Before Yesterday'), Agnon's heroes tend to be Galicians. In his *Fantasy Stories* he writes of the Hassidic mystic rabbi Nachman of Bratislav with an air of nostalgia, but as his subject comes nearer to the contemporary scene, so does the element of realism increase, with almost an undertone of asperity in dealing with the present. [R F H]

Kol Sippurav shel Shemuel Yoseph Agnon (Berlin, 1931–5, Jerusalem, 1950–62; collected novels and short stories in Hebrew); *In the Heart of the Seas,* tr. I. M. Lask (New York, 1948); *Tehilla,* tr. I. M. Lask (London and New York, 1956).

E. Tsoreph, *Shay Agnon* (Tel-Aviv, 1957) (in Hebrew).

'Ahikar, Story of'. An ancient work of Near Eastern wisdom literature. Ahikar was one of the wise men of antiquity, in whose name proverbs were handed down from generation to generation. As counsellor to Kings Sennacherib and Esarhaddon of Assyria, he chose his nephew Nadan to succeed him in his old age. After Nadan took his uncle's place, he accused Ahikar of betraying Assyria. Ahikar was saved from death by a faithful friend, and restored to the King's grace when Assyria was in dire need of his advice; Nadan was chastised and put to death. The proverbs are presented in the tale as lessons and admonitions to Nadan, whose failure to heed them and base ingratitude brought him to a bad end.

'Ahikar the counsellor' is referred to in a late Neo-Babylonian tablet from Erech. The tale and proverbs are preserved first in Aramaic among the Elephantine papyri. Ahikar is mentioned in the book of Tobit, as is also Nadan, and some of the proverbs are repeated there. Democritus (*c.*460 B.C.) is said to have used the works of an Akikaros in his writings and Theophrastus (*c.*370 B.C.) is said to have written a book called Akicharos. Material from Ahikar also entered the Aesopian corpus. Versions of Ahikar, preserved in Syriac, Armenian, Slavonic, Turkic and Neo-Aramaic, attest to the great popularity of the tale, which was also known to the writers of The Koran [J C G/D J W]

The Story of Ahikar, ed. F. C. Conybeare, J. R. Harris and A. S. Lewis (2nd edn, 1913); ed. and tr. A. E. Cowley in *Aramaic Papyri of the Fifth Century B.C.* (1923); tr. H. L. Ginsberg, in *Ancient Near Eastern Texts*, ed. J. B. Pritchard (Princeton, 1955); *Documents from Old Testament Times*, ed. D. Winton Thomas (1958).

Akutagawa Ryūnosuke (1892–1927). Japanese novelist. He studied English at Tokyo University and was a member of a literary group centred upon it, under the influence of ◊ Natsume Sōseki. He was the Japanese intellectual *par excellence* and apart from a little teaching and some journalism, spent his whole life in literary production. The best-known side of this consists of short stories the material of which came, or purported to come, from old collections of tales such as ◊ *Konjaku-monogatari*. His method was to give the old material a twist, assigning to his characters a new cynical psychological slant. Some outstanding examples of these are *Rashōmon* (1915) (tr. Kojima – see below), *Hana* (1916) (*The Nose*, tr. Shaw – see below), *Kesa to Moritō* (1918) (*Kesa and Moritō*, Keene, *MJL*), *Jigokuhen* (1918) (*Hell Screen*, tr. W. H. H. Norman, Tokyo, 1948; Keene, *MJL*), *Yabu no naka* (1922) (*In a Grove*, tr. Kojima – see below). He was also interested in the so-called Christian era in Japan (second half of 16th century), which he appears to have seen as a time of great picturesqueness. The story *Tabako to akuma* (1917) (*Tobacco and the Devil*, tr. Shaw – see below) illustrates this interest. His detached attitude contrasts with that of the proletarian and naturalist novelists of his time, preoccupied respectively with politics and morbid self-portrayal. His style, over which he probably took more trouble than almost any modern author, is elegant and clear. He shows wit, penetration and intelligence, and a predilection for the macabre. In 1927 appeared *Kappa* (tr. S. Shiojiri, Tokyo, 1949), a novel of political and social satire of the sort of *Gulliver's Travels*, in which a man finds himself in the world of the *kappa*, or water-sprites, a topsy-turvy version of our own. In the same year he committed suicide, feeling that the world had no more to offer him. Many of his stories have been translated, and the modernity and the universality of his approach make them readily appreciated by Western readers. [C J D]

Rashomon and Other Stories, tr. Kojima Takashi (1952); *Tales Grotesque and Curious*, tr. G. W. Shaw (Tokyo, 1938).

Alagiyavanna (fl. 1590–1620). Sinhalese poet. He held the office of *mukaväṭi* or *mohoṭṭāla* (clerk), which is sometimes referred to as if it were his name. During this period there was an independent Sinhalese king (Rājasiṃha I) at Sītāvaka, 30 miles inland from Colombo, while the Portuguese held the coastal areas and controlled the nominal Sinhalese king there. Alagiyavanna served under Rājasiṃha, and possibly under the Portuguese also. His principal works are *Kusadā-kava*, recounting the story of the Kusa jātaka, one ◊ *sandēsa* poem called *Sävul-sandēsa* ('The Cock's Message'), and a book of versified moral maxims entitled *Subhāṣita*. The best known of these is the first, which is written in an easy style with much action and comparatively little descriptive padding. It was translated by T. Steele (1871) into Victorian-type verse. [C H B R]

M. Wickramasinghe (tr. E. R. Sarathchandra), *Sinhalese Literature* (Colombo, 1950); S. G. Perera and M. E. Fernando, *Kustantinu Haṭana* (Colombo, 1932; introduction).

al-Bîrûnî. ⇨ under Bîrûnî.

al-Ghazālī. ⇨ under Ghazālī.

al-Hamadhānī. ⇨ under Hamadhānī.

al-Harīrī. ⇨ under Harīrī.

al-Jāhiz. ⇨ under Jāhiz.

al-Maqrīzī. ⇨ under Maqrīzī.

al-Mutanabbī. ⇨ under Mutanabbī.

al-Tabarī. ⇨ under Tabarī.

Ali, Ahmad (1906–). Pakistani writer. He first attracted attention in the thirties as a writer of Urdu short stories strongly socialist in tendency, but most of his subsequent work has been in English. *Twilight in Delhi* (1940) is a novel, a portrayal of Muslim domestic life in Delhi at the beginning of the present century, tinged with a bitter awareness of the decline of Muslim fortunes in India. *The Falcon and the Hunted Bird* (Karachi, 1950) is a small volume of English verse translations from the classical Urdu poets. The selection is good, but the translations uneven in quality. [R R]

Ali Haji, Raja (*c.* 1808–68+). ⇨ Malay historian. The son of a Muslim Bugis ruler in the Riau Archipelago south of Singapore, he was brought up in court circles and appears later to have played the role of diplomat, civil servant and court historian.

His best-known work is *Tuhfat al-Nafis* (Singapore, 1932), begun in 1865, and there are some grounds for regarding this as the first proper Malay history. Its early portions contain the usual legendary material, but the author strikes a new note by criticizing the status and value of his traditional sources. His other main historical work, perhaps earlier, is *Silsilah Melayu dan Bugis* (Johore Bahru, 1956), which deals primarily with Bugis infiltration from the Celebes into the Malay world in the 18th century.

Raja Ali knew Arabic and his Malay style is adequate if undistinguished. He also wrote some verse; in 1857 an early Malay grammar, *Bustan al-Katibin* (Singapore, 1872); and in 1858 a discursive, encyclopedic dictionary *Kitab Pengetahuan Bahasa* (Singapore, 1928). [J C B]

Winstedt, *C M L*; J. C. Bottoms, 'Malay Historical Works', in *Malaysian Historical Sources*, ed. K. G. Tregonning (Singapore, 1962).

Āḻvār. The name collectively applied to the 12 Vaishnava *bhakti* poets (devotees of the god Viṣṇu) of Tamil, who flourished between A.D. 600 and 900. Later their hymns were collected into the *Nālāyirappirapantam* (the 'Four Thousand *Prabandha*' or poems), the fourth part of which is made up of the profoundly mystical *Tiruvāymoḻi* of Nammāḻvār, the greatest of the 12. The number also included a poetess (Āṇṭāḷ), her father (Periyāḻvār), a Chera prince (Kulacēkarar) and an untouchable (Tiruppāṇāḻvār). [R E A]

Hymns of the Āḻvārs, ed. and tr. J. S. M. Hooper (i, 1929).
Āḻkondavilli Govíndāchārya, *The Holy Lives of the Āzhvārs or the Drāvida Saints* (Mysore, 1902); S. Vaiyapuri Pillai, *History of Tamil Language and Literature* (Madras, 1956).

'Amaru'. ⇨ Śaṅkara.

Amir Hamzah (1911–46). ⇨ Indonesian lyric poet. Although a man of modern education he was a traditionalist. A member of the family of the Sultan of Langkat in East Sumatra he loved ancient Malay vocabulary, culture, history and verse forms, and was a staunch Muslim. His poem on the Malay hero Hang Tuah is in the form of a simplified but very colourful *shaer* and brings to mind a European ballad. His earliest poems – published in 1941 under the title *Buah Rindu* ('Fruit of Longing') – are sad songs of a lonely wanderer. In his later poems, published in 1937 as *Njanji Sunji* ('Songs of Solitude'), he shows strong religious feeling and addresses himself to God as the God of Love. He was killed in the disturbances in East Sumatra that preceded independence. [E C G B]

Amru'u'l-Qais. ⇨ Imru'u'l-Qais.

Āṇṭāḷ. ⇨ Āḻvār.

Appar. ⇨ Nāyaṉmār.

Arabian Nights. This celebrated collection of stories, more correctly known as *The Thousand and One Nights* (Arabic: *Alf laila wa-laila*), is only partly Arab in origin. The romances woven into it are from all the leading civilizations of the East, largely from Persia.

The individual stories are arranged in a narrative framework calculated to hold the reader's (or rather the listener's, since the stories were originally the property of storytellers) attention from one instalment to the next. This framework is as follows: The Persian monarch Shahriyār has, because of his unfortunate marital experiences, so little faith in woman's fidelity that he has adopted the habit of taking a new wife each night and putting her to death next morning. The ingenious Shahrāzād (Scheherezade), however, keeps Shahriyār amused from one night to the next by telling him stories that he cannot bear to bring to an end by killing her. Thus, each story leads into the next, without the reader's noticing the division.

The basis of the collection was an ancient Persian book known as the *Thousand Stories* (Hazār Afsāna), which was translated into Arabic not later than the 10th century. Many of the tales come from India, just as the stories in the book of *Kalila wa-Dimna*, a book of fables largely about animals, stem from the Sanskrit *Fables of Bidpai*. Other stories were added to this original collection; one early series concerns Harun al-Rashid and his court poet ⇨ Abu Nuwās. The collection was further expanded during the Mamlūk period in Egypt. Snatches of verse are interpolated into the prose narrative, as in many types of Arabic literature, often without much relevance.

There was no standard text of the work until about the 15th century. Muslim scholars regarded it as fit only for the coffee-house storyteller, and took no interest in it as literature; medieval editors and scribes were therefore free to collect as many tales as they liked from various manuscripts. The work is written mostly in simple Arabic, with many traces of the Egyptian colloquial; this contrasts strongly with the complicated idiom of the acknowledged masters of artistic prose in classical Arabic.

The *Nights* were introduced to the western world by the French orientalist Antoine Galland (1646–1715). There have been a number of English translations, one of the most remarkable of which is that of Sir Richard Burton (16 vols., 1885–8). Burton uses his own style of archaic English to translate the *Nights*, a style that may be found slightly wearing to read, but one that has dignity and is not inappropriate to romance. Burton's footnotes and Terminal Essay contain much information of anthropological interest. After his death, his wife published an expurgated edition of his translation. More recent translators include A. J. Arberry (*Scheherezade. Tales from the Thousand and One Nights*, 1953). [A S T]

The Book of the Thousand Nights and One Night, tr. E. Powys Mathers (16 vols., 1923; repr. 1929); *The Thousand and One Nights, or Arabian Nights Entertainments*, tr. E. W. Lane (many edns; repr. 1925–8, 1930, etc.).
N. Elisséeff, *Thèmes et motifs des Mille et une nuits* (Beirut, 1949); *E of I*.

Ariwara Narihira (825–880). Japanese court poet. Little is known of his life except that he was the grandson of an emperor by both parents, and that he was sent into exile on one occasion for an unwise love affair. Otherwise, legend has made him the type of the courtly amorous adventurer. His poems are all *tanka* (of 31 syllables), and are mainly to be found in the *Kokinshū* (a poetry collection published in *c.*905), and in the *Ise-monogatari* ('Tales of Ise'), which describe generally erotic incidents involving the hero, who is Ariwara himself and whose poems accompany the stories. His verse shows signs of sincere feeling and a good knowledge of the psychology of the lover, both male and female, which are often accompanied by a pleasant wit. [C J D]

Keene, *A J L*; *Ise-monogatari*, ed. and tr. Fritz Vos (The Hague, 1957).
Brower and Miner, *J C P*.

'Arthaśāstra'. ⇨ Kauṭilya.

Aśvaghoṣa (1st cent. A.D.). The first known writer of classical Sanskrit poetry. He is said to have been born a brahmin, but to have later embraced Buddhism. Aśvaghoṣa's work is a great distance from that of his successors, both in time and content. His 2 epic poems celebrate the life of the Buddha (*Buddhacarita*) and the conversion of the Buddha's half-brother, Nanda (*Saundaryananda*). The former constitutes a major source for the traditional history of the Buddha's early life, wanderings and illumination, but is unfortunately incomplete; the last half is known only through Chinese and Tibetan translations.

Both works are didactic and religiously inspired; nevertheless, they have much in common stylistically with later Sanskrit poetry, and it even seems likely that Aśvaghosa knew a rudimentary form of poetic theory, judging by his use of several complicated figures of speech. His work has little of the brilliance of ◊ Kālidāsa's and none of the baroque of later writers. [E G]

Buddhacarita, tr. E. B. Cowell (Calcutta, 1935–6); *Saundaryananda*, tr. E. B. Cowell (1928).

Winternitz, *G I L*, ii.

'Atâ Malik. ◊ Juwaynî.

'Attâr, Farîd al-Dîn (fli. *c*.1180–*c*.1220). Persian mystic poet. He was born and spent most of his long life at Nîshâpûr in north-east Persia. By profession a pharmacist (Arabic *'attâr*) and physician, he spent many years collecting the tales and sayings of Muslim mystic saints, putting together 97 biographies in his one prose-work, *Tadhkirat al-Awliyâ* (German tr. of some *vitae* by P. Klappstein, *Vier turkestanische Heilige . . .*, Berlin, 1920, and J. Hallauer, *Die Vita des Ibrahim b. Edhem*, Leipzig, 1925; French tr. of a version in Eastern Turkish, by Pavet de Courteille, Paris, 1889–90). His principal poetical work, much imitated and commented on in the Muslim world, is *Mantiq al-Tayr* ('The Conference of the Birds'), an elaborate allegory with numerous digressions ('Attâr is a born storyteller) describing in some 5,000 couplets how all the birds (i.e. human souls) set out in search of the Sîmurgh (a mythical bird, i.e. the Godhead): all but thirty die, and the survivors realize that they (Persian *sî murgh* = 'thirty birds') are themselves the Sîmurgh (abridged tr. E. FitzGerald, Boston, 1899, and R. P. Masani, 1924; S. C. Nott, 1954, from the French of Garcin de Tassy, 1863).

'Attâr's other chief works are *Ilâhî-nâma* ('The Book of The Divine'), the parable of the quest for happiness of a king's six sons (French tr. F. Rouhani, 1961); *Musîbat-nâma* ('The Book of Affliction'), an allegory of the soul's ascent to God; and *Asrâr-nâma* ('The Book of Secrets'). Many of the 20 other surviving works ascribed to 'Attâr are now rejected as spurious. [V L M]

Browne, *L H P*, ii; M. Smith, *The Persian Mystics: 'Attâr* (W E S, 1932); Arberry, *C P L*; Rypka, *I L*; *E of I*; H. Ritter, *Das Meer der Seele* (Leiden, 1955) (analysis of poems).

Avesta. The name, probably meaning 'Injunction', given to the holy books of the Zoroastrians, composed in an otherwise unrecorded eastern Iranian language, closely akin to Sanskrit. The texts are in many places obscure, because of unknown words and the corruptions of long oral transmission. They were probably first written down in Persia proper in the 3rd–6th centuries A.D. Only a small part of the original Avesta survives, divisible into the following sections: (1) The *Gathas*, generally dated to *c*. 600 B.C., hymns composed by Zoroaster himself in traditional style but highly individual idiom, moving because of the intensity of the thought and feeling, but largely obscure because of difficulties of content and language. (2) The *Yashts*, hymns to individual gods of the later Zoroastrian pantheon, preserved in a more recent version of the language but embodying much pre-Zoroastrian material. They contain some beautiful ancient invocations, and fragments of a mythology also found in the Indian Vedas. (3) The *Yasna* and *Visperad*, liturgical texts in verse and prose, of different dates and varying literary quality. (4) The *Vendidad*, a miscellaneous collection of prose writings, largely concerned with ritual but with some interesting legendary material. It is written in a late form of the language, which is often halting.

Several translations of the *Gathas* exist, but none can be regarded as authoritative, while all translations of Younger Avestan texts can be challenged on individual points, arising from the obscurity of some of the verses. [E M B]

The Gathas, tr. M. W. Smith (Linguistic Society of America, 1929); *The Hymns of Zarathustra*, ed. J. Duchesne-Guillemin, tr. M. Henning (1952); *Avesta*, German tr. F. Wolff (Strassburg, 1910); *Die Yashts des Awesta*, German tr. H. Lommel (Göttingen, Leipzig, 1927); *The Zend-Avesta*, tr. J. Darmester and L. Mills (Sacred Books of the East, 3 vols., 1883–7).

Avicenna (ibn Sīnā, Husain ibn 'Abdullāh) (980–1037). Arabic physician and philosopher. He was of Persian origin, born near Bukhara, and educated as an Ismā'īlī. He was, it seems, a precocious student, and gained early recognition as a physician. He was forced to flee from Khwārizm to escape from Sultan Mahmūd of Ghazna, who wished to add him to the circle of famous men detained at his court; he then travelled, sometimes accepting important posts from the rulers he visited.

Avicenna adopted and developed the Aristotelian philosophy (as interpreted by the neo-Platonists), which was the basis of most Muslim philosophy at that period, and made use of the work of the celebrated Arab philosopher al-Fārābī (*c.* 870–950). Avicenna's *Kitāb al-Shifā'* ('Book of Healing') is an encyclopedia with sections on logic, physics, metaphysics, psychology and natural history. Much of the material is Aristotelian. *Kitāb al-Najāt* ('Book of Salvation') is a compendium of this work. In spite of Avicenna's interest in metaphysics, he remained an orthodox Muslim, and wrote a number of books on theology. In his later years he also wrote some allegorical mystical works, important in the development of 'Illuminationist' Sufism.

Avicenna is important in the history of medicine. His *Qānūn* or Canon of Medicine is an encyclopedia which long remained the standard text book in Europe. He wrote many other minor works, and put much of his scientific and medical information into rather crude verse; these versions, in an early Arabic metre not much used for artistic verse, were presumably intended more as *aides-mémoire* than as literary compositions. Avicenna also wrote a number of books in Persian. [A S T]

Avicenna's Psychology, tr. F. Rahman (1952); *Avicenna on Theology*, tr. A. J. Arberry (W E S, 1951).

S. M. Afnan, *Avicenna: His Life and Works* (1958); *Avicenna Commemoration Volume* (Calcutta, 1956); E. G. Browne, *Arabian Medicine* (1921); H. Corbin, *Avicenna and the Visionary Recital* (1960); O. C. Gruner, *A Treatise on the Canon of Medicine of Avicenna* (1930); G. M. Wickens, ed., *Avicenna: Scientist and Philosopher. A Millenary Symposium* (1952).

B

'Babad'. ◊ Javanese literary genre, literally 'a clearing' (of a plot in the forest). A generic name for metrical treatises on the history of Java, either dealing with a local province such as *Babad Banyumas* or (like the best-known example *Babad Tanah Jawi* composed in 17th and 18th centuries) with the whole country. This latter is a typical mythological blend of native, Hindu and Muslim elements. It has been condensed into Javanese prose (J. J. Meinsma, in Javanese script: The Hague, 1874; later printed in Latin script) and translated into Dutch (W. L. Olthof, The Hague, 1941). These later forms are often quoted by historians. Parts have proved reliable, but others seem rather to be dynastic fiction or to reflect the individual attitudes of the author or a later editor. What the *babad* lack in historicity, however, they make up for by their unconscious revelation of Javanese ways of life and thought. During the thirties Balé Poestaka, the Government literature agency in Batavia, reprinted the Javanese text of *Babad Tanah Jawi* and *Babad Gianti* in Javanese script in some 30 100-page pamphlets. [C H]

Bâbur (1483–1530). Founder of the Mogul dynasty of India, poet and autobiographer. He was born at Ferghana in Turkestan. A descendant of Timur (Tamerlane), at the age of 11 he succeeded to his father's small principality and to his struggles with other Timurid princes. The rise of the Uzbek Khan Shaybânî obliged him in 1504 to flee over the Hindu Kush to Kabul, from where, after repeated failures to conquer Samarkand and Transoxania, he turned his eyes south. Invited into India in 1524 by one faction of warring Muslim rulers, he occupied in succession Lahore, Delhi, Agra and Lucknow, to make himself master of Hindustan. A born leader, shrewd and determined, convinced he was born to greatness, he was also chivalrous, tolerant and cultured. His great literary work is the *Bâbur-nâma*, written in Eastern ('Chaghatay') Turkish, in which he records, frankly and modestly, the events of his stormy life; its unaffected style and vivid descriptions make it not only a valuable historical source but one of the finest examples of Turkish prose literature (*The Babur-nama in English*, tr. A. S. Beveridge, 2 vols., 1922, with full introduction and notes).

Bâbur left also a collection of poems

(*dîwân*) in Chaghatay Turkish (with a score or so in Persian), mostly written in the classical tradition, i.e. in various quantitative metres, but with a few in the popular syllabic metre; technically skilful, they are fresh and sincere in tone. Among his minor works is a treatise on prosody. [V L M]

Browne, *L H P*, iii; W. Erskine, *History of India under the First Two Sovereigns of the House of Taimur* (2 vols., 1854); *Cambridge History of India*, iv (1937); Harold Lamb, *Babur the Tiger* (1961); *E of I*; *Philologiae Turcicae Fundamenta*, ii (Wiesbaden, 1964).

Bakin. ◊ Kyokutei Bakin.

Balagtas, Francisco (1788–1862). By common consent the prince of Tagalog poets. Tagalog, the language of the central provinces of Luzon Island, has of all ◊ Philippine languages the most highly developed literature. Balagtas, a native of Bulacan Province, received a college education in Manila and was employed in various minor municipal posts. His principal work, *Ang pinagdaanang buhay ni Florante at Laura sa kahariang Albanya* ('Of What Befell Florante and Laura in the Kingdom of Albania'), was first published in 1838 (ed. J. R. de Leon, Manila, 1950; tr. G. St Clair, 1950) and has been frequently re-edited since. It is a narrative poem (*awit*) whose merits lies not so much in the story – an improbable tale borrowed from Spanish sources – as in the technical perfection of the verse, aphorisms memorably stated, and descriptive and reflective passages of great beauty. The dedicatory poem 'Kay Selya' ('To Celia') is with reason considered one of the finest lyrics in the language. [H C]

Balinese Literature. The inhabitants (under 2 million) of the small island of Bali were never converted to Islam, like their neighbours in Java, and remain Hindu to this day. They have thus preserved the greater part of Old ◊ Javanese Literature in manuscripts which are still both respected and popular.

The Balinese have produced lengthy writings of their own in modern Javanese metres and in prose, on religious, philosophical and metaphysical subjects. Formerly available only in manuscript, these are now stencilled and made available in both romanized and Balinese scripts (the latter similar to Javanese script).

The literary language is strongly influenced by Javanese: courtly and heroic Old Javanese poems are often translated into the Balinese language, while Balinese poems are nowadays translated, in turn, into Indonesian. One popular and sentimental poem, the *Jaya Prana*, has been translated into English (C. Hooykaas, 1958); and perhaps no other literature in a Malayo-Polynesian language has a comparable number of folk-tales, some of which ridicule the common man, some the Brahmin priests, some even the magician. Generally, indigenous Balinese writing now has to struggle to maintain itself against the influence of modern Indonesian. [C H]

C. Hooykaas, 'Books Made in Bali', in Felicitation Volume in honour of Dr K. M. Munshi (Bombay, 1962) (also in *Bijdragen tot de Taal-, Land- en Volkenkunde*, Vol. 119, The Hague, 1963).

Bāṇa. Sanskrit author. Court poet of Harṣadeva, King of Thanesvar (A.D. 606–47) and author of two important Sanskrit prose works, a novel *Kādambarī* and the only 'history' surviving from the classical period, the *Harṣacarita*, celebrating the accession of his patron to the throne.

The *Harṣacarita* is apparently incomplete, for it stops abruptly before Harṣa is completely successful in his enterprise. As history its value is limited by the obvious deference Bāṇa pays to Harṣa.

The *Kādambarī* is, like the *Kathāsaritsāgara* (◊ Somadeva), a love intrigue and a frame story, but of a more complicated kind: the series of narrators are themselves actors in the story and their narrations often function as flashbacks. The plot has the curious quality of ending, after many involutions, at precisely the point where it began. The *Kādambarī* is by Indian standards a *chef d'œuvre* of the prose art; indeed its style of language and story reaches a complexity which is almost a caricature of the Indian literary genius.

King Harṣa is himself reputed to be the author of 3 not unworthy dramas – the *Ratnāvalī*, the *Priyadarśikā* (both taking themes from the Bṛhatkathā) and the 'Buddhist' *Nāgānanda*. [E G]

Harṣacarita, tr. E. B. Cowell and F. W. Thomas (1897); *Kādambarī*, tr. C. M. Ridding (1896); *Priyadarśikā*, tr. Nariman, Jackson and Ogden (New York, 1923).

T. Watters, *On Yuan Chwang's Travels in India* (1904–5); Winternitz, *G I L*, iii.

Bar Hebraeus (Abu'l-Faraj, Gregory) (1226–86). Syriac historian and philosopher. He came of a Jewish family, hence his name of Bar Hebraeus. He was the son of a physician of Malatia on the upper Euphrates. He knew Arabic, Syriac and Greek. While studying medicine in Tripoli, he was ordained and became bishop of Malatia a year later at the age of 20. In 1253 he was translated to the see of Aleppo, and in 1264 appointed *maphrian* or Catholicos-Patriarch of the Jacobite Church. He died at Maragha in Persia.

Bar Hebraeus was a prolific writer. He wrote a commentary on the Bible in Syriac, two works on the doctrines of the Jacobite Church, a book on ecclesiastical and civil law, and another on morals, which owed much to ◊ al-Ghazālī. He composed a *summa* of Aristotelian philosophy in four parts: logic, natural philosophy, metaphysics, and practical philosophy (i.e. ethics, economics and politics). He also wrote a Syriac grammar, but his medical writings have perished. His Church history deals with both the Jacobites and the Nestorians. He compiled a secular history, beginning as was customary with Adam and Eve; one sixth of the work is given up to pre-Islamic history, and the other five sixths treat of the Near East up to his own day. This book made a great name for itself, and the author was asked to translate it into Arabic: this he did, adapting the text to his new Muslim readers. He died soon after finishing this, having foretold that his end was near. His most readable work is his collection of sometimes improper 'laughable stories' (ed. and tr. E. A. Wallis Budge, 1897–9).

Simple and uncritical in his modes of thought, Bar Hebraeus commands respect as one of the most industrious compilers of knowledge who ever lived. [D M L]

Bar Hebraeus's Book of the Dove, tr. A. J. Wensinck (Leiden, 1919); *The Chronography*, tr. E. A. Wallis Budge (2 vols., 1932).
W. Wright, *A Short History of Syriac Literature* (1894).

Barash, Asher (1889–1952). Hebrew novelist and short-story writer. Born in Poland, he went to Palestine as a young man and settled in Tel Aviv. He depicts the life of Jews in Galicia chiefly in his novels *Tmunot Mibet Mivshal-Haschechar* (1928); and *Ahava Zara* (1938). His later novels and short stories describe the new life in Israel in a simple, realistic style. He also edited an anthology of modern Hebrew poetry under the title *Mivchar Ha-shirah Ha-ivrit Hachadasha* (1938). [E E]

Klausner, *H M H L*; Waxman, *H J L*.

'Barlaam and Josaphat'. The story of Barlaam and Josaphat, one of the most popular tales of medieval Christendom, purports to tell of the conversion of the Indians to Christianity by the holy ascetic Barlaam and his disciple, the Indian prince Josaphat. In reality the book is a Christian romance, based ultimately on the legendary life of Gautama Buddha.

The work presents Josaphat (=the Bodhisattva, or Buddha elect) as son of a pagan king of India named Abenner. At the prince's birth, an astrologer declares that his greatness will not be of this world but of eternity. Abenner tries to shield his son from all knowledge of the harsh realities of human life. Josaphat grows up and insists on venturing out of the palace. He sees a cripple, a blind man, and another ancient and infirm: these represent three of the Four Omens of Buddhist tradition. The hermit Barlaam appears and preaches to Josaphat in a series of parables. He converts the prince to Christianity and they exchange raiment, Josaphat receiving the ascetic's hair apron. King Abenner is furious, but cannot prevail against his son's decision. In the end Abenner is himself converted before he dies. Josaphat abdicates and departs into the wilderness, where he is reunited with Barlaam. The two saints end their lives together in the odour of sanctity.

The story first assumed its narrative shape among the Manichaeans of Central Asia, who transmitted it to the Arabs. The first Christian version was made in Georgian about the 9th century (*The Wisdom of Balahvar*, tr. D. M. Lang, 1957), and from this the standard Greek text (ed. and tr. G. R. Woodward and H. Mattingly, Loeb, 1914) was adapted by St Euthymius the Georgian and his disciples on Mount Athos early in the 11th century. From the Greek, the Barlaam and Josaphat legend spread throughout Christendom (e.g. Ethiopic version, ed. and tr. E. A. Wallis Budge, 2 vols., 1923). Several leading Churches numbered the two heroes among their saints. [D M L]

Bashō (1644–94). Japanese poet and diarist. He was born in Iga-Ueno, near Kyoto, and in his youth was companion to the son of the local lord. With him he studied the writing of 17-syllable verse, a form which had developed from the 31-syllable *tanka* through the intermediary of *renga* (linked songs) in which *tanka* had been divided into units of 17 and 14 syllables, composed by different authors. The *hokku* (starting verse) of a *renga* came to exist separately, and until the mid 17th century tended to be comic or satirical. Bashō's master died in 1666, and in 1667 he moved to Edo (now Tokyo). There he continued to compose *hokku* (the present name, *haiku*, is 19th-century) in the Danrin style, which still favoured the comic, and to take part in *renga* composition. About 1680 he made his home in a typical recluse's hut on the outskirts of Edo, and from a *bashō* (banana) tree that grew at the door he named it the Bashō retreat, using the same name himself. His *hokku* now became more original. They occur in collections which appeared from 1684 until his death, and in diaries of his journeys of this period. The object of these travels, in which he followed the example of the Chinese poet ⇨ Li Po and the Japanese ⇨ Saigyō-hōsi, was to visit famous places and observe nature, taking only the barest essentials, and relying on the hospitality of temples and of fellow-poets. He records his impressions both in verse and in direct and telling prose. The best known of these journals is *Oku no hosomichi* (*The Narrow Road of Oku*, Keene, *AJL*).

Buddhism played a large part in his life, and to the teachings of the Zen sect may be ascribed his quiet style, his avoidance of the over-picturesque and grandiose, and his liking for scenes in which an incisive or momentary feature stands out against a continuous backcloth, similar to the flash of enlightenment against the background of meditation. But his work can also be appreciated without any appeal to Buddhist thought; his *haiku* are a series of superb pictures in which whole landscapes, whole seasons, are evoked by the description of the crucial details. His poetry shows little interest in his fellow human beings. After his time, *haiku* changed, almost certainly for the worse. [C J D]

Donald Keene, 'Bashō's Journey of 1684', in *Asia Major*, VII, pts 1/2 (Dec. 1959); Donald Keene, 'Bashō's Journey to Sarashina', *Transactions of the Asiatic Society of Japan*, 3rd series, No. 5 (1957).

Keene, *A J L*; *Haiku*, ed. R. H. Blyth (4 vols., Tokyo, 1949–52); A. G. Henderson, *An Introduction to Haiku* (Garden City, N.Y., 1958).

Ben-Yehudah, Eliezer (1858–1922). Hebrew lexicographer. Jewish nationalist and the pioneer of Modern Hebrew as a spoken language. Born in Lithuania, he received his early education at a talmudic academy in Polotzk and at the grammar school of Dinaburg. In 1878 he went to Paris to study medicine with the purpose of settling in Palestine. His literary activity began in Paris with an article in a Hebrew journal advocating a return to Palestine as the solution of the Jewish problem. Owing to tuberculosis he was forced to give up his medical studies and went to Algeria and thence to Palestine. He took up residence in Jerusalem in 1881, where he lived but for a few years in the U.S.A. (1915–19) until his death.

Ben-Yehudah's greatest achievement was his Hebrew dictionary. It covers the Hebrew of all ages and literary genres and includes many words that he himself coined to meet modern needs. It is the most comprehensive Hebrew dictionary, although the language has developed so rapidly since his death that its usefulness for the Hebrew of today is fairly limited. He covered about half the alphabet in his lifetime, and the work was carried on by his wife and other scholars, reaching completion in 1959. The acceptance of Hebrew as the modern spoken language of the Jews in Palestine was largely due to the enthusiasm of Eliezer Ben-Yehudah. He would speak no other language, not even in the family. He edited many Hebrew journals, and in 1888 helped found the Hebrew Language Council. [R F H]

Eliezer Ben Yehuda of Jerusalem, *A Complete Dictionary of Ancient and Modern Hebrew* (17 vols., Berlin-Jerusalem, 1908–59).

Waxman, *H J L*, iv.

'Bhagavadgītā' (*c.*200 B.C.). One of the holiest works of popular Hinduism; a short poem of seven hundred verses and the most famous of the later interpolations in the ⇨ *Mahābhārata.* The anonymous poem records a sermon delivered by Kṛṣṇa to Arjuna as the two armies are drawn up for their climactic battle. At first only an exhortaton by Kṛṣṇa, his friend and charioteer, that Arjuna be brave and do battle, even at the risk of fratricide, the poem ultimately becomes a theophany of Kṛṣṇa as Viṣṇu, the all-high God. In its former aspect, the *Gītā* is a philosophical defence of action at the expense of contemplative withdrawal from the world's affairs; in its latter, it is a religious document central to the devotional worship of Kṛṣṇa, whose cult is perhaps the most widespread of any Hindu deity. The *Gītā* marks the historical turning point between the older Hindu religion, based on the Vedic sacrifice and its brahminical monopoly of ritual functions, and the later theistic, devotional and soteriological Hinduism based on worship of the great gods Śiva and Viṣṇu, and open to all Hindus regardless of caste. The *Gītā* has continued to influence Indian society profoundly, and even modern political doctrines have been referred to it by Gandhi, Aurobindo, Tilak and others. [E G]

Tr. Charles Wilkins (1785) (the first translation of an Indian literary work into a western language); tr. Edwin Arnold (Boston, 1885); tr. Franklin Edgerton (Cambridge, Mass., 1944): tr. S. Radhakrishnan (New York, 1948); tr. Juan Mascaró (Penguin Classics, 1962).

F. Edgerton, The *Bhagavadgītā* (1944); R. G. Bhandarkar, *Śaivism, Vaiṣṇavism and Minor Religious Systems* (Strassburg, 1913).

Bharata. ⇨ *Nāṭyaśāstra.*

'Bhārata Yuddha'. A 12th-century Old-Javanese ⇨ *kakawin*, composed by Mpu Sēḍah and Mpu Panuluh, dealing with the final stage of the war between the Pāndawa and Kaurawa (two sets of cousins, descendants of Bhārata). Their feud is the main theme of the world's longest epic, the ⇨ *Mahābhārata,* a Sanskrit poem dating from perhaps the 4th century B.C. and consisting of 100,000 stanzas. The *Bhārata Yuddha,* of 722 stanzas, passes over the long introductory books dealing with the former exploits of the heroes and their ancestors. It starts with the last effort towards a reconciliation, vividly depicts the tragic battle scenes and omits the final redemption of the slain warriors. The Old-Javanese epic was also recast into a Modern-Javanese metrical form at the 18th-century Muslim court in Surakarta by Yosodipuro. Both versions have been translated into Dutch. [C H]

Bhārati. ⇨ Subrahmaṇya Bhārati.

Bhartṛhari (7th cent.). Classical Sanskrit poet. Author of 3 collections of short verses on the topics of love, justice and final liberation. An excellent practitioner of the lyric style, Bhartṛhari's 'hundred' verses on love are touched with a deep understanding of the sweet passion as well as a certain sceptical view of its consequences; the other 'hundreds' are more gnomic, and the last especially reveals a mind evidently greatly deceived by that love which was so admirably depicted in the first.

Bhartṛhari has been reasonably identified with a famous grammarian of the same name, of whom the Chinese pilgrim I-Tsing reports that he adopted the ascetic's robes seven times only to return to the joys of householding. [E G]

Selected verses, considerably expurgated: *Śatakas,* tr. B. Hale Wortham (1886); *A Century of Indian Epigrams,* tr. Paul E. More (New York, 1899).

Winternitz, *G I L,* iii.

Bhavabhūti (8th cent.). Indian dramatist. Second only to ⇨ Kālidāsa in general estimation. He lived at the court of King Yaśovarman of Kanauj (720–50). His 3 dramas are unsurpassed in their mastery of Sanskrit, and his style is marked by a sense of pathos rare in classical poetry. The *Mahāvīracarita* (tr. J. Pickford, 1871) and the *Uttararāmacarita* (tr. S. K. Belvalkar, Cambridge, Mass., 1915) ('Acts of Rāma' and 'Later Acts of Rāma') are based on the Rāma cycle, and the *Mālatīmādhava* (Fr. tr. G. Strehley, Paris, 1885) is a secular play based partly on the *Bṛhatkathā* (⇨ Somadeva). [E G]

Winternitz, *G I L,* iii.

Bialik, Chaim Nachman (1873–1934). Hebrew poet. Born near Zhitomir in the

Ukraine, he was the youngest child of a large and poor family. When his widowed mother could no longer support him, he went to live with his grandfather, who though severe gave him good opportunities of education and reading. In his teens he was able to study by himself in the local synagogue – a lonely kind of life reflected in several poems. At 17 he was sent to the Talmudic Academy at Volozhin, where he stayed for about a year and a half, developing an interest in modern literature. He then went on to Odessa, a centre of literary activity at the time. Here he was noticed and encouraged by Asher Ginzberg (pseud. Achad ha-Am), who helped him to get his poem *El ha-Tsippor* published. He returned to Zhitomir, married, and tried to settle down to the life of a lumber merchant. Some of his most impressive poems date from this period – several nature poems and *Al Saf Beth ha-Midrash* ('On the Threshold of the House of Study'). The long narrative *Ha-Matmid* ('The Perpetual Student') was also largely written in this period, and is one of Bialik's best poems. It is about the almost tragic tenacity of the youth who abandons all interest in life to study the Talmud. 'To what end is this mighty sacrifice?' asks the poet.

The sufferings of the Jewish people figure largely in Bialik's poetry. The Kishinev pogrom of 1903 inspired the anguish and fury of *Be-Ir ha-Haregah* ('In the City of Slaughter'), a poem which stirred Jewish youth to Zionist activity.

Undoubtedly the greatest modern Hebrew poet and literary figure, Bialik was a notable anthologist and translator of numerous world classics into Hebrew. In 1921 he founded the *Devir* publishing house in Berlin. It was later transferred to Tel-Aviv, where he himself spent the last ten years of his life. [R F H]

Kithve Ch. N. Bialik (Tel-Aviv, 1926–38) (selected works in Hebrew); *Poems from the Hebrew*, ed. L. V. Snowman (1924); *Halachah and Aggadah*, tr. L. Simon (1944). M. Ungerfeld, *Ch. N. Bialik vitsirotav* (Tel-Aviv, 1960) (Hebrew bibliography); Waxman, *H J L*, iv.

Bidyalankarana, Prince (1876–1945). Thai writer and literary historian. His work bridges the traditional and the new in Thai literature. His chief work is *Sam Krung*, a historical poem on three Thai capitals, Ayuthaya, Thonburi and Bangkok. One of the early writers of prose fiction, he produced many short stories which are distinguished for their wit. An important work is *Ĉhotmai Changwang Ram*, the fictional correspondence of a Thai official to his son studying abroad, and one of the earliest literary works to deal with the human and social aspects of the impact of the West on Thailand. [E H S S]

al-Bîrûnî, Abu'l-Rayhân Muhammad (973–1051). Muslim scholar. The most original scholar of medieval Islam, eminent in the fields of mathematics, geography, astronomy and the natural sciences. Born in Khwârazm (now Soviet Karakalpakistan), where he began his scientific studies. For some years from about 998 he was at the court of the local ruler of Jurjân, south-east of the Caspian Sea, where in 1000 he completed his first great work (in Arabic) *al-Âthâr al-Bâqiya* (*The Chronology of Ancient Nations*, tr. E. Sachau, 1879), on calendars and eras and the related astronomical problems. He was back in Khwârazm from 1009 until the district was conquered in 1017 by Sultan Mahmûd of Ghazna, who removed the learned men, al-Bîrûnî among them, to his capital in Afghanistan. Thenceforth al-Bîrûnî remained with Mahmûd and his successors, perhaps as court astrologer. Accompanying Mahmûd on his Indian campaigns, he learned Sanskrit and studied Indian scientific and religious literature: his second major work, *Ta'rîkh al-Hind* ('History of India'), completed in 1030 (tr. E. Sachau, *Al-Beruni's India*, 2 vols., 1888, new ed. 1910), is a penetrating and detailed description of the greatest value and remarkable for its objectivity. He spent the rest of his life at Ghazna engaged on scientific and literary works.

Of the 180 works – many only short treatises – with which al-Bîrûnî is credited, some 25 survive. Here may be mentioned a work on the mathematical elements of astrology (*The Book of Instruction . . .*, ed. and tr. R. Ramsey Wright, 1934), the astronomical *Tamhîd al-Mustaqarr* (*Al-Biruni on Transits*, tr. M. Saffouri and A. Ifram, Beirut, 1959), and the astronomical *al-Qânûn al-Masʿûdî*, written for Mahmûd's son Masʿûd. [V L M]

Carra de Vaux, *Les penseurs de l'Islam*, ii (Paris, 1921–6); G. Sarton, *Introduction to the History of Science*, i (Washington, 1927); *Al-Biruni Commemoration Volume* (Calcutta, 1951); *E of I*; J. D. Pearson, *Index Islamicus 1906–55*, nos. 4638–4703, and *Supplement 1956–60*, nos. 1326–1340.

Bluvstein, Rahel (1890–1931). Hebrew poetess. Born in Poltava, she came to Palestine from the Ukraine as a pioneer in 1908. Her poetry has no trace of diaspora life but is pervaded by a love for the land of Israel and its people. [E E]

Shirat Rahel (Tel Aviv, 1954).
D. Kobler, *Four Rahels* (1947).

'Book of Odes'. Collection of 305 ancient Chinese songs, composed between about 1000 B.C. and 700 B.C. Few of them are accurately datable. Traditionally these songs were collected from all parts of the country by special court officials, to be used as a gauge of the people's feelings. If so, they must have been edited by musicians for court entertainment, for they contain few localisms. ◊ Ssu-ma Ch'ien records that originally there were more than 3,000 songs, from which Confucius selected the present collection. There is no evidence to support these theories, but as Confucius several times referred to the '300 Songs', it is likely that they had been arranged in their present form by his time. The traditional connexion with Confucius made the *Book of Odes* a sacred classic, committed to memory by the literati, and preserved for posterity.

The songs are grouped in sections. One contains 160 folk songs and ballads. These include love songs, work songs, songs of forsaken wives etc. Another contains court songs about feasting and hunting, sacrifices, campaigns, legends etc. The third section contains 40 hymns, songs sung as accompaniment for ritual dancing, performed at court in rites to the royal ancestors.

Some of the songs probably represent the oldest extant Chinese poetry, dating back to the beginning of the Chou Dynasty (1122–219 B.C.). Most of the poems were meant to be sung, but although the music was already lost by the end of the Chou Dynasty, the words survive as an important source of knowledge of ancient Chinese civilization. They contain some of the earliest known uses of rhyme in world literature and have exerted a great influence on later Chinese poetry. [J D C]

Tr. Arthur Waley, *The Book of Songs* (1937).

Bose, Buddhadeva (1908–). Bengali poet, novelist and short-story writer. One of the most outstanding and original of contemporary Bengali writers. He has long been a controversial figure, as leader of a literary movement anti-traditionalist in style, language and subject matter. As editor of the journal *Pragati*, a short-lived literary progressive journal published in Dacca, and then of the influential literary magazine *Kavita* (founded 1935), he has defended his position in essays and in exemplary pieces.

Bose is not often translated into English, although his short stories have appeared in such magazines as *Dial* (1960, No. 3) and his poems in collections and anthologies such as *Green and Gold* (ed. Humayun Kabir, New York, 1960). Of a great many volumes of his poetry published in Bengali, perhaps the most representative is *Srestha kavita* ('Best Poetry', Calcutta, 1957); he has also written over 40 novels and has published a number of volumes of essays of considerable power and craftsmanship. He is former Professor and Head of the Department of Comparative Literature at Jadavpur University in Calcutta and the editor of *Kavita*. [E C D]

'Brāhmaṇa' (relating to, or derived from *brahman*, the sacred utterance or 'logos' of the Veda). A group of texts (*c.* 1000–800 B.C.) constituting the second period of the ◊ Veda, wherein are described and discussed the techniques and materials of the sacrifice. Though the *Brāhmaṇas* are ostensibly based on the *Saṃhitas*, they represent a radical revision of the earlier religion, emphasizing the precise control of those forces which in the Veda appear mysterious. The *Brāhmaṇas* are the first 'genuine' Hindu texts and consecrate the pre-eminence of the sacrificial priest, or *brāhmaṇa* (*brahmin*).

The fundamental doctrine of the *Brāhmaṇas* is the functional identity of the macrocosm and the microcosm – the objective universe and the sacrifice. The sacrificial act (*karman*) becomes identified with its correlative: the world becomes a sacrifice. The Indian preoccupation with the inevitable fruit of acts, as well as the extreme importance of verbal technique (◊ Pāṇini), can be traced to this nexus of word and deed. [E G]

Śatapathabrāhmaṇa, tr. J. Eggeling (Sacred Books of the East, 5 vols., 1882) (the longest and most important *Brāhmaṇa*, belonging to the school of the *Yajurveda*); *Aitareya Brāhmaṇas*, tr. A. B. Keith (Harvard Oriental Series, 1920).

A. B. Keith, *The Religion and Philosophy of the Vedas and Upaniṣads* (Harvard Oriental Series, 2 vols., 1925); H. Oldenberg, *Die Weltanschauung der Brāhmaṇatexte* (Göttingen, 1919).

Brenner, Joseph Hayyim (1881–1921). Hebrew novelist. Born in Novi Malini, Bulgaria, he came from the ghetto, studied in Yeshivah and privately in high school, enlisted and served in the Russian army but at the outbreak of the Japanese war in 1905 escaped to London where he lived in abject poverty editing the Hebrew periodical, *Hamoeorer* ('The Awakener'). Like most of his contemporaries he was attracted to Socialism and for a time became an adherent of the *Bund* (the Jewish Socialist Movement). Soon, however, he found that he could not reconcile his deep-rooted Jewishness and love for the Hebrew language with the extreme tendencies of the movement and he became a Zionist. In 1908 he settled in Palestine, where he became leader of the pioneer groups and a founder of the *Histadruth* (General Confederation of Labour). Having seen the beginning of the realization of Zionist dreams he was killed in Jaffa in the Arab riots in 1921. The stormy life he led is reflected in his writing which is chaotic, turbulent, yet full of compassion for his heroes. His novels are full of often irrelevant detail, rather a series of episodes than a coherent narrative; still they show a deep understanding of the varied situations of life. The novels portray life as he saw it in Russia and the London East End and later the struggles of early Jewish settlement in Palestine. His short stories (collected edn, 1898) are rooted in the poverty, misery and darkness of the ghetto. [E E]

Kolkitve (Tel Aviv, 1953 ff.).

D. A. Friedman, *Iosef Hayyim Brenner* (Berlin, 1923).

'Bṛhatkathā'. ◊ Somadeva.

Burmese Literature. The earliest surviving records of written Burmese are found in the large body of stone inscriptions from the early 12th century A.D. onwards. They record acts of merit such as the building of Buddhist pagodas and monasteries, and sometimes contain moving passages describing the aspirations of the dedicator. The first surviving literary texts, written on processed palm-leaf, date from the mid 15th century. From this time till 1752 may be called the 'classical' period. Its literature is very largely in verse, in lines of 4 syllables, with rhymes moving from the end towards the beginning of successive lines in a number of different patterns. It was written by and for members of the royal courts, who were learned in the Buddhist scriptures and in Burmese literature, and so is highly esoteric, containing allusions and points of fine artistry which often baffle or escape the notice of the outsider. The dominant themes were religious exhortation and advice on virtuous conduct (◊ *pyo*) mainly written by Buddhist monks acting as the king's preceptors; glorification of the king written by court poets (◊ *maw-gun; e-gyin*); and sadness, love and longing (◊ Shin Raṭṭhasāra; Shin Sīlavaṁsa; Pade-tha-ya-za).

Burmese historical literature in prose begins with the 'Celebrated Chronicle' (*Ya-zawin-gyaw*), A.D. 1520, by Shin Sīlavaṁsa. It is an adaptation of the *Mahāvaṁsa* (a Pali chronicle of Ceylon) with short notes appended on some Burmese kings. The next history of note is the 'Great Chronicle' (*Maha Ya-zawin-gyi*) by U Kala (fl. 1714–33), who incorporated much of Shin Sīlavaṁsa's material and added a section at the beginning on the formation of the world, but most of his work recounts events in the reigns of Burmese kings up to the year 1728. The 'Glass Palace Chronicle' (*Hman-nan Ya-zawin*), written by a group of scholars at the command of King Ba-gyi-daw (1819–37) and completed in 1832, is a revised edition of U Kala's history brought nearly up to date; and the sequel, up to the end of the Burmese monarchy in 1886, was written in two stages: in the reign of King Mindon (1853–78), and in 1909. The latter part of the 'Glass Palace Chronicle', together with its sequel, covering the period 1752–1886, is known as 'The Chronicle of the Konbaung Dynasty' (*Kon-baung-zet Ya-zawin*). Some historical data are also to be found in the *e-gyin* and *maw-gun* poems. Part of the 'Glass Palace Chronicle' has been translated, under this title, by Pe Maung Tin and G. H. Luce (Rangoon University Press, 1960).

A new phase in Burmese literary history began with the founding of a new dynasty (Kon-baung) in 1752 and the conquest of Ayuthaya, the then capital of Thailand, in 1767. The old forms were still written, but many new ones emerged in a renewal of literary activity. Among them were songs, a verse form called ◊ *yagan* and the drama. These new forms all employed freer rhyme patterns and line lengths than the 'classical' verse, and their themes were often drawn from non-Buddhist sources (such as the ◊ *Rāmāyaṇa*) which entered Burma from Thailand. Though literature was still centred on the court, it now began to be written for entertainment as well as for edification. (◊ Let-wè Thondara; Kin-wun Min-gyi.)

The modern period in Burmese literature may be said to begin with the abrupt changes brought about by the completion of the British annexation, the fall of the monarchy (in 1886), and the spread of printing at about the same time. Literature was no longer for the court but for the public, and the old verse forms soon died out. A spate of printed plays was followed by novels and short stories, which are still written in large numbers, ranging from cheap love stories to serious novels with a social purpose. This increased the use of prose, which had been restricted before to such subjects as translations from the scriptures, histories and legal works. At the same time much of the old literature was printed. Almost all of it is available today. The ◊ Khit-san movement, begun in the 1930s, aimed at improving the standards of contemporary writing by combining modernity with traditional features. Since Burma attained independence in 1948 Burmese has almost been re-instated, in place of English, as the official language and the medium of instruction at all levels, but it is still too early for the effects on literature of the political change to have become fully apparent. (◊ Nu, U.)

The Burmese theatre deserves special mention. The earliest known plays are the long and formal 'palace plays' (*nan-dwin zat-taw-gyi*) about the adventures of princes and princesses written at the end of the 18th century on Thai models (◊ Pade-tha-ya-za). Early in the 19th century 'stage plays' (*pya-zat*), based on ◊ *jātaka* stories and Hindu and other legends, were popular up and down the country. The playwrights U ◊ Pon-nya and U Kyin U (*c.*1819–53) were both patronised by the king and provincial governors and perhaps for this reason the texts of some of their plays have survived. They are mostly in freely flowing rhymed prose, with the action interrupted by songs. With the spread of printing in the 1870s the texts of plays became available to the public as reading matter, complete with songs and stage directions, and the whole play was rhymed. After 1883 output increased and quality declined. Stage plays are still popular, but are improvised according to a pre-arranged sequence of scenes, so the written play with its rhymed prose has died out and its place was taken, early in the 20th century, by the novel and the short story. See *Burmese Drama* by Maung Htin Aung (1937), and *Konmara Pya Zat* (translation of a play, with an introduction) by Hla Pe (1952). [J W A O]

Minn Latt, 'Mainstreams in Burmese Literature', in *New Orient*, Prague, Vols. 1 (1960) and 2 (1961); G. E. Harvey, *History of Burma* (1925); Hla Pe, 'Dawn Songs', in *O A S*, X X (1958).

C

Cantu Mēnōn, O. (1846–99). Indian novelist. His reputation rests solely on *Indulekha* (1889; tr. W. Dumergue, Madras, 1890), the first novel of any importance in Malayalam. It is a story of the impact of western ideas on an orthodox family of South Malabar, and something of a feminist tract. Cantu Mēnōn's only other novel, *Śārada*, was never completed. [R E A]

Cāttaṉār (2nd cent. A.D.?; 5th cent. A.D.?). Tamil poet. Author of *Maṇimēkalai*. This poem of 30 cantos is the sequel to ⇨ Iḷankō's *Cilappatikāram*, although considered by some to be earlier. Maṇimēkalai is the daughter of the hero of *Cilappatikāram*, Kōvalan, and his mistress Mātavi. She resists the suit of a Chola prince and, after visiting a number of holy places and studying the various religious systems, renounces the world to become a Buddhist ascetic. Though Cāttaṉār's complex narrative is not lacking in variety and vigour, his poem, with its elaborate yet lucid exposition of the doctrines of Buddhism, is important above all as the only extant Buddhist 'epic' in Tamil. [R E A]

S. Krishnaswami Aiyangar, *Manimekhalai in Its Historical Setting* (1928); S. Vaiyapuri Pillai, *History of Tamil Language and Literature* (Madras, 1956).

Chairil Anwar (1922–49). ⇨ Indonesian poet. A member of a family from Medan, East Sumatra, which had moved to Djakarta, he started writing in 1942 soon after the Japanese occupation. Although a vagabond by nature and with little formal education, he translated the poems of Rilke and the Dutch writers Marsman and Slauerhoff, and modelled his Indonesian poems on them. With his burning vitality and poetic feeling he is regarded as the principal figure of the *Angkatan Empatpuluh Lima* ('Generation of 1945') and the greatest of Indonesian poets. He has described his approach as follows: 'In Art, vitality is the chaotic initial state; beauty the cosmic final state.' In his hands the developing Indonesian language at last attained equality with other languages as a literary medium. Chairil Anwar's collections of poems were all published in Djakarta after his early death – *Deru tjampur Debu* ('Cries in the Dust') in 1949, and *Kerikil Tadjam* ('Sharp Gravel') and *Jang Terampas dan Jang Putus* ('The Robbed and the Broken') in 1951. [E C G B]

A. Teeuw, *Pokok dan Tokoh*, ii (5th edn, Djakarta, 1959); H. B. Jassin, *Chairil Anwar* (Djakarta, 1956).

Chatterji, Bankimchandra (1838–94). Bengali novelist. He wrote many novels, essays and short stories, and is usually considered the first writer of the true novel in India. In 1872 he began the journal *Baṅgadarśana*, in which most of his work appeared in serial form. One of the first graduates of Calcutta University, Bankimchandra's work is greatly influenced by British novelists, especially Scott. His novels are primarily romances, with domestic theme and moral overtone, against a background of social orthodoxy (he stood, for example, against widow remarriage). He was a storyteller of some ingenuity and charm; this made his work immediately popular, as, in some quarters, it is today. Stylistically, Bankimchandra was imaginative, though not experimentalist – his style moves back from the novelties introduced by Pyarichand Mitra and Kaliprasanna Sinha toward the elegant and dignified prose of earlier decades. Bankimchandra's political and historical views were also orthodox, and he was a proponent of Hindu nationalism as against Islam. Many of his novels have been translated into English. [E C D]

Krishnakanta's Will, tr. J. C. Ghosh (New York, 1962); *The Abbey of Bliss* (*Anandamath*), tr. Nares Chandra Sen-Gupta (Calcutta, 1906).

Chavchavadze, Ilia (1837–1907). Georgian novelist, poet and essayist. He came of an ancient princely family, and was born at the small town of Kvareli. In 1857 he went to St Petersburg University, where he came under the influence of contemporary Russian radicals such as Dobrolyubov and Chernyshevsky. For his participation in the student riots of 1861, Chavchavadze was sent back to Georgia, where he worked for the liberation of the Georgian peasantry from serfdom. He founded a political movement known as the Pirveli Dasi or First Group, helped to found the Society for the Spreading of Literacy among the Georgians and revive the Georgian Dramatic Society, and edited the journal *Iveria*. Following the first Russian revolution of 1905, he was elected to represent Georgia in the Council of State at St Petersburg. He was murdered near his home at Saguramo in 1907 by unidentified assassins, thought to be acting under the orders of the tsarist secret police.

Ilia Chavchavadze's literary and public career covered half a century. He is linked with the poet Akaki Tsereteli (1840–1915) and the pedagogue Iakob Gogebashvili (1840–1912) as one of the foremost leaders of Georgia's cultural and social revival of the second half of the 19th century.

Chavchavadze's devastating novel of Georgian country life, *Katsia adamiani?* ('Do You Call This a Man?') (1863), recalls the savage satire of Gogol or Saltykov-Shchedrin, and jolted his fellow-countrymen out of their complacency. His considerable poetic output included a number of lyrics, a historical poem on the theme of the 13th-century Georgian hero King Dimitri the Devoted, who died for his people at the time of the Mongol invasions, and a philosophical poem of great power, *The Hermit* (tr. Marjory Wardrop, 1895). [DML]

Anthology of Georgian Poetry, ed. V. Urushadze (2nd edn, Tbilisi, 1958).

D. M. Lang, *A Modern History of Georgia* (1962).

'Chĕnṭini' ('Tjĕnṭini'). An anonymous 18th-century ◊ Javanese poem. This long metrical narrative may almost be called an encyclopedia of 18th-century Javanese religion and philosophy, and of cultural life at both court and village level and in the widespread and thriving theological colleges. It is accessible in print and in a detailed résumé in Dutch, but still awaits closer study to evaluate its treasures. [CH]

Sĕrat Tjĕnṭini, ed. Bataviaasch Genootschap van Kunsten en Wetenschappen, I–VIII (4 vols., 1912).

T. Pigeaud, *De Serat Tjabolang en de Serat Tjentini*, Verhandelingen van het Koninklijk Bat. Gen. v. K. en W., LXXII/2 (1933).

Chikamatsu Monzaemon (1653–1725). Japanese dramatist. Details of his early life are unknown, but he is believed to have come of warrior stock, and to have spent some time in a Buddhist monastery. By 1676 he was in Kyoto, writing plays for the *kabuki*, the live popular drama which had continued to develop, in spite of government opposition, since its emergence at the beginning of the 17th century; he also wrote plays for the puppet theatre, which had been going for about the same period but had suffered from fewer government restrictions. In 1686 he became associated with Takemoto Gidayū, a chanter in the puppet theatre in Osaka, and between them they developed an advanced style of puppet play. Up to then these had often been crude melodramas, and had existed in various styles each with its own particular tradition of chanting. Gidayū combined the best elements of previous styles, and Chikamatsu refined the crude playbooks, without however yet departing from the traditional legendary, historical and religious themes that had always formed its material. In 1703 however Chikamatsu wrote *Sonezaki shinjū* (*Love Suicides at Sonezaki*), the first of his domestic pieces, dealing with the love affairs of the now important merchant classes. The greatest of these is probably *Shinjū Ten no Amijima* (1721; tr. D. H. Shively, *The Love Suicide at Amijima*, 1953). Its theme is the suicide of a paper merchant, ruined by his love for the courtesan Koharu, and seeking escape, in death with her, from this troubled world to everlasting peace in a Buddhist paradise. These domestic pieces were founded on actual incidents, and in them Chikamatsu reached a standard of acute observation and realistic characterization in depth that was new in Japan and hardly equalled after his time until the coming of the modern novel. Though the theme of ruin for love was the one he treated most frequently and powerfully, he also wrote up at least one murder for robbery; he also used historical themes, which he turned into long pieces of great complexity remarkable for intricate staging and elements of fantasy. He was perhaps in advance of his times, for in spite of his great contemporary reputation his domestic plays did not survive his death unmodified but were altered to a more stylized pattern.

His puppet play-books, which include all his important works, are in the form of a continuous text incorporating dialogue and descriptive material. They were chanted to musical accompaniment, by one artiste usually, but sometimes by more, and the puppets were manipulated so that their actions followed the chanting.

Major Plays of Chikamatsu (1961) contains translations of his important domestic pieces and of his outstanding historical play *Kokusen-ya kassen* (*The Battles of Coxinga*, tr. Donald Keene, 1951). The other works mentioned have important introductory material. [CJD]

'Chin P'ing Mei'. An anonymous Chinese novel of the late 16th century. It takes an episode from the 'Shui-hu chuan', the seduction of Golden Lotus by Hsi-men Ch'ing, as its point of departure and then unfolds the lurid career of the concupiscent Hsi-men, and the fate of his wives after his death. The motive power of the society the novel portrays is greed and vanity in their diverse forms, but *Chin P'ing Mei* is no moralizing tract; indeed, its popularity rests chiefly on its eroticism. Although the author was only too anxious to borrow from a multiplicity of literary sources, a good part of the novel at least must have derived from his own experience, for this was the first considerable work of fiction which was anchored to observable, day-to-day, rather than extraordinary, happenings. This involved a continuous rather than episodic plan, and more attention to character and its machinations. Dialogues are exceptionally lengthy. [D E P]

The Golden Lotus, tr. Clement Egerton (1939) (the most complete translation).

P. D. Hanan, in *Asia Major*, Vol. I X, Pt 1, Vol. x, Pt 1 (1962–3).

Chou Shu-jen (pseud. **Lu Hsün**) (1881–1936). Chinese story-writer and essayist. Regarded by many as the most important literary figure of modern China. He was born into a well-to-do family in Shaohsing, Chekiang Province, but his family's fortunes declined during his boyhood. In 1898 he entered a 'modern' type school in Nanking and in 1902 he went to Japan to study medicine. While there he became convinced that China's soul was even more in need of a cure than her body and he embarked upon a literary career as a means to this end. His early writings include articles for Chinese student journals in Japan on scientific and literary topics, and some translations of Russian and other East European short stories, which made no impact at the time. The 1911 Revolution found him teaching in his native Shaohsing, but its failure to improve the lot of the Chinese people disillusioned him, and he took a post in Peking, where he kept out of contemporary literary activity until the New Culture Movement was under way in 1918. Then the movement for a vernacular literature initiated by Hu Shih, Ch'en Tu-hsiu and others induced him to write his first story, 'Diary of a Madman', which was published in the magazine *New Youth*. This was the first work of fiction of the new movement. Later stories were collected into the anthologies *Battle Cries* (1923) and *Hesitation* (1926).

Chou Shu-jen's long story 'Ah Q cheng-chuan' (tr. Yang, 'The True Story of Ah Q', in *Selected Works of Lu Hsün*, Vol. 1, Peking, 1956) was written in 1921. Ah Q is a village odd-job man who personifies the 'diseases of the spirit' from which, according to the author's diagnosis, China was suffering. Sustained by a feeling of 'spiritual superiority', he stumbles from one misadventure to another to his tragicomic end at the hands of the executioner.

Chou Shu-jen published one other collection, *Old Tales Retold*, consisting of traditional stories with a modern twist, a number of translations including Gogol's *Dead Souls* and essays on a wide range of subjects, usually polemical and concerned with the reform of Chinese society and literature and published in numerous literary journals, some of which he helped to found.

During his last few years spent in Shanghai, he sympathized with the Chinese Communist Party, having given up any hope of saving China by non-revolutionary means, and cooperated with the Communists in a number of literary activities. [J D C]

Huang Sung-k'ang, *Lu Hsün and the New Culture Movement of Modern China* (Amsterdam, 1957).

Chuang Tzu (*c.* 369–286 B.C.). Chinese Taoist philosopher. The authorship of the work bearing his name is not definitely established, but seven chapters seem to be by the hand of one literary genius.

The book of Chuang Tzu is outstanding among early Chinese philosophical works for the wit and imagination of its content, which are matched by the qualities of its style. Unlike other early works it is not concerned with the problems of government so much as the individual human spirit. It contains parables and anecdotes which brilliantly question the validity of conventional morality, inviting the reader to free his mind from the fetters it imposes and to step into the limitless world beyond, harmonizing himself with the Tao, the principle which underlies the universe. In addition to fantasy and allegory, the *Chuang Tzu* contains an abundance of satire in which Confucius and his disciples are lampooned. [J D C]

Tr. Herbert A. Giles (1926).

'Ch'u Elegies'. An anthology of Chinese poetry, collected and edited by Wang I in A.D. 125. The earlier poems date back to the 3rd century B.C., and all originate from the state of Ch'u, which lay on the Yangtze River far to the south of the area which produced most of the songs of the ◊ *Book of Odes*. The poems are grouped under 17 titles and are written in two different styles, one style being originally set to music, while the other was that of the longest poem in the collection, the *Li Sao* or *Encountering Sorrow*. About half the poems are traditionally ascribed to Ch'ü Yüan (313?–290? B.C.), and if he did write at least some of them he is the earliest named Chinese poet.

Ch'ü Yüan was a nobleman of the state of Ch'u who for a few years held high rank at court, but, calumniated by other officials, he was banished to the South, where, traditionally, he drowned himself in the Milo River, a Yangtze tributary. The supposed date of his death is celebrated in China as the Dragon Boat Festival. The *Li Sao* is a lament describing the author's own noble qualities, and his vain search for someone who will appreciate them. It is full of allegory and lavish description and is quite different in spirit from anything in the *Book of Odes*. Apart from the *Li Sao* the *Elegies* also contain the *Nine Songs* (actually numbering 11), which were shamanistic invocations; an enigmatic poem known as the *Heavenly Questions*, which consists of a series of questions on the origin of the universe, the dynasty, etc.; a group of poems called the *Nine Poems*, attributed to Ch'ü Yüan but probably of later origin; another group called the *Nine Arguments*, attributed to Sung Yü, and a number of later poems, some by Wang I himself.

The *Elegies* rival the *Book of Odes* in importance for their influence on later Chinese poetry. The song style, much of which was pentasyllabic, was the precursor of much of T'ang poetry, whilst the Sao style developed into a form of prose-poem known as the *'fu'*. [JDC]

Ch'u Tz'u, The Songs of the South, tr. David Hawkes (1959); *The Nine Songs*, tr. A. Waley (1955).

Ch'ü Yüan. ◊ *Ch'u Elegies*.

'Cilappatikāram'. ◊ Iḷankō.

Confucius (K'ung Ch'iu) (*c.* 551–*c.* 479 B.C.). Chinese philosopher. The historical Confucius must be distinguished from the Confucius of tradition. Modern scholarship has shown that of the many historical sources of information only the *Analects*, a collection of his sayings made fairly soon after his death, gives a reliable account of his philosophy, and that much of that – especially in the last five books – is suspect. It is unlikely that he wrote or edited anything.

Confucius was born in rather humble circumstances in the state of Lu, in east central China, at a time when the Chou dynasty, once a comparatively unified feudal regime, had been broken up by internal wars. Confucius's ambition was to restore the supposedly peaceful conditions of earlier centuries, and his plan for achieving this was to introduce men of wisdom and virtue into government service, where they would guide the hereditary rulers along the right paths. He believed that a virtuous government produced a virtuous people. It was as a teacher that he was most successful. He wished to influence affairs of state directly, and with that end in view spent a decade or so travelling through China, but it is fairly certain that though he tried hard he never obtained any influential post. His pupils, however, did. He taught them 'the Way' (*tao*), the course to be followed by men of virtue and integrity, who would be unconcerned with material reward and loyal to their rulers yet fearlessly critical of them. He seems to have taught by debate and by appeals to reason rather than to authority, and there was little book-learning. He taught them *li* (etiquette, ceremonial), which was an integral part of court procedure and which he seems to have valued for its own sake as a sort of emotional restraint. Musical training was considered important. Religion and metaphysics played no part in his philosophy. He was revolutionary in his respect for the common people and in his belief that the state existed for the people, not the people for the state. But he also saw the necessity for strict authority and discipline, in the state as in the family, and this aspect of his philosophy was later abused by totalitarian governments. He accepted pupils from every class, if necessary without payment, the only qualifications being enthusiasm and intelligence.

At the end of his life Confucius believed that he had failed. But in fact, through his disciples, Confucianism spread, and in the 2nd century B.C. it became the official state doctrine. By then however the facts of his life and teachings had become distorted out of recognition. Elements of supernaturalism, even of magic, were introduced. Works were attributed to him which he could not possibly have written. Bad governments manipulated his ideas to support their evil ends. It was only in the 17th century that a slow start was made to reinstate his original doctrines, a process which has continued, with considerable controversy, to the present day. (⇨ *Book of Odes*.) [D L D]

Analects, tr. Arthur Waley (1938, last reprinted 1964).
H. G. Creel, *Confucius: The Man and the Myth* (1951).

D

Daṇḍin (fl. 7th cent.) A classical Indian author and master of Sanskrit prose. His work, the *Daśakumāracarita* or 'History of the Ten Princes', is marked by narrative terseness and characteristic (but not overwhelming) use of long compound words in description. The milieu of Daṇḍin's stories is that of the urban and sophisticated India of Gupta and pre-Hun times – classical India *par excellence*. With wit and a superb taste for the bizarre and the dramatic, Daṇḍin conducts his heroes through a breathtaking sequence of adventures where the characters are not only kings and princesses, but the *demi-monde* of courtesans, gamblers, ascetics *cum* pimps and thieves.

Another work, the *Avantisundarīkathā*, has been attributed to Daṇḍin, and there is no reason to doubt the traditional identification of Daṇḍin the 'novelist' with Daṇḍin the author of the *Kāvyādarśa*, the most brilliant early work of poetics. [E G]

Dasha-kumara-charita or the Ten Princes, tr. Arthur Ryder (Chicago, 1927); *Kāvyādarśa*, German tr. O. Böhtlingk (Leipzig, 1890).

Dazai Osamu (1909–48). Japanese novelist. He was the sixth son of a rich family of landowners in northern Japan. Even before entering University he started literary production, and the suicide of ⇨ Akutagawa Ryūnosuke is said to have made a considerable impression on him. He became a student of French literature at Tokyo University, but spent all his time on such extra-curricular activities as left-wing politics, and did not graduate. His life until 1938 is marked on the one hand by considerable dissipation and instability, with three attempts at suicide, and on the other by the development of his literary ability under the guidance of several novelists, of whom the most distinguished was ⇨ Ibuse Masuji. Conflict between his left-wing opinions and his membership of a rich family engendered in him sentiments of guilt and indebtedness to society. He was also unlucky in his love affairs. These influences shaped his works of this period, which are numerous. The two that established his reputation as a brilliant writer of despairing novels were *Gyakkō* ('Retrogression') and *Dōke no hana* ('A Clown's Flowers'), both written in 1935. In 1937 appeared *Ningen shikkaku* (*No Longer Human*, tr. D. Keene, 1958).

His second period, until the end of the war, was one of comparative contentment. In 1939 he married and for a time he was free from anxiety about love affairs. It was a time of governmental restriction on artistic activity, and he was one of those who tried to resist by continuing to produce novels of merit not connected with the war effort.

After the war, he became something of a hero, symbolizing the return to a cultural existence that many Japanese were yearning for. The relaxation of wartime restrictions and his new popularity were to prove his undoing. His suicidal tendencies returned and in 1948 his fourth attempt at self-destruction was successful.

In the previous year had appeared his masterpiece *Shayō* (*The Setting Sun*, tr. D. Keene, 1950), the study of an aristocratic family forced at the end of the war to cope with a new situation in which money and prestige were no longer theirs. The delicate yet penetrating characterization, the atmospheric descriptions of the post-war scene, and the reflections of their own straits that its readers saw in this novel ensured its success. So representative were its characters that the new poor were known as *shayō-zoku* (*Setting Sun* people). It is one of the greatest Japanese post-war novels. [C J D]

A Visitor, tr. I. Morris, in Morris, *M J S*; *Villon's Wife*, tr. D. Keene, in Keene, *M J L*.

'Dhammapada'. A collection of 423 aphorisms which, in Pali verse form, are revered by southern Buddhists as illustrative of the Buddhist *dhamma* or moral system. Similar collections occur in other languages of Buddhism. This book was incorporated before the beginning of the Christian era into the fifth section (*nikāya*) of the Pali *sutta-piṭaka*, or collection of sermons, and has exercised a remarkable influence on the thoughts of faithful Buddhists, which its purely literary merits can perhaps hardly account for (tr. Babbett, 1936).

Later, each aphorism had attached to it a story supposedly illustrative of the sentiment expressed; the collection of these stories, called *Dhammapadaṭṭhakathā* or Dhammapada commentary, was made about the 5th century A.D. (tr. E. W. Burlingame, *Buddhist Legends* 3 vols., Cambridge, Mass., 1921). [C H B R]

'Dharmaśāstra'. ⇨ *Manu.*

Doan Thi Diem (1705–46). ⇨ Vietnamese poetess. Doan Thi Diem wrote poetry in both Chinese and Nom (i.e. Vietnamese) characters, but is better known for the latter. Her finest work, *Chinh-phu-ngam* ('Lament of a Soldier's Wife') (Saigon, 1950; Fr. tr. Bui Van Lang, Hanoi, 1943), is a translation into Nom characters from a Chinese-style poem by another Vietnamese poet, Dang Tran Con, and is immeasurably superior to the original. It is considered the perfect poem of its type in Nom characters. [P J H]

Dọk Mai Sot (1906–63). Thai novelist. Pseudonym of Mọm Luang Bubpa Sukich Nimmanheminda. She wrote her first novel in 1929. In the following two decades, she established a commanding position among the women writers who played an important part in the development of the novel and the short story. Her characters are drawn from the Thai official classes. One important theme in her work is the defence of ideal Thai virtues against cruder social influences deriving from contact with the West. Despite a certain melodramatic quality in her earlier work she expounds her socio-moral lessons, through the interplay of character and incident, with maturity and quiet humour. Of her 10 novels, *Ni lae Lok* ('Thus the World Is'), 1935, and *Phu Di* ('The Noble One'), 1937, exhibit these characteristics at their best. [E H S S]

'The Good Citizen', in *Span*, ed. Lionel Wigmore (1959) (short story).

Dun Karm. ⇨ Psaila.

E

Edogawa Rampo (1894–). Japanese short-story writer. He was born in Mie prefecture but spent most of his childhood in Nagoya. A student of economics at Waseda University in Tokyo, he won a precarious livelihood from various trades in the six years following graduation. In 1923, he started writing mystery and thriller stories, the first modern Japanese writer to do so, although there were, and are, many translations from western writers of the genre. Since then he has concentrated, quite successfully, on this output. His name is a pseudonym, echoing the Japanese pronunciation of Edgar Allan Poe, upon whom he has modelled his plots and style, though usually with an authentic Japanese background and the brutally realistic description typical of much modern Japanese writing. [C J D]

Japanese Tales of Mystery and Imagination, tr. James B. Harris (Tokyo, 1957).

'E-Gyin'. A type of ⇨ Burmese poem in the 'classical' quadri-syllabic line, in the form of an address to a child of the royal family, recounting the noble deeds of the child's ancestors and glorifying the reigning king. The most famous *e-gyin* is the *Paleik-sa* (A.D. 1774), by U Hpyaw. [J W A O]

Ethiopic Literature. Apart from a number of inscriptions, some perhaps dating back to the 5th century B.C., there is no record of a literature proper in Ethiopia till after the introduction of Christianity to the Court at Aksum in the 4th century A.D. Shortly after, the Old and New Testaments and a number of other Christian works, notably the Physiologus, were translated from Greek or Syriac into the official language of the Court, Geʿez. With the decline of Aksum there followed several centuries of political obscurity from which no literary works are extant, though they may have existed. The 'restoration' of the Solomonic dynasty in 1270 ushered in a new era of literary activity in Geʿez, by now no longer the language of the people. Since then there has been a continuous production of works, with periods of high attainment in the reigns of the emperors Amda Sion (1314–44) and Zar'a Yaʿqob (1434–68).

Ethiopic writing is almost entirely Christian in character and purpose. It includes numerous hagiographical, didactic and apocalyptic works and there is a large body of literature connected with the Virgin Mary. Some works of more general interest exist, such as the *Kebra Nagast,* a collection of traditions relating to the Queen of Sheba and the early history of the country. Though they can often be traced back to Coptic-Arabic originals, such works are none the less interesting for that since, even translated, they tended to be moulded to the spirit and character of Ethiopian Christianity. Original composition is primarily represented by the royal chronicles (14th century onwards). Some works, not extant in other languages, have been preserved solely through the medium of Geʿez, notably the *Book of Enoch* (tr. R. H. Charles, 2nd edn, 1912). Translations of Ethiopic works of all types were published by the late Sir E. A. Wallis Budge. [A K I]

E. Ullendorff, *The Ethiopians* (1960).

Evliyâ Chelebi (1614–after 1683). Ottoman traveller. He was born in Istanbul, the son of the Palace goldsmith. His skill as a Koran-reciter having brought him to the notice of Murâd IV (1623–40), he completed his education in the Palace School, passing out as a cadet in the cavalry. He felt a continued urge to travel. A dream prompted him to compose (1640) a detailed description of Istanbul (only in parts original); thereafter, thanks to his mother's connexions and probably his own charm, he attached himself to the suites of successive dignitaries, to spend the rest of his life on military campaigns and civil errands which took him throughout the Ottoman Empire – then at its greatest extent – and beyond. He left a 10-volume *Seyâhat-nâme* ('Book of Travels'), never finally revised, which describes minutely the monuments of the towns he visited, the customs, dress and language of the inhabitants, and the scenery and crops of each district, giving a unique picture of everyday life. A taste for tales of wonder and a tendency to exaggerate caused his work to be undervalued, but it was finally printed, in a poor (and in part censored) edition between 1896 and 1938. The first two volumes (Istanbul, Anatolia) were translated into English by J. von Hammer, the first to appreciate the value of the work (*Narrative of Travels . . . ,* London, 1834, 1850), and the material of the first is attractively digested in A. Pallis's *In the Days of the Janissaries* (1951). No full translation has been made in English or any other language, though numerous monographs and articles deal with Evliyâ's descriptions of different areas; the most substantial is R. Kreutel's *Im Reiche des goldenes Apfels* (description of Vienna, etc.; Graz, 1957). [V L M]

F. Babinger, *Die Geschichtsschreiber der Osmanen und ihre Werke* (Leipzig, 1927); A. Bombaci, *Storia della letteratura turca* (Milan, 1956); *E of I.*

Ezuttacchan. ⇨ Tuñcatt' Ezuttacchan.

F

Firdawsî, Mansûr(?) Abu'l-Qâsim (*c.* 935–*c.* 1020). The great epic poet of Persia. He was born of a family of land-owners near Tûs, where his tomb is now a national shrine. Almost every 'fact' reported about his life is contested, so that very little is known for certain. His fame rests upon his *Shâh-nâma* ('Book of the Kings'), of over 50,000 couplets, which relates in 50 chapters the traditional history of the Iranian kings from the legendary Kayûmard to the fall of the Sassanian dynasty in A.D. 641. It is mainly based on a 10th-century prose compilation, the versification of which had been begun by a certain Daqîqî (d. *c.* 980), whose verses Firdawsî incorporated into his own poem. The *Shâh-nâma,* finally completed in 1010 (whether there were earlier recensions and, if so, when and for whom they were composed are questions still unresolved), was presented to Sultan Mahmûd of Ghazna (997–1030); legend recounts that Firdawsî, dissatisfied with his reward, betook himself to Herât and thence to Mâzandarân, where he wrote a savage satire on Mahmûd. Firdawsî's masterpiece was the model and inspiration for most later Muslim epic poetry (English tr. A. G. and E. Warner, 9 vols., 1905–25; J. Atkinson's abridged tr. of 1832 inspired Matthew Arnold's *Sohrab and Rustum*).

The attribution to Firdawsî of a romantic epic *Yûsuf and Zulaykhã* (based on the Biblical story of Joseph and Potiphar's wife as it is recounted in the Koran) is now contested (German tr. O. Schlechta-Wssehrd, Vienna, 1889). [V L M]

Browne, *LHP*, i, ii; Arberry, *CPL*; Rypka, *IL*; *E of I*.

Futabatei Shimei (1864–1909). Japanese novelist. He was born in Tokyo, the son of an ex-*samurai* government official, and lived in various parts of Japan in his boyhood. After an unsuccessful attempt to enter the army, he started to study Russian in the Foreign Languages School in Tokyo. He was soon publishing translations of Russian authors, and these were followed by original novels. For a period he was an official translator, and for three years (1899–1902) he was professor of Russian at his old school. A further period of literary production followed an unsuccessful attempt to get to Russia in 1902. In 1908 he went to St Petersburg, Berlin and London; but his health failed and he died on the way home. His 3 original novels are *Ukigumo* (*The Drifting Cloud,* tr. D. Keene, in Keene, *MJL*) (1887), *Sono Omokage* (*An Adopted Husband,* tr. Buhachiro Mitsui and G. M. Sinclair, 1920) (1906) and *Heibon* (*Mediocrity,* tr. Glenn Shaw, Tokyo, 1927) (1907). All, and in particular the last, may be seen as partly autobiographical. They catch the indecision and lack of direction of Futabatei and many of his contemporaries with great skill and careful observation. His hero is the prototype of so many unsatisfactory characters who were to appear in later Japanese novels. His diffidence may be contrasted with the energy of ⇨ Mori Ōgai or ⇨ Tsubouchi Shōyō, with whom, at the same time, he forms an innovating group, each with a different foreign affiliation. As a novelist he was the most talented of them. He was outstanding for his clear vision and honest observation. His realism is enhanced by lifelike conversations, for which he used a language far nearer real speech than that of the dignified Mori or Tsubouchi. [C J D]

G

Gamsakhurdia, Konstantine (1891–). Leading contemporary novelist and man of letters of Soviet Georgia. He was educated at the Kutaisi Gymnasium (West Georgia). Prior to the Russian Revolution of 1917, he continued his University studies in Western Europe. In 1915, while living in Munich, he started work on his poetic novel *Dionisos ghimili* ('The Smile of Dionysus', 1925). Between 1916 and 1919, he travelled about Western Europe, visiting Berlin, Geneva and Paris, his experiences there being subsequently mirrored in his novels and essays.

After the occupation of independent Georgia by the Red Army in 1921, Gamsakhurdia was viewed with suspicion by the Communist regime, as a 'decadent' and a potential ideological adversary. His novel *Mtvaris motatseba* ('The Rape of the Moon', 1935–6) gives a symbolic picture of the collapse of the old order of Georgian society under the impact of Russian Communism. During the Stalin-Beria purges, Gamsakhurdia turned to the more favoured genre of historical and patriotic fiction, embarking on a great trilogy on the life of the Georgian King, David the Builder (1089–1125). Artistically among the most successful of Gamsakhurdia's novels is *Didostatis Konstantines marjvena* ('The Right Hand of Grand Master Constantine', 1939; English tr. V. Eristavi, *The Hand of a Great Master,* Moscow, 1959), set in the medieval Georgian kingdom in the 11th century. The book centres round the building of the Cathedral of the Wonder-working Pillar at Mtskheta, and the tragic love of the architect Konstantine Arsakidze for the captive princess Shorena, which leads to his mutilation and death at the hand of the jealous King Giorgi. Distinguished in parts by brutal realism, in others by tender poetic vision, the novel contains character portrayals of great psychological insight.

Since Stalin's death, Gamsakhurdia has been restored to his rightful place in Georgian literary life, though his shattered health prevents him from active participation in public affairs. His 70th birthday was celebrated in 1961 on a national scale. In 1963, he began to publish his revealing autobiography in the Tbilisi literary journal *Mnatobi* ('The Beacon'), but publication was suspended after the first two instalments, which deal with his early life and experiences up to 1914. [D M L]

Gandhi, Mohandas Karamchand (1869–1948). He is too well known for his life to need detailed mention here. It is not always appreciated though that nearly all his published works were first written in his mother tongue, Gujarati. His style is very simple, appropriately for one whose main purpose was social propaganda, and a work such as his autobiography, *Satyanā prayogo* (1927–9; tr. Mahadev Desai, *An Autobiography or the Story of My Experiments with Truth,* 1949), has become a model for a pure Gujarati prose style.

Apart from this his main works in Gujarati are the *History of Satygraha in South Africa* (Ahmedabad, 1924–5; tr. V. G. Desai, Madras, 1928), the countless articles written for the periodical *Navajivan* which he edited until 1932, as well as later articles and pamphlets, and his Letters, still not all published in Gujarati. There have been many selections in English from all these minor writings and the Government of India are now engaged in publishing his complete works, in Hindi and in English. The first 12 volumes (New Delhi, 1958–64) have reached December 1914. [I M P R]

H. A. Jack, ed., *The Gandhi Reader* (1958) (good bibliography).

'Geser Khan'. Of the many heroic epics of the Mongols (◊ Mongolian Literature), the best known, through the medium of I. J. Schmidt's German translation (Berlin, 1925), is that of *Geser Khan.* Geser Khan is born with the divine mission of pacifying and ruling the world. As a child he is persecuted by his uncle Chotong, but subsequently fulfils his various missions, subduing hostile kings and giants, restoring order to the kingdom of China, rescuing his mother from the underworld and so on. Versions of the Geser epic are to be found not only in several Mongolian dialects, Khalkha, Buriat, Monguor in Kansu province and Kalmuck, but also in Tibetan and other central Asian languages. Hence, efforts to interpret the epic as a national monument of the Mongols, similar to the *Secret History*, and depicting popular opposition to the oppressive regime of princes and lamas, must be disregarded. The version translated by Schmidt was printed from wooden blocks in Peking in 1716. The Chinese bookseller's reference-title *San Kuo-chih* (*Romance of the Three Kingdoms*) which appears on this print is evidence of the early identification by Mongols and Chinese of Geser Khan with the hero Kuan-yü of the Chinese romance, canonized as the Chinese god of war. Until recent years temples of Geser Khan in his quality of god of war among the Mongols were to be found attached to many lamaseries, and in at least one of these the printed version of the epic was being used as a liturgy as late as 1943. Geser Khan also figures as one of several divine patrons of fortune-telling among the Mongols. [C B]

N. Poppe, *Mongolische Volksdichtung* (Wiesbaden, 1955); R. Stein, *Recherches sur l'épopée et le barde au Tibet* (Paris, 1959); A. David-Neel, *The Superhuman Life of Gesar of Ling* (1959).

Ghālib, Asadullah Khān (1797–1869). Urdu and Persian poet and wit. He was born in an aristocratic family in Agra, India, and spent his childhood there. Married at the early age of 13, he soon after moved to Delhi, then the centre of a remarkable intellectual renaissance. He became deeply attached to it, and except for a period (1827–9) in Calcutta, remained there. He had begun writing Urdu and Persian verse in his childhood. Up to 1857 most of his work was in Persian, and he always declared his Urdu verse to be beneath all comparison with his Persian. Yet it is his Urdu verse that has always been the basis of his poetic fame. It is written in the strict classical forms, yet bears his individual stamp. His verse is the first in classical Urdu poetry with an unmistakably modern ring. He himself foresaw that it might not be fully appreciated until after his death. He is now the one poet of Urdu whose popularity rivals that of ◊ Iqbāl. An unyielding adherence to his own values, a humorous distrust of dogmas, and an ability to look at himself through others' eyes were expressed in his verse as in his life. The well-known anecdotes of him recorded by his younger friend Hālī in his (Urdu) *Memoir of Ghālib*, illuminate these qualities, and his cheerfully avowed laxity in religious matters. Though he reverenced God and His prophet, he never fulfilled the more irksome requirements of Islam.

Ghālib was in Delhi throughout the revolt of 1857 and suffered deeply. Many of his friends, both British and Indian, lost their lives. To alleviate his loneliness he began corresponding with his friends outside Delhi, and these frank, self-revelatory letters were later published, the first volume appearing just before his death. They are unique in Urdu literature, and would themselves have assured his fame. [R R]

J. L. Kaul, *Interpretations of Ghālib* (Delhi, 1957); P. L. Lakhanpal, *Ghālib, the Man and His Verse* (Delhi, 1960).

Ghazal. A short lyric poem on themes of earthly or mystic love, or both. Though these themes predominate, many others do occur. The ghazal form originated in Arabic literature. It occupied a less prominent place there than in the literatures to which the spread of Islam brought the Arabic literary forms. First in Persian, later in Turkish, and later still in Urdu, it came to assume a pre-eminent position among the classical forms. Its greatest exponent is considered to be the 14th-century Persian poet ◊ Hâfiz. All subsequent ghazal-writers owe much to him. The unity of the ghazal is one not of content but of form. Every couplet is an independent entity, and very often there is not even unity of mood between the couplets which compose the poem. But they are bound together by a strict rhyme-scheme – AA, BA, CA, DA etc. – and by the use of a single, strictly defined metre throughout the poem, though any one of a very wide range of such metres may be selected for any particular ghazal. The last couplet must introduce the *nom de plume* of the poet. [R R]

al-Ghazālī, Muhammad ibn Muhammad (1059–1111). Arab mystical philosopher. Born in Tūs in Persia. He was for a while in the entourage of ◊ Nizām al-Mulk, who presumably gave him his post as a teacher of theology at the Nizāmiyya College in Baghdād. While there he suffered a severe mental crisis which resulted in the breakdown of his health and the loss of his faith in Orthodox Islam. He resigned in 1095, and for the next 10 years led a wandering life, visiting Mecca, Alexandria, Jerusalem (which he left shortly before its capture by the Crusaders) and Damascus. During these years he decided that Sufism (Islamic mysticism) was the only tenable creed; he recovered his health and taught for a short time in Nīshāpūr in Persia.

Al-Ghazālī records his spiritual pilgrimage in a short work, *The Deliverer from Error*. In this he describes his examination of Kalām (orthodox Muslim scholasticism), Falsafa (metaphysics based on those of the Greeks) and T'lîm (the doctrine of those who accept, without criticism, the teaching of an infallible Imām) before deciding for Sufism. His great work is *The Revivification of the Religious Sciences* (Book 20 tr. L. Zolondek, Leiden, 1963), in which he examines theology and ethics from a moderate Sufi standpoint. He also wrote *The Incoherence of the Philosophers* (tr. Sabih Ahmad Kamali, 1958: Pakistan Philos. Congress Pub. No. 3) in which he attacked all philosophical systems, from those of Plato and Aristotle to those of his own day. This work was answered by Ibn Rushd (Averroes) in *The Incoherence of the Incoherence* (tr. S. van der Bergh, 2 vols., 1954). [A S T]

Book of Fear and Hope, tr. W. McKane (Leiden, 1962); *Confessions of Al Ghazzali*, tr. C. Field (Wisdom of the East Series, 1909); *The Niche for Lights*, tr. W. T. H. Gairdner (1924); *Worship in Islam*, tr. and comm. E. E. Calverley (2nd edn, 1957); *O Youth*, tr. G. H. Scherer (Beirut, 1933).

Nicholson, *L H A*; Margaret Smith, *Al-Ghazali the Mystic* (1944); W. Montgomery Watt, *The Faith and Practice of al-Ghazâlî* (1953), *Muslim Intellectual: A Study of Al-Ghazali* (1963).

'Gilgamesh, Epic of'. An important poetic cycle of ancient Sumeria, later expanded in the Akkadian language of Babylonia. The hero, a half-historical, half-legendary demigod, is identified with the Gilgamesh who ruled at Uruk (Warka) in Babylonia about 2700 B.C. The name Gilgamesh in Sumerian signifies 'father, hero' or 'the old one, the hero'. In the stories, he has a boon companion, Enkidu, a wild man tamed by a courtesan. Among their adventures together is a journey to subdue the dread Huwawa, guardian of the cedar forest. Ishtar, goddess of love, proposes marriage to Gilgamesh, who spurns her advances. When the two friends destroy the divine bull which Ishtar sends to punish them, the gods avenge themselves by killing Enkidu. Afterwards Gilgamesh travels to the Babylonian 'Noah' Utnapishtim, survivor of the Great Flood, to learn the secret of immortality. Utnapishtim shows Gilgamesh a magic plant which renews youth, but this is stolen by a serpent as Gilgamesh washes at a well. Finally Enkidu's shade returns to tell Gilgamesh the secrets of the gloomy world of the departed. Elements from these stories have been detected in the *Odyssey*, the *Aeneid* and other epics and sagas of the Classical and also of the medieval world.

Apart from its Sumerian prototype, the work is preserved in Akkadian in 12 tablets from the library of King Ashurbanipal of Assyria (669–630 B.C.), and also fragments in Hittite and Hurrian. A fragment dating from about 1400 B.C. has been found at Megiddo in Palestine, so it is not surprising to find resemblances between the eleventh tablet of Gilgamesh, which describes the Flood and the Ark, and the Hebrew narrative in Genesis.

Timeless and philosophically profound, the epic of Gilgamesh is impregnated with deep pessimism. The adventures of Gilgamesh and Enkidu transcend the confines of time and space, for they revolve about elemental forces and about human problems common to mankind throughout the ages. Dignified and enigmatic, and yet wonderfully warm and immediate in their appeal, these stories are essential to the understanding of civilized man at an early, critical stage of world history. [D M L]

Ed. and tr. R. Campbell Thompson (2 vols., 1928, 1930); tr. Samuel Noah Kramer and E. A. Speiser, in James B. Pritchard, *Ancient Near Eastern Texts Relating to the Old Testament* (2nd edn, Princeton, 1955); tr. N. K. Sandars (Penguin Classics, 1960).
Alex. Heidel, *The Gilgamesh Epic and Old Testament Parallels* (Chicago, 1946); S. N. Kramer, *History Begins at Sumer* (2nd edn, 1962); S. N. Kramer, *Sumerian Mythology* (New York, 1961).

Greenberg, Uri Zevi (1891–). Hebrew writer. Born in Galicia and spending his youth among the poorest and most oppressed Jews of Eastern Europe, he became embittered by the fate of his people and settled in Palestine in 1923. He borrows the style of the ancient Hebrew prophets and exhorts his people by pouring invective upon them for having brought the spirit of slavery to the land of redemption. His attacks upon the great powers who he thinks have betrayed the Jewish people are of equal fierceness but lack the mature technique of his contemporaries. [E E]

Eima pedolah ve-yareach (Tel Aviv, 1925); *Rechovot ha-nahar* (Jerusalem/Tel Aviv, 1951).
Waxman, *H J L.*

Güntekin, Reshad Nuri (1892–1956). Turkish novelist, journalist and playwright. Educated at a French school at Izmir (Smyrna) and at Istanbul University, he became a teacher and a school inspector. A very prolific writer, he began his literary career after the First World War as a playwright; his first novel, *Çalıkuşu* ('The Wren', 1922; tr. Sir Wyndham Deedes, *Autobiography of a Turkish Girl*, 1949), won him fame and immense popularity. His novels and short stories owe their success to a clear style, a fecund gift of narration pointed by realistic detail, and a sympathetic, rather sentimental, exploration of character. *Akşam Güneşi* (1926) is also accessible in English (tr. Sir W. Deedes, *Afternoon Sun*, 1951). [V L M]

O. Spies, *Die türkische Prosaliteratur der Gegenwart* (Leipzig, 1943); *Enc. Brit.* (1961); *Philologiae Turcicae Fundamenta*, ii (Wiesbaden, 1964).

H

Hâfiz, Shams al-Dîn Muhammad (?1326–1390). The greatest lyric poet of Persia. He was born in poverty in Shîrâz, where he spent nearly all his life. He seems to have made a living as a teacher and perhaps also as a professional copyist of manuscripts, until his poems won him fame and the patronage of the local Muzaffarid rulers. His works consist almost entirely of about 500 short lyrics (◊ ghazals) on the conventional themes of love and wine, and using – though not to excess – the conventional figures of paronomasia, metonymy, etc. They have traditionally been interpreted as mystical allegories, to such an extent that his poems, like Virgil's in Europe, were opened at random in search of a guide to conduct; but Western scholarship now inclines to take them literally, i.e. the 'Beloved' of the love-poems stands not for God but for a human beauty or a princely patron, and the bacchanalian tone of others merely reflects a carefree and optimistic outlook on a turbulent world.

From the 17th century onwards European scholars and poets have attempted translations of Hâfiz's lyrics, into Latin, French, English, German (Goethe), and even Greek (for the history of these studies, with quotations, see Arberry, *CPL*). The whole of his *Dîvân* ('Collected Works') was translated into German prose by J. von Hammer-Purgstall (Tübingen, 1812–13), into German verse by V. von Rosenzweig (Vienna, 1858–64), and into French verse by A. Guy (Paris, 1927); the English prose translation by H. W. Clarke (Calcutta, 1891) is 'curious rather than reliable' (Arberry). The most successful renderings into English verse are those of Gertrude Bell (*Poems from the Divan of Hafiz,* 1897, 1928) and those in A. J. Arberry's anthologies (*Fifty Poems,* 1947 and 1953, and *Immortal Rose,* 1948). [V L M]

Browne, *L H P*, iii; Rypka, *I L*; *E of I*.

Hâjji Khalfa, by-name of **Mustafâ ibn 'Abdullâh,** also known as **Kâtib Chelebi** (1609–57). Ottoman polymath and encyclopedist. The son of a soldier (perhaps a renegade), he was apprenticed to one of the government accounts departments and accompanied the army on various Eastern campaigns. In about 1635 legacies enabled him to devote most of his time to study, and the rest of his short life was spent in Istanbul composing works on nearly every branch of learning. His monumental bibliography of Moslem literature, in Arabic (ed. with Latin tr. G. Flügel, *Lexicon bibliographicum . . .,* 7 vols., Leipzig, 1835–58), is still an indispensable work of reference. He wrote a Universal History in Arabic from the Creation to his own day, a more detailed chronicle of the years 1591–1655 in Turkish, and a history of Ottoman naval campaigns (partial tr. J. Mitchell, *The History of the Maritime Wars of the Turks,* 1831).

Hâjji Khalfa was one of the first Ottoman scholars to be eager to learn the sciences of infidel Europe: helped by a renegade French priest he translated into Turkish a Latin edition of Johann Carion's *Chronicle,* selections from the 1587 reprint of the *Corpus universae historiae praesertim byzantinae,* and the *Atlas minor* of Mercator and Hondius; the last enabled him to embark on a new version of a great geographical work *Jihân-numâ,* 'Cosmorama' – of which he had had to leave the first version unfinished for lack of material on Western Europe. His last work, *Mîzân al-Haqq* (tr. G. L. Lewis, *The Balance of Truth,* 1957), is a collection of eirenic essays seeking to reconcile the contradictions between orthodox dogma and popular practice. [V L M]

F. Babinger, *Die Geschichtsschreiber der Osmanen und ihre Werke* (Leipzig, 1927); A. Adıvar, *La science chez les turcs ottomans* (Paris, 1939); *E of I*.

al-Hamadhānī, Ahmad ibn al-Husain (967–1007). Arab writer. Known as 'Badī' al-Zamān' (Wonder of the Age). He was a native of Hamadhān in Persia, but wrote in Arabic. After a restless youth, he settled at Herāt in Afghanistan under the patronage of Sultan Mahmūd of Ghazna.

Al-Hamadhānī and ◊ al-Harīrī were the great exponents of the literary genre known as the *maqāma* (pl. *maqāmāt,* usually tr. 'Seances' or 'Sessions'). The *maqāma* is a kind of short story, or episode, written in rhymed prose, an old literary device, much used in the Koran, but subsequently rather out of favour. Al-Hamadhānī's *Maqāmāt* (tr. W. J. Prendergast, 1915) represent the adventures of an unscrupulous vagabond, Abu'l-Fath of Alexandria; the narrator continually meets him in unexpected situations, and finds him earning his living by imposing on good nature and gullibility. These stories act as a frame for the author's virtuosity in word manipulation, his use of elaborate figures of speech and his placing of an apposite quotation or allusion.

These *Maqāmāt,* not perhaps easy for us to appreciate, constitute the only prose fiction in classical Arabic literature, apart from popular romances such as the ◊ *Arabian Nights* and the *Romances of the Banī Hilāl,* and philosophical parables such as those written by ◊ Avicenna and Ibn Tufail's *Hayy ibn Yaqdhān* ('Alive Son of Awake'). The *Maqāmāt* resemble the 'picaresque' novel, for example the *Satyricon* of Petronius, but they are shorter self-contained units, and depend, as has been said, largely upon the author's skill with language. ◊ Al-Harīrī is generally considered in the East to be al-Hamadhānī's superior as a writer of Maqāmāt. [A S T]

Nicholson, *L H A*; *E of I.*

Hamdullâh Mustawfî (?1281–1350). Persian geographer and historian. He came of a family of Arab origin, long settled at Qazwîn, which had produced a succession of high-ranking civil servants, he himself being promoted a Superintendent of Finances (*mustawfî*) by the vizier and historian ◊ Rashîd al-Dîn in about 1311. His three great works, all of the first importance, are (1) *Ta'rîkh-i Guzîda* ('The Select History'), a universal history, very simply written, from the Creation to the year 1329 (abridged tr. E. G. Browne and R. A. Nicholson, 1913); (2) *Zafar-nâma* ('The Book of Victory'), a heroic poem of 75,000 couplets, intended as a continuation of the *Shâh-nâma* of ◊ Firdawsî, which relates the history of the Muslim world down to the year of its completion, 1335; and (3) *Nuzhat al-Qulûb* ('The Delight of Hearts'), a geographical and cosmographical treatise completed in 1340 (tr., geographical section, G. Le Strange, 1919, zoological section, J. Stephenson, 1928). [V L M]

Browne, *L H P*, iii; Arberry, *C P L*; C. A. Storey, *Persian Literature: A Bio-Bibliographical Survey*, i (1927–); *E of I.*

Hameiri, Avigdor, pseud. of **Emil Feuerstein** (1886–). Hebrew poet. He was raised in a traditional Jewish atmosphere in Hungary, where he was born, but was deeply influenced by the Hungarian poet Ady. In 1910 he founded the short-lived Hebrew periodical *Hayehudi.* He translated many Hungarian poets into Hebrew, among them *Tragedy of Man* by Madach, which has become compulsory reading in Israeli schools. During the First World War he served in the Austro-Hungarian Army and fell prisoner of the Russians. His war-time novel *Hashigaon Hagadol* left a deep impression on modern Hebrew writers. After the war, he settled in Palestine and, upon the establishment of the State of Israel, became first editor of the Israeli equivalent of Hansard. [E E]

Belivnat has'appi-t (Jerusalem, 1962) (poems); *Hamaschiach halevan* (Tel Aviv, 1948) (novel); *Hamsked haran* (Tel Aviv, 1944) (short stories); *Mivha-t sippurei A. H.* (Tel Aviv, 1954) (short stories).

Waxman, *H J L.*

Hamzah Fansuri (or **Hamzah of Barus;** fl. *c.*1550–1600). Malay Sufi poet and writer. He was probably born at Ayuthaya in Thailand, but his family evidently came from Barus in North Sumatra, where he himself subsequently settled. In his travels he visited Arabia, Iraq, the Malay peninsula and Java. He was initiated in Baghdad into the *Qādiriyyah* religious order. He adhered to the so-called *Wujūdiyyah* school of Sufis, who affirm the doctrine of Oneness of Being.

Hamzah Fansuri wrote in Malay, but knew Arabic and Persian well; he was much influenced by ◊ Ibn al-ʿArabī, Jīlī as well as other classical Sufi writers and poets, among whom are ◊ al-Ghazālī, ◊ ◊ ʿAttâr, ◊ Jalâl al-Dîn Rûmî, ◊ Saʿdî and ◊ Jâmî. So far as is known, he was the first to write a systematic and definitive account of the Sufi doctrines in the Malay tongue. He thus introduced Muslim philosophical and mystical terminology into the Malay language. He is also to be credited with introducing the poetic verse genre of the *rubāʿī* (quatrain), which in Malay literature became popularly known as the *shaʿir.* His ideas have always been very much misunderstood and misrepresented, even up to the present day. One of his most assiduous and potent accusers was ◊ Nuruddin Ar-Raniri, who wrote several polemical treatises charging Hamzah Fansuri with heresy. In 1637, his works were ceremonially burnt by order of the Sultan of Acheh. In the passionate intensity of his verse, and his intellectual and imaginative approach to his religion, Hamzah Fansuri is sometimes reminiscent of John Donne. [S M N A]

S. M. N. al-Attas, *The Mysticism of Hamzah Fansuri* (1967).

Han Yü (768–824). Chinese essayist. Born in present-day Honan Province in North China, he was orphaned at 3 and brought up by a cousin, Han Hui, whose literary views were to influence him strongly, but who died when Han Yü was still young. Fired with ambition, he made many attempts to gain, by examination or patronage, official appointment in the capital, Ch'ang-an. These having failed, he sought employment in various parts of the Empire. In 802 he returned to Ch'ang-an, where, apart from a period of exile in the South, he served in various official capacities until his death.

Han Yü's passion for government service exemplified the Confucian ideals for which he fought throughout his life. He believed it to be his mission to restore Confucian orthodoxy and to destroy what he regarded as the baleful influences of Buddhism and Taoism. He expressed these views forthrightly in such essays as *Yüan-tao* ('On the True Way). In harmony with this aim was his antagonism to the florid style of parallel prose which was fashionable in his time, and which contrasted with the plain style of the early Confucian philosophers. His own prose is based on classical style, but also borrows from the vernacular of his day. Thus his works are no mere imitations of the old writers, but possess a clarity and simplicity for which he is regarded as one of the great masters of Chinese prose. [J D C]

Gems of Chinese Literature, Prose, ed. H. A. Giles (1926).

al-Harīrī, Abu Muhammad al-Qāsim (1054–1122). Arab philologist. A native of Basra in Iraq, where he held a small administrative post. He produced a volume of 50 *maqāmāt*, which, although often longer and more elaborate than those of ♢ al-Hamadhānī, follow almost exactly the same pattern. Their hero is another witty vagabond, Abu Zaid of Sarūj, they are written in rhymed prose, with interpolated passages of verse, and they are designed principally to exhibit the author's skill in the manipulation of the Arabic language, the depth of his erudition in all branches of learning, and his adeptness at refined obscurity of allusion. In all of these al-Harīrī is al-Hamadhānī's superior. Al-Hamadhānī perhaps tells a better story than al-Harīrī, but in this, too, the latter is by no means deficient. Indeed, his *Maqāmāt* could hardly have remained so popular had they not possessed the power of entertaining as well as that of exercising the learned. Chenery (*The Assemblies of al-Harīrī*, tr. Chenery and Steingass, 2 vols., 1869–98) says, 'For more than seven centuries his work has been esteemed as, next to the Koran, the chief treasure of the Arabic tongue.'

The *Maqāmāt* of both al-Harīrī and al-Hamadhānī are particularly interesting to us as representing, no doubt in a somewhat romanticized form, a picture of life in a Muslim community in the 10th–12th centuries A.D. [A S T]

Nicholson, *L H A*; *E of I*.

Harṣa. ♢ Baṇa.

Hayashi Fumiko (1904–51). Japanese novelist. Hers is the literature of the struggling poor. Though her father is said to have been an itinerant pedlar she was educated up to high-school level, but from the age of 18 she had a precarious existence, struggling to live by literary work and by a series of short-lived jobs. Her associates were mainly among the 'proletarian' and other left-wing writers, though she herself was not one of these. Her works include a series of novels entitled *Hōrōki* ('Journal of a Vagabond', 1922–7). This is somewhere between fiction and autobiography, and is in diary form. Her descriptions of the life of the down-trodden have great realism and compassion. Her heroine (like herself) has considerable strength of will and even optimism, and a never-failing attachment to literary pursuits. Her post-war novels, including *Shita-machi* (*Tokyo*, tr. I. Morris, in Keene, *MJL*) (1948) and *Ukigumo* (*Floating Cloud*, tr. Y. Koitabashi, Tokyo, 1957 – not to be confused with the novel with the same title by Futabatei Shimei), contain moving descriptions of the Tokyo of the time. [C J D]

'Heike-monogatari'. Japanese historical romance. It was composed in the first half of the 13th century, but exists in many forms. It tells of the 12th-century conflict between the great families of the Minamoto (Genji) and Taira (Heike). The title is equivalent to 'Tales of the Heike'. It relates how the Heike, at first all-powerful in Japan, were brought low, and it provides a vast illustration of the Buddhist view of the transience of human life and achievement. The work was recited by blind minstrel-priests in the following centuries, and some episodes have become extremely famous. Its influence on later literature has been immense: firstly, its stories have provided material for the *nō* plays and later drama; secondly, its language is an early example of a prose style which developed into that of the normal novel, a combination of Japanese and Chinese elements, in contrast to the fundamentally Japanese language of earlier novels like ◊ Murasaki Shikibu's *Genji-monogatari*. Its style is varied and it employs a large vocabulary enriched with technical military terms and Buddhist phraseology. [C J D]

'Heike Monogatari', tr. A. L. Sadler, *Transactions of the Asiatic Society of Japan*, XLVI, 2 (1918), and XLIX, 1 (1921); Keene, *A J L*; *Tales of the Heike and the Four Square Hut*, tr. A. L. Sadler (Sydney, 1928).

Higuchi Ichiyō (1872–96). Japanese novelist. An outstanding writer in the early days of the modern novel in Japan. Born of warrior stock reduced to shopkeeping in the East End of Tokyo, she was trained, typically, to become a dutiful wife, but her father died when she was 17. She supported the family herself by writing stories, a task which she tackled just as she had her polite female attainments – she went to a teacher of novel-composition. They became lovers but separated some time before she died. She may have owed something to him, but her observation and background were her own. Most of her work dates from the last two or three years of her life: her masterpiece is *Takekurabe* (tr. Edward Seidensticker, in Keene, *MJL*), a study of adolescence in the kind of district she knew well. Her sharpness of vision and the skill with which she recorded that vision account for her great reputation. She was influenced by ◊ Ihara Saikaku.

She wrote for ordinary people, and so stands outside the main stream of the Japanese novel, and apart from the theorists who proliferated in the early days of its development. Her reputation rests partly on what she might have achieved had she lived longer. [C J D]

'Hikayat Hang Tuah'. Anonymous, probably 17th-century, quasi-historical prose work in ◊ Malay, which would today be described as a picaresque novel. It recounts the adventures of the Malay warrior hero Hang Tuah, one of the great figures of the Malay Kingdom of Malacca in the second half of the 15th century, and has thus become a national epic. It is unhistorical, part-legend, part-fantasy, but lively – with a notable tragic element in one of the main episodes. It provides a vivid picture of the material and conceptual background of the Malay world of that time, and of relations between Malacca, South India, Thailand, Java, Sumatra and China.

There are many manuscripts, and several published versions (best: Djakarta, 1956). There is a German translation (H. Overbeck, *Die Geschichte von Hang Tuah*, 2 vols., Munich, 1922) but no English, though M. C. ff. Sheppard, *The Adventures of Hang Tuah* (Kuala Lumpur, 1957), provides a simplified abridgement and a fair flavour of the original. [J C B]

Hikmet, Nazim (1902–63). Turkish radical poet and dramatist. Born in Salonika of a family of Ottoman officials, he became a cadet in the Turkish navy and began to write poems, the first being published when he was 15. In 1921 he went to Moscow, remaining in the Soviet Union until 1928. He adopted Marxist ideas and became greatly influenced by the futurist poetry of Vladimir Mayakovsky. In 1928 he returned to Turkey, having joined the Turkish Communist Party in 1924. He published books of verse, seeking to free Turkish poetry from the hitherto dominant stylized classical metres. With lively eloquence, vigour and vivid, satiric humour, Hikmet tackled many social problems of the Kemalist Turkey of his day, though he also wrote love and nature poems. Among his early books of verse are *835 Satır* ('835 Lines', 1929), *1+1=1* (1930), *Gece Gelen Telgraf* ('Night Wire', 1932), *Benerci kendini nicin öldürdü?* ('Why did Benerci Kill Himself?', 1932) and *The Lay of Simavneli Kadıoğlu Bedrettin* (1936).

In 1938 Hikmet was arrested on charges of sedition and sentenced to 28 years' imprisonment. He was released in 1950 as a result of an international campaign of protest against this treatment. He soon escaped to the Soviet Union, where many of his poems and plays have been published in Russian and Azerbaijan Turki translation. Some of his verse has also been translated into Greek and French. His last important work was a powerful semi-autobiographical novel, first published in Russian at Moscow in 1962, and then in a French version, by Munevver Andaç, under the title *Les romantiques* (Paris, 1964). Hikmet's writings were formerly banned in his native Turkey. [D M L]

E. Saussey, *Prosateurs turcs contemporains* (Paris, 1935); *The Times*, 7 June 1963 (obituary notice); *Great Soviet Encyclopaedia*, 2nd edn, vol. 46 (in Russian; with portrait and extensive bibliography); O. Spies, in *Handbuch der Orientalistik*, V, i.

Hino Ashihei (1907–61). Japanese novelist. He was born at Wakamatsu in Kyūshū, and studied English at Waseda University in Tokyo. As a student he contributed short stories to a student magazine. In 1937 his novel *Funnyō-tan* ('Sanitary Tales'), a humorous account of local government affairs in his native Kyūshū, earned him an Akutagawa Prize and he became famous overnight. He was now serving with the Japanese army in China, and was appointed war correspondent of a prominent monthly magazine. Then appeared a series of works with the fighting in China as a background – *Mugi to Heitai* (*Barley and Soldiers*, tr. K. and L. W. Bush, Tokyo, 1939) and *Tsuchi to Heitai* (*Earth and Soldiers*, part tr. S. Ishimoto, in Keene, *MJL*) in 1938, and *Hana to Heitai* ('Flowers and Soldiers') in 1939. Although these can easily be dismissed as mere reporting, they show an ability to write about real people and an appreciation of the individual soldier's point of view that make them sympathetic reading. Their popularity was increased by the absence of any other worthwhile fiction at a time when government control over the arts was very strict.

After the war he was for a while 'purged' – forbidden to take part in public life. After he was freed from restriction, he resumed literary activities. He wrote stories about his home province, and in particular a long novel *Hana to Ryū* ('Flower and Dragon', 1952), which tells the story of his parents' life. This is considered his best work. [C J D]

Hitomaro. ⇨ Kakinomoto Hitomaro.

Ho Xuan Huong (fl. end of 18th cent.). ⇨ Vietnamese poetess. She composed poetry in Nom (i.e. non-Chinese) characters. In the simplicity of its language, the perfection of its rhythms, and its portrayal of the life of ordinary Vietnamese people, her work is unmatched. She has frequently been criticized on account of the erotic, even obscene, nature of some of her poems, but her position among the greatest of the Vietnamese poets is unchallenged. [P J H]

Ho Xuan Huong, Nha Tho Cach Mang ('Ho Xuan Huong: A Revolutionary Poet'), ed. Hoa Bang (Saigon, 1950).

Hsi-K'ang (223–63). Chinese scholar, poet, musician and painter. He lived at the time of political and philosophical disarray after the end of the Han dynasty. He married a member of the Wei Imperial family, but was not active in their contest for actual power with the military strongmen of the Ssu-ma clan, preferring self-cultivation after the Taoist model. He refused office from Generalissimo Ssu-ma, and when later he involved himself in a morality case by testifying for a friend he was executed. According to legend he calmly played a rare tune on his beloved lute before going to his death.

Hsi-k'ang was famous as the leader, with Juan Chi, of the 'Seven Sages of the Bamboo Grove', a group that used to seek periodic seclusion to pursue the more ethereal pleasures. In his political essays he derided Confucian state practice from a Taoist standpoint. His most famous essay is 'On the Lute' (tr. R. van Gulik, Tokyo, 1941), whose notes could carry him into communion with the Tao. In poetry his strength was in the 4-word line, which he helped to establish. His style is characteristically 'aloof' and 'unsullied'. [D E P]

Hsü Chih-mo (1896–1931). Chinese poet. He was born in Chekiang province, went to Peking University, and set off in 1916 on extensive travels abroad. He first went to the U.S.A., where he studied banking and politics, and then crossed to England, where he was taught by Laski. His friendship with H. G. Wells encouraged him to turn to literature, which he pursued at Cambridge, a place he celebrated in prose and verse. He returned to China in 1924, taught English Literature at Peking, won fame as the editor of the literary supplement of the newspaper *Chʿen Pao* in the next year, and interpreted for Tagore on his Chinese tour. His *Poems of Chih-mo* was published in 1925. Hsü was later on one of the mainstays of the Crescent Moon Society, which generally speaking upheld the values of the cultivated bourgeoisie. He died in an aeroplane crash.

Hsü was extravagant in his personal life – he called himself 'a wild horse without a halter' – and extravagant too in his poetry, assaulting the peaks of emotion, often vicarious emotion. His idol was Keats, though many strains of European Romanticism were present in his work. He does manage to transfer his own love of beauty to his poems. In technique, he went further than anyone else in using English metres, and was a fecund experimenter in verse forms. He also contributed to the new literature through his translations. [D E P]

Kai-yu Hsu, *Twentieth Century Chinese Poetry* (1965) (selection).
Cyril Birch, 'English and Chinese Metres in Hsu Chih-mo', *Asia Major* VIII, 2 (1961).

Hsüeh-chʿin. ⇨ Tsʿao Chan.

'Hua-Pen'. The form that the vernacular short story took in China. The term means 'story book', but has been translated as 'prompt book', on the ground that the texts were originally the written versions of the professional storytellers' recitations. By the time of the Ming dynasty (1368–1644), however, the form – which originated in Sung (960–1279) – was established as a pastime of the literati.

Of the formal characteristics of the *hua-pen*, some of the most notable are: the author calling himself 'storyteller' and assuming audience reaction; illustrative verses interspersed in the prose narrative; the customary inclusion of a prologue (either a poem or an anecdote); and the use of the speech of the streets. Themes are drawn frequently from classical and Buddhist literature, but also from contemporary urban (and often low) life.

The earliest existing collections of *hua-pen* date from the 16th century; individually some may go back to Sung times. The best-known collections are those of Feng Meng-lung (1574–1646) (selection tr. Cyril Birch, *Stories from a Ming Collection*, 1958). For some other accurate translations, see *The Courtesan's Jewel Box* (Peking, 1957). [D E P]

John L. Bishop, *The Colloquial Short Story in China* (Harvard, 1956).

Hung Sheng (1646–1704). Chinese poet and dramatist. He came from a well-known family which had moved to Peking from the provinces. His wife, a granddaughter of a former Grand Secretary, was an accomplished musician who accompanied Hung Sheng as he sang. Hung Sheng became a student of the Imperial Academy and some of the most prominent men of letters of his day were his friends. He achieved fame when an early version of *The Palace of Eternal Youth* (tr. Yang, Peking, 1955) was first performed in *c.* 1684. The play remained popular until 1689, when a performance at a time of Imperial Mourning drew it to the attention of the censors. The Emperor ordered playwright, actors and audience to be punished and Hung Sheng was expelled from the Imperial Academy. He returned to his native province, ending his days in poverty. In 1704 he fell overboard while drunk on a pleasure trip and was drowned.

The Palace of Eternal Youth, one of China's best lyric dramas, treats a theme which had been used many times by poets and dramatists – the love of the Lady Yang and Ming Huang, Emperor of the Tang Dynasty. At its tragic climax the Emperor is forced by his soldiers to make the Lady Yang commit suicide when a rebellion causes them to flee the capital. Hung Sheng rejected the traditional interpretation of this episode, which put responsibility for the rebellion on the shoulders of Lady Yang. Instead he wrote a poignant love-story which has remained popular in China for three centuries. He wrote a number of other plays, mainly on historical themes, but none reached the same high standard. [J D C]

Hung Shen, 'The Palace of Eternal Youth and its Author', *Chinese Literature*, 1954, 4.

I

Ibn al-ʿArabī, Muhammad ibn ʿAlī, called **Muhyi al-Din** (1165–1240). Arab mystical writer. He was born at Murcia in Spain.

He spent his youth in Seville, and then travelled extensively in the East, finally settling in Damascus, where he died.

Ibn al-ʿArabī composed 2 great mystical treatises, *Meccan Revelations* and *Fusūs al-Hikam* (tr. as 'Wisdom of the Prophets', Khan Sahib Khaja Khan, Madras, 1929). He is, however, best known for his mystical odes (tr. R. A. Nicholson, 1911). In these odes Ibn al-ʿArabī, like all Sufis, expresses his longing for Union with God in terms of passionate human love; many critics, indeed, have been uncertain whether his poetry is in fact religious or erotic, a difficulty also encountered in the poetry of ◊ Hâfiz. The philosophy of Ibn al-ʿArabī's poetry appears to combine, as does that of most Sufi poets, elements of Muslim Orthodoxy, Manichaeanism, Gnosticism, neo-Platonism and Christianity. Later Sufi poets, particularly Persians, can scarcely be called Muslims at all; their beliefs appear to coalesce into an indefinite pantheism.

Ibn al-ʿArabī is said also to have made the Muwashshah a respectable literary form. This is a type of poem, apparently native to Moorish Spain, which ends with a couplet in the colloquial language, and sometimes even in Spanish. It was long despised by Arab literary circles, but after Ibn al-ʿArabī had established it, many of the finest love poems in Arabic literature were written in this form. [A S T]

A. E. Affifi, *The Mystical Philosophy of Muhyiddin Ibnul ʿArabi* (1939); M. Asín Palacios, *Islam and the Divine Comedy* (1926); Rom Landau, *The Philosophy of Ibn ʿArabî* (1959); R. A. Nicholson, *Studies in Islamic Mysticism* (1921); A. R. Nykl, *Hispano-Arabic Poetry* (Baltimore, 1946).

Ibn Baṭṭūṭa (Baṭūṭah), Muhammad ibn ʿAbdullāh (1304–*c.* 1377). Arab voyager and geographer. He was actually a Berber from Morocco, and belonged to a family of lawyers. At the age of 21 he went on the pilgrimage to Mecca to fulfil his religious obligation and to add to his qualifications as a lawyer by consulting the scholars he met. While at Mecca he was seized by a desire for further travel, and for the next 25 years he wandered from Constantinople to China, and from the Crimea to the Maldive Islands. He served as a judge in India, and was sent on a mission to China. He served again as a judge, for 18 months, in the Maldive Islands, where he objected to the women's scanty dress, which did not conform to Muslim standards. He was interested in everything he saw, but seems to have been remarkably casual in practical matters – in one place he married a wife who gave him a daughter, but soon set off again and severed all connexion with them.

Ibn Baṭṭūṭa retired to Fez in 1354 to put together the narrative of his travels. His contemporaries regarded him as a romancer, but his reports, where they can be checked, are accurate. He dictated the outlines of his story to a pupil, who put it into literary shape. After his first great journey, he visited Spain, and afterwards travelled south to the African kingdom of Mali. At this professedly Muslim court he saw the king present a delegation of visiting cannibals with an attractive young girl, who was promptly cut up and publicly eaten by the guests. He is said to have died in Morocco in 1377 (or 1369, according to other authorities). [A S T]

Rehla of Ibn Battûta (Travels in India, Maldive Islands and Ceylon), tr. Mahdi Husain, (Gaekwad's Oriental Series, No. 122, Baroda, 1953); *Travels in Asia and Africa*, tr. and selected by H. A. R. Gibb (1929); *Travels*, tr. H. A. R. Gibb (Hakluyt Society ed., 4 vols., Vol. i 1958, Vol. ii 1962).

W. Boulting, *Four Pilgrims* (1920); H. F. Janssens, *Ibn Batouta, 'Le Voyageur de l'Islam'* (Brussels, 1948); *E of I.*

Ibn Ezra, Abraham Ben Meir (1093–1167). Hebrew poet and scholar. Born in Toledo, he lived mainly in Spain until about 1140, from when he travelled extensively in North Africa, England, France, Italy and possibly Palestine. It is from the period of his travels that nearly all his writings date. There were said to be 108 books of these, covering such diverse subjects as Biblical exegesis, Hebrew grammar, philosophy, astrology and secular and religious poetry. His fame rests on his Bible commentaries, representing the Spanish school of exegesis at its best. They are based on linguistic and factual examinations of the text, with sometimes a hint of criticism foreshadowing the more modern approach. Although critically acute and often scintillating and witty, Ibn Ezra here employed a style which is scarcely lucid and frequently mystical. He is supposed to have written commentaries on all the books of the Hebrew Bible, but not all have survived.

The range of Ibn Ezra's poetry includes penitential poems (some are to be found in the liturgy), love poems, wine ditties and even a long poem on the game of chess, giving all its intricate rules. The *Divan* is his well-known collection of poems, riddles and epigrams, edited notably by D. Kahana (*Kovets chokhmath ha-Rava*, Warsaw, 1922). In these poems he shows his mastery of the Hebrew language, which is also exhibited by his acrostic-style poems in peculiar shapes. His biting sense of humour finds expression in some satiric poems, and he also wrote semi-poetic treatises in rhymed prose, of which the best is the letter of *Chay ben Mekits*, a treatise of philosophical theology. [R F H]

The Commentary . . . on Isaiah, ed. and tr. M. Friedländer (1872–7); *The Beginning of Wisdom. An Astrological Treatise . . .*, ed. and tr. R. Levy and F. Cantera (Baltimore, 1939).

Waxman, *H J L*, i.

Ibn Hazm, 'Ali ibn Ahmad (994–1064). Arab writer. Grandson of a Spanish convert to Islam. He was chief minister at Cordoba, but was forced to withdraw from public life by the odium that his bitter attacks on his theological opponents aroused.

Ibn Hazm was perhaps the greatest figure in 11th-century Hispano-Arab prose literature. He began as a poet, but he is now best known for his book on chivalrous love, *Tauq al-Hamāma* (*The Ring of the Dove*, tr. A. J. Arberry, 1953; German tr. M. Weisweiler, 42 edns; also tr. into French, Spanish and Russian), a vivid picture of life in Muslim Spain, describing some of the more intimate experiences of Ibn Hazm himself.

Ibn Hazm belonged to the Zāhirī school of Islam. This was a strict sect, which interpreted the Koran literally, and which recognized no precedent except that based either on the Koran or on the well-attested customs of the Prophet. He did, however, write an important book on comparative religion, *The Book of Religious and Philosophical Sects*, where he examines and refutes the claims made by the various non-Muslim faiths – he deals at length with inconsistencies in the Old and New Testaments. He attacked many of the most revered authorities of Islam, and his books were once publicly burned in Seville. He himself commemorated this event in an epigram. [A S T]

M. Asín Palacios, *Abenházam de Córdoba* (5 vols., Madrid, 1927–32); I. Friedlaender, *The Heterodoxies of the Shiites according to Ibn Hazm* (New Haven, 1909); Nicholson, *L H A*; *E of I.*

Ibn Khaldūn, 'Abd al-Raḥmān ibn Muḥammad (1332–1406). Arab philosopher and historian. He came of an aristocratic family long resident in Muslim Spain. He himself was born in Tunis, had a good education, and held various official posts in North Africa and in Spain, where he had gone in 1362. The Sultan of Granada sent him as an ambassador to Pedro the Cruel of Castile in 1364. He was later disgraced and imprisoned, then retired to Egypt, where he became chief judge. He was sent on an embassy to Tamerlane, described in his autobiography. He died in Cairo.

Ibn Khaldūn's principal work was *The Book of Examples*, a general history of the Muslims, especially the North African dynasties. His real fame rests on its Introduction, which forms the first systematic treatise on the philosophy of history (*The Muqaddimah*: *An Introduction to History*, tr. F. Rosenthal, 3 vols., 1958). Ibn Khaldūn sees man as a social animal, conditioned by his surroundings and the climate he lives in. Man starts as a nomad, of pure and simple manners, loyal to his tribe, and eventually settles down to an urbanized, sedentary life. This is both an advance and a regression, for although the arts and sciences can flourish only in urban communities, the townsman loses the virtues of the nomad, and his tribal spirit turns into national patriotism. Nations become corrupted by luxury, and are eventually swept away by a ruder, more vigorous people. As more and more men are contained within city walls, its ruler has to devote more and more attention to keeping the peace and maintaining justice; as his realm grows greater, it needs more and more the unifying force of religion. Events in North African history gave Ibn Khaldūn the theory that a dynasty normally lasts four generations. He concludes his Introduction with an account of the various Muslim systems of government, and a short survey of the arts and sciences, of education, magic and literature, which constitutes a summary of the extent of knowledge at that period. [A S T]

An Arab Philosophy of History: Selections from the Prolegomena, tr. C. Issawi (W E S, 1950).

M. A. Enan, *Ibn Khaldun: His Life and Work* (Lahore, 1941); W. J. Fischel, *Ibn Khaldun and Tamerlane: Their Historic Meeting in Damascus* (Berkeley, Cal., 1952); Muhsin Mahdi, *Ibn Khaldun's Philosophy of History* (1957).

Ibn Khallikān, Aḥmad ibn Muḥammad (1211–82). Arab biographer. In their studies of the Prophet, Muslims attached great importance to the men who reported, directly or indirectly, his words and acts, and they collected biographical information concerning them. In the same way, historians would later include information concerning the notable men of Islam in their chronicles, adding the obituaries of those who had died in a certain year as an appendix to the annals of that year. Often, too, such information would be made into a separate biographical dictionary. Such dictionaries were arranged on various principles; some dealt exclusively with poets, some with lawyers, some with grammarians, some with scholars; others would include all those who died in a particular century, or all those connected with particular cities.

Ibn Khallikān occupies the leading place in this literary genre. He was born at Arbela, studied there and at Aleppo, then went to Egypt, where he became a deputy judge and professor. In 1261 he was made chief judge at Damascus, but was dismissed after 10 years, and returned to his professorship in Egypt. He was reappointed to Damascus in 1278, but was again dismissed shortly before his death.

Ibn Khallikān began his great work in 1256 and finished it in 1274 (*Ibn Khallikān's Biographical Dictionary*, tr. Baron MacGuckin de Slane, 4 vols., Paris, 1842–71). It is more comprehensive than any other Arab biographical dictionary, for it includes entries relating to rulers, soldiers, scholars, judges, statesmen and poets, arranged in alphabetical order. It is written in simple but elegant language, and is enriched by many pleasing anecdotes of Muslim life. [A S T]

E. V. Lucas, *A Boswell of Baghdad* (1917); *E of I*.

Ibn Sīnā. ⇨ Avicenna.

Ibuse Masuji (1898–). Japanese novelist. He was born in Hiroshima prefecture and went to Tokyo for courses in French literature and in art. He did not complete his studies, but became a professional writer. Between 1923 and 1940 he wrote many novels. They were of two sorts: novels describing the contemporary scene, full of humour, not to say whimsy, but at the same time compassionate; and historical novels, particularly of the period just before the Meiji Restoration.

He served with the army in south-east Asia, but was writing again as soon as the war was over. He still writes novels of both kinds. Two in particular are well regarded in Japan: *Honjitsu Kyūshin* (1949; tr. E. Seidensticker, *No Consultation Today*, in *Japan Quarterly* (Tokyo), VIII, i, 1961), which cleverly portrays a whole town by the accounts it gives of the patients treated by a police-doctor, and *Yōhai Taishō* (1950; tr. J. Bester, in *Japan Quarterly* (Tokyo), I, i, 1954, *A Far-Worshipping Commander*), the story of an ex-officer who believes that the war is still on. The background of his work is realistic, but his human beings tend to be treated symbolically or even fantastically, tending some critics to call him a poet at heart. In this he stands apart from most of his contemporaries, for whom thorough-going realism is essential. [C J D]

The Charcoal Bus, tr. I. Morris, in Morris, *M J S*.

Ihara Saikaku (1642–93). Japanese novelist. He was one of the three great writers of the end of the 17th century (the others being ⇨ Bashō and ⇨ Chikamatsu Monzaemon). Little is known of his life. He was born in Osaka, probably of merchant stock, and until he was 40 his literary production was confined to poetry. He showed great facility in 17-syllable poems and chain poems, but his poetic reputation rests more upon the originality of his style and the speed of composition (his record was 23,500 verses in 24 hours) than on literary merit. In 1682 he started writing the prose fiction for which he is justly famous. This can be divided into 3 broad periods: 1682–6, the erotic period; 1685–9, miscellaneous works; 1688–93, tales of merchants. The first of his erotic novels was *Kōshoku Ichidai Otoko* (1682; tr. K. Hamada, *The Life of an Amorous Man*, 1964), the biography, in 54 episodes, of one Yonosuke, who enjoyed the love of women of all kinds, and who, at the end, is sailing off to a land inhabited entirely by women to spend there his declining years. The book has echoes of Murasaki Shikibu's *Tale of Genji* and might almost be taken as its bourgeois counterpart. Saikaku's next important work, *Kōshoku Gonin Onna* (1686; tr. Theodore de Bary, *Five Women Who Loved Love*, 1956), has 5 stories of respectable girls who fall victim to love, the stories being based on actual events. The same year saw *Kōshoku Ichidai Onna* (*Life of an Amorous Woman*, tr. I. Morris, 1963), in which the main character appears at the beginning as an old woman in Buddhist retirement; she gives to some young men the account of her many erotic adventures, either as a prostitute or without pay, her decline from her position high in the courtesan hierarchy to that of a mere street-walker, her earning a living in the various occupations available to a woman making her own way. The miscellaneous works include collections of stories from various parts of Japan, stories of vendettas and loyalties among warriors, and a collection of tales of male homosexual love. The third period is represented by 2 collections of tales, *Nippon Eitai-gura* ('The Eternal Storehouse of Japan', 1688) and *Seken Mune-san-yō* ('Mental Arithmetic to Get You Through the World', 1692). The first consists of 30 lively stories describing methods of making money by industry or imagination. The second has stories telling how hard-pressed merchants plot to circumvent the bill-collectors at the end of the year. Saikaku died shortly after the publication of the last work.

The characteristic feature of Saikaku's writing is the liveliness of his prose; he made it a supple instrument, full of vigour and overtones of meaning. We can see the influence of his training in 17-syllable poems, in which the same qualities are found. Even his works which have a unified theme, like *The Life of an Amorous Man*, are anecdotal. The stories in the collections have little in common except their background.

Of the available translations, Morris's selection contains a majority of the chapters of the *Amorous Woman*, and 3 of the 5 who loved love, as well as 8 of the merchant stories. Its translations and explanatory material are excellent, as are those of Sargent, whose work includes the whole of *Nippon Eitai-gura*, and de Bary. [C J D]

The Japanese Family Storehouse, tr. G. W. Sargent (1959).
Howard Hibbert, *The Floating World in Japanese Fiction* (1959).

Iḷangō-Aḍigaḷ. ⇨ Iḷankō.

Iḷankō (2nd cent. A.D.?; 5th cent. A.D.?). Author of the Tamil verse romance *Cilappatikāram* (tr. V. R. Ramachandra Dikshitar, Madras, 1939; Alain Daniélou, New York, 1965). This 'Story of the Anklet' is divided into three parts, set in the different capitals of the three great Tamil kingdoms of antiquity. It tells of the life of a merchant, Kōvalan, married to Kaṇṇaki. A rapturous affair with a courtesan, Mātavi, ends with his return to his faithful wife and their journey together to seek a renewal of their fortunes in Maturai, capital of the Pandyas. There an attempt to sell one of Kaṇṇaki's anklets results in Kōvalan's being falsely accused of stealing the queen's anklet, which it resembled, and in his consequent execution on the orders of the king. His widow cursed the city, which was consumed by fire. In telling his story Iḷankō skilfully mixes dramatic and descriptive sections with lyrical songs and occasional passages of rhetorical prose. A sequel to the story is found in *Maṇimēkalai* by ⇨ Cāttaṉār. [R E A]

Imru'u'l-Qais or **Amru'u'l-Qais, ibn Hujr** (d. *c.* 540). Arab poet. He is said to have been a Beduin chief's son, and to have led a wandering (probably criminal) life attempting to recover his patrimony, lost at the dissolution of the confederation which his father headed. The Emperor Justinian summoned him to Constantinople, to employ him in mobilizing the Arabs for war against Persia, but he died at Ankara, on his way back to Arabia. He is said to have been poisoned by the Emperor because of a liaison with a Byzantine princess.

Imru'u'l-Qais is regarded as the greatest of the poets of the Jāhiliyya (Ignorance), as the Muslims call the pre-Islamic period. He is credited with a large body of poetry, among which is his celebrated *Muʿallaqa*. This is a *qasīda* (ode), and forms part of the collection of 7 odes (actually 10, as different odes are included in different texts) known as the *Muʿallaqāt*. The significance of this name, literally 'suspended', is unknown.

In any one poem a pre-Islamic poet has one basic object; it may be to praise himself, to praise his tribe or his patron, to beg for a reward, to taunt his enemies, or something else of this sort. Before doing so, however, he will give a lengthy description of the desert, a journey, his camel or his horse, and of other places, objects and situations familiar to his audience which will awaken response in them. Since his aim is to describe in new ways objects and situations similar to those described by his contemporaries, it is very difficult to translate the pre-Islamic poems satisfactorily.

The poetry of this period was later considered by the Arabs to be the only suitable model for their own. Poets would learn by heart an enormous amount of it, and would produce something almost indistinguishable from it. Poems of this sort continued to be composed long after the appearance of the 'Modern' school, in spite of the criticism and ridicule of the 'Moderns' and their partisans. Books like the *Kitāb al-Aghānī* ('Book of Songs'; ⇨ Abu'l-Faraj al-Isfahānī) must have served as valuable reference works for would-be poets of the period. [A S T]

The Poem of Amriolkais, tr. Sir William Jones (repr. Shaftesbury, 1930); C. J. Lyall, *Translations of Ancient Arabian Poetry* (1885, repr. 1930); *The Seven Golden Odes of Pagan Arabia*, tr. Lady Anne Blunt and W. S. Blunt (1930); *The Seven Odes*, ed. and tr. A. J. Arberry (1957).

'Inao'. The author of the complete version of this Thai poem, intended for theatrical presentation, is reputed to have been King Rama II (1809–24). The story derives from the Javanese ⇨ *Panji* cycle of tales and deals with the picaresque adventures of the hero Inao. It probably arrived in Thailand through the Malay states and two versions, long and short, are traditionally ascribed to the daughters of King Boromakot (1733–59). [E H S S]

Indonesian Literature. This entry deals only with literature in the modernized form of Malay now called the 'Indonesian language'. Literature in other languages of the Republic of Indonesia will be found under the names of those languages, e.g. Balinese, Javanese. (⇨ Malay.)

The foundations of the Indonesian language and its literature were laid at the end of the 19th and the beginning of the 20th century when the Christian Missions and the Government of Netherlands India opened Malay schools not only in Malay-speaking territories but also in areas with no written language of their own. The use of written Malay in these schools and their adoption of romanized script necessitated some Europeanization of the traditional language.

Further modification gradually took place after 1908 when the Government founded a publishing bureau, later called the *Balai Pustaka*. It first published local folk tales and legends in Malay; continued with translations of literary works from European languages and monthly cultural journals; and, when modern-minded men of letters wished to write original works in Malay, did much to encourage them. In 1922 the *Balai Pustaka* published the first modern novel in Malay – *Sitti Nurbaya* by Marah Rusli, a member of the Minangkabau community of West Sumatra, which took the lead in the development of the Malay language and its literature. In the same year another Minangkabau, Muhammad ⇨ Yamin, published the first collection of modern poems to appear in Malay. From then until 1933 ⇨ Roestam Effendi, Sanusi ⇨ Pané and more especially Sutan ⇨ Takdir Alisjahbana were the principal shapers of the language and its literature.

In 1928 Malay, in the stage of development it had then reached, was adopted as the future national language and renamed 'Indonesian' by a congress of young nationalists from all parts of Netherlands India. It continued, however, to be called 'Malay' by most of the world until Indonesian independence was acknowledged after the Second World War. In 1933 Alisjahbana and Armijn ⇨ Pané with the assistance of the outstanding poet, ⇨ Amir Hamzah, founded a cultural journal called *Pudiangga Baru* ('The New Man of Letters'). This was the focus of Indonesian literature until the Japanese invasion, and, with the *Balai Pustaka*, it was largely instrumental in giving the Indonesian nationalists a language sufficiently developed for what was to come – its sudden adoption in place of Dutch for all governmental purposes, and the flowering of the literature of the *Angkatan Empatpuluh Lima* ('Generation of 1945'). The difference between the *Pudjangga Baru* generation and that of 1945 was the difference between hope and careful approach on the one hand and, on the other, the impetuosity that goes with a feeling of sudden national awakening. The *Angkatan Empatpuluh Lima* produced many writers, ⇨ Chairil Anwar and Pramoedya Ananta ⇨ Toer deserving special mention. The output of poetry and of short stories in Indonesian continues to be considerable. [E C G B]

Indonesian Writing in Translation, ed. John M. Echols (Ithaca, N.Y., 1956).

A. Teeuw, *Pokok dan Tokoh dalam Kesusasteraan Indonesia Baru* (Djakarta, 1955).

Iqbāl, Sir Muhammad (1873–1938). Urdu and Persian poet and thinker. He was born in Sialkot, now in West Pakistan, where he was educated in English, Arabic and Persian. In 1895 he left for Lahore, where he was in 1899 appointed to a lectureship in philosophy. He went abroad in 1905, and studied philosophy at Cambridge, and at Heidelberg and Munich, where he was awarded a doctorate for his thesis, *The Development of Metaphysics in Persia* (published 1908). In the same period he qualified in law, and in 1908 returned to India.

From his childhood he had written poetry with facility. His earliest verse shows many influences – of classical Persian and Urdu, of the English romantics, and of contemporary Muslim Indian thought – of the Aligarh movement, with its emphasis on the need to embrace the learning and the values of the West, of that movement's more socially conservative critics, of the Muslim revivalism common to both trends, and of Indian nationalism, with its stress on harmony between the different Indian communities. Criticism of modern Western civilization becomes more pronounced from the time of his visit to England. About 1910 he resigned his lectureship because he did not feel free to speak his mind in government service. Though he took no part in political activities he was deeply affected by the rising feeling against the West amongst Indian Muslims, and by the consequent growth of Pan-Islamic feeling culminating in the Khilafat movement of the early 1920s. The influence of socialist ideas also becomes discernible. His first Urdu collection, *The Call of the Road*, was published at this stage (1924). Despite these feelings he had in 1922 accepted a knighthood.

His positive theories are elaborated more fully in long poems in Persian. All represent a revived and revitalized Islam as the hope of the world. The first of these works, *The Secrets of the Self*, appeared in 1915 (tr. R. A. Nicholson, 1920). In it Iqbāl attacked Islam's long tradition of contemplative passivity and other-worldliness, declaring that man's destiny is to be God's vicegerent on earth, and that so far from seeking the annihilation of the self, this requires man to develop all the potentialities of the self and to struggle to change the world. In 1917 came *The Mysteries of Selflessness* (tr. A. J. Arberry, 1953), which seeks to show how man's individual role harmonizes with his social role in a dynamic society. Two volumes of shorter poems 'poetically, the best of his work in Persian' (Kiernan) developed these and other themes; these were *The Message of the East* in 1923 (tr. of the first part, *The Tulip of Sinai*, by A. J. Arberry, 1947) and *Psalms of the East* in 1927. Iqbal asserts that a true interpretation of Islam compels the conclusions he sets forth; but this imposes the task of 'the reconstruction of religious thought in Islam', and a series of 6 lectures in English, delivered in 1928, were revised and published under this title in 1934. The last of his major Persian works, *The Pilgrimage of Eternity* (tr. Shaikh Mahmud Ahmad, Lahore, 1961), was published in 1932. It tells of the poet's journey through the universe with the great Persian poet ⇨ Jalâl al-Dîn as his guide.

Within India most people's acquaintance with Persian was too slight for them to read these works, and they continued to look to his Urdu for their inspiration. A second (probably his best) Urdu collection, *Gabriel's Wing*, appeared in 1935. *The Rod of Moses* followed in 1936, and *The Gift of Hejaz*, containing both Urdu and Persian poems, appeared posthumously in 1938, the year of his death.

From 1930 onwards his political writings foreshadow many of the ideas which were subsequently to find expression in the formation of Pakistan. His appeal has been enormous, and has given rise to a voluminous literature, mostly in Urdu. Pakistanis (especially West Pakistanis) claim him with justification as their national poet, but his popularity has always extended far beyond their ranks. His verse is occasionally turgid and bombastic, but at its best it is strikingly powerful, and though his message is expressed in Islamic terms, not only Muslims but Indian nationalists, socialists, and communists have acknowledged his inspiration. [R R]

Poems from Iqbal, tr. V. G. Kiernan (Bombay, 1947; revised edn, London, 1955); *Complaint and Answer*, tr. Altaf Husain (Lahore, 1943).

Iqbal Singh, *The Ardent Pilgrim* (1951); S. A. Vahid, *Iqbal: His Art and Thought* (1959); Annemarie Schimmel, *Gabriel's Wing*, a study on the religious ideas of Sir Muhammad Iqbal (Leiden, 1963).

Ishikawa Takuboku (1885–1912). Japanese poet. The son of an impoverished Buddhist priest, he was born in the prefecture of Iwate, in north Japan. At school he composed poetry and submitted work, most often unsuccessfully, to the magazine *Myōjō*, run by Yosano Hirosho. In 1902 he went to Tokyo to study under Yosano, but illness forced him back home. His early, unsuccessful, poems had been *tanka*, a traditional form in 31 syllables, but he now started to write modern free-style verse, and had some published in *Myōjō* – sufficient to form a collection which appeared in 1905. In 1906 he married, and in the ensuing period of privation and illness his sister and father died, his wife bore him two children, one of which died, his mother died, and his wife developed tuberculosis. He himself, after years of unemployment or poorly paid jobs, died of the same disease. Apart from the collection of modern verse, he left two of *tanka*: *Ichiaku no suna* (1910; tr. S. Sakanishi, *A Handful of Sand*, Boston, 1934) and *Kanashiki gangu* (*A Sad Toy*), published posthumously.

His poetry, although often in *tanka* form, is modern in content, having none of the themes long associated with that form. He pours into his verse all his suffering, and often appears in it in his favourite guise, that of a man defiantly facing the whole universe, bound to be defeated in the end but not begging for mercy. He appeals particularly to Western readers for his lyricism, for the direct expression of sincere sentiments. Equally revealing is his *Romaji Diary*, written in 1909 (tr. D. Keene, in Keene, *MJL*). [C J D]

The Poetry of Ishikawa Takuboku, ed. and tr. H. H. Honda (Tokyo, 1959).

J

al-Jāhiz (*c.* 780–869). Arab writer. Al-Jāhiz ('The Goggle-Eyed') was the nickname of 'Amr ibn Bahr of Iraq, the grandson of a Negro slave. He held Muʿtazilite views (the Muʿtazilites were a powerful rationalist sect of the period), but apparently of a remarkably broad and unbigoted nature.

Al-Jāhiz was a theologian – some of his theological treatises survive – but is better known as an exponent of belles-lettres, and was one of the first writers of what came to be known as 'Adab' ('Culture') literature. This genre originated for the purpose of providing handbooks of etiquette and useful information for court secretaries, but it quickly developed, and 'Adab' works became encyclopedias of useful and entertaining knowledge for the educated man.

Arabic literature is very largely compilatory; a great number of books consist almost entirely of quotations from other authors. This reflects, in other fields, the importance attached by Muslims to a reliable authority for any religious tradition. Thus, al-Jāhiz's greatest works, *The Book of Eloquence and Exposition* and *The Book of Animals*, are large compilations containing a quantity of more or less related information concerning, in the first case, the Arabic language, in the second, animals. Information of scientific value is interspersed with anecdotes, scraps of verse and frequent scarcely relevant digressions. The object of these works seems to be as much to entertain as to instruct, but they did provide a mass of information otherwise difficult to find, since manuscripts of certain works might not be readily available, and there was, in any case, no way of referring to a page when the pagination of no two manuscripts corresponded.

Al-Jāhiz's books, like those of so many Arab authors, seem to us to be formless. Little importance seems to have been attached to form, in a book, or even in a sentence. It is considered only when a work of conscious artistry is being composed, such as the *Maqāmāt* of ◊ al-Hamadhānī or ◊ al-Harīrī. Even then the artistic unit is very small, and the author is concerned only with the arrangement of his words and figures of speech in a sentence, or at most in a paragraph. Digression is always likely; Arab writers seem far more interested in imparting information than in composing an artistic whole.

Al-Jāhiz is often considered one of the most entertaining of Arab authors. Among the many shorter treatises that are attributed to him are *The Book of Misers* (Fr. tr., *Le livre des avares,* C. Pellat, Paris, 1951), *The Merits of the Turks, The Superiority of Speech to Silence* and *The Book of the Crown* (Fr. tr., *Le livre de la couronne,* C. Pellat, Paris, 1954). [A S T]

C. Pellat, *Le milieu basrien et la formation de Ǧāhiz* (Paris, 1953); *E of I.*

Jalâl al-Dîn known as **Rûmî** (i.e. of Rûm, Asia Minor) and **Mawlânâ** ('our Master') (1207–73). The greatest Persian mystic poet, and founder of the Mevlevî Order (the 'Dancing Dervishes'). He was born at Balkh in north Afghanistan. When he was still a child his father left home (perhaps before the threat of the Mongol invasions) and embarked on long wanderings, to settle finally, in about 1228, at Konya (Iconium), the seat of the Seljuq dynasty of Asia Minor. After his father's death in 1230, Jalâl al-Dîn succeeded him as an orthodox professor of theology and a noted public preacher. His initiation into the secrets of the mystic 'way' was begun by an old student of his father, but the great turning-point in his life came in 1244, when he encountered the wandering dervish Shams al-Dîn of Tabrîz – a spiritual director who aroused his passionate devotion and from whom, to the jealousy of his own disciples, he remained inseparable until the dervish's unexplained disappearance in 1247. This devotion released a stream of rapturous lyric poems, many written in the name of the vanished dervish, with whom, as the 'mirror' reflecting the Godhead, Jalâl al-Dîn had come to identify himself; hence the collection of Jalâl al-Dîn's lyrics (*ghazals*) and quatrains (*rubâ'īs*) is known as *Dîvâni-i Shams-i Tabrîz* (selections tr. R. A. Nicholson, 1898, and Sir Colin Garbett, Cape Town, 1956; *The Rubâ'îyât . . .*, tr. A. J. Arberry, 1949). The same passion was lavished in succession on two favoured disciples; the second of them, Husâm al-Dîn, succeeded Jalâl al-Dîn as head of the new Order, which received its systematic organization at the hands of Jalâl al-Dîn's son Sultân Walad. Jalâl al-Dîn was buried beside his father at Konya; his shrine, around which the Mevlevî conventicle grew up, remains even under the secular Turkish republic a revered place of pilgrimage. Jalâl al-Dîn's great work is the *Mathnawî-i Ma'nawî,* in some 27,000 couplets, 'an unsystematized 6-volume exposition in fables, stories and reflections cast in highly poetical language of the basic ideas of mysticism' (Brockelmann), dictated over the years to Husâm al-Dîn (abridged tr. E. H. Whinfield, 1887–98; ed. with tr. and commentary, R. A. Nicholson, 1924–40; A. J. Arberry, *Tales from the Masnavi,* 1961).

One of Jalâl al-Dîn's disciples recorded 71 of his short prose 'meditations' on the mystical life (tr. A. J. Arberry, *The Discourses of Rûmî,* 1961). Seven (early?) sermons and a collection of 147 letters also survive. [V L M]

Browne, *L H P*, ii; F. Hadland Davis, *The Persian Mystics: Jalálu'd-dín Rúmí* (W E S 1907); H. Ritter, 'Maulânâ Ǧalâladdîn Rûmî und sein Kreis', in *Der Islam*, xxvi (1942); R. A. Nicholson, *Rúmí, Poet and Mystic* (1950); Arberry, *C P L*; Rypka, *I L*; *E of I.*

Jâmî, Nûr al-Dîn 'Abd al-Rahmân (1414–92). Persian poet, scholar and mystic. The last great figure of the Golden Age of Persian literature. After studying for a theological career at Samarkand and Herât, he embraced the mystical life, but without lapsing into heterodoxy. Winning the patronage and friendship of Sultan Husayn Bayqara (Timurid ruler of Herât, 1469–1506), who appointed him professor of a college founded expressly for him, and of Husayn's adviser ◊ Nawâ'î, he enjoyed immense fame and authority as an exponent of the mystical 'way', as a teacher and as a prolific writer in verse and prose. His most famous work is the

Haft Awrang ('Seven Thrones'), a set of 7 long poems modelled on the 'Quintet' of ◊ Nizâmî, of which two, love-stories expounding allegorically the mystic's quest for God, have been translated: *Salâmân and Absâl* (Fr. tr. A. Bricteux, Paris, 1911; Eng. tr. Edward Fitzgerald, 1856 etc., new ed. A. J. Arberry, *Fitzgerald's S. and A.*, 1956), and *Yûsuf and Zulaykhâ*, his most celebrated work (Fr. tr. A. Bricteux, Paris, 1927; Eng. tr. R. T. H. Griffith, 1882).

Of his prose works, generally written in a direct and unaffected style, the best known are: *Nafahât al-Uns* ('Breaths of Friendship'), the biographies of some 600 saints (extracts tr. R. A. Nicholson, *Eastern Poetry and Prose*, 1922); *Bahâristân* ('Land of Spring'), a sophisticated imitation of the *Gulistân* of ◊ Sa'dî (Fr. tr. H. Massé, Paris, 1925; Eng. tr. E. Rehatsek, Benares, 1887, and (Book 6) C. E. Wilson, *Persian Wit and Humour*, 1883); and *Lawâ'ih* ('Effulgences'), a treatise on mysticism (ed. and tr. E. H. Whinfield and Muhammad Qazwînî, 1906). [V L M]

Browne, *L H P*, iii; F. Hadland Davis, *The Persian Mystics: Jámí* (W E S, 1908); Arberry, *C P L*; J. Rypka, *I L*; *E of I*.

'Jātaka' ('Birth-story'). A well-known type of moralistic tale, in which the principal character (sometimes human, but frequently an animal) is afterwards identified with the Buddha in a previous incarnation. These were collected together by A.D. 400 at the latest in a volume containing 547 such stories in Pali, which forms part of the canonical corpus of Southern Buddhism; but many of the tales themselves are pre-Buddhistic (i.e. before 500 B.C.). The Pali *jātaka* in its literary form begins with the 'Present Story', recounting an occasion in the Buddha's earthly life which reminded him of a previous existence, followed by the 'Past Story' or *jātaka*-tale proper, and finishing with an identification of the characters in the past story with those of the present story. The narrative is mainly in prose, interspersed with stanzas of ancient verse, to which the prose is considered as an *aṭṭhakathā* or commentary. (Complete Pali collection tr. in 3 vols., ed. Cowell, 1957.)

Other stories outside this collection were also recognized as *jātaka*-stories; some are found in Sanskrit collections, some in the vernacular literature of Buddhist countries. They were extremely popular among Buddhists from the earliest times.

The *jātaka* have had a profound religious and literary influence in Thailand. Complete translations from the Pali exist; nos. 538–47 have been the most popular. The Vessantara Jātaka (No. 547) exists in many versions from the 15th century onwards. Incidents from *jātaka* tales occur in popular preaching texts such as *Phra Malai Thewathera* and have provided an important inspiration for mural and miniature painting. The non-canonical Paṇṇasa Jātaka is the source of the ancient *lakọn chatri* themes (◊ Thai Literature) and of many narrative romances, frequently dramatized, such as *Samutthakhot* and *Su'a Kho* (17th century) or *Sang Thong* (18th century).

Motifs and incidents from the *jātakas* are also found in beast fables and other traditional didactic materials in Malay and related languages both in the Malay Peninsula and in Sumatra, Java and the neighbouring archipelago. (◊ Pañcatantra.) [C H B R/E H S S]

M. Winternitz, article 'Jātaka' in *Encyclopedia of Religion and Ethics*, vii (1914); *Buddhist Birth Stories*, tr. T. W. Rhys Davids (1925), introduction.

Javanese Literature. Javanese literature began, a thousand years ago, in following both the Hindu and Buddhist content, and the style, of Indian models. The language (Old Javanese, or *Kawi*) was written in an Indian-type script, employed Indian verse metres and contained many Sanskrit words (◊ *Kakawin*).

Though some Buddhist treatises have survived, most Old Javanese literature, which is very varied, is based on Hindu works, especially the two great Indian epics, the ◊ *Rāmāyaṇa* and ◊ *Mahābhārata*. The former is the longest poem (*Rāmāyaṇa*) in Old Javanese literature and the closest to a Sanskrit model. The latter has been condensed into prose for use in the Javanese shadow-play (*wayang*) and into a version of the central books of ◊ *Bhārata Yuddha*. The *Nāgarakretagama* by ◊ Prapañcha and contemporary law books and treatises on religious foundations give a good picture of the 14th-century empire of Majapahit. (◊ *Pararaton*.)

Later literature uses indigenous metres and includes sung romances, based on the adventures of Raden ◊ Panji, a popular hero, also borrowed by Malay and other Indonesian literatures. From the 15th century (when Middle Javanese succeeded Old Javanese), Java was gradually converted to Islam and the literature adapted Arabic-Persian romances, e.g. of the hero Amir Hamzah in ◊ *Ménak*. Another remarkable work, encyclopedic in character, is the 18th-century ◊ *Chěṇṭini*. Hindu-Javanese mythology, however, continued to exert its influence in the early portions of historical works (◊ *Babad*) and in poems, manuals for shadow-play performers, and a great variety of other writings.

Most of this literature is still in manuscript – some is still being published in the Javanese and roman scripts, but most modern authors use ◊ Indonesian. [C H]

R. M. Ng. Poerbatjaraka and Tardjan Hadidjaya, *Kepustakaan Djawa* (Jakarta and Amsterdam, 1957); Prapañcha, *Nāgarakretagama*, tr. and ed. T. G. T. Pigeaud, *Java in the 14th Century*, iii (The Hague, 1960).

Jayadeva (fl. 12th cent.). Author of the *Gītagovinda*, an erotico-religious poem on the amours of Radhā and Kṛṣṇa, one of the finest lyric pieces of Sanskrit literature (tr. George Keyt, Bombay, 1947). Jayadeva is one of the most original Indian poets; his poem finds little stylistic affinity in the earlier lyric, being a far more unitary, and indeed almost dramatic work. The very marked element of *bhakti* worship (strong emotional devotion to a personal God) has suggested to many historians that Jayadeva's poem originated from a more popular milieu and was only later given a Sanskrit revision. This argument insists too strongly on the opposition of popular and Sanskritic. [E G]

Indian Poetry, tr. Edwin Arnold (1881). Winternitz, *G I L*, iii.

Jippensha Ikku (1765–1831). Japanese comic novelist. He was born in what is now Shizuoka prefecture and was brought up in Edo (now Tokyo), remaining there until 1791, when he obtained a post with a magistrate in Osaka. While there he may have written some plays. He later returned to Edo and devoted himself to writing comic stories and verse. These had no success until 1802, when he began to publish *Hizakurige* (*Shank's Mare*, tr. T. Satchell, 1960). Travel, in particular to holy or otherwise famous places, had long been popular in Japan, and there were many guidebooks for the various great highways. The *Hizakurige* series was a comic version of these. From 1802 to 1809 appeared the section devoted to the most famous road of all, that from Edo to Osaka, with a diversion to Ise on the way. Further journeys were described in books appearing at intervals until 1820, but the first instalment was the most successful. Various stories of the author's fondness for practical joking – that, for example, he had fireworks placed beneath his shroud so that his cremation should go off with a bang – are now discounted.

The works take two picaresque characters, Yajirobei and Kitahachi, along the various routes. Being Edo-born, they despise the provincials they meet but they are continually tricked and cheated. The humour is crude but universal; the two main characters endearingly take their misfortunes in good part. The writing gives a vivid, if rosy, picture of the times. The series enjoyed great popularity in Japan, and the journeys were extended, by another author, after the Meiji restoration, to allow the heroes to visit the West. The translation is worth sampling (though repetitiveness may make it irksome to read all through), if only for the humanity of its ribaldry. Jippensha's humour, as well as being concerned with cozening, is sometimes bawdy or scatological. It forms one link in a long chain which includes the comic interludes to *nō* plays, and the *rakugoka*, or comic storytellers of today. [C J D]

Jnāneśvar (1271–1296?). Indian religious poet. Author of *Jnāneśvarī*, a verse commentary on the *Bhagavadgītā* and one of the earliest and most important works of the Marathi literature of India (tr. R. K. Bhagvat, Poona, 1953–4; new UNESCO tr. by H. M. Lambert in preparation). It is an exposition of the path of *bhakti*, personal devotion to God, in direct simple verse with an abundance of earthy metaphors and similes from everyday life. Its literary and religious influence continues to the present time. Its traditional date, 1290, agrees with the stage of developments of the language, but nothing certain is known of its author. There are numerous traditions about his life and miraculous powers among his devotees, and his tomb at Alandi, near Poona, is a place of pilgrimage. A more learned philosophical poem, the *Amṛtānubhava*, and many devotional songs (*abhangs*) are more or less plausibly attributed to Jnāneśvar. [I M P R]

J. F. Edwards, *Dnyaneshwar the Out-Caste Brahmin* (Poona, 1941); N. MacNicol, *Psalms of Maratha Saints* (Calcutta, 1919).

Joaquín, Nick (1917–). ◊ Philippine writer in English. He began writing short stories at 20. He also began studies for the priesthood, which explains in part the Christian setting of his stories and his almost pastoral preoccupation with the paraliturgical practices and superstitions of his characters.

His *Prose and Poems* (Manila, 1952) was quickly followed by the Barangay Theatre Guild's production of his play, *Portrait of the Artist as Filipino*. Both deal with the passing of one world into another, and of the conflicts that the transition engenders. Joaquín's prize-novel, *The Woman Who Had Two Navels* (Manila, 1961), is a more ample statement of the tensions between illusion and reality against a setting in which past and present interpenetrate. It won the first Stonehill Award, a yearly grant. He is at present a staff member of a Manila magazine, for which he writes under the pseudonym Quijano de Manila. Joaquín has been taken to task for his 'lack of serenity', due in part to his lush, exotic manner. Certainly, however, he can evoke vividly the mixture of bravery and hope, trepidation and nostalgia, that accompanies life's more moving experiences. [A P G M]

Miguel A. Bernad, 'Haunted Intensity', in *Bamboo and the Greenwood Tree* (Manila, 1961); Josefina D. Constantino, 'Review Article: The Woman Who Had Two Navels', in *Philippine Studies*, ix (Manila, 1961); Lourdes Busuego-Pablo, 'The Spanish Tradition in Nick Joaquín', in *Philippine Studies*, iii (Manila, 1955); Harry B. Furay, 'The Stories of Nick Joaquín', in *Philippine Studies*, i (Manila, 1953).

Juwaynî, by-name of **'Alâ al-Dîn 'Atâ Malik** (1226–83). Persian historian of the Mongols. He came of a distinguished family of public servants, his father being Minister of Finance to the Mongol governor of the western territories of the empire and his brother Grand Vizier to Abaqa Khan (1265–82). Juwaynî began his career as private secretary to the Mongol governor Arghun, whom he accompanied on official missions to Mongolia; while at Karakorum in 1252–3 he conceived the idea of writing the history of the Mongol conquests. After accompanying Hulagu in the campaigns against the Assassins and the caliph of Baghdad, he was appointed governor of Baghdad and Lower Mesopotamia, where he ruled justly for over 20 years. By 1281 however he was under a cloud, repelling with difficulty charges of peculation and of treasonable correspondence with the Sultan of Egypt. He died in disgrace, and is buried at Tabrîz.

Juwaynî's *Ta'rîkh-i Jihân-gushâ* (tr. J. A. Boyle, *The History of the World-Conqueror*, 2 vols., 1958) was composed piecemeal from 1252 until about 1260. Though written in very elaborate and euphuistic style, it is an invaluable source, by one who was at the centre of affairs and had an intimate knowledge of the Mongol Empire. The first book relates the history of Jenghiz Khan and his successors, the second and third the history of his principal opponents, the Khwârazmshâhs and the 'Assassins' of Alamut.

Juwaynî composed 2 short tracts rebutting the calumnies directed against him (summarized in E. G. Browne's Introduction, cited below). Some of his letters and state papers also survive. [V L M]

E. G. Browne, Introduction to Mirza Muhammad's edition, Gibb Memorial Series, 1912; Arberry, *C P L*; *E of I*.

K

Kabīr (d. 1518). Indian poet and Hindu sectarian reformer. The little that is known of his life derives mainly from traditions handed down by his sect. He was born at Banaras and probably brought up by Muslim foster-parents. He was early attracted to the devotional worship of the Vaiṣṇava avatar Rām, which had recently acquired a footing in northern

India, but was also powerfully influenced by other current Hindu and Muslim doctrines. Traditions of the yogī Gorakhnāth and his successors' teaching strengthened his conviction of the value of subjective experience of God, and of the uselessness of esoteric theory and outward observances. He was led to reject the doctrine of Rām as an avatar of Viṣṇu and to see in Rām rather a divine principle, independent of creed, with which all other gods might be equated. The influence of Muslim Ṣūfī mysticism is also evident in Kabīr's thought, where it reinforces the spirit of *bhakti* or loving devotion to the divine which he had inherited from Vaiṣṇavism.

Kabīr's poetry is the expression of his religious eclecticism. He probably taught only orally, and the canon of his works is uncertain. Three collections written in a mixture of Hindi dialects are generally considered authentic: the *Bījak* ('Account Book'), a collection in the Sikh *Ādi granth*, and the *Granthāvalī* ('Collected Writings'). These are in rhyming couplets and a variety of other stanzas; their style is often rough and their themes obscure in detail, but they can express their author's broad religious convictions with great effectiveness. [R S M]

Au cabinet de l'amour, tr. Ch. Vaudeville (Paris, 1959) (selected verse with introductions and notes).

Ch. Vaudeville, *Kabīr Granthavali* (Pondicherry, 1957); F. E. Keay, *A History of Hindi Literature* (Calcutta, 1920).

'Kakawin'. A type of old Javanese court poem of epic or didactic content. The earliest and best-known example is the *Rāmāyaṇa Kakawin* (◊ *Rāmāyaṇa*) of the 10th century. The form is still in use in the adjacent island of Bali. The metres, often frequently changed throughout the poem, are Indian not Indonesian and the lines, which were meant to be sung, may be of differing lengths. Rhyme is optional. [C H]

C. Hooykaas, *The Old-Javanese Rāmāyaṇa Kakawin, with special reference to the problem of interpolation in kakawins*, Verhandelingen, Koninklijk Instituut voor Taal-, Land- en Volkenkunde XVI (The Hague, 1955); C. Hooykaas, *The Old-Javanese Rāmāyaṇa, an Exemplary Kakawin as to Form and Content*, Verhandelingen, Koninklijke Nederlandsche Akademie van Wetenschappen, Afd. Letterkunde, Nieuwe Reeks, Deel LXV/1 (Amsterdam, 1958).

Kakinomoto Hitomaro (fl. *c.*700), Japanese poet. His life is known only from his poetry. This is preserved in the *Man-yō-shū* ('Collection for a Myriad Ages', *c.*760), the earliest surviving poetry collection in Japan. He was a low-ranking court official, and appears to have died in the province of Iwami, near the western tip of the main island. He is generally considered the best poet of this collection, and certainly he is the greatest of its earlier poets. He has left several hundred *tanka* ('short poems' of 31 syllables) and many *chōka* ('long poems'). The 'long poems' of the *Man-yō-shū* were a highly developed form of great potentiality, and their elevation to great poetry can be credited to Hitomaro. He was no slavish imitator of Chinese originals, even though some of his inspiration must have come from China. His work is very Japanese, both in language and in his adherence to the Shintō religion. A favourite theme was death: he wrote moving elegies for imperial personages as well as for more humble people, such as his wife and an unknown man whose body he found on a beach. However, he wrote also court poems for more auspicious occasions, and some tender love poetry. He had still much contact with the native spirit of Early Japan, and Brower and Miner compare him with the Elizabethan poets: a stage between the primitive poets and the refined courtiers of Nara. (It was here that the Japanese court found a settled home in 710, after the earlier period in which the capital had changed with the change of emperor.) [C J D]

Nippon Gakujutsu Shinkōkai, *The Manyōshū, One Thousand Poems* (1965); Brower and Miner, *J C P*.

Kālidāsa (fl. A.D. 400). The greatest Indian classical poet. Nothing is known of his personal life save that he was probably a brahmin and a worshipper of Śiva. Tradition associates his name with that of the legendary King Vikramāditya, now supposed to have been the greatest of the Gupta monarchs, Chandragupta II, who reigned in Ujjain from A.D. 375 to 413.

Kālidāsa excelled in all literary genres except the prose novel, which apparently he did not attempt. The best of his works is the *Śakuntalā*, last of 3 dramas (◊ *Nāṭyaśāstra*). Based on an old epic tale, it recounts serenely and elegantly the love of King Duśyanta and Śakuntalā, a semi-divine nymph. The curse of an irascible holy man causes Duśyanta to forget his promise to marry Śakuntalā. He spurns her, but then discovers a ring which restores his memory of her. His great sadness is assuaged by their reunion in heaven. Of Kālidāsa's other dramas, the *Vikramorvaśīya*, based on a legend found in the Veda, is also a love story involving human and divine actors – the King Purūravas and the nymph Urvaśi. The *Mālavikāgnimitra* is a harem comedy.

Kālidāsa also excelled in the epic genre. His *Raghuvaṃśa* retells the history of the dynasty whose greatest hero was Rāma (◊ *Rāmāyaṇa*). The *Kumārasaṃbhava* preserves the vigorous and sometimes risqué myth of the conquest of the ascetic Śiva by the lovely Pārvatī. Besides the famous *Meghadūta*, the lyrics *Śṛṅgāratilaka* and *Ṛtusaṃhara* are also attributed to Kālidāsa.

Kālidāsa's style is marked by a quality rare in Sanskrit poetry – clarity, by which is not meant simplicity; yet the careful discipline of sympathetic descriptions is never overpowered by a false sense of elegance. His language sets the standard of purity in Sanskrit. [E G]

Śakuntalā: tr. Sir William Jones (1789); tr. Arthur Ryder (Everyman, 1912); tr. M. Monier-Williams (1855); tr. Murray Emeneau (Berkeley, 1962); *Raghuvaṃśa*: tr. P. D. L. Johnstone (1902); Fr. tr. L. Renou (Paris, 1928); *Meghadūta*: tr. G. H. Rooke (1935); tr. H. H. Wilson (1843).
Winternitz, *G I L*, 3.

'Kāmasūtra' of Vātsyāyana. An ancient Hindu text on erotics (*kāma* or 'love'), the most representative text from the third of the traditional three disciplines relating to the 'goods' of human action: *dharma*, the religious law (◊ *Manu*), *artha*, profit, material advantage (◊ Kauṭilya), and *kāma*, pleasure. It is thus as an important element of general ethics that 'erotics' are to be judged. With masterly straightforwardness, Vātsyāyana pursues the consequences of the proposition that, though pleasure is not an adequate goal by itself, no life can be complete without it. With candour and a scholarly rigour which avoids any suggestion of obscenity, he defines the conditions and techniques of the supreme pleasure, and discusses such ancillary topics as how to approach a woman socially, how to court the unmarried or seduce the married. One chapter deals with the ethics of the prostitute, distinct from other women not only by her livelihood but by her cultural attainments, which included mastery of the '64 arts'. Also noteworthy is the detailed description of the person, apartments and daily routine of the man about town.

Written in the concise, technical style of the legal literature, the *Kāmasūtra* evidently has much in common with the opportunistic ethics of the *Arthaśāstra*; a knowledge of *kāmasūtra* was presumed by all the classical poets, and their works show familiarity with its precepts. To understand fully Indian erotics, the importance of erotic imagery in later religious practices (◊ Jayadeva) must be appreciated. [E G]

Tr. Sir Richard Burton (repr. 1962).
R. Schmidt, *Beiträge zur Indischen Erotik* (Leipzig, 1902); J. J. Meyer, *Sexual Life in Ancient India* (2nd edn, 1952).

Kamo Chōmei (1153–1216). Japanese critic and essayist. His family were the hereditary priests of the Kamo shrine in Kyoto. Until about 1205 he was at court, and served as an official in the Poetry Department. He was also a noted performer on the *biwa*, the oriental lute. In about 1205 he retired from the world, taking the Buddhist tonsure and living in mountain hermitages. The reason usually given for this is that his hopes of assuming the priesthood of the family shrine were disappointed. However, he continued his literary work, and also visited Kamakura, seat of the then military rulers of Japan. His best-known work is *Hōjōki* (*Record of a Ten-foot Square Hut*), written in 1212. This description of his hermitage life contains moving passages on the mutability of human life, with graphic accounts of earthquake and famine. He describes his desire to separate himself from the turbulence of the times. Buddhist sentiment pervades the work.

Of his other writings, perhaps the most interesting is *Mumyōshō* ('Nameless Notes'), a miscellany of poetry criticism in which he advocates the style of *yūgen*, the mysterious or symbolic element in poetry which suggests a meaning beyond that of the mere words. It is written in the obscure style normally used for criticism of this sort. [C J D]

Tales of the Heike and the Four Square Hut, tr. A. L. Sadler (Sydney, 1928); Keene, *M J L.*

Kampaṉ (probably between 9th cent. and 12th cent.). Tamil poet. He composed the principal Tamil version of the ◊ *Rāmāyaṇa*. Though the main outline of the original Sanskrit story is the same, Kampaṉ's version differs considerably in feeling. The hero, Rāma, is regarded as a god, as in most of the 'vernacular' versions of the story in India. He is an incarnation of the god Viṣṇu. The Tamil version consequently has those special qualities of vivid tenderness and pathos (peculiar perhaps to the followers of Viṣṇu) especially noteworthy in the Kṛṣṇa-literature. The tale is moreover presented in a South Indian guise as being more appealing to Tamil readers. It was submitted to the followers of Viṣṇu at their centre in Srīrangam for their *imprimatur*. Kampaṉ's epic was entitled *Irāmāvatāram*, the Rāma Incarnation. It was completed by *Uttarakāṇṭam*, composed by Oṭṭakkūttar, Kampaṉ's contemporary. [J R M]

The Ayodhya Canto of the Ramayana, tr. C. Rajagopalachari (London, for UNESCO, 1961).
V. V. S. Aiyar, *Kamba Ramayanam – A Study* (Delhi, 1949).

Karaosmanoğlu, Yakub Kadri (1888–). Turkish writer. The leading Turkish novelist of the republican period. Born in Cairo and educated at a French school there. Coming to Istanbul in 1908, he attracted attention with mannered 'prose-poems' and a collection of short stories, *Bir Serencam* (1914; German tr. H. W. Duda, *Eine Weibergeschichte und andere Novellen*, Leipzig, 1923), whose dominant theme of hostility to religious fanaticism reappeared in his controversial *Nur Baba* (1922), a detailed picture of life in a decadent dervish convent (German tr. A. Schimmel, *Flamme und Falter*, 1947). An enthusiastic supporter of the Kemalist movement, but no chauvinist, he became a deputy and served for many years from 1934 as a diplomat. Strongly influenced by the French realists, he has produced a series of powerful novels depicting, with sympathy but without false sentiment, the psychological crises of individuals in the contexts of the successive crises of modern Turkey: the decay of Ottoman society during the despotism of Abdulhamid, in *Kiralık Konak* (1922), the bewilderment of a young exile in Paris at the same period, in *Bir Sürgün* (1938), the party struggles of 1908–18, in *Hüküm Gecesi* (1927), the cosmopolitan world of occupied Istanbul at the end of the First World War, in *Sodom ve Gomore* (1928; Fr. tr. R. Marchand, *Leila, fille de Gomorrhe*, 1934), the brutish life of the Anatolian peasantry during the War of Independence, in *Yaban* (1932; German tr. M. Schultz, *Der Fremdling*, 1939; Ital. tr. A. Scalero, 1941), and the triumph of the young republic, in *Ankara* (1934); while *Panorama* (1953) portrays the corrupting influence of self-interest on the reformers' ideals. He has written 2 books of memoirs: the account of his early years in *Anamın Kitabı* (1957), and his experiences during the War of Independence, in *Vatan Yolunda* (1958). [V L M]

O. Spies, *Die türkische Prosaliteratur der Gegenwart* (Leipzig, 1943); *Anthologie des écrivains turcs d'aujourd'hui* (Ankara, 1948); A. Bombaci, *Storia della letteratura turca* (Milan, 1956); *Enc. Brit.* (1961); *Philologiae Turcicae Fundamenta*, ii (Wiesbaden, 1964).

Kâtib Chelebi. ◊ Hâjji Khalfa.

Kauṭilya. The supposed author of the *Arthaśāstra*, an Indian textbook of practical politics. By tradition Kauṭilya is identified with Cāṇakya, prime minister of Candragupta Maurya (322–298 B.C.), King of Magadha (Bihar), but the text of the *Arthaśāstra* is not concerned with the problems of a great kingdom extending over all of North India. It discusses in Machiavellian detail the techniques of power of the petty prince in the fluid society of a decentralized period (perhaps that following the collapse of the Maurya-Śuṅga dynasties, 1st century B.C.).

The *Arthaśāstra* ('Treatise on the (Political) Good'; tr. R. Shamasastry, Mysore, 1961) was rediscovered only in 1909 and altered considerably certain views previously held concerning the high morality and other-worldliness of classical Indian society. The text is completely devoted to the idea of maintaining stability in the kingdom and power for the king, whether by policy or subterfuge. The one virtue accepted without question is that of the oath: the minister who has sworn allegiance is completely faithful to his master.

In the social philosophy of Hinduism, three 'goals' are generally admitted: *dharma* (religious duty), *kāma* (pleasure), and *artha*. The *Arthaśāstra* figures as the standard formulation of the latter (◊ *Manu* and *Kāmasūtra*).

Kauṭilya is also the subject of one of the more famous plays of Indian antiquity, the *Mudrārāksasa* of Viśakhadatta, which purports to recount the intrigue surrounding Candragupta's revolt against his predecessor, the last Nanda king. [E G]

N. N. Law, *Studies in Ancient Indian Polity* (1914), and *Inter-State Relations in Ancient India* (Calcutta and London, 1920).

Kawabata Yasunari (1899–). Japanese novelist. Born in Osaka and orphaned while still a child, he nevertheless had a good education – he went to high school and university in Tokyo, studying English and Japanese literature. While still a student, he was appointed in 1923 to the staff of Kikuchi Kan's magazine, *Bungei shunjū*. Since then his whole life has been wrapped up in literature. He has kept clear of the schools and schisms so characteristic of Japanese artistic life, and in his support of his fellow artists he has followed the example of his patron, Kikuchi Kan.

His first important work, *Izu no odoriko* (1926; *The Izu Dancer*, tr. E. Seidensticker, *Atlantic Monthly* 195, 1955), was a nostalgic treatment of his encounter, while on holiday from school, with a troupe of dancers, one of whom aroused a shadowy infatuation in him. The ability to create an atmosphere, using soft colours and a tinge of melancholy, can already be seen. In 1937 came *Yukiguni* (*The Snow Country*, tr. E. Seidensticker, 1957). In this description of a winter resort and one of its *geisha* can be sensed the passage of time since his boyhood, for although nostalgia is still there, it is rather for the traditional Japan. The author seems less involved than in the earlier work. The war interrupted his writing, but in 1947 appeared *Semba-zuru* (*Thousand Cranes*, tr. E. Seidensticker, 1959), in which his objective eye is turned to post-war Japan. He continues writing in the same vein, and remains extremely Japanese – any Western influence is well below the surface. He is clearly interested in the individual, and not in generalization or ideologies. [C J D]

The Mole, tr. E. Seidensticker, in Keene, *M J L*; *The Moon on the Water*, tr. George Saitō in Morris, *M J S*.

Kenkō-hōshi. ◊ Yoshida Kenkō.

Khit-san ('Experiment for a New Age'). The name of a ◊ Burmese literary movement, begun in the 1930s. Its leading figures were Sein Tin, Thein Han, Maung Wun, E Maung and Toe Aung (writing under the names Theip-pan Maung Wa, Zaw-gyi, Min Thu-wun, Maung Thant Zin and Ku-tha respectively), who, with other enterprising members of Rangoon University, deliberately adopted a style in which the new ideas and words from the West were not allowed to swamp tradition. Their verse was brief and simple, and they wrote many novels and short stories, both original and translated or adapted from Western literature. A selection of their short stories was published in *Khit-san Pon-byin* (2 vols.: 1934 and 1938), and a collection of poems in *Khit-san Kabya* (1934). They have influenced later writers strongly. [J W A O]

Khmer Literature. The classical Khmer literature of Cambodia consists largely of works derived from India. These include learned treatises on medicine, augury and astronomy, many in verse; translations of the Buddhist Canon; lives of the Buddha in prose and verse; and moral poems or treatises of Buddhist origin. There are many dramatic poems based on the Rama cycle; among them is the most renowned work of Khmer literature, the *Ream-Ker* (◊ *Rāmāyaṇa*). There is no question of mere translation. Incidents and conversations are added, details are altered and a Cambodian flavour is given by the rambling narrative style. The literature not of Indian derivation includes long verse-novels and court- and love-poetry of the 19th century.

A self-consciously elevated style of language, characterized by frequent alliteration and reduplicative word-sequences, is employed. Verse-metres have an internal rhyme probably of native origin, but the syllable-structure may be derived from Indian versification.

Most of the literature may still be read only on anonymous, undated palm-leaf manuscripts. The Buddhist Institute of Phnom Penh is gradually publishing and editing the more important texts. Translations into French may be found in *Cambodge: contes et légendes recueillis et publiés en Français* by A. Leclère (Paris, 1895) and *Contes Khmers traduits du Cambodgien* by G. H. Monod (Mouans-Sartoux, 1944).

Modern Cambodian authors are either imitating the Western detective or romantic novel or writing more serious works such as nationalist poems and religious treatises. [J M J]

Khu'krit Pramoj, Mọm Ratchawong (1912–). Thai writer and journalist. Founder (1950) and editor of the leading Bangkok daily paper, *Sayam Rat*. He is a liberal politician, and a key figure in contemporary journalism and literary activity, and a satirical writer of great power. He has handled important social topics in novels, short stories, essays and plays for radio and television.

His long novel *Si Phaen Din* ('Four Reigns') (1953) exhibits a sophisticated nationalism together with a respect for tradition. The novel *Lại Chiwit* ('Many Lives') investigates the lives of many types of Thai people, following the drowning of the characters concerned in a river-boat accident, rather in the manner of Thornton Wilder's *The Bridge of San Luis Rey*. *Phai Daeng* (*Red Bamboo*, tr. Bangkok, 1955), dealing with Communist agitation in a village, is a satire on Thai political fiction-writing. [E H S S]

'Khun Chang, Khun Phaen'. A popular Thai narrative epic-romance some 20,000 lines long, concerning two noblemen and their rivalry in the royal service and over the hand of Phim, the heroine. Scholars in Thailand relate the poem to events of the early 16th century. Relations between the sexes are fully explored in the context of official life. Recital by court bards of episodes from the poem took place at such ceremonies as the tonsurate or head-shaving of royal children.

The earliest manuscript record dates from the reign of Rama II (1809–24) and the first printed episodes from 1873, but this anonymous story has long been known to country bards in Central Thailand. [E H S S]

J. Kasem Sibunruang, *La femme, le héros et le vilain* (Paris, 1960) (contains summary in French).

E. H. S. Simmonds, 'Thai Narrative Poetry: Palace and Provincial Texts of an Episode from *Khun Chang, Khun Phaen*', in *Asia Major*, 1964.

Ki Tsurayuki (*c.* 870–946). Japanese poet and diarist. Little definite information is available about his life. He appears to have held a succession of posts in the government. In 905 the *Kokin-wakashū* (or *Kokinshū*), a collection of old and new poems, appeared with Ki Tsurayuki as one of 5 compilers. This collection, the first major one since the *Man-yō-shū* (◊ Ōtomo Yakamochi), and the first of a series of anthologies prepared by order of the emperor in a special department of the government, contained work by many famous poets, including ◊ Ono Komachi and ◊ Ariwara Narihira. The poems in this collection number just over 1,000 and, although written over a long period, have characteristics which distinguish them from the *Man-yō-shū* and also from later collections. There are virtually no long poems, the authors come from the narrow circle of court officials and aristocracy, and the themes are love, nature and the passage of time. The first is dominant, partly because much of the poet's time was taken up with love – for its successful pursuit a poetical talent was essential. Poetry competitions led to increasing artificiality, yet the collection contains much good poetry, Ki Tsurayuki's being above average, if not very distinguished. His most important contribution, apart from his work as compiler, was the writing of the Japanese preface (there is another, in Chinese). This short piece, which shows signs of Chinese influence and may be adapted from the Chinese preface, is the earliest piece of literary criticism in Japanese. Its poetical aesthetics were to be influential for centuries to come.

One of Ki Tsurayuki's later appointments was to the governorship of Tosa, in Shikoku. He wrote a diary of his return journey to the capital in 936. This is not quite a straightforward chronicle, for he pretends that it was written by one of the women of the governor's train.

He could thus use a fairly simple Japanese, and portray emotions, such as a fear of pirates, that a man should not have confessed to. Its directness and simplicity, and the hints it gives of conditions of the time, make it well worth reading.

Apart from the translations listed below, Brower and Miner, *JCP*, should be consulted for the poetry of the *Kokinshū*. [C J D]

The Tosa Diary, tr. William N. Porter (1912); tr. G. W. Sargent, in Keene, *A J L* (extracts).
Georges Bonneau, *Le monument poétique de Heian: Le Kokinshū*, i (Paris, 1933), ii (Paris, 1934).

Kikuchi Kan (1888–1948). Japanese novelist, playwright and journalist. He was born in Shikoku, and attended (and was asked to leave) schools in Tokyo. He eventually graduated from Kyoto University, but retained from his schooldays in the capital a friendship for ◊ Akutagawa Ryūnosuke. His early works, and perhaps the most satisfying as literature, were some plays written about 1916 – they include *Okujō no kyōjin* (*The Madman on the Roof*, tr. Iwasaki and Shaw; also Keene, *MJL*) and *Chichi kaeru* (*The Father Returns*), translated by Shaw. Later he wrote other plays, and unlike that of some other authors, all his dramatic work was for performance and has been played with considerable success. He also wrote innumerable short stories and serials, believing that he ought to cater for the man in the street, not just the intellectual. He is often described as a neo-realist – his writing is down-to-earth, without tricks of style and pretension. But his original work alone would not explain the great position he held in pre-war Japanese literature. He was also a patron of young novelists, particularly after 1923 when he founded the monthly *Bungei shunjū*, a literary and artistic review which still publishes original work, and it is as editor of this that his name will go down to history. [C J D]

Tōjurō's Love and Four Other Plays, tr. Glenn W. Shaw (Tokyo, 1925).

Kinoshita Junji (1914–). Japanese dramatist. He was born in Tokyo and received the academic's normal education, in his case a specialization in English literature at Tokyo University. Throughout his career he has been a professor at various universities in the capital. His English studies led him to Shakespeare and the drama. Whereas many modern Japanese dramatists have had little experience of the theatre, using drama as a literary form without necessarily envisaging its performance, Kinoshita is a practical dramatist and has long been a leader, with the great actress Yamamoto Yasue, of a left-wing theatre group, the *Budō no kai*. He is particularly interested in Japanese folk tales, and has written many plays incorporating such material, including, in 1947, *Hata no oto* ('The Sound of the Loom') and *Kikimimi zukin* ('The Magic Hearing Cap'). In 1949 appeared *Yūzuru* (*Twilight Crane*, tr. A. C. Scott, in *Playbook*, Norfolk, Conn., 1956), the legend of a crane-wife who wove fine cloth from her feathers, but who was forced to give up human form by the greed of her husband and his associates. Although it appears slight in print, performances have been widely acclaimed, and it has been staged in Russia and America. He always places social criticism in his work against a strong background of local life and tradition. Kinoshita has travelled widely on both sides of the iron curtain, and is one of the liveliest minds, in spite of his engagement, in the Japanese literary sphere. He continues to write plays for stage and broadcasting, has done much translating from Western dramatists, and has written a great quantity of dramatic criticism. [C J D]

Mori Arimasa, *Le dramaturge japonais: Kinoshita Junji*, in *Les théâtres d'Asie* (Paris, 1961).

Kin-wun Min-gyi U Kaung (1821–1908). ◊ Burmese court minister and writer, later adviser to the British Government of Burma. He wrote many poems and some 'letters' (◊ Pon-nya), but is perhaps best known in the West for his 'London Diary' (*Lan-dan Thwa Ne-zin Hmat-tan*) and 'Paris Diary' (*Pè-rit Thwa Ne-zin Hmat-tan*), day-by-day accounts in prose of what he saw and did on two missions (1871 and 1873) to the governments of Italy, Britain and France. [J W A O]

Kobayashi Takiji (1903–33). Japanese novelist. He was born in Akita prefecture, in North Japan, and later moved to Hokkaidō, the northern island. He had a commercial training and worked as a bank employee, and at the same time began to express his left-wing views in his writings. He went to Tokyo in 1930, and became a leading member of the Proletarian School of authors, as a theorist as well as a writer, and later a member of the communist party. From 1928 to his death (presumably in prison some time after his arrest in 1933) he wrote a number of political novels. The one with most literary merit is *Kani-kōsen* (1929; tr., *The Cannery Boat*, 1933), which describes the conditions aboard a crab-canning ship, dominated by a sadistic 'superintendent'. Some of the crew are driven by a storm on to the Russian coast, and return full of glowing stories of the life there. Mutiny follows, suppressed by a naval party from a destroyer. In spite of the naïve political expression, the novel exposed a real scandal, and is technically interesting for its preoccupation not with an individual, as with most novelists of the time, but with a group. [C J D]

'Kojiki' ('Records of Ancient Matters'). Japanese chronicle compiled by imperial order and presented to the court in 712. It is an account of the creation of the world, and of the Japanese imperial line from the beginnings of Japan down to the Empress Suiko (592–628). Much of the later material is a monotonous catalogue of emperors and their progeny, but there is much of interest in the earlier chapters, where myths and legends from this very early stage of Japanese development are recorded. It was compiled when the Chinese ideographic system was beginning to be used for writing Japanese and the reading of the text of *Kojiki* (tr. B. H. Chamberlain, Kobe, 1932; Keene, *AJL*) has not been definitely established; it is, however, almost certainly in Japanese, and thus is the earliest book in that language. It contains a number of poems of a primitive type, but foreshadowing later development. It was followed in 720 by *Nihongi* (*Nihonshoki*) (tr. W. G. Aston, 1956) a chronicle in Chinese, covering the period from the beginning up to 697 [C J D]

Brower and Miner, *J C P.*

'Konjaku-monogatari' ('Tales of Long Ago') (*c.* 1050). Japanese story collection. Two books of the original 31 have been lost, the remainder being divided into 3 sections – India (Books I–V) (187 tales), China (VI–X) (180 tales) and Japan (XI–XXXI) (736 tales). The first section has tales of the Buddha and Buddhism in India; the second is partly Buddhist and partly concerned with typical Chinese themes, such as filial piety; the third has a very wide selection of themes, ranging from the introduction of Buddhism to Japan, to comical obscenities. These tales have their sources in earlier Japanese collections written in Chinese and, farther back, in the ◊ *jātaka* stories and in many hitherto unrecorded Japanese legends and traditions. The style forms an interesting contrast with that of *Genji-monogatari*: the latter has an allusive, aesthetic tone, using as far as possible a purely Japanese vocabulary not derived from Chinese; *Konjaku-monogatari* uses plain, generally lucid, constructions, with many words of Chinese origin (possibly this language was the one used by the ordinary Japanese of the time). It can also be considered as an ancestor of that of modern Japanese literature, through such intermediaries as ◊ *Heike-monogatari*. The sentiments of the stories match the style, being earthy and practical, more interested in deeds than in motives. They counterbalance the refinement and introspection of court literature, and provide a source of all sorts of information about the society of the period. Unfortunately there are very few stories translated. [C J D]

S. W. Jones, *Ages Ago* (1959).

Koran (Qur'ān). The Holy Koran is the sacred book of Islam. It is part of the Muslim creed that the Koran was dictated by God to Muhammad at intervals throughout the latter's life and mission. The 114 separate Sūras or chapters which make up the book are said first of all to have been written down 'on pieces of paper (papyrus?), stones, palm-leaves, rib-bones, pieces of leather, as well as upon the hearts of men'. After the Prophet's death in A.D. 632, the book was edited and arranged (according to tradition) by Muhammad's secretary Zaid ibn Thābit, on the orders of the Caliph Abu Bakr.

The Koran develops with the development of Muhammad's missionary life. At first he was a voice crying in a social wilderness, and his message was delivered in short passages of oracular poetry, similar, it seems, to the utterances of the tribal 'poets' or sooth-sayers, from whom he was at great pains to dissociate himself; his message was concerned principally with the judgement to come. At a somewhat later stage, it is the unity of God that is emphasized.

The tone of the Sūras changes greatly after the Hijra (the flight from Mecca to Medina in 622, from which the beginning of the Muslim era is dated), and the establishment of Muhammad's rule in Medina. Muhammad was now preoccupied with legal and moral pronouncements, including the laying down of the laws of marriage and inheritance. He was also obliged to issue political statements, in order to explain, for instance, the defeat of the Muslims by the Meccans at Uhud in 625, and to defend the continuance of fighting during the sacred months.

The early Sūras are written in rhymed prose; the later Sūras, which were intended to deal with specific legal or moral problems, are in a more straightforward prose style.

The theology of the Koran is strictly monotheistic. God (Al-Lāh) is one: 'There is none like Him'. Complete obedience to God's will is enjoined. In spite of the Koran's attacks on Jews and unbelievers, it has much in common with the Bible, the Apocrypha and the Midrash. The Christian doctrine of the Trinity, however, and the ancient polytheism of the Arabs are alike rejected. There is one true religion; Moses, Christ and Muhammad himself are among the prophets sent by the one God to bring man back to the truth. Muhammad is the 'Seal of the Prophets'. [A S T]

Tr. G. Sale (1734, etc.); tr. J. M. Rodwell (Everyman's Library, 1876, etc.); tr. E. H. Palmer (1880, etc.); tr. Muhammad ʿAli (1917, etc.); tr. M. Pickthall (1930, etc.); tr. R. Bell (1937–39); tr. A. J. Arberry (1955). A. J. Arberry, *The Holy Koran* (1953); A. Guillaume, *Islam* (Penguin Books, 1954); W. Montgomery Watt, *Muhammad at Mecca* (1953), and *Muhammad at Medina* (1956).

Kuan Han-chʿing (*c.* 1220–*c.* 1300). Chinese dramatist. Little is definitely known about his life, except that he lived at the Yüan (Mongol) capital Cambulac (present-day Peking) and was a member of the Imperial Academy of Physicians. He appears to have been proficient in music, dancing and singing and also at a kind of football. He was certainly one of the earliest and most prolific of the famous Yüan dramatists. Some 65 plays have been attributed to him, though of these only 18 are extant, and some of these are of doubtful authorship.

Kuan Han-chʿing's plays are notable for their humanity and strong sense of justice. He was particularly skilled in portraying female characters. His plots are well constructed and his lyrics are not stereotyped, as they so often seem to be in Chinese plays. His themes are varied and include tragedies, comedies and crime mysteries. Often the plot is based on older stories but Kuan Han-chʿing revitalizes them and enriches the characters psychologically. *Snow in Midsummer* (tr. Yang, *Selected Plays of Kuan Han-chʿing*, Peking, 1958) is the best of his tragedies. Its heroine is a young widow who defies the attempts of the villain to force her to marry him. The latter with the connivance of a corrupt official finally secures her execution for a crime he himself has committed. Before her execution she swears that after her death, Heaven will send snow in midsummer. [J D C]

Wang Chi-ssu, 'Kuan Han-chʿing, Outstanding Dramatist of the Yüan Dynasty', in *Chinese Literature*, 1957, 1.

Kulacēkarar. ◊ Āḻvār.

Kulap Saipradit. ◊ Si Burapha.

'Kuraḷ'. ◊ Vaḷḷuvar.

Kyokutei Bakin (1767–1848). Japanese novelist. Born in Edo of a family of *samurai* rank, he was orphaned at an early age. He is said to have spent his youth reading classical and popular literature, and composing 17-syllable poems (*haiku*). After much travel and many literary masters, he became in 1790 the pupil of the successful novelist Santō Kyōden, and under his guidance wrote his first book. He soon became more famous than his master. He wrote many short illustrated stories, and works of a historical or antiquarian nature (some still of use today), but he is best known for his *yomi-hon*, 'reading books', a genre of which ◊ Ueda Akinari had been an earlier master. In Bakin's hands these became stories full of fantastic incident. Some are adaptations of Chinese novels, some are stories of Japan. All are very long, have an exceedingly ornate and involved style, and are unrelievedly moralistic. The most famous is *Nansō Satomi Hakkenden* (*The Biographies of Eight Dogs*, extract tr. Keene, *AJL*) which appeared in parts between 1814 and 1841. They recount the exploits of eight heroes who have the same noble dog as their spiritual ancestor. At one time Bakin was thought of as one of Japan's two greatest novelists (the other being ⇨ Murasaki Shikibu). Now few read his works, but he is still very important as a typical moralizing novelist of the late Tokugawa period, and for the great influence he exerted. [C J D]

A Captive of Love, tr. E. Greey (1912); *Two Wives Exchange Spirits and Other Tales*, tr. A. L. Gowans (1930).

L

Lao Literature. Laos, in the Indo-Chinese peninsula, possesses a rich literature in the form of palm-leaf manuscripts of which very few have been printed.

Religious literature comprises canonical Buddhist texts and commentaries. Buddhist teaching also reaches the people through stories of Indra, an important protective figure, and Thep Malai, the monk who visited heaven and hell. ⇨ *Jātaka* tales have always occupied a key place in Lao literature and form a link between religious and secular branches in that many popular romances derive from *jātaka* sources. The 10 great *jātaka* (*Sip Sat*) are the most popular, and the non-canonical *Paṇṇāsajātakam* (*Ha Sip Sat*) is the source of many poetic romances intended for recitation, such as *Sang Sin Sai* and *Kalaket*. These tales describe the adventures of princely heroes and heroines in an atmosphere of magic and mystery: enchanted forests, hermits or ogres, flying steeds and the like.

The Indian ⇨ *Pañcatantra* is the source of many moral fables. These were supposedly related by a princess, Tantai Mahathewi, on the principle of *The Thousand and One Nights*. A parallel tradition exists in Cambodia, Java and Thailand. There is also a genre of comic tales of which *Ai Chet Hai* ('Brother Seven Jars'), the adventures of a super-human giant, is a good example.

Drama in Laos is little developed but localized versions of the Indian Rāma epic have long been known and episodes are performed at Luang Prabang, the royal capital, by a troupe maintained by the King of Laos.

Unchanging social conditions have inhibited the rise of a modern literature, but some short-story writers are now beginning to publish work in the few existing magazines. [E H S S]

Bernard-Thierry, Solange, 'Littérature laotienne', in *Histoire des littératures*, Vol. 1 (*Encyclopédie de la Pléiade*, Paris, 1955); Finot, Louis, 'Recherches sur la littérature laotienne', in *Bulletin de l'école française d'extrême orient*, 17/5, 1917 (list of manuscripts, summaries in French of *Kalaket* and other tales).

Lao She. ⇨ Shu Chʻing-chʻun.

Lao Tzu (*c.* 570 B.C.). Chinese philosopher. Author of the book bearing his name which later also became known as the *Tao te ching* ('The Classic of the Way and its Power'; tr. D. C. Lau, Penguin Classics, 1964). According to tradition, Lao Tzu was born in the State of Ch'u. His family name was Li and his personal name Tan, and he was for a while the Keeper of the Archives in the Eastern Chou capital. He is said to have instructed Confucius. Many modern scholars think that the book was written after the death of Confucius in the 3rd century B.C., and that Lao Tzu himself lived in the 4th century B.C., thus having no connexion with the book. It is also possible that a philosopher by the name Li Tan was a contemporary of Confucius and that, whether he was or not, the *Tao te ching* may contain some of his sayings.

The *Tao te ching* has been traditionally regarded as the oldest of the Taoist classics, but this is doubtful. It is also not certain that the book has a single author. The Tao (Way) is described as being unnamable, the Non-Being that came before Being, and the Te is the nature, or power that is inherent in each thing. The philosophy advocated is naturalism, i.e. following one's own nature without distinguishing between what is good and what is evil, but accepting both as being part of the Way. It advocates the feminine virtues of yielding and passivity, which it likens to water, which flows in a soft and yielding manner and yet is powerful. The book is full of such paradoxes, written in a cryptic verse form interspersed with a prose commentary, the latter having possibly been added by later editors. Some of the rhymes appear to be old sayings. Such is the enigmatic nature of the writing that while some scholars claim that it is a blue-print for the life of a recluse, others feel that at least in part it is a political work, advocating a *laissez-faire* government, or even a form of anarchism, and that it was written in opposition to the prevailing Confucian and paternalistic ideas of the time. Both as a poetic and as a philosophic work the *Tao te ching* has exerted a profound influence throughout Chinese history. [J D C]

Fung Yu-lan, *A History of Chinese Philosophy: The Period of the Philosophers* (1937).

Le Tac (fl. 13th cent.). ◊ Vietnamese historian. The deputy-governor of Nghe-an Province during the Mongol invasion of Central Vietnam in 1284/5, Le Tac deserted his compatriots and offered his services to the enemy. After the defeat of the Mongols in 1285, he retreated with them into China for the remainder of his life. There, about 1300, he wrote the *Annam Chi-luoc* ('Concise History of Vietnam') in 20 chapters; this is the oldest surviving historical work by a Vietnamese writer (Hue, 1961). One of the three extant manuscripts of this book is in the Library of the British Museum. [P J H]

Let-wè Thon-dara (fl. 1752–83). ◊ Burmese court minister and poet. Composer of many poems including 2 famous ◊ *yadu* written in exile at Mè-za in northern Burma, and describing his unhappiness in terms of such pathos that the king is said to have ordered his immediate recall (some tr. in *Journal of the Burma Research Society*, XXV, 1935). [J W A O]

Li Chʻing-chao (Li I-an) (1084–1151?). Chinese poetess. She was born in Shantung province of parents who were both accomplished literary stylists. She married her soul-mate Chao Ming-chʻeng at 17. Her blissful life was disrupted when the Chin barbarians invaded north China; she fled south with her husband in 1127, but he died shortly afterwards at Nanking, and thereafter she drifted haplessly from place to place in south-east China.

Most of the little of her work that remains consists of poems in the *tzʻu* style – verses composed to conform to the notation and line-length of popular tunes, in any language that approached the vernacular. Li Chʻing-chao adopted the orthodox mellifluous, subdued style of *tzʻu*, as opposed to the bold and vigorous style championed by ◊ Su Tung-pʻo. For this reason her embittered and scornful patriotic poems are composed in the traditional *shih* form. The *tzʻu* of her early period are concerned with both the sheltered domestic wife and the immortal longings of a romantic young woman; the ingenuous expression of her thirst for love in these poems earned her a rebuke for licentiousness. Her distress after the flight south is reflected in the poetry of her later period, which is imbued with a feeling of desolation. [D E P]

Tr. in *The White Pony*, ed. Robert Payne (Mentor, 1960); *Anthologie de la poésie classique chinoise*, ed. Paul Demiéville (Paris, 1962).

Li Fei-kan (pseud. **Pa Chin**) (1904–). Chinese novelist. Born in Chengtu, capital of Szechwan province. His unhappy childhood gave him an intense hatred of the traditional family system. When quite young he became an anarchist and while studying in France (1927–9) he translated Kropotkin's *Ethics*. His pen name, Pa Chin, is composed of the first and last syllables of the Chinese transcription of the names Bakunin and Kropotkin.

Li Fei-kan wrote a number of works in France, but his best-known novels are the trilogy *Torrent*, consisting of *Family* (1933) (tr. Shapiro, Peking, 1958), *Spring* (1938) and *Autumn* (1940). In these he drew on his boyhood experiences to depict the struggle between the older and younger generations in a large family. This theme aroused memories in the minds of many young Chinese, and *Family* became a best-seller, later being dramatized by ◊ Wan Chia-pao and filmed. It remains popular among the young, its diffuse romantic style marring it somewhat for more mature readers. Li Fei-kan's other works include his earlier trilogy *Love* and his later novels *Fire*, *Garden of Leisure* and *Cold Nights*. He also wrote a number of short stories, the most celebrated being

Dog (tr. in Snow, *Living China*, 1936). Since 1949 he has written little other than reportage. [J D C]

Li I-an. ⇨ Li Chʻing-chao.

Li Ju-chen (1763–1830?). Chinese novelist. Born in Peking, Li showed great intellectual promise in his youth. He had his success in scholarship, not in an official career. His *Mirror of Sounds*, printed in 1810, was an original contribution to phonology, but he only held minor official posts. Towards the end of his life he lived in severely reduced circumstances.

Li's one novel, *Ching hua yuan* ('Flowers in the Mirror'), was printed in 1828; it had taken him 20 years to complete, not surprisingly, considering the erudition that went into it. The 'flowers' of the title are 100 flower-spirits relegated to earthly existence because they obey an edict of Empress Wu of the Tʻang dynasty and so neglect their duty. They show extraordinary talent in all fields of endeavour and so justify the author's plea for the elevation of woman in the public esteem. The most popular sections are those describing the travels of Tʻang Ao and his friends to imaginary lands which serve to illustrate the injustices and depravities of society, or, as in 'The Country of Gentlemen', the author's ideal. Li Juchen shows himself the complete moralist in the final allegorical section, where the effects of vices are illustrated in the mazes the heroes have to penetrate. [D E P]

Chang Hsin-chang, *Allegory and Courtesy in Spenser* (1955).

Li Po (701–762). Chinese poet. He grew up in Szechwan province, where his life was unconstrained, his education erratic and his interests inclined to the arcane. Before he left his home province at 25 he had spent a few years as a hermit and trained himself in the arts of the 'knight-errant', or selfless avenger of injustices. He wandered widely, making many friends among officials, recluses and fellow poets, building his own reputation as he went. On the recommendation of the famous Taoist Wu Yun he was summoned to court in 742, and was retained as a sort of court poet; he led a wild life there for three years until he fell out of favour. He continued his wandering, sometimes riding high with singing girls in train, never it appears deprived for very long. In 757 he entered the service of Prince Lin, who was making a bid for the throne; the prince was defeated and Li Po was banished, but reprieved on his way to exile. He died three years later, still a *Taugenichts*. He took four wives, but none detained him for very long.

Li Po's addiction to wine is legendary, and many are the poems which revel in it. But his poems show a man of many parts: he nourished romantic political ambitions as well as an interest in alchemy and a love for Taoist 'spirit journeys'. His contemporaries seem to have been most impressed by his genius and his personal appearance – the term 'banished immortal' is used of him. He could turn his hand effortlessly to any kind or length of poem, and his richly varied experiences provided inexhaustible subject-matter; he has provided verbal paintings of most of China's famous mountains and streams. Familiarity with the folk song probably contributed to the vigour and fluency of his style. He preferred simple to ornate language and paid little heed to formal rules. His name is often coupled with that of ⇨ Tu Fu as the greatest of Chinese poets. He is now praised in China for his 'positive Romanticism'. [D E P]

Arthur Waley, *The Poetry and Career of Li Po* (1958).

Lieh Tzu (possibly fl. *c.* 500 B.C.). Chinese philosopher. His full name was Lieh Yü-kʻou. He is traditionally regarded as author of the book bearing his name, but as the latter shows signs of Buddhist influence, it was probably not written until about A.D. 300. Some scholars feel that it may have been written earlier, and that parts bearing evidence to the contrary were only added in later editions.

The *Lieh Tzu* is one of the three major Taoist works. It is arranged in 8 chapters, 7 of which express a philosophy similar to that of the ⇨ *Lao Tzu* and ⇨ *Chuang Tzu*. The writing is mostly in the form of parables and sayings with occasional verses, and is on the whole clearer and easier to understand than the other two works. Chapter 7, which purports to express the ideas of a philosopher called Yang Chu, propounds a form of hedonism, and appears to have been written by a different hand. The rest may well be the work of one author, although some passages are borrowed from earlier Taoist works, notably the *Chuang Tzu*. The whole is suffused with a sense of fatalism and the idea of the relativity of values, and the Yang Chu chapter, though not truly Taoist in content, could be said to be a possible corollary of Taoism. As life is short, and man should not meddle with the natural course of things, is it not best to enjoy himself while he may? Taoism is, however, generally opposed to excess, which it maintains will harm the body and shorten life.

The *Lieh Tzu*, together with the other Taoist works, has had a profound influence on Chinese art. Chinese landscape painting, which portrays man as an insignificant part of nature, is an expression of the naturalism first expounded by the Taoists. The *Lieh Tzu* is also an important work of literature in its own right. [J D C]

A. C. Graham, *The Book of Lieh-tzu* (1960).

Liu E (1857–1909). Chinese novelist and reformer. Born in Kiangsu Province, East China. While young he cultivated many interests, including medicine, flood control, poetry and music, most of them reflected in his novel. He joined a society which sought to fuse Confucian, Buddhist and Taoist teachings. For a time he practised medicine, and in 1888 helped to control a Yellow River flood. As a reformer he attempted to establish several modern business enterprises in China, but they failed. While the foreign armies occupied Peking in 1900 he procured the imperial grain, which at the time was controlled by the Russians, for distribution to the people. This act was later utilized by his enemies to bring about his banishment. He died in exile.

His best known work, *Lao Tsʻan yu-chi* (*The Travels of Lao Tsʻan*, tr. H. Shadick, 1952), was one of a spate of novels published serially in the new journals of the last decade of the Chʻing Dynasty. It appeared between 1904 and 1907. The hero, Lao Tsʻan, is an itinerant scholar who travels the Shantung countryside practising medicine and acting in a philanthropic manner. He rescues victims of tyrannical officials, whom the author regards as a greater curse than the corrupt inefficient ones. Though loosely constructed, in the traditional Chinese manner, and relying to some extent on hackneyed themes, *The Travels of Lao Tsʻan* is imbued with the humanity, learning and power of observation of its author. It contains descriptions of scenery and musical performances which critics attest to have few equals in Chinese literature. [J D C]

Lo Kuan-Chung (*c.* 1400). Chinese novelist. Supposed author of *San-kuo-chih-yen-i* (tr. Brewitt-Taylor, *San Kuo, or Romance of the Three Kingdoms*, 1925). The original material of this novel is contained in the standard history of the Three Kingdoms, and concerns the exploits and stratagems of the generals and statesmen of the period A.D. 184–280. But the original has been embellished by the author, or authors, probably with the aid of story-tellers' versions of the same events, so that the novel has been described as being three parts fiction and seven parts fact. The narrative is disjointed and the style alternates between literary and colloquial; nevertheless the characters are sharply delineated and much of the incident dramatically unfolded, and the work is regarded as one of the great Chinese novels. Part of its popularity is due to the fact that much of it has been dramatized, so that it is familiar even to the illiterate. It has served as a popular handbook of chivalry and military strategy for several centuries. [J D C]

Lu Hsün. ⇨ Chou Shu-jen.

M

Mādhava Paṇikkar, Kavalam (1895–1964). Indian statesman and writer. He is known in the west for his achievements as a statesman – he was at different times Indian ambassador to the United Nations, China and France – and as a historian. Noteworthy among many distinguished historical works are *A Survey of Indian History* (1947) and *Asia and Western Dominance* (1952). At home he is esteemed also as a prolific and important writer in Malayalam of poetry, plays, autobiography and historical novels. Of these the best known is perhaps *Kērala simham* (1942), set in Kerala at the time of the 1857 Mutiny. [R E A]

'Mahābhārata' (*c.*400 B.C.–A.D. 200). The great epic of India, said to be the longest poem in the world. The work is attributed to Vyāsa, compiler of the ◊ Veda, but is evidently the product of several centuries. The main story celebrates a fratricidal war fought by the sons of two half-brothers over the succession to the kingdom of the Bhāratas, whose founder is eponymous hero of India. Blind Dhṛtarāṣṭra, though elder, is prohibited from reigning, and Pāṇḍu accepts sovereignty. The 100 sons of the former, led by Duryodhana, do not accept the succession, and entice Yudhiṣṭhira, the eldest son of Pāṇḍu, to gamble away his birthright in a rigged dice game. The exiled Yudhiṣṭhira and his four brothers, Bhīma, Arjuna, Nakula and Sahadeva, ally with God Kṛṣṇa and determine to reclaim their kingdom. The great 18-day battle results in the total victory of the Pāṇḍavas.

But the main story occupies half of the *Mahābhārata*; interspersed is a veritable encyclopedia of folklore, story, myth, and philosophy, often bearing little relation to the tale. The older courtly epic has been made the vehicle for conveying a great mass of other material generally inculcating a brahminical ethic. Such additions are the famous religious poem, the ◊ *Bhagavadgītā,* the stories of Nala and Sāvitrī, and an abridgement of the ◊ *Rāmāyaṇa.* [E G]

Tr. P. C. Roy (Calcutta, 1887–96).
E. W. Hopkins, *The Great Epic of India* (New York, 1901), and *Legends of India* (New Haven, 1928).

'Mahāvaṃsa'. The Great Chronicle of Ceylon. A dynastic history of Ceylon from the 5th century B.C. onwards, written in Pali verse of an epic literary quality. The original was compiled by a Ceylonese monk named Mahānāma in the 5th century A.D., but this was added to at various subsequent times down to the 19th century. The latter portions are sometimes called the *Cūlavaṃsa,* or Lesser Chronicle. This work, noteworthy for being one of the very few Indian historical records, is translated by W. Geiger (1912 and 1930; reprinted 1950 and 1958). The greater part is in the form of two epic chronicles, the heroes of which are the kings Duṭṭhagāmani (161–137 B.C.) and Parkramabāhu I (1153–86) respectively. The writers' interests are predominantly religious, and events unimportant from this point of view, such as the activities of the Portuguese and Dutch invaders in the latter sections, are touched on only briefly. [C H B R]

Malay Literature. The Malays of the Malay Peninsula, of Eastern Sumatra and to a lesser extent of Indonesia and the whole Archipelago share a literature in common. Though there are few manuscripts extant written before 1600, there is other evidence that written literature existed in the 15th and probably in the 14th century, and the mythical and legendary material which forms a great part of the literature unquestionably goes back at least 1,000, and perhaps 2,000 years before 1600.

Malaya's geographical position on the central trade routes between the Middle and Far East has been reflected in the variety of cultural influences seen in the literature, especially from the Arabic-speaking countries, Persia and India, Sumatra and Java, and to a lesser extent China. There are many Indian-type romances as well as versions of the *Rāmāyaṇa* and ◊ *Mahābhārata* picaresque works based on the Javanese ◊ *Panji* tales and Muslim theological treatises as well as popular missionary writing. Most of this is adapted rather than translated.

The best genres of Malay literature, however, are the most typically indigenous: the beast stories and folk-romances still told by illiterate story-tellers (◊ Penglipor Lara) in the up-country villages (many of these are still unrecorded); the historical works, e.g. the ◊ *Sejarah Melayu*; and the poetry, especially the typical Malay 4-line verse called ◊ *pantun, sha'er* and a type of rhapsodic blank verse often of very high quality sometimes called *gurindam.*

Characteristics of early Malay literature (say, up to 1800) are anonymity of authorship; many differing versions of the texts through constant and arbitrary copying of manuscripts through the centuries; lack of sophistication (to the western mind); a significant difference between court (written) and rural (oral) materials; and the embodiment of group and social attitudes rather than individual. Much of this literature is still in manuscript in libraries in Djakarta, Singapore, London and Leiden.

In the early 17th century a group of Sumatran writers representing Sufi religious teaching and thought from India and Persia (though they wrote in Malay) made a valuable contribution in religious and historical works (◊ Abdul Rauf Singkel, Shams'uddin Pasai, and Nuruddin ar-Raniri) and in mystical poetry (◊ Hamzah Fansuri).

A great advance was signalled early in the 19th century by ◊ Abdullah bin Abdul Kadir, usually known as Munshi Abdullah, whose intelligence and original ideas of life and society, showing a strong contrast with older literature, eased the Malay transition into the modern world with its increased Western influences.

The period of more intensive colonial influence in Malaya (*c.* 1870–1957) seems to have inhibited indigenous literary effort – higher education was almost entirely in English during this period – and little of value was written. There have been signs of a renaissance in the last 10 years or so, much of it following on the notable post-war ◊ Indonesian literary achievement which has been an important stimulus to peninsular writers.

The total output of Malay literature may be said to be relatively small. Yet an immense amount of research and study remains to be done and it is proper at present to speak of the poverty of our own knowledge rather than the paucity of writings. The more it becomes possible to relate the literature to its society and environment, the more important and significant it becomes and the more impressive its qualities. A romanized script is now normally used, though the Arabic-type script (called *Jawi*) formerly used for older literature is still used for religious and some other writings. [J C B]

Winstedt, *C M L*; C. Hooykaas, *Perintis Sastra* (Kuala Lumpur, 1963) (in Malay).

Maltese Literature. ◊ Psaila.

Māṇikkavācakar. ◊ Nāyaṉmār.

'Maṇimēkalai'. ◊ Cāttaṉār.

Mantu, Sa'adat Hasan (1912–55). Urdu short-story writer. He was born in Sambālpūr, in the Amritsar district of Panjāb, India, and educated at Amritsar and later at the Muslim University, Aligarh. He then worked in Lahore, Bombay and Delhi in journalism, films and broadcasting. His literary activity began early. His first works included translations from Victor Hugo, Tolstoy, Gorki, Oscar Wilde and other Europeans; but most of his work is original. Short stories (from 1940 he published more than 20 collections) comprise the greater part of his output, but he also wrote numbers of radio dramas, sketches and essays. His preoccupation with sexual themes and with eccentricities of behaviour led to prosecutions for obscenity, but most were unsuccessful. There is little which European taste would find obscene. His best writing is frank, realistic and informed by a deep but unobtrusive sympathy. After the formation of Pakistan he settled in Lahore. Heavy drinking in his later years hastened his death. [R R]

Black Milk, tr. Hāmid Jalāl (Karachi, 1955) (11 stories).

'Manu' ('Manusmṛti') (probably compiled 200 B.C.–A.D. 200). The best-known ancient Indian treatise on religious law and social obligation (*dharma* and caste); the work itself is only one specimen of a vast literature, termed *dharmaśātra*, and is neither the oldest nor the most authoritative.

'Manu' is the eponymous ancestor of the human race (cognate with the English *man*); the 'law book' attributed to him is in fact a compilation or 'recollection' (*smṛti*) of prescriptions and observances relating to various previous (Vedic) schools and attempts to generalize and systematize those rules of conduct to all of Indian society. It constitutes a principal source for what is known of the everyday life and custom during the epic and early classical period.

The 'laws of Manu' are primarily concerned with regulation of the two highest castes, brahmin (priestly) and kṣatriya (princely), for the former regulating the various sacraments, notably the *upanayana* (or initiation to Vedic study), kinds of marriage, daily rituals and offerings of the householder, permitted foods, kinds of ritual impurity and their expiations, etc.; for the latter, duties and rights of the king, administration of justice, especially relating to the collection of taxes, payment of debts, sale of property, litigation, rights of succession, etc.

The impression left by the *Manusmṛti* is

that of a work of theory; classifications and distinctions abound and little attention is paid to the practical problems of evidence and judgement. There is little indication that the text was ever strictly applied as a statute (◊ Kauṭilya), despite the English title 'laws'. [E G]

The Laws of Manu, tr. G. Bühler (Sacred Books of the East, 1886).

J. Jolly, *Hindu Law and Custom*, tr. B. Ghosh (Calcutta, 1928); P. V. Kane, *History of Dharmaśāstra* (5 vols., Bombay, 1930–35); J. D. Mayne, *A Treatise on Hindu Law and Usage* (Madras, 1938).

Man-yō-shu. ◊ Ōtomo Yakamochi.

Mao Tun. ◊ Shen Yen-ping.

al-Maqrīzī, Ahmad ibn 'Alī (1364–1442). Egyptian historian. He came of a family of scholars. His first public appointment was that of a deputy judge in Cairo, where he also lectured on Tradition (the science of the Traditions of the Prophet has always been extremely important in Islam, for determining both religious and legal precedent). In 1408 he was sent to Damascus as controller of a hospital, where he taught in several colleges. He returned to Cairo some ten years later, and remained there, apart from five years' residence in Mecca, for the rest of his life, devoting himself to scholarship.

Al-Maqrīzī produced histories of the Fātimid caliphs of Egypt and of the Ayyūbids, the dynasty of Salāh al-Dīn (Saladin). He also wrote a detailed topographical description of Egypt, which catalogues the physical features and towns, mosques, churches, etc., of the country, and contains accounts of the various peoples, their customs, systems of taxation, calendars, and a large amount of other historical, political and theological information. He also planned a vast biographical dictionary, left unfinished. Al-Maqrīzī composed a number of monographs on historical subjects, and also on Islamic coins, weights and measures, and bees.

Like the works of many Arab authors, those of al-Maqrīzī are largely compilations from other books; as most of these are now lost, however, al-Maqrīzī's works are particularly valuable. [A S T]

Histoire des Sultans Mamlouks, tr. M. Quatremère (2 vols., Paris, 1837–44); *Livre des admonitions et de l'observation*, tr. P. Casanova (Cairo, 1906, etc.); *Le traité des famines*, tr. G. Wiet (Leiden, 1962).
E of I.

Matsuo Bashō. ◊ Bashō.

'Maw-gun'. A type of ◊ Burmese poem in the 'classical' quadri-syllabic line. The typical *maw-gun* glorifies the king on the occasion of some achievement such as the conquest of new territory, the building of a pagoda, the construction of a canal, etc. Its greatest exponent was Nawade II (1755–1840), a courtier who wrote over 14 *maw-gun*, including the famous *Vilāsinī* on the acquisition by the king of a white elephant, considered in Burma a symbol of power. [J W A O]

Mawlânâ. ◊ Jalâl al-Dîn.

'Ménak' ('Nobleman') or **'Sĕrat Ménak'** ('The Book of the Nobleman'). One of the best known and most voluminous ◊ Javanese poems. It deals with the chivalrous exploits of Amir Hamzah, the uncle of the Prophet Muhammad. It is not an original Javanese work, but an enlargement of the Malay *Hikayat Amir Hamzah*, which in its turn was an adaptation of a Persian work brought from India, whence the *Sufi* mystics introduced their particular form of Islam. The *Ménak* has been published, but not in any European translation. [C H]

Ed. in Javanese script (8 vols., Bataira and Semarang, 1854–87); reprint in forty 100-page pamphlets by Balé Pustaka, Batavia, during the thirties; contents in Dutch in A. C. Vreede, 'Catalogus van de Javaansche, en Madoereesche Handschriften der Leidsche Universiteits-Bibliotheek' (Leiden, 1892).

'Milinda-Pañha' ('The Questions of Milinda'). A lengthy Buddhist text in Pali (perhaps originally in some other Prakrit), containing a philosophical dialogue between the sage Nāgasena and the Greco-Bactrian king 'Milinda' (Menander), who ruled in north-west India about 100 B.C. The book as we have it has been added to later, but the original portions (roughly the first 3 of its 7 books) are one of the finest examples of early Indian literary prose. In Burma, though not in Ceylon, this work is accounted a canonical book of the fifth *nikāya* of the *suttapiṭaka* (collection of discourses). [C H B R]

Tr. I. B. Horner (Sacred Books of the Buddhists, 1963–4).
Winternitz, *G I L*, ii; B. C. Law, *History of Pali Literature* (1933).

Minangkabau Literature. The Minangkabau are a vigorous and highly intelligent people of West Sumatra who have a peculiar matrilineal social organization. Their speech differs from standard ◊ Malay more in pronunciation than in structure and vocabulary. They have therefore been able to share in, and contribute to, the literary heritage of the Malay-speaking world as a whole. In addition they have a considerable literature in their own dialect – *pantun* (quatrains), *ibarat* (short parables in verse), *talibun* and *padato* (odes), riddles and, the most important, *kaba* (stories told in rhythmic prose). The oldest and major work in the latter form is the *Kaba Tjindue Mato*, a state myth justifying the balance and harmony of Islam and of Minangkabau matrilineal custom. Modern Minangkabau writers write in ◊ Indonesian, a language they have taken the lead in fashioning out of the older form of standard Malay, and which has thereby acquired many Minangkabau words and turns of phrase. [E C G B]

Rantjak dilabueh, a Minangkabau kaba, ed. and tr. A. E. Johns (Cornell, 1958).
A. L. van Hasselt, *De Talen en Letterkunde van Midden-Sumatra* (Leiden, 1881).

Mishima Yukio (1925–). Japanese novelist. He was born in Tokyo, where his father was a senior government official. By the time of his graduation in law from Tokyo University in 1947, he had established a considerable reputation as a writer by his contributions to literary reviews. As early as in 1944 a collection of his stories had appeared. He entered the civil service, but resigned shortly afterwards and has since devoted himself entirely to writing.

He has an absorbing interest in psychopathic states, derived it is said, from the influence of the French psycho-analytical method. Yet he has certainly not cut himself off completely from Japanese models. He covers a broader range of subjects than the Japanese Naturalists and autobiographical novelists. He has none of their sentimentality and maintains a sophisticated objectivity. His characters are often young post-war Japanese, with only loose connexions with the past, and uncertainty in the present. *Kamen no Kokuhaku* (1949; tr. M. Weatherby, *Confessions of a Mask*, 1960) is a study of the sexual awakening of its hero, and his realization of his perversion. *Ai no kawaki* ('The Thirst for Love') (1951) is a tragic tale of a woman's search for happiness. *Kinjiki* ('Forbidden Pleasure') (1952) describes an old scholar's craving for a handsome youth. *Kinkakuji* (*The Temple of the Golden Pavilion*) (1956) is a fictional account of an actual incident, the principal character being a trainee-priest who becomes obsessed with the temple and finally burns it down. The translation of this novel has drawn reluctant praise from Western reviewers, who contrast the brilliance of the author's methods with the unpleasantness of the theme. A different sort of novel is *Shiosai* (1954; tr. M. Weatherby, *The Sound of Waves*, 1956), which describes a modern idyll on an island in the Inland Sea. Here Western technique is employed without particular success.

Mishima is also a dramatist, writing plays in both modern and traditional form and, most notably, some interesting modern versions of *nō* plays.

Whether his reputation will be a lasting one in Japan is not sure. Much of his writing is superficial and his themes are often sordid. But there is no doubt that he excels at describing the post-war generation, and because of this and his intelligibility to Western readers, translations of his works seem to have made their mark in America, where he is taken as typifying the modern Japanese literary scene. [C J D]

Five Modern Noh Plays, tr. D. Keene (1957); *The Temple of the Golden Pavilion*, tr. I. Morris (1957); *After the Banquet*, tr. D. Keene (1963).

Mishnah. A compilation of Jewish law, next in authority to the Hebrew scriptures. It contains the core of the Oral Law, traditionally believed to have been received by Moses from God along with the Written Law, and forms the basis of the ◊ Talmud. In the Mishnah, the substance of the Oral Law is presented in 6 main sections (*sedarim*): *Zeraim* deals with laws of agriculture and the harvest share of the priests, the levites and the poor; *Moed* with the Sabbath and set feasts; *Nashim* with laws affecting women (marriage and divorce); *Nezikin* with property rights and legal proceedings; *Kodashim* with the vows, ritual slaughter, and sacrifices of the Temple; and *Toharot* with the laws of uncleanness. Each *seder* is divided into subsections called *massek·toth*, or tractates, 63 in number, in turn divided into chapters and paragraphs (*misnayyoth*).

The Mishnah was codified in the second century A.D. by Rabbi Judah the Patriarch, though when exactly it was written down is disputed. Basically it embodies the religious traditions and beliefs of the Pharisees of the time of Christ, certain sayings and interpretations being attributed to particular teachers (*Tannaim*) going back possibly to the third century B.C.

The language is Hebrew, and the style mostly the dry preciseness expected of a catalogue of laws. Occasionally there is a more narrative tone, but more often a brevity which is obscure without previous knowledge of the subject.

There are several complete manuscripts of the Mishnah, and innumerable editions of the *textus receptus* based on the edition of Prague, 1614–17. A scholarly edition of the Mishnah, with German translation and commentary, was commenced in Berlin in 1912 by G. Beer and O. Holtzmann and is still in progress. There is a very thorough English translation with good Introduction and notes by H. Danby (1933). [R F H]

H. L. Strack, *Introduction to the Talmud and Midrash* (Philadelphia, 1931).

Mon Literature. 11th-century inscriptions show the language of the Mons, a Buddhist people of Lower Burma and the Menam Valley, as a fully developed literary vehicle, and from then on there is a continuous tradition, submerged but not broken in times of political eclipse. The literature began with translations, and then adaptations, of Pali texts, and religious works have always dominated. Even in the secular field factual compilations of various kinds overshadow legend and epic; drama and the novel have never been greatly cultivated.

To the 16th century belong two notable biographies of hero-kings, *Rajadhiraj* and *Bayinnaung*. The first celebrates the passing of the heroic age, the second hails the new epoch of mass armies and international military adventures. *Rajadhiraj* is ascribed to Bayinnaung's general the Duke of Dala, who may have written its companion also. Most early authors, however, remain anonymous, the first name to achieve general renown being *Athwa Sayadaw* (fl. 1740–75), a prolific monk whose *History of Kings* (tr. R. Halliday, *Journal of the Burma Research Society*, xiii, 1, 1923) incidentally recounts the fortunes of the Shwe Dagon pagoda in Rangoon. Another monk, Nandasara, was the author of *Prince Asah* (1825; tr. R. Halliday, Rangoon, 1923), a long narrative poem on a theme from the legendary beginnings of the Pegu kingdom in Lower Burma.

Though the printing press now sustains a modest output, small editions and a reverence for the literature of the past have combined to prevent any great contemporary flowering. [H L S]

R. Halliday, *The Talaings* (Rangoon, 1917).

Mongolian Literature. Mongolian literary history opens with the mid-13th-century *Secret History of the Mongols*, an account more epic than strictly historical of the genealogy and life of Jenghiz Khan. It preserves a great deal of older folklore and legend, much in alliterative verse form, and is uninfluenced by the lamaist Buddhism which coloured most later chronicles, notably the 17th-century *Precious Summary* of Sanang Setsen and the *Golden Summary*.

Few literary texts survive from the 13th–16th centuries, though fragments of poetry have been discovered, notably a version of the Alexander epic and, written on birch bark, a poetic dialogue, a genre frequently occurring in Mongolian folk literature. Later works – chronicles, epics, collections of legends, popular religious rituals – incorporate much traditional material relating to early social customs and preserving episodic and didactic literature associated with the name of Jenghiz Khan. Mongolia's final conversion to Buddhism in the late 16th century, followed by her subjugation by China, opened the way to overwhelming literary influence from abroad, and translations from Tibetan lamaist literature – religious and medical treatises, rituals, prayers and hagiography, as well as collections of tales – form the bulk of printed literature of the 17th and 18th centuries. Translations of many of the popular Chinese novels also circulated in manuscript, while episodes from them were worked into poetical form and sung by bards to instrumental accompaniment. Printing was practically a monopoly of the lamaseries, both in Mongolia and also in Peking, the great centre of the Mongolian book trade, so that indigenous secular literature – epics, ballads, lyrics, song-dramas, ceremonial improvisations, proverbs and the like – was transmitted orally for the most part.

The year 1921, the year of the successful Soviet-supported revolution against the Chinese, marks a definitive new departure in Mongol literature. Mongol authors stand henceforth completely under the influence of Soviet literature and follow the line of 'socialist realism'. The most important work of this period is probably B. Rintchen's historical novel *Dawn on the Steppes* (1951–5). No modern literature appears to have been published in Europe in translation, but a few stories by the well-known scholar and writer Ts. Damdinsuren (b. 1908) and others have appeared in New Delhi in English. [C B]

Die Geheime Geschichte der Mongolen, tr. Erich Haenisch (Leipzig, 1948).

W. Heissig, 'Mongolische Literatur', in *Handbuch der Orientalistik*, I, v (Leiden/Cologne, 1964); L. K. Gerasimovich, *Literatura Mongol'skoi Narodnoi Respubliki 1921–1964* (Leningrad, 1965).

Mori Ōgai (1862–1922). Japanese novelist. He was born at Tsuwano, in Shimane prefecture, and studied medicine and German. From 1884 to 1888 he continued his studies in Germany. Later he was to rise to the highest rank available to a military health expert. There was another side to his life, however, for he produced a large number of translations from European languages, mainly German, some poetry and drama and, above all, many novels and short stories. It is for his novels that he is remembered. His work falls into three periods. During the first, as a result of his stay in Germany, the influence of the German Romantics was very strong: a typical product of this period is *Maihime* ('The Dancing Girl') (1890), set in Europe and telling of a tragic love affair. The second period is characterized by his opposition to the Naturalist school of writers, who were preoccupied with their art to the exclusion of other livelihood and with the influence of carnal appetites upon human character. For Mori Ōgai writing was a leisure occupation, its aim being to entertain both reader and author. He saw self-discipline as a cure for the Naturalists' preoccupation with sex and squalor. Products of this period are *Vita sexualis* (1909) in which he seeks to show that sex is only one ingredient of the full life, and *Gan* (1913; tr. Goldstein and Ochiai, *The Wild Geese*, 1959), a romantic tale of tragic love. Finally, Mori Ōgai turned to modern versions of legends and historical incidents, with obvious admiration for the old military virtues. Examples are *Sakai jiken* ('The Sakai Incident') (1914); *Sanshō-dayū* (1915; tr. T. Fukude, Tokyo, 1952); and *Takasebune* (1916; tr. G. W. Paschall, in *The Heart is Alone*, Tokyo, 1957).

His style is always a little heavy, partly, perhaps, owing to his German training, and his unbending dignity and seriousness of tone both perhaps contributed to the ponderous effect of his manner. As time went on, however, there was an increasing flexibility. Though his work has aged, many present-day Japanese have a nostalgic admiration for him. [C J D]

Mowlavi. ⇨ Jalâl al-Dîn.

Munshi, Kanaiyalāl Maniklāl (1887–). Indian statesman and writer. The elder statesman of Gujarati literature. He has written over 70 books including drama, fiction and history, but is chiefly known as a historical novelist and a historian of Gujarati literature. He was a friend and supporter of Gandhi from the beginning, played a leading role in Congress and since independence has been a minister in the central government of India and a governor of the state of Uttar Pradesh (1952–7). [I M P R]

K. M. Munshi, *Gujarat and Its Literature* (Bombay, 1935).

Munshi Abdullah. ⇨ Abdullah bin Abdul Kadir Munshi.

Murasaki Shikibu (*c.* 980–*c.* 1030). Japanese novelist and diarist. She lived during the so-called Fujiwara period, when the family of this name had a powerful hold over the imperial court in Kyoto. Her father was a member of a minor branch of the family, and had a normal government career, finishing as a provincial governor before his retirement from the world in 1016. She eavesdropped upon her brother's Chinese lessons and, though such knowledge was considered most unladylike at the time, acquired some ability herself. She married just before the turn of the century and had children, but her husband died in 1001. When her father was posted to a distant province, rather than take her with him and deprive her of a chance of a decent re-marriage, he found her a position in the service of the Empress Akiko, where she remained until her death. Her diary (tr. Annie S. Omori and Kochi Doi, in *Diaries of Court Ladies of Old Japan*, 1921), which closes in 1010, gives us much information about the life and people at her mistress's court. Akiko was a serious-minded woman who deplored the frivolities that she saw in the entourage of other imperial ladies, and although Murasaki writes longingly in her diary of the gaiety to be found elsewhere, the impression remains that it was at Akiko's court that she was most at home. She has left miniature descriptions of some of her famous contemporaries. She forms an interesting contrast with the witty, frivolous, ◊ Sei Shōnagon.

It was at Akiko's court that she wrote the great novel *Genji-monogatari* (*The Tale of Genji*, tr. Arthur Waley, 1935). The exact date of writing, and how long it took to write, is uncertain. It is a work of considerable length (54 chapters) and a development of style that can be discerned in its course may be due either to the author's increasing maturity, or to different authorship of the last 10 chapters. It was probably written to be read out aloud for the entertainment of Akiko, and its writing may have taken years. It was certainly complete by 1022. The first 44 chapters tell the story of Prince Genji, against an imaginary court background, very similar to the one Murasaki served in. Genji's adventures are all amorous, but the work is of great subtlety and charm, and not at all indecent. Its delicate, allusive style reflects the intricacies of motive and thought of the participants. The last 10 chapters deal with some adventures of Genji's putative son, and have an interest all of their own. The work is certainly the greatest achievement of Japanese literature, and is among the mighty novels of the world. Waley's translation is faithful, though some consider that it does the original more than justice. [C J D]

Ivan Morris, *The World of the Shining Prince* (1964).

Mushakōji Saneatsu (1885–). Japanese novelist and dramatist. He was born in Tokyo, and has spent his life in literature and in humanitarian enterprises. Believing in the fundamental goodness of human beings, he has twice tried to establish model village communities. He has been strongly influenced by Christianity. From the first he has opposed Naturalism in his writings and to this end founded in 1910 with ◊ Shiga Naoya and other novelists a literary magazine *Shirakaba* ('White Birch'). His plays can be considered with his stories, for they were probably not written to be performed but to be read. Both often demonstrate the author's view of the refining influence of life's misfortunes, as distinct from the Naturalist attitude that suffering brings a demoralization. His work suffers from a sameness of theme and style, and should therefore be read in small quantities, but it has considerable interest. [C J D]

Friendship, tr. R. Matsumoto (Tokyo, 1958); *Judas' Explanation* and *John, On Hearing Judas' Explanation*, tr. R. N. McKinnon, in *The Heart is Alone* (Tokyo, 1957).

al-Mutanabbī, Ahmad ibn al-Husain (915–965). Arab poet. Born in Kūfa. In 928 he went to Syria and studied at Damascus. His ambition was to be a professional poet, and since the necessary patrons proved slow in coming forward, he set himself up as a prophet and led an unsuccessful political–religious revolt. After two years' imprisonment he returned to poetry, and led a wandering life, earning small rewards from men of little importance. After some success in Damascus, he was received at the courts of rulers in Aleppo, Egypt and Shiraz. He was killed by Beduin when travelling from Persia to Baghdad.

The Arabs regard al-Mutanabbī as one of their greatest poets. He is the principal figure of the 'Modern' school, which began to break away from the traditional themes and ways of expression of the Pre-Islamic poets, long regarded as the only ones suitable for poetry. The

'Moderns' made considerable use of Badī' (Innovation) – their new, and, to conservative poets and critics, shocking images, figures of speech and plays on words. The old type of poetry, in which poets who had scarcely ever seen the desert wept over the deserted camping-sites of their loved ones, and described in painstaking detail the points of their camels, continued to be written, side by side with the 'Modern' type. Al-Mutanabbī did not abandon the *qasīda* (ode), but transformed it, and made it into an organic whole, with theme leading naturally to theme, instead of a series of almost unconnected lines.

Unfortunately the poetry of the 'Moderns' degenerated as that of the older poets had. The 'Moderns' were educated more as philologists than as poets, and their poetry tended to concern itself more with extravagance of language than with feeling. Western readers find some of this bombast already present in the work of al-Mutanabbī, but ◊ Abu'l-'Alā al-Ma'arrī once said of him, 'I should sometimes have liked to change a word in his poems, but could never think of a better.' [A S T]

Tr. A. J. Arberry (1967).
R. Blachère, *Un poète arabe du IVe siècle de l'Hégire* (Paris, 1935); Nicholson, *L H A; E of I.*

N

Nagai Kafū (1879–1959). Japanese novelist. He was born in Tokyo. His family was of warrior descent. In his younger days he acquired a considerable knowledge and taste for all the entertainments which had survived from feudal Japan, especially the popular drama – *kabuki.* At the same time he learned novel-writing, like ◊ Higuchi Ichiyō and ◊ Tayama Katai, from a master, in his case Hirotsu Ryūrō, a writer of tragic realist novels. Nagai Kafū became involved in the Naturalist craze, and in 1902 wrote *Jigoku no hana* ('Flowers of Hell'), avowedly influenced by Zola, to demonstrate man's animal nature. From 1903 to 1908 he was travelling in America and France. On his return, Tokyo apparently disgusted him with its brash modernity, compared with the old-fashioned city it was when he left, and compared, also, with the charms of Paris. At all events, after some sketches and short stories describing his travels, he started again to write novels with a Japanese background, into which he puts all his nostalgia for the past. They are almost all stories of *geisha* and their misfortunes, for in spite of his romantic view of the past, he does not make it out to be a golden age. On the contrary, he tells with calm objectivity of the tragic lives of his heroines. Perhaps the best of the novels of this period is *Sumida-gawa* (1909; tr. D. Keene, *The River Sumida*, in Keene, *MJL*). Subsequently he transferred his interest to bar-waitresses, prostitutes, and to dancers and performers of Asakusa, one of the pleasure quarters of Tokyo. After *Sumida-gawa* his best-known work is *Bokutō kidan* (*Strange Tale from East of the River*, tr. E. Seidensticker, see below), written in 1937, in his 'prostitute period'. Again nostalgic for old survivals, it depicts a novelist at work, looking for material for a story to be set in the sordid surroundings he so faithfully describes. It is the work of a great literary artist, but is spoilt for some Western readers by the author's apparent lack of feeling for his characters. [C J D]

Hydrangea, tr. I. Morris, in Morris, *M J S*; *Kafū the Scribbler*, tr. E. Seidensticker (1965).

'Nagarakrĕtāgama'. ◊ Prapañcha.

'Nālaṭiyār'. ◊ Vaḷḷuvar.

'Nālāyirappirapantam'. ◊ Āḷvār.

Nammāḷvār. ◊ Āḷvār.

Nārāyaṇa Mēnōn, Vaḷḷattōḷ (1879–1958). Indian poet. Like so many of the Indian poets of his day, Vaḷḷattōḷ found his inspiration in his compatriots' struggle for self-rule. He wrote in his mother tongue, Malayalam, the language of the state of Kerala. Previously he had translated the ◊ *Rāmāyaṇa* from Sanskrit and written a long poem in the style of the Sanskrit poets. A third period found him the poet of social justice. In old age he translated the ◊ *Ṛgveda.*

Though a Hindu, he showed a tolerant sympathy for the messages of Islam, Buddhism, Jainism and Christianity. His poem on Mary Magdalene is so far his only work to appear in English translation (Erik de Mauny, 1952). [R E A]

K. M. Panikkar, 'Vallothol of Kerala', in *Indian Literature*, I, 1, New Delhi, Oct. 1957; V. K. Narayana Menon, 'Vallathol', in *Indian Literature*, I, 2, Apr.–Sept. 1958.

Natsume Sōseki (1867–1926). Japanese novelist. He was born in Tokyo and graduated in English at Tokyo University in 1893. He then taught at schools in different parts of Japan, and wrote *haiku* as a hobby. From 1900 to 1902 he studied in London. His return to Japan was followed by a productive period of novel writing. Two which appeared in 1905 are well known: *Rondon-tō* ('The Tower of London'), a romantic tale in which the history of the Tower is set against realistic descriptions of London; and *Waga hai wa neko de aru* (*I Am a Cat*, tr. K. Shibata and M. Kai, Tokyo, 1961), a witty, satirical description of the world of the author seen through the eyes of his cat. It is said that the success of *I Am a Cat* caused him to take up literary work as a career. In *Botchan* (1906; tr. Mori Yasutarō, Tokyo, 1924) he makes use of his experiences as a schoolmaster. He describes with realism and humour the encounter between a new teacher in a provincial school and the rest of the staff, whose integrity leaves much to be desired. *Kusamakura* ('With Grass for Pillow', 1906; tr. A. Turney as *The Three-Cornered World*, 1965) is usually held to be his best work. It presents the mind of an artist who is attempting to apply to himself an aesthetic discipline of non-feeling, and the conflict which arises between this effort at detachment and the emotions which he cannot stifle. Sōseki's attitude is quite different from that of the Naturalists with their humourless descriptions of squalor and lust. In these novels he shows his interest in the problems of ethics and idealism. But overlying all is an objective, humorous tone and a realism that may well have been derived from English originals.

He gave up academic life in 1907, and joined a national newspaper as literary editor. In 1911, illness interrupted his writing. When he resumed, his work had a sombreness in marked contrast to the cheerful tone of earlier novels: this was due partly to his personal suffering, but also to the ebbing away of the optimism that had pervaded Japan after her victory over the Russians, when equality with the West seemed attained. In his last novels, Sōseki shows a developed power of psychological analysis, *Kokoro* (*Heart*; tr. E. McClellan, Chicago, 1956) is typical of this last period. His death occurred while he was working on a long novel, *Meian* ('Light and Darkness').

Sōseki's style is polished, and his observation of human character of the highest order. His novels bear the stamp of authority which leaves the reader with a feeling of satisfaction, though they use no facile devices to arouse interest or excitement. [C J D]

'Nāṭyaśāstra'. The oldest and most authoritative treatise on Indian dramatic art (mainly 500–700?; some parts much older); it is attributed to Bharata Muni. The drama, as a poetic style, is as old as the 1st century A.D.; fragments of dramas attributable to ⇨ Aśvaghoṣa have been recently discovered.

The *Nāṭyaśāstra* is a compendium designed for the various participants in the dramatic craft, from carpenter to critic. It is important for its theory of dramatic delectation (*rasa*), by which poet, actor and critic participate in an affective emotional unity which transcends their particular states and resembles, according to Abhinavagupta, the freedom of ultimate release (*mokṣā*). The drama and the dance are in India closely linked (in Sanskrit, the two terms are etymologically related), and the *Nāṭyaśāstra* is also the source of that tradition which survived in the so-called nautch (*nāṭya*) and was recently given a classical revival as 'Bhārata Nāṭyam'. ⇨ Kālidāsa, Bhavabhūti. [E G]

Tr. Manomohan Ghosh (Calcutta, 1950–). A. B. Keith, *The Sanskrit Drama* (1924); S. Levi, *Le théâtre indien* (Paris, 1890); Sten Konow, *Das Indische Drama* (Berlin, 1920).

Nawâ'î, poetical nom-de-plume of **Mîr 'Alî Shîr** (1441–1501). Turkish poet. The greatest poet of classical eastern ('Chaghatay') Turkish literature. He was born of an aristocratic family at Herât. After studying at Mashhad and spending some years, perhaps in exile, at Samarkand, he returned to Herât in 1469 when his old school-fellow Sultan Husayn Bayqara made himself master of the town, to establish there a brilliant and profligate court. With a short intermission when he was out of favour (1487–94), he lived there as the Sultan's honoured friend and adviser, a patron of learning and literature (among his protégés were the historians Mîrkhônd and Khwândemîr and the artist Bihzâd) and a founder of charitable institutions. Nawâ'î composed a mass of occasional verse, finally arranged in 1 volume of Persian and 4 volumes of Turkish poems. Between 1483 and 1485 he wrote a set of 5 romantic epics, modelled in subject-matter and metre on the *Khamsa* of ◊ Nizâmî, but written in Turkish (Eng. tr. planned by UNESCO), and a *Lisân al-tayr*, 'The Language of the Birds', inspired by the *Mantiq al-Tayr* of ◊ 'Attâr. He translated, with additions, under the title *Nasâ'im al-Mahabba*, the *Nafahât al-Uns* of ◊ Jâmî, who had initiated him into the Naqshbandî dervish-order.

His *Mahbûb al-Qulûb* ('The Hearts' Beloved'), in rhyming prose, reminiscent in style of Jâmî's *Bahâristân*, contains a satirical description of contemporary society; *Majâlis al-Nafâ'is* is a collection of biographies of contemporary writers; and *Khamsat al-Mutahayyirîn*, a memoir of his friendship with Jâmî (selections from these three tr. by A. Belin in *Journal Asiatique*, 1861, 1866). His short prose *Muhâkamat al-Lughatayn* ('Contention of the Two Languages') is a landmark in literature, a comparison as literary languages of Persian, the classic language for belles-lettres, and Turkish, becoming accepted as a literary language only in Nawâ'î's day, and largely thanks to his skilful use of it. [VLM]

Browne, *LHP* iii; A. Bombaci, *Storia della letteratura turca* (Milan, 1956); *E of I*; V. V. Barthold, 'Mîr Alî-Shîr', tr. V. and T. Minorsky, in *Four Studies on the History of Central Asia*, iii (Leiden, 1962); *Philologiae Turcicae Fundamenta*, ii (Wiesbaden, 1964).

Nāyaṉmār. The collective name given to 63 devotees of Śiva; their poems have been collected into the first 11 books of the Śaiva 'canon', *Tirumuṟai*. The twelfth and last book of the *Tirumuṟai*, Cēkkiḻar's *Periyapurāṇam*, contains stories in verse about these poets.

The most important of the 63 are Tiruñāṉacampantar, Tirunāvukkaracu (Appar) and Cuntarar, the 3 authors of *Tēvāram*, the collective name of the first 7 books of *Tirumuṟai*. *Tēvāram* are hymns on Śiva at many of his shrines in South India. Also important is Māṇikkavācakar, who wrote 2 works in the *Tirumuṟai*, *Tiruvācakam*, a lyrical poem in praise of Śiva, and *Tirukkōvaiyār*, a long mystical poem. [JRM]

Hymns of the Tamil Śaivite Saints, ed. and tr. F. Kingsbury and G. E. Phillips (Calcutta, 1921); *The Tiruvāçagam or 'Sacred Utterances' of . . .* tr. G. U. Pope (Oxford, 1900; repr. Madras, *c.* 1960).

Nazim Hikmet. ◊ Hikmet, Nazim.

Nguyen Du (1765–1820). ◊ Vietnamese poet. Nguyen Du is considered the greatest of the Vietnamese poets who wrote in Nom (i.e. non-Chinese) characters. His masterpiece, *Kim Van Kieu* (Fr. tr. Nguyen Van Vinh, Hanoi, 1943), is a narrative poem about the lovers Kim and Kieu written in couplets of 6 and 8 syllables. Almost a verse novel, this work embodies much Confucian teaching. It is universally loved by Vietnamese and has come to be regarded as Vietnam's national poem. Two of Nguyen Du's other poems are also highly regarded, but his work in Chinese characters is less well known. [PJH]

Nguyen Trai (1380–1442). ◊ Vietnamese statesman, scholar and poet. Friend and companion of Le Loi, who liberated Vietnam from Chinese domination, he was a most gifted verse and prose writer. He is credited with the composition of Le Loi's proclamations, which are prose masterpieces, and was the first Vietnamese to write a geography book. Nguyen Trai wrote in Chinese characters and observed Chinese literary conventions. No published edition of his work is available. [PJH]

'Nirat'. A genre of long reflective love poetry in Thai literature. The writer addresses a loved one from whom he is absent on, for example, a pilgrimage, or a royal embassy. The expression of amorous thoughts and of the pain of separation is inspired by the sensations he experiences during his journey (the sight of the moon, or the calling of birds), or, particularly, by place names.

The earliest poem distinguished by the

title is the 17th-century *Nirat Hariphunchai,* but similar characteristics are found in the poetry of ◊ Si Prat and in the earlier *Thawathotsamat* ('The Twelve Months'). The genre was developed extensively during the 18th and 19th centuries, notably by ◊ Sunthọn Phu. *Nirat Lọndọn,* written by Mọm Ratchothai, on the visit of a Thai embassy to the court of Queen Victoria in 1857, provides an interesting view of England at that time. The genre has survived into the modern period, becoming more of a travel account than an expression of love-longing.

Nirat contain much valuable information on topography, ceremonies, customs and the way of life both urban and rural, of the Thai people. [E H S S]

Schweisguth, P., 'Les nirat ou poèmes d'adieu dans la littérature siamoise', in *Journal of the Siam Society,* Vol. 38, 1950.

Nizâm al-Mulk, title of Hasan b. 'Alî (1018–92). Persian statesman and writer on the art of government. Born near Tûs, where his father was a minor official, he served the Seljuq prince Chaghri Beg and gained the regard of his son Alp Arslan, then governing Khorasan for his father. He was Alp Arslan's right-hand man throughout his reign (1063–72), and upon the accession of his young son Malik-shâh (1072–92) became the virtual ruler of the empire. He was a champion of orthodoxy and a generous patron of learning, fostering both by founding the Nizâmiyya College in Baghdad. His vigorous repression of heresy led to his murder by an emissary of the 'Assassins' of Alamut. His *Siyâsat-nâma,* written in unadorned Persian prose in 1091 at the invitation of Malik-shâh and somewhat expanded by a later editor, is a practical manual of statecraft, illustrated by historical anecdotes (Fr. tr. C. Schefer, 1893; Eng. tr. H. Darke, *The Book of Government or Rules for Kings,* 1960). [V L M]

Browne, *L H P,* ii; Arberry, *C P L; E of I.*

Nizâmî, Ilyâs ibn Yûsuf (?1140–1209). Persian poet. The master of romantic epic. Little is known of his life. Born at Ganja (now Kirovabad in Soviet Azerbaijan), he was orphaned at an early age. Of wide learning, pious and tolerant, he seems to have led a retired life, perhaps supported by the patrons to whom he dedicated his poems. His fame rests on 5 epic poems, written in a highly allusive style abounding in metonymy; later denominated the *Khamsa* ('Quintet'), they served as a model for numerous later poets. (1) *Makhzan al-Asrâr* ('The Treasury of Secrets'), composed *c.*1175, is a series of 20 discourses on ethical topics, each illustrated by an anecdote (Eng. tr. G. H. Dârâb, 1945); (2) *Khusraw and Shîrîn* (1180) is the legend of the Sassanian monarch Khusraw II's love for the princess Shîrîn; (3) *Laylâ and Majnûn* (1188) is a Bedouin love-story, the most popular romance in Muslim literature (abridged paraphrase by J. Atkinson, 1836); (4) *Iskandar-nâma* ('The Book of Alexander') relates in 2 parts (1191 and *c.*1200) the medieval legend of Alexander the Great, warrior, philosopher and prophet (Pt 1 tr. H. W. Clarke, 1881); (5) *Haft Paykar* ('The Seven Portraits') (1197), so named from one incident in the story, recounts the legendary history of the Sassanian monarch Bahrâm Gûr (tr. C. E. Wilson, 1924).

Nizâmî is said to have left also many odes and lyrics, of which only a few, much inferior to his epics, survive. [V L M]

Browne, *L H P,* ii; Arberry, *C P L;* Rypka, *I L; E of I.*

Nō Drama. ◊ Zeami Motokiyo.

Noma Hiroshi (1915–). Japanese novelist. He was born in Kobe and educated in Kyoto. At the university there he specialized in French literature. He also became a devoted Marxist, an allegiance which has dominated his career. After a period of employment in the Osaka city administration, he was conscripted into the army in 1941, but was imprisoned and later dismissed the service for his left-wing activities. This experience provided him with material for his undoubted masterpiece, *Shinkū-chitai* (1952; tr. B. Fretchman, *Zone of Emptiness,* 1956), a powerful and bitter picture of life in the Japanese army. His work rises above the normal run of mere propaganda, and displays considerable artistic merit. [C J D]

Nu, U (1907–). ◊ Burmese writer and former Prime Minister. A nationalist leader who helped to achieve independence for Burma, U Nu's many publications include political and religious (Buddhist) pamphlets, translations of Western left-wing literature, public speeches, and some Western-type plays. His *Nga Hnit Ya-thi* has been translated into English as *Burma under the Japanese* (1954), and his play *Lu-du Aung-than* as *The People Win Through* (Rangoon, 1953). [J W A O]

Nuruddin Ar-Raniri, Shaikh (fl. 1621–44). Sumatran ◊ Malay theologian and Muslim historian. Born in Gujerat, West India, of South Arabian origin. He went to Mecca in 1621, travelled perhaps to Malaya, and then to Acheh where he arrived in 1637. He enjoyed royal patronage there for seven years before returning to India, where he died.

His most popular works were theological in content, e.g. *Sirat al-Mustakim* (1634–44), *Asrar al-insan fi ma'rifat al-ruh wa'l rahman* (*c.* 1640) and *Akhbar al-'akhirah fi ahwal al-kiamah* (1642). He attacked the religious views of ◊ Hamzah Fansuri and ◊ Shamsu'ddin Pasai. His most valuable work is now considered to be *Bustan a's-Salatin* (1638), in 7 parts and based on Persian models, containing popularized accounts of Muslim cosmology, some historical material on Acheh, Malacca and Pahang, and many ethical examples and precepts. His Malay is normally easy and fluent in spite of some imperfections of idiom and many Arabicisms. Nuruddin was a highly educated man of his time and fully conversant with the works of the orthodox Muslim mystics. [J C B]

Bustan a's-Salatin, ed. R. J. Wilkinson (2 vols., Singapore, 1899–1900); *Twee Maleise Geschriften van Nuruddin ar-Raniri*, tr. P. Voorhoeve (Leiden, 1955).

O

'Omar Khayyâm (d. ?1122). Persian poet and mathematician. Famous in the West, thanks to Edward Fitzgerald, as author of the *Rubâ'îyât*, in the East as as astronomer and mathematician, he was born (the date is unknown) near Nîshâpûr in north-east Persia. His fame as a mathematician prompted the Seljuq Sultan Malikshâh and his vizier ◊ Nizâm al-Mulk to invite him in 1074 to undertake astronomical research at a new observatory and serve on a commission for calendar reform. His *rubâ'îs* ('quatrains') are a series of independent epigrammatic stanzas, composed perhaps as the outlet for a pessimistic and cynical rationalism which in his strictly orthodox day it was not politic to teach openly.

Fitzgerald did not pretend to make a close translation: 'Those [stanzas] here selected are strung into something of an Eclogue' (preface to 1st edn, 1859). His first edition, published anonymously, was remaindered; but it later caught the attention of Swinburne and Rossetti, who launched the work, well attuned to the *fin-de-siècle* mood, on its career of fantastic and unabated popularity. After this success, critics began whittling down – even to as few as 12 – the number of *rubâ'îs* to be regarded as 'Omar's authentic work, but the traditional canon seems now to have been rehabilitated by the appearance of two 13th-century manuscripts, one in the Chester Beatty collection (ed. with literal tr. A. J. Arberry, 1949), the other now at Cambridge (verse tr. A. J. Arberry, 1952).

'Omar was one of the greatest mathematicians of the Middle Ages, but seems to have written little. His principal scientific work is an algebra (Fr. tr. F. Woepcke, Paris, 1851); he also wrote treatises on physics and metaphysics. [V L M]

Browne, *L H P*, ii; Rypka, *I L*; *E of I*; G. Sarton, *Introduction to the History of Science*, i (Washington, 1927); A. G. Potter, *A Bibliography of the Rubáiyát* (1929); A. J. Arberry, *The Romance of the Rubáiyát* (1959) (centenary reprint of 1st edn with introduction and select bibliography).

Ono Komachi (fl. *c.* 850). Japanese poetess. Her life survives only in legend: it is reported that she was a court lady of great beauty, famous for her love affairs; when her beauty started to fade she atoned for her former worldliness by becoming a beggar and died in poverty.

Her *tanka* (short 31-syllable poems) are nearly all in *Kokinshū* (a collection of poetry presented in 905). They deal with sexual passion and increasing age. As she sees her grey hairs increase, she looks back with guilty regret on time wasted in dissolute pleasure. Her love poems are of great intensity, heightened by her skilful use of *kakekotoba* ('pivot words'), a device based on homonyms: this deliberate use of ambiguity enabled her to pack her short poems with concentrated feeling. [C J D]

Le monument poétique de Heian: le Kokinshû, ed. and tr. Georges Bonneau (3 vols., Paris, 1933–5); Keene, *A J L*.
Brower and Miner, *J C P*.

Ōoka Shōhei (1909–). Japanese novelist, whose interest in literature began at primary school and led to a special study of Stendhal at Kyoto University where he graduated in French literature. Until he joined the army in 1944 he was mainly occupied with translation of the master's works, and critical studies of them. His military service was in the Philippines, where his experiences were all of defeat and imprisonment. These gave him materials for many novels. First was *Furyoki* ('Records of Imprisonment') (1948), a study of prisoner-of-war psychology. Others with similar themes are *Rēte no ame* ('Rain at Leyte') (1948), and *Ikite iru horyo* ('Living Prisoners') (1949). His best work to date is *Nobi* (1951; tr. I. Morris, *Fire on the Plain*, 1957), a terrible account of the sufferings and degradation of a soldier trying to survive in the jungle when his army was facing defeat. The objectivity and the interest in psychological study in these works surely derive from the Western traditions that were so familiar to Ōoka, and at the same time go back to some aspects of Japanese Naturalism (as exemplified by ⇨ Tayama Katai's *Ippeisotsu*). They also reflect the revulsion against war and military glory which was typical of Japan in the immediate post-war period and which was strengthened by the war in Korea.

Ōoka has used his skill in depicting characters under stress in descriptions of more normal life. Of these, the best-known is his *Musashino fujin* ('The Lady from Musashino') (1950), which deals with the adultery of an otherwise respectable woman. [C J D]

Orbeliani, Sulkhan-Saba (1658–1725). Georgian fabulist and lexicographer. He belonged to a leading princely family of Kartli (Eastern Georgia). As a young man he took part in court affairs at Tbilisi and was appointed tutor to Prince Vakhtang. In 1698 he retired to a monastery and took holy orders. He had marked Roman Catholic leanings. His former pupil Vakhtang became king of Kartli in 1711 and two years later sent Sulkhan-Saba to Europe on a diplomatic mission to King Louis XIV of France and to the Pope. After a Turkish invasion, King Vakhtang was forced to leave Georgia together with his followers, and Sulkhan-Saba Orbeliani died in exile in Moscow in 1725.

Sulkhan-Saba composed the first systematic Georgian dictionary, under the title of *Sitqvis-kona* or *Bouquet of Words*; containing over 17,000 entries, it is used by scholars to this day. In *Travels in Europe*, he describes his mission to France and Italy (1713–16); much of it, including the section on Versailles, is lost.

Most famous of his books is *Dsigni sibrdzne-sitsruisa* or *The Book of Wisdom and Lies* (tr. J. O. Wardrop, published by William Morris, Kelmscott Press, 1894; other versions in Russian and German), a story book in which edifying tales and amusing Oriental anecdotes are set in a narrative framework concerning the education of a king's son. A verbal duel takes place between the prince's tutor Leon, who discourses on the aims of education and the duties of princes, and the cynical court eunuch Ruka. Some of the fables and tales, both frivolous and profound, derive from Persian and Turkish sources, others from Georgian folk-lore and Orbeliani's own fertile imagination. [D M L]

D. M. Lang, '"Wisdom and Lies": Variations on a Georgian Literary Theme', in *O A S*, XVIII, 1956.

Osaragi Jirō (1897–). Japanese novelist. He was born in Yokohama, and graduated in law at Tokyo University in 1921. At first he worked in the Foreign Office, but later became a professional writer. He is classified in Japan as a 'popular novelist'. This means that he writes mainly historical romances, typically appearing in instalments in daily newspapers. His first novel of this sort was *Kurama tengu* ('Goblin from Kurama') (1942). He has continued writing in this style, but dealing with subjects which the normal popular novel would not aspire to, such as the Dreyfus affair (*Dreyfus jihen*) (1930) and the Opium War (*Ahen sensō*) (1942).

However, he will be remembered, at

least in the West, more for his novels of contemporary life. He has been writing them since the 1930s, but it was the stimulus of the post-war period that resulted in *Kikyō* (1948; tr. B. Horowitz, *Homecoming*, 1955), the story of a Japanese expatriate who had long lived in Malaya, but who returned to Japan after the war. One feels that its tidy structure, efficient characterization, and clarity of style, not to say slickness, is derived much more from the West than from Japan. In fact the novel might well have been written by a Westerner. [C J D]

Ōtomo Yakamochi (718–85). Japanese poet and anthologist. He was the son of Ōtomo Tabito, himself a famous poet. His family was one of the oldest in the legendary history of Japan. He was a court official like his father, but his career was chequered. He left the capital to govern a province at the age of 29, and returned in 751. For a while he had success and promotion, but in 758 he was posted again to the provinces. No work of his later than 759 survives, perhaps because, soon after his death, the Ōtomo family was broken up, he himself being deprived posthumously of office and rank, all because of a crime committed by a distant relative. His poetry remains in the *Man-yō-shū* (*Collection for a Myriad Ages*), the earliest surviving collection of Japanese poetry, which dates from the second half of the 8th century. Ōtomo Yakamochi was probably one of the compilers. He has more poems (some 500) than any other contributor, and the latest of them is dated 759, which is also the latest date mentioned in the whole collection. He is notable for the variety of styles that he is able to adopt with great skill. Some of his work seems superficial and this is no doubt partly due to the fact that he was so prolific. He demonstrates the tendency, which was to develop more and more in Japanese poetry, for poets to write about fictitious sentiments, taking on various roles, but he does it with immense skill.

The *Man-yō-shū* contains about 4,500 poems, and about 450 poets are named. It is in 20 books, and the earliest poems are assigned by scholars to the 5th century. Its fascination lies not only in the historical value of its material, but also, and chiefly, in the very high quality of much of the poetry. There is often to be found in it an apparent freshness and sincerity of sentiment that was to become rarer as poetry became more and more a polite pursuit. The authors come from a wider range of social class than was common later. It is the only collection which contains a significant number of 'long poems' (as distinct from the 31- syllable 'short poems' which were to become the standard of the next eight centuries). Many of these are of great value, showing a power of sustained development that is necessarily absent from the shorter form. The other outstanding poets of the *Man-yō-shū* are Kakinomoto Hitomaro, Yamanoe Okura (d. 733), who had been to China and who wrote philosophical poems and also some on his children, and Yamabe Akahito (d. 736), famous for his short nature poems.

The *Man-yō-shū* contains much that can be read with enjoyment even in translation, and the two works listed for further reading are strongly recommended. [C J D]

Nippon Gakujutsu Shinkōkai, *The Manyōshu, One Thousand Poems* (1965); Brower and Miner, *J C P*

P

Pa Chin. ◊ Li Fei-kan.

Pade-tha-ya-za (fl. 1684–1754). ◊ Burmese court minister and poet, and a great innovator, whose literary work anticipated developments some 50 years after his death. This chief works are ◊ *pyo* poems, including the unorthodox *Sūjā* (or *Thuza*), dated 1691, on a non-Buddhist theme, and one on the arrival of Thai envoys at the Burmese court; the *Mani-ket Zat-taw-gyi*, written between 1733 and 1752, the first known palace play; and some of the earliest classical songs, including four on the happy life of simple villagers, a theme unconventional in the court-dominated literature of the time. For a translation of one of these songs see 'Country Life in Burmese Literature' by Dunn, Hla Pe and Stewart, in *OAS*, XII (1948). [J W A O]

Pahlavi. An adjective (meaning 'Parthian', but secondarily 'ancient, heroic') applied in later times to the Middle Persian writings of the Zoroastrians, *c.* 3rd–9th centuries A.D., preserved in a difficult script, with fossilized Aramaic words occurring as ideograms. No manuscript is earlier than the 14th century, and a poor scribal tradition adds to textual problems.

The writings have more theological and antiquarian than literary value, part of their interest being that they represent the transition in Persia from oral to written literature (the secular literature of this period has almost all perished). They fall into the following categories: (1) The translation of the ◊ Avesta, with commentaries, known as the *Zand* (probably 'Elucidation'). (2) Compilations from the *Zand* on specific themes, notably the *Bundahishn* ('Creation'). (3) Apologetic writings, some by individuals, others, like the encyclopedic *Denkard,* by several hands. These contain much traditional material. (4) Texts representing well-known categories of oral literature, e.g. wisdom-texts (*handarz* or gnomes, riddles, a contest-poem); mantic works (spells and visionary texts, such as the *Arda Viraf Namag,* with Dantesque vision of heaven and hell); a fragment of heroic verse (*Ayadgar-i Zareran*), mutilated but with glimpses of splendour; a prose romance (*Karnamag-i Ardashir*). The few verse texts are in unrhymed stress metres, which lend themselves to scribal corruption.

The translations by E. West in Sacred Books of the East (ed. F. Max Müller) are antiquated but the only extensive renderings. For later translations of individual works see M. Boyce 'Middle Persian Literature' in *Handbuch der Orientalistik,* ed. B. Spuler, IV, ii (1943). [E M B]

'Pañcatantra'. The best-known Indian collection of didactic stories. The 'five chapters' of the work deal with the five principal topics of courtly policy as defined by the *Arthaśātra* (◊ Kauṭilya): the losing, and winning, of friends; war and peace; loss of property; and precipitate conduct. It was thus intended as an easy introduction to government for the young prince; but the stories themselves, often animal fables, were of much wider application, and it is more as a treatise on the ethics of success that the *Pañcatantra* gained renown. The virtues recommended are those of everyday advantage, and the only vice is stupidity; the jackal is often the hero.

The *Pañcatantra* draws upon a considerable body of 'folk literature' and 'legend' which has inspired several other compilations, notably the ◊ *jātaka* stories, and the famous but now lost *Bṛhatkathā*, or 'great story' (◊ Somadeva), where the value of the story as entertainment is emphasized.

The influence of the *Pañcatantra* on world literature is perhaps greater than that of any other Indian composition; it had a genuinely world-wide reputation before the advent of techniques of mass communication. It was translated into all the major languages of Europe and western Asia by the 17th century via a chain of intermediate translations which began with a 6th-century Pahlavi version. The fairy tales of Hans Christian Andersen show motifs which can be clearly traced back to the Indian source; the 'Princess and the Pea' is one such. Tales and precepts from the *Pañcatantra* are also met with all over South-East Asia. [E G]

Gold's Gloom: Tales from the Pancatantra, tr. Arthur Ryder (Chicago, 1925).

J. Hertel, *Das Pancatantra, seine Geschichte und seine Verbreitung* (Leipzig und Berlin, 1914); F. Edgerton, *Pancatantra Reconstructed* (New Haven, 1924).

Pané, Armijn (1908–). ◊ Indonesian novelist, essayist, critic, dramatist and poet. He was the most westernized of the principal figures of the *Pudjangga Baru* generation – even more truly western in spirit than the prophet of westernization, ◊ Takdir Alisjahbana, himself. His prose, in hybrid 'European Malay', is lively, full of subtleties and sometimes brilliant. In his poetry he fails to make use of the beauty of the older elements of the language. His principal work is the novel *Belenggu* ('Shackles') originally published episodically in *Pudjangga Baru* in 1940 and republished since the war by Pustaka Rakjat. This is a genuine psychological study and very different from any earlier novel in Indonesian. Much of his work, like that of many Indonesian writers, has appeared in periodicals. In 1953 many of his short stories were collected and republished under the title *Kisah antara Manusia* ('Stories of Humanity'). [E C G B]

Pané, Sanusi (1905–). ◇ Indonesian poet, dramatist and literary editor. The elder brother of Armijn ◇ Pané. Sanusi Pané originated from the west coast of Sumatra, but while still young was taken to Java. His first poem was published in 1921 when he was only 16. During the following nine years he wrote the poems contained in his 3 volumes of poetry – *Pantjaran Tjinta* ('Outpouring of Love'), 1926, also containing lyric prose; *Puspa Mega* ('Flowers and Clouds'), 1927, containing sonnets, and *Madah Kelana* ('Verses of a Wanderer'), 1930, containing his most mature verse. A romantic, Sanusi Pané had a great love for Indian and Indo-Javanese culture and was the champion of tradition and 'art for art's sake' in public controversy with ◇ Takdir Alisjahbana. After 1930 he ceased to write verse but wrote a number of dramas, mainly set in ancient Java. In 1941 he became Chief Editor of the *Balai Pustaka*. [E C G B]

Paṇikkar. ◇ Mādhava Paṇikkar.

Pāṇini (fl. 4th cent. B.C.). Indian grammarian. His importance is threefold: (a) His method of description is remarkably like that of contemporary structural linguistics. (b) In classical Indian scholarship, grammar enjoys among the sciences the architectonic position which we attribute to mathematics. As the standard grammarian, Pāṇini becomes in a way the methodological authority for any scholarly investigation. His influence on logic, ritual exegesis, poetics and abstract philosophy is incalculable. (c) Finally, it was his grammar which fixed for all time the form of Sanskrit, the 'perfect' language.

Pāṇini's grammar, in 8 chapters and 32 sections, is a model of economy. Rules are formulated with laconic brevity. Grammatical categories are defined formally, and roots, stems and affixes are recognized as the analytical units of word-formation.

Pāṇini himself refers to several of his predecessors, and his own work is in part only a compilation and a completing of various theories. The science of grammar, like other early Hindu learning, had its roots in the early brahmanical ritual and reflected, in origin, a need to preserve correctly the sacred texts which were by late Vedic times no longer understandable. [E G]

The Ashtadhyāyī of Pāṇini, tr. S. C. Vasu (2 vols., Allahabad, 1891–8); *La grammaire de Pāṇini*, Fr. tr. L. Renou (Paris, 1847–54); *Grammatik*, German tr. O. Böhtlingk (Leipzig, 1887).

B. Liebich, *Zur Einführung in die indische einheimische Sprachwissenschaft* (Heidelberg, 1919–20); L. Renou, *L'Inde classique* (Paris, 1953).

'Panji'. Name of a genre of ◇ Javanese chevaleresque love-romance perhaps dating from the 12th century in pre-Muslim as well as in Muslim Java, in Javanized Bali, Lombok, Malaya and throughout the Malay-speaking areas of the Indonesian Archipelago (also *'Panji Tales'*, *'Panji Cycle'*). Panji, known as Ino Kertapati or Raden Mantri, prince of Koripan, is in search of his cousin and bride Galuh Daha; Koripan and Daha were two of the four East Javan kingdoms unified by the Majapahit empire of the 14th century. Panji is an accomplished courtier and lover, an intrepid traveller and, if need be, hero, who undertakes endless wanderings and adventures.

These stories present a vivid picture of medieval Javanese court life. They form part of the traditional literature of Java and are also staged in both dramatic and shadow-play performances. They are accessible in Javanese printed books, Malay and Balinese manuscripts and Dutch extracts. [C H]

R.M. Ng. Dr Poebatjaraka, 'Pandji-verhalen onderling vergeleken', Bibliotheca Javanica 9, *Bataviaasch Genootschap van Kunsten en Wetenschappen*, Batavia, 1940; H. Overbeck, *'Java in de Maleische Literatuur* (*Hikajat Galoeh di-gantoeng*)', Djawa XII, 1932; XIII, 1933.

Pantun. A ◇ Malay and ◇ Indonesian verse-form, usually of 4 lines. There are a thousand or more of these pithy but imaginative verses, which may be sung as well as spoken, and which have for at least four centuries been a popular delight of the Malays as well as forming a treasury of erotic, philosophical and traditional ideas and sentiments.

The usual pattern is a verse of 4 lines, each with 8 or 10 syllables (i.e. 4 stresses), and rhyming *abab*. Rarer forms contain 6 or 8 lines with an *abcabc* or *abcd abcd* rhyme scheme. *Pantun berkait* ('connected *pantuns*') are longer and have an alternate arrangement of lines in which lines 2 and 4 of the first quatrain become lines 1 and 3 of the second, and so on to a length of 20 or more lines.

The first two lines of the normal *pantun* have as their main object the establishment of the sound pattern that follows in the last two lines. Sometimes they also suggest, in an allusive way, the particular theme of the last two lines which, however, always bear the kernel of the thought to be communicated. Under the name *pantoum,* this form also achieved a certain vogue in Europe in the 19th century and was used by Victor Hugo. (⇨ Achehnese Literature; Minangkabau Literature.) [J C B]

Malay Pantuns, tr. A. W. Hamilton (Sydney, 1944).

R. J. Wilkinson and R. O. Winstedt, *Pantun Melayu* (Singapore, 1914); K. Sim, *Flowers of the Sun* (Singapore, 1957).

'Pararaton'. 16th-century anonymous ⇨ Javanese historical chronicle (lit. 'The Book of Kings'). Written in an earlier form of the language, known as Middle-Javanese, this book (also known as *Ken Arok* or *Ken Angrok* after the chief character) is a prose chronicle of the kingdoms of Tumapĕl and Majapahit which flourished in East Java during the 13th and 14th centuries. The work is part picaresque novel, dealing with the founder of the dynasty, and part history, though as a historical source it is considered less valuable than stone and copper inscriptions or the *Nāgarakrĕtāgama* (⇨ Prapañcha). No English translation has yet been made. [C H]

Dutch tr. J. Brandes, re-edited N. J. Krom, Verhandelingen Bataviaasch Genootschap, Vol. 62 (2nd edn, The Hague, 1920).

Patañjali. ⇨ *Yogasūtra.*

Peddana. 16th-century Telugu poet. He was the chief poet at the court of Kṛṣṇadēvarāya, ruler of Vijayanagar from 1509 to 1530. He composed *Manucaritra,* an epic developing an episode in the *Mārkaṇḍeya Purāṇa.* A pious brahman youth, Pravara, loved by a heavenly damsel Varudhini, rejects her; meanwhile a heavenly youth whose love Varudhini had spurned succeeds in winning her by assuming the form of Pravara. [J R M]

P. T. Raju, *Telugu Literature (Andhra Literature)* (Bombay, 1944).

Penglipor Lara (lit. 'soother of cares'). The traditional ⇨ Malay village bard who recites popular tales based on the adventures of a romantic hero. The same phrase is also applied to the stories themselves. The description 'folk-romance' is specially apt since these prose tales (often containing short passages of fine poetry) have for centuries formed the staple literary diet of the Malay villagers, and provide, in some measure, a rural and oral counterpart to the written and more sophisticated *hikayat* of the Court.

Among the best-known folk-romances are *Cheritera Sri Rama* (ed. W. E. Maxwell, 1886), *Hikayat Malim Deman* and *Hikayat Malim Dewa* (both Kuala Lumpur, 1963) and *Hikayat Anggun Che Tunggal* (Singapore, 1960). Their plots are often loosely based on Indian themes and there are superficial Muslim touches though a sub-stratum of animistic and Hindu-Buddhist beliefs suggests an older source for them.

The form of these stories (which are usually sung), the frequent verse interpolations, the relatively undeveloped characters and stock situations – often described in formulaic stereotyped phrases – are reminiscent of much other oral literature in many parts of the world, though here the local background from Malaya and Sumatra (whence some of the stories derive) is particularly vivid and characteristic. [J C B]

Winstedt, *C M L.*

Periyāḷvār. ⇨ Āḷvār.

Petrus Ky. ⇨ Truong Vinh Ky.

Philippine Literature. The migration of Malayo-Polynesian peoples at different periods to relatively isolated regions of an archipelago composed of 7,000-odd islands resulted in a great diversity of Philippine languages, of which the principal ones are Ilokano (northern Luzon Island), Tagalog (central and southern Luzon) and Binisaya (Visayan Islands). Before the Spanish conquest (1565) the literature in these languages consisted chiefly of poetry, either recited or sung. The principal forms were sayings and proverbs (*sabi, sawikain*), sea shanties (*soliranin*), love songs (*kundiman*), odes (*kumintang*) and ballads (*awit*). Little of this archaic poetry remains, for although

Filipinos were literate in a script of their own, they used writing for letters rather than literature.

The Spaniards introduced, besides the romanized alphabet, new themes and new forms. New themes: Spanish tales of chivalry (*corridos*) were adapted, chiefly by Tagalog poets, to the *awit* (12-syllable line, in stanzas of 4 assonanced verses); an outstanding example is ♢ Balagtas's *Florante at Laura.* The Roman Catholic liturgy gave rise to the choral chanting during Holy Week of an Ilokano *Lamentations of Jeremias,* and versions in other Philippine languages of the Bible story of the Fall and Redemption. Of this last, one of the finest is Aquino de Belen's Tagalog *Pasion,* published in 1703. New forms: the drama, introduced by Jesuit missionaries (1598), was composed at first for performance at religious festivals and state occasions, and in Spanish; but Filipino playwrights were soon writing plays in their respective languages, using Spanish models. A standard plot was evolved based on the conflict between Christians and Moors, hence the popular name, *moro-moro,* for such plays. An indigenous prose literature did not develop until the 19th century; an early example is Modesto de Castro's *Urbana at Felisa,* a collection of moral essays in letter-form.

Filipino literaure in Spanish was also a late development; its first exponents were the nationalist leaders, the greatest being ♢ Rizal. The bulk of this literature appeared in the early part of this century, when poets such as Apostol and Guerrero wrote in French symbolist style, and essayists such as Briones and Recto became corresponding members of the Spanish Academy.

With the American occupation of the Archipelago in 1898, English became the official medium of instruction in a system of popular education far more extensive than had been realized under Spanish rule. The rapidity and relative thoroughness of this development brought a linguistic curtain down between the writers of one generation and the reading public of the next: the elegant writers in Spanish, from authors as widely circulated as Rizal to the '*mocerío del "Ateneo"*' (young men of promise, in a college noted for its literary alumni), had soon to give way to a new breed of writers in English.

Making this new language yield a respectable if not significant literature was largely the work of short-story writers. They included José García ♢ Villa, who has since turned his best efforts to poetry, and the short-lived Manuel Arguilla. The short story has remained the most developed literary genre.

This interest in prose soon extended to the novel, though at first the shape of the Philippine novel was much influenced by the years of practice with the short story. Significant names are Stevan Javellana, N. V. M. Gonzalez, Nick ♢ Joaquín, Celso Al. Carunungan, and Kerima Polotan Tuvera.

While the prose practitioners have busied themselves addressing a public almost exclusively Filipino, one poet has demonstrated that the country's writers in English might have something to say to the English-speaking world outside the islands. Villa's experiments in the technique of poetry and the statements of his individual *angst* have elicited critical studies from Dame Edith Sitwell, David Daiches and Marianne Moore. A group of young poets from several different literary coteries also publish an occasional anthology entitled *Signatures* (ed. Leonidas V. Benesa).

Writing in English for the Philippine theatre has not produced a body of works as important as that in the other genres. Criticism is largely confined to the writing of journalistic reviews. Two collections of critical essays about Filipino writing in English have, however, appeared in book form: Salvador P. Lopez's *Literature and Society* (Manila, 1940) and Miguel A. Bernad's *Bamboo and the Greenwood Tree* (Manila, 1961). [H C]

Epifanio de los Santos, *Literatura tagala* (Madrid, 1909); W. E. Retana, *El teatro en Filipinas* (Madrid, 1909); *Higher Education and Philippine Culture*, ed. James B. Reuter and others (Manila, 1960).

'Phra Lọ'. An anonymous Thai epic romance originating earlier than the 17th century, probably in a northern Thai state, and a source for several later narratives. The story concerns the magically induced and disastrous love of the hero-prince Phra Lọ for the two daughters of a neighbouring ruler, for whose sake he deserts his own family and state. The two feuding principalities are only reconciled after the death in battle of the three lovers. Buddhist ideas of causation and retribution are worked into the genuinely tragic narrative. [E H S S]

Dhani Nivat, Prince, 'The Date and Authorship of the Romance of Phra Lọ', *Journal of the Siam Society*, Vol. 41, 1954.

'Pien-wen'. A Chinese literary genre. Some of the stories and ballads found at the turn of the present century among a mass of heterogeneous material in the Thousand Buddha Caves at Tun-huang, Kansu, are entitled '*pien-wen*', and that term has been used loosely to describe them all. The Tun-huang material as a whole is thought to date from the 6th to the 10th centuries.

Buddhist stories and popularizations form the core of the collection of vulgar literature. Some of the Buddhist *pien-wen* could well have provided the text for the persuasive oral performances by priests so popular in T'ang times (A.D. 618–907). Their distinctive feature, connected with public presentation, is alternation between prose and verse, a characteristic of almost all *pien-wen*, which was to stay with Chinese fiction until recent times.

Particularly interesting, however, are those pieces which belong to the indigenous Chinese tradition, for these contribute much to the knowledge of the evolution of Chinese popular literature. The *pien-wen* in this category are greatly varied in form, style and thought, and their subject-matter includes Confucian parables, historical anecdotes, popular legends, stories of romance, adventure and politics, and animal and ghost stories. Some are entirely in verse, some entirely in prose; some are stiff and learned in style, others vulgar and racy; some piously orthodox in thought, others rudely plebeian. Their literary value can be considerable: most impressively there is to be found a directness and depth of feeling of a kind present in the poems of the Exeter Book. [D E P]

Arthur Waley, *Ballads and Stories from Tun-huang* (1961).

Pinski, David (1872–1960). Yiddish playwright and novelist. Born at Mohilev, he lived in Switzerland and Germany, then settled in America in 1899, but finally emigrated to Israel in 1950. His stories reflect the socialist ideas he embraced early on and to which he devoted most of his public activities. But in later years he turned to Jewish folklore and legends for his source material. He wrote several novels, the last being *Der Zurissener Mensch*, dealing with American Jewish life during the war. His plays include: *Isaac Sheftel* (1899); *Di Muter* (1901); *Familie Ts'vi* (1905); *Der Oitzer* (tr. L. Lewisohn, *The Treasure*, 1905). His essays on Yiddish drama, *Das Yiddishe Drama*, were published in 1909. [E E]

In Yisroël, ed. J. Leftwich (London, 1960). Waxman, *H J L*.

Po Chü-i (772–846). Chinese poet. He was born in a small town in Honan Province. When about 10 or 11, he moved nearer the capital, Ch'ang-an. In 785 there was a drought, and the family were again forced to move, this time to Soochow and Hangchow. Thus many of his early poems are about parting and the death of friends. They are rather formal, and contain many quotations and clichés. In 799 he passed the provincial examinations and the following year the metropolitan examinations with high honours. He left the capital and stayed for a while at a Buddhist monastery, where he received instructions from a monk. The next year he returned to the capital to embark upon the career of an official. In 807 he became a member of the Hanlin Academy, and subsequently married. He opposed the power of the Palace Eunuchs and the requisitioning of goods for the Palace Armies and the Palace Ladies, and wrote poems on these subjects. Although not opposed to philosophical Taoism, he attacked magical Taoism and the taking of longevity pills, and he wrote a poem and a ballad opposing this custom. He made proposals on tax reform and protested to the throne against the whipping of peasants.

In 815 Po Chü-i was sent into exile as a punishment for an indiscretion, and though he lived fairly comfortably during exile and wrote many poems describing the scenery, he seems to have been greatly intimidated in later life by the thought of another banishment. Recalled to the capital in 820 he kept out of politics thereafter, and his poetry became more influenced by Buddhism. He said of himself that he was lazy by nature, hating office routine, and preferring countryside rambles. He wished to retire early, but was always short of money, and was eventually retired at 70 on half pay.

Po Chü-i's poetic output was prolific. He wrote many poems in the formal style demanded for the official examinations, which were studied by the young as models. He also wrote many 'regulated poems' which demanded great skill in fitting the words into prescribed patterns. Following fashion, he exchanged these poems with acquaintances as a literary game, the most famous of his 'opponents' being Yüan Chen, the two men being celebrated all over China for the elegance of these verses. Po regarded his political ballads, intended to be sung in order to influence the Emperor and court officials, as his best works. It was said that he used to read his poems to an old peasant woman, and delete anything she did not understand. It was owing to this lucidity of language that he earned the greatest popularity in his own time of any Chinese poet. [J D C]

A. Waley, *The Life and Times of Po Chü-i* (1948).

Polynesian Literature. The cultural area of Polynesia embraces all the islands situated within a roughly triangular area bounded by New Zealand, Hawaii and Easter Island. In addition, the Ellice Islands, the Lau group of Fiji and a number of scattered and isolated communities as far west as the Solomons and the Carolines are Polynesian, either wholly or partly, in language and culture. In contrast to their Melanesian and Micronesian neighbours, whose languages and cultures are discrete, the Polynesians speak closely related languages and have evolved relatively homogeneous institutions. Religion, technology and language, however, make it convenient to distinguish the central cultures (Samoa, Tonga and neighbouring islands) from the peripheral cultures (Society Islands, Austral Islands, Marquesas, Tuamotu Archipelago, Easter Island, and to the north and south-west, Hawaii, the Cook Islands and New Zealand).

With the sole exception of the Easter Island script, writing was apparently not known until the 19th century, when missionary activity introduced the Roman alphabet and literacy spread rapidly. A considerable body of unwritten literature is known to have existed in all the main island groups and much has been recorded. The coming of Christianity to all parts of Polynesia has put an end to the high achievements of heathen poetry.

In Eastern Polynesian society, the accurate transmission of sacred lore from one generation to the next was often institutionalized in special schools for carefully selected and initiated pupils. The latter when fully proficient became bards and minstrels who attached themselves to the retinue of a chief. The natural aptitude of Polynesians for dancing, poetry and singing, and the high honour in which a successful poet, composer, dancing master or performer was held, kept up the standard of accomplishment and helped to maintain a steady flow of material. Many literary forms were known.

In poetry, the open syllables of Polynesian languages, the high frequency of vowels, together with the absence of consonant clusters, were utilized for special effects and rhyming patterns.

In addition to the principal gods (Tangaroa, Tu, Tane, Rongo and others), whose activities were the inspiration of much epic prose and poetry, the Polynesian pantheon included demigods, the fame of whose exploits have spread to parts of Micronesia and Melanesia and who are remembered in the literature of many island groups. By far the most famous one is Maui, the hero of a cycle of legends and myths, who obtained fire for man from the underworld and who brought up New Zealand from the deep with his magic fish-hook. Almost equally famous are other cycles associated with Tinirau and Hina (the prototype pair of lovers who meet from far across the sea, are separated and reunited), with Tafaki and with Rata.

Much of Polynesian poetry consists of epics. Nobility of character, loyalty to one's kinsmen, maritime travel, war and conquest are some of its recurring themes. A great deal of lyrical poetry is also on record. The handling of the twin themes of landscape and love is of special interest in that the language varies from considerable reticence, with a wealth of esoteric allusion and metaphor, to almost complete absence of restraint in the poetic treatment of sex. [G B M]

K. Luomala, *Voices on the Wind* (Honolulu, 1955); C. R. H. Taylor, *A Pacific Bibliography* (2nd edn, 1965); Gambier Islands, Tuamotu Archipelago: P. H. Buck, *Ethnology of Mangareva* (Honolulu, 1938);

Tonga: E. E. V. Collocott, *Tales and Poems of Tonga* (Honolulu, 1928); Cook Islands: W. W. Gill, *Myths and Songs from the South Pacific* (1876); New Zealand: Sir George Grey, *Polynesian Mythology* (Auckland, New Zealand, 1885); Hawaii: N. B. Emerson, *Unwritten Literature of Hawaii* (Washington, 1909).

Pon-nya, U (*c.* 1807–66). ⇨ Burmese author. He wrote several kinds of poem, but is best known for his 'letters' (*myit-taza*) and plays. U Pon-nya's letters were a new departure in this form, as they were often written by him on behalf of ordinary people on everyday matters instead of being edifying homilies addressed to the king. The texts of 5 of his plays are extant: *Paduma, Ye-thè, Kosala, Vessantara* and *Vijaya* (the last 3 are also spelt *Kaw-thala, We-than-daya* and *Wi-zaya* respectively). His style is lively, with deft rhymes and clever puns. His plays became the model for later playwrights. [J W A O].

Prapañcha (14th cent.). ⇨ Javanese author. His only known work, the epic poem *Nāgarakrĕtāgama* dated 1365, is the most important work in Old-Javanese literature and also supplies the only information we have about the author. As son of the Buddhist chaplain (*adhyakṣa*) to the Majapahit king of East Java, Prapañcha accompanied him on his travels round the kingdom and his descriptions are a valuable historical and sociological source. As well as a practising priest and a student of history, he was also a highly talented poet. [C H]

T. G. T. Pigeaud, *Java in the 14th Century* (5 vols., The Hague, 1960–3).

Prem Cand. ⇨ Śrīvāstav.

Psaila, Monsignor Carmelo, known as **Dun Karm** (1871–1961). Maltese poet and lexicographer. He was born at the small town of Żebbug, his father being a seafaring man serving on a little cargo vessel trading between Malta and Greece. He received his primary education at the local government school, from which he moved on to the Diocesan Grammar School and then to the Theological Seminary at Floriana. He was ordained priest at the age of 23, and appointed lecturer at the Seminary and teacher at the Diocesan Grammar School. In 1921 the Apostolic Visitor, Cardinal La Fontaine, arbitrarily dismissed Dun Karm from his teaching posts, but he was immediately appointed Assistant Director of the National Library of Malta. Retiring in 1936, he was then commissioned to work on the official English-Maltese dictionary, which he brought successfully to completion. Dun Karm was awarded the degree of Litt. D. by the Royal University of Malta in 1945. His last years were spent in tranquil retirement, amid the veneration of the Maltese people.

Two phases may be distinguished in Dun Karm's literary career. During the first, he wrote verse in Italian, which already placed him in the forefront of the contemporary Maltese literary world. In the later phase he abandoned Italian poetry for Maltese. It is to be noted that Maltese is a Semitic language, having affinities with the Arabic of Tunisia and traces of the ancient Phoenician tongue. It has however a considerable Romance element, perhaps up to 20 per cent of the vocabulary being of Sicilian origin. Not until 1934 did Maltese replace Italian as the official language of Malta, side by side with English. When Dun Karm was persuaded as early as 1912 to change over from Italian to Maltese verse, he was ahead of his time and his untiring zeal in fostering his country's national idiom made him many enemies.

Dun Karm has been truly characterized as 'Romantic in thought and sentiment . . . classical in relation to his own literature'. His poems treat of the beauties of nature, of love of fatherland, of religious experience, of his own deeply felt spiritual struggles and anguish. Thanks to the work of A. J. Arberry and Father P. Grech, it need no longer be feared, in the words of a Maltese compatriot of Dun Karm's, that 'this great man must forever remain unappreciated beyond his island home because only a few hundred thousand people are able to understand his language.' [D M L]

Dun Karm: Poet of Malta, tr. A. J. Arberry, introd., notes and glossary P. Grech (1961).

P'u Sung-ling (1640–1715). Chinese story-writer and novelist. Author of *Liao-chai-chih-i* (*Strange Stories from a Chinese Studio*, tr. H. Giles, 1916). He came from a cultured Shantung family, his father having been a merchant and scholar. He passed the local examination in 1658, but had no further academic success. After serving for a time as secretary to a magistrate, he spent 20 years, from 1672 onwards, as secretary to a wealthy friend. Thereafter he spent most of his remaining years at home, attending to family business and acting as tutor to the sons of the gentry.

The first edition of *Liao-chai-chih-i* (1766) contained 431 stories, but more have since been recovered from older manuscripts. They are in the T'ang and Sung tradition of 'strange tales' and comprise legends and short stories in which fact and fiction, the natural and the supernatural, are closely interwoven. They abound with fox fairies and spirits, usually disguised as women and endowed with human attributes. Most stories have a moral, and rewards and punishments are meted out in strict accordance with deserts. Written in 'literary style', they are outstanding among the stories of this genre for their poetical language and rich vocabulary.

P'u Sung-ling also wrote a novel in the vernacular, *Hsing-shih-in-yüan-chuan*, in which the main characters are a shrew and a hen-pecked husband, and also narrative ballads and poetry. [J D C]

'Purāṇa'. A class of texts of popular Hinduism, dating from the time of the epic or slightly thereafter, and continuing to be written or enlarged upon throughout the medieval period.

According to tradition, a *Purāṇa* deals with 5 subjects: the creation of the world, periodic dissolution and recreation of the world, genealogy of gods and saints, the eras or epochs into which each creation is divided, and the histories of royal dynasties. But the actual texts conform to this pattern irregularly or imperfectly. The *Purāṇas* are in fact encyclopedias of folk religion and englobe in large part the traditions central to the great cults of Śiva and Viṣṇu. As with the epics, an older, secular or princely, tradition seems to have been appropriated to the uses of popular belief.

The canonical *Purāṇas* are 18 in number, of which the best known in the west are (a) the *Viṣṇu* (tr. H. H. Wilson, 1864–77), which celebrates Kṛṣṇa according to the Pāñcarātra sect; (b) the relatively late *Bhāgavata* (tr. J. M. Sanyal, Calcutta, 1952–4), by far the most famous but least characteristic *Purāṇa*, written in a uniform and consciously archaizing style and devoted to the propagation of the *bhakti* cult. The tenth book is the standard biography of Kṛṣṇa; (c) *Mārkaṇḍeya* (tr. F. E. Pargiter, Calcutta, 1904), one of the oldest *Purāṇas*, parts of which predate Śaivite or Vaiṣṇnavite sectarianism; (d) *Agni* (tr. M. N. Dutt, Calcutta, 1903–4); and (e) *Garuḍa* (tr. E. Wood, Allahabad, 1911). The last two carry the encyclopedic tendency to the extreme and include résumés of grammar, medicine, poetics, etc., as well as extensive treatments of religious topics.

Like the epics, the *Purāṇas* contain much historical material, principally king lists but also descriptions of cities and holy places, though the form of presentation, mixed with legends and uncritical traditions, makes their use as history quite hazardous. It was the *Bhāgavata Purāṇa's* mention of Candragupta Maurya (*c.* 322–298 B.C.) which permitted the identification of that legendary sovereign with the Sandracottos known to the Greeks and thus supplied the key to the early chronology of India. [E G]

W. Kirfel, *Das Purāṇapañcalakṣaṇa* (Bonn, 1927); F. E. Pargiter, *Ancient Indian Historical Tradition* (1922); ◊ *Mahābhārata*; A. Barth, *Religions of India* (1889); E. W. Hopkins, *Religions of India* (Boston, 1895).

'Pyo'. A type of ◊ Burmese poem in the 'classical' quadri-syllabic line, often as long as a small book. The essence of the early *pyo* (15–16th century A.D.) lies in their religious teaching. Some simply offer precepts for virtuous conduct, others – more interesting as literature – are set in the framework of a ◊ *jātaka* or of an episode from the life of the Buddha retold in verse. The latter contain extended passages employing all the arts of Burmese poetry on the doctrinal points which arise in the course of the story. [J W A O]

R

Rāhula, Śrī (fl. 1430–60). Sinhalese poet. He was connected with the royal family of Ceylon, and was the principal poet of the reign of King Parākramabāhu VI at

Kōṭṭē, near Colombo. He was a Buddhist monk, and held the position of Sangharāja or head of the Buddhist Order in Ceylon. His principal works are *Kāvyaśēkhara,* recounting the story of the Sattubhasta Jātaka, and two ◊ *sandēsa* poems, *Parevisandēsa* (*The Dove's Message*, ed. and tr. S. de Silva, Colombo, 1873) and *Sälalihini-sandēsa* ('The Starling's Message', tr. W. C. Macready, as *The Sela's Message*, Colombo, 1865). Rāhula's style is classical, in the Sanskrit tradition. [C H B R]

C. E. Godakumbura, *Sinhalese Literature* (Colombo, 1955).

Raja Rao (1909–). Indian writer of novels and short stories in English. His mother tongue is Kanarese, but his post-graduate education was in France, and all his publications in book form have been in English. *Kanthapur* (1938) is an account of the impact of Gandhi's teaching on a Mysore village, told with considerable sophistication of technique. *Cow of the Barricades* (1947) is a collection of short stories, and his latest novel, *The Serpent and the Rope* (1960), written after a long silence in which Raja Rao returned to India and renewed connexion with his roots, is an ambitious study of the interpenetration of Indian and Western culture in a semi-autobiographical framework. [I M P R]

K. R. Srinivasa Iyengar, *Indian Writing in English* (Bombay, 1962).

Rājagōpālāchāri, Chakravarti (1879–). Indian statesman and man of letters. A close associate of Gandhi, he has in his time been Chief Minister of Madras, Governor of West Bengal and Governor-General of India.

Entirely bilingual, he has made a considerable contribution both to Indian writing in English and to Tamil prose and is a brilliant orator in both languages. Most of his English works are concerned with the exposition of Hindu texts and beliefs, but they also include a verse translation of part of a Tamil epic, *The Ayodhya Canto of the Ramayana as Told by Kamban* (1961) (◊ Kampaṉ). Among his short stories in Tamil are *Kaṟpaṉaikkāṭu* (1957), a collection of fables for children, and *The Fatal Cart and Other Stories* (tr. C. R. Ramaswami, New Delhi, 1946). His Tamil prose versions of the ◊ *Mahābhārata* (author's tr. Bombay, 1951) and the ◊ *Rāmāyaṇa* (tr. Bombay, 1957) were also written for children but have had a much wider success. Like all of Rājagōpālāchāri's best work they combine simplicity with profundity. [R E A]

Rajaji's Speeches (2 vols., Bombay, 1958).
Monica Felton, *I Meet Rajaji* (1962); K. S. Krisnan, 'Chakravarti Thirumagan by C. Rajagopalachari', *Indian Literature,* I, 2, New Delhi, Apr.–Sept. 1959.

Rajaji. ◊ Rājagōpālāchāri.

Rājam Ayyar, B. R. (1872–98). Tamil novelist. Author of one of the earliest novels in Tamil, *Kamalambal, or the Fatal Rumour*, the story of a South Indian brahmin family, published serially 1893–5. His unfinished novel in English, *True Greatness, or Vasudeva Sastri,* gives quite a good impression of the pleasantly humorous style and the philosophical import of his Tamil work. For the last two years of his life Rājam Ayyar was editor of an English-language monthly, *Prabuddha Bharata.* Most of his own contributions, including *Vasudeva Sastri* and a number of stories, were later reprinted in book form as *Rambles in Vedanta* (Madras, 1905), which also contains a brief sketch of his life. [R E A]

'Ramakian'. ◊ *Rāmāyaṇa.*

Rāmānuja (11th cent. B.C.). Indian philosopher. Chief rival of ◊ Śaṅkara within the Vedānta. He tried to reconcile the doctrine of liberation with a view that the world is in some respects real (qualified non-dualism or *viśiṣṭādvaita*). His commentary on the *Brahmasūtras* is often more faithful to the original than is Śaṅkara's more doctrinaire version. Rāmānuja was a Vaiṣṇava and a devotee of Rāma; his school, now a sect (the caste of Śrīvaiṣṇavas) likewise combine elements of Vedic orthodoxy with popular religious practice. [E G]

The Vedântasûtras, tr. G. Thibaut (Sacred Books of the East, 3 vols., 1890–1904).
P. N. Srinivasachari, *The Philosophy of Viśiṣṭādvaita* (Madras, 1946).

'Rāmāyaṇa'. The shorter epic of India (◊ *Mahābhārata*). It recounts the adventures of Rāma, King of Ayodhyā (Oudh), who, like the Kṛṣṇa of the *Mahābhārata,* has become one of the favourite deities of popular Hinduism. The poem, attributed to Vālmīki (who may very well have been the author), comprises 7 books, of which the first and last are later additions. The remaining 5 tell, with poetic ability and few digressions, of Rāma's courtship of Sītā; his marriage; the abduction of Sītā by Rāvaṇa, a demon and rival whom Rāma had bested by bending a great bow; Rāma's alliance with the monkey king Hanuman and their invasion of Laṅka (said to be Ceylon), the island kingdom of Rāvaṇa; the war and rescue of Sītā. The last book, probably added later, concerns Rāma's jealousy and banishment of Sītā (whom he suspects of having encouraged Rāvaṇa), the birth of Rāma's twin sons, and the happy reunion of the family.

Dating the epic is difficult; the style and content suggest that it is younger than the *Mahābhārata*, yet the *Mahābhārata* contains a condensed version of the *Rāmāyaṇa*. The events of the *Mahābhārata* are older, yet its redaction took place over a longer period of time. Perhaps the *Rāmāyaṇa* was complete by the beginning of the Christian era.

The adventures of Rāma have enjoyed an unparalleled popularity in India. The epic itself has been adapted in most of the vernacular languages, including two famous medieval versions in Hindi (⇨ Tulsī Dās) and Tamil (⇨ Kampaṉ). The story has been made the subject of innumerable literary and popular works: dramas by Bhāsa and Bhavabhūti, epic poems by ⇨ Kālidāsa and Bhāravi, folk plays and recitations in every part of India. Rāma, a deity more ideal than the unpredictable Kṛṣṇa, is adored in temples everywhere.

The Thai version of the *Rāmāyaṇa* exhibits marked differences from the Sanskrit epic. Episodes known from Sinhalese, southern Indian and Bengali versions are included, while Khmer and Javanese versions have also influenced its development in Thailand. In turn, Thai texts and techniques of production have had an influence on Cambodian and Lao performances. Early in the formation of the local tradition ancient Buddhist versions probably played an important part.

The only complete Thai version is the *Ramakian* of Rama I (1782–1809). Invocations and texts of episodes, some intended for performance as dance-drama, are known from the 18th century. Despite the relatively late date of such manuscripts, the epic has a long history in Thailand. (⇨ Thai Literature; Javanese Literature.) [E G]

Tr. R. T. H. Griffith (5 vols., 1870–89); tr. M. L. Sen (3 vols., Calcutta, 1927).

H. Jacobi, *Das Rāmāyana, Geschichte und Inhalt* (Bonn, 1893); (⇨ *Mahābhārata*); Swami Satyananda Puri and Charoen Sarahiran, *The Ramakirti* (*Ramakian*) *or the Thai Version of the Ramayana* (Bangkok, 1949); Dhani Nivat, Prince, 'The Rama Jataka, a Lao Version of the story of Rama', in *Journal of the Siam Society*, 36, 1947.

Rashîd al-Dîn Fadlullâh (*c.*1247–1318). Muslim statesman and historian. Perhaps of Jewish descent. Beginning his career as the court-physician of the Mongol Sultan Abaqa Khan, in 1298 he was appointed vizier by Abaqa's successor Ghâzân (1295–1304) and continued to hold office under Uljâytû (1304–16). The envy aroused by his great wealth and grandiose benefactions enabled his enemies, early in the reign of the young Abu Saʿîd, to procure first his deposition from office and then his execution on the charge of having poisoned Uljâytû. His great history, *Jâmi ʿal-Tawârîkh* ('Collection of Chronicles'), was begun as a history of the Mongols at the invitation of Ghâzân Khan, who put the state archives at his disposal, and continued, as a universal history, for Uljâytû. The work is notable for impartiality, clarity of style, and the wide range and authority of its sources. Rashîd al-Dîn took great pains to ensure its transmission to posterity, in two versions, one Persian and one Arabic, but it was never completed. The manuscripts vary much in content, and the whole of the surviving text has not yet been published. The work falls into two parts: the first, known as *Ta'rîkh-i Ghâzânî*, comprises an account of the Turkish and Mongol tribes and the reigns of Jenghiz Khan and his successors down to Ghâzân, with an uncompleted section on Uljâytû; the second is a general history of the world – from China to Europe – in 12 sections; a geographical third part was planned, but perhaps never written. Of the first part, the account of the tribes has been translated into German by F. von Erdmann (*Vollständige Übersicht . . .*, Kazan, 1841) and by C. Saleman (in W. Radloff, *Das Kudatku Bilig . . .*, i, St Petersburg, 1891), and the history of Hûlâgû was edited with French translation by E. Quatremère (Paris, 1836); of part two, the history of the 'Franks' – largely based on the chronicle of Martinus Oppaviensis (d. 1278) – is edited with French translation by K. Jahn (Leiden, 1951). There are besides extensive translations into Russian. [V L M]

Browne, *L H P*, iii; Arberry, *C P L*; *E of I*; C. A. Storey, *Persian Literature: a Bio-bibliographical Survey*, i (1927–).

'Ṛgveda' ('Rigveda') (*veda*, Sanskrit 'lore'). The oldest Indian text (*c.* 1500–1000 B.C.) and the first extensive composition in any Indo-European tongue (an archaic form of Sanskrit); a collection of 1,028 hymns (*ṛk*) celebrating various natural and ethical deities. The chief and most sacred authority of orthodox Hinduism, the *Ṛgveda* was communicated from teacher to pupil within the priestly class of brahmins through a technique of pronunciation and memorization so explicit that the text extant has altered not at all in nearly 3,500 years.

The hymns of the *Ṛgveda* were composed during nearly half a millennium which coincided with the Indo-Europeans' (or *āryans*, as they called themselves) conquest of north India. The hymns are our only historical sources for this epoch. They reveal a stage of Indian society and religion more Indo-European than Hindu, are permeated with a sense of the awesome and grand in nature, and show man concerned with propitiating the violent forces around him or securing the favour of those lovely and beneficent. Certain hymns are martial in tone, while others, to the dawn and the sun, are justly renowned for their serene inspiration.

In time, the sanctity of the *Ṛgveda* became a matter of its outward form, little being understood of its meaning or significance, and it was as a collection of esoteric formulae, attributed to divine authorship, that the *Ṛgveda* was accommodated to the vastly different religion of later India. Its original meaning is still often disputed by philologists. (⇨ Veda, *Brāhmaṇa*, *Upaniṣad*.) [E G]

Tr. R. T. H. Griffith (2 vols., Benares, 1896–97); German tr. K. F. Geldner (Harvard Oriental Series, Cambridge, Mass., 1951). H. Oldenberg, *Die Religion des Veda* (Berlin, 1894); A. A. Macdonnell, *Vedic Mythology* (Strassburg, 1897); A. Bergaigne, *La religion védique* (Paris, 1878–83).

Rizal, José (1861–96). ⇨ Philippine patriot, novelist and poet. He was a Tagalog, with some admixture of Chinese blood. After receiving a classical education at the Jesuit college in Manila, he went to Spain for medical studies, and there took an active part in the campaign for colonial reforms being carried on by Filipino students and expatriates. He contributed political tracts to *La solidaridad*, the organ of the movement, while corresponding with German scholars on scientific and anthropological questions; but two novels in sequence, *Noli me tángere* (1886; tr. Camilo Osias, 1956, and L. Guerrero, 1961) and *El filibusterismo* (1891; tr. C. Derbyshire, *The Reign of Greed*, 1912) are his major literary works. They are written in Spanish, of which he had full command. They present with passionate indignation – and so not always fairly – the abuses of Spanish rule and the supineness of Filipinos in knuckling under it: 'there would be no tyrants, if there were no slaves.' The books, published in Europe, were banned in the Philippines, but contributed significantly nevertheless to a separatist movement which resulted in revolution when the Spanish government executed Rizal on a charge of treason (1896). Before he was killed, he wrote a poem – untitled, but commonly known as *El último adiós* ('Last Farewell') – which may well be considered as one of the most moving expressions of patriotism as Asians understand it. [H C]

Poesías de Rizal, ed. J. C. de Veyra (Manila, 1946).

Austin Craig, *Lineage, Life and Labors of Dr José Rizal* (Manila, 1913); F. C. Laubach, *Rizal: Man and Martyr* (Manila, 1936); Camilo Osias, *José Rizal: His Life and Times* (Manila, 1948).

Roestam Effendi (1903–). ⇨ Indonesian lyric poet and literary pioneer. His collection of poems – *Pertjikan Permenungan* ('Thoughts at Random') – appeared in 1924. Always an innovator and rebel – he was once a Communist Deputy in the Dutch Parliament – Roestam Effendi experimented extensively with new forms of verse and successfully adapted European forms to the natural rhythms of the Malay language. His meaning is often obscured by his use of unusual words from his native Minangkabau dialect. He also wrote a play called *Bébasari* (1928). [E C G B]

Rûmî. ◊ Jalâl al-Dîn.

Rustaveli, Shota (fl. *c.*1200?). National bard of Georgia in the Caucasus. Traditionally, Rustaveli lived and wrote at the court of Queen Tamar (1184–1213), under whom Georgia enjoyed its Golden Age. Nothing concrete is known of his life. He is said to have studied in Athens, fallen hopelessly in love with his sovereign Tamar, and died a pilgrim in Jerusalem. Some critics dispute the traditional dating of Rustaveli and his work, and assign them to a later period.

Rustaveli's sole surviving work is the great romantic epic *Vepkhis-tqaosani* or *The Man in the Panther's Skin* (tr. Marjory Wardrop, 1912, repr. Moscow, 1938; other versions in French, German, Russian, Czech, Japanese, etc.). The poem's setting is exotic. The Arabian paladin Avtandil falls in love with Princess Tinatin, daughter of his liege lord King Rostevan. Frustrated in his passion, he swears eternal comradeship with the Indian knight Tariel, and joins with him in quest of the fair Nestan-Darejan, who has been abducted to the land of the *kajebi,* who are demons or *jinn* after the fashion of the *Arabian Nights.* After many fantastic adventures, the two pairs of lovers are reunited.

Much of the poem is allegorical, giving a vivid portrayal of the manners and ideals of medieval Georgia. The cults of chivalry and courtly love are much in evidence, and parallels have been drawn with the poetry of the Troubadours in the West. Influenced by neo-Platonism, Rustaveli shows profound psychological insight and philosophical wisdom. Many of his aphorisms have become Georgian proverbs. Though professing respect for Christianity, Rustaveli is alien to medieval scholasticism. Some churchmen regarded his poem as pagan and profane and burnt the manuscripts which fell into their hands. No manuscript copy earlier than the 17th century is known to survive. [D M L]

C. M. Bowra, *Inspiration and Poetry* (1955); D. M. Lang, *Landmarks in Georgian Literature* (1966).

S

Sa'dî (Musharrif al-Dîn b. Muslih) of Shîrâz (*c.*1215–?1292). Persian poet and popular moralist. His works have always been esteemed and much quoted in the Muslim world for their homely and practical wisdom. Little is known for certain of his life, as the autobiographical references he makes in his writings are not all to be taken seriously. Orphaned at an early age, he began his studies in his native Shîrâz but later attended the Nizâmiyya College at Baghdad (◊ Nizâm al-Mulk). He then took to a wandering life, visiting Asia Minor, Syria and Egypt, and making the Pilgrimage to Mecca (he claims also to have been for a time the prisoner of the Crusaders and to have visited Kâshghar and India). One year after his return to Shîrâz in 1256, he presented to the local ruler his didactic poem *Bûstân* ('The Orchard'), consisting of 'dissertations on justice, good government, beneficence, earthly and mystic love, humility, submissiveness, contentment and other excellences' (R. Levy) (Eng. tr. G. S. Davie, 1882), and in 1258 his *Gulistân* ('The Rose-garden'), a collection of gnomic anecdotes written in rhyming prose with verse-passages interspersed (numerous translations into most European languages; in English, among others: E. B. Eastwick, Hertford, 1852; J. T. Platts, 1873; Sir Richard Burton, 1928; A. J. Arberry (chaps. 1 and 2), *Kings and Beggars,* 1945). The rest of his life was spent at Shîrâz, where his tomb is still revered.

Sa'dî was also a prolific writer of occasional verse – panegyric, elegies, facetiae, and particularly of lyrics (*ghazals*), two cycles of which have been translated (Sir L. W. King, *Badâ'i',* Berlin, 1925, and *Taiyibât,* London, 1926); as the popularizer of the *ghazal*-form he paved the way for ◊ Hâfiz. The attribution to Sa'dî of the *Pand-nâma,* a short verse-treatise on ethics (ed. and tr. A. N. Wollaston, 1906), is now generally rejected. [V L M]

Browne, *LHP*, ii; H. Massé, *Essai sur le poète Saadi* (Paris, 1919); R. A. Nicholson, *Eastern Poetry and Prose* (Cambridge, 1922); *E of A*; Arberry, *CPL*; Rypka, *IL.*

Saigyō-hōsi (1118–90). Japanese poet. He was a member of an important family moving in court circles, but at the age of 23 abandoned wife, family and worldly life to become a priest. He spent the rest of his days travelling throughout Japan, composing *tanka*, 'short poems' of 31 syllables. In this way of life he was following Chinese precedents – and he also wanted to escape from the Japanese civil wars. Many of his compositions were selected for imperial poetry collections, in particular for the *Senzaishū* (1183) and *Shinkokinshū* (1206).

His work is of great importance because his most characteristic poems express a new spirit, different from that of the love poetry of the Heian court. Buddhist thought pervades his writing, as does melancholy, partly a product of his times. His travels brought him closer to nature than many of the poets that preceded him. In the development of Japanese poetry, he seems to form a link between *mono no aware*, the sense of sympathy felt by the author for the rest of creation, and *yūgen*, the inclusion of a deeper, symbolic, ingredient into literature. He wrote occasional verse which is no better than the compositions of lesser men, but his best nature poetry is still very moving. He is the spiritual ancestor of ◊ Bashō. [C J D]

Keene, *A J L*.
Brower and Miner, *J C P*.

Saikaku. ◊ Ihara Saikaku.

'Śakuntalā'. ◊ Kālidāsa.

'Sandēsa'. 'Message-poem'; a well-known type of poem in Sinhalese, the first surviving example dating from the 14th century. The Sanskrit word *sandeśa* means 'message', and such poems are based on the *Meghadūta* of ◊ Kālidāsa. The essential feature is the entrusting of a message to a chosen messenger, usually a bird; but the actual message is unimportant, being usually a prayer for prosperity. The chief portion of the poem consists of elaborate descriptions of the route to be followed by the messenger. Thus in Śrī ◊ Rāhula's *Sälalihini-sandēsa* there are 6 introductory verses in praise of the chosen bird-messenger, 13 verses describing the capital city of Ceylon from which his journey is to start, 32 verses describing the journey, 39 verses describing the temple where he is to deliver his message, and finally 16 verses disclosing the message itself (tr. in *Marg*, v, 3, Bombay, 1952).

This type of poem had its period of greatest popularity in the 15th century, but has continued to be written down to the present day. It is the only truly secular genre in classical Sinhalese literature. [C H B R]

Sangam Literature (Tamil). A legend of three successive literary academies (Sangam) first appears in a medieval commentary to *Kaḷaviyal*, a work on poetics. No work of the first two is extant. These academies are stated to have lasted thousands of years and to have perished in a flood together with their cities. Among the works of the third academy listed, the Eight Anthologies (*Eṭṭuttokai*) and a 'grammar' (*Tolkāppiyam*) have survived.

With the exception of the anthology *Paripāṭal*, the *Eṭṭuttokai* are collections of discontinuous non-religious poems, grouped broadly into collections of bardic poetry, *puṟam*, and courtly love poetry, *akam*. Most famous of the former is *Puṟanāṉūṟu*, an anthology of 400 poems praising various kings and chieftains of the early Tamil country. Both this and *Patiṟṟupattu*, which deals with the early kings of Kerala, in south-west India, bear out a number of points raised in the classical geographies of Ptolemy and others. *Akanāṉūṟu*, an anthology of 400 poems, is one of the better-known collections of love poetry. *Paripāṭal* uniquely among these eight is an anthology of religious poetry, possibly the earliest of this genre in Tamil. The date of these poems and of the large number of poets is uncertain, but they may safely be ascribed to the first five centuries A.D.

Tolkāppiyam has sections on phonetics, word-structure, grammar, prosody and poetics.

Sometimes included in Sangam Literature are the Ten Songs (*Pattuppāṭṭu*). These seem to relate to the same period as the anthology poems and to some of the heroes therein, but are considerably larger works of 300 to 700 lines each. [J R M]

Two Thousand Years of Tamil Literature: An Anthology with Studies and Translations, ed. J. M. Somasundaram Pillai (Madras, 1959).
V. R. Ramachandra Dikshitar, *Studies in*

Tamil Literature and History (2nd edn, Madras, 1936); K. N. Sivaraja Pillai, *The Chronology of the Early Tamils* (Madras, 1932); Xavier S. Thani Nayagam, *Nature in Ancient Tamil Poetry* (Tuticorin, 1953).

Śaṅkara (8th cent A.D.). Indian philosopher and mystic. The chief architect of the Vedānta. It would appear that he was born in Malabar, spent some time at Śṛṅgeri in Mysore, travelled extensively, and died (at 32?) at Kedarnāth in the Himālaya.

His commentary on the *Brahmasūtras* (the summary of Upaniṣadic speculation, which became the canonical text of Vedānta), is the oldest still preserved (◊ *Upaniṣad* and Rāmānuja).

Śaṅkara founds his doctrine upon an uncompromising interpretation of the unity of *ātman* and *brahman*; his non-dualism (*advaita*) emphasizes the unreality of the world of appearance (*māyā*) and asserts that salvation is a function of intellection alone, irrelevant to tradition, birth or idolatry.

The intellectual inheritance of modern India in a way begins with Śaṅkara. The philosophy which preceded him is now mostly vestige, but his name is still at the centre of lively sectarian controversy, and it is his doctrines that other schools must first dispute. The most orthodox caste of brahmins, the *smārta*, who consider the ◊ Veda their only authority, look to Śaṅkara as the founder of their order. Rāmānuja and Madhva, the other great Vedāntins, are more influenced by the popular *bhakti* cults of the day. (◊ *Bhagavadgītā*.)

Besides his scholarly commentary, Śaṅkara is said also to have composed more popular versions of his doctrine, particularly as commentaries on the *Bhagavadgītā* (not a congenial text for his ideas) and older *Upaniṣads*. His *Upadeśasāhasrī* (attribution contested) serves as an introduction to his *Brahmasūtrabhāṣya*. Such is the fame of Śaṅkara that devotional poems (as *Saundaryalaharī*) and even secular love lyrics (*Amaruśataka*) have been credited to him. [E G]

The Vedântasûtras, tr. G. Thibaut (Sacred Books of the East, 3 vols., 1890–1904); *Self-ledge* (*Ātmabodha*), tr. Swami Nikhilananda (New York, 1946); *Saundaryalaharī*, tr. W. N. Brown (Cambridge, Mass., 1958).

P. Deussen, *System of the Vedānta*, tr. C. Johnston (Chicago, 1932); O. Lacombe, *L'Absolu selon le Vedānta* (Paris, 1937); S. N. Dasgupta, *History of Indian Philosophy* (5 vols., 1922–55).

Sāttaṉār. ◊ Cāttaṉār.

Seami Motokiyo. ◊ Zeami Motokiyo.

Sei Shōnagon (fl. 1000). Japanese authoress. All that is known of her life is that she was the daughter of Kiyowara Motosuke, himself a noted wit, was a contemporary of the novelist ◊ Murasaki Shikibu and was lady-in-waiting to the Empress Sadako, who, in contrast to Murasaki's mistress, the Empress Akiko, liked her courtiers to be witty, not to say frivolous. Sei Shōnagon's literary production is in the form of a 'pillow book' – a collection of notes, observations and categories, the usual aim of which is to classify scenes, human types, events, natural phenomena and so on under such headings as 'amusing', 'annoying', 'moving'. Her vivid and often scathing comments on the people about her, written with a malice and a polished indelicacy that would have fitted her for a successful career at Versailles, still make good reading. [C J D]

The Pillow-Book of Sei Shōnagon, tr. Arthur Waley (1928) (selections); *Les notes de chevet de Séi Shōnagon*, Fr. tr. André Beaujard (Paris, 1934) (complete).

'Sejarah Melayu' ('The Malay Annals'), An anonymous ◊ Malay history, probably written about A.D. 1535. This prose work (ed. R. O. Winstedt, 1938), of which there are several published (and many unpublished manuscript) versions, is considered the finest work in Malay literature (tr. C. C. Brown, 1952).

Some think that the original nucleus was re-written later by Tun Seri Lanang (fl. A.D. 1611), Bendahara (Chief Minister) of the former Muslim Malacca sultanate then in Johore. The intelligent, educated and cosmopolitan personality of the writer and the complete (albeit unhistorical) familiarity with both Court and foreign circles and political events over a long period of time, support this view, though it is difficult to know how much to attribute to the original 16th-century writer and how much to a 17th-century 'editor'.

The power of observation and description displayed here, and the use of a clear, lively and succinct style of Malay has led to this particular form of the language being regarded by some as 'classical' Malay.

There are few dates in the *Sejarah Melayu*, much legend and anecdote; yet liveliness of observation and variety of interest have together made this the chief historical source for the customs and events of the heyday of the Malay kingdom of Malacca (A.D. *c.* 1450–1511). [J C B]

Winstedt, *C M L*; C. C. Brown, 'A Malay Herodotus', *O A S*, XII, 3 and 4, 1948.

Shamsu'ddin (of) Pasai (or **al-Sumatrani**) (?–1630). ◊ Malay theologian. Lived and worked in Java and Sumatra. He was a heterodox Muslim mystic who enjoyed high favour during the reign of Mahkota Alam in Acheh (A.D. 1607–36) but whose works, like those of ◊ Hamzah Fansuri, were later condemned to be burnt. One that survived is his *Mir'at al-mu'min* (1601). His favourite subjects were the doctrine of existence and the recitation of religious formulae, while his mysticism was speculative rather than emotional. He also wrote a commentary on Hamzah Fansuri's poems *Kitab Sharh ruba'i Hamzah Fansuri*, and an Arabic work *Jauhar al Ḥaḳā'iḳ* (ed. C. A. O. van Nieuwenhuijze, see below). [J C B]

C. A. O. van Nieuwenhuijze, *Samsu'l-Dīn van Pasai* (Leiden, 1945).

Shen Yen-ping (pseud. **Mao Tun**) (1896–). Chinese novelist, critic and pioneer of the New Literature Movement. He was born in a small town in Chekiang province, the eldest son of a large family. His father, a supporter of the Reform Party, died when he was 10, and he was eventually forced by poverty to curtail his education and work in the Commercial Press in Shanghai. In 1921–3 he edited *The Short Story*, published by the same firm, where he wrote extensively on modern European literature, particularly of the naturalist and realist schools. From 1923 to 1927 he became involved in revolutionary politics, which provided the material for his first work of fiction *The Eclipse*, a trilogy of short novels, published 1928, acclaimed for the honesty with which it dealt with the theme of the individual in a revolution. This was followed by *Wild Roses* and *Rainbow*, two novels published in 1929, and his most ambitious work, *Midnight* (1933).

Midnight (tr. Hsü and Barnes, Peking, 1957) depicts the complicated interrelationship between town and country and between foreign and Chinese business in the Shanghai of the Depression. Its hero is an industrialist whose attempts to build Chinese industry end in bankruptcy at the hands of a foreign-backed financier. Though somewhat uneven, this work has been acclaimed in China as a masterpiece of neo-realism. Shen Yen-ping has also written numerous stories, essays and reminiscences and one play. The best of his stories display the same meticulous attention to physical detail and atmosphere as his novels, notable among them being *Spring Silkworms* and *The Lin Family's Shop* (tr. Shapiro, *Spring Silkworms and Other Stories*, Peking, 1956).

Since 1949 Shen Yen-ping, who holds the position of Minister of Culture of the People's Republic of China, has confined his literary activity largely to criticism. Many of his articles have appeared in the journal *Chinese Literature*, which he edits. [J D C]

Shiga Naoya (1883–). Japanese novelist. He was brought to Tokyo from the provinces for education, but did not complete his course at Tokyo University. He worked with ◊ Mushakōji Saneatsu to form the anti-Naturalist *Shirakaba* ('White Birch') association of writers, and his early stories show the influence of this connexion. But his forceful personality did not permit him to subject himself to a group, and it is as an individualist that he is known in Japan. His personal style became apparent in 1913, when he wrote *Han no hanzai* (*Han's Crime*, tr. I. Morris, in Keene, *MJL*), in which a Chinese juggler kills his wife during his knife-throwing act, after years of conflict with her. Conflict was indeed the theme of much of his work, possibly as a result of a long quarrel with his father. This quarrel is described in an autobiographical novel, *Wakai* ('Reconciliation', 1917). It is generally thought that his writings from 1912–17 are his best. He has produced one long novel, *An-ya Kōrō* ('Journey into the Dark'), which is in several parts and took 25 years to write (1912–37). Although the incidents in the story are not autobiographical, yet the hero's search for happiness, and the suffering he encounters are typical of the life of the author. In some ways he can be compared with ◊ Natsume Sōseki – for his humour, for his apparently simple but really very subtle style, for his deep penetration into human psychology and for his independence from literary schools. But he is even more of an individualist than Natsume. Since the war he has lent his name to some left-wing activities, but has not written anything to equal his earlier novels. [C J D]

At Kinosaki, tr. E. Seidensticker, in Keene, *M J L*; *The Artist*, tr. Ivan Morris, in Morris, *M J S*.

Shih Nai-an (probably 14th cent.). Chinese novelist. Of Shih Nai-an nothing substantial is known; his name is only a useful peg on which to hang the novel *Shui-hu Chuan* (best known to English speakers in Pearl Buck's translation called *All Men are Brothers*). The novel seems to have originally been put together by a sort of literary committee. It dates probably from the late 14th century, though earliest extant editions are of the 16th century.

The novel has its origins in the historical rebellion of 'Sung Chiang and his Thirty-six', recorded in the history of the Sung Dynasty. This band soon evolved in popular literature as larger-than-life revolutionary heroes. It can be deduced from its structure that the novel incorporated fully written-up accounts of their exploits in story-teller fashion, while its grand lines were taken from 'Tales of the Hsuan-ho period of the Sung dynasty' of Yuan times (1279–1386), which set the seal of sidereal divinity on the Thirty-six and disclosed their mission – to 'spread abroad chivalry and exterminate treachery and evil'.

The *Shui-hu Chuan* has gone through transformations under various editors, but is restored in the modern edition to something near its original form. It is as perfect an example of the story-teller's art as can be found anywhere; it has bounding vitality and a genius for the right phrase in dialogue and for the striking gesture. The populist outlook of the novel – the assumption that justice is never done to the common people – accounts for the regard in which it is held in China today. [D E P]

Richard Irwin, *The Evolution of a Chinese Novel* (Harvard, 1953).

Shimazaki Tōson (1872–1943). Japanese poet and novelist. Born in Nagano, a mountainous and, until recently, remote district in the main island of Japan, he was educated in Tokyo, and became a Christian in 1888. Until 1896 he led a restless life and his literary output was mainly in the form of poems in a new verse-form, which constitute some of the earliest serious modern poetry in Japan. They were idealistic and romantic in sentiment, and appeared in 1907 in a collection entitled *Wakanashū* ('Collection of Young Leaves'). From 1896 he pursued the profession of schoolmaster, first at Sendai, then at Komoro in his native province. His interests moved from poetry to the novel, in which field his idealism combined with the dominant theories of the period to produce one of the few Naturalist novels in Japan to tackle a social theme: *Hakai* (1906; *The Broken Promise*, one chapter tr. E. Seidensticker, in *MJL*). This deals with the problem of the *eta* or outcastes in Japan, represented by one of them, a schoolteacher, who conceals his origins but finally breaks his promise made to his father and discloses his secret. In 1906 Shimazaki abandoned teaching and henceforward lived by the pen. After the death of his wife he was in France from 1913 to 1916, and then returned to Tokyo. Finally, from 1929 to 1935 appeared his most important work, *Yoake-mae* ('Before the Dawn'), a long historical novel of the period just before and including the Meiji Restoration. It is set in his native province, and the central character is a last representative of a long line of provincial scholars, a portrait which has much in common with the author's father. The novel reflects the nationalistic and anti-foreign sentiments that were growing in Japan at the time. [C J D]

Poem tr. D. Keene, in Keene, *MJL*.

Shin Raṭṭhasāra (1468–1530). Buddhist monk and ◊ Burmese poet. (Also spelt Rat-htat-tha-ra etc.). He is held to be the greatest writer of ◊ *pyo*, and of his 5 surviving works in this form the *Hatthipāla* (or *Ko-gan*) *Pyo* in his masterpiece. He also wrote ◊ *maw-gun* and a moving poem (in a form called *taw-la*) on his thoughts as he walked through the forest on a pilgrimage. His evocative description of the sights and sounds of the forest was imitated by many later writers in the ◊ *yadu* form. Several *yadu* are ascribed to him, including a unique poem in which conventional lines of 4 syllables alternate with lines of 5 syllables. [J W A O]

Shin Sīlavaṁsa (1453–1518). ◊ Burmese Buddhist monk and author. (Also spelt Thi-lawun-tha etc.). The contemporary and rival of ◊ Shin Raṭṭhasāra. His poems in the ◊ *pyo* form are valued less for their artistic merit than for their religious profundity. Like his rival, he wrote ◊ *maw-gun*, one of which, the *Ratanā Vimān* (or *Yadana Beik-man*), about a monastery built for him by the king, was inscribed on stone (A.D. 1497). Several ◊ *yadu* poems are ascribed to him, and he wrote two of the earliest prose works in Burmese: the *Pārāyana-vatthu* ('Stories about the Way to the Other Side' – i.e. to Nirvana) and a history called the *Ya-zawin-gyaw*, both of which were adapted from Pali Buddhist texts. [J W A O]

Shlonsky Avraham (1900–). Hebrew poet. Born in Russia, went to Palestine in 1921 and, although he became one of its most virile poets, whose lightness of form and magical rhythm grips the reader, he clearly shows the influence of Soviet Russian poets. In 1925, with Steinmann, he edited a literary periodical which marked the first revolt in Hebrew literature. He translated Pushkin, Shakespeare, Romain Rolland and modern Russian poets and founded *Sifriat Poalim* ('Workers' Library'). [E E]

Waxman, *H J L*; Klausner, *H M H L*.

Shu Chʻing-chʻun (pseud. **Lao She**) (1898–). Chinese novelist and playwright. He was born of Manchu ancestry in Peking, his early life being a struggle against poverty. After teaching in China for some years he came to England, where he studied and taught from 1924 to 1930. It was while in England, and under the influence of English novelists, especially Dickens, that he began his literary career. His first two novels, *The Philosophy of Old Chang* and *Chao Tzu-yüeh*, show this influence most clearly. His third novel, *The Two Mas*, is one of the few Chinese works of fiction set outside China, its chief characters being a Chinese curio-dealer and his son living in London.

Shu Chʻing-chʻun's best-known novel, *Lo-tʻo hsiang-tzu* (tr. King, *Rickshaw Boy*, 1945), was written after the author's return to China, where he became a professional writer. Its hero is a young Peking rickshaw puller, whose ambition to own his own rickshaw and to become independent is constantly frustrated by his environment, in spite of the tenacity with which he pursues his goal. The dignity of the hero in adverse circumstances has been compared to that of characters in Hardy, though his misfortunes are attributed not to fate but to the evils of society. The happy ending of the English version has been added by the translator.

Shu Chʻing-chʻun published his long novel *Four Generations under One Roof* in 1946, but most of his output in the war and post-war periods have been plays and narrative ballads. Notable among his plays are *Dragon Beard Ditch* (tr. Liao Hung-ying, Peking, 1956) which depicts the changes in the life of a Peking slum brought about by the 1949 revolution and *Tea House* (1958), in which modern history is reflected in the changing scene in a Peking tea house. [J D C]

C. T. Hsia, *A History of Modern Chinese Fiction* (New Haven, 1961).

Si Burapha (pseud. for **Kulap Saipradit**) (*c.*1905–). Thai novelist. Si Burapha's first, and immediately successful novel, *Luk Phu Chai* ('A Man Indeed'), 1928, already showed his interest in social problems. The subject is the struggle of a man of humble birth to reach high position despite social barriers. In *Khang lang phap* ('Behind the Picture'), 1938, and *Songkhram Chiwit* ('The Struggle of Life') he treats themes of love with great literary skill, introducing a degree of introspection rare in Thai writing. In 1954 he criticized contemporary romantic writing in an essay on the purpose of the novel inspired, partly, by Marxist ideas. Such influences affect his later work which, however, is not of the same quality as that of his middle period. [E H S S]

Si Prat (17th cent.). Thai poet. The son of a court poet, Si Prat had a brief but brilliant career in the reign of Phra Narai (1657–88). He was exiled to Nakhọn Si Thammarat, in south Thailand, under suspicion of indiscreet behaviour with ladies of the palace and, later, was executed there for a repetition of the offence.

His masterpiece, *Kamsuan Si Prat* ('The Mourning of Si Prat'), is a prototype of the ◊ *nirat* and was probably written during his journey into exile. With exquisite skill, he blends his sentiments on leaving behind his beloved lady and his native city, Ayuthaya, with descriptions of nature. He also wrote *Anirut*, a narrative romance deriving from Buddhist and Puranic sources. [E H S S]

Siamese Literature. ◊ Thai Literature.

'Śilappadikāram'. ◊ Iḷankō.

Śivaśankara Piḷḷa, Takazi (1914–). Indian novelist. Before his time novels in Malayalam had tended to have a relatively prosperous middle-class setting. Takazi (the name of his native village, by which he is generally known), after a false start as a poet, has written a large number of novels and short stories with a humbler background. The best known are *Tōṭṭiyuṭe makan* ('The Scavenger's Son', 1948), *Raṇṭiṭaṅṅazi* ('Two Measures', a story of landless agricultural labourers, 1949) and *Cemmīn* ('Prawns', 1956, tr. Narayana Menon as *Chemmeen*, 1962). For the last of these, dealing with the life of the fishermen of Kerala, the author received the President's Award. [R E A]

Somadeva (11th cent.). Indian poet. The author of the *Kathāsaritsāgara* (*Ocean of the Streams of Story*, tr. C. H. Tawney, 10 vols., 1924–8), the best-known collection of folk tales in Sanskrit literature. Somadeva was a Kashmiri Brahmin who lived during the reign of King Ananta (11th century). His work is one of the treasures of Indian poetry; it is written in a simple yet elegant style and is one of the best accounts of Indian customs and life during the classical period.

The *Kathāsaritsāgara* is one of the three known Sanskrit versions of the lost vernacular *Bṛhatkathā* ('Great Story') of Guṇāḍhya. This vast collection of fable and romance, built around the adventure of Udayana, king of Vatsa and the typical hero of Indian folklore, has inspired many of the best works of Indian literature, from the plays of Bhāsa to the novel of Subandhu. Somadeva's Sanskrit rendering shows a considerable brahminization of the Bṛhatkathā's largely secular milieu, which is better represented in the novel of ◊ Daṇḍin. The *Kathāsaritsāgara* is a 'frame story', in which the principal story serves as cadre to a great number of subsidiary stories; a striking example is the 'Twenty-five Tales of a Vampire' (*Vetālapancaviṃsatika*, tr. as *Vikram and the Vampire*, R. Burton, 1893), which, itself a frame story, is often cited as a separate work. As in the *Arabian Nights* the minor stories constitute the principal interest. [E G]

C. H. Tawney, introduction to translations mentioned; F. Lacote, *Essai sur Guṇāḍhya et la Bṛhatkathā* (Paris, 1908); Winternitz, *G I L*, iii.

Sot Kuramarohit (1908–). Thai novelist. Sot Kuramarohit began writing short-stories as a youth and turned to political journalism during a period of further education at Peking University (1931–5). He became a fierce critic of the Japanese and German militarist regimes and regularly contributed articles on anti-war and democratic themes to Bangkok journals. In his novels from the later 1930s, and in his short stories, radio plays and film scripts, he adopts a socialist standpoint. Important works are *Peking* (1943), on social conditions in China, and *Raya* (1955), on the Japanese occupation of Thailand. [E H S S]

Śrīvāstav, Dhanpat Rāy (Prem Cand) (1880–1936). Indian novelist and short-story writer. His work was almost all written under the pen-name Prem Cand. He was born near Banaras and spent most of his life in the United Provinces, working first as a schoolmaster and sub-inspector. In 1921 he withdrew from teaching under the influence of Gandhi's non-cooperation movement, and devoted the rest of his life mainly to Hindi literature. Till *c.* 1914 most of his writing was in Urdu, and it was chiefly through this medium that he acquired his literary background in short story and novel. These genres he established in Hindi on a genuine literary level. His 250-odd short stories (collected in 8 vols. under the title *Mānasarovar*, 'The Holy Lake') depict a wide cross-section of northern Indian life and contain much of his best work. They are compact and predominantly realistic, though sometimes marred by uncritical approval of ideal standards of conduct and social service, a tendency almost always latent in Prem Cand's work, and more pronounced in his full-scale novels. His last complete novel, *Godān* (1936), is his best, and is distinguished for its realistic description of Indian village life and its brilliant characterization of the peasant Hori. But Prem Cand fails to portray his urban characters with the same sympathy, and the work suffers from his evident desire to denigrate the values of urban life.

Prem Cand wrote 11 other complete novels between *c.* 1904 and 1936, dealing largely with social and political questions. Though unequal as literature, they are valuable as presenting a comprehensive picture of the life and mood of the northern India of his day. [R S M]

The Secret of Culture and Other Stories, tr. Madan Gupta (Bombay, 1960); *A Treasury of Modern Asian Stories*, ed. Daniel L. Milton and William Clifford (New York, 1961) (episode from *Godān* and a short story); *Short Stories of Premchand*, tr. Gurdial Mallik (Bombay, 1946); *A Premchand Reader*, ed. N. H. Zide and others (Honolulu, 1962).

Ssu-ma Ch'ien (145–*c.* 86 B.C.). Chinese annalist. Author of *Shih-chi* (*Historical Records*). He came from a long line of 'historians', his father Ssu-ma Tan having been chief astronomer and official historian in the court of the Western Han Dynasty. He began his study of history at the age of 10 and at 20 was sent by his father on an extensive tour of the Emperor's domains. On his return he was appointed attendant to the Han Emperor Wu Ti, and subsequently accompanied the Emperor on many tours, making notes on the history, geography and customs of the places he visited. In 107, soon after his father's death, he became official court historian. This gave him access to the imperial library, of great use to him when in 104 he began his great task. His work was interrupted when he incurred the Emperor's displeasure for defending a defeated general: he was castrated and thrown into prison. Three years later he was released and continued his work. The exact date of his death is not known, but appears to have been when he was about 60 years old.

The *Historical Records* are history conceived on a grand scale, covering the period from the time of the legendary Yellow Emperor (2697 B.C.) up to the author's own time. The work was partly based on traditional histories, but incorporated important new developments in historical writing. It comprises the following sections: The *Basic Annals*, mainly centred on the court, giving detailed accounts of the Emperors' life and administration, in most cases accurately dated; the *Tables of Events*, which are chronologies of members of the imperial family, officials holding office, etc.; the *Records*, which deal separately with different aspects of government, such as court ceremony, music, finance, water conservancy; *Noble Families*, which consists of the family histories of the feudal princes; and the *Biographies*, which deal with the lives of famous men, including officials, philosophers, men of letters, merchants and knights-errant.

Recent archaeology has testified to the accuracy of much of the *Historical Records'* early chronology. In addition to its value as a history, it has long been a model of classical Chinese style. [J D C]

Burton Watson, *Ssu-ma Ch'ien, Grand Historian of China* (New York, 1958).

Steinberg, Judah (1861–1908). Hebrew story-writer. Born in a small Bessarabian town, Lipcani, of Hassidic family, he spent the greater part of his life teaching Hebrew. He found his way to the movement of enlightenment and gradually acquired recognition as a writer. Living close to the people, full of sympathy for the dwellers of the ghetto, he excelled in a kind of short sharp sketch of the simple people who bear their hard lot with dignity and even joy. The peculiar situation of Jews in a hostile environment and the psychological stresses imposed on them are mirrored in his stories like *Asher ben Asher*, *Teshuvah*, *Nizoz Kadosh* and *Brit Milah*. Of his novels, *Ba-Yomin ha-Hem* (tr. G. Yeshurun, *In Those Days*, Philadelphia, 1915) was the only success. It is a simple story of Jewish soldiers press-ganged into military service during the reign of Nicolas I. [E E]

Kolkitve J. S. (Tel Aviv, 1959); *Zichronot*, tr. E. Solis Cohen, jr, *The Breakfast of the Birds* (Philadelphia, 1917).

Klausner, *H M H L*; Waxman, *H J L*.

Steinman, Eliezer (1892–). Hebrew novelist and short-story writer. Born in Russia. He presents the problems of the modern Jew torn between his heritage and the vicissitudes of modern civilization. Influenced by both Gorky and other Russian writers and by Freud, his novels, *Zugot* (Berlin/Tel Aviv, 1930) and *Dudaim* (Tel Aviv, 1931) are much concerned with the sexual problems of their heroes. [E E]

Waxman, *H J L.*

Su Shih. ◊ Su Tung-pʻo.

Su Tung-pʻo (Su Shih) (1036–1101). Chinese poet, essayist, painter etc. His collected works carry an Imperial preface, a rare distinction in itself, praising his genius, integrity and statesmanship. Su Tung-pʻo, his father Su Hsun, and brother Su Che together made up the 'Su trio' from Szechwan, whose prose styles were models for later ages.

Something of a child prodigy, Su Tung-pʻo passed the highest state examination in 1057 and then, as a conservative in opposition to Wang An-shih's reform party, entered on a hazardous political career. In 1079 he was thrown into gaol for his satirical verses, and he was banished twice, but enjoyed, too, periods of high office. Dedicated to the welfare of the people, Su was one of the numerous officials described as 'Confucian on the outside, and Taoist on the inside', for he explored Taoism, and Buddhism too, for an answer to the problem of life and death.

Su was equally famous for his prose and poetry, both in the traditional *shih* form and the newer *tzʻu* form, a type of verse with lines of unequal length and prescribed tone pattern based on popular melodies. In *shih,* Su's natural medium was the 7-word line; some are poems of protest, but typically they are descriptive or express his private feelings. As for *tzʻu,* Su is credited with extending its scope, previously confined to sentimental themes to include both grave and gay. His shorter prose pieces afford vivid glimpses of this vital man in his endless variety of moods. [D E P]

Su Tung-pʻo, tr. Burton Watson (1965) (selections).
Lin Yutang, *The Gay Genius* (1948).

Subrahmaṇya Bhārati, C. (1882–1921). Tamil poet. He is generally regarded as the outstanding Tamil poet of modern times and the major figure of the renaissance in Tamil letters. As a young man he was deeply involved in the struggle for the independence of British India, though his active political career effectively ended in 1908 when he went into exile in Pondicherry. In his verse (a selection of which has been published in English translation by S. Prema, Madras, 1958) his commonest concerns are the greatness of the Tamil poets of two millennia ago and the need for freedom from foreign rule. His range also covers lyrical verse, devotional poetry and the epic. Of his longer poems the best known is his *Kaṇṇan pāṭṭu,* a picture of the many aspects of Krishna.

Though Bhārati will be remembered above all as a poet, he is important in the development of Tamil prose, not widely used as a literary medium until the end of the last century. The bulk of his prose writings are on political or social topics. He wrote a number of short novels and stories and translated some from Tagore.

Like many of his contemporaries in India Bhārati was fluent in English, as the posthumous collections, *Essays and Other Prose Fragments* and *Agni and Other Poems* (Madras, 1937), show.

Throughout the Tamil-speaking world Bhārati societies exist, and one of these, the Calcutta Bharati Tamil Sangam, has published a useful set of *Essays on Bharati* (1958). [R E A]

P. Mahādēvan, *Subrahmaṇya Bhārati: Patriot and Poet* (Madras, 1957); Prema Nandakumar, *Subramanīa Bharati* (Mysore, 1964).

Śūdraka. Classical Indian dramatist. Author of the *Mṛcchakaṭika* (*Little Clay Cart*). So little is known of Śūdraka that it has been suggested that the name is a pesudonym of a perhaps better-known personage. The play itself claims that he was a king and lived for over one hundred years.

The *Mṛcchakaṭika* is very popular in the West, but it is not typical of the best Indian drama (◊ Kālidāsa). The principal characters are the noble Cārudatta, a penniless Brahmin, the prostitute Vasantasenā, and the thief Śarvilaka. The intrigue is half love story and half political plot. For all its realistic air, the play satisfies the major conventions of the dramatic style, and a happy resolution is provided. Among the famous passages are the description of the prostitute's palace, and the minute account of the technique of housebreaking, taken almost verbatim from the *śāstra* of thievery. Oddly, the first 4 acts (of 10) are modelled closely on an unfinished play of Bhāsa, the *Dāridracārudatta.* [E G]

The Little Clay Cart, tr. Revilo Oliver (Urbana, Ill., 1938); tr. Arthur Ryder (Harvard Oriental Series, Cambridge, Mass., 1905).
Winternitz, *G I L*, iii; introduction by Oliver to *The Little Clay Cart,* mentioned above.

Sunthọn Phu (*c.*1786–*c.*1855). ⇨ Thai poet. He is one of Thailand's most popular poets. Though a court scribe, he was of provincial origin and retained the common touch in his verses. He served at court during the reigns of Rama I, II and III and received the title Phra Sunthọn Wohan, but his career was interrupted by periods of poverty and disgrace due to personal indiscretions.

His most famous work, *Phra Aphaimani,* is an epic-romance some 30,000 lines long with incident derived from many sources, in which the hero is involved at the climax with European rivals. The last of the poetic romances, it demonstrates perfectly both the eclectic tendencies in Thai literature and the inventive genius of its best poets. *Phra Aphaimani* has retained its popularity and summary dramatizations are still performed. Sunthọn Phu also composed parts of ⇨ *Khun Chang, Khun Phaen,* other popular narratives, didactic poetry, and 5 ⇨ *nirat* which provide valuable biographical material. [E H S S]

'Suttanipāta'. Text of the Pali Buddhist canon, now forming part of the fifth *nikāya* of the *sutta-piṭaka* (collection of discourses). It consists of a number of discourses, partly in prose and partly in verse. It was not composed as a unity, but it contains some of the oldest Buddhist compositions (which, though the Buddha died about 480 B.C., were not systematically written down till the 1st century B.C.). It has been second only to the *Dhammapada* in popular esteem among southern Buddhists. [C H B R]

Tr. E. M. Hare, *Woven Cadences* (Sacred Books of the Buddhists, 1948).
Winternitz, *G I L*, ii.

T

al-Tabarī, Muhammad ibn Jarīr (838–923). Arab historian. Born south of the Caspian Sea, in Tabaristān. He travelled in Egypt and Syria, lectured on poetry in Cairo, and finally settled in Baghdad. Here he provoked the enmity of the Muslim orthodox by attempting to found a legal sect of his own.

Al-Tabarī wrote one of the 2 principal commentaries on the Koran, and a Universal History, the *Annals,* from the Creation to the year 915, in 15 volumes (an abridgement of the work as originally planned). When his students protested at its length, he consented to shorten it, but remarked sadly, 'Enthusiasm for learning is dead.'

Al-Tabarī's policy is to reproduce as many conflicting accounts of the same event as possible, gathered from traditions whose authority goes back to eye-witnesses. This makes his history a valuable and comparatively reliable document; it is especially useful for the history of Sasanid Persia and the early caliphate – no other early sources exist. [A S T]

The Reign of Al'Mu'tasim, 833–842, tr. Elma Marin (New Haven, 1951).
Nicholson, *L H A*; *E of I.*

Tagore, Rabindranath (1861–1941). Bengali (Indian) poet, novelist, essayist, dramatist. Although in the West his fame rests primarily upon his translations and versions of such mystical verse as *Gitanjali,* which were brought to the attention of the West by W. B. Yeats and Ezra Pound in London and which won him the Nobel Prize in 1913, in India and particularly in his native Bengal he is noted equally for his other achievements. In the course of his long and productive life Rabindranath produced over 1,000 poems, about 24 plays, 8 novels, at least 8 volumes of short stories, over 2,000 songs, and an immense number of essays and other types of prose writing. In addition, he was an educator with great originality and imagination, as his school and university at

Santiniketan witness, a musician of sufficient stature to have his own style of music accepted and named after him, and a painter acclaimed by some critics as the best that modern India has produced.

As a writer, Rabindranath had a rare feeling for the potentiality of his native language, and he used it as an innovator: with his novel *Gharer baire* (1916), he began to move away from the traditional literary Bengali toward the more lively spoken language in his writing, and this began a literary controversy which still continues in Bengal. His poetry is characterized by simplicity of emotion and lyric dignity of language, his essays by power and clarity of thought, and his novels by social consciousness. His social awareness and the originality of his vision are seen in his protest resignation of his knighthood and his unpopular controversy with Gandhi over freedom and the ways it should be gained. Born into the aristocratic and talented Tagore family of Calcutta, Rabindranath's idea was that of personal freedom, which he felt must be realized before national freedom could be won. Much of his work contains a rich and ironic humour, directed toward the stultifying influences of tradition and toward those who confuse a basic humanity with values of wealth and authority. [E C D]

Collected Poems and Plays of Rabindranath Tagore (New York, 1961); *A Tagore Reader*, ed. Amiya Chakravarty (New York, 1961).

Tâhâ Ḥusayn (1889–). Egyptian man of letters and humanist. He was born in Upper Egypt of farming stock. Though blind since youth, he had a brilliant academic career, and was appointed in 1925 to the chair of Arabic literature at Cairo University, and in 1942 to the rectorship of Alexandria University. He was twice Minister of Education in the Wafdist government of Nahas Pasha.

Married to a Frenchwoman, Tâhâ Ḥusayn is a man of international outlook and universal sympathies, a determined fighter against bigotry and obscurantism. His colourful autobiography has been translated into English (*An Egyptian Childhood*, tr. E. H. Paxton, 1932; *The Stream of Days: A Student at the Azhar*, tr. H. Wayment, 2nd edn, 1948). His essays on classical Arabic literature are highly esteemed, and he has written a numbers of novels. He is a brilliant orator and can speak extempore in polished classical Arabic.

Among his many honours, Tâhâ Ḥusayn is a Corresponding Member of the School of Oriental and African Studies, University of London. He is held in great respect throughout the Muslim world, as one of the intellectual leaders of the Arab cultural and national revival of our time. [D M L]

The Future of Culture in Egypt, tr. S. Glazer (Washington, 1954).
P. Cachia, *Tâhâ Husain, His Place in the Egyptian Literary Renaissance* (1956).

'Taiheiki'. Japanese historical romance in 40 chapters. Literally entitled 'Record of the Great Peace', this work is concerned with the period from 1319 to 1368, when the Emperor Go-Daigo was seeking to shake off the military dictatorship. It is attributed in one source to a certain Kojima, a priest who died in 1374, but of whom nothing else is known. The title is something of a riddle, since violence is almost unbroken throughout. The construction is loose, the influence of Chinese considerable, and the inspiration is Confucian, with emphasis on the warrior code. The language is a development of that of ◊ *Heike-monogatari*, being more pretentious and decorated. As a historical document it is of no great value; its contribution to Japanese literature lies partly in its being a source of themes which were to be used again and again in later works, but mainly in the highly developed intricacy of its *michi-yuki*, descriptions of journeys told poetically, with the names of the places passed through, and their literary connotations, worked into the narrative. The *michi-yuki* was to become an important ingredient of dramatic works. [C J D]

Tr. Helen Craig McCullough (1959) (first 12 chapters only).

Takdir Alisjahbana, Sutan (1908–). ◊ Indonesian essayist, poet, moralist, grammarian, novelist, sociologist, politician and patron of literature. He has always had an intense desire to raise Indonesia in all respects to the level of the advanced nations, and his contribution has been mainly in language and literature. He was the chief driving force behind the cultural journal *Pudjangga Baru* until its closure at the time of the Japanese invasion in 1942. His many essays of this period, concise and simple in style, preached a 'dynamism' intended to vitalize the calm world of pre-war Indonesia. He considered that ideas of 'art for art's sake' should be subordinated to this aim and he had much controversy with the traditionalists. Since the Japanese invasion his career has embraced the secretaryship of the Indonesian language commission (1942–5); the preparation of a 2-volume dictionary of technical terms, *Kamus Istilah*; the editorship of a monthly magazine called *Pembangunan*, of a language journal and of a scientific monthly; a professorship of the Indonesian language and, later, a professorship of philosophy. [E C G B]

Novels: *Ta' Putus Dirundung Malang* ('Misfortune Without End') (1929); *Dian yang Ta' Kundjung Padam* ('The Everburning Candle') (1932); *Lajar Terkembang* ('With Full Sail Set') (1937); *Anak Perawan Disarang Penjamun* ('A Girl in a Bandit Lair') (1941); Poems: *Tebaran Mega* ('Scattered Clouds') (1935).

Takeda Izumo (1690–1756). Japanese dramatist. He can be regarded as the successor to ⇨ Chikamatsu Monzaemon, for when the master was no longer writing, Takeda Izumo became the leader of a group of collaborators composing new plays. These had historical themes, and were very lengthy, with intricate plots and sub-plots. The two best are *Sugawara denju tenarai kagami* ('Sugawara's Secrets of Penmanship', translated as *The House of Sugawara* in Ernst – see below) (1746), and *Kanadehon Chūshingura* ('The Loyal League') (1748). The first is a fantastic account of the downfall of Sugawara Michizane, a minister of the early 10th century, and of the fortunes of triplet brothers, two of whom served him openly, and the third in secret, while appearing to aid his enemy. The most famous scene is *Terakoya*, or the Temple School, in which the third triplet sacrifices his own son to save that of Sugawara Michizane. This scene has become a classic instance of the conflict between duty and affection, the theme of innumerable puppet and live plays. *Kanadehon Chūshingura* is the staging, modified to comply with legislation prohibiting the showing of contemporary events, of a vendetta carried out in 1701 by the retainers of a certain lord when their master was provoked to draw his sword against a court official (the eventual victim of the plot), and as a result was ordered to take his own life. Although historical, these plays include love scenes more typical of domestic drama, and thus combine the two standard types of Chikamatsu's day. Both plays became important items of the repertory of the live popular theatre (*kabuki*), even though they had originally been written for puppets. They are, however, so long and complex that complete performances have been rare in modern times, audiences being satisfied with the showing of separate acts or scenes. [C J D]

Three Japanese Plays, tr. Earle Ernst (1959). Shioya Sakae, *Chushingura, an Exposition* (Tokyo, 1956).

Takizawa Bakin. ⇨ Kyokutei Bakin.

Talmud. Two large works of traditional Jewish religious literature are referred to by this name. The Palestinian Talmud is the lesser of the two both in size and in importance to the Jewish religion, the word Talmud normally referring to the Babylonian work. Both Talmuds consist of the ⇨ Mishnah with additional material (Gemara) in the form of extensions and applications of laws (Halakhah) and pious anecdotes and words of advice (Aggadah), being the teachings of rabbis, known as Amoraim, and the discussions in rabbinic academies over several centuries from the completion of the Mishnah (A.D. *c.* 200). The Talmuds are written in Hebrew and Aramaic, the Palestinian Talmud using the Western or Palestinian dialect of Aramaic, and the Babylonian, the Eastern dialect. The Babylonian Talmud is more than three times as long as the Palestinian.

The early history of the Palestinian Talmud is very obscure. The authorities mentioned by name all lived before the 5th century, and by the 11th century it is quoted by commentators on the Babylonian Talmud, being used as an aid to its study. Only one complete manuscript of it is now extant (in Leiden), but there are numerous ancient manuscript fragments to witness the text, which is an important source for the study of Palestinian Aramaic. The first printed edition was that of Daniel Bomberg (Venice, 1522), and the Vilna edition (1926) contains all the important commentaries to that date. It was translated into French by M. Schwab (11 vols., Paris 1871–90).

The Babylonian Talmud was more or less complete by the middle of the 8th century. Only one complete manuscript is known to survive persistent Christian destruction during the Middle Ages, a 14th-century codex in Munich, though much has come down in the way of single tractates. The first complete printed edition was that of Bomberg (Venice, 1520–23). The best-known edition of our time is the Vilna edition of 1902. In 1960 the first part of a vast critical edition (Gemara Shelemah) being prepared in Jerusalem, appeared. [R F H]

The Soncino Talmud, ed. I. Epstein (35 vols., 1935–52) (English translation).

H. L. Strack, *Introduction to the Talmud and Midrash* (Philadelphia, 1931); Z. H. Chajes, *The Student's Guide Through the Talmud* (London, 1952).

Tanizaki Jun-ichirō (1886–1965). Japanese novelist. He was a member of a merchant-class family in Tokyo, his father being a rice-broker. He attended Tokyo University, where he studied Japanese literature and also started his literary career. At this stage of his development he was deeply affected by the West and fell under the influence of Edgar Allan Poe and Oscar Wilde. He was opposed to the Naturalists, and favoured as a theme the description of fantastic sensuality with a strong tendency towards writing about sadistic women and masochistic men. An example is the story *Irezumi* (or *Shisei*) (tr. I. Morris, in Morris, *MJS*, as *The Victim*, but whose title is equivalent to 'The Tattooing'); in this an expert in the art is so attracted by the beauty of a girl's skin that he induces her to allow him to tattoo a design on her back. He imprints on it the shape of a spider, and the girl's hidden cruelty is brought to the surface. He maintained this brilliant style until 1923, when he left Tokyo after the great earthquake and moved to Kyoto, the old capital. This move was accompanied by an increasing interest in the traditional aspects of Japanese life. The conflict between East and West that he felt strongly at the time is shown in the novel *Tade kuu muhi* (1928; tr. E. Seidensticker, *Some Prefer Nettles*, 1955), a delicately-drawn picture of a husband and wife no longer attracted by each other, yet not energetic enough to separate. There followed stories with traditional themes, represented by *Ashikari* (1932) and *Shunkinshō* (1933; *Ashikari and the Story of Shunkin*, tr. R. Humpherson and H. Okita, Tokyo, 1936). The next ten years, when Japanese literary production was cramped by government control, Tanizaki spent on his adaptation of *Genji-monogatari*, the famous 11th-century novel by ◊ Murasaki Shikibu. The subtle descriptions and characterization of this classic are generally held to have influenced the long novel *Sasame-yuki* ('Light Snow', but translated as *The Makioka Sisters*, tr. E. Seidensticker, 1957) which appeared, with interruptions, between 1943 and 1948. This is a delicate and satisfying depiction of the affairs of a family, the Makioka sisters and their connexions, in Osaka. Although the sentiments of his characters are all Japanese, the means he used to describe them owe much to Western literature. Tanizaki continued to write until his death; his novel, *Kagi* (*The Key*, tr. H. Hibbett, 1961), a well-written but sordid story of an elderly couple, harks back to his youthful themes. [C J D]

Seven Japanese Tales, tr. H. Hibbett (1964).

Tʻao Chʻien. ◊ Tʻao Yuan-ming.

Tʻao Yuan-ming (Tʻao Chʻien) (365–427). Chinese poet. Now (though not in his own time) generally regarded as the outstanding poet of his age. He came of a poor gentry family from the present province of Kiangsi. At the age of 28 he held the post of libationer, and thereafter a succession of other minor posts. Disgusted with the bowing and scraping of officialdom, he retired finally to cultivate his land at the age of 40. The simple life of his homestead was a source of great happiness to him, but was clearly very strenuous too. Never able to earn more than a modest living, his economic condition progressively declined and he had occasionally to beg for food.

Tʻao's name is now a by-word for close-to-the-earth simplicity; many of his poems express a feeling of affinity with nature in contrast to disgust with the world of affairs; and in his utopia, depicted in the prose piece *Peach-Blossom Fountain*, the people are content with rustic life, live by their own hands, and support no government. T'ao aspired to attune himself to the cycle of nature in Taoist fashion, but also felt, true to the Confucian tradition, that he had a political destiny to fulfil; much of the poignancy of his poetry lies in the fact that he was not finally reconciled to either way. Of T'ao's poems 120-odd are extant. They are mostly in 5-word lines, using plain language. [D E P]

Tr. William Acker (1952).

Tayama Katai (1871–1930). Japanese novelist. He was born in Gumma prefecture, where his father was a police official. At 11 he was working in Tokyo as a messenger boy for a bookshop, but he returned to his native village for a time. There he started studying English with an old scholar dating from the feudal period, from whom also he acquired a taste for literature. His first efforts in that direction were some poems and prose in Chinese, published in a magazine for the young. His father had died and the whole family returned to Tokyo, under his elder brother, when Katai was 16. He spent his time in odd literary activity and in the study of English from private teachers. He read Dickens, Thackeray, and English translations of Hugo, Goethe, and, above all, Zola. He also read the Japanese classics. It was the time of the early modern novelists in Japan – ◊ Futabatei and ◊ Tsubouchi in particular – and he went to another of them, Ozaki Kōyō, for instruction in novel-writing, and was allowed to work under one of that master's pupils. His first novel appeared in 1891, but that and many subsequent ones had no success and are now forgotten. He continued his patient reading of Western novels, and his acquaintances grew more numerous among Japanese writers. But his best work was not to appear until after the Russo-Japanese war, in which he was a newspaper correspondent, and after his marriage. Perhaps these experiences provided him with the materials which had hitherto been lacking. In 1907 appeared *Futon* ('The Mattress'), a sensational tale of a novelist's love for a beautiful pupil, and said to be, at least in part, autobiographical. This work is taken as the typical product of the Japanese Naturalist movement, with its frank realism and its concentration on the sordid side of human nature. In the next year appeared an equally remarkable work, *Ippeisotsu* (*One Soldier*, tr. G. W. Sargent, in Keene, *MJL*), a harrowing account of the death from beri-beri of a soldier, reflecting the misery of war and looking forward to the bitterly anti-war novels of the 1950s. A trilogy *Sei* ('Life') (1908), *Tsuma* ('Wife') (1908) and *Enishi* ('Ties') (1909) continued his autobiographical works. He wrote until his death, but his later production did not attain the brilliance of his middle period.

Katai is different from so many other Japanese novelists in that he had no academic training, but was a working novelist. The vigour and realism of his work, coinciding with the vogue for Naturalism, ensured his success. He can be thought of as a pioneer of a whole genre, that of the sordid, sentimental, self-pitying autobiographical novel, the so-called I-novel, which is still very much alive in Japan. [C J D]

Tchernichowski, Shaul (1873–1943). Hebrew poet. His chief characteristic is that he brought a quality until then unknown to Hebrew poetry, a secular tendency emphasizing the will of Jews to be like all other nations, an emancipation from the ghetto, and sometimes even from Jewish tradition. There is a degree almost of paganism in his poetry. He does not find a conflict between his Judaism and the world at large. He was born in the Crimea, i.e. outside the Pale of Settlement, and although his parents were observant Jews, his early years were spent with his gentile contemporaries. He was 7 when he first became acquainted with the Hebrew language, and indeed it was his first teacher who implanted in him his deep love of it. His first composition was a long Hebrew Biblical poem; at 15 he went to Odessa to attend a commercial high school and after graduation prepared for university entrance examinations to be able to study medicine. Having failed these, he left Russia in 1899 and entered the University of Heidelberg. Already in Odessa he came into contact with the Chovevei Zion (Lovers of Zion) movement and the many writers and thinkers around it, among them the then young essayist Josef Klausner, who induced him never to write in any language but Hebrew. He stayed four years in Heidelberg and went on to Lausanne where he studied for another three years.

As a young man of fine physique and vivacity he led a gay life and was continuously entangled with women. All this is reflected in his poetry. In 1907 he returned to Russia and was employed as an itinerant doctor. When war broke out he was drafted as an army doctor. After the war he settled in Berlin and went to Palestine in 1930.

His poetry differs greatly from his predecessors' – indeed he is unique in Hebrew poetry for the sensuous beauty of his love lyrics and nature poems. His songs are singing of a fleeting love that knows no disappointment and is ever ready for a new adventure. After the love-lyrics came the pantheistic songs to heathen gods. He was even nicknamed 'Hellene' and 'Heathen'; but he also sang of Biblical themes, choosing chiefly heroic themes, and he also wrote 'Idylls' describing the life of the Jews in his native Crimea. Although he wrote prose, in this he never achieved the stature of his poetry. He was an unrivalled translator, especially in the accomplished, metrically true, translations of the *Epic of* ⇨ *Gilgamesh*, the *Kalevala*, the *Iliad* and *Odyssey*. [E E]

Shirim (Tel Aviv, 1950).

L. Snowman, *Tchernichowski and His Poetry* (1929); Waxman, *H J L*; Klausner, *H M H L*.

Tenāli Rāmuḍu (Tenāli Rāma, Tenāli Rāmakṛṣṇa) (17th cent.). Telugu poet. He flourished at the court of Vēṅkaṭapati Rāja who, after the fall of Vijanagar, changed his capital to Candragiri. Rāmuḍu is most famous for his practical jokes at court, especially at the expense of his Vaiṣṇava teacher, Tātacāri. He also wrote an epic about Pāṇḍuraṅga, a form of Viṣṇu, in more serious vein. [J R M]

P. T. Raju, *Telugu Literature* (*Andhra Literature*) (Bombay, 1944); A. S. Panchapakesa Ayyar, *Tenali Rama* (Madras, 1947).

Thai Literature. The earliest Thai literary remains are those of the kingdom of Sukhothai (from A.D. *c.* 1250). They comprise historical inscriptions, didactic poetry, moral sayings and cosmological treatises.

Traditional poetic literature developed during the Ayuthaya period (1350–1767). Two forms of drama, the popular *lakhọn chatri*, and episodes from the story of Rāma, existed at least as early as the 15th century. The former consists of popular plays performed by strolling troupes of three male actors and accompanying musicians, with themes drawn from Paṇṇasa ⇨ Jātaka. *Lakhọn chatri*, known as *nora* in south Thailand, is still performed. It has a quasi-religious function.

Court drama used naturalized versions of the Rāma epic (⇨ Rāmāyaṇa). The story was enacted as a shadow play (*nang yai*) with huge, highly decorative, static figures cut out of hide, or as the masked play (*khon*) with masked male actors. A popular form of shadow play (*nang talung*) employing semi-articulated puppets, survives in the southern provinces.

Dance-drama (*lakhọn*) divided into two types possibly as early as the 17th century. *Lakhọn nai* was performed inside the palace using female players only, while *lakhọn nọk* developed as a semi-popular form, especially during the late 18th and early 19th centuries. It drew widely on ⇨ *jātaka* tales and indigenous Thai stories. Glove and figure puppets are also known.

The literature of Ayuthaya reached its full flowering in the reign of King Narai (1657–88), mainly in lengthy narrative historical poems and heroic epic-romances.

The epic-romances, though they originate in different periods of Thai history, share important common features. All are long narrative poems with a primarily secular function: the purpose is entertainment rather than religious instruction. All are concerned with the lives of Thai heroes. Though these heroes are not actual historical personages, they are solely human, not divine incarnations. An epic impulse is interwoven with an element of romance in the atmosphere of magic, mystery and love. The best-known epic-romances are: ⇨ *Phra Lọ*, ⇨ *Khun Chang, Khun Phaen* and *Phra Aphaimani* (⇨ Sunthọn Phu). Associated with this genre are historical poems such as *Yuan Phai* (?16th century), and *Taleng Phai* (19th century) in which the heroes are figures in history. Epic-romance stands midway, as it were, between the romances developed from Buddhist *jātaka* tales and the historical narratives.

In the 17th century, reflective poetry is represented by the love-songs of ⇨ Si Prat and poems inspired by the changing seasons or by absence from a loved one. Reflective poetry was also written in the 18th century – a period of considerable dramatic activity. Further Buddhist stories were adapted and ⇨ *Inao* made its first appearance.

When Ayuthaya was sacked by the Burmese in 1767 much literary material was lost. A revival took place after the founding of the new capital at Bangkok by Rama I (1782–1809), who produced a full version of the Rāma epic. Texts of *Inao* date from this reign and from that of Rama II (1809–24) when episodes from *Khun Chang, Khun Phaen* were also written down. About 1830, Sunthọn Phu wrote *Phra Aphaimani,* and he and others composed many ⇨ *nirat.*

Although brahmanical influences in court and country were strong, religious literature of all periods is based mainly on Buddhist ideas and consists of translations and adaptations of Buddhist tales, commentaries on canonical works, popular compilations and didactic poetry.

Hindu and Buddhist influences on secular and religious literature reached the Thai states through the ancient Khmer and Mon civilizations and directly from Bengal and Ceylon. They affect deeply vocabulary, versification, imagery and themes. Thai literature is typically a synthesis of these influences with native psychological attitudes, personal expression or local settings.

Prose, though developed early, became the dominant literary medium with the emergence of the modern state. From about 1850 traditional poetic literature began to decline as it lost its social functions. Religious literature and the secondary genres such as elegiac poetry and the lyric were less affected and popular forms, folk songs, plays and tales, continue to the present day.

King ⇨ Vajiravudh, Prince ⇨ Bidyalankarana and their literary circle introduced new western-influenced genres with their prose plays and stories. From the later 1920s women novelists and short-story writers became prominent. Themes were, and are, often of a simple romantic nature, but K. Surangkhanang introduced a note of realism in her novels. Concern with the impact of the West appears in the work of ⇨ Dọk Mai Sot and Prince Akat Damkoeng.

Radio and television have given a new lease of life to the short prose play and some writers, including ⇨ Si Burapha, ⇨ Sot Kuramarohit and ⇨ Khu'krit Pramoj, in dealing with social and political questions, have furthered the development of the novel and short story. [E H S S]

Dhanit Yupho, *Classical Siamese Theatre,* tr. P. S. Sastri (Bangkok, 1952); Schweisguth, P. *Étude sur la littérature siamoise* (Paris, 1951); *Journal of the Siam Society* (Bangkok) (articles in English and French; see especially work of Princes Damrong Rajanubhab, Dhani Nivat and Bidyalankarana); Chatra Books (Bangkok) publish some paperback English translations.

Thakasi Sivasankara Pillai. ⇨ Śivaśankara Piḷḷa.

'Thērī-Gāthā' ('Thēra-Gatha'). 'Songs of the Sisters and of the Brethren'. A collection of Pali poems, each of which is assigned to a particular monk or nun of the early days of the Buddhist order. The whole collection now forms part of the fifth *nikāya* of the *sutta-piṭaka* (collection of discourses). These hymns are not all of the same date, but many of them are among the oldest surviving Buddhist writings. The Buddha died about 480 B.C., and some of the songs may go back to a time not long after. They are remarkable in particular for their refreshing appreciation of nature, an appreciation which is not much in evidence in ancient Indian writings generally. [C H B R]

Tr. C. A. F. Rhys Davids (1909, 1913).

Tibetan Literature. Tibetan was developed as a literary language from the 7th century onwards, mainly because of the interest of some of its rulers in introducing Buddhism. A syllabary of 30 letters was devised by adapting a 7th-century (Indian) Gupta syllabary. A considerable proportion of the works produced from the 7th to the 13th century were skilfully methodical translations of Buddhist works, largely from Sanskrit, on which Indian scholars and Tibetan translators worked side by side. But indigenous literature was already being produced, namely chronicles and legendary and liturgical works, representing the remains of ancient oral traditions, the bulk of which were soon submerged in the rising flood of Buddhist literature.

The Tibetan Buddhist Canon was

finally fixed in the 13th century; it consists of two parts, the 'Kanjur' ('translated word', namely the teachings of the Buddhas themselves), and the 'Tenjur' ('translated treatises', which are mainly commentaries by Indian teachers). By this time there already existed some Buddhist works of Tibetan origin proper (e.g. *Mi-la Ras-pa* or Milarepa and *sGam-po-pa,* as listed below), but from the 13th century onwards under the impetus given by a large number of religious houses and orders, Tibetan literature developed into the large collections of historical and biographical works, treatises and commentaries, liturgy and religious drama, which still await the interest of foreign scholars in spite of the amount of work already done in the Tibetan field.

Much material was undoubtedly lost as a result of Chinese Communist savagery in 1959. Since printing from wood-blocks (xylographs) has been in use in the main religious centres for several centuries, the final loss may not prove to be so great as once feared. There is also a considerable amount of literature still in manuscript form, especially in the outlying districts where block-prints have not been easily available. Collections of Tibetan works, mostly in block-print form, exist in the main libraries of Europe, notably London, Paris and Rome. [D L S]

Trois mystères tibétains, tr. J. Bacot (Paris, 1921); *Tibet's Great Yogi Milarepa*, tr. W. Y. Evans-Wentz (1928); *History of Buddhism by Bu-ston*, tr. E. Obermiller (2 vols., Heidelberg, 1931–2); *The Tibetan Book of the Dead*, tr. Evans-Wentz (new edn, 1957); *sGam-po-pa's Jewel Ornament of Liberation*, tr. H. V. Guenther (1959); *The Hevajra Tantra*, ed. and tr. D. L. Snellgrove (2 vols., 1959); *The Message of Milarepa*, tr. Sir Humphrey Clarke (W E S, 1958); *The Hundred Thousand Songs. Selections from Milarepa, Poet-Saint of Tibet*, tr. Antoinette K. Gordon (Rutland, Vermont, and Tokyo, 1961).

G. Tucci, *Tibetan Painted Scrolls* (3 vols., Rome, 1949); D. L. Snellgrove, *Buddhist Himâlaya* (1957); H. Hoffmann, *The Religions of Tibet* (1961); R. A. Stein, *Recherches sur l'épopée et le barde au Tibet* (Paris, 1959).

T'ien Han (1898–). Chinese dramatist. He came from a peasant family in Hunan province, studied in Japan, joined the Young China Association and the Creation Society, and taught drama at various universities. He led an extraordinarily active life; he founded and managed the South Country Society, the most important progressive drama group in South China in the nineteen-twenties. To this early period belong such plays as *A Night in the Café* and *The Night the Tiger was Captured*, among many others; they were mostly concerned with sensitive youths whose love lives were frustrated by parents. The themes later changed to anti-imperialism and resistance to Japanese aggression.

After 1930 T'ien Han threw himself into the proletarian drama movement, organized by the Left-Wing Dramatists' League. He was arrested in 1935, but released the next year. During the war against Japan he was engaged in propaganda work. Since 1949 he has been preoccupied with administering the new national drama organizations, and has been a deputy for his home region. His latest plays, in 1958, centred respectively on Kuan Han-ch'ing, a 'people's dramatist' of the Yuan dynasty, and the building of the Ming Tombs reservoir.

He first wrote western-style one-act plays, but then abandoned this mode and went on to make some interesting technical innovations in western-style drama, incorporating such features of the traditional drama as music and song and the episodic arrangement. He has always worn his heart on his sleeve, the result once being 'sentimentalism', and now 'revolutionary optimism'. [D E P]

'Tirukkuṟal', 'Tiruvaḷḷuvar'. ◊ Vaḷḷuvar.

Tiruppāṇāḻvār. ◊ Āḻvār.

'Tjĕṇṭini'. ◊ *Chĕṇṭini.*

Toer, Pramoedya Ananta (1925–). ◊ Indonesian novelist. He was a soldier in the war of independence and was captured by the Dutch and imprisoned for over two years, an experience that has coloured his writing. Without taking sides politically he deals powerfully and realistically with human problems arising out of the brutalities and cruel necessities of the Japanese occupation and the war of independence. His most important novels are *Keluarga Gerilja* ('A Guerilla

Family'), *Perburuan* ('Hunting'), *Mereka Jang dilumpuhkan* ('The Paralysed') and *Bukan Pasarmalam* ('No Fun Fair'). He has also published several collections of short stories. [E C G B]

Totovents, Vahan (1889–1937). Armenian novelist and memoirist. He was born in the small country town of Mezré in the province of Kharput. His first literary effort appeared in 1907 in a Smyrna weekly paper. In the following year Totovents went to Constantinople and then proceeded abroad to Paris and to New York. He attended the University of Wisconsin, returning to the Caucasus in 1915 to fight for the defence of Armenia against the Turks. In 1917–18 he edited a daily newspaper in Tbilisi, and wrote numerous short stories and literary studies. In 1920 he again left for America but returned in 1922 to settle in the newly founded Armenian Soviet Socialist Republic, where he developed into a leading writer of fiction, poetry and plays. When barely 48 years told, he fell victim to the Stalin-Beria terror and was put to death.

Totovents is best known for his autobiographical *Life on the Old Roman Road*, published in 1930 (tr. M. Kudian, *Scenes from an Armenian Childhood*, 1962), which tells in lyrical prose of life in Turkish Armenia prior to 1915, when the Turks killed or deported his fellow countrymen, and 'the blue canopy of heaven collapsed like the turquoise dome of an ancient church during an earthquake'. From Totovents' house, which lay on an ancient Roman highway, he could see oxen passing by with almond blossom decorating their horns; a camel caravan on its way from Mesopotamia; or on one occasion, a mob of children pursuing the president of the town council as he emerged from the local whore's abode. The book is rich in glimpses of Turkish provincial life before the First World War, and has many skilfully drawn character sketches, as of Totovents' own father carefully trying on his tailor-made coffin shortly before his death. Nor does Totovents conceal the poverty and violence he witnessed in his childhood – the beggars asleep on refuse heaps, the public executions, the lunatics beaten by their relatives to 'cure' them. Such grim touches set off the general impression of a lovable people living out their last years, before they fell victim to Turkish brutality and the horrors of war. [D M L]

Truong Vinh Ky (Petrus Ky) (1837–98). ◊ Vietnamese writer. The great pioneer of Quoc Ngu (Romanized script), Truong Vinh Ky was a prolific writer and produced works ranging from Vietnamese folk tales and accounts of his own travels to a history of Vietnam. In addition, he translated several works from Nom (Vietnamese) and Chinese characters into Quoc Ngu script, making them widely available for the first time. It is largely due to his efforts that the Quoc Ngu writing of the Vietnamese language has been universally adopted today. [P J H]

Chuyen Doi Xua ('Tales of Long Ago') (Saigon, 1897).

Ts'ao Chan (Hsüeh-ch'in) (1716?–64). Chinese novelist. He was born into the family which held the hereditary office of Commissioner of Imperial Textiles in Nanking, a family so wealthy that they were able to entertain the K'ang-hsi Emperor four times. But calamity overtook them and their property was confiscated. Ts'ao Chan was living in poverty in Peking when he wrote his famous novel, *The Dream of the Red Chamber*, in his last years.

The *Dream* (tr. Wang Chi-chen, 1959) stands out as the only great novel of manners in Chinese literature. It describes lingeringly and in perfect detail the glory and decline of the great Chia family, while in the foreground the childhood lovers Pao-yu and Tai-yu play out their tragic destiny. In that the novel was written directly and fully from the author's experience, it expanded the range and realism of character delineation in Chinese fiction. But it also transcends the ordinary plane of existence, referring insistently to the supernatural world where a grander scheme prevails: the pervading theme is in fact distinctly Buddhist.

The last third of the novel is by another hand, that of Kao Eh, and this has led to great controversy about Ts'ao Chan's original intentions. [D E P]

Wu Shih-ch'ang, *On the Red Chamber Dream* (1961).

Tsao Yu. ◊ Wan Chia-pao.

Tsubouchi Shōyō (1859–1935). Japanese literary theorist, novelist and dramatist. He was the youngest of ten children of a former feudal official turned farmer near Nagoya. As a boy he was an avid reader of traditional literature. In 1867 he was sent up to Tokyo to study in the school which later became Tokyo University. It was there that he acquired a taste for English literature and became, in particular, an admirer of Shakespeare. His earliest publication was a translation of *The Bride of Lammermoor,* and in 1884 appeared an adaptation into a traditional Japanese dramatic form of *Julius Caesar.* In the following year came his most influential work, *Shōsetsu-shinzui* (*The Essence of the Novel,* preface tr. D. Keene, in Keene, *MJL*), a plea for realism and the rejection of a didactic or moral purpose in fiction. In his novel *Tōsei shosei katagi* ('Present-Day Students') (1886), he tried to apply his teaching to a realistic description of student life. In the event, he could not rid himself of the influence of the works he had read as a boy, and the plot is as involved and unlikely as any of theirs. However he was a great teacher, and the work of ◇ Futabatei Shimei, who was greatly under his influence, is the most successful application of his doctrines. Tsubouchi wrote no more novels, but more and more concerned himself with drama, both as a translator of Shakespeare, and also as a patron of the theatre in Japan. For a while he ran a stage company; and also wrote plays, of which the most successful was *Kiri hitoha* ('A Pawlonia Leaf') (1896). In this historical drama, partly influenced by Shakespeare, he tried to use the resources of the traditional *kabuki* to produce a modern theatre. Once again, his language was too elegant and his thoughts too noble, and his dramatic writing was not a great success, although *Kiri hitoha* is still in the *kabuki* repertoire. For more than forty years until his death Tsubouchi taught at Waseda University and many great writers and scholars have been his students. A fine theatre museum, its exterior imitating an Elizabethan playhouse, stands there to his memory. [C J D]

Tu Fu (712–770). Chinese poet. His mother died when he was young and he was brought up by an aunt. At 15 he was already celebrated among the local poets in Loyang. In 731 he began to travel, returning home in 735 to take the imperial examination. Having failed he set off on another tour. Not many of his earlier poems are extant, but we know from his later poems that his youth was a time of hopeful confidence and that he dreamed of advising the emperor, so that he should become like the sage kings of antiquity. In 744 Tu Fu met the poet Li Po in Loyang and was much influenced by him, joining a drinking set. His poem *Eight Immortals of Drinking* reflects the spirit of freedom current at that time of prosperity. Unlike Li Po, Tu Fu was unable to withdraw from official life, and he proceeded to the capital to seek appointment. He was again unsuccessful, and his poems expressed his disappointment. In 751, however, three compositions on imperial ceremonies which he submitted to the emperor attracted the latter's attention and he was given a minor post.

Hitherto Tu Fu's poems had dealt mainly with the beauties of nature and the poet's sorrows, but at about this time his humanism became apparent in such poems as *The Army Carts,* about conscription, and *The Beauties,* in which he contrasts the pomp of the emperors with the lot of the poor.

In 755 the rebellion of An Lu-shan broke out, and once more Tu Fu was forced to set out on his travels. Although only in his forties, his hair was already white and his health was poor. In 757 he reached the emergency capital, where he offered his services to the new emperor and for a while held a minor post, but before long was suspended for speaking his mind. From 760 to 765 he lived in Chengtu, patronised by an old friend who had been appointed governor, but on the latter's death he travelled again in Szechuan and Honan, finally dying in Hangchow at the age of 58.

In this second period of his life, Tu Fu's poetry reached its full maturity. After his arrival at Fenghsiang in 757, he found that his son had starved to death and his poetry now reflected the tragic desolation of the chaotic times. His poetry is concise and at the same time extraordinarily evocative, which makes it extremely difficult to render it in foreign languages. He carried the poetry of the

Tang period to the highest peak of its achievement. [J D C]

W. Hung, *Tu Fu, China's Greatest Poet* (1952) (biography with translations).

Tukārām (1598–1649). Marathi poet of India. A low-caste poet who lived and died at Dehu near Poona, the major exponent of the *abhang*, a short devotional and lyrical poem. Tukārām was a devotee of the god Vithobā at Pandharapur, the most famous holy place in Maharashtra, and his 'psalms' are constantly sung by the Vārkari pilgrims who attend the festivals there. Over 4,000 *abhangs* are attributed to him. [I M P R]

The Poems of Tukārām, tr. J. Nelson Fraser and K. B. Marathe (3 vols., Madras, 1909–15); *Psaumes du pèlerin*, Fr. tr. G. A. Deleury (Paris: Collection UNESCO, 1956); *Psalms of Maratha Saints*, tr. N. Macnicol (Calcutta, 1919).

Tulsī Dās (A.D. 1532?–1623). Indian poet. Little is known with certainty about his life. He was a Brahman, was probably born in Rājāpur, U.P., and lived most of his adult life in Banaras as a devotee of the Vaiṣṇava avatar Rām. He began his most famous poem, the *Rāmcaritmānas* (*The Holy Lake of the Acts of Rāma*, tr. W. D. P. Hill, 1952), in 1574; it is the finest achievement of medieval Hindi literature and has had incalculable influence on the Hindu population of northern India ever since. It inculcates above all the sentiment of *bhakti* or loving devotion to Rām as a means to salvation, while setting forth as models of conduct the main figures of the story, Rām in his human form, his wife Sītā, and his brothers. The poem is written in an eastern Hindi dialect and arranged in 7 cantos; the predominant stanza form is a series of rhyming quatrains concluded with a shorter couplet. It draws on many sources for its material, notably a medieval recasting of the Sanskrit epic ◊ *Rāmāyaṇa* in which the spiritual significance of Rām's deeds had been emphasized. While Tulsī Dās was pre-eminently a devotee of Rām he gave an honoured place in his work both to the brahmanical doctrine of monism and to the polytheistic mythology of Hinduism. This eclecticism meant that he was able to enlist a maximum of support for the worship of Rām in Northern India, where the great success of the *Rāmcaritmānas* has led to the cult of Rām replacing that of the rival avatar Kṛṣṇa as the dominant religious influence.

Twelve other works of varying length are attributed with some certainty to Tulsī Dās. Notable are the *Vinay pattrikā*, a long series of verses in honour of Hindu sacred places and deities, especially Rām and Sītā; the *Gītāvalī*, a series of verses on aspects of the story of Rām, intended to be sung; and the *Kṛṣṇa gītāvalī*, a similar series in honour of Kṛṣṇa, written in the Braj *Bhāṣā* dialect. [R S M]

C. Vaudeville, *Étude sur les sources et la composition du Rāmāyaṇa de Tulsī Dās* (Paris, 1955); F. E. Keay, *A History of Hindi Literature* (Calcutta, 1920); J. M. Macfie, *The Ramayana of Tulsi Das* (1930); tr. F. R. Allchin, *Kavitāvalī* (1964).

Tu-Luc Van-Doan. ◊ Vietnamese literary group. The Tu-Luc Van-Doan was an association of Vietnamese writers which flourished during the 1930s and exercised a major influence upon modern Vietnamese prose writing. The members of this association were themselves heavily influenced by western novelists, particularly the French, and introduced a completely new style of writing. Lively narrative style, familiar everyday language, long passages of dialogue and introspection combined to change radically the form of the Vietnamese novel. Vietnamese writing has never been the same since the publication of the work of this association. [P J H]

Nhat linh, *Hai Buoi, Chieu Vang* ('Two Golden Afternoons') (Saigon, 1952); Khai Hung, *Dep* ('Beauty') (Saigon, 1952).

Tuñcatt' Ezuttacchan (early 16th cent. ?). Indian (Malayalam) poet. Much legend has grown up round him: little is known about his life. Ezuttacchan ('Father of Letters') would appear to have been a title rather than a personal name; Tuñcattu is probably his family name; his first name is a subject of controversy. Ezuttacchan is the outstanding Malayalam poet and religious teacher. He was an exponent of *bhakti* (personal devotion to God) and glorified the god Viṣṇu.

His first work, *Adhyātma Rāmāyaṇam*, differs from the Sanskrit ◊ *Rāmāyaṇa* in making the hero an ideal figure both as a man and as a god. Ezuttacchan also wrote a Malayalam version of the ◊ *Mahābhārata* in his *Mahābhāratam*, again with considerable originality. Far shorter than the Sanskrit poem, it has greater unity. On the assumption that the vital part was the story of the Pāṇḍavas, Ezuttacchan made this the centre of his *Bhāratam* and included other episodes only if relevant to this main theme.

A number of shorter works are attributed to Ezuttacchan with varying degrees of probability. Among them is a heroic poem *Brahmāṇḍa purāṇam*, based on the Sanskrit *purāṇa* of the same title. [R E A]

Chelnat Acyuta Menon, *Eżuttaccan and His Age* (Madras, 1940).

Tyāgarāja (1767–1847). Indian bard and composer. He was born into a musical family at Tiruvārūr, a small town in Tanjore District, South India, famous for its temple of a form of Śiva called Tyāgarāja, after whom the composer was named. In his youth, his family moved to Tiruvaiyāṟu, north of Tanjore, where the composer spent the rest of his life apart from pilgrimages to many shrines in the south. His death there is annually commemorated by an important music festival.

The inspiration of most of his work was Śri Rāma, regarded as a form of the god Viṣṇu, and he stressed the devotional function of music. Most of his 800 surviving compositions are discontinuous songs called *Kīrtana*, comparable in function to the motet, divided into three according to the pattern of subjects, *a, b, cb*. Tyāgarāja also wrote two works similar to oratorios. His compositions were imparted to various groups of disciples, and three such groups have preserved his work in the Umayāḷpuram, Tillaisthānam and Walajapet collections of manuscripts.

Tyāgarāja's Telugu diction, direct and colloquial, reflects the fact that he came from a Telugu-speaking family long resident in the Tamil country. In style his songs range from simple pieces owing something to tunes popularized by European bands in Tanjore to highly involved compositions employing many variants of each phrase. [J R M]

V. Raghavan, 'Introductory Thesis' to C. Ramanujachari, *The Spiritual Heritage of Tyagaraja* (Madras, 1957).

U

Ueda Akinari (1734–1809). Japanese novelist. He was born in a brothel district in Osaka, and at the age of three was adopted into a family of oil merchants. He led a more or less dissolute life until his marriage in about 1760, when he settled down and worked in the family business. His first literary activity had been the composition of *haiku*, and in 1766 he took up writing as a profession, producing stories in various genres; in 1768 appeared his masterpiece, *Ugetsu-monogatari* ('Tales of the Rainy Moon'), a collection of stories from Japanese and Chinese sources (tr. W. Whitehouse, *Monumenta nipponica*, I, i, ii, and IV, i, Tokyo, 1938 and 1941; Fr. tr. R. Sieffert, *Contes de pluie et de lune*, Paris, 1956). There followed a period of twelve years when medicine was his main occupation. During this time and his subsequent retirement, he enjoyed the friendship of many of Japan's leading scholars and writers. He lived to what was at the time an advanced old age, keeping up his literary studies to the end. Apart from his fame as a novelist he was also well-known as a student of 'Japanese learning', i.e. the elucidation and criticism of the early chronicles, poetry, and novels written in Japanese (as distinct from Chinese).

Ugetsu-monogatari is an early example of *yomihon*, which are novels or stories using historical, legendary or didactic material, in a style which varies from the picturesque to the turgid, but always has a certain weightiness arising from the use of constructions and locutions derived from Chinese – a comparable effect to the use of Latin or Greek forms of expression in English. Ueda Akinari's style is simple compared with that of later *yomihon* writers like ◊ Kyokutei Bakin, but his material in *Ugetsu-monogatari* has all the fantastic elements that characterize the form. [C J D]

P. Humbertclaude, 'Essai sur la vie et l'œuvre de Ueda Akinari (1734–1809)', in *Monumenta nipponica*, III, ii; IV, i, ii; V, i (Tokyo, 1940–42).

'Upaniṣad' (intimate, hence esoteric 'session' or instruction of a pupil by his master). A class of texts of *c.* 800–500 B.C. constituting the last stage or 'end' of the ◊ Veda, wherein the deeper cosmological and personal significance of the by now elaborately ritualized religion (◊ *Brāhmaṇa*) is explored. The foundation of most later Indian philosophy and one of the evident intellectual forerunners of Buddhism, the *Upaniṣads* are among the most significant religious writings of mankind, and they remain today a basic tenet of Hinduism. Though over 200 compositions have been called '*upaniṣads*', the name applies *par excellence* only to those of the oldest stratum, properly 'Vedic'. Deussen identifies 14 such works – the 6 oldest, in prose; *Bṛhadāraṇyaka, Chāndogya, Taittirīya, Aitareya, Kauṣītakī* and *Kena*; then 5 less old, in verse: *Kaṭha, Īśa, Śvetāśvatara, Muṇḍaka* and *Mahānārayaṇa*; finally the 3 youngest, again in prose: *Praśna, Maitrāyanīya* and *Māṇḍukya.*

These are mostly apophthegmatic accounts of the teaching of renowned sages; they are not works of speculative philosophy, though in them many problems are for the first time posed in strictly philosophical terms. The overriding concern of the ancient teachers was the place of the individual self, or soul (*ātman*), in the structure of the cosmos, represented by the sacrifice and termed *brahman* ('*Weltgeist*') after its principle of reality. On one level, the soul is bound to existence, to the enjoyment of the fruits of its actions, doomed to relive an indefinite cycle of birth and death. But on the other, the soul can, by knowing its identity with the *brahman* which underlies all appearance, choose to liberate itself from that cycle. Yājñavalkya, the teacher of the *Bṛhadāraṇyaka,* asserts the identity of *brahman* and *ātman* as unqualified universals. Others, like Uddālaka in the *Chāndogya*, employ the realistic analogy of the organic whole: the *ātman* and the *brahman* are identical, as 'selves' implied by structural relationships amongst the various visible 'parts' of the human form, on the one hand, and the cosmos on the other.

Many related topics are discussed: the journey of the soul after death (in the *Kaṭha, Chāndogya*); the 'self' of deep sleep (*Bṛhadāraṇyaka, Chāndogya*); the doctrine of the five sheathes, wherein the highest reality is said to be *ānanda* ('joy') (*Taittirīya*).

Much social history is gleaned from the *Upaniṣads*; indeed little is known of the period save what can be got from them. Two widely held theories can be mentioned: (a) The *Upaniṣads,* with their closely related predecessor texts, the *āraṇyakas* (forest-books), represent the speculations of a small but advanced group of thinkers who withdrew from the highly complicated urban life of the time, with its costly and intellectually barren ritualism (◊ *Brāhmaṇa*), into the 'forest', where they established 'secret' retreats and concerned themselves and their students with the *meaning* of the rituals; (b) Since many of these teachers are not brahmins, indeed are represented as teachers of brahmins, the *Upaniṣads* testify to a 'revolt' among the princely class, dissatisfied with the barren ritualism of the brahminical sacrifice. The *Upaniṣads* thus anticipate the evident 'anti-brahminism' of early Buddhism, which itself is but an extension of upaniṣadic doctrines of individual salvation.

However this may be, the *Upaniṣads* were soon understood as the essence, as well as the end, of the Veda (Vedānta), and the doctrines taught therein are taken as theological necessities by the representatives of the most orthodox school of Hindu philosophy, itself called Vedānta (◊ Śaṅkara). [E G]

Thirteen Principal Upaniṣads, tr. R. E. Hume (1921); *The Principal Upaniṣads*, tr. S. Radhakrishnan (1953).

P. Deussen, *The Philosophy of the Upaniṣads*, tr. A. S. Geden (2nd edn, Edinburgh, 1906); H. Oldenberg, *Die Lehre der Upaniṣaden und die Anfänge des Buddhismus* (Göttingen, 1915); A. B. Keith (cited under *Brāhmaṇa*); S. N. Dasgupta, *History of Indian Philosophy* (1922-5).

V

Vajiravudh (Rama VI), King (1881–1925). Thai monarch (1910–25) and writer, educated at Oxford and Sandhurst. In his efforts to develop Thailand as a modern state he became a pioneer of political journalism. He was a prolific writer and a skilled dramatist. He put into excellent Thai a number of classical English and French dramatic works, including *The Merchant of Venice* and other Shakespeare plays. He wrote many short comedies in the genre of spoken drama, new to Thailand, and encouraged the production of plays with mixed casts. *Hua Chai Chai Num* ('The Heart of a Young Man') is a novel in epistolary form, the first of its kind, demonstrating the impact of western social ideas and manners in Thailand. [E H S S]

Vaḷḷattōḷ. ◊ Nārāyaṇa Mēnōn.

Vaḷḷuvar (3rd or 4th cent. A.D.?). Tamil poet. The author of the Tamil classic *Tirukkuṟaḷ* (*tiru* 'sacred'; *kuṟaḷ* in Tamil prosody is a particular kind of couplet). Little certain is known of his life. His *Kuṟaḷ* has 133 chapters, each of 10 verses. The major division is into 3 books, on virtue, on government and society and on love. The poet's outlook is such that all religions of the Tamil country have at one time or another claimed him as their own. Numerous attempts, none entirely successful, have been made to translate his aphorisms into the languages of western Europe. English translations with lengthy commentaries include those by G. U. Pope (1886), A. Chakravarti (Madras, 1953) and K. M. Balasubram (Madras, 1962).

Kuṟaḷ is conventionally grouped with a number of other (mainly ethical) compositions as one of the Eighteen Minor Works (*Patiṉeṇkīḻkkaṇakku*) of Tamil. The next most important of these is the *Nālaṭiyār*, a Jain anthology of 400 quatrains (tr. G. U. Pope, 1893). Its subject matter has much in common with *Kuṟaḷ*. [R E A]

V. R. Ramachandra Dikshitar, *Studies in Tamil Literature and History* (2nd edn, Madras, 1936); Francis Whyte Ellis, *Tirukkural: Ellis' Commentary*, ed. R. P. Sethu Pillai (Madras, 1955).

Vālmīki ◊ *Rāmāyaṇa*.

Vātsyāyana. ◊ *Kāmasūtra*.

Veda. Those sacred writings of orthodox Hinduism termed *Śruti* ('revealed' knowledge), as opposed to *smṛti* or 'tradition'. A vast and varied literature, covering the millennium 1500–500 B.C., the Veda represents the slow accretion of sacred lore centring about the sacrifice. The Veda traditionally comprises 4 schools, the oldest of which is that the *Ṛg* (sacred formulae), the other being the *Sāmaveda* (chants), *Yajurveda* (sacred technique), and *Atharvaveda* (corrective magic). Within each school a uniform (also 4-fold) development occurs, based on a traditional 'collection' (*saṃhitā*) of original texts, which itself forms the 'first' layer (◊ *Ṛgveda*, the 'collection' of the *Ṛg* school). The second stage is that of voluminous exegetical commentaries testifying to an elaboration of sacrificial procedure (◊ *Brāhmaṇas*) of *c.* 1000–800 B.C., followed by *Āraṇyakas* (forest-books) and ◊ *Upaniṣads*, in which the esoteric meaning of the sacrifice is taught. These last may be dated at 800–500 B.C.

The *Ṛgveda*, as the oldest and most authoritative part of the Veda, is often referred to loosely as the 'Veda'. [E G]

Vedānta. ◊ Śaṅkara.

Vidyāpati (15th cent.). Indian poet. The greatest Indian love poet of his time. By 1400 he had already attained fame and the patronage of the King of Mithila. He was born at Bisapi, a village in the Mithila region on the eastern side of North Bihar.

During the Muslim invasion of Mithila he sought refuge in Nepal for a few years where he wrote some of his Sanskrit treatises. During the last phase of his life he retired from the Court and returned to his village where he died, it is believed, in his nineties.

He wrote many Sanskrit works, principally the *Purusa pariksa*, the *Durgābhakti taraginī*, the *Dānavākyāvali*, the *Vivada Sāra*, and the *Gayā pattana*. But it is for his matchless love songs in Maithili dialect that he is outstanding. Some deal allegorically with the relations of the soul to God under the form of the love which Radha bore to Lord Krishna. Indian literature on love and sex has a long history, but earlier poets had made only a robustly male approach to sex. Vidyāpati's approach was almost feminine. He loved and admired female temperament and nature and believed that sexual love was the greatest need and experience in life, as much for women as for men. His religious love-sonnets were adopted and recited by the Hindu reformer, Chaitanya, the first propounder of modern Vaishnavism in eastern India (this sect regards Radha-Krishna as the highest deity) and through him became the house-poetry of Bihar and Bengal. Even today his love songs are most popular. [B N P]

Love Songs of Vidyapati, tr. Deben Bhattacharya (1963).
Subadra Jha, *The Songs of Vidyapati* (Benaras, 1954).

Vietnamese Literature. Writing was brought to Vietnam from China before the beginning of the Christian era and the earliest Vietnamese literary compositions, both verse and prose, were written in Chinese characters according to Chinese rules and conventions. (◊ Nguyen Trai and Le Tac.) The tradition of writing in Chinese persisted in Vietnam until late in the 19th century, Vietnamese works being distinguishable from Chinese more by subject-matter than style.

A system of writing the Vietnamese language in Chinese-style characters was developed later. These characters, unintelligible to Chinese, were called Chu Nom and they gave rise to a second *genre* of Vietnamese literature. Writing in Nom characters is known to have existed as early as the 13th century, although the oldest surviving fragments date only from the 14th century. As it developed, Nom literature moved gradually away from Chinese forms until it assumed a distinctive character of its own. The finest period of Vietnamese literature in Nom characters was that of the late 18th and early 19th centuries.

Christian missionaries from Europe, who first reached Vietnam early in the 17th century, found writing in characters inconvenient and time-consuming. They therefore devised a Romanized script known as Quoc Ngu which could be learned by any speaker of the language in a very short time. For a long period the writing of Quoc Ngu was confined to Vietnamese Christians but, after the arrival of the French during the 19th century, it spread to all sections of the population and has today replaced characters entirely. Virtually all Vietnamese literature during the 20th century has been written in Quoc Ngu. [P J H]

Villa, José García (1914–). Filipino poet and short-story writer. Perhaps the best-known ◊ Philippine writer in English. The stern family discipline of his boyhood influenced some of his early short stories (*Footnote to Youth*, New York, 1933). These deal with rejection and with the veil that must always divide any two beings. Villa was beginning to probe into what he now calls 'the ethic-philosophic force behind all essential living'.

At the University of New Mexico (where Villa enrolled in 1930), while editing the magazine *Clay*, he attracted the attention of Edward J. O'Brien, editor of the *Best Short Stories* annuals, who encouraged him. Villa went on to postgraduate study at Columbia University, where he worked seriously on his poetry. He chose to remain in exile in New York after his studies, rather than to fall back on the materially comfortable but confining (and family-centred) social structure of his homeland. Only in 1959 did he return for a brief visit. Villa still lives in New York. He has been honoured with the Shelley Memorial Award and a Guggenheim Fellowship.

During his exile, he described in poetry his 'search for the metaphysical meaning of man's life in the Universe – the finding of man's selfhood and identity in the mystery of Creation'. The most important of these poems are in *Have Come, Am Here* (New York, 1942) and *Volume Two* (New York, 1949). The former received the poetry award of the American Academy of Arts and Letters. In it, Villa experimented with a new rhyming method which he called 'reversed consonance'. The other book introduced a genre which the author termed 'comma poems'.

In 1953, Villa began work on a 'theory of poetry'. This work has yet to be published, but 3 new books have appeared since: *Selected Poems and New* (New York, 1958), with an introduction by Dame Edith Sitwell; *Poems 55* (Manila, 1962); and *Selected Short Stories* (Manila, 1962). The last two contain previously published material. [A P G M]

Twentieth Century Authors, 1st Supplement, ed. Stanley J. Kunitz et al. (New York, 1955); Salvador P. Lopez, 'So No: A Theory of Poetry' and 'The Poetry of José

García Villa', in *Literature and Society* (Manila, 1940); Rolando S. Tinio, 'Trying to Read Villa', in *Philippine Studies*, vii (Manila, 1959); Arturo G. Roseburg, *Pathways to Philippine Literature in English* (Manila, 1958).

Viśakhadatta. ◊ Kauṭilya.

W

Wan Chia-pao (Tsao Yu) (1910–). Chinese dramatist. He was born in Hopei province of fairly well-to-do parents, and was educated at the American-sponsored Nankai school and Tsinghua University. He was a research student at Tsinghua when he published his first play, *Thunderstorm* (tr. Wang and Barnes, Peking, 1958); it was warmly welcomed by progressive critics. There fellowed a regular succession of plays until *Family* (1942), when he laid down his pen for several years because he was too depressed to write.

He held a succession of teaching posts after leaving Peking, travelling to South and West China with the refugee universities. After the war he went to the U.S.A for one year. He willingly accommodated himself to Communist rule and has been director of the People's National Theatre. In recent years he has written *Bright Skies* (tr. Chang, Peking, 1960), a fairly conventional propagandist play.

Thunderstorm (1934) was not far removed in design from Greek tragedy: it aimed to awe the audience with the violence of the disruptive powers that are active in the world, and death and madness are the lot of his characters; but because of its setting it was generally received as an attack on the tyranny of the traditional family system. *Sunrise* (1936) still presented life as cruel, but the forces of darkness were social rather than elemental capitalists and racketeers. He tried to give all characters equal weight, in the manner of 'those Impressionist paintings composed of dots'. *Wilderness* (1937) showed distinct Shakespearean influence. *Transformation, Peking Man* and *Family* followed, the last two direct attacks on the 'feudal' way of life that had to give way to the new. [DEP]

Wen I-tuo (1899–1946). Chinese poet and scholar. Born into a wealthy family in Hupei, he was a studious youth, but the May Fourth upheaval stirred his enthusiasm and he was won over to the cause of the 'new literature'. He was in America from 1922 to 1925 studying art and – privately – literature, immersing himself particularly in the English Romantic poets – but also in some of the more plangent Chinese poets. His first collection of poems, published in China in 1923 under the title of *Red Candle*, reflects these tastes. He considered himself a sort of martyr to art, but found that the hard facts of life dragged him down from the poetic world to the 'dusty world'; one of these hard facts was the slighting of the Chinese by Americans, the theme of his 'Laundry Song'.

After his return to China Wen held posts in various universities before settling at Tsinghua again. In 1926 he founded with Hsu Chih-mo and others the influential *Poetry Supplement*. His second collection of poems, *Dead Water*, was published in 1928. In the same year he helped edit the *Crescent Monthly*, but subsequently withdrew into his classical studies, which were to be very productive. The chaos and injustices of the war administration forced him out to join the Democratic League. For his pains he was assassinated.

One of the best modern Chinese poets, he was an early exponent of the theory of 'dancing in fetters' in vernacular poetry, having real success in creating natural but regular and strong rhythms. [DEP]

Hsu Kai-yu, 'The Poetry and Career of Wen I-tuo', in *Harvard Journal of Asiatic Studies* (1958).

Wu Chʻeng-en (*c.*1510–80). Chinese novelist. Author of *Hsi-yu chi* (tr. A. Waley, *Monkey*, 1942). Little is known about him, but he is said to have held the post of District Magistrate for a time and to have been a good poet, though of his writing nothing of much value, apart from the novel, survives.

Hsi-yu chi is based on the story of the Chinese Buddhist priest Tripitaka's journey to India to obtain sacred texts. In the novel, however, the character of Tripitaka is overshadowed by that of his assistant, Monkey, whose resourcefulness and magic powers enable them to overcome all kinds of natural and supernatural obstacles and finally reach their goal. The novel is episodic in the Chinese tradition and rich in incident, which makes it extremely popular with Chinese children. Others find in it a deeper significance. It has been described as allegorical of human endeavour, Monkey symbolizing man's intelligence, and one of Tripitaka's other companions, Pigsy, man's physical desires. It also contains anti-bureaucratic satire, the hierarchy of gods in heaven corresponding to the earthly Chinese bureaucratic system. [J D C]

Wu Ching-tzu (1701–54). Chinese novelist. Author of *Ju-lin wai-shih* (tr. Yang, *The Scholars*, Peking, 1957). He was a native of Anhwei Province in east China, his family being fairly well-to-do and having the reputation for success in the civil-service examinations. He himself, however, never proceeded beyond the local examinations, and though at the age of 36 he was recommended to compete in a special examination, illness prevented him from taking part. By this time, because of criticism of his prodigality, he had moved to Nanking, where he spent the rest of his days in poverty.

Ju-lin wai-shih is a satirical novel, which exposes the empty formalism of the examination system and the mentality of those whose sole ambition in life is to succeed in the examinations in order to qualify for office, using abject flattery to gain their ends, and having attained office, immediately starting to lord it over others. The author's ideal character, Wang Mien, refuses office and lives as a hermit in the mountains. The characters and incidents are extremely well observed, and the satire is never allowed to go beyond the bounds of credibility. Yet although there is unity of theme, the construction of the novel is panoramic rather than concentrated.

Ju-lin wai-shih is generally considered to be China's best satirical novel. It influenced a great many other novels written later in the Ch'ing Dynasty, but none rival it in quality.

Wu Ching-tzu wrote a number of works on the Classics, which have not survived, and nearly 200 poems which have been reprinted in recent years. [J D C]

Wu Tsu-hsiang, 'The Realism of Wu Ching-tzu', in *Chinese Literature*, 1954, No. 4.

Y

'Yadu'. A type of ◊ Burmese poem, better transcribed *ra tu* – to be derived from Sanskrit *ṛtu 'season'* – written in the 'classical' quadrisyllabic line and usually of three stanzas. The golden age of the *yadu* was between about A.D. 1550 and 1630, when its dominant theme was the mood of wistful sadness evoked by contemplation of the beauties of nature and the effects of the changing seasons in the forest, or the longing and yearning of one separated from loved ones or from home. Nawade I (1545–1600) wrote over 300 *yadu* of high quality, and Prince Natshin-naung (1578–1619) had a long-drawn-out and tragic love which moved him to write *yadu* of great pathos. ◊◊ Let-wè Thon-dara. [J W A O]

'Yagan'. A type of ◊ Burmese poem which first appears in the mid 18th century A.D. It has a freer syllable structure than the 'classical' verse, and ostensibly tells a story from the ◊ *jātaka* or from Hindu and other legends, but its characteristic feature is witty and scurrilous abuse of contemporary figures, especially other writers. The most highly esteemed *yagan* is the *Ya-ma* (based on part of the ◊ *Rāmāyaṇa*) by U Toe (fl. 1751–96). [J W A O]

Yamin, Muhammad (1903–62). ◊ Indonesian lyric poet, literary pioneer, historian and elder statesman. His *Tanah Air* ('Fatherland') published in 1922 was the first collection of modern Malay verse to be published. The 'fatherland' to which he there referred was Sumatra, not Indonesia. A further volume of verse, *Indonesia, Tumpah Darahku* ('Indonesia, My Homeland'), appeared on 28 October 1928, the day Muhammad Yamin and his fellow nationalists resolved to revere a single – Indonesian – homeland, race and language. Muhammad Yamin's play on a Javanese historical subject – *Ken Arok dan Ken Dedes* – also appeared in 1928. Although a pioneer in literary form, his language remains much closer to classical Malay than that of younger writers. [E C G B]

Yāqūt ibn ʿAbdullāh (1179–1229). Muslim geographer. A Greek, born in Asia Minor. He was captured as a child, and sold as a slave in Baghdad to a merchant who had him educated, and who later sent him as his agent to the Persian Gulf and to Syria. He was freed in 1199 and became a scribe and bookseller. In 1213 he set out again to travel in Syria, Egypt, Iraq and Khurāsān (north-east Persia). He spent two years working in libraries at Merv, in Central Asia. In 1218 he went on to Khiva, but had to leave, in order to escape the Mongol invasion. He arrived in Mosul destitute, but was given assistance in reaching Aleppo. He returned to Mosul two years later in order to finish his *Geographical Dictionary*; this task lasted until 1224. While he was in Damascus he only narrowly escaped death at the hands of the Shīʿite Muslims for his Sunnite views.

Yāqūt's geographical work is extremely important, and contains not only topographical but also historical and biographical information. His other great book is his *Dictionary of Learned Men*, which contains biographies of all those who were in any way connected with Arabic literature. Some sections are now lost. Yāqūt's works, like those of most Arab compilers, are full of anecdotes and digressions; there is, for instance, in the *Dictionary of Learned Men*, a long discussion between a Christian philosopher and a Muslim theologian. [A S T]

The Introductory Chapters of Yāqūt's Mu'jam al-Buldān, tr. Wadie Jwaideh (Leiden, 1959). G. Le Strange, *The Lands of the Eastern Caliphate* (1905); *E of I.*

'Yogasūtra'. The basic text of the yoga, one of the six traditional schools of Indian philosophy. Attributed to Patañjali (perhaps the famous grammarian of the 1st or 2nd century B.C.), the *Yogasūtra* teaches a method of liberation (*mokṣā*) distinguished by its emphasis on bodily and mental discipline. The Yoga (from the root *yuj* – 'to join, yoke') adopts the theoretical position of the Sāṃkhya – a strict dualism of matter and mind – and builds upon it a technique for eliminating the influence of the senses and passions upon consciousness. This is the doctrine of classical Yoga (*rājayoga* or *jñānayoga*). The ◊ *Bhagavadgītā* attempts to modify the theory so as not to imply the abandonment of social duties, while still maintaining the aspect of a selfless discipline (*karmayoga*, or yoga of action). Certain medieval practices involving extreme self-torture (such as continually looking at the sun) constitute a third type of yoga (*haṭha*, of violence).

Although the Yoga is counted as one of the orthodox systems of philosophy, in that it does not reject the authority of the Veda, it is, like Buddhism, one of the intellectual descendants of the Upaniṣadic speculations which have no place for Brāhminical ritualism. [E G]

The Yoga System of Patañjali, tr. J. H. Woods (Harvard Oriental Series, Cambridge, Mass., 1914).
M. Eliade, *Yoga: Immortality and Freedom*, tr. W. R. Trask (1958); S. N. Dasgupta, *Yoga, the Method of Reintegration* (1924).

Yokomitsu Riichi (1898–1947). Japanese novelist. Born in Ueno in Mie prefecture, where ◊ Bashō had spent his youth, Yokomitsu had from his early days an interest in literature. He studied at Waseda University in Tokyo, first in the English department and later in that of economics, probably with more interest in the former, for he was devoted to Western literature. His first collection of short stories appeared in 1923 and founded his reputation as a writer of great imagination and style. He was also a literary theorist, and joined and left several schools of novelists. He is associated in particular with the *Shin-kankakuha* ('New Sensationalism'), and in collaboration with ◊ Kawabata Yasunari published a review *Bungei-jidai* ('The Literary Age'). Among Japanese novelists he owed a great deal to ◊ Shiga Naoya. In a period when the proletarian writers, with their emphasis on the propaganda value of the novel, and the autobiographists with their self-pitying 'I-novels', were flourishing, he was one of those who stood out for novel-writing as an artistic pursuit. His thoughts run on illness, death, and man's unavailing struggle with the forces that dominate his life, but there is a sharpness of observation, and an ironical objectivity that keeps him from sentimentality and vain protests. [C J D]

Machine, tr. E. Seidensticker in Morris, *M J S*; *Spring Came on a Horse-drawn Cart*, tr. Mary M. Suzuki, in *The Heart is Alone* (Tokyo, 1957); *Time*, tr. D. Keene, in Keene, *M J L*.

Yosano Akiko (1878–1942). Japanese poetess. She was born at Sakai, near Osaka, the daughter of the proprietor of a cake-shop. Her early interest in poetry was heightened when a monthly magazine *Myōjō* ('Morning Star') began to be published in 1900 by the poet Yosano Hiroshi. She sent him samples of her work, mainly passionate love poems, and her first collection (of 400 poems), *Midaregami* (*Tangled Hair*, tr. S. Sakanishi, Boston, 1935), came out early in 1901. She married Yosano in the autumn of the same year. She published many other collections, but her work very often declined into cheap sentimentality. *Midaregami* is usually reckoned her best. The verse-form she generally used was the traditional *tanka* (of thirty-one syllables). Among her other literary productions was a modern adaptation of *Genji-monogatari*. Her chief claim to literary fame is that she was one of the first women since the 11th century to express her emotions for all to read. [C J D]

H. H. Honda, *The Poetry of Yosano Akiko* (Tokyo, 1957).

Yoshida Kenkō (1283–1350). Japanese writer. A courtier and Shintō shrine official, he retired from the world in 1323, and in about 1330, or perhaps later, wrote a series of essays, observations, notes and anecdotes which were collected into *Tsurezure-gusa* (*Essays in Idleness*; tr. George Sansom, in *Transactions, Asiatic Society of Japan*, 39, Tokyo, 1911; extracts in Keene, *AJL*). These earned him enduring fame as one of Japan's great authors. Before his retirement from court and shrine, he was well known as a poet. He probably retired mainly to get away from the disturbed conditions in Japan at the time. He became a Buddhist priest and spent some time in travel and living as a hermit, but it seems that he did not entirely disappear from his old haunts, and was still prominent in poetic circles. His becoming a Buddhist priest did not amount to anything like a conversion, for the Shintō and Buddhist religions were at the time integrated, and his action constituted the normal way of getting away from it all.

Tsurezure-gusa has 243 sections of various lengths. They include philosophical and religious statements, views of love, observations of nature, comments upon the times. He is worldly-wise and shows a gentle melancholy. He looks back with nostalgia on earlier times in Japan, in particular on the Heian period before the civil wars, when the world seemed to centre around the court, whose manners and ideals were supreme, and before the warrior became the universal hero. *Tsurezure-gusa* is comparable with ◊ Sei Shōnagon's *Pillow Book*, but there are obvious differences between the witty woman and the melancholy recluse, although each is characterized by a diversity of form and style. [C J D]

Yüan Mei (1716–97). Chinese poet. Yüan retired early in life from his official post and settled in his famous Sui Garden in Nanking, from which he sallied forth on long journeys even in great old age. The most acclaimed poet of his age, he was also a great liver, a self-professed hedonist, notorious for his roving eye. Though he was a prolific writer of occasional verse, he did not approve of poetizing where no genuine emotion was present: ' "Where two hearts join" is my guide.' He belonged to the 'Individualist' school of Chinese poetry which refused to let the individual's inspiration be crabbed by customary literary usage and prohibitions (see his 'Talks on Poetry'). His own style is clear and fluent, his phrasing felicitous. But his thought, though fresh, was not very profound. Apart from his poetry and criticism he also compiled a collection of tales of the supernatural. [D E P]

Arthur Waley, *Yuan Mei* (1956).

'Yüeh-fu'. Chinese poetic genre. The term *Yüeh-fu* means 'music bureau' and originally referred to a department established in about 120 B.C. to provide court music, train musicians and collect songs. As applied to poetry, the term probably first designated the ritual hymns etc. produced by this bureau, but its meaning was gradually extended to cover the whole of the surviving ballad literature of the Han dynasty as well as post-Han imitations of these ballads and original poems written in the same style.

Surviving *Yüeh-fu* poetry includes love songs, military songs and the complaints of orphans, lonely wives and the poor and homeless. Most are shorter lyrical poems, but included in the *Yüeh-fu* collections are the few longer narrative poems and ballads of the period: *Chiao-Chung-ch'ing's Wife*, the *Song of Lo-fu* and *The Ballad of Mulan* (tr. A. Waley, in *The Temple*, 1923). The predominant metre of the *Yüeh-fu* poems is the 5-syllable line, which from the 3rd century A.D. until the time of the great T'ang poets was the dominant verse form in Chinese poetry. [J D C]

J. R. Hightower, *Topics in Chinese Literature* (1950).

Z

Zeami Motokiyo (1363–1443). Japanese dramatist and actor. At the age of 7, he appeared with his father Kan-ami in a performance of what is now called *nō* drama and attracted the attention of the *shōgun* Yoshimitsu, whose favour he enjoyed until his death in 1409. From then till his own death his fortunes fluctuated with changing rulers; for a period he was exiled to the island of Sado, but seems to have returned to the capital for his last years. He and his father fashioned the *nō* play from various popular entertainments into the form still seen today. It is performed with no scenery and only rudimentary properties on a wooden stage, by male actors in magnificent costume, who wear a mask when they portray a woman, a supernatural being, or an old man. The acting style is formal and symbolic, and uses the dance to help express emotion. There is an orchestra of two or three drums and a flute, playing on the stage at the back, and a chorus to comment upon the action and take over the principal actor's words when he is busy with his dancing. A normal *nō* programme used to consist of five plays, separated by comic interludes (*kyōgen*). The plays are very often in two acts, with the principal actor taking a major role in each part. These roles generally show two aspects of the same character. Zeami himself is credited with having written some 240 plays, of which 100 still survive and include very many of the great plays of the present repertory – *Hagoromo, Kantan, Aoi no ue, Takasago*, to mention only a few.

Important though his compositions are, they are not obviously distinguishable from those of his father or of his successors. Perhaps his true greatness lies in his aesthetic theories, recorded in his notebooks. Like most Japanese writing on aesthetics, they are not easy to understand, but clearly he set great store on the one hand on realism of acting, and on the other, on *yūgen*, a term of great difficulty of interpretation, which seems to have meant for Zeami elegance, beauty and symbolic depth. [C J D]

P. G. O'Neill, *Early Nō Drama* (1958); Noel Peri, *Le nô* (Tokyo, 1944); Shidehara Michitaro and Wilfred Whitehouse, 'Seami's Sixteen Treatises', in *Monumenta nipponica*, IV, 2 and V, 2 (Tokyo, 1941, 1942); Arthur Waley, *The Nō Plays of Japan* (1921).

Zoroaster, Zoroastrian Literature. ⇨ Avesta; Pahlavi.

RECOMMENDED READING*

Arabic: R. A. Nicholson, *A Literary History of the Arabs* (1903, reissued 1953)
R. A. Nicholson, *Studies in Islamic Poetry* (1921)
Chinese: Fung Yu-lan, *A History of Chinese Philosophy* (1937)
C. T. Hsia, *A History of Modern Chinese Fiction* (New Haven, Conn., 1961)
H. A. Giles, *A History of Chinese Literature* (1901)
Georgian: D. M. Lang, *The Georgians* (1966).
Gujarati: K. M. Munshi, *Gujarat and its Literature* (Bombay, 1935)
Hebrew: M. Waxman, *A History of Jewish Literature* (4 vols, 2nd edn, New York, 1947)
Hindi: F. E. Keay, *A History of Hindi Literature* (Calcutta, 1920)
Indian: M. Winternitz, *Geschichte der Indianischen Literatur* (3 vols., 1905–20; tr. S. Ketkar, 2 vols., Calcutta, 1927–33)
Japanese: R. H. Brower and E. Miner, *Japanese Court Poetry* (Stanford University, Calif., 1961)
K. B. Shinkōkai, *Introduction to Classic Japanese Literature* (Tokyo, 1948)
K. B. Shinkōkai, *Introduction to Contemporary Japanese Literature* (Tokyo, 1939)
Malay: Sir Richard Winstedt, *A History of Classical Malay Literature*, Journal of the Malayan Branch of the Royal Asiatic Society, Vol. 31, pt 3 (Singapore, 1961)
Pali: B. C. Law, *History of Pali Literature* (1933)
Persian: A. J. Arberry, *Classical Persian Literature* (1958)
E. G. Browne, *A Literary History of Persia* (4 vols., 1906–24)
J. Rypka, *Iranische Literaturgeschichte* (Leipzig, 1959)
C. A. Storey, *Persian Literature: A Bio-Bibliographical Survey* (1927)
Siamese: P. Schweisguth, *Étude sur la littérature siamoise* (Paris, 1951)
Sinhalese: C. E. Godakumbura, *Sinhalese Literature* (Colombo, 1955)
M. Wickramasinghe, *Sinhalese Literature* (tr. E. R. Sarathchandra, Colombo, 1950)
Syriac: W. Wright, *A Short History of Syriac Literature* (1894)
Tagalog: E. de los Santos, *Literatura tagala* (Madrid, 1909)
Tamil: S. V. Pillai, *History of Tamil Language and Literature* (Madras, 1956)
Telugu: P. T. Raju, *Telugu Literature* (Bombay, 1944)
Turkish: A. Bombaci, *Storia della letteratura turca* (Milan, 1956)

* As the Oriental section of this Companion covers such a wide field, it has been necessary to restrict this reading list to standard histories – where they exist – of the relevant literatures.

A

'Abdillaahi Muuse (*c.*1880–). Somali oral poet and man of religion. Known for his wisdom and piety. Author of various topical and didactic poems. He is particularly remembered for the saying used in one of his poems: 'He who speaks to termite hills will not get any sense out of them.' [B W A]

Andrzejewski and Lewis, *S P I.*

Achebe, Chinua (1930–). Nigerian novelist. His father was a mission teacher in Ogidi. He was among the first to follow a full degree course at the University College of Ibadan. Having toured in Africa and America, he joined the Nigerian Broadcasting Corporation in 1954 and later became Director of External Broadcasting. He has now resigned.

His first novel, *Things Fall Apart* (1958), deals with the impact on tribal life of the white man's arrival. It is a book of impressive neutrality. Achebe makes no decisions for us. His cool, terse prose, illuminated in the dialogues by the proverbial imagery of the Ibo language, distances the author, leaving room for irony and a meaningful ambiguity. *No Longer at Ease* (1960) turns to modern Lagos and the temptations confronting a young Nigerian with a Western education when given responsibility in his own country. Again the excessive demands made on the individual in an uneasy society are presented without bias and economically. *Arrow of God* (1964) returns to the theme of civilization's threat to traditional village life. The detailed documentation of tribal customs, gay and sinister, gives an equivocal dignity to the hero, the chief priest of Ulu, whose means of life they are. [P T]

Moore, *S A W.*

Alcantara, Osvaldo. ⇨ Lopes, Baltasar.

'Ali Duuh (b. probably mid 19th cent., d. shortly before Second World War). Somali oral poet. Some of his poems have been written down by Somali private collectors, and one has been published with English translation and notes. He is renowned for his wit, invective and forcefulness. As one of the elders of his clan he was involved in various interclan disputes and intrigues and used his poetry powerfully as propaganda. [B W A]

Andrzejewski and Galaal, *S P C*, i.

Aluko, T. M. (1920–). Nigerian novelist. Born in Ilesha, Nigeria, and studied engineering at the Yaba Higher College. Went to London to study in 1946, returned in 1950, and in 1956 became Town Engineer in Lagos. He now works for the University of Ibadan.

He started writing short stories in his twenties and continued in Britain. Some have been published in *West African Review* and broadcast on the BBC 'Calling West Africa'. His first novel, *One Man One Wife* (Lagos, 1959), tells the story of the conflict of values in a family. His second novel, *One Man, One Matchet* (1964), also deals with a conflict of ideals. He often utilizes folklore. He describes situation and custom accurately, but relies heavily on documentary, as is also evident in his third novel. [J A R]

Andrade, Mário Pinto de (1928–). Angolan poet and critic. Born in Golungo Alto. He studied in Luanda, Mozambique, in Lisbon and in Paris, where he studied Sociology. He has contributed critical articles and articles of sociological interest to journals in Angola, Portugal and Brazil. He was once with *Présence africaine* in Paris. He now lives in Rabat, Morocco, and is still active with the Angolan Liberation Movement. He writes in Portuguese. He has compiled *Caderno de poesia negra de expressão portuguesa* with Francisco José Tenreiro (Lisbon, 1953) and an anthology of Negro verse in Portuguese, *Antologia da poesia negra de expressão portuguesa* (Paris, 1958) [O R D]

Armattoe, R. E. G. (1913–53). Ghanaian poet. Born in Denu. He was an anthropologist, historian, doctor and politician. He worked in Ireland for 10 years, returned to Ghana, but left again. He was accidentally killed in Hamburg. He published two volumes of verse in English, *Between the Forest and the Sea* (Londonderry, Ireland, 1950) and *Deep Down the Black Man's Mind* (Ilfracombe, Devon, 1953). His poetry is limited, expressing attitudes towards race that have become a commonplace. [J A R]

Reed and Wake, *B A V*.

Awoonor-Williams, George (1935–). Ghanaian poet. Born in Wheta, in the Volta region of Ghana, and educated at Achimota College and the University of Ghana. He is now director of the Ghana Film Institute and was an editor of *Okyeame*, a recent Ghanaian literary publication, now defunct.

He has published a volume of poetry, *Rediscovery* (Mbari, Ibadan, 1964), and his poems have appeared in *Okyeame* and *Black Orpheus*. His poetry is among the most exciting to come out of Africa. He unifies his local view of people and events with a universal one of spiritual dichotomy and the dilemma of physical isolation, making a composite picture of the conflicts of life and the omnipresence of death. [O R D]

Reed and Wake, *B A V*; Moore and Beier, *M P A*.

B

Beti, Mongo. ◊ Biyidi, Alexandre.

Bhély-Quenum, Olympe (1928–). French West African novelist. Born at Cotonu in Dahomey and educated in Dahomey. In 1942–5 he roamed about Dahomey, Togo and the Gold Coast, where he learnt English, and then worked for the firm of John Walkden and Co. until 1948. He then went to Avranches (France), where he studied for the *baccalauréat classique*. In 1954 he won first prize in the Zellidja scholarship competition, which enabled him to travel through French Equatorial Africa. The following year, he passed the second part of the *baccalauréat*, in philosophy, and entered the University of Caen. He won two diplomas, and then taught at the Paul Langevin Lycée at Suresnes. In 1962, he received a certificate in diplomatic studies from the Institut des Hautes Études d'Outre-mer, and has been studying for a degree in social psychology at the Sorbonne.

Bhély-Quenum's literary activity began with the novel *Un piège sans fin* (Paris, 1960), in which the Negro soul's emotional sensibility finds powerful expression. In 1961 he published a story in the magazine *Bingo*, and became literary critic of *La vie africaine*, of which he is now chief editor and managing director. Bhély-Quenum is accredited to UNESCO as a professional journalist. He contributes to various French, Italian, Canadian and Swiss magazines. New novels in preparation include *La vague déferlée*, *Forces obscures* and *Les Amazones*. His most recent novel is *Le chant du lac* (Paris, 1965). [G T A]

Biyidi, Alexandre (pseud. **Mongo Beti** and **Eza Boto**) (1932–). French West African novelist. Biyidi was born near Yaundé in the Cameroons. He was educated at Yaundé, Aix-en-Provence, and Paris.

Under the pseudonym Eza Boto, Biyidi's literary career began in 1953 with a tale, *Sans amour et sans haine*, followed soon after by his first novel, *Ville cruelle*. Under the nom-de-plume of Mongo Beti he wrote *Le pauvre Christ de Bomba* (1956), *Mission terminée* (1957; tr. Peter Green, *Mission to Kala*, 1958) and *Le roi miraculé* (1958; tr. *King Lazarus*, 1961), which won the 1957 Sainte-Beuve prize. He is outstanding among French-speaking African novelists for originality of style, and his work is admired and enjoyed for its exuberance, satirical verve and disarming humour. His novels form a psychological and social document on life in the Cameroons during the colonial period. [G T A]

Moore, *S A W*.

Blay, J. Benibengor (*c.* 1900–). Ghanaian writer. Born in Ghana and educated there. He has travelled in Europe and America and was a member of Parliament in Ghana. He writes in English. His works include booklets and radio-plays. Among his works of fiction are *Dr Bengta Wants a Wife* (1953), *Emilia's Promise* (Ghana, n.d.) and *After the Wedding* (Ghana, n.d.), a sequel to *Emilia's Promise*. He has published 3 books of poetry and his collected poems are in *Thoughts of a Youth* (Ghana, 1961). His poetry is conventional in subject-matter, and his novelettes are greatly influenced by popular European fiction. But he is one of the few African writers who have created a popular home-market of readers. [O R D]

Bolamba, Antoine-Roger (1913–). Congolese poet. Born in Boma, Congo. He has worked in the Information Service in Leopoldville and is editor of *La voix du Congolais*. He writes in French. He has published two volumes of poetry, *Premiers Essais* (Elisabethville, Congo, 1947) and *Eszano, chants pour mon pays* (Paris, 1955), and a book of social studies on the evolution of the black woman. His poetry has an intense patriotic flavour which enfeebles his theme, as very often the diction becomes trite, the thought commonplace, reducing it to apparent attitudinizing. [J A R]

Moore and Beier, *M P A*.

Boto, Eza. ⇨ Biyidi, Alexandre.

Brew, Kwesi (1928–). Ghanaian novelist and poet. Born in Cape Coast, Ghana. He is a graduate of Ghana University. He joined the Public Service in 1953, spent some time in Bonn and now works for the Foreign Office of the Ghana government in Accra.

He writes both poetry and prose. A novel of his has recently been accepted for publication in England. He has published poetry in *Okyeame*, the Ghana literary journal, and in *Voices of Ghana* (1958), ed. H. Swaazy. His poetry has a tender lyricism often concerned with love and religion. In it one finds the extolling of the individual above the community, an interesting development in African literature. [O R D]

Reed and Wake, *B A V*; Moore and Beier, *M P A*.

Brink, André Philippe (1935–). South African novelist and playwright. Editor of the avant-garde periodical *Sestiger* (1963–65). Profoundly influenced by a two-year stay in Paris, he is now the most prolific and versatile of the younger generation of South African writers. *Pot-pourri* (1961), *Sempre diritto* (1963) and *Olé* (1965) give an account of his 'Latin' travelling experiences. A study of the 'Shakespearian' tragic, *Orde en chaos* (1962), was accompanied by his blank-verse drama *Caesar* (1961). Then followed by the first attempts at 'absurdist' theatre in Afrikaans: *Bagasie* (1965), a trilogy of one-act plays. A play in three acts, *Elders mooiweer en warm* (1965; 'Elsewhere Fair and Warm') challenges both the Sartrean 'in camera' thesis and De Sade's amoralism: it investigates man's predicament in an existence which cannot be but fraught with personal guilt but is yet endowed with the power of self-deliverance.

The greatest stir Brink has made is with his novels: *Lobola vir die lewe* (1962; 'Lobola for Life'), *Die ambassadeur* (1963; tr. the author, *The Ambassador*, 1964), *Orgie* (1964; 'Orgy') and *Terugkeer na die son* (1966; 'Return to the Sun'), which in essence belong to the psychological literature of confession. A virtuoso style and technique, an at first bewildering, then highly revealing construction, and a perspicacious treatment of sexual love as 'a form of metaphysical enquiry' (Lawrence Durrell, quoted in the second novel) command their recognition as the most able novels so far written in Afrikaans. [R A]

R. Antonissen, *Kern en tooi* (Pretoria, 1963), and *Spitsberaad* (Pretoria, 1966).

Brutus, Dennis (1924–). South African poet. He taught English in South Africa for 10 years, then worked in Johannesburg and began studying Law at Witwatersrand University. Government suspicion made him plan to come to Europe, but he was detained and severely wounded in an alleged attempt to escape. He was released from prison in 1965 and now teaches in London.

He has published *Sirens Knuckles Boots* (Mbari, Ibadan, 1963), a volume of poems written against the background of racial repression which nevertheless have a humour and solemnity that prevent them from being mere racialist pamphleteering. [J A R]

C

Casely-Hayford, Gladys M. (Aquah Laluah) (1904–50). Ghanaian writer. Born in Axim, of a well-known literary family. Her godfather was Coleridge-Taylor, the musician. After education in Britain she taught in Sierra Leone, where she died.

She wrote both prose and verse. Some of her poetry has recently been reprinted in *Poems from Black Africa* (ed. Langston Hughes, Indiana University Press, 1963). Her earliest poems, published under the pen name of Aquah Laluah, appeared in the *Atlantic Monthly*. Her poetry shows deep religious awareness and moral conviction. Although she wrote mostly in standard English she also experimented with Krio in occasional verse. Her short stories and sketches in *West African Review* show a close observation of and sympathy with West African life. [J A R]

Clark, John Pepper (1935–). Nigerian poet and playwright. Born in Ijaw country of the Nigerian Delta. He graduated in 1960 at Ibadan University. He has worked as a journalist and went to America for a year. He was at the Institute of African Studies, University of Ibadan, doing research on Ijaw epic, and now lectures at the University of Lagos.

He has published poems in *Black Orpheus*, and in a volume published by Mbari, Ibadan, 1962. His first play, *Song of a Goat* (Mbari, Ibadan, 1961), poses the problem of the stigma of barrenness in a rural community. His second, *The Masquerade*, is a sequel, and his third and most recent, *The Raft*, is about four men drifting in the Niger, uncertain whether they will live or die. All three have been published as *Three Plays* (1964). He has written a book of reportage called *America Their America* (1964), a short story for *Black Orpheus*, and a recent play, *Ogidi* (1967). His plays suffer from one vital weakness – they are obsessed with unrelated sex themes and cumbersome imagery. His dialogue very often lacks the vigour to carry forward his ideas. His poems are more successful, utilizing indigenous myth and social matter. [O R D]

Reed and Wake, *B A V*; Moore and Beier, *M P A*.

Conton, William (1925–). Sierra Leonean novelist. Born in Bathurst, and educated in West Africa and England. He was principal of the Government Secondary School in Bo, Sierra Leone, and is now Chief Education Officer in Freetown.

His only novel, *The African* (1960; extract in Rive, *MAP*), is biographical. It is the story of Kisimi Kamara, who after a thwarted love affair in England, returns to Africa, to bring about the freedom of his people and the equality of black and white. The novel is moving and tender in parts. Its opening chapters are overloaded with documentary detail, but the pace quickens after the meeting with Greta and her death; which gives the hero's political motives a personal as well as national intensity. Conton has written a history of West Africa for schools. [O R D]

D

Dadié, Bernard (1916–). French West African poet and novelist. Born at Assini on the Ivory Coast and educated in Senegal, he is Director of Fine Arts at the Dakar Institut Français d'Afrique Noire.

Dadié first became known as a poet with *Afrique debout* (1950), verses dedicated to his native land and people; this was followed by *La ronde des jours* (1956). But he is renowned above all as a subtle and profound storyteller. His psychological novels have a strong poetic, fairy-tale flavour, whether they deal with the daily life of a young African, as does *Climbié* (1956), or with the pressing current problems of emergent Africa and the clash of African and European social and spiritual values and standards, as does *Un nègre à Paris* (1959). Dadié has also collected and adapted many African stories and folk-tales, published in his *Légendes africaines* (1953) and *Le pagne noir* (1955), as well as in the Paris magazine *Présence africaine* (1958–60, etc.), to which he also contributes articles on African literary history and criticism. [G T A]

Hughes and Reygnault, *A A M.*

Dei-Anang, M. F. (1909–). Ghanaian poet and dramatist. Born in Mampong-Akwapim, and educated at Achimota College and the University of London. From 1938 he worked in various ministries in Ghana and attended the Bandung Conference in 1954 as a delegate of his country. He is head of the Secretariat for African Affairs in Accra.

He has written poetry and drama. Among his verse publications are *Wayward Lines from Africa* (1946) and *Africa Speaks* (Accra, 1959), the latter with an introduction on poetry in Africa. He has also published poetry in *Okyeame. Cocoa Comes to Mampong* (Cape Coast, 1949) contains brief dramatic sketches based on the story of cocoa in Ghana. *Okomfo Anokye's Golden Stool* (1960) is a 3-act play based on a heroic legend of the Ashanti in which the destiny of two royal lovers is influenced by tribal gods. Patriotism and dedication informs all his work. Occasional archaisms often offend the modern reader. His art is limited by its principally didactic function. [J A R]

Dempster, Roland T. (1910–65). Liberian poet. Born in Tosoh, near Robertsport. He graduated at Liberia College. He was qualified in Business Studies and Literature. He worked in various government departments before taking up a Professorship first at Liberia College and then at the University of Liberia. He published essays and patriotic verse. His poetic publications include *The Mystical Reformation of Gondolia* (1953 and Liberia, 1961), *To Monrovia Old and New* (1958) and *A Song out of Midnight* (1959 and Liberia, n.d.). There is much attitudinizing in his verse and an over-rigid adherence to the conventional forms of versification. [J A R]

Dhlomo, H. I. E. (1905–57). South African playwright. Educated in South Africa. He was a book-keeper by profession and wrote in the vernacular and in English. He was editor of a Durban African weekly journal till his death.

He published 14 plays in English, dealing with historical heroes like Shaka, Moshoeshoe, Catewayo and Dingane. *The Girl Who Killed to Save* (Lovedale, South Africa, 1935), perhaps his best-known play, is the story of Nongqause, a prophetess and daughter of a witch-doctor. He is also known for *The Valley of a Thousand Hills* (Durban, 1941), a long poem of epic grandeur which bemoans the fall of the black race in South Africa. Both in drama and poetry, he achieved the glorification of his race by a passionate reliving of history within a rigid artistic form. [J A R]

Dhlomo, R. R. R. (?–). South African writer, born in the second half of the 19th century. Educated in South Africa. He contributed to, then edited, *Ilanga Lase-Natal*, a Zulu weekly, founded by ◊ Dube.

He wrote in Zulu and English. His Zulu publications include *Ushaka* (1937), the familiar story of Shaka, in dialogue, with some description. Professor Jabavu finds this melodramatic and overdone. Dhlomo is also the author of *U Dingane ka Senzangakhona* (1936) ('Dingane, the Son of Senzangakhona'), a horror story, *U Mpande ke Senzangakhona* (1938) ('Umpande, the Son of Senzangakhona'), an anthology, *Ujeqe, u kwazi kuyathuthukisa* (1937) ('Knowledge Makes One Happy') and *Izikhali zanamuhla* ('Present-Day Weapons'), these last two being didactic in tone. (All were published in Pietermaritzburg.) His best-known English publication is a novelette, *An African Tragedy* (Lovedale, South Africa, 1928), a heavily sententious tale of Robert Zulu's unfortunate introduction to city life. [O R D]

Diop, Birago (1906–). French West African short-story writer and poet. Born at Dakar into a middle-class Wolof family from Senegal. He had a brilliant school career, then qualified as a veterinary surgeon at the Toulouse Veterinary School. In 1945 he became head of the Zoo-Technical services of the Haute-Volta. After Senegal became independent (1960), he was appointed Senegalese ambassador in Tunis.

Birago Diop showed early literary aptitude, and wrote poems inspired by the esoteric African circumcision rites. But it was not until 1960 that he published his first book of verse, *Leurres et lueurs*, a sort of anthology of his experiences.

His real fame rests on his short stories, *Contes d'Amadou Koumba* (Paris, 1947; also tr. into Russian), and *Nouveaux contes d'Amadou Koumba* (Paris, 1958) with a preface by L. S. ◊ Senghor. While posing modestly as a mere interpreter of the naïve tales of his village *griot* or storyteller, he cleverly evokes the poetic inspiration of his native land. The stories are characterized by subtle evocation of nature and daily life, vivacity of imagery, and common sense shot through with humour. Local expressions impart a truly African flavour to the stories, which provide an outlet for the wit and wisdom of the African peasant. While his tales allow the European reader to make intimate and personal contact with Africa, they also reveal how much the African peasant resembles other peasants all over the world. This is one of many factors which give these stories their universal appeal. [G T A]

Rutherfoord, *D L*; Hughes and Reygnault, *A A M*; Moore and Beier, *M P A*.

Diop, David (1927–60). French West African poet. Born in Bordeaux, France, of African parents. During his short life he was often in poor health. He was killed in an aeroplane crash near Dakar. He frequently contributed poems to *Présence africaine* and was published in Senghor's anthology. His only volume of poems was *Coups de pilon* (Paris, 1956). They were for the most part passionate poems in the *négritude* vein but infused with a warmth and a generosity that was distinctly his own. [O R D]

Moore and Beier, *M P A*.

Diop, Sheikh Anta (1923–). French West African literary and social theorist. Born at Diurbel in Senegal. He showed early literary promise, combining qualifications in physics with the degree of Doctor of Letters. He is on the staff of the Institut Français d'Afrique Noire at Dakar.

Diop is noted as a tireless scholar, not afraid of bold hypotheses. While trying to demonstrate the basic unity of the Negro world, and even to prove the African origin of all human civilizations, he draws on a wide range of historical, cultural and linguistic data. Among his most significant works are *Nations nègres et cultures* (1954), *Unité culturelle de l'Afrique noire* (1960) and *Afrique noire pré-coloniale* (1960). These books, together with others devoted to the comparative study of African and European cultural and political systems, have established Diop's ability and audacity. [G T A]

Dube, John (?–). South African writer. Born in Natal, South Africa, in the latter half of the 19th century. He is a minister of religion and has a doctorate. In 1904 he began *Ilanga Lase-Natal*, a Zulu weekly. He founded the Ohlange Institute near Durban. He was the first Zulu to publish a novel in Zulu: *Insila ka Shaka* ('Shaka's Bodyguard') (Marianhill, Natal, 1930 and 1951), which Professor C. L. S. Nyembezi called 'a lively story told in Dube's gripping style'. Other works include *U shembe* (Pietermaritzburg, 1936) and *Jege the Body Servant of King Tschaka* (Lovedale, South Africa, 1951), a historical novel. [O R D]

E

Ekwensi, Cyprian O. D. (1921–). Nigerian novelist. Educated in Nigeria where he taught for a while, in Ghana and at London University where he studied Pharmacy. He is now Director of Information Services to the Nigerian Federal Government. With his stimulating and colourful personality, he is one of the leading public figures of modern Nigeria.

Ekwensi has written 4 novels, many stories and childrens' book, including *An African Night's Entertainment* (1962). *People of the City* (1954) was journalistic and melodramatic, but it is nevertheless a fine account of Lagos's uncomfortably sophisticated life. *Jagua Nana* (1961) is better constructed, but still flawed by an incomplete assimilation of American language and characterization. In *Burning Grass* (1962) Ekwensi settles into his own austerer style, and *Beautiful Feathers* (1963) maintains the new level of achievement despite some careless narration. Though Ekwensi's devices are often overobvious, he knows how to disturb a

Western reader. In the Lagos of *Beautiful Feathers* Western-style broken homes add to the strain of Western-style marriages. Ekwensi's Nigeria is almost as uneasy at that of ◊ Achebe. [P T]

Elmi Bonderi. ◊ 'Ilmi Bownderi.

Eybers, Elisabeth (1915–). Afrikaans poet. The sudden transition, in her sixteenth year, from the quiet little village where her father was minister of religion to the disorienting life of Johannesburg resulted in her first collection of poems, *Belydenis in die Skemering* (1936), a poetry of yearning strongly influenced by the English Victorians and Georgians. Her next volumes – *Die Stil Avontuur* (1939) (*The Quiet Adventure*, 1948) and *Die Vrou* (1945) – contain poetry of fulfilment, deriving from her pregnancy, which led her thoughts to dwell lovingly, in warmly biotic terms, on the intimate relationship between mother and child, time and eternity. Her later work – *Die Ander Dors* (1946) etc. – insists on the purification attained through suffering; here the portrayal of man's and woman's relationship, most often in sonnet form, reaches a climax. This leads to the irony of her most important work, *Die Helder Halfiaar* (1956), in which the disillusioned middle-aged woman either desperately tries to escape into a child's life of wonder, or cynically accepts reality and mortality. After her divorce from her husband, an eminent businessman, she emigrated to Holland, where her latest work, *Balans* (1962), was compiled. These poems are often more resigned, more metallic in quality, and movingly reflect the fragility of human relationships, contrasted with the lasting value and purity – but also the rigidness – of art. [A P B]

Gedigte (1958).
D. J. Opperman, *Digters van Dertig* (Kaapstad, 1953).

F

Faarah Nuur (b. *c.* mid. 19th cent., d. before Second World War). Somali oral poet and clan leader. Much of his poetry concerns the conflict between his own clan and another which extorted a tribute from them. Some of his poetry deals also with the partitions of the Somali nation by foreign powers. [B W A]

Andrzejewski and Lewis, *S P I.*

Fagunwa, Daniel O. (*c.* 1910–63). Nigerian novelist. Started work as a teacher and subsequently worked with the Ministry of Education at Ibadan. His works, all in Yoruba, have drawn on the traditions of Yoruba oral narrative. His first book, *Ogboju-ode ninu igbó Irunmale* ('The Skilful Hunter in the Forest of Spirits'), was published in 1939, and was followed by several others which enjoyed great popularity. Of these, *Igbo Olodumare* ('Forest of the Lord') published in 1945, is perhaps the most popular. [W H W]

Fodeba, Keita (1921–). French West African poet and director of Ballets Africains. Born in Guinea, educated at Dakar, and later went to Paris. He has worked as a teacher, directed the Troupe du Théâtre Africain, founded by himself, and held the portfolio for Economic Affairs in the Government of Guinea.

His creative work is strongly influenced by the traditional literature and art of his native land. His published works include 3 collections of verse: *Poèmes africains* (Paris, 1950), *Le maître d'école* and *Minuit* (Paris, 1953) and the preface to Michel Huet's *Les hommes de la dance* (Lausanne, 1954). More recently he has dedicated himself to making known and interpreting the art of his people, especially the superb dances of Guinea, to the outside world. The startling vigour, originality and beauty of the Ballets Africains under his directorship has brought this company international success. [J A R]

Fonseca, Aguinaldo (1922–). Journalist and poet, born in Cape Verde Islands. He writes in Portuguese. He has worked for many literary reviews and had a poem in ◊ Andrade's anthology. He has published a volume of poems, *Linha do horizonte* (Lisbon, 1951). His poems have a quick, snappy diction and say a great deal in a few terse words. [O R D]

Moore and Beier, *M P A.*

G

Galaal. ⇨ Musa Hajji Ismail Galaal.

Gicaru, Muga (1920–). Kenyan (Kikuyu) writer. He attended mission school and then went to Nairobi, where he worked and attended evening classes. He then went to England to study, and in the fifties returned to Kenya. His *Land of Sunshine* (London, 1958) is an autobiography, describing the situation in Kenya before the Mau-Mau uprising. It contains much political propaganda and is episodic in parts. But the author has the ability to describe suffering and the disgusting aspects of torture. There is some romanticizing of the African and African ways of life [J A R]

I

'Ilmi Bowndheri (Elmi Bonderi) (b. *c.* 1908, d. probably *c.* 1938). Somali oral poet. His many love poems gained him a wide reputation in north-western Somaliland. According to popular tradition he died of love for a woman he could not marry. Rejected by the woman's relatives as too poor he had gone away to earn money and on his return found her married. During the illness which preceded his death he recited many poems which those around him learnt by heart and passed on to others. His poems are characterized by a majestic power of diction and by images drawn from the history of Somali clans and Islamic tradition. Some have been written down by private collectors. [B W A]

A Tree for Poverty: Somali Poetry and Prose, ed. Margaret Laurence (Nairobi, 1954) (tr. of one poem).

Mohamed Farah Abdillahi and B. W. Andrzejewski, 'The Life of 'Ilmi Bowndheri, a Somali Oral Poet Who is Said to Have Died of Love', *Journal of the Folklore Institute*, Indiana University, 1967.

Ismaaʿiil Mire (1884–*c.* 1950). Somali oral poet. One of the war leaders in the Somali insurrection against the British administration and a close friend of ⇨ Mahammed ʿAbdille Hasan. His poems give a first-hand account of that period and are thus an important historical source. After the insurrection he composed poems connected with interclan affairs and also turned to religious and reflective themes. His poem with the refrain 'Know that through pride men fall' is particularly widely known among the Somalis and so is his observation on success: 'Keep silent, oh Muslims, for he who becomes successful loses his soul.' [B W A]

Andrzejewski and Lewis, *SPI*.

J

Jabavu, D. D. T. (1885–1959). South African scholar. Born in Cape Province and died there. He was Professor of Latin and Bantu Languages at Fort Hare University. He wrote mostly in Xhosa.

His 1943 address to the Fort Hare branch of the English Association, afterwards published under the title *The Influence of English on Bantu Literature* (Lovedale, South Africa, n.d.), is a useful guide to vernacular literature. Besides two travel books, *E Jerusalem* ('In Jerusalem') and *E America* ('In America'), he has published *Imbumba Yama Nyama* ('Selections') (Lovedale, South Africa, 1953), *Isithuko* ('Insult') (Lovedale, South Africa, 1954), and *Izidunsulwana* ('Small Mounds') (Cape Town, 1958). In Jabavu's writings there is a balance between Western European method and Bantu thought. His achievement lies in reconciliation and in his broad nationalism. [O R D]

Jabavu, Noni (1920–). South African writer. Born in Cape Province, the daughter of ⇨ D. D. T. Jabavu. She came to England at 14. The war interrupted her music studies at the Royal Academy and she became a technician. She married an English film director and travelled widely in Mozambique, Kenya and South Africa. She lived for some time in Uganda with her husband but they are now in England.

Her first book, *Drawn in Colour* (London, 1960), is a personal documentary account of differences between East and South Africa in their contact with the Western world. Her second, *The Ochre People* (London, 1963), is also autobiographical, each of its three parts dealing with a different geographical area. It is less successful than her first book because it is too heavily documented and contains an over-abundance of Xhosa words which do little to promote her theme. [O R D]

Jolobe, J. R. (1902–). South African writer. Born in Indwe, Cape Province. He took an Arts degree at Fort Hare, is a Presbyterian minister and has taught in South African schools. Since 1958 he has been at the Lovedale Mission School. He writes in English and Xhosa.

Um yezo ('An Orchard') (Johannesburg, 1936) is a collection of his poetry in Xhosa which he later translated into English as *Poems of an African* (Lovedale, S.A., 1946). It includes a sonnet 'To Light', a poem of consolation 'To the Fallen', a poem of remembrance 'In Memory', and a long narrative poem 'Thuthula' (shortened form in Reed and Wake, *BAV*). Other works include *A mavo* ('Personal Impressions') (Johannesburg, 1951), essays on the social life of the Xhosa; *Lovedale Xhosa Rhymes* (Lovedale, S.A., 1957), an anthology; and *Uzagula* (Lovedale, S.A., 1923), which takes its name from the heroine, and a translation of Aesop's fables into Xhosa. [J A R]

Jordan, A. C. (1906–). South African scholar and novelist. Born in Cape Province. Was lecturer in Bantu Languages at the University of Cape Town. He recently went to California and now lectures at the University of Wisconsin.

His novel *Ingqumbo Yeminyanya* ('The Wrath of the Ancestors') (Lovedale, S.A., 1939 and 1961) was recently dramatized. It is the story of a Lovedale–Fort Hare student born into a royal family. He disappears at four but grows up in a village nearby and finally returns to claim his throne. He insists on marrying the woman of his choice, someone who flouts local traditions and kills a snake, the messenger of the ancestors. The tribe is divided into factions, and at the end the queen and her son die and the chief kills himself. From 1957 Jordan has written a series of articles for *Africa South* on the theme 'Towards an African Literature'. These are of great value to anyone interested in the vernacular literature of South Africa [J A R]

K

Kagame, Abbé Alexis or **Alegisi** (1912–). Ruandan poet, historian and ethnographer. One of the leading intellectual figures of Ruanda-Urundi, he was born at Kiyanza in the chieftainship of Buriza. His father, Pierre Bitahurwina, a member of the Tutsi tribe, was deputy chief. Kagame was educated first at the state school in Ruhengeri, then at the Kabgayi seminary school. After studying philosophy and theology at the main seminary at Kabgayi, he was ordained priest in 1941. His first publication, *Inganji Karinga* ('The Victorious Drum') (Kabgayi, 1943), was devoted to the ancient history of Ruanda. He later took his Ph.D. at the Pontifical Gregorian University in Rome.

He has published an epic in 3 parts on the evangelization of Ruanda, *Isoko y'amajyambere* (Kabgayi, 1949–51). He translated portions of his second Oluruanda religious epic into French as *La divine pastorale* (Brussels, 1952). This was followed by *La naissance de l'Univers* (1955).

Though Father Kagame has devoted himself untiringly to pastoral work in Ruanda-Urundi, he has maintained his literary and scientific endeavours. He is an associate of the Institut pour la Recherche Scientifique en Afrique Centrale, and a Corresponding Member of the Belgian Académie Royale des Sciences d'Outre-mer, which has sponsored some 10 major studies by Father Kagame on the history, literature and civilization of Ruanda-Urundi. [G T A]

Preface to Kagame, *La divine pastorale* (Brussels, 1952); *Travaux publiés par l'Académie Royale des Sciences d'Outre-mer* (1952–61, etc.).

Kane, Sheikh Hamidou (1928–). French West African novelist. Born at Matam in Senegal. A Muslim by faith, he is a native of the Futa mountains, and a representative of the Fula language and culture. After receiving traditional instruction in the Koran, he attended French schools in Senegal. He then went to Paris University to study philosophy and law, before entering the École Nationale de la France d'Outre-mer. In July 1959 he returned to Senegal as an official in the French overseas administration. He was appointed deputy to the director of development projects, then head of chancery to the Minister of Development and Planning of independent Senegal. From 1960 to 1963 he was governor of the district of Thiès.

Sheikh Hamidou has been aptly called 'a true witness of Islam in its modern African guise'. His first book, *L'aventure ambiguë* (pref. by Vincent Monteil, Paris, 1961), is a romantic autobiography, which tells of the encounter of two worlds of experience, Black Africa and Western Europe, by a young African, brutally initiated by a Muslim teacher into Islamic mysticism, then remoulded by the French educational system. It is a story of spiritual fidelity and of intellectual uprooting, a penetrating and sophisticated critique of the doubtful values implicit in Western civilization. [G T A]

Krige, Uys (1910–). Bilingual South African poet, playwright, novelist and critic. He went to England as a journalist in 1931, and later travelled widely in France and Spain (see *Sol y Sombra*, 1948). During the war he was a correspondent in North Africa and Europe, and a prisoner in Italy. Since then he has devoted himself to writing.

Krige's best work is in Afrikaans. A sense of ephemeral beauty dominates his early poetry, notably *Rooidag* (1940). In the war years, the conflict between brutal force and the joy of living prompted some of his best writings, while *Die Groue Kring* (1956) contrasts the glowing warmth of life and the omnipotence of death. Krige's insight into foreign literatures is considerable, his translation of Lorca's lament being probably the finest in Afrikaans (*Vir die Luit en die Kitaar*, 1950). He has edited collections of the poetry of Roy Campbell and Guy Butler. Among Krige's English writings, the war novel *The Way Out* (1946) and the stories of *The Dream and the Desert* (1953) share a strangely sensuous and poetic prose style. His latest publication in English is *The Sniper and Other One Act Plays* (1962). [D D]

Oorlogsgedigte (1942); *Alle Paaie Gaan na Rome* (1949); *Ballade van die Groot Begeer* (1960); *Gedigte 1927–40* (1961).

Roy MacNab and Charles Gulston, *South African Poetry* (1948); D. J. Opperman, *Digters van Dertig* (1953); R. Antonissen, *Die Afrikaanse Letterkunde* (Pretoria, 1955).

L

La Guma, Alex (1925–). South African short-story writer. Born in Cape Town. Son of Jimmy La Guma, the president of the South African Coloured People's Congress. He was among the accused in the South African 'Treason Trials'. He was a columnist for a weekly Cape Town paper, but now lives in London.

Two of his short stories, *A Glass of Wine* and *Slipper Satin*, have been published by *Black Orpheus*. Both concern mixed marriage in South Africa. In *Africa South* he published *Out of Darkness*, the story of Old Cockroach, a prisoner serving a long-term sentence for culpable homicide. The theme is the same, involving a quarrel brought about by the racial relationships of two lovers. His most recent story, also published by *Black Orpheus*, is *Tattoo Marks and Tails*, about prison life. His novelette, *A Walk in the Night* (Mbari, Ibadan, 1962), is a story of colour relationships, violence and murder. It is told in terse language with passionate precise descriptions of night and the city. [O R D]

Ladipo, Duro (*c.*1930–). Nigerian playwright. Attended primary school in Nigeria and then taught. He formed the Duro Ladipo Theatre in 1962 for Mbari Mbayo, Oshogbo. He has written Yoruba folk operas, usually staged by himself and his company. Among his most successful are *Enia soro* ('The Unreliable'), a story of misplaced trust; *Oba koso* ('The King Does Not Hang'), the story of two rival generals in King Shango's armies; *Oba moro* ('The Ghost King'); and *Oba waja* ('The King is Dead'), which highlights the tragedy of Westernization and its effects on the old ways. All of these plays have been translated and have been published by Mbari, Ibadan. [J A R]

Laluah, A. ◊ Casely-Hayford.

Laye, Camara (1928–). Contemporary French West African novelist. Comes of a Malinke family from Kouroussa, Upper Guinea. His father was a jeweller and goldsmith, his mother a smith's daughter. A Muslim by faith, Camara Laye attended a Koranic school, then the French primary school at Kouroussa. At Conakry technical college, he received a first-class proficiency certificate in mechanical engineering. He was sent to France to the Central School of Automobile Engineering at Argenteuil. On his own initiative he entered the École Ampère in Paris, working for the diploma in industrial instruction. To gain a living, he had to work for eight months as a mechanic at the Simca works, while following evening courses at the National Conservatory of Arts and Crafts. He finally studied for a specialized diploma in engineering at the Technical College for Aeronautics and Automobile Construction.

Camara Laye's literary career began in his Paris student days. Unlike most other African writers – some of whom have adversely criticized him for this – he is politically non-partisan, and remarkable rather for his psychological insight. His first book, *L'enfant noir* (1953; tr. J. Kirkup et al., *The Dark Child*, 1954), is an autobiographical novel for which Camara Laye, still a student in Paris, was awarded the Charles Veillon prize; it is remarkable for its picture of the traditions of Malinke civilization. His second novel, *Le regard du roi* (1954; tr. James Kirkup, *The Radiance of the King*, 1956), is an allegory about man's search for God, written in a colloquial *griot* style, in which the adventures of the hero are developed in a narrative sometimes comic, sometimes touching, and always with immense verve.

On his return from France, Camara Laye was attached for a time to the Guinea Ministry of Youth, and then went back to his native Upper Guinea. [G T A]

Rutherfoord, *D L*; Moore, *S A W*.

Leipoldt, C. Louis (1880–1947). Afrikaans poet and playwright. After a lonely childhood with nature as his refuge, he became a journalist and during the Boer War acted as correspondent for pro-Boer newspapers in The Hague, Brussels, Chicago and Manchester. The war, and nature, formed the mainspring of his early poems, *Oom Gert Vertel en ander Gedigte* (1911), the first of his more than 40 publications (including essays, and narrative and biographical prose). Unlike his contemporaries he revealed no chauvinism or conventional calvinism: to him the war was a revelation of the human conflict between blind force and defencelessness. From 1903 he studied medicine in England, Germany and the U.S.A. and afterwards worked in hospitals in Dulston and Chelsea; in 1912 he visited Borneo, Java and Sumatra, an experience which may have been at the root of his eventual conversion to Buddhism. In 1914 he returned to South Africa as a child specialist, with a deep interest in botany and gastronomy. His contact with Europe and the Far East had made him a true cosmopolitan, which is also reflected in his choice of material for his plays *Die Heks* (1923), the first tragedy in Afrikaans, which is situated in mediæval Germany, and *Die Laaste Aand* (1930), the first Afrikaans verse play, which takes place in East India and the early Cape. Leipoldt's poetry is characterized by its spontaneity to the point of carelessness and exaggeration, its hedonistic exuberance and its dramatic qualities; his war poems are a violent outcry against brutal force causing innocent suffering. But his vehemence is always balanced by reconciliation, especially in his later work – *Skoonheidstroos* (1932) etc. A few long poems in *Uit Drie Wêrelddele* (1923) reveal an unexpectedly strong undercurrent of philosophical speculation which suggests that his *joie de vivre* is really the surface of a deeply tragic and at times fatalistic approach to life and an acute sense of transitoriness. [A P B]

Vyftig Gedigte (2nd edn, 1956); *Afrikaans Poems With English Translations*, ed. A. P. Grove and C. J. D. Harvey (1962).
M. P. O. Burgers, *C. L. Leipoldt* (1960).

Leroux, Étienne (1922–). South African novelist. His debut at 34 with *Die eerste lewe van Colet* (1956; 'Colet's First Life'), a psycho-analysis of sexual growth from childhood to manhood in existentialist perspective, marked the beginning of the new novel in Afrikaans. The 'story' was continued in *Hilaria* (1957), in which the pathological condition of an individual becomes the pathetic index of modern existence depleted of all sense by a vulgarly commercialized society. In *Die Mugu* (1959) the individuality of man appeared to be an absurdity doomed to obliteration in the grotesque mosaic of Western welfare-togetherness, which is in dire need of a 'living myth'. Such a myth is frantically desired in *Sewe Dae by die Silbersteins* (1962; tr. C. Eglington, *Seven Days at the Silbersteins*, 1964) and *Een vir Azazel* (1964; 'One for Azazel') – which are shortly to be completed by *Die Derde Oog* ('The Third Eye') to form a trilogy of 'phantasmal' novels. [R A]

R. Antonissen, *Kern en tooi* (Pretoria, 1963), and *Spitsberaad* (Pretoria, 1966).

Lopes, Baltasar (pseud. **Osvaldo Alcantara**) (1904–). Novelist and poet, born in the Cape Verde Islands. He is lawyer and rector at the Liceu de S. Vincente, Cape Verde Islands. He writes in Portuguese.

He appeared in Mario de Andrade's *Antologia* (Paris, 1958) with his poem 'Mamãe'. His publications include *O dialecto Crioulo* (Lisbon, 1958), *Chiquinho* (Cape Verde, 1947, and Lisbon, 1961) (a novel), and an *Antologia da ficcão Cabo-Verdiana*. His work often describes the poor earth and the absence of rain, symbolizing physical and spiritual exile, or what has aptly been described as 'a calvary of bodily and mental agony'.
[O R D]

Louw, N. P. van Wyk (1906–). Afrikaans poet, dramatist and essayist. From the outset his poetry is characterized by a transposition of all events to a level of metaphysical conflict between light and darkness, good and evil, concepts which grow increasingly complex and subtle while the poet's language becomes more and more sober. During the years he spent in Cape Town, first as a student and later as lecturer in Education, his poetry developed from experiments with traditional forms to intensely dramatic and eminently personal expressions of passionate thought. After his epic poem *Raka* (1941) he created an overawing series of figures in various forms and stages of disintegration, enabling him to penetrate all layers of the human personality (*Gestaltes en Diere*, 1942); this was often accompanied by a keen historical sense which first found dramatic expression in *Die Dieper Reg* (1938); this was followed, in 1951, by *Dias*, a study of the irrationality of human will and divine providence; in 1956 by his verse player *Germanicus*, a new 'tragedy of inaction'; and in 1966 by *Die Pluimsaad Waai Ver*, based on the Anglo-Boer War. He also wrote several important radio plays. In 1950 he was appointed Professor of Afrikaans Literature, Culture and History in the University of Amsterdam, and during his years of 'exile' (before he acceded to the chair of Afrikaans Literature in the Witwatersrand University in 1958) his poetry turned to basic South African motives, becoming much more concrete and chiselled (*Nuwe Verse*, 1954). He identified himself with the exiled Ovid and in his latest work, *Tristia* (1962), his penetrating quest for truth beneath everyday appearance assumes a moving irony. He is not only the major poet of Afrikaans literature but also the leading essayist on cultural, literary and political problems (*Lojale Verset*, 1939; *'n Wêreld deur Glas*, 1958; *Liberale Nasionalisme*, 1958). He is the only writer who has received the Hertzog Prize (the highest South African literary award) five times: for poetry, drama and essays.
[A P B]

Gedigte (1960); *Afrikaans Poems with English Translations*, ed. A. P. Grove and C. J. D. Harvey (1962).
D. J. Opperman, *Digters van Dertig* (1953).

M

Mahammed 'Abdille Hasan (1864–1920). Somali oral poet. Muslim religious leader and the founder of modern Somali nationalism. His alliterative poems, like all poetry in Somali, were composed and handed down orally. From youth he showed great zeal for religious studies and at the age of 19 had already gained the title of sheikh for his learning. He travelled to religious centres outside his country and in Mecca met Sayyid Muhammad Saalih, a religious reformer, and joined his religious fraternity, the Saalihiya. On his return he started a religious campaign, advocating a puritanical and austere adherence to Islam, and in 1899 declared a holy war against the infidels, which he conducted with skill, courage and ferocity. It won him the nickname 'Mad Mullah' from his opponents. In 1920 he was finally defeated by the British forces and died in exile in Ethiopia. Throughout his active life as a preacher and war leader he used his poetry to propagate his religious doctrine, publicize his political views, attack his enemies and win allies. His poetry is characterized by a fiery imagination, and by religious and patriotic fervour. He compared the power of his diction to the waves of the sea and to torrential rain. His imagery is rooted in the everyday life of the nomadic pastoralists in the prairies and deserts of the arid country which he loved passionately. He is well known for the passages vividly depicting African scenery and wild life. Particularly striking are his lament on parting with his favourite horse and the poetic message to the Ogaden clan asking for their support in his insurrection. He also composed hymns and poems in Arabic. There are several private collections of his poems, of which the most reliable and extensive are those of Sheikh Jama Umar Ise and ◊ Musa H. I. Galaal, both of Mogadishu. Seven of his poems, with notes and English translations, have been published in *Somali Poetry* (see below). [B W A]

Enrico Cerulli, 'Muhammad B. 'Abd Allah Hassan', *E of I*; D. Jardine, *The Mad Mullah of Somaliland* (1923); Andrzejewski and Lewis, *S P I*; I. M. Lewis, *The Modern History of Somaliland – From Nation to State* (1965).

Maimane, J. Arthur (1932–). South African short-story writer. He has worked for newspapers in South Africa but in 1958 left for Ghana, then London, where he now lives.

An early story, *Just a Tsotsi*, tells of a white police constable who mistakenly shoots a former black playmate. *The Hungry Boy*, published in *Following the Sun* (Berlin, 1960), is a story of the effects of poverty. Other short stories are *The Note*, in which a liberal lawyer defends an African, and *The Madness*, in which an ageing white woman commands her servant to make love to her. He is hanged for rape. In *A Kaffer Woman*, published in *Black Orpheus*, the opposite happens and a white farmer takes a black mistress. When discovered, he shoots himself. His stories seem to protest against the sexual restrictions due to South African racial laws. [O R D]

Malangatana, Valente (1936–). Poet, born in Marracuene, Mozambique. He had an informal education and took an early interest in drawing and painting. Since 1959 he has worked as painter and artist. He writes poetry (some has been published in *Black Orpheus*), and he has recently completed an autobiography. [O R D]

Malonga, Jean (1907–). Congolese novelist. Born in Brazzaville, Congo. He attended local mission school and high school. He went to France in 1948 as a member of the French National Assembly. He has published *Cœur d'Aryenne*, a novelette, in *Trois écrivains noirs* (Paris, 1954), and a novel *La légende de M'Pfoumou Ma Mazono* (Paris, 1954). [O R D]

Marais, Eugène (1871–1936). Afrikaans poet and naturalist. In 1897, after a few turbulent years as editor-owner of an influential pro-Afrikaans Transvaal newspaper, and the death of his wife after one year of marriage, he went to England to study law, medicine and Egyptology. Towards the end of the Boer War he joined an unsuccessful expedition to the Transvaal, via Mozambique. His deep concern for his people resulted in a few conventionally patriotic poems and in the delicate melancholy of 'Winternag' (1905), the first important poem in Afrikaans. Soon afterwards he abandoned his legal and journalistic work in Pretoria and took refuge in the Waterberg district, where he first became interested in the 'communal mind' of termites and baboons; his experiments led to the publication of the important bio-psychological studies *Die Siel van die Mier* (1934) and *Burgers van die Berge* (1938), of which the former influenced Maeterlinck. This contact with nature and his acquaintance with an old Bushman storyteller prompted his *Dwaalstories* (1927), primitive, mythical tales with a simplicity and musicality unrivalled in Afrikaans prose. His most important poems form part of these tales. They are characterized by their peculiar paratactic construction, concrete imagery and primitive rhythm. Marais' eventual return to Pretoria to resume his legal practice, and his increasing addiction to drugs, aggravated the pessimism expressed in such poems as 'Skoppensboer'. The last years of his life, which ended in suicide in 1936, were devoted to the revision and extension of his small volume of poetry, *Gedigte* (which had first been published by a friend in 1925), the systematizing of his scientific theories and discoveries, and the writing of magazine articles, short stories and a few inferior melodramas. [A P B]

Gedigte – Poems, tr. A. E. Thorpe (1956); *The Soul of the White Ant*, tr. Winifred de Kock (1937).

F. G. M. du Toit, *Eugène Nielen Marais* (Amsterdam, 1940).

Matip, Benjamin (1932–). Camerounian novelist. Born in Eseka, Cameroun, studied Political Economy and Law in Paris, and from 1955 practised law in Paris. In 1958 he was a Camerounian delegate to the Afro-Asian Writers' Conference and in 1959 he was a member of the Permanent Secretariat of Afro-Asian writers in Colombo. He writes in French and has published a novel, *Afrique nous t'ignorons* (Paris, 1956), partly autobiographical and dealing in part with the excitement caused in Cameroun by the outbreak of the last war, and *À la belle étoile* (Paris, 1962), a collection of fables. [J A R]

Matshikiza, Todd (*c.* 1924–). South African journalist. Born in Queenstown, and educated in South Africa, at one time at Lovedale Institute, where he later taught. He taught also in St Peter's and worked in broadcasting. He wrote the music for *King Kong* and in 1960 came to London with that show. In South Africa he was a journalist and ran a monthly column in *Drum* called *With the Lid Off*. He is now working for the radio station in Malawi. In his column he adopted a snappy style full of what Langston Hughes called 'ironic humour', also present in his only book so far, *Chocolates for my Wife* (London, 1961), a chatty account of his experiences in South Africa and England. [O R D]

Mbiti, John (1931–). Kenyan writer. Born in Kitui, Kenya, where he attended primary school and high-school. After taking a degree at Makerere College, Uganda, he studied theology in the U.S.A. before returning to Kenya as a teacher and minister of religion. In 1961 he went to Cambridge, where he wrote a thesis. He has compiled an English-Kamba vocabulary and translated folk-tales into English. His article 'Reclaiming the Vernacular Literature of the Akamba Tribe' appeared in *Présence africaine* and he has contributed poems and short stories to various periodicals in Europe. He has a poem, 'New York Skyscrapers', in Moore and Beier, *MPA*. Other works include *Mutunga na ngewa yake*, in the vernacular (Edinburgh, 1954), and *Over the Fence* (1954). [J A R]

Modisane, Bloke (1923–). South African writer. Born in Sophiatown, Johannesburg. Educated in South Africa, living there until the Sophiatown disaster. He was a reporter, feature writer, theatre and music critic for *Drum*, and did some acting. In 1959 he came to England, where he has continued to write and to act at the Royal Court Theatre and on B.B.C. television. In 1963 he went to America to lecture on African music and literature.

One of his best-known articles is that on the colour bar in *Twentieth Century*; another, 'Why I Ran Away', appeared in Langston Hughes's *An African Treasury* (1961) (previously published in the *New Statesman*). He has also published short stories. Other works are *The Professional Beggar*, a beggar's view of his social problems, *All Langa Was Quiet*, about a strike, and *The Situation*, which describes the predicament of the educated African. He has written poems, mainly about colour. His first and only book so far is *Blame Me on History* (1963), an autobiographical reconstruction of his years in South Africa. The writing is full of pathos, humour and warmth, but above all there is a vigorous and terse condemnation of apartheid. [O R D]

Mofolo, Thomas (1877–1948). South African novelist. Father of Sotho as a literary language. He was successively student, teacher, clerk and proof-reader at a South African mission school at Morija before becoming a land agent in the Basutoland gold-mines. In sudden prosperity he opened a mill in Basutoland, but was later contented with the ownership of a small store there.

Mofolo's novels show the effect on a patriotic tribesman of the European impact. Their influence, in this respect, on later African writers has been freely acknowledged. All three are in Sotho. *Moeti oa bochabela* (1912), translated as *The Traveller of the East,* and *Pitseng* ('At the Pot', 1934) are less often read than *Chaka* (1925; tr. F. H. Dutton, 1931) which has also been translated into French, German and also Ibo, the native language of an important group of Nigerian writers. It is a historical romance about the Zulu warrior-king whose exploits Rider Haggard describes in *Nada the Lily* (1892). Mofolo's conscious handling of Chaka's reign as part of a national mythology is given weight by a portentous prose-style, the result of an unembarrassed delight in heroic elevation. [P T]

Rutherfoord. *D L.*

Mopeli-Paulus, A. S. (1913–). Lesotho writer. He studied Medicine at Witwatersrand University, taught for a period, and later served in the Second World War in East Africa and Egypt. He lives in Johannesburg, works in a lawyer's office and is a chief of Basutoland. He has published stories and a travel book in the vernacular and written 2 other books which have been translated into English: *Blanket Boy's Moon* (1953) with Peter Lanham, the partly autobiographical story of Monare, torn between tribals laws and government authority; and *Turn to the Dark* (1956), with Miriam Basner. [J A R]

Mphahlele, Ezekiel (1919–). South African writer. Born in Pretoria. His autobiography, *Down Second Avenue* (1959), combines documentary precision with the structure and style of a novel. Inevitably it is a story of struggle and setback. In 1932 Mphahlele was brought to live in a Pretoria slum. He went through High School, then Teacher Training College in Natal. In 1941–5 he worked at an institute for the African blind. Seven years as a schoolmaster ended in 1952 when he was dismissed and banned from teaching in the Union as a result of agitation against the Bantu Education Act. In 1955 he joined the staff of *Drum,* but disliked journalism. His Syndicate of Artists was formed to meet higher cultural standards among Africans. In 1957 he went to teach in Nigeria. His book *The African Image* (1962) is partly an explanation of his voluntary exile, partly a record of a visit to England and partly a reworking of a degree thesis on the non-white in fiction. He is now living in America.

Mphahlele has an easy mastery of prose style, but has not so far written fiction to equal his autobiography. His second collection of stories, *The Living and Dead* (Ibadan, 1961), is erratic, but in at least two stories he has found the balance he seeks – 'the ironic meeting between protest and acceptance in their widest terms'. [P T]

Man Must Live (Cape Town, 1946).
Moore, *S A W.*

Mqhayi, S. E. K. (1875–1945). South African writer. He worked for some time for Xhosa newspapers. He did a great deal to show the strength of Xhosa as a medium for literature.

He wrote 2 volumes of poetry, *Imihobe nemibongo* (1927) ('Song of Praise') and *Inzuzu* ('Gain'). There is some poetry as well in his prose works. He translated 2 books into Xhosa: *Ulimo* ('The Science of Agriculture'), an agricultural book, and *U Aggrey um Afrika* ('Aggrey of Africa'), a biography. He wrote biographies of J. K. Bokwe and Nathaniel Umhalla and an autobiography, *U Mqhayi wase Ntabozuko* ('Mquayi of Mount Glory') (Lovedale, S.A., 1912). His two best-known works of fiction are *Ityala lama wele* ('The Case of the Twins') (Lovedale, S.A., 1912) a story of twins who rivalled each other on the basis of who was firstborn, and *U don jadu* (Lovedale, S.A., 1929) which, according to Professor Jabavu (who translated it into English), is about Xhosa court-life before the coming of the Europeans. Jabavu found the latter cumbersome in parts. Both works have become classics in the Xhosa language. [ORD]

Musa Hajji Ismail Galaal (Musa Galaal) (1914–). Somali prose writer, poet and collector of oral literature. He spent his youth as a camel-herder of the nomadic interior and became a teacher after the Second World War. From 1951 to 1954 he worked at the School of Oriental and African Studies, University of London. After the independence of the Somali Republic in 1960, he became the chairman of the Linguistic Committee concerned with the introduction of a national orthography for Somali, and afterwards the head of the Cultural Relations Division in the Ministry of Education in Mogadishu. In 1956 he published a collection of traditional stories and poems in Somali under the title *Hikmad Soomaali* (1956) (some translated in *A Selection from African Prose*, 1. *Traditional Oral Texts*, 1964). He has written a novel in Somali, as yet unpublished, depicting the traditional way of life in his country. [BWA]

Andrzejewski and Galaal, *SPC*.

Muyaka b. Haji al-Ghassaniy (1776–1840). Swahili poet. He was a friend of the Mazrui governors of Fort Jesus, Mombasa. He wrote prolifically in verse on contemporary affairs. More than any other Swahili writer, Muyaka succeeded in transferring Swahili poetry from the mosque to the market-place. An anthology of his poems, *Diwani ya Muyaka*, ed. W. Hichens, was published by the University of Witwatersrand Press in 1940. [LPH]

Harries, *SP*.

Mwana Kupona (1810–60). Swahili poetess. Wife of Bwana Mataka, Shaikh of Siu in Kenya, who for 20 years carried on a guerrilla warfare against Saiyid Said, Sultan of Zanzibar. She wrote one very well-known poem called *Utendi wa Mwana Kupona* ('The Homiletic of Mwana Kupona'). [LPH]

Harries, *SP*.

N

Naigiziki, J. V. S. (1915–). Ruandese writer. Born in Mwulire-Busanga. He worked there as a schoolmaster, translator, printer, assistant chauffeur and import agent's clerk. He lives in Astrida in Ruanda and writes in French. He has written *Escapade ruandaise* (Brussels, 1950), an autobiographical journal; *L'optimiste* (Astride, Ruanda, 1954), a play; and *Mes transes à trente ans* (Astrida, Ruanda, 1955), a novel which exploits his paramystical experiences and includes *Escapade ruandaise*. [JAR]

Rutherfoord, *DL*.

Neto, Agostinho (1922–). Angolan patriotic poet. Born at Icola e Bengo in Portuguese West Africa. He went to Lisbon to study medicine and returned to Angola to practise. He became associated with the movement for the rediscovery of Angola's indigenous culture, led by Viriato da Cruz, and in 1960 was elected president of the Angolan Liberation Movement. Arrested and taken to Portugal for imprisonment, he escaped in 1962. Neto's poems, strongly coloured by political and social protest, have appeared in Portuguese in two anthologies edited by Mário de ◊ Andrade (1953, 1958), as well as in Portuguese and Angolan reviews. [ORD]

Moore and Beier, *MPA*.

Ngugi, James (1938–). Kenyan novelist and playwright. Born in Limuru, Kenya. He read English at Makerere University College. He has written 3 novels, the first of which won the highest award of the East African Literature Bureau, and a play, produced by the Uganda National Theatre for Independence. He has edited *Penpoint*, the journal of Makerere Department of English, in which some of his short stories have appeared. He frequently writes for the *Sunday Nation*, Kenya, on literary and political matters.

His play, *The Black Hermit*, partly in verse and not yet published, is about an educated young man who, shirking responsibility at first, slowly learns its meaning. His first published novel, *Weep Not Child* (1964), is the story of a young boy growing up amidst the Mau-Mau struggle. It describes its shattering effect on his family life. A short story, *The Return*, appeared in *Transition*, No. 3, and a second novel, *The River Between* (1965), has also appeared. [O R D]

Nicol, Abioseh (1924–). Short-story writer and poet, born in Sierra Leone. Educated in Nigeria and Sierra Leone. He studied at Cambridge, took a first-class honours in Natural Sciences and was a Research Fellow in Biochemistry. He returned to Sierra Leone as a senior pathologist in the Sierra Leonean Medical Service. He is now principal of Fourah Bay College, University of Sierra Leone, and in 1961 was a delegate to the UNESCO conference in Boston.

His short stories, poems and articles have been published in America and Europe. In England he has written on African affairs and literature for *Encounter, The Times,* the *Economist,* and the *Guardian.* His poetry has a strong religious flavour. In neither his poetry nor his prose has he ever indulged in narrow racialist pamphleteering; he has always expanded his vision to deal with wider and more universal aspects of life. There is often a satirical twist to his humour. [O R D]

Africa: A Subjective View (1964); Reed and Wake, *B A V*; *Poems from Black Africa* (Indiana U.P., 1963); *An African Treasury*, ed. Langston Hughes (1960) (short story).

Nketia, J. H. (1921–). Ghanaian musicologist and writer. Born in Ashanti Mampong, Ghana. He was once attached to the Department of Sociology, University of Ghana, as a musicologist, but is now with the Institute of African Studies, University of Ghana. He has written 12 books in Twi and is an internationally known musicologist. He has written widely on African music. Among his publications are *Kwabena Amoa* (1953), a book of fiction; *Funeral Dirges of the Akan People* (Achimota, Ghana, 1955); and *Folk Songs of Ghana* (Legon, Ghana, 1963), with music and texts in vernacular and English. [J A R]

Nyembezi, C. L. S. (?–). South African poet and novelist. He attended Witwatersrand University and was at one time Professor of Bantu languages at the University College of Fort Hare. He writes in English and Zulu and has published poems in the vernacular. He has written 2 novels and translated Alan Paton's *Cry the Beloved Country* into Zulu. He has also collected *Zulu Proverbs* (Johannesburg, 1954) and published *A Review of Zulu Literature* (Pietermaritzburg, 1961), based on a lecture at Natal University. One novel, *Mtanami, mtanami* ('My Child! My Child!') (Pietermaritzburg, 1950), is about young people changing the old life of the town. [O R D]

Nzekwu, Onuora (1928–). Nigerian novelist. Born in Kafanchan, Northern Nigeria. He taught for several years before becoming a journalist with *Nigeria Magazine*. He was formerly editor.

He has published 3 novels. *Wand of Noble Wood* (1961) is centred upon a Lagos journalist, by intellectual conviction a Westerner but by emotional persuasion a man subject to the traditions of his people. He is strongly opposed when he wants to marry the woman of his choice. Jan Carew, the West Indian novelist, found it gave 'profound insights into the shifting social patterns of modern West Africa'. In *Blade Among the Boys* (1962), his hero is again divided, this time between tribal religion and church. When he decides he wants to become a priest, his mother is horrified, since celibacy and consequent childlessness are not qualities his tribe admires. His novels have a direct approach. His most recent is *Highlife for Lizards* (1966). There is too heavy a reliance on the main character, but Nzekwu skilfully integrates elements of Ibo life and folklore. [J A R]

O

Ogot, Grace (1930–). Kenyan short-story writer. Born in Butere, Nyanza, Kenya. She was self-taught and became a nurse. She went to London in 1955, where she wrote articles and broadcast on the B.B.C.'s East African Service. She left England in 1958, married in 1959, and returned to England with her husband, a historian, remaining until 1961. They now live at Makerere College, Kampala, Uganda, where she is an official in community development.

She has written short stories and children's stories. One of her stories has been translated into German as 'Die Getötete Zauberkatze' and is about a farmer who killed a magic cat and went mad as a result. Another story, 'The Year of the Sacrifice', published by *Black Orpheus*, is about the virgin daughter of a chief about to sacrifice herself to abate the drought and saved just in time by her lover. [O R D]

Ogunde, Herbert (1916–). Nigerian playwright. He became a school teacher, and later a policeman, before forming a professional theatre company 20 years ago in Nigeria. He has composed over 15 operatic plays. The lyrics and dialogue are, however, largely improvised on the stage. Some of the songs have been published. Among his best-known plays is *Yoruba ronu* (Yaba, Nigeria, 1964) ('Yorubas Must Think'), banned by the West Nigerian Government in 1965. [J A R]

Ogunmola, E. Kolawole (1925–). Nigerian playwright. He became a primary school teacher and studied at the University of Ibadan Drama Department on a Rockefeller grant for 6 months. He had been a professional writer and actor before and has continued since. He writes in Yoruba.

His 12 or more plays are really folk-operas. Among the best known are *They Were Enemies*, involving the betrayal of a friend, *Love of Money* (1954), about a man who gives in to the greedy demands of his second wife and suffers accordingly, and *Agbaraj' agbara* ('The Reign of the Mighty'), about power. The latter was produced in 1962 at the University of Ibadan Arts Theatre. His dramatized version of Amos ◊ Tutuola's *Palm Wine Drinkard* has been performed all over West Africa. A strong didacticism runs throughout his work. Often his plays have biblical themes; always they show the triumph of good over evil. [O R D]

Okara, Gabriel (1921–). Nigerian writer. Born in Bumodi. Educated in Umahia, Nigeria, and in 1959 went to America and studied journalism at Northwestern University. He is now Information Officer with the Eastern Regional Government in Enugu.

His first literary attempts were plays and broadcast talks. He has published some poetry in *Black Orpheus* (Nos. 1, 3 and 6). His attempts to translate Ijaw idiom directly into English have produced an exciting language which is used in a work recently published as a novel, *The Voice* (1964). He has also written about Ijaw myth and folklore. He shows an interest in indigenous culture and the impact of this and western culture on the modern urbanized African. He romanticizes the African past as being free from the complexities of present-day civilization. [J A R]

Reed and Wake, *B A V*; Moore and Beier, *M P A*.

Okigbo, Christopher (1932–). Nigerian poet. Born near Onitsha, Eastern Nigeria. He graduated at the University of Ibadan in Classics in 1956. He worked in government service, then taught for 2 years and afterwards joined the library staff of the University of Nigeria. He was West African representative of the Cambridge University Press.

He has published 2 volumes of poetry: *Hevensgate* (Mbari, Ibadan, 1962) and *Limits* (Mbari, Ibadan, 1964). He has also published 'Silences' in *Transition* No. 8. He is one of the most exciting poets now writing in Africa. Strongly influenced by T. S. Eliot, his poetry is concerned with the ritualistic exploration of being. Through sharp imagery the protagonist in his poetry explores various states of consciousness and unconsciousness to attain a universality with the world. [J A R]

Reed and Wake, *B V A*; Moore and Beier, *M P A*.

Opperman, D. J. (1914–). Afrikaans poet and dramatist. His familiarity with the Zulu language and people may explain the peculiar nature of his work: a poetry of the concrete, with a mythical power of incantation, and an ability to render delicate spiritual conflicts in almost tangible language. After university education in Natal, and a few years as teacher and journalist, he became first lecturer and afterwards Professor of Afrikaans Literature in the universities of Cape Town and Stellenbosch. He is also a critic of note and his 'Poets of the Thirties' (*Digters van Dertig*, 1953) is a standard work of reference. His first volume, *Heilige Beeste* (1945), awarded the Hertzog Prize for Literature, was already centred in primitive symbols: earth, woman and the supernatural. In *Negester oor Nineve* (1947) it deepens into a contrast between magical creativity and the sterility of the human city. In his later work (the brilliant epic poem *Joernaal van Jorik*, 1949; and *Engel uit die Klip*, 1950) his attention is increasingly focused on basic conflicts arising from the South African scene; this often assumes the form of an adjustment of medieval legends to his immediately surrounding reality, in such a way that a subtle pattern of allusions is created. His poetry culminates in *Blom en Baaierd* (1956) and *Dolosse* (1963), presenting the conflicts between order and chaos, creation and disintegration, a mythical, primitive past and a civilized present. In his 2 verse plays, *Periandros van Korinthe* (1954) and the less convincing *Vergelegen* (1956), both of which approach the problem of a man with absolute aims in his fatal struggle with reality which admits only relative values, he proves himself, with N. P. van Wyk ◊ Louw, the leading Afrikaans dramatist. [A P B]

Gedigte (1960); *Afrikaans Poems with English Translations*, ed. and tr. A. P. Grove and C. J. D. Harvey (1962).
Ernst van Heerden, *Rekenskap* (1963).

Osadaby, Dennis (1911–). Nigerian poet. Born in Asaba. He studied Law in England and while there started writing poetry late published in West Africa, England and India and broadcast by the B.B.C. He has been a government clerk, a solicitor, journalist, lawyer and member of Parliament. He has represented Nigeria at many Congresses in Europe and was formerly President of the Senate. He was Premier of the newly created state of the Mid-West in Nigeria.

He works in English. Most of his poetry was written between 1930 and 1950 and published in a volume called *Africa Sings* (1952). It has a strong nationalistic fervour and is often didactic in tone but stems from the poet's personal experiences. The topics he chooses often suggest a measure of attitudinizing, but his poetry springs from deep conviction. [J A R]

Ousmane, Sembene. ◊ Sembene Ousmane.

Oyono, Ferdinand (1929–). French West African novelist. Born at Ngulemakong in the Cameroons. In Paris he obtained his *licence* in law at the University Law Faculty. His first novel, *Une vie de Boy* (Paris, 1956), was soon followed by *Le vieux nègre et la médaille* (1956) and *Chemin d'Europe* (1960). One of his stories, 'Un lépreux sur une tombe', has appeared in the magazine *Hommes sans épaules* (1958). His work, satirical in parts, and imbued with both humour and pathos, depict in masterly fashion the life of ordinary people in the Cameroons during the colonial period. (Translations of Oyono's writings have appeared in Germany, Holland, Czechoslovakia, Norway and the U.S.A.

Oyono has shown much interest in the stage, and in 1959 created the role of 'Papa Bon Dieu' at the theatre of the Alliance Française in Paris. He is a member of the executive of the National Committee of French Writers. Later on Oyono was called upon to follow a diplomatic career, as Minister Plenipotentiary of the Cameroons accredited to the Common Market, and then Ambassador of the Cameroons at Monrovia (Liberia). [G T A]

Hughes and Reygnault, *A A M*.

P

Peters, Leurie (1932–). Gambian poet. Born in Bathurst, he was educated in Gambia and Sierra Leone and studied medicine in Cambridge, qualifying in 1959. He now lives in London. He is versatile and an able singer. He has taken part in B.B.C. programmes, was Chairman of 'Africa Forum' and took part in 'Calling West Africa'.

He has written a novel but is known mainly for his poetry. This has appeared in *Black Orpheus* (Nos. 11 and 14). A volume of his poetry has been published by Mbari (Ibadan, 1964). His poetry has to a large extent freed itself of the trammels of race and colour. He is essentially an urbanized poet who writes within the tradition of European verse. When there is a reference to Africa it is in the nature of a flashback, closely interwoven but never forced. [O R D]

Plaatje, Sol. T. (1877–1932). South African writer. He was educated only up to primary level but supplemented this by private study. He was employed as a court-interpreter and spoke Dutch, English, German, Afrikaans and four Bantu languages.

He wrote 2 books in English: *Native Life in South Africa,* a political attack on government policy and the South African Land Act of 1913, and *Mhudi* (Lovedale, S.A., 1930), a novel. The novel is a historical romance about Mzilikazi, Tshaka's lieutenant. The Boers defeat Mzilikazi and he goes to the north with what is left of his army. The novel shows a considerable depth of characterization, especially as regards his female characters, and a great measure of compassion. His style, which uses pathetic fallacy and incorporates songs, is in keeping with the traditions of Bantu oral literature.

Besides this he wrote three books in Tswana and collected 732 proverbs in his *Sechuana Proverbs* and translated them into English, Latin, French, German and Italian. He also translated *The Comedy of Errors* (*Diphoshophosho*) (Morija, Lesotho, 1930) and *Julius Caesar* (*Dintshontsho tsa Bo-Juliuse Kesara*) (Johannesburg, 1937), and *The Merchant of Venice, Othello,* and *Much Ado about Nothing.*

Professor Jabavu thought highly of his work. He felt that his achievement was two-way and that he was able to convey foreign English ideas into the esoteric medium of the vernacular. As Mphahlele wrote, Plaatje writes 'as a politician and a historian, not like Mofolo as a moralist'. [O R D]

Q

Qamaan Bulhan (b. probably mid 19th century, d. shortly before Second World War). Somali oral poet. Of the Ogaden clan, he lived mainly in Eastern Ethiopia. His poems achieved fame throughout Somali-speaking territories. He acted as spokesman of his clan in several interclan conflicts, defending his position and publicizing his views in the form of alliterative poems. Qamaan is also well known for his philosophical and reflective turn of mind and some lines from his poems have become proverbial expressions. Many of his poems have been written down by Somali private collectors, and one has been published with English translation and notes. [B W A]

Andrzejewski and Galaal, *SPC*, ii.

R

Raage Ugaas (probably 18th cent.). Somali oral poet. Of the Ogaden clan, with a strong orthodox Muslim background, he gained a wide reputation owing to the purity of his language and his gentle wisdom and piety. Two of his poems have so far been published, and a large number of them can be found in private collections in the Somali Republic. [B W A]

Andrzejewski and Lewis, *SPI*; B. W. Andrzejewski and Musa H. I. Galaal, 'The Art of the Verbal Message in Somali Society', *Neue Afrikanistische Studien*, Hamburger Beiträge zur Afrika-Kunde, 5, Deutsches Institut für Afrika-Forschung (Hamburg, 1966).

Rabéarivelo, Jean-Joseph, originally **Joseph-Casimir** (1901–37). Malagasy poet. Founder of the modern literature of Madagascar, he was born at Antananarivo of a poor but noble family. He was an only son; his affectionate and understanding mother encouraged his poetic vocation in every way. However, his early years were full of hardship. He was taken away from the Collège Saint-Michel at Amparibe when only 13, and contracted a very early marriage. He drifted from one job to another. In spite of appeals to the French colonial administration, he never secured permanent and adequately paid employment and spent his last months as a proof-reader in a printing works at Antananarivo. Local French officials thwarted his great ambition to visit France, which he considered his spiritual home. Worn out by frustration and domestic troubles, his health undermined by drug addiction, his mind obsessed by unfulfilled literary aspirations, he committed suicide on 22 June 1937, just as his poetic talent was attaining maturity.

Rabéarivelo was a man of frail physique but passionate nature. A pure Malagasy by descent, he became virtually a complete *assimilé,* which helped to hasten the final tragedy of his life. Poetry was his dominant passion. When he left school prematurely, his command of French was faulty. He set to work with a will and soon invented a distinctive poetic idiom of his own, though using French as a medium. His first book of poems, *La coupe de cendres*, appeared in 1924, and was followed by *Sylves* (1927), *Volumes* (1928), *Presque-Songes* (1934) and *Traduit de la nuit* (Tunis, 1935). A posthumous collection, *Vieilles chansons du pays d'Imérina,* was published under the editorship of Robert Boudry at Antananarivo in 1939.

Rabéarivelo's first poems betray the influence of the French Symbolist poets. Later he gave full rein to the rich spontaneity of his ardent and sensitive temperament. The brilliant intensity of his imagery, which has been likened to Leconte de Lisle's, marks him as a child of the tropics. He was so successful in utilizing the vernacular ballad forms of Madagascar, especially that called 'hainteny', that some of his most original lyrics – 'chants frais et harmonieux', as they have been justly called – seem like translations from popular poetry. Rabéarivelo is venerated as the father of Madagascar's literary culture, and exercised a profound influence on other Malagasy poets, such as ⇨ Ranaivo and ⇨ Rabemananjara. [G T A]

Senghor, *P N M*; Rutherfoord, *D L*; Moore and Beier, *M P A.*

Rabemananjara, Jean-Jacques (1913–). Malagasy poet, dramatist and statesman. Born at the coastal town of Tamatave in Madagascar, of a Betsimisaraka family. He completed his secondary education at the Jesuit college in Antananarivo, where he founded a literary magazine called *Revue des jeunes.* He then entered the French colonial administration and in 1939 came to Paris for a tour of duty at the Ministry of the Colonies. The outbreak of the Second World War and the German occupation prevented him from returning to Madagascar. He studied for an Arts degree at Paris University and passed with high distinction. He frequented Paris literary circles and proclaimed himself the disciple of the famous Malagasy bard ⇨ Rabéarivelo. His first collections of poems, *L'éventail de rêve* and *Au confins de la nuit,* published in Madagascar, were followed by *Sur les marches du soir* (Gap, 1940). In 1942 he brought out a play, *Les dieux malgaches* (Paris, 1947), which narrowly failed to secure performance at the Odéon.

As editor of the *Revue des jeunes,* Rabemananjara had adopted the motto: '*Devenir français tout en restant malgache.*' He began by imitating the French Romantics, the Parnassians and the Symbolists, though even his early poems show promise of original talent. He abandoned the popular balladry of the 'hain-teny' for the more grandiose, rhetorical style characteristic of his later poems collected in *Rites millénaires* (1955), *Lamba* (1956), *Antsa* (1956) and *Antidotes* (1961) (all published in Paris). He recently published 2 new tragedies, *Les boutriers de l'aurore* (Paris, 1957) and *Les agapes des dieux* (Paris 1962), and has also written a short history of Madagascar (Gentilly, 1952).

After the Second World War, Rabemananjara was caught up in the spiritual and ideological movement known as *négritude.* He took part in the Madagascar liberation movement and was imprisoned for some years after the abortive 1947 revolt. When Madagascar became independent in 1960, Rabemananjara became Minister of National Economy in the new republic. [G T A]

Senghor, *P N M*; Rutherfoord, *D L*; Hughes and Reygnault, *A A M.*

Rabie, Jan Sebastiaan (1920–). South

African short-story writer, novelist and free-lance journalist. After his debut with four traditionalist novels in the forties, he spent several years in Paris and, in 1956, shocked his Afrikaans readers with a volume of surrealist 'prose-poems', *Eenen-twintig* ('Twenty-one'). These bore the stamp of 'engaged literature', to which Rabie has vowed himself ever since. *Mens-alleen* ('Man Alone'), written in 1950–5 but not published until 1963, evoked in the only vaguely defined framework of a 'Latin' civil war between democratic and totalitarian powers the miserable plight of modern man hunted down and harassed by political forces beyond his control. *Ons, die Afgod* (1958; 'We, the Idol') was the first outspokenly anti-racist novel in Afrikaans. This was recently followed up with the first two volumes of the *Bolandia*-series, *Eiland voor Afrika* (1964; 'Island off Africa') and *Die Groot Anders-Maak* (1964; 'The Great Commutation'), which trace the present white–coloured relationship back to the earliest decades of the Dutch settlement at the Cape of Good Hope.

Rabie's style is often metaphorically overloaded; but every now and then he achieves passages of a dramatic, though sometimes somewhat sensational, dynamism and a human tenderness which are unsurpassed in Afrikaans literature. [R A]

R. Antonissen, *Kern en tooi* (Pretoria, 1963), and *Spitsberaad* (Pretoria, 1966).

Ranaivo, Flavien (1914–). Malagasy poet. Born at Arivonimamo near Antananarivo, in the Imerina country which has been celebrated in the verse of his compatriot ⇨ Rabéarivelo. His father was for some years governor of Arivonimamo. Ranaivo spent his youth at Antananarivo, and passed happy days wandering through the countryside round the capital. He learnt music before he learnt the alphabet, and did not attend school until he was eight.

In Ranaivo's poetry, one feels an effort to bring out the hidden depths of his inner personality. Like Rabéarivelo before him, Ranaivo exploits the vernacular song and ballad form, especially that known as 'hain-teny', but he is even more original and authentic than his predecessor. His poetic work first became known on the publication of his *L'ombre et le vent* (pref. by O. Monnoni, illustrations by Andriamampianina, Antananarivo, 1947) and obtained wider recognition when some of his verses were included in Senghor's *Anthologie de la nouvelle poésie nègre et malgache* (Paris, 1948). Ranaivo has since published *Mes chansons de toujours* (Paris, 1955), with a preface by L. S. ⇨ Senghor. His close-knit poetic style still retains elements of French thought and literary technique, but all his poetry is marked by a generous flow of inspiration and bold flashes of imagery. [G T A]

Rutherfoord, *D L*; Moore and Beier, *M P A*.

Ribas, Óscar (1909–). Angolan writer. The most eminent and also the most versatile and productive writer in Portuguese Africa. He was born of mixed parentage in Luanda, Angola. His eyesight began to fail at the age of 21 and he became totally blind. He is the author of a novel and several collections of short stories and ethnographic texts. All his works are published in Portuguese. They depict the life and thought of the Kimbundu people.

He published a collection of poems, essays and short stories, entitled *Flores e espinhos* (Luanda, 1948). In 1951 he published *Uanga* (Lello, Luanda), a novel, which is shortly to appear in a German translation. This was followed by a collection of short stories, *Ecos da minha terra* (Lello, Luanda, 1952). One of the stories in this volume, *A Praga*, was awarded the Margaret Wrong Literary Prize in London in 1952.

Óscar Ribas has devoted the last ten years to a study of the religious beliefs, oral literature and folklore of his people, resulting in a series of collected essays: *Ilundo* (Museu de Angola, Luanda, 1958) and *Missosso* (Tipografia Angolana, Luanda, I, 1961; II, 1962; III in preparation). He has been working on a historical novel from the period of Queen Jinga and preparing a dictionary of regional idioms. [G A]

Rive, Richard (1931–). South African short-story writer. Born in District Six in Cape Town. His father was an American Negro and his mother a coloured South African. He studied locally and went to the University of Cape Town. Afterwards he taught in a training college and now teaches English and Latin in a large Cape Town school.

He started writing as a student and his early stories appeared in South African periodicals and afterwards in European and American journals. Some have been collected in *African Songs* (Berlin, 1963). They are largely stories of protest that describe in Rive's persistent style the effects of black, white and coloured people living in South Africa. He is able to balance humour and passionate insight and blend them into impressive stories of spiritual triumph over physical limitations. A short story has also been published in *Transition* 8 and a poem appears in Langston Hughes's *Poems from Black Africa* (Indiana University Press, 1963). He has edited an anthology, *Modern African Prose* (1964). [J A R]

Robert, Shaaban (1909–62). Tanzanian poet and essayist. Born near Tanga and educated at Dar-es-Salaam. He spent all his life on or near the East African coast, much of the time in Government service. His output, all in Swahili, includes a wide variety of prose and verse. His contribution to modern Swahili literature was recognized in 1960 by the award of the Margaret Wrong Medal and Prize.

Shaaban Robert's early published works include *Pambo la lugha* ('The Embellishment of Language', Witwatersrand, 1947) and the autobiographical *Maisha yangu* ('My Life', 1949). These were followed by *Kusadikika* (1951), an allegory after the style of *Gulliver's Travels* of present-day political trends as seen by a Tanzanian; this is perhaps his best work. In 1952, Shaaban Robert brought out a Swahili translation of the *Rubaiyat* of Omar Khayyam. His later publications comprise *Adili na nduguze* ('Adili and his Brothers', 1952), *Kielezo cha insha* (a collection of essays, Witwatersrand, 1954), *Siti bint saad* (2nd edn, Tanga, 1960) and the didactic *Masomo yenye adili* ('Readings in Behaviour', Tanga, 1959); also *Almasi za Afrika* ('African Diamonds', Tanga, 1960) and *Insha na mashairi* ('Essays and Poems', Tanga, 1961). His longest verse epic, *Vita vya uhuru* ('The War for Freedom'), was still in manuscript form at his death. Shaaban Robert was a pious Muslim, and some of his prose writing is marred by an excess of moralization. [W H W]

Harries, *S P.*

Rubadiri, David (1930–). Malawi poet. He attended Makerere College, Kampala, Uganda. During the 1959 emergency he was arrested, then he went to Cambridge to read English, and did some writing and broadcasting. On his return he taught, continued writing and was recently appointed his country's ambassador to the United States. He teaches at Makerere.

His work has been published in recent African anthologies. He also has a poem in *Transition* 12. He is a poet of the social conscience and often, as in 'Stanley Meets Mutesa' and the more recent 'On Parting from a First "White" Love', he writes about the meeting of two worlds. [O R D]

Rutherfoord, *D L.*
Moore and Beier, *M P A.*

S

Sadji, Abdoulaye (1910–61). French West African writer. Born in Rufisque, Senegal. He went to the Koranic Schools until 11 then to the French elementary school and finally to a teachers' training college, obtaining his diploma in 1929. In 1932 he obtained his baccalaureate. He worked for radio, then became an inspector of elementary schools in Senegal.

He published a school reader with ⇨ Senghor, *La belle histoire de Leuk-le-Lièvre* (Paris, 1953), and a novelette in *Trois écrivains noirs* (Paris, 1954) about Nini, a child of a mixed union. His only full-length novel is *Maimouna* (Dakar, 1953), the story of a Senegalese woman. He has also written a volume of tragical short stories, *Tounka* (Dakar, n.d.). He shows a passionate love of country in his books, is at home in describing the violence and warmth of big-city life, and has an ability to portray women unequalled by any other African writer. [O R D]

Saiyid Abdallah b. Ali b. Nasir of Lamu (*c.*1720–1810). Swahili poet. Like at least four other leading Swahili poets, he came of the line of Shaikh Abu Bakr b. Salim who was born at Tarim in the Hadramawt in 1584. His celebrated poem *al-Inkishafi* ('Self-examination'; tr. and ed. W. Hichens, *The Soul's Awakening*, 1939) is a soliloquy on the inevitability of death, inspired by the passing of the old Arab citadels of the East African coast. He also wrote *Takhmis ya Liyongo* ('Poem of Liyongo'), based on traditional songs concerning the legendary Swahili hero of that name. The manuscript of this is in the British Museum. [L P H]

Harries, *S P.*

Saiyid Abu Bakr b. Abd al-Rahman (Saiyid Mansab) (1828–1922). Swahili poet. Born at Lamu in Kenya, he studied law and theology at Mecca. He served as *kadhi* or judge at Zanzibar during the sultanate of Saiyid Majid. He composed the Swahili abridgement of *Maulid al-Barzanji*, a poem on the birth of the Prophet Muhammad, and a long romantic poem called *Utendi wa Akida tu 'l-Awami*, embodying a homiletic on religious duties. [L P H]

Harries, *S P.*

Saiyid Umar b. Amin b. Nasir al-Ahdal (1800–70), Swahili poet. He served as *kadhi* or judge of Siu, north of Mombasa in Kenya. He specialized in acrostic poems on religious themes, among the best known of which are *Wajiwaji* and *Dura Mandhuma* ('The String of Pearls'). [L P H]

Harries, *S P.*

Salaan 'Arrabey (b. mid 19th cent., d. soon after Second World War). Somali oral poet. He was known for his versatility and humour and was skilled in influencing important events by composing poems appropriate to the situation. It is said that he could cause an interclan war or stop it. He travelled widely and in his poems numerous innovations and foreign borrowings can be found. His familiarity with English, Swahili, Arabic and Hindustani brought him success both as a merchant and an interpreter. Many of his poems are found in ⇨ Musa H. I. Galaal's private collection. [B W A]

Andrzejewski and Lewis, *S P I*; Andrzejewski and Galaal, *S P C*, iii.

Santos, Arnaldo (1936–). Angolan poet. Born in Luanda, and went to school locally. He now works as an official in the Health Service. He writes in Portuguese and is one of the younger, most exciting poets. His poetry is protest poetry, identifying itself with the poor and the downtrodden. Two of his poems appeared in the *London Magazine* (October 1962); in an introduction it was said that his poetry is 'of a more intimate tone and attachment to nature', though one finds in it the same desperate hope. [J A R]

Sembene Ousmane (1923–). French West African novelist. Born at Ziguinchor in Senegal. His family lived by fishing, and Ousmane too was brought up to be a fisherman. But after three years at a technical school in Marsassoum, he left for Dakar where he did a variety of manual jobs before being called up during the Second World War. He took part in the Allied invasion of Italy and finished up as a docker on the quayside at Marseilles. All this time he was reading and writing whenever he had the chance. From his life and experiences at Marseilles, his first novel, *Le docker noir* (Paris, 1956), was born. Then he fell ill. His spine was seriously affected and he was debarred from all physical labour. From this time on, he has devoted himself to literature, as well as making an extended tour of the countries of Europe. He subsequently returned to his native Senegal where, as he says, 'so much remains to do and to write'.

Ousmane won international renown with his second novel, *Ô pays, mon beau peuple* (Paris, 1957), which has been translated into Slovak, Hungarian, Rumanian, German and Bulgarian. It tells the tragic story of a young Negro married to a white girl and returning to his native village after eight years of absence; the hero perishes in an attempt to implant in his old community an alien outlook which it cannot tolerate or comprehend. Ousmane's reputation was further strengthened by *Les bouts de bois de Dieu* (Paris, 1960), which describes the struggle of the strikers of the 'Dakar-Niger' between October 1947 and March 1948; this work has been translated into English in the United States, as well as into Dutch, Hungarian and Italian. Ousmane's latest book, *Voltaïque*, was published in 1962. Always in touch with human reality, this self-taught novelist and courageous social observer is notable for his profound respect for the individual human conscience. [G T A]

Senghor, Léopold Sédar (1906–). French West African poet, philosopher and statesman. Born at Joal, an old Portuguese settlement about 100 kilometres south of Dakar. He is of the Serer tribe, his father being a rich groundnut merchant. He was educated locally by the Catholic Fathers of the Holy Spirit, who taught him the Wolof and French languages, and then completed his schooling at the Libermann College in Dakar. In 1928 he went on to the Lycée Louis-le-Grand in Paris and five years later completed his *agrégation* at the Sorbonne, the first West African to do so. While living at the Cité Universitaire, Senghor made the acquaintance of his '*ami fraternel et témoin d'élection*', the Martinique poet Aimé Césaire, with whom he worked out the principles of the famous literary and ideological movement known as *négritude*. After *agrégation* in 1933, Senghor was appointed a master at the Lycée Descartes at Tours and afterwards at the Lycée Marcelin Berthelot at Saint-Maur des Fosses. During the German occupation, he took an active part in the French Resistance.

Senghor's career as poet and politician began on the liberation of France in 1944. He was appointed to a chair at the École Nationale de la France d'Outremer, and elected Deputy for Senegal in the French National Assembly. His first collection of poems, *Chants d'ombre,* appeared in 1945, and was followed by *Hosties noires* (1948), *Chants pour Naëtt* (1949), *Éthiopiques* (1956) and *Nocturnes* (1961). In 1948 Senghor brought out an important anthology of modern African and Malagasy poetry written in French, with a long introductory essay by Jean-Paul Sartre, setting out the intellectual and spiritual claims of the peoples of resurgent Africa. This anthology, translated into several languages, is a basic source-book for modern African poetry and literature. Senghor has also published important essays stressing the specific contribution of the African mind to world culture and human experience generally; several of these have appeared in the journal *Présence africaine* (Paris), others as prefaces to books by African writers such as F. ⇨ Ranaivo and Birago ⇨ Diop. In 1955 Senghor became a Minister in the French government, and in 1960 was unanimously elected the first President of the Republic of Senegal. His political convictions have found expression in articles on social theory, tinged with an individual form of Socialism.

Unlike that of his friend Césaire, Senghor's verse is often grave and meditative in mood. He sees himself as an ambassador-at-large of the world of Africa, whose beauty he exalts with a profound and ardent tenderness. Among the familiar themes of *négritude* which appear one by one in Senghor's poetry are the pervasive presence of the dead and their protective guiding influence upon the living; the devastation of ancient Africa and its culture by white Europe; the harsh rigidity of the modern West and its desperate need for the complementing qualities of Africa; and the warm triumphant beauty of African women. [G T A]

Selected Poems, tr. John Reed and Clive Wake (1964); *Anthologie de la nouvelle poésie nègre et malgache, précédée de Orphée Noir par Jean-Paul Sartre* (Paris, 1948); *La belle histoire de Leuk-le-lièvre, en collaboration avec Abdoulaye Sadji* (Paris, 1953); Moore and Beier, *M P A*.
Moore, *S A W*.

Shaikh Muhyi 'l-Din al-Waili (1778–1869). Swahili poet. He was *kadhi,* or chief judge, of Zanzibar. He wrote the copy of the *Kitab al-Sulwa* now in the British Museum, and many Swahili poems, the best known of which is perhaps *Dua ya Kuombea Mvua* ('Prayer for Rain'). [L P H]

Harries, *S P*.

Sinxo, G. B. (1902–62). South African novelist and poet. Born in Cape Province, South Africa. He wrote in Xhosa and published 3 novels: *Unomsa* (after the name of his heroine) (Lovedale, S.A., 1922), *Umfundisi* ('The Minister of Religion') (Lovedale, S.A., 1927), and *U mzali wohahleko* ('The Prodigal Parent') (Lovedale, S.A., 1939), about a mother who spoilt her own child and punished her step-child with obvious consequences. He also wrote a book of poems, *Thoba sikutyele* ('Come Let Me Tell You') (Lovedale, S.A., n.d.), a Xhosa drama, *Imfene ka Debeza* ('Dabeza's Baboon') (Lovedale, S.A., 1925), a story of witchcraft, and other novelettes. [O R D]

Socé, Ousmane (1911–). French West African poet and novelist. Born in

Rufisque. He went to local schools and afterwards studied to be a veterinary surgeon. He is at the moment Senegal's ambassador to the United States and the United Nations. He writes in French and has published poetry and fiction. His novels are *Karim* (Paris, 1934), about a young man in Senegal, and *Mirages de Paris* (Paris, 1937). His poems are in a volume called *Les rhythmes du Khalam* (Paris, 1962). [J A R]

Soga, T. B. (1831–71). South African writer. He wrote in Xhosa. Among his best-known work is *Intlalo ka Xosa* ('The Way of Life of the Xhosas') (Lovedale, S.A.). This is an attempt at writing Xhosa folklore or history. According to Professor Jabavu the book was the first attempt made in the Xhosa language to explain the customs and traditions of the Xhosa people. He found that the author wrote with a sound sense of history as well as a knowledge of present-day events. Soga also translated the Bible and *Pilgrim's Progress* into Xhosa. He wrote many essays (see *Africa South,* Oct. 1958, p. 114), all on serious topics and with didactic intent. His work was strongly influenced by Christianity. [O R D]

Soyinka, Wole (1934–). Nigerian playwright and poet. Born in Abeokuta, the son of a schools' supervisor, he attended the universities of Ibadan and Leeds. He then spent eighteen months studying the theatre in London. He was attached to the Royal Court Theatre, where his play *The Invention* was produced experimentally. In 1960 he returned to Ibadan to study indigenous drama forms at University College. He is now Director of the School of Drama, University of Ibadan, and manages a touring company of players in his spare time.

Soyinka's ambition to develop a Nigerian theatre is apparent in his own plays, several of which have been produced in Nigeria. *The Trials of Brother Jero, The Swamp Dwellers* and *The Strong Breed* were collected in *Three Plays* (Ibadan, 1963), and he has also published *The Dance of the Forests* (1963) and a satirical comedy, *The Lion and the Jewel* (1963), in which he presents the imposition of modern civilization on Africa as a threat to the African villagers' individuality. Soyinka's proverbial style, and the strong rhythmic rather than visual quality of his prose and poetry, share with many of his themes a source in Nigerian folklore. This much is apparent in his latest play, *The Road* (1965). Several poems and some criticism of his work have appeared in the Nigerian magazine *Black Orpheus*. He has also published a novel, *The Interpreters*. [P T]

Hughes and Reygnault, *A A M*; Moore and Beier, *M P A*.

Swahili Literature. From the 16th century onwards, Hadrami Saiyids brought with them to the East African coast didactic and homiletic verse in Arabic, which was paraphrased in Swahili, the Swahili versions being often written down together with the Arabic originals in the form of interlinear insertion. This type of verse was supplemented by free Swahili renderings of popular Islamic tales from the Arabic *maghazi* literature. The earliest original Swahili poem known to scholars is the *Utendi wa Tambuka* ('Lay of Tabuk'), an anonymous work the manuscript of which, dated A.D. 1728, is preserved in the library of the Seminar für Afrikanische Sprachen, Hamburg.

In the 19th century, the use of the Swahili-Arabic script was extended to include ritual songs of Bantu origin, together with many original compositions unrelated to any Arabic original. The poet ◊ Muyaka b. Haji wrote verse which was a commentary on the Mazrui struggle against the Sultan of Muscat. Other prominent poets were ◊ Saiyid Abdallah of Lamu, ◊ Shaikh Muhyi 'l-Din al-Waili, ◊ Mwana Kupona, ◊ Saiyid Umar b. Amin and ◊ Saiyid Abu Bakr.

Modern poetry in Swahili seldom achieves the technical efficiency of the earlier work and the themes are often trite, though exceptions have come from the work of Shaaban ◊ Robert of Tanga. Verse in the traditional manner, religious in character, is still written [L P H]

Harries, *S P*.

T

Tchicaya, u Tam'si (nom-de-plume of **Felix Tchicaya)** (1931–). Congolese poet, journalist and raconteur. Born at

Mpili in the Middle Congo. In 1946 he accompanied his father, then Deputy for the Moyen Congo, to Europe, and studied at the Orleans Lycée and then at the Lycée Janson de Sailly in Paris. His first book of verse, *Le mauvais sang* (1955), was followed by *Feu de brousse* (1957), *À triche-cœur* (1958) and *Épitomé* (1962). From 1957 to 1960, Tchicaya worked in Paris as a producer for the French radio, for which he adapted over a hundred African stories and legends. He contributed frequently to the Paris review *Vie africaine* and in 1960 became chief editor of the journal *Congo* (Leopoldville).

Tchicaya has latterly been an official of UNESCO, and belongs to several French literary societies and committees. Extracts from his works have been translated into Polish, Czech and Hungarian, as well as appearing in English in the magazine *Atlantic Monthly*. [G T A]

Brush Fire (Ibadan, 1964); Moore and Beier, *M P A*.

Themba, Can (1924–). South African journalist and short-story writer. He took a degree at Fort Hare with a distinction in English. He is a journalist and was at one time with *Drum*. He is now an assistant editor of the weekly, *The Golden City Post*. He lives in South Africa.

He has written a number of short stories. Among the best known is 'Mob Passion' (in Rutherfoord, *DL*), which won a short-story competition in *Drum* in 1953. In it he describes the violence of an inter-tribal feud. Mphahlele did not like the story, however, and considered it 'a poor Hollywood imitation'. He has also published two sketches: *The Bottom of the Bottle*, nostalgic recollections of Sophiatown, and *Requiem for Sophiatown*, on the same theme but with a greater element of protest. His writing is in general vigorous protest writing but he achieves in large measure a tone of cynical detachment. [O R D]

Tutuola, Amos (1920–). Nigerian novelist. Born of Christian parents in Abeokuta. Tutuola had only a few years' schooling. He has worked as a coppersmith, a Government messenger in Lagos, and is now a storekeeper with the Nigerian Broadcasting Service in Ibadan.

His best book was his first, *The Palm-Wine Drinkard* (1952), though there is evidence of renewed vitality in his fifth and latest, *Feather Woman of the Jungle* (1962). His books defy categorization. They combine elements of myth, fairy-tale and tall story in a style that is oral and ungrammatical. Narrative energy puts pressure on the tangled, rhythmic sentences, and Gargantuan fantasy tumbles endearingly into empirical fact, or is illustrated by a startling analogy drawn from the apparatus of modern life. A grotesque exploitation of magic's scorn for probability, a perception of humour in horror, and an intuitive treatment of myth are the staple of his work, which is closer to epic than to the novel. [P T]

My Life in the Bush of Ghosts (1954); *Simbi and the Satyr of the Dark Jungle* (1955); *The Brave African Huntress* (1958).

Moore, *S A W*; Harold R. Collins, 'The Ghost Novels of Amos Tutuola', in *Critique*, Autumn/Winter, 1960–61.

V

Vilakazi, B. W. (1905–47). South African poet and novelist. He was appointed to the staff of the University of the Witwatersrand and was Senior Language Assistant in the Department of Bantu Languages until his death.

He wrote 3 novels and poetry in Zulu and collaborated with Professor Doke on a Zulu-English dictionary. His novels are *Noma Nini* ('Any Time') (Marianhill, 1935), which tells of the Zulu reaction to the missionaries at Groutville, *U Dingiswayo ka Jobe* ('Dingiswayo, Son of Jobe') (London, 1939), about Chief Dingswayo, Shaka's guardian, and *Nje nempela* ('As a Positive Fact') (Marianhill, 1955), based on the Bambatha rebellion of 1906.

Professor Jabavu felt that his first book of poems, *Inkondlo ka Zulu* ('Zulu Horizons') (Johannesburg, 1935), attained to the level of a classic. He found in it a variety of metres and verse-forms influenced by English literature and listed Keats and Gray among Vilakazi's influences. According to Professor Nyembezi he is more important as a poet than as a prose writer, since his poetry developed from traditional praise-songs and he adopted European forms and experimented with stanza and rhyme (a difficult thing in Zulu). Consequently Professor Nyembezi found that in *Inkondlo ka Zulu* he used rhyme but discarded it later.

Some of his poems have been translated into English by Malcolm and Friedman under the title *Zulu Horizons* (Capetown, 1962). A translation appears also in *Darkness and Light* (ed. Peggy Rutherfoord, 1963) and a critique and translation of 'In the Gold Mines' (about the injustices of mine labour) in *Africa South* and *The African Image* (1962) by Ezekiel ⇨ Mphahlele. [O R D]

RECOMMENDED READING

Books

Beier, Ulli, ed., *Introduction to African Literature* (1967)
Brown, Lalage and Crowder, Michael, ed., *The Proceedings of the First International Congress of Africanists* (1964)
Cook, Mercer, *Five French Negro Authors* (Washington, 1943)
Dathorne, O. R., *African Literature* (1968)
African Poetry for Schools and Training Colleges (1967) (with a historical and critical introduction)
Gleason, Judith Illsley, *This Africa: Novels by West Africans in English and French* (Evanston, Ill. 1965)
Jahn, Janheinz, *Muntu* (1961)
Kesteloot, Lilyan, *Les écrivains noirs de langue française: naissance d'une littérature* (Brussels, 1963)
Krog, E. W., ed., *African Literature in Rhodesia* (Rhodesia, 1966)
McLeod, A. L., ed., *The Commonwealth Pen* (Ithaca, New York, 1961)
Melone, Thomas, *De la négritude dans la littérature négro-africaine* (Paris, 1962)
Moore, Gerald, ed., *African Literature and the Universities* (Ibadan, 1965)
Seven African Writers (1962)
Mphahlele, Ezekiel, *The African Image* (1962)
Nathan, Ferdinand, *Littérature africaine* (Paris, 1964) (studies of eight French African writers)
Nicol, Davidson, *Africa: A Subjective View* (1964)
Nketia, J. H., *Folk Songs of Ghana* (Ghana, 1963)
Nkosi, Lewis, *Home and Exile* (1965)
Sartre, Jean-Paul, *Black Orpheus* (Paris, n.d.) (Introduction to L. S. Senghor's anthology, 1948)
Shepherd, R. H. W., *Lovedale and Literature for the Bantu* (Lovedale, South Africa, 1945)
Tibble, Anne, *African/English Literature* (1966)
Wauthier, Claude, *The Literature and Thought of Modern Africa* (1966)

Journals

Abbia, Yaounde, Cameroon
African Forum, American Society of African Culture, New York
Black Orpheus, ed. Ulli Beier, O. R. Dathorne and Wole Soyinka, Ibadan, Nigeria
Bulletin of the Association for African Literature in English, ed. Eldred Jones, Fourah Bay College, Freetown, Sierra Leone
The Classic, ed. Nathaniel Nakasa, Johannesburg, South Africa
Cultural Events in Africa, London
Journal of Commonwealth Literature, ed. Arthur Ravenscroft, University of Leeds
The New African, ed. Randolph Vigne, London
Nigeria Magazine, Marina, Lagos
Présence Africaine, Société Africaine de Culture, Paris
Transition, ed. Rajat Neogy, Kampala, Uganda

MORE ABOUT PENGUINS

Penguin Book News, which appears every month, contains details of all the new books issued by Penguins as they are published. From time to time it is supplemented by *Penguins in Print*, which is a complete list of all books published by Penguins which are in print. (There are nearly three thousand of these.)

A specimen copy of *Penguin Book News* will be sent to you free on request, and you can become a subscriber for the price of the postage – 4s. for a year's issues (including the complete lists). Just write to Dept EP, Penguin Books Ltd, Harmondsworth, Middlesex, enclosing a cheque or postal order, and your name will be added to the mailing list.

Some other books published by Penguins are described on the following pages.

Note: *Penguin Book News* and *Penguins in Print* are not available in the U.S.A. or Canada

THE PELICAN GUIDE TO ENGLISH LITERATURE

EDITED BY BORIS FORD

What this work sets out to offer is a guide to the history and traditions of English Literature, a contour-map of the literary scene. It attempts, that is, to draw up an ordered account of literature that is concerned, first and foremost, with value for the present, and this as a direct encouragement to people to read for themselves.

Each volume sets out to present the reader with four kinds of related material:

(i) An account of the social context of literature in each period.

(ii) A literary survey of the period.

(iii) Detailed studies of some of the chief writers and works in the period.

(iv) An appendix of essential facts for reference purposes.

The *Guide* consists of seven volumes, as follows:

1. *The Age of Chaucer*
2. *The Age of Shakespeare*
3. *From Donne to Marvell*
4. *From Dryden to Johnson*
5. *From Blake to Byron*
6. *From Dickens to Hardy*
7. *The Modern Age*

WAITING FOR THE END

LESLIE A. FIEDLER

The American Literary Scene
from Hemingway to Baldwin

In *Love and Death in the American Novel* Leslie Fiedler created a new kind of criticism, urgent and outspoken, provoking rage in some, reverence in others. In this more recent survey of the American literary scene he sees many contemporary novels as expressions of American myths, old and new – from the Old South, as represented by Faulkner, and the towering self-created myth that was Ernest Hemingway, through the sex-and-whisky revolt of the twenties and thirties (Fitzgerald and Henry Miller), to the drug culture of Kerouac, Ginsberg and today's 'beats'. He argues that the new prominence in American writing of Jewish and Negro authors (Bellow, Mailer, Malamud, and Baldwin) reflects a wider search for identity throughout America.

Whether he is discussing the revolt of the academics or the 'Hollywood novel', Professor Fiedler is the most maddeningly stimulating guide to 'the world's first post-literate culture'.

THE THEATRE OF THE ABSURD

MARTIN ESSLIN

The theatre is no longer a middle-class drawing room. Ever since sophisticated European audiences exploded in near-riots at the first performances of *Waiting for Godot* avant-garde playwrights have been breaking through the crust of stage conventions to the shifting core of psychological reality present in human hopes, fears and dreams. In plays by such writers as Beckett, Ionesco, Genet and Pinter language gutters, communication falters, character and personality disintegrate, the very sequence of time and laws of physics may go by the board. Shorn of all certainties these dramatists are confronting a world in which God is dead, a world which, in the Existentialist sense, is *absurd*.

Martin Esslin's classic study of the dramatists of the Absurd has been fully revised for this Pelican edition. In it he examines the origins, nature and future of a movement whose significance transcends the bounds of the stage and influences the whole intellectual climate of our time.

THE NEW POETIC

Yeats to Eliot

C. K. STEAD

By the end of the nineteenth century the Romantic movement had split into two opposed impulses, producing on the one hand the popular discursive poet in the manner of Kipling and Newbolt and on the other the aesthete-poet in search of 'Beauty'. In this highly original study Professor Stead re-examines the experiments of the Georgian school and those of their more radical successors, Ezra Pound and the Imagists, and contends that it has been the function of poetry since Yeats to restore a wholeness of sensibility and to readjust the relations between the poet, his audience, and his experience. In his survey of this 'new poetic' Professor Stead offers a radical re-appraisal of the poetry and criticism of T. S. Eliot, whom he places in a tradition running unbroken from the great Romantics. As a result he not only re-discovers the essential 'newness' of the major poetry of our age, but stimulates insight into the essential nature of all great poetry.